E-commerce

business. technology. society.

GLOBAL EDITION

SIXTEENTH EDITION

Kenneth C. Laudon
New York University

Carol Guercio Traver
Azimuth Interactive, Inc.

Harlow, England • London • New York • Boston • San Francisco • Toronto
Sydney • Dubai • Singapore • Hong Kong • Tokyo • Seoul • Taipei
New Delhi • Cape Town • Sao Paulo • Mexico City • Madrid • Amsterdam
Munich • Paris • Milan

Microsoft and/or its respective suppliers make no representations about the suitability of the information contained in the documents and related graphics published as part of the services for any purpose. All such documents and related graphics are provided "as is" without warranty of any kind. Microsoft and/or its respective suppliers hereby disclaim all warranties and conditions with regard to this information, including all warranties and conditions of merchantability, whether express, implied or statutory, fitness for a particular purpose, title and non-infringement. In no event shall Microsoft and/or its respective suppliers be liable for any special, indirect or consequential damages or any damages whatsoever resulting from loss of use, data or profits, whether in an action of contract, negligence or other tortious action, arising out of or in connection with the use or performance of information available from the services. The documents and related graphics contained herein could include technical inaccuracies or typographical errors. Changes are periodically added to the information herein. Microsoft and/or its respective suppliers may make improvements and/or changes in the product(s) and/or the program(s) described herein at any time. Partial screen shots may be viewed in full within the software version specified.

Microsoft® Windows® and Microsoft Office® are registered trademarks of Microsoft Corporation in the U.S.A. and other countries. This book is not sponsored or endorsed by or affiliated with Microsoft Corporation.

Acknowledgments of third-party content appear on the appropriate page within the text, which constitute an extension of this copyright page.

Pearson Education Limited
KAO Two
KAO Park
Hockham Way
Harlow
Essex
CM17 9SR
United Kingdom

and Associated Companies throughout the world

Visit us on the World Wide Web at: www.pearsonglobaleditions.com

© Kenneth C. Laudon and Carol Guercio Traver 2021

The rights of Kenneth C. Laudon and Carol Guercio Traver to be identified as the authors of this work have been asserted by them in accordance with the Copyright, Designs and Patents Act 1988.

Authorized adaptation from E-commerce 2019: business. technology. society., *15th edition, ISBN 978-0-13-499845-9, by Kenneth C. Laudon and Carol Guercio Traver, published by Pearson Education.*

All rights reserved. No part of this publication may be reproduced, stored in a retrieval system, or transmitted in any form or by any means, electronic, mechanical, photocopying, recording or otherwise, without either the prior written permission of the publisher or a license permitting restricted copying in the United Kingdom issued by the Copyright Licensing Agency Ltd, Saffron House, 6–10 Kirby Street, London EC1N 8TS.

All trademarks used herein are the property of their respective owners. The use of any trademark in this text does not vest in the author or publisher any trademark ownership rights in such trademarks, nor does the use of such trademarks imply any affiliation with or endorsement of this book by such owners. For information regarding permissions, request forms, and the appropriate contacts within the Pearson Education Global Rights and Permissions department, please visit www.pearsoned.com/permissions.

British Library Cataloguing-in-Publication Data
A catalogue record for this book is available from the British Library

ISBN 10: 1-292-34316-8
ISBN 13: 978-1-292-34316-7

Typeset in ITC New Veljovic Pro Book by Azimuth Interactive, Inc.
Printed and bound by Vivar in Malaysia.

PREFACE

E-commerce 2020–2021: business. technology. society, 16E, Global Edition provides you with an in-depth introduction to the field of e-commerce. We focus on key concepts, and the latest empirical and financial data, that will help you understand and take advantage of the evolving world of opportunity offered by e-commerce, which is dramatically altering the way business is conducted and driving major shifts in the global economy. The Global Edition is aimed at students and professionals in the European Union, the Middle East, Asia-Pacific, Australia, and South Africa. Case studies reflect e-commerce firms in these regions, and figures and tables relate to these regional sources wherever possible.

Just as important as our global orientation, we have tried to create a book that is thought-provoking and current. We use the most recent data available, and focus on companies that you are likely to encounter on a daily basis in your everyday life, such as Facebook, Google, Twitter, Amazon, YouTube, Pinterest, eBay, Uber, WhatsApp, Snapchat, and many more that you will recognize, as well as some exciting startups that may be new to you. Global Edition cases include Puma, Scratch, Canva, InMobi, Spotify, Deezer, Souq, Alibaba, OVH, ASOS, MADE.COM, Brut, and Rocket Internet, among others. We also have up-to-date coverage of the key topics in e-commerce today, from privacy and piracy, to government surveillance, cyberwar, fintech, social-local-mobile marketing, Internet sales taxes, intellectual property, and more. You will find here the most up-to-date and comprehensive overview of e-commerce today.

The e-commerce concepts you learn in this book will make you valuable to potential employers. The e-commerce job market is expanding rapidly. Many employers expect new employees to understand the basics of e-commerce, online marketing, and how to develop an e-commerce presence. Every industry today is touched in at least some way by e-commerce. The information and knowledge you find in this book will be valuable throughout your career, and after reading this book, we expect that you will be able to participate in, and even lead, management discussions about e-commerce for your firm.

WHAT'S NEW IN THE 16TH EDITION

Careers in E-commerce

In this edition, at the end of every chapter, we feature a section on careers in e-commerce that examines a job posting by an online company for an entry-level position. We provide a brief overview of the field and company, some details about the position, a list of the qualifications and skills that are typically required, and then some tips about how to prepare for an interview, as well as showing how the concepts learned in each chapter can help students answer some possible interview questions.

Currency

The 16th Global Edition features all new or updated opening, closing, and "Insight on" cases. The text, as well as all of the data, figures, and tables in the book, have been updated through February 2020, with the latest marketing and business intelligence available from eMarketer, Pew Research Center, Forrester Research, comScore, Gartner Research, and other industry and government sources.

In addition, we have added new, expanded, and/or updated material throughout the text on a number of e-commerce topics that have appeared in the headlines during 2019 and early 2020, including the following:

- The latest developments with respect to on-demand service companies such as Uber; updates on the challenges that mobile apps pose to the Web's dominance of the Internet ecosphere, including progressive web apps (PWAs), Rocket Internet's results as an e-commerce incubator and Puma's efforts to become an omni-channel retailer (Chapter 1)
- Internet access in rural India; 5G and new Wi-Fi standards; new Internet access technologies such as drones, balloons, and white space; developments in IoT, wearable computing devices such as the Apple Watch; virtual and augmented reality (including their use by IKEA and Natuzzi Italia), artificial intelligence, and intelligent assistants (Chapter 2)
- Analysis of Scratch's success as a start-up subscription service; France's OVHcloud; alternative web development methodologies such as agile development, DevOps, component-based development, and the use of web services; DHTML, AngularJS, D3; jQuery; increasing focus on online accessibility; mobile-first and responsive design, including Klook Travel; update on Dick's Sporting Goods' effort to reclaim its e-commerce infrastructure (Chapter 3)
- New cyberwarfare threats; new security threats (such as the growth of cryptojacking, malvertising, ransomware (including WannaCry), business e-mail compromise (BEC) and W-2 phishing, data breaches at Marriott; IoT botnet DDoS attacks, newly discovered software vulnerabilities, and smartphone security issues; biometric security techniques such as Apple's Face ID; FTC enforcement actions with respect to data security; mobile wallets; Bitcoin and blockchain technology; P2P (Venmo, Facebook Messenger, Zelle); and mobile payment systems including Alipay and WeChat Pay (Chapter 4)
- How Canva leveraged a successful business model; MADE.COM's crowdsourcing-based business model; use of initial coin offerings (ICOs) by startups; new issues surrounding crowdfunding; connected cars as a new platform for e-commerce; how Dollar Shave Club used a viral video and subscription-based business model to go from small startup to being acquired for $1 billion in just five years (Chapter 5)
- Updates on InMobi's mobile advertising platform; Google search engine algorithm updates; new IAB guidelines, ad fraud, and viewability issues; the continuing rise in usage of ad blocking software; industry and FTC guidelines on cross-device tracking; Apple's Intelligent Tracking Prevention (ITP); issues with programmatic advertising (Chapter 6)

- Update on the use of Pinterest as a social marketing and social e-commerce platform; new social marketing and social e-commerce tools from Facebook, Twitter, Pinterest, Instagram, LinkedIn, and Snapchat; Accuracast (social media marketing analysis); the issues and opportunities presented by social marketing on TikTok; use of 3D mobile marketing; proximity marketing; BLE (Chapter 7)

- Update on the right to be forgotten, privacy issues associated with digital assistant devices, facial recognition, and IoT technology; issues with persistent location tracking; FTC privacy enforcement actions; new EU General Data Protection Regulation (GDPR); Apple/U.S. government iPhone privacy fight; new technological privacy protections; privacy as a business; updates on DMCA litigation; the new EU Copyright Directive; the new EU Trade Secrets Directive; online sales tax developments in the United States and Europe; net neutrality developments; online fantasy sports gambling issues; Big Tech and antitrust issues in the United States and Europe (Chapter 8)

- Update on Spotify and Deezer; industry structure convergence continues; updates on newspaper Digital First business models; native digital news sites such as France's Brut; update on e-books; streaming music and television services; the impact of Pokemon GO and emergence of e-sports (Chapter 9)

- Update on LinkedIn; use of algorithms by social networks, such as Facebook; the dark side of social networks; Facebook fake news controversy; Yahoo Japan's acquisition of Line; update on eBay (Chapter 11)

- Updates on Souq.com, Amazon, and OpenTable; ASOS's use of big date; digital native verticals (manufacturer-direct); fintech startups; the impact of phony online reviews; updates on on-demand service companies, including Bawiq and Careem in the Middle East (Chapter 10)

- Update on Alibaba; the rise of B2B sell-side marketplaces; supply chain visibility; blockchain in the food supply chain; cloud-based B2B; mobile B2B; B2B marketing; update on Walmart supply chain issues (Chapter 12)

FEATURES AND COVERAGE

Strong Conceptual Foundation: Business, Technology, Society The book emphasizes the three major driving forces that permeate all aspects of e-commerce: business development and strategy, technological innovations, and social and legal issues and impacts. In each chapter, we explore how these forces relate to the chapter's main topic, which provides students with a strong and coherent conceptual framework for understanding e-commerce.

Currency Important new developments happen almost every day in e-commerce and the Internet. We try to capture as many of these important new developments as possible in each annual edition. You will not find a more current book for 2020–2021. Many other texts are already six months to a year out of date before they even reach the printer. This text, in contrast, reflects extensive research through February 2020.

Real-World Business Firm Focus and Cases From Akamai Technologies to Google, Microsoft, Apple, and Amazon; to Facebook, Twitter, and Snapchat; to Netflix, YouTube, and Pinterest, this book contains hundreds of real-company examples and over 60 more-extensive cases that place coverage in the context of actual e-commerce businesses. You'll find these examples in each chapter, as well as in special features such as chapter-opening, chapter-closing, and "Insight on" cases. The book takes a realistic look at the world of e-commerce, describing what's working and what isn't, rather than presenting a rose-colored or purely "academic" viewpoint. We strive to maintain a critical perspective on e-commerce and avoid industry hyperbole.

In-depth Coverage of Marketing and Advertising The text includes two chapters on marketing and advertising, both traditional online marketing and social, mobile, and local marketing. Marketing concepts, including market segmentation, personalization, clickstream analysis, bundling of digital goods, long-tail marketing, and dynamic pricing, are used throughout the text.

In-depth Coverage of B2B E-commerce We devote an entire chapter to an examination of B2B e-commerce. In writing this chapter, we developed a unique and easily understood classification schema to help students understand this complex arena of e-commerce. This chapter covers e-distributors, e-procurement companies, exchanges, and industry consortia, as well as the development of private industrial networks and collaborative commerce.

Current and Future Technology Coverage Internet and related information technologies continue to change rapidly. The most important changes for e-commerce include dramatic price reductions in e-commerce infrastructure (making it much less expensive to develop a sophisticated e-commerce presence), the explosive growth in the mobile platform, and expansion in the development of social technologies, which are the foundation of online social networks. While we thoroughly discuss the current Internet environment, we devote considerable attention to describing emerging technologies and applications such as the Internet of Things, blockchain, augmented and virtual reality, and 5G, among others.

Up-to-Date Coverage of the Research Literature This text is well grounded in the e-commerce research literature. We have sought to include, where appropriate, references to and analysis of the latest e-commerce research findings, as well as many classic articles, in all of our chapters. We have drawn especially on the disciplines of economics, marketing, and information systems and technologies, as well as law journals and broader social science research journals including sociology and psychology. Figures and tables sourced to "authors' estimates" reflect analysis of data from the U.S. Department of Commerce, estimates from various research firms, historical trends, revenues of major online retailers, consumer online buying trends, and economic conditions.

Special Attention to the Social and Legal Aspects of E-commerce We have paid special attention throughout the book to the social and legal context of e-commerce. Chapter

8 is devoted to a thorough exploration of ethical dimensions of e-commerce, including information privacy, intellectual property, governance, and protecting public welfare on the Internet.

Writing That's Fun to Read Unlike some textbooks, we've been told by many students that this book is actually fun to read and easy to understand. This is not a book written by committee—you won't find a dozen different people listed as authors, co-authors, and contributors on the title page. We have a consistent voice and perspective that carries through the entire text and we believe the book is the better for it.

OVERVIEW OF THE BOOK

The book begins with an introduction to the major themes of the book. Chapter 1 defines e-commerce, distinguishes between e-commerce and e-business, and defines the different types of e-commerce. Chapter 2 traces the historical development of the Internet and thoroughly describes how the Internet, Web, and mobile platform work. Chapter 3 focuses on the steps managers need to follow in order to build an e-commerce presence. This chapter covers the process that should be followed in building an e-commerce presence; the major decisions regarding outsourcing site development and/or hosting; how to choose software, hardware, and other tools that can improve website performance; and issues involved in developing a mobile website and mobile applications. Chapter 4 focuses on e-commerce security and payments, building on the e-commerce infrastructure discussion of the previous chapter by describing the ways security can be provided over the Internet. This chapter defines digital information security, describes the major threats to security, and then discusses both the technology and policy solutions available to business managers seeking to secure their firm's sites. This chapter concludes with a section on e-commerce payment systems. We identify the various types of online payment systems (credit cards, stored value payment systems such as PayPal, digital wallets, and others), the development of mobile and social payment systems such as Alipay, WeChat Pay, Apple Pay, Venmo, Zelle, and Facebook Messenger, as well as a section on cryptocurrencies and blockchain, the technology underlying them.

The next four chapters focus directly on the business concepts and social-legal issues that surround the development of e-commerce. Chapter 5 introduces and defines the concepts of business model and revenue model, describes the major e-commercebusiness and revenue models for both B2C and B2B firms, and introduces the basic business concepts required throughout the text for understanding e-commerce firms including industry structure, value chains, and firm strategy. Chapter 6 focuses on e-commerce consumer behavior, the Internet audience, and introduces the student to the basics of online marketing and branding, including traditional online marketing technologies and marketing strategies. Topics include the website as a marketing platform, search engine marketing and advertising, display ad marketing, e-mail campaigns, affiliate and lead generation marketing programs, multichannel marketing, and various customer retention strategies such as personalization (including interest-based advertising, also known as behavioral targeting) and customer service tools. The chapter also covers other marketing strategies such as pricing and long-tail marketing. Internet marketing technologies (web transaction logs, tracking files, data mining, and big data) and marketing automation and CRM systems are also explored. The chapter concludes with a section on understanding the costs and benefits of various types of online marketing, including a section on marketing analytics software. Chapter 7 is devoted to an in-depth analysis of social, mobile, and local marketing. Topics include Facebook, Twitter, Pinterest, and other social media marketing platforms such as Instagram, Snapchat, LinkedIn, and TikTok, the evolution of mobile marketing, and the growing use of geo-aware technologies to support proximity marketing. Chapter 8 provides a thorough introduction to the social and legal environment of e-commerce. Here, you will find a description of the ethical and legal dimensions of e-commerce, including a thorough discussion of the latest developments in personal information privacy, intellectual property, Internet governance, questions surrounding Big Tech and compeittion, jurisdiction, and public health and welfare issues such as pornography, gambling, and health information.

The final four chapters focus on real-world e-commerce experiences in retail and services, online media, auctions, portals, and social networks, and business-to-business e-commerce. These chapters take a sector approach rather than the conceptual approach used in the earlier chapters. E-commerce is different in each of these sectors. Chapter 9 explores the world of online content and digital media and examines the enormous changes in online publishing and entertainment industries that have occurred over the last two years, including streaming movies, e-books, and online newspapers and magazines. Chapter 10 explores the online world of social networks, auctions, and portals. Chapter 11 takes a close look at the experience of firms in the retail marketplace for both goods and services, as well as on-demand service companies such as Uber and Airbnb. Chapter 11 also includes an "E-commerce in Action" case that provides a detailed analysis of the business strategies and financial operating results of Amazon, which can be used as a model to analyze other e-commerce firms. Chapter 12 concentrates on the world of B2B e-commerce, describing both Net marketplaces and the less-heralded, but very large arena of private industrial networks and the movement toward collaborative commerce.

PEDAGOGY AND CHAPTER OUTLINE

The book's pedagogy emphasizes student cognitive awareness and the ability to analyze, synthesize, and evaluate e-commerce businesses. While there is a strong data and conceptual foundation to the book, we seek to engage student interest with lively writing about e-commerce businesses and the transformation of business models at traditional firms.

Each chapter contains a number of elements designed to make learning easy as well as interesting.

Learning Objectives A list of learning objectives that highlights the key concepts in the chapter guides student study.

Chapter-Opening Cases Each chapter opens with a story about a leading e-commerce company that relates the key objectives of the chapter to a real-life e-commerce business venture.

Everything on Demand:
The "Uberization" of E-commerce

If you were asked to pick iconic examples of e-commerce in the two decades since it began in 1995, it is likely that companies such as eBay, Google, Apple, and Facebook would be high on your list. But today, a new breed of e-commerce company is muscling its way to the forefront. Uber and other firms with similar business models, such as Lyft (a ride service similar to Uber's), Airbnb (rooms for rent), Instacart (grocery shopping), Trusk (movers), Deliveroo (grocery shopping), and ZipJet (laundry service), are the pioneers of an on-demand service e-commerce business model that is sweeping up billions of investment dollars and disrupting major industries, from transportation to hotels, real estate, house cleaning, maintenance, and grocery shopping.

Uber is perhaps the most well-known, as well as the most controversial, company that uses the on-demand service model. Uber offers a variety of different services. The two most common are UberX, which uses compact sedans and is the least expensive, and UberBlack, which provides higher-priced town car service. UberPool is a ride-sharing service that allows users to share a ride with another person who happens to be going to the same place. Uber is also attempting to leverage its business model by expanding into several related areas, with UberRush, a same-day delivery service; UberCargo, a trucking service; and UberEats, a food delivery service.

Uber, headquartered in San Francisco, was founded in 2009 by Travis Kalanick and Garrett Camp, and has grown explosively since then to over 600 cities in 65 countries. Uber currently has over 3 million drivers worldwide and 75 million riders who made 4 billion trips in 2017. In 2017, riders spent $37 billion on the Uber platform, generating $7.5 billion in revenue for Uber, but it still lost $4.5 billion, with losses in developing markets swallowing up profits being generated in North America, Europe, and elsewhere. That trend has continued in 2018, with a reported loss of $2 billion through the first three quarters of 2018. Uber's strategy has been to expand as fast as possible while foregoing short-term profits in the hope of long-term returns. As of November 2018, Uber had raised over $24 billion from venture capital investors. Uber is currently valued at around $72 billion, more than all of its

© Lenscap/Alamy

Preface

"Insight on" Cases Each chapter contains three real-world cases illustrating the themes of technology, business, and society. These cases take an in-depth look at relevant topics to help describe and analyze the full breadth of the field of e-commerce. The cases probe such issues as the ability of governments to regulate Internet content, how to design websites for accessibility, the challenges faced by luxury marketers in online marketing, and smartphone security.

Margin Glossary Throughout the text, key terms and their definitions appear in the text margin where they are first introduced.

Real-Company Examples Drawn from actual e-commerce ventures, well over 100 pertinent examples are used throughout the text to illustrate concepts.

Chapter-Closing Case Studies Each chapter concludes with a robust case study based on a real-world organization. These cases help students synthesize chapter concepts and apply this knowledge to concrete problems and scenarios such as Dick's Sportings Goods efforts to take control of its e-commerce operations, ExchangeHunterJumper's efforts to build a brand, and the evolution of eBay.

Chapter-Ending Pedagogy Each chapter contains extensive end-of-chapter materials designed to reinforce the learning objectives of the chapter.

Key Concepts Keyed to the learning objectives, Key Concepts present the key points of the chapter to aid student study.

Review Questions Thought-provoking questions prompt students to demonstrate their comprehension and apply chapter concepts to management problem solving.

Projects At the end of each chapter are a number of projects that encourage students to apply chapter concepts and to use higher-level evaluation skills. Many make use of the Internet and require students to present their findings in an oral or electronic presentation or written report. For instance, students are asked to evaluate publicly available information about a company's financials at the SEC website, assess payment system options for companies across international boundaries, or search for the top 10 cookies on their own computer and the sites they are from.

Web Resources Web resources that can extend students' knowledge of each chapter with projects, exercises, and additional content are available at E-commerce2020global.com. The website contains the following content provided by the authors:
- Additional projects, exercises, and tutorials
- Information on how to build a business plan and revenue models
- Essays on careers in e-commerce

INSTRUCTOR RESOURCES

At the Instructor Resource Center, www.pearsonglobaleditions.com, instructors can easily register to gain access to a variety of instructor resources available with this text in downloadable format. If assistance is needed, our dedicated technical support team is ready to help with the media supplements that accompany this text. Visit support.pearson.com/getsupport for answers to frequently asked questions and toll-free user support phone numbers.

The following supplements are available with this text:

- **Instructor's Resource Manual**
- **Test Bank**
- **TestGen® Computerized Test Bank**
- **PowerPoint Presentation**
- **Image Library**
- **Video Cases and Learning Tracks.** The authors have created a collection of video case studies that integrate short videos, supporting case study material, and case study questions. Video cases can be used in class to promote discussion or as written assignments. There are 29 video cases for the 16th edition, all with updated supporting case study material. There is also a collection of Learning Tracks: additional essays, created by the authors, that provide instructors and students with more in-depth content on selected topics in e-commerce.

ACKNOWLEDGMENTS

Pearson Education has sought the advice of many excellent reviewers, all of whom have strongly influenced the organization and substance of this book. The following individuals provided extremely useful evaluations of this and previous editions of the text:

Deniz Aksen, Koç University (Istanbul)
Carrie Andersen, Madison Area Technical College
Subhajyoti Bandyopadhyay, University of Florida
Christine Barnes, Lakeland Community College
Reneta Barneva, SUNY Fredonia
Rathin Basu, Ferrum College
Dr. Shirley A. Becker, Northern Arizona University
Prasad Bingi, Indiana-Purdue University, Fort Wayne
Joanna Broder, Pima Community College
Lisa Bryan, Southeastern Community College
James Buchan, College of the Ozarks
Ashley Bush, Florida State University
Cliff Butler, North Seattle Community College
Carl Case, St. Bonaventure University
Teuta Cata, Northern Kentucky University
Adnan Chawdhry, California University of Pennsylvania
Mark Choman, Luzerne City Community College
Andrew Ciganek, Jacksonville State University
Daniel Connolly, University of Denver
Tom Critzer, Miami University
Dr. Robin R. Davis, Claflin University
Dursan Delen, Oklahoma State University
Abhijit Deshmukh, University of Massachusetts
Brian L. Dos Santos, University of Louisville
Robert Drevs, University of Notre Dame
Akram El-Tannir, Hariri Canadian University, Lebanon
Kimberly Furumo, University of Hawaii at Hilo
John H. Gerdes, University of California, Riverside
Gurram Gopal, Illinois Institute of Technology
Philip Gordon, University of California at Berkeley
Allan Greenberg, Brooklyn College
Bin Gu, University of Texas at Austin
Norman Hahn, Thomas Nelson Community College
Peter Haried, University of Wisconsin-La Crosse
Sherri Harms, University of Nebraska at Kearney
Sharon Heckel, St. Charles Community College
David Hite, Virginia Intermont College
Gus Jabbour, George Mason University
Thaddeus Janicki, University of Mount Olive
Kevin Jetton, Texas State University, San Marcos
Jim Keogh, Saint Peter's University
Ellen Kraft, Georgian Court University
Gillican Lee, Lander University
Zoonky Lee, University of Nebraska, Lincoln
Andre Lemaylleux, Boston University, Brussels
Haim Levkowitz, University of Massachusetts, Lowell
Yair Levy, Nova Southeastern University
Richard Lucic, Duke University
Brenda Maynard, University of Pikeville

Vincent McCord, Foothill College
John Mendonca, Purdue University
John Miko, Saint Francis University
Dr. Abdulrahman Mirza, DePaul University
Natalie Nazarenko, SUNY - Fredonia
Barbara Ozog, Benedictine University
Kent Palmer, MacMurray College
Karen Palumbo, University of St. Francis
James Pauer, Lorain County Community College
Wayne Pauli, Dakota State University
Sam Perez, Mesa Community College
Jamie Pinchot, Thiel College
Selwyn Piramuthu, University of Florida
Kai Pommerenke, University of California at Santa Cruz
Barry Quinn, University of Ulster, Northern Ireland
Mahesh (Michael) Raisinghani, TWU School of Management, Executive MBA Program
Michelle Ramim, Nova Southeastern University
Jay Rhee, San Jose State University
Jorge Romero, Towson University
John Sagi, Anne Arundel Community College
Carl Saxby, University of Southern Indiana
Patricia Sendall, Merrimack College
Dr. Carlos Serrao, ISCTE/DCTI, Portugal
Neerja Sethi, Nanyang Business School, Singapore
Amber Settle, DePaul CTI
Vivek Shah, Texas State University-San Marcos
Wei Shi, Santa Clara University
Seung Jae Shin, Mississippi State University

Sumit Sircar, University of Texas at Arlington
Toni Somers, Wayne State University Mike Ilitch School of Business
Hongjun Song, University of Memphis
Pamela Specht, University of Nebraska at Omaha
Esther Swilley, Kansas State University
Tony Townsend, Iowa State University
Bill Troy, University of New Hampshire
Susan VandeVen, Southern Polytechnic State University
Hiep Van Dong, Madison Area Technical College
Michael Van Hilst, Nova Southeastern University
Mary Vitrano, Palm Beach Community College
Andrea Wachter, Point Park University
Nitin Walia, Ashland University
Catherine Wallace, Massey University, New Zealand
Biao Wang, Boston University
Haibo Wang, Texas A&M International University
Harry Washington, Lincoln University
Irene Wheeler, CVCC
Rolf Wigand, University of Arkansas at Little Rock
Erin Wilkinson, Johnson & Wales University
Alice Wilson, Cedar Crest College
Dezhi Wu, Southern Utah University
Gene Yelle, SUNY Institute of Technology
Kaimei Zheng, Isenberg School of Management, University of Massachusetts, Amherst
David Zolzer, Northwestern State University

GLOBAL EDITION ACKNOWLEDGMENTS

Pearson would like to thank the following people for their work on the Global Edition:

Contributors
June Clarke, Sheffield Hallam University
Fiona Ellis-Chadwick, Loughborough University
Graham Jones, The University of Buckingham

Reviewers
Eddren Law Yi Feng, Universiti Tenaga Nasional
George Mickhail, Bryant University
Krish Saha, Birmingham City University
Petter Terenius, Lancaster University and University of Borås
Tuan Yu, University of Kent

We would like to thank eMarketer, Inc. and David Iankelevich for their permission to include data and figures from their research reports in our text. eMarketer is one of the leading independent sources for statistics, trend data, and original analysis covering many topics related to the Internet, e-business, and emerging technologies. eMarketer aggregates e-business data from multiple sources worldwide.

In addition, we would like to thank all those who have worked so hard to make sure this book is the very best it can be, including Steven Jackson, Managing Editor, Global Editions, and Daniel Luiz, Senior Project Editor, Global Editions, for all their help and support in creating this Global Edition. Very special thanks to Megan Miller and Will Anderson at Azimuth Interactive, Inc., for all their hard work on the production of, and supplements for, this book.

Finally, last but not least, we would like to thank our family and friends, without whose support this book would not have been possible.

Kenneth C. Laudon
Carol Guercio Traver

Brief Contents

1	INTRODUCTION TO E-COMMERCE	38
2	E-COMMERCE INFRASTRUCTURE	90
3	BUILDING AN E-COMMERCE PRESENCE	166
4	E-COMMERCE SECURITY AND PAYMENT SYSTEMS	232
5	E-COMMERCE BUSINESS STRATEGIES	322
6	E-COMMERCE MARKETING AND ADVERTISING	378
7	SOCIAL, MOBILE, AND LOCAL MARKETING	464
8	ETHICS, LAW, AND E-COMMERCE	536
9	ONLINE MEDIA	632
10	ONLINE COMMUNITIES	700
11	E-COMMERCE RETAIL AND SERVICES	744
12	B2B E-COMMERCE	810

Contents

1 INTRODUCTION TO E-COMMERCE 38

Learning Objectives   38

Everything on Demand: The "Uberization" of E-commerce   39

1.1 The First Thirty Seconds: Why You Should Study E-commerce   44

1.2 Introduction to E-commerce   44

What Is E-commerce?   45
The Difference Between E-commerce and E-business   45
Technological Building Blocks Underlying E-commerce: the Internet, Web, and Mobile Platform   46
Major Trends in E-commerce   48

Insight on Technology: Will Apps Make the Web Irrelevant?   49

1.3 Unique Features of E-commerce Technology   52

Ubiquity   54
Global Reach   54
Universal Standards   54
Richness   55
Interactivity   55
Information Density   56
Personalization and Customization   56
Social Technology: User-Generated Content and Social Networks   57

1.4 Types of E-commerce   58

Business-to-Consumer (B2C) E-commerce   58
Business-to-Business (B2B) E-commerce   59
Consumer-to-Consumer (C2C) E-commerce   60
Mobile E-commerce (M-commerce)   60
Social E-commerce   61
Local E-commerce   62

1.5 E-commerce: A Brief History   63

E-commerce 1995–2000: Invention   64
E-commerce 2001–2006: Consolidation   67

E-commerce 2007–Present: Reinvention   67
Assessing E-commerce: Successes, Surprises, and Failures   68
Insight on Business: Rocket Internet   69

1.6   *Understanding E-commerce: Organizing Themes*   73
Technology: Infrastructure   73
Business: Basic Concepts   75
Society: Taming the Juggernaut   75
Insight on Society: Facebook and the Age of Privacy   76

1.7   *Academic Disciplines Concerned with E-commerce*   78
Technical Approaches   78
Behavioral Approaches   78

1.8   *Careers in E-commerce*   79
The Company   79
Position: Category Specialist in the e-Commerce Retail Program   79
Qualifications/Skills   80
Preparing for the Interview   80
Possible First Interview Questions   80

1.9   *Case Study: Puma Goes Omni*   82

1.10   *Review*   85
Key Concepts   85
Questions   87
Projects   88
References   88

2   E-COMMERCE INFRASTRUCTURE   90

Learning Objectives   90

Tech Titans Target a Prize: Bringing Internet Access to Rural India   91

2.1   *The Internet: Technology Background*   94
The Evolution of the Internet: 1961—The Present   96
The Internet: Key Technology Concepts   100
  Packet Switching   100
  Transmission Control Protocol/Internet Protocol (TCP/IP)   102
  IP Addresses   102
  Domain Names, DNS, and URLs   104
  Client/Server Computing   104
The Mobile Platform   106

The Internet "Cloud Computing" Model: Hardware and Software as a Service   107
Other Internet Protocols and Utility Programs   111

2.2 Internet Infrastructure and Access   113

The Internet Backbone   115
Internet Exchange Points   117
Tier 3 Internet Service Providers   117
Campus/Corporate Area Networks   120
Mobile Internet Access   121
    Telephone-based versus Computer Network-based Wireless Internet Access   121
Other Innovative Internet Access Technologies: Drones, Balloons, and White Space   124
The Internet of Things   125
Insight on Business:** The Apple Watch: Bringing the Internet of Things to Your Wrist   **127
Who Governs the Internet?   129
Insight on Society:** Government Regulation and Surveillance of the Internet   **131

2.3 The Web   134

Hypertext   135
Markup Languages   137
    HyperText Markup Language (HTML)   137
    eXtensible Markup Language (XML)   139
Web Servers and Clients   140
Web Browsers   142

2.4 The Internet and the Web: Features and Services   142

Communication Tools   142
    E-mail   143
    Messaging Applications   143
    Online Message Boards   143
    Internet Telephony   144
    Video Conferencing, Video Chatting, and Telepresence   144
Search Engines   145
Downloadable and Streaming Media   146
Web 2.0 Applications and Services   149
    Online Social Networks   149
    Blogs   149
    Wikis   149
Virtual Reality and Augmented Reality   150
Insight on Technology:** Leaping into the Future with AR and VR   **151
Intelligent Digital Assistants   153

2.5 Mobile Apps: The Next Big Thing Is Here   153

Platforms for Mobile Application Development   154
App Marketplaces   154

2.6 Careers in E-commerce   155
   The Company   155
   Position: E-commerce Specialist   155
   Qualifications/Skills   156
   Preparing for the Interview   156
   Possible First Interview Questions   156

2.7 Case Study: Akamai Technologies: Attempting to Keep Supply Ahead of Demand   158

2.8 Review   161
   Key Concepts   161
   Questions   162
   Projects   163
   References   163

3 BUILDING AN E-COMMERCE PRESENCE   166

Learning Objectives   166

Scratch Builds an E-commerce Presence from "Scratch"   167

3.1 Imagine Your E-commerce Presence   170
   What's the Idea? (The Visioning Process)   170
   Where's the Money: Business and Revenue Model   170
   Who and Where Is the Target Audience?   171
   What Is the Ballpark? Characterize the Marketplace   171
   Where's the Content Coming From?   172
   Know Yourself: Conduct a SWOT Analysis   173
   Develop an E-commerce Presence Map   174
   Develop a Timeline: Milestones   175
   How Much Will This Cost?   175

3.2 Building an E-commerce Presence: A Systematic Approach   176
   The Systems Development Life Cycle   178
      Systems Analysis/Planning: Identify Business Objectives, System Functionality, and Information Requirements   179
      System Design: Hardware and Software Platforms   180
      Building the System: In-house Versus Outsourcing   180
   Insight on Business: OVH Takes E-commerce to the Clouds   185
      Testing the System   187
      Implementation, Maintenance, and Optimization   188
   Alternative Web Development Methodologies   190

3.3 Choosing Software   191
   Simple Versus Multi-Tiered WebSite Architecture   191

Web Server Software   193
    Site Management Tools   194
    Dynamic Page Generation Tools   194
Application Servers   196
E-commerce Merchant Server Software Functionality   197
    Online Catalog   197
    Shopping Cart   197
    Credit Card Processing   197
Merchant Server Software Packages (E-commerce Software Platforms)   197
    Choosing an E-commerce Software Platform   199

3.4 Choosing Hardware   200
Right-sizing Your Hardware Platform: The Demand Side   200
Right-sizing Your Hardware Platform: The Supply Side   201

3.5 Other E-commerce Site Tools   204
WebSite Design: Basic Business Considerations   205
Tools for Search Engine Optimization   205
Tools for Interactivity and Active Content   206
    Common Gateway Interface (CGI)   207
    Active Server Pages (ASP) and ASP.NET   207
    Java, Java Server Pages (JSP), and JavaScript   208
    ActiveX and VBScript   209
    ColdFusion   209
    PHP, Ruby on Rails (RoR), and Django   209
    Other Design Elements   210
Personalization Tools   211
The Information Policy Set   211

Insight on Society: Designing for Accessibility   **212**

3.6 Developing a Mobile Website and Building Mobile Applications   214
Planning and Building a Mobile Presence   215
Mobile Presence: Design Considerations   216
Cross-platform Mobile App Development Tools   217
Mobile Presence: Performance and Cost Considerations   218

3.7 Careers in E-commerce   219
The Company   219
Position: UX Designer   219

Insight on Technology: Klook Sets Its Sights on New Vistas   **220**

Qualifications/Skills   222
Preparing for the Interview   222
Possible First Interview Questions   223

3.8 Case Study: Dick's Sporting Goods: Taking Control of Its E-commerce Operations   225

3.9 *Review* 228
　　Key Concepts　228
　　Questions　230
　　Projects　231
　　References　231

4　E-COMMERCE SECURITY AND PAYMENT SYSTEMS　232

　　Learning Objectives　232

　　The Rise of the Global Cyberattack: WannaCry and NotPetya　*233*

4.1 *The E-commerce Security Environment*　236
　　The Scope of the Problem　237
　　　The Underground Economy Marketplace: The Value of Stolen Information　238
　　What Is Good E-commerce Security?　240
　　Dimensions of E-commerce Security　241
　　The Tension Between Security and Other Values　242
　　　Security versus Ease of Use　242
　　　Public Safety and the Criminal Uses of the Internet　243

4.2 *Security Threats in the E-commerce Environment*　244
　　Malicious Code　244
　　Potentially Unwanted Programs (PUPs)　248
　　Phishing　250
　　Hacking, Cybervandalism, and Hacktivism　252
　　Data Breaches　253

　　Insight on Society: The Marriott Data Breach　*254*
　　Credit Card Fraud/Theft　256
　　Identity Fraud　257
　　Spoofing, Pharming, and Spam (Junk) Websites　257
　　Sniffing and Man-in-the-Middle Attacks　258
　　Denial of Service (DOS) and Distributed Denial of Service (DDOS) Attacks　259
　　Insider Attacks　260
　　Poorly Designed Software　260
　　Social Network Security Issues　261
　　Mobile Platform Security Issues　262
　　Cloud Security Issues　263

　　Insight on Technology: Think Your Smartphone Is Secure?　*264*
　　Internet of Things Security Issues　266

4.3 *Technology Solutions*　267
　　Protecting Internet Communications　267
　　Encryption　268

Symmetric Key Cryptography   269
Public Key Cryptography   270
Public Key Cryptography Using Digital Signatures and Hash Digests   270
Digital Envelopes   273
Digital Certificates and Public Key Infrastructure (PKI)   274
Limitations of PKI   276
Securing Channels of Communication   277
Secure Sockets Layer (SSL) and Transport Layer Security (TLS)   277
Virtual Private Networks (VPNs)   278
Wireless (Wi-Fi) Networks   279
Protecting Networks   279
Firewalls   279
Proxy Servers   280
Intrusion Detection and Prevention Systems   281
Protecting Servers and Clients   281
Operating System Security Enhancements   281
Anti-Virus Software   282

4.4 Management Policies, Business Procedures, and Public Laws   282
A Security Plan: Management Policies   282
Insight on Business: Are Biometrics the Solution for E-commerce Security?   285
The Role of Laws and Public Policy   287
Private and Private-Public Cooperation Efforts   289
Government Policies and Controls on Encryption   289

4.5 E-commerce Payment Systems   290
Online Credit Card Transactions   292
Credit Card E-commerce Enablers   293
PCI-DSS Compliance   294
Limitations of Online Credit Card Payment Systems   294
Alternative Online Payment Systems   295
Mobile Payment Systems: Your Smartphone Wallet   296
Blockchain and Cryptocurrencies   297

4.6 Electronic Billing Presentment and Payment   302
Market Size and Growth   303
EBPP Business Models   303

4.7 Careers in E-commerce   305
The Company   305
The Position: Cybersecurity Threat Management Team Trainee   305
Qualifications/Skills   306
Preparing for the Interview   306
Possible First Interview Questions   307

4.8   Case Study: Alipay and WeChat Pay Lead in Mobile Payments   309

4.9   Review   314
    Key Concepts   314
    Questions   317
    Projects   317
    References   318

5 E-COMMERCE BUSINESS STRATEGIES   322

    Learning Objectives   322

    Australia's Canva Grows from Startup to Super Unicorn   *323*

5.1   E-commerce Business Models   326
    Introduction   326
    Eight Key Elements of a Business Model   326
        Value Proposition   326
        Revenue Model   328
        Market Opportunity   329
    Insight on Society: MADE.COM: Furniture for the Crowd   *330*
        Competitive Environment   332
        Competitive Advantage   333
        Market Strategy   334
        Organizational Development   335
        Management Team   335
    Raising Capital   336
    Categorizing E-commerce Business Models: Some Difficulties   338
    Insight on Business: Crowdfunding Takes Off   *339*

5.2   Major Business-to-Consumer (B2C) Business Models   341
    E-tailer   341
    Community Provider   344
    Content Provider   345
    Insight on Technology: Connected Cars and the Future of E-commerce   *346*
    Portal   348
    Transaction Broker   348
    Market Creator   349
    Service Provider   350

5.3   Major Business-to-Business (B2B) Business Models   351
    E-distributor   351

E-procurement 352
Exchanges 353
Industry Consortia 353
Private Industrial Networks 354

5.4 How E-commerce Changes Business: Strategy, Structure, and Process 354
Industry Structure 355
Industry Value Chains 358
Firm Value Chains 359
Firm Value Webs 360
Business Strategy 361
E-commerce Technology and Business Model Disruption 363

5.5 Careers in E-commerce 366
The Company 366
Position: Assistant Manager of E-business 366
Qualifications/Skills 367
Preparing for the Interview 367
Possible First Interview Questions 367

5.6 Case Study: Dollar Shave Club: From Viral Video to $1 Billion in Just Five Years 370

5.7 Review 374
Key Concepts 374
Questions 375
Projects 376
References 376

6 E-COMMERCE MARKETING AND ADVERTISING 378

Learning Objectives 378

InMobi's Global Mobile Ad Network 379

6.1 Consumers Online: The Internet Audience and Consumer Behavior 382
Internet Traffic Patterns: The Online Consumer Profile 382
- Intensity and Scope of Usage 383
- Demographics and Access 383
- Type of Internet Connection: Broadband and Mobile Impacts 384
- Community Effects: Social Contagion in Social Networks 385

Consumer Behavior Models 386
The Online Purchasing Decision 387
Shoppers: Browsers and Buyers 389
What Consumers Shop for and Buy Online 390

Intentional Acts: How Shoppers Find Vendors Online   391
Why Some People Don't Shop Online   391
Trust, Utility, and Opportunism in Online Markets   391

6.2 Digital Commerce Marketing and Advertising Strategies and Tools   392

Strategic Issues and Questions   392
The Website as a Marketing Platform: Establishing the Customer Relationship   394
Traditional Online Marketing and Advertising Tools   395
    Search Engine Marketing and Advertising   397
    Display Ad Marketing   401
    E-mail Marketing   407
    Affiliate Marketing   409
    Viral Marketing   410
    Lead Generation Marketing   410
Social, Mobile, and Local Marketing and Advertising   411
Multi-channel Marketing: Integrating Online and Offline Marketing   412
Other Online Marketing Strategies   413
    Customer Retention Strategies   413

Insight on Business: Are the Very Rich Different from You and Me?   *414*

    Pricing Strategies   420
    Long Tail Marketing   425

Insight on Technology: The Long Tail: Big Hits and Big Misses   *426*

6.3 Internet Marketing Technologies   428

The Revolution in Internet Marketing Technologies   428
Web Transaction Logs   428
Supplementing the Logs: Cookies and Other Tracking Files   430
Databases, Data Warehouses, Data Mining, and Big Data   432
    Databases   432

Insight on Society: Every Move You Take, Every Click You Make, We'll Be Tracking You   *433*

    Data Warehouses and Data Mining   435
    The Challenge of Big Data   436
Marketing Automation and Customer Relationship Management (CRM) Systems   437

6.4 Understanding the Costs and Benefits of Online Marketing Communications   440

Online Marketing Metrics: Lexicon   440
How Well Does Online Advertising Work?   443
The Costs of Online Advertising   445
Marketing Analytics: Software for Measuring Online Marketing Results   447

6.5 Careers in E-commerce   449

The Company   449
The Position: Digital Marketing Assistant   450
Qualifications/Skills   450
Preparing for the Interview   451

Possible First Interview Questions   451

6.6 *Case Study: Programmatic Advertising: Real-Time Marketing*   453

6.7 *Review*   458
Key Concepts   458
Questions   459
Projects   460
References   460

7 SOCIAL, MOBILE, AND LOCAL MARKETING   464

Learning Objectives   464

Pinterest Expands Around the Globe   465

7.1 *Introduction to Social, Mobile, and Local Marketing*   468
From Eyeballs to Conversations   468
From the Desktop to the Smartphone and Tablet   468
The Social, Mobile, Local Nexus   469

7.2 *Social Marketing*   470
Social Marketing Players   471
The Social Marketing Process   472
Facebook Marketing   473
   Basic Facebook Features   474
   Facebook Marketing Tools   474
   Starting a Facebook Marketing Campaign   478
   Measuring Facebook Marketing Results   480
Twitter Marketing   482

Insight on Technology: Optimizing Social Marketing with Accuracast   483

   Basic Twitter Features   485
   Twitter Marketing Tools   485
   Starting a Twitter Marketing Campaign   487
   Measuring Twitter Marketing Results   488
Pinterest Marketing   489
   Basic Pinterest Features   490
   Pinterest Marketing Tools   490
   Starting a Pinterest Marketing Campaign   493
   Measuring Pinterest Marketing Results   495
Marketing on Other Social Networks: Instagram, Snapchat, and Linkedin   496
The Downside of Social Marketing   490

7.3 *Mobile Marketing*   498
Overview: M-commerce Today   498

Insight on Society: Social Marketing on Tik Tok: Worth the Risk?   *499*
    How People Actually Use Mobile Devices   501
    In-App Experiences and In-App Ads   502
    How the Multi-Screen Environment Changes the Marketing Funnel   503
Basic Mobile Marketing Features   504
    The Technology: Basic Mobile Device Features   505
Mobile Marketing Tools: Ad Formats   507
Starting a Mobile Marketing Campaign   508
Insight on Business: Mobile Marketing Revs Up with 3D and Augmented Reality   *509*
Measuring Mobile Marketing Results   511

7.4 Local and Location-Based Mobile Marketing   **513**
The Growth of Local Marketing   513
The Growth of Location-Based (Local) Mobile Marketing   514
Location-Based Marketing Platforms   515
Location-Based Mobile Marketing: The Technologies   515
Why Is Location-based Mobile Marketing Attractive to Marketers?   517
Location-Based Marketing Tools   517
    A New Lexicon: Location-Based Digital Marketing Features   518
    Proximity Marketing with Beacons   519
Starting a Location-Based Marketing Campaign   520
Measuring Location-Based Marketing Results   521

7.5 Careers in E-commerce   **521**
The Company   522
The Position: Social Media Associate   522
Qualifications/Skills   522
Preparing for the Interview   523
Possible First Interview Questions   523

7.6 Case Study: ExchangeHunterJumper.com: Building an International Brand with Social Marketing   **525**

7.7 Review   **531**
Key Concepts   531
Questions   533
Projects   534
References   534

8   ETHICS, LAW, AND E-COMMERCE   536

Learning Objectives   536

The Right to Be Forgotten: Europe Leads on Internet Privacy   *537*

8.1 Understanding Ethical, Social, and Political Issues in E-commerce   **540**

    A Model for Organizing the Issues   541
    Basic Ethical Concepts: Responsibility, Accountability, and Liability   543
    Analyzing Ethical Dilemmas   545
    Candidate Ethical Principles   546

8.2 Privacy and Information Rights   **547**

    What Is Privacy?   547
    Privacy in the Public Sector: Privacy Rights of Citizens   548
    Privacy in the Private Sector: Privacy Rights of Consumers   549
        Information Collected by E-commerce Companies   553
        Key Issues in Online Privacy of Consumers   555
        Marketing: Profiling, Behavioral Targeting, and Retargeting   555
        Social Networks: Privacy and Self Revelation   558
        Mobile Devices: Privacy Issues   559
        Consumer Privacy Regulation and Enforcement: The FTC   560
        Consumer Privacy Regulation: The U.S. Federal Communications Commission (FCC)   564
        Privacy and Terms of Use Policies   564
        Privacy Protection in Europe: The General Data Protection Regulation (GDPR)   566
        Industry Self-Regulation   568
        Technological Solutions   569
    Privacy Protection as a Business   572
    Privacy Advocacy Groups   573
    Limitations on the Right to Privacy: Law Enforcement and Surveillance   574
    Insight on Technology: Apple: Defender of Privacy?   ***576***

8.3 Intellectual Property Rights   **579**

    Types of Intellectual Property Protection   580
    Copyright: the Problem of Perfect Copies and Encryption   581
        Fair Use Doctrine   582
        The Digital Millennium Copyright Act of 1998   583
        Copyright Protection in the European Union   587
    Patents: Business Methods and Processes   588
        E-commerce Patents   589
    Trademarks: Online Infringement and Dilution   590
        Trademarks and the Internet   593
        Cybersquatting and Brandjacking   593
        Cyberpiracy   595
        Metatagging   595
        Keywording   596
        Linking   597
        Framing   597
    Trade Secrets   598
    Challenge: Balancing the Protection of Property with Other Values   598

8.4 Governance   599
  Can the Internet Be Controlled?   599
  Taxation   600
  Net Neutrality   601
  Insight on Business: New Rules Extend EU Taxation of E-commerce   *602*
  Antitrust, Monopoly, and Market Competition in the Internet Era   605

8.5 Public Safety and Welfare   605
  Protecting Children   606
  Cigarettes, Gambling, and Drugs: Is the Web Really Borderless?   608
  Insight on Society: The Internet Drug Bazaar Operates Around the Globe   *609*

8.6 Careers in E-commerce   612
  The Company   612
  Position: E-commerce Privacy Research Associate   613
  Qualifications/Skills   613
  Preparing for the Interview   614
  Possible First Interview Questions   614

8.7 Case Study: Are Big Tech Firms Getting "Too Big"?   616

8.8 Review   623
  Key Concepts   623
  Questions   625
  Projects   626
  References   626

9 ONLINE MEDIA   632

  Learning Objectives   632
  Spotify and Deezer: European Streaming Music Services Spread Around the Globe   *633*

9.1 Online Content   636
  Content Audience: Where Are the Eyeballs?   636
  Content Market: Entertainment and Media Industry Revenues   639
  Insight on Society: Are Millennials Really All That Different?   *640*
  Online Content: Consumption, Revenue Models, and Revenue   643
  Digital Rights Management (DRM) and Walled Gardens   645
  Media Industry Structure   645
  Media Convergence: Technology, Content, and Industry Structure   646
    Technological Convergence   646
    Content Convergence   646
    Industry Structure Convergence   648

9.2 The Online Publishing Industry   649

    Online Newspapers   649

        From Print-centric to Digital First: The Evolution of Newspaper Online Business Models, 1995–2017   651

        Online Newspaper Industry: Strengths and Challenges   654

    Insight on Business: Brut: Native Digital News   *660*

    Magazines Rebound on the Digital Platform   662

    E-Books and Online Book Publishing   663

        Amazon and Apple: The New Digital Media Ecosystems   665

        E-book Business Models   666

        Interactive Books: Converging Technologies   667

9.3 The Online Entertainment Industry   667

    Home Entertainment: Television and Movies   671

    Insight on Technology: Hollywood and Big Tech: Let's Have Lunch   *677*

    Music   680

    Games   683

9.4 Careers in E-commerce   687

    The Company   687

    Position: Digital Audience Development Specialist   687

    Qualifications/Skills   688

    Preparing for the Interview   688

    Possible First Interview Questions   689

9.5 Case Study: Netflix: How Does This Movie End?   691

9.6 Review   695

    Key Concepts   695

    Questions   697

    Projects   697

    References   698

10   ONLINE COMMUNITIES   700

    Learning Objectives   700

    LinkedIn: A Tale of Two Countries   *701*

10.1 Social Networks and Online Communities   703

    What Is an Online Social Network?   704

    The Growth of Social Networks and Online Communities   705

    Turning Social Networks into Businesses   707

    Types of Social Networks and Their Business Models   709

    Insight on Society: The Dark Side of Social Networks   *710*

Social Network Technologies and Features 713

10.2 Online Auctions 715

Insight on Technology: Trapped Inside the Facebook Bubble? 716

Benefits and Costs of Auctions 720
    Benefits of Auctions 720
    Risks and Costs of Auctions 720
Auctions as an E-commerce Business Model 721
Types and Examples of Auctions 722
When to Use Auctions (and for What) in Business 723
Auction Prices: Are They the Lowest? 724
Consumer Trust in Auctions 725
When Auction Markets Fail: Fraud and Abuse in Auctions 725

10.3 E-commerce Portals 726

The Growth and Evolution of Portals 727
Types of Portals: General-Purpose and Vertical Market 728
Insight on Business: Yahoo Japan Merges with Line to Create Mega Portal 729
Portal Business Models 732

10.4 Careers in E-commerce 733

The Company 733
Position: Social Marketing Specialist 733
Qualifications/Skills 734
Preparing for the Interview 734
Possible First Interview Questions 734

10.5 Case Study: eBay Evolves 736

10.6 Review 740

Key Concepts 740
Questions 741
Projects 742
References 742

11   E-COMMERCE RETAIL AND SERVICES   744

Learning Objectives 744

Souq.com: The Amazon of the Middle East Gets Acquired by Amazon 745

11.1 The Online Retail Sector 748

The Retail Industry 749
Online Retailing 750
    E-commerce Retail: The Vision 751

The Online Retail Sector Today   752

11.2 Analyzing the Viability of Online Firms   757

    Strategic Analysis   758
    Financial Analysis   759

11.3 E-commerce in Action: E-tailing Business Models   760

    Virtual Merchants   760
    Amazon   762
       The Vision   762
       Business Model   762
       Financial Analysis   764
       Strategic Analysis—Business Strategy   764
       Strategic Analysis—Competition   767
       Strategic Analysis—Technology   768
       Strategic Analysis—Social and Legal Challenges   768
       Future Prospects   769
    Omni-Channel Merchants: Bricks-and-Clicks   769
    Catalog Merchants   771
    Manufacturer-Direct   772
    Common Themes in Online Retailing   773

11.4 The Service Sector: Offline and Online   775

    Insight on Technology: ASOS Uses Big Data to Find Its Most Valuable Customers   776

11.5 Online Financial Services   778

    Fintech   779
    Online Banking and Brokerage   779
       Multi-Channel vs. Pure Online Financial Services Firms   780
       Financial Portals and Account Aggregators   781
    Online Mortgage and Lending Services   781
    Online Insurance Services   782
    Online Real Estate Services   784

11.6 Online Travel Services   785

    Why Are Online Travel Services So Popular?   785
    The Online Travel Market   786
    Online Travel Industry Dynamics   786

11.7 Online Career Services   788

    Insight on Society: Phony Reviews   789
    It's Just Information: The Ideal Web Business?   791
    Online Recruitment Industry Trends   792

11.8 On-Demand Service Companies   794

    Insight on Business: Food Delivery on Demand in the Middle East   795

11.9 *Careers in E-commerce*   798
  The Company   798
  Position: Associate, e-Commerce Initiatives   798
  Qualifications/Skills   799
  Preparing for the Interview   799
  Possible First Interview Questions   800

11.10 *Case Study: OpenTable: Your Reservation Is Waiting*   801

11.11 *Review*   804
  Key Concepts   804
  Questions   807
  Projects   807
  References   808

12 B2B E-COMMERCE   810

Learning Objectives   810

Alibaba: China's E-commerce King   811

12.1 *An Overview of B2B E-commerce*   815
  Some Basic Definitions   817
  The Evolution of B2B E-commerce   817
  The Growth of B2B E-commerce   819
  Potential Benefits and Challenges of B2B E-commerce   821

12.2 *The Procurement Process and Supply Chains*   822
  Insight on Society: Where's My iPad? Global Supply Chain Risk and Vulnerability   823
  Steps in the Procurement Process   825
  Types of Procurement   825
  Multi-Tier Supply Chains   826
  Visibility and Other Concepts in Supply Chain Management   827
  The Role of Existing Legacy Computer Systems and Enterprise Systems in Supply Chains   828

12.3 *Trends in Supply Chain Management and Collaborative Commerce*   828
  Just-in-Time and Lean Production   829
  Supply Chain Simplification   829
  Supply Chain Black Swans: Adaptive Supply Chains   830
  Accountable Supply Chains: Labor Standards   831
  Sustainable Supply Chains: Lean, Mean, and Green   832
  Electronic Data Interchange (EDI)   833
  Mobile B2B   835
  B2B in the Cloud   836
  Supply Chain Management Systems   838

Blockchain and Supply Chain Management   839
Collaborative Commerce   840

Insight on Technology: Blockchain Improves the Food Supply Industry   841

    Collaboration 2.0: Cloud, Web, Social, and Mobile   844

Social Networks and B2B: The Extended Social Enterprise   844

B2B Marketing   845

12.4 *Net Marketplaces: The Selling Side of B2B*   846

Characteristics of Net Marketplaces   846

Types of Net Marketplaces   847

    E-distributors   847

    E-procurement   849

    Exchanges   851

    Industry Consortia   853

12.5 *Private Industrial Networks*   856

Objectives of Private Industrial Networks   857

Private Industrial Networks and Collaborative Commerce   858

Insight on Business: Walmart's Private Industrial Network Supports Omni-channel Growth   859

Implementation Barriers   861

12.6 *Careers in E-commerce*   862

The Company   862

Position: Junior Supply Chain Analyst   862

Qualifications/Skills   863

How to Prepare for the Interview   863

Possible First Interview Questions   863

12.7 *Case Study: Elemica: Cooperation, Collaboration, and Community*   865

12.8 *Review*   870

Key Concepts   870

Questions   873

Projects   874

References   874

Index   877

CHAPTER 1

Introduction to E-commerce

LEARNING OBJECTIVES

After reading this chapter, you will be able to:

- Understand why it is important to study e-commerce.
- Define e-commerce, understand how e-commerce differs from e-business, identify the primary technological building blocks underlying e-commerce, and recognize major current themes in e-commerce.
- Identify and describe the unique features of e-commerce technology and discuss their business significance.
- Describe the major types of e-commerce.
- Understand the evolution of e-commerce from its early years to today.
- Describe the major themes underlying the study of e-commerce.
- Identify the major academic disciplines contributing to e-commerce.

Everything on Demand:
The "Uberization" of E-commerce

If you were asked to pick iconic examples of e-commerce in the 25 years since it began in 1995, it is likely that companies such as Amazon, Google, Apple, and Facebook would be high on your list. But over the last few years, a different breed of e-commerce company has muscled its way to the forefront. Uber and other firms with similar business models, such as Taxify (a ride service similar to Uber's), Airbnb (rooms for rent), Takeaway and JustEat (food delivery), Movinga (movers), and Zipjet (laundry service), are the pioneers of an on-demand service e-commerce business model that has swept up billions of investment dollars and disrupted major industries, from transportation to hotels, real estate, house cleaning, maintenance, and grocery shopping.

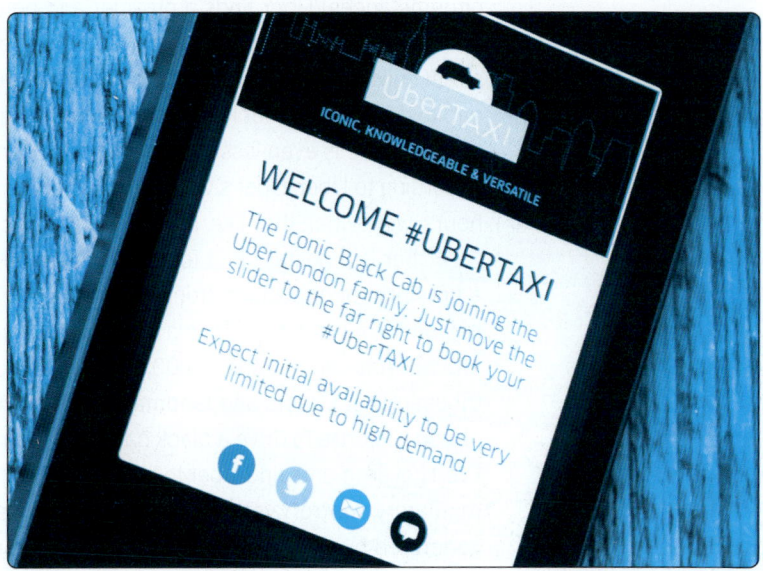
© Lenscap/Alamy

Uber is perhaps the most well-known, as well as the most controversial, company that uses the on-demand service model. Uber offers a variety of different services. The two most common are UberX, which uses compact sedans and is the least expensive, and UberBlack, which provides a higher-priced town car service. UberPool is a ride-sharing service that allows users to share a ride with another person who happens to be going to the same place. Uber is also attempting to leverage its business model by expanding into several related areas with UberRush, a same-day delivery service; UberCargo, a trucking service; and UberEats, a food delivery service.

Uber, headquartered in San Francisco, was founded in 2009 by Travis Kalanick and Garrett Camp, and has grown explosively since then to over 700 cities in 69 countries. Uber currently has almost 4 million drivers worldwide and over 90 million riders, who made over 5 billion trips in 2018. In the same year, riders spent $50 billion on the Uber platform, generating $11.3 billion in revenue for Uber, but it still lost $1.8 billion, with losses in developing markets swallowing up profits being generated in North America, Europe, and elsewhere. That trend continued in 2019, with a loss of a whopping $7.4 billion through the first three quarters of 2019. Uber's strategy has been to expand as fast as possible while forgoing short-term profits in the hope of long-term returns. In the last several years, Uber has sold

39

its operations in China, Southeast Asia, and Russia, where it had been engaged in costly turf wars with other competitors, reportedly to free up capital to invest in other emerging markets such as India, Latin America, and the Middle East.

Despite the fact that it thus far has not been able to operate at a profit, Uber offers a compelling value proposition for both customers and drivers. Customers can sign up for free, request a pickup using his or her smartphone, and nearly instantly (under the best of circumstances) Uber finds a provider and notifies the customer of the estimated time of arrival and price. Riders can accept the price or find an alternative. No need to stand on a street corner frantically waving, competing with others, or waiting endlessly for an available cab to drive by, without knowing when that might happen. With UberPool ride-sharing, the cost of a ride is even less, making it cost-competitive with owning a car in an urban area, according to Uber. Uber's value proposition for drivers is that it allows them to set their own hours, work when they like, and put their own cars to use generating revenue.

Uber is a poster child for "digital disruption." It is easy to see why Uber has ignited a firestorm of opposition from existing taxi services around the world. If you've paid $1 million for a license to drive a taxi in New York City, what is it worth now that Uber has arrived? Answer: less than $200,000. Taxi drivers in London typically invest years learning thousands of streets and landmarks before they are able to pass the tests necessary to obtain a license to drive a black cab there, something Uber drivers are not required to do. Even governments find Uber to be a disruptive threat. Governments do not want to give up regulatory control over passenger safety, driver training, nor the healthy revenue stream generated by charging taxi firms for a taxi license and sales taxes.

Uber's business model differs from traditional retail e-commerce. Uber doesn't sell goods. Instead it has created a smartphone-based platform that enables people who want a service—like a taxi—to find a provider with the resources, such as a personal automobile and a driver with available time, to fill the demand. It's important to understand that although Uber and similar firms are often called "sharing economy" companies, this is a misnomer. Uber drivers are selling their services as drivers and the temporary use of their car. Uber itself is not in the sharing business either: it charges a 25% commission on every transaction on its platform. Uber is not an example of true "peer-to-peer" e-commerce because Uber transactions involve an online intermediary: a third party that provides a platform for, and takes a cut of, all transactions.

Uber has disrupted the traditional taxi business model because it offers a superior, fast, convenient taxi-hailing service when compared to traditional taxi companies. With a traditional taxi service, there is no guarantee you will find a cab. Uber significantly reduces that uncertainty. Uber's business model is also much more efficient than a traditional taxi firm. Uber does not own taxis and has no maintenance and financing costs. Uber calls its drivers "independent contractors," not employees. Doing so enables Uber to avoid costs for workers' compensation, minimum wage requirements, driver training, health insurance, and commercial licensing.

Quality control should be a nightmare with almost 4 million contract drivers. But Uber relies on user reviews to identify problematic drivers and driver reviews to identify problematic passengers. Drivers are evaluated by riders on a 5-point scale. Drivers that fall below 4.5 are warned and may be dropped if they don't improve. Customers are also rated with a

5-point system. Drivers can refuse to pick up troublesome customers, and the Uber server can delay service to potential customers with low ratings or ban them entirely. Uber does not publicly report how many poorly rated drivers or passengers there are in its system. Academic articles have found that in similar on-demand companies, such as Airbnb, there is a built-in bias for both sellers and buyers to give good reviews regardless of the actual experience. If you routinely give low reviews to sellers (drivers), they will think you are too demanding and not service you in the future. If a driver gives low reviews to passengers, they might not rate you highly in return.

Rather than having a dispatcher in every city, Uber has an Internet-based app service running on cloud servers located throughout the world. It does not provide radios to its drivers, who instead must use their own smartphones and cell service, which the drivers pay for. It does not provide insurance or maintenance for its drivers' cars. Uber has shifted the costs of running a taxi service entirely to the drivers. Uber charges prices that vary dynamically with demand: the higher the demand, the greater the price of a ride. Therefore, it is impossible, using public information, to know if Uber's prices are lower than traditional taxis. Clearly, in high-demand situations they are higher, sometimes ten times higher, than a regulated taxi. There is no regulatory taxi commission setting uniform per-mile fares. Consumers do face some traditional uncertainties regarding availability: during a rain storm, a convention, or a sports event, when demand peaks, not enough drivers may be available at any price.

If Uber is the poster child for the on-demand service economy, it's also an iconic example of the social costs and conflicts associated with this kind of e-commerce. Uber has been charged in many countries with misclassifying its drivers as contractors as opposed to employees, thereby denying the drivers the benefits of employee status, such as minimum wages, social security, workers' compensation, and health insurance. Uber has also been the target of numerous lawsuits filed on behalf of its drivers, accusing the company of mistreatment, lack of due process, underpayment, and violation of state employment laws.

Uber has been accused of violating public transportation laws and regulations throughout the world; abusing the personal information it has collected on users of the service; seeking to use personal information to intimidate journalists; failing to protect public safety by refusing to do adequate criminal, medical, and financial background checks on its drivers; taking clandestine actions against its chief U.S.-based competitor Lyft in order to disrupt its business; and being tone-deaf to the complaints of its own drivers against the firm's efforts to reduce driver fees. Uber has been banned in several European cities. For instance, in London, Transport for London, the regulatory body that governs taxi services in London, refused in 2017 to renew Uber's license, based, it said, on concerns about user safety. Uber was allowed to continue operating while it appealed the ruling and in June 2018 was granted a 15-month probationary license. Uber then sought a five-year renewal upon expiration of the probationary license in September 2019 but was once again unsuccessful, with Transport for London denying them a license to operate. As in 2017, Uber is appealing the ruling and continues to operate in the interim. More significantly, in 2017, the European Court of Justice, the European Union's most powerful court, ruled that Uber should be treated as a transportation service, subject to all of the existing laws and regulations of the EU member countries in which it operates that apply to such services, rather than as a digital platform not subject to such laws and regulations, as Uber had been attempting to assert. Uber claims that the ruling will not have much impact

SOURCES: "Uber Loses License to Operate in London, *Wall Street Journal*, December 6, 2019; "Uber Shares Have the Potential to Double, Barclay's Says," by Esha Day, Bloomberg.com, November 15, 2019; "Uber's Dara Khosrowshahi Is Making Some Headway," by Davey Alba, *New York Times*, November 11, 2019; "Uber Technologies, Inc. Quarterly Report for the Quarter Ended September 30, 2019," filed with the Securities and Exchange Commission, November 5, 2019; "Uber Unveils New Safety Features Amid Scathing Report," Cbsnews.com, September 26, 2019; "Culture Crossover: Uber Impact: The Cost and Disruption and Monopoly," by Somrata Sarkar, Techworld.com, May 17, 2019; "How the Promise of a $120 Billion Uber IPO Evaporated," by Mike Isaac, Michael J. de la Merced, and Andrew Ross Sorkin, *New York Times*, May 15, 2019; "Uber Is Selling Its Southeast Asia Business

on it, however, as it claims that it now operates in accordance with transportation laws and regulations of most European counties in which it does business.

Critics also fear the long-term impact of on-demand service firms because of their potential for creating a society of part-time, low-paid temp work, displacing traditionally full-time, secure jobs—the so-called "uberization" of work. As one critic put it, Uber is not the Uber for rides so much as it is the Uber for low-paid jobs. A study by the MIT Center for Energy and Environmental Policy Research found that after taking into account costs such as fuel, insurance, maintenance, and repairs, Uber drivers' median profit was only $3.37 per hour. Uber responds to this fear by claiming that it is lowering the cost of transportation, making better use of spare human and financial resources, expanding the demand for ride services, and expanding opportunities for car drivers, whose pay it claims is about the same as other taxi drivers.

Over the last several years, Uber has been hit by a series of continuing controversies and scandals, creating a public relations nightmare for the company and culminating in the resignation of a number of board members, senior executives, and finally its co-founder and CEO, Travis Kalanick. It was charged with corporate mismanagement and misconduct (including using a secret program known as Greyball to track and evade regulators and other law enforcement officials), workplace discrimination and sexual harassment, and violation of the privacy of its customers through the use of its mobile app to track the location of those customers at all times, even when the app was not in use. In 2019, a *Washington Post* report raised serious questions about how Uber handles passenger safety.

Despite the controversy surrounding it, Uber has become entrenched in the everyday life of millions of people around the globe and continues to attract drivers, customers, and additional investors. In May 2019, Uber went public, raising over $8 billion at a valuation of about $82 billion, which, although a staggering amount, was well below the $120 billion value initially floated by its investment bankers. During 2019, Uber's stock price declined significantly, losing almost half its value since the IPO. Nonetheless, Uber's CEO, Dara Khosrowshahi, believes Uber remains well-positioned going forward, characterizing Uber's business model as upscale and global. Uber has stated it expects to be profitable by 2021, and as of the end of 2019, most Wall Street analysts remained positive on its prospects.

to Competitor Grab," by Johana Bhuiyan, Recode.net, March 25, 2018; "MIT Study Shows How Much Driving for Uber or Lyft Sucks," by Natasha Lomas, Yahoo.com, March 2, 2018; "Uber Dealt Setback After European Court Rules It Is a Taxi Service," by Liz Alderman, *New York Times*, December 20, 2017; "Uber Request to Take Drivers' Rights Case Directly to Top UK Court Rejected," by Hannah Boland, Telegraph.co.uk, December 4, 2017; "Here's All the Shady Stuff Uber's Been Accused of So Far," by Joe McGauley, Thrillist.com, March 7, 2017; "Even Uber Couldn't Bridge the China Divide," by Farhad Manjoo, *New York Times*, August 1, 2016; "Uber Sells China Operations to Didi Chuxing," by Alyssa Abkowitz and Rick Carew, *Wall Street Journal*, August 1, 2016; "An Uber Shakedown," *Wall Street Journal*, April 24, 2016; "Uber Settlement Takes Customers for a Ride," by Rob Berger, *Forbes*, April 22, 2016; "Twisting Words to Make 'Sharing' Apps Seem Selfless," by Natasha Singer, *New York Times*, August 9, 2015; "The $50 Billion Question: Can Uber Deliver?," by Douglas Macmillan, *Wall Street Journal*, June 15, 2015; "How Everyone Misjudges the Sharing Economy," by Christopher Mims, *Wall Street Journal*, May 25, 2015; "The On-Demand Economy Is Reshaping Companies and Careers," *The Economist*, January 4, 2015; "The On-Demand Economy: Workers on Tap," *The Economist,* January 3, 2015.

In 1994, e-commerce as we now know it did not exist. In 2019, 25 years later, over 2 billion consumers worldwide spent around $4.3 trillion, and businesses around $27 trillion, purchasing goods and services via a desktop computer or mobile device. There have been significant changes in the e-commerce environment during this time period.

The early years of e-commerce, during the late 1990s, were a period of business vision, inspiration, and experimentation. It soon became apparent, however, that establishing a successful business model based on those visions would not be easy. There followed a period of retrenchment and reevaluation, which led to the stock market crash of 2000–2001, with the value of e-commerce, telecommunications, and other technology stocks plummeting. After the bubble burst, many people were quick to write off e-commerce. But they were wrong. The surviving firms refined and honed their business models, and the technology became more powerful and less expensive, ultimately leading to business firms that actually produced profits. Between 2002–2007, retail e-commerce grew at more than 25% per year.

Then, in 2007, Apple introduced the first iPhone, a transformative event that marked the beginning of yet another new era in e-commerce. In the last ten years, mobile devices, such as smartphones and tablet computers, and mobile apps have supplanted the traditional desktop/laptop platform and web browser as the most common method for consumers to access the Internet. Facilitated by technologies such as cellular networks, Wi-Fi, and cloud computing, mobile devices have become advertising, shopping, reading, and media viewing machines, and in the process, have transformed consumer behavior yet again. During the same time period, social networks such as Facebook, Twitter, YouTube, Pinterest, Instagram, and Snapchat, which enable users to distribute their own content (such as videos, music, photos, personal information, commentary, blogs, and more), rocketed to prominence. The mobile platform infrastructure also gave birth to another e-commerce innovation: on-demand services that are local and personal. From hailing a taxi, to food delivery, to washing your clothes, on-demand services have created a marketspace that enables owners of resources such as cars, spare bedrooms, and spare time to find a market of eager consumers looking to buy a service in a few minutes using their smartphones. Uber, profiled in the opening case, is a leading example of these on-demand service firms that are disrupting traditional business models. Today, mobile, social, and local are the driving forces in e-commerce.

But while the evolution of e-commerce technology and business over the past quarter-century has been a powerful and mostly positive force in our society, it is becoming increasingly apparent that it also has had, and continues to have, a serious societal impact, from promoting the invasion of personal privacy, aiding in the dissemination of false information, enabling widespread security threats, and facilitating the growth of business titans, such as Amazon, Google, and Facebook, that dominate their fields, leading to a decimation of effective competition. As a result, it is likely that the Internet and e-commerce are entering a period of closer regulatory oversight that may have a significant impact on the conduct of e-commerce as it enters its second quarter-century.

1.1 THE FIRST THIRTY SECONDS: WHY YOU SHOULD STUDY E-COMMERCE

The rapid growth and change that has occurred in the first quarter-century of e-commerce represents just the beginning—what could be called the first 30 seconds of the e-commerce revolution. Technology continues to evolve at exponential rates. This underlying ferment presents entrepreneurs with opportunities to create new business models and businesses in traditional industries and in the process, disrupt, and in some instances, destroy existing business models and firms. The rapid growth of e-commerce is also providing extraordinary growth in career and employment opportunities, which we describe throughout the book.

Improvements in underlying information technologies and continuing entrepreneurial innovation in business and marketing promise as much change in the next decade as was seen in the previous two decades. The twenty-first century will be the age of a digitally enabled social and commercial life, the outlines of which we can still only barely perceive at this time. Analysts estimate that by 2023, consumers worldwide will be spending almost $7.3 trillion and businesses around $34 trillion in digital transactions. It appears likely that e-commerce will eventually impact nearly all commerce, and that most commerce will be e-commerce by the year 2050, if not sooner.

Business fortunes are made—and lost—in periods of extraordinary change such as this. The next five years hold exciting opportunities—as well as risks—for new and traditional businesses to exploit digital technology for market advantage. For society as a whole, the next few decades offer the possibility of significant gains in social welfare, as well as signifcant challenges, as the digital revolution works its way through larger and larger segments of the world's economy.

It is important to study e-commerce in order to be able to perceive and understand the opportunities and risks that lie ahead. By the time you finish this book, you will be able to identify the technological, business, and social forces that have shaped, and continue to shape, the growth of e-commerce, and be ready to participate in, and ultimately guide, discussions of e-commerce in the firms where you work. More specifically, you will be able to analyze an existing or new idea for an e-commerce business, identify the most effective business model to use, and understand the technological underpinnings of an e-commerce presence, including the security and ethical issues raised, as well as how to optimally market and advertise the business, using both traditional e-marketing tools and social, mobile, and local marketing.

1.2 INTRODUCTION TO E-COMMERCE

In this section, we'll first define e-commerce and then discuss the difference between e-commerce and e-business. We will also introduce you to the major technological building blocks underlying e-commerce: the Internet, Web, and mobile platform. The section concludes with a look at some major current trends in e-commerce.

WHAT IS E-COMMERCE?

E-commerce involves the use of the Internet, the World Wide Web (Web), and mobile apps and browsers running on mobile devices to transact business. Although the terms Internet and Web are often used interchangeably, they are actually two very different things. The *Internet* is a worldwide network of computer networks, and the *Web* is one of the Internet's most popular services, providing access to billions of web pages. An *app* (short-hand for application) is a software application. The term is typically used when referring to mobile applications, although it is also sometimes used to refer to desktop computer applications as well. A *mobile browser* is a version of web browser software accessed via a mobile device. (We describe the Internet, Web, and mobile platform more fully later in this chapter and in Chapters 2 and 3) More formally, e-commerce can be defined as digitally enabled commercial transactions between and among organizations and individuals. Each of these components of our working definition of e-commerce is important. *Digitally enabled transactions* include all transactions mediated by digital technology. For the most part, this means transactions that occur over the Internet, the Web, and/or via mobile devices. *Commercial transactions* involve the exchange of value (e.g., money) across organizational or individual boundaries in return for products and services. Exchange of value is important for understanding the limits of e-commerce. Without an exchange of value, no commerce occurs.

The professional literature sometimes refers to e-commerce as digital commerce. For our purposes, we consider e-commerce and digital commerce to be synonymous.

e-commerce
the use of the Internet, the Web, and mobile apps and browsers running on mobile devices to transact business. More formally, digitally enabled commercial transactions between and among organizations and individuals

THE DIFFERENCE BETWEEN E-COMMERCE AND E-BUSINESS

There is a debate about the meaning and limitations of both e-commerce and e-business. Some argue that e-commerce encompasses the entire world of electronically based organizational activities that support a firm's market exchanges—including a firm's entire information system infrastructure. Others argue, on the other hand, that e-business encompasses the entire world of internal and external electronically based activities, including e-commerce.

We think it is important to make a working distinction between e-commerce and e-business because we believe they refer to different phenomena. E-commerce is not "anything digital" that a firm does. For purposes of this text, we will use the term **e-business** to refer primarily to the digital enabling of transactions and processes *within* a firm, involving information systems under the control of the firm. For the most part, in our view, e-business does not include commercial transactions involving an exchange of value across organizational boundaries. For example, a company's online inventory control mechanisms are a component of e-business, but such internal processes do not directly generate revenue for the firm from outside businesses or consumers, as e-commerce, by definition, does. It is true, however, that a firm's e-business infrastructure provides support for online e-commerce exchanges; the same infrastructure and skill sets are involved in both e-business and e-commerce. E-commerce and e-business systems blur together at the business firm boundary, at the point where internal business systems link up with suppliers or customers (see **Figure 1.1**). E-business applications turn into e-commerce precisely when an exchange of value occurs. We will examine this intersection further in Chapter 12.

e-business
the digital enabling of transactions and processes within a firm, involving information systems under the control of the firm

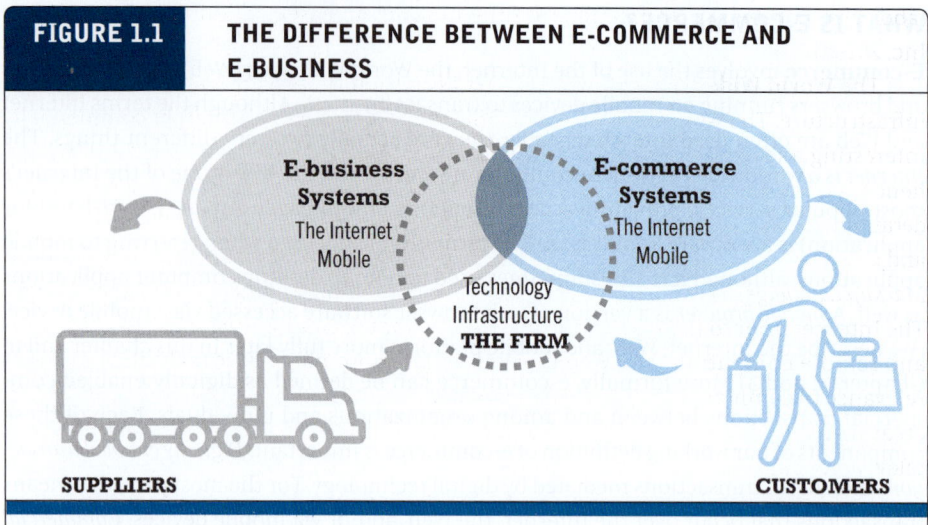

FIGURE 1.1 THE DIFFERENCE BETWEEN E-COMMERCE AND E-BUSINESS

E-commerce primarily involves transactions that cross firm boundaries. E-business primarily involves the application of digital technologies to business processes within the firm.

TECHNOLOGICAL BUILDING BLOCKS UNDERLYING E-COMMERCE: THE INTERNET, WEB, AND MOBILE PLATFORM

The technology juggernauts behind e-commerce are the Internet, the Web, and increasingly, the mobile platform. We describe the Internet, Web, and mobile platform in some detail in Chapter 2. The **Internet** is a worldwide network of computer networks built on common standards. Created in the late 1960s to connect a small number of mainframe computers and their users, the Internet has since grown into the world's largest network. It is impossible to say with certainty exactly how many computers and other mobile devices such as smartphones and tablets, as well as other Internet-connected consumer devices, such as smartwatches, connected TVs, and remotes such as Amazon's Echo are connected to the Internet worldwide at any one time, but some experts estimate that by 2019, the number had reached 22 billion, growing to an estimated 38.6 billion by 2025 (Strategy Analytics, 2019). The Internet links businesses, educational institutions, government agencies, and individuals together, and provides users with services such as e-mail, document transfer, shopping, research, instant messaging, music, videos, and news.

One way to measure the growth of the Internet is by looking at the number of Internet hosts with domain names. (An *Internet host* is defined by the Internet Systems Consortium as any IP address that returns a domain name in the in-addr.arpa domain, which is a special part of the DNS namespace that resolves IP addresses into domain names.) In January 2019, there were more than 1 billion Internet hosts in over 245 countries, up from just 72 million in 2000 (Internet Systems Consortium, 2019).

The Internet has shown extraordinary growth patterns when compared to other electronic technologies of the past. It took radio 38 years to achieve a 30% share of U.S. households. It took television 17 years to achieve a 30% share. It took only 10 years for the Internet/Web to achieve a 53% share of U.S. households once a graphical user interface was invented for the Web in 1993. In the United States, over 280 million people of all ages

Internet
worldwide network of computer networks built on common standards

(about 85% of the U.S. population) use the Internet at least once a month (eMarketer, Inc. 2019a).

The **World Wide Web (the Web)** is an information system that runs on the Internet infrastructure. The Web was the original "killer app" that made the Internet commercially interesting and extraordinarily popular. The Web was developed in the early 1990s and hence is of much more recent vintage than the Internet. We describe the Web in some detail in Chapter 2. The Web provides access to billions of web pages indexed by Google and other search engines. These pages are created in a language called *HTML (HyperText Markup Language)*. HTML pages can contain text, graphics, animations, and other objects. The Internet prior to the Web was primarily used for text communications, file transfers, and remote computing. The Web introduced far more powerful capabilities of direct relevance to commerce. In essence, the Web added color, voice, and video to the Internet, creating a communications infrastructure and information storage system that rivals television, radio, magazines, and libraries.

World Wide Web (the Web)
an information system running on Internet infrastructure that provides access to billions of web pages

There is no precise measurement of the number of web pages in existence, in part because today's search engines index only a portion of the known universe of web pages. Google has identified over 130 trillion individual web pages, up from 30 trillion in 2013, although many of these pages do not necessarily contain unique content (Schwartz, 2016). In addition to this "surface" or "visible" Web, there is also the so-called deep Web that is reportedly 500 to 1,000 times greater than the surface Web. The deep Web contains databases and other content that is not routinely identified by search engines such as Google (see **Figure 1.2**). Although the total size of the Web is not known, what is indisputable is that web content has grown exponentially since 1993.

The mobile platform has become a significant part of Internet infrastructure. The **mobile platform** provides the ability to access the Internet from a variety of mobile

mobile platform
provides the ability to access the Internet from a variety of mobile devices such as smartphones, tablets, and other ultra-lightweight laptop computers

FIGURE 1.2   THE DEEP WEB

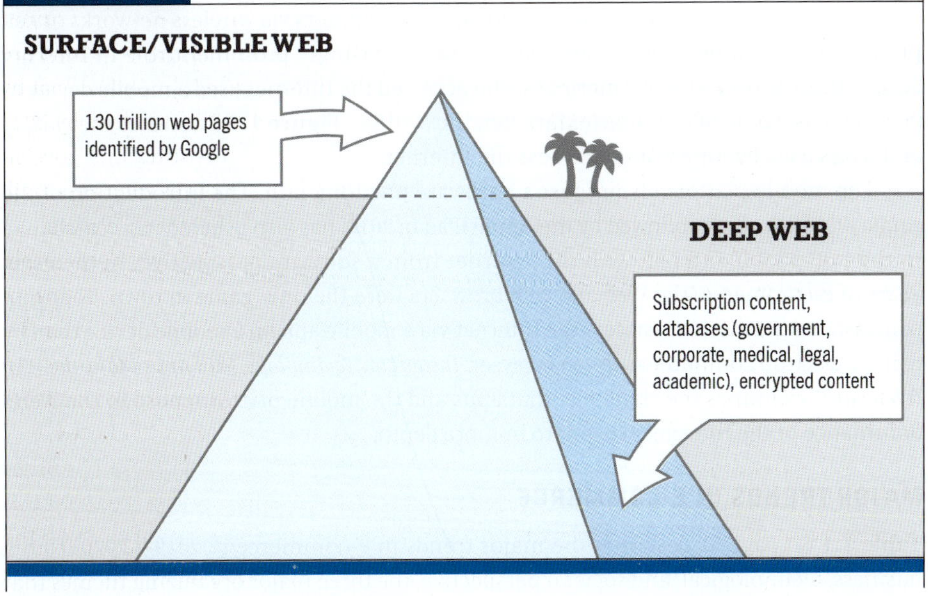

SURFACE/VISIBLE WEB

130 trillion web pages identified by Google

DEEP WEB

Subscription content, databases (government, corporate, medical, legal, academic), encrypted content

The surface web is only a small part of online content.

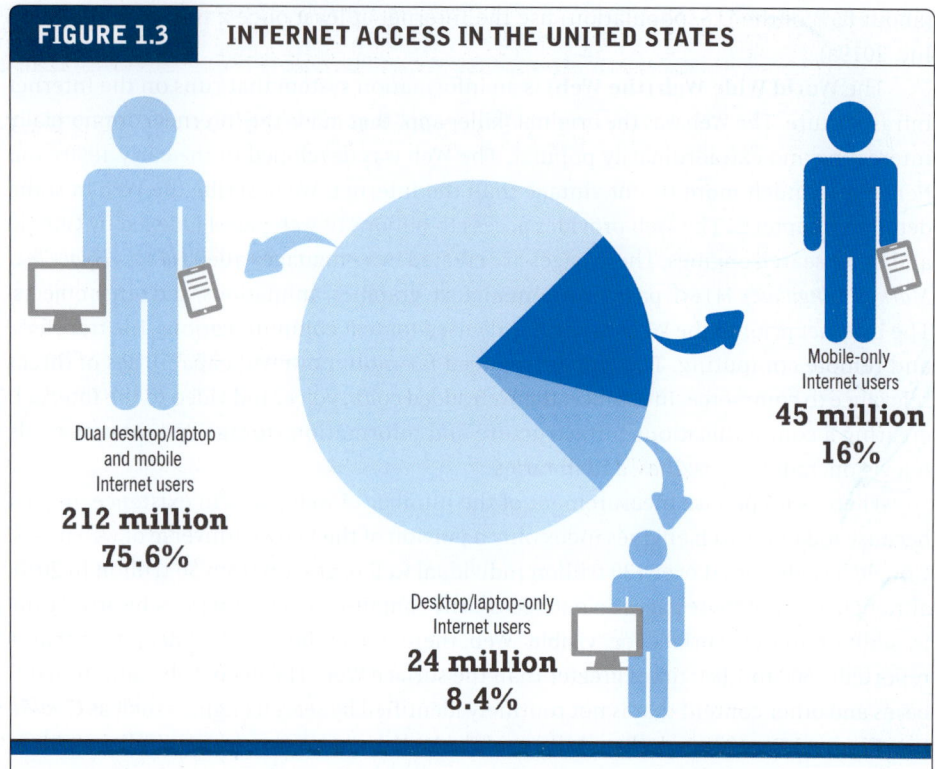

FIGURE 1.3 INTERNET ACCESS IN THE UNITED STATES

Over 75% of all Internet users in the United States (about 212 million people in 2018) went online using both a desktop/laptop and mobile device. Almost 16% (about 45 million) only went online by using a mobile device. Just 8.4% (about 24 million) used only a desktop or laptop computer to access the Internet.
SOURCE: Based on data from eMarketer, Inc., 2018a.

devices such as smartphones, tablets, and laptop computers via wireless networks or cell phone service. Mobile devices are playing an increasingly prominent role in Internet access. In 2018, over 91% of Americans who accessed the Internet used a mobile device to do so at least some of the time (eMarketer, Inc., 2018a). **Figure 1.3** illustrates the variety of devices used by Americans to access the Internet.

The mobile platform is not just a hardware phenomenon. The introduction of the Apple iPhone in 2007, followed by the Apple iPad in 2010, has also ushered in a sea-change in the way people interact with the Internet from a software perspective. In the early years of e-commerce, the Web and web browsers were the only game in town. Today, in contrast, more Americans access the Internet via a mobile app on a mobile device than by using a desktop computer and web browser. *Insight on Technology: Will Apps Make the Web Irrelevant?* examines the challenge that apps and the mobile platform pose to the Web's dominance of the Internet ecosphere in more depth.

MAJOR TRENDS IN E-COMMERCE

Table 1.1 on page 51 describes the major trends in e-commerce in 2019—2020 from a business, technological, and societal perspective, the three major organizing themes that we use in this book to understand e-commerce (see Section 1.6).

INSIGHT ON TECHNOLOGY

WILL APPS MAKE THE WEB IRRELEVANT?

Nowadays, it's hard to recall a time before the Web. How did we get along without the ability to go online to search for an item, learn about a topic, play a game, or watch a video? Though the Web has come a remarkably long way from its humble beginnings, some experts think that the Web's best days are behind it. Opinions vary about the future role of the Web in a world where apps have become a dominant force in the Internet ecosystem. In 10 years, will the Web be a forgotten relic? Or will the Web and apps coexist peacefully as vital cogs in the Internet ecosystem? Will the app craze eventually die down as users gravitate back toward the Web as the primary way to perform online tasks?

Apps have grown into a disruptive force ever since Apple launched its App Store in 2008. The list of industries apps have disrupted is wide-ranging: communications, media and entertainment, logistics, education, healthcare, and most recently, with Uber and Airbnb, the taxi and hotel industries. Despite not even existing prior to 2008, in 2018, sales of apps accounted for over $100 billion in revenues worldwide, and the app economy is continuing to show robust growth, with estimates that revenue will reach over $155 billion by 2022. More of those revenues are likely to come from in-app purchases than from paid app downloads.

Although usage of apps tends to be highly concentrated, with nearly 90% of smartphone app minutes spent on an individual's top five apps, consumers are trying new apps all the time and typically use about 20 different apps per month, leaving room for new app developers to innovate and create successful apps. Users are downloading an increasing number of apps, with the number reaching over 194 billion worldwide during 2018, according to research firm App Annie.

In 2014, for the first time ever, Americans used mobile devices more than desktop computers to access the Internet. The time U.S. adults are spending using mobile devices has exploded, now accounting for over 63% of total time spent on the Internet. Of the time spent using mobile devices, over 85% is spent using mobile apps and less than 15% using mobile browsers. In 2019, according to consulting firm eMarketer, adult mobile Internet users in the United States were expected to spend an average of almost 3 hours a day within apps on their smartphones and tablet computers compared to just over 25 minutes a day using a mobile browser.

Consumers have gravitated to apps for several reasons. First, smartphones and tablet computers enable users to use apps anywhere, instead of being tethered to a desktop or having to lug a heavy laptop around. Of course, smartphones and tablets enable users to use the Web too, but apps are often more convenient and boast more streamlined, elegant interfaces than mobile web browsers.

Not only are apps more appealing in certain ways to consumers, they are much more appealing to content creators and media companies. Apps are much easier to control and monetize than websites, not to mention they can't be crawled by Google or other services. On the Web, the average price of ads per thousand impressions is falling, and many content providers are still mostly struggling to turn the Internet into a profitable content delivery platform. Much of software and media companies' focus has shifted to developing mobile apps for this reason.

In the future, some analysts believe that the Internet will be used to transport data, but individual app interfaces will replace the web

(continued)

browser as the most common way to access and display content. Even the creator of the Web, Tim Berners-Lee, feels that the Web as we know it is being threatened.

But there is no predictive consensus about the role of the Web in our lives in the next decade and beyond. Although apps may be more convenient than the Web in many respects, the depth of the web browsing experience trumps that of apps. The Web is a vibrant, diverse array of sites, and browsers have an openness and flexibility that apps lack. The connections between websites enhance their usefulness and value to users, and apps that instead seek to lock users in cannot offer the same experience. In addition, the size of the mobile web audience still exceeds that of the mobile app audience. And when it comes to making purchases online, using a web browser on a desktop computer still handily beats mobile devices. Retail purchases made on desktops still account for over 55% of all online retail purchases.

Other analysts who are more optimistic about the Web's chances to remain relevant in an increasingly app-driven online marketplace feel this way because of the emergence of HTML5 and progressive web apps (PWAs). HTML5 is a markup language that enables more dynamic web content and allows for browser-accessible web apps that are as appealing as device-specific apps. A PWA combines the best elements of mobile websites and native mobile apps. A PWA functions and feels like a native app, but it does not need to be downloaded from an app store, and so does not take up any of the mobile device's memory. Instead, it runs directly in a mobile web browser, but is able to load instantly, even in areas of low connectivity. Some people think that a good PWA can ultimately function as a total replacement for a company's mobile website, native app, and even possibly its desktop website.

The shift towards apps and away from the Web is likely to have a significant impact on the fortunes of e-commerce firms. As the pioneer of apps and the market leader in apps, smartphones, and tablet computers, Apple stands to gain from a shift towards apps, and although it also faces increasing competition from other companies, including Google, the established success of the App Store will make it next to impossible to dethrone Apple. For instance, while Google's Google Play store had almost three times the number of downloads compared to Apple's App Store in 2018, the App Store still made nearly twice the amount of revenue ($46.6 billion) than Google Play ($24.8 billion). Google hopes that PWAs are at least a partial answer to the problem presented to it by native apps, because the more activity that occurs on native apps, which Google cannot crawl, the less data Google has access to, which impacts its web-based advertising platform.

Ultimately, most marketers see the future as one in which the Web and mobile apps work together, with each having an important role in serving different needs.

SOURCES: "US Desktop/Laptop Retail Ecommerce Sales," eMarketer, Inc., October 2019; "US Time Spent with Mobile 2019: Smartphones Gain Minutes, but New Challengers Emerge," by Yoram Wormser, eMarketer, Inc., May 30, 2019; "App Store Made Almost Twice as Much as Google Play in 2018," by Killian Bell, Cultofmac.com, January 18, 2019; "The State of Mobile in 2019—The Most Important Trends to Know," Appannie.com, January 16, 2019; "2019 Report: The Global State of Mobile," comScore, Inc., 2019; "Progressive Web Apps: What They Are and Why They Matter," by Wilson Kerr, Digitalcommerce360.com, May 28, 2018; "App Market Growth Is Global as U.S. Market Stabilizes: App Annie," by Nate Swanner, Insights.dice.com, May 14, 2018; "The Data Behind 10 Years of the iOS App Store, 2018," by App Annie, May 2018; "App Annie Forecast 2017–2022," by App Annie, May 2018; "Why Progressive Web Apps Will Replace Native Mobile Apps," by Andrew Gazdecki, Forbes.com, March 9, 2018; "Mobile's Hierarchy of Needs," comScore, March 2017; "Publishers Straddle the Apple-Google, App-Web Divide," by Katie Benner and Conor Dougherty, *New York Times*, October 18, 2015; "Mobile Addicts Multiply Across the Globe," by Simon Khalaf, Flurrymobile.tumblr.com, July 15, 2015; "How Apps Won the Mobile Web," by Thomas Claburn, Informationweek.com, April 3, 2014; "Mobile Apps Overtake PC Internet Usage in U.S.," by James O'Toole, Money.cnn.com, February 28, 2014; "Is The Web Dead In the Face of Native Apps? Not Likely, But Some Think So," by Gabe Knuth, Brianmadden.com, March 28, 2012; "The Web Is Dead. Long Live the Internet," by Chris Anderson and Michael Wolff, Wired.com, August 17, 2010; "The Web Is Dead? A Debate," by Chris Anderson, Wired.com, August 17, 2010.

TABLE 1.1   MAJOR TRENDS IN E-COMMERCE, 2019–2020

BUSINESS

- Retail e-commerce continues to grow worldwide, with a global growth rate of over 20%, and even higher in Asia-Pacific.
- Retail m-commerce sales skyrocket, reaching over $2.2 trillion in 2019.
- The mobile app ecosystem continues to grow, with over 2.5 billion people worldwide using mobile apps in 2019.
- Social e-commerce, based on social networks and supported by advertising, emerges and continues to grow, generating an estimated $16.5 billion from social commerce in the United States in 2018.
- Local e-commerce, the third dimension of the mobile-social-local e-commerce wave, is also growing, fueled by an explosion of interest in on-demand services such as Uber.
- B2B e-commerce revenues continue to expand, reaching about $27 trillion worldwide in 2019.
- On-demand service firms like Uber and Airbnb attract billions in capital, garner multi-billion dollar valuations, and show explosive growth.
- Mobile advertising continues growing at astronomical rates, accounting for over 70% of all digital ad spending.
- Small businesses and entrepreneurs continue to flood into the e-commerce marketplace, often riding on the infrastructures created by industry giants such as Apple, Facebook, Amazon, Google, and eBay.

TECHNOLOGY

- A mobile computing and communications platform based on smartphones, tablet computers, wearable devices, and mobile apps becomes a reality, creating an alternative platform for online transactions, marketing, advertising, and media viewing. The use of mobile messaging services such as Facebook Messenger, WhatsApp, and Snapchat continues to expand, and these services are now used by almost two-thirds of smartphone users.
- Smart speakers such as Amazon Echo and Google Home become increasingly popular, providing an additional platform for e-commerce.
- Cloud computing completes the transformation of the mobile platform by storing consumer content and software on "cloud" (Internet-based) servers and making it available to any consumer-connected device from the desktop to a smartphone.
- The Internet of Things (IoT), comprised of billions of Internet-connected devices, continues to grow exponentially.
- As firms track the trillions of online interactions that occur each day, a flood of data, typically referred to as big data, is being produced.
- In order to make sense out of big data, firms turn to sophisticated software called business analytics (or web analytics) that can identify purchase patterns as well as consumer interests and intentions in milliseconds.

SOCIETY

- User-generated content, published online as social network posts, tweets, blogs, and pins, as well as video and photo-sharing, continues to grow and provides a method of self-publishing that engages millions.
- Social networks encourage self-revelation, threatening privacy, as Facebook comes under fire for allowing third parties such as Cambridge Analytica to mine its database of user information without user consent.
- The EU General Data Protection Regulation takes effect, impacting all companies that operate in any of the EU member nations.
- Concerns increase about the increasing market dominance of Facebook, Amazon, and Google, leading to calls for government regulation in both the European Union and United States.
- Conflicts over copyright management and control continue, but there is substantial agreement among online distributors and copyright owners that they need one another.
- Surveillance of online communications by both repressive regimes and Western democracies grows.
- Concerns over commercial and governmental privacy invasion increase.
- Online security continues to decline as major companies are hacked and lose control over customer information.
- Spam remains a significant problem.
- On-demand service e-commerce produces a flood of temporary, poorly paid jobs without benefits.

From a business perspective, one of the most important trends to note is that all forms of e-commerce continue to show very strong growth. Retail e-commerce has been growing worldwide at over 20% a year for the last few years and in 2019 reached around $3.5 trillion. Retail m-commerce is growing at an even faster rate and increased to over $2.2 trillion in 2019. Social networks such as Facebook, Pinterest, and Instagram are enabling social e-commerce by providing advertising, search, and Buy buttons that enable consumers to actually purchase products. Local e-commerce is being fueled by the explosion of interest in on-demand services such as Uber and Airbnb. B2B e-commerce, which dwarfs all other forms, is also continuing to strengthen and grow.

From a technology perspective, the mobile platform based on smartphones and tablet computers has finally arrived with a bang, driving astronomical growth in mobile advertising and making true mobile e-commerce a reality. The use of mobile messaging services such as Facebook Messenger, WhatsApp, and Snapchat has created an alternative communications platform that is beginning to be leveraged for commerce as well. Cloud computing is inextricably linked to the development of the mobile platform by enabling the storage of consumer content and software on cloud (Internet-based) servers, and making it available to mobile devices as well as desktops. Other major technological trends include the increasing ability of companies to track and analyze the flood of online data (typically referred to as big data) being produced. The Internet of Things (IoT), comprised of billions of Internet-connected devices, continues to grow exponentially, and will only add to this flood of data in the years to come.

At the societal level, other trends are apparent. The Internet and mobile platform provide an environment that allows millions of people to create and share content, establish new social bonds, and strengthen existing ones through social network, photo- and video-posting, and blogging sites and apps, while at the same time creating significant privacy issues. Privacy seems to have lost some of its meaning in an age when millions create public online personal profiles, while at the same time concerns over commercial and governmental privacy invasion continue to increase. The major digital copyright owners have increased their pursuit of online piracy with mixed success, while reaching agreements with the big technology players such as Apple, Amazon, and Google to protect intellectual property rights. Governments have successfully moved toward taxation of e-commerce sales. Sovereign nations have expanded their surveillance of, and control over, online communications and content as a part of their anti-terrorist activities and their traditional interest in law enforcement. Online security, or lack thereof, remains a significant issue, as new stories about security breaches, malware, hacking, and other attacks emerge seemingly daily.

1.3 UNIQUE FEATURES OF E-COMMERCE TECHNOLOGY

Figure 1.4 illustrates eight unique features of e-commerce technology that both challenge traditional business thinking and help explain why we have so much interest in e-commerce. These unique dimensions of e-commerce technologies suggest many new possibilities for marketing and selling—a powerful set of interactive, personalized, and rich messages are available for delivery to segmented, targeted audiences.

FIGURE 1.4 — EIGHT UNIQUE FEATURES OF E-COMMERCE TECHNOLOGY

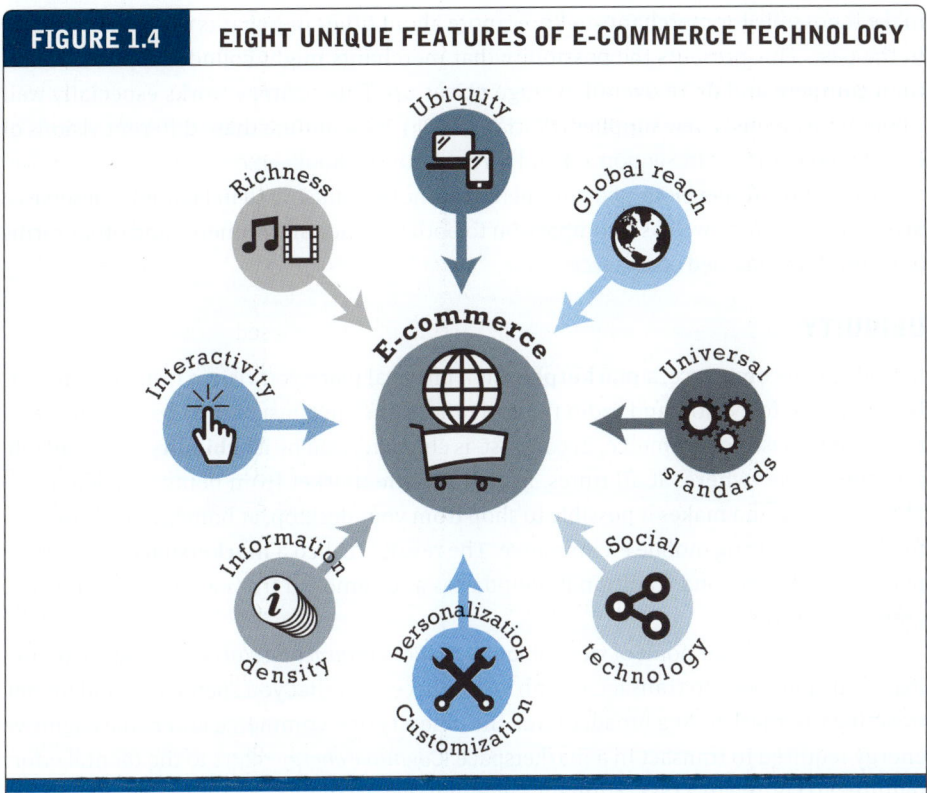

E-commerce technologies provide a number of unique features that have impacted the conduct of business.

Prior to the development of e-commerce, the marketing and sale of goods was a mass-marketing and salesforce–driven process. Marketers viewed consumers as passive targets of advertising campaigns and branding "blitzes" intended to influence their long-term product perceptions and immediate purchasing behavior. Companies sold their products via well-insulated channels. Consumers were trapped by geographical and social boundaries, unable to search widely for the best price and quality. Information about prices, costs, and fees could be hidden from the consumer, creating profitable information asymmetries for the selling firm. **Information asymmetry** refers to any disparity in relevant market information among parties in a transaction. It was so expensive to change national or regional prices in traditional retailing (what are called *menu costs*) that one national price was the norm, and dynamic pricing to the marketplace (changing prices in real time) was unheard of. In this environment, manufacturers prospered by relying on huge production runs of products that could not be customized or personalized.

E-commerce technologies make it possible for merchants to know much more about consumers and to be able to use this information more effectively than was ever true in the past. Online merchants can use this information to develop new information asymmetries, enhance their ability to brand products, charge premium prices for high-quality service, and segment the market into an endless number of subgroups, each receiving a different price. To complicate matters further, these same technologies also

information asymmetry

any disparity in relevant market information among parties in a transaction make it possible for merchants to know more about other merchants than was ever true in the past. This presents the possibility that merchants might collude on prices rather than compete and drive overall average prices up. This strategy works especially well when there are just a few suppliers (Varian, 2000a). We examine these different visions of e-commerce further in Section 1.4 and throughout the book.

Each of the dimensions of e-commerce technology illustrated in Figure 1.4 deserves a brief exploration, as well as a comparison to both traditional commerce and other forms of technology-enabled commerce.

UBIQUITY

In traditional commerce, a **marketplace** is a physical place you visit in order to transact. For example, television and radio typically motivate the consumer to go someplace to make a purchase. E-commerce, in contrast, is characterized by its **ubiquity**: it is available just about everywhere, at all times. It liberates the market from being restricted to a physical space and makes it possible to shop from your desktop, at home, at work, or even from your car, using mobile e-commerce. The result is called a **marketspace**—a marketplace extended beyond traditional boundaries and removed from a temporal and geographic location.

From a consumer point of view, ubiquity reduces *transaction costs*—the costs of participating in a market. To transact, it is no longer necessary that you spend time and money traveling to a market. At a broader level, the ubiquity of e-commerce lowers the cognitive energy required to transact in a marketspace. *Cognitive energy* refers to the mental effort required to complete a task. Humans generally seek to reduce cognitive energy outlays. When given a choice, humans will choose the path requiring the least effort—the most convenient path (Shapiro and Varian, 1999; Tversky and Kahneman, 1981).

marketplace
physical space you visit in order to transact

ubiquity
available just about everywhere, at all times

marketspace
marketplace extended beyond traditional boundaries and removed from a temporal and geographic location

GLOBAL REACH

E-commerce technology permits commercial transactions to cross cultural, regional, and national boundaries far more conveniently and cost-effectively than is true in traditional commerce. As a result, the potential market size for e-commerce merchants is roughly equal to the size of the world's online population (over 3.8 billion in 2019) (eMarketer, Inc., 2019b). More realistically, the Internet makes it much easier for startup e-commerce merchants within a single country to achieve a national audience than was ever possible in the past. The total number of users or customers an e-commerce business can obtain is a measure of its **reach** (Evans and Wurster, 1997).

In contrast, most traditional commerce is local or regional—it involves local merchants or national merchants with local outlets. Television, radio stations, and newspapers, for instance, are primarily local and regional institutions with limited but powerful national networks that can attract a national audience. In contrast to e-commerce technology, these older commerce technologies do not easily cross national boundaries to a global audience.

reach
the total number of users or customers an e-commerce business can obtain

UNIVERSAL STANDARDS

One strikingly unusual feature of e-commerce technologies is that the technical standards of the Internet, and therefore the technical standards for conducting e-commerce, are

universal standards—they are shared by all nations around the world. In contrast, most traditional commerce technologies differ from one nation to the next. For instance, television and radio standards differ around the world, as does cell phone technology.

The universal technical standards of e-commerce greatly lower *market entry costs*—the cost merchants must pay just to bring their goods to market. At the same time, for consumers, universal standards reduce *search costs*—the effort required to find suitable products. And by creating a single, one-world marketspace, where prices and product descriptions can be inexpensively displayed for all to see, *price discovery* becomes simpler, faster, and more accurate (Banerjee et al., 2016; Bakos, 1997; Kambil, 1997). Users, both businesses and individuals, also experience *network externalities*—benefits that arise because everyone uses the same technology. With e-commerce technologies, it is possible for the first time in history to easily find many of the suppliers, prices, and delivery terms of a specific product anywhere in the world, and to view them in a coherent, comparative environment. Although this is not necessarily realistic today for all or even most products, it is a potential that will be exploited in the future.

universal standards
standards that are shared by all nations around the world

RICHNESS

Information **richness** refers to the complexity and content of a message (Evans and Wurster, 1999). Traditional markets, national sales forces, and retail stores have great richness: they are able to provide personal, face-to-face service using aural and visual cues when making a sale. The richness of traditional markets makes them a powerful selling or commercial environment. Prior to the development of the Web, there was a trade-off between richness and reach: the larger the audience reached, the less rich the message.

E-commerce technologies have the potential for offering considerably more information richness than traditional media such as printing presses, radio, and television because they are interactive and can adjust the message to individual users. Chatting with an online sales person, for instance, comes very close to the customer experience in a small retail shop. The richness enabled by e-commerce technologies allows retail and service merchants to market and sell "complex" goods and services that heretofore required a face-to-face presentation by a sales force to a much larger audience.

richness
the complexity and content of a message

INTERACTIVITY

Unlike any of the commercial technologies of the twentieth century, with the possible exception of the telephone, e-commerce technologies allow for **interactivity**, meaning they enable two-way communication between merchant and consumer and among consumers. Traditional television or radio, for instance, cannot ask viewers questions or enter into conversations with them, or request that customer information be entered into a form.

Interactivity allows an online merchant to engage a consumer in ways similar to a face-to-face experience. Comment features, community forums, and social networks with social sharing functionality such as Like and Share buttons all enable consumers to actively interact with merchants and other users. Somewhat less obvious forms of interactivity include responsive design elements, such as websites that change format depending on what kind of device they are being viewed on, product images that change as a mouse hovers over them, the ability to zoom in or rotate images, forms that notify the user of a problem as they are being filled out, and search boxes that autofill as the user types.

interactivity
technology that allows for two-way communication between merchant and consumer

INFORMATION DENSITY

information density
the total amount and quality of information available to all market participants

E-commerce technologies vastly increase **information density**—the total amount and quality of information available to all market participants, consumers and merchants alike. E-commerce technologies reduce information collection, storage, processing, and communication costs. At the same time, these technologies greatly increase the currency, accuracy, and timeliness of information—making information more useful and important than ever. As a result, information becomes more plentiful, less expensive, and of higher quality.

A number of business consequences result from the growth in information density. One of the shifts that e-commerce is bringing about is a reduction in information asymmetry among market participants (consumers and merchants). Prices and costs become more transparent. *Price transparency* refers to the ease with which consumers can find out the variety of prices in a market; *cost transparency* refers to the ability of consumers to discover the actual costs merchants pay for products. Preventing consumers from learning about prices and costs becomes more difficult with e-commerce and, as a result, the entire marketplace potentially becomes more price competitive (Sinha, 2000). But there are advantages for merchants as well. Online merchants can discover much more about consumers; this allows merchants to segment the market into groups willing to pay different prices and permits them to engage in *price discrimination*—selling the same goods, or nearly the same goods, to different targeted groups at different prices. For instance, an online merchant can discover a consumer's avid interest in expensive exotic vacations, and then pitch expensive exotic vacation plans to that consumer at a premium price, knowing this person is willing to pay extra for such a vacation. At the same time, the online merchant can pitch the same vacation plan at a lower price to more price-sensitive consumers. Merchants also have enhanced abilities to differentiate their products in terms of cost, brand, and quality.

PERSONALIZATION AND CUSTOMIZATION

personalization
the targeting of marketing messages to specific individuals by adjusting the message to a person's name, interests, and past purchases

customization
changing the delivered product or service based on a user's preferences or prior behavior

E-commerce technologies permit **personalization**: merchants can target their marketing messages to specific individuals by adjusting the message to a person's name, interests, and past purchases. Today this is achieved in a few milliseconds and followed by an advertisement based on the consumer's profile. The technology also permits **customization**—changing the delivered product or service based on a user's preferences or prior behavior. Given the interactive nature of e-commerce technology, much information about the consumer can be gathered in the marketplace at the moment of purchase.

With the increase in information density, a great deal of information about the consumer's past purchases and behavior can be stored and used by online merchants. The result is a level of personalization and customization unthinkable with traditional commerce technologies. For instance, you may be able to shape what you see on television by selecting a channel, but you cannot change the contents of the channel you have chosen. In contrast, the online version of the *Financial Times* allows you to select the type of news stories you want to see first, and gives you the opportunity to be alerted when certain events happen. Personalization and customization allow firms to precisely identify market segments and adjust their messages accordingly.

SOCIAL TECHNOLOGY: USER-GENERATED CONTENT AND SOCIAL NETWORKS

In a way quite different from all previous technologies, e-commerce technologies have evolved to be much more social by allowing users to create and share content with a worldwide community. Using these forms of communication, users are able to create new social networks and strengthen existing ones.

All previous mass media in modern history, including the printing press, used a broadcast model (one-to-many): content is created in a central location by experts (professional writers, editors, directors, actors, and producers) and audiences are concentrated in huge aggregates to consume a standardized product. The telephone would appear to be an exception but it is not a mass communication technology. Instead the telephone is a one-to-one technology. E-commerce technologies have the potential to invert this standard media model by giving users the power to create and distribute content on a large scale, and permit users to program their own content consumption. E-commerce technologies provide a unique, many-to-many model of mass communication.

Table 1.2 provides a summary of each of the unique features of e-commerce technology and their business significance.

TABLE 1.2 BUSINESS SIGNIFICANCE OF THE EIGHT UNIQUE FEATURES OF E-COMMERCE TECHNOLOGY

E-COMMERCE TECHNOLOGY DIMENSION	BUSINESS SIGNIFICANCE
Ubiquity—E-commerce technology is available everywhere: at work, at home, and elsewhere via mobile devices, anytime.	The marketplace is extended beyond traditional boundaries and is removed from a temporal and geographic location. "Marketspace" is created; shopping can take place anywhere. Customer convenience is enhanced, and shopping costs are reduced.
Global reach—The technology reaches across national boundaries, around the earth.	Commerce is enabled across cultural and national boundaries seamlessly and without modification. "Marketspace" includes potentially billions of consumers and millions of businesses worldwide.
Universal standards—There is one set of technology standards.	There is a common, inexpensive, global technology foundation for businesses to use.
Richness—Video, audio, and text messages are possible.	Video, audio, and text marketing messages are integrated into a single marketing message and consuming experience.
Interactivity—The technology works through interaction with the user.	Consumers are engaged in a dialog that dynamically adjusts the experience to the individual and makes the consumer a co-participant in the process of delivering goods to the market.
Information density—The technology reduces information costs and raises quality.	Information processing, storage, and communication costs drop dramatically, while currency, accuracy, and timeliness improve greatly. Information becomes plentiful, cheap, and accurate.
Personalization/Customization—The technology allows personalized messages to be delivered to individuals as well as groups.	Enables personalization of marketing messages and customization of products and services based on individual characteristics.
Social technology—User-generated content and social networks.	Enables user content creation and distribution and supports development of social networks.

1.4 TYPES OF E-COMMERCE

There are a number of different types of e-commerce and many different ways to characterize them. For the most part, we distinguish different types of e-commerce by the nature of the market relationship—who is selling to whom. Mobile, social, and local e-commerce can be looked at as subsets of these types of e-commerce.

BUSINESS-TO-CONSUMER (B2C) E-COMMERCE

business-to-consumer (B2C) e-commerce
online businesses selling to individual consumers

The most commonly discussed type of e-commerce is **business-to-consumer (B2C) e-commerce**, in which online businesses attempt to reach individual consumers. B2C e-commerce includes purchases of retail goods, travel, financial, real estate, and other types of services, and online content. B2C has grown exponentially since 1995 and is the type of e-commerce that most consumers are likely to encounter (see **Figure 1.5**).

Within the B2C category, there are many different types of business models. Chapter 5 has a detailed discussion of seven different B2C business models: online retailers, service providers, transaction brokers, content providers, community providers/social networks, market creators, and portals. Then we look at each of these business models in action. In Chapter 11, we examine online retailers, service providers, including on-demand services,

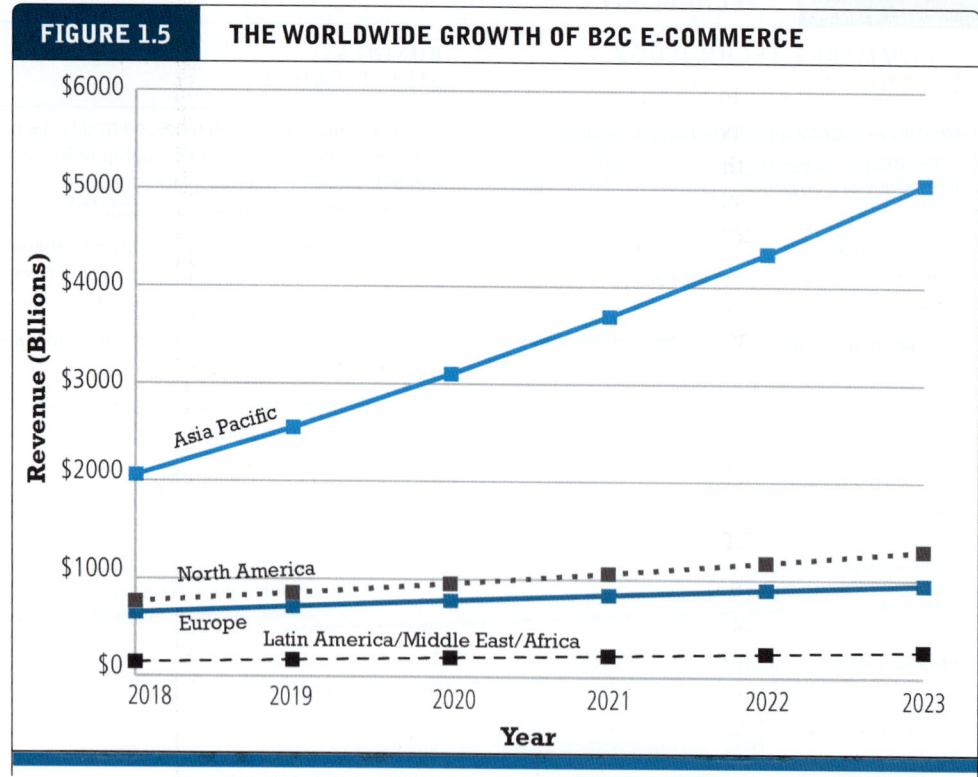

FIGURE 1.5 — THE WORLDWIDE GROWTH OF B2C E-COMMERCE

B2C e-commerce is growing in all regions. Overall global growth is over 20% and is even higher in Asia-Pacific.
SOURCES: Based on data from eMarketer, Inc., 2019c; 2019d.

FIGURE 1.6 ROOM TO GROW: WORLDWIDE RETAIL E-COMMERCE, 2019

The retail e-commerce market is still just a small part of the overall global retail market, but with much room to grow in the future.

and transaction brokers. In Chapter 9, we focus on content providers. In Chapter 10, we look at community providers (social networks), market creators (auctions), and portals.

The data suggests that, over the next five years, B2C e-commerce worldwide will continue to grow by over 20% annually. There is tremendous upside potential. Today, for instance, retail e-commerce (which currently comprises the majority of B2C e-commerce revenues) is still a very small part (around 14%) of the overall $25 trillion retail market worldwide. There is obviously much room to grow (see **Figure 1.6**). However, it's not likely that B2C e-commerce revenues will continue to expand forever at current rates. As online sales become a larger percentage of all sales, online sales growth will likely eventually decline. However, this point still appears to be a long way off. Online content sales, involving everything from music, to video, games, and entertainment, have an even longer period to grow before they hit any ceiling effects.

BUSINESS-TO-BUSINESS (B2B) E-COMMERCE

Business-to-business (B2B) e-commerce, in which businesses focus on selling to other businesses, is the largest form of e-commerce, with around $6.5 trillion in transactions in the United States in 2019 (see **Figure 1.7**) and about $27 trillion worldwide (U.S. Census Bureau, 2019; UNCTAD, 2019). This is a small portion of total B2B commerce (which remains largely non-automated), suggesting that B2B e-commerce has significant growth potential. The ultimate size of B2B e-commerce is potentially huge.

There are two primary business models used within the B2B arena: Net marketplaces, which include e-distributors, e-procurement companies, exchanges, and industry

business-to-business (B2B) e-commerce
online businesses selling to other businesses

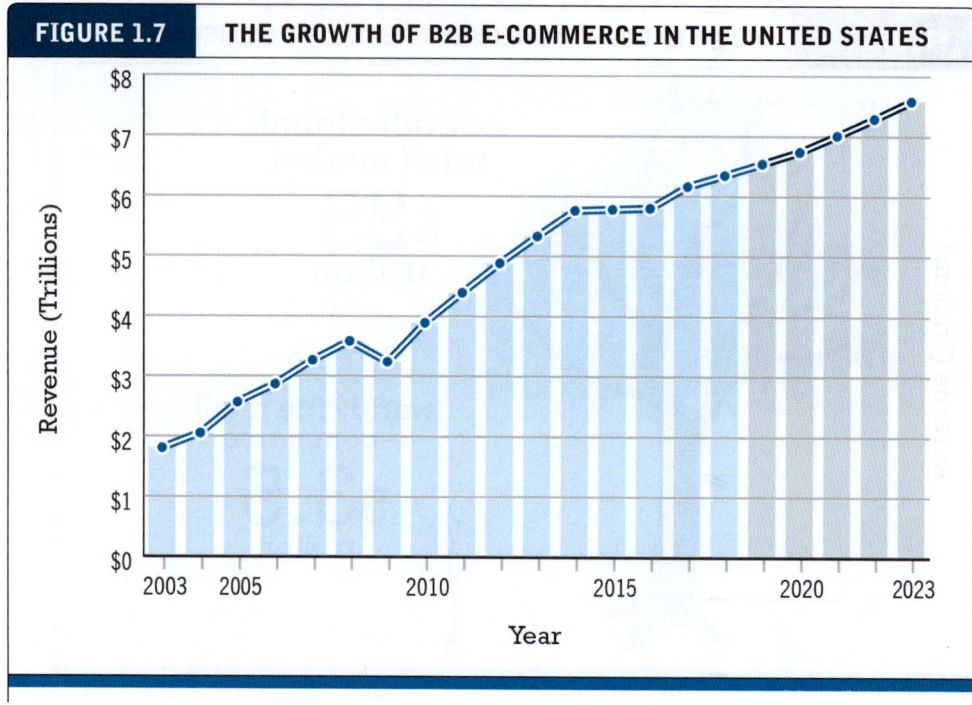

FIGURE 1.7   THE GROWTH OF B2B E-COMMERCE IN THE UNITED STATES

B2B e-commerce in the United States is about six times the size of B2C e-commerce. In 2023, B2B e-commerce is projected to be reach around $7.6 trillion. (Note: Does not include EDI transactions.)
SOURCES: Based on data from U.S. Census Bureau, 2019; authors' estimates.

consortia, and private industrial networks. We review various B2B business models in Chapter 5 and examine them in further depth in Chapter 12.

CONSUMER-TO-CONSUMER (C2C) E-COMMERCE

consumer-to-consumer (C2C) e-commerce
consumers selling to other consumers

Consumer-to-consumer (C2C) e-commerce provides a way for consumers to sell to each other, with the help of an online market maker (also called a platform provider). In C2C e-commerce, the consumer prepares the product for market, places the product for auction or sale, and relies on the market maker to provide catalog, search engine, and transaction-clearing capabilities so that products can be easily displayed, discovered, and paid for. eBay, Craigslist, and Etsy were the original C2C platform provider pioneers in the United States, but today they face significant competition. For instance, third-party sales on Amazon have skyrocketed. Facebook has also entered the arena with Facebook Marketplace. There are also a number of new entrants focused on the C2C market, such as Gumtree, Quikr, Depop, and Vinted. On-demand service companies such as Uber and Airbnb can also be considered as C2C platform providers.

MOBILE E-COMMERCE (M-COMMERCE)

mobile e-commerce (m-commerce)
use of mobile devices to enable online transactions

Mobile e-commerce (m-commerce) refers to the use of mobile devices to enable online transactions. M-commerce involves the use of cellular and wireless networks to connect

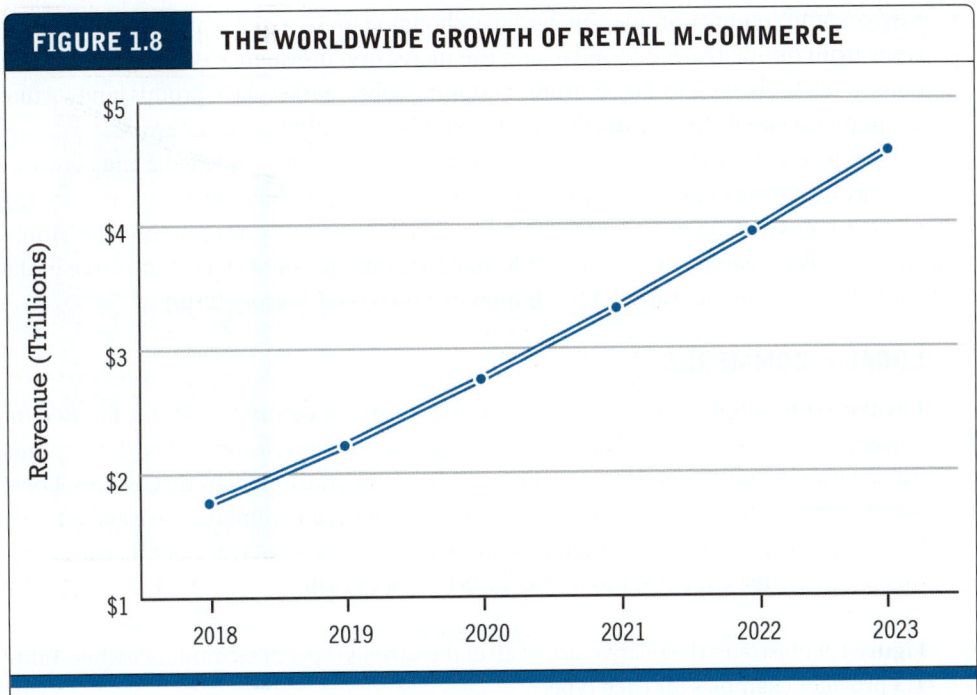

FIGURE 1.8 THE WORLDWIDE GROWTH OF RETAIL M-COMMERCE

It is anticipated that retail m-commerce will continue to grow by over 20% a year through the next several years as consumers become more and more accustomed to using mobile devices to purchase products and services.
SOURCES: Based on data from eMarketer, Inc., 2019e.

smartphones and tablet computers to the Internet. Once connected, mobile consumers can purchase products and services, make travel reservations, use an expanding variety of financial services, access online content, and much more.

Retail m-commerce purchases reached over $2.2 trillion worldwide in 2019 and are expected to continue to grow rapidly over the next five years (see **Figure 1.8**). Factors that are driving the growth of m-commerce include the increasing amount of time consumers are spending using mobile devices, larger smartphone screen sizes, greater use of responsive design enabling websites to be better optimized for mobile use and mobile checkout and payment, and enhanced mobile search functionality (eMarketer, Inc., 2018e). A variation of m-commerce known as *conversational commerce* involves the use of chatbots on mobile messaging apps such as Facebook Messenger, WhatsApp, Snapchat, and Slack as a vehicle for companies to engage with consumers.

SOCIAL E-COMMERCE

Social e-commerce is e-commerce that is enabled by social networks and online social relationships. Social e-commerce is often intertwined with m-commerce, particularly as more and more social network users access those networks via mobile devices. The growth of social e-commerce is being driven by a number of factors, including the increasing popularity of social sign-on (signing onto websites using your Facebook or other social network ID), network notification (the sharing of approval or disapproval of products,

social e-commerce
e-commerce enabled by social networks and online social relationships

services, and content), online collaborative shopping tools, social search (recommendations from online trusted friends), and the increasing prevalence of integrated social commerce tools such as Buy buttons, Shopping tabs, marketplace groups, and virtual shops on Facebook, Instagram, Pinterest, YouTube, and other social networks.

Social e-commerce is still in its relative infancy, but with social media and networks playing an increasingly important role in influencing purchase decisions and driving sales, it is continuing to grow. According to Policy Factory, a series produced by Think-Tanks+, a Paris-based news agency dedicated to think-thanks, social e-commerce in the United States generated about $16.5 billion in 2018 (Policy Factory, 2019).

LOCAL E-COMMERCE

local e-commerce
e-commerce that is focused on engaging the consumer based on his or her current geographic location

Local e-commerce, as its name suggests, is a form of e-commerce that is focused on engaging the consumer based on his or her current geographic location. Local merchants use a variety of online marketing techniques to drive consumers to their stores. Local e-commerce is the third prong of the mobile-social-local e-commerce wave and is being fueled by an explosion of interest in local on-demand services such as Uber. Local e-commerce grew in the United States to over $125 billion in 2019.

Figure 1.9 illustrates the relative size of all of the various types of e-commerce while **Table 1.3** provides examples for each type.

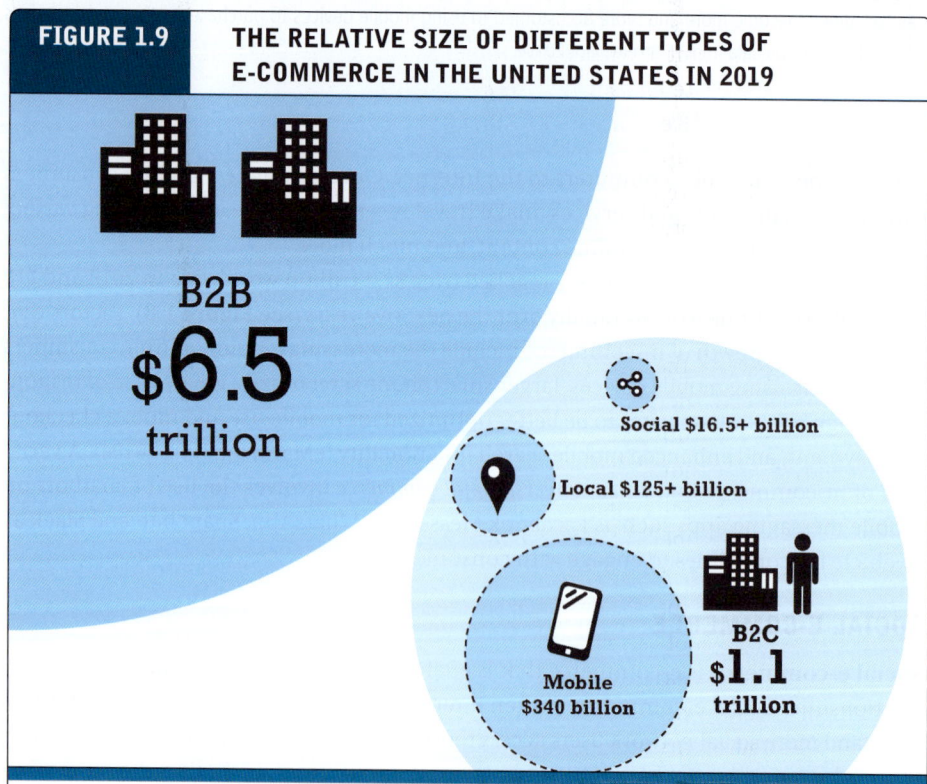

FIGURE 1.9   THE RELATIVE SIZE OF DIFFERENT TYPES OF E-COMMERCE IN THE UNITED STATES IN 2019

B2B $6.5 trillion
Social $16.5+ billion
Local $125+ billion
Mobile $340 billion
B2C $1.1 trillion

B2B e-commerce dwarfs all other forms of e-commerce; mobile, social, and local e-commerce, although growing rapidly, are still relatively small in comparison to "traditional" e-commerce.

TABLE 1.3	MAJOR TYPES OF E-COMMERCE
TYPE OF E-COMMERCE	EXAMPLE
B2C—business-to-consumer	Amazon is a general merchandiser that sells consumer products to retail consumers.
B2B—business-to-business	Metalshub is an independent third-party marketplace that serves the paper industry.
C2C—consumer-to-consumer	Online platforms such as eBay, Etsy, and Gumtree enable consumers to sell goods directly to other consumers. Airbnb and Uber provide similar platforms for services such as room rental and transportation.
M-commerce—mobile e-commerce	Mobile devices such as tablet computers and smartphones can be used to conduct commercial transactions.
Social e-commerce	Facebook is both the leading social network and social e-commerce platform.
Local e-commerce	Groupon offers subscribers daily deals from local businesses in the form of Groupons, discount coupons that take effect once enough subscribers have agreed to purchase.

1.5 E-COMMERCE: A BRIEF HISTORY

It is difficult to pinpoint just when e-commerce began. There were several precursors to e-commerce. In the late 1970s, a pharmaceutical firm named Baxter Healthcare initiated a primitive form of B2B e-commerce by using a telephone-based modem that permitted hospitals to reorder supplies from Baxter. This system was later expanded during the 1980s into a PC-based remote order entry system and was widely copied throughout the United States long before the Internet became a commercial environment. The 1980s saw the development of Electronic Data Interchange (EDI) standards that permitted firms to exchange commercial documents and conduct digital commercial transactions across private networks.

In the B2C arena, the first truly large-scale digitally enabled transaction system was the Minitel, a French videotext system that combined a telephone with an 8-inch screen. The Minitel was first introduced in 1981, and by the mid-1980s, more than 3 million had been deployed, with more than 13,000 different services available, including ticket agencies, travel services, retail products, and online banking. The Minitel service continued in existence until December 31, 2006, when it was finally discontinued by its owner, France Telecom.

However, none of these precursor systems had the functionality of the Internet. Generally, when we think of e-commerce today, it is inextricably linked to the Internet. For our purposes, we will say e-commerce begins in 1995, following the appearance of the first banner advertisements placed by AT&T, Volvo, Sprint, and others on Hotwired in late October 1994, and the first sales of banner ad space by Netscape and Infoseek in early 1995.

Although e-commerce is not very old, it already has a tumultuous history, which can be usefully divided into three periods: 1995–2000, the period of invention; 2001–2006, the period of consolidation; and 2007–present, a period of reinvention with social, mobile, and local expansion. The following examines each of these periods briefly, while **Figure 1.10** places them in context along a timeline.

E-COMMERCE 1995–2000: INVENTION

The early years of e-commerce were a period of explosive growth and extraordinary innovation. During this Invention period, e-commerce meant selling retail goods, usually quite simple goods, on the Internet. There simply was not enough bandwidth for more complex products. Marketing was limited to unsophisticated static display ads and not very powerful search engines. The web policy of most large firms, if they had one at all, was to have a basic static website depicting their brands. The rapid growth in e-commerce was fueled by over $125 billion in venture capital. This period of e-commerce came to a close in 2000 when stock market valuations plunged, with thousands of companies disappearing (the "dot-com crash").

The early years of e-commerce were one of the most euphoric of times in commercial history. It was also a time when key e-commerce concepts were developed. For computer scientists and information technologists, the early success of e-commerce was a powerful vindication of a set of information technologies that had developed over a period of 40 years—extending from the development of the early Internet, to the PC, to local area networks. The vision was of a universal communications and computing environment that everyone on Earth could access with cheap, inexpensive computers—a worldwide universe

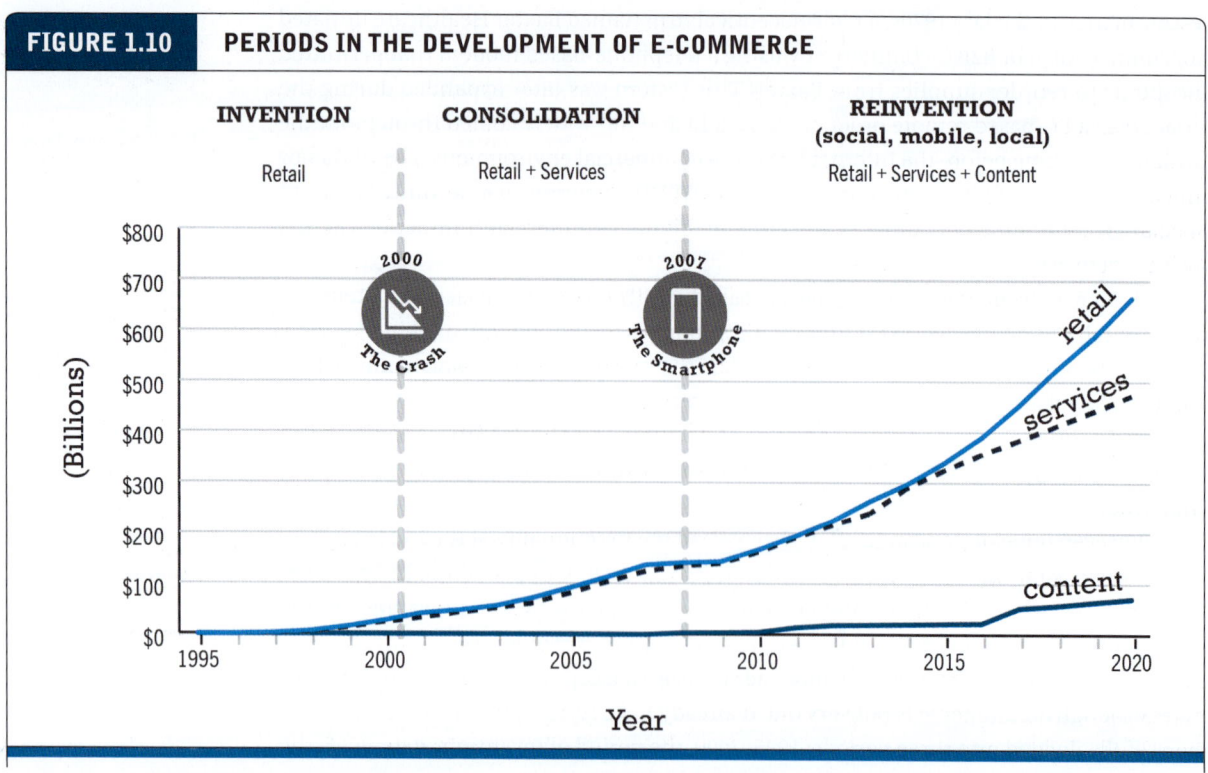

FIGURE 1.10 PERIODS IN THE DEVELOPMENT OF E-COMMERCE

of knowledge stored on HTML pages created by hundreds of millions of individuals and thousands of libraries, governments, and scientific institutes. Technologists celebrated the fact that the Internet was not controlled by anyone or any nation, but was free to all. They believed the Internet—and the e-commerce that rose on this infrastructure—should remain a self-governed, self-regulated environment.

For economists, the early years of e-commerce raised the realistic prospect of a nearly perfect competitive market: where price, cost, and quality information are equally distributed, a nearly infinite set of suppliers compete against one another, and customers have access to all relevant market information worldwide. The Internet would spawn digital markets where information would be nearly perfect—something that is rarely true in other real-world markets. Merchants in turn would have equal direct access to hundreds of millions of customers. In this near-perfect information marketspace, transaction costs would plummet because search costs—the cost of searching for prices, product descriptions, payment settlement, and order fulfillment—would all fall drastically (Bakos, 1997). For merchants, the cost of searching for customers would also fall, reducing the need for wasteful advertising. At the same time, advertisements could be personalized to the needs of every customer. Prices and even costs would be increasingly transparent to the consumer, who could now know exactly and instantly the worldwide best price, quality, and availability of most products. Information asymmetry would be greatly reduced. Given the instant nature of Internet communications, the availability of powerful sales information systems, and the low cost involved in changing online prices (low menu costs), producers could dynamically price their products to reflect actual demand, ending the idea of one national price, or one suggested manufacturer's list price. In turn, market middlemen—the distributors and wholesalers who are intermediaries between producers and consumers, each demanding a payment and raising costs while adding little value—would disappear (**disintermediation**). Manufacturers and content originators would develop direct market relationships with their customers. The resulting intense competition, the decline of intermediaries, and the lower transaction costs would eliminate product brands, and along with these, the possibility of *monopoly profits* based on brands, geography, or special access to factors of production. Prices for products and services would fall to the point where prices covered costs of production plus a fair, "market rate" of return on capital, plus additional small payments for entrepreneurial effort (that would not last long). Unfair competitive advantages (which occur when one competitor has an advantage others cannot purchase) would be reduced, as would extraordinary returns on invested capital. This vision was called **friction-free commerce** (Smith et al., 2000).

For real-world entrepreneurs, their financial backers, and marketing professionals, e-commerce represented a tremendous opportunity to earn far above normal returns on investment. This is just the opposite of what economists hoped for. The e-commerce marketspace represented access to millions of consumers worldwide who used the Internet and a set of marketing communications technologies (e-mail and web pages) that was universal, inexpensive, and powerful. These new technologies would permit marketers to practice what they always had done—segmenting the market into groups with different needs and price sensitivity, targeting the segments with branding and promotional messages, and positioning the product and pricing for each group—but with even more precision. In this new marketspace, extraordinary profits would go to **first movers**—those

disintermediation
displacement of market middlemen who traditionally are intermediaries between producers and consumers by a new direct relationship between producers and consumers

friction-free commerce
a vision of commerce in which information is equally distributed, transaction costs are low, prices can be dynamically adjusted to reflect actual demand, intermediaries decline, and unfair competitive advantages are eliminated

first mover
a firm that is first to market in a particular area and that moves quickly to gather market share

firms who were first to market in a particular area and who moved quickly to gather market share. In a "winner take all" market, first movers could establish a large customer base quickly, build brand name recognition early, create an entirely new distribution channel, and then inhibit competitors (new entrants) by building in *switching costs* for their customers through proprietary interface designs and features available only on one platform. The idea for entrepreneurs was to create near monopolies online based on size, convenience, selection, and brand. Online businesses using the new technology could create informative, community-like features unavailable to traditional merchants. These "communities of consumption" also would add value and be difficult for traditional merchants to imitate. The thinking was that once customers became accustomed to using a company's unique web interface and feature set, they could not easily be switched to competitors. In the best case, the entrepreneurial firm would invent proprietary technologies and techniques that almost everyone adopted, creating a network effect. A **network effect** occurs where all participants receive value from the fact that everyone else uses the same tool or product (for example, a common operating system, telephone system, or software application such as a proprietary instant messaging standard or an operating system such as Windows), all of which increase in value as more people adopt them.[1]

network effect
occurs where users receive value from the fact that everyone else uses the same tool or product

To initiate this process, entrepreneurs argued that prices would have to be very low to attract customers and fend off potential competitors. E-commerce was, after all, a totally new way of shopping that would have to offer some immediate cost benefits to consumers. However, because doing business on the Web was supposedly so much more efficient when compared to traditional "bricks-and-mortar" businesses (even when compared to the direct mail catalog business) and because the costs of customer acquisition and retention would supposedly be so much lower, profits would inevitably materialize out of these efficiencies. Given these dynamics, market share, the number of online visitors ("eyeballs"), and gross revenue became far more important in the earlier stages of an online firm than earnings or profits. Entrepreneurs and their financial backers in the early years of e-commerce expected that extraordinary profitability would come, but only after several years of losses.

Thus, the early years of e-commerce were driven largely by visions of profiting from new technology, with the emphasis on quickly achieving very high market visibility. The source of financing was venture capital funds. The ideology of the period emphasized the ungoverned "Wild West" character of the Web and the feeling that governments and courts could not possibly limit or regulate the Internet; there was a general belief that traditional corporations were too slow and bureaucratic, too stuck in the old ways of doing business, to "get it"—to be competitive in e-commerce. Young entrepreneurs were therefore the driving force behind e-commerce, backed by huge amounts of money invested by venture capitalists. The emphasis was on *disrupting* (destroying) traditional distribution channels and disintermediating existing channels, using new pure online companies who aimed to achieve impregnable first-mover advantages. Overall, this period of e-commerce was characterized by experimentation, capitalization, and hypercompetition (Varian, 2000b).

---

[1] The network effect is quantified by Metcalfe's Law, which argues that the value of a network grows by the square of the number of participants.

E-COMMERCE 2001–2006: CONSOLIDATION

In the second period of e-commerce, from 2000 to 2006, a sobering period of reassessment of e-commerce occurred, with many critics doubting its long-term prospects. Emphasis shifted to a more "business-driven" approach rather than being technology driven; large traditional firms learned how to use the Web to strengthen their market positions; brand extension and strengthening became more important than creating new brands; financing shrunk as capital markets shunned startup firms; and traditional bank financing based on profitability returned.

During this period of consolidation, e-commerce changed to include not just retail products but also more complex services such as travel and financial services. This period was enabled by widespread adoption of broadband networks in American homes and businesses, coupled with the growing power and lower prices of personal computers that were the primary means of accessing the Internet, usually from work or home. Marketing on the Internet increasingly meant using search engine advertising targeted to user queries, rich media and video ads, and behavioral targeting of marketing messages based on ad networks and auction markets. The web policy of both large and small firms expanded to include a broader "web presence" that included not just websites, but also e-mail, display, and search engine campaigns; multiple websites for each product; and the building of some limited community feedback facilities. E-commerce in this period was growing again by more than 10% a year.

E-COMMERCE 2007–PRESENT: REINVENTION

Beginning in 2007 with the introduction of the iPhone, to the present day, e-commerce has been transformed yet again by the rapid growth of **Web 2.0** (a set of applications and technologies that enable user-generated content, such as that posted on online social networks, blogs, wikis, and video- and photo-sharing websites and apps; widespread adoption of mobile devices such as smartphones and tablet computers; the expansion of e-commerce to include local goods and services; and the emergence of an on-demand service economy enabled by millions of apps on mobile devices and cloud computing. This period can be seen as both a sociological, as well as a technological and business phenomenon.

The defining characteristics of this period are often characterized as the "social, mobile, local" online world. Entertainment content has developed as a major source of e-commerce revenues and mobile devices have become entertainment centers, as well as on-the-go shopping devices for retail goods and services. Marketing has been transformed by the increasing use of social networks, word-of-mouth, viral marketing, and much more powerful data repositories and analytic tools for truly personal marketing. Firms have greatly expanded their online presence by moving beyond static web pages to social networks such as Facebook, Twitter, Pinterest, and Instagram in an attempt to surround the online consumer with coordinated marketing messages. These social networks share many common characteristics. First, they rely on user-generated content. "Regular" people (not just experts or professionals) are creating, sharing, and broadcasting content to huge audiences. They are inherently highly interactive, creating new opportunities for people to socially connect to others. They attract extremely large audiences (over 2 billion

Web 2.0

set of applications and technologies that enable user-generated content

TABLE 1.4 — EVOLUTION OF E-COMMERCE

1995–2000 INVENTION	2001–2006 CONSOLIDATION	2007–PRESENT REINVENTION
Technology driven	Business driven	Mobile technology enables social, local, and mobile e-commerce
Revenue growth emphasis	Earnings and profits emphasis	Audience and social network connections emphasis
Venture capital financing	Traditional financing	Return of venture capital financing; buy-outs of startups by large firms
Ungoverned	Stronger regulation and governance	Extensive government surveillance
Entrepreneurial	Large traditional firms	Entrepreneurial social, mobile, and local firms
Disintermediation	Strengthening intermediaries	Proliferation of small online intermediaries renting business processes of larger firms
Perfect markets	Imperfect markets, brands, and network effects	Continuation of online market imperfections; commodity competition in select markets
Pure online strategies	Mixed "bricks-and-clicks" strategies	Return of pure online strategies in new markets; extension of bricks-and-clicks in traditional retail markets
First-mover advantages	Strategic-follower strength; complementary assets	First-mover advantages return in new markets as traditional web players catch up
Low-complexity retail products	High-complexity retail products and services	Retail, services, and content

users worldwide as of December 2019 in the case of Facebook). These audiences present marketers with extraordinary opportunities for targeted marketing and advertising.

More recently, the reinvention of e-commerce has resulted in a set of on-demand, personal service businesses such as Uber, Airbnb, Instacart, and Deliveroo. These businesses have been able to tap into a large reservoir of unused assets (cars, spare rooms, and personal spare time) and to create lucrative markets based on the mobile platform infrastructure. The *Insight on Business* case, *Rocket Internet*, takes a look at Rocket Internet, which has invested in and mentored a number of startups.

Table 1.4 summarizes e-commerce in each of these three periods.

ASSESSING E-COMMERCE: SUCCESSES, SURPRISES, AND FAILURES

Looking back at the evolution of e-commerce, it is apparent that e-commerce has been a stunning technological success, ramping up from a few thousand to trillions of e-commerce transactions per year. In 2019 it generated about $4.2 trillion in retail and travel

INSIGHT ON BUSINESS

ROCKET INTERNET

By now most people have all heard the story of Mark Zuckerberg dropping out of college to start Facebook. These days, tech startup founders are less likely to build businesses on their own, and instead often seek the help of an incubator. Incubators have become essential in helping new tech startups grow from the kernel of a great idea into an established, vibrant business. Rocket Internet is one such incubator.

Founded in 2007 by German entrepreneurs Oliver Samwer and his brothers Alexander and Marc, Rocket Internet launches e-commerce and other Internet startups in emerging markets, with the goal of becoming the world's largest Internet platform outside the United States and China. Headquartered in Berlin and with offices around the globe, Rocket Internet has launched over 200 companies with more than 42,000 employees in 120 countries. In 2014, Rocket went public on the Frankfurt Stock Exchange in the largest German technology IPO in the past decade. The initial pricing valued the company at around €6.5 billion. Since its IPO, the company's stock price has steadily fallen from a high of nearly €60 before settling in at approximately €23 per share for most of 2019, and the company's market capitalization is now down to about €3.6 billion. Rocket's struggles illustrate the perils of chasing growth at all costs above profitability.

Rocket bills itself as more than a venture capital firm or typical incubator. Rocket has a variety of teams that work closely with each of its ventures, including teams focused on engineering and product development, online marketing, CRM, business intelligence, operations, HR, and finance. Rocket also helps its startups by providing access to centralized logistics and other back-office functions to help them cut down on operational costs. Rocket also handles the acquisition of venture capital on behalf of its startup companies, freeing them to focus on rapidly growing the business. Rocket is a data-driven company and its startups collect and analyze as much data as possible on their markets and customers, allowing them to quickly make changes to spur growth. In many emerging markets, the most talented workers end up in established industries, but Rocket is ensuring that e-commerce also captures top talent in those regions. Prominent companies launched via Rocket Internet include Germany's Zalando, India's Jabong, Russia's Lamoda, Australia's The Iconic and Zanui, Pakistan's Daraz, and Southeast Asia's Zalora.

However, critics of Rocket Internet claim that the company is less concerned with innovation than it is with launching clones of successful United States–based businesses in other markets. Rocket counters that it improves upon established businesses by refining their business processes and by localizing them to better fit specific areas. Investors have also long been concerned about the profitability of Rocket's portfolio. Many of Rocket's companies have market-leader status in their respective areas, but few of them are profitable. Rocket has contended that by focusing on growth in emerging markets first, profits would come in time. In 2018, the company finally made good on that promise, recording a net profit of €196 million for the year, up dramatically from a loss of €6 million in 2017. It continued in that vein in 2019, generating a profit of over €548 million for the first six months of the year. However, those profits were largely due to the successful IPOs of a number of its most prominent startups, including food delivery companies Delivery Hero and HelloFresh; home goods retailers Home24 and WestWing; African e-commerce retailer Jumia; and Global Fashion Group. For

(continued)

investors seeking exposure to e-commerce startup companies in emerging markets, opportunities can be scarce, since most of those companies are privately held. Rocket represents one of the few opportunities to invest in a portfolio dominated by these types of companies.

Rocket has had the most success launching companies modeled after established businesses in emerging markets and then selling these ventures to those established businesses. eBay's acquisition of Germany's leading auction site, Alando, where the Samwers got their start, is an example, and the company sold a controlling stake in Southeast Asian Amazon clone Lazada to Alibaba for $1 billion in 2016, a price exceeding investor valuations of the company and representing a profit of over 20 times its initial investment. In 2017, Rocket sold half of its shares of Delivery Hero for €660 million, as well as Germany-based beauty retailer Glossybox and Dubai-based fashion retailer Namshi. These sales and the IPOs have helped Rocket stay afloat as it continues to support its other businesses. In 2019, the company had a massive €3.3 billion in cash on hand. Many investors are still betting that with time and growth, more of Rocket's portfolio of companies will become profitable. In 2018, Rocket announced its plans to use its cash on hand to buy back up to €150 million of its own stock as well as to make more traditional investments in other startup companies. In the future, Rocket may begin to resemble something closer to a typical venture capital firm.

Rocket still understands that above all, it needs more of its stable of companies to become profitable. To that end, Rocket is focusing more on sustainable companies and less on selling their companies to market leaders Oliver Samwer believes that in the past, it may have sold some businesses, such as Alando, too early, but that it was necessary in order for Rocket to build a track record. Now that it has one, it can afford to take a longer-term view. Rocket is increasingly liquidating many of its smaller companies, especially in food delivery, with the sale of companies at a loss in Spain, Italy, Brazil, and Mexico. Rocket's Airbnb clone, Wimdu, closed down at the end of 2018 as well. Still, as the global economy continues to rely more on the Internet and Internet-based services, accelerators like Rocket Internet will have a prominent role in markets around the world.

SOURCES: "Rocket Internet Sits on $3.3 Billion Cash Pile after IPOs," by Stefan Nicola, Bloomberg.com, September 19, 2019; "Rocket Internet Set to Found More Companies in 2019," Reuters.com, April 4, 2019; "Rocket Internet Annual Report 2018," Rocket-internet.com, April 4, 2019; "Rocket Internet: Organizing a Startup Factory," by Oliver Baumann et al., Link.springer.com, December 2018; "Wimdu, Rocket Internet's Airbnb Clone, To Shut Down This Year 'Facing Significant Business Challenges,'" by Ingrid Lunden, Techcrunch.com, September 27, 2018; "Cash-flush Rocket Internet Lifted by $175 Million Buyback Plan," by Emma Thomasson, Reuters.com, September 20, 2018; "Rocket Internet CEO Samwer Looks at Crafting New Strategies for Success," by Stefan Nicola, Bloomberg, August 27, 2018; "Rocket Internet – Providing Access to Up and Coming Companies in the Emerging Markets," by Kevin Carter, Seekingalpha.com, June 10, 2018; "Rocket Internet's Spectacular Display," by Leila Abboud, Bloomberg.com, September 28, 2017; "Start-ups Giant Rocket Internet Offloads Glossybox to UK Rival," by Mark Kleinman, News.sky.com, August 14, 2017; "Rocket Internet's Trajectory Shift," by Leila Abboud, Bloomberg.com, November 23, 2016; "German Tech Incubator Rocket Internet to Focus on Biggest Companies," Nasdaq.com, November 16, 2016; "Rocket Internet Leaves Us Groping in the Dark," by Leila Abboud, Bloomberg.com, October 12, 2016; "Inside Rocket Internet's Ailing Startup Factory," by Jeremy Kahn, et al., Bloomberg.com, October 7, 2016; "Rocket Internet's Deal with Alibaba Validates Its Opaque, Unproven Model," by Joon Ian Wong, Qz.com, April 13, 2016; "Rocket Internet Drops 13% in Debut," by Chase Gummer, *Wall Street Journal*, October 2, 2014; "Rocket Internet's Marc Samwar on Cloning: We Make Business Models Better Because We Localize," by Leena Rao, Techcrunch.com, October 28, 2013; "eBay Acquires Germany's Leading Onine Person-to-Person Trading Site – Alando.de AG," Prnewswire.com, June 22, 2013.

B2C revenues from over 2 billion online buyers worldwide and around $27 trillion in B2B revenues. With enhancements and strengthening, described in later chapters, it is clear that e-commerce's digital infrastructure is solid enough to sustain significant growth in e-commerce during the next decade. The Internet scales well. The "e" in e-commerce has been an overwhelming success.

From a business perspective, though, the early years of e-commerce were a mixed success, and offered many surprises. Only a very small percentage of dot-coms formed in those early years have survived as independent companies. Yet online retail sales of goods and services are still growing very rapidly. Contrary to economists' hopes, however, online sales are increasingly concentrated. For instance, according to the *Internet Retailer Top 1000 Report*, in the United States, the top 1000 retailers accounted for almost 90% of all U.S. online retail sales in 2018. No one foresaw that Google and Facebook would dominate the online advertising marketplace, accounting for over 60% of U.S. digital advertising revenues, or that one firm, Amazon, would account for 37% of all U.S. online sales via direct sales and sales by third-party sellers using Amazon's platform, as well as more than 45% of the growth of U.S. e-commerce retail sales in 2018 (Digitalcommerce360.com, 2019; eMarketer, Inc., 2019f; Pymnts, 2019).

So thousands of firms have failed, and those few that have survived dominate the market. The idea of thousands of suppliers competing on price has been replaced by a market dominated by giant firms. Consumers use the Web as a powerful source of information about products they often actually purchase through other channels, such as at a traditional bricks-and-mortar store, a practice sometimes referred to as "webrooming," "ROBO" (research online, buy offline), or O2O (online-to-offline). One survey found that 80% of consumers said they had webroomed in the past 12 months. This is especially true of expensive consumer durables such as automobiles, appliances, and electronics (Netsertive, 2018). This offline "Internet-influenced" commerce is very difficult to estimate, but definitely significant. For instance, Forrester Research estimates that half of all U.S. retail sales in 2018 were influenced by consumers' use of digital devices prior to or during a physical shopping trip and expects this percentage to grow to almost 60% by 2023 (Forrester Research, 2018). The "commerce" in e-commerce is basically very sound, at least in the sense of attracting a growing number of customers and generating revenues and profits for large e-commerce players.

Although e-commerce has grown at an extremely rapid pace in customers and revenues, it is clear that many of the visions, predictions, and assertions about e-commerce developed in the early years have not been fulfilled. For instance, economists' visions of "friction-free" commerce have not been entirely realized. Prices are sometimes lower online, but the low prices are sometimes a function of entrepreneurs selling products below their costs. In some cases, online prices are higher than those of local merchants, as consumers are willing to pay a small premium for the convenience of buying online (Cavallo, 2016). Consumers are less price sensitive than expected; surprisingly, the websites with the highest revenue often have the highest prices. There remains considerable persistent and even increasing price dispersion: online competition has lowered prices, but price dispersion remains pervasive in many markets despite lower search costs (Levin, 2011,

Ghose and Yao, 2010). In a study of 50,000 goods in the United Kingdom and the United States, researchers found Internet prices were sticky even in the face of large changes in demand, online merchants did not alter prices significantly more than offline merchants, and price dispersion across online sellers was somewhat greater than traditional brick and mortar stores (Gorodnichenko et al., 2014). The concept of one world, one market, one price has not occurred in reality as entrepreneurs discover new ways to differentiate their products and services. Merchants have adjusted to the competitive Internet environment by engaging in "hit-and-run pricing" or changing prices every day or hour (using "flash pricing" or "flash sales") so competitors never know what they are charging (neither do customers); and by making their prices hard to discover and sowing confusion among consumers by "baiting and switching" customers from low-margin products to high-margin products with supposedly "higher quality." Finally, brands remain very important in e-commerce—consumers trust some firms more than others to deliver a high-quality product on time and they are willing to pay for it (Rosso and Jansen, 2010).

The "perfect competition" model of extreme market efficiency has not come to pass. Merchants and marketers are continually introducing information asymmetries. Search costs have fallen overall, but the overall transaction cost of actually completing a purchase in e-commerce remains high because users have a bewildering number of new questions to consider: Will the merchant actually deliver? What is the time frame of delivery? Does the merchant really stock this item? How do I fill out this form? Many potential e-commerce purchases are terminated in the shopping cart stage because of these consumer uncertainties. Some people still find it easier to call a trusted catalog merchant on the telephone than to order online.

Finally, intermediaries have not disappeared as predicted. Although many manufacturers do sell online directly to consumers, they typically also make use of major e-commerce marketplaces, such as Amazon, eBay, Walmart, Jet, and Wish.com. If anything, e-commerce has created many opportunities for middlemen to aggregate content, products, and services and thereby introduce themselves as the "new" intermediaries. Third-party travel sites such as Travelocity, Orbitz, and Expedia are an example of this kind of intermediary.

The visions of many entrepreneurs and venture capitalists for e-commerce have not materialized exactly as predicted either. First-mover advantage appears to have succeeded only for a very small group of companies, albeit some of them extremely well-known, such as Google, Facebook, Amazon, and others. Getting big fast sometimes works, but often not. Historically, first movers have been long-term losers, with the early-to-market innovators usually being displaced by established "fast-follower" firms with the right complement of financial, marketing, legal, and production assets needed to develop mature markets, and this has proved true for e-commerce as well. Many e-commerce first movers, such as eToys, FogDog (sporting goods), Webvan (groceries), and Eve.com (beauty products), failed. Customer acquisition and retention costs during the early years of e-commerce were extraordinarily high, with some firms, such as E*Trade and other financial service firms, paying up to $400 to acquire a new customer. The overall costs of doing business online—including the costs of technology, site and mobile app design and maintenance, and warehouses for fulfillment—are often no lower than the costs faced by the most efficient bricks-and-mortar stores. A large warehouse costs tens of millions of dollars regardless of a firm's online presence. The knowledge of how to run the warehouse is priceless, and not easily moved. The startup costs can be staggering. Attempting to achieve or enhance profitability by raising prices has often led to large customer defections. From the e-commerce merchant's perspective, the "e" in e-commerce does not stand for "easy."

On the other hand, there have been some extraordinary and unanticipated surprises in the evolution of e-commerce. Few predicted the impact of the mobile platform. Few anticipated the rapid growth of social networks or their growing success as advertising platforms based on a more detailed understanding of personal behavior than even Google has achieved. And few, if any, anticipated the emergence of on-demand e-commerce, which enables people to use their mobile devices to order up everything from taxis, to groceries, to laundry service.

1.6 UNDERSTANDING E-COMMERCE: ORGANIZING THEMES

Understanding e-commerce in its totality is a difficult task for students and instructors because there are so many facets to the phenomenon. No single academic discipline is prepared to encompass all of e-commerce. After teaching the e-commerce course for a number of years and writing this book, we have come to realize just how difficult it is to "understand" e-commerce. We have found it useful to think about e-commerce as involving three broad interrelated themes: technology, business, and society. We do not mean to imply any ordering of importance here because this book and our thinking freely range over these themes as appropriate to the problem we are trying to understand and describe. Nevertheless, as in previous technologically driven commercial revolutions, there is a historic progression. Technologies develop first, and then those developments are exploited commercially. Once commercial exploitation of the technology becomes widespread, a host of social, cultural, and political issues arise, and society is forced to respond to them.

TECHNOLOGY: INFRASTRUCTURE

The development and mastery of digital computing and communications technology is at the heart of the newly emerging global digital economy we call e-commerce. To understand the likely future of e-commerce, you need a basic understanding of the information technologies upon which it is built. E-commerce is above all else a technologically driven phenomenon that relies on a host of information technologies as well as fundamental concepts from computer science developed over a 50-year period. At the core of e-commerce are the Internet and the Web, which we describe in detail in Chapter 2. Underlying these technologies are a host of complementary technologies: cloud computing, desktop computers, smartphones, tablet computers, local area networks, relational and non-relational databases, client/server computing, data mining, and fiber-optic switches, to name just a few. These technologies lie at the heart of sophisticated business computing applications such as enterprise-wide information systems, supply chain management systems, manufacturing resource planning systems, and customer relationship management systems. E-commerce relies on all these basic technologies—not just the Internet. The Internet,

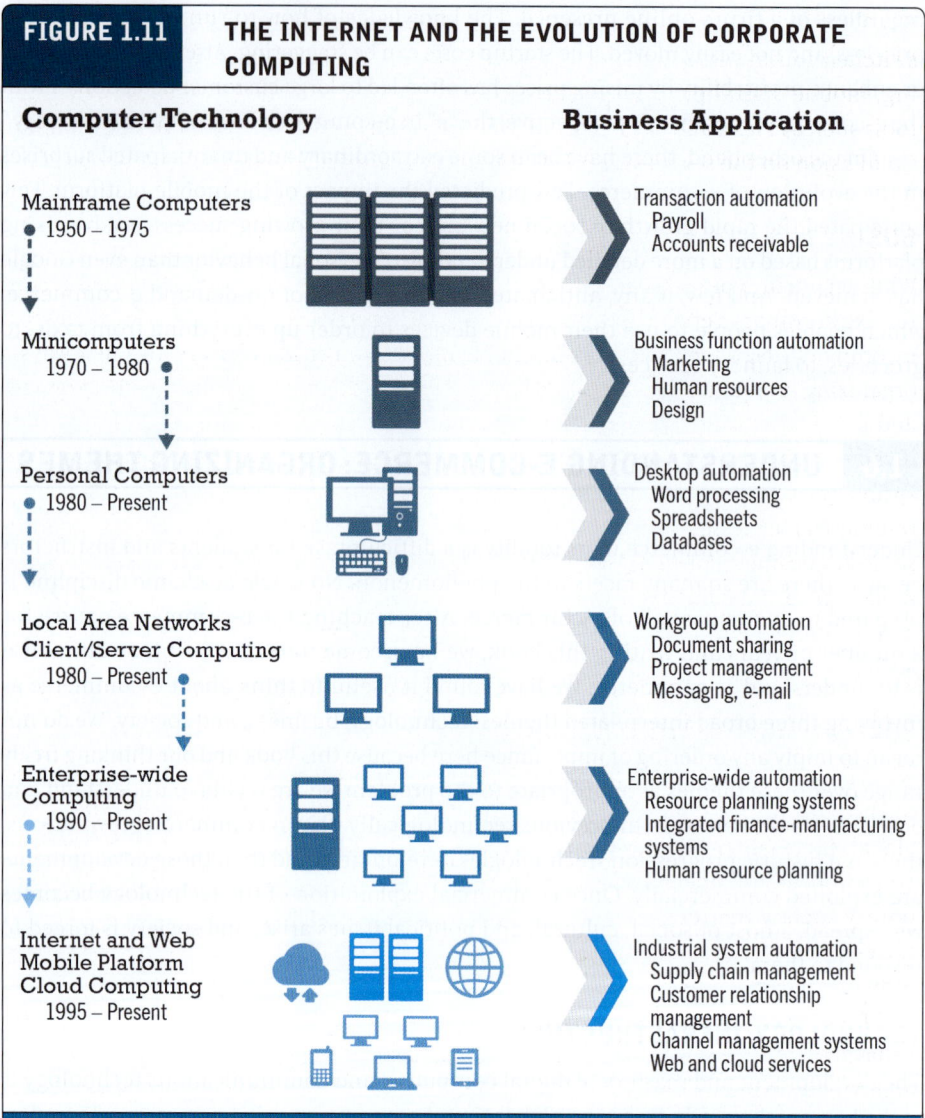

FIGURE 1.11 THE INTERNET AND THE EVOLUTION OF CORPORATE COMPUTING

The Internet and Web, and the emergence of a mobile platform held together by the Internet cloud, are the latest in a chain of evolving technologies and related business applications, each of which builds on its predecessors.

while representing a sharp break from prior corporate computing and communications technologies, is nevertheless just the latest development in the evolution of corporate computing and part of the continuing chain of computer-based innovations in business. **Figure 1.11** illustrates the major stages in the development of corporate computing and indicates how the Internet and the Web fit into this development trajectory.

To truly understand e-commerce, you will need to know something about packet-switched communications, protocols such as TCP/IP, client/server and cloud computing, mobile digital platforms, web servers, HTML5, CSS, and software programming tools such as Flash and JavaScript on the client side, and Java, PHP, Ruby on Rails, and ColdFusion on the server side. All of these topics are described fully in chapters 2–4.

BUSINESS: BASIC CONCEPTS

While technology provides the infrastructure, it is the business applications—the potential for extraordinary returns on investment—that create the interest and excitement in e-commerce. New technologies present businesses and entrepreneurs with new ways of organizing production and transacting business. New technologies change the strategies and plans of existing firms: old strategies are made obsolete and new ones need to be invented. New technologies are the birthing grounds where thousands of new companies spring up with new products and services. New technologies are the graveyard of many traditional businesses. To truly understand e-commerce, you will need to be familiar with some key business concepts, such as the nature of digital markets, digital goods, business models, firm and industry value chains, value webs, industry structure, digital disruption, and consumer behavior in digital markets, as well as basic concepts of financial analysis. We'll examine these concepts further in Chapters 5, 6, 7, and 9 through 12.

SOCIETY: TAMING THE JUGGERNAUT

With around 3.8 billion people worldwide now using the Internet, many for e-commerce purposes, the impact of the Internet and e-commerce on society is significant and global. Increasingly, e-commerce is subject to the laws of nations and global entities. You will need to understand the pressures that global e-commerce places on contemporary society in order to conduct a successful e-commerce business or understand the e-commerce phenomenon. The primary societal issues we discuss in this book are individual privacy, intellectual property, and public policy.

Because the Internet and the Web are exceptionally adept at tracking the identity and behavior of individuals online, e-commerce raises difficulties for preserving privacy—the ability of individuals to place limits on the type and amount of information collected about them, and to control the uses of their personal information. Read the *Insight on Society* case, *Facebook and the Age of Privacy*, to get a view of some of the ways e-commerce sites use personal information.

Because the cost of distributing digital copies of copyrighted intellectual property— tangible works of the mind such as music, books, and videos—is nearly zero on the Internet, e-commerce poses special challenges to the various methods societies have used in the past to protect intellectual property rights.

The global nature of e-commerce also poses public policy issues of equity, equal access, content regulation, and taxation. For instance, in the United States, public telephone utilities are required under public utility and public accommodation laws to make basic service available at affordable rates so everyone can have telephone service. Should these laws be extended to the Internet and the Web? If goods are purchased by a

INSIGHT ON SOCIETY

FACEBOOK AND THE AGE OF PRIVACY

Ever play a game or fill out a form or survey on Facebook or sign into a website with your Facebook credentials? When you did or used any of several million apps on the Facebook platform between 2007 and 2015, you probably were not aware that Facebook was giving unfettered access to both your own and your friends' personal information to third-party app developers and websites. The third-party developers could do whatever they wanted with that information. Although Facebook cut off that kind of third-party access in 2015, it recently revealed that it had lost control of that information and was unable to track how it had been used by third-party developers. The privacy preferences of users were ignored. Surprised? You shouldn't be: it's been standard business practice at Facebook for many years.

In a 2010 interview, Mark Zuckerberg, the founder of Facebook, proclaimed that the age of privacy had to come to an end. According to Zuckerberg, people were no longer so worried about sharing their personal information with friends, friends of friends, or even the online universe. Supporters of Zuckerberg's viewpoint believed that the twenty-first century would be a new era of openness and transparency. However, not everyone is a true believer. Privacy—limitations on what personal information government and private institutions can collect and use—is a founding principle of democracies. A decade's worth of privacy surveys in the United States show that well over 80% of the American public fear the Internet is a threat to their privacy. Today, Zuckerberg's remarks are haunting Facebook as the company faces its largest existential crisis in its brief history precisely over the issue of privacy.

Facebook's business model is based on building a database of billions of users who are encouraged, or even perhaps deceived, into relinquishing control over personal information, which is then sold to advertisers and other third-party developers who use the Facebook platform to sell services. The less privacy Facebook's users want or have, the more Facebook profits. Eliminating personal information privacy is built into Facebook's DNA and business model.

Third-party developers, advertisers, and Facebook employees and executives have known for years of Facebook's practice of sharing deep personal information with whomever would pay, but little of this was known by the public until the so-called Cambridge Analytica scandal that first came to light in early 2018. Cambridge Analytica was a political consulting and data analytics firm that obtained data on several hundred thousand Facebook users from Aleksandr Kogan, a psychology professor at Cambridge University. Kogan had obtained permission from Facebook to use the personal information of Facebook users as part of a research project on psychological profiles. Kogan used a personality quiz app that was downloaded by around 300,000 participants to collect the data, which included not only information about the participants, but also their friends, as well as their friends' friends. The result was a database of usable profiles of over 87 million Facebook users! Cambridge Analytica then used these profiles from Kogan to target political ads, initially in 2015 to support Senator Ted Cruz's presidential campaign, and later to support Donald Trump's campaign.

These revelations led to congressional hearings in which Zuckerberg and other executives apologized for Facebook's failure to enforce its own privacy policies, its failure to recognize the massive drain of personal information on 87 million users, and its failure to protect the privacy of its users. It was a mistake, the company said, and a breach of Facebook policies. Millions of users joined the Delete Facebook movement as a result of these revelations, although this has not had significant impact on Facebook's revenues. Facebook for its part has initiated a number of large-scale internal efforts to clarify its policies, restrict unlimited access to user information by advertisers and third-party developers, and make it easier for users to control how their personal information is used and by whom. No one knows if these efforts will succeed, and there are many skeptics given Facebook's past promises related to user privacy that have largely gone unfulfilled.

The Cambridge Analytica affair seriously damaged Facebook's long-standing claims that it would protect users' personal information from abuse by third-party developers. It also appears to violate the terms of a 2011 settlement with the U.S. Federal Trade Commission that required Facebook to obtain user consent before overriding their privacy preferences, stop making false statements about how much information was shared with third-party developers, stop falsely claiming users could restrict sharing of data to limited audiences, such as only a user's friends, and stop falsely claiming that it did not share deep personal information with advertisers.

Public confidence in Facebook's claims that it would protect users' privacy was further shaken in 2018 when Facebook revealed that it also had data-sharing agreements with at least 60 phone and device makers, including Apple, Amazon, BlackBerry, Microsoft, and Samsung, that allowed these firms access to virtually all the personal information on Facebook users. These agreements allowed device makers to offer their customers Facebook features such as Like buttons, games, address books and calendars, and messaging. In addition, the personal data on users' friends was also shared, even when these friends had explicitly chosen not to have their data shared using Facebook's privacy controls. According to Facebook, these device manufacturers are not considered third parties, but rather as device partners, and their use of this information is regulated by so-called strict agreements. In 2018 a *New York Times* reporter tested a BlackBerry app called The Hub that lets users view all of their messages and social media counts in one location. After connecting, the Hub app retrieved detailed data on the reporter and 556 of her friends, and 294,000 friends of the reporter's friends. So one user account generated data on hundreds of thousands of other Facebook users without their consent and without regard to their privacy settings in Facebook. The BlackBerry Hub app was able to access more than 50 types of personal information about users and friends. The data is stored on the device provider's servers. Spokespersons for the device makers either declined to comment or claimed they used the information solely to provide an effective user experience. Facebook claims it is reducing this program, but it is unclear what information, if any, will continue to be shared.

■ **SOURCES:** "Facebook's Latest Problem: It Can't Track Where Much of the Data Went," by Deepa Seetharaman, *Wall Street Journal*, June 27, 2018; "Facebook Gave Device Makers Deep Access to Data on Users and Friends," by Gabriel Dance, Nicholas Confessore, and Michael LaForgian, *New York Times*, June 3, 2018; "Facebook Says Cambridge Analytica Harvested Data of Up to 87 Million Users," by Cecilia Kang and Sheera Frenkel, *New York Times*, April 24, 2018; "Facebook Introduces Central Page for Privacy and Security Settings," by Sheera Frenkel and Natasha Singer, *New York Times*, March 28, 2018; "FTC Probing Facebook Over Data Use by Cambridge Analytica," by John D. McKinnon, *New York Times*, March 20, 2018; "Facebook's Role in Data Misuse Sets Off Storms on Two Continents," by Matthew Rosenberg and Sheera Frenkel, *New York Times*, March 18, 2018; "How Trump Consultants Exploited the Facebook Data of Millions," by Matthew Rosenberg, Nicholas Confessore, and Carole Cadwalladr, *New York Times*, March 17, 2018; "Experimental Evidence of Massive-scale Emotional Contagion Through Social Networks," by Adam D. I. Kramera, Jamie E. Guillory, and Jeffrey T. Hancock, Proceedings of the National Academy of Sciences, March 25, 2014; "Facebook Settles FTC Charges That It Deceived Consumers By Failing to Keep Privacy Promises," Federal Trade Commission, November 29, 2011.

New York State resident from a website in California, shipped from a center in Illinois, and delivered to New York, what state has the right to collect a sales tax? Should some heavy Internet users who consume extraordinary amounts of bandwidth by streaming endless movies be charged extra for service, or should the Internet be neutral with respect to usage? What rights do nation-states and their citizens have with respect to the Internet, the Web, and e-commerce? We address issues such as these in Chapter 8, and also throughout the text.

1.7 ACADEMIC DISCIPLINES CONCERNED WITH E-COMMERCE

The phenomenon of e-commerce is so broad that a multidisciplinary perspective is required. There are two primary approaches to e-commerce: technical and behavioral.

TECHNICAL APPROACHES

Computer scientists are interested in e-commerce as an exemplary application of Internet technology. They are concerned with the development of computer hardware, software, and telecommunications systems, as well as standards, encryption, and database design and operation. Operations management scientists are primarily interested in building mathematical models of business processes and optimizing these processes. They are interested in e-commerce as an opportunity to study how business firms can exploit the Internet to achieve more efficient business operations. The information systems discipline spans the technical and behavioral approaches. Technical groups within the information systems specialty focus on data mining, search engine design, and artificial intelligence.

BEHAVIORAL APPROACHES

From a behavioral perspective, information systems researchers are primarily interested in e-commerce because of its implications for firm and industry value chains, industry structure, corporate strategy, and online consumer behavior. Economists have focused on online consumer behavior, pricing of digital goods, and on the unique features of digital electronic markets. The marketing profession is interested in marketing, brand development and extension, online consumer behavior, and the ability of e-commerce technologies to segment and target consumer groups, and differentiate products. Economists share an interest with marketing scholars who have focused on e-commerce consumer response to marketing and advertising campaigns, and the ability of firms to brand, segment markets, target audiences, and position products to achieve above-normal returns on investment.

Management scholars have focused on entrepreneurial behavior and the challenges faced by young firms who are required to develop organizational structures in short time spans. Finance and accounting scholars have focused on e-commerce firm valuation and accounting practices. Sociologists—and to a lesser extent, psychologists—have focused on general population studies of Internet usage, the role of social inequality in skewing Internet benefits, and the use of the Web as a social network and group communications tool. Legal scholars are interested in issues such as preserving intellectual property, privacy, and content regulation.

No one perspective dominates research about e-commerce. The challenge is to learn enough about a variety of academic disciplines so that you can grasp the significance of e-commerce in its entirety.

1.8 CAREERS IN E-COMMERCE

At the beginning of this chapter, in Section 1.1, we explained why studying e-commerce can help you take advantage of future opportunities. The digital Internet/e-commerce economy is growing rapidly, and is expected to continue to do so, and prospects for employment are promising. Employers in this sector are looking for a wide variety of skills, and having a familiarity with the vocabulary, as well as the concepts, underlying e-commerce can help you as you interview, as well as on the job.

To illustrate, we will conclude each chapter with a section that examines a job posting by an Internet/e-commerce company for an entry-level position. We will give you a brief overview of the company, some details about the position, a list of the qualifications and skills that are typically required, and then give you some tips about how to prepare for an interview, as well as show you how concepts you've learned in the chapter can help you answer some possible interview questions. In this chapter, we'll look at a job posting from one of the most familiar types of e-commerce companies: an online retailer.

THE COMPANY

The company is a large global retailer that is rapidly expanding its online and mobile operations. The company is seeking to develop omni-channel e-commerce capabilities based on world-class pricing technology, automated warehouses, and an advanced fulfillment program that combines its retail stores with online and mobile sales. The company has hundreds of different product categories and operates multiple branded websites.

POSITION: CATEGORY SPECIALIST IN THE E-COMMERCE RETAIL PROGRAM

You will manage the performance of your category of products across the firm's websites and apps. More specifically, you will:

- Manage and monitor the introduction of new products, and establish processes to ensure they are available at stores and online.
- Improve the online user experience browsing and searching for products.
- Manage item and category pages including graphics, customer reviews, and content. Find new ways in which our customers can discover products online.
- Optimize pricing of our products and benchmark competitor prices.
- Analyze product performance, identify key trends, and suggest how the firm can improve its revenues, customer service, and margins.
- Work with cross-functional teams in marketing, customer relationship management, and supply chain management to execute initiatives to optimize category performance.

QUALIFICATIONS/SKILLS

- Bachelor's degree with a strong academic background
- An entrepreneurial attitude
- Strong attention to detail
- Strong communication and teamwork skills
- Strong analytical and critical thinking skills
- Ability to work in an ambiguous environment, face challenges, and solve problems
- Negotiation and persuasion skills
- Fast learner, with an ability to absorb information and experiences and apply them

PREPARING FOR THE INTERVIEW

The first step in preparing for an interview is to do some background research about the company you will be interviewing with, as well as the industry in general. Visit their websites, apps, and social media presence. It would also be helpful to review Sections 1.2 and 1.3, so that you can demonstrate an understanding of the basic concepts underlying e-commerce, and show that you know about some of the major trends that will be impacting e-commerce in the coming year, and that you have a familiarity with the basic features underlying e-commerce technology. Being able to converse about the different types of e-commerce, covered in Section 1.4, especially the growing importance of m-commerce, should also be helpful. Before the interviews, you should also think about where your background such as courses taken, outside activities, and personal interests can be useful to the company's business objectives. Re-read the position description and identify where you may have unique skills.

POSSIBLE FIRST INTERVIEW QUESTIONS

1. We hope to build an omni-channel web presence where consumers can buy our products online or in physical stores, which will also have in-store kiosks where customers can explore and order products. What challenges do you think you will face when introducing products to an omni-channel store?

You can prepare for this type of question by visiting national retail stores that already have an omni-channel presence and be prepared to report on your experience as a consumer. Some of the key challenges include providing a consistent customer experience across channels, coordinating pricing, and integrating physical store sales teams with efforts from online marketing teams.

2. Based on what you already know about our online presence, how do you think we should expand our online activities?

You could reference the explosive growth in smartphones and m-commerce, as well as the growth in social networks, and suggest the firm expand its mobile and social network presence.

3. We're finding that quite a few of our customers come to our website to see our offerings and then buy on Amazon. How do you think our firm can respond to this situation?

You could approach this question by explaining why so many people use Amazon: great product search engine, an interface that's easy to use, convenient payment, Prime shipping, and low prices. This suggests that the firm should develop websites and a mobile app that match Amazon's features.

4. How can our company use social networks such as Facebook, Twitter, and Pinterest to expand our business?

You could respond to this by noting that social networks are excellent branding and product introduction tools, but purchases are more likely to take place on the company's website.

5. We gather a tremendous amount of personal information about our online customers. What kinds of issues do you think this poses for our company?

You could address this question by referencing the concerns that people have that their private communications, online transactions, and postings be kept private, unless they grant permission for the release of this personal information. You may have had some personal experiences online where you felt your privacy was being invaded. Talk about these experiences.

6. Our online sales have grown at about 20% a year for several years. Yet many of our customers also buy from our retail stores located in malls, sometimes based on what they see online. And vice versa: some come to our websites and apps and then try it out and buy in the stores. Do you think our e-commerce channel will continue expanding at this rate in the future?

You can address this question by pointing out that e-commerce currently is a very small part of total retail commerce, and therefore you believe there is plenty of room for e-commerce to keep growing rapidly in the future. The firm's online presence will likely drive in-store purchases.

7. Have you worked on the development of a website or app for a business or started an online business yourself? How did it work out?

Here, you will have to draw on your personal experiences, or those of friends, in using the web to promote a business. If you've had some experience you can share, be prepared to identify what made these efforts successful, as well as what the challenges were, and the mistakes you made. Failure is a valuable experience to share with interviewers. It shows you tried. If you have no experience, you can talk about an idea for an e-commerce company that you have thought about, and how you would turn it into a successful business.

1.9 CASE STUDY

Puma
Goes Omni

When Puma, one of the world's top sports footwear, apparel, and accessories brands, conceived its Love=Football campaign, the goal was to create a memorable tagline in a language that would be understood the world over—pictures. In the process, the company stumbled upon the power of social marketing. Puma's ad agency, Droga5, filmed a light-hearted commercial featuring scruffy everyday men in a Tottenham pub singing love songs to their Valentines. The video went viral, garnering more than 130 million impressions and spawning hundreds of homemade response videos. Today, Puma's marketing campaigns are branded with the slogan "Forever Faster," which, according to Ruth How, Puma's Head of Marketing and Communications at Puma UK, Ireland & Benelux, is a sentiment that applies not only to its marketing message to consumers but also to Puma's approach to marketing itself. As How notes, since so much of Puma's target market lives and breathes in the digital space, it is imperative for Puma to fuse marketing with technology to reach those consumers.

© René van den Berg/Alamy Stock Photo

Puma maintains an extensive presence on Facebook, Twitter, Instagram, Pinterest, Snapchat, and YouTube and closely integrates its social strategy with its other marketing channels to deepen its engagement with consumers. It uses social media in part to better understand the different regional and sub-brand audiences within the over 120 countries in which it operates. Not all content is suitable for every one of its over 20 million global Facebook fans. Dedicated sport, country, region, and product category pages were created for each social network. For several years, Puma took a trial-and-error approach, focusing on building its follower base. Today, Puma uses a data-driven approach, geo-targeting posts tailored to specific social network audiences at the appropriate times of the day to maximize fan engagement and generate the right mix of online content to best drive sales. The company also sends personalized messages based on customers' website activity, using items abandoned in shopping carts and other information to generate customized messages and surveys. This integration of channels into a cohesive customer acquisition strategy is in fact a key element of the emerging world of omni-channel retailing.

The advent of the term "omni-channel" signals the evolution of multi-channel or cross-channel retailing to encompass all digital and social technologies. The idea is that customers can examine, access, purchase, and return goods from any channel, even change channels during the process, and receive timely and relevant product information at each step along the way and in each channel. The rise of social networks and the personalized retail it engenders is a primary driver of omni-channel—the complete integration of the shopping and brand experience. Marketing efforts combine offline events, sales and online promotions and brand building across all available channels. For a company like Puma, with e-commerce sites in the United States, Russia, Canada, China, India, Malaysia Switzerland, Germany, France, the United Kingdom, and a European site that serves multiple countries in multiple languages, this presents quite a challenge.

To meet that challenge, Puma, aided by Astound Commerce, a leading e-commerce consultancy firm, undertook a complete restructuring of its e-commerce business. One hundred team members working on the project for nine months completed the restructuring, which included coordinating warehouses, PayPal, and credit card companies with all of Puma's different localized sites. Puma felt it needed to shake things up to compete with Adidas, Nike, and other sports apparel companies in a global market that was rapidly shifting away from mature Western markets and desktop commerce. To coordinate market rollouts and ensure a unified brand image, a command center took over brand strategy and investment decisions, leaving daily operational and locality-based decision-making to the regional teams. One central website, powered by Salesforce Commerce Cloud, Puma's main e-commerce platform, was used to simplify managing global e-commerce operations from a central digital platform, and the company now uses Informatica database technology to manage its 20,000 products centrally, reducing costs and streamlining inventory management. Puma also began to use the AutoStore inventory automation system in some of its warehouses. The system uses a series of bins and robotic handlers to improve storage density, energy efficiency, and the capability to ship items same-day to customers. Puma's goal was to overhaul its e-commerce operations from the ground up to ensure that all of its teams were on the same page and that it was using top-end technology in every area to power its business.

SOURCES: "Reinventing the Customer Experience for a Legacy Brand," Astoundcommerce.com, accessed December 2019; "Puma's New Flagship Brings Products to Life with Digitization," by Dan Berthianume, September 3, 2019; "Puma Launches Own E-commerce Platform," Focusmalaysia.com, April 22, 2019; "Puma Delivers Strong Growth in Sales and Profitability in 2018," About.puma.com, February 14, 2019 "Puma Leverages the Power of Salesforce to Relaunch Its Mobile Sites and Speed Past Customer Expectations," Salesforce.com, accessed January 2019; "Puma, Nike Top List of Most-mentioned Brands on Instagram," by Robert Williams, Mobilemarketer.com, December 21, 2018; "Puma Set to Dethrone Nike in NBA & Culture Push," by Kori Hale, Forbes.com, December 20, 2018; "Selena Gomez Resurfaces on Social Media, Teases New Collaboration with Puma," by Monica R. Lopez, Sunstar.com, November 28, 2018; "Puma Is Rare Brand to Take True Mobile-First Approach to E-commerce," by Lisa Lee, Salesforce.com, June 7, 2018; "Puma Marketer on Why Retail Is Still a Priority, Despite Massive E-commerce Push," by Vivienne Tay, Marketing-interactive.com, June 13, 2018; "Puma Sees India in Top 5 in 3 Years," by John Sarkar and Digbijay Mishral, Timesofindia.indiatimes.com, September 8, 2017; "Sports Brand PUMA Europe to Engage Consumers at a Personal Level," by Paul Skeldon, Internetretailing.net, September 5, 2017; "Puma's Online Business Grows 15 Times in the Last 5 Years," by Sneha Jha, Economictimes.indiatimes.com, August 30, 2017; "Puma Goes Even More Mobile with Its New Online Store," Puma-catchup.com, August 18, 2017; "Puma's Data-Driven Digital Transformation with Informatica," by Antonia Renner, Blogs.informatica.com, May 31, 2017; "Puma Autostore," Autostoresystem.com/Cases/Puma, 2017; "Puma Overhauls Site, Breaks All Records," Demandware.com, November 2016; "What Puma Is Doing Right in Asia," by Byravee Iyer, Campaignasia.com, October 12, 2016; "Puma Personalizes Targeted Messages Based on

Puma assigned the overhaul of its websites to Viget, a web design firm. It created templates to unite several Puma sites into one and unify the look across numerous categories and content types. Puma also modeled its physical stores after the design updates made to its websites, laying out items in similar arrangements. A dozen category sites now complement Puma.com, with a custom-built content management system (CMS) ensuring that consistent Puma branding and navigation are maintained across all sub-sites and pages. Category managers can customize home pages outside of the template layout. The flexibility to roll out local, regional, and global campaigns is thus built into the website design. What's more, the CMS integrates with a language translation tool, a Storefinder tool that helps visitors locate Puma stores, and Puma's product inventory manager. These design changes improved site visualization and navigation, prompting customers to spend twice as much time on the site and raising the order rate. Other features like the ability to design Puma shoes from the ground up using a built-in web app across all of its sites have made Puma's online presence even more compelling.

Puma then turned to the mobile platform, first incorporating Storefinder into its mobile site interface. Using the GPS capability of the mobile device, Puma stores nearest to the user can be located along with address and contact information. Puma's mobile sites were rebuilt using responsive design features, enabling users to experience the same content and appearance as on a desktop or laptop, managed by the same CMS. Puma also incorporated mobile into its omni-channel marketing strategy. In fact, whereas most mobile sites are scaled down from the desktop version, Puma's sites are the opposite—the desktop site is an enlarged version of the mobile site, which has all the functionality of a typical desktop site, including speed. Puma also developed PUMATRAC, a mobile app that automatically analyzes environmental conditions to give runners feedback on how these variables impact their performance. The app offers multiple options to share statistics and routes with other runners. Puma has since overhauled its mobile sites in 24 separate markets, customizing features for each one, ensuring that mobile customers can access items they place in their shopping cart on other platforms, and allowing its web and mobile sites to load 69% faster than previous iterations. Puma's mobile traffic accounts for 70% of all site traffic in many markets, and all of Puma's sites can now handle large traffic spikes when new products hit the market. Overall, Puma has seen its mobile conversion rates improve from less than 1% to approximately 1.5%; though this sounds modest, the increase has resulted in a significant increase in sales and profits for the company.

In addition to focusing on unifying its branding efforts and e-commerce websites, Puma has also streamlined its e-commerce teams. In the past, Puma maintained nine independent e-commerce teams on five continents. Currently, it has teams divided into the three major segments that comprise the majority of its sales—North America, Europe, and Asia-Pacific—as well as a global unit that operates at a level above these regional segments. At the same time, the company is also pursuing a strategy that is flexible and focused on the precise local needs in individual markets, despite reducing the number of individual e-commerce teams. For example, Puma found that in the Asia-Pacific region, traditional paid media advertising was very ineffective compared to social marketing, particularly social media ads featuring compelling influencers like Selena Gomez, whom the company partnered with in 2018, and 2018 World Cup stars like Romelu Lukaku.

Over the past several years, Puma has gained invaluable omni-channel experience and laid the groundwork for resurgent success. In 2019, Puma opened its first-ever North American flagship store in New York City. The digital-centric store is intensely focused on delivering an innovative, interactive, and personalized customer experience using augmented reality and Internet of Things technologies.

Puma's ability to adapt its strategy to individual areas has also helped the company advance into India, where it was given the right to sell to customers directly as well as via popular e-commerce portal Flipkart, and China, a growing market where Puma has traditionally had minimal presence. Puma believes that India will become one of the company's top five markets in the near future. Puma entered the market for NBA player endorsements in 2018, both because the NBA culture meshes well with Puma's and because the NBA is extremely popular in China. Many top young NBA players inked agreements to wear Puma footwear during games in 2019 and beyond.

Implementing a successful omni-channel strategy is a monumental task. Puma's fortunes did not improve overnight. Puma CEO Bjorn Gulden believes that 2015 represented a turning point for the Puma brand back to profitability. By 2018, Puma's e-commerce sales had risen to more than 15 times what they had been in 2012. The company's stock price has more than tripled over the past three years, and its sales have continued to grow across all of its segments, leading to sales growth of over 17% and a significant gain in net earnings from €136 million in 2017 to €188 million in 2018. The company's credits its e-commerce strategy as the main driver of its turnaround and continued success.

SOURCES: "Site Visits, Cart Abandonment," by Laurie Sullivan, Mediapost.com, June 15, 2016; "Which Sneaker Brand Wins the E-commerce Foot Race?" by Zach Blatt, Internetretailer.com, May 17, 2016; "How Puma Is Turning to Startups to Become 'the Fastest Sports Brand in the World'," by Natalie Mortimer, Thedrum.com, March 29, 2016; "Puma and Adidas to Start Their Own E-commerce Portals in India," Businessinsider.in, March 7, 2016; "Inside Puma's Branded Content Strategy," by Lucia Moses, Digiday.com, December 15, 2014; "Puma Understands the Importance of Local Needs in a Global E-commerce Rollout," by Derek Du Preez, Diginomica.com, June 24, 2014; "How Puma Is Improving Sales Operations Through E-commerce," by Paul Demery, Internetretailer.com, May 20, 2014; "Puma's Unified Approach to Global E-commerce," Ecommerce-facts.com, August 5, 2013; "Puma's Head of E-Commerce: Changes and Challenges of Customization in the Apparel Industry," Masscustomization.de, July 16, 2013; "Puma: Challenges in an Omni-channel World," Embodee.com, May 3, 2013.

Case Study Questions

1. What is the purpose of Puma's content management system?
2. Why did Puma build a single centralized website rather than continue with multiple websites serving different countries and regions?
3. What social media sites does Puma use, and what do they contribute to Puma's marketing effort?

1.10 REVIEW

KEY CONCEPTS

Understand why it is important to study e-commerce.

- The next five years hold out exciting opportunities—as well as risks—for new and traditional businesses to exploit digital technology for market advantage. It is important to study e-commerce in order to be able to perceive and understand these opportunities and risks that lie ahead.

- **Define e-commerce, understand how e-commerce differs from e-business, identify the primary technological building blocks underlying e-commerce, and recognize major current themes in e-commerce.**
  - E-commerce involves digitally enabled commercial transactions between and among organizations and individuals.
  - E-business refers primarily to the digital enabling of transactions and processes within a firm, involving information systems under the control of the firm. For the most part, unlike e-commerce, e-business does not involve commercial transactions across organizational boundaries where value is exchanged.
  - The technology juggernauts behind e-commerce are the Internet, the Web, and increasingly, the mobile platform.
  - From a business perspective, one of the most important trends to note is that all forms of e-commerce continue to show very strong growth. From a technology perspective, the mobile platform has finally arrived with a bang, driving astronomical growth in mobile advertising and making true mobile e-commerce a reality. At a societal level, major issues include privacy and government surveillance, protection of intellectual property, online security, and governance of the Internet.

- **Identify and describe the unique features of e-commerce technology and discuss their business significance.**

There are eight features of e-commerce technology that are unique to this medium:
- *Ubiquity*—available just about everywhere, at all times, making it possible to shop from your desktop, at home, at work, or even from your car.
- *Global reach*—permits commercial transactions to cross cultural and national boundaries far more conveniently and cost-effectively than is true in traditional commerce.
- *Universal standards*—shared by all nations around the world, in contrast to most traditional commerce technologies, which differ from one nation to the next.
- *Richness*—enables an online merchant to deliver marketing messages in a way not possible with traditional commerce technologies.
- *Interactivity*—allows for two-way communication between merchant and consumer and enables the merchant to engage a consumer in ways similar to a face-to-face experience, but on a much more massive, global scale.
- *Information density*—is the total amount and quality of information available to all market participants. The Internet reduces information collection, storage, processing, and communication costs while increasing the currency, accuracy, and timeliness of information.
- *Personalization* and *customization*—the increase in information density allows merchants to target their marketing messages to specific individuals and results in a level of personalization and customization unthinkable with previously existing commerce technologies.
- *Social technology*—provides a many-to-many model of mass communications. Millions of users are able to generate content consumed by millions of other users. The result is the formation of social networks on a wide scale and the aggregation of large audiences on social network platforms.

- **Describe the major types of e-commerce.**

There are six major types of e-commerce:
- *B2C e-commerce* involves businesses selling to consumers and is the type of e-commerce that most consumers are likely to encounter.
- *B2B e-commerce* involves businesses selling to other businesses and is the largest form of e-commerce.
- *C2C e-commerce* is a means for consumers to sell to each other. In C2C e-commerce, the consumer prepares the product for market, places the product for auction or sale, and relies on the market maker to provide catalog, search engine, and transaction clearing capabilities so that products can be easily displayed, discovered, and paid for.
- *Social e-commerce* is e-commerce that is enabled by social networks and online social relationships.
- *M-commerce* involves the use of wireless digital devices to enable online transactions.

- *Local e-commerce* is a form of e-commerce that is focused on engaging the consumer based on his or her current geographic location.

■ **Understand the evolution of e-commerce from its early years to today.**

E-commerce has gone through three stages: innovation, consolidation, and reinvention.
- The early years of e-commerce were a technological success, with the digital infrastructure created during the period solid enough to sustain significant growth in e-commerce during the next decade, and a mixed business success, with significant revenue growth and customer usage, but low profit margins.
- E-commerce entered a period of consolidation beginning in 2001 and extending into 2006.
- E-commerce entered a period of reinvention in 2007 with the emergence of the mobile digital platform, social networks, and Web 2.0 applications that attracted huge audiences in a very short time span.

■ **Describe the major themes underlying the study of e-commerce.**

E-commerce involves three broad interrelated themes:
- *Technology*—To understand e-commerce, you need a basic understanding of the information technologies upon which it is built, including the Internet, the Web, and mobile platform, and a host of complementary technologies—cloud computing, desktop computers, smartphones, tablet computers, local area networks, client/server computing, packet-switched communications, protocols such as TCP/IP, web servers, HTML, and relational and non-relational databases, among others.
- *Business*—While technology provides the infrastructure, it is the business applications—the potential for extraordinary returns on investment—that create the interest and excitement in e-commerce. Therefore, you also need to understand some key business concepts such as electronic markets, information goods, business models, firm and industry value chains, industry structure, and consumer behavior in digital markets.
- *Society*—Understanding the pressures that global e-commerce places on contemporary society is critical to being successful in the e-commerce marketplace. The primary societal issues are intellectual property, individual privacy, and public policy.

■ **Identify the major academic disciplines contributing to e-commerce.**

There are two primary approaches to e-commerce: technical and behavioral. Each of these approaches is represented by several academic disciplines.
- On the technical side, this includes computer science, operations management, and information systems.
- On the behavioral side, it includes information systems as well as sociology, economics, finance and accounting, management, and marketing.

QUESTIONS

1. What does omni-channel mean in terms of e-commerce presence?
2. What is the deep Web?
3. What are some of the unique features of e-commerce technology?
4. What are some of the factors driving the growth of social e-commerce?
5. Why is it likely that the Internet and e-commerce are entering a period of closer regulatory oversight?
6. How does the ubiquity of e-commerce impact consumers?
7. What impact does the increased interactivity provided by e-commerce technologies have on business?
8. What difficulties are presented in trying to measure the number of web pages in existence?
9. Why is the mobile platform not just a hardware phenomenon?
10. What is conversational commerce and how does it relate to m-commerce?
11. Describe the three different stages in the evolution of e-commerce.

12. Define disintermediation and explain the benefits to Internet users of such a phenomenon. How does disintermediation impact friction-free commerce?
13. What is the difference between a PWA and a regular app?
14. What is driving the growth of social e-commerce?
15. Discuss the ways in which the early years of e-commerce can be considered both a success and a failure.
16. What are five of the major differences between the early years of e-commerce and today's e-commerce?
17. How do the Internet and the Web fit into the development of corporate computing?
18. Why is the term "sharing economy" a misnomer?
19. What are those who take a technical approach to studying e-commerce interested in?
20. What have been some of the surprises that have occurred in the evolution of e-commerce?

PROJECTS

1. Choose an e-commerce company and assess it in terms of the eight unique features of e-commerce technology described in Table 1.2. Which of the features does the company implement well, and which features poorly, in your opinion? Prepare a short memo to the president of the company you have chosen detailing your findings and any suggestions for improvement you may have.

2. Search online for an example of each of the major types of e-commerce described in Section 1.4 and listed in Table 1.3. Create a presentation or written report describing each company (take a screenshot of each, if possible), and explain why it fits into the category of e-commerce to which you have assigned it.

3. Given the development and history of e-commerce in the years 1995–2019, what do you predict we will see during the next five years of e-commerce? Describe some of the technological, business, and societal shifts that may occur as the Internet continues to grow and expand. Prepare a brief presentation or written report to explain your vision of what e-commerce will look like in 2024.

4. Prepare a brief report or presentation on how companies are using Instagram or another company of your choosing as a social e-commerce platform.

5. Follow up on events at Uber since December 2019 (when the opening case was prepared). Prepare a short report on your findings.

REFERENCES

Bakos, Yannis. "Reducing Buyer Search Costs: Implications for Electronic Marketplaces." *Management Science* (December 1997).

Banerjee, Suman, and Chakravarty, Amiya. "Price Setting and Price Discovery Strategies with a Mix of Frequent and Infrequent Internet Users." Stevens Institute of Technology School of Business Research Paper (April 15, 2016).

Cavallo, Alberto F. "Are Online and Offline Prices Similar? Evidence from Large Multi-Channel Retailers." NBER Working Paper No. 22142. (March 2016).

Digital Commerce 360. "Internet Retailer 2019 Top 500 Report." (2019).

eMarketer, Inc. "US Internet Users and Penetration." (April 2019a).

eMarketer, Inc. "Internet Users and Penetration Worldwide." (April 2019b).

eMarketer, Inc. "Retail Ecommerce Sales, by Country," (December 2019c).

eMarketer, Inc. "Digital Travel Sales, by Country." (July 2019d).

eMarketer, Inc. "Retail Mcommerce Sales, by Country, 2018–2020." (December 2019e).

eMarketer, Inc. "US Net Digital Ad Revenue Share, by Company, 2019." (October 1, 2019f).

eMarketer, Inc. (Corey McNair). "US Digital Users: eMarketer's Estimates for 2018." (March 2018).

Evans, Philip, and Thomas S. Wurster. "Getting Real About Virtual Commerce." *Harvard Business Review* (November–December 1999).

Evans, Philip, and Thomas S. Wurster. "Strategy and the New Economics of Information." *Harvard Business Review* (September–October 1997).

Forrester Research (Satish Meena). "Forrester Analytics: Digital-Influenced Retail Sales Forecast, 2018 to 2023 (US)." (December 10, 2018).

Ghose, Anindya, and Yuliang Yao. "Using Transaction Prices to Re-Examine Price Dispersion in Electronic Markets." *Information Systems Research*, Vol. 22 No. 2 (June 2011).

Gorodnichenko, Yuriy, et al. "Price Setting in Online Markets: Does IT Click?" NBER Working Paper No. 20819 (December 2014).

Internet Systems Consortium, Inc. "ISC Internet Domain Survey." (January 2019).

Kambil, Ajit. "Doing Business in the Wired World." *IEEE Computer* (May 1997).

Levin, Jonathon. "The Economics of Internet Markets." NBER Working Paper No 16852 (February 2011).

Netsertive. "2018 Local Consumer Survey." (April 23, 2018).

Policy Factory. "Social Commerce—China Ahead of the Game." Ceoworld.biz (September 2, 2019).

Pymnts. "Amazon's Share of Total eComm Sales: Now 37%?" Pymnts.com (June 14, 2019).

Rosso, Mark, and Bernard Jansen. "Smart Marketing or Bait & Switch: Competitors' Brands as Keywords in Online Advertising." Proceedings of the 4th Workshop on Information Credibility. ACM (2010).

Schwartz, Barry. "Google Knows of 130 Trillion Pages on the Web—100 Trillion More in 4 Years." Seroundtable.com (November 14, 2016).

Shapiro, Carl, and Hal R. Varian. *Information Rules. A Strategic Guide to the Network Economy*. Cambridge, MA: Harvard Business School Press (1999).

Sinha, Indrajit. "Cost Transparency: The Net's Threat to Prices and Brands." *Harvard Business Review* (March-April 2000).

Smith, Michael, Joseph Bailey, and Erik Brynjolfsson. "Understanding Digital Markets: Review and Assessment." In Erik Brynjolfsson and Brian Kahin (eds.), *Understanding the Digital Economy*. Cambridge, MA: MIT Press (2000).

Strategy Analytics. "Strategy Analytics: Internet of Things Now Numbers 22 Billion Devices But Where is the Revenue?" Strategyanalytics.com (May 16, 2019).

Tversky, A., and D. Kahneman. "The Framing of Decisions and the Psychology of Choice." *Science* (January 1981).

UNCTAD (United Nations Conference on Trade and Development.) "Digital Economy Report 2019: Value Creation and Capture: Implications for Developing Countries." (2019).

U.S. Census Bureau. "E-Stats 2017: Measuring the Electronic Economy." (September 23, 2019).

Varian, Hal R. "When Commerce Moves On, Competition Can Work in Strange Ways." *New York Times* (August 24, 2000a).

Varian, Hal R. "5 Habits of Highly Effective Revolution." *Forbes ASAP* (February 21, 2000b).

CHAPTER 2

E-commerce Infrastructure

LEARNING OBJECTIVES

After reading this chapter, you will be able to:

- Discuss the origins of, and the key technology concepts behind, the Internet.
- Explain the current structure of the Internet.
- Understand how the Web works.
- Describe how Internet and web features and services support e-commerce.
- Understand the impact of mobile applications.

Tech Titans Target a Prize:
Bringing Internet Access to Rural India

Half of the world's population does not have access to the Internet. India is arguably among the least Internet-connected populations, with the majority of its citizens living in widely dispersed rural areas largely without Internet service. Among the 500 million Indian Internet users (mostly in large urban areas), over 460 million use mobile phones to access the Internet. Most continent-size countries have difficulties serving their rural populations. In China, for instance, about 40% of its estimated 1.4 billion people, living mostly in dispersed rural regions, have no Internet access. Of China's estimated 870 million Internet users, 90% use their mobile phones for access, relying on Wi-Fi hotspots provided by telecommunications companies.

While Internet growth in the industrial world has reached a saturation point, with limited prospects for rapid expansion, India represents an untapped potential growth asset for telecommunications and technology providers. India has one of the fastest-growing Internet and smartphone populations in the world.

© dpa picture alliance/ Alamy Stock Photo

In 2014, the government of India launched its Digital India project with the objective of building high-speed networks and improving digital literacy in rural areas. A part of this program was called Digital Village, an effort to connect an estimated 1,000 of 250,000 rural villages to the Internet by expanding existing private Wi-Fi networks as well as government-developed networks. In 2019, the Indian government announced plans to expand the project. However, connecting all of the rural villages in India would be a massive task from a financial perspective and also hampered by the limits of current Wi-Fi technology. Wi-Fi hotspots, which use radio signals, have a limited reach of about 100 meters (300 feet), making them suitable for individual buildings, but not for large regions. WiMax (Worldwide Interoperability for Microwave Access) using microwave line of sight frequencies has a range of only 30 miles.

Other technologies are needed that can cover a continent and yet provide affordable service to a rural population. One solution is something that flies above the rural areas and provides both upload and download of Internet access requests. Geosynchronous satellites would be ideal, but they are very expensive to build and launch, and it would take 10 to 15 such satellites to cover India's land mass.

Enter the tech giants from Silicon Valley looking for new audiences to support their advertising models: Google, Facebook, and Microsoft. Both Facebook and Google have

SOURCES: "Facebook Users, by Country," eMarketer, Inc., November 2019; "Microsoft's Airband International Aims to Bring Internet to 40 Million People," by Sean Endicott, Windowscentral.com, October 7, 2019; "DMs Honoured for Pioneering Work," by Press Trust of India, Thehindu.com, August 23, 2019; "Google's Project Loon Is About to Start Commercial Testing," by Chris Merriman, Theinquirer.net, July 2, 2019; "Modi Govt to Scale Up Digital Village 2.0," by S. Ronendra Singh, Thehindubusinessline.com, May 28, 2019; "Amazon Constellation Sends Number of Planned Communications Satellites Soaring Above 20,000," by Doug Messier, Parabolicarc.com, April 5, 2019; "Digital India: Technology to Transform a Connected Nation," by Noshir Kaka et al., McKinsey Global Institute, Mckinsey.com, March 2019; "Internet Users, by Country," eMarketer, Inc., April 2019; "Mobile Phone Internet Users and Penetration in India," eMarketer, Inc., April 2019; "Facebook Is Developing an Internet Satellite After Shutting Down Drone Project," by Nick Statt, Theverge.com, July 21, 2018; "Facebook Confirms It's Working on a New Internet Satellite," by Louise Matsakis, Wired.com, July 20, 2018; "Project Loon Signs Its First Deal for Internet-delivering Balloons—in Kenya," by Nathan Mattise, Arstechnica.com, July 19, 2018; "Facebook's Express Wi-Fi Now Has Its Own Android App," by Shannon Liao, Theverge.com, March 15, 2018; "Alphabet's X Division Is Setting Up Cable-less Internet in Rural India," by Abhimanyu Ghoshal, Thenextweb.com, December 15, 2017; "Google Is Using Light Beam Tech to Connect Rural India to the Internet" by Jon Russell, Techcrunch.com, December 15, 2017; "Facebook, Other Social Media Giants Won't Get Net Exclusivity: Government," by Pankaj Doval, Timesofindia.indiatimes.com, November 24, 2017; "Google's Project Loon: DGCA to Study Balloon-Powered Internet Project from Next Month," by Pranav Mukul, Indianexpress.com, October 11, 2017; "Security Agencies Red Flag Microsoft's White Space

announced a goal to sign up another billion people to the Internet. India already has the largest Facebook audience in the world, and Google Search is the dominant search engine; there are more users in India than anywhere else.

Google's solution is a balloon network called Project Loon, formally announced in 2013, though research on the project started in 2008. This project is a part of Google's Next Billion Users initiative. After five years of development, in 2013 Google's "moonshot" division, Alphabet X, announced a pilot experiment near Christchurch, New Zealand, to deliver Internet service. The ultimate goal is to create a balloon network of thousands of balloons floating in the stratosphere, flying at an elevation of 18–20 kilometers (9–10 miles). The first step in large-scale deployment is to launch 300 balloons in the southern hemisphere at the 40th parallel south, providing Internet access to Australia, New Zealand, the Pacific Ocean, and southern Latin America. The balloons use high-speed LTE cell phone technology to beam signals to cell ground stations connected to the Internet provided by local Internet service providers. The same technology is used to connect the balloons to one another. Individuals with Google SIM cards connect directly to the balloons overhead. The location of the balloons is controlled by a Google global flight control system that can change the altitude of the balloons and take advantage of wind patterns in the stratosphere to keep them in the correct locations. Currently, the balloons have a service life of six months to a year and can be lowered to the ground gently, so the equipment can be retrieved and re-used. In 2018, Project Loon announced its first commercial agreement when it partnered with Kenya to improve Internet penetration in the country and in 2019 began the first commercial testing of the technology. The Indian government has tested and studied Project Loon for several years, and India and Google may soon move forward on the initiative.

In 2017, in separate effort from Project Loon, Google began a project with the South Indian state of Andhra Pradesh to create a high-speed Internet network for homes in rural areas. The project employed free space optical communications (FSOC), which uses optical beams from lasers or LEDs to connect with local FSOC receivers that transmit LTE signals to local users. In 2019, District Magistrate Kartikeya Mishra was honored with an Indian Express Excellence in Governance award for his role in bringing the project about, However, this technology has a number of limitations: fog, clouds, and rain impair its functions, and keeping the light beams aimed properly can be a challenge.

Facebook and Google are direct competitors for Internet audiences in India who can be shown ads. In 2013, Facebook launched Internet.org, a consortium involving Facebook, Samsung, Ericsson, MediaTek, Opera Software, Nokia, and Qualcomm, with the goal of bringing affordable Internet access to less-developed countries. The consortium produced a smartphone app named Free Basics to provide an interface for the Internet. Working with existing ISPs and cellular telecommunications companies, the service offered limited cellular Internet service for news, maternal health, travel, and sports along with Facebook. The Indian Government banned the service in February 2016 because it discriminated against other services and violated India's net neutrality laws, which prohibit exclusive Internet services and discriminatory pricing. In late 2016 Facebook launched Express Wi-Fi, which offers low-cost Internet access to customers of local cellular phone providers, who then re-distribute this to public Wi-Fi hotspots. In effect, Facebook is subsidizing Internet access provided by local cell companies who currently provide only cell service. In 2018, Facebook created an app that Express Wi-Fi users can use to pay and locate nearby hotspots.

Through its Connectivity Lab, Facebook has developed a number of wide area technologies to deliver broadband service to rural areas, from satellites and lasers to drones. In 2018, Facebook shut down one such initiative—its Aquila project, which featured solar-powered drones and lasers that beamed Internet to remote areas. Facebook will still create software to achieve these goals, but the company will no longer create its own aircraft. Instead, the company is putting its energy behind launching Internet satellites at lower orbits, just like Project Loon, to provide broadband at a wide scale. Facebook's satellite effort is called Project Athena.

Microsoft has also entered the market and in 2016 began a test program in Harasil village, in the state of Maharashtra, that used white space technology to deliver Internet access to rural areas. Microsoft has deployed this technology in the United States, Singapore, Kenya, Tanzania, South Africa, and the Philippines. White space broadband enables wide-area wireless networking using the unused space between older television channels, achieving broadband data speeds that can be transmitted up to 10 kilometers at a very low cost without any additional cabling or new transmission towers. However, in 2017, India's Telecom Ministry withdrew Microsoft's license due to opposition from cellular operators who wanted an auction for the spectrum rather than an exclusive grant to one company, and from the National Intelligence Agency, who viewed the technology as a threat to national security because use of this spectrum was unregulated and communications could not be monitored by authorities. Currently the villagers rely on the much slower Internet service from local cell companies. In the meantime, Microsoft continues to expand its efforts to bring Internet access to underserved area such as Latin America and Sub-Saharan Africa using whitespace technology.

As to the future, Amazon, SpaceX, OneWeb, SES, Intelsat, Boeing, ViaSat, Telesat, Audacy, Karousel LLC, Space Norway, Theia Holdings, and LeoSat are all hoping to establish networks of low and medium earth orbit satellites to provide Internet access. With so many technology companies vying to bring Internet access to India, its citizens may not have to wait long for universal Internet access.

Technology for Rural Internet," by Krishna Kumar, Economictimes. indiatimes.com, October 5, 2017; "India Declines Microsoft a White Spaces Internet License," by Surur, Mspoweruser.com, July 5, 2017; "No, Google's Not a Bird: Bringing the Internet to Rural India," by Ellen Barry, *New York Times*, May 21, 2017; "Facebook Offers India Cheap WiFi via 20,000 Hotspots," by Rishi Iyengar, Money.com, May 4, 2017; "SpaceX Plans to Launch First Internet-Providing Satellites in 2019," by Rich McCormick, Theverge.com, May 4, 2017; "India Says It Will Roll Out Free Wi-Fi In 1,000 Rural Villages," by Joseph Hincks, *Fortune*, January 31, 2017; "Facebook Is Testing a New Wi-Fi Service in India. It's Not Free This Time," by Nick Statt, Theverge.com, August 8, 2016; "Facebook Moves One Step Closer to Light-Based Wireless Communication," by Steph Yin, *New York Times*, July 21, 2016; "Performance Analysis of Free Space Optical Communication in Open-Atmospheric Turbulence Conditions with Beam Wandering Compensation Control," by Arockia Bazil, *IET Communications*, June 16, 2016; "Google in Talks with Telecoms to Pilot Project Loon in India," by Catherine Shu, Techcrunch.com, March 8, 2016; "Inside Facebook's Ambitious Plan to Connect the Whole World," by Jessi Hempel, Wired.com, January 19, 2016; "Google Parent Company Alphabet Targeting India for Stratospheric Internet Balloons" by Newley Purnell, *Wall Street Journal*, November 3, 2015.

This chapter examines the Internet, Web, and mobile platform of today and tomorrow, how they evolved, how they work, and how their present and future infrastructure enable new business opportunities.

The opening case illustrates the importance of understanding how the Internet and related technologies work, and being aware of what's new. The Internet and its underlying technology are not static phenomena, but instead continue to change over time. Computers have merged with cell phone services; broadband access in the home and broadband wireless access to the Internet via smartphones, tablet computers, and laptops are expanding rapidly; self-publishing via social networks and blogging now engages millions of Internet users; and software technologies such as cloud computing and smartphone apps are revolutionizing the way businesses are using the Internet. Looking forward a few years, the business strategies of the future will require a firm understanding of these technologies and new ones, such as the use of artificial intelligence, the Internet of Things, the "smart/connected" movement (smart homes, smart TVs, and connected cars), augmented and virtual reality, and artificial intelligence to deliver products and services to consumers. **Table 2.1** summarizes some of the most important developments in e-commerce infrastructure for 2019–2020.

2.1 THE INTERNET: TECHNOLOGY BACKGROUND

What is the Internet? Where did it come from, and how did it support the growth of the Web? What are the Internet's most important operating principles? How much do you really need to know about the technology of the Internet?

Let's take the last question first. The answer is: it depends on your career interests. If you are on a marketing career path, or general managerial business path, then you need to know the basics about Internet technology, which you'll learn in this and the following chapter. If you are on a technical career path and hope to become a web designer, or pursue a technical career in web infrastructure for businesses, you'll need to start with these basics and then build from there. You'll also need to know about the business side of e-commerce, which you will learn about throughout this book.

As noted in Chapter 1, the **Internet** is an interconnected network of thousands of networks and millions of computers (sometimes called *host computers* or just *hosts*), linking businesses, educational institutions, government agencies, and individuals. The Internet provides approximately 3.8 billion people around the world with services such as e-mail, apps, newsgroups, shopping, research, instant messaging, music, videos, and news (eMarketer, Inc., 2019a). No single organization controls the Internet or how it functions, nor is it owned by anybody, yet it has provided the infrastructure for a transformation in commerce, scientific research, and culture. The word *Internet* is derived from the word *internetwork*, or the connecting together of two or more computer networks. The **Web** is one of the Internet's most popular services, providing access to billions, perhaps trillions, of web pages, which are documents created in a programming language called HTML that

Internet
an interconnected network of thousands of networks and millions of computers linking businesses, educational institutions, government agencies, and individuals

Web
one of the Internet's most popular services, providing access to billions, and perhaps trillions, of web pages

TABLE 2.1   TRENDS IN E-COMMERCE INFRASTRUCTURE 2019–2020

BUSINESS

- Mobile devices become the primary access point to the Internet, provide a rapidly expanding social marketing and advertising platform, and create a foundation for location-based web services and business models.
- Explosion of Internet content services and mobile devices strains the business models of Internet backbone providers (the large telecommunication carriers).
- The growth in cloud computing and bandwidth capacity enables new business models for distributing music, movies, and television.
- Search becomes more social and local, enabling social and local commerce business models.
- Big data produced by the Internet creates new business opportunities for firms with the analytic capability to understand it.

TECHNOLOGY

- Mobile devices such as smartphones and tablet computers have become the dominant mode of access to the Internet.
- The explosion of mobile apps threatens the dominance of the Web as the main source of online software applications.
- Cloud computing reshapes computing and storage, and becomes an important force in the delivery of software applications and online content.
- The Internet runs out of IPv4 addresses; the transition to IPv6 continues.
- The decreased cost of storage and advances in database software lead to explosion in online data collection known as big data, and creates new business opportunities for firms with the analytic capability to understand it.
- The Internet of Things, with millions of sensor-equipped devices connecting to the Internet, starts to become a reality, and is powering the development of smart connected "things" such as televisions, houses, cars, and wearable technology.
- Interest in and funding of artificial intelligence technologies explode, with potential applications ranging from supply chain logistics, to self-driving cars, to consumer-oriented personal assistants.
- Augmented reality applications such as Pokemon GO, and virtual reality hardware such as Facebook's Oculus Rift, Google's Cardboard, and Samsung's Gear VR, begin to gain traction.
- HTML5 grows in popularity among publishers and developers and makes possible web applications that are just as visually rich and lively as native mobile apps.

SOCIETY

- Governance of the Internet becomes more involved with conflicts between nations; the United States gives up control over IANA, which administers the Internet's IP addressing system.
- Government control over, and surveillance of, the Internet is expanded in most advanced nations, and in many nations the Internet is nearly completely controlled by government agencies.
- The growing infrastructure for tracking online and mobile consumer behavior conflicts with individual claims to privacy and control over personal information.

can contain text, graphics, audio, video, and other objects, as well as "hyperlinks" that permit users to jump easily from one page to another. Web pages are navigated using web browser software.

THE EVOLUTION OF THE INTERNET: 1961—THE PRESENT

Although journalists talk glibly about "Internet" time—suggesting a fast-paced, nearly instant, worldwide global change mechanism—in fact, today's Internet had its start almost 69 years ago and evolved slowly in its first few decades, before accelerating with the development of the Web and mobile platform.

The history of the Internet can be segmented into three phases (see **Figure 2.1**). During the *Innovation Phase*, from 1961 to 1974, the fundamental building blocks of the Internet—packet-switching hardware, a communications protocol called TCP/IP, and client/server computing (all described more fully later in this section)—were conceptualized and then implemented in actual hardware and software. The Internet's original purpose was to link large mainframe computers on different college campuses. This kind of one-to-one communication between campuses was previously possible only via the telephone system or private networks owned by the large computer manufacturers.

During the *Institutionalization Phase*, from 1975 to 1995, large institutions such as the U.S. Department of Defense (DoD) and the National Science Foundation (NSF) provided funding and legitimization for the fledging Internet. Once the concepts behind the Internet had been proven in several government-supported demonstration projects, the DoD contributed $1 million to further develop them into a robust military communications system. This effort created what was then called ARPANET (Advanced Research Projects Agency Network). In 1986, the NSF assumed responsibility for the development of a civilian Internet (then called NSFNET) and began a 10-year-long $200 million expansion program.

During the *Commercialization Phase*, from 1995 to the present, the U.S. government encouraged private corporations to take over and expand the Internet backbone as well as local service beyond military installations and college campuses to the rest of the population around the world. See **Table 2.2** for a closer look at the development of the Internet from 1961 on.

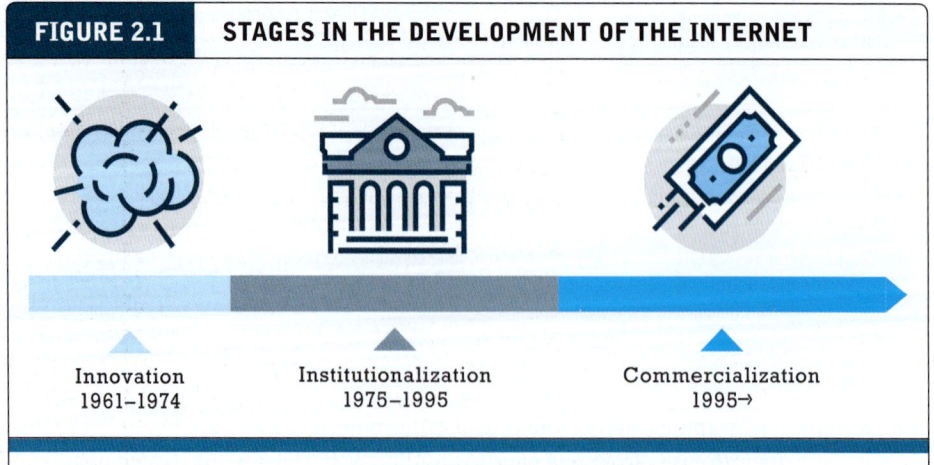

FIGURE 2.1 STAGES IN THE DEVELOPMENT OF THE INTERNET

Innovation 1961–1974
Institutionalization 1975–1995
Commercialization 1995→

The Internet has developed in three stages from 1961 to the present. In the Innovation stage, basic ideas and technologies were developed; in the Institutionalization stage, these ideas were brought to life; in the Commercialization stage, once the ideas and technologies had been proven, private companies brought the Internet to millions of people worldwide.

TABLE 2.2 DEVELOPMENT OF THE INTERNET TIMELINE

YEAR	EVENT	SIGNIFICANCE
INNOVATION PHASE 1961–1974		
1961	Leonard Kleinrock (MIT) publishes a paper on "packet switching" networks.	The concept of packet switching is born.
1962	J. C. R. Licklider (MIT) writes memo calling for an "Intergalactic Computer Network."	The vision of a global computer network is born.
1969	BBN Technologies awarded ARPA contract to build ARPANET.	The concept of a packet-switched network moves closer toward physical reality.
1969	The first packet-switched message is sent on ARPANET from UCLA to Stanford.	The communications hardware underlying the Internet is implemented for the first time. The initial ARPANET consisted of four routers (then called Interface Message Processors (IMPs)) at UCLA, Stanford, UCSB, and the University of Utah.
1972	E-mail is invented by Ray Tomlinson of BBN. Larry Roberts writes the first e-mail utility program permitting listing, forwarding, and responding to e-mails.	The first "killer app" of the Internet is born.
1973	Bob Metcalfe (Xerox PARC Labs) invents Ethernet and local area networks.	**Client/server computing is invented.** Ethernet permitted the development of local area networks and client/server computing in which thousands of fully functional desktop computers could be connected into a short-distance (<1,000 meters) network to share files, run applications, and send messages.
1974	"Open architecture" networking and TCP/IP concepts are presented in a paper by Vint Cerf (Stanford) and Bob Kahn (BBN).	**TCP/IP invented.** The conceptual foundation for a single common communications protocol that could potentially connect any of thousands of disparate local area networks and computers, and a common addressing scheme for all computers connected to the network, are born. Prior to this, computers could communicate only if they shared a common proprietary network architecture. With TCP/IP, computers and networks could work together regardless of their local operating systems or network protocols.
INSTITUTIONALIZATION PHASE 1975–1995		
1976	The Apple I is released.	The first computer, in kit form, developed by Apple.
1977	Lawrence Landweber envisions CSNET (Computer Science Network).	CSNET is a pioneering network for U.S. universities and industrial computer research groups that could not directly connect to ARPANET, and was a major milestone on the path to the development of the global Internet.
1980	TCP/IP is officially adopted as the DoD standard communications protocol.	The single largest computing organization in the world adopts TCP/IP and packet-switched network technology.
1981	IBM introduces IBM PC, its first personal computer.	Personal desktop computers begin to become popular, forming the foundation for today's Internet and affording millions of people access to the the Internet and Web.
1984	Apple Computer releases the HyperCard program as part of its graphical user interface operating system called Macintosh.	The concept of "hyperlinked" documents and records that permit the user to jump from one page or record to another is commercially introduced.

(continued)

TABLE 2.2 — DEVELOPMENT OF THE INTERNET TIMELINE (CONTINUED)

YEAR	EVENT	SIGNIFICANCE
1984	Domain Name System (DNS) introduced.	DNS provides a user-friendly system for translating IP addresses into words that people can easily understand.
1989	Tim Berners-Lee of CERN in Switzerland proposes a worldwide network of hyperlinked documents based on a common markup language called HTML—HyperText Markup Language.	**The concept of an Internet-supported service called the World Wide Web based on HTML pages is born**. The Web would be constructed from "pages" created in a common markup language, with "hyperlinks" that permitted easy access among the pages.
1990	NSF plans and assumes responsibility for a civilian Internet backbone and creates NSFNET.[1] ARPANET is decommissioned.	The concept of a "civilian" Internet open to all is realized through nonmilitary funding by NSF.
1993	The first graphical web browser called Mosaic is invented by Marc Andreessen and others at the National Center for Supercomputing Applications at the University of Illinois.	Mosaic makes it very easy for ordinary users to connect to HTML documents anywhere on the Web. The browser-enabled Web takes off.
1994	Andreessen and Jim Clark form Netscape Corporation.	The first commercial web browser—Netscape—becomes available.
1994	The first banner advertisements appear on Hotwired.com in October 1994.	**The beginning of e-commerce**.
COMMERCIALIZATION PHASE 1995–PRESENT		
1995	NSF privatizes the backbone, and commercial carriers take over backbone operation.	**The fully commercial civilian Internet is born**. Major long-haul networks such as AT&T, Sprint, GTE, UUNet, and MCI take over operation of the backbone. Network Solutions (a private firm) is given a monopoly to assign Internet addresses.
1995	Jeff Bezos founds Amazon; Pierre Omidyar forms AuctionWeb (eBay).	E-commerce begins in earnest with pure online retail stores and auctions.
1998	The U.S. federal government encourages the founding of the Internet Corporation for Assigned Names and Numbers (ICANN).	Governance over domain names and addresses passes to a private nonprofit international organization.
1999	The first full-service Internet-only bank, First Internet Bank of Indiana, opens for business.	Business on the Web extends into traditional services.
2003	The Internet2 Abilene high-speed network is upgraded to 10 Gbps.	A major milestone toward the development of ultra-high-speed transcontinental networks several times faster than the existing backbone is achieved.
2005	NSF proposes the Global Environment for Network Innovations (GENI) initiative to develop new core functionality for the Internet.	Recognition that future Internet security and functionality needs may require the thorough rethinking of existing Internet technology.
2006	The U.S. Senate Committee on Commerce, Science, and Transportation holds hearings on "Network Neutrality."	The debate grows over differential pricing based on utilization that pits backbone utility owners against online content and service providers and device makers.

[1] "Backbone" refers to the U.S. domestic trunk lines that carry the heavy traffic across the nation, from one metropolitan area to another. Universities are given responsibility for developing their own campus networks that must be connected to the national backbone.

TABLE 2.2 DEVELOPMENT OF THE INTERNET TIMELINE (CONTINUED)

YEAR	EVENT	SIGNIFICANCE
2007	The Apple iPhone is introduced.	The introduction of the iPhone represents the beginning of the development of a viable mobile platform that will ultimately transform the way people interact with the Internet.
2008	Internet "cloud computing" becomes a billion-dollar industry.	Internet capacity is sufficient to support on-demand computing resources (processing and storage), as well as software applications, for large corporations and individuals.
2009	Internet-enabled smartphones become a major new online access platform.	Smartphones extend the reach and range of the Internet to more closely realize the promise of the Internet anywhere, anytime, anyplace.
2010	The U.S. Federal Communications Commission (FCC) launches National Broadband Plan.	FCC-led initiative to promote the goal of achieving universal, affordable Internet access by 2020.
2011	ICANN expands domain name system.	ICANN agrees to permit the expansion of generic top-level domain names from about 300 to potentially thousands using any word in any language.
2012	World IPv6 Launch day.	Major Internet service providers (ISPs), home networking equipment manufacturers, and online companies begin to permanently enable IPv6 for their products and services as of June 6, 2012.
2013	The Internet of Things (IoT) starts to become a reality.	Internet technology spreads beyond the computer and mobile device to anything that can be equipped with sensors.
2014	Apple introduces Apple Pay and Apple Watch.	Apple Pay aims to become the first widely adopted mobile payment system; Apple Watch ushers in a new era of wearable Internet-connected technology and is a further harbinger of the Internet of Things.
2015	FCC adopts regulations mandating net neutrality.	ISPs are required to treat all data on the Internet equally and are not allowed to discriminate or charge differentially based on user, content, site, platform, application, type of equipment, or mode of communication.
2017	FCC broadband consumer privacy rules aimed at ISPs are repealed.	ISPs remain able to collect, share, and sell consumer data such as Web browsing history without consumer consent.
2018	FCC officially rescinds net neutrality regulations in June 2018; in response, a number of states take steps via legislation or executive order to mandate net neutrality.	Net neutrality continues to be the subject of political controversy.
2019	The commercial availability of 10 Gpbs Internet access increases.	Advanced technologies such as virtual reality, augmented reality, artificial intelligence, and 4k streaming drive demand for higher broadband access speeds.

SOURCES: Based on Leiner et al., 2000; Zakon, 2005; Gross, 2005; Geni.net, 2007; ISOC.org, 2010; Arstechnica.com, 2010; ICANN, 2011a; Internet Society, 2012; IEEE Computer Society, 2013; Craig, 2016; NCTA, 2019.

THE INTERNET: KEY TECHNOLOGY CONCEPTS

In 1995, the U.S. Federal Networking Council (FNC) passed a resolution formally defining the term *Internet* as a network that uses the IP addressing scheme, supports the Transmission Control Protocol (TCP), and makes services available to users much like a telephone system makes voice and data services available to the public (see **Figure 2.2**).

Behind this formal definition are three extremely important concepts that are the basis for understanding the Internet: packet switching, the TCP/IP communications protocol, and client/server computing. Although the Internet has evolved and changed dramatically in the last 35 years, these three concepts are at the core of the way the Internet functions today and are the foundation for the Internet of the future.

Packet Switching

packet switching
a method of slicing digital messages into packets, sending the packets along different communication paths as they become available, and then reassembling the packets once they arrive at their destination

packets
the discrete units into which digital messages are sliced for transmission over the Internet

Packet switching is a method of slicing digital messages into discrete units called **packets**, sending the packets along different communication paths as they become available, and then reassembling the packets once they arrive at their destination (see **Figure 2.3**). Prior to the development of packet switching, early computer networks used leased, dedicated telephone circuits to communicate with terminals and other computers. In circuit-switched networks such as the telephone system, a complete point-to-point circuit is put together, and then communication can proceed. However, these "dedicated" circuit-switching techniques were expensive and wasted available communications capacity—the circuit would be maintained regardless of whether any data was being sent. For nearly 70% of the time, a dedicated voice circuit is not being fully used because of pauses between

FIGURE 2.2   RESOLUTION OF THE U.S. FEDERAL NETWORKING COUNCIL

"The Federal Networking Council (FNC) agrees that the following language reflects our definition of the term 'Internet.'

'Internet' refers to the global information system that—

(i) is logically linked together by a globally unique address space based on the Internet Protocol (IP) or its subsequent extensions/follow-ons;

(ii) is able to support communications using the Transmission Control Protocol/Internet Protocol (TCP/IP) suite or its subsequent extensions/follow-ons, and/or other IP-compatible protocols; and

(iii) provides, uses or makes accessible, either publicly or privately, high level services layered on the communications and related infrastructure described herein."

Last modified on October 30, 1995.

SOURCE: Federal Networking Council, 1995

FIGURE 2.3 PACKET SWITCHING

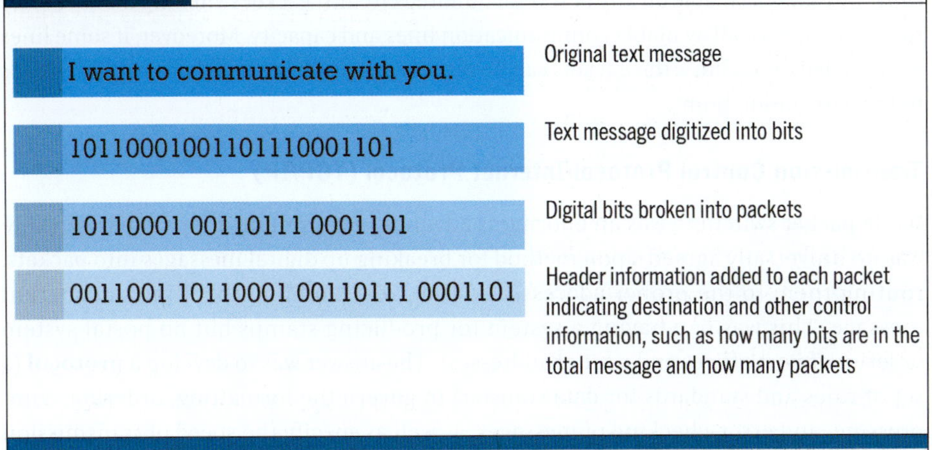

I want to communicate with you.	Original text message
1011000100110111 0001101	Text message digitized into bits
10110001 00110111 0001101	Digital bits broken into packets
0011001 10110001 00110111 0001101	Header information added to each packet indicating destination and other control information, such as how many bits are in the total message and how many packets

In packet switching, digital messages are divided into fixed-length packets of bits (generally about 1,500 bytes). Header information indicates both the origin and the ultimate destination address of the packet, the size of the message, and the number of packets the receiving node should expect. Because the receipt of each packet is acknowledged by the receiving computer, for a considerable amount of time, the network is not passing information, only acknowledgments, producing a delay called latency.

words and delays in assembling the circuit segments, both of which increase the length of time required to find and connect circuits. A better technology was needed.

The first book on packet switching was written by Leonard Kleinrock in 1964 (Kleinrock, 1964), and the technique was further developed by others in the defense research labs of both the United States and England. With packet switching, the communications capacity of a network can be increased by a factor of 100 or more. (The communications capacity of a digital network is measured in terms of bits per second.[2]) Imagine if the gas mileage of your car went from 15 miles per gallon to 1,500 miles per gallon—all without changing too much of the car!

In packet-switched networks, messages are first broken down into packets. Appended to each packet are digital codes that indicate a source address (the origination point) and a destination address, as well as sequencing information and error-control information for the packet. Rather than being sent directly to the destination address, in a packet network, the packets travel from computer to computer until they reach their destination. These computers are called routers. A **router** is a special-purpose computer that interconnects the different computer networks that make up the Internet and routes packets along to their ultimate destination as they travel. To ensure that packets take the best available path toward their destination, routers use a computer program called a **routing algorithm**.

router
special-purpose computer that interconnects the computer networks that make up the Internet and routes packets to their ultimate destination as they travel the Internet

routing algorithm
computer program that ensures that packets take the best available path toward their destination

[2] A bit is a binary digit, 0 or 1. A string of eight bits constitutes a byte. A home telephone dial-up modem connects to the Internet usually at 56 Kbps (56,000 bits per second). Mbps refers to millions of bits per second, whereas Gbps refers to billions of bits per second.

protocol
set of rules and standards for data transfer

Transmission Control Protocol/Internet Protocol (TCP/IP)
core communications protocol for the Internet

TCP
establishes connections among sending and receiving computers and handles assembly and reassembly of packets

IP
provides the Internet's addressing scheme and is responsible for delivery of packets

Network Interface Layer
responsible for placing packets on and receiving them from the network medium

Internet Layer
responsible for addressing, packaging, and routing messages on the Internet

Transport Layer
responsible for providing communication with other protocols within TCP/IP suite

Application Layer
includes protocols used to provide user services or exchange data

Border Gateway Protocol (BGP)
enables exchange of routing information among systems on the Internet

Packet switching does not require a dedicated circuit, but can make use of any spare capacity that is available on any of several hundred circuits. Packet switching makes nearly full use of almost all available communication lines and capacity. Moreover, if some lines are disabled or too busy, the packets can be sent on any available line that eventually leads to the destination point.

Transmission Control Protocol/Internet Protocol (TCP/IP)

While packet switching was an enormous advance in communications capacity, there was no universally agreed-upon method for breaking up digital messages into packets, routing them to the proper address, and then reassembling them into a coherent message. This was like having a system for producing stamps but no postal system (a series of post offices and a set of addresses). The answer was to develop a **protocol** (a set of rules and standards for data transfer) to govern the formatting, ordering, compressing, and error-checking of messages, as well as specify the speed of transmission and means by which devices on the network will indicate they have stopped sending and/or receiving messages.

Transmission Control Protocol/Internet Protocol (TCP/IP) has become the core communications protocol for the Internet (Cerf and Kahn, 1974). **TCP** establishes the connections among sending and receiving computers, and makes sure that packets sent by one computer are received in the same sequence by the other, without any packets missing. **IP** provides the Internet's addressing scheme and is responsible for the actual delivery of the packets.

TCP/IP is divided into four separate layers, with each layer handling a different aspect of the communication problem (see **Figure 2.4**). The **Network Interface Layer** is responsible for placing packets on and receiving them from the network medium, which could be a LAN (Ethernet) or Token Ring network, or other network technology. TCP/IP is independent from any local network technology and can adapt to changes at the local level. The **Internet Layer** is responsible for addressing, packaging, and routing messages on the Internet. The **Transport Layer** is responsible for providing communication with other protocols (applications) within the TCP/IP protocol suite by acknowledging and sequencing the packets to and from the applications. The **Application Layer** includes a variety of protocols used to provide user services or exchange data. One of the most important is the **Border Gateway Protocol (BGP)**, which enables the exchange of routing information among different autonomous systems on the Internet. BGP uses TCP as its transport protocol. Other important protocols included in the Application layer include HyperText Transfer Protocol (HTTP), File Transfer Protocol (FTP), and Simple Mail Transfer Protocol (SMTP), all of which we will discuss later in this chapter.

IP Addresses

The IP addressing scheme answers the question "How can billions of computers attached to the Internet communicate with one another?" The answer is that every computer connected to the Internet must be assigned an address—otherwise it cannot send or

FIGURE 2.4 THE TCP/IP ARCHITECTURE AND PROTOCOL SUITE

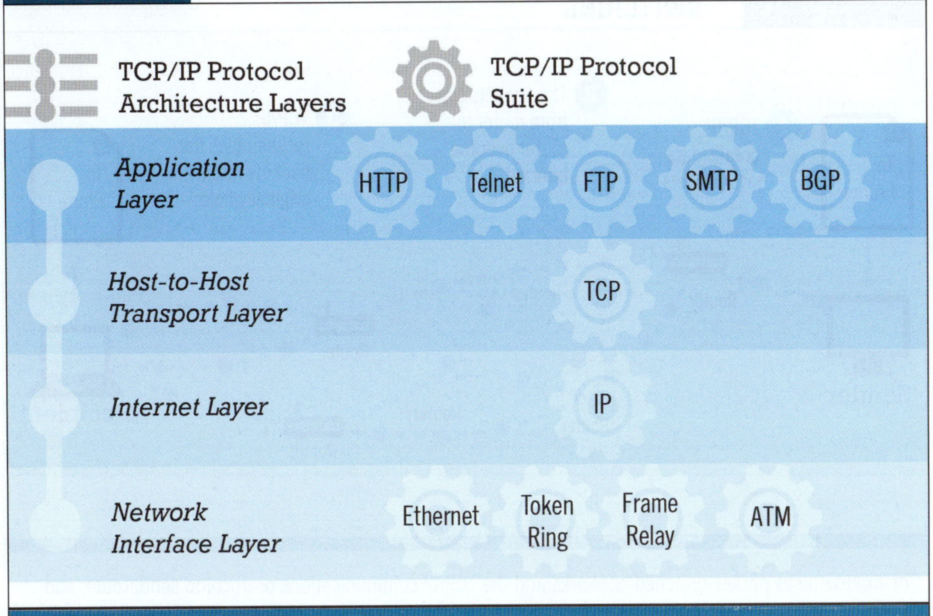

TCP/IP Protocol Architecture Layers	TCP/IP Protocol Suite
Application Layer	HTTP, Telnet, FTP, SMTP, BGP
Host-to-Host Transport Layer	TCP
Internet Layer	IP
Network Interface Layer	Ethernet, Token Ring, Frame Relay, ATM

TCP/IP is an industry-standard suite of protocols for large internetworks. The purpose of TCP/IP is to provide high-speed communication network links.

receive TCP packets. For instance, when you sign onto the Internet using a dial-up, DSL, or cable modem, your computer is assigned a temporary address by your Internet Service Provider. Most corporate and university computers attached to a local area network have a permanent IP address.

There are two versions of IP currently in use: IPv4 and IPv6. An **IPv4 Internet address** is a 32-bit number that appears as a series of four separate numbers marked off by periods, such as 64.49.254.91. Each of the four numbers can range from 0–255. This "dotted quad" addressing scheme supports up to about 4 billion addresses (2 to the 32nd power). In a typical Class C network, the first three sets of numbers identify the network (in the preceding example, 64.49.254 is the local area network identification) and the last number (91) identifies a specific computer.

Because many large corporate and government domains have been given millions of IP addresses each (to accommodate their current and future work forces), and with all the new networks and new Internet-enabled devices requiring unique IP addresses being attached to the Internet, the number of IPv4 addresses available to be assigned has shrunk significantly. Registries for North America, Europe, Asia, and Latin America have all essentially run out. IPv6 was created to address this problem. An **IPv6 Internet address** is 128 bits, so it can support up to 2^{128} (3.4×10^{38}) addresses, many more than IPv4. According to Akamai, in the United States, about 50% of Internet traffic now occurs over IPv6. India leads the way globally, with over 60% of Internet traffic converted to IPv6 (Akamai, 2019a).

IPv4 Internet address
Internet address expressed as a 32-bit number that appears as a series of four separate numbers marked off by periods, such as 64.49.254.91

IPv6 Internet address
Internet address expressed as a 128-bit number

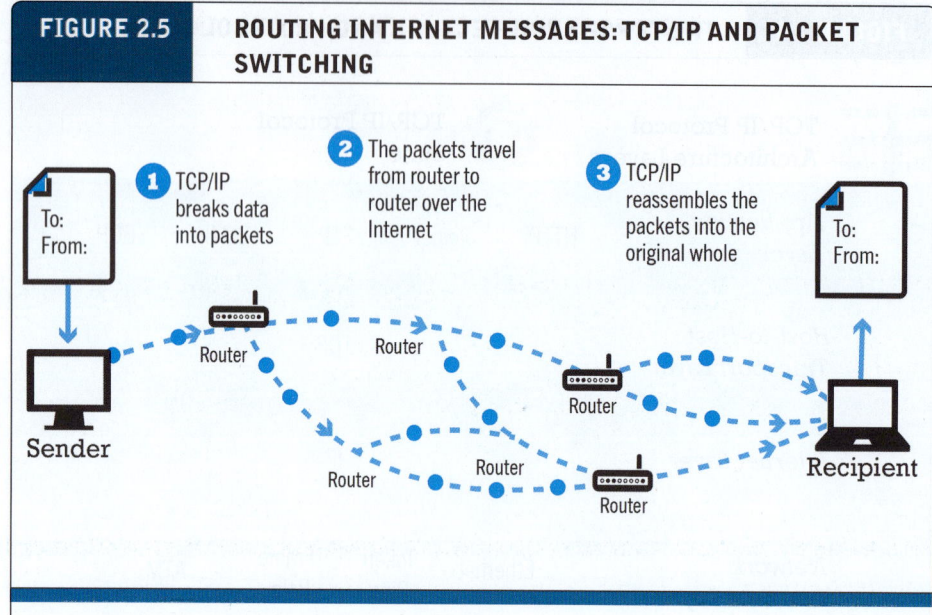

The Internet uses packet-switched networks and the TCP/IP communications protocol to send, route, and assemble messages. Messages are broken into packets, and packets from the same message can travel along different routes.

Figure 2.5 illustrates how TCP/IP and packet switching work together to send data over the Internet.

Domain Names, DNS, and URLs

Most people cannot remember 32-bit numbers. An IP address can be represented by a natural language convention called a **domain name**. The **Domain Name System (DNS)** allows expressions such as Google.com to stand for a numeric IP address (google.com's numeric IP is 172.217.12.206).[3] A **Uniform Resource Locator (URL)**, which is the address used by a web browser to identify the location of content on the Web, also uses a domain name as part of the URL. A typical URL contains the protocol to be used when accessing the address, followed by its location. For instance, the URL https://www.pearson.com refers to the IP address 159.182.41.80 with the domain name pearson.com and the protocol being used to access the address, HTTPS. A URL can have from two to four parts; for example, name1.name2.name3.org. We discuss domain names and URLs further in Section 2.4. **Figure 2.6** illustrates the Domain Name System and **Table 2.3** summarizes the important components of the Internet addressing scheme.

Client/Server Computing

While packet switching exploded the available communications capacity and TCP/IP provided the communications rules and regulations, it took a revolution in computing

---

domain name
IP address expressed in natural language

Domain Name System (DNS)
system for expressing numeric IP addresses in natural language

Uniform Resource Locator (URL)
the address used by a web browser to identify the location of content on the Web

---

[3] You can check the IP address of any domain name on the Internet. If using a Windows operating system, open the command prompt. Type ping <Domain Name>. You will receive the IP address in return.

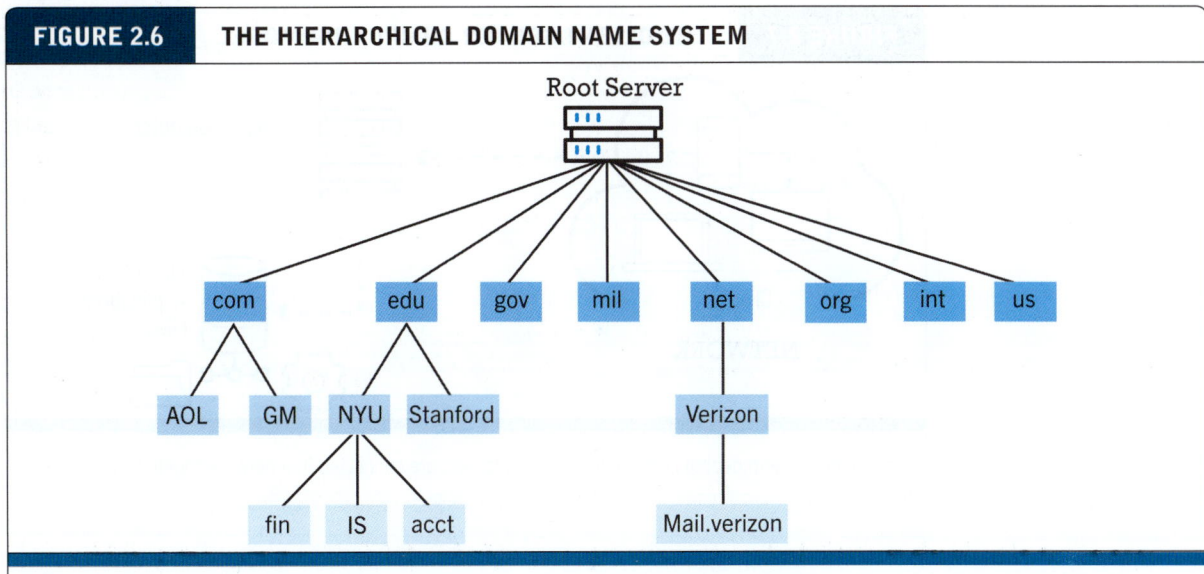

FIGURE 2.6 THE HIERARCHICAL DOMAIN NAME SYSTEM

The Domain Name System is a hierarchical namespace with a root server at the top. Top-level domains appear next and identify the organization type (such as .com, .gov, .org, etc.) or geographic location (such as .uk [Great Britain] or .ca [Canada]). Second-level servers for each top-level domain assign and register second-level domain names for organizations and individuals such as IBM.com, Microsoft.com, and Stanford.edu. Finally, third-level domains identify a particular computer or group of computers within an organization, e.g., www.finance.nyu.edu.

to bring about today's Internet and the Web. That revolution is called client/server computing and without it, the Web—in all its richness—would not exist. **Client/server computing** is a model of computing in which **client** computers are connected in a network with one or more **servers**, which are computers that are dedicated to performing common functions that the client computers on the network need, such as file storage, software applications, printing, and Internet access. The client computers are themselves sufficiently powerful to accomplish complex tasks. Servers are networked computers dedicated to common functions that the client computers on the network need, such as file storage, software applications, utility programs that provide web connections, and printers (see **Figure 2.7**). The Internet is a giant example of client/server computing in which millions

client/server computing
a model of computing in which client computers are connected in a network together with one or more servers

client
a powerful desktop computer that is part of a network

server
networked computer dedicated to common functions that the client computers on the network need

TABLE 2.3 PIECES OF THE INTERNET PUZZLE: NAMES AND ADDRESSES

IP addresses	Every device connected to the Internet must have a unique address number called an Internet Protocol (IP) address.
Domain names	The Domain Name System allows expressions such as Pearsoned.com (Pearson Education's website) to stand for numeric IP locations.
DNS servers	DNS servers are databases that keep track of IP addresses and domain names on the Internet.
Root servers	Root servers are central directories that list all domain names currently in use for specific domains; for example, the .com root server. DNS servers consult root servers to look up unfamiliar domain names when routing traffic.

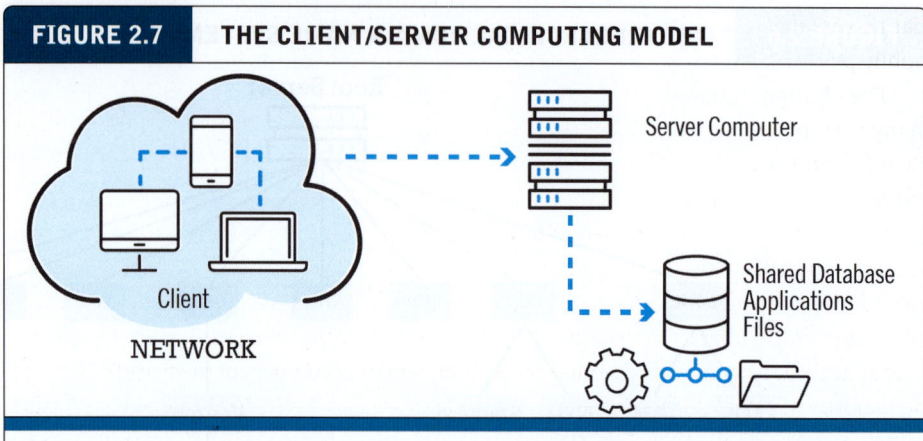

FIGURE 2.7 THE CLIENT/SERVER COMPUTING MODEL

In the client/server model of computing, client computers are connected in a network together with one or more servers.

of web servers located around the world can be easily accessed by millions of client computers, also located throughout the world.

To appreciate what client/server computing makes possible, you must understand what preceded it. In the mainframe computing environment of the 1960s and 1970s, computing power was very expensive and limited. For instance, the largest commercial mainframes of the late 1960s had 128k of RAM and 10-megabyte disk drives, and occupied hundreds of square feet. There was insufficient computing capacity to support graphics or color in text documents, let alone sound files, video, or hyperlinked documents. In this period, computing was entirely centralized: all work was done by a single mainframe computer, and users were connected to the mainframe using terminals.

With the development of personal computers and local area networks during the late 1970s and early 1980s, client/server computing became possible. Client/server computing has many advantages over centralized mainframe computing. For instance, it is easy to expand capacity by adding servers and clients. Also, client/server networks are less vulnerable than centralized computing architectures. If one server goes down, backup or mirror servers can pick up the slack; if a client computer is inoperable, the rest of the network continues operating. Moreover, processing load is balanced over many powerful smaller computers rather than concentrated in a single huge computer that performs processing for everyone. Both software and hardware in client/server environments can be built more simply and economically.

In 2019, there were an estimated 1 billion to 1.5 billion "traditional" personal computers in use around the world (Bott, 2019). Personal computing capabilities have also moved to smartphones and tablet computers (all much "thinner" clients with a bit less computing horsepower, and limited memory, but which rely on Internet servers to accomplish their tasks). In the process, more computer processing will be performed by central servers.

THE MOBILE PLATFORM

Today, the primary means of accessing the Internet worldwide is through highly portable smartphones and tablet computers, and not traditional desktop or laptop PCs. This means that the primary platform for e-commerce products and services is also changing to a mobile platform.

The change in hardware has reached a tipping point. The form factor of PCs has changed from desktops to laptops and tablet computers such as the iPad (and more than 100 other competitors). Tablets are lighter, do not require a complex operating system, and rely on the Internet cloud to provide processing and storage.

Smartphones are a disruptive technology that radically alters the personal computing and e-commerce landscape. Smartphones have created a major shift in computer processors and software that has disrupted the dual monopolies long established by Intel and Microsoft, whose chips, operating systems, and software applications began dominating the PC market in 1982. Few smartphones use Intel chips, which power 90% of the world's PCs, and the majority of smartphones use either Google's Android or Apple's iOS operating systems rather than Microsoft Windows, the dominant operating system for desktop computers. Smartphones do not use power-hungry hard drives but instead use flash memory chips with storage up to 256 gigabytes that also require much less power. In 2019, about 3.3 billion people worldwide used a mobile phone to access the Internet (eMarketer, Inc., 2019b).

The mobile platform has profound implications for e-commerce because it influences how, where, and when consumers shop and buy. We discuss mobile access to the Internet further in Section 2.2.

THE INTERNET "CLOUD COMPUTING" MODEL: HARDWARE AND SOFTWARE AS A SERVICE

Cloud computing is a model of computing in which computer processing, storage, software, and other services are provided as a shared pool of virtualized resources over the Internet. These "clouds" of computing resources can be accessed on an as-needed basis from any connected device and location. **Figure 2.8** illustrates the cloud computing concept.

cloud computing

model of computing in which computer processing, storage, software, and other services are provided as a shared pool of virtualized resources over the Internet

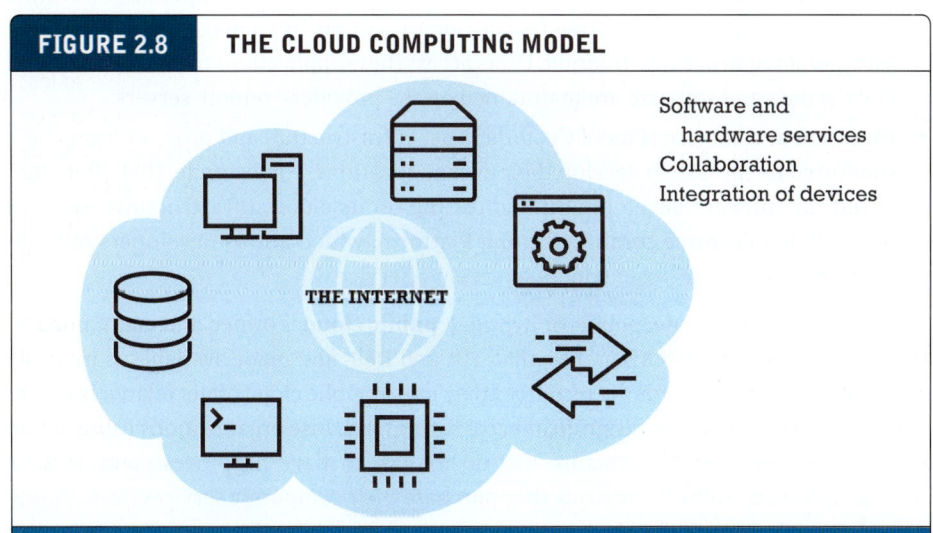

FIGURE 2.8 THE CLOUD COMPUTING MODEL

Software and hardware services
Collaboration
Integration of devices

THE INTERNET

In the cloud computing model, hardware and software services are provided on the Internet by vendors operating very large server farms and data centers.

The U.S. National Institute of Standards and Technology (NIST) defines cloud computing as having the following essential characteristics:

- **On-demand self-service:** Consumers can obtain computing capabilities such as server time or network storage as needed automatically on their own.
- **Ubiquitous network access:** Cloud resources can be accessed using standard network and Internet devices, including mobile platforms.
- **Location-independent resource pooling:** Computing resources are pooled to serve multiple users, with different virtual resources dynamically assigned according to user demand. The user generally does not know where the computing resources are located.
- **Rapid elasticity:** Computing resources can be rapidly provisioned, increased, or decreased to meet changing user demand.
- **Measured service:** Charges for cloud resources are based on the amount of resources actually used.

Cloud computing consists of three basic types of services:

- **Infrastructure as a service (IaaS):** Customers use processing, storage, networking, and other computing resources from third-party providers called cloud service providers (CSPs) to run their information systems. For example, Amazon used the spare capacity of its information technology infrastructure to develop Amazon Web Services (AWS), which offers a cloud environment for a myriad of different IT infrastructure services. See **Table 2.4** for a description of the range of services that AWS offers, such as its Simple Storage Service (S3) for storing customers' data and its Elastic Compute Cloud (EC2) service for running applications. Users pay only for the amount of computing and storage capacity they actually use.
- **Software as a service (SaaS):** Customers use software hosted by the vendor on the vendor's cloud infrastructure and delivered as a service over a network. Leading SaaS examples includes G Suite, which provides common business applications online, and Salesforce.com, which provides customer relationship management and related software services over the Internet. Users access these applications from a web browser, and the data and software are maintained on the providers' remote servers.
- **Platform as a service (PaaS):** Customers use infrastructure and programming tools supported by the CSP to develop their own applications. For example, IBM offers IBM Cloud for software development and testing on its cloud infrastructure. Another example is Salesforce.com's Lightning Platform, which allows developers to build applications that are hosted on its servers as a service.

public cloud

third-party service providers that own and manage large, scalable data centers that offer computing, data storage, and high-speed Internet to multiple customers who pay for only the resources they use

A cloud can be private, public, or hybrid. A **public cloud** is owned and maintained by CSPs, such as Amazon Web Services, IBM, HP, and Dell, and made available to multiple customers, who pay only for the resources they use. A public cloud offers relatively secure enterprise-class reliability at significant cost savings. Because organizations using public clouds do not own the infrastructure, they do not have to make large investments in their own hardware and software. Instead, they purchase their computing services from remote providers and pay only for the amount of computing power they actually use (utility computing) or are billed on a monthly or annual subscription basis. The term *on-demand computing* is also used to describe such services. As such, public clouds are ideal

TABLE 2.4 AMAZON WEB SERVICES

NAME	DESCRIPTION
COMPUTING SERVICES	
Elastic Compute Cloud (EC2)	Scalable cloud computing services
Elastic Load Balancing (ELB)	Distributes incoming application traffic among multiple EC2 instances
STORAGE SERVICES	
Simple Storage Service (S3)	Data storage infrastructure
Glacier	Low-cost archival and backup storage
DATABASE SERVICES	
DynamoDB	NoSQL database service
Redshift	Petabyte-scale data warehouse service
Relational Database Service (RDS)	Relational database service for MySQL, Oracle, SQL Server, and PostgreSQL databases
ElastiCache	In-memory cache in the cloud
SimpleDB	Non-relational data store
NETWORKING AND CONTENT DELIVERY SERVICES	
Route 53	DNS service in the cloud, enabling business to direct Internet traffic to web applications
Virtual Private Cloud (VPC)	Creates a VPN between the Amazon cloud and a company's existing IT infrastructure
CloudFront	Content delivery services
Direct Connect	Provides alternative to using the Internet to access AWS cloud services
ANALYTICS	
Elastic MapReduce (EMR)	Web service that enables users to perform data-intensive tasks
Kinesis	Big data service for real-time data streaming ingestion and processing
APPLICATION SERVICES	
AppStream	Provides streaming services for applications and games from the cloud
CloudSearch	Search service that can be integrated by developers into applications
MESSAGING SERVICES	
Simple Email Service (SES)	Cloud e-mail sending service
Simple Notification Service (SNS)	Push messaging service
Simple Queue Service (SQS)	Queue for storing messages as they travel between computers

(continued)

TABLE 2.4	AMAZON WEB SERVICES (CONT.)
DEPLOYMENT AND MANAGEMENT SERVICES	
Identity and Access Management (IAM)	Enables securely controlled access to AWS services
CloudWatch	Monitoring service
Elastic Beanstalk	Service for deploying and scaling web applications and services developed with Java, .Net, PHP, Python, Ruby, and Node.js
CloudFormation	Service that allows developers an easy way to create a collection of related AWS resources
MOBILE	
Cognito	Allows developers to securely manage and synchronize app data for users across mobile devices
Mobile Analytics	Can collect and process billions of events from millions of users a day
PAYMENT SERVICES	
Flexible Payment Service (FPS)	Payment services for developers
DevPay	Online billing and account management service for developers who create an Amazon cloud application
MISCELLANEOUS	
Amazon Mechanical Turk	Marketplace for work that requires human intelligence
Alexa Web Information Service	Provides web traffic data and information for developers

environments for small and medium-sized businesses who cannot afford to fully develop their own infrastructure; for applications requiring high performance, scalability, and availability; for new application development and testing; and for companies that have occasional large computing projects. Gartner estimates that spending on public cloud services worldwide (not including cloud advertising) will grow by 17% in 2020, to over $266 billion (Gartner, Inc., 2019a). Companies such as Google, Apple, Dropbox, Box, and others also offer public clouds as a consumer service for online storage of data, music, and photos. Google Drive, Dropbox, and Apple iCloud are leading examples of this type of consumer cloud service.

A **private cloud** provides similar options as a public cloud but is operated solely for the benefit of a single tenant. It might be managed by the organization or a third party and hosted either internally or externally. Like public clouds, private clouds can allocate storage, computing power, or other resources seamlessly to provide computing resources on an as-needed basis. Companies that have stringent regulatory compliance or specialized licensing requirements that necessitate high security, such as financial services or healthcare companies, or that want flexible information technology resources and a cloud service model while retaining control over their own IT infrastructure, are gravitating toward these private clouds.

Large firms are most likely to adopt a **hybrid cloud** computing model, in which they use their own infrastructure for their most essential core activities and adopt public cloud

private cloud
provides similar options as a public cloud but only to a single tenant

hybrid cloud
offers customers both a public cloud and a private cloud

computing for less-critical systems or for additional processing capacity during peak business periods. **Table 2.5** compares the three cloud computing models. Cloud computing will gradually shift firms from having a fixed infrastructure capacity toward a more flexible infrastructure, some of it owned by the firm, and some of it rented from giant data centers owned by CSPs.

Cloud computing has some drawbacks. Unless users make provisions for storing their data locally, the responsibility for data storage and control is in the hands of the provider. Some companies worry about the security risks related to entrusting their critical data and systems to an outside vendor that also works with other companies. Companies expect their systems to be available 24/7 and do not want to suffer any loss of business capability if cloud infrastructures malfunction. Nevertheless, the trend is for companies to shift more of their computer processing and storage to some form of cloud infrastructure.

Cloud computing has many significant implications for e-commerce. For e-commerce firms, cloud computing radically reduces the cost of building and operating websites because the necessary hardware infrastructure and software can be licensed as a service from CSPs at a fraction of the cost of purchasing these services as products. This means firms can adopt "pay-as-you-go" and "pay-as-you-grow" strategies when building out their websites. For instance, according to Amazon, hundreds of thousands of customers use Amazon Web Services. For individuals, cloud computing means you no longer need a powerful laptop or desktop computer to engage in e-commerce or other activities. Instead, you can use much less-expensive tablet computers or smartphones that cost a few hundred dollars. For corporations, cloud computing means that a significant part of hardware and software costs (infrastructure costs) can be reduced because firms can obtain these services online for a fraction of the cost of owning, and they do not have to hire an IT staff to support the infrastructure.

OTHER INTERNET PROTOCOLS AND UTILITY PROGRAMS

There are many other Internet protocols and utility programs that provide services to users in the form of Internet applications that run on Internet clients and servers. These Internet

TABLE 2.5   CLOUD COMPUTING MODELS COMPARED

TYPE OF CLOUD	DESCRIPTION	MANAGED BY	USES
Public cloud	Third-party service offering computing, storage, and software services to multiple customers	Third-party service providers (CSPs)	Companies without major privacy concerns Companies seeking pay-as-you-go IT services Companies lacking IT resources and expertise
Private cloud	Cloud infrastructure operated solely for a single organization and hosted either internally or externally	In-house IT or private third-party host	Companies with stringent privacy and security requirements Companies that must have control over data sovereignty
Hybrid cloud	Combination of private and public cloud services that remain separate entities	In-house IT, private host, third-party providers	Companies requiring some in-house control of IT that are also willing to assign part of their IT infrastructures to a public cloud partition on their IT infrastructures

services are based on universally accepted protocols—or standards—that are available to everyone who uses the Internet. They are not owned by any organization, but they are services that have been developed over many years and made available to all Internet users.

HyperText Transfer Protocol (HTTP) is the Internet protocol used to transfer web pages (described in the following section). HTTP was developed by the World Wide Web Consortium (W3C) and the Internet Engineering Task Force (IETF). HTTP runs in the Application Layer of the TCP/IP model shown in Figure 2.4 on page 103. An HTTP session begins when a client's browser requests a resource, such as a web page, from a remote Internet server. When the server responds by sending the page requested, the HTTP session for that object ends. Because web pages may have many objects on them—graphics, sound or video files, frames, and so forth—each object must be requested by a separate HTTP message. For more information about HTTP, you can consult RFC 2616, which details the standards for HTTP/1.1, the version of HTTP most commonly used today (Internet Society, 1999). (An RFC is a document published by the Internet Society [ISOC] or one of the other organizations involved in Internet governance that sets forth the standards for various Internet-related technologies. You will learn more about the organizations involved in setting standards for the Internet later in the chapter.) An updated version of HTTP, known as HTTP/2, was published as RFC 7540 in May 2015 (IETF, 2015). HTTP/2 addresses a number of HTTP 1.1 shortcomings and is designed to enhance performance by eliminating the need to open multiple TCP connections between a client and server (known as multiplexing), allowing servers to push resources to a client without the client having to request them (known as server push), and reducing the HTTP header size (header compression). HTTP/2 will also have security benefits, with improved performance for encrypted data running over HTTP/2. HTTP/2 is supported by almost all the leading web browsers, but as of November 2019, it had only been adopted by around 40% of all websites, in part due to the challenges involved for organizations in transitioning their applications from HTTP to HTTP/2 (W3techs.com, 2019).

E-mail is one of the oldest, most important, and frequently used Internet services. Like HTTP, the various Internet protocols used to handle e-mail all run in the Application Layer of TCP/IP. **Simple Mail Transfer Protocol (SMTP)** is the Internet protocol used to send e-mail to a server. SMTP is a relatively simple, text-based protocol that was developed in the early 1980s. SMTP handles only the sending of e-mail. To retrieve e-mail from a server, the client computer uses either **Post Office Protocol 3 (POP3)** or **Internet Message Access Protocol (IMAP)**. You can set POP3 to retrieve e-mail messages from the server and then delete the messages on the server, or retain them on the server. IMAP is a more current e-mail protocol. IMAP allows users to search, organize, and filter their mail prior to downloading it from the server.

File Transfer Protocol (FTP) is one of the original Internet services. FTP runs in TCP/IP's Application Layer and permits users to transfer files from a server to their client computer, and vice versa. The files can be documents, programs, or large database files. FTP is the fastest and most convenient way to transfer files larger than 1 megabyte, which some e-mail servers will not accept. More information about FTP is available in RFC 959 (Internet Society, 1985).

Telnet is a network protocol that also runs in TCP/IP's Application Layer and is used to allow remote login on another computer. The term Telnet also refers to the Telnet

---

HyperText Transfer Protocol (HTTP)
the Internet protocol used for transferring web pages

Simple Mail Transfer Protocol (SMTP)
the Internet protocol used to send mail to a server

Post Office Protocol 3 (POP3)
a protocol used by the client to retrieve mail from an Internet server

Internet Message Access Protocol (IMAP)
a more current e-mail protocol that allows users to search, organize, and filter their mail prior to downloading it from the server

File Transfer Protocol (FTP)
one of the original Internet services. Part of the TCP/IP protocol that permits users to transfer files from the server to their client computer, and vice versa

Telnet
a terminal emulation program that runs in TCP/IP

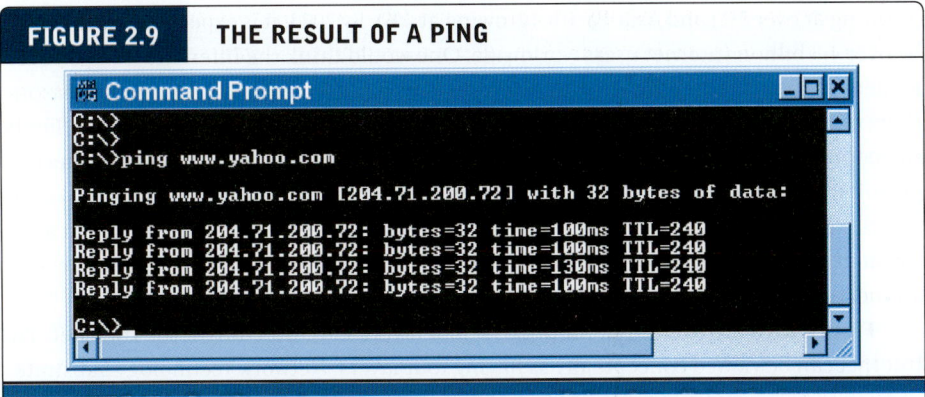

FIGURE 2.9   THE RESULT OF A PING

A ping is used to verify an address and test the speed of the round trip from a client computer to a host and back.
SOURCE: Command Prompt, Microsoft Windows, Microsoft Corporation.

program, which provides the client part of the protocol and enables the client to emulate a mainframe computer terminal. You can then attach yourself to a computer on the Internet that supports Telnet and run programs or download files from that computer. Telnet was the first "remote work" program that permitted users to work on a computer from a remote location.

Secure Sockets Layer (SSL)/Transport Layer Security (TLS) are protocols that operate between the Transport and Application Layers of TCP/IP and secure communications between the client and the server. SSL/TLS helps secure e-commerce communications and payments through a variety of techniques, such as message encryption and digital signatures, that we will discuss further in Chapter 5.

Packet InterNet Groper (Ping) is a utility program that allows you to check the connection between a client computer and a TCP/IP network (see **Figure 2.9**). Ping will also tell you the time it takes for the server to respond, giving you some idea about the speed of the server and the Internet at that moment. You can run Ping from the command prompt on a personal computer with a Windows operating system by typing: ping <domain name>. Ping can also be used to slow down or even crash a domain server by sending it millions of ping requests.

Tracert is one of several route-tracing utilities that allow you to follow the path of a message you send from your client to a remote computer on the Internet.

Secure Sockets Layer (SSL)/Transport Layer Security (TLS)
protocols that secure communications between the client and the server

Ping
a program that allows you to check the connection between your client and the server

Tracert
one of several route-tracing utilities that allow you to follow the path of a message you send from your client to a remote computer on the Internet

2.2   INTERNET INFRASTRUCTURE AND ACCESS

In 2019, there were an estimated 3.8 billion Internet users worldwide, up from 100 million users at year-end 1997. While this is a huge number, it still represents only about 50% of the world's population (eMarketer, Inc., 2019a). Although Internet user growth slowed in the United States and Western Europe in 2019 to only 1% to 1.5%, the growth rate worldwide was an estimated 4.6%, with the highest growth areas being the Middle East/Africa (growing at over 5%) and Asia-Pacific (growing at 6%). By 2023, it is expected that there will be over 4.3 billion Internet users worldwide. One would think the Internet would be overloaded with such incredible growth; however, this has not been true for several reasons. First, client/server computing is highly extensible. By simply adding servers and clients, the population of Internet users can grow indefinitely. Second, the Internet architecture is built in layers so that each layer can change without disturbing developments in other layers. For instance, the technology used to move messages through the Internet can go through radical changes to make service faster without being disruptive to your desktop applications running on the Internet.

Figure 2.10 illustrates the "hourglass" and layered architecture of the Internet. The Internet can be viewed conceptually as having four layers: Network Technology Substrates,

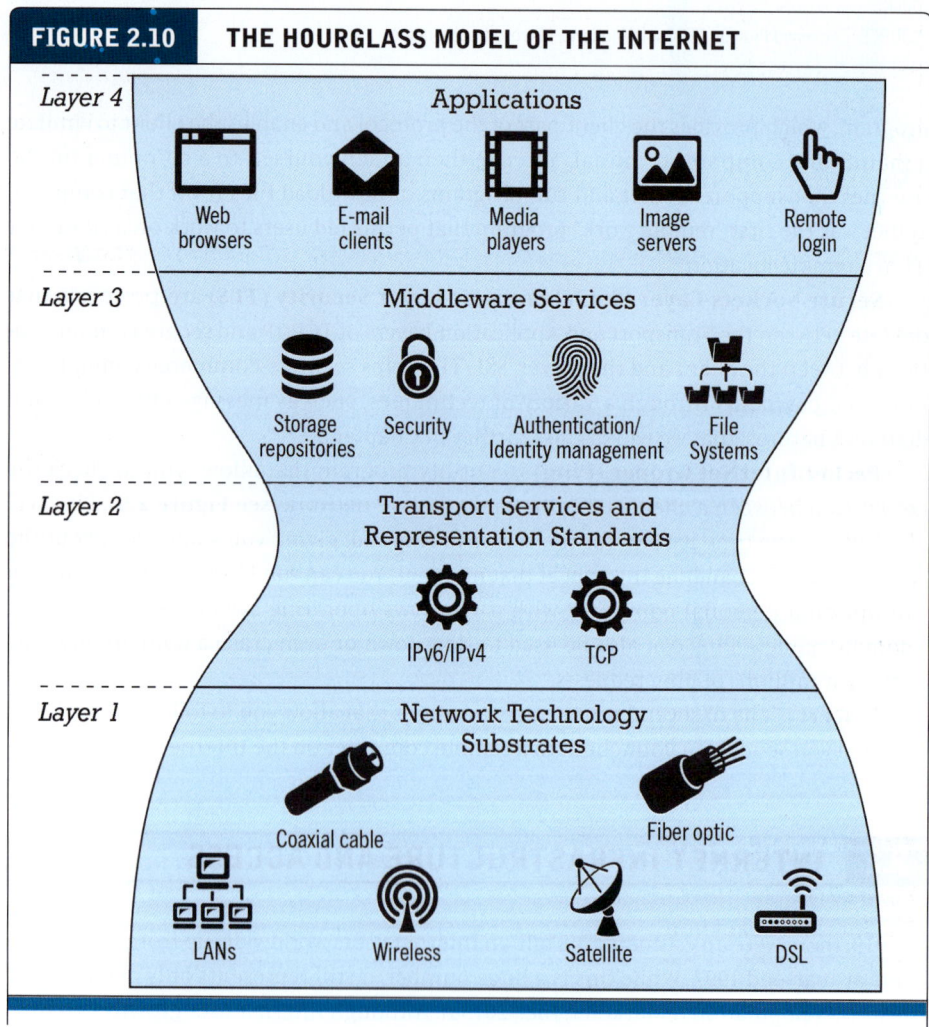

FIGURE 2.10 THE HOURGLASS MODEL OF THE INTERNET

The Internet can be characterized as an hourglass modular structure with a lower layer containing the bit-carrying infrastructure (including cables and switches) and an upper layer containing user applications such as e-mail and the Web. In the narrow waist are transportation protocols such as TCP/IP.

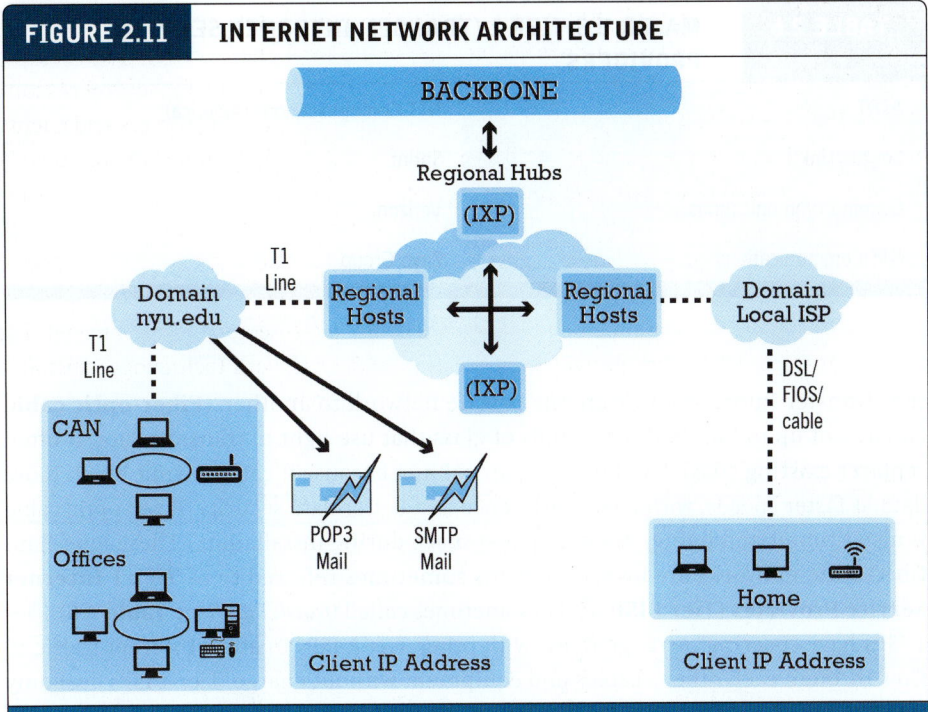

FIGURE 2.11 INTERNET NETWORK ARCHITECTURE

Today's Internet has a multi-tiered open network architecture featuring multiple backbones, regional hubs, campus/corporate area networks, and local client computers.

Transport Services and Representation Standards, Middleware Services, and Applications.[4] The **Network Technology Substrate layer** is composed of telecommunications networks and protocols. The **Transport Services and Representation Standards layer** houses the TCP/IP protocol. The **Applications layer** contains client applications such as the Web, e-mail, and audio or video playback. The **Middleware Services layer** is the glue that ties the applications to the communications networks and includes such services as security, authentication, addresses, and storage repositories. Users work with applications (such as e-mail) and rarely become aware of middleware that operates in the background. Because all layers use TCP/IP and other common standards linking all four layers, it is possible for there to be significant changes in the Network Technology Substrate layer without forcing changes in the Applications layer.

THE INTERNET BACKBONE

Figure 2.11 illustrates some of the main physical elements of today's physical Internet. The Internet's **backbone** is created by numerous privately owned networks comprised of high-bandwidth fiber-optic cable that are physically connected with each other and

Network Technology Substrate layer
layer of Internet technology that is composed of telecommunications networks and protocols

Transport Services and Representation Standards layer
layer of Internet architecture that houses the TCP/IP protocol

Applications layer
layer of Internet architecture that contains client applications

Middleware Services layer
the "glue" that ties the applications to the communications networks and includes such services as security, authentication, addresses, and storage repositories

backbone
high-bandwidth fiber-optic cable networks that transport data around the world

---

[4] Recall that the TCP/IP communications protocol also has layers, not to be confused with the Internet architecture layers.

TABLE 2.6	MAJOR U.S. TIER 1 (TRANSIT) INTERNET SERVICE PROVIDERS
AT&T	NTT Communications (America)
CenturyLink	Sprint
Cogent Communications	Verizon
GTT Communications	Zayo Group

fiber-optic cable

consists of up to hundreds of strands of glass or plastic that use light to transmit data

Tier 1 Internet Service Providers (Tier 1 ISPs)

own and control the major long-haul fiber-optic cable networks comprising the Internet's backbone

bandwidth

measures how much data can be transferred over a communications medium within a fixed period of time; is usually expressed in bits per second (bps), kilobits per second (Kbps), megabits per second (Mbps), or gigabits per second (Gbps)

redundancy

multiple duplicate devices and paths in a network

that transfer information from one private network to another. (**Fiber-optic cable** consists of up to hundreds of strands of glass that use light to transmit data. It often replaces existing coaxial and twisted pair cabling because it can transmit much more data at faster speeds, with less interference and better data security. Fiber-optic cable is also thinner and lighter, taking up less space during installation.) These long-haul fiber-optic networks are owned by firms sometimes referred to as **Tier 1 Internet Service Providers (Tier 1 ISPs)** (also sometimes called *transit ISPs*) (see **Table 2.6**). Tier 1 ISPs have "peering" arrangements with other Tier 1 ISPs to allow Internet traffic to flow through each other's cables and equipment without charge. Tier 1 ISPs deal only with other Tier 1 or Tier 2 ISPs (described in the next section) and not with end consumers. For the sake of simplicity, we will refer to these networks of backbones as a single "backbone." **Bandwidth** measures how much data can be transferred over a communications medium within a fixed period of time and is usually expressed in bits per second (Bps), kilobits (thousands of bits) per second (Kbps), megabits (millions of bits) per second (Mbps), or gigabits (billions of bits) per second (Gbps). In the United States, the backbone can carry data at rates of up to 100 Gbps.

Connections to other continents are made via a combination of undersea fiber-optic cable and satellite links. Increasingly, rather than leasing bandwidth from Tier 1 ISPs, Internet giants such as Google, Microsoft, and Facebook are laying down their own fiber-optic networks. For instance, Google has one cable stretching from California to Japan and another connecting the United States to Brazil, and added additional submarine cables in 2019, while Facebook and Microsoft have allied to lay a cable across the Atlantic, connecting Virginia to Spain. The backbone in foreign countries typically is operated by a mixture of private and public owners. The backbone has built-in redundancy so that if one part breaks down, data can be rerouted to another part of the backbone. **Redundancy** refers to multiple duplicate devices and paths in a network. A recent study of the Internet's physical structure in the United States has created one of the first maps of the Internet's long-haul fiber network as it currently exists. The map reveals that, not surprisingly, there are dense networks of fiber in the Northeast and coastal areas of the United States, while there is a pronounced absence of infrastructure in the Upper Plains and Four Corners regions. The U.S. Department of Homeland Security has made the map, as well as the data that underlies it, available to government, private, and public researchers, believing that doing so could make the Internet more resilient by improving knowledge (Simonite, 2015; Durairajan et al., 2015).

INTERNET EXCHANGE POINTS

Regional hubs where Tier 1 ISPs physically connect with one another and/or with regional (Tier 2) ISPs were originally called Network Access Points (NAPs) or Metropolitan Area Exchanges (MAEs), but now are more commonly referred to as **Internet Exchange Points (IXPs)** (see **Figure 2.12**). Tier 2 ISPs exchange Internet traffic both through peering arrangements as well as by purchasing Internet transit, and they connect Tier 1 ISPs with Tier 3 ISPs, which provide Internet access to consumers and business. Tier 3 ISPs are described further in the next section.

TIER 3 INTERNET SERVICE PROVIDERS

The firms that provide the lowest level of service in the multi-tiered Internet architecture by leasing Internet access to home owners, small businesses, and some large institutions are sometimes called **Tier 3 Internet Service Providers (ISPs)**. Tier 3 ISPs are retail providers. They deal with "the last mile of service" to the curb—homes and business offices. Tier 3 ISPs typically connect to IXPs with high-speed telephone or cable lines (45 Mbps and higher).

There are a number of major ISPs throughout Europe, such as Plusnet, Sky Broadband, Virgin Media, and TalkTalk in the UK; Orange, SFR, Bouyges Telecom, and Free Mobile in France; and Tiscali, BT Italia, and Fastweb in Italy. If you have home or small business Internet access, a Tier 3 ISP likely provides the service to you. (It's important to note that many Tier 3 ISPs are also Tier I ISPs; the two roles are not mutually exclusive.) Satellite firms also offer Internet access, especially in remote areas where broadband service is not available.

Table 2.7 on page 119 summarizes the variety of services, speeds, and costs of Internet access available to consumers and businesses. There are two types of service: narrowband and broadband. **Narrowband** service is the traditional telephone modem connection now operating at 56.6 Kbps (although the actual throughput hovers around 30 Kbps due to line noise that causes extensive resending of packets). This used to be the most common form of connection worldwide but it has been largely replaced by broadband connections in the United States, Europe, and Asia. Broadband service is based on DSL (including high speed fiber-optic service), cable, telephone (T1 and T3 lines), and satellite technologies. **Broadband**, in the context of Internet service, refers to any communication technology that permits clients to play streaming audio and video files at acceptable speeds. In the United States, broadband users surpassed dial-up users in 2004, and although the rate of broadband adoption has slowed in recent years, the number of broadband households has grown to about 73% of all households, up from 68% in 2012 (Singer, Naef, and King, 2017). In 2015, the U.S. Federal Communications Commission updated its broadband benchmark speeds to 25 Mbps for downloads and 3 Mbps for uploads. The FCC has found that over 10 million Americans lack access to 25 Mbps/3 Mbps service, and that rural America is particularly underserved, with more than half lacking such access. In addition, over 46 million U.S. homes are served by only one provider offering 25 Mbps broadband (Broadkin, 2017, Federal Communications Commission, 2015). According to Cable.co.uk and M-Lab, an open source project, the global average broadband speed in 2019 was 11.03 Mbps, an increase of over 20% compared to 2018.

Internet Exchange Point (IXP)
hub where the backbone intersects with local and regional networks and where backbone owners connect with one another

Tier 3 Internet Service Provider (Tier 3 ISP)
firm that provides the lowest level of service in the multi-tiered Internet architecture by leasing Internet access to home owners, small businesses, and some large institutions

narrowband
the traditional telephone modem connection, now operating at 56.6 Kbps

broadband
refers to any communication technology that permits clients to play streaming audio and video files at acceptable speeds

FIGURE 2.12 — SOME MAJOR U.S. INTERNET EXCHANGE POINTS (IXPs)

Region	Name	Location	Operator
EAST	Boston Internet Exchange (BOSIX)	Boston	Markley
	New York International Internet Exchange (NYIIX)	New York	Telehouse
	Peering and Internet Exchange (PAIX)	New York, Virginia, Atlanta	Equinix
	NAP of the Americas	Miami	Verizon Terremark
CENTRAL	Any2 Exchange	Chicago	CoreSite
	Peering and Internet Exchange (PAIX)	Dallas	Equinix
	Midwest Internet Cooperative Exchange (MICE)	Minneapolis	Members
WEST	Peering and Internet Exchange (PAIX)	Seattle, Palo Alto	Equinix
	Los Angeles International Internet Exchange (LAIIX)	Los Angeles	Telehouse
	Any2 Exchange	San Jose, Los Angeles	CoreSite
	Seattle Internet Exchange (SIX)	Seattle	Members

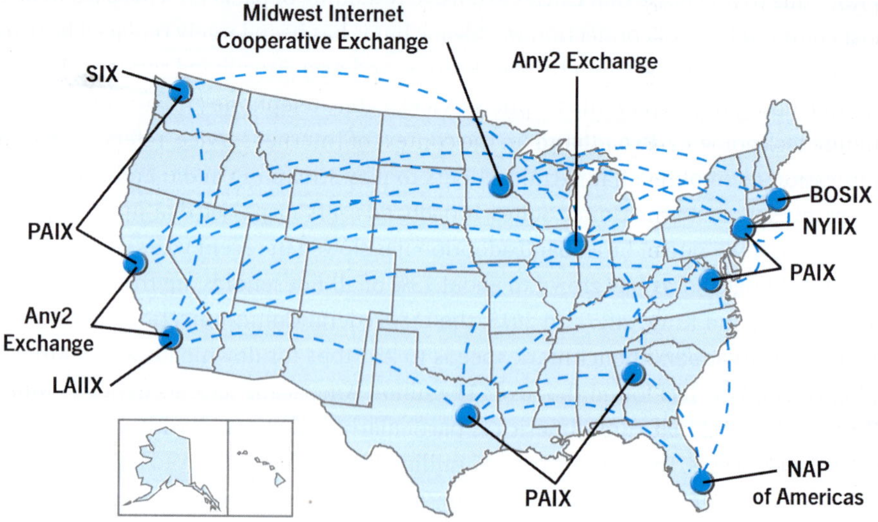

TABLE 2.7 INTERNET ACCESS SERVICE LEVELS AND BANDWIDTH CHOICES IN THE UNITED STATES

SERVICE	COST/MONTH	DOWNLOAD SPEED
Telephone modem	$10–$25	30–56 Kbps
DSL	$20–$30	1–15 Mbps
FiOS	$50–$300	25 Mbps–500 Mbps
Cable Internet	$35–$199	15 Mbps–300 Mbps
Satellite	$39–$129	5–15 Mbps
T1	$200–$300	1.54 Mbps
T3	$2,500–$6,000	45 Mbps

Taiwan leads in average download speed, at 28.1 Mbps. However, of the top 50 countries, 37 are in Europe. Not surprisingly, countries in Africa continue to lag (Cable.co.uk, 2019).

The actual throughput of data will depend on a variety of factors including noise in the line and the number of subscribers requesting service. Service-level speeds quoted are typically only for downloads of Internet content; upload speeds tend to be slower, although a number of broadband ISPs have plans that offer the same upload as download speed. T1 and T3 lines are publicly regulated utility lines that offer a guaranteed level of service, but the actual throughput of the other forms of Internet service is not guaranteed.

Digital Subscriber Line (DSL) service is a telephone technology that provides high-speed access to the Internet through ordinary telephone lines found in a home or business. Service levels typically range from about .5 to 15 Mbps. DSL service requires that customers live within two miles (about 4,000 meters) of a neighborhood telephone switching center. In order to compete with cable companies, telephone companies now also offer an advanced form of DSL called **FiOS (fiber-optic service)** that provides up to 500 Mbps to homes and businesses.

Cable Internet refers to a cable television technology that piggybacks digital access to the Internet using the same analog or digital video cable providing television signals to a home. Cable Internet is a major broadband alternative to DSL service, generally providing faster speeds and a "triple play" subscription: telephone, television, and Internet for a single monthly payment. However, the available bandwidth of cable Internet is shared with others in the neighborhood using the same cable. When many people are attempting to access the Internet over the cable at the same time, speeds may slow and performance will suffer. Cable Internet services typically range from 15 Mbps up to 300 Mbps. Deutsche Telekom, Vodafone, Telefonica, and Liberty Global are some of the major cable Internet providers in Europe.

T1 and T3 are international telephone standards for digital communication. **T1** lines offer guaranteed delivery at 1.54 Mbps, while **T3** lines offer 45 Mbps. T1 lines cost about $200–$300 per month, and T3 lines around $2500–$6000 per month. These are leased,

Digital Subscriber Line (DSL)
delivers high-speed access through ordinary telephone lines found in homes or businesses

FiOS (fiber-optic service)
a form of DSL that provides speeds of up to 500 Mbps

cable Internet
piggybacks digital access to the Internet on top of the analog video cable providing television signals to a home

T1
an international telephone standard for digital communication that offers guaranteed delivery at 1.54 Mbps

T3
an international telephone standard for digital communication that offers guaranteed delivery at 45 Mbps

dedicated, guaranteed lines suitable for corporations, government agencies, and businesses such as ISPs requiring high-speed guaranteed service levels.

Satellite Internet is offered by satellite companies that provide high-speed broadband Internet access primarily to homes and offices located in rural areas where DSL or cable Internet access is not available. Access speeds and monthly costs are comparable to DSL and cable, but typically require a higher initial payment for installation of a small (18-inch) satellite dish. Upload speeds tend to be slower, typically 1–5 Mbps. Satellite providers typically have policies that limit the total megabytes of data that a single account can download within a set period, usually monthly. Major satellite providers in Europe include Hughes, Telefonica, Europasat, and Bentley Walker, among others. In 2016, Facebook announced plans to launch a satellite aimed at bringing Internet connectivity to parts of sub-Saharan Africa, but those plans were put on hold when the SpaceX rocket that was to launch the satellite exploded while being tested during pre-launch activities. In 2019, Facebook moved ahead with plans for a new low-orbit satellite system code-named Athena. SpaceX, Boeing, and OneWeb (backed by Softbank) are also working on similar Internet satellite efforts (Matsakis, 2018).

Nearly all business firms and government agencies have broadband connections to the Internet. Demand for broadband service has grown so rapidly because it greatly speeds up the process of downloading web pages and large video and audio files (see **Table 2.8**). As the quality of Internet service offerings continues to expand, the demand for broadband access will continue to swell.

satellite Internet
high-speed broadband Internet access provided via satellite

CAMPUS/CORPORATE AREA NETWORKS

Campus/corporate area networks (CANs) are generally local area networks operating within a single organization—such as New York University or Microsoft Corporation. In fact, most large organizations have hundreds of such local area networks. These organizations are sufficiently large that they lease access to the Web directly from regional and national carriers. These local area networks generally are running Ethernet (a local area network protocol) and have network operating systems such as Windows Server or Linux

campus/corporate area network (CAN)
generally, a local area network operating within a single organization that leases access to the Web directly from regional and national carriers

TABLE 2.8	TIME TO DOWNLOAD A 10-MEGABYTE FILE BY TYPE OF INTERNET SERVICE
TYPE OF INTERNET SERVICE	TIME TO DOWNLOAD
NARROWBAND SERVICES	
Telephone modem	25 minutes
BROADBAND SERVICES	
DSL @ 1 Mbps	1.33 minutes
Cable Internet @ 10 Mbps	8 seconds
T1 @ 1.54 Mpbs	52 seconds
T3 @ 45 Mbps	2 seconds

that permit desktop clients to connect to the Internet through a local Internet server attached to their campus networks. Connection speeds in campus area networks are in the range of 10–100 Mbps to the desktop.

MOBILE INTERNET ACCESS

Fiber-optic networks carry the long-haul bulk traffic of the Internet and play an important role in bringing high-speed broadband to the household and small business. The goal is to bring gigabit and ultimately terabit bandwidth to the household over the next 20 years. But along with fiber optics, arguably the most significant development for the Internet and Web has been the emergence of mobile Internet access.

Wireless Internet is concerned with the last mile of Internet access to the user's home, office, car, smartphone, or tablet computer, anywhere they are located. Up until 2000, the last-mile access to the Internet—with the exception of a small satellite Internet connect population—was bound up in land lines of some sort: copper coaxial TV cables or telephone lines or, in some cases, fiber-optic lines to the office. Today, in comparison, high-speed cell phone networks and Wi-Fi network hotspots provide a major alternative.

Today, sales of desktop computers have been eclipsed by sales of smartphones and tablet and ultramobile laptop computers with built-in wireless networking functionality. Clearly, a large part of the Internet is now mobile, access-anywhere broadband service for the delivery of video, music, and web search. According to eMarketer, there were about 3.3 billion mobile Internet users worldwide in 2019 (eMarketer, Inc., 2019b).

Telephone-based versus Computer Network-based Wireless Internet Access

There are two different basic types of wireless Internet connectivity: telephone-based and computer network-based systems.

Telephone-based wireless Internet access connects the user to a global telephone system (land, satellite, and microwave) that has a long history of dealing with millions of users simultaneously and already has in place a large-scale transaction billing system and related infrastructure. Cellular telephones and the telephone industry are currently the largest providers of wireless access to the Internet today. Around 1.38 billion smartphones were expected to be sold worldwide in 2019 (IDC, 2019). Smartphones combine the functionality of a cell phone with that of a laptop computer with Wi-Fi capability. This makes it possible to combine in one device music, video, web access, and telephone service. Tablet computers can also access cellular networks. **Table 2.9** summarizes the various telephone technologies currently being used and under development for wireless Internet access. 5G wireless is the next frontier.

5G provides for high-bandwidth mobile broadband with speeds reaching 10 Gbps or more, support for up to 100,000 connections per square kilometer (known as massive machine-to-machine (M2M) connections), and ultra low-latency (less than 10 milliseconds) communications. Full deployment of 5G is expected to take a number of years, utilizing a new part of the wireless spectrum (shorter millimeter waves in the 30 GHz to 300 GHz range), and including the development of a transmission infrastructure involving tens of thousands of small cell and distributed antenna systems installed on utility poles, as well as additional investments in fiber optic networks. Telecommunications companies are expected to invest up to $5 billion. The first pre-official 5G devices began to launch in 2018, with more being deployed in 2019.

5G
cellular standard for high-bandwidth mobile broadband

TABLE 2.9 WIRELESS INTERNET ACCESS TELEPHONE TECHNOLOGIES

TECHNOLOGY	SPEED	DESCRIPTION
3G (THIRD GENERATION)		
CDMA2000 EV-DO HSPA (W-CDMA)	144 Kbps–2 Mbps	High-speed, mobile, always on for e-mail, browsing, and instant messaging. Implementing technologies include versions of CDMA2000 EV-DO (used by CDMA providers) and HSPDA (used by GSM providers). Nearly as fast as Wi-Fi.
3.5G (3G+)		
CDMA2000 EV-DO, Rev.B	Up to 14.4 Mbps	Enhanced version of CDMA 2000 EV-DO.
HSPA+	Up to 11 Mbps	Enhanced version of HSPA.
4G (FOURTH GENERATION)		
Long-Term Evolution (LTE)	Up to 100 Mbps	True broadband on cell phone; lower latency than previous generations.
5G (FIFTH GENERATION)		
Standards under development	Up to 10 Gbps	Goals include 1–10 Gbps connectivity; sub-10 millisecond latency enabling services such as autonomous driving, augmented reality, virtual reality, and immersive/tactile Internet.

Wi-Fi
Wireless standard for Ethernet networks with greater speed and range than Bluetooth

Wireless local area network (WLAN)-based Internet access derives from a completely different background from telephone-based wireless Internet access. Popularly known as **Wi-Fi**, WLANs are based on computer local area networks where the task is to connect client computers (generally stationary) to server computers within local areas of, say, a few hundred meters. Wi-Fi functions by sending radio signals that are broadcast over the airwaves using certain radio frequency ranges (2.4 GHz to 5.875 GHz, depending on the type of standard involved). The major technologies here are the various versions of the Wi-Fi standard, WiMax, and Bluetooth (see **Table 2.10**).

In a Wi-Fi network, a *wireless access point* (also known as a "hot spot") connects to the Internet directly via a broadband connection (cable, DSL telephone, or T1 line) and then transmits a radio signal to a transmitter/receiver installed in a tablet or laptop computer or smartphone. **Figure 2.13** illustrates how a Wi-Fi network works.

Wi-Fi provided under the 802.11 a/b/g/n specifications offers high-bandwidth capacity from 11 Mbps up to a theoretical maximum of 600 Mbps—far greater than any 3G or 4G service currently in existence—but has a limited range of 100 meters (about 300 feet), with the exception of WiMax discussed below. Wi-Fi is also exceptionally inexpensive. The cost of creating a corporate Wi-Fi network in a single 14-story building with an access point for each floor is less than $100 an access point. It would cost well over $500,000 to wire the same building with Ethernet cable. IEEE 802.11ac is a version of the 802.11 specification adopted in 2013 that provides for effective throughputs of 500 Mbps to over 1 Gbps. IEEE 802.11ad, sometimes referred to as short-range wi-fi, provides for theoretical maximum throughput up to 7 Gbps. The first 802.11ad devices began shipping at the beginning of 2016. Next-generation Wi-Fi standards currently being worked on by the

TABLE 2.10 — WIRELESS NETWORK INTERNET ACCESS TECHNOLOGIES

TECHNOLOGY	RANGE/SPEED	DESCRIPTION
Wi-Fi (IEEE 802.11 a/b/g/n)	100 meters/11–70 Mbps	Evolving high-speed, fixed broadband wireless local area network for commercial and residential use
802.11ac	50 meters/ 500 Mbps–1 Gbps	Enhanced version of 802.11n that provides higher throughput
802.11ad	less than 10 meters/up to 7 Gbps	High-speed short-range Wi-Fi
WiMax (IEEE 802.16)	30 miles/50–70 Mbps	High-speed, medium-range, broadband wireless metropolitan area network
Bluetooth (wireless personal area network)	1–30 meters/1–3 Mbps	Modest-speed, low-power, short-range connection of digital devices

IEEE 802.11 Working Group include 802.11ay, a follow-up to 802.11ad that also uses 60 GHz wireless, and will provide for data rates of up to 20 Gbps, and 802.11ax, aimed at high-efficiency WLANs used for stadiums and other areas where many people want to access a Wi-Fi network at the same time. A next-generation 802.11ah standard, sometimes referred to as HaLow and aimed at the Internet of Things, is also being developed. Another Wi-Fi standard, 802.11af (sometimes referred to as White-Fi or Super Wi-Fi), is a Wi-Fi variant

FIGURE 2.13 — WI-FI NETWORKS

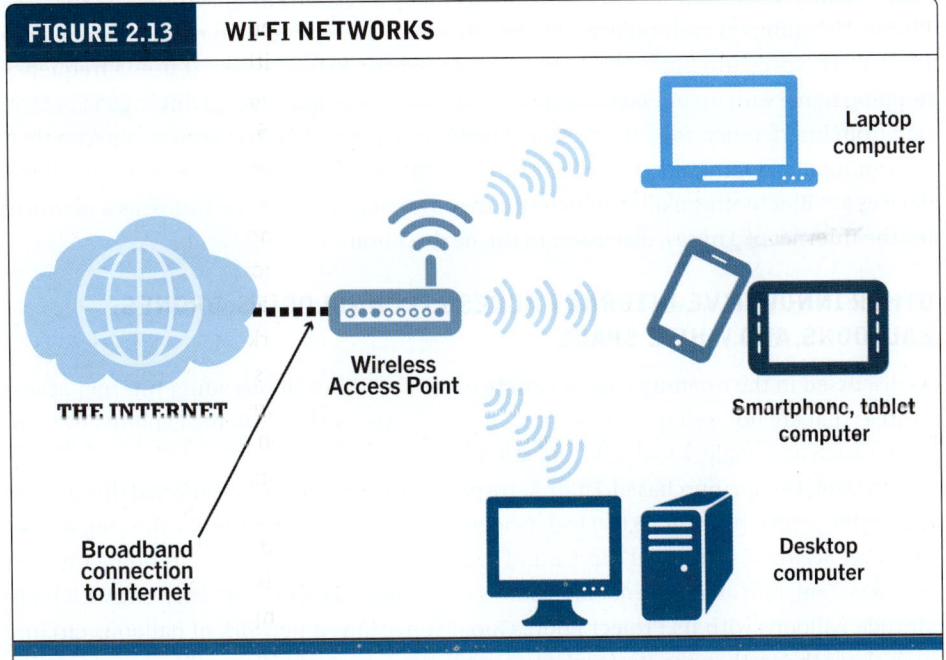

In a Wi-Fi network, wireless access points connect to the Internet using a land-based broadband connection. Clients, which could be desktops, laptops, tablet computers, or smartphones, connect to the access point using radio signals.

designed to use parts of the spectrum left underutilized when television broadcasting switched from analog to digital.

While initially a grass roots, "hippies and hackers" public access technology, billions of dollars have subsequently been poured into private ventures seeking to create for-profit Wi-Fi networks. One of the most prominent networks has been created by Boingo Wireless with more than 1 million hotspots around the globe. Optimum WiFi (available to Optimum Online customers for free) also offers over 2 million hotspots around the world. AT&T Wi-Fi Services (formerly Wayport) has another large network that provides Wi-Fi service at hotels, airports, McDonald's, IHOP restaurants, and Hertz airport rental offices, with thousands of hotspots throughout the United States and access to Boingo's wireless network internationally. T-Mobile and Sprint also have Wi-Fi services at Starbucks coffee shops and thousands of other public locations in the United States. Apple, in turn, has made Wi-Fi automatically available to iPhone and iPad devices as an alternative to the more expensive and much slower cellular systems. The number of public Wi-Fi hotspots is expected to grow from 124 million in 2017 to about 550 million by 2022. It is expected that Wi-Fi will be carrying over 55% of all Internet traffic by 2022 (Cisco, 2019).

A second WLAN technology for connecting to the Internet, and for connecting Internet devices to one another, is called Bluetooth. **Bluetooth** is a personal connectivity technology that enables links between mobile devices and connectivity to the Internet (Bluetooth.com, 2019). Bluetooth is the universal cable cutter, promising to get rid of the tangled mess of wires, cradles, and special attachments that plague the current world of personal computing. With Bluetooth, users can wear a wireless earbud, share files in a hallway or conference room, synchronize their smartphone with their laptop without a cable, send a document to a printer, and even pay a restaurant bill from the table to a Bluetooth-equipped cash register. Bluetooth is also an unregulated media operating in the 2.4 GHz spectrum but with a very limited range of 30 feet or less. It uses a frequency hopping signal with up to 1,600 hops per second over 79 frequencies, giving it good protection from interference and interception. Bluetooth-equipped devices constantly scan their environments looking for connections to compatible devices. Today, almost all mobile devices are Bluetooth-enabled. Bluetooth may also play a role in the future as a platform for the Internet of Things, discussed in the next section.

Bluetooth
technology standard for short-range wireless communication under 30 feet

OTHER INNOVATIVE INTERNET ACCESS TECHNOLOGIES: DRONES, BALLOONS, AND WHITE SPACE

As discussed in the opening case, a variety of new methods of providing Internet access to areas that are not well served by wired or cellular networks are being explored by companies such as Google, Facebook, and Microsoft.

In 2014, Google purchased Titan Aerospace, which makes solar-powered drones that can fly for several years at 65,000 feet. Google has been experimenting with using drones to deliver 5G wireless Internet service and in 2018 spun off Project Wing, its drone Internet access system, into an independent business unit. Google is also experimenting with high-altitude balloons with its Project Loon. Google envisions a network of balloons circling high above the earth in the stratosphere, establishing a ring of uninterrupted connectivity. In 2014, Google sent a prototype of a networked hot-air balloon around the world in 22 days, even taking photos for its Street View program, and in 2015, the government of Sri

Lanka announced that Sri Lanka would be the first country to use Project Loon to provide universal Internet access across Sri Lanka. Project Loon is now part of Alphabet (Google's parent company) and in 2017 was deployed in Peru to provide Internet access to thousands of Peruvians whose homes were destroyed by flooding and mudslides. In 2018, Project Loon passed a significant test, demonstrating its ability to transfer Internet data across a 621 mile span (1,000 kilometers) using seven different balloons, and in 2019, it began commercial trials in Kenya (Merriman, 2019; D'Onfro, 2018; Reisinger, 2018; Westgarth, 2017).

In a similar effort, Facebook has put together the Facebook Connectivity Lab, where engineers are focusing on solar-powered drones, tether-tenna (small helicopters connected to an Internet cable and power source), satellites, and infrared lasers capable of providing Internet access. To propel that effort, Facebook purchased the British company Ascenta, whose founders helped create the world's longest flying solar-powered drone. In 2016, Facebook completed a full-scale test flight of its first Internet access solar-powered drone, Aquila. Created from carbon fiber, the drone has the wingspan of a Boeing 737 but weighs less than a small car, and is designed to fly at 60,000 to 90,000 feet for up to three months at a time. It reportedly uses a laser communications system that can beam data from the sky. Although Facebook announced in 2018 that it would no longer build the aircraft for the project, it will continue to develop software and other related technology (Matsakis, 2018).

In 2017, Microsoft announced a pilot program called the Airband Initiative to provide access to rural areas that lack broadband via unused frequencies previously used for analog television signals, known as white spaces. The project faces opposition from television broadcasters, who have concern that using unused airwaves may interfere with broadcasts on nearby channels, as well the costs of developing devices compatible with the technology using the 802.11af Wi-Fi standard. Since then, Microsoft has entered into a number of agreements with various providers of broadband networks to advance the project (Alleven, 2018; Tam, 2017; Kang, 2017).

THE INTERNET OF THINGS

No discussion of the Internet would be complete without mentioning the **Internet of Things (IoT)**, also sometimes referred to as the Industrial Internet. Internet technology is spreading beyond the desktop, laptop, and tablet computer, and beyond the smartphone, to consumer electronics, electrical appliances, cars, medical devices, utility systems, machines of all types, even clothing—just about anything that can be equipped with sensors that can collect data and connect to the Internet, enabling the data to be analyzed with data analytics software.

IoT builds on a foundation of existing technologies, such as radio frequency identification (RFID) tags, and is being enabled by the availability of low-cost sensors, the drop in price of data storage, the development of big data analytics software that can work with trillions of pieces of data, as well as implementation of IPv6, which will allow Internet addresses to be assigned to all of these new devices. Although IoT devices don't necessarily have to be wireless, most use wireless communications technology previously discussed, such as cellular networks, Wi-Fi, Bluetooth, or other wireless protocols such as ZigBee or Z-Wave, to connect either directly or via a mobile app to the Internet (often a cloud service).

IoT technology is powering the development of "smart" connected "things"— televisions, houses, and cars, as well as wearable technology—clothing and devices like the

Internet of Things (IoT)
Use of the Internet to connect a wide variety of devices, machines, and sensors

Apple Watch. Internet-connected television devices, such as smart televisions, streaming media players, and video game consoles that actively deliver Internet connectivity to the television screen have become very popular, with 210 million such devices installed in American homes at the beginning of 2018, which is estimated to grow to 275 million by the end of 2021 (NPD Group Inc, 2018). Smart houses have attracted even more interest, fueled by Google's purchase of Nest Labs for $3.2 billion. Nest Labs makes smart thermostats, home security cameras, and smoke and carbon monoxide alarms and has made Nest Weave, a protocol it developed that enables appliances, thermostats, door locks, and other devices to communicate with each other and other Nest products, available to third-party developers and manufacturers. Google Home, a digital speaker that works with Google Assistant, Google's intelligent digital voice assistant, is also part of Google's smart home strategy. Apple has a similar smart home platform that it calls HomeKit. HomeKit is a framework and network protocol for controlling devices in the home that is programmed directly into Apple's iOS software for iPhones and iPads, and is integrated with Siri, Apple's voice-activated artificial intelligence assistant. A number of devices are designed specifically for use with HomeKit, such as a smart thermostat, a smart deadbolt lock, a home sensor that provides temperature, humidity, and air quality readings, and an iDevices switch that enables you to turn electronic devices on and off using Siri, as well as Apple's smart speaker, HomePod. Many cable companies such as Charter Spectrum, Comcast, and AT&T also offer connected home systems that include appliances and lights. All in all, the global market for smart house products is expected to grow from about $75 billion in 2018 to over $150 billion by 2024 (Research and Markets, 2019).

In 2014, Apple introduced the Apple Watch. The Apple Watch features a fitness/activity tracker similar to offerings from Fitbit, is able to access a wide variety of apps, and also works with Apple Pay, Apple's mobile payment service. A number of other manufacturers, such as Samsung, Garmin, and Fossil, have also introduced smartwatches. According to Gartner, consumer spending worldwide on wearable devices is expected to grow to $52 billion by 2020 (Gartner, Inc., 2019b). The *Insight on Business* case, *The Apple Watch: Bringing the Internet of Things to Your Wrist*, provides a more in-depth examination of the Apple Watch.

Connected cars that have built-in Internet access have also arrived (see the *Insight on Technology* case, *Connected Cars and the Future of E-commerce* in Chapter 5). Here too, Google and Apple are major players. Google has developed Android Auto, a smartphone-based car interface, as well as Android Automotive, a version of its Android operating system designed specifically for cars. Apple has developed CarPlay, a software platform that synchronizes iPhones to the car's infotainment system. Connected cars are likely to be integrated with smart home initiatives in the future. The next frontier on the connected car front is the the self-driving car, combining IoT and artificial intelligence technologies. Many Internet technology companies, such as Google, Baidu (China's version of Google), Uber, and Intel, have jumped into the fray alongside automotive companies such as Tesla, BMW, Volvo, GM, Ford, and others.

Despite all of the IoT activity, however, interoperability remains a major concern. As with many technologies in the early stages of development, many organizations are fighting to create the standards that participants in the market will follow. The AllSeen Alliance, formed by Qualcomm in 2013 with 50 other companies, including Microsoft and Cisco, was one group that hoped to create an open source standard. Membership in the

INSIGHT ON BUSINESS

THE APPLE WATCH: BRINGING THE INTERNET OF THINGS TO YOUR WRIST

Apple has a rich history of disrupting the technology landscape. When Apple first unveiled its Apple Watch, the company hoped it would follow in the footsteps of its iPod, iPhone, and iPad. So far, the Watch has not been a smash hit, but it is selling relatively well with strong growth potential.

The Apple Watch is a prominent example of wearable technology, a fast-developing field with potential applications in healthcare, medicine, fitness, and many other areas. Examples of wearable technology include wristbands and watches, smart clothing and footwear, and smart glasses. The proliferation of smaller, more compact, more powerful devices and the resulting improvements in computing power have made wearable computing possible.

Analysts view wearable computing as an industry primed for growth in the near future. Over 220 million wearable devices were expected to be shipped in 2019; that number is projected to grow to over 300 million units by 2023. However, the market for wearable computing is evolving so quickly that even these projections could quickly become obsolete. Apple ended 2017 as the industry leader in wearable computing for the first time and has established a dominant position in this market, with almost 50% of the global smart watch market as of 2019.

Apple originally conceived of the Watch as a filter for the iPhone, only notifying users when truly critical information required attention. The Apple Watch prioritizes speed and simplicity above depth of engagement. Apple also placed its typical emphasis on elegant design when developing the Watch, which features a scrolling wheel called the Digital Crown and a screen that senses different levels of force applied by the user's touch and responds accordingly. On the back of the watch are sensors that can monitor the user's vital signs and movements. Movement is used to control many functions of the Watch; for example, lifting an arm to view an incoming text message, and lowering it again to hide it, saving it for later.

Perhaps the most unique component of the Apple Watch is the Taptic Engine, a feature that applies gentle pressure to the skin to deliver information and alerts to the user. Watch wearers are alerted to different types of incoming information depending on the number, cadence, and force of the taps. Different taps designate incoming phone calls, upcoming meetings, text messages, and news alerts. The Apple Watch might someday tap you to let you know that you're leaving the house without a winter coat on a cold day, or that your blood sugar is low and you need to eat.

The Watch launched with 3,500 apps available and has continued to add more apps focused on fitness, sleep tracking, weather, music and entertainment, travel, productivity tools, finance, and even some simple games. Major online retailers have also sought to create apps for the Watch, such as eBay and Amazon, as well as bricks-and-mortar retailers like JCPenney, Kohl's, and Target. The latter group hopes to add features that improve the in-store shopping experience for Watch wearers. Users might be able to use a retailer's Watch app to

(continued)

avoid long lines in stores, find items more efficiently with interactive store maps, and pay for their purchases with Apple Pay using the phone's built-in Apple Pay button on the underside of the phone. However, in 2018, Apple announced a change to its operating system requiring that apps no longer require an iPhone to refresh data or perform key functions, disabling many prominent apps in the process. Instagram, Slack, eBay, and Amazon's apps were all discontinued due to the change, and while many of these companies are working to develop new versions, some may decide that the Apple Watch is not the ideal interface for the service they provide.

In 2019, Apple released its watchOS 6 operating system, which adds another set of useful features. Most significantly, watchOS 6 allows users to access the App Store directly from the Watch, rather than having to install apps from an iPhone. These improvements followed others Apple had previously made, including updates to Siri, peer-to-peer payments with Apple Pay, upgrades to Apple Music for the Watch, the ability to automatically detect when its user is exercising, better tracking of calorie consumption, the ability to listen to podcasts without the involvement of another device, and the the ability to connect to a Wi-Fi network without the use of an iPhone.

Apple has also released several medical applications for the device, including apps that measure heart rate, heart rhythm and ECG, a fall detection app, and an app that measures noise levels. It is also working on a non-invasive glucose monitor for diabetics. FDA rules now allow Apple to more easily market the Watch as a health device, which could dramatically increase the Watch's target audience. A common criticism of the Watch in the early going was that anything it can do, the iPhone could do faster and better. But Apple has placed a clear emphasis on promoting features and apps that run natively on the Watch, and as Apple continues to work on biometric features in addition to its entertainment offerings, the Watch could become a must-have device for many different types of consumers.

Apple released a new version of the Watch in September 2019, the Apple Watch Series 5. The most attention-grabbing features were the ability to access the App Store directly from the Watch, an always-on display that shows the time, international SOS capability, a new built-in compass and updated Maps app, and up to 32GB of storage.

Apple will face continued opposition from other wearable manufacturers such as Samsung with its Galaxy series of smart watches, Fitbit, and manufacturers who use Google's Wear OS, such as Fossil, LG, and Huawei, but Apple has rapidly gained market share and overtaken its competitors by making constant improvements to the Watch's battery life, weight, speed, and other features. Although some analysts feel the Watch has been a disappointment by Apple's lofty standards, in a few years' time the Watch may emphatically prove its doubters wrong.

SOURCES: "Healthcare-Apple Watch-Apple," Apple.com, accessed December 2, 2019; "Best Wear OS Watch 2019: Our List of the Top Ex-Android Wear Smartwatches," by James Peckham, Techrader.com, November 21, 2019; "Apple Watch Share Grew in Q3, Delivering More than 2.5 Times Second Place Samsung," Patentlyapple.com, November 8, 2019; "Apple Watch 5 Review," by Gareth Beavis, Techrader.com, September 18, 2019; "Earwear and Watches Expected to Drive Wearables Market at a CAGR of 7.9%, Says IDC," Idc.com, June 19, 2019; "WWDC: When Apple Watch Became a Platform," by Jonny Evans, Computerworld.com, June 11, 2018; "watchOS 5 Adds Powerful Activity and Communications Features to Apple Watch," Apple.com, June 4, 2018; "The Best Apple Watch Apps," by Andy Boxall, Digitaltrends.com, May 27, 2018; "The Apple Watch Has a Secret Weapon That Helps It Dominate the Market," by Tonya Riley, Cnbc.com, May 4, 2018; "Instagram Is No Longer Available on the Apple Watch," by Emily Price, Fortune.com, April 4, 2018; "Apple Watch Appears on Its Way to Becoming a $6 Billion Business," by Eric Jhonsa, Realmoney.thestreet.com, June 6, 2017; "watchOS 4 Brings More Intelligence and Fitness Features to Apple Watch," Apple.com, June 5, 2017.

Alliance soared after its initial founding and by 2016, it had over 200 members. Another group, the Open Interconnect Consortium, formed in 2014 by Intel, Broadcom, Dell, and others apparently not happy with the AllSeen effort, also reached over 200 members. In late 2016, these two groups put their differences aside and merged to create the Open Connectivity Foundation. A different group, the Industrial Internet Consortium, has been formed by AT&T, Cisco, GE, IBM, and Intel to focus on engineering standards for industrial assets. And as with many other types of Internet-related technology, Google with its Android operating system and Apple with the AirPlay wireless streaming protocol may be trying to create their own standards.

Other concerns include security and privacy. Security experts believe that IoT devices could potentially be a security disaster, with the potential for malware being spread through a connected network, and difficulty in issuing patches to devices, leaving them vulnerable (Internet Society, 2015). Data from stand-alone smart devices can reveal much personal detail about a consumer's life, and if those devices are all ultimately interconnected, there will be little that is truly private.

Although challenges remain before the Internet of Things is fully realized, it is coming closer and closer to fruition. Experts estimate that as of 2019, there were anywhere from 10 billion to 25 billion IoT devices already installed (not including smartphones, tablets, or desktop computers), with some projecting as many as 100 billion connected IoT devices and a global economic impact of up to over $1.5 trillion by 2025 (Ranger, 2018; Columbus, 2018).

WHO GOVERNS THE INTERNET?

Aficionados and journalists often claim that the Internet is governed by no one, and indeed cannot be governed, and that it is inherently above and beyond the law. What these people forget is that the Internet runs over private and public telecommunications facilities that are themselves governed by laws, and subject to the same pressures as all telecommunications carriers. In fact, the Internet is tied into a complex web of governing bodies, national governments, and international professional societies. There is no one single governing organization that controls activity on the Internet. Instead, there are a number of organizations that influence the system and monitor its operations. Among the governing bodies of the Internet are:

- The *Internet Corporation for Assigned Names and Numbers (ICANN)*, which coordinates the Internet's systems of unique identifiers: IP addresses, protocol parameter registries, and the top-level domain systems. ICANN was created in 1998 as a nonprofit organization and manages the *Internet Assigned Numbers Authority (IANA)*, which is in charge of assigning IP addresses.
- The *Internet Engineering Task Force (IETF)*, which is an open international community of network operators, vendors, and researchers concerned with the evolution of the Internet architecture and operation of the Internet. The IETF has a number of working groups, organized into several different areas, that develop and promote Internet standards, which influence the way people use and manage the Internet.
- The *Internet Research Task Force (IRTF)*, which focuses on the evolution of the Internet. The IRTF has a number of long-term research groups working on various topics such as Internet protocols, applications, and technology.

- The *Internet Engineering Steering Group (IESG)*, which is responsible for technical management of IETF activities and the Internet standards process.
- The *Internet Architecture Board (IAB)*, which helps define the overall architecture of the Internet and oversees the IETF and IRTF.
- The *Internet Society (ISOC)*, which is a consortium of corporations, government agencies, and nonprofit organizations that monitors Internet policies and practices.
- The *Internet Governance Forum (IGF)*, which is a multi-stakeholder open forum for debate on issues related to Internet governance.
- The *World Wide Web Consortium (W3C)*, which is a largely academic group that sets HTML and other programming standards for the Web.
- The *Internet Network Operators Groups (NOGs)*, which are informal groups that are made up of ISPs, IXPs, and others that discuss and attempt to influence matters related to Internet operations and regulation.

While none of these organizations has actual control over the Internet and how it functions, they can and do influence government agencies, major network owners, ISPs, corporations, and software developers with the goal of keeping the Internet operating as efficiently as possible. ICANN comes closest to being a manager of the Internet and reflects the powerful role that the U.S. Department of Commerce has played historically in Internet governance. The United States has been responsible for the IANA function since the beginning of the Internet. After the creation of ICANN, however, the expectation was the function would eventually be transferred out of the U.S. government's control. In 2006, however, the U.S. Department of Commerce announced that the U.S. government would retain oversight over the root servers, contrary to initial expectations. There were several reasons for this move, including the use of the Internet for basic communications services by terrorist groups and the uncertainty that might be caused should an international body take over. In 2008, the Department of Commerce reaffirmed this stance, stating that it did not have any plans to transition management of the authoritative root zone file to ICANN (U.S. Department of Commerce, 2008). At the same time, growing Internet powers China and Russia were lobbying for more functions of the Internet to be brought under the control of the United Nations, raising fears that governance of the Internet could become even more politicized (Pfanner, 2012). In 2014, the United States, under continued pressure from other countries, finally announced its willingness to transition control of IANA, provided that certain stipulations are met, including that the organization managing the IANA functions not be specifically controlled by any other government or inter-governmental organization (such as the United Nations). The transition took place on October 1, 2016.

In addition to these professional bodies, the Internet must also conform to the laws of the sovereign nation-states in which it operates, as well as the technical infrastructures that exist within each nation-state. Although in the early years of the Internet there was very little legislative or executive interference, this situation is changing as the Internet plays a growing role in the distribution of information and knowledge, including content that some find objectionable.

Read *Insight on Society: Government Regulation and Surveillance of the Internet* for a further look at the issue of censorship of Internet content and substance.

INSIGHT ON SOCIETY

GOVERNMENT REGULATION AND SURVEILLANCE OF THE INTERNET

In the early years of the Internet and the Web, many people assumed that because the Internet is so widely dispersed, it would be impossible to control or monitor. But the reality is quite different. All governments assert some kind of control and surveillance over Internet content and messages, and in many nations this control and surveillance is very extensive.

While the Internet is a decentralized network, Internet traffic runs through fiber-optic trunk lines that are controlled by national authorities or private firms. In China, for instance, there are three such lines, and China requires the companies that own them to configure their routers for both internal and external service requests. When a request originates in China for a web page in Chicago, Chinese routers examine the request to see if the site is on a blacklist, and then examine words in the requested web page to see if it contains blacklisted terms. The system is often referred to as "The Great Firewall of China" (but by China as the "Golden Shield") and was implemented with the assistance of a number of U.S. technology firms such as Cisco Systems (the largest manufacturer of routers in the world), Juniper Networks, and Blue Coat (which provides deep packet inspection software), among others.

Over the past several years, China has strengthened and extended its regulation of the Internet. In 2017, China created a new government organization to draft cyber policy and passed a comprehensive law governing cybersecurity. The purported major goals of the new policy are to defend against cyberattacks and protect its citizens' data, to shift away from foreign technology towards domestic alternatives, and to expand the government's ability to control information. The law requires that data relating to Chinese citizens must be stored on Chinese servers and that firms must submit to a security review before moving data out of China. Other legislation provides that web users may be jailed for up to three years if they post "defamatory rumors" that are read by more than 5,000 people. China has also issued rules to restrict the dissemination of political news and opinions on messaging applications such as WeChat and now uses image filtering technology that enables it to erase images sent on those apps in mid-transmission, before they are ever received. Users are required to post political opinions and news only to state-authorized media outlets and are required to use their own names when establishing accounts. China has also formed agreements with countries such as Tanzania, Nigeria, Thailand, Sri Lanka, and Ethiopia to provide surveillance and content censorship technology along with tech support in exchange for political influence.

In 2017, China blocked the messaging service WhatsApp, which had appealed to many Chinese citizens because of its robust message encryption and subsequent ability to evade the government's content censorship techniques. China pressured Apple to remove WhatsApp and similar services such as Skype, as well as many popular virtual private network (VPN) apps that approximately 100 million Chinese citizens used to circumvent the firewall, from its App Store. In past years, the government had turned a blind eye to services like WhatsApp and VPNs as they pursued economic growth, but China has now shifted its focus to consolidating technological and social control of the Internet within their borders. China also asked Google to take down thousands of items that it characterized

(continued)

as endangering national interests and even forced Mercedes-Benz to take down an Instagram post quoting the Dalai Lama, whom it views as a dangerous revolutionary. In the meantime, Apple has agreed to build its first data center within Chinese borders in partnership with Guizhou-Cloud Big Data, a government-controlled Chinese tech company. The data center will be built in such a way that the government will have full access to all user data. Chinese tech companies Alibaba, Tencent, and Baidu all have similar arrangements with the government, even helping to track down content critical of the government. Although Apple and Google have stated that they are uncomfortable with Chinese censorship, critics charge that the 800 million potential customers in China have led them to compromise their principles.

China is often criticized for its extensive Internet controls, but other countries have similar policies. Iran's Internet surveillance of its citizens is considered by security experts to be one of the world's most sophisticated mechanisms for controlling and censoring the Internet, allowing it to examine the content of individual online communications on a massive scale. The Iranian system goes beyond merely preventing access to specific sites such as Google, Twitter, and Facebook. The government also uses deep packet inspection to read messages, alter their contents for disinformation purposes, and identify senders and recipients. Computers installed in the line between users and ISPs open up every digitized packet, inspecting for keywords and images, reconstructing the message, and then sending it on. In 2016, Iran completed the first stage of establishing an isolated, domestic version of the Internet that it calls The National Information Network, one that purportedly is faster and less costly, but which controls what users can and cannot see and subjects its users to even more heightened surveillance. In 2017, it launched the second phase of the Network, which consists of 500 government-approved sites. In 2019, amid widespread protests that originated due to rising gasoline prices, the Iranian government instituted a wide-scale Internet and mobile data shutdown, blocking both inbound and outbound connections.

Russia also has rules to control online speech, including forcing bloggers to register with the government and the ability to take websites down at its discretion. Russia also has a law similar to China's requiring Internet companies to store their data on Russian soil, as well as additional laws that require mandatory data retention by ISPs and telecommunications providers for between 6 months and three years, access to all such data without a warrant, and the creation of a government backdoor that will enable it to access all encrypted communications. In 2017, Russia enacted a law banning the use of virtual private networks (VPNs) and anonymizers, tools that can be used to establish a secure and anonymous connection to the Internet, and in 2018 Russia banned the popular messaging service Telegram when the company refused to give the government access to encrypted messages. Russia also banned 16 million IP addresses used by Amazon Web Services and Google Cloud that Telegram had been using to skirt the ban. However, despite the ban, Telegram still remains in use in Russia, apparently in part due to difficulties in effectively implementing the ban.

But it is not just totalitarian nations that have sought to regulate and surveil the Internet. Both Europe and the United States have, at various times, also taken steps to control access to certain websites, censor web content, and engage in extensive surveillance of communications. For instance, Great Britain has a list of blocked sites, as do Germany, France, and Australia. Even in South Korea, one of the world's most wired countries, there are restrictions on content that is deemed subversive and harmful to the public order. Typically, these blocked sites contain truly objectionable content such as child pornography or Nazi memorabilia.

In response to terrorism threats and other crimes, European governments and the U.S. government also perform deep packet inspection on e-mail and text communications of terrorist suspects. This surveillance is not limited to cross-border international data flows and includes large-scale domestic surveillance and analysis of routine e-mail, tweets, and other messages. In 2013, National Security Agency (NSA) contractor Edward Snowden made headlines by leaking classified NSA documents shedding light on the NSA's PRISM program, which allowed the agency access to the servers of major Internet companies such as Facebook, Google, Apple, Microsoft, and many others. Additionally, the documents revealed the existence of the NSA's XKeyscore program, which allows analysts to search databases of e-mails, chats, and browsing histories of individual citizens without any authorization. Warrants, court clearance, or other forms of legal documentation are not required for analysts to use the technology. Snowden's documents also showed spy agencies were tapping data from smartphone apps and that the NSA was tapping the flow of personal user information between Google and Yahoo. The NSA claimed that the program was only used to monitor foreign intelligence targets and that the information it collects has assisted in apprehending terrorists.

Many European powers have also moved ahead with plans to fortify their online surveillance. In response to multiple terrorist attacks, France has passed rules that force ISPs to maintain browsing data, as well as additional provisions for surveillance of phone calls, e-mails, and all mobile phone communications. The Investigatory Powers Act 2016 gives the British government some of the world's strongest powers to conduct online surveillance, including the bulk interception of overseas-related communications. In 2019, the UK High Court dismissed a challenge to the Act, concluding that the law did not violate the Human Rights Act 1998. In Germany, the Communications Intelligence Gathering Act authorizes Germany's Federal Intelligence Service to gather and process communications of foreign nationals, including communications flowing through Internet Exchange Points (IXPs) located within Germany.

In the United States, the Trump administration has signed a bill that allows the NSA to continue foreign intelligence collection that also gathers incidental information on the entire American population. President Trump has also taken a combative stance towards Chinese tech companies ZTE and Huawei. As tensions between world powers continue to simmer, governments are likely to double down on their control of the content that passes across their online borders.

SOURCES: "How the Iranian Government Shut Off the Internet," by Lily Hay Newman, Wired.com, November 17, 2019; "China's Global Reach: Surveillance and Censorship Beyond the Great Firewall," by Danny O'Brien, Eff.org, October 10, 2019; "UK High Court Rules for Government in Investigatory Powers Act Case," by Tim Zubizarreta, Jurist.org, July 30, 2019; "Apple Speeds Up Construction of First China Data Center, by Xinhau, Global.chinadaily.com, April 27, 2019; "Outlawed App Telegram Emerges as Key Tool for Russian Protesters," by Francesca Ebel, Denverpost.com, September 15, 2019; "US Companies Help Censor the Internet in China, Too," by Tom Simonite, Wired.com, June 3, 2019; "Beijing Wants to Rewrite the Rules of the Internet," by Samm Sacks, *The Atlantic*, June 18, 2018; "Russia Blocks Millions of IP Addresses in Battle Against Telegram App," by Andrew Roth, *The Guardian*, April 17, 2018; "China Presses Its Internet Censorship Efforts Across the Globe," by Paul Mozur, *New York Times*, March 2, 2018; "Russia Threatens to Block YouTube and Instagram, After Complaints from an Oligarch," by Matthew Luxmoore, *New York Times*, February 12, 2018; "Iran Deploys 'Halal' Internet in Latest Bid to Rein In Citizens' Web Freedoms," by Jon Gambrell, Independent.co.uk, January 29, 2018; "Apple Can't Resist Playing by China's Rules," by Chen Guangcheng, *New York Times*, January 23, 2018; "Trump Signs Bill Renewing NSA's Internet Surveillance Program," by Dustin Volz, Reuters.com, January 19, 2018; "Why China's Internet Censorship Model Will Prevail Over Russia's," by Valentin Weber, Cfr.org, December 12, 2017; "China's Tech Giants Have a Second Job: Helping Beijing Spy on Its People," by Liza Lin and Josh Chin, *Wall Street Journal*, November 30, 2017; "Microsoft's Skype Pulled from Apple, Android China App Stores," Keith Bradsher and Cate Cadell, Reuters.com, November 21, 2017; "Facebook, Take Note: In China's 'New Era,' the Communist Party Comes First," by Li Yuan, *Wall Street Journal*, November 2, 2017; "China Blocks WhatsApp, Broadening Online Censorship," *New York Times*, September 25, 2017; "China's Internet Censors Play a Tougher Game of Cat and Mouse," by Paul Mozur, *New York Times*, August 3, 2017; "Russia VPN Ban: What Tech Pros and Business Travelers Need to Know," by Conner Forrest, Techrepublic.com, July 31, 2017; "China's Stopchat: Censors Can Stop Images Mid-Transmission," by Eva Dou, *Wall Street Journal*, July 18, 2017; "After Terror Attacks, Britain Moves to Police the Web," by Mark Scott, *New York Times*, June 19, 2017; "China's New Cybersecurity Law Takes Effect Today, and Many Are Confused," by Sophia Yan, Cnbc.com, June 1, 2017; "A New Era of Mass Surveillance Is Emerging Across Europe," by Asaf Lubin, Justsecurity.org, January 9, 2017.

2.3 THE WEB

Without the Web, there would be no e-commerce. The invention of the Web brought an extraordinary expansion of digital services to millions of amateur computer users, including color text and pages, formatted text, pictures, animations, video, and sound. In short, the Web makes nearly all the rich elements of human expression needed to establish a commercial marketplace available to nontechnical computer users worldwide.

While the Internet was born in the 1960s, the Web was not invented until 1989–1991 by Dr. Tim Berners-Lee of the European Particle Physics Laboratory, better known as CERN (Berners-Lee et al., 1994). Several earlier authors—such as Vannevar Bush (in 1945) and Ted Nelson (in the 1960s)—had suggested the possibility of organizing knowledge as a set of interconnected pages that users could freely browse (Bush, 1945; Ziff Davis Publishing, 1998). Berners-Lee and his associates at CERN built on these ideas and developed the initial versions of HTML, HTTP, a web server, and a browser, the four essential components of the Web.

First, Berners-Lee wrote a computer program that allowed formatted pages within his own computer to be linked using keywords (hyperlinks). Clicking on a keyword in a document would immediately move him to another document. Berners-Lee created the pages using a modified version of a powerful text markup language called Standard Generalized Markup Language (SGML).

Berners-Lee called this language HyperText Markup Language, or HTML. He then came up with the idea of storing his HTML pages on the Internet. Remote client computers could access these pages by using HTTP (introduced earlier in Section 2.1 and described more fully in the next section). But these early web pages still appeared as black and white text pages with hyperlinks expressed inside brackets. The early Web was based on text only; the original web browser only provided a line interface.

Information shared on the Web remained text-based until 1993, when Marc Andreessen and others at the National Center for Supercomputing Applications (NCSA) at the University of Illinois created a web browser with a graphical user interface (GUI) called **Mosaic** that made it possible to view documents on the Web graphically—using colored backgrounds, images, and even primitive animations. Mosaic was a software program that could run on any graphically based interface such as Macintosh, Windows, or Unix. The Mosaic browser software read the HTML text on a web page and displayed it as a graphical interface document within a GUI operating system such as Windows or Macintosh. Liberated from simple black and white text pages, HTML pages could now be viewed by anyone in the world who could operate a mouse and use a Macintosh or PC.

Aside from making the content of web pages colorful and available to the world's population, the graphical web browser created the possibility of **universal computing**, the sharing of files, information, graphics, sound, video, and other objects across all computer platforms in the world, regardless of operating system. A browser could be made for each of the major operating systems, and the web pages created for one system, say, Windows, would also be displayed exactly the same, or nearly the same, on computers running the Macintosh or Unix operating systems. As long as each operating system had a Mosaic browser, the same web pages could be used on all the different types of computers

Mosaic
Web browser with a graphical user interface (GUI) that made it possible to view documents on the Web graphically

universal computing
the sharing of files, information, graphics, sound, video, and other objects across all computer platforms in the world, regardless of operating system

and operating systems. This meant that no matter what kind of computer you used, anywhere in the world, you would see the same web pages. The browser and the Web have introduced us to a whole new world of computing and information management that was unthinkable prior to 1993.

In 1994, Andreessen and Jim Clark founded Netscape, which created the first commercial browser, **Netscape Navigator**. Although Mosaic had been distributed free of charge, Netscape initially charged for its software. In 1995, Microsoft Corporation released its own free version of a browser, called **Internet Explorer**. In the ensuing years, Netscape fell from a 100% market share to less than .5% in 2009. The fate of Netscape illustrates an important e-commerce business lesson. Innovators usually are not long-term winners, whereas smart followers often have the assets needed for long-term survival. Much of the Netscape browser code survives today in the Firefox browser produced by the Mozilla Foundation, a nonprofit organization dedicated to Internet openness.

Netscape Navigator
the first commercial web browser

Internet Explorer
Microsoft's web browser

HYPERTEXT

Web pages can be accessed through the Internet because the web browser software on your PC can request web pages stored on an Internet host server using the HTTP protocol. **Hypertext** is a way of formatting pages with embedded links that connect documents to one another and that also link pages to other objects such as sound, video, or animation files. When you click on a graphic and a video clip plays, you have clicked on a hyperlink. For example, when you type a web address in your browser such as http://www.sec.gov, your browser sends an HTTP request to the sec.gov server requesting the home page of sec.gov.

HTTP is the first set of letters at the start of every web address, followed by the domain name. The domain name specifies the organization's server computer that is housing the document. Most companies have a domain name that is the same as or closely related to their official corporate name. The directory path and document name are two more pieces of information within the web address that help the browser track down the requested page. Together, the address is called a Uniform Resource Locator, or URL. When typed into a browser, a URL tells it exactly where to look for the information. For example, in the following URL:

hypertext
a way of formatting pages with embedded links that connect documents to one another, and that also link pages to other objects such as sound, video, or animation files

> http://www.megacorp.com/content/features/082602.html
>
> http = the protocol used to display web pages
>
> www.megacorp.com = domain name
>
> content/features = the directory path that identifies where on the domain web server the page is stored
>
> 082602.html = the document name and its format (an HTML page)

The most common domain extensions (known as general top-level domains, or gTLDs) currently available and officially sanctioned by ICANN are shown in **Table 2.11**. Countries also have domain names, such as .uk, .au, and .fr (United Kingdom, Australia, and France, respectively). These are sometimes referred to as country-code top-level

TABLE 2.11 EXAMPLES OF TOP-LEVEL DOMAINS

GENERAL TOP-LEVEL DOMAIN (GTLD)	YEAR(S) INTRODUCED	PURPOSE	SPONSOR/OPERATOR
.com	1980s	Unrestricted (but intended for commercial registrants)	VeriSign
.edu	1980s	U.S. educational institutions	Educause
.gov	1980s	U.S. government	U.S. General Services Administration
.mil	1980s	U.S. military	U.S. Department of Defense Network Information Center
.net	1980s	Unrestricted (but originally intended for network providers, etc.)	VeriSign
.org	1980s	Unrestricted (but intended for organizations that do not fit elsewhere)	Public Interest Registry (was operated by VeriSign until December 31, 2002)
.int	1998	Organizations established by international treaties between governments	Internet Assigned Numbers Authority (IANA)
.aero	2001	Air-transport industry	Société Internationale de Telecommunications Aeronautiques SC (SITA)
.biz	2001	Businesses	NeuLevel
.coop	2001	Cooperatives	DotCooperation LLC
.info	2001	Unrestricted use	Afilias LLC
.museum	2001	Museums	Museum Domain Name Association (MuseDoma)
.name	2001	For registration by individuals	Global Name Registry Ltd.
.pro	2002	Accountants, lawyers, physicians, and other professionals	RegistryPro Ltd
.jobs	2005	Job search	Employ Media LLC
.travel	2005	Travel search	Tralliance Corporation
.mobi	2005	Websites specifically designed for mobile phones	mTLD Top Level Domain, Ltd.
.cat	2005	Individuals, organizations, and companies that promote the Catalan language and culture	Fundació puntCAT
.asia	2006	Regional domain for companies, organizations, and individuals based in Asia	DotAsia Organization
.tel	2006	Telephone numbers and other contact information	ICM Registry
.xxx	2010	Top level domain for pornographic content	ICM Registry

SOURCE: Based on data from ICANN, 2011b.

domains, or ccTLDs. In 2008, ICANN approved a significant expansion of gTLDs, with potential new domains representing cities (such as .berlin), regions (.africa), ethnicity (.eus), industry/activities (such as .health), and even brands (such as .deloitte). In 2009, ICANN began the process of implementing these guidelines. In 2011, ICANN removed nearly all restrictions on domain names, thereby greatly expanding the number of different domain names available. As of 2019, over 1,230 gTLDs have been applied for, acquired, and launched, with over 23 million domain registrations using those gTLDs (Verisign, 2019). The new gTLDs are in multiple languages and scripts/characters (including Arabic, Chinese, Japanese, and Russian) and include geographic place names such as .nyc, .london, and .paris; business identifiers such as .restaurant, .realtor, .technology, and .lawyer; brand names such as .bmw and .suzuki; and a whole host of other descriptive names.

MARKUP LANGUAGES

Although the most common web page formatting language is HTML, the concept behind document formatting actually had its roots in the 1960s with the development of Generalized Markup Language (GML).

HyperText Markup Language (HTML)

HyperText Markup Language (HTML) is a GML that is relatively easy to use. HTML provides web page designers with a fixed set of markup "tags" that are used to format a web page. When these tags are inserted into a web page, they are read by the browser and interpreted into a page display. All web browsers allow you to view the source HTML code for a web page, with the particular method depending on the web browser being used. For instance, if you are using the Firefox web browser, all you need to do is press the Control key on the keyboard at the same time as pressing the U key. In **Figure 2.14**, the HTML code in the first screen produces the display in the second screen.

HTML defines the structure of a document, including the headings, graphic positioning, tables, and text formatting. HTML is used in conjunction with **Cascading Style Sheets (CSS)**, which tells a web browser how to display the HTML elements on the screen. HTML provides the structure of the page, while CSS provides the style. HTML web pages can be created with any text editor, such as Notepad or WordPad, using Microsoft Word (simply save the Word document as a web page), or any one of several web page development tools such as Microsoft Expression Web or Adobe Dreamweaver CC.

The most recent version of HTML is **HTML5**. HTML5 has become the de facto web page development standard, providing functionality that in the past was provided by plug-ins such as Adobe Flash. HTML enables not only video but also animations and interactivity with the assistance of CSS3, JavaScript, and HTML5 Canvas, an element used to draw graphics using JavaScript. HTML5 is also used in the development of mobile websites and mobile apps, and is an important tool in both responsive web design and adaptive web delivery, all of which are discussed more fully in Chapter 4. HTML5 apps work just like web pages, with page content, including graphics, images, and video, loaded into the browser from a web server, rather than residing in the mobile device hardware. This device-independence has been embraced by mobile developers. HTML5 can also access built-in features of mobile devices, like GPS and swiping. The rise of HTML5 as the preferred media delivery platform

HyperText Markup Language (HTML)
GML that is relatively easy to use in web page design. HTML provides web page designers with a fixed set of markup "tags" that are used to format a web page

Cascading Style Sheets (CSS)
tells a web browser how to display the HTML elements on the screen

HTML5
most recent version of HTML

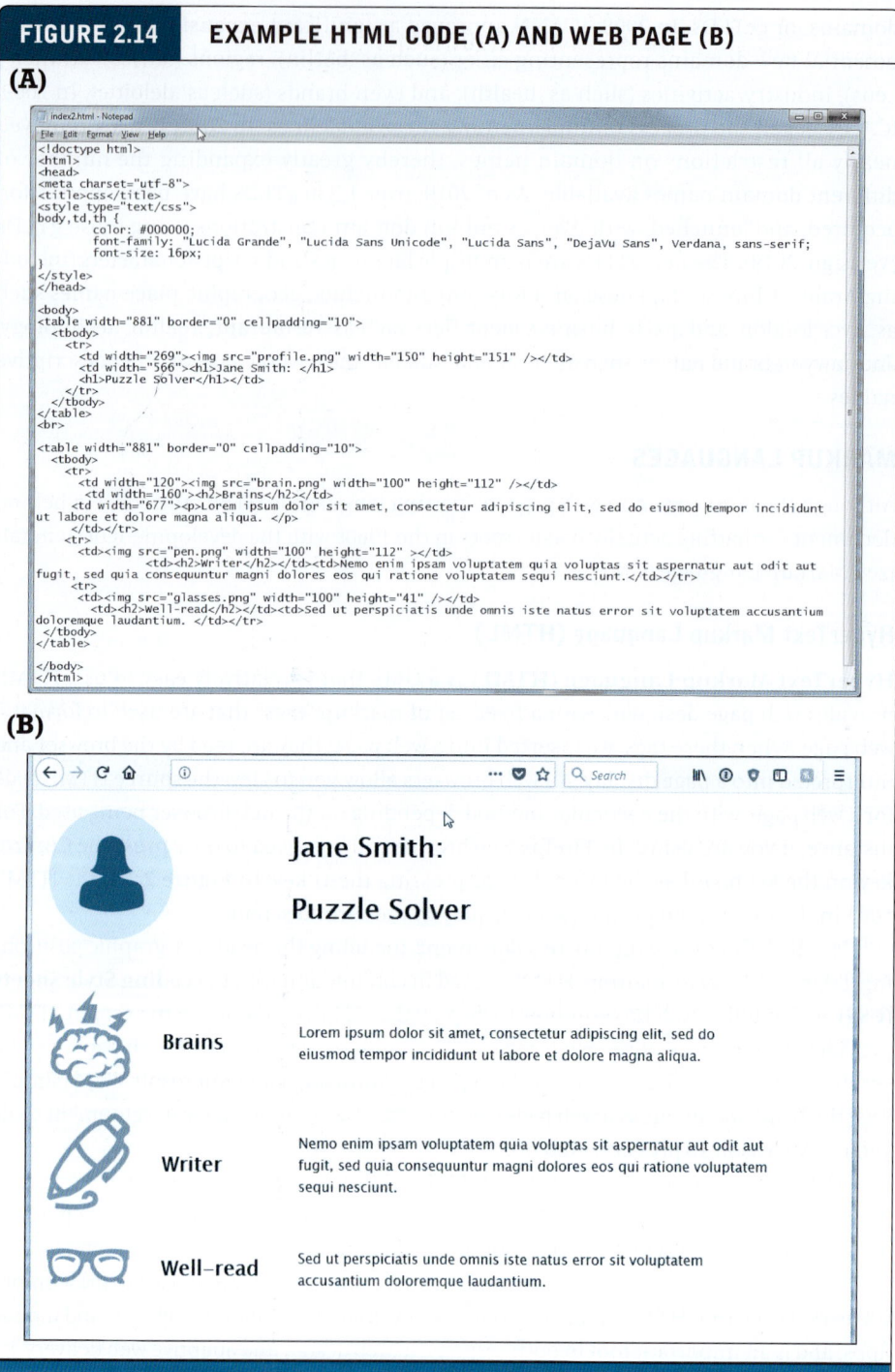

FIGURE 2.14 EXAMPLE HTML CODE (A) AND WEB PAGE (B)

HTML is a text markup language used to create web pages. It has a fixed set of "tags" that are used to tell the browser software how to present the content on screen. The HTML shown in Figure 2.14 (a) creates the web page seen in Figure 2.14 (b).

SOURCES: (A) Notepad, Microsoft Windows, Microsoft Corporation; (B) Internet Explorer, Microsoft Windows, Microsoft Corporation.

FIGURE 2.15 A SIMPLE XML DOCUMENT

```
<?xml version="1.0"?>
<note>
<to>George</to>
<from>Carol</from>
<heading>Just a Reminder</heading>
<body>Don't forget to order the groceries from FreshDirect!</body>
</note>
```

The tags in this simple XML document, such as <note>, <to>, and <from>, are used to describe data and information, rather than the look and feel of the document.

for the Web has mirrored the growth of the mobile platform and has hastened the demise of Adobe Flash, which was developed for the desktop.

eXtensible Markup Language (XML)

eXtensible Markup Language (XML) takes web document formatting a giant leap forward. XML is a markup language specification developed by the W3C that is similar to HTML, but has a very different purpose. Whereas the purpose of HTML is to control the "look and feel" and display of data on the web page, XML is designed to describe data and information. For example, consider the sample XML document in **Figure 2.15**. The first line in the sample document is the XML declaration, which is always included; it defines the XML version of the document. In this case, the document conforms to the 1.0 specification of XML. The next line defines the first element of the document (the root element): <note>. The next four lines define four child elements of the root (to, from, heading, and body). The last line defines the end of the root element. Notice that XML says nothing about how to display the data, or how the text should look on the screen. HTML is used for information display in combination with XML, which is used for data description.

Figure 2.16 shows how XML can be used to define a database of company names in a company directory. Tags such as <Company>, <Name>, and <Specialty> can be defined for a single firm, or an entire industry. On an elementary level, XML is extraordinarily easy to learn and is very similar to HTML except that you can make up your own tags. At a deeper level, XML has a rich syntax and an enormous set of software tools, which make XML ideal for storing and communicating many types of data on the Web.

XML is "extensible," which means the tags used to describe and display data are defined by the user, whereas in HTML the tags are limited and predefined. XML can also transform information into new formats, such as by importing information from a database and displaying it as a table. With XML, information can be analyzed and displayed selectively, making it a more powerful alternative to HTML. This means that business firms, or entire industries, can describe all of their invoices, accounts payable, payroll records, and financial information using a web-compatible markup language. Once described, these business documents can be stored on intranet web servers and shared throughout the corporation.

eXtensible Markup Language (XML)

a markup language specification developed by the World Wide Web Consortium (W3C) that is designed to describe data and information

FIGURE 2.16   SAMPLE XML CODE FOR A COMPANY DIRECTORY

```xml
<?xml version="1.0"?>
<Companies>
    <Company>
          <Name>Azimuth Interactive Inc.</Name>
        <Specialties>
                <Specialty>HTML development</Specialty>
                  <Specialty>technical documentation</Specialty>
               <Specialty>ROBO Help</Specialty>
               <Country>United States</Country>
        </Specialties>
        <Location>
               <Country>United States</Country>
             <State />
             <City>Chicago</City>
        </Location>
             <Telephone>301-555-1212</Telephone>
    </Company>
    <Company>
       ...
    </Company>
    ...
</Companies>
```

This XML document uses tags to define a database of company names.

Really Simple Syndication (RSS)

program that allows users to have digital content, including text, articles, blogs, and podcast audio files, automatically sent to their computers over the Internet

Really Simple Syndication (RSS) is an XML format that allows users to have digital content, including text, articles, blogs, and podcast audio files, automatically sent to their computers over the Internet. An RSS aggregator software application that you install on your computer gathers material from the websites and blogs that you tell it to scan and brings new information from those sites to you. Sometimes this is referred to as "syndicated" content because it is distributed by news organizations and other syndicators (or distributors). Users download an RSS aggregator and then "subscribe" to the RSS "feeds." When you go to your RSS aggregator's page, it will display the most recent updates for each channel to which you have subscribed. RSS has rocketed from a "techie" pastime to a broad-based movement. Although Google has closed down Google Reader, a popular RSS product, a number of other RSS reader options remain, including Feedly, Reeder, and NewsBlur.

WEB SERVERS AND CLIENTS

We have already described client/server computing and the revolution in computing architecture brought about by client/server computing. You already know that a server is a computer attached to a network that stores files, controls peripheral devices, interfaces with the outside world—including the Internet—and does some processing for other computers on the network.

But what is a web server? **Web server software** refers to the software that enables a computer to deliver web pages written in HTML to client computers on a network that request this service by sending an HTTP request. Apache, which works with Linux and Unix operating systems, is the most commonly used type of web server software in terms

web server software

software that enables a computer to deliver web pages written in HTML to client computers on a network that request this service by sending an HTTP request

of number of active websites. Microsoft's Internet Information Services (IIS) also has significant market share along with Nginx, an open source web server (Netcraft, 2019).

Aside from responding to requests for web pages, all web servers provide some additional basic capabilities such as the following:

- *Security services*—These consist mainly of authentication services that verify that the person trying to access the site is authorized to do so. For websites that process payment transactions, the web server also supports SSL and TLS, the protocols for transmitting and receiving information securely over the Internet. When private information such as names, phone numbers, addresses, and credit card data needs to be provided to a website, the web server uses SSL and TLS to ensure that the data passing back and forth from the browser to the server is not compromised.
- *FTP*—This protocol allows users to transfer files to and from the server. Some sites limit file uploads to the web server, while others restrict downloads, depending on the user's identity.
- *Search engine*—Just as search engine sites enable users to search the entire Web for particular documents, search engine modules within the basic web server software package enable indexing of the site's web pages and content and permit easy keyword searching of the site's content. When conducting a search, a search engine makes use of an index, which is a list of all the documents on the server. The search term is compared to the index to identify likely matches.
- *Data capture*—Web servers are also helpful at monitoring site traffic, capturing information on who has visited a site, how long the user stayed there, the date and time of each visit, and which specific pages on the server were accessed. This information is compiled and saved in a log file, which can then be analyzed. By analyzing a log file, a site manager can find out the total number of visitors, the average length of each visit, and the most popular destinations, or web pages.

The term *web server* is also used to refer to the physical computer that runs web server software. Leading manufacturers of web server computers include Lenovo, Dell, and Hewlett-Packard. Although any desktop computer can run web server software, it is best to use a computer that has been optimized for this purpose. To be a web server, a computer must have web server software installed and be connected to the Internet. Every public web server computer has an IP address. For example, if you type http://www.pearson.com/laudon in your browser, the browser software sends a request for HTTP service to the web server whose domain name is pearson.com. The server then locates the page named "laudon", sends the page back to your browser, and displays it on your screen.

Aside from the generic web server software packages, there are actually many types of specialized servers on the Web, from **database servers** that access specific information within a database, to **ad servers** that deliver targeted banner ads, to **mail servers** that provide e-mail messages, and **video servers** that provide video clips. At a small e-commerce site, all of these software packages might be running on a single computer, with a single processor. At a large corporate site, there may be hundreds or thousands of discrete server computers, many with multiple processors, running specialized web server functions. We discuss the architecture of e-commerce sites in greater detail in Chapter 4.

A **web client**, on the other hand, is any computing device attached to the Internet that is capable of making HTTP requests and displaying HTML pages. The most common

database server
server designed to access specific information within a database

ad server
server designed to deliver targeted banner ads

mail server
server that provides e-mail messages

video server
server that serves video clips

web client
any computing device attached to the Internet that is capable of making HTTP requests and displaying HTML pages, most commonly a Windows PC or Macintosh

client is a Windows or Macintosh desktop computer, with various flavors of Unix/Linux computers a distant third. However, the fastest growing category of web clients is not computers at all, but mobile devices. In general, a web client can be any device—including a printer, refrigerator, stove, home lighting system, or automobile instrument panel—capable of sending and receiving information from a web server.

WEB BROWSERS

web browser
software program whose primary purpose is to display web pages

A **web browser** is a software program whose primary purpose is to display web pages. Browsers also have added features, such as e-mail and newsgroups (an online discussion group or forum). The leading U.S. desktop web browser is Google's Chrome, a small, yet technologically advanced open source browser, with about 67% of the market as of October 2019. Chrome is also the leading mobile browser, with about a 64% share of that market. The second most popular desktop browser is Mozilla Firefox, with about a 9% share. However, Firefox's share of the mobile/tablet market is very small, with only about a 1% share. Firefox is a free, open source web browser for the Windows, Linux, and Macintosh operating systems, based on Mozilla open source code (which originally provided the code for Netscape). It is small and fast and offers many features such as pop-up blocking and tabbed browsing. Microsoft's Internet Explorer is in third place in the desktop browser marketplace, with about an 8% share. It also has less than a 1% share of the mobile browser market. Microsoft's Edge browser is in fourth place, with about 5% of the desktop browser market. Microsoft introduced Edge, an entirely new browser bundled with its Windows 10 operating system in 2015. Edge was designed to replace Internet Explorer but thus far still trails Internet Explorer in terms of popularity as a desktop browser. Apple's Safari browser has only about a 4% share of the desktop browser market, but is the second most popular mobile browser, with a 27% share, due in large part to its use on iPhones and iPads (Marketshare.hitslink.com, 2019a, 2019b).

2.4 THE INTERNET AND THE WEB: FEATURES AND SERVICES

The Internet and the Web have spawned a number of powerful software applications upon which the foundations of e-commerce are built. You can think of all these as web services, and it is interesting as you read along to compare these services to other traditional media such as television or print media. If you do, you will quickly realize the richness of the Internet environment.

COMMUNICATION TOOLS

The Internet and Web provide a number of communication tools that enable people around the globe to communicate with one another, both on a one-to-one basis as well as a one-to-many basis. Communication tools include e-mail, messaging applications, online message boards (forums), Internet telephony applications, and video conferencing, video chatting, and telepresence. We'll look at each of these in a bit more depth in the following sections.

E-mail

Since its earliest days, **electronic mail**, or **e-mail**, has been the most-used application of the Internet. Worldwide, there are over 3.9 billion e-mail users, over half of the world's total population, sending over 293 billion e-mails a day (Radicati Group, 2019). Estimates vary on the amount of spam, ranging from 40% to 90%. E-mail marketing and spam are examined in more depth in Chapter 6.

E-mail uses a series of protocols to enable messages containing text, images, sound, and video clips to be transferred from one Internet user to another. Because of its flexibility and speed, it is now the most popular form of business communication—more popular than the phone, fax, or snail mail (the U.S. Postal Service). In addition to text typed within the message, e-mail also allows **attachments**, which are files inserted within the e-mail message. The files can be documents, images, sounds, or video clips.

Messaging Applications

Instant messaging (IM) allows you to send messages in real time, unlike e-mail, which has a time lag of several seconds to minutes between when messages are sent and received. IM displays text entered almost instantaneously. Recipients can then respond immediately to the sender the same way, making the communication more like a live conversation than is possible through e-mail. To use IM, users create a buddy list they want to communicate with, and then enter short text messages that their buddies will receive instantly (if they are online at the time). And although text remains the primary communication mechanism in IM, more advanced systems also provide voice and video chat functionality. Instant messaging over the Internet competes with cell phone Short Message Service (SMS) and Multimedia Messaging Service (MMS) texting, which is far more expensive than IM. Major IM systems include Skype and Google Hangouts. (Both AIM (AOL Instant Messenger) and Yahoo Messenger have recently been discontinued.) IM systems were initially developed as proprietary systems, with competing firms offering versions that did not work with one another. Today, there still is no built-in interoperability among the major IM systems.

Mobile messaging apps, such as Facebook Messenger, WhatsApp (purchased by Facebook for $22 billion in 2014), Snapchat (which allows users to send pictures, videos, and texts that will disappear after a short period of time), Kik, Viber, and others have also become wildly popular, providing competition for both traditional desktop IM systems and SMS text messaging. Over 2.5 billion worldwide (over 65% of all Internet users) use mobile messaging apps, and companies are increasingly turning their attention to using these apps to market their brands (eMarketer, Inc., 2019c, 2019d).

Online Message Boards

An **online message board** (also referred to as a forum, bulletin board, discussion board, discussion group, or simply a board or forum) is a web application that enables Internet users to communicate with each other, although not in real time. A message board provides a container for various discussions (or "threads") started (or "posted") by members of the board, and, depending on the permissions granted to board members by the board's administrator, enables a person to start a thread and reply to other people's threads. Most message board software allows more than one message board to be created. The board

---

electronic mail (e-mail)
the most-used application of the Internet. Uses a series of protocols to enable messages containing text, images, sound, and video clips to be transferred from one Internet user to another

attachment
a file inserted within an e-mail message

instant messaging (IM)
displays text entered almost instantaneously. Recipients can then respond immediately to the sender the same way, making the communication more like a live conversation than is possible through e-mail

online message board
a web application that allows Internet users to communicate with each other, although not in real time

administrator typically can edit, delete, move, or otherwise modify any thread on the board. Unlike an electronic mailing list (such as a listserv), which automatically sends new messages to a subscriber, an online message board typically requires that the member visit the board to check for new posts. Some boards offer an "e-mail notification" feature that notifies users that a new post of interest to them has been made.

Internet Telephony

If the telephone system were to be built from scratch today, it would be an Internet-based, packet-switched network using TCP/IP because it would be less expensive and more efficient than the alternative existing system, which involves a mix of circuit-switched legs with a digital backbone. Likewise, if cable television systems were built from scratch today, they most likely would use Internet technologies for the same reasons.

IP telephony is a general term for the technologies that use **Voice over Internet Protocol (VoIP)** and the Internet's packet-switched network to transmit voice, fax, and other forms of audio communication over the Internet. VoIP can be used over a traditional handset as well as over a mobile device. VoIP avoids the long distance charges imposed by traditional phone companies.

In the United States, more than half of residential customers are now using VoIP, and this number is expanding rapidly as cable systems provide telephone service as part of their "triple play": voice, Internet, and TV as a single package. This number is dwarfed, however, by the number of mobile VoIP subscribers, which has grown explosively over the last several years, fueled by the rampant growth of mobile messaging apps that now also provide free VoIP services, such as Skype, Facebook Messenger, WhatsApp (also owned by Facebook), Viber (owned by Japanese e-commerce giant Rakuten), WeChat, Line, Kakao-Talk, and others (Bar, 2019; BuddeComm, 2018).

VoIP is a disruptive technology. In the past, voice and fax were the exclusive provenance of the regulated telephone networks. With the convergence of the Internet and telephony, however, this dominance is already starting to change, with local and long distance telephone providers and cable companies becoming ISPs, and ISPs getting into the phone market. Key players in the VoIP market include independent service providers such as VoIP pioneers Vonage and Skype (now owned by Microsoft), as well as traditional players such as telephone and cable companies that have moved aggressively into the market. Skype currently dominates the international market. Skype carries over 3 billion minutes per day (translating into about 90 billion minutes per month) from 300 million users around the world (Greig, 2019; Perez, 2017).

Video Conferencing, Video Chatting, and Telepresence

Internet video conferencing is accessible to anyone with a broadband Internet connection and a web camera (webcam). The most widely used web conferencing suite of tools is WebEx (now owned by Cisco). Slack, a cloud-based team collaboration tool that includes video conferencing and chatting, is another popular option. VoIP companies such as Skype and ooVoo also provide more limited web conferencing capabilities, commonly referred to as video chatting. Apple's FaceTime is another video chatting technology available for iOS mobile devices with a forward-facing camera and Macintosh computers equipped with Apple's version of a webcam, called a FaceTime camera.

IP telephony
a general term for the technologies that use VoIP and the Internet's packet-switched network to transmit voice and other forms of audio communication over the Internet

Voice over Internet Protocol (VoIP)
protocol that allows for transmission of voice and other forms of audio communication over the Internet

Telepresence takes video conferencing up several notches. Rather than single persons "meeting" by using webcams, telepresence creates an environment in a room using multiple cameras and screens, which surround the users. The experience is uncanny and strange at first because as you look at the people in the screens, they are looking directly at you. Broadcast quality and higher screen resolutions help create the effect. Users have the sensation of "being in the presence of their colleagues" in a way that is not true for traditional webcam meetings. Providers of telepresence software and hardware include Cisco, LifeSize, BlueJeans Network, and Polycom.

SEARCH ENGINES

Search engines identify web pages that appear to match keywords, also called queries, entered by a user and then provide a list of the best matches (search results). Over 85% of U.S. Internet users regularly use search engines from either desktop or mobile devices, and they generate around 18.5 billion queries a month on desktop computers, about 11.7 billion of which are conducted using Google. Desktop search volume is declining, as more and more search activity moves to mobile devices. In fact, Google reported that mobile search queries exceeded desktop queries in the United States and numerous other countries for the first time in 2015. There are hundreds of different search engines, but in the United States, the vast majority of the search results are supplied by the top three providers: Google, Microsoft's Bing, and Yahoo (Verizon Media). Google, Bing, and Yahoo are also major search providers in Europe. Other European search providers include T-Online (Germany) and Qwant (France). In China, Baidu, Qihoo 360, and Sohu Sogou are major search engine providers (eMarketer, Inc., 2019e; comScore, Inc., 2018a, 2018b).

Web search engines started out in the early 1990s shortly after Netscape released the first commercial web browser. Early search engines were relatively simple software programs that roamed the nascent Web, visiting pages and gathering information about the content of each web page. These early programs were called variously crawlers, spiders, and wanderers; the first full-text crawler that indexed the contents of an entire web page was called WebCrawler, released in 1994. AltaVista (1995), one of the first widely used search engines, was the first to allow "natural language" queries such as "history of web search engines" rather than "history + web + search engine."

The first search engines employed simple keyword indexes of all the web pages visited. They would count the number of times a word appeared on the web page, and store this information in an index. These search engines could be easily fooled by web designers who simply repeated words on their home pages. The real innovations in search engine development occurred through a program funded by the Department of Defense called the Digital Library Initiative, designed to help the Pentagon find research papers in large databases. Stanford, Berkeley, and three other universities became hotbeds of web search innovations in the mid-1990s. At Stanford in 1994, two computer science students, David Filo and Jerry Yang, created a hand-selected list of their favorite web pages and called it "Yet Another Hierarchical Officious Oracle," or Yahoo!. Yahoo initially was not a real search engine, but rather an edited selection of web sites organized by categories the editors found useful. Yahoo later developed "true" search engine capabilities.

In 1998, Larry Page and Sergey Brin, two Stanford computer science students, released their first version of the Google search engine. This search engine was different: not only

search engine
identifies web pages that appear to match keywords, also called queries, entered by the user and then provides a list of the best matches

did it index each web page's words, but Page had discovered that the AltaVista search engine not only collected keywords from sites but also calculated what other sites linked to each page. By looking at the URLs on each web page, they could calculate an index of popularity. AltaVista did nothing with this information. Page took this idea and made it a central factor in ranking a web page's appropriateness to a search query. He patented the idea of a web page ranking system (PageRank System), which essentially measures the popularity of the web page. Brin contributed a unique web crawler program that indexed not just keywords on a web page, but combinations of words (such as authors and their article titles). These two ideas became the foundation for the Google search engine (Brandt, 2004). **Figure 2.17(A)** illustrates how Google indexes the Web. **Figure 2.17(B)** shows you what happens when you enter a search query.

Initially, few understood how to make money from search engines. That changed in 2000 when Goto.com (later Overture) allowed advertisers to bid for placement on their search engine results, and Google followed suit in 2003 with its AdWords program, which allowed advertisers to bid for placement of short text ads on Google search results. The spectacular increase in Internet advertising revenues has helped search engines transform themselves into major shopping tools and created an entire new industry called "search engine marketing."

When users enter a search term at Google, Bing, Yahoo, or any of the other websites serviced by these search engines, they receive two types of listings: sponsored links, for which advertisers have paid to be listed (usually at the top of the search results page), and unsponsored "organic" search results. Advertisers can also purchase small text ads on the right side of the search results page. In addition, search engines have extended their services to include news, maps, satellite images, computer images, e-mail, group calendars, group meeting tools, and indexes of scholarly papers.

Although the major search engines are used for locating general information of interest to users, search engines have also become a crucial tool within e-commerce sites. Customers can more easily search for the product information they want with the help of an internal search program; the difference is that within websites, the search engine is limited to finding matches from that one site. For instance, online shoppers more often use Amazon's internal search engine to look for products than conducting a product search using Google (Scott, 2017). Pinterest is challenging Google in the realm of visual search, as discussed in the opening case in Chapter 7.

DOWNLOADABLE AND STREAMING MEDIA

download
transfers a file from a web server and stores it on a computer for later use

streaming media
enables video, music, and other large-bandwidth files to be sent to a user in a variety of ways that enable the user to play the files as they are being delivered

When you **download** a file from the Web, the file is transferred from a web server and is stored on your computer for later use. With the low-bandwidth connections of the early Internet, audio and video files were difficult to download, but with the huge growth in broadband connections, these files are not only commonplace but today constitute the majority of web traffic. **Streaming media** is an alternative to downloaded media and enables video, music, and other large-bandwidth files to be sent to a user in a variety of ways that enable the user to play the files as they are being delivered. In some situations, the files are broken into chunks and served by specialized video servers to client software that puts the chunks together and plays the video. In other situations, a single large file is delivered from a standard web server to a user who can begin playing the video before

FIGURE 2.17 HOW GOOGLE WORKS

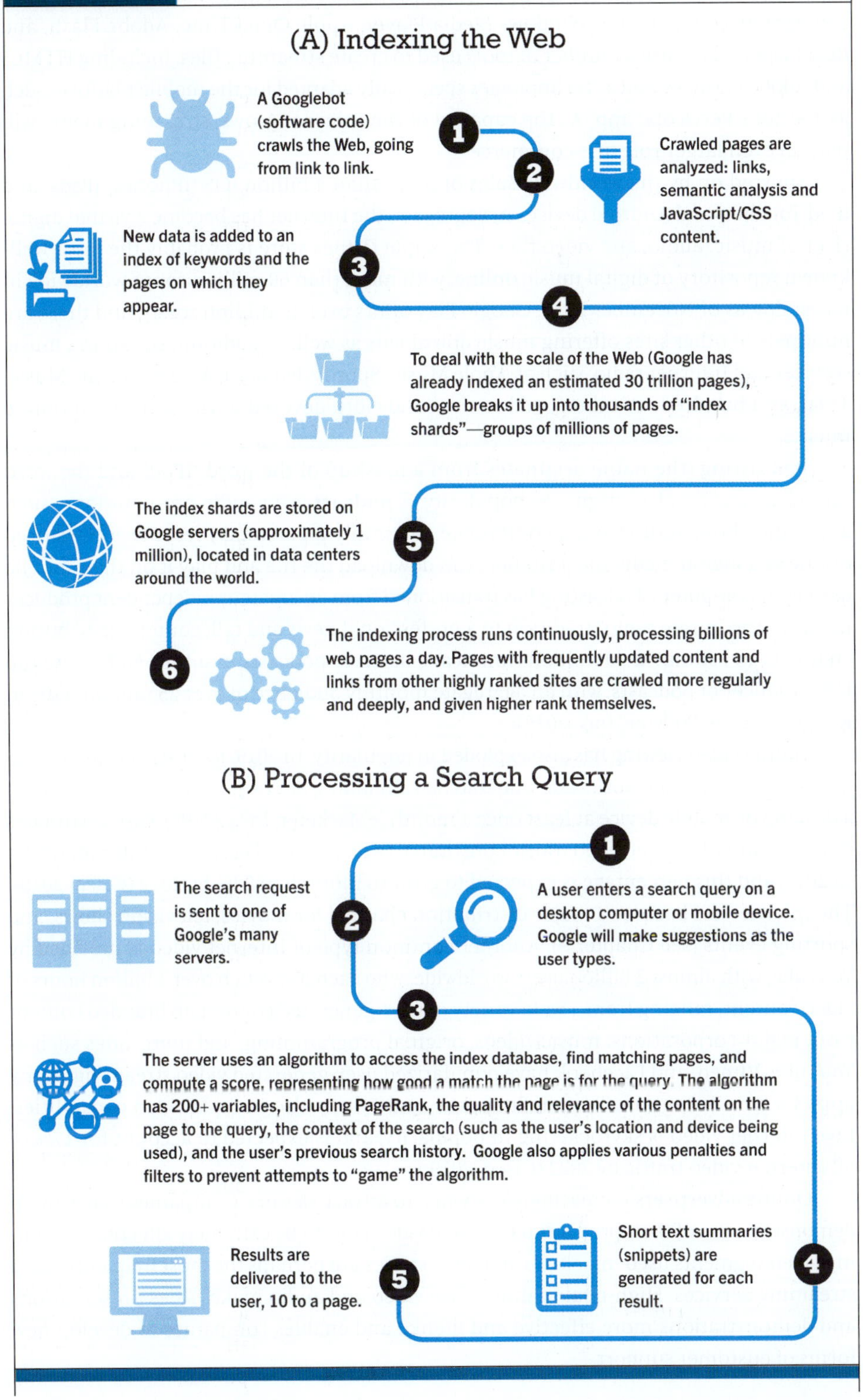

(A) Indexing the Web

1. A Googlebot (software code) crawls the Web, going from link to link.

2. Crawled pages are analyzed: links, semantic analysis and JavaScript/CSS content.

3. New data is added to an index of keywords and the pages on which they appear.

4. To deal with the scale of the Web (Google has already indexed an estimated 30 trillion pages), Google breaks it up into thousands of "index shards"—groups of millions of pages.

5. The index shards are stored on Google servers (approximately 1 million), located in data centers around the world.

6. The indexing process runs continuously, processing billions of web pages a day. Pages with frequently updated content and links from other highly ranked sites are crawled more regularly and deeply, and given higher rank themselves.

(B) Processing a Search Query

1. A user enters a search query on a desktop computer or mobile device. Google will make suggestions as the user types.

2. The search request is sent to one of Google's many servers.

3. The server uses an algorithm to access the index database, find matching pages, and compute a score, representing how good a match the page is for the query. The algorithm has 200+ variables, including PageRank, the quality and relevance of the content on the page to the query, the context of the search (such as the user's location and device being used), and the user's previous search history. Google also applies various penalties and filters to prevent attempts to "game" the algorithm.

4. Short text summaries (snippets) are generated for each result.

5. Results are delivered to the user, 10 to a page.

the entire file is delivered. Streamed files must be viewed in real time; they cannot be stored on client hard drives without special software. Streamed files are "played" by a software program such as Windows Media Player, Apple QuickTime, Adobe Flash, and Real Player. There are a number of tools used to create streaming files, including HTML5 and Adobe Flash, as well as technologies specifically adapted for the mobile platform such as Twitter's Periscope app. As the capacity of the Internet grows, streaming media will play an even larger role in e-commerce.

Spurred on by the worldwide sales of more than 4 billion iOS (iPhones, iPads, and iPod Touches) and Android devices in aggregate, the Internet has become a virtual digital river of music, audio, and video files. The Apple iTunes store is probably the most well-known repository of digital music online, with more than 60 million songs worldwide in its catalog as of November 2019. Google Play offers over 40 million songs, and there are hundreds of other sites offering music downloads as well. In addition, streaming music services and Internet radio, such as Apple Music, Spotify, Pandora, Amazon Prime Music, Tidal, and hundreds of others, add to the bandwidth devoted to the delivery of online music.

Podcasting (the name originates from a mashup of the word "iPod" and the word "broadcasting") is also surging in popularity. A **podcast** is an audio presentation—such as a radio show, audio from a conference, or simply a personal presentation—stored online as a digital media file. Listeners can download the file and play it on their mobile devices or computers. Podcasting has transitioned from an amateur independent producer media in the "pirate radio" tradition to a professional news and talk content distribution channel. An estimated 90 million Americans listen to podcasts monthly. NPR is the top U.S. producer of podcasts, with an aggregate monthly audience of over 25 million (Edison Research, 2019; Podtrac, Inc., 2019).

Online video viewing has also exploded in popularity. In 2019, for instance, there were over 2.6 billion people worldwide who watched streaming or downloaded video content on a desktop or mobile device at least once a month (eMarketer, Inc., 2019f). Cisco estimates that consumer Internet video traffic constituted over 75% of all consumer Internet traffic in 2019, and this percentage is expected to grow to more than 82% by 2022 (Cisco, 2019). The Internet has become a major distribution channel for movies, television shows, and sporting events (see Chapter 9). Another common type of Internet video is provided by YouTube, with almost 2 billion users worldwide, who each day watch over 1 billion hours of video content, ranging from a wide variety of user-generated content, to branded content from major corporations, music videos, original programming, and more. Sites such as YouTube, Vimeo, and Facebook have popularized user-generated video streaming. Many apps such as Instagram, Twitter, Snapchat, and others also include video capabilities. Live Internet video is skyrocketing in popularity, and is expected to account for 17% of all Internet video traffic by 2022 (Cisco, 2019.)

Online advertisers increasingly use video to attract viewers. Companies that want to demonstrate use of their products have found video clips to be extremely effective. Streaming video segments used in web ads and news stories are perhaps the most frequently used streaming services. High-quality interactive video and audio makes sales presentations and demonstrations more effective and lifelike and enables companies to develop new forms of customer support.

podcast

an audio presentation—such as a radio show, audio from a movie, or simply a personal audio presentation—stored online as a digital media file

WEB 2.0 APPLICATIONS AND SERVICES

Today's broadband Internet infrastructure has greatly expanded the services available to users. These capabilities have formed the basis for new business models. Web 2.0 applications and services are "social" in nature because they support communication among individuals within groups or social networks.

Online Social Networks

Online social networks are services that support communication within networks of friends, acquaintances, people with similar interests, colleagues, and even entire professions. Online social networks have developed very large worldwide audiences (over 2.9 billion people in 2019, over one-third of the world's population) and form the basis for advertising platforms and social e-commerce (see Chapters 6, 7, and 10). The largest social networks are Facebook (over 2.4 billion monthly active users worldwide), Instagram (over 1 billion members worldwide), LinkedIn (more than 660 million members worldwide), Twitter (around 320 million active users worldwide), and Pinterest (over 300 million active users). These networks rely on user-generated content (messages, photos, and videos) and emphasize sharing of content. All of these features require significant broadband Internet connectivity and equally large cloud computing facilities to store content.

Blogs

A **blog** (originally called a **weblog**) is a personal web page that typically contains a series of chronological entries (newest to oldest) by its author, and links to related web pages. The blog may include a blogroll (a collection of links to other blogs) and trackbacks (a list of entries in other blogs that refer to a post on the first blog). Most blogs allow readers to post comments on the blog entries as well. The act of creating a blog is often referred to as "blogging." Blogs are either hosted by a third-party site such as WordPress, Tumblr, Blogger, LiveJournal, TypePad, and Xanga, or prospective bloggers can download software such as Movable Type to create a blog that is hosted by the user's ISP. Blog pages are usually variations on templates provided by the blogging service or software and hence require no knowledge of HTML. Therefore, millions of people without HTML skills of any kind can post their own web pages, and share content with friends and relatives. The totality of blog-related websites is often referred to as the "blogosphere."

Blogs have become hugely popular. In 2019, Tumblr and Wordpress together hosted over 510 million blogs, so it is likely that the total number is significantly higher. According to eMarketer, there are an estimated 31 million active U.S. bloggers, and 85 million U.S. blog readers (eMarketer, Inc., 2016a, 2016b). No one knows how many of these blogs are kept up to date or are just yesterday's news. And no one knows how many of these blogs have a readership greater than one (the blog author). In fact, there are so many blogs you need a search engine just to find them, or you can just go to a list of the most popular 100 blogs and dig in.

Wikis

A **wiki** is a web application that allows a user to easily add and edit content on a web page. (The term wiki derives from the "wiki wiki" (quick or fast) shuttle buses at Honolulu

blog
personal web page that is created by an individual or corporation to communicate with readers

wiki
web application that allows a user to easily add and edit content on a web page

Airport.) Wiki software enables documents to be written collectively and collaboratively. Most wiki systems are open source, server-side systems that store content in a relational database. The software typically provides a template that defines layout and elements common to all pages, displays user-editable source code (usually plain text), and then renders the content into an HTML-based page for display in a web browser. Some wiki software allows only basic text formatting, whereas others allow the use of tables, images, or even interactive elements, such as polls and games. Because wikis by their very nature are very open in allowing anyone to make changes to a page, most wikis provide a means to verify the validity of changes via a "Recent Changes" page, which enables members of the wiki community to monitor and review the work of other users, correct mistakes, and hopefully deter "vandalism."

The most well-known wiki is Wikipedia, an online encyclopedia that contains more than 51 million articles in over 300 different languages on a variety of topics. The Wikimedia Foundation, which operates Wikipedia, also operates a variety of related projects, including Wikibooks, a collection of collaboratively written free textbooks and manuals; Wikinews, a free content news source; and Wiktionary, a collaborative project to produce a free multilingual dictionary in every language, with definitions, etymologies, pronunciations, quotations, and synonyms.

VIRTUAL REALITY AND AUGMENTED REALITY

In 2016, virtual reality and augmented reality technologies began to enter the consumer market and attract significant attention and since that time, they have continued to gain further traction. **Virtual reality (VR)** involves fully immersing users within a virtual world, typically through the use of a head-mounted display (HMD) connected to headphones and other devices that enable navigation through the experience and allowing users to feel as if they are actually present within the virtual world. High-end VR devices designed to be used with PCs or gaming systems include Facebook's Oculus Rift, HTC's Vive, and Sony's PlayStation VR. Samsung's Gear VR, Google Cardboard, and Google DayDream View are examples of lower-cost, mobile, entry-level devices. A number of publishers are experimenting with VR content that can use these lower-cost devices. For example, the New York Times has a VR mobile app that viewers can use with Google Cardboard to view VR films and advertisements that feature 360-degree video. Immersive 360-degree video and photos are the most frequently viewed types of VR content. eMarketer estimates that there were almost 43 million virtual reality users in the United States in 2019, and this number is expected to increase to over 57 million by 2021. **Augmented reality (AR)** involves overlaying virtual objects over the real world, via smartphones, tablets, or HMDs. Among the highest profile uses of AR thus far has been in Nintendo's Pokemon GO game. Other uses include Snapchat's Lenses feature, which uses facial recognition technology and 3-D models that allow users to augment their selfies by overlaying animations or other images on top of them, and "try-before-you-buy" apps created for beauty and fashion brands. eMarketer estimates that there were about 69 million augmented reality users in the United States in 2019, expected to grow to 85 million by 2021 (eMarketer, Inc., 2019g, 2019h). The *Insight on Technology* case, *Leaping into the Future with VR and AR*, examines the possibilities for mixing VR and AR with e-commerce.

virtual reality (VR)
involves fully immersing users within a virtual world, typically through the use of a head-mounted display (HMD) connected to headphones and other devices

augmented reality (AR)
involves overlaying virtual objects over the real world, via smartphones, tablets, or HMDs

INSIGHT ON TECHNOLOGY

LEAPING INTO THE FUTURE WITH AR AND VR

Initially characterized by some as a solution in search of a problem, virtual reality (VR) and augmented reality (AR) applications that engage users in an immersive experience are likely to become mainstream within the next five to ten years. Right now there are still hurdles to widespread adoption of VR in particular. But as VR headset hardware evolves and high-speed 5G cellular networks become widely available, consumers are likely to become much more interested in VR. AR applications, in contrast, do not require special hardware or very-high-speed networks, are on the shelf now, and work well with existing technologies. Today, the number of AR business applications is increasing and this will drive consumers to be exposed to AR environments and eventually scale up to a mass consumer platform.

Magic Leap, a Florida-based startup, is one example of the future of VR/AR. Magic Leap has raised $3 billion from venture capital investors including Google and in 2018 released its first product, Magic Leap One, which includes VR goggles that look like big swim goggles. The platform puts virtual objects into the real world (think Pokemon GO on steroids), unlike virtual reality headware that blocks out the real world with a virtual reality. Yes, the goggles look clunky, weigh nearly a pound (14 ounces), and are pricy at $2,295. They are at the same stage of development as the first PCs. But investors believe their future will follow the same trajectory.

Virtual tourism is one application of VR that is starting to catch on. TimeLooper, a startup VR firm, uses a VR headset to explore historical moments around the world, such as the fall of the Berlin Wall in 1989, the Great Fire of London in 1660, and the experiences of immigrants at New York's Ellis Island in the 1880s. Another firm, Zreality, uses VR goggles to take tourists on a 50-minute VR tour of Luxembourg. Applications such as these allow tourists to walk through history—virtually—using a VR device as a way to get a visceral feel for what it was like to actually experience the event.

E-commerce marketers are expanding their use of VR/AR apps to provide users with an enhanced customized experience. According to the VR/AR Association, the retail industry is already spending more than $1 billion annually on VR/AR, growing at over 200% annually. For instance, in 2018 Ikea, the Swedish furniture company, launched Ikea Place, which permits users to scan a room in their homes with their smartphones, select a piece of furniture online, and see how it will look in their room. Lowe's has a similar application called View in Your Space, which enables customers to virtually place Lowe's products, from tile to flooring, furniture, and carpets, into a room in real time. Lowe's app uses the ARKit development environment to develop these capabilities. The goal is a seamless, omni-channel shopping experience that integrates online products with physical stores in a personalized manner.

Natuzzi Italia, one of the world's largest furniture brands, has also been testing augmented and virtual reality tools, and expects to install Microsoft HoloLens 2 headsets in 300 of its stores by the end of 2020. In a one-month pilot program at Natuzzi's London flagship store, over 80% of purchasing customers used the headset to view 3D digital models of its furniture.

(continued)

One of the most sophisticated AR e-commerce applications is Sephora's Virtual Artist app. Sephora is one of the largest specialty retailers of beauty products in the world, with 2,300 stores in 33 countries. Virtual Artist, developed by Sephora's Innovation Lab in San Francisco, allows online customers to try out thousands of shades of lipstick, eye shadow, lashes and 20,000 other cosmetic products and color variations using their smartphones. Based on facial recognition and AI software, customers take a selfie, and the app allows them to see how products will change their looks. The software identifies and measures where lips, eyes, and other facial features are, and then knows exactly where to place the products being tested. By 2019, over 8.5 million people had used the app.

One hindrance to widespread adoption of VR and AR is the lack of developer tools. This is changing rapidly. While the successful experience of early adopters is encouraging, what will really drive VR/AR are the billions being invested in hardware and software by Facebook, Apple, Alphabet (Google), Microsoft, and especially Amazon. They see big opportunities. Facebook is doubling down on AR efforts with its Spark AR Studio development platform. According to Facebook, since its launch, the Spark AR Studio platform has powered AR experiences for over 1 billion people. Zuckerberg sees AR as the next big thing, a technology that will have an impact equal to Apple iPhones. In 2014 Facebook purchased Oculus, which makes VR goggles, for an astounding $3 billion, despite the fact that a similar earlier effort by Google (Google Glass) failed in the marketplace. Facebook is investing millions in a VR/AR app ecosystem similar to Apple's App Store that will develop thousands of VR/AR experiences, all on the Facebook platform. Google has launched its ARCore development environment and has invested heavily in Magic Leap. For Facebook and Google, VR/AR will provide more screens where ads can be shown. For Apple, VR/AR is another source of content, a new app environment that will make its devices more appealing and that users will pay for and use to make in-app purchases. Apple's iOS 11 and beyond operating systems include ARKit, a feature that allows developers and consumers to easily create AR experiences for the iPhone or iPad. For Amazon and Microsoft, big players in cloud computing, VR/AR apps are a large potential cloud market. Amazon has created a cloud-based development platform called Sumerian, which will allow developers to create immersive 3D virtual environments in an easy-to-use interface that run on Amazon Web Services (AWS) cloud servers. One thing for sure is that mass consumer VR/AR apps will require extraordinary amounts of new cloud computing capacity as well as a similar increase in cellular network capacity. As a result, AT&T, Verizon, T-Mobile, Sprint, and other telecommunications companies that provide cellular service also have an iron in the VR/AR fire because mass consumer use of these apps will require extraordinary cellular bandwidth to support meaningful consumer interactions without latency delays.

With all of these big technology companies invested in the development of VR and AR, chances are good that these technologies will be making their presence felt in the e-commerce arena in the not-too-distant future.

SOURCES: "Forget Digital Versus Physical: The Future Is Programmable," by Maghan McDowell, Voguebusiness.com, June 3, 2019; "Facebook Shares Major Spark AR Studio Update," by Michael Slater, Developers.facebook.com, April 30, 2019; "Magic Leap Raises $280 Million from NTT DoCoMo," by Michael J. de la Merced, *New York Times*, April 26, 2019; "Magic Leap Headset Test Drive: Off Your Phone and Into Your World," by Joanna Stern, *New York Times*, August 8, 2018; "For Tourists, the Berlin Wall Can (Virtually) Fall Again," by Caitlin Ostroff, *New York Times*, June 27, 2018; "5G Can Reinvent Ecommerce With VR and AR—If Policymakers Allow," by Roslyn Layton, Forbes.com, June 6, 2018; "How Sephora Is Leveraging AR and AI to Transform Retail and Help Customers Buy Cosmetics," By Alison DeNisco Rayome, Techrepublic.com, May 17, 2018; "Inside Sumerian, Amazon's Big Bet on Augmented and Virtual Reality," by Rob Marvin, Pcmagazine.com, April 16, 2018; "Virtual Reality: Beyond Gaming," by Victoria Petrock, eMarketer, Inc., April 2018; "Retail E-commerce: How AR and VR Can Transform Shopping," Computerworld.com, February 1, 2018; "Lowe's Lands Top Spot on Most Innovative Companies in AR/VR List," by Amy Kreis, Lowes.com, February 20, 2018; "AR/VR Startups Raised $3 Billion Last Year Led by a Few Industry Juggernauts," by Lucas Matney, Techcrunch.com, January 5, 2018; "Mark Zuckerberg Sees Augmented Reality Ecosystem in Facebook," by Mike Isaac, *New York Times*, April 18, 2017; "How Augmented Reality (AR) Is Shaping Content Marketing Experiences," by Anastasia Dyakovskaya, Insight News Cred, October 9, 2017.

INTELLIGENT DIGITAL ASSISTANTS

The idea of having a conversation with a computer, having it understand you and be able to carry out tasks according to your direction, has long been a part of science fiction, from the 1968 Hollywood movie *2001: A Space Odyssey*, to an old Apple promotional video depicting a professor using his personal digital assistant to organize his life, gather data, and place orders at restaurants. That was all fantasy. But Apple's Siri, billed as an intelligent personal assistant and knowledge navigator and released in 2011, has many of the capabilities of the computer assistants found in fiction. Siri has a natural-language, conversational interface, situational awareness, and is capable of carrying out many tasks based on verbal commands by delegating requests to a variety of different web services. For instance, you can ask Siri to find a restaurant nearby that serves Italian food. Siri may show you an ad for a local restaurant in the process. Once you have identified a restaurant you would like to eat at, you can ask Siri to make a reservation using OpenTable. You can also ask Siri to place an appointment on your calendar, search for airline flights, and figure out what is the fastest route between your current location and a destination using public transit. The answers are not always completely accurate, but critics have been impressed with its uncanny abilities. Siri is currently available on the Apple Watch, the iPhone 4S and later versions, iPads with Retina display, the iPad Mini, and iPod Touches (fifth generation and later versions).

In 2012, Google released Google Now, its version of an intelligent digital assistant for Android-based smartphones. Google Now was part of the Google Search mobile application. While Google Now had many of the capabilities of Apple's Siri, it attempted to go further by predicting what users might need based on situational awareness, including physical location, time of day, previous location history, calendar, and expressed interests based on previous activity, as described in its patent application (United States Patent Office, 2012). In 2016, Google supplanted Google Now with Google Assistant, a similar virtual assistant integrated into its Google Home products and Pixel phones. Other intelligent digital assistants include Amazon's Alexa, Samsung's S Voice, LG's Voice Mate, and Microsoft's Cortana.

2.5 MOBILE APPS: THE NEXT BIG THING IS HERE

When Steve Jobs introduced the iPhone in January 2007, no one, including himself, envisioned that the device would launch a software revolution or become a major e-commerce platform, let alone a game platform, advertising platform, and general media platform for television shows, movies, videos, and e-books. The iPhone's original primary functions, beyond being a cell phone, were to be a camera, text messaging device, and web browser. What Apple initially lacked for the iPhone were software applications ("apps") that would take full advantage of its computing capabilities. The solution was apps developed by outside developers. In July 2008, Apple introduced the App Store, which provides a platform for the distribution and sale of apps by Apple as well as by independent developers. Around the same time, Google was developing Android as an open source operating system for mobile devices. In October 2008, the first smartphone using Android was released, and Google launched the Android Market (now called Google Play) as the official app store for Android. In 2010, tablet computers such as Apple's iPad and the Samsung Galaxy Tab, which provided additional platforms for mobile apps, were introduced.

In 2018, 105 billion apps were downloaded from Apple's App Store and Google's Play Store worldwide. There are currently over 3 million apps available for download in the Apple App Store and a similar number for Android devices on Google Play as well.

The mobile app phenomenon has spawned a new digital ecosystem: tens of thousands of developers, a wildly popular hardware platform, and millions of consumers now using a mobile device to replace their clunky desktop-laptop computer and act as a digital media center as well. More consumers are opting to consume media on their phones and tablet computers than ever before, which is more good news for app developers.

The implications of the app ecosystem for e-commerce are significant. The smartphone in your pocket or the tablet computer on your lap becomes not only a general-purpose computer, but also an always-present shopping tool for consumers, as well as an entirely new marketing and advertising platform for vendors. Early e-commerce applications using desktops and laptops were celebrated as allowing people to shop in their pajamas. Smartphones and tablets extend this range from pajamas to office desktops to trains, planes, and cars, all while you are on the move. You can shop anywhere, shop everywhere, and shop all the time, in between talking, texting, watching videos, and listening to music. Almost all of the top 100 brands have a presence in at least one of the major app stores, and more than 90% have an app in the Apple App Store. Retail m-commerce generated about $2.2 trillion in 2019 worldwide (eMarketer, Inc., 2019i).

PLATFORMS FOR MOBILE APPLICATION DEVELOPMENT

Unlike mobile web sites, which can be accessed by any web-enabled mobile device, native apps, which are designed specifically to operate using the mobile device's hardware and operating system, are platform-specific. Applications for the iPhone, iPad, and other iOS devices can be written in Swift, a programming language introduced Apple in 2014 specifically for developing iOS applications, or the Objective-C programming language using the iOS SDK (software developer kit). Applications for Android operating system–based phones typically are written using Java, although portions of the code may be in the C or C++ programming language. In addition to creating native apps using a programming language such as Objective C or Java, there are also hundreds of low-cost or open source app development toolkits that make creating cross-platform mobile apps relatively easy and inexpensive without having to use a device-specific programming language. See Section 3.6 in Chapter 3 for more information.

APP MARKETPLACES

Once written, applications are distributed through various marketplaces. Android apps for Android-based phones are distributed through Google Play, which is controlled by Google. iPhone applications are distributed through Apple's App Store. Apps can also be purchased from third-party vendors such as Amazon's Appstore. It is important to distinguish "native" mobile apps, which run directly on a mobile device and rely on the device's internal operating system, from web apps, which install into your browser, although these can operate in a mobile environment as well.

2.6 CAREERS IN E-COMMERCE

In this section, we'll examine a job posting by a company looking to fill a position that requires an understanding of the basic technologies underlying the Internet, the Web, and the mobile platform.

THE COMPANY

The firm was one of the first companies in Europe to target the replacement battery market for digital and personal devices, such as PCs, laptops, and smartphones. The company distributes batteries, lights, and support services for digital devices through franchised retail stores, websites, and sales to businesses (B2B). It also operates Amazon and eBay stores. It has expanded into emergency power systems for hospitals, industry, and government agencies. More recently it entered the tablet and personal computer repair and maintenance, battery recycling, and lighting markets. Starting with a single store in Iowa in 1988, it began a franchising business in 1992. Today the company has over 600 franchised retail stores and several websites. The company has an inventory of over 50,000 types of batteries, light bulbs, and accessories. The company has recently formed an E-commerce Department, with broad responsibilities to integrate its multiple e-commerce efforts to support the firm's future expansion.

POSITION: E-COMMERCE SPECIALIST

You will work with a team of employees in the E-commerce Department with the mission of coordinating multiple websites serving different product lines and market channels, and recommending new technologies to the firm, including cloud computing, Software-as-a-Service, mobile channel development, virtual reality techniques, and video tools. The company is looking for a person who is passionate about its business, with a knack for technology, the Internet, and mobile devices, and how they can be used in business. Responsibilities include:

- Introducing new applications of Internet, web, and mobile technology to other departments and preparing reports for their managers on new opportunities to apply these technologies to business opportunities and challenges.
- Collaborating with product line and marketing departments to develop a common understanding of the importance of an integrated online and mobile e-commerce presence.
- Working with franchise retail stores to inform them of new technology initiatives that the firm will be launching, preparing presentations to franchisees, and gathering feedback.
- Collaborating with the IT Department to develop more cost-effective e-commerce technology and enterprise platforms, including cloud computing infrastructure and Software-as-a-Service (SaaS).
- Developing strategic plans, roadmaps, and budgets to help guide the firm's e-commerce efforts over the next five years.

- Marketing and general Internet research.

QUALIFICATIONS/SKILLS

- Bachelor's degree in computer science, management information systems, and/or business administration, with e-commerce and digital marketing courses.
- Background understanding and experience with e-commerce, content management, and database-driven applications.
- Basic knowledge of Internet, web technology and mobile devices/platforms, and their use in e-commerce
- Demonstrated awareness of how the Internet and mobile platforms may change in the near future
- Basic knowledge of cloud computing, both hardware and software
- Basic knowledge and understanding of interactive media, tools, and technologies
- Ability to work with a variety of teams in IT, marketing, and supply chain management
- Excellent verbal and written communication skills
- Strong focus, self-discipline, and time management skills

PREPARING FOR THE INTERVIEW

To prepare for this interview, review Sections 2.1, 2.2, and 2.3 to make sure that you understand and are able to appropriately use the basic terminology that describes Internet/Web infrastructure. Pay particular attention to the material about cloud computing in Section 2.1, including being able to discuss the various services offered by Amazon Web Services (Table 2.4), as well as the material about wireless/mobile Internet access in both that section and Section 2.2. It would be helpful for you to be able to discuss forthcoming trends in e-commerce infrastructure detailed in Table 2.1. Be aware of trends such as the Internet of Things and be able to discuss its potential impact on the business. Finally, review Sections 2.4 and 2.5 so that you are able to discuss how Internet/Web technology is put to work to benefit a business. You should be familiar with all of the various software applications and tools discussed in those sections, ranging from mobile apps, to communication tools, search engines, different types of media, various Web 2.0 applications and services, as well as tools that are just starting to make their mark, such as virtual reality, augmented reality, and intelligent digital assistants.

POSSIBLE FIRST INTERVIEW QUESTIONS

1. Currently our e-commerce operations are spread across various product lines (batteries, lights, and industry power solutions) and different marketing channels. What ideas do you have for integrating these diverse web activities into a coherent online and mobile presence?

You could salute the efforts of the firm to bring all its e-commerce and online operations into a single e-commerce department. Bringing all the major e-commerce players in the company together and having them collaborate on a company policy seems to be a good starting point. It is important to develop a consistent online brand.

2. We're using smartphones for everything from store checkout, to customer management, to logistics. But we don't really have a consumer-oriented mobile strategy. How do you suggest we develop mobile into a consumer sales tool?

You might inquire about the percentage of the company's sales that originate from mobile devices. The future is increasingly mobile. Most consumer purchases are still done with desktop, laptops, and tablets, but mobile devices now account for more and more search and browsing activities. The firm should focus on developing its mobile search capabilities, and build mobile sites and/or a mobile app that allow users to browse and purchase the company's products.

3. What ideas do you have for applying the Internet of Things (IoT) to our business?

One possibility is to have sensors record the movements of customers in stores, and suggest purchase opportunities based on the customers' store location—a kind of very local geo-marketing. Perhaps certain products could have sensors built into them and be capable of sending data, such as battery charge levels, back to the firm's data centers. Consumers could be alerted to when their batteries are losing the ability to recharge and therefore should be replaced.

4. Currently we have most of our computer operations located in a company data center. The software we use for logistics, supply chain management, and customer data is a collection of software tools developed over many years. What suggestions do you have for using cloud computing and Software-as-a-Service?

You can note that cloud computing comes in a variety of forms, and that there are multiple vendors. Cloud computing includes renting infrastructure, software, database, and networking services. In almost all cases, a firm can reduce its infrastructure costs and get to market much faster than when operating its own data centers.

5. How can we use video and streaming media to connect with our retail customers?

You could remark that video is becoming almost as important as text for developing a brand and attracting customers. The firm should consider building a YouTube channel to market its products, and show people how to use the products. What kinds of YouTube business videos have you experienced, and why did you find them helpful?

2.7 CASE STUDY

Akamai Technologies:
Attempting to Keep Supply Ahead of Demand

In 2019, the amount of Internet traffic generated by YouTube alone was greater than the amount of traffic on the entire Internet in 2000. Because of video streaming and the explosion in mobile devices demanding high-bandwidth applications, Internet traffic has more than quadrupled since 2011 and is predicted to double from 2019 to 2022 (see **Figure 2.18**). Internet video is now a majority of Internet traffic and will reach over 82% by 2022, according to Cisco. Mobile platform traffic is expected to grow sevenfold between 2017 and 2022. Cisco estimates that annual global Internet traffic will be around 4.8 zettabytes in 2022: that's 4,800 exabytes, or, in other words, 48 with 19 zeroes behind it!

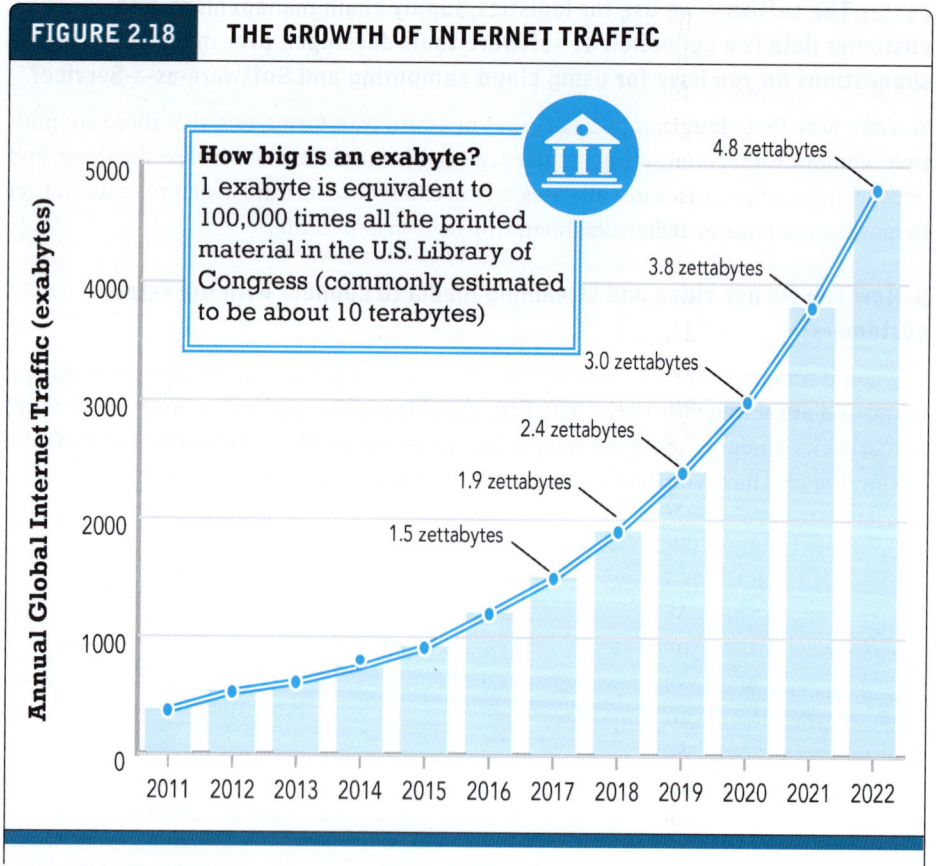

FIGURE 2.18 THE GROWTH OF INTERNET TRAFFIC

Sources: Based on data from Cisco, 2019.

In today's broadband environment, the threshold of patience is very low. Over 50% of mobile users will leave a page that takes more than three seconds to load. Increased video and audio customer expectations are bad news for anyone seeking to use the Web for delivery of high-quality multimedia content and high-definition video. Akamai is one of the Web's major helpers, and an overwhelming majority of the Web's top companies use Akamai's services to speed delivery of content. Akamai serves more than 30 terabits of web traffic per second.

Slow-loading web pages and content sometimes result from poor design, but more often than not, the problem stems from the underlying infrastructure of the Internet. The Internet is a collection of networks that has to pass information from one network to another. Sometimes the handoff is not smooth. Every 1,500-byte packet of information sent over the Internet must be verified by the receiving server and an acknowledgment sent to the sender. This slows down not only the distribution of content such as music, but also slows down interactive requests, such as purchases, that require the client computer to interact with an online shopping cart. Moreover, each packet may go through many different servers on its way to its final destination, multiplying by several orders of magnitude the number of acknowledgments required to move a packet from New York to San Francisco. The Internet today spends much of its time and capacity verifying packets, contributing to a problem called "latency" or delay. For this reason, a single e-mail with a 1-megabyte attached PDF file can create more than 50 megabytes of Internet traffic and data storage on servers, client hard drives, and network backup drives. Web page load times for desktops have also increased significantly as pages become laden with more content of various types. Load times increased by over 60% from 2013 to 2015 and have continued to rise since that time, further complicating content distribution.

Akamai Technologies was founded by Tom Leighton, an MIT professor of applied mathematics, and Daniel Lewin, an MIT grad student, with the idea of expediting Internet traffic to overcome these limitations. Lewin's master's thesis was the theoretical starting point for the company. It described storing copies of web content such as pictures or video clips at many different locations around the Internet so that one could always retrieve a nearby copy, making web pages load faster.

Officially launched in August 1998, Akamai's current products are based on its Akamai Intelligent Edge Platform, a cloud platform made up of approximately 265,000 servers in over 135 countries within nearly 1,500 networks around the world, and all within a single network hop of 85% of all Internet users. Akamai software on these servers allows the platform to identify and block security threats and provide comprehensive knowledge of network conditions, as well as instant device-level detection and optimization. Akamai's site performance products allow customers to move their online content closer to end users so a user in New York City, for instance, will be served L.L.Bean pages from the New York metro area Akamai servers, while users of the L.L.Bean site in San Francisco will be served pages from Akamai servers in San Francisco. Akamai has a wide range of large corporate and government clients: about 55% of Fortune Global 500 companies, 19 of the top 20 U.S. e-commerce retailers, 8 of the top 10 European e-commerce retailers, all of the top 5 travel websites, 7 of the top 10 largest global banks, and so on. In 2019, Akamai typically delivered more than 50 terabits per second (Tbps) in daily web traffic. In October 2019, it announced that traffic on its network had hit a new peak of 107 Tbps.

It also supported more than 25 million concurrent viewers of the 2019 Cricket World Cup, a new world record for live streaming.

Accomplishing this daunting task requires that Akamai monitor the entire Internet, locating potential sluggish areas and devising faster routes for information to travel. Frequently used portions of a client's website, or large video or audio files that would be difficult to send to users quickly, are stored on Akamai's servers. When a user requests a song or a video file, his or her request is redirected to an Akamai server nearby and the content is served from this local server. Akamai's servers are placed in Tier 1 backbone supplier networks, large ISPs, universities, and other networks. Akamai's software determines which server is optimal for the user and then transmits the content locally. Web sites that are "Akamaized" can be delivered anywhere from 4 to 10 times as fast as non-Akamaized content. In 2018, Akamai released an improved Image Manager tool, which automates image conversion of large image files to speed load times on image-heavy webpages, as part of a partnership with the BigCommerce e-commerce platform. Akamai has developed a number of other business services based on its Internet savvy, including targeted advertising based on user location and zip code, content security, business intelligence, disaster recovery, on-demand bandwidth and computing capacity during spikes in Internet traffic, storage, global traffic management, and streaming services. Akamai announced it would launch a blockchain-based payment network for credit cards and other financial transactions. The network is expected to perform one million transactions per second at latencies of less than two seconds, which compares very favorably to Bitcoin's seven transactions per second and latency of sixty minutes per transaction.

The shift toward cloud computing and the mobile platform as well as the growing popularity of streaming video have provided Akamai with new growth opportunities. As more businesses and business models are moving to the Web, Akamai has seen its client base continue to grow beyond the most powerful Internet retailers and online content providers.

However, the growth of streaming video has also created new challenges for Akamai, including increased competition from Comcast and Amazon, which have built competing content delivery services as well as Amazon's Cloudfront content delivery network. Many of Akamai's largest clients, including Apple, Facebook, Google, Microsoft, and Netflix, are also increasingly shifting their content delivery operations away from Akamai's platforms and onto in-house content delivery networks. Amazon in particular continues to make inroads against Akamai in addition to bringing its own content delivery nearly entirely in-house. Other competitors in content delivery, such as Cloudflare, Fastly, and StackPath, also represent threats to Akamai's continued dominance.

Akamai is also acutely aware of the increase in cybercrime as more traffic migrates to the Internet. Growth in Internet traffic is good news for Akamai, but the company must also now deal with politically motivated cyberattacks, organized crime online, and state-sponsored cyberwarfare, not just against its clients, but against CDNs like Akamai itself. Akamai has continued to improve its Kona Site Defender tool, which offers a variety of security measures for Akamai clients. The tool protects against Distributed Denial of Service (DDoS) attacks and includes a firewall for web applications. In 2018, Akamai rolled out new improvements to Kona's ability to automate app security. With DDoS attacks against CDNs on the rise, Akamai has also taken precautions to ensure that it can

SOURCES: "Facts & Figures," Akamai.com, accessed December 2, 2019; "Akamai Reaches New Milestone for Web Traffic Delivered, Akamai.com, October 21, 2019; "Akamai, Mitsubishi UFJ Financial Announce Blockchain-based Payment Network," by Asha McLean, Zdnet.com, May 22, 2018; "Akamai Announces New Enhancements to World's Largest and Most Trusted Cloud Delivery Platform," Prnewswire.com, April 16, 2018; "BigCommerce Begins Offering Akamai Image Optimization Tool to Sellers," by Natalie Gagliordi, Zdnet.com, January 30, 2018; "Discontent and Disruption in the World of Content Delivery Networks," by Mahendra Ramsinghani, Techcrunch.com, June 1, 2017; Michael Kerner, "Akamai CSO Detailers Cyber-Security Challenges and Improvements," Eweek.com, May 15, 2017; "Akamai Buys Software Startup Soasta," by Natalie Gagliordi, Zdnet.com, March 29, 2017; "Akamai Security Business Shines, Offsets Apple, Facebook Shift," by Reinhardt Krause, *Investor's Business Daily*, October 26, 2016; "Amazon, Comcast Content Delivery Network Push Could Hurt

withstand an attack against its infrastructure. With so many businesses now dependent on the uninterrupted flow of content over the Internet, Akamai is in a very strong position to sell security services and analytics to its customers. Akamai has partnered with security companies such as Trustwave and China Unicom to sell products jointly and has also set itself up for future growth by moving into areas of the world with less developed broadband infrastructure, such as the Middle East. In 2017, Akamai acquired SOASTA, whose flagship product, CloudTest, allows companies to test and analyze the performance of their websites and website applications and is used by Apple, Target, and Walmart. The move will add a valuable new offering to Akamai's Web Performance Solutions group of tools. In 2019, it acquired Exceda, Akamai's largest channel partner in Latin America.

The improvements in Akamai's security businesses have offset much of the slowdown in its content delivery business. Akamai's Cloud Security Solutions business segment grew 36% in 2018. In 2019, increases in revenues from its Cloud Security Solutions division continued to drive Akamai's performance, enabling it to beat Wall Street estimates and raise its overall revenue forecasts.

Akamai," by Reinhardt Krause, Investors.com, May 11, 2016; "Google and Akamai Partner on Speeding Up Cloud Network," by Steven J. Vaughan-Nichols, Zdnet.com, November 20, 2015; "Microsoft and Akamai Bring CDN to Azure Customers," by Sudheer Sirivara, Azure.microsoft.com, September 29, 2015; "Akamai, Trustwave to Promote, Sell Each Other's Security Services," by Sean Michael Kerner, Eweek.com, June 1, 2015; "Akamai and China Unicom Establish Strategic Cloud Services Partnership," Akamai.com, May 26, 2015; "To Cash In on Wave of Web Attacks, Akamai Launches Standalone Security Business," by Andy Greenberg, Forbes.com, February 21, 2012.

Case Study Questions

1. Why does Akamai need to geographically disperse its servers to deliver its customers' web content?

2. If you wanted to deliver software content over the Internet, would you sign up for Akamai's service? Why or why not?

3. Do you think Internet users should be charged based on the amount of bandwidth they consume, or on a tiered plan where users would pay in rough proportion to their usage?

2.8 REVIEW

KEY CONCEPTS

- Discuss the origins of, and the key technology concepts behind, the Internet.
  - The Internet has evolved from a collection of mainframe computers located on a few U.S. college campuses to an interconnected network of thousands of networks and millions of computers worldwide.
  - The history of the Internet can be divided into three phases: the Innovation Phase (1961–1974), the Institutionalization Phase (1975–1995), and the Commercialization Phase (1995 to the present).
  - Packet switching, TCP/IP, and client/server technology are key technology concepts behind the Internet.
  - The mobile platform has become the primary means for accessing the Internet.

- Cloud computing refers to a model of computing in which firms and individuals obtain computing power and software applications over the Internet, rather than purchasing the hardware and software and installing it on their own computers.
- Internet protocols and utility programs such as BGP, HTTP, SMTP and POP, SSL and TLS, FTP, Telnet, Ping, and Tracert provide a number of Internet services.

■ **Explain the current structure of the Internet.**

- The main structural elements of the Internet are the backbone (composed primarily of high-bandwidth fiber optic cable), IXPs (hubs that use high-speed switching computers to connect to the backbone), CANs (campus/corporate area networks), ISPs (which deal with Internet access of service to homes and offices), and the mobile platform, which provides Internet access via cellular telephone networks and Wi-Fi networks.
- The Internet of Things (IoT) builds on a foundation of existing technologies, such as RFID tags, low-cost sensors, inexpensive data storage, big data analytics software, and IPv6, to power the development of a host of smart connected "things."
- *Governing bodies*, such as IAB, ICANN, IESG, IETF, ISOC, and W3C, have influence over the Internet and monitor its operations, although they do not control it.

■ **Understand how the Web works.**

- The Web was developed during 1989–1991 by Dr. Tim Berners-Lee, who created a computer program that allowed formatted pages stored on the Internet to be linked using keywords (hyperlinks). In 1993, Marc Andreessen created the first graphical web browser, which made it possible to view documents on the Web graphically and created the possibility of universal computing.
- The key concepts you need to be familiar with in order to understand how the Web works are hypertext, HTTP, URLs, HTML, CSS, XML, web server software, web clients, and web browsers.

■ **Describe how Internet and web features and services support e-commerce.**

- Together, the Internet and the Web make e-commerce possible by allowing computer users to access product and service information and to complete purchases online.
- Some of the specific features that support e-commerce include communication tools such as e-mail, messaging applications, online message boards, Internet telephony, video conferencing, video chatting, and telepresence; search engines; and downloadable and streaming media.
- Web 2.0 applications and services include social networks, blogs, and wikis.
- Virtual reality, augmented reality, and artificial intelligence technologies have begun to enter the consumer market and attract significant attention.

■ **Understand the impact of mobile applications.**

- The mobile app phenomenon has spawned a new digital ecosystem.
- Smartphone and tablet users spend the majority of their time using mobile apps rather than the mobile Web.
- There are a variety of different platforms for mobile application development including Swift and Objective-C for iOS devices and Java (and C and C++ for certain elements) for Android smartphone devices.
- Mobile apps for the iPhone are distributed through Apple's App Store and for Android devices through Google Play. There are also third-party vendors such as Amazon's Appstore.

QUESTIONS

1. What advantages does client/server computing have over mainframe computing?
2. What are three different types of cloud computing models that have been developed?
3. Why is packet switching so essential to the Internet?

4. What are four Internet protocols besides HTTP (the Web) and sending e-mail (SMTP)?
5. What are the three main phases in the evolution of the Internet? Briefly describe each.
6. How does virtual reality differ from augmented reality?
7. Why is VoIP considered to be a disruptive technology?
8. How is Microsoft aiming to provide Internet access to remote areas?
9. Identify the various types of narrowband and broadband ISP Internet connections. Of all, which is the fastest and which is the slowest?
10. What is the Internet of Things and how is it being created and enabled?
11. Explain what domain names, URLs, and IP addresses are and provide an example of each. How are they used when a user is browsing the Web?
12. How does 5G differ from 4G?
13. How does HTTP/2 improve on HTTP? Why isn't it being used by more websites?
14. Identify the layers used in Internet technology. What is their importance to Internet communications?
15. Why does the mobile platform have profound implications for e-commerce?
16. What is the difference between Tier 1, Tier 2, and Tier 3 Internet Service Providers?
17. What are three concerns about the Internet of Things?
18. What is the difference between HTML and XML?
19. What is podcasting?
20. What are the implications of the app ecosystem for e-commerce?

PROJECTS

1. Review the *Insight on Business* case on Apple Watch. What developments have occurred since this case was written in December 2019?

2. Call or visit the websites of a cable provider, a DSL provider, and a satellite provider to obtain information on their Internet services. Prepare a brief report summarizing the features, benefits, and costs of each. Which is the fastest? What, if any, are the downsides of selecting any of the three for Internet service (such as additional equipment purchases)?

3. Select two countries (excluding the United States) and prepare a short report describing their basic Internet infrastructure. Are they public or commercial? How and where do they connect to backbones within the United States?

4. Investigate the Internet of Things. Select one example and describe what it is and how it works.

REFERENCES

Akamai Inc. "IPV6 Adoption Visualization." (accessed November 20, 2019).

Alleven, Monica. "Microsoft Keeps White Spaces on the Front Burner." Fiercewireless.com (June 7, 2018).

Arstechnica.com. "Capitol Hill, The Internet, and Broadband: An Ars Technica Quarterly Report." (September 2010).

Bar, Ofir Eyal. "The Current State of the VoIP Market." Benzinga.com (August 7, 2019).

Berners-Lee, Tim, Robert Cailliau, Ari Luotonen, Henrik Frystyk Nielsen, and Arthur Secret. "The World Wide Web." *Communications of the ACM* (August 1994).

Bluetooth SIG, Inc. "Bluetooth Technology." (Accessed November 21, 2019).

Bott, Ed. "As the PC Market Continues to Shrink Slowly, Guess Which OEMs Are Still Thriving?," Zdnet.com (January 24, 2019).

Brandt, Richard. "Net Assets: How Stanford's Computer Science Department Changed the Way We Get Information." *Stanford Magazine* (November/December 2004).

Brodkin, Jon. "50 Million US Homes Have Only One 25Mbps Internet Provider or None at All." Arstechnica.com (June 30, 2017).

BuddeCom. "BuddeCom Intelligence Report—Global OTT VoIP and Mobile Messaging Services Market." (June 27, 2018).

Bush, Vannevar. "As We May Think." *Atlantic Monthly* (July 1945).

Cable.co.uk. "Worldwide Broadband Speed League 2019." (Accessed November 21, 2019).

Cerf, V., and R. Kahn, "A Protocol for Packet Network Intercommunication." *IEEE Transactions on Communications*, Vol. COM-22, No. 5, pp. 637–648 (May 1974).

Cisco. "Cisco Visual Networking Index: Forecast and Trends, 2017–2022." (February 27, 2019).

Columbus, Louis. "2018 Roundup of Internet of Things Forecasts and Market Estimates." Forbes.com (December 13, 2018).

comScore, Inc. "Explicit Core Search Share Report July 2018." (September 2018).

comScore, Inc. "Exolicit Core Search Query Report July 2018." (September 2018b).

Craig, Caroline. "Sorry ISPs: The FCC Finally Has the Dopes on the Ropes." Infoworld.com (June 17, 2016).

D'Onfro, Jillian. "Alphabet Spins Drone and Internet Balloon Projects into Independent Companies." Cnn.com (July 11, 2018).

Durairajan, Ramakrishnan, Paul Barford, Joel Sommers, and Walter Willinger. "InterTubes: A Study of the US Long-haul Fiber-optic Infrastructure." SIGCOMM '15 (August 17–21, 2015).

Edison Research. "The Podcast Consumer 2019." (April 5, 2019).

eMarketer, Inc. "Internet Users and Penetration Worldwide." (April 2019a).

eMarketer, Inc. "Mobile Phone Internet Users and Penetration, Worldwide." (April 2019b).

eMarketer, Inc., "Mobile Phone Messaging App Users, by Country." (November 2019c).

eMarketer, Inc. "Mobile Phone Messaging App User Penetration, by Country." (November 2019d).

eMarketer, Inc. "US Search Users and Penetration." (March 2019e).

eMarketer, Inc. "Digital Video Viewers by Country." (August 2019f).

eMarketer, Inc. "US Augmented Reality Users." (March 2019g).

eMarketer, Inc. "US Virtual Reality Users." (March 2019h).

eMarketer, Inc. "Retail Mcommerce Sales, by Country." (October 2019i).

eMarketer, Inc., "US Bloggers and Penetration, 2015–2020." (August 3, 2016a).

eMarketer, Inc. "US Blog Readers and Penetration, 2015–2020." (August 3, 2016b).

Federal Communications Commission. "FCC Finds U.S. Broadband Deployment Not Keeping Pace." (January 29, 2015).

Federal Networking Council. "FNC Resolution: Definition of 'Internet.'" (October 24, 1995).

Gartner, Inc. "Gartner Forecasts Worldwide Public Cloud Revenue to Grow 17% in 2020." (November 19, 2019a).

Gartner, Inc. "Gartner Says Global End-User Spending on Wearable Devices to Total $52 Billion in 2020." (October 30, 2019).

Grieg, Jonathan. "Can Skype Still Please Its Consumer Users As It Embraces Business." Download.cnet.com (February 18, 2019).

Gross, Grant. "NSF Seeks Ambitious Next-Generation Internet Project." *Computerworld* (August 29, 2005).

IDC. "Worldwide Smartphone Forecast Update, 2019–2023." (June 2019).

IEEE Computer Society. "Top Trends for 2013." (2013).

Internet Corporation for Assigned Names and Numbers (ICANN). "ICANN Approves Historic Change to Internet's Domain System." (June 20, 2011a).

Internet Corporation for Assigned Names and Numbers (ICANN). "Top-Level Domains (gTLDs)." (2011b).

Internet Engineering Task Force (IETF). "RFC 7540: Hypertext Transfer Protocol Version 2 (HTTP/2)." (May 2015).

Internet Society. "The Internet of Things: An Overview." (October 2015).

Internet Society. "World IPv6 Launch on June 6, 2012, To Bring Permanent IPv6 Deployment." (January 2012).

Internet Society. "ISOC's Standards Activities." (September 2010).

Internet Society. "RFC 2616: Hypertext Transfer Protocol-HTTP/1.1." (June 1999).

Internet Society. "RFC 0959: File Transfer Protocol." (October, 1985).

Kang, Cecilia. "To Close Digital Divide, Microsoft to Harness Unused Television Channels." *New York Times* (July 11, 2017).

Kleinrock, Leonard. *1964 Communication Nets: Stochastic Message Flow and Delay*. New York: McGraw-Hill (1964).

Leiner, Barry M., Vinton G. Cerf, David D. Clark, Robert E. Kahn, Leonard Kleinrock, Daniel C. Lynch, Jon Postel, Larry G. Roberts, and Stephen Wolff. "All About the Internet: A Brief History of the Internet." *Internet Society* (ISOC) (August 2000).

Matsakis, Louise. "Facebook Confirms Its Working on a New Internet Satellite." Wired.com (July 20, 2018).

Merriman, Chris. "Google's Project Loon Is About to Start Commercial Testing," Theinquirer.net (July 2, 2019).

National Research Foundation. "NSP Leadership in Discovery and Initiative Sparks White House US Ignite Initiative." (June 13, 2012).

NCTA.com "The Future of Super Fast Internet is 10G." (accessed December 2, 2019).

Netcraft. "October 2019 Web Server Survey." (October 24, 2019).

Netmarketshare. "Desktop Browser Market Share." Marketshare.hitslink.com. (Accessed November 22, 2019a).

Netmarketshare. "Mobile Browser Market Share." Marketshare.hitslink.com. (Accessed November 22, 2019b).

NPD Group. "Seven Percent Compound Annual Growth Expected for Internet-Connected TV Devices in the U.S. Through 2021, Forecasts NPD." Npd.com (September 6, 2018).

Perez, Sarah. "Skype/s Big Redesign Publicly Launches to Desktop Users." Techcrunch.com (October 30, 2017).

Pfanner, Eric. "Ethics Fight Over Domain Names Intensifies." *New York Times* (March 18, 2012).

Podtrac, Inc. "Podcast Industry Ranking Highlights, Top 10 Podcast Publishers, US Audience: October 2019." (accessed November 22, 2019).

Radicati Group. Email Statistics Report, 2019–2023—Executive Summary." (February 2019).

Ranger, Steven. "What Is the IoT? Everything You Need to Know About the Internet of Things Right Now." Zdnet.com (August 21, 2018).

Reisinger, Don. "Alphabet's Loon Just Beamed the Internet Over 621 Miles." Fortune.com (September 11, 2018).

Research and Markets. "Smart Home Market by Product (Lighting Control, Security & Access Control, HVAC, Entertainment, Smart Speaker, Home Healthcare, Smart Kitchen, Home Appliances, and Smart Furniture), Software & Services, and Region - Global Forecast to 2024." (January 2019).

Scott, Terri. "How Amazon Outmuscled Google for eRetail Product Search Results." Ecommerceinsiders.com (February 20, 2017).

Simonite, Tom. "First Detailed Public Map of U.S. Internet Backbone Could Make It Stronger." Technologyreview.com (September 15, 2015).

Singer, Hal, Ed Naef, and Alex King. "Assessing the Impact of Removing Regulatory Barriers on Next Generation Wireless and Wireline Broadband Infrastructure Investment." Economists Incorporated (June 2017).

Tam, Pui-Wing. "Daily Report: A Technology to Close the Digital Divide." *New York Times* (July 11, 2017).

U.S. Department of Commerce. "Letter to ICANN Chairman." Ntia.doc.gov (July 30, 2008).

Verisign. "The Verisign Domain Name Industry Brief Q2 2019." (Accessed November 22, 2019).

W3Techs.com. "Usage of HTTP/2 for Websites." (Accessed November 21, 2019).

Westgarth, Alastair. "Helping Out in Peru." Blog.x.company (May 17, 2017).

Zakon, Robert H. "Hobbes' Internet Timeline v8.1." Zakon.org (2005).

Ziff-Davis Publishing. "Ted Nelson: Hypertext Pioneer." Techtv.com (1998).

CHAPTER 3

Building an E-commerce Presence

LEARNING OBJECTIVES

After reading this chapter, you will be able to:

- Understand the questions you must ask and answer, and the steps you should take, in developing an e-commerce presence.
- Explain the process that should be followed in building an e-commerce presence.
- Identify and understand the major considerations involved in choosing web server and e-commerce merchant server software.
- Understand the issues involved in choosing the most appropriate hardware for an e-commerce site.
- Identify additional tools that can improve website performance.
- Understand the important considerations involved in developing a mobile website and building mobile applications.

Scratch Builds an E-commerce Presence

From "Scratch"

Building an e-commerce presence from "scratch" can seem like a daunting task. But that's the challenge that Mike Halligan and Doug Spiegelhauer took on when they decided to band together to create an Australian-based dog food subscription service, aptly named Scratch.

Halligan originally had the idea for the company when his family dog fell ill and he began to research foods to help improve her quality of life. He found that the dog food market was confusing, poorly regulated, and overpriced. This type of revelation is repeated often in the founding stories of many e-commerce companies.

Halligan's background was in marketing, initially creating customized blogs for clients that weren't able to pay the prices charged by major marketers and then running an e-commerce agency that worked with brands on e-commerce strategy. He also spent time as a general manager for The 5th, a direct-to-consumer e-commerce brand selling watches, bags, and frames. Although Halligan had ample experience in digital marketing, he lacked first-hand experience in the pet food industry. While researching the way dog food ingredients were developed and labeled on packaging, he met Spiegelhauer, who ran a company in the pet food industry.

The state of the dog food market in Australia was ripe for disruption. Regulation of the industry is nearly nonexistent. In fact, there are laws that absolve pet food companies of the obligation to disclose how much of each ingredient listed on the packaging actually goes into the food. Ingredients like gelling agents, coloring agents, and processed cereals are routinely found in dog food, and many companies remove grains to achieve the 'grain-free' designation, but instead substitute less healthy products. The markup for pet food was roughly 80%, with only 10% to 15% of the final retail price representing the actual ingredients used to make the food. Consumers have been long uneasy, with major pet food brands earning poor marks for trustworthiness. Furthermore, only 5% of pet food sales in Australia were taking place online at the time Scratch was founded, presenting a tremendous opportunity.

The direct-to-consumer e-commerce business model, which allows a company to bypass traditional distribution pathways, avoiding the inevitable price markups that occur at each point in the supply chain, has seen a number of major successes in the past several years. Consumers reap the benefits, saving money without having to sacrifice product quality. Depending on the type of product offered, a direct-to-consumer e-commerce company may offer individual purchases of items, or it may instead be a subscription service, where customers receive products on a regular basis, typically monthly. Given the rapid emergence of this business model, many other startups are seeking to replicate this type of success. Halligan and Spiegelhauer saw a golden opportunity to seize on that customer dissatisfaction and create a direct-to-consumer alternative that dog lovers would appreciate. Australia also happens to have 4.8 million dogs, more dogs per capita than any other place on the planet.

Halligan and Spiegelhauer launched Scratch in early 2018 with three overarching goals. First, they wanted to eliminate the secrecy seemingly omnipresent in the dog food industry. Second, they wanted to bring an element of joy and fun to their customers' experience buying dog food—in short, to "make customers smile." Lastly, they wanted to be an environmentally friendly business however possible, both in the materials and ingredients used. Scratch uses the savings it obtains from shipping direct-to-consumer to offer ethically sourced kangaroo meat, broad beans and chickpeas, omega-3 salmon oil for brain and joint health as well as shinier coats of fur, and other essential vitamins and minerals.

Scratch's value proposition to Australian consumers was simple—buying pet food the traditional way pales in comparison to receiving a much better product shipped directly to your door with superior customer service. Scratch started with enough capital investment to operate for a year, offering just one product to customers in its home city of Melbourne. The company has since grown to Sydney, Brisbane, Adelaide, and Canberra, and is developing a second product geared for large dog breed puppies.

Scratch prepared for its launch by creating an online quiz to test whether dog owners knew what was in their current pet food, with the hope that once pet owners realized how unhealthy some of the ingredients included in existing brands might be, they would see the value in Scratch as an alternative. They also put out a casting call for dogs in Melbourne to use in its advertising. In the process, Scratch gained a valuable list of contacts for future marketing efforts. It also has plans for lighthearted local events, such as a partnership with dating service Bumble for mixers where single dog owners can meet; this is consistent with the founders' second goal of creating fun experiences for their customers.

Scratch had some tough choices to make with its e-commerce setup. The company knew it wanted to offer a subscription service, but providing the same amount of food to all dogs each month didn't make sense. Instead, Scratch wanted to allow dog owners to customize their subscription frequency based on their dog's precise nutritional requirements. A large dog, for example, might need a new box of food every 20 days; a smaller dog might need one every 60 days. In the world of subscription services, this type of arrangement is extremely unusual, requiring Scratch to develop an e-commerce platform that could provide these highly customizable subscription options.

For that reason, Scratch ultimately settled on WordPress and WooCommerce to provide its marketing and e-commerce functions. Many businesses choose Shopify for e-commerce due to its ease of use, but it lacked the customizability that Scratch required as a result of its unusual variable-frequency subscription model. WooCommerce was founded in 2008 by three WordPress enthusiasts who had shared ideas for commercial WordPress themes for years. The company is now a major e-commerce player that powers 30% of all online stores and had already been downloaded over 10 million times prior to the company's purchase by Automattic, the company that owns and operates WordPress.

WooCommerce Subscriptions' customizability allows Scratch to offer individualized subscription plans based on the weight, age, and activity level of each dog. Scratch's standard 7.5kg box is then sent at a fixed interval to the customer, but WooCommerce also offers the option to send highly targeted e-mails to these customers; for example, after a customer's first order, they receive an e-mail explaining how the system works and when they're going to get a new box; once they renew and order a second time, they receive a different, more streamlined e-mail. Customers receive options that allow them to delay orders based on the quantity of food remaining. An Australian company named Metorik, also based out of Melbourne, provides further customizability to WooCommerce, allowing Scratch to dive deep into company data to answer questions about how customers differ in purchasing habits from city to city; for example, the company can find out how their average subscription frequencies differ in their more suburban markets compared to urban centers like Melbourne.

WooCommerce allowed Scratch to set up its warehouse integration immediately and seamlessly. When Scratch receives orders, the company doesn't actively manage them; instead, its food manufacturer is automatically prompted to make more food using Scratch's precise recipe, orders are automatically filled at the company's warehouse, and they are shipped directly to the consumer. Although much of the savings from the direct-to-consumer model were used to improve the ingredients of the food, they're also used for environmentally-friendly and attractive packaging. The box zips tight to preserve the smell and nutrition of the food, and WooCommerce even allows the company to customize its packaging with each dog's name on the box.

The automation of order fulfillment allows Scratch to focus much more time on customer service and customer retention efforts. Scratch plans to allow live customer service chat via WooCommerce using Facebook Messenger or Intercom in the near future. Scratch also does Facebook retargeting when a potential customer adds a product to their cart but doesn't buy it, YouTube marketing, and search engine optimization for specific searches indicating a high degree of involvement in pets' well-being, such as "pet daycare" or "pet hotel." The company also devotes significant energy to their social media presence. The company's Facebook page already has 2,000 followers and its Instagram feed has over 11,000, which makes sense given how popular dogs and pets in general can be on such a visual platform. Scratch's Instagram feed features dogs happily greeting their shipments of Scratch food, dog-themed jokes and tweets, and positive customer testimonials. The company website features a simplistic, fun design, with a whimsical sense of humor.

Halligan and Spiegelhauer hope that their company continues to grow, but they plan on doing so responsibly and sustainably. These values are what differentiate the company from its large competitors in the dog food market and may yet make them the latest direct-to-consumer e-commerce company to become a customer's best friend.

SOURCES: "About," Woocommerce.com/accessed December 2019; "Mike Halligan," Michaelhalligan.com.au/scratch-dog-food, accessed December 2019; "About," Scratchpetfood.com.au/about, accessed December 2019; "GoDaddy Gives Merchants Online Boost with WooCommerce Integration," Pymnts.com, October 22, 2019; "Scratch: Subscription Dog Food Ruffling up the Pet Food Industry," by Eric Berkhinfand, Metorik.com, August 6, 2019; "Dog Lovers Assemble: You Need This New Subscription Service," Theurbanlist.com, June 24, 2019; "Scratch Case Study: Changing The Dry Pet Food Business For The Better," by Marina Pape, woocommerce.com, November 2018; "Woof! Why Scratch Is the Must-Try Dog Food for your Mate," Ellaslist.com, November 29, 2018; Gina Baldassarre, "Melbourne's Scratch Has Created a Dog Food Subscription Service for 'Pet Parents,'" Startupdaily.net, November 28, 2018.

In Chapter 2, you learned about e-commerce's technological foundation: the Internet, the Web, and the mobile platform. In this chapter, you will examine the important factors that a manager needs to consider when building an e-commerce presence. The focus will be on the managerial and business decisions you must make before you begin, and that you will continually need to make. Although building a sophisticated e-commerce presence isn't easy, today's tools are much less expensive and far more powerful than they were during the early days of e-commerce. At the same time, the proliferation of mobile devices and social networks adds complexity because firms need to build a presence on three platforms: the Web, mobile, and social networks. In this chapter, we focus on both small and medium-sized businesses as well as much larger corporate entities that serve thousands of customers a day, or even an hour. As you will see, although the scale may be very different, the principles and considerations are basically the same.

3.1 IMAGINE YOUR E-COMMERCE PRESENCE

Before you begin to build a website or app of your own, there are some important questions you will need to think about and answer. The answers to these questions will drive the development and implementation of your e-commerce presence.

WHAT'S THE IDEA? (THE VISIONING PROCESS)

Before you can plan and actually build an e-commerce presence, you need to have a vision of what you hope to accomplish and how you hope to accomplish it. The vision includes not just a statement of mission, but also identification of the target audience, characterization of the market space, a strategic analysis, a marketing matrix, and a development timeline. It starts with a dream of what's possible, and concludes with a timeline and preliminary budget for development.

If you examine any successful website, you can usually tell from the home page what the vision that inspires the site is. If the company is a public company, you can often find a succinct statement of its vision or mission in the reports it files with the Securities and Exchange Commission. For Amazon, it's to become the largest marketplace on earth. For Facebook, it's to make the world more open and connected. For Google, it's to organize the world's information and make it universally accessible and useful. The e-commerce presence you want to build may not have such all-encompassing ambitions, but a succinct statement of mission, purpose, and direction is the key factor in driving the development of your project. For instance, the mission of TheKnot is to be the Internet's comprehensive, one-stop wedding planning solution.

WHERE'S THE MONEY: BUSINESS AND REVENUE MODEL

Once you have defined a mission statement, a vision, you need to start thinking about where the money will be coming from. You will need to develop a preliminary idea of your business and revenue models. You don't need detailed revenue and cost projections at this point. Instead, you need a general idea of how your business will generate revenues. The basic choices will be described in Chapter 5. Basic business models include portal, e-tailer, content provider, transaction broker, market creator, service provider, and community provider (social network).

The basic revenue model alternatives are advertising, subscriptions, transaction fees, sales, and affiliate revenue. There's no reason to adopt a single business or revenue model, and in fact, many firms have multiple models. For instance, the *Financial Times* digital business model is to both sell subscriptions and sell ad space. In addition, it sells unique photographs and gifts. At TheKnot, a vertical portal for the wedding industry, you will find ads, affiliate relationships, and sponsorships from major creators of wedding products and services, including a directory to local wedding planners, all of which produce revenue for TheKnot. PetSmart, the most popular pet website in the United States, has a more focused sales revenue model, and presents itself almost entirely as an e-tailer of pet supplies.

WHO AND WHERE IS THE TARGET AUDIENCE?

Without a clear understanding of your target audience, you will not have a successful e-commerce presence. There are two questions here: who is your target audience and where can you best reach them? Your target audience can be described in a number of ways: demographics, behavior patterns (lifestyle), current consumption patterns (online vs. offline purchasing), digital usage patterns, content creation preferences (blogs, social networks, sites like Pinterest), and buyer personas (profiles of your typical customer). Understanding the demographics of your target audience is usually the first step. Demographic information includes age, income, gender, and location. In some cases, this may be obvious, and in others, much less so. For instance, Harley-Davidson sells motorcycles to a very broad demographic range of varying ages, incomes, and locations, from 34-year-olds to 65-year-olds. Although most of the purchasers are middle-aged men, with middle incomes, many of the men ride with women, and the Harley-Davidson website has a collection of women's clothing and several web pages devoted to women riders. While the majority of men who purchase Harley-Davidsons have modest incomes, a significant group of purchasers are professionals with above-average incomes. Hence, the age and income demographic target is quite broad. What ties Harley-Davidson riders together is not their shared demographics, but their love of the motorcycles and the brand, and the lifestyle associated with touring the highways of America on a powerful motorcycle that sounds like a potato popper. In contrast, a company like TheKnot is aimed at women in the 18-year-old to 34-year-old demographic who are in varying stages of getting married, with lifestyles that include shopping online, using smartphones and tablets, downloading apps, and using Facebook. This audience is technologically hip. These women read and contribute to blogs, comment on forums, and use Pinterest to find ideas for fashion. A "typical" visitor to TheKnot would be a 28-year-old woman who has an engagement ring, is just starting the wedding planning process, has an income of $45,000, lives in the Northeast, and is interested in a beach wedding. There are, of course, other "typical" profiles. For each profile for your website you will need to develop a detailed description.

WHAT IS THE BALLPARK? CHARACTERIZE THE MARKETPLACE

The chances of your success will depend greatly on the characteristics of the market you are about to enter, and not just on your entrepreneurial brilliance. Enter into a declining market filled with strong competitors, and you will multiply your chances of failure. Enter into a market that is emerging, growing, and has few competitors, and you stand a better chance. Enter a market where there are no players, and you will either be rewarded handsomely with a profitable monopoly on a successful product no one else thought of (Apple) or you will be quickly forgotten because there isn't a market for your product at this point in time (the Franklin e-book reader circa 1999).

Features of the marketplace to focus on include the demographics of the market and how an e-commerce presence fits into the market. In addition, you will want to know about the structure of the market: competitors and substitute products.

What are the features of the marketplace you are about to enter? Is the market growing, or receding in size? If it's growing, among which age and income groups? Is the marketplace shifting from offline to online delivery? If so, is the market moving toward traditional websites, mobile, and/or tablets? Is there a special role for a mobile presence in this market? What percentage of your target audience uses a website, smartphone, or tablet? What about social networks? What's the buzz on products like yours? Are your potential customers talking about the products and services you want to offer on Facebook, Twitter, Pinterest, Instagram, or blogs? How many blogs focus on products like yours? How many Twitter posts mention similar offerings? How many Facebook Likes (signs of customer engagement) are attached to products you want to offer?

The structure of the market is described in terms of your direct competitors, suppliers, and substitute products. You will want to make a list of the top five or ten competitors and try to describe their market share, and distinguishing characteristics. Some of your competitors may offer traditional versions of your products, while others will offer new renditions or versions of products that have new features. You need to find out everything you can about your competitors. What's the market buzz on your competitors? How many unique monthly visitors (UMVs) do they have? How many Facebook Likes, Twitter followers, and/or Pinterest followers? How are your competitors using social sites and mobile devices as a part of their online presence. Is there something special you could do with social networks that your competitors do not? Do a search on customer reviews of their products. You can find online services (some of them free) that will measure the number of online conversations about your competitors, and the total share of Internet voice each of your competitors receives. Do your competitors have a special relationship with their suppliers that you may not have access to? Exclusive marketing arrangements would be one example of a special supplier relationship. Finally, are there substitutes for your products and services? For instance, your site may offer advice to the community of pet owners, but local pet stores or local groups may be a more trusted source of advice on pets.

WHERE'S THE CONTENT COMING FROM?

Websites are like books: they're composed of a lot of pages that have content ranging from text, to graphics, photos, and videos. This content is what search engines catalog as they crawl through all the new and changed web pages on the Internet. The content is why your customers visit your site and either purchase things or look at ads that generate revenue for you. Therefore, the content is the single most important foundation for your revenue and ultimate success.

There are generally two kinds of content: static and dynamic. Static content is text and images that do not frequently change, such as product descriptions, photos, or text that you create to share with your visitors. Dynamic content is content that changes regularly, say, daily or hourly. Dynamic content can be created by you, or increasingly, by bloggers and fans of your website and products. User-generated content has a number of advantages: it's free, it engages your customer fan base, and search engines are more likely to catalog your site if the content is changing. Other sources of content, especially photos, are external websites that aggregate content such as Pinterest, discussed in the closing case study in Chapter 1.

KNOW YOURSELF: CONDUCT A SWOT ANALYSIS

A **SWOT analysis** is a simple but powerful method for strategizing about your business and understanding where you should focus your efforts. In a SWOT analysis you describe your strengths, weaknesses, opportunities, and threats (SWOT). In the example SWOT analysis in **Figure 3.1**, you will see a profile of a typical startup venture that includes a unique approach to an existing market, a promise of addressing unmet needs in this market, and the use of newer technologies (social and mobile platforms) that older competitors may have overlooked. There are many opportunities to address a large market with unmet needs, as well as the potential to use the initial website as a home base and spin-off related or nearby sites, leveraging the investment in design and technology. But there are also weaknesses and threats. Lack of financial and human resources are typically the biggest weakness of startup companies. Threats include competitors that could develop the same capabilities as you, and low market entry costs, which might encourage many more startups to enter the marketplace.

Once you have conducted a SWOT analysis, you can consider ways to overcome your weaknesses and build on your strengths. For instance, you could consider hiring

SWOT analysis

describes a firm's strengths, weaknesses, opportunities, and threats

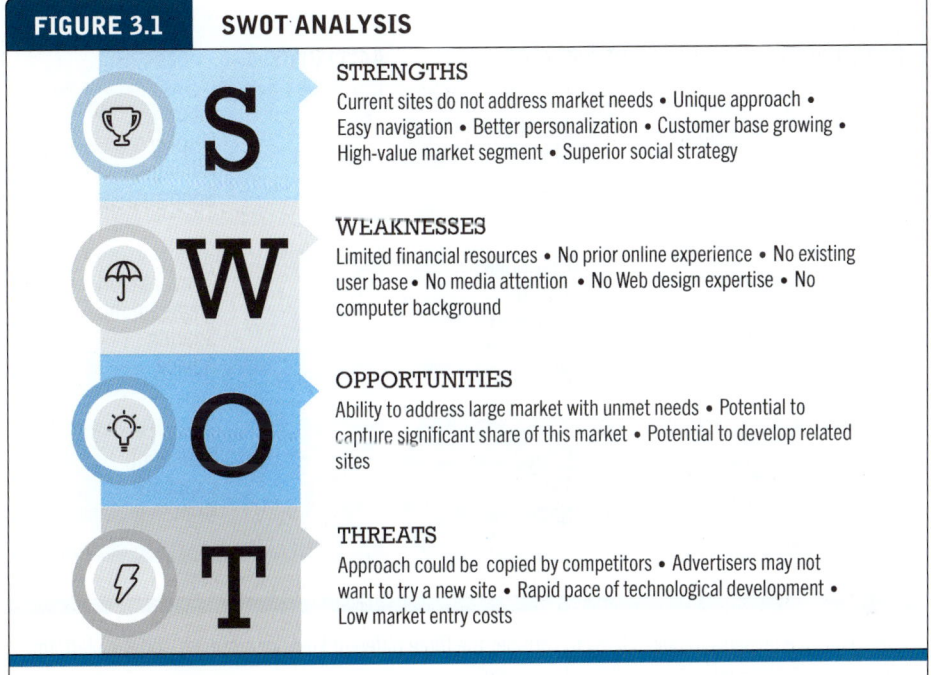

FIGURE 3.1 SWOT ANALYSIS

STRENGTHS
Current sites do not address market needs • Unique approach • Easy navigation • Better personalization • Customer base growing • High-value market segment • Superior social strategy

WEAKNESSES
Limited financial resources • No prior online experience • No existing user base • No media attention • No Web design expertise • No computer background

OPPORTUNITIES
Ability to address large market with unmet needs • Potential to capture significant share of this market • Potential to develop related sites

THREATS
Approach could be copied by competitors • Advertisers may not want to try a new site • Rapid pace of technological development • Low market entry costs

A SWOT analysis describes your firm's strengths, weaknesses, opportunities, and threats.

or partnering to obtain technical and managerial expertise, and looking for financing opportunities (including friends and relatives).

DEVELOP AN E-COMMERCE PRESENCE MAP

E-commerce has moved from being a PC-centric activity on the Web to a mobile and tablet-based activity as well. While around 70% of e-commerce retail and travel revenues are still generated by purchases made from a desktop computer, increasingly smartphones and tablets are being used for purchasing. Smartphones and tablets are also used by a majority of Internet users in the United States to shop for goods and services, explore purchase options, look up prices, and access social sites. Your potential customers use these various devices at different times during the day, and involve themselves in different conversations depending on what they are doing—touching base with friends, viewing photos on Instagram, tweeting, or reading a blog. Each of these are "touch points" where you can meet the customer, and you have to think about how you develop a presence in these different virtual places. **Figure 3.2** provides a roadmap to the platforms and related activities you will need to think about when developing your e-commerce presence.

Figure 3.2 illustrates three different kinds of e-commerce presence: website/app, social media, and offline media. For each of these types there are different platforms that you will need to address. For instance, in the case of websites and/or apps, there are three different platforms: traditional desktop, tablets, and smartphones, each with different capabilities. And for each type of e-commerce presence there are related activities

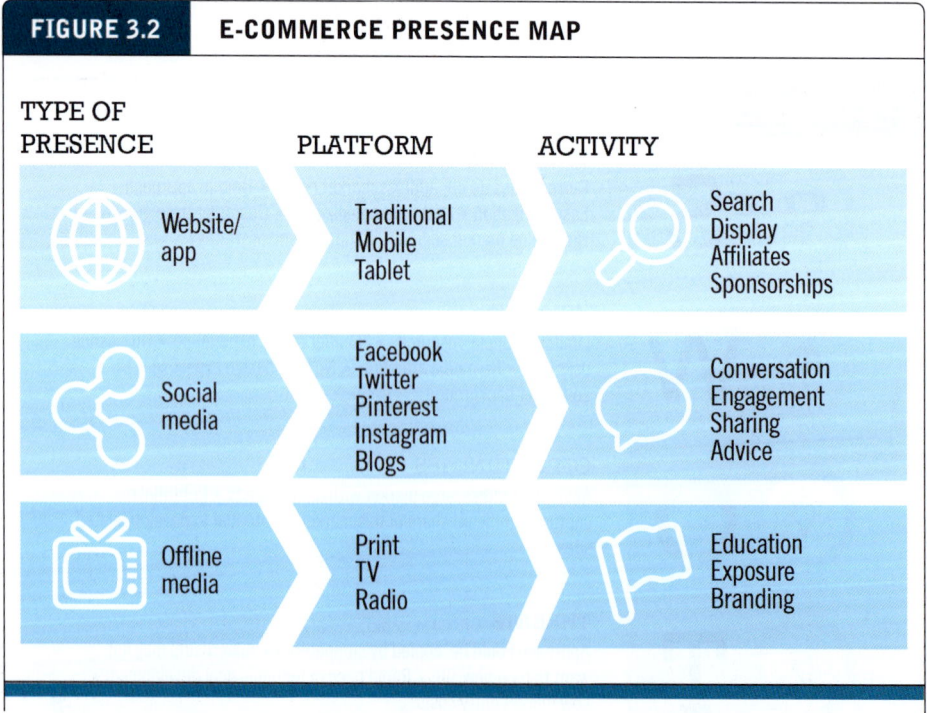

FIGURE 3.2 E-COMMERCE PRESENCE MAP

TYPE OF PRESENCE	PLATFORM	ACTIVITY
Website/app	Traditional Mobile Tablet	Search Display Affiliates Sponsorships
Social media	Facebook Twitter Pinterest Instagram Blogs	Conversation Engagement Sharing Advice
Offline media	Print TV Radio	Education Exposure Branding

An e-commerce presence requires firms to consider the three different kinds of presence, and the platforms and activities associated with each type of presence.

you will need to consider. For instance, in the case of websites and apps, you will want to engage in search engine marketing, display ads, affiliate programs, and sponsorships. Offline media, the third type of e-commerce presence, is included here because many firms use multiplatform or integrated marketing where print, television, or radio ads refer customers to websites and apps. The marketing activities in Figure 3.2 are described in much greater detail in Chapters 6 and 7.

DEVELOP A TIMELINE: MILESTONES

Where would you like to be a year from now? It's a good idea for you to have a rough idea of the time frame for developing your e-commerce presence when you begin. You should break your project down into a small number of phases that could be completed within a specified time. Six phases are usually enough detail at this point. **Table 3.1** illustrates a one-year timeline for the development of a startup e-commerce company.

Note that this example timeline defers the development of a mobile plan until after a website and social media plan have been developed and implemented. There is a growing trend, however, to flip this timeline around, and begin with a mobile plan instead (sometimes referred to as mobile first design). Mobile first design has both advantages and disadvantages that will be examined more fully in Section 3.6.

HOW MUCH WILL THIS COST?

It's too early in the process to develop a detailed budget for your e-commerce presence, but it is a good time to develop a preliminary idea of the costs involved. How much you spend on a website, for instance, depends on what you want it to do. Simple websites can be built and hosted with a first-year cost of $5,000 or less if all the work is done in-house by yourself and others willing to work without pay. A more reasonable budget for a small startup using available tools and design services such as WordPress might be $10,000 to

TABLE 3.1	E-COMMERCE PRESENCE TIMELINE	
PHASE	ACTIVITY	MILESTONE
Phase 1: Planning	Envision e-commerce presence; determine personnel	Mission statement
Phase 2: Website development	Acquire content; develop a site design; arrange for hosting the site	Website plan
Phase 3: Web implementation	Develop keywords and metatags; focus on search engine optimization; identify potential sponsors	A functional website
Phase 4: Social media plan	Identify appropriate social platforms and content for your products and services	A social media plan
Phase 5: Social media implementation	Develop Facebook, Twitter, and Pinterest presence	Functioning social media presence
Phase 6: Mobile plan	Develop a mobile plan; consider options for porting your website to mobile devices	A mobile plan

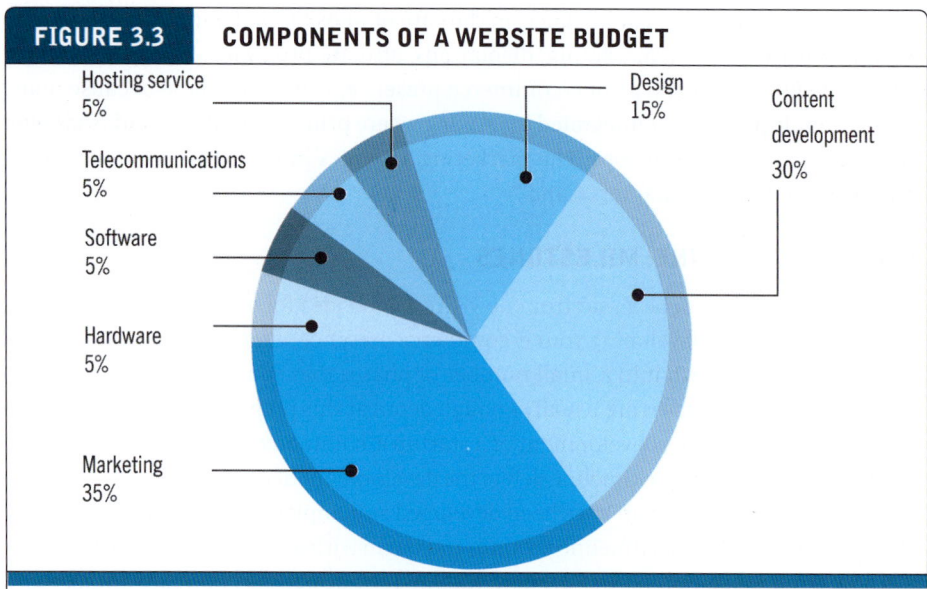

FIGURE 3.3 COMPONENTS OF A WEBSITE BUDGET

While hardware and software costs have fallen dramatically, websites face significant design, content development, and marketing costs.

$25,000. Here the firm owner would develop all the content at no cost, and a web designer and programmer would be hired to implement the initial website. As discussed later, the website would be hosted on a cloud-based server. The websites of large firms that offer high levels of interactivity and linkage to corporate systems can cost several hundred thousand to millions of dollars a year to create and operate. Large firms often outsource their web development and hosting entirely, although many large firms have recently changed and brought the entire web effort in-house (see the closing case study, *Dick's Sporting Goods: Taking Control of Its E-commerce Operations*).

While how much you spend to build a website depends on how much you can afford, and, of course, the size of the opportunity, **Figure 3.3** provides some idea of the relative size of various website costs. In general, the cost of hardware, software, and telecommunications for building and operating a website has fallen dramatically (by over 50%) in the last decade, making it possible for very small entrepreneurs to build fairly sophisticated sites. At the same time, while technology has lowered the costs of system development, the costs of marketing, content development, and design have risen to make up more than half of typical website budgets. The longer-term costs would also have to include site and system maintenance, which are not included here. The costs of developing a mobile site and apps are discussed in Section 3.6.

3.2 BUILDING AN E-COMMERCE PRESENCE: A SYSTEMATIC APPROACH

Once you have developed a vision of the e-commerce presence you want to build, it's time to start thinking about how to build and implement that presence. Building a successful e-commerce presence requires a keen understanding of business, technology, and social issues, as well as a systematic approach. E-commerce is just too important to be left totally to technologists and programmers.

The two most important management challenges are (1) developing a clear understanding of your business objectives and (2) knowing how to choose the right technology to achieve those objectives. The first challenge requires you to build a plan for developing your firm's presence. The second challenge requires you to understand some of the basic elements of e-commerce infrastructure. Let the business drive the technology.

Even if you decide to outsource the development effort and operation to a service provider, you will still need to have a development plan and some understanding of the basic e-commerce infrastructure issues such as cost, capability, and constraints. Without a plan and a knowledge base, you will not be able to make sound management decisions about e-commerce within your firm.

Let's assume you are a manager for a medium-sized industrial parts firm in the United States. You have been given a budget of $100,000 to develop an e-commerce presence for the firm. The purpose will be to sell and service the firm's customers, who are mostly small machine and metal fabricating shops, and to engage your customers through the website, perhaps via a blog and user forum. Where do you start? In the following sections, we will examine developing an e-commerce website, and then, at the end of the chapter, discuss some of the more specific considerations involved in developing a mobile site and building mobile applications.

First, you must be aware of the main areas where you will need to make decisions (see **Figure 3.4**). On the organizational and human resources fronts, you will have to bring together a team of individuals who possess the skill sets needed to build and manage a successful e-commerce presence. This team will make the key decisions about business objectives and strategy, technology, design, and social and information policies. The entire development effort must be closely managed if you hope to avoid the disasters that have occurred at some firms.

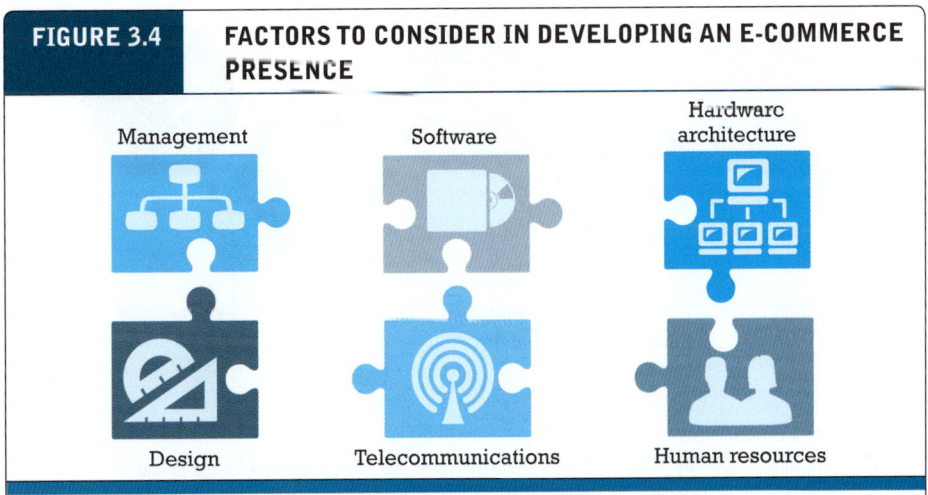

FIGURE 3.4 FACTORS TO CONSIDER IN DEVELOPING AN E-COMMERCE PRESENCE

Building an e-commerce presence requires that you systematically consider the many factors that go into the process.

You will also need to make decisions about hardware, software, and telecommunications infrastructure. The demands of your customers should drive your choices of technology. Your customers will want technology that enables them to find what they want easily, view the product, purchase the product, and then receive the product from your warehouses quickly. You will also have to carefully consider design. Once you have identified the key decision areas, you will need to think about a plan for developing the project. There are a number of different methodologies for building information systems such as websites. One of the most traditional methods is the systems development life cycle, described in the following section.

THE SYSTEMS DEVELOPMENT LIFE CYCLE

systems development life cycle (SDLC)

a methodology for understanding the business objectives of any system and designing an appropriate solution

The **systems development life cycle (SDLC)** is a methodology for understanding the business objectives of any system and designing an appropriate solution. Adopting a life cycle methodology does not guarantee success, but it is far better than having no plan at all. The SDLC method also helps in creating documents that communicate objectives, important milestones, and the uses of resources to management. **Figure 3.5** illustrates the five major steps involved in the systems development life:

- Systems analysis/planning
- Systems design
- Building the system
- Testing
- Implementation and maintenance

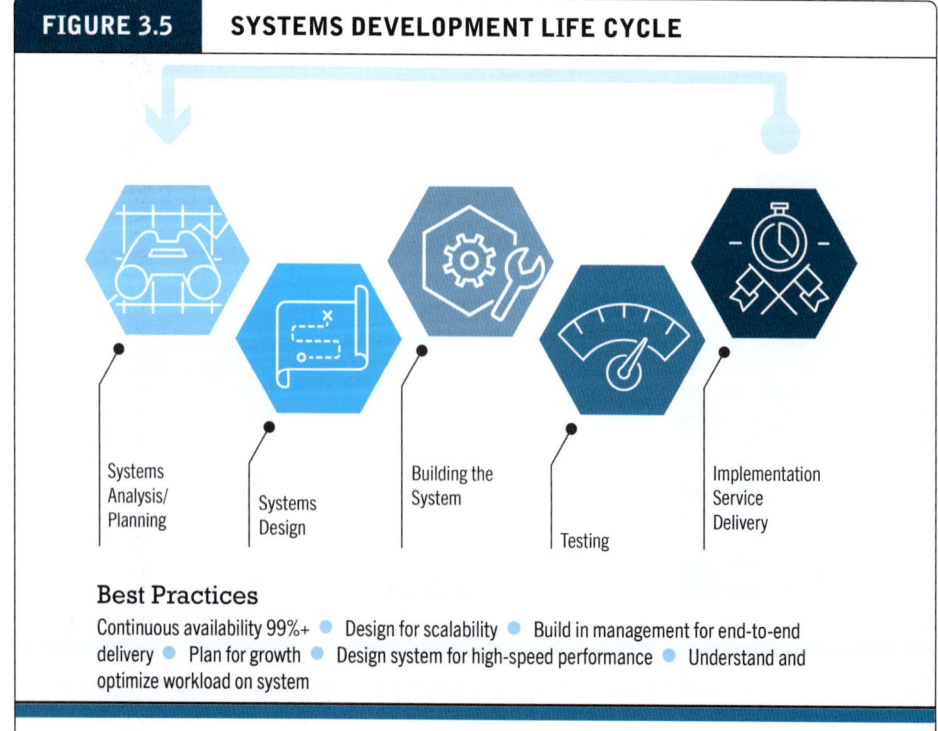

FIGURE 3.5 SYSTEMS DEVELOPMENT LIFE CYCLE

Systems Analysis/Planning: Identify Business Objectives, System Functionality, and Information Requirements

In the systems analysis/planning step of the SDLC, you try to answer the question, "What do we want this e-commerce site or app to do for our business?" The key point is to let the business decisions drive the technology, not the reverse. This will ensure that your technology platform is aligned with your business. We will assume here that you have identified a business strategy and chosen a business model to achieve your strategic objectives (see Chapter 5). But how do you translate your strategies, business models, and ideas into a working e-commerce website?

One way to start is to identify the specific business objectives for your site, and then develop a list of system functionalities and information requirements. **Business objectives** are simply capabilities you want your site to have.

System functionalities are types of information systems capabilities you will need to achieve your business objectives. The **information requirements** for a system are the information elements that the system must produce in order to achieve the business objectives. You will need to provide these lists to system developers and programmers so they know what you as the manager expect them to do.

Table 3.2 describes some basic business objectives, system functionalities, and information requirements for a typical e-commerce site. As shown in the table, there are ten basic business objectives that an e-commerce site must deliver. These objectives must be

business objectives
capabilities you want your site to have

system functionalities
types of information systems capabilities you will need to achieve your business objectives

information requirements
the information elements that the system must produce in order to achieve the business objectives

TABLE 3.2 SYSTEM ANALYSIS: BUSINESS OBJECTIVES, SYSTEM FUNCTIONALITIES, AND INFORMATION REQUIREMENTS FOR A TYPICAL E-COMMERCE SITE

BUSINESS OBJECTIVE	SYSTEM FUNCTIONALITY	INFORMATION REQUIREMENTS
Display goods	Digital catalog	Dynamic text and graphics catalog
Provide product information (content)	Product database	Product description, stocking numbers, inventory levels
Personalize/customize product	Customer on-site tracking	Site log for every customer visit; data mining capability to identify common customer paths and appropriate responses
Engage customers in conversations	On-site blog; user forums	Software with blogging and community forum functionality
Execute a transaction	Shopping cart/payment system	Secure credit card clearing; multiple payment options
Accumulate customer information	Customer database	Name, address, phone, and e-mail for all customers; online customer registration
Provide after-sale customer support	Sales database	Customer ID, product, date, payment, shipment date
Coordinate marketing/advertising	Ad server, e-mail server, e-mail campaign manager, ad banner manager	Site behavior log of prospects and customers linked to e-mail and banner ad campaigns
Understand marketing effectiveness	Site tracking and reporting system	Number of unique visitors, pages visited, products purchased, identified by marketing campaign
Provide production and supplier links	Inventory management system	Product and inventory levels, supplier ID and contact, order quantity data by product

translated into a description of system functionalities and ultimately into a set of precise information requirements. The specific information requirements for a system typically are defined in much greater detail than Table 3.2 indicates. To a large extent, the business objectives of an e-commerce site are not that different from those of an ordinary retail store. The real difference lies in the system functionalities and information requirements. In an e-commerce site, the business objectives must be provided entirely in digital form without buildings or salespeople, 24 hours a day, 7 days a week.

System Design: Hardware and Software Platforms

Once you have identified the business objectives and system functionalities, and have developed a list of precise information requirements, you can begin to consider just how all this functionality will be delivered. You must come up with a **system design specification**—a description of the main components in the system and their relationship to one another. The system design itself can be broken down into two components: a logical design and a physical design. A **logical design** includes a data flow diagram that describes the flow of information at your e-commerce site, the processing functions that must be performed, and the databases that will be used. The logical design also includes a description of the security and emergency backup procedures that will be instituted, and the controls that will be used in the system.

A **physical design** translates the logical design into physical components. For instance, the physical design details the specific model of server to be purchased, the software to be used, the size of the telecommunications link that will be required, the way the system will be backed up and protected from outsiders, and so on.

Figure 3.6(a) presents a data flow diagram for a simple high-level logical design for a very basic website that delivers catalog pages in HTML in response to HTTP requests from the client's browser, while **Figure 3.6(b)** shows the corresponding physical design. Each of the main processes can be broken down into lower-level designs that are much more precise in identifying exactly how the information flows and what equipment is involved.

Building the System: In-house Versus Outsourcing

Once you have a clear idea of both the logical and physical designs for your site, you can begin considering how to actually build the site. You have many choices, and much depends on the amount of money you are willing to spend. Choices range from outsourcing everything (including the actual systems analysis and design) to building everything yourself (in-house). **Outsourcing** means that you will hire an outside vendor to provide the services involved in building the site rather than using in-house personnel. You also have a second decision to make: will you host (operate) the site on your firm's own servers or will you outsource the hosting to a web host provider? These decisions are independent of each other, but they are usually considered at the same time. There are some vendors who will design, build, and host your site, while others will either build or host (but not both). **Figure 3.7** on page 182 illustrates the alternatives.

Build Your Own versus Outsourcing Let's take the building decision first. If you elect to build your own site, there are a range of options. Unless you are fairly skilled, you should use a pre-built template to create the website. For example, Yahoo Small Business provides

---

system design specification
description of the main components in a system and their relationship to one another

logical design
describes the flow of information at your e-commerce site, the processing functions that must be performed, the databases that will be used, the security and emergency backup procedures that will be instituted, and the controls that will be used in the system

physical design
translates the logical design into physical components

outsourcing
hiring an outside vendor to provide the services you cannot perform with in-house personnel

FIGURE 3.6 A LOGICAL AND A PHYSICAL DESIGN FOR A SIMPLE WEBSITE

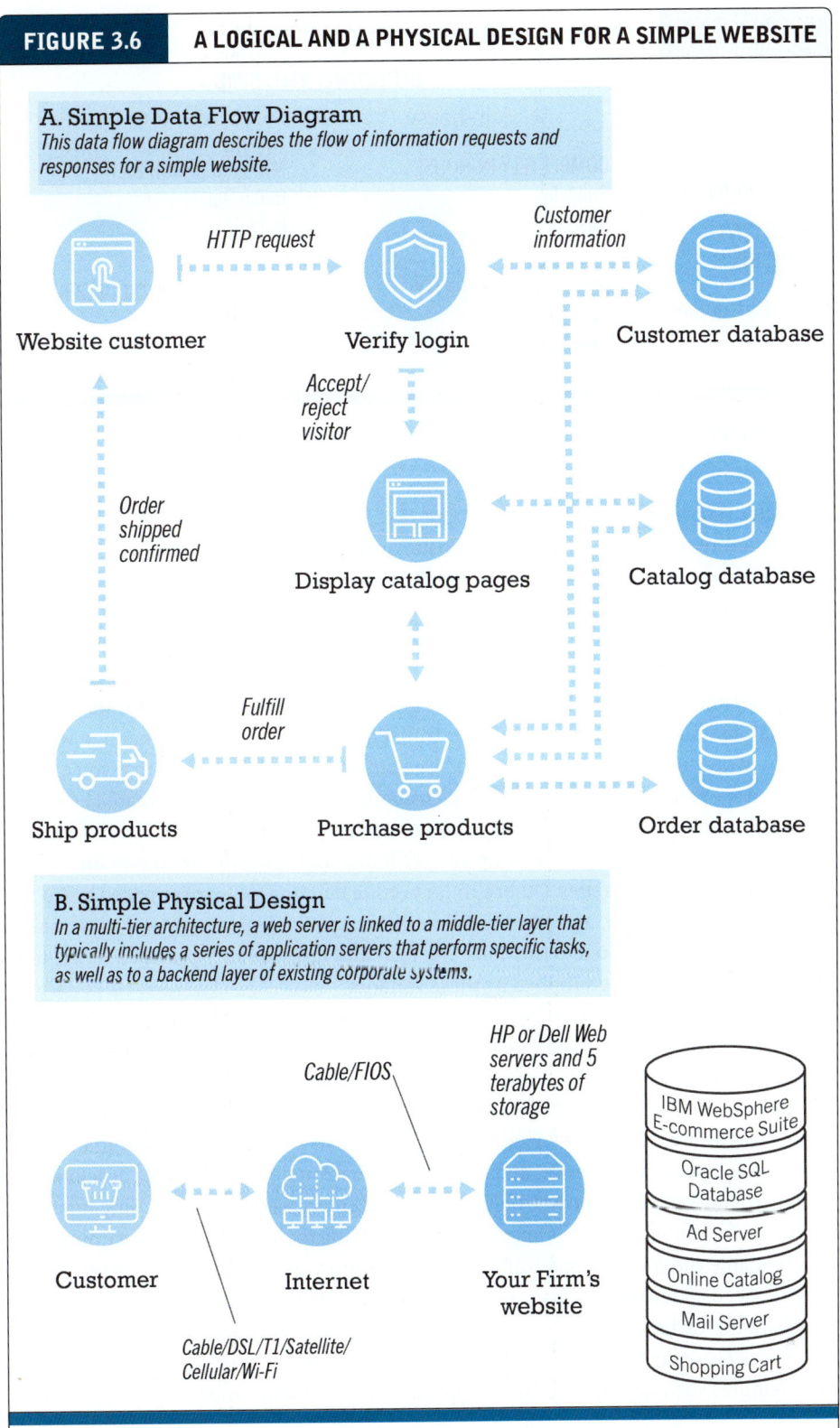

FIGURE 3.7 CHOICES IN BUILDING AND HOSTING

	BUILDING THE SITE	
HOSTING THE SITE	**In-house**	**Outsource**
In-house	COMPLETELY IN-HOUSE Build: In Host: In	MIXED RESPONSIBILITY Build: Out Host: In
Outsource	MIXED RESPONSIBILITY Build: In Host: Out	COMPLETELY OUTSOURCED Build: Out Host: Out

You have a number of alternatives to consider when building and hosting an e-commerce site.

templates that merely require you to input text, graphics, and other data, as well as the infrastructure to run a sales-oriented website once it has been created.

If your website is not a sales-oriented site requiring a shopping cart, one of the least expensive and most widely used site building tools is WordPress. **WordPress** is a website development tool with a sophisticated content management system. A **content management system (CMS)** is a database software program specifically designed to manage structured and unstructured data and objects in a website environment. A CMS provides web managers and designers with a centralized control structure to manage website content. WordPress also has thousands of user-built plug-ins and widgets that you can use to extend the functionality of a website. Websites built in WordPress are treated by search engines like any other website: their content is indexed and made available to the entire web community. Revenue-generating ads, affiliates, and sponsors are the main sources of revenue for WordPress sites. Other similar website building tools are provided by Google Sites, Wix, Squarespace, and Weebly. While these are the least costly ways to create a website, you will be limited to the "look and feel" and functionality provided by the templates and infrastructure supplied by these vendors.

If you want more customization than using a pre-built template can provide and have some programming experience, you can build the site yourself. Here too, there are a variety of options. You can choose to build the site truly "from scratch," coding it using HTML and CSS (see Chapter 2), and adding interactivity with CGI scripts, JavaScript and other programming tools (see pages 206–211). You can also use web development tools such as Adobe Dreamweaver CC and Microsoft Visual Studio, which enable developers to quickly create web pages and websites,. On a larger, enterprise-wide scale, companies may choose to use top-of-the-line prepackaged site-building tools such as Sitecore Commerce, which enable them to create a sophisticated e-commerce presence truly customized to specific needs. **Figure 3.8** illustrates the spectrum of tools available. We will look more closely at the variety of e-commerce software available in Section 3.3.

The decision to build a website on your own has a number of risks. Given the complexity of features such as shopping carts, credit card authentication and processing, inventory

WordPress
open source content management and website design tool

content management system (CMS)
organizes, stores, and processes website content

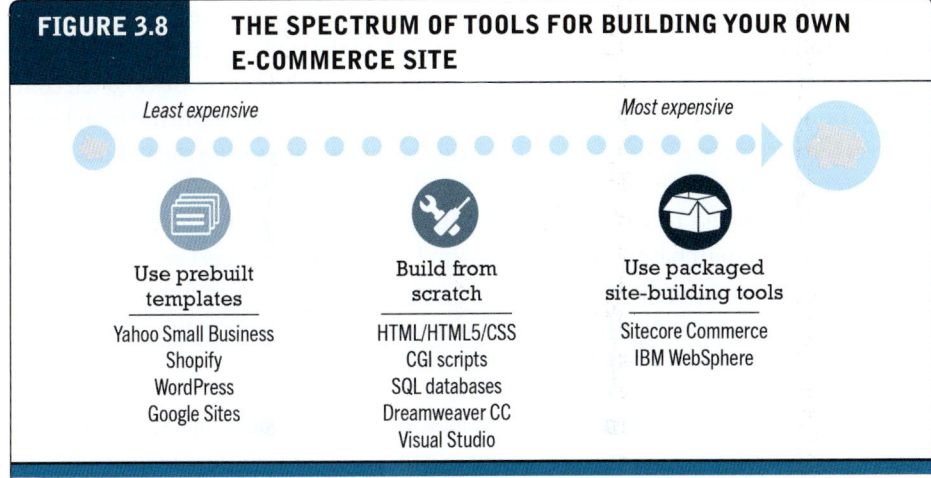

FIGURE 3.8 THE SPECTRUM OF TOOLS FOR BUILDING YOUR OWN E-COMMERCE SITE

management, and order processing, the costs involved are high, as are the risks of doing a poor job. You will be reinventing what other specialized firms have already built, and your staff may face a long, difficult learning curve, delaying your entry to market. Your efforts could fail. On the positive side, you may be better able to build a site that does exactly what you want, and, more importantly, develop the in-house knowledge to allow you to change the site rapidly if necessary due to a changing business environment.

If you choose more expensive site-building packages, you will be purchasing state-of-the art software that is well tested. You could get to market sooner. However, to make a sound decision, you will have to evaluate many different packages, and this can take a long time. You may have to modify the package to fit your business needs and perhaps hire additional outside vendors to do the modifications. Costs rise rapidly as modifications mount. A $4,000 package can easily become a $40,000 to $60,000 development project (see **Figure 3.9**).

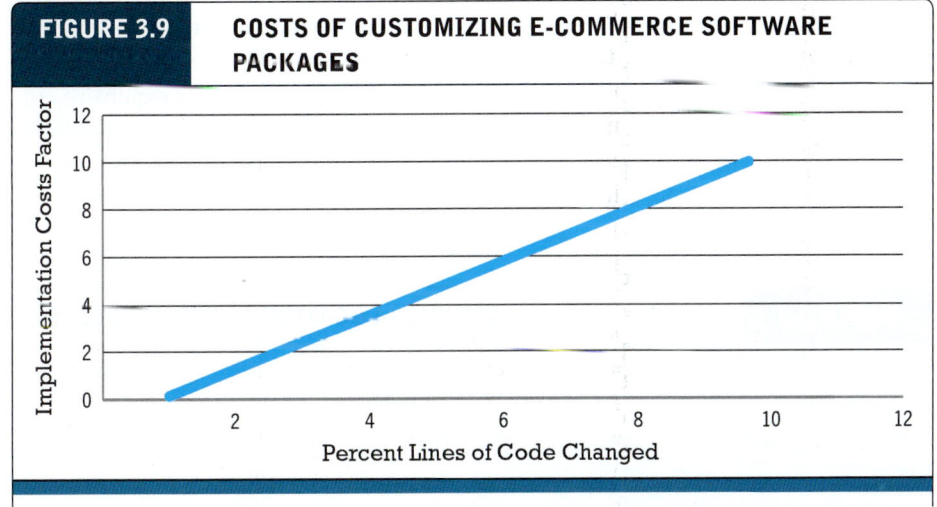

FIGURE 3.9 COSTS OF CUSTOMIZING E-COMMERCE SOFTWARE PACKAGES

While sophisticated site development software packages appear to reduce costs and increase speed to market, as the modifications required to fit the package to your business needs rise, costs rise rapidly.

In the past, bricks-and-mortar retailers in need of an e-commerce site typically designed the site themselves (because they already had the skilled staff in place and had extensive investments in information technology capital such as databases and telecommunications). However, as web applications have become more sophisticated, larger retailers today rely heavily on vendors to provide sophisticated website capabilities, while also maintaining a substantial internal staff. Small startups may build their own sites from scratch using in-house technical personnel in an effort to keep costs low. Medium-size startups will often purchase a website design and programming expertise from vendors. Very small mom-and-pop firms seeking simple storefronts will use templates like WordPress. For e-commerce sites, the cost of building has dropped dramatically in the last five years, resulting in lower capital requirements for all players.

Host Your Own versus Outsourcing Now let's look at the hosting decision. Most businesses choose to outsource hosting and pay a company to host their website, which means that the hosting company is responsible for ensuring the site is "live," or accessible, 24 hours a day. By agreeing to a monthly fee, the business need not concern itself with many of the technical aspects of setting up a web server and maintaining it, telecommunications links, nor with staffing needs.

You can also choose to *co-locate*. With a **co-location** agreement, your firm purchases or leases a web server (and has total control over its operation) but locates the server in a vendor's physical facility. The vendor maintains the facility, communications lines, and the machinery. Co-location has expanded with the spread of virtualization where one server has multiple processors and can operate multiple websites at once with multiple operating systems. In this case, you do not buy the server but rent its capabilities on a monthly basis, usually at one-quarter of the cost of owning the server itself. See **Table 3.3** for a list of some of the major hosting/co-location/cloud providers. There is an extraordinary range of prices for co-location, ranging from $4.95 a month, to several hundred thousand dollars per month depending on the size of the website, bandwidth, storage, and support requirements.

While co-location involves renting physical space for your hardware, you can think of using a cloud service provider as renting virtual space in your provider's infrastructure. Cloud services are rapidly replacing co-location because they are less expensive, and arguably more reliable. Unlike with co-location, your firm does not own the hardware. Cloud service providers offer a standardized infrastructure, virtualization technology, and employ a pay-as-you-go billing system. (See *Insight on Business: OVH Takes E-commerce to the Clouds*).

co-location

when a firm purchases or leases a web server (and has total control over its operation) but locates the server in a vendor's physical facility. The vendor maintains the facility, communications lines, and the machinery

TABLE 3.3	KEY PLAYERS: HOSTING/CO-LOCATION/CLOUD SERVICES
Amazon Web Services (AWS) EC2	IBM Bluemix
CenturyLink	Microsoft
Digital Realty Trust	OVH
Fujitsu	Rackspace
Google Cloud	Virtualstream

INSIGHT ON BUSINESS

OVH TAKES E-COMMERCE TO THE CLOUDS

OVH is the largest European-based provider of website hosting and other cloud computing services. Based in Roubaix, France, OVH (which recently changed its name to OVHcloud) ranks as one of the top 10 cloud service providers in the world, and offers firms an alternative to Amazon Web Services (AWS), Google Cloud, and Microsoft Azure. OHV operates 30 data centers in 19 countries on four continents (Europe, North America, Asia, and Australia) and has its own global fiber optic network. OVH provides website hosting, helps companies expand their existing data center capacity without having to invest heavily in their own infrastructure, and also provides disaster recovery capabilities. Founded in 1999 by Polish-born entrepreneur Octave Klaba, OVH has over 1.5 million customers worldwide and claims revenue of more than $500 million, with 20% annual growth.

For traditional manufacturing and retailing firms trying to quickly develop an online presence, cloud computing services can provide an easy and much less expensive path than building their own infrastructure from scratch. For example, Villeroy and Boch is one of the largest manufacturers of porcelain products in the world. Starting out in 1748 in a small town in France, the company has continually evolved and adapted to keep up with changes in production and marketing technologies. Currently based in Metlach, Germany, Villeroy and Boch sells tableware and wellness products throughout the world to department stores and specialty retail shops. In 2019, it generated just under $1 billion in revenue.

When Villeroy and Boch decided to enter the online marketplace, it needed to build a new digital infrastructure that would provide a seamless customer experience—from viewing its procelain creations to submitting an order, as well as payment options. Customer support, e-mail, and an online customer chat functionality also needed to be built. Customers who wanted to pick up orders in their retail outlets also needed to be served. Rather than build its own e-commerce platform, Villeroy and Boch turned to OVH to build a hosted private cloud to provide fast response times, flexibility, and the ability to scale up as e-commerce visitors and transactions grew. One of the attractions of OVH's private cloud is on-demand computing resources, where the firm is charged only for the computing power it actually uses. As online transactions peak in holiday periods, or even during the day, OVH provides all the computing power needed. This greatly reduced the amount of IT hardware that Villeroy and Boch needed to purchase. Another advantage of using OVH is the ability to integrate the online e-commerce system with its existing data centers and systems.

Sainsbury's is another of OVH's high-profile customers and provides a good example of how cloud computing can be used to selectively expand a firm's existing digital infrastructure to handle an expanding number of online customers without disruption. Founded in London in 1869, Sainsbury's is a multi-brand, multi-product merchandiser. With over 1,400 stores, including 280 Argos general merchandise stores, Sainsbury's is the third largest supermarket retailer in the United Kingdom as well as one of its largest retailers. Sainsbury's website is the third-most visited website in the United Kingdom. Customers ordering via the website can have their groceries and merchandise delivered within four

(continued)

hours of purchase online or can be picked up immediately at a local Sainsbury's store. Over 130 million customers shop at Sainsbury's online and offline stores. However, the growth of its online business began to tax the ability of Sainsbury's corporate data centers to manage its loyalty programs across all its online transactions. Rather than add to its existing data center infrastructure, Sainsbury's turned to OHV to handle the loyalty program. Doing so has enabled Sainsbury's to handle the growth in transactions without further taxing its own data centers. Speed of deployment was a major factor in the decision to use a cloud service in addition to the ability to mirror Sainsbury's existing loyalty program software and infrastrucure while also providing security and data integrity, and other management services.

Cloud computing can also provide rapidly growing firms with a disaster recovery safety net. For example, The Hut Group (THG) is an e-commerce company that sells beauty, lifestyle, sports and wellness products produced by major global brands. The Hut maintains more than 160 websites worldwide and has 30 million visitors a month to its sites. Founded in 2004 and located in Manchester, UK, THG is now valued at more than $2.5 billion. In 2018, its revenue grew 28% to over $1.2 billion.

THG has grown so explosively by developing new websites and aqcuiring other online firms and partners. However, THG's disaster recovery solutions were less than optimal, requiring more than three days to recover from a disaster and using processes that involved extensive manual processing and testing. If a disaster occurred, managers estimated the firm would lose up over $500,000 a day. THG decided to turn to OHV to implement a robust disaster recovery system that replicated the firm's data and transaction processing systems. The OHV system uses over 850 virtual machines to back up THG existing systems. As a result, THG can recover from a disaster in three hours, and it saved more than $950,000 in capital expenditures.

Cloud computing can also provide smaller firms with a nearly complete replacement digital infrastructure to reduce the complexity and cost of operating their own systems. For example, NextRadioTV is a media company located in Paris, France, that operates TV and radio stations, websites, and magazines across France. After a period of aggressive growth in its online media offerings, the firm was operating 80 physical servers across France and serving over 9 million visitors daily. Managing 80 physical servers, responding to unpredictable demand, and round-the-clock alerts from its servers was taxing the firm's resources. The firm decided to turn to OVH to provide a scalable, secure, and reliable cloud-based solution. OVH implemented a dedicated cloud service for NextRadioTV that uses 80 virtual machines that can reliably service 9 million customers daily and expand to handle sudden surges in web traffic within 15 minutes. The OVH solution reduced the cost of the NextRadioTV's digital infrastructure by 40%.

The versatility, scalability, and power of cloud computing as well as its ability to reduce a firm's digital infrastructure costs are the leading reasons why Gartner, a leading research and advisory firm, forecasted global public cloud revenues to grow at 17% to $266 billion in 2020.

SOURCES: "About Us," Ovhcloud.com, accessed December 19, 2019; "Case Study: NextRadioTV—Delivering the Digital Experience Customers," OVHcloud.com, accessed December 19, 2019; "Case Study: The Hut Group—All E-commerce, All the Time," OVHcloud.com, accessed December 19, 2019; "Case Study: Sainsbury's—Streamlining and Securing Online Sales," OVHcloud.com, accessed December 19, 2019; "Case Study: Villeroy & Boch—Tradition Meets E-Commerce Innovation," OVHcloud.com, accessed December 19, 2019; "Viva La Difference!," by Peter Judge, Datacenterdynamics.com, November 29, 2019; "Gartner Forecasts Worldwide Public Cloud Revenue to Grow 17% in 2020," Gartner.com, November 13, 2019 "OVH Rebrands to Take Its European Cloud to the World," by Peter Judge, Datacenterdynamics.com, October 10, 2019; "France's OVH to Triple Spending to Take on Google, Amazon in Cloud Computing," by Mathieu Rosemain and Gwénaëlle Barzic, Reuters.com. October 18, 2018.

Hosting, co-location, and cloud services have become a commodity and a utility: costs are driven by very large providers (such as Amazon, Microsoft, IBM, and Google) who can achieve large economies of scale by establishing huge "server farms" located strategically around the country and the globe. This means the cost of pure hosting has fallen as fast as the fall in server prices, dropping about 50% every year. Telecommunications costs have also fallen. As a result, most hosting services seek to differentiate themselves from the commodity hosting business by offering extensive site design, marketing, optimization, and other services. Small, local ISPs also can be used as hosts, but service reliability is an issue. Will the small ISPs be able to provide uninterrupted service, 24 hours a day, 7 days a week, 365 days a year? Will they have service staff available when you need it?

There are several disadvantages to outsourcing hosting. If you choose a vendor, make sure the vendor has the capability to grow with you. You need to know what kinds of security provisions are in place for backup copies of your site, internal monitoring of activity, and security track record. Is there a public record of a security breach at the vendor? Many Fortune 500 firms have their own private cloud data centers so they can control the web environment. On the other hand, there are risks to hosting your own site if you are a small business. Your costs will be higher than if you had used a large outsourcing firm because you don't have the market power to obtain low-cost hardware and telecommunications. You will have to purchase hardware and software, have a physical facility, lease communications lines, hire a staff, and build security and backup capabilities yourself.

Testing the System

Once the system has been built and programmed, you will have to engage in a testing process. Depending on the size of the system, this could be fairly difficult and lengthy. Testing is required whether the system is outsourced or built in-house. A complex e-commerce site can have thousands of pathways through the site, each of which must be documented and then tested. It is important to note that testing is generally under-budgeted. As much as 50% of the budget can be consumed by testing and rebuilding (usually depending on the quality of the initial design). **Unit testing** involves testing the site's program modules one at a time. **System testing** involves testing the site as a whole, in the same way a typical user would when using the site. Because there is no truly "typical" user, system testing requires that every conceivable path be tested. Final **acceptance testing** requires that the firm's key personnel and managers in marketing, production, sales, and general management actually use the system as installed on a test Internet or intranet server. This acceptance test verifies that the business objectives of the system as originally conceived are in fact working.

Another form of testing is called **A/B testing** (or **split testing**). This form of testing involves showing two versions (A and B) of a web page or website to different users to see which one performs better. There are several different types of A/B testing that can be used for a website design project. A *template test* compares the same general page content using two different layouts and or design treatments. A *new concept test* compares a control page with one that is very different. A *funnel test* compares the flow through a series of pages (such as a product page, to a registration page, to a shopping cart page, versus skipping the registration page) to see which one results in a higher percentage of

unit testing
involves testing the site's program modules one at a time

system testing
involves testing the site as a whole, in a way the typical user will use the site

acceptance testing
verifies that the business objectives of the system as originally conceived are in fact working

A/B testing (split testing)
involves showing two versions of a web page or website to different users to see which one performs better

multivariate testing
involves identifying specific elements, creating versions for each element, and then creating a unique combination of each element and version to test

conversions. **Multivariate testing** is a much more sophisticated form of testing than A/B testing. Multivariate testing involves identifying specific elements, or variables, on a web page, such as a headline, image, button, and text, creating versions for each element, and then creating a unique combination of each element and version to test. So, for example, if there are three elements and two versions of each, there will be eight possible combinations (2*2*2 = 8) to test. When used correctly, multivariate testing enables designers to identify the most optimal layout, color, content, and format.

Implementation, Maintenance, and Optimization

Most people unfamiliar with systems erroneously think that once an information system is installed, the process is over. In fact, while the beginning of the process is over, the operational life of a system is just beginning. Systems break down for a variety of reasons—most of them unpredictable. Therefore, they need continual checking, testing, and repair. Systems maintenance is vital but sometimes not budgeted for. In general, the annual system maintenance cost will roughly parallel the development cost. An e-commerce site that cost $40,000 to develop is likely to require a $40,000 annual expenditure to maintain. Very large e-commerce sites experience some economies of scale so that, for example, a site that costs $1 million to develop is likely to require an annual maintenance budget of perhaps half to three-quarters of that cost.

Why does it cost so much to maintain an e-commerce site? Unlike payroll systems, for example, e-commerce sites are always in a process of change, improvement, and correction. Studies of traditional systems maintenance have found 20% of the time is devoted to debugging code and responding to emergency situations (for example, a new server was installed by your ISP, and all your hypertext links were lost and CGI scripts disabled—the site is down!). Another 20% of the time is concerned with changes in reports, data files, and links to backend databases. The remaining 60% of maintenance time is devoted to general administration (making product and price changes in the catalog) and making changes and enhancements to the system. E-commerce sites are never finished: they are always in the process of being built and rebuilt. They are dynamic—much more so than payroll systems.

The long-term success of an e-commerce site will depend on a dedicated team of employees (the web team) whose sole job is to monitor and adapt the site to changing market conditions. The web team must be multi-skilled; it will typically include programmers, designers, and business managers drawn from marketing, production, and sales support. One of the first tasks of the web team is to listen to customers' feedback on the site and respond to that feedback as necessary. A second task is to develop a systematic monitoring and testing plan to be followed weekly to ensure all the links are operating, prices are correct, and pages are updated. A large business may have thousands of web pages, many of them linked, that require systematic monitoring. Other important tasks of the web team include **benchmarking** (a process in which the site is compared with those of competitors in terms of response speed, quality of layout, and design) and keeping the site current on pricing and promotions. The Web is a competitive environment where you can very rapidly frustrate and lose customers with a dysfunctional site.

benchmarking
a process in which the site is compared with those of competitors in terms of response speed, quality of layout, and design

FIGURE 3.10 FACTORS IN WEBSITE OPTIMIZATION

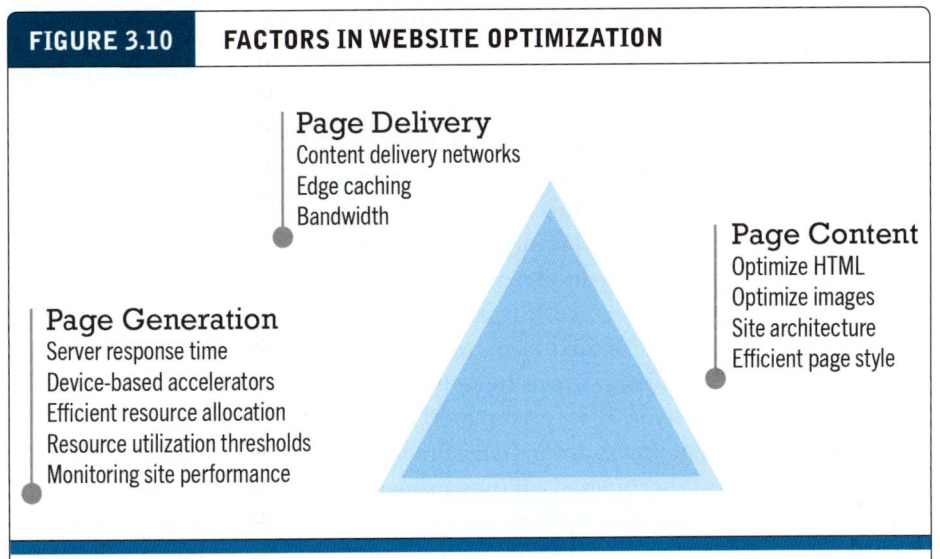

Website optimization requires that you consider three factors: page content, page generation, and page delivery.

Factors in Optimizing Website Performance If you are a small firm using one of the available design and hosting sites like WordPress, you do not have to worry about hardware, software, and website optimizing techniques because the vendor will provide this expertise. However, if you are developing your firm's website in-house, you will need to consider these issues. The purpose of a website is to deliver content to customers and to complete transactions. The faster and more reliably these two objectives are met, the more effective the website is from a commerce perspective. If you are a manager or marketing executive, you will want the website operating in a way that fulfills customers' expectations. You'll have to make sure the website is optimized to achieve this business objective. The optimization of website performance is more complicated than it seems and involves a number of factors, including page content, page generation, and page delivery (see **Figure 3.10**). In this chapter, we describe the software and hardware choices you will need to make in building an e-commerce site; these are also important factors in website optimization.

Using efficient styles and techniques for *page design* and *content* can reduce response times by two to five seconds. Simple steps include reducing unnecessary HTML comments and white space, using more efficient graphics, and avoiding unnecessary links to other pages in the site. *Page generation* speed can be enhanced by segregating computer servers to perform dedicated functions (such as static page generation, application logic, media servers, and database servers), and using various devices from vendors to speed up these servers. Using a single server or multiple servers to perform multiple tasks reduces throughput by more than 50%. *Page delivery* can be sped up by using specialized content delivery networks such as Akamai, or by increasing local bandwidth. We will discuss some of these factors throughout the chapter, but a full discussion of optimizing website performance is beyond the scope of this text.

ALTERNATIVE WEB DEVELOPMENT METHODOLOGIES

Today, in addition to the traditional systems life cycle development process, there are a number of alternative development methodologies intended to expedite the process. Although a detailed examination of these methodologies is beyond the scope of this text, it is helpful to be familiar with some of the basic terms and concepts.

Prototyping consists of building a sample or model rapidly and inexpensively to test a concept or process. The initial prototype can be iteratively refined based on feedback until it satisfies user requirements. Prototyping is particularly useful for user interface design (often referred to as *front end design*). There are various ways to prototype, ranging from simple paper sketches, to *wireframing* (creating a "skeleton" version that focuses on functionality rather than design), to using software tools to create clickable mockups, to building an actual prototype in, for example, HTML, CSS, and JavaScript.

Agile development breaks down a large project into a series of smaller subprojects that are completed in short periods of time using iteration and continuous feedback. Improvement or addition of new functionality takes place within the next iteration as developers clarify requirements. This helps to minimize the overall risk and allows the project to adapt to changes more quickly. Agile methods emphasize face-to-face communication over written documents, encouraging people to collaborate and make decisions quickly and effectively. **Scrum** is a type of agile development that provides a framework for managing the development process. The Scrum process typically involves a cross-functional team headed by a "coach" known as the Scrum master and uses the concept of a "sprint," during which the team takes a small set of features of the project from idea to code to tested functionality and integrates them into the end product.

DevOps also builds on agile development principles as an organizational strategy to create a culture and environment that further promote rapid and agile development practices. DevOps stands for "development and operations" and emphasizes close collaboration between the developers who create applications and the operational staff that run and maintain the applications. DevOps aims to promote better and more frequent communication and collaboration between systems development and operations groups and a fast and stable workflow throughout the entire development life cycle. With this type of organizational change along with agile techniques, standardized processes, and more powerful automated software creation and testing tools, it is possible to release more reliable applications more rapidly and more frequently.

Component-based development takes advantage of the functionality offered by object-oriented programming tools. **Component-based development** enables a system to be built by assembling and integrating various software components that already have been assembled and which provide common functions such as a user interface or online ordering capability. Businesses are using component-based development to create their e-commerce applications by combining commercially available components for shopping carts, user authentication, search engines, and catalogs with pieces of software for their own unique business requirements.

Web services are loosely coupled, reusable software components using Extensible Markup Language (XML) and other open protocols and standards that enable one application to communicate with another with no custom programming required to share data

---

prototyping
consists of building a sample or model rapidly and inexpensively to test a concept or process

agile development
breaks down a large project into a series of smaller subprojects that are completed in short periods of time using iteration and continuous feedback

Scrum
type of agile development that provides a framework for managing the development process

DevOps
builds on agile development principles as an organizational strategy to create a culture and environment that further promote rapid and agile development practices

component-based development
enables a system to be built by assembling and integrating various software components that already have been assembled and which provide common functions

web services
loosely coupled, reusable software components using XML and other open protocols and standards that enable one application to communicate with another with no custom programming required to share data and services

and services. In addition to supporting internal and external integration of systems, web services can be used as tools for building new information system applications or enhancing existing systems. Because these software services use a universal set of standards, they can be less expensive and less difficult to weave together than proprietary components. Web services can perform certain functions on their own and can also engage other web services to complete more complex transactions, such as checking credit, procurement, or ordering products. By creating software components that can communicate and share data regardless of the operating system, programming language, or client device, web services can provide significant cost savings in systems building while opening up new opportunities for collaboration with other companies.

3.3 CHOOSING SOFTWARE

Along with telecommunications, software and hardware constitute the infrastructure of an e-commerce presence. Although today, many businesses choose to outsource their e-commerce infrastructure to cloud providers, it is still very important to have a basic understanding of the underlying software and hardware components that comprise that presence.

SIMPLE VERSUS MULTI-TIERED WEBSITE ARCHITECTURE

Prior to the development of e-commerce, websites simply delivered web pages to users who were making requests through their browsers for HTML pages with content of various sorts. Website software was appropriately quite simple—it consisted of a server computer running basic web server software. We might call this arrangement a single-tier system architecture. **System architecture** refers to the arrangement of software, machinery, and tasks in an information system needed to achieve a specific functionality (much like a home's architecture refers to the arrangement of building materials to achieve a particular functionality). Many websites started this way—there are no monetary transactions. Tens of thousands of sites still perform this way. Orders can always be called in by telephone and not taken online.

However, the development of e-commerce required a great deal more interactive functionality, such as the ability to respond to user input (name and address forms), take customer orders for goods and services, clear credit card transactions on the fly, consult price and product databases, and even adjust advertising on the screen based on user characteristics. This kind of extended functionality required the development of web application servers and a multi-tiered system architecture to handle the processing loads. *Web application servers*, described more fully later in this section, are specialized software programs that perform a wide variety of transaction processing required by e-commerce.

In addition to having specialized application servers, e-commerce sites must be able to pull information from and add information to pre-existing corporate databases. These older databases that predate the e-commerce era are called *backend* or *legacy* databases. Corporations have made massive investments in these systems to store their information on customers, products, employees, and vendors. These backend systems constitute an additional layer in a multi-tiered site.

system architecture
the arrangement of software, machinery, and tasks in an information system needed to achieve a specific functionality

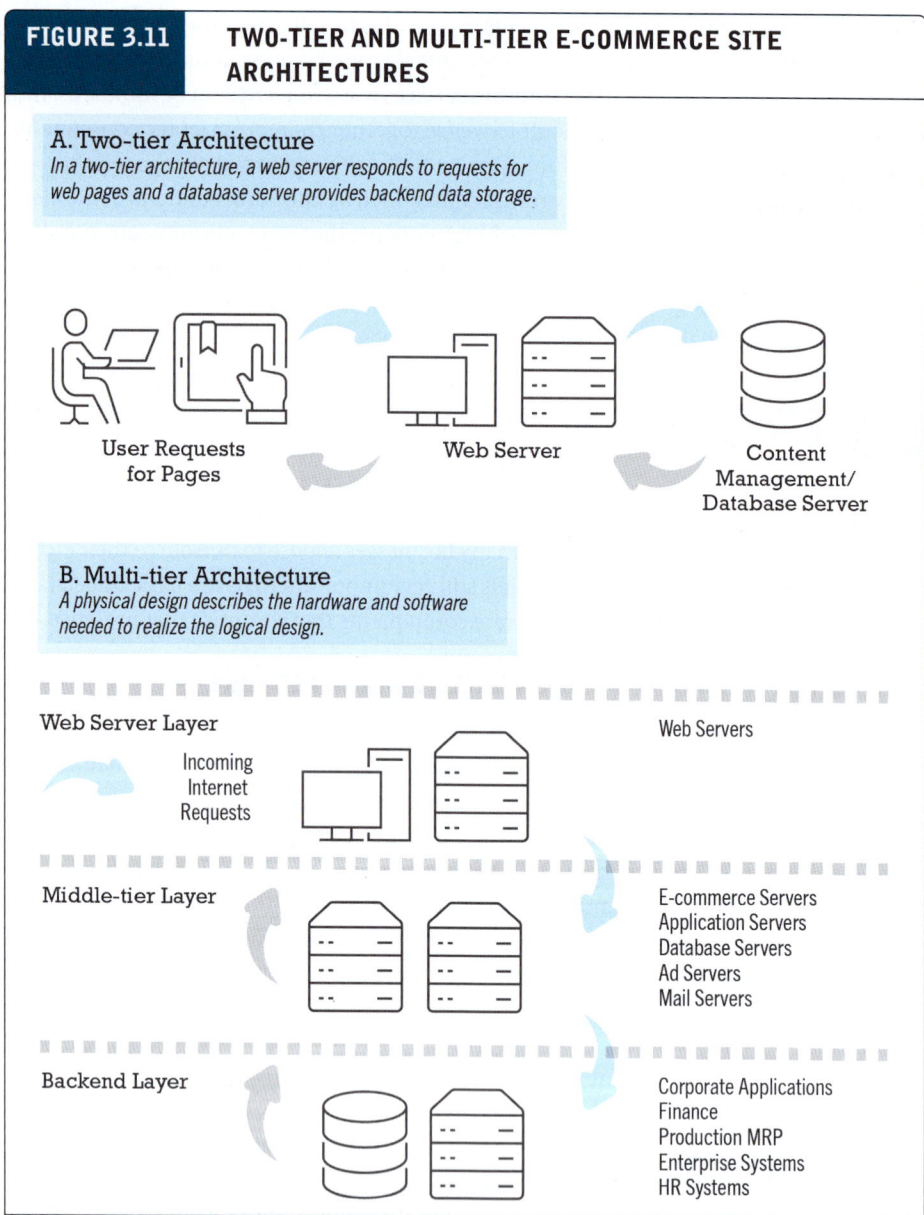

FIGURE 3.11 TWO-TIER AND MULTI-TIER E-COMMERCE SITE ARCHITECTURES

two-tier architecture
e-commerce system architecture in which a web server responds to requests for web pages and a database server provides backend data storage

multi-tier architecture
e-commerce system architecture in which the web server is linked to a middle-tier layer that typically includes a series of application servers that perform specific tasks as well as a backend layer of existing corporate systems

Figure 3.11 illustrates a simple two-tier and a more complex multi-tier e-commerce site architecture. In **two-tier architecture**, a web server responds to requests for web pages and a database server provides backend data storage. In a **multi-tier architecture**, in contrast, the web server is linked to a middle-tier layer that typically includes a series of application servers that perform specific tasks, as well as to a backend layer of existing corporate systems containing product, customer, and pricing information. A multi-tiered site typically employs several physical computers, each running some of the software applications and sharing the workload across many physical computers.

The remainder of this section describes basic web server software functionality and the various types of web application servers.

WEB SERVER SOFTWARE

All e-commerce sites require basic web server software to answer requests from customers for HTML and XML pages.

When you choose web server software, you will also be choosing an operating system for your site's computers. Apache, which works with Linux and Unix operating systems, is the leading web server software (Netcraft, 2019). Unix is the original programming language of the Internet and Web, and Linux is a derivative of Unix designed for the personal computer. Apache was developed by a worldwide community of Internet innovators. Apache is free and can be downloaded from many sites on the Web; it also comes installed on most IBM web servers. Literally thousands of programmers have worked on Apache over the years; thus, it is extremely stable. There are thousands of utility software programs written for Apache that can provide all the functionality required for a contemporary e-commerce site. In order to use Apache, you will need staff that is knowledgeable in Unix or Linux.

Microsoft Internet Information Services (IIS) is another popular type of web server software. IIS is based on the Windows operating system and is compatible with a wide selection of Microsoft utility and support programs.

There are also many other smaller providers or open source versions of web server software. Note that the choice of web server has little effect on users of your system. The pages they see will look the same regardless of the development environment. There are many advantages to the Microsoft suite of development tools—they are integrated, powerful, and easy to use. The Unix operating system, on the other hand, is exceptionally reliable and stable, and there is a worldwide open software community that develops and tests Unix-based web server software.

Table 3.4 shows the basic functionality provided by all web servers.

TABLE 3.4	BASIC FUNCTIONALITY PROVIDED BY WEB SERVERS
FUNCTIONALITY	DESCRIPTION
Processing of HTTP requests	Receive and respond to client requests for HTML pages
Security services (Secure Sockets Layer)/ Transport Layer Security	Verify username and password; process certificates and private/public key information required for credit card processing and other secure information
File Transfer Protocol	Permits transfer of very large files from server to server
Search engine	Indexing of site content; keyword search capability
Data capture	Log file of all visits, time, duration, and referral source
E-mail	Ability to send, receive, and store e-mail messages
Site management tools	Calculate and display key site statistics, such as unique visitors, page requests, and origin of requests; check links on pages

Site Management Tools

In Chapter 2, we described most of the basic functionality of the web servers listed in Table 3.4. Another functionality not described previously is site management tools. **Site management tools** are essential if you want to keep your site working, and if you want to understand how well it is working. Site management tools verify that links on pages are still valid and also identify orphan files, or files on the site that are not linked to any pages. By surveying the links on a website, a site management tool can quickly report on potential problems and errors that users may encounter. Your customers will not be impressed if they encounter a "404 Error: Page Does Not Exist" message on your website. Links to URLs that have moved or been deleted are called dead links; these can cause error messages for users trying to access that link. Regularly checking that all links on a site are operational helps prevent irritation and frustration in users who may decide to take their business elsewhere to a better functioning site.

Even more importantly, site management tools can help you understand consumer behavior on your website. Site management software and services, such as those provided by Webtrends, can be purchased in order to more effectively monitor customer purchases and marketing campaign effectiveness, as well as keep track of standard hit counts and page visit information. These services can track your e-commerce presence on the Web, mobile, and social network platforms.

Dynamic Page Generation Tools

One of the most important innovations in website operation has been the development of dynamic page generation tools. Prior to the development of e-commerce, websites primarily delivered unchanging static content in the form of HTML pages. While this capability might be sufficient to display pictures of products, consider all the elements of a typical e-commerce site today by reviewing Table 3.2 (on page 179), or visit what you believe is an excellent e-commerce site. The content of successful e-commerce sites is always changing, often day by day. There are new products and promotions, changing prices, news events, and stories of successful users. E-commerce sites must intensively interact with users who not only request pages but also request product, price, availability, and inventory information. One of the most dynamic sites is eBay—the auction site. There, the content is changing minute by minute. E-commerce sites are just like real markets—they are dynamic. News sites, where stories change constantly, also are dynamic.

The dynamic and complex nature of e-commerce sites requires a number of specialized software applications in addition to static HTML pages. **Dynamic HTML (DHTML)** is a term used to refer to a collection of technologies, including HTML, CSS, Javascript, and the Document Object Model (DOM) (an application programing interface) that can be used together to create interactive websites. DHTML can used to change the way a page looks when it is used, but does not actually generate a unique page. Dynamic web page generation is more complex. With **dynamic page generation**, the contents of a web page are stored as objects in a database, rather than being hard-coded in HTML. When the user requests a web page, the contents for that page are then fetched from the database. The objects are retrieved from the database using Common Gateway Interface (CGI), Active Server Pages (ASP), Java Server Pages (JSP), or other server-side programs. CGI, ASP, and

JSP are described in Section 3.5. This technique is much more efficient than working directly in HTML code. It is much easier to change the contents of a database than it is to change the coding of an HTML page. A standard data access method called *Open Database Connectivity (ODBC)* makes it possible for applications written in the C programming language to access data from any database regardless of the database and operating system software being used via an ODBC driver that serves as a translator between the application and the database. ODBC drivers are available for most of the major database management systems offered by companies such as Oracle, SAP, Sybase, and IBM. Java Database Connectivity (JDBC) is a version of ODBC that provides connectivity between applications written in the Java programming language and a wide range of databases. However, while ODBC remains the de facto standard for cross-platform data access, today many web development platforms provide functionality that allows a programmer to directly link to a target database, making ODBC/JDBC drivers unnecessary.

Dynamic page generation gives e-commerce several significant capabilities that generate cost and profitability advantages over traditional commerce. Dynamic page generation lowers *menu costs* (the costs incurred by merchants for changing product descriptions and prices). Dynamic page generation also permits easy online *market segmentation*—the ability to sell the same product to different markets. For instance, you might want variations on the same banner ad depending on how many times the customer has seen the ad. In the first exposure to a car ad, you might want to emphasize brand identification and unique features. On the second viewing you might want to emphasize superlatives like "most family friendly" to encourage comparison to other brands. The same capability makes possible nearly cost-free *price discrimination*—the ability to sell the same product to different customers at different prices. For instance, you might want to sell the same product to corporations and government agencies but use different marketing themes. Based on a cookie you place on client computers, or in response to a question on your site that asks visitors if they are from a government agency or a corporation, you would be able to use different marketing and promotional materials for corporate clients and government clients. You might want to reward loyal customers with lower prices, say on DVDs or musical tracks, and charge full price to first-time buyers. Dynamic page generation allows you to approach different customers with different messages and prices.

Dynamic page generation also enables the use of a content management system (CMS). As previously described, a CMS is used to create and manage web content. A CMS separates the design and presentation of content (such as HTML documents, images, video, audio) from the content creation process. The content is maintained in a database and dynamically linked to the website. A CMS usually includes templates that can be automatically applied to new and existing content, WYSIWYG editing tools that make it easy to edit and describe (tag) content, and collaboration, workflow, and document management tools. Typically, an experienced programmer is needed to install the system, but thereafter, content can be created and managed by non-technical staff. There are a wide range of commercial CMSs available, from top-end enterprise systems offered by OpenText, IBM, Adobe, and Oracle, to mid-market systems by Sitecore, PaperThin, and Episerver, as well as hosted software as a service (SaaS) versions by Acquia, Clickability (Upland), and Crownpeak among others. There are also several open source content management systems available, such as WordPress, Joomla, Drupal, OpenCms, and others.

APPLICATION SERVERS

web application server
software program that provides specific business functionality required of a website

Web application servers are software programs that provide the specific business functionality required of a website. The basic idea of application servers is to isolate the business applications from the details of displaying web pages to users on the front end and the details of connecting to databases on the back end. Application servers are a kind of middleware software that provides the glue connecting traditional corporate systems to the customer as well as all the functionality needed to conduct e-commerce. In the early years, a number of software firms developed specific separate programs for each function, but increasingly, these specific programs are being replaced by integrated software tools that combine all the needed functionality for an e-commerce site into a single development environment, a packaged software approach.

Table 3.5 illustrates the wide variety of application servers available in the marketplace. The table focuses on "sell-side" servers that are designed to enable selling products on the Web. So-called "buy-side" and "link" servers focus on the needs of businesses to connect with partners in their supply chains or find suppliers for specific parts and

TABLE 3.5	APPLICATION SERVERS AND THEIR FUNCTION
APPLICATION SERVER	FUNCTIONALITY
Catalog display	Provides a database for product descriptions and prices
Transaction processing (shopping cart)	Accepts orders and clears payments
List server	Creates and serves mailing lists and manages e-mail marketing campaigns
Proxy server	Monitors and controls access to main web server; implements firewall protection
Mail server	Manages Internet e-mail
Audio/video server	Stores and delivers streaming media content
Chat server	Creates an environment for online real-time text and audio interactions with customers
News server	Provides connectivity and displays Internet news feeds
Fax server	Provides fax reception and transmission using a web server
Groupware server	Creates workgroup environments for online collaboration
Database server	Stores customer, product, and price information
Ad server	Maintains web-enabled database of advertising banners that permits customized and personalized display of advertisements based on consumer behavior and characteristics
Auction server	Provides a transaction environment for conducting online auctions
B2B server	Implements buy, sell, and link marketplaces for commercial transactions

assemblies. There are several thousand software vendors that provide application server software. For Linux and Unix environments, many of these capabilities are available free on the Internet from various sites. Most businesses—faced with this bewildering array of choices—choose to use integrated software tools called merchant server software.

E-COMMERCE MERCHANT SERVER SOFTWARE FUNCTIONALITY

E-commerce merchant server software provides the basic functionality needed for online sales, including an online catalog, order taking via an online shopping cart, and online credit card processing.

Online Catalog

A company that wants to sell products online must have a list, or **online catalog**, of its products, available on its website. Merchant server software typically includes a database capability that will allow for construction of a customized online catalog. The complexity and sophistication of the catalog will vary depending on the size of the company and its product lines. Small companies, or companies with small product lines, may post a simple list with text descriptions and perhaps color photos. A larger site might decide to add sound, animations, or videos (useful for product demonstrations) to the catalog, or interactivity, such as customer service representatives available via instant messaging to answer questions. Today, larger firms make extensive use of streaming video.

Shopping Cart

Online **shopping carts** are much like their real-world equivalent; both allow shoppers to set aside desired purchases in preparation for checkout. The difference is that the online variety is part of a merchant server software program residing on the web server, and allows consumers to select merchandise, review what they have selected, edit their selections as necessary, and then actually make the purchase by clicking a button. The merchant server software automatically stores shopping cart data.

Credit Card Processing

A site's shopping cart typically works in conjunction with credit card processing software, which verifies the shopper's credit card and then puts through the debit to the card and the credit to the company's account at checkout. Integrated e-commerce software suites typically supply the software for this function. Otherwise, you will have to make arrangements with a variety of credit card processing banks and intermediaries.

MERCHANT SERVER SOFTWARE PACKAGES (E-COMMERCE SOFTWARE PLATFORMS)

Rather than build your site from a collection of disparate software applications, it is easier, faster, and generally more cost-effective to purchase a **merchant server software package** (also called an **e-commerce software platform**). Merchant server software offers an integrated environment that promises to provide most or all of the functionality and capabilities you will need to develop a sophisticated, customer-centric site. An important element of merchant sofware packages is a built-in shopping cart that can display

e-commerce merchant server software
software that provides the basic functionality needed for online sales, including an online catalog, order taking via an online shopping cart, and online credit card processing

online catalog
list of products available on a website

shopping cart
allows shoppers to set aside desired purchases in preparation for checkout, review what they have selected, edit their selections as necessary, and then actually make the purchase by clicking a button

merchant server software package (e-commerce software platform)
offers an integrated environment that provides most or all of the functionality and capabilities needed to develop a sophisticated, customer-centric site

TABLE 3.6 OPEN SOURCE SOFTWARE OPTIONS

FUNCTIONALITY	OPEN SOURCE SOFTWARE
Web server	Apache (the leading web server for small and medium businesses)
Shopping cart, online catalog	Many providers: osCommerce, Zen Cart, AgoraCart, X-cart, AspDotNetStorefront
Credit card processing	Credit card acceptance is typically provided in shopping cart software but you may need a merchant account from a bank as well.
Database	MySQL (the leading open source SQL database for businesses)
Programming/scripting language	PHP is a scripting language embedded in HTML documents but executed by the server, providing server-side execution with the simplicity of HTML editing. Perl is an alternative language. JavaScript programs are client-side programs that provide user interface components. Ruby on Rails (RoR, Rails) and Django are other popular open source web application frameworks.
Analytics	Analytics keep track of your site's customer activities and the success of your web advertising campaign. You can also use Google Analytics if you advertise on Google, which provides good tracking tools; most hosting services will provide these services as well. Other open source analytic tools include Matomo, CrawlTrack, and Open Web Analytics.

merchandise, manage orders, and clear credit card transactions. E-commerce software platforms come in three general ranges of price and functionality.

While existing firms often have the financial capital to invest in commercial merchant server software, many small firms and startup firms do not. There are really two options here, the key factor being how much programming experience and time you have. One option is to utilize the e-commerce merchant services provided by sites that makes it easy to create an e-commerce website with customizable templates, such as Yahoo Small Business, which offers a Starter plan for $10.95 a month and a 1.5% transaction fee for each transaction processed through the store. An e-commerce template is a predesigned website that allows users to customize the look and feel of the site to fit their business needs and provides a standard set of functionalities. Most templates today contain ready-to-go site designs with built-in e-commerce functionality like shopping carts, payment clearance, and site management tools. The Starter plan also includes a mobile storefront, search engine optimization tools, and a variety of other marketing tools. Many others, such as Bigcommerce, Vendio, and Shopify, offer similar services.

If you have considerable, or at least some, programming background, you can consider open source merchant server software. **Open source software** is software developed by a community of programmers and designers, and is free to use and modify. **Table 3.6** provides a description of some open source options. The advantage of using open source web building tools is that you get exactly what you want, a truly customized unique website. The disadvantage is that it will take several months for a single programmer to develop the site and get all the tools to work together seamlessly. How many months do you want to wait before you get to market with your ideas?

open source software
software that is developed by a community of programmers and designers, and is free to use and modify

Midrange e-commerce software platforms include IBM WebSphere Commerce Express Edition and Sitecore Experience Commerce. High-end enterprise solutions for large global firms are provided by IBM Websphere Professional and Enterprise Editions, SAP Hybris, Oracle ATG Web Commerce, Magento, and others. Many of these e-commerce software platforms, such as IBM Commerce on Cloud, SAP Hybris Commerce Cloud, Salesforce Commerce Cloud (formerly Demandware), Oracle Commerce Cloud, and Net-Suite SuiteCommerce (now also owned by Oracle), among others, are now available on a software-as-a-service (SaaS) basis, a model in which the software is hosted in the cloud and run by the client via a web browser. This model enables a firm to launch an e-commerce site very quickly. There are several hundred software firms that provide e-commerce software, which raises the costs of making sensible decisions on this matter.

Choosing an E-commerce Software Platform

With all of these vendors, how do you choose the right one? Evaluating these tools and making a choice is one of the most important and uncertain decisions you will make in building an e-commerce site. The real costs are hidden—they involve training your staff to use the tools and integrating the tools into your business processes and organizational culture. The following are some of the key factors to consider:

- Functionality, including availability on an SaaS basis
- Support for different business models, including m-commerce
- Business process modeling tools
- Visual site management tools and reporting
- Performance and scalability
- Connectivity to existing business systems
- Compliance with standards
- Global and multicultural capability
- Local sales tax and shipping rules

For instance, although e-commerce software platforms promise to do everything, your business may require special functionality—such as streaming audio and video. You will need a list of business functionality requirements. Your business may involve several different business models—such as a retail side and a business-to-business side; you may run auctions for stock excess as well as fixed-price selling. Be sure the package can support all of your business models. You may wish to change your business processes, such as order taking and order fulfillment. Does the platform contain tools for modeling business process and work flows? Understanding how your site works will require visual reporting tools that make its operation transparent to many different people in your business. A poorly designed software package will drop off significantly in performance as visitors and transactions expand into the thousands per hour, or minute. Check for performance and scalability by stress-testing a pilot edition or obtaining data from the vendor about performance under load. You will have to connect the e-commerce platform to your traditional business systems. How will this connection to existing systems be made, and is your staff skilled in making the connection? Because of the changing technical environment—in particular, changes in m-commerce platforms—it is important to document exactly what standards the platform supports now, and what the migration path will be toward the future. Finally, your e-commerce site may have to work both globally and locally. You may need a foreign language edition using foreign currency denominations. And you will have to collect sales taxes across many local, regional, and national tax systems. Does the e-commerce platform support this level of globalization and localization?

3.4 CHOOSING HARDWARE

Whether you host your own site or outsource the hosting and operation of your site, you will need to understand certain aspects of the computing hardware platform. The **hardware platform** refers to all the underlying computing equipment that the system uses to achieve its e-commerce functionality. Your objective is to have enough platform capacity to meet peak demand (avoiding an overload condition), but not so much platform that you are wasting money. Failing to meet peak demand can mean your site is slow, or actually crashes. How much computing and telecommunications capacity is enough to meet peak demand? How many hits per day can your site sustain?

To answer these questions, you will need to understand the various factors that affect the speed, capacity, and scalability of an e-commerce site.

hardware platform
refers to all the underlying computing equipment that the system uses to achieve its e-commerce functionality

RIGHT-SIZING YOUR HARDWARE PLATFORM: THE DEMAND SIDE

The most important factor affecting the speed of your site is the demand that customers put on the site. **Table 3.7** lists the most important factors to consider when estimating the demand on a site.

Demand on a website is fairly complex and depends primarily on the type of site you are operating. The number of simultaneous users in peak periods, the nature of customer requests, the type of content, the required security, the number of items in inventory, the number of page requests, and the speed of legacy applications that may be needed to supply data to the web pages are all important factors in overall demand on a website system.

Certainly, one important factor to consider is the number of simultaneous users who will likely visit your site. In general, the load created by an individual customer on a server is typically quite limited and short-lived. A web session initiated by the typical user is **stateless**, meaning that the server does not have to maintain an ongoing, dedicated interaction with the client. A web session typically begins with a page request, then a server replies, and the session is ended. The sessions may last from tenths of a second to a minute per user. Nevertheless, system performance does degrade as more and more simultaneous users request service. Fortunately, degradation (measured as "transactions per second" and "latency" or delay in response) is fairly graceful over a wide range, up until a peak load is reached and service quality becomes unacceptable (see **Figure 3.12**).

stateless
refers to the fact that the server does not have to maintain an ongoing, dedicated interaction with the client

Serving up static web pages is **I/O intensive**, which means it requires input/output (I/O) operations rather than heavy-duty processing power. As a result, website performance is constrained primarily by the server's I/O limitations and the telecommunications connection, rather than the speed of the processor.

I/O intensive
requires input/output operations rather than heavy-duty processing power

TABLE 3.7 FACTORS IN RIGHT-SIZING AN E-COMMERCE PLATFORM

SITE TYPE	PUBLISH/ SUBSCRIBE	SHOPPING	CUSTOMER SELF-SERVICE	TRADING	WEB SERVICES/ B2B
Examples	WSJ.com	Amazon	Travelocity	E*Trade	Ariba e-procurement exchanges
Content	Dynamic Multiple authors High volume Not user-specific	Catalog Dynamic items User profiles with data mining	Data in legacy applications Multiple data sources	Time sensitive High volatility Multiple suppliers and consumers Complex transactions	Data in legacy applications Multiple data sources Complex transactions
Security	Low	Privacy Nonrepudiation Integrity Authentication Regulations	Privacy Nonrepudiation Integrity Authentication Regulations	Privacy Nonrepudiation Integrity Authentication Regulations	Privacy Nonrepudiation Integrity Authentication Regulations
Percent secure pages	Low	Medium	Medium	High	Medium
Cross session information	No	High	High	High	High
Searches	Dynamic Low volume	Dynamic High volume	Nondynamic Low volume	Nondynamic Low volume	Nondynamic Moderate volume
Unique items (SKUs)	High	Medium to high	Medium	High	Medium to high
Transaction volume	Moderate	Moderate to high	Moderate	High to extremely high	Moderate
Legacy integration complexity	Low	Medium	High	High	High
Page views (hits)	High to very high	Moderate to high	Moderate to low	Moderate to high	Moderate

Other factors to consider when estimating the demand on a website are the user profile and the nature of the content. If users request searches, registration forms, and order taking via shopping carts, then demands on processors will increase markedly.

RIGHT-SIZING YOUR HARDWARE PLATFORM: THE SUPPLY SIDE

Once you estimate the likely demand on your site, you will need to consider how to scale up your site to meet demand. We have already discussed one solution that requires very little thought: outsource the hosting of your website to a cloud-based service. You can also engage the services of a content delivery network (CDN) such as Akamai. See Chapter 2 for a discussion of cloud-based computing services and a case study on

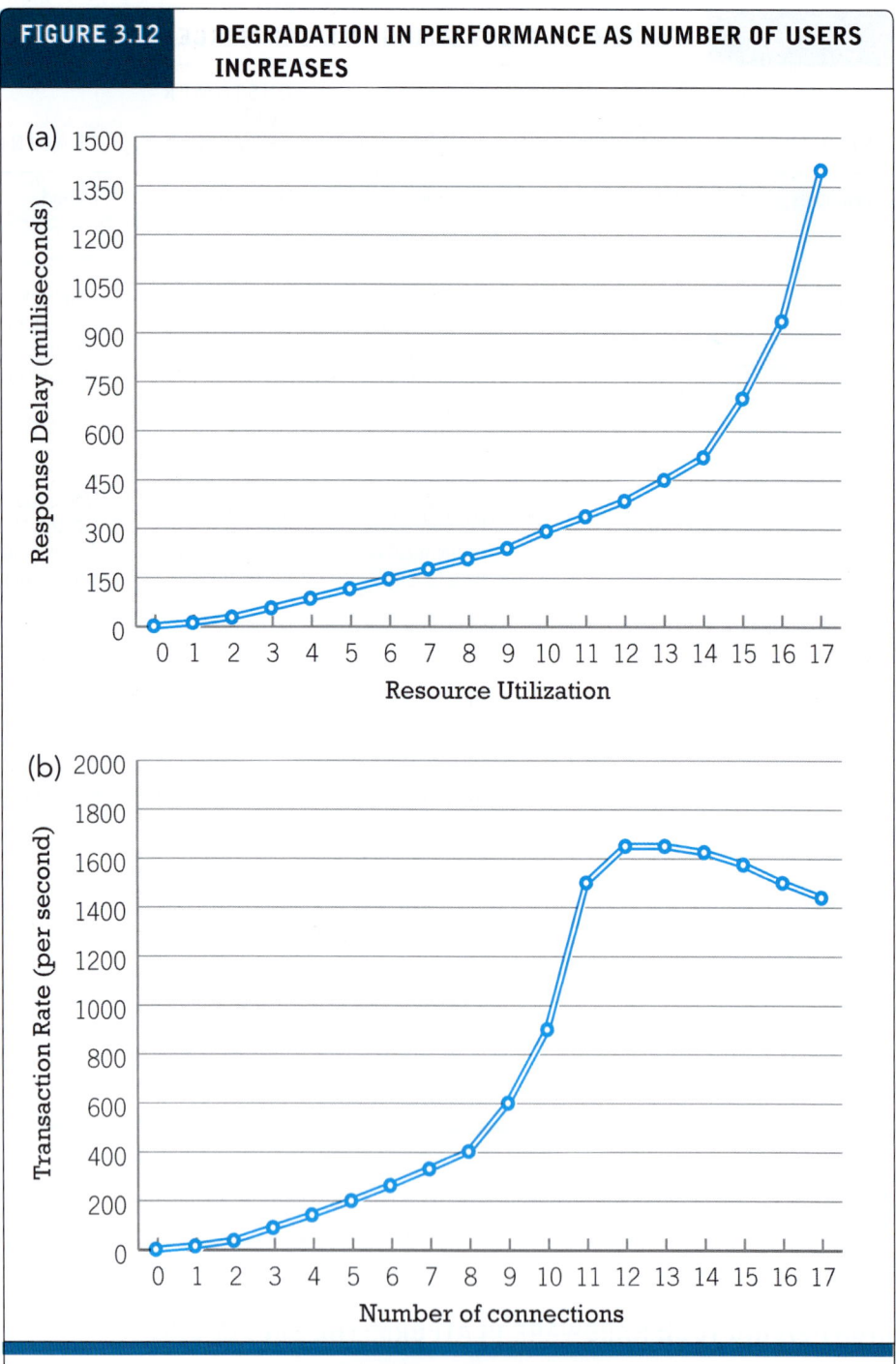

FIGURE 3.12 DEGRADATION IN PERFORMANCE AS NUMBER OF USERS INCREASES

Degradation in web server performance occurs as the number of users (connections) increases, and as the system's resources (processors, disk drives) become more utilized. In (a), user-experienced delay rises gracefully until an inflection point is reached, and then delay rises exponentially to an unacceptable level. In (b), the transaction rate rises gracefully until the number of users rapidly escalates the transaction rate, and at a certain inflection point, the transaction rate starts declining as the system slows down or crashes.

TABLE 3.8	VERTICAL AND HORIZONTAL SCALING TECHNIQUES
TECHNIQUE	APPLICATION
Use a faster computer	Deploy edge servers, presentation servers, data servers, etc.
Create a cluster of computers	Use computers in parallel to balance loads.
Use appliance servers	Use special-purpose computers optimized for their task.
Segment workload	Segment incoming work to specialized computers.
Batch requests	Combine related requests for data into groups, process as group.
Manage connections	Reduce connections between processes and computers to a minimum.
Aggregate user data	Aggregate user data from legacy applications in single data pools.
Cache	Store frequently used data in cache rather than on the disk.

Akamai. However, if you decide to host your own website, scalability is an important consideration. **Scalability** refers to the ability of a site to increase in size as demand warrants. There are three steps you can take to meet the demands for service at your site: scale hardware vertically, scale hardware horizontally, and/or improve the processing architecture of the site (see **Table 3.8**). **Vertical scaling** refers to increasing the processing power of individual components. **Horizontal scaling** refers to employing multiple computers to share the workload and increase the "footprint" of the installation (IBM, 2002).

You can scale your site vertically by upgrading the servers from a single processor to multiple processors. You can keep adding processors to a computer depending on the operating system and upgrade to faster chip speeds as well.

There are two drawbacks to vertical scaling. First, it can become expensive to purchase additional processors with every growth cycle, and second, your entire site becomes dependent on a small number of very powerful computers. If you have two such computers and one goes down, half of your site, or perhaps your entire site, may become unavailable.

Horizontal scaling involves adding multiple single-processor servers to your site and balancing the load among the servers. You can then partition the load so some servers handle only requests for HTML or ASP pages, while others are dedicated to handling database applications. You will need special load-balancing software (provided by a variety of vendors such as Cisco, Microsoft, and IBM) to direct incoming requests to various servers.

There are many advantages to horizontal scaling. It is inexpensive and often can be accomplished using older PCs that otherwise would be disposed of. Horizontal scaling also introduces redundancy—if one computer fails, chances are that another computer can pick up the load dynamically. However, when your site grows from a single computer to perhaps 10 to 20 computers, the size of the physical facility required (the "footprint") increases and there is added management complexity.

scalability
the ability of a site to increase in size as demand warrants

vertical scaling
increasing the processing power of individual components

horizontal scaling
employing multiple computers to share the workload

TABLE 3.9	IMPROVING THE PROCESSING ARCHITECTURE OF YOUR SITE
ARCHITECTURE IMPROVEMENT	DESCRIPTION
Separate static content from dynamic content	Use specialized servers for each type of workload.
Cache static content	Increase RAM to the gigabyte range and store static content in RAM.
Cache database lookup tables	Use cache tables to look up database records.
Consolidate business logic on dedicated servers	Put shopping cart, credit card processing, and other CPU-intensive activity on dedicated servers.
Optimize ASP code	Examine your code to ensure it is operating efficiently.
Optimize the database schema	Examine your database search times and take steps to reduce access times.

A third alternative—improving the processing architecture—is a combination of vertical and horizontal scaling, combined with artful design decisions. **Table 3.9** lists some of the more common steps you can take to greatly improve performance of your site. Most of these steps involve splitting the workload into I/O-intensive activities (such as serving web pages) and CPU-intensive activities (such as taking orders). Once you have this work separated, you can fine-tune the servers for each type of load. One of the least expensive fine-tuning steps is to simply add RAM to a few servers and store all your HTML pages in RAM. This reduces load on your hard drives and increases speed dramatically. RAM is thousands of times faster than hard disks, and RAM is inexpensive. The next most important step is to move your CPU-intensive activities, such as order taking, onto a high-end, multiple-processor server that is dedicated to handling orders and accessing the necessary databases. Taking these steps can permit you to reduce the number of servers required to service 10,000 concurrent users from 100 down to 20, according to one estimate.

3.5 OTHER E-COMMERCE SITE TOOLS

Now that you understand the key factors affecting the speed, capacity, and scalability of your website, we can consider some other important requirements. You will need a coherent website design that makes business sense—not necessarily a site to wow visitors or excite them, but to sell them something. You will also need to know how to build active content and interactivity into your site—not just display static HTML pages. You must be able to track customers who come, leave, and return to your site in order to be able to greet return visitors ("Hi Sarah, welcome back!"). You will also want to track customers throughout your site so you can personalize and customize their experience. You will definitely want the ability for customers to generate content and feedback on your site to increase their engagement with your brand. Finally, you will need to establish a set of information policies for your site—privacy, accessibility, and access to information policies.

TABLE 3.10 E-COMMERCE WEBSITE FEATURES THAT ANNOY CUSTOMERS

- Requiring user to view ad or intro page before going to website content
- Pop-up and pop-under ads and windows
- Too many clicks to get to the content
- Links that don't work
- Confusing navigation; no search function
- Requirement to register and log in before viewing content or ordering
- Slow loading pages
- Content that is out of date
- Inability to use browser's Back button
- No contact information available (web form only)
- Unnecessary splash/flash screens, animation, etc.
- Music or other audio that plays automatically
- Unprofessional design elements
- Text not easily legible due to size, color, format
- Typographical errors
- No or unclear returns policy

In order to achieve these business capabilities, you will need to be aware of some design guidelines and additional software tools that can cost-effectively achieve the required business functionality.

WEBSITE DESIGN: BASIC BUSINESS CONSIDERATIONS

This is not a text about how to design websites. (In Chapter 6, we discuss website design issues from a marketing perspective.) Nevertheless, from a business manager's perspective, there are certain design objectives you must communicate to your website designers to let them know how you will evaluate their work. At a minimum, your customers will need to find what they need at your site, make a purchase, and leave. A website that annoys customers runs the risk of losing the customer forever. See **Table 3.10** for a list of the most common consumer complaints about websites.

Some critics believe poor design is more common than good design. It appears easier to describe what irritates people about websites than to describe how to design a good website. The worst e-commerce sites make it difficult to find information about their products and make it complicated to purchase goods; they have missing pages and broken links, a confusing navigation structure, and annoying graphics or sounds that you cannot turn off. **Table 3.11** restates these negative experiences as positive goals for website design.

TOOLS FOR SEARCH ENGINE OPTIMIZATION

A website is only as valuable from a business perspective as the number of people who visit. The first stop for most customers looking for a product or service is to start with a search engine, and follow the listings on the page, usually starting with the top three to five listings, then glancing to the sponsored ads to the right. The higher you are on the search engine pages, the more traffic you will receive. Page 1 is much better than Page 2. So how do you get to Page 1 in the natural (unpaid) search listings? While every search engine is different, and none of them publish their algorithms for ranking pages, there are some basic ideas that work well:

- **Metatags, keywords, titles, page contents:** Search engines "crawl" your site and identify keywords as well as title pages and then index them for use in search arguments. Pepper your pages with keywords that accurately describe what you say you do in your

TABLE 3.11	THE EIGHT MOST IMPORTANT FACTORS IN SUCCESSFUL E-COMMERCE SITE DESIGN
FACTOR	DESCRIPTION
Functionality	Pages that work, load quickly, and point the customer toward your product offerings
Informational	Links that customers can easily find to discover more about you and your products
Ease of use	Simple foolproof navigation
Redundant navigation	Alternative navigation to the same content
Ease of purchase	One or two clicks to purchase
Multi-browser functionality	Site works with the most popular browsers
Simple graphics	Avoids distracting, obnoxious graphics and sounds that the user cannot control
Legible text	Avoids backgrounds that distort text or make it illegible

metatag site "description" and "keywords" sections of your source code. The goal is to find a balance of the different type of keywords, including shorter head keywords that may be more generic (such as "car"), body keywords that may be slightly more specific (such as "British sports car"), and long-tail keywords that are much more detailed, such as "1968 red Jaguar XKE convertible").

- **Offer expertise:** White papers, industry analyses, FAQ pages, guides, and histories are excellent ways to build confidence on the part of users and to encourage them to see your website as the place to go for help and guidance.
- **Get linked up:** Encourage other sites to link to your site; build a blog that attracts people and who will share your URL with others and post links in the process. Build a Facebook page for your company, and think about using Instagram or Pinterest to develop a following or fan base for your products.
- **Buy ads:** Complement your natural search optimization efforts with paid search engine keywords and ads. Choose your keywords and purchase direct exposure on web pages. You can set your budget and put a ceiling on it to prevent large losses. See what works, and observe the number of visits to your site produced by each keyword string.
- **Local e-commerce:** Developing a national market can take a long time. If your website is particularly attractive to local people, or involves products sold locally, use keywords that connote your location so people can find you nearby. Town, city, and region names in your keywords can be helpful, such as "Vermont cheese" or "San Francisco blues music."

TOOLS FOR INTERACTIVITY AND ACTIVE CONTENT

The more interactive a website is, the more effective it will be in generating sales and encouraging return visitors. Although functionality and ease of use are the supreme objectives in site design, you will also want to interact with users and present them with a lively, "active" experience. You will want to personalize the experience for customers by addressing their individual needs, and customize the content of your offerings based on their behavior or expressed desires. In order to achieve these business objectives, you will need to consider carefully the tools necessary to build these capabilities. Simple interactions such as a customer submitting a name, along with more complex interactions involving credit cards, user preferences, and user responses to prompts, all require special programs. The following sections provide a brief description of some commonly used software tools for achieving high levels of site interactivity.

Common Gateway Interface (CGI)

Common Gateway Interface (CGI) is a set of standards for communication between a browser and a program running on a server that allows for interaction between the user and the server. CGI permits an executable program to access all the information within incoming requests from clients. The program can then generate all the output required to make up the return page (the HTML, script code, text, etc.), and send it back to the client via the web server. For instance, if a user clicks the My Shopping Cart button, the server receives this request and executes a CGI program. The CGI program retrieves the contents of the shopping cart from the database and returns it to the server. The server sends an HTML page that displays the contents of the shopping cart on the user's screen. Notice that all the computing takes place on the server side (this is why CGI programs and others like them are referred to as "server-side" programs).

CGI programs can be written in nearly any programming language as long as they conform to CGI standards. Currently, Perl is one of the most popular languages for CGI scripting. Generally, CGI programs are used with Unix servers. CGI's primary disadvantage is that it is not highly scalable because a new process must be created for each request, thereby limiting the number of concurrent requests that can be handled. CGI scripts are best used for small to medium-sized applications that do not involve a high volume of user traffic. There are also web server extensions available, such as FastCGI, that improve CGI's scalability and SCGI, which is a simpler version of FastCGI (Doyle and Lopes, 2005).

CGI scripts also face security issues. In 2014, a major security hole in the command-line shell used by many Linux and Unix operating systems was discovered. Nicknamed Shellshock, the hole allowed hackers to target vulnerable CGI scripts on Apache web servers. These types of security issues have resulted in some web hosting services requiring their customers to use alternatives to CGI.

Active Server Pages (ASP) and ASP.NET

Active Server Pages (ASP) is Microsoft's original version of server-side programming for Windows. Invented by Microsoft in late 1996, ASP grew rapidly to become the major technique for server-side web programming in the Windows environment. ASP enables developers to easily create and open records from a database and execute programs within an HTML page, as well as handle all the various forms of interactivity found on e-commerce sites. Like CGI, ASP permits an interaction to take place between the browser and the server. ASP uses the same standards as CGI for communication with the browser. ASP programs are restricted to use on Windows servers running Microsoft's IIS web server software. **ASP.NET**, first released in January 2002, and part of Microsoft's .NET framework,

Common Gateway Interface (CGI)
a set of standards for communication between a browser and a program running on a server that allows for interaction between the user and the server

Active Server Pages (ASP)
a proprietary software development tool that enables programmers using Microsoft's IIS package to build dynamic pages

ASP.NET
successor to ASP

is the successor to ASP. ASP.NET Core 2.1 is the most current version of ASP.NET. ASP.NET Core 2.1 features an improved, modern, cross-platform web framework for cloud and regular application servers.

Java, Java Server Pages (JSP), and JavaScript

Java is a programming language that allows programmers to create interactivity and active content on the client computer, thereby saving considerable load on the server. Java was initially developed by Sun Microsystems as a platform-independent programming language for consumer electronics. The idea was to create a language whose programs (so-called Write Once Run Anywhere [WORA] programs) could operate on any computer regardless of operating system. This would be possible if every operating system at the time (Macintosh, Windows, Unix, DOS, and mainframe MVS systems) had a Java Virtual Machine (VM) installed that would interpret the Java programs for that environment.

By 1995, however, when Sun Microsystems released Java 1.0, the first public version of the language, it had become clear that Java was more applicable to the Web than to consumer electronics. Java programs (known as Java applets) could be downloaded to the client over the Web and executed entirely on the client's computer. Applet tags could be included in an HTML page. To enable this, each browser would have to include a Java VM. Today, the leading browsers include a VM to run Java programs. When the browser accesses a page with an applet, a request is sent to the server to download and execute the program and allocate page space to display the results of the program. Java can be used to display interesting graphics, create interactive environments (such as a mortgage calculator), and directly access the web server. The most current versions of Java, JDK (Java Development Kit) 10 and JRE (Java Runtime Environment) 10 (for running Java applications), were released in early 2018. Today, Java remains one of the most popular programming languages, with many critical technologies, such as the Google Android mobile platform (although not Apple's iOS), leveraging aspects of the language. However, Java does face some challenges. In recent years, it has been plagued by security flaws, which Oracle has been attempting to address with the frequent release of new versions and security patches (Krill, 2015).

Java Server Pages (JSP), like CGI and ASP, is a web page coding standard that allows developers to use a combination of HTML, JSP scripts, and Java to dynamically generate web pages in response to user requests. JSP uses Java "servlets," small Java programs that are specified in the web page and run on the web server to modify the web page before it is sent to the user who requested it. JSP is supported by most of the popular application servers on the market today.

JavaScript is a programming language invented by Netscape that is used to control the objects on an HTML page and handle interactions with the browser. It is most commonly used on the client side to handle verification and validation of user input, as well as to implement business logic. For instance, JavaScript can be used on customer registration forms to confirm that a valid phone number, zip code, or even e-mail address has been given. Before a user finishes completing a form, the e-mail address given can be tested for validity. JavaScript appears to be much more acceptable to corporations and other environments in large part because it is more stable and also it is restricted to the

---

Java
a programming language that allows programmers to create interactivity and active content on the client computer, thereby saving considerable load on the server

Java Server Pages (JSP)
like CGI and ASP, a web page coding standard that allows developers to dynamically generate web pages in response to user requests

JavaScript
a programming language invented by Netscape that is used to control the objects on an HTML page and handle interactions with the browser

operation of requested HTML pages. JavaScript is also used as part of Node.js, a cross-platform environment for server-side applications (including mobile), which has been used by companies such as PayPal, Walmart, and LinkedIn. In 2015, Node.js v4.0 was released, combining Node.js and io.js, a variant of the JavaScript platform built on V8, the JavaScript virtual machine used in Google Chrome, into a single codebase for the first time. Node.js has become one of the most popular server-side developer frameworks, resulting in JavaScript remaining a vital language not just for web development, but also for platform-as-a-service (PaaS) application (Vaughan-Nichols, 2017).

There are also a number of other tools based on JavaScript that help automate the process of creating web applications. AngularJS (sometimes also referred to as Angular.js) is a Javascript-based open source front-end web application framework that extends the functionality of HTML. D3.js (short for Data Driven Documents) is a JavaScript library for visualizing data with HTML, SVG, and CSS. jQuery is a cross-platform JavaScript library designed to simplify the client-side scripting of HTML. *Ajax (asynchronous JavaScript and XML)* uses a variety of different tools, including JavaScript, to allow web pages to be updated asynchronously (i.e., updating only parts of the page rather than having to reload the entire page to change just part of the content).

ActiveX and VBScript

Microsoft invented the **ActiveX** programming language to compete with Java and **VBScript** to compete with JavaScript. When a browser receives an HTML page with an ActiveX control (comparable to a Java applet), the browser simply executes the program. Unlike Java, however, ActiveX has full access to all the client's resources—printers, networks, and hard drives. VBScript performs in the same way as JavaScript. ActiveX and VBScript work only if you are using Internet Explorer. Otherwise, that part of the screen is blank. However, the days of ActiveX and VBScript are numbered. Microsoft has dropped support for both in Microsoft Edge, the browser that has replaced Internet Explorer in the Windows 10 operating system. Microsoft believes that the need for ActiveX and VBScript has been significantly reduced given the capabilities of HTML5, and that eliminating them will enhance browser security.

ActiveX
a programming language created by Microsoft to compete with Java

VBScript
a programming language invented by Microsoft to compete with JavaScript

ColdFusion

ColdFusion is an integrated server-side environment for developing interactive web and mobile applications. Originally developed by Macromedia and now offered by Adobe, ColdFusion combines an intuitive tag-based scripting language and a tag-based server scripting language (CFML) that lowers the cost of creating interactive features. ColdFusion offers a powerful set of visual design, programming, debugging, and deployment tools including the ability to create mobile apps, robust security features and support for interoperability. The most recent version, released in 2018, offers a more intuitive user interface, performance monitoring tools, and programming language enhancements.

ColdFusion
an integrated server-side environment for developing interactive web applications

PHP, Ruby on Rails (RoR), and Django

PHP is an open source, general-purpose scripting language that is most frequently used in server-side web applications to generate dynamic web page content, although it can

PHP
open source, general-purpose scripting language

also be used for client-side graphical user interface applications. PHP is also a part of many web application development frameworks, such as CakePHP, CodeIgniter, and others, and is also part of the LAMP (Linux, Apache, MySQL, PHP) open source web development model for building dynamic websites and web applications (Perl and Python are sometimes substituted for PHP in some LAMP projects). According to W3Techs, PHP is, by far and away, the most commonly used server-side scripting language (used by almost 79% of the websites whose server-side programming language it was able to identify), with ASP.NET a distant second, used by around 10.6%, followed by Java, with only about 3.7%, and Ruby on Rails at 2.9%. ColdFusion, Perl, JavaScript, and Python were all less than 2% (W3techs.com, 2019). PHP is also popular with hackers, and is frequently used in phishing attacks (RSA FraudAction Intelligence, 2016).

Ruby on Rails (Ruby, RoR, or Rails) is an open source web application framework based on the Ruby programming language. RoR is based on a philosophy known as convention over configuration, or coding by convention (CoC), which means that the framework provides a structured layout that minimizes the number of decisions that the programmer needs to make, thereby simplifying and speeding development. JavaScript and Ajax are highly integrated into RoR, which makes it easy to handle Ajax requests for page updates. Ruby was very popular in the early 2000s, but in the last several years has fallen out of favor somewhat. Some well-known websites based on RoR include Shopify, Groupon, Kickstarter, and Airbnb (Korkishko, 2017; DeNisco, 2017).

Django is also an open source web application framework. It is based on the Python programming language. Django is optimized for the creation of complex, database-driven websites. It allows for fast development, focuses on automating as much as possible, emphasizes the reusability of various components, and follows the DRY (Don't Repeat Yourself) programming principle. Some well-known websites based on Django include Instagram, Pinterest, and NASA (Panal, 2017).

Other Design Elements

One easy way to pump up the energy on your website is to include some appropriate widgets (sometimes called gadgets, plug-ins, or snippets). **Widgets** are small chunks of code that execute automatically in your HTML web page. They are prebuilt and many are free. Social networks and blogs use widgets to present users with content drawn from around the Web (news headlines from specific news sources, announcements, press releases, and other routine content), calendars, clocks, weather, live TV, games, and other functionality. You can copy the code to an HTML web page. You can find widgets at Apple's Dashboard Widgets, Wolfram|Alpha Widgets, and SIMILE Widgets. There are also widgets for specific platforms such as WordPress, Amazon Widgets, and Pinterest's Widget Builder.

Mashups are a little more complicated and involve pulling functionality and data from one program and including it in another. The most common mashup involves using Google Maps data and software and combining it with other data. For instance, if you have a local real estate website, you can download Google Maps and satellite image applications to your site so visitors can get a sense of the neighborhood. There are thousands of Google Map mashups, from maps of Myanmar political protests, to maps of the Fortune

500 companies, all with associated news stories and other content. Other mashups involve sports, photos, video, shopping, and news.

PERSONALIZATION TOOLS

You will definitely want to know how to treat each customer on an individual basis and emulate a traditional face-to-face marketplace. *Personalization* (the ability to treat people based on their personal qualities and prior history with your site) and *customization* (the ability to change the product to better fit the needs of the customer) are two key elements of e-commerce that potentially can make it nearly as powerful as a traditional marketplace, and perhaps even more powerful than direct mail or shopping at an anonymous suburban shopping mall. Speaking directly to the customer on a one-to-one basis, and even adjusting the product to the customer is quite difficult in the usual type of mass marketing, one-size-fits-all commercial transaction that characterizes much of contemporary commerce.

There are a number of methods for achieving personalization and customization. For instance, you could personalize web content if you knew the personal background of the visitor. You could also analyze the pattern of clicks and sites visited for every customer who enters your site. We discuss these methods in later chapters on marketing. The primary method for achieving personalization and customization is through the placement of cookie files on the user's client computer. A cookie is a small text file placed on the user's client computer that can contain any kind of information about the customer, such as customer ID, campaign ID, or purchases at the site. And then, when the user returns to the site, or indeed goes further into your site, the customer's prior history can be accessed from a database. Information gathered on prior visits can then be used to personalize the visit and customize the product.

For instance, when a user returns to a site, you can read the cookie to find a customer ID, look the ID up in a database of names, and greet the customer ("Hello Mary! Glad to have you return!"). You could also have stored a record of prior purchases, and then recommend a related product ("How about the wrench tool box now that you have purchased the wrenches?"). And you could think about customizing the product ("You've shown an interest in the elementary training programs for Word. We have a special 'How to Study' program for beginners in Office software. Would you like to see a sample copy online?").

We further describe the use of cookies in Chapter 6.

THE INFORMATION POLICY SET

In developing an e-commerce site, you will also need to focus on the set of information policies that will govern the site. You will need to develop a **privacy policy**—a set of public statements declaring to your customers how you treat their personal information that you gather on the site. You also will need to establish **accessibility rules**—a set of design objectives that ensure users with disabilities can effectively access your site. There are more than 650 million people worldwide who have a disability, many of whom may require special help in order to be able to access computers or mobile devices (see *Insight on Society: Designing for Accessibility*). E-commerce information policies are described in greater depth in Chapter 8.

privacy policy
a set of public statements declaring to your customers how you treat their personal information that you gather on the site

accessibility rules
a set of design objectives that ensure disabled users can effectively access your site

INSIGHT ON SOCIETY

DESIGNING FOR ACCESSIBILITY

About 10% of the population worldwide has a disability that affects their ability to use the Internet. There are approximately 360 million people worldwide with hearing loss and 285 million with significant vision loss. Although these and other disabilities, such as motor and mobility impairments, can be addressed with intelligent software and hardware design, oftentimes, they are not. As a result, the Internet and mobile devices are unfriendly places for many people with disabilities.

How can designers build in accessibility for the blind? One tool is screen-reader software. A blind person navigates a web page by checking the hypertext links on the page, usually by jumping from link to link with the Tab key; the screen-reader software automatically reads the highlighted text as the focus moves from link to link. The screen-reader software is looking for ASCII text, which it can convert to speech or Braille. Examples of such software include Freedom Scientific's Job Access with Speech (JAWS) and MacForTheBlind's VoiceOver.

There are also several simple strategies web designers can use to improve accessibility. Embedding text descriptions behind images is one example that allows screen readers to announce those descriptions. Allowing users to set the color and font schemes also can make a difference for the visually impaired. Adding screen magnification tools and sound labels where hyperlinks appear are two additional ways to increase accessibility. For those who are hearing impaired, access to close-captioned video with subtitles can also be helpful.

These are examples of "equivalent alternatives" that disability advocates suggest should be required for both visual and auditory content to ensure that individuals with disabilities have equal access to information that appears on-screen. Guidelines for creating accessible web pages include ensuring that text and graphics are understandable when viewed without color, using features that enable activation of page elements via a variety of input devices (such as keyboard, head wand, and Braille reader), and providing clear navigation mechanisms (such as navigation bars or a site map) to aid users.

The World Wide Web Consortium (W3C)'s Web Content Accessibility Guidelines (WCAG) also provide organizations with strategies in web design for accommodating people with many different kinds of disabilities. The current version of WCAG is WCAG 2.1, released in June 2018, and the first update of WCAG standards since WCAG 2.0, which went into effect in 2008.

Ensuring accessibility of mobile devices has its own set of issues, in many instances even more challenging than those associated with the Web. There is only a limited selection of mobile devices with built-in accessibility features. The small size of the device, screen, and keypad presents its own problems. Third-party applications, such as text-to-speech/screen readers and screen magnifiers, are now becoming available, but much work still needs to be done. For instance, many mobile devices come equipped with voice control capabilities and audio alerts, which could be helpful to those with vision or motor difficulties, but in most cases, these are still limited to simple tasks and do not provide access to the full functionality of the device. In addition, the deaf community cannot rely on audio content or alerts, so developers need to provide text or other alternatives for auditory information. Those with impaired motor functionality also face great challenges in dealing with input to mobile devices. To deal with these challenges, WCAG 2.1 provides a number of additional guidelines for mobile accessibility.

Web accessibility is also a matter of government policy. Article 9 of the United Nations' *Convention on the Rights of Persons with Disabilities* requires that appropriate measures must be taken to ensure access to information and communications technologies for persons with disabilities on an equal basis with others as a matter of basic human rights. As of 2019, 180 countries had ratified the Convention. Despite this, actual accessibility of both government and private websites remains quite low. For instance, a European Commission report on monitoring accessibility found that only one-third of the content generated by public authorities was accessible. In 2015, the European Commission proposed a European Accessibility Act (EAA), which will set accessibility requirements for certain products and services, including computers and operating systems, banking services, smartphones, digital television services, transportation services, e-books, and e-commerce. The requirements set forth what features must be accessible, such as a user interface, but do not mandate specific technical solutions. In May 2019, the European Parliament approved a final version of the EAA, followed by approval by the EU Council. In June 2019, the EAA was published in the Official Journal of the EU, which begins a three-year transition period during which nation states enact specific versions into their national laws.

Various countries have also implemented accessibility legislation. In many cases, standards apply only to government agency websites and not private websites. For example, French law requires all French public websites to comply with its standard, RGAA 3, which is based on WCAG 2. In Germany, all government websites must comply with BITV 2 (also based on WCAG 2). One exception is Australia, which requires non-government as well as government websites to comply with WCAG 2. In the United Kingdom, service providers must make reasonable adjustments to ensure that their websites are accessible to all users. In determining what is reasonable, the Statutory Code of Practice indicates that factors to be taken into account include the service provider's financial and other resources, the amount of resources already spent on making adjustments, and the extent of any disruption that it would cause the service provider. Large companies will clearly have a more difficult time justifying any failure to make their websites accessible. In the United States, several statutes, including the Rehabilitation Act (Section 508), the Americans with Disabilities Act (the ADA), and the 21st Century Communications and Video Accessibility Act, impose various obligations with respect to accessibility.

Disability advocates are also using lawsuits as a way to advance their cause. For instance, the Royal National Institute of the Blind brought a court case against BMI Baby, a British travel agency. BMI Baby ultimately agreed to make changes to its website to enable the blind to book flights. Other similar cases have been settled out of court. Despite these successes, however, much remains to be done to make websites, mobile sites, and apps fully accessible.

▬ **SOURCES:** "European Accessibility Act: Final Steps on the European Level—First Steps on the National Level," by David Hay, Eud.eu, March 13, 2019; "Web Content Accessibility Guidelines (WCAG) 2.1: W3C Recommendation 05 June 2018," W3.org, accessed December 31, 2018; "Government Accessibility Standards and WCAG 2," by Mark Rogers, Powermapper.com, November 28, 2017; "European Accessibility Act/After 2015-12," Europarl.europa.eu, accessed November 11, 2017; "EU Ready to Set Laws for Accessibility Testing," Qa-financial.com, December 9, 2016; "Proposal for a Directive of the European Parliament and of the Council on the Approximation of the Laws, Regulations, and Administrative Proposals of the Member States as Regards the Accessibility Requirements for Products and Services—Progress Report," Council of the European Union, November 18, 2016; "Commission Proposes to Make Products and Services More Accessible," European Commission, December 2, 2015; "Tough New EU Public Sector Web Accessibility Rules Take Shape," by Dan Jellinek, UKAuthority.com, March 4, 2014; "Digital Britain 2: Putting Users at the Heart of Government's Digital Services," National Audit Office, March 28, 2013.

3.6 DEVELOPING A MOBILE WEBSITE AND BUILDING MOBILE APPLICATIONS

Today, building a website is just one part of developing an e-commerce presence. Given that over 85% of all Internet users worldwide access the Web at least part of the time from mobile devices, businesses today need to develop mobile websites, and mobile web apps, native apps, or hybrid apps, in order to interact with customers, suppliers, and employees. Deciding which of these extended web presence tools to use is a first step.

There are different kinds of m-commerce platform offerings to consider, each with unique advantages and costs. A **mobile website** is a version of a regular website that is scaled down in content and navigation so that users can find what they want and move quickly to a decision or purchase. You can see the difference between a regular website and a mobile site by visiting the Amazon website from your desktop computer and then a smartphone or tablet computer. Amazon's mobile site is a cleaner, more interactive site suitable for finger navigation, and efficient consumer decision making. Like traditional websites, mobile websites run on a firm's servers, and are built using standard web tools such as server-side HTML, Linux, PHP, and SQL. Like all websites, the user must be connected to the Web and performance will depend on bandwidth. Generally, mobile websites operate more slowly than traditional websites viewed on a desktop computer connected to a broadband office network. Most large firms today have mobile websites.

A **mobile web app** is an application built to run on the mobile web browser built into a smartphone or tablet computer. In the case of Apple, the native browser is Safari. Generally it is built to mimic the qualities of a native app using HTML5 and Java. Mobile web apps are specifically designed for the mobile platform in terms of screen size, finger navigation, and graphical simplicity. Mobile web apps can support complex interactions used in games and rich media, perform real-time, on-the-fly calculations, and can be geo-sensitive using the smartphone's built-in global positioning system (GPS) function. Mobile web apps typically operate faster than mobile websites but not as fast as native apps.

A **native app** is an application designed specifically to operate using the mobile device's hardware and operating system. These stand-alone programs can connect to the Internet to download and upload data, and can operate on this data even when not connected to the Internet. Download a book to an app reader, disconnect from the Internet, and read your book. Because the various types of smartphones have different hardware and operating systems, apps are not "one size fits all" and therefore need to be developed for different mobile platforms. An Apple app that runs on an iPhone cannot operate on Android phones. As you learned in Chapter 2, native apps are built using different programming languages depending on the device for which they are intended, which is then compiled into binary code, and which executes extremely fast on mobile devices, much faster than HTML or Java-based mobile web apps. For this reason, native apps are ideal for games, complex interactions, on-the-fly calculations, graphic manipulations, and rich media advertising.

---

mobile website
version of a regular desktop website that is scaled down in content and navigation

mobile web app
application built to run on the mobile web browser built into a smartphone or tablet computer

native app
application designed specifically to operate using the mobile device's hardware and operating system

Increasingly, developers are combining elements of native apps and mobile web apps into hybrid apps. A **hybrid app** has many of the features of both a native app and a mobile web app. Like a native app, it runs inside a native container on the mobile device and has access to the device's APIs, enabling it to take advantage of many of the device's features, such as a gyroscope, that are normally not accessible by a mobile web app. It can also be packaged as an app for distribution from an App store. Like a mobile web app, it is based on HTML5, CSS3, and JavaScript, but uses the device's browser engine to render the HTML5 and process the JavaScript locally.

hybrid app

has many of the features of both a native app and a mobile web app

PLANNING AND BUILDING A MOBILE PRESENCE

What is the "right" mobile presence for your firm? The answer depends on identifying the business objectives, and from these, deriving the information requirements of your mobile presence. The same kind of systems analysis and design (SAD) reasoning described earlier in the chapter is needed for planning and building a mobile presence, although there are important differences.

The first step is to identify the business objectives you are trying to achieve. **Table 3.12** illustrates the thought process for the analysis stage of building a mobile presence. Why are you developing a mobile presence? Is it to drive sales by creating an easily browsed catalog where users can shop and purchase? Strengthen your brand by creating an engaging, interactive experience? Enable customers to interact with your customer community? How are your competitors using their mobile presence? Once you have a clear sense of business objectives, you will be able to describe the kind of system functionality that is needed and specify the information requirements for your mobile presence.

After you have identified the business objectives, system functionality, and information requirements, you can think about how to design and build the system. Now is the time to consider which to develop: a mobile website, a mobile web app, or a native app.

TABLE 3.12	SYSTEMS ANALYSIS FOR BUILDING A MOBILE PRESENCE	
BUSINESS OBJECTIVE	SYSTEM FUNCTIONALITY	INFORMATION REQUIREMENTS
Driving sales	Digital catalog; product database	Product descriptions, photos, SKUs, inventory
Branding	Showing how customers use your products	Videos and rich media; product and customer demonstrations
Building customer community	Interactive experiences, games with multiple players	Games, contests, forums, social sign-up to Facebook
Advertising and promotion	Coupons and flash sales for slow-selling items	Product descriptions, coupon management, and inventory management
Gathering customer feedback	Ability to retrieve and store user inputs including text, photos, and video	Customer sign-in and identification; customer database

TABLE 3.13 UNIQUE FEATURES THAT MUST BE TAKEN INTO ACCOUNT WHEN DESIGNING A MOBILE PRESENCE

FEATURE	IMPLICATIONS FOR MOBILE PLATFORM
Hardware	Mobile hardware is smaller, and there are more resource constraints in data storage and processing power.
Connectivity	The mobile platform is constrained by slower connection speeds than desktop websites.
Displays	Mobile displays are much smaller and require simplification. Some screens are not good in sunlight.
Interface	Touch-screen technology introduces new interaction routines different from the traditional mouse and keyboard. The mobile platform is not a good data entry tool but can be a good navigational tool.

For instance, if your objective is branding or building community, a native app might be the best choice because it enables you to deliver a rich, interactive, and immersive experience that can strengthen the emotional connection with the brand. Because native apps are stored locally on the device, they can be accessed even when the user is offline, enabling the user to more deeply engage. In addition, native apps can take advantage of the mobile device's unique characteristics, such as using the gyroscope to deliver a 360-degree view. If your objective, on the other hand, is to create broad awareness, provide specific information on particular products, or drive sales, then a mobile website or mobile web app makes more sense, because it is relatively easy and inexpensive to simply publish information to the mobile Web and consumers are still most comfortable completing transactions on the Web (although this is changing as more and more retailers add e-commerce functionality directly into apps). Increasingly, however, the choice will not be an either/or decision. Mobile apps and mobile websites each offer distinct benefits, and in most cases, the best strategy will be to plan to deliver compelling content across all devices.

MOBILE PRESENCE: DESIGN CONSIDERATIONS

Designing a mobile presence is somewhat different from traditional desktop website design because of different hardware, software, and consumer expectations. **Table 3.13** describes some of the major differences.

Designers need to take mobile platform constraints into account when designing for the mobile platform. Mobile page load speed has been shown to be a signficant factor in conversion rates (Moffat, 2017). File sizes should be kept smaller and the number of files sent to the user reduced. Focus on a few, powerful graphics, and minimize the number of images sent to the user. Prioritize the loading of critical content first, and while the user is processing that content, start to load the next layer of content. Simplify choice boxes and lists so the user can easily scroll and touch-select the options.

Mobile presence has become so important that it is fueling a growing trend to flip the traditional e-commerce development process and begin instead with development of a mobile presence rather than a desktop website (known as **mobile first design**). Mobile first design has several advantages. Instead of creating a full-featured design for a desktop website that then needs to be scaled back, mobile first design focuses on creating the best possible experience given mobile platform constraints and then adding back elements for the desktop platform, progressively enhancing the functionality of the site. Proponents of mobile first design argue that it forces designers to focus on what is most important, and this helps create a lean and efficient mobile design that functions much better than a design that begins with a traditional platform that must be stripped down to work on mobile. Mobile first design is not without its challenges, however. It can be more difficult for designers who are more comfortable with the more traditional process (Byers, 2013).

Other important trends in the development of mobile websites include responsive web design and adaptive web design.

Responsive web design (RWD) tools and design techniques make it possible to design a website that automatically adjusts its layout and display according to the screen resolution of the device on which it is being viewed, whether a desktop, tablet, or smartphone. RWD tools include HTML5 and CSS3, and its three key design principles involve using flexible grid-based layouts, flexible images and media, and media queries. RWD uses the same HTML code and design for each device, but uses CSS (which determines the layout of the web page) to adjust the layout and display to the screen's form factor. RWD sites typically work well for sites with relatively simple functionality (i.e., sites that primarily deliver content) and that users engage with in a similar manner no matter the device being used. However, using RWD can be costly, often requiring a complete redesign of the website's interface. Another problem with RWD, particularly if not coupled with mobile first design, is that the responsive website still has the size and complexity of a traditional desktop site, sometimes making it slow to load and perform on a mobile device. Another technique, known as adaptive web design, has been developed to deal with this issue.

With **adaptive web design (AWD)** (sometimes also referred to as *adaptive delivery* or *responsive web design with server-side components (RESS)*), the server hosting the website detects the attributes of the device making the request and, using predefined templates based on device screen size along with CSS and JavaScript, loads a version of the site that is optimized for the device. AWD has a number of advantages, including faster load times, the ability to enhance or remove functionality on the fly, and typically a better user experience, particularly for businesses where user intent differs depending on the platform being used. For example, creating its mobile website with AWD enabled Lufthansa to focus on actions its mobile users are most likely to take, such as checking in, getting flight status information, and looking up travel itineraries, and to provide a differentiated experience from its traditional desktop site (Pratap, 2013). A variation on AWD uses a cloud-based platform to provide similar functionality.

CROSS-PLATFORM MOBILE APP DEVELOPMENT TOOLS

In addition to creating native apps from scratch using a programming language such as Objective C or Java (as described in Chapter 2), there are hundreds of low-cost or open

---

mobile first design
beginning the e-commerce development process with a mobile presence rather than a desktop website

responsive web design (RWD)
tools and design principles that automatically adjust the layout of a website depending on the screen resolution of the device on which it is being viewed

adaptive web design (AWD)
server-side technique that detects the attributes of the device making the request and, using predefined templates based on device screen size along with CSS and JavaScript, loads a version of the site that is optimized for the device

source app development toolkits that make creating cross-platform mobile apps relatively easy and inexpensive without having to use a device-specific programming language.

Tools include Appery.io, a cloud-based platform that enables you to use a drag-and-drop visual builder tool to create HTML5 apps using jQuery Mobile. Appery.io supports Android, iOS, and Windows Phone applications. Codiqa is a similar tool that is even easier to use. It also provides a drag-and-drop interface and builds an app with 100% HTML5 components, without the need to do any coding. For those who are even less technical, Swiftic is a free mobile app builder that allows you to include a variety of functionality, including e-commerce, notifications, and a social feed.

On the more technical side, PhoneGap is a mobile development framework that uses software called Apache Cordova to enable building hybrid mobile applications using HTML, CSS, and JavaScript. Axway Appcelerator is a similar, less technical tool for creating and managing hybrid mobile apps.

MOBILE PRESENCE: PERFORMANCE AND COST CONSIDERATIONS

If you don't have an existing website, the most efficient process may be to use a mobile first design philosophy and design a mobile site first. Alternatively, you may choose to build a traditional website using RWD or AWD techniques. If you already have a website that you don't want to totally redevelop, the least expensive path is to resize it to create a smartphone-friendly mobile site. Doing so typically will not require a complete redesign effort. You will need to reduce the graphics and text, simplify the navigation, and focus on improving the customer experience so you do not confuse people. Because your customers might still need to use a relatively slow cell connection at times, you will need to lighten up the amount of data you send. Also, given the difficulty of customer data entry on a mobile device, you cannot expect customers to happily enter long strings of numbers or text characters. For marketing clarity, make sure the brand images used on the mobile website match those on the traditional website. The cost of developing a mobile website can range widely, from upwards of $1 million for a custom-designed site for a large global enterprise to well under $1,000 for a small business who chooses a company such as Wix or MoFuse that offers a template or mobile website creator.

Building a mobile web app that uses the mobile device's browser requires more effort and cost than developing a mobile website and suffers from the same limitations as any browser-based application. However, it does offer some advantages such as better graphics, more interactivity, and faster local calculations as, for instance, in mobile geo-location applications like Foursquare that require local calculations of position and then communication with the site's web server.

The most expensive path to a mobile presence is to build a native app. Native apps can require more programming expertise, although there are many new development packages that can build mobile native apps with minimal programming expertise. In addition, virtually none of the elements used in your existing website can be reused, and you will need to redesign the entire logic of the interface and carefully think out the customer experience. For instance, there is a fairly stable HTML traditional website interface with buttons, graphics, videos, and ads that has developed over the last decade. This is not true for apps. There is no set of standards or expectations even on the part of users—every app looks different from every other app. This means the user confronts large variations in app design, so your interface must be quite simple and obvious. Many of the bells and whistles found on the large desktop website screen cannot be used in mobile apps. You'll need even greater simplification and focus. These weaknesses are also native apps' greatest strength: you have the opportunity to create a really stunning, unique customer experience where users can interact with your brand. If you want an intense branding experience with your customers, where interaction between your brand and customers is effortless and efficient, then native apps are the best choice. The *Insight on Technology* case, *Klook Sets Its Sights on New Vistas*, takes a look at a travel tech company's development of a mobile-first strategy and the steps it has taken to grow its e-commerce presence.

3.7 CAREERS IN E-COMMERCE

The material in this chapter provides foundational information for a number of different careers. Job titles include web developer/programmer (including front end developer/front end engineer; full stack developer; and titles that focus on a particular technology such as JavaScript developer/engineer or similar), web designer (including user interface (UI) designer, user experience (UX) designer, and interaction designer), and webmasters. Many of these positions, although labeled as "web," involve working with mobile applications as well. In this section, we'll examine a job posting by a company looking for a UX designer.

THE COMPANY

The company is a restaurant chain known for its Italian dishes, such as pizza, pasta, heroes, and desserts. The company has over 11,000 locations worldwide. Much of its growth in the past five years has resulted from global expansion including in China, Japan, India, and the Middle East. The company uses three different formats: family-style locations, storefront delivery and carryout, and locations that do both sit-down dinners and carryout. The company has developed a robust web presence that enables customers to order meals either on the company website or via an app. The company's strategy is to leverage its investment in physical locations by expanding its online ordering, pick-up, and delivery business. To carry out this strategy, the company is aiming for continuous improvement of the customer experience on the firm's websites, mobile apps, and social network sites.

POSITION: UX DESIGNER

You will be working with the UX Group, which reports to the Chief E-commerce Officer. The UX Group creates intuitive and engaging online experiences for the company's customers throughout its digital and mobile ecosystem, including social media. You will work on developing business processes, online roadmaps, and analytic models of consumer behavior. You will be working with product managers, online developers, and analysts to create engaging digital experiences for our customers. Responsibilities include:

INSIGHT ON TECHNOLOGY

KLOOK SETS ITS SIGHTS ON NEW VISTAS

Klook Travel Technology Ltd. is a travel tech company founded in 2014 and based in Hong Kong. The company's main audience is in Southeast Asia, where the online booking markets largely bypassed the PC and went straight to mobile. As user access to PCs as a means of making bookings is likely to be limited while traveling, if available at all, Klook has a mobile-first strategy that is based on a localized approach adapted to the different marketplaces it operates in.

Klook, which stands for "keep looking," provides a tourism app with a simple value proposition: it does away with the inconveniences of pre-trip and in-destination planning. It effectively provides an online concierge service that makes the travel experience as enjoyable and hassle-free for its user base as possible. There is also a clear focus on affordability and competitive pricing. A direct link to in-destination attractions and services means that prices are considerably lower, as no commission is added to the sale cost.

Initially focused on its home market of Southeast Asia, Klook targeted customers looking for adventure and things to do, the so-called free and independent travelers, but it has grown rapidly since and now offers its 350 destinations to a sizable sector of international tourists. Starting the business involved a fundamental challenge: Klook needed merchants providing attractive offers to attract customers, but it had to convince merchants that the user numbers would be worth it too. The company managed to assemble a wide array of suppliers through old-fashioned cold-calling, and over time, as brand awareness grew, it was able to build on its initial focus on local partnering to grow strategic partnerships with many big names in the tourism sector among transportation companies, tourist attractions, and hoteliers. Its offerings have steadily increased to include over 100,000 things to do, from food-themed excursions, to adventure expeditions, to sightseeing tours.

What market strategy does Klook use to grow its customer base? Local marketing teams provide feedback on any regional and local trends to the company's headquarters so that offers can be based on themes such as the season or a local festival. Klook actively uploads blogposts on seasonal offerings, informative updates, and recommendations for its users, and a section on its website is dedicated to affiliates and influencers, whose image posts fuel their followers' fear of missing out (FOMO).

Expanding one's offering comes at a price, of course; a hefty investment is needed to scale up and digitize the available content and develop the app and associated systems for increased traffic. Klook has succeeded in raising $520 million from investors such as Sequoia Capital, Softbank Vision Fund, TCV, and Goldman Sachs so far, and the company has now expanded into Europe, North America, and Australia. Its ever-increasing range of partnerships means that Klook can offer its customers the best available prices while focusing on the best-possible experience for its users, further securing its long-term market position.

The Klook app has an intuitive layout that is ordered by destination and things to do. The user can add filters for dates and availability, and the price offers combine attractions, activities, food tours, and sightseeing, with transportation links also included. The design won Best of Year awards from the Google Play and Apple app stores in 2015, 2017, and 2018, and the consumer response has been just as positive: 75% of Klook's bookings in 2018 were made by mobile, and the company anticipates triple-digit growth in both revenue and bookings in 2019.

In what was a fragmented marketplace, Klook was able to successfully leverage available technology to provide digital solutions and make connections between the user and the provider by working directly with attraction owners and managers. Klook has focused on deepening key partnerships while growing and diversifying the offers on available destinations and activities. The Klook Partner App allows merchants to easily manage bookings, enabling local merchants and smaller attractions to attract tourists from a wider customer base. Klook's custom-built enterprise software allows even small-scale merchants to accept digital bookings and payments, and the data it captures allows its partners to get a good sense of the different nationalities' preferences.

Instant confirmation for same-day bookings is part of Klook's value proposition; it enhances the travel experience for the user and makes it more likely that they will become repeat customers. However, last-minute bookings require instant confirmation and ticket access, so the company uses QR code technology that enables tickets to be delivered to a user's device as e-vouchers, and these can be easily accessed even offline.

One of the challenges of the in-destination travel market has been connectivity integration, and Klook has also taken on the task of using its internally developed technology to digitize in-destination supply. Operational procedures—from the customer's initial browsing, to booking their choice, to booking confirmation and ticketing—have to be seamless; in a socially connected world, customer reviews quickly highlight any issues to a global audience. Klook seeks to use data analytics to improve the overall experience for all stakeholders, and the millions of monthly visitors on the platform across its website, mobile web, and app now gives the company access to enormous data sets. The insights gleaned from the data allows for more personalized targeted recommendations based on search and booking behavior.

For the longer term, the company is investing in AI and machine-learning systems, and it has plans for connectivity to AI voice-powered assistants to cater to an audience that is increasingly using Amazon's Alexa, Google Assistant, and Apple's Siri. Klook will have to improve search and user recommendations to fit both voice searching and image recognition technology.

Klook has ambitious expansion plans, including growth in European markets and an increase in its workforce from 1,800 in 2019 to 2,500 by the end of 2020. Serving those customers in Europe means adding French, Italian, Russian, German, and Spanish to the languages currently on offer. Klook's ambitions are also firmly fixed on the Japanese market for the Summer Olympics in 2020, which is expected to attract 40 million foreign tourists. This growth will have to overcome technology challenges such as the existing Japanese legacy systems, including paper train tickets. Klook's experience in the use of QR codes to provide tickets and vouchers via mobile devices will be very welcome in this marketplace. Klook has also recently launched China Rail on its platform, leveraging the experience it has gained while working with the Hong Kong airport express and railways in Southeast Asia.

■ **SOURCES:** "Klook Celebrates 5th Anniversary and Will Surpass 60 Million Trip Bookings in 2019, Outlines Global Expansion Plan," Klook.com, September 12, 2019; "How This Hong Kong-based Travel Unicorn Is Planning to Make Its Mark in the Asian Market," by Nidhi Singh, Entrepreneur.com, April 10, 2019; "Hong Kong Travel Startup Klook to Focus on Expansion, COO Says," Bloomberg Daybreak: Asia, Bloomberg.com, April 10, 2019; "Klook Receives $225 Million SoftBank Investment in Nod to Tours and Activities," by Raini Hamdi, Skift.com, April 09, 2019; "Klook Completes US$425M Series D Funding with New Capital Raise Led by Softbank Vision Fund," by Chin Yung Lu, April 9, 2019, Startmeup.hk; "The Insider Secrets & Story of Hong Kong Traveltech Startup Klook Discovered," by Heather Lo, Medium.com, December 4, 2017; "Klook Banking on AI to Beef Up Travel Services," by Trevor Tan, Straitstimes.com, November 1, 2017; "Klook, an App for Booking Travel Activities Across Asia, Raises $5M," by Jon Russell, TechCrunch.com, October 16, 2015.

Case contributed by June Clarke, Sheffield Business School

- Contributing to the development of an entrepreneurial, cross-disciplinary UX team that embraces creativity, data, and a constant focus on the customer.
- Implementing the company's UX approach and best practices throughout the firm.
- Creating and directing the creation of customer journey maps, navigation flows, prototypes, wireframes, and interactions that are customer-centric.
- Working with data analysts to continuously improve the user experience by testing, prototyping, and analyzing customer behavior and business results.
- Contributing to UX and design thought leadership by working with product, engineering, and marketing teams to develop new products and services throughout the digital ecosystem.

QUALIFICATIONS/SKILLS

- Bachelor's degree in computer science, information science, management information systems, humanities, and/or equivalent experience
- Coursework or experience in e-commerce, human-computer interaction, web design, front-end mobile web development, UX design, statistics and data analysis, and/or marketing
- Knowledge of UX tools such as Axure, Balsamiq, Sketch, and/or Adobe CC
- Knowledge of current user experience and design methodologies
- Demonstrated ability to identify solutions to business problems using a design perspective
- A desire to work in a multitasking, fast-paced environment and to collaborate as a member of the e-commerce digital experience team
- Ability to look for solutions and information in creative ways and convey complicated results and insights to people of varying backgrounds
- Intensely curious with an intrinsic love for excellent user experience
- Strong written and spoken communication skills

PREPARING FOR THE INTERVIEW

As noted above in the list of qualifications/skills, a UX designer position requires a number of technical skills that you will need to have acquired via various coursework or from practical experience. You should be prepared to demonstrate that you have these basic technical skills. In addition, you are likely to be asked some questions that require you to show that you have a broader-based understanding of the process of establishing an e-commerce presence via the development of websites, mobile sites, and mobile applications. To do so, review the material in Sections 3.2, 3.3, and 3.4, which will allow you to show that you understand how the overall pieces of the effort fit together. Also review Section 3.6, which specifically focuses on some basics of mobile website and mobile application development. You can use Section 3.5 to review some basic website design features that both annoy (Table 3.10) and are appreciated by (Table 3.11) users, as well to refresh your memory about various software tools for interactivity, active content, and personalization. Finally, reread the *Insight on Society* case, *Designing for Accessibility*.

Showing that you understand the importance of accessible design will be one way to help you distinguish yourself!

POSSIBLE FIRST INTERVIEW QUESTIONS

1. What is your favorite e-commerce website or mobile app, in terms of user experience, and why do you like it? What do you think are the characteristics of a really effective e-commerce experience?

Apple is frequently viewed as a paragon of user experience. Amazon also obviously comes to mind. Why is this so? "User friendliness" is not a specific-enough answer. Focus instead on specific qualities such as ease of search (finding what you want quickly), coherent roadmap or path through the content to the purchase, fast payment, and speed and responsiveness of the screens. And of course, "design" is important. Design includes the use of images, colors, font, and icons.

2. We're in the food service business, delivering our products to consumers no matter where or when they want to consume our food. What would your vision be for an effective e-commerce experience for our customers?

You can expand on your answer above. Your vision might be one where consumers can go online to the company's website or apps and find exactly what they want (everything from a seat at a table to takeout and delivery) and do so in an acceptable time frame and price, using a visually pleasing and effective e-commerce presence.

3. How can an e-commerce presence help meet our customers' needs?

You can suggest that the traditional ways of buying a pizza (showing up at the location, or ordering by telephone) can lead to customer annoyance: long waits at the physical location, long order and/or delivery time, and dropped orders. Having an effective digital presence is likely to reduce order time, increase accuracy, and provide a more predictable outcome. For instance, digital customers can be given a pick-up time at the store or arrange a definite delivery time. You might suggest an Uber like app for mobile users.

4. How can we personalize our e-commerce presence for each consumer?

You can suggest that prior purchase records could be kept to identify customer preferences. Returning customers can be asked if they want to reorder what they ordered during their previous visit. The digital platform needs to be able to recognize returning customers and suggest menu items they are likely to want, rather than have them follow a long roadmap through the site.

5. Have you had any experience in designing a website or mobile app? What did you learn from that experience?

If you've had some experience designing a website, talk about the design issues you dealt with, and how you solved them. If you have no experience, talk about your experience with websites that are difficult to use, provide a poor user experience, and have poor design qualities.

6. Do you think we should use a native mobile app or a browser-based mobile app? What about adaptive design techniques?

You could suggest that native apps are much faster, and have simple designs suited to mobile devices. A separate design is needed, and this adds to the cost of a digital presence. Browser-based apps are slower, but much of the design and code of the firm's websites can be re-used. Adaptive designs, which adjust the display to the device being used, work well with scrolling lists, but do not work so well with the complicated roadmap of choices found on most websites.

3.8 CASE STUDY

Dick's Sporting Goods:
Taking Control of Its E-commerce Operations

Founded in 1948 by Dick Stack in Binghamton, New York, Dick's Sporting Goods has grown from a small local business selling fishing and camping supplies into a Fortune 500 business with stores throughout the United States. After Stack's retirement in 1984, his son Edward bought the business with his siblings and took over as president. Edward spearheaded the company's growth from a handful of local stores into a sporting goods powerhouse. The company sells athletic apparel, outerwear, sportswear, a variety of shoes, fitness equipment, and outdoor equipment. Now headquartered in Pennsylvania, Dick's also runs two smaller franchises: its Field & Stream outdoor goods division, and Golf Galaxy for golfing supplies. Dick's prides itself on combining small-business customer service with big-box retailer selection and values, and routinely outperforms competitors in customer service metrics such as phone and e-mail response time and delivery speed.

© Ian Dangall/Alamy Stock Photo

Unlike some of its competitors, Dick's was quick to embrace the online channel and has maintained very strong e-commerce sales relative to its competitors in the sporting goods industry. Dick's increased its e-commerce revenue by 40% from 2010 to 2015, whereas its competitors' revenues increased by only 20% over that span. For most of that period, Dick's relied on external vendors for its IT and e-commerce needs. eBay handled Dick's back-end fulfillment processes and most aspects of their e-commerce presence for approximately 10 successful years.

However, by 2015, Dick's had grown to a size where its agreement with eBay was costing the company significant revenue. eBay collected a fixed commission on all items Dick's sold online, no matter how big, despite the fact that expensive items cost no more for eBay to process than cheaper ones. As Dick's e-commerce sales continued to grow, its deal with eBay was costing it more and more money.

Many bigger businesses have moved their e-commerce operations away from external vendors and back within the control of the company to avoid these types of expenses. Also, customizing pre-made software and services from external vendors can be difficult. However, once in-house, companies can more easily differentiate their web presences from competitors and adjust their software and services to best suit their capabilities. Companies that reclaim their e-commerce operations also maintain easier access to their proprietary customer data.

Facing pressure to slow down physical growth and reduce the high cost of maintaining physical real estate, and sensing the trend towards e-commerce at the expense of in-store sales, Dick's made the difficult decision to follow suit and formulated a plan to take over its own e-commerce operations. The company's rapidly increasing online sales gave Dick's both the incentive and the budget to undertake the transition. Edward Stack explained that the money the company was going to recoup from no longer paying transaction commissions to eBay would pay for the temporary increase in expenditure required to build and maintain an e-commerce infrastructure. Stack estimated that the company stood to immediately save between $20 and $25 million per year, and with a total expenditure relating to the switch of about $80 million, the move would pay for itself within four years.

Having control of its e-commerce operations allows Dick's to provide better support for unique omnichannel features, such as shipping online orders from physical Dick's stores. To that end, Dick's has also begun to convert its stores into distribution centers as well as traditional retail showrooms. This will increase efficiency and improve delivery times, turning its perceived weakness of excessive bricks-and-mortar infrastructure into a strength. Approximately 80% of Dicks' e-commerce orders are shipped within the geographical area of a physical store. In addition, customers can order online and pickup orders at local stores. Customizing its infrastructure and website capabilities to capitalize on this unusual arrangement was one of the reasons it wanted to reclaim operation of its e-commerce platform.

To carry out this strategy, Dick's began development of its proprietary e-commerce platform and integrating its existing systems in 2014. In 2015, Dick's began moving two of its lesser brands, Field & Stream and Golf Galaxy, onto the platform to ensure that there were no major issues with it, and continued development work. In 2017, the company completed the launch of the new platform, which it credited with strong online sales during the year-ending holiday season, despite some isolated glitches. For example, after the Houston Astros won the World Series, Dick's erroneously displayed commemorative baseball jerseys typically priced at $140 for just $9.98 and sparked a furor when they were forced to cancel thousands of orders. Overall, the company considers the new platform to be a major success.

Dick's selected IBM Websphere Commerce Suite for its e-commerce technology stack because of its emphasis on omnichannel shopping and fulfillment capability. Core components of the stack also include Apache ServiceMix service-oriented architecture, Manhattan Associates Order Management System for supply chain management, JDA Software Group software for merchandising, allocation, and replenishment, Oracle PeopleSoft for human resource management, IBM hardware, and Cisco networking technology. Manhattan Associates runs Dick's four Pittsburgh distribution centers, and JDA Software Group data is directed into a data warehouse that allows Dick's to access real-time information from any area of their business.

Specific features of the new e-commerce platform that Dick's has prioritized include the ability to buy online and pick up items at a store, the ability to ship from or to a store, and its associate ordering system. The platform also features the ability to break down and test different pricing and marketing approaches by region, an improved search function, and better analytics capabilities. Dick's has found that e-commerce sales double in regions where it opens new stores, and that multichannel customers spend three times as much as single-channel customers. That's why Dick's has focused so much on integrating physical and virtual sales and omnichannel features. Bringing all of its e-commerce infrastructure in house also gives the company better control over development cycles and speeds up its testing and implementation time frames. Dick's has also used the mobile platform to drive brand loyalty. Dick's uses piloting beacons, or physical sensors in stores that respond to incoming customers' smartphones, to produce customers' company rewards cards as they approach the store, offering promotions and other customized deals. The company has also integrated its own mobile app with popular fitness trackers like FitBit and MapMyRun to encourage its customers to live a healthy lifestyle, awarding rewards card points for consistent physical activity.

The process wasn't without risk. Installing a completely new e-commerce platform is no easy task. It involves integrating legacy systems and new systems without losing access to information, hiring a slew of new employees to manage the system, and avoiding implementation delays, cost overruns, outages, and other delays. Shifting much of its focus to the lower-margin online channel with extremely experienced competitors like Amazon lurking is also a challenge. Dick's has capitalized on the failures of its retail competitors, acquiring the leases on 30 Sports Authority retail locations at a steep discount after its bankruptcy, as well as all of the assets of GolfSmith after it went out of business as well. Dick's also acquired the intellectual property and customer data of both franchises. While the bankruptcies of Sports Authority, GolfSmith, and other bricks-and-mortar franchises caused problems in the short term for Dick's, due to the needs of those firms to liquidate their inventories at low prices, they have also given Dick's more market share. Although Dick's overall net income for the fiscal year ending February 2, 2019 dropped slightly, e-commerce sales grew to over $1.2 billion, an increase of 17%. In 2019, Dick's e-commerce sales continued to increase, and it had its best quarterly growth in six years in the third quarter of 2019.

SOURCES: "Dick's Sporting Goods Share Skyrocket on Earnings Beat, Raised Outlook," by Lauren Thomas, Cnbc.com, November 26, 2019; "Roundup: Ecommerce Sales Spike 15% at Dick's Sporting Goods," by Stephanie Crets, Digitalcommerce360.com; "Dick's Tech Chief Goes All Out on In-House Software," by Sara Castellanos, *Wall Street Journal*, March 26, 2019; "Know Why You Should Hold on to DICK'S Sporting (DKS) Stock," Nasdaq.com, April 12, 2018; "Fulfillment Costs Cut into Profits for Omnichannel Retailers," by James Risley, Digitalcommerce360.com, March 16, 2018; "After Website Hiccup, Dick's Sporting Goods Using Tax Break to Add Retail Tech Jobs," by Jamie Grill-Goodman, Risnews.com, March 14, 2018; "Dick's Sporting Goods Apologizes for Astros Jersey Price Glitch," by Taylor Berry, Cw39.com, December 28, 2017; "Scrambling to Respond to a Market That's in Panic Mode," by Andria Cheng, Fmarketer.com, August 15, 2017; "Dick's Sporting Goods Shakes Up Leadership Team," by Daphne Howland, Retaildive.com, May 15, 2017; "Dick's Sporting Goods Partners with CommerceHub to Propel E-commerce Growth," Digitalcommerce360.com, November 9, 2016; "Dick's Digital Strategy Is on the Move," by C. D. Lewis, Risnews.com, October 17, 2016; "Why Dick's Sporting Goods Decided to Play Its Own Game in E-commerce," by Larry Dignan, Techrepublic.com, April 21, 2016; "Dick's Sporting Goods Touts Omnichannel Success and New Store Growth," by Mike Troy, Chainstoreage.com, March 8,

2016; "Dick's Sporting Goods Opens a New Online Store," by Matt Lindner, Internetretailer.com, November 12, 2015; "Dick's Sporting Goods Could Get a Boost From E-commerce," by Chris Laudani, Thestreet.com, September 30, 2015; "Dick's Sporting Goods Aims to Control Its E-commerce Destiny," by Larry Dignan, Zdnet.com, May 21, 2015.

In 2019, Dick's focused on finishing the transition to in-house software for all its e-commerce platforms, which Dick's management believes has given it a significant strategic advantage. It launched a new search engine that improved page load times for search results on both its desktop and mobile platforms. It also launched new software for inventory tracking, which enables it to list products online within 30 minutes of a major event, instead of the three-to-five days it previously required. Future plans include overhauling how products are displayed and how search, checkout, and shipping estimates work on its website, and re-platforming its mobile and tablet sites.

Case Study Questions

1. Why did Dick's decide to leave eBay and take over its own e-commerce operations?
2. What is Dick's omnichannel strategy?
3. What are the three steps in Dick's migration to its new website?
4. What are the primary benefits of Dick's new system?

3.9 REVIEW

KEY CONCEPTS

- **Understand the questions you must ask and answer, and the steps you should take, in developing an e-commerce presence.**
  - Questions you must ask and answer when developing an e-commerce presence include:
    - What is your vision and how do you hope to accomplish it?
    - What is your business and revenue model?
    - Who and where is the target audience?
    - What are the characteristics of the marketplace?
    - Where is the content coming from?
    - Conduct a SWOT analysis.
    - Develop an e-commerce presence map.
    - Develop a timeline.
    - Develop a detailed budget.

- **Explain the process that should be followed in building an e-commerce presence.**
  - Factors you must consider when building an e-commerce site include hardware, software, telecommunications capacity, website and mobile platform design, human resources, and organizational capabilities.
  - The systems development life cycle (a methodology for understanding the business objectives of a system and designing an appropriate solution) for building an e-commerce website involves five major steps:
    - Identify the specific business objectives for the site, and then develop a list of system functionalities and information requirements.
    - Develop a system design specification (both logical design and physical design).
    - Build the site, either by in-house personnel or by outsourcing all or part of the responsibility to outside contractors.

- Test the system (unit testing, system testing, acceptance testing, A/B (split) testing, and multivariate testing).
- Implement and maintain the site.
- The basic business and system functionalities an e-commerce site should contain include a digital catalog, a product database, customer tracking, shopping cart/payment system, an on-site blog, a customer database, an ad server, a site tracking and reporting system, and an inventory management system.
- Advantages of building a site in-house include the ability to change and adapt the site quickly as the market demands and the ability to build a site that does exactly what the company needs.
- Disadvantages of building a site in-house include higher costs, greater risks of failure, a more time-consuming process, and a longer staff learning curve that delays time to market.
- Using design templates cuts development time, but preset templates can also limit functionality.
- A similar decision is also necessary regarding outsourcing the hosting of the site versus keeping it in-house. Relying on an outside vendor places the burden of reliability on someone else in return for a monthly hosting fee. The downside is that if the site requires fast upgrades due to heavy traffic, the chosen hosting company may or may not be capable of keeping up. Reliability versus scalability is the issue in this instance.

■ **Identify and understand the major considerations involved in choosing web server and e-commerce merchant server software.**

- Early websites used single-tier system architecture and consisted of a single-server computer that delivered static web pages to users making requests through their browsers. The extended functionality of today's websites requires the development of a multi-tiered systems architecture, which utilizes a variety of specialized web servers, as well as links to pre-existing backend or legacy corporate databases.
- All e-commerce sites require basic web server software to answer requests from customers for HTML and XML pages. When choosing web server software, companies are also choosing what operating system the site will run on. Apache, which runs on the Unix system, is the market leader.
- Web servers provide a host of services, including processing user HTML requests, security services, file transfer, a search engine, data capture, e-mail, and site management tools.
- Dynamic server software allows sites to deliver dynamic content, rather than static, unchanging information. Web application server programs enable a wide range of e-commerce functionality, including creating a customer database, creating an e-mail promotional program, and accepting and processing orders, as well as many other services.
- E-commerce merchant server software is another important software package that provides catalog displays, information storage and customer tracking, order taking (shopping cart), and credit card purchase processing. E-commerce software platforms can save time and money, but customization can significantly drive up costs. Factors to consider when choosing an e-commerce software platform include its functionality, support for different business models, visual site management tools and reporting systems, performance and scalability, connectivity to existing business systems, compliance with standards, and global and multicultural capability.

■ **Understand the issues involved in choosing the most appropriate hardware for an e-commerce site.**

- Speed, capacity, and scalability are three of the most important considerations when selecting an operating system, and therefore the hardware that it runs on.
- To evaluate how fast the site needs to be, companies need to assess the number of simultaneous users the site expects to see, the nature of their requests, the type of information requested, and the bandwidth available to the site. The answers to these questions will provide guidance regarding the processors necessary to meet customer demand. In some cases, additional processing power can increase capacity, thereby improving system speed.

- Scalability is also an important issue. Increasing processing supply by scaling up to meet demand can be done through vertical or horizontal scaling or by improving processing architecture.

■ **Identify additional tools that can improve website performance.**

- In addition to providing a speedy website, companies must also strive to have a well-designed site that encourages visitors to buy. Building in interactivity improves site effectiveness, as do personalization techniques.
- Commonly used software tools for achieving high levels of website interactivity and customer personalization include Common Gateway Interface (CGI) scripts, Active Server Pages (ASP) and ASP.NET, Java applets, JavaScript, ActiveX and VBScript, Ajax, PHP, Ruby on Rails (RoR or Rails), and Django.

■ **Understand the important considerations involved in developing a mobile website and building mobile applications.**

- When developing a mobile presence, it is important to understand the difference between a mobile website, mobile web apps, native apps, and hybrid apps.
- The first step is to identify business objectives, because they help determine which type of mobile presence is best.
- Design should take into account mobile platform constraints. Recent trends include mobile first design, responsive web design, and adaptive web design.
- Developing a mobile website is likely to be the least expensive option; mobile web apps require more effort and cost; native apps are likely to be the most expensive to develop.

QUESTIONS

1. What are the main factors to consider when developing an e-commerce presence?
2. What elements do you need to address when developing a vision for an e-commerce presence?
3. Name the main kinds of e-commerce presence and the different platforms for each type.
4. Identify the different phases used in a one-year timeline for the development of an e-commerce presence and the related milestones for each phase.
5. What are the major advantages and disadvantages of deciding to build an e-commerce site in-house?
6. What are the various components of a website budget?
7. What is multivariate testing and how does it differ from A/B testing (split testing)?
8. What are the disadvantages of outsourcing hosting? What risks does a small business face when hosting its own website?
9. What is a content management system and what function does it serve?
10. What is open source software and how can it be used in creating an e-commerce presence?
11. What is a SWOT analysis?
12. What are some methods for achieving personalization and customization?
13. Discuss some of the ways that you can optimize a website so that it will appear higher up in search engine listings.
14. What is CGI and how does it enable interactivity?
15. What is Ruby on Rails? What role does it play in website design?
16. How does agile development enable the release of applications more rapidly than the traditional systems development life cycle?
17. Why is building a native app the most expensive method of creating a mobile presence?
18. What unique features must be taken into account when designing a mobile presence?
19. What is a mashup and what are they used for?
20. What are web services and how are they used?

PROJECTS

1. Go to the website of Wix, Weebly, or another provider of your choosing that allows you to create a simple e-tailer website for a free trial period. Create a website. The site should feature at least four pages, including a home page, product page, shopping cart, and contact page. Extra credit will be given for additional complexity and creativity. Come to class prepared to present your e-tailer concept and website.

2. Visit several e-commerce sites, not including those mentioned in this chapter, and evaluate the effectiveness of the sites according to the eight basic criteria/functionalities listed in Table 3.11. Choose one site you feel does an excellent job on all the aspects of an effective site and create a PowerPoint or similar presentation, including screen shots, to support your choice.

3. Imagine that you are in charge of developing a fast-growing startup's e-commerce presence. Consider your options for building the company's e-commerce presence in-house with existing staff, or outsourcing the entire operation. Decide which strategy you believe is in your company's best interest and create a brief presentation outlining your position. Why choose that approach? And what are the estimated associated costs, compared with the alternative? (You'll need to make some educated guesses here—don't worry about being exact.)

4. Choose two e-commerce software packages and prepare an evaluation chart that rates the packages on the key factors discussed in the section "Choosing an E-commerce Software Platform." Which package would you choose if you were developing a website of the type described in this chapter, and why?

5. Choose one of the open source web content management systems such as WordPress, Joomla, or Drupal or another of your own choosing and prepare an evaluation chart similar to that required by Project 4. Which system would you choose and why?

REFERENCES

Byers, Josh. "Three Reasons a 'Mobile First' Philosophy Is Critical to Achieving Your Business Goals." Copyblogger.com (May 11, 2013).

DeNisco, Alison. "The Death of Ruby? Developers Should Learn These Languages Instead." Techrepublic.com (August 7, 2017).

Doyle, Barry, and Cristina Videira Lopes. "Survey of Technologies for Web Application Development." *ACM*, Vol. 2, No. 3 (June 2005).

IBM (High Volume Web Sites Team). "Best Practices for High-Volume Web Sites." *IBM Redbooks* (December 2002).

Korkishko, Iryna. "Well-known Sites Built With Ruby on Rails." Synicode.co (June 20, 2017).

Krill, Paul. "Java at 20: The Programming Juggernaut Rolls On." Infoworld.com (May 18, 2015).

Moffat, Branwell. "E-commerce: Perception of Website Speed Makes All the Difference for Sales." The-future-of-commerce.com (May 25, 2017).

Netcraft. "December 2019 Web Server Survey." (December 10, 2019).

Panal, Carolina. "Top 5 Sites Built with Django." Bedjango.com (February 1, 2017).

Pratap, Ravi. "Responsive Design vs. Adaptive Delivery: Which One's Right for You?" Venturebeat.com (November 19, 2013).

RSA FraudAction Intelligence. "A Decade of Phishing." Rsa.com (November 2016).

Vaughan-Nichols, Steven. "JavaScript Explodes on the Server Side with the Growth of Node.js." Zdnet.com (July 27, 2017).

W3Techs. "Usage of Server-side Programming Languages for Websites." W3techs.com (accessed December 16, 2019).

CHAPTER 4

E-commerce Security and Payment Systems

LEARNING OBJECTIVES

After reading this chapter, you will be able to:

- Understand the scope of e-commerce crime and security problems, the key dimensions of e-commerce security, and the tension between security and other values.
- Identify the key security threats in the e-commerce environment.
- Describe how technology helps secure Internet communications channels and protect networks, servers, and clients.
- Appreciate the importance of policies, procedures, and laws in creating security.
- Identify the major e-commerce payment systems in use today.
- Describe the features and functionality of electronic billing presentment and payment systems.

The Rise of the Global Cyberattack:

WannaCry and NotPetya

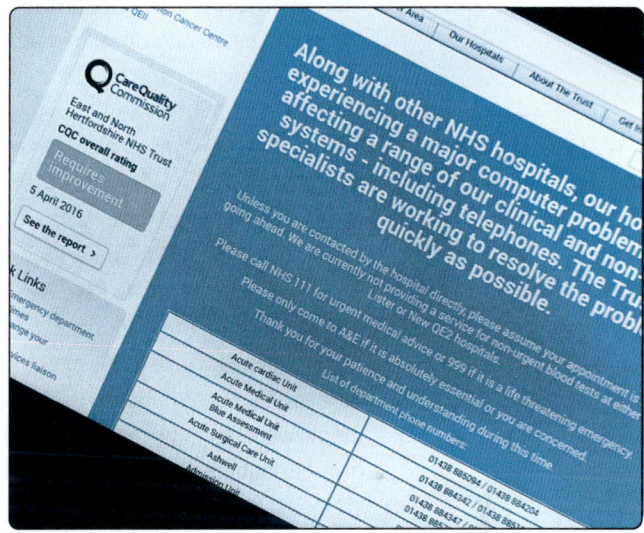

©Jeffrey Blackler/Alamy Stock Photo

The Internet is many things to many people: a vibrant marketplace for buyers and sellers of all shapes and sizes; a multifaceted, rapidly expanding entertainment platform; and a critical tool for nearly every modern business. However, the Internet has also become a battlefield where individuals, corporations, and nations must all guard against attacks from malicious actors and sometimes one another. As more and more business and personal information moves online, cybercriminals are also improving their techniques for wreaking havoc on targets without the proper level of security, whether they are individual users or government agencies. The recent proliferation of dangerous ransomware throughout Great Britain, Europe, Asia, and the United States has proved that many organizations lack the level of online security required to guard against the latest malware threats.

Ransomware is a type of malware that completely blocks access to a computer system until a "ransom" is paid by the user, most commonly in bitcoin, which are difficult to trace. To execute this type of attack, hackers have to lure users into downloading software onto their device, usually by duping them into clicking a link. Then, that software completely encrypts the files on the computer and only displays a screen demanding payment. While anti-virus software and firewalls can often prevent these types of attacks, cybercriminals are always on the hunt for new techniques to breach different operating systems. In 2015, less than 1% of spam emails contained ransomware, but since then, that number has skyrocketed. In 2019, Europol identified ransomware as the top threat in its annual *Internet Organized Crime Threat Assessment* report, noting that while the volume of attacks had declined, the attacks that continued to be perpetrated were more targeted and likely to case greater damage.

Cybercriminals aren't the only ones looking for an edge on this emerging new battlefield. National governments have also poured money and manpower into improving their cyberwarfare capabilities, not just to defend themselves, but also to improve their ability to attack targets. In 2017, a cybercriminal group based in Russia known as the Shadow Brokers claimed that it had stolen a "cyber weapon" from the National Security Agency (NSA) of the United States. Known as EternalBlue, this "weapon" was actually a security flaw the NSA had identified in various versions of the Windows operating system. Using the flaw, attackers could exploit the Server Message Block (SMB) protocol of Windows, allowing them to execute code on a target computer. While the NSA was able to warn Microsoft that the EternalBlue vulnerability had been stolen, and Microsoft subsequently released a patch fixing the vulnerability for some variations of Windows, the Shadow Brokers still released EternalBlue publicly in April 2017.

Just one month later, in May 2017, WannaCry ransomware spread like wildfire through more than 300,000 computers in 150 countries. While most ransomware requires tricking individual users into downloading software, the WannaCry ransomware was especially effective because it used the EternalBlue vulnerability to find its way onto targeted computers. Not only that, but while Microsoft made patches available that would fix the problem in more recent versions of Windows, it did not do so for some of the older versions of Windows still in use, such as Windows XP and Windows 8. Additionally, many users of the computers running newer versions of Windows failed to apply the patch and were equally vulnerable. WannaCry initially demanded $300 in Bitcoin to restore the files but soon doubled that to $600 and set a deadline for payment of one week.

In England, the National Health Service (NHS) was ravaged by WannaCry shortly after the attack began. All forms of computerized communication were disabled, forcing healthcare staff to use WhatsApp on their phones to communicate. Over 19,000 medical appointments were canceled and several hospitals were so badly disrupted that they were forced to divert ambulances to other locations. WannaCry spread via the N3 broadband network that connects NHS sites and was most effective against Windows 7 machines, which are used to some degree by approximately 90% of NHS divisions. Windows XP machines simply crashed instead of continuing the spread of the infection, but further contributed to the outages. The attack exposed the NHS's inability to respond to an attack of this magnitude. While it did have a plan in place to respond to attacks like this at both the national and local level, the NHS had never tested their plan at the local level, leaving many offices helpless to respond to such a devastating attack. According to a report issued by the Department of Health in October 2018, WannaCry cost the NHS £92 million.

WannaCry continued its spread into Russia, where it wreaked havoc on the Interior Ministry and hundreds of other companies; Germany, where it crippled the ticket vending machines on the national railway, Deutsche Bahn; and China, where pirated versions of Windows, which are especially vulnerable, are common. Spanish telecom company Telefonica, Danish shipping company and FedEx subsidiary TNT Express, French automaker Renault, Japanese tech titan Hitachi, and several leading Chinese universities all reported being hit hard by WannaCry. Although a very low number of affected companies actually paid the ransom, it did hundreds of millions of dollars in damage to companies such as FedEx, Renault, Hitachi, and others due to service delays and IT repairs. Many of these companies are prominent multi-national corporations with significant cybersecurity operations. The WannaCry attack proved that even the biggest companies are not invulnerable to attack. Overall, the damage caused by WannaCry has been estimated at as high as $8 billion.

If a virus running rampant through the computer networks of some of the world's biggest companies and organizations wasn't stunning enough, the WannaCry story continued to take several shocking twists. Marcus Hutchins, a 23-year-old British cybersecurity expert and founder of the popular blog MalwareTech, discovered a "killswitch" that helped to stop

SOURCES: "IOCTA Internet Organised Crime Threat Assessment, 2019," by Europol, October 9, 2019; "U.S. Treasury Sanctions North Korean Cyber Groups," by Ian Talley and Dustin Volz, *Wall Street Journal*, September 13, 2019; "NHS Must Take Urgent Steps to Defend Against Hackers, Says White Paper," by Kate Wighton, Imperial.ac.uk, July 2, 2019; "The EU Cybersecurity Act Is Now Applicable," Jonesday.com, June 2019; "Two Years after Wanna Cry, a Million Computers Remain at Risk," by Zack Whittaker, Techcrunch.com, May 12, 2019; "UK.gov Joins Microsoft in Fingering North Korea for WannaCry," by John Leyden, Theregister.co.uk, October 27, 2017; "British Security Minister Says North Korea Was Behind WannaCry Hack on NHS," by Adam Withnall, Indepen-

the spread of the malware. But just a few months later, Hutchins was arrested in the United States at the DEF CON cybersecurity conference in Las Vegas and charged with six counts of hacking-related charges for malware that steals online banking information known as Kronos, which he allegedly developed as a teenager. His malware had been a frequent seller on the darknet marketplace AlphaBay, which U.S. law enforcement dismantled in July 2017. Hutchins eventually pled guilty to the charges. Hutchins' rapid rise and fall is a reminder that the lines on the battlefield of cyberwar are often blurred, with former criminals changing sides and vice versa.

In June 2017, a second strain of ransomware began to propagate that lacked the killswitch of WannaCry. Known as NotPetya, this newer variation also used EternalBlue to gain access to targets and was tougher to shut down, spreading through its victims' networks with devastating speed. The malware was initially identified as a strain that has been active since 2016 called Petya, but it was later found to have several significant upgrades over that malware, which led to its designation as NotPetya. NotPetya affected many infrastructural institutions in Ukraine, including power companies, airports, public transit systems, and the country's central bank, as well as Danish shipping company Maersk (costing it between $250 million and $300 million), Russian oil company Rosnoft, global pharmaceutical giant Merck ($870 million), FedEx's European subsidiary TNT Express ($400 million), French construction company Saint-Gobain ($384 million), U.S. food producer Mondelez ($188 million), and UK manufacturer Reckitt Benckiser ($129 million). The total overall damages from NotPetya are estimated to be $10 billion. In February 2018, the United States and United Kingdom jointly identified Russia as the perpetrator of the attack as part of Russia's efforts to destabilize the Ukraine.

The role of the Shadow Brokers in leaking EternalBlue to the public is well documented, but they were not the perpetrators of the WannaCry attacks. Intelligence from the NSA and the United Kingdom's National Cyber Security Centre indicated that a North Korean hacking group known as Lazarus was behind the attack and that it was likely a state-sponsored operation. In 2018, the U.S. Department of Justice formally charged a North Korean programmer, reportedly an intelligence officer for North Korea's intelligence agency, as one of the persons who perpetrated the attack. North Korea continues to deny not only involvement in the attack, but also the existence of the person indicted by the U.S. government. In September 2019, the U.S. Treasury Department imposed sanctions on the Lazarus Group and two associated subgroups, known as Bluenoroff and Andariel, freezing any assets they might have in the United States. In the wake of WannaCry and NotPetya, the EU governing bodies reached initial agreement in December 2018 on the Cybersecurity Act, strengthening and extending the powers of the European Union Agency for Network and Information Security (ENISA), and creating a certification process for online services and consumer devices. The Act went into effect in June 2019. However, such legislation is only a small part in protecting against future cyberattacks. Security analyst firm Check Point noted that a year after the attacks, most companies are still not at all prepared to deal with such attacks. In 2019, according to one report, almost 1 million devices are still vulnerable to EternalBlue exploits. In the United Kingdom, for example, experts claim that NHS Trusts are still ignoring cybersecurity, and in July 2019, researchers at Imperial College presented a report to the House of Lords warning that the NHS remained very vulnerable to cyberattacks. Under the circumstances, the likelihood of similar attacks occurring in the future is extremely high.

dent.co.uk, October 27, 2017; "NHS Could Have Avoided WannaCry Simply by Patching Windows 7 or Securing Firewalls, Claims NAO," by Graeme Burton, Computing.co.uk, October 27, 2017, "NHS Didn't Know How to Respond to WannaCry, Claims National Audit Office in Investigation into the Ransomware Outbreak," by Graeme Burton, Computing.co.uk, October 27, 2017; "North Korea Behind Devastating 'WannaCry' Cyberattack That Hit NHS and Systems Across US, Says Microsoft Head," by Jon Sharman, Independent.co.uk, October 14, 2017; "FedEx Cuts Profit Forecast on $300 Million Hit from Cyberattack," by Mary Schlangenstein, Bloomberg.com, September 19, 2017; "Who Is Marcus Hutchins?" by Brian Krebs, Krebsonsecurity.com, September 17, 2017; "New Ransomware Attack Is Infecting Airlines, Banks, and Utilities Across Europe," by Russell Brandom, Theverge.com, June 27, 2017; "A Scary New Ransomware Outbreak Uses WannaCry's Old Tricks," by Lily Hay Newman, *Wired*, June 27, 2017; "WannaCry Outbreak Halted When Infosec Pro Bought Domain for £8," by Carly Page, V3.co.uk, May 15, 2017; "The Fallout from a Global Cyberattack: 'A Battle We're Fighting Every Day,'" by Steve Lohr and Liz Alderman, *New York Times*, May 15, 2017; "Ransomware 'WannaCry' Attack: Asia Reports Thousands of New Cases," by Yuri Kageyama and Louise Watt, *USA Today*, May 15, 2017; "Cyber Attack Hits German Train Stations as Hackers Target Deutsche Bahn," by Chris Graham, Telegraph.co.uk, May 13, 2017; "Russian-linked Cyber Gang Blamed for NHS Computer Hack Using Bug Stolen from US Spy Agency," by Robert Mendick, James Titcomb, Ben Farmer, and Cara McGoogan, Telegraph.co.uk, May 12, 2017; "Telefonica, Other Spanish Firms Hit in 'Ransomware' Attack," Reuters.com, May 12, 2017; "UK Hospitals Hit with Massive Ransomware Attack," by Russell Brandom, Theverge.com, May 12, 2017; "Windows SMB Zero-Day Exploit Goes Live on Github After Microsoft Fails to Fix," by Graeme Burton, Theinquirer.net, February 6, 2017.

As *The Rise of the Global Cyberattack: WannaCry and NotPetya* illustrates, the Internet and Web are increasingly vulnerable to large-scale attacks and potentially large-scale failure. Increasingly, these attacks are led by organized gangs of criminals operating globally—an unintended consequence of globalization. Even more worrisome is the growing number of large-scale attacks that are funded, organized, and led by various nations against the Internet resources of other nations. Anticipating and countering these attacks has proved a difficult task for both business and government organizations. However, there are several steps you can take to protect your websites, your mobile devices, and your personal information from routine security attacks. Reading this chapter, you should also start thinking about how your business could survive in the event of a large-scale "outage" of the Internet.

In this chapter, we will examine e-commerce security and payment issues. First, we will identify the major security risks and their costs, and describe the variety of solutions currently available. Then, we will look at the major payment methods and consider how to achieve a secure payment environment. **Table 4.1** highlights some of the major trends in online security in 2019–2020.

TABLE 4.1 WHAT'S NEW IN E-COMMERCE SECURITY 2019–2020

- Large-scale data breaches continue to expose data about individuals to hackers and other cybercriminals.
- Mobile malware presents a tangible threat as smartphones and other mobile devices become more common targets of cybercriminals, especially as their use for mobile payments rises.
- Malware creation continues to skyrocket and ransomware attacks rise.
- The astronomical rise in the price of cryptocurrencies leads to cryptomining, where coin-mining software that steals computer processing power in order to use it to mine cryptocurrencies, is installed on computers without their users' knowledge.
- Distributed Denial of Service (DDoS) attacks are now capable of slowing Internet service within entire countries.
- Nations continue to engage in cyberwarfare and cyberespionage.
- Hackers and cybercriminals continue to focus their efforts on social networks to exploit potential victims through social engineering and hacking attacks.
- Politically motivated, targeted attacks by hacktivist groups continue, in some cases merging with financially motivated cybercriminals to target financial systems with advanced persistent threats.
- Software vulnerabilities, such as the Heartbleed bug and other zero day vulnerabilities, continue to create security threats.
- Software supply chain attacks, where hackers target development environments to infect software that is then downloaded by end users, increase in frequency.

4.1 THE E-COMMERCE SECURITY ENVIRONMENT

For most law-abiding citizens, the Internet holds the promise of a huge and convenient global marketplace, providing access to people, goods, services, and businesses worldwide, all at a bargain price. For criminals, the Internet has created entirely new—and lucrative—ways to steal from the more than 2 billion online consumers worldwide today. From products and services, to cash, to information, it's all there for the taking on the Internet.

It's also less risky to steal online. Rather than rob a bank in person, the Internet makes it possible to rob people remotely and almost anonymously. Rather than steal a CD at a local record store, you can download the same music for free and almost without risk from the Internet. The potential for anonymity on the Internet cloaks many criminals in legitimate-looking identities, allowing them to place fraudulent orders with online merchants, steal information by intercepting e-mail, or simply shut down e-commerce sites by using software viruses and swarm attacks. The Internet was never designed to be a global marketplace with billions of users and lacks many basic security features found in older networks such as the telephone system or broadcast television networks. By comparison, the Internet is an open, vulnerable-design network. The actions of cybercriminals are costly for both businesses and consumers, who are then subjected to higher prices and additional security measures. The costs of malicious cyberactivity include not just the cost of the actual crime, but also the additional costs that are required to secure networks and recover from cyberattacks, the potential reputational damage to the affected company, as well as reduced trust in online activities, the loss of potentially sensitive business information, including intellectual property and confidential business information, and the cost of opportunities lost due to service disruptions. Ponemon Institute estimates that the average total cost of a data breach to corporations worldwide in 2018 was $3.92 million (Ponemon Institute/IBM Security, 2019).

THE SCOPE OF THE PROBLEM

Cybercrime is becoming a more significant problem for both organizations and consumers. Bot networks, DDoS attacks, Trojans, phishing, ransomware, data theft, identity fraud, credit card fraud, and spyware are just some of the threats that are making daily headlines. Social networks also have had security breaches. But despite the increasing attention being paid to cybercrime, it is difficult to accurately estimate the actual amount of such crime, in part because many companies are hesitant to report it due to the fear of losing the trust of their customers, and because even if the crime is reported, it may be difficult to quantify the actual dollar amount of the loss. A joint study by McAfee and the Center for Strategic and International Studies examined the difficulties in accurately estimating the economic impact of cybercrime and cyberespionage, with its research indicating a range of $445 billion to $600 billion worldwide. Further research is planned to try to help determine an even more accurate estimate (McAfee/Center for Strategic and International Studies, 2018).

One source of information is a survey conducted by Ponemon Institute of 355 companies in various industries in 11 countries. The 2019 survey found that the average annualized cost of cybercrime for all organizations in the study was $13 million, representing a 12% increase from the previous year and a 72% increase over the previous five years. U.S. companies had the highest total average cost, at $27.4 million, followed by Japan, at $13.6 million. The United Kingdom experienced the greatest percentage increase in the annual average cost, increasing by 31% to $11.5 million, followed closely by utility companies, at $17 million. The average cost also varied by industry segment, with companies in the banking sector reporting the highest average cost, more than $18 million. The number of successful cyberattacks increased, by 11% from the previous year, and by 67% over a five-year period.

The most costly cybercrimes were those caused by malware, web-based attacks, denial of service, and malicious insiders (Ponemon Institute/Accenture, 2019).

Reports issued by security product providers, such as Symantec, Webroot, Cisco, and others, are another source of data. Symantec issues an *Internet Security Threat Report* based on more than 123 million sensors monitoring Internet activity around the globe. Advances in technology have greatly reduced the entry costs and skills required to enter the cybercrime business. Low-cost and readily available web attack kits enable hackers to create malware without having to write software from scratch. In addition, there has been a surge in polymorphic malware, which enables attackers to generate a unique version of the malware for each victim, making it much more difficult for pattern-matching software used by security firms to detect (Webroot, 2018). According to Symantec, one in ten URLs are malicious, with a significant increase in formjacking (the use of malicious code to steal credit card information from checkout web pages). Web attacks overall increased by 56%. (Symantec, 2019). However, these sorts of reports typically do not attempt to quantify actual crimes and/or losses related to these threats.

Online credit card fraud is one of the most high-profile forms of e-commerce crime. Although the average amount of credit card fraud loss experienced by any one individual is typically relatively small, the overall amount is substantial. Juniper Research predicts that retailers will lose about $130 billion in revenue worldwide between 2018 and 2023 due to card-not-present online payment fraud (Juniper Research, 2019). The nature of credit card fraud has changed greatly from the theft of a single credit card number and efforts to purchase goods at a few sites, to the simultaneous theft of millions of credit card numbers and their distribution to thousands of criminals operating as gangs of thieves. The emergence of identity fraud, described in detail later in this chapter, as a major online/offline type of fraud may well markedly increase the incidence and amount of credit card fraud, because identity fraud often includes the use of stolen credit card information and the creation of phony credit card accounts.

The Underground Economy Marketplace: The Value of Stolen Information

Criminals who steal information on the Internet do not always use this information themselves, but instead derive value by selling the information to others on the so-called underground or shadow economy market. Data is currency to cybercriminals and has a "street value" that can be monetized. For example, in 2013, Vladislav Horohorin (alias "BadB") was sentenced to over 7 years in U.S. federal prison for using online criminal forums to sell stolen credit and debit card information (referred to as "dumps"). At the time of his arrest, Horohorin possessed over 2.5 million stolen credit and debit card numbers. There are several thousand known underground economy marketplaces around the world that sell stolen information, as well as malware, such as exploit kits, access to botnets, and more. **Table 4.2** lists some recently observed prices for various types of stolen data, which typically vary depending on the quantity being purchased, supply available, and "freshness." For example, when credit card information from the Target data breach first appeared on the market, individual card numbers went for up to $120 each. After a few

TABLE 4.2 THE CYBER BLACK MARKET FOR STOLEN DATA

DATA	PRICE*
Individual U.S. card number with expiration date and CVV2 (the three-digit number printed on back of card) (referred to as a CVV)	$5–$8
Individual U.S. card number with full information, including full name, billing address, expiration date, CVV2, date of birth, mother's maiden name, etc. (referred to as a Fullz or Fullzinfo)	$20–$60
Dump data for U.S. card (the term "dump" refers to raw data such as name, account number, expiration data, and CVV encoded on the magnetic strip on the back of the card)	$60–$100
Bank account login credentials	$80–$700
Online payment service accounts (PayPal, etc.)	$20–$300
Drivers license information	$20
Online account login credentials (Facebook, Twitter, eBay, Apple)	$10–$15
Medical information/health credentials	$10–$20
1,000 e-mail addresses	$1–$10
Scan of a passport	$1–$25
Social security number	$1

SOURCES: Based on data from Symantec, 2019; Stack, 2018; Osborne, 2018.
*Prices vary based on supply and quality (freshness of data, account balances, validity, etc.).

weeks, however, the price dropped dramatically (Leger, 2014). Experts believe the cost of stolen information has generally fallen as the tools of harvesting have increased the supply. On the demand side, the same efficiencies and opportunities provided by new technology have increased the number of people who want to use stolen information. It's a robust marketplace.

Finding these marketplaces and the servers that host them can be difficult for the average user (and for law enforcement agencies), and prospective participants are typically vetted by other criminals before access is granted. This vetting process takes place through Twitter, Tor, and VPN services, and sometimes e-mail exchanges of information, money (often Bitcoins, a form of digital cash that we discuss further in Section 4.5), and reputation. There is a general hierarchy of cybercriminals in the marketplace, with low-level, nontechnical criminals who frequent "carder forums," where stolen credit and debit card data is sold, aiming to make money, a political statement, or both, at the bottom; resellers in the middle acting as intermediaries; and the technical masterminds who create malicious code at the top.

So, what can we can conclude about the overall size of cybercrime? Cybercrime against e-commerce sites is dynamic and changing all the time, with new risks appearing often. The amount of losses to businesses is significant and growing. The managers of e-commerce sites must prepare for an ever-changing variety of criminal assaults, and keep current in the latest security techniques.

WHAT IS GOOD E-COMMERCE SECURITY?

What is a secure commercial transaction? Anytime you go into a marketplace you take risks, including the loss of privacy (information about what you purchased). Your prime risk as a consumer is that you do not get what you paid for. As a merchant in the market, your risk is that you don't get paid for what you sell. Thieves take merchandise and then either walk off without paying anything, or pay you with a fraudulent instrument, stolen credit card, or forged currency.

E-commerce merchants and consumers face many of the same risks as participants in traditional commerce, albeit in a new digital environment. Theft is theft, regardless of whether it is digital theft or traditional theft. Burglary, breaking and entering, embezzlement, trespass, malicious destruction, vandalism—all crimes in a traditional commercial environment—are also present in e-commerce. However, reducing risks in e-commerce is a complex process that involves new technologies, organizational policies and procedures, and new laws and industry standards that empower law enforcement officials to investigate and prosecute offenders. **Figure 4.1** illustrates the multi-layered nature of e-commerce security.

To achieve the highest degree of security possible, new technologies are available and should be used. But these technologies by themselves do not solve the problem. Organizational policies and procedures are required to ensure the technologies are

FIGURE 4.1   THE E-COMMERCE SECURITY ENVIRONMENT

E-commerce security is multi-layered, and must take into account new technology, policies and procedures, and laws and industry standards.

not subverted. Finally, industry standards and government laws are required to enforce payment mechanisms, as well as to investigate and prosecute violators of laws designed to protect the transfer of property in commercial transactions.

The history of security in commercial transactions teaches that any security system can be broken if enough resources are put against it. Security is not absolute. In addition, perfect security of every item is not needed forever, especially in the information age. There is a time value to information—just as there is to money. Sometimes it is sufficient to protect a message for a few hours or days. Also, because security is costly, we always have to weigh the cost against the potential loss. Finally, we have also learned that security is a chain that breaks most often at the weakest link. Our locks are often much stronger than our management of the keys.

We can conclude then that good e-commerce security requires a set of laws, procedures, policies, and technologies that, to the extent feasible, protect individuals and organizations from unexpected behavior in the e-commerce marketplace.

DIMENSIONS OF E-COMMERCE SECURITY

There are six key dimensions to e-commerce security: integrity, nonrepudiation, authenticity, confidentiality, privacy, and availability.

Integrity refers to the ability to ensure that information being displayed on a website, or transmitted or received over the Internet, has not been altered in any way by an unauthorized party. For example, if an unauthorized person intercepts and changes the contents of an online communication, such as by redirecting a bank wire transfer into a different account, the integrity of the message has been compromised because the communication no longer represents what the original sender intended.

Nonrepudiation refers to the ability to ensure that e-commerce participants do not deny (i.e., repudiate) their online actions. For instance, the availability of free e-mail accounts with alias names makes it easy for a person to post comments or send a message and perhaps later deny doing so. Even when a customer uses a real name and e-mail address, it is easy for that customer to order merchandise online and then later deny doing so. In most cases, because merchants typically do not obtain a physical copy of a signature, the credit card issuer will side with the customer because the merchant has no legally valid proof that the customer ordered the merchandise.

Authenticity refers to the ability to identify the identity of a person or entity with whom you are dealing on the Internet. How does the customer know that the website operator is who it claims to be? How can the merchant be assured that the customer is really who she says she is? Someone who claims to be someone he is not is "spoofing" or misrepresenting himself.

Confidentiality refers to the ability to ensure that messages and data are available only to those who are authorized to view them. Confidentiality is sometimes confused with **privacy**, which refers to the ability to control the use of information a customer provides about himself or herself to an e-commerce merchant.

E-commerce merchants have two concerns related to privacy. They must establish internal policies that govern their own use of customer information, and they must protect that information from illegitimate or unauthorized use. For example, if hackers break into an e-commerce site and gain access to credit card or other information, this

integrity
the ability to ensure that information being displayed on a website or transmitted or received over the Internet has not been altered in any way by an unauthorized party

nonrepudiation
the ability to ensure that e-commerce participants do not deny (i.e., repudiate) their online actions

authenticity
the ability to identify the identity of a person or entity with whom you are dealing on the Internet

confidentiality
the ability to ensure that messages and data are available only to those who are authorized to view them

privacy
the ability to control the use of information about oneself

TABLE 4.3 — CUSTOMER AND MERCHANT PERSPECTIVES ON THE DIFFERENT DIMENSIONS OF E-COMMERCE SECURITY

DIMENSION	CUSTOMER'S PERSPECTIVE	MERCHANT'S PERSPECTIVE
Integrity	Has information I transmitted or received been altered?	Has data on the site been altered without authorization? Is data being received from customers valid?
Nonrepudiation	Can a party to an action with me later deny taking the action?	Can a customer deny ordering products?
Authenticity	Who am I dealing with? How can I be assured that the person or entity is who they claim to be?	What is the real identity of the customer?
Confidentiality	Can someone other than the intended recipient read my messages?	Are messages or confidential data accessible to anyone other than those authorized to view them?
Privacy	Can I control the use of information about myself transmitted to an e-commerce merchant?	What use, if any, can be made of personal data collected as part of an e-commerce transaction? Is the personal information of customers being used in an unauthorized manner?
Availability	Can I get access to the site?	Is the site operational?

violates not only the confidentiality of the data, but also the privacy of the individuals who supplied the information.

Availability refers to the ability to ensure that an e-commerce site continues to function as intended.

Table 4.3 summarizes these dimensions from both the merchants' and customers' perspectives. E-commerce security is designed to protect these six dimensions. When any one of them is compromised, overall security suffers.

availability
the ability to ensure that an e-commerce site continues to function as intended

THE TENSION BETWEEN SECURITY AND OTHER VALUES

Can there be too much security? The answer is yes. Contrary to what some may believe, security is not an unmitigated good. Computer security adds overhead and expense to business operations, and also gives criminals new opportunities to hide their intentions and their crimes.

Security versus Ease of Use

There are inevitable tensions between security and ease of use. When traditional merchants are so fearful of robbers that they do business in shops locked behind security gates, ordinary customers are discouraged from walking in. The same can be true with respect to e-commerce. In general, the more security measures added to an e-commerce site, the more difficult it is to use and the slower the site becomes. As you will discover reading this chapter, digital security is purchased at the price of slowing down processors and adding significantly to data storage demands on storage devices. Security is a technological and business overhead that can detract from doing business. Too much security can harm profitability, while not enough security can potentially put you out of business. One solution is to adjust security settings to the user's preferences. A McKinsey report found that when consumers find authentication at websites easy, they purchased 10% to 20% more (Hasham et al., 2016). Over the last few years, with the occurrence of so many high-profile data breaches, consumers' tolerance for enhanced security has increased. A recent IBM study found that security is at the forefront of users' concerns, with over 50% of those surveyed stating that they would never trade convenience for security. Almost three-quarters of consumers said that they would prefer additional security, even if they required additional steps in order to be able to access accounts (IBM Security, 2018).

Public Safety and the Criminal Uses of the Internet

There is also an inevitable tension between the desires of individuals to act anonymously (to hide their identity) and the needs of public officials to maintain public safety that can be threatened by criminals or terrorists. This is not a new problem, or even new to the electronic era. The U.S. government began tapping telegraph wires during the Civil War in the mid-1860s in order to trap conspirators and terrorists, and the first police wiretaps of local telephone systems were in place by the 1890s—20 years after the invention of the phone (Schwartz, 2001). No nation-state has ever permitted a technological haven to exist where criminals can plan crimes or threaten the nation-state without fear of official surveillance or investigation. In this sense, the Internet is no different from any other communication system. Drug cartels make extensive use of voice, fax, the Internet, and encrypted e-mail; a number of large international organized crime groups steal information from commercial websites and resell it to other criminals who use it for financial fraud. Over the years, the U.S. government has successfully pursued various "carding forums" (websites that facilitate the sale of stolen credit card and debit card numbers), such as Shadowcrew, Carderplanet, and Cardersmarket, resulting in the arrest and prosecution of a number of their members and the closing of the sites. However, other criminal organizations have emerged to take their place.

The Internet and mobile platform also provide terrorists with convenient communications channels. In an effort to combat such terrorism, the U.S. government has significantly ramped up its surveillance of communications delivered via the Internet. The extent of that surveillance created a major controversy with National Security Agency contractor Edward Snowden's release of classified NSA documents that revealed that the NSA had obtained access to the servers of major Internet companies such as Facebook, Google, Apple, Microsoft, and others, as well as that NSA analysts have been searching e-mail, online chats, and browsing histories of U.S. citizens without any court approval. Security agencies have shifted from mass surveillance to smaller, targeted surveillance of terrorists and terrorist groups, and the use of predictive algorithms to focus their efforts (N. F. Johnson et al., 2016). The proper balance between public safety and privacy in the effort against terrorism has proven to be a very thorny problem for the U.S. government.

4.2 SECURITY THREATS IN THE E-COMMERCE ENVIRONMENT

From a technology perspective, there are three key points of vulnerability when dealing with e-commerce: the client, the server, and the communications pipeline. **Figure 4.2** illustrates a typical e-commerce transaction with a consumer using a credit card to purchase a product. **Figure 4.3** illustrates some of the things that can go wrong at each major vulnerability point in the transaction—over Internet communications channels, at the server level, and at the client level.

In this section, we describe a number of the most common and most damaging forms of security threats to e-commerce consumers and site operators: malicious code, potentially unwanted programs, phishing, hacking and cybervandalism, credit card fraud/theft, spoofing, pharming, spam (junk) websites (link farms), identity fraud, Denial of Service (DoS) and DDoS attacks, sniffing, insider attacks, poorly designed server and client software, social network security issues, mobile platform security issues, and finally, cloud security issues.

MALICIOUS CODE

malicious code (malware)
includes a variety of threats such as viruses, worms, Trojan horses, and bots

Malicious code (sometimes referred to as "malware") includes a variety of threats such as viruses, worms, Trojan horses, ransomware, and bots. Some malicious code, sometimes

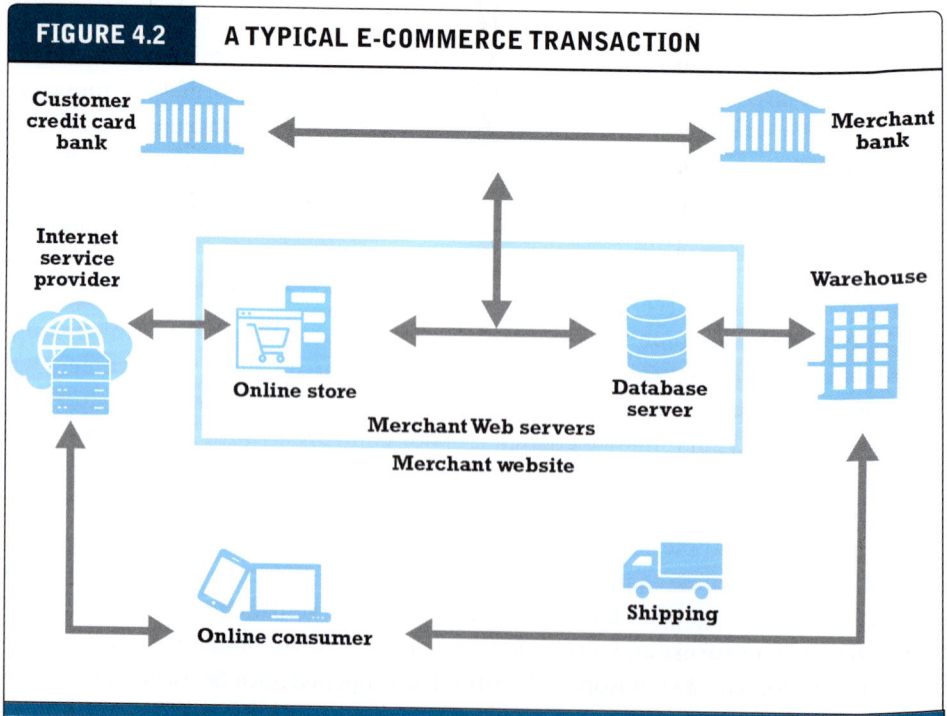

FIGURE 4.2 A TYPICAL E-COMMERCE TRANSACTION

In a typical e-commerce transaction, the customer uses a credit card and the existing credit payment system.

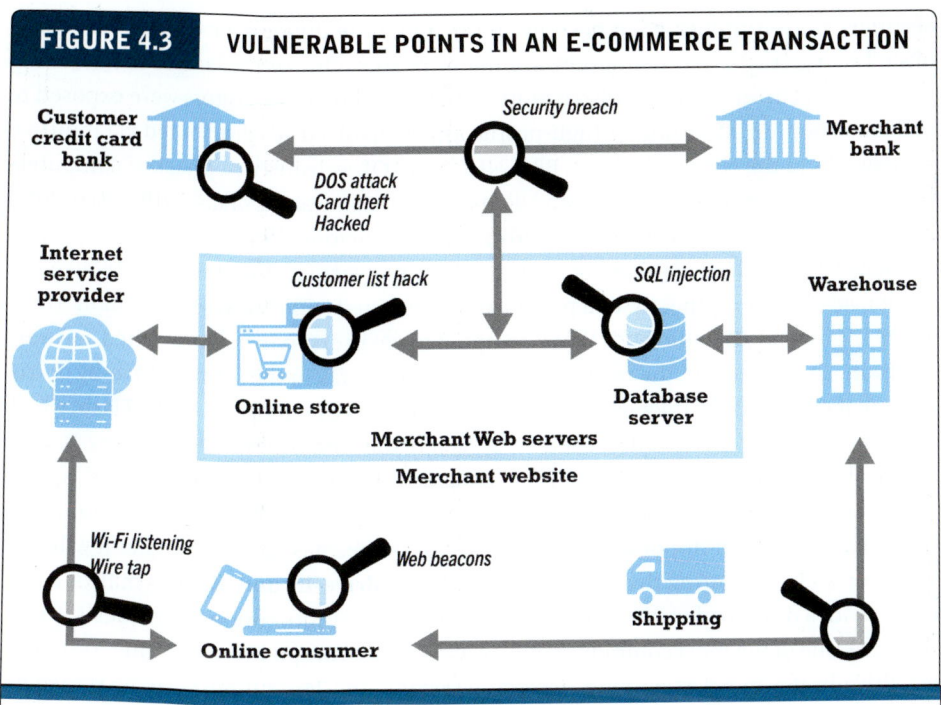

FIGURE 4.3 VULNERABLE POINTS IN AN E-COMMERCE TRANSACTION

There are three major vulnerable points in e-commerce transactions: Internet communications, servers, and clients.

referred to as an *exploit*, is designed to take advantage of software vulnerabilities in a computer's operating system, web browser, applications, or other software components. **Exploit kits** are collections of exploits bundled together and rented or sold as a commercial product, often with slick user interfaces and in-depth analytics functionality. Use of an exploit kit typically does not require much technical skill, enabling novices to become cybercriminals. Exploit kits typically target software that is widely deployed, such as Microsoft Windows, Internet Explorer, Adobe Flash and Reader, and Oracle Java. According to Symantec, about 246 million new variants of malware were created in 2018 (Symantec, 2019). In the past, malicious code was often intended to simply impair computers, and was often authored by a lone hacker, but increasingly it involves a small group of hackers or a nation-state supported group, and the intent is to steal e-mail addresses, logon credentials, personal data, and financial information. It's the difference between petty crime and organized crime.

Malware is often delivered in the form of a malicious attachment to an email or embedded as a link in the email. Malicious links can also be placed in innocent-looking Microsoft Word or Excel documents. The links lead directly to a malicious code download or websites that include malicious code (Symantec, 2017). One of the latest innovations in malicious code distribution is to embed it in the online advertising chain (known as **malvertising**), including in Google, and other ad networks. As the ad network chain

exploit kit
collection of exploits bundled together and rented or sold as a commercial product

malvertising
online advertising that contains malicious code

becomes more complicated, it becomes more and more difficult for websites to vet ads placed on their sites to ensure they are malware-free. One of the largest malvertising infections occurred at Yahoo where more than 6.9 million daily visitors were exposed to malicious pop-up ads. Another high-profile attack involved ads distributed via multiple ad networks to the New York Times, BBC, NFL, and AOL websites that hijacked computers when clicked, encrypted user data, and demanded ransomware (Zurkas, 2018; Cisco, 2017; Blue, 2016; Vuijsje, 2016; Zarras et al., 2014). These malicious ads can be stopped by using ad blockers. Google is also taking steps to block malvertising, and in 2017, blocked 79 million ads for attempting to send people to sites infested with malware, 66 million "trick-to-click" ads, and 48 million ads that attempted to get users to install unwanted software (Sullivan, 2018). Much of the malvertising in past years was in the form of drive-by downloads that exploited the frequent zero-day vulnerabilities that plagued Adobe Flash, which was often used for online advertisements. As a result, the Internet Advertising Bureau urged advertisers to abandon Adobe Flash in favor of HTML5, and Mozilla Firefox, Apple's Safari, and Google's Chrome browser all now block Flash advertisements from autoplaying. Amazon has also stopped accepting Flash ads. Adobe has announced that it will stop updating and distributing the Flash Player in 2020. A **drive-by download** is malware that comes with a downloaded file that a user intentionally or unintentionally requests. Drive-by is now one of the most common methods of infecting computers. According to Symantec, drive-by download exploit kits, including updates and 24/7 support, can be rented for between $100 to $700 per week. Malicious code embedded in PDF files also is common. Equally important, there has been a major shift in the writers of malware from amateur hackers and adventurers to organized criminal efforts to defraud companies and individuals. In other words, it's now more about the money than ever before.

A **virus** is a computer program that has the ability to replicate or make copies of itself, and spread to other files. In addition to the ability to replicate, most computer viruses deliver a "payload." The payload may be relatively benign, such as the display of a message or image, or it may be highly destructive—destroying files, reformatting the computer's hard drive, or causing programs to run improperly.

Viruses are often combined with a worm. Instead of just spreading from file to file, a **worm** is designed to spread from computer to computer. A worm does not necessarily need to be activated by a user or program in order to replicate itself. The Slammer worm is one of the most notorious. Slammer targeted a known vulnerability in Microsoft's SQL Server database software and infected more than 90% of vulnerable computers worldwide within 10 minutes of its release on the Internet; crashed Bank of America cash machines, especially in the southwestern part of the United States; affected cash registers at supermarkets such as the Publix chain in Atlanta, where staff could not dispense cash to frustrated buyers; and took down most Internet connections in South Korea, causing a dip in the stock market there. The Conficker worm (also known as Downad), which first appeared in 2008, is the most significant worm since Slammer, and reportedly infected 11 million computers worldwide (Microsoft, 2015). Originally designed to establish a global botnet, a massive industry effort has defeated this effort, but in 2017, Conficker was resurrected by hackers to aid in infecting computers with WannaCry ransomware, described below. It is still one of the most prevalent malware threats on the Internet (Scmagazine.com, 2017; TrendMicro, 2017).

drive-by download
malware that comes with a downloaded file that a user requests

virus
a computer program that has the ability to replicate or make copies of itself, and spread to other files

worm
malware that is designed to spread from computer to computer

Ransomware is a type of malware (often a worm) that locks your computer or files to stop you from accessing them. Ransomware will often display a notice that says an authority such as the FBI, Department of Justice, or IRS has detected illegal activity on your computer and demands that you pay a fine in order to unlock the computer and avoid prosecution. One type of ransomware is named CryptoLocker. CryptoLocker encrypts victims' files with a virtually unbreakable asymmetric encryption and demands a ransom to decrypt them, often in Bitcoins. If the victim does not comply within the time allowed, the files are rendered immune to decryption. Other variants include CryptoDefense and Cryptowall. The growth of ransomware is also related to the growth of the virtual currency Bitcoin. Hackers often demand victims pay using Bitcoin so their transactions are hidden from authorities. As discussed in the opening case, in 2017, WannaCry, the most widespread ransomware attack to date, occurred, followed shortly thereafter by NotPetya, another ransomware attack very similar to WannaCry. Although the overall incidence of ransomware attacks decreased in 2018, ransomware continues to pose a significant threat, particularly ransomware targeting organizations, which increased by 12% (Symantec, 2019).

A **Trojan horse** appears to be benign, but then does something other than expected. The Trojan horse is not itself a virus because it does not replicate, but is often a way for viruses or other malicious code such as bots or *rootkits* (a program whose aim is to subvert control of the computer's operating system) to be introduced into a computer system. The term *Trojan horse* refers to the huge wooden horse in Homer's *Iliad* that the Greeks gave their opponents, the Trojans—a gift that actually contained hundreds of Greek soldiers. Once the people of Troy let the massive horse within their gates, the soldiers revealed themselves and captured the city. In today's world, a Trojan horse may masquerade as a game, but actually hide a program to steal your passwords and e-mail them to another person. Miscellaneous Trojans and Trojan downloaders and droppers (Trojans that install malicious files to a computer they have infected by either downloading them from a remote computer or from a copy contained in their own code) are a common type of malware. In 2011, Sony experienced the largest data breach in history up to that time when a Trojan horse took over the administrative computers of Sony's PlayStation game center and downloaded personal and credit card information involving 77 million registered users (Wakabayashi, 2011). Trojan horses are often used for financial malware distributed via botnets. One example is Zeus, which steals information by keystroke logging and has infected over 10 million computers since it first became known in 2007. Other examples include Tinba, a Trojan that sells user credentials via a web injection attack as users attempt to log into their bank website; Ramnit, which is designed to steal banking, FTP passwords, session cookies, and personal data; and Emotet, a banking Trojan that reemerged in 2017 and aggressively expanded in 2018 (Symantec, 2019; Checkpoint Research Team, 2017). In 2018, banking trojans continued to pose a significant threat, with underground interest and development activity surging. For instance, security researchers identified a new variant of the Kronos banking trojan, nicknamed Osiris, being used against users in Germany, Japan, and Poland. As noted in the opening case, British security researcher Marcus Hutchins, who was credited with stopping the WannaCry ransomware outbreak, has been accused of developing and distributing Kronos and is currently awaiting trial in the United States. The new variant is very similar to the original version of

ransomware

malware that prevents you from accessing your computer or files and demands that you pay a fine

Trojan horse

appears to be benign, but then does something other than expected. Often a way for viruses or other malicious code to be introduced into a computer system

Kronos but uses the Tor anonymizing network to hide its command-and-control server (Vijayan, 2018).

A **backdoor** is a feature of viruses, worms, and Trojans that allows an attacker to remotely access a compromised computer. Downadup is an example of a worm with a backdoor, while Virut, a virus that infects various file types, also includes a backdoor that can be used to download and install additional threats.

Bots (short for robots) are a type of malicious code that can be covertly installed on your computer when attached to the Internet. Once installed, the bot responds to external commands sent by the attacker; your computer becomes a "zombie" and is able to be controlled by an external third party (the "bot-herder"). **Botnets** are collections of captured computers used for malicious activities such as sending spam, participating in a DDoS attack or credential stuffing campaign (malicious login attempts), stealing information from computers, and storing network traffic for later analysis. The number of botnets operating worldwide is not known but is estimated to be well into the thousands, controlling millions of computers. Bots and bot networks are an important threat to the Internet and e-commerce because they can be used to launch very large-scale attacks using many different techniques. In 2011, federal marshals accompanied members of Microsoft's digital crimes unit in raids designed to disable the Rustock botnet, at that time the leading source of spam in the world with nearly 500,000 slave PCs under the control of its command and control servers located at six Internet hosting services in the United States. Officials confiscated the Rustock control servers at the hosting sites, which claimed they had no idea what the Rustock servers were doing. The actual spam e-mails were sent by the slave PCs under the command of the Rustock servers (Wingfield, 2011). In 2013, Microsoft and the FBI engaged in another aggressive botnet operation, targeting 1,400 of Zeus-derived Citadel botnets, which had been used in 2012 to raid bank accounts at major banks around the world, netting over $500 million (Chirgwin, 2013). In 2015, an international cybersquad took down the Beebone botnet, made up of 12,000 computers that had been infecting about 30,000 computers a month around the world via drive-by downloads with Changeup, a polymorphic worm used to distribute Trojans, worms, backdoors, and other types of malware (Constantin, 2015). The FBI and British police were also able to stop a botnet that had stolen over $10 million from banks (Pagliery, 2015). As a result of efforts such as these, the number of bots has significantly declined, especially in the United States, although they still continue to pose a threat (Symantec, 2019).

Malicious code is a threat at both the client and the server levels, although servers generally engage in much more thorough anti-virus activities than do consumers. At the server level, malicious code can bring down an entire website, preventing millions of people from using the site. Such incidents are infrequent. Much more frequent malicious code attacks occur at the client level, and the damage can quickly spread to millions of other computers connected to the Internet. **Table 4.4** lists some well-known examples of malicious code.

POTENTIALLY UNWANTED PROGRAMS (PUPS)

In addition to malicious code, the e-commerce security environment is further challenged by **potentially unwanted programs (PUPs)**, also sometimes referred to as potentially

TABLE 4.4		NOTABLE EXAMPLES OF MALICIOUS CODE
NAME	TYPE	DESCRIPTION
Emotet	Botnet/Ransomware	Largest botnet that delivers various malicious payloads, including ransomware. First appeared in 2017, became the most prevalent malware in 2018, and continued to have an impact in 2019.
WannaCry	Ransomware/worm	First appeared in 2017. Exploits vulnerabilities in older versions of Windows operating systems, encrypts data, and demands a ransom payment to decrypt them.
Cryptolocker	Ransomware/Trojan	Hijacks users' photos, videos, and text documents, encrypts them with virtually unbreakable asymmetric encryption, and demands ransom payment for them.
Citadel	Trojan/botnet	Variant of Zeus Trojan, focuses on the theft of authentication credentials and financial fraud. Botnets spreading Citadel were targets of Microsoft/FBI action in 2012.
Zeus	Trojan/botnet	Sometimes referred to as king of financial malware. May install via drive-by download and evades detection by taking control of web browser and stealing data that is exchanged with bank servers.
Ramnit	Trojan/botnet	One of the most prevalent malicious code families still active. In operation since 2010, but largely disappeared in 2015 after the botnet that spread it was taken down. Reemerged in 2016 to become one of the most common financial trojans.
Conficker	Worm	First appeared in 2008. Targets Microsoft operating systems. Uses advanced malware techniques. Largest worm infection since Slammer in 2003. Used in 2017 in conjunction with various ransomware attacks.
Netsky.P	Worm/Trojan	First appeared in early 2003. It spread by gathering target e-mail addresses from the computers, then infected and sent e-mail to all recipients from the infected computer. It was commonly used by bot networks to launch spam and DoS attacks.
Storm (Peacomm, NuWar)	Worm/Trojan	First appeared in 2007. It spread in a manner similar to the Netsky.P worm. Could also download and run other Trojan programs and worms.
Nymex	Worm	First discovered in 2006. Spread by mass mailing; activated on the 3rd of every month, and attempted to destroy files of certain types.
Zotob	Worm	First appeared in 2005. Well-known worm that infected a number of U.S. media companies.
Mydoom	Worm	First appeared in 2004. One of the fastest spreading mass-mailer worms.
Slammer	Worm	Launched in 2003. Caused widespread problems.
Melissa	Macro virus/worm	First spotted in 1999. At the time, the fastest spreading infectious program ever discovered. It attacked Microsoft Word's Normal.dot global template, infecting all newly created documents and also mailed an infected Word file to the first 50 entries in each user's Microsoft Outlook Address Book.

unwanted applications (PUAs), such as adware, browser parasites, spyware, and other applications that install themselves on a computer, such as rogue security software, toolbars, and PC diagnostic tools, typically without the user's informed consent. Such programs are increasingly found on social network and user-generated content sites where users are fooled into downloading them. Once installed, these applications are usually exceedingly difficult to remove from the computer. One example of a PUP is PCProtect, which infects PCs running Windows operating systems. PCProtect poses as a legitimate anti-malware program when in fact it is malware.

adware
a PUP that serves pop-up ads to your computer

browser parasite
a program that can monitor and change the settings of a user's browser

Adware is typically used to call for pop-up ads to display when the user visits certain sites. It is increasingly being used as a tool by cybercriminals. According to Malwarebytes, the volume of adware is on the rise, and now accounts for 40% of event detections on systems protected by the Malwarebytes program (Malwarebytes, 2018). A **browser parasite** (also sometimes referred to as a browser-setting hijacker) is a program that can monitor and change the settings of a user's browser, for instance, changing the browser's home page, or sending information about the sites visited to a remote computer. Browser parasites are often a component of adware. In 2015, Lenovo faced a barrage of criticism when it became known that it had been shipping its Windows laptops with Superfish adware preinstalled. Superfish injected its own shopping results into the computer's browser when the user searched on Google, Amazon, or other websites. In the process, Superfish created a security risk by enabling others on a Wi-Fi network to silently hijack the browser and collect anything typed into it. Lenovo ultimately issued a removal tool to enable customers to delete the adware. Microsoft and legitimate security firms have redefined adware programs to be malware and discourage manufacturers from shipping products with adware programs (Loeb, 2016). **Coin/cryptocurrency miners**, which facilitate cryptojacking, are a new form of potentially unwanted program. For example, Coinhive is a service that can be deployed on websites using JavaScript. Users who visit such sites are at risk for having the script suck up their computer processing power, which is then used to mine cryptocurrencies.

coin/cryptocurrency miners
used to facilitate cryptojacking

spyware
a program used to obtain information such as a user's keystrokes, e-mail, instant messages, and so on

Spyware can be used to obtain information such as a user's keystrokes, copies of e-mail and instant messages, and even take screenshots (and thereby capture passwords or other confidential data).

PHISHING

social engineering
exploitation of human fallibility and gullibility to distribute malware

Social engineering relies on human curiosity, greed, and gullibility in order to trick people into taking an action that will result in the downloading of malware. Kevin Mitnick, until his capture and imprisonment in 1999, was one of America's most wanted computer criminals. Mitnick used simple deceptive techniques to obtain passwords, social security, and police records, all without the use of any sophisticated technology (Mitnick, 2011).

phishing
any deceptive, online attempt by a third party to obtain confidential information for financial gain

BEC (business e-mail compromise) phishing
variation of Nigerian letter scams in which an attacker poses as a high-level employee of a company and requests that another employee transfer funds to a fraudulent account

Phishing is any deceptive, online attempt by a third party to obtain confidential information for financial gain. Phishing attacks typically do not involve malicious code but instead rely on straightforward misrepresentation and fraud, so-called "social engineering" techniques. One of the most popular phishing attacks is the e-mail scam letter. The scam begins with an e-mail: a rich former oil minister of Nigeria is seeking a bank account to stash millions of dollars for a short period of time, and requests your bank account number where the money can be deposited. In return, you will receive a million dollars. This type of e-mail scam is popularly known as a "Nigerian letter" scam (see **Figure 4.4**). **BEC (business e-mail compromise) phishing** is a variation of Nigerian letter scams. In BEC phishing, an attacker poses as a high-level employee of a company and requests that another employee transfer funds to a fraudulent account. One specific type of BEC phishing that has become very prevalent involves requests for employee W-2 information from payroll or human resources personnel by scammers impersonating high-level company executives (Crowe, 2017). According to Symantec, almost half of the

FIGURE 4.4 AN EXAMPLE OF A NIGERIAN LETTER E-MAIL SCAM

This is an example of a typical Nigerian letter e-mail scam.
© keith morris / Alamy Stock Photo

e-mail addresses involved in this type of phishing that it analyzed had Nigerian IP addresses. According to the U.S. FBI, over $12.5 billion worldwide was reported stolen during the period from October 2013 to May 2018 as a result of BEC phishing (Federal Bureau of Investigation, 2018).

Thousands of other phishing attacks use other scams, some pretending to be eBay, PayPal, or Citibank writing to you for account verification (known as *spear phishing*, or targeting a known customer of a specific bank or other type of business). Click on a link in the e-mail and you will be taken to a website controlled by the scammer, and prompted to enter confidential information about your accounts, such as your account number and PIN codes. On any given day, millions of these phishing attack e-mails are sent, and, unfortunately, some people are fooled and disclose their personal account information.

Phishers rely on traditional "con man" tactics, but use e-mail or other forms of online communication, such as social media or SMS messaging, to trick recipients into voluntarily giving up financial access codes, bank account numbers, credit card numbers, and other personal information. Often, phishers create (or "spoof") a website that purports to be a legitimate institution and cons users into entering financial information, or the site downloads malware such as a keylogger to the victim's computer. For instance, a 2018 report found that the number of fake retail website designed to phish for customer information rose by almost 300% from the third quarter of 2017 to the third quarter of 2018 (Zhou, 2018). Phishers use the information they gather to commit fraudulent acts such as charging items to your credit cards or withdrawing funds from your bank account, or in other ways "steal your identity" (identity fraud). Symantec reported that in 2018, about 1 in every 3,207 e-mails contained a phishing attack, a slight decrease in the rate compared to 2017. Although more and more people are becoming alert to the dangers of phishing, Verizon found that on average, 4% of people in any given phishing campaign will still click on it (Symantec, 2019; Verizon, 2018). However, certain types of phishing, such as BEC phishing and spear phishing, continue to grow. In perhaps one of the most notorious examples of spear phishing, e-mails that appeared to be legitimate Gmail password account reset requests enabled hackers to gain access to the Gmail account of John Podesta, Hillary Clinton's campaign chairman, as well as a number of other members of the Democratic National Committee, during the 2016 election (Symantec, 2018, 2017).

To combat phishing, in 2012, leading e-mail service providers, including Google, Microsoft, Yahoo, and AOL, as well as financial services companies such as PayPal, Bank of America, and others, joined together to form DMARC.org, an organization aimed at dramatically reducing e-mail address spoofing, in which attackers use real e-mail addresses to send phishing e-mails to victims who may be deceived because the e-mail appears to originate from a source the receiver trusts. DMARC (Domain-based Message Authentication, Reporting, and Conformance) offers a method of authenticating the origin of the e-mail and allows receivers to quarantine, report, or reject messages that fail to pass its test. Yahoo and AOL have reported significant success against email fraud as a result of using DMARC, and in 2016 Google joined them in implementing a stricter version of DMARC, in which e-mail that fails DMARC authentication checks will be rejected. As of 2019, over 80% of all federal domains and over 50% of Fortune 500 companies used DMARC, up from just one-third in 2017 (Garcia-Tobar, 2019).

HACKING, CYBERVANDALISM, AND HACKTIVISM

A **hacker** is an individual who intends to gain unauthorized access to a computer system. Within the hacking community, the term **cracker** is typically used to denote a hacker with criminal intent, although in the public press, the terms hacker and cracker tend to be used interchangeably. Hackers and crackers gain unauthorized access by finding weaknesses in the security procedures of websites and computer systems, often taking advantage of various features of the Internet that make it an open system that is easy to use. In the past, hackers and crackers typically were computer aficionados excited by the challenge of breaking into corporate and government websites. Sometimes they were satisfied merely by breaking into the files of an e-commerce site. Today, hackers have malicious intentions to disrupt, deface, or destroy sites (**cybervandalism**) or to steal personal or corporate information they can use for financial gain (data breach).

Hacktivism adds a political twist. Hacktivists typically attack governments, organizations, and even individuals for political purposes, employing the tactics of cybervandalism, distributed denial of service attacks, data thefts, and doxing (gathering and exposing personal information of public figures, typically from emails, social network posts, and other documents). The most prominent hacktivist organization is Wikileaks, founded by Julian Assange and others, which released documents and e-mails of the U.S. Department of State, U.S. Department of Defense, and Democratic National Committee in 2016. LulzSec and Anonymous are two other prominent hacktivist groups. Another group, known as the Shadow Brokers, was responsible for releasing a number of hacking tools

hacker
an individual who intends to gain unauthorized access to a computer system

cracker
within the hacking community, a term typically used to denote a hacker with criminal intent

cybervandalism
intentionally disrupting, defacing, or even destroying a site

hacktivism
cybervandalism and data theft for political purposes

from the NSA and information about major software vulnerabilities, including the EternalBlue flaw used for the WannaCry ransomware attack.

Groups of hackers called *tiger teams* are sometimes used by corporate security departments to test their own security measures. By hiring hackers to break into the system from the outside, the company can identify weaknesses in the computer system's armor. These "good hackers" became known as **white hats** because of their role in helping organizations locate and fix security flaws. White hats do their work under contract, with agreement from the target firms that they will not be prosecuted for their efforts to break in. Hardware and software firms such as Apple, Microsoft, Intel, HP, and many others pay bounties of $25,000 to $250,000 to white hat hackers for discovering bugs in their software and hardware (Warren, 2018).

white hats
"good" hackers who help organizations locate and fix security flaws

In contrast, **black hats** are hackers who engage in the same kinds of activities but without pay or any buy-in from the targeted organization, and with the intention of causing harm. They break into websites and reveal the confidential or proprietary information they find. These hackers believe strongly that information should be free, so sharing previously secret information is part of their mission.

black hats
hackers who act with the intention of causing harm

Somewhere in the middle are the **grey hats**, hackers who believe they are pursuing some greater good by breaking in and revealing system flaws. Grey hats discover weaknesses in a system's security, and then publish the weakness without disrupting the site or attempting to profit from their finds. Their only reward is the prestige of discovering the weakness. Grey hat actions are suspect, however, especially when the hackers reveal security flaws that make it easier for other criminals to gain access to a system.

grey hats
hackers who believe they are pursuing some greater good by breaking in and revealing system flaws

DATA BREACHES

A **data breach** occurs whenever organizations lose control over corporate information to outsiders. The Identity Theft Resource Center recorded 1,244 breaches in 2018, a decrease of 23% compared to 2017, but the number of consumer records exposed in those breaches increased by 126%. Breaches involving the business sector had the highest impact, representing 46% of all breaches, followed by the medical/healthcare industry, representing about 29%, and the banking/credit/financial sector rounding out the top three, at 11%. Hackers were the leading cause of data breaches, responsible for almost 40% of breaches, followed by unauthorized access (30%), and employee error (12%). Almost 50% of the breaches involved social security numbers, and about 20% included credit and debit card information (Identity Theft Resource Center, 2019). Two of the most notorious data breaches that have recently come to light include the Yahoo data breach, believed to be the largest breach at a single company in history, exposing the identity of every single user of Yahoo's email service (a total of 3 billion people), and the Equifax data breach, where hackers accessed and downloaded the personal data files of approximately 148 million U.S. consumers, or roughly 45% of the U.S. population. Another huge data breach occurred in late 2018, when Marriott International revealed that a breach of its Starwood guest reservation system exposed the personal data of up almost 400 million people. Read the *Insight on Society* case, *The Marriott Data Breach*, for more information. In 2019, the trend has continued, with financial services firm Capitol One announcing the exposure of data of over 100 million customers in the United States and Canada who had applied for credit cards (Frias, 2019).

data breach
occurs when an organization loses control over its information to outsiders

INSIGHT ON SOCIETY

THE MARRIOTT DATA BREACH

In November 2018, Marriott, the world's largest hotel company, announced that one of its reservation systems had been hacked. With over 7,000 properties and more than 1 million hotel rooms worldwide, Marriott manages a very large and detailed database on the movements of millions of people that is a valuable target of hackers. In what is believed to have been the second-largest data breach in history, an estimated 500 million guest records were downloaded by hackers, including credit cards, addresses, phone numbers, and passport information. Marriott has estimated that credit card information on 327 million individual customers was involved, along with 25 million passports, 5 million of which were not encrypted. The system involved was the reservation system for Starwood Hotels, which includes the Westin, Sheraton, St. Regis, and W hotels. After purchasing Starwood in 2016, Marriot continued to operate the Starwood system independently because Marriott's own reservation system was not capable of taking on the additional load of Starwood. This turned out to be a major factor in the data breach.

How the breach occurred is still not completely understood by Marriott or the authorities. An initial investigation by Marriot found that the Starwood legacy system was likely breached in 2014 but Starwood systems personnel did not detect the malware installed for a period of four years. When Marriott purchased Starwood, it purchased a reservation that was already compromised. To make matters worse, shortly after the acquisition, Marriott laid off many of the Starwood system's staff in an effort to cut costs via consolidation, which often occurs in mergers and acquisitions. Subsequently, several class action law suits have been filed claiming that Marriott did not conduct sufficient due diligence when purchasing Starwood and that management allowed a compromised reservation system to continue operating.

Company and government investigators did find a remote access trojan that could send any data it found to external servers, along with MimiKatz, malware for finding the data. MimiKatz is a tool that can search username and password combinations in large databases. How the trojan and MimiKatz got access to the Starwood servers is not known, but one likely candidate was phishing emails sent to Starwood employees who had legitimate access to its reservation system. The weakest link in systems is at the end point, through users of a system who have legitimate access to it.

If the guest information had been properly encrypted, it might have been useless to hackers. Unfortunately, this was not the case. The credit card information was indeed encrypted, but the hackers also likely stole the encryption keys that were stored on the same hacked server. This is a fatal flaw in many corporate systems: best practices call for installing the encryption keys that unlock encrypted data on separate servers which are isolated from main transaction systems in the firm and, ideally, stored on separate secure networks. Encryption alone is not a "bullet proof" guarantee of cyber security but rather a basic first step that can work if it is properly installed and managed. Unfortunately, passport numbers were stored "in the open" and not encrypted at all.

Who actually led the hacking effort, and for what purpose, remains a mystery, although there are a few clues. Hacks of large databases with credit card information usually result in that information being sold quickly to other hackers on the dark web or being used to conduct fraudulent credit card purchases. However, this spurt in illegal activity did not occur in Marriott hack, and none of the stolen information has appeared on the dark web.

U.S. government investigators believe this was not a hack done for commercial reasons; instead, they point to Chinese intelligence agencies as the likely source, because the hackers used cloud servers associated with Chinese state hackers, along with other details of the hack that, to date, remain undisclosed. One theory is that the stolen passport numbers may be the most valuable aspect of the hack: Marriott is one of the main providers to U.S. government armed forces and government personnel. The data on government guests could be useful for tracking the movements of military and intelligence employees and building dossiers on individuals. In congressional testimony in Washington, however, Marriott's CEO denied the Chinese were involved.

Marriott has announced in 2019 that it has incurred $128 million in expenses as a result of the breach. It has also been fined $120 million by the U.K.'s Information Commissioner's Office (ICO) for violating U.K. privacy laws, which are derived from the EU's General Data Protection Regulation (GDPR). The ICO claims that Marriott failed to undertake adequate due diligence when it acquired Starwood.

Marriott's 2018 revenues were just over $20 billion. Hence, $250 million in fines to Marriott constitute about 1% of its revenues and about 11% of its $2.2 billion in earnings—a substantial loss of earnings but a minor part of its overall revenue. However, loss of reputation and potential loss of customers including government agencies is also a risk for Marriott that could amount to much more than government fines.

Marriott responded to the breach by offering guests compensation for costs associated with obtaining a new passport as well as for credit card losses if fraud occurred as a result of the breach. Several class action lawsuits have been filed again Marriott as well as the consulting and service company Accenture, to whom Starwood had outsourced their security. The City of Chicago sued the company in 2019 for failing to protect the personal information of Chicago residents, claiming that Marriott had allowed criminals to copy extensive personal information for a period of over four years and failed to implement reasonable safeguards that could have prevented the data breach. Even worse, so the suit claims, firm managers knew of the security risks for four years.

SOURCES: "Why Encryption Is Failing Us," by Tom Kellermann, Techradar.com, November 30, 2019; "Marriott Data Breach FAQ: How Did It Happen and What Was the Impact?," by Josh Fruhlinger, CSOonline.com, September 30, 2019; "Marriott Takes $126 Million Charge Related to Data Breach," by Maria Armental, *Wall Street Journal*, August 5, 2019; "Marriott To Be Fined Nearly £100m over GDPR Breach," by Mark Sweeney, Theguardian.com, July 9, 2019; "Chicago Sues Marriott over Data Breach Claiming Hotel Chain Failed to Protect Personal Information," by Gabriel Neves, Legalnewsline.com, April 8, 2019; "Marriott CEO Reveals New Details About Mega Breach," by Kate O'Flaherty, Forbes.com, March 11, 2019; "2018 Annual Report on Form 10-K, for the Fiscal Year ended December 31, 2018," Marriott International, Inc., February 20, 2019; "Marriott's Data Breach May Be the Biggest in History. Now It's Facing Multiple Class-action Lawsuits," by Gaby Del Valle, Vox.com, January 11, 2019; "Marriott Now Says 5 Million Unencrypted Passport Numbers Were Stolen in Starwood Hotel Data Breach," by Zach Whittaker, Techcrunch.com, January 4, 2019.

CREDIT CARD FRAUD/THEFT

Theft of credit card data is one of the most feared occurrences on the Internet. Fear that credit card information will be stolen prevents users from making online purchases in many cases. Online merchants use a variety of techniques to combat credit card fraud, including using automated fraud detection tools, manually reviewing orders, rejection of suspect orders, and requiring additional levels of security such as email address, zip code, and CVV security codes.

U.S. federal law limits the liability of individuals to $50 for a stolen credit card. For amounts more than $50, the credit card company generally pays the amount, although in some cases, the merchant may be held liable if it failed to verify the account or consult published lists of invalid cards. Banks recoup the cost of credit card fraud by charging higher interest rates on unpaid balances, and by merchants who raise prices to cover the losses. In 2015, the U.S. credit card system began a shift to EMV credit cards, also known as smart cards or chip cards. Already widely used in Europe, EMV credit cards have a computer chip instead of a magnetic strip that can be easily copied by hackers and sold as dump data (see Table 4.2). While EMV technology cannot prevent data breaches from occurring, it has made it harder for criminals to profit from the mass theft of credit card numbers (Riley, 2018).

In the past, the most common cause of credit card fraud was a lost or stolen card that was used by someone else, followed by employee theft of customer numbers and stolen identities (criminals applying for credit cards using false identities). Today, the most frequent cause of stolen cards and card information is the systematic hacking and looting of a corporate server where the information on millions of credit card purchases is stored.

International orders have a much higher risk of being fraudulent, with fraud losses twice those of domestic orders. If an international customer places an order and then later disputes it, online merchants often have no way to verify that the package was actually delivered and that the credit card holder is the person who placed the order. As a result, most online merchants will not process international orders.

A central security issue of e-commerce is the difficulty of establishing the customer's identity. Currently there is no technology that can identify a person with absolute certainty. For instance, a lost or stolen EMV card can be used until the card is cancelled, just like a magnetic strip card. Until a customer's identity can be guaranteed, online companies are at a higher risk of loss than traditional offline companies. The federal government has attempted to address this issue through the Electronic Signatures in Global and National Commerce Act (the "E-Sign" law), which gives digital signatures the same authority as hand-written signatures in commerce. This law also intended to make digital signatures more commonplace and easier to use. Similar laws on the state level have been adopted using the framework provided by the Uniform Electronic Transaction Act (UETA). Although the use of e-signatures is still uncommon in the B2C retail e-commerce arena, many businesses are starting to implement e-signature solutions, particularly for B2B contracting, financial services, insurance, health care, and government and professional services. DocuSign, Adobe Sign, Citrix RightSignature, and OneSpan Sign are currently among the most widely adopted e-signature solutions.

They use a variety of techniques, such as remote user identification through third-party databases or personal information verification such as a photo of a driver's license; multi-factor user authentication methods (user ID and password, e-mail address verification, secret question and answer); and public/private key encryption to create a digital signature and embedded audit trail that can be used to verify the e-signature's integrity. The use of fingerprint identification is also one solution to positive identification, but the database of print information can be hacked. Mobile e-signature solutions are also beginning to be adopted.

IDENTITY FRAUD

Identity fraud involves the unauthorized use of another person's personal data, such as social security, driver's license, and/or credit card numbers, as well as user names and passwords, for illegal financial benefit. Criminals can use such data to obtain loans, purchase merchandise, or obtain other services, such as mobile phone or other utility services. Cybercriminals employ many of the techniques described previously, such as spyware, phishing, data breaches, and credit card theft, for the purpose of identity fraud. Data breaches, in particular, often lead to identity fraud.

Identity fraud is a significant problem throughout the world. In 2018, according to Javelin Strategy & Research, 14.4 million U.S. consumers suffered identity fraud. The total dollar losses as a result of identity fraud were approximately $14.7 billion (Javelin Research & Strategy, 2019).

identity fraud
involves the unauthorized use of another person's personal data for illegal financial benefit

SPOOFING, PHARMING, AND SPAM (JUNK) WEBSITES

Spoofing involves attempting to hide a true identity by using someone else's e-mail or IP address. For instance, a spoofed e-mail will have a forged sender e-mail address designed to mislead the receiver about who sent the e-mail. IP spoofing involves the creation of TCP/IP packets that use someone else's source IP address, indicating that the packets are coming from a trusted host. Most current routers and firewalls can offer protection against IP spoofing. Spoofing a website sometimes involves **pharming**, automatically redirecting a web link to an address different from the intended one, with the site masquerading as the intended destination. Links that are designed to lead to one site can be reset to send users to a totally unrelated site—one that benefits the hacker.

Although spoofing and pharming do not directly damage files or network servers, they threaten the integrity of a site. For example, if hackers redirect customers to a fake website that looks almost exactly like the true site, they can then collect and process orders, effectively stealing business from the true site. Or, if the intent is to disrupt rather than steal, hackers can alter orders—inflating them or changing products ordered—and then send them on to the true site for processing and delivery. Customers become dissatisfied with the improper order shipment, and the company may have huge inventory fluctuations that impact its operations.

In addition to threatening integrity, spoofing also threatens authenticity by making it difficult to discern the true sender of a message. Clever hackers can make it almost impossible to distinguish between a true and a fake identity or web address.

spoofing
involves attempting to hide a true identity by using someone else's e-mail or IP address

pharming
automatically redirecting a web link to an address different from the intended one, with the site masquerading as the intended destination

spam (junk) websites
also referred to as link farms; promise to offer products or services, but in fact are just collections of advertisements

Spam (junk) websites (also sometimes referred to as *link farms*) are a little different. These are sites that promise to offer some product or service, but in fact are just a collection of advertisements for other sites, some of which contain malicious code. For instance, you may search for "[name of town] weather," and then click on a link that promises your local weather, but then discover that all the site does is display ads for weather-related products or other websites. Junk or spam websites typically appear on search results, and do not involve e-mail. These sites cloak their identities by using domain names similar to legitimate firm names, and redirect traffic to known spammer-redirection domains such as topsearch10.com.

SNIFFING AND MAN-IN-THE-MIDDLE ATTACKS

sniffer
a type of eavesdropping program that monitors information traveling over a network

A **sniffer** is a type of eavesdropping program that monitors information traveling over a network. When used legitimately, sniffers can help identify potential network troublespots, but when used for criminal purposes, they can be damaging and very difficult to detect. Sniffers enable hackers to steal proprietary information from anywhere on a network, including passwords, e-mail messages, company files, and confidential reports. For instance, in 2013, five hackers were charged in another worldwide hacking scheme that targeted the corporate networks of retail chains such as 7-Eleven and the French retailer Carrefour SA, using sniffer programs to steal more than 160 million credit card numbers (Voreacos, 2013).

E-mail wiretaps are a variation on the sniffing threat. An e-mail wiretap is a method for recording or journaling e-mail traffic generally at the mail server level from any individual. E-mail wiretaps are used by employers to track employee messages, and by government agencies to surveil individuals or groups. E-mail wiretaps can be installed on servers and client computers. In the United States, the USA PATRIOT Act permits the FBI to compel ISPs to install a black box on their mail servers that can impound the e-mail of a single person or group of persons for later analysis. In the case of American citizens communicating with other citizens, an FBI agent or government lawyer need only certify to a judge on the secret 11-member U.S. Foreign Intelligence Surveillance Court (FISC) that the information sought is relevant to an ongoing criminal investigation to get permission to install the program. Judges have no discretion. They must approve wiretaps based on government agents' unsubstantiated assertions. In the case of suspected terrorist activity, law enforcement does not have to inform a court prior to installing a wire or e-mail tap. A 2007 amendment to the 1978 Foreign Intelligence Surveillance Act, known as FISA, provided new powers to the National Security Agency to monitor international e-mail and telephone communications where one person is in the United States, and where the purpose of such interception is to collect foreign intelligence (Foreign Intelligence Surveillance Act of 1978; Protect America Act of 2007). The FISA Amendments Reauthorization Act of 2017 extends the provisions of FISA until the end of 2023. NSA's XKeyscore program, revealed by Edward Snowden, is a form of "wiretap" that allows NSA analysts to search through vast databases containing not only e-mail, but online chats, and browsing histories of millions of individuals (Wills, 2013).

The U.S. Communications Assistance for Law Enforcement Act (CALEA) requires all communications carriers (including ISPs) to provide near-instant access to law enforcement agencies to their message traffic. Many Internet services (such as Facebook and LinkedIn) that have built-in ISP services technically are not covered by CALEA. One can only assume these non-ISP e-mail operators cooperate with law enforcement. Unlike the past where wiretaps required many hours to physically tap into phone lines, in today's digital phone systems, taps are arranged in a few minutes by the large carriers at their expense.

A **man-in-the-middle (MitM) attack** also involves eavesdropping but is more active than a sniffing attack, which typically involves passive monitoring. In a MitM attack, the attacker is able to intercept communications between two parties who believe they are directly communicating with one another, when in fact the attacker is controlling the communications. This allows the attacker to change the contents of the communication.

DENIAL OF SERVICE (DOS) AND DISTRIBUTED DENIAL OF SERVICE (DDOS) ATTACKS

In a **Denial of Service (DoS) attack**, hackers flood a website with useless pings or page requests that inundate and overwhelm the site's web servers. Increasingly, DoS attacks involve the use of bot networks and so-called "distributed attacks" built from thousands of compromised client computers. DoS attacks typically cause a website to shut down, making it impossible for users to access the site. For busy e-commerce sites, these attacks are costly; while the site is shut down, customers cannot make purchases. And the longer a site is shut down, the more damage is done to a site's reputation. Although such attacks do not destroy information or access restricted areas of the server, they can destroy a firm's online business. Often, DoS attacks are accompanied by attempts at blackmailing site owners to pay tens or hundreds of thousands of dollars to the hackers in return for stopping the DoS attack.

A **Distributed Denial of Service (DDoS) attack** uses hundreds or even thousands of computers to attack the target network from numerous launch points. DoS and DDoS attacks are threats to a system's operation because they can shut it down indefinitely. Major websites have experienced such attacks, making the companies aware of their vulnerability and the need to continually introduce new measures to prevent future attacks. According to Neustar, the number of both large- and small-scale DDoS attacks continued to increase in 2019. Attacks are also increasing in power. For instance, the largest DDoS attack in the Internet's history was launched against GitHub, the open-source software development platform in February 2018.

The growth of the Internet of Things (IoT), with billions of Internet-connected things from refrigerators to security cameras that can be used to launch service requests against servers, also poses a new threat (Cisco, 2018). In 2016, the Mirai botnet launched a large scale DDoS attack using Internet devices such as these against an Internet domain resolving firm, Dyn. Twitter, Amazon, Netflix, Airbnb, the New York Times, and many other sites across the country were affected. Hackers were able to guess the administrator passwords of common devices (often set to factory defaults like admin, or 12345), and then insert instructions to launch an attack against Dyn servers (Sanger and Perlroth, 2016). DDoS attacks are typically isolated to a single firm, but in the Dyn attack, the firm attacked happened to be one of the switchboards for a large part of the Internet in the United States. According to Netscout/Arbor, IoT botnets have become the preferred platform for launching DDoS attacks (Netscout/Arbor, 2018).

man-in-the-middle (MitM) attack
attack in which the attacker is able to intercept communications between two parties who believe they are directly communicating with one another, when in fact the attacker is controlling the communications

Denial of Service (DoS) attack
flooding a website with useless traffic to inundate and overwhelm the network

Distributed Denial of Service (DDoS) attack
using numerous computers to attack the target network from numerous launch points

In another measure of the prevalence of DDoS attacks, in a Netscout survey of ISP and network operators around the world, respondents noted that the number of DDoS attacks against SaaS services increased from 13% to 41% and those against third party data centers and cloud services increased from 11% to 34% during the survey period. Netscout also reported that the size and complexity of reported DDoS attacks rose dramatically, with attacks reaching over 1 terabit in size in terms of bandwidth and using multiple vectors of attack (Netscout, 2019). Another trend is DDoS smokescreening, in which attackers use DDoS as a distraction while they also insert malware or viruses or steal data. In a recent bi-annual global DDoS attack survey Neustar reported that 90% of companies that experienced a DDoS attack also reported some form of breach or associated actitivity with the breach (Neustar, 2017). And not surprisingly, now that mobile data connections have become faster and more stable, hackers are beginning to harness mobile devices for mobile-based DDoS attacks. An attack originating from China used malicious ads loaded inside mobile apps and mobile browesrs as the attack mechanism (Majkowski, 2015).

INSIDER ATTACKS

We tend to think of security threats to a business as originating outside the organization. In fact, the largest financial threats to business institutions come not from robberies but from embezzlement by insiders. Bank employees steal far more money than bank robbers. The same is true for e-commerce sites. Some of the largest disruptions to service, destruction to sites, and diversion of customer credit data and personal information have come from insiders—once trusted employees. A 2019 survey of insider threats found that 70% of organizations surveyed had experienced an insider attack within the past 12 months (Cybersecurity Insiders, 2019). IBM Security found that in the financial services and health care industries, there has been a greater percentage of attacks resulting from the actions of insiders (either malicious or inadvertent) than from outsiders (Cybersecurity Insiders, 2019; IBM Security, 2017). Employees have access to privileged information, and, in the presence of sloppy internal security procedures, they are often able to roam throughout an organization's systems without leaving a trace. Research from Carnegie Mellon University documents the significant damage insiders have done to both private and public organizations (Software Engineering Institute, 2012). In some instances, the insider might not have criminal intent, but inadvertently exposes data that can then be exploited by others. Companies are equally worried about accidental/unintentional data breaches due to user carelessness as they are about malicious insiders (Cybersecurity Insiders, 2019).

POORLY DESIGNED SOFTWARE

SQL injection attack
takes advantage of poorly coded web application software that fails to properly validate or filter data entered by a user on a web page

Many security threats prey on poorly designed software, sometimes in the operating system and sometimes in the application software, including browsers. The increase in complexity and size of software programs, coupled with demands for timely delivery to markets, has contributed to an increase in software flaws or vulnerabilities that hackers can exploit. For instance, **SQL injection attacks** take advantage of vulnerabilities in poorly coded web application software that fails to properly validate or filter data entered by a user on a web page to introduce malicious program code into a company's systems and networks. An attacker can use this input validation error to send a rogue SQL query to the underlying database to access the database, plant malicious code, or access other systems on the network. Large web applications have hundreds of places for inputting user data, each of which creates an opportunity for an SQL injection attack. A large number of web-facing applications are believed to have SQL injection vulnerabilities, and tools are available for hackers to check web applications for these vulnerabilities.

Each year, security firms identify thousands of software vulnerabilities in web browsers, PC, Macintosh, and Linux software, as well as mobile device operating systems and applications. A **zero-day vulnerability** is one that has been previously unreported and for which no patch yet exists. According to Ponemon Institute's *2018 State of Endpoint Security Risk* report, 76% of attacks on organization endpoints in 2018 were thought to be zero-day attacks (Ponemon Institute, 2018). The very design of the personal computer includes many open communication ports that can be used, and indeed are designed to be used, by external computers to send and receive messages. Ports that are frequently attacked include TCP port 445 (Microsoft-DS), port 80 (WWW/HTTP), and 443 (SSL/HTTPS). Given their complexity and design objectives, all operating systems and application software, including Linux and Macintosh, have vulnerabilities. For example, a vulnerability in Apache Struts, an open-source framework used to build Java web applications, was exploited in the Equifax data breach. In October 2018, Google announced that it was shutting down its social network, Google +, after it was revealed that a software flaw had given outside developers access to the personal information of its users (Corbett, 2018).

zero-day vulnerability
software vulnerability that has been previously unreported and for which no patch yet exists

In 2014, a flaw in the OpenSSL encryption system, used by millions of websites, known as the **Heartbleed bug**, was discovered (see Section 4.3 for a further discussion of SSL). The vulnerability allowed hackers to decrypt an SSL session and discover user names, passwords, and other user data, by using OpenSSL in combination with a communications protocol called the RFC6520 heartbeat that helps a remote user remain in touch after connecting with a website server. In the process a small chunk of the server's memory content can leak out (hence the name heartbleed), potentially large enough to hold a password or encryption key that would allow a hacker to exploit the server further. The Heartbleed bug also affected over 1,300 Android apps. Later in 2014, another vulnerability known as ShellShock or BashBug that affected most versions of Linux and Unix, as well as Mac OS X, was revealed. ShellShock enabled attackers to use CGI (see Chapter 3) to add malicious commands. In 2015, researchers announced that they had discovered a new SSL/TLS vulnerability that they named FREAK (Factoring RSA Export Keys) that allows man-in-the-middle attacks that enable the interception and decryption of encrypted communications between clients and servers, which would then allow the attackers to steal passwords and other personal information. More than 60% of encrypted websites were reportedly open to attack via this security vulnerability, including those for the White House, the FBI, and the National Security Agency (Hackett, 2015; Vaughan-Nichols, 2015).

Heartbleed bug
flaw in OpenSSL encryption system that allowed hackers to decrypt an SSL session and discover user names, passwords, and other user data

SOCIAL NETWORK SECURITY ISSUES

Social networks like Facebook, Twitter, LinkedIn, Pinterest, and Tumblr provide a rich and rewarding environment for hackers. Viruses, site takeovers, identity fraud, malware-loaded apps, click hijacking, phishing, and spam are all found on social networks. Common types of scams on social networks include manual sharing scams, where victims unwittingly share videos, stories, and pictures that include links to malicious sites and fake offerings that invite victims to join a fake event or group with incentives such as free gift cards and that require a user to share his or her information with the attacker. Other techniques include fake Reactions buttons that, when clicked, install malware and post updates to the user's Newsfeed, further spreading the attack, and fake apps. By sneaking in among our friends, hackers can masquerade as friends and dupe users into scams.

Social network firms have thus far been relatively poor policemen because they have failed to aggressively weed out accounts that send visitors to malware sites. Social networks are open: anyone can set up a personal page, even criminals. Most attacks are social engineering attacks that tempt visitors to click on links that sound reasonable. Social apps downloaded from either the social network or a foreign site are not certified by the social network to be clean of malware. It's "clicker beware."

MOBILE PLATFORM SECURITY ISSUES

The explosion in mobile devices has broadened opportunities for hackers. Mobile users are filling their devices with personal and financial information, and using them to conduct an increasing number of transactions, from retail purchases to mobile banking, making them excellent targets for hackers. In general, mobile devices face all the same risks as any Internet device as well as some new risks associated with wireless network security. For instance, public Wi-Fi networks that are not secured are very susceptible to hacking. For example, in 2017, researchers announced that they had discovered a flaw in the WPA2 Wi-Fi security protocol that allows hackers to intercept passwords, e-mail, and other traffic on Wi-Fi networks. Over 40% of all Android devices were found to be vulnerable to an exceptionally devastating variant of the attack (Ricker, 2017). While most PC users are aware their computers and websites may be hacked and contain malware, most cell phone users believe their cell phone is as secure as a traditional landline phone. As with social network members, mobile users are prone to thinking they are in a shared, trustworthy environment.

Mobile cell phone malware (sometimes referred to as malicious mobile apps (MMAs) or rogue mobile apps) was developed as early as 2004 with Cabir, a Bluetooth worm affecting Symbian operating systems (Nokia phones) and causing the phone to continuously seek out other Bluetooth-enabled devices, quickly draining the battery. The iKee.B worm, first discovered in 2009, only two years after the iPhone was introduced, infected jailbroken iPhones, turning the phones into botnet-controlled devices. An iPhone in Europe could be hacked by an iPhone in the United States, and all its private data sent to a server in Poland. IKee.B established the feasibility of cell phone botnets.

In 2017, Symantec blocked an average of over 10,500 malicious mobile apps per day. Mobile ransomware attacks increased by 33% in 2018. The majority of mobile malware still targets the Android platform. For instance, Symantec has already discovered Android malware that can intercept text messages with bank authentication codes and forward them to attackers, as well as fake versions of legitimate mobile banking applications.

However, the Apple iPhone platform is beginning to be increasingly targeted as well (Symantec, 2019). And it is not just rogue applications that are dangerous, but also popular legitimate applications that simply have little protection from hackers. For instance, in 2014, security researchers revealed that the Starbucks mobile app, the most used mobile payment app in the United States, was storing user names, e-mail addresses, and passwords in clear text, in such a way that anyone with access to the phone could see the passwords and user names by connecting the phone to a computer. According to researchers, Starbucks erred in emphasizing convenience and ease of use in the design of the app over security concerns (Schuman, 2014).

Vishing attacks target gullible cell phone users with verbal messages to call a certain number and, for example, donate money to starving children in Haiti. *Smishing* attacks exploit SMS/text messages. Compromised text messages can contain e-mail and website addresses that can lead the innocent user to a malware site. Criminal SMS spoofing services have emerged, which conceal the cybercriminal's true phone number, replacing it with a false alpha-numeric name. SMS spoofing can also be used by cybercriminals to lure mobile users to a malicious website by sending a text that appears to be from a legitimate organization in the From field, and suggesting the receiver click on a malicious URL hyperlink to update an account or obtain a gift card. A small number of downloaded apps from app stores have also contained malware. *Madware*—innocent-looking apps that contain adware that launches pop-up ads and text messages on your mobile device—is also becoming an increasing problem (Cody, 2017).

Read the *Insight on Technology* case, *Think Your Smartphone Is Secure?*, for a further discussion of some of the issues surrounding smartphone security.

CLOUD SECURITY ISSUES

The move of so many Internet services into the cloud also raises security risks. From an infrastructure standpoint, DDoS attacks threaten the availability of cloud services on which more and more companies are relying. For instance, as previously noted, the DDoS attack on Dyn caused a major disruption to cloud services across the United States. According to Alert Logic, which analyzed over 32 million security events in the IT environments of more than 3,000 enterprise customers from August 2015 to January 2017, companies with hybrid networks, with their applications scattered among public clouds, private clouds, and on-premises systems, are the most at risk (Alert Logic, 2017). Safeguarding data being maintained in a public cloud environment is also a major concern (Cybersecurity Insiders/Alert Logic, 2018). For example, researchers identified several ways data could be accessed without authorization on Dropbox, which offers a popular cloud file-sharing service. In 2014, compromising photos of as many as 100 celebrities such as Jennifer Lawrence were posted online, reportedly stolen from Apple's iCloud. Although initially it was thought that the breach was made possible by a vulnerability in Apple's Find My iPhone API, it instead apparently resulted from lower-tech phishing attacks that yielded passwords that could be used to connect to iCloud. These incidents highlight the risks involved as devices, identities, and data become more and more interconnected in the cloud. A 2019 Thales/Ponemon Insititute survey of over 3,300 information security and information technology personnel found that over 55% believed using cloud services

INSIGHT ON TECHNOLOGY

THINK YOUR SMARTPHONE IS SECURE?

Many people believe their smartphones are unlikely to be hacked because Apple and Google are protecting them from malware, and that cell phone networks are just as secure as the land-line phone system. But hackers can do to a smartphone just about anything they can do to any Internet device: request malicious files without user intervention, delete files, transmit files, install programs running in the background that can monitor user actions, and potentially convert the smartphone into a robot that can be used in a botnet to send e-mail and text messages to anyone. There are about 2.9 billion smartphone users worldwide using their phones for work, shopping, and paying bills. The size and richness of the smartphone target for hackers has never been bigger, and the number of attacks is on the rise.

Apps are the most common avenue for potential security breaches. Apple and Google now offer over 5 million apps collectively. Apple claims that it examines every app to ensure that each one plays by Apple's App Store rules, but risks remain. In 2014, the first attack on iPhones that were not jailbroken (altered to allow hacked versions of iOS to install third-party apps) occurred, via malware known as Wirelurker. In 2016, malware called AceDeceiver infected non-jailbroken Apple devices by scanning the App Store for other corrupted apps and automatically downloading them. Hackers frequently download apps and republish those same apps to the App Store with malware embedded. They also buy apps from their original developers and embed malware in a similar manner.

Apple's iOS operating system has also been subject to breaches. Updates to iOS in 2016 exposed a series of vulnerabilities, collectively known as Trident, that allowed attackers to take complete control of a phone remotely, using malware called Pegasus. Though Apple quickly scrambled to fix the vulnerability, releasing an operating system update in ten days, Trident and Pegasus showed that the iOS operating system was not as impervious to malware as many users believe. Fewer than 40 devices in total were attacked by Pegasus, but the malware is proof of concept for this type of attack. In 2018, Apple also moved to fix a security flaw in its phones that had allowed both law enforcement and cybercriminals to access locked phones.

Although iOS malware is becoming more prevalent, it still affects less than 1% of all iOS devices. Android devices, in contrast, are fifty times more likely to be infected with malware compared to iOS devices. This is due in part to the fact that Android users can download apps from third-party stores that are poorly regulated, whereas Apple users are confined to the more tightly controlled App Store. For example, in China, where Google Play does not operate, there are 386 million active Android users, many of whom use these third-party app stores. In 2018, security researchers revealed the existence of a years-long coordinated spyware campaign called Dark Caracal. Hackers associated with Dark Caracal had created spoofed versions of real apps, including messaging apps Signal and WhatsApp, and placed them on third-party app stores. They then sent phishing e-mails to potential victims. Once downloaded, these apps installed malware called Pallas, which allowed the hackers to access photos, location, record audio, and a trove of personal information. Android devices represented over 60% of Dark Caracal's targets, and the hackers behind the campaign have stolen hundreds of gigabytes of data from thousands of victims.

Similarly to Apple, Google uses an automated screening technique called Google Play Protect to detect malicious apps and wipe them from the Google Play store. Google can also perform a remote wipe of offending apps from Android phones without user intervention. In 2018, Google rolled out a new feature called Project Treble. Treble is a reorganization of the Android operating system that separates hardware-specific code from the rest of Android, allowing Google to patch vulnerabilities and other security issues more quickly. Still, Treble only helps users get rid of malware faster; it can't stop Android phones from being infected.

Beyond the threat of rogue apps, smartphones of all stripes are also susceptible to browser-based malware, often received via unsafe wireless networks. In addition, most smartphones, including the iPhone, permit manufacturers to remotely download configuration files to update operating systems and security protections. Unfortunately, flaws in the public key encryption procedures that permit remote server access to iPhones have been discovered, raising further questions about the security of such operations. Attackers have also developed methods of hijacking phones using weaknesses in SIM cards. There are at least 500 million vulnerable SIM cards in use today, and the defects allow hackers to obtain the encryption key that guards users' personal information, granting them nearly complete access over the phone in the process. Many users don't even take advantage of the security features they have available to them, such as the use of a lock screen, which only one-third of Android users have enabled.

Some smartphone manufacturers are developing new approaches to security, such as HTC, whose Exodus phone takes security a step even further than Treble. The phone has a data partition intended for the storage of cryptocurrency and other sensitive data that cannot be accessed by the Android operating system at all. If the Exodus and other similar prototypes are successful, smartphone users may gravitate towards phones that keep their most sensitive data out of the reach of Apple and Google; but hackers will undoubtedly do their best to find vulnerabilities in these approaches as well.

SOURCES: "Google Says Project Treble Has Massively Accelerated Android Updates," by Ryan Whitwam, Extremetech.com, October 24, 2019; "Android-powered Connected Devices Are Fifty Times More Likely to Be Infected with Malware When Compared to iOS," Pandasecurity.com, January 14, 2019; "HTC's Blockchain Phone Will Push the Boundary of Smartphone Security," by Sarang Sheth, Yankodesign.com, October 24, 2018; "What Is Project Treble? The Android Upgrade Fix, Explained," by J.R. Raphael, Computerworld.com, September 20, 2018; "Android Pie and Project Treble: Assessing Google's Grand Upgrade Fix," by J.R. Raphael, Computerworld.com, August 30, 2018; "Apple to Close iPhone Security Hole That Law Enforcement Uses to Crack Devices," by Jack Nicas, New York Times, June 13, 2018; "How to Fight the Threat of Malware on Mobile Devices," by Jason Glassberg, Bizjournals.com, May 9, 2018; "Your Smartphones Are Getting More Valuable for Hackers," by Alfred Ng, Cnet.com, March 8, 2018; "FTC Recommends Steps to Improve Mobile Device Security Update Practices," Ftc.gov, February 28, 2018; "Dark Caracal Hacking Group Has Stolen Hundreds of Gigabytes of Data from 21 Countries," by Brandon Vigliarolo, Techrepublic.com, January 23, 2018; "Dark Caracal: Good News and Bad News," by Gennie Gebhart, Eff.org, January 19, 2018; "Which Phone Protects Your Security the Best? We Asked the Experts," by Lucinda Shen, Time.com, September 25, 2017; "Smartphones Under Fire: Why We Need to Keep Our Android Devices Safe," by Michael Miley, Blog.trendmicro.com, September 6, 2017; "New Malware Turns Smartphones into Cyberattackers," by Hiawatha Bray, Bostonglobe.com, August 30, 2017; "Here's How Malware Gets Inside Your Phone's Apps," by Peter Hannay, Businessinsider.com, June 23, 2017; "Pegasus: The Ultimate Spyware for iOS and Android," by John Snow, Kaspersky.com, April 11, 2017; "Trident iOS Flaws; Researchers Detail How the Spyware Stayed Hidden," by Danny Palmer, Zdnet.com, November 7, 2016; "Beware, iPhone Users: Fake Retail Apps Are Surging Before Holidays," by Vindu Goel, New York Times, November 6, 2016; "iPhone Malware That Steals Your Data Proves No Platform Is Truly Secure," by Liam Tung and Raymond Wong, Mashable.com, August 26, 2016; "XAgent iPhone Malware Attack Steals Data Without Jailbreaking," by Jeff Gamet, Macobserver.com, February 5, 2015; "Apple Blocks Apps Infected with WireLurker Malware Targeting iPhones and iPads," by Carly Page, Theinquirer.net, November 6, 2014.

made it more difficult to protect sensitive data. The survey also found most organizations were not taking full responsibility for the security of their data in the cloud, instead looking to their cloud providers to provide that security (Thales/Ponemon Institute, 2019).

INTERNET OF THINGS SECURITY ISSUES

As you learned in Chapter 2, the Internet of Things (IoT) involves the use of the Internet to connect a wide variety of sensors, devices, and machines, and is powering the development of a multitude of smart connected things, such as home electronics (smart TVs, thermostats, home security systems, and more), connected cars, medical devices, and industrial equipment that supports manufacturing, energy, transportation, and other industrial sectors. IoT raises a host of security issues that are in some ways similar to existing security issues, but even more challenging, given the need to deal with a wider range of devices, operating in a less controlled, global environment, and with an expanded range of attack. In a world of connected things, the devices, the data produced and used by the devices, and the systems and applications supported by those devices, can all potentially be attacked. **Table 4.5** takes a closer look at some of the unique security challenges posed

TABLE 4.5 INTERNET OF THINGS SECURITY CHALLENGES

CHALLENGE	POSSIBLE IMPLICATIONS
Many IoT devices, such as sensors, are intended to be deployed on a much greater scale than traditional Internet-connected devices, creating a vast quantity of interconnected links that can be exploited.	Existing tools, methods, and strategies need to be developed to deal with this unprecedented scale.
Many instances of IoT consist of collections of identical devices that all have the same characteristics.	Magnifies the potential impact of a security vulnerability.
Many IoT devices are anticipated to have a much longer service life than typical equipment.	Devices may "outlive" the manufacturer, leaving them without long-term support, which creates persistent vulnerabilities.
Many IoT devices are intentionally designed without the ability to be upgraded, or the upgrade process is difficult.	Raises the possibility that vulnerable devices cannot or will not be fixed, leaving them perpetually vulnerable.
Many IoT devices do not provide the user with visibility into the workings of the device or the data being produced, nor alert the user when a security problem arises.	Users may believe an IoT device is functioning as intended when, in fact, it may be performing in a malicious manner.
Some IoT devices, such as sensors, are unobtrusively embedded in the environment such that a user may not even be aware of the device.	Security breach might persist for a long time before being noticed.

by IoT identified by the Internet Society (ISOC), a consortium of corporations, government agencies, and nonprofit organizations that monitors Internet policies and practices (Internet Society, 2016, 2015).

Already, alarming reports of hacked IoT devices are starting to pop up in the popular press. For example, in 2015, researchers demonstrated the ability to hack into a Jeep Cherokee through its entertainment system, sending commands to the dashboard, steering, brakes, and transmission system from a remote laptop that turned the steering wheel, disabled the brakes, and shut down the engine (Greenberg, 2015). Fiat Chrysler Automobiles immediately issued a recall notice to fix the software vulnerability involved, but it is almost certain that such incidents will continue to occur, as auto manufacturers add more and more wireless "connected car" features to automobiles. Other reports have surfaced of wireless baby monitors being hacked, as well as medical devices such as hospital lab blood gas analyzers, radiology picture archive and communication systems, drug infusion pumps, and hospital x-ray systems (Storm, 2015a, 2015b). The previously mentioned DDoS 2016 attack on Dyn launched by the Mirai botnet relied in part on more than 500,000 IoT devices such as Internet-connected security cameras (Sanger and Perlroth, 2016). In 2017, a botnet known as Reaper or IoTroop formed, with security analysts warning that it was recruiting IoT devices such as routers, webcams, and DVRs at a faster pace and with the potential to cause more damage than the Mirai botnet (Kan, 2017).

4.3 TECHNOLOGY SOLUTIONS

At first glance, it might seem like there is not much that can be done about the onslaught of security breaches on the Internet. Reviewing the security threats in the previous section, it is clear that the threats to e-commerce are very real, widespread, global, potentially devastating for individuals, businesses, and entire nations, and likely to be increasing in intensity along with the growth in e-commerce and the continued expansion of the Internet. But in fact a great deal of progress has been made by private security firms, corporate and home users, network administrators, technology firms, and government agencies. There are two lines of defense: technology solutions and policy solutions. In this section, we consider some technology solutions, and in the following section, we look at some policy solutions that work.

The first line of defense against the wide variety of e-commerce security threats is a set of tools that can make it difficult for outsiders to invade or destroy a site. **Figure 4.5** illustrates the major tools available to achieve e-commerce security.

PROTECTING INTERNET COMMUNICATIONS

Because e-commerce transactions must flow over the public Internet, and therefore involve thousands of routers and servers through which the transaction packets flow, security experts believe the greatest security threats occur at the level of Internet communications. This is very different from a private network where a dedicated communication line is established between two parties. A number of tools are available to protect the security of Internet communications, the most basic of which is message encryption.

There are a number of tools available to achieve e-commerce security.

ENCRYPTION

Encryption is the process of transforming plain text or data into **cipher text** that cannot be read by anyone other than the sender and the receiver. The purpose of encryption is (a) to secure stored information and (b) to secure information transmission. Encryption can provide four of the six key dimensions of e-commerce security referred to in Table 4.3 on page 242:

- *Message integrity*—provides assurance that the message has not been altered.
- *Nonrepudiation*—prevents the user from denying he or she sent the message.
- *Authentication*—provides verification of the identity of the person (or computer) sending the message.
- *Confidentiality*—gives assurance that the message was not read by others.

This transformation of plain text to cipher text is accomplished by using a key or cipher. A **key** (or **cipher**) is any method for transforming plain text to cipher text.

Encryption has been practiced since the earliest forms of writing and commercial transactions. Ancient Egyptian and Phoenician commercial records were encrypted using substitution and transposition ciphers. In a **substitution cipher**, every occurrence of a given letter is replaced systematically by another letter. For instance, if we used the cipher "letter plus two"—meaning replace every letter in a word with a new letter two places forward—then the word "Hello" in plain text would be transformed into the following cipher text: "JGNNQ." In a **transposition cipher**, the ordering of the letters in each word

encryption
the process of transforming plain text or data into cipher text that cannot be read by anyone other than the sender and the receiver. The purpose of encryption is (a) to secure stored information and (b) to secure information transmission

cipher text
text that has been encrypted and thus cannot be read by anyone other than the sender and the receiver

key (cipher)
any method for transforming plain text to cipher text

substitution cipher
every occurrence of a given letter is replaced systematically by another letter

transposition cipher
the ordering of the letters in each word is changed in some systematic way

is changed in some systematic way. Leonardo Da Vinci recorded his shop notes in reverse order, making them readable only with a mirror. The word "Hello" can be written backwards as "OLLEH." A more complicated cipher would (a) break all words into two words and (b) spell the first word with every other letter beginning with the first letter, and then spell the second word with all the remaining letters. In this cipher, "HELLO" would be written as "HLO EL."

Symmetric Key Cryptography

In order to decipher (decrypt) these messages, the receiver would have to know the secret cipher that was used to encrypt the plain text. This is called **symmetric key cryptography** or **secret key cryptography**. In symmetric key cryptography, both the sender and the receiver use the same key to encrypt and decrypt the message. How do the sender and the receiver have the same key? They have to send it over some communication media or exchange the key in person. Symmetric key cryptography was used extensively throughout World War II and is still a part of Internet cryptography.

symmetric key cryptography (secret key cryptography) both the sender and the receiver use the same key to encrypt and decrypt the message

The possibilities for simple substitution and transposition ciphers are endless, but they all suffer from common flaws. First, in the digital age, computers are so powerful and fast that these ancient means of encryption can be broken quickly. Second, symmetric key cryptography requires that both parties share the same key. In order to share the same key, they must send the key over a presumably *insecure* medium where it could be stolen and used to decipher messages. If the secret key is lost or stolen, the entire encryption system fails. Third, in commercial use, where we are not all part of the same team, you would need a secret key for each of the parties with whom you transacted, that is, one key for the bank, another for the department store, and another for the government. In a large population of users, this could result in as many as $n^{(n-1)}$ keys. In a population of billions of Internet users, billions of keys would be needed to accommodate all e-commerce customers. Clearly this situation would be too unwieldy to work in practice.

Modern encryption systems are digital. The ciphers or keys used to transform plain text into cipher text are digital strings. Computers store text or other data as binary strings composed of 0s and 1s. For instance, the binary representation of the capital letter "A" in ASCII computer code is accomplished with eight binary digits (bits): 01000001. One way in which digital strings can be transformed into cipher text is by multiplying each letter by another binary number, say, an eight-bit key number 0101 0101. If we multiplied every digital character in our text messages by this eight-bit key and sent the encrypted message to a friend along with the secret eight-bit key, the friend could decode the message easily.

The strength of modern security protection is measured in terms of the length of the binary key used to encrypt the data. In the preceding example, the eight-bit key is easily deciphered because there are only 2^8 or 256 possibilities. If the intruder knows you are using an eight-bit key, then he or she could decode the message in a few seconds using a modern desktop PC just by using the brute force method of checking each of the 256 possible keys. For this reason, modern digital encryption systems use keys with 56, 128, 256, or 512 binary digits. With encryption keys of 512 digits, there are 2^{512} possibilities to

Data Encryption Standard (DES)

developed by the National Security Agency (NSA) and IBM. Uses a 56-bit encryption key

Advanced Encryption Standard (AES)

the most widely used symmetric key algorithm, offering 128-, 192-, and 256-bit keys

public key cryptography

two mathematically related digital keys are used: a public key and a private key. The private key is kept secret by the owner, and the public key is widely disseminated. Both keys can be used to encrypt and decrypt a message. However, once the keys are used to encrypt a message, that same key cannot be used to unencrypt the message

check out. It is estimated that all the computers in the world would need to work for 10 years before stumbling upon the answer.

The **Data Encryption Standard (DES)** was developed by the National Security Agency (NSA) and IBM in the 1950s. DES uses a 56-bit encryption key. To cope with much faster computers, it has been improved by the *Triple DES Encryption Algorithm (TDEA)*—essentially encrypting the message three times, each with a separate key. Today, the most widely used symmetric key algorithm is **Advanced Encryption Standard (AES)**, which offers key sizes of 128, 192, and 256 bits. AES had been considered to be relatively secure, but in 2011, researchers from Microsoft and a Belgian university announced that they had discovered a way to break the algorithm, and with this work, the "safety margin" of AES continues to erode. There are also many other symmetric key systems that are currently less widely used, with keys up to 2,048 bits.[1]

Public Key Cryptography

In 1976, a new way of encrypting messages called **public key cryptography** was invented by Whitfield Diffie and Martin Hellman. Public key cryptography (also referred to as *asymmetric cryptography*) solves the problem of exchanging keys. In this method, two mathematically related digital keys are used: a public key and a private key. The private key is kept secret by the owner, and the public key is widely disseminated. Both keys can be used to encrypt and decrypt a message. However, once the keys are used to encrypt a message, the same key cannot be used to unencrypt the message. The mathematical algorithms used to produce the keys are one-way functions. A *one-way irreversible mathematical function* is one in which, once the algorithm is applied, the input cannot be subsequently derived from the output. Most food recipes are like this. For instance, it is easy to make scrambled eggs, but impossible to retrieve whole eggs from the scrambled eggs. Public key cryptography is based on the idea of irreversible mathematical functions. The keys are sufficiently long (128, 256, and 512 bits) that it would take enormous computing power to derive one key from the other using the largest and fastest computers available. **Figure 4.6** illustrates a simple use of public key cryptography and takes you through the important steps in using public and private keys.

Public Key Cryptography Using Digital Signatures and Hash Digests

In public key cryptography, some elements of security are missing. Although we can be quite sure the message was not understood or read by a third party (message confidentiality), there is no guarantee the sender really is the sender; that is, there is no authentication of the sender. This means the sender could deny ever sending the message (repudiation). And there is no assurance the message was not altered somehow in transit. For example, the message "Buy Cisco @ $16" could have been accidentally or intentionally altered to read "Sell Cisco @ $16." This suggests a potential lack of integrity in the system.

---

[1] For instance: DESX, GDES, and RDES with 168-bit keys; the RC Series: RC2, RC4, and RC5 with keys up to 2,048 bits; and the IDEA algorithm, the basis of PGP, e-mail public key encryption software described later in this chapter, which uses 128-bit keys.

FIGURE 4.6 PUBLIC KEY CRYPTOGRAPHY—A SIMPLE CASE

STEP	DESCRIPTION
1. The sender creates a digital message.	The message could be a document, spreadsheet, or any digital object.
2. The sender obtains the recipient's public key from a public directory and applies it to the message.	Public keys are distributed widely and can be obtained from recipients directly.
3. Application of the recipient's key produces an encrypted cipher text message.	Once encrypted using the public key, the message cannot be reverse-engineered or unencrypted using the same public key. The process is irreversible.
4. The encrypted message is sent over the Internet.	The encrypted message is broken into packets and sent through several different pathways, making interception of the entire message difficult (but not impossible).
5. The recipient uses his/her private key to decrypt the message.	The only person who can decrypt the message is the person who has possession of the recipient's private key. Hopefully, this is the legitimate recipient.

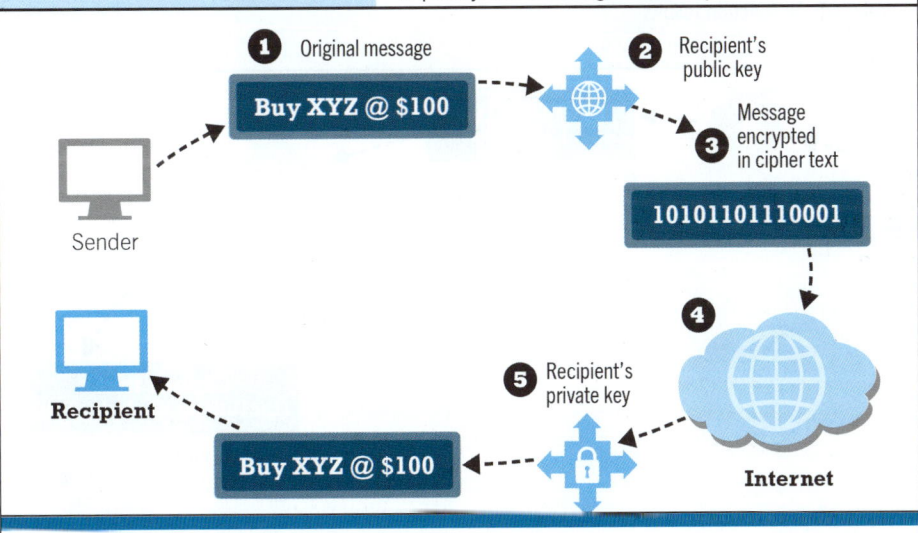

In the simplest use of public key cryptography, the sender encrypts a message using the recipient's public key, and then sends it over the Internet. The only person who can decrypt this message is the recipient, using his or her private key. However, this simple case does not ensure integrity or an authentic message.

A more sophisticated use of public key cryptography can achieve authentication, nonrepudiation, and integrity. **Figure 4.7** illustrates this more powerful approach.

To check the integrity of a message and ensure it has not been altered in transit, a hash function is used first to create a digest of the message. A **hash function** is an algorithm that produces a fixed-length number called a *hash* or *message digest*. A hash function can be simple, and count the number of digital 1s in a message, or it can be more complex, and produce a 128-bit number that reflects the number of 0s and 1s, the number of 00s and 11s, and so on. Standard hash functions are available (MD4 and MD5 produce 128- and 160-bit

hash function

an algorithm that produces a fixed-length number called a hash or message digest

FIGURE 4.7   PUBLIC KEY CRYPTOGRAPHY WITH DIGITAL SIGNATURES

STEP	DESCRIPTION
1. The sender creates an original message.	The message can be any digital file.
2. The sender applies a hash function, producing a 128-bit hash result.	Hash functions create a unique digest of the message based on the message contents.
3. The sender encrypts the message and hash result using the recipient's public key.	This irreversible process creates a cipher text that can be read only by the recipient using his or her private key.
4. The sender encrypts the result, again using his or her private key.	The sender's private key is a digital signature. There is only one person who can create this digital mark.
5. The result of this double encryption is sent over the Internet.	The message traverses the Internet as a series of independent packets.
6. The receiver uses the sender's public key to authenticate the message.	Only one person can send this message, namely, the sender.
7. The receiver uses his or her private key to decrypt the hash function and the original message. The receiver checks to ensure the original message and the hash function results conform to one another.	The hash function is used here to check the original message. This ensures the message was not changed in transit.

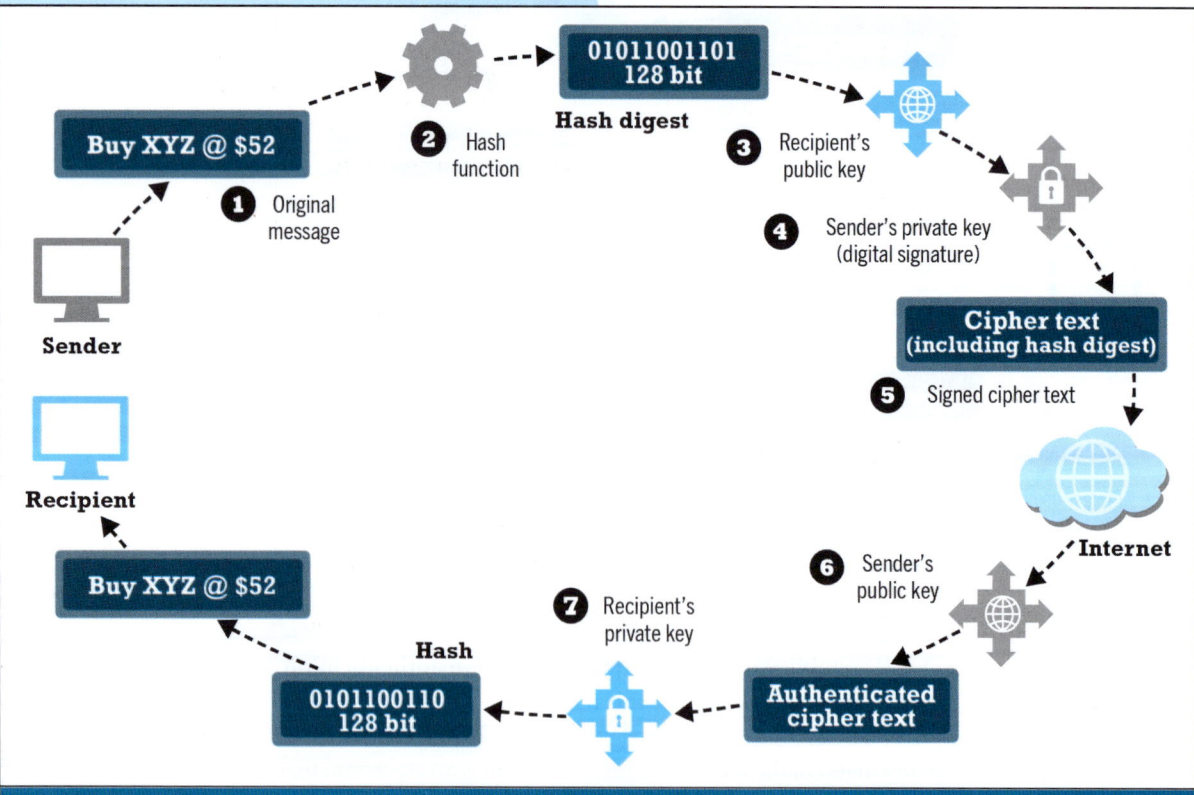

A more realistic use of public key cryptography uses hash functions and digital signatures to both ensure the confidentiality of the message and authenticate the sender. The only person who could have sent the above message is the owner or the sender using his/her private key. This authenticates the message. The hash function ensures the message was not altered in transit. As before, the only person who can decipher the message is the recipient, using his/her private key.

hashes) (Stein, 1998). These more complex hash functions produce hashes or hash results that are unique to every message. The results of applying the hash function are sent by the sender to the recipient. Upon receipt, the recipient applies the hash function to the received message and checks to verify the same result is produced. If so, the message has not been altered. The sender then encrypts both the hash result and the original message using the recipient's public key (as in Figure 4.6 on page 271), producing a single block of cipher text.

One more step is required. To ensure the authenticity of the message and to ensure nonrepudiation, the sender encrypts the entire block of cipher text one more time using the sender's private key. This produces a **digital signature** (also called an *e-signature*) or "signed" cipher text that can be sent over the Internet.

A digital signature is a close parallel to a handwritten signature. Like a handwritten signature, a digital signature is unique—only one person presumably possesses the private key. When used with a hash function, the digital signature is even more unique than a handwritten signature. In addition to being exclusive to a particular individual, when used to sign a hashed document, the digital signature is also unique to the document, and changes for every document.

The recipient of this signed cipher text first uses the sender's public key to authenticate the message. Once authenticated, the recipient uses his or her private key to obtain the hash result and original message. As a final step, the recipient applies the same hash function to the original text, and compares the result with the result sent by the sender. If the results are the same, the recipient now knows the message has not been changed during transmission. The message has integrity.

Early digital signature programs required the user to have a digital certificate, and were far too difficult for an individual to use. Newer programs are Internet-based and do not require users to install software, or understand digital certificate technology. DocuSign, Adobe Sign, and Sertifi are among a number of companies offering online digital signature solutions. Many insurance, finance, and surety companies now permit customers to electronically sign documents.

Digital Envelopes

Public key cryptography is computationally slow. If one used 128 or 256-bit keys to encode large documents—such as this chapter or the entire book—significant declines in transmission speeds and increases in processing time would occur. Symmetric key cryptography is computationally faster, but as we pointed out previously, it has a weakness—namely, the symmetric key must be sent to the recipient over insecure transmission lines. One solution is to use the more efficient symmetric encryption and decryption for large documents, but public key cryptography to encrypt and send the symmetric key. This technique is called using a **digital envelope**. See **Figure 4.8** for an illustration of how a digital envelope works.

In Figure 4.8, a diplomatic document is encrypted using a symmetric key. The symmetric key—which the recipient will require to decrypt the document—is itself encrypted, using the recipient's public key. So we have a "key within a key" (a *digital envelope*). The encrypted report and the digital envelope are sent across the Web. The recipient first uses his/her private key to decrypt the symmetric key, and then the recipient uses the

digital signature (e-signature)
"signed" cipher text that can be sent over the Internet

digital envelope
a technique that uses symmetric encryption for large documents, but public key cryptography to encrypt and send the symmetric key

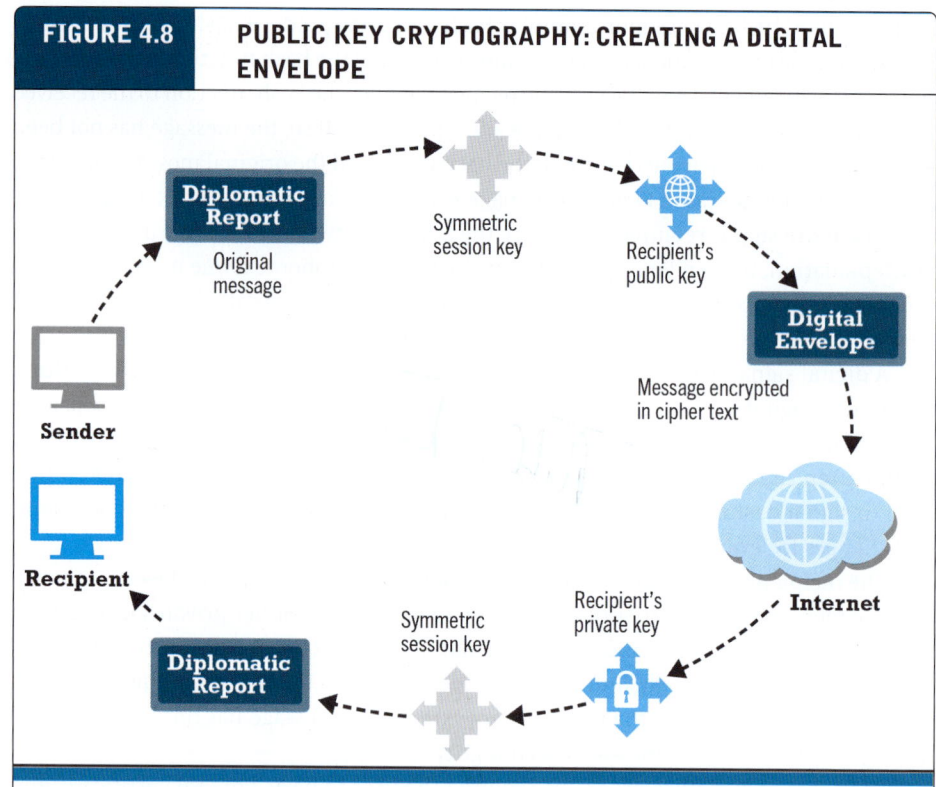

FIGURE 4.8 PUBLIC KEY CRYPTOGRAPHY: CREATING A DIGITAL ENVELOPE

A digital envelope can be created to transmit a symmetric key that will permit the recipient to decrypt the message and be assured the message was not intercepted in transit.

symmetric key to decrypt the report. This method saves time because both encryption and decryption are faster with symmetric keys.

Digital Certificates and Public Key Infrastructure (PKI)

There are still some deficiencies in the message security regime described previously. How do we know that people and institutions are who they claim to be? Anyone can make up a private and public key combination and claim to be someone they are not. Before you place an order with an online merchant such as Amazon, you want to be sure it really is Amazon you have on the screen and not a spoofer masquerading as Amazon. In the physical world, if someone asks who you are and you show a social security number, they may well ask to see a picture ID or a second form of certifiable or acceptable identification. If they really doubt who you are, they may ask for references to other authorities and actually interview these other authorities. Similarly, in the digital world, we need a way to know who people and institutions really are.

Digital certificates, and the supporting public key infrastructure, are an attempt to solve this problem of digital identity. A **digital certificate** is a digital document issued by a trusted third-party institution known as a **certification authority (CA)** that contains the name of the subject or company, the subject's public key, a digital certificate serial

digital certificate
a digital document issued by a certification authority that contains a variety of identifying information

certification authority (CA)
a trusted third party that issues digital certificates

Technology Solutions 275

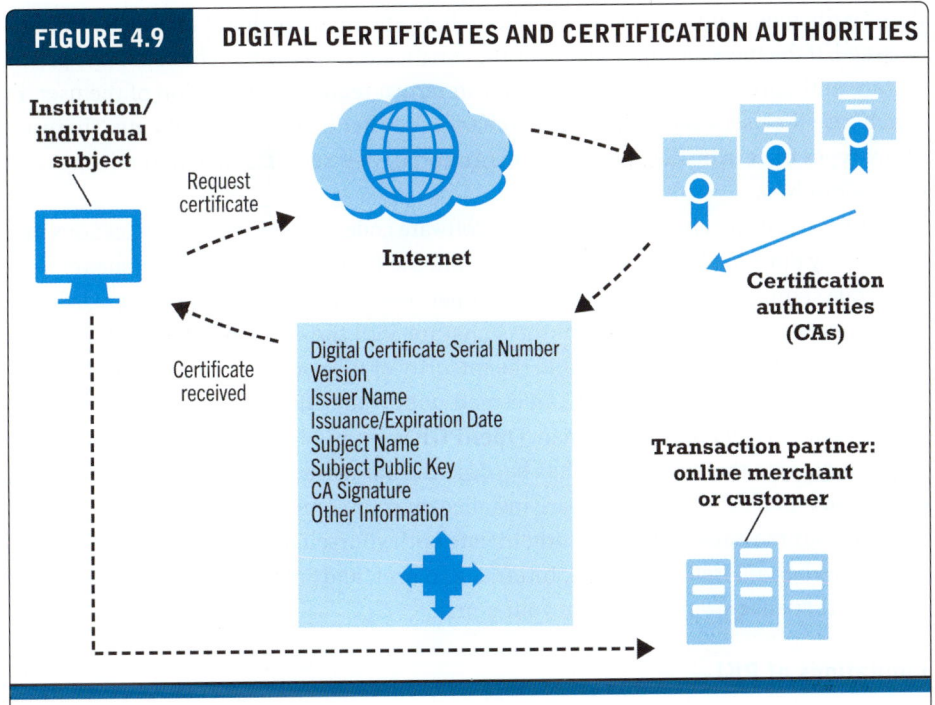

FIGURE 4.9 DIGITAL CERTIFICATES AND CERTIFICATION AUTHORITIES

The PKI includes certification authorities that issue, verify, and guarantee digital certificates that are used in e-commerce to assure the identity of transaction partners.

number, an expiration date, an issuance date, the digital signature of the certification authority (the name of the CA encrypted using the CA's private key), and other identifying information (see **Figure 4.9**).

Worldwide, thousands of organizations issue CAs. GlobalSign was the first certification authority created in Europe. EU member states and other European nations maintain lists of approved CAs. A hierarchy of CAs has emerged with less-well-known CAs being certified by larger and better-known CAs, creating a community of mutually verifying institutions. **Public key infrastructure (PKI)** refers to the CAs and digital certificate procedures that are accepted by all parties. When you sign into a "secure" site, the URL will begin with "https" and a closed lock icon will appear on your browser. This means the site has a digital certificate issued by a trusted CA. It is not, presumably, a spoof site.

To create a digital certificate, the user generates a public/private key pair and sends a request for certification to a CA along with the user's public key. The CA verifies the information (how this is accomplished differs from CA to CA). The CA issues a certificate containing the user's public key and other related information. Finally, the CA creates a message digest from the certificate itself (just like a hash digest) and signs it with the CA's private key. This signed digest is called the *signed certificate*. We end up with a totally unique cipher text document—there can be only one signed certificate like this in the world.

There are several ways the certificates are used in commerce. Before initiating a transaction, the customer can request the signed digital certificate of the merchant and decrypt

public key infrastructure (PKI)
CAs and digital certificate procedures that are accepted by all parties

it using the merchant's public key to obtain both the message digest and the certificate as issued. If the message digest matches the certificate, then the merchant and the public key are authenticated. The merchant may in return request certification of the user, in which case the user would send the merchant his or her individual certificate. There are many types of certificates: personal, institutional, web server, software publisher, and CAs themselves.

PKI and CAs can also be used to secure software code and content for applications that are directly downloaded to mobile devices from the Internet. Using a technique referred to as code signing, mobile application developers use their private key to encrypt a digital signature. When end users decrypt the signature with the corresponding public key, it confirms the developer's identity and the integrity of the code.

Pretty Good Privacy (PGP), an e-mail public key encryption software tool, was invented in 1991 by Phil Zimmerman. **OpenPGP** is a non-proprietary protocol based on PGP, which over the past decade has become the standard for nearly all of the world's encrypted e-mail. Using PGP software installed on your computer, you can compress and encrypt your messages as well as authenticate both yourself and the recipient. There are also a number of Firefox, Chrome, Internet Explorer, and Safari add-ons, extensions, or plug-ins that enable you to encrypt your e-mail.

Pretty Good Privacy (PGP)
e-mail public key encryption software tool

OpenPGP
non-proprietary protocol based on PGP

Limitations of PKI

PKI is a powerful technological solution to security issues, but it has many limitations, especially concerning CAs. PKI applies mainly to protecting messages in transit on the Internet and is not effective against insiders—employees—who have legitimate access to corporate systems including customer information. Most e-commerce sites do not store customer information in encrypted form. Other limitations are apparent. For one, how is your private key to be protected? Most private keys will be stored on insecure desktop or laptop computers.

There is no guarantee the person using your computer—and your private key—is really you. For instance, you may lose your laptop or smartphone, and therefore lose the private key. Likewise, there is no assurance that someone else in the world cannot use your personal ID papers, such as a social security card, to obtain a PKI authenticated online ID in your name. If there's no real world identification system, there can be no truly secure Internet identification system. Under many digital signature laws, you are responsible for whatever your private key does even if you were not the person using the key. This is very different from mail-order or telephone order credit card rules, where you have a right to dispute the credit card charge. Second, there is no guarantee the verifying computer of the merchant is secure. Third, CAs are self-selected organizations seeking to gain access to the business of authorization. They may not be authorities on the corporations or individuals they certify. For instance, how can a CA know about all the corporations within an industry to determine who is or is not legitimate? A related question concerns the method used by the CA to identify the certificate holder. Was this an e-mail transaction verified only by claims of the applicants who filled out an online form? For instance, VeriSign acknowledged in one case that it had mistakenly issued two digital certificates to someone fraudulently claiming to represent Microsoft. Digital certificates have been hijacked by hackers, tricking consumers into giving up personal information. For example, in 2014, India's National Informatics Centre, an intermediate CA that was trusted by the Indian Controller of Certifying Authorities, whose certificates were included in the Microsoft Root Store and thus trusted by the vast majority of programs running on Windows, including Internet Explorer and Chrome, was hacked and a number of unauthorized digital certificates were issued for domains operated by Google and Yahoo (Datta, 2014). Last, what are the policies for revoking or renewing certificates? The expected life of a digital certificate or private key is a function of the frequency of use and the vulnerability of systems that use the certificate. Yet most CAs have no policy or just an annual policy for reissuing certificates. If Microsoft, Apple, or Cisco ever rescinded a number of CAs, millions of users would not be able to access sites. The CA system is difficult and costly to police.

SECURING CHANNELS OF COMMUNICATION

The concepts of public key cryptography are used routinely for securing channels of communication.

Secure Sockets Layer (SSL) and Transport Layer Security (TLS)

The most common form of securing channels is through the *Secure Sockets Layer (SSL)* and *Transport Layer Security (TLS)* protocols. When you receive a message from a server on the Web with which you will be communicating through a secure channel, this means you will be using SSL/TLS to establish a secure negotiated session. (Notice that the URL changes from HTTP to HTTPS.) A **secure negotiated session** is a client-server session in which the URL of the requested document, along with the contents, contents of forms, and the cookies exchanged, are encrypted (see **Figure 4.10**). For instance, your credit card number that you entered into a form would be encrypted. Through a series of handshakes and communications, the browser and the server establish one another's identity by exchanging digital certificates, decide on the strongest shared form of encryption, and then proceed to communicate using an agreed-upon session key. A **session key** is a unique symmetric encryption key chosen just for this single secure session. Once used, it is gone forever. Figure 4.10 shows how this works.

In practice, most private individuals do not have a digital certificate. In this case, the merchant server will not request a certificate, but the client browser will request the merchant certificate once a secure session is called for by the server.

SSL/TLS provides data encryption, server authentication, optional client authentication, and message integrity for TCP/IP connections. SSL/TLS addresses the issue of authenticity by allowing users to verify another user's identity or the identity of a server. It also protects the integrity of the messages exchanged. However, once the merchant receives the encrypted credit and order information, that information is typically stored in unencrypted format on the merchant's servers. While SSL/TLS provides secure transactions between merchant and consumer, it only guarantees server-side authentication. Client authentication is optional.

secure negotiated session
a client-server session in which the URL of the requested document, along with the contents, contents of forms, and the cookies exchanged, are encrypted

session key
a unique symmetric encryption key chosen for a single secure session

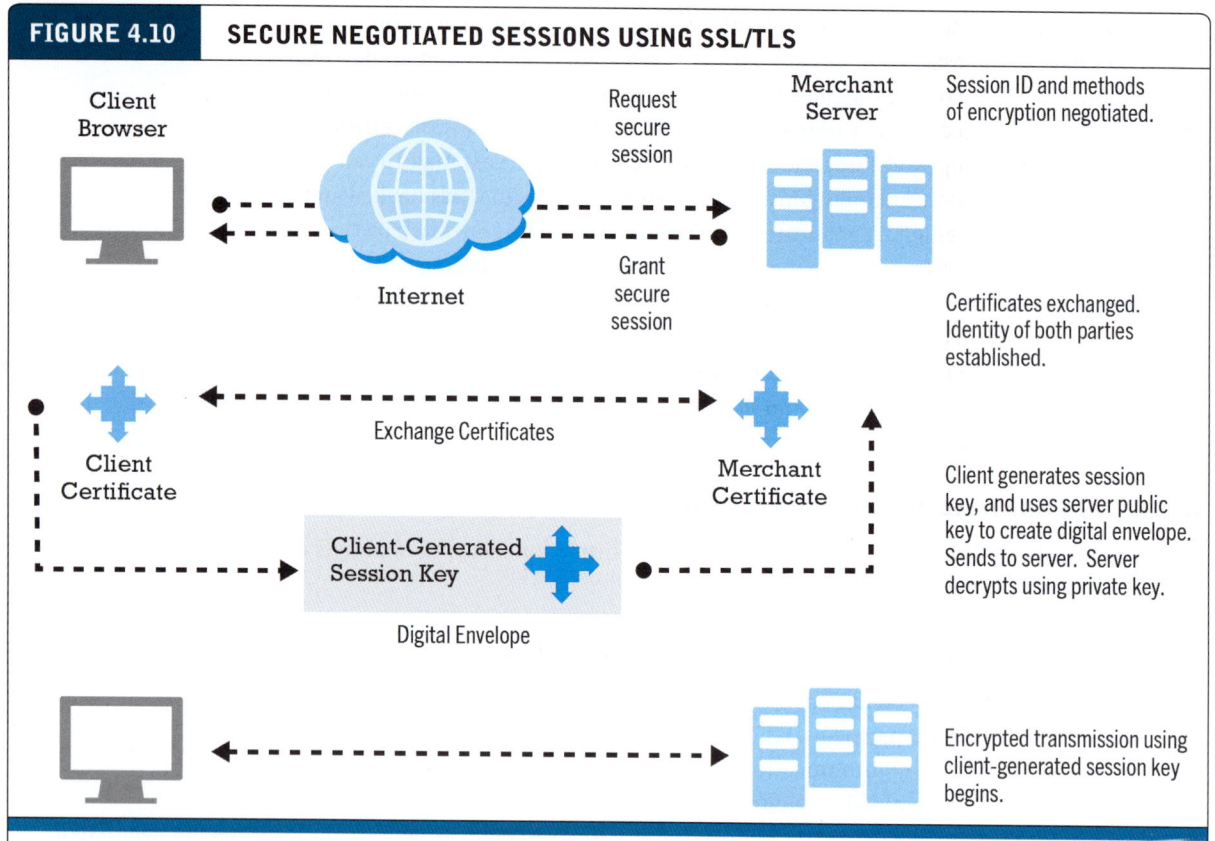

FIGURE 4.10 SECURE NEGOTIATED SESSIONS USING SSL/TLS

Certificates play a key role in using SSL/TLS to establish a secure communications channel.

In addition, SSL/TLS cannot provide irrefutability—consumers can order goods or download information products, and then claim the transaction never occurred. Recently, social network sites such as Facebook and Twitter have begun to use SSL/TLS for a variety of reasons, including the ability to thwart account hijacking using Firesheep over wireless networks. Firesheep, an add-on for Firefox, can be used by hackers to grab unencrypted cookies used to "remember" a user and allow the hacker to immediately log on to a website as that user. SSL/TLS can thwart such an attack because it encrypts the cookie. In 2015, the White House's Office of Management and Budget issued a memorandum requiring that all publicly accessible federal websites and web services use HTTPS by December 31, 2016. HTTPS encrypts user requests to website servers. It is implemented by the server adopting the HTTP Strict Transport Security (HSTS) feature that forces browsers to only access the server using HTTPS (CIO.gov, 2016).

Virtual Private Networks (VPNs)

A **virtual private network (VPN)** allows remote users to securely access a corporation's local area network via the Internet, using a variety of VPN protocols. VPNs use both authentication and encryption to secure information from unauthorized persons (providing confidentiality and integrity). Authentication prevents spoofing and misrepresentation

virtual private network (VPN)
allows remote users to securely access internal networks via the Internet, using the Point-to-Point Tunneling Protocol (PPTP)

of identities. A remote user can connect to a remote private local network using a local ISP. The VPN protocols will establish the link from the client to the corporate network as if the user had dialed into the corporate network directly. The process of connecting one protocol through another (IP) is called *tunneling,* because the VPN creates a private connection by adding an invisible wrapper around a message to hide its content. As the message travels through the Internet between the ISP and the corporate network, it is shielded from prying eyes by an encrypted wrapper.

A VPN is "virtual" in the sense that it appears to users as a dedicated secure line when in fact it is a temporary secure line. The primary use of VPNs is to establish secure communications among business partners—larger suppliers or customers, and employees working remotely. A dedicated connection to a business partner can be very expensive. Using the Internet and VPN as the connection method significantly reduces the cost of secure communications.

Wireless (Wi-Fi) Networks

Accessing the Internet via a wireless (Wi-Fi) network has its own particular security issues. Early Wi-Fi networks used a security standard called Wired Equivalent Privacy (WEP) to encrypt information. WEP was very weak, and easy for hackers to crack. An alternative standard, Wi-Fi Protected Access (WPA), was developed that provided a higher standard of protection, but this too soon became vulnerable to intrusion. **WPA2**, introduced in 2004, uses the AES algorithm for encryption, and CCMP, a more advanced authentication code protocol. In June 2018, the Wi-Fi Alliance, the trade group that oversees the WPA protocol, announced the next generation of the protocol, **WPA3**, which implements a more robust key exchange protocol and a more secure way to connect IoT devices. It also features expanded encryption for public networks. However, even the updated WPA3 standard still has vulnerabilities that could allow attackers to recover passwords (Barnett, 2018, Kan, 2019).

PROTECTING NETWORKS

Once you have protected communications as well as possible, the next set of tools to consider are those that can protect your networks, as well as the servers and clients on those networks.

Firewalls

Firewalls and proxy servers are intended to build a wall around your network and the attached servers and clients, just like physical-world firewalls protect you from fires for a limited period of time. Firewalls and proxy servers share some similar functions, but they are quite different.

A **firewall** refers to either hardware or software that filters communication packets and prevents some packets from entering or exiting the network based on a security policy. The firewall controls traffic to and from servers and clients, forbidding communications from untrustworthy sources, and allowing other communications from trusted sources to proceed. Every message that is to be sent or received from the network is processed by the firewall, which determines if the message meets security guidelines established by the business. If it does, it is permitted to be distributed, and if it doesn't, the message is blocked. Firewalls can filter traffic based on packet attributes such as source

WPA2
wireless security standard that uses the AES algorithm for encryption and CCMP, a more advanced authentication code protocol

WPA3
Next generation WPA protocol, expected to begin being implemented in 2019

firewall
refers to either hardware or software that filters communication packets and prevents some packets from entering the network based on a security policy

IP address, destination port or IP address, type of service (such as WWW or HTTP), the domain name of the source, and many other dimensions. Most hardware firewalls that protect local area networks connected to the Internet have default settings that require little if any administrator intervention and employ simple but effective rules that deny incoming packets from a connection that does not originate from an internal request—the firewall only allows connections from servers that you requested service from. A common default setting on hardware firewalls (DSL and cable modem routers) simply ignores efforts to communicate with TCP port 445, the most commonly attacked port. The increasing use of firewalls by home and business Internet users has greatly reduced the effectiveness of attacks, and forced hackers to focus more on e-mail attachments to distribute worms and viruses.

There are two major methods firewalls use to validate traffic: packet filters and application gateways. *Packet filters* examine data packets to determine whether they are destined for a prohibited port or originate from a prohibited IP address (as specified by the security administrator). The filter specifically looks at the source and destination information, as well as the port and packet type, when determining whether the information may be transmitted. One downside of the packet filtering method is that it is susceptible to spoofing, because authentication is not one of its roles.

Application gateways are a type of firewall that filters communications based on the application being requested, rather than the source or destination of the message. Such firewalls also process requests at the application level, farther away from the client computer than packet filters. By providing a central filtering point, application gateways provide greater security than packet filters but can compromise system performance.

Next-generation firewalls use an application-centric approach to firewall control. They are able to identify applications regardless of the port, protocol, or security evasion tools used; identify users regardless of device or IP address; decrypt outbound SSL; and protect in real-time against threats embedded in applications.

Proxy Servers

proxy server (proxy)
software server that handles all communications originating from or being sent to the Internet, acting as a spokesperson or bodyguard for the organization

Proxy servers (proxies) are software servers (often a dedicated computer) that handle all communications originating from or being sent to the Internet by local clients, acting as a spokesperson or bodyguard for the organization. Proxies act primarily to limit access of internal clients to external Internet servers, although some proxy servers act as firewalls as well. Proxy servers are sometimes called *dual-home systems* because they have two network interfaces. To internal computers, a proxy server is known as the *gateway*, while to external computers it is known as a *mail server* or *numeric address*.

When a user on an internal network requests a web page, the request is routed first to the proxy server. The proxy server validates the user and the nature of the request, and then sends the request onto the Internet. A web page sent by an external Internet server first passes to the proxy server. If acceptable, the web page passes onto the internal network web server and then to the client desktop. By prohibiting users from communicating directly with the Internet, companies can restrict access to certain types of sites, such as pornographic, auction, or stock-trading sites. Proxy servers also improve web performance by storing frequently requested web pages locally, reducing upload times, and hiding the internal network's address, thus making it more difficult for hackers to monitor.

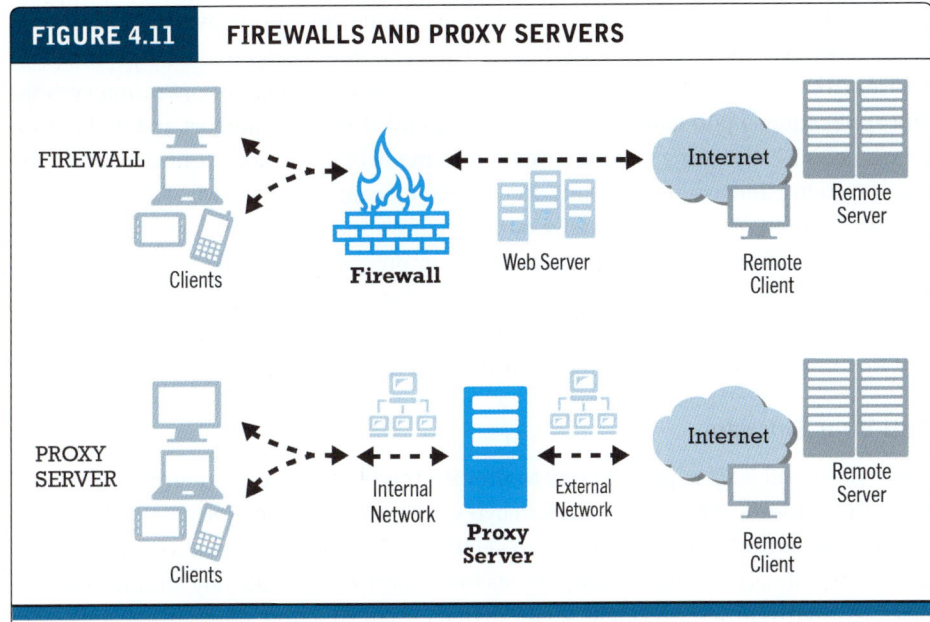

FIGURE 4.11 FIREWALLS AND PROXY SERVERS

The primary function of a firewall is to deny access by remote client computers to local computers. The primary purpose of a proxy server is to provide controlled access from local computers to remote computers.

Figure 4.11 illustrates how firewalls and proxy servers protect a local area network from Internet intruders and prevent internal clients from reaching prohibited web servers.

Intrusion Detection and Prevention Systems

In addition to a firewall and proxy server, an intrusion detection and/or prevention system can be installed. An **intrusion detection system (IDS)** examines network traffic, watching to see if it matches certain patterns or preconfigured rules indicative of an attack. If it detects suspicious activity, the IDS will set off an alarm alerting administrators and log the event in a database. An IDS is useful for detecting malicious activity that a firewall might miss. An **intrusion prevention system (IPS)** has all the functionality of an IDS, with the additional ability to take steps to prevent and block suspicious activities. For instance, an IPS can terminate a session and reset a connection, block traffic from a suspicious IP address, or reconfigure firewall or router security controls.

PROTECTING SERVERS AND CLIENTS

Operating system features and anti-virus software can help further protect servers and clients from certain types of attacks.

Operating System Security Enhancements

The most obvious way to protect servers and clients is to take advantage of automatic computer security upgrades. The Microsoft, Apple, and Linux/Unix operating systems are continuously updated to patch vulnerabilities discovered by hackers. These patches are autonomic; that is, when using these operating systems on the Internet, you are

intrusion detection system (IDS)

examines network traffic, watching to see if it matches certain patterns or preconfigured rules indicative of an attack

intrusion prevention system (IPS)

has all the functionality of an IDS, with the additional ability to take steps to prevent and block suspicious activities

prompted and informed that operating system enhancements are available. Users can easily download these security patches for free. The most common known worms and viruses can be prevented by simply keeping your server and client operating systems and applications up to date. In 2014, Microsoft ended security support and updates for its Windows XP operating system. Despite this, many organizations continue to use XP-based systems, and as a result, many security experts anticipate a wave of strikes against such systems. In 2017, after a massive outbreak of WannaCry ransomware that exploited Windows XP vulnerabilities, Microsoft took an unprecedented step of issuing additional security patches for Windows XP in an effort to stem further outbreaks (Warren, 2017). Application vulnerabilities are fixed in the same manner. For instance, most popular Internet browsers are updated automatically with little user intervention.

Anti-Virus Software

The easiest and least expensive way to prevent threats to system integrity is to install anti-virus software. Programs by Malwarebytes, McAfee, Symantec (Norton AntiVirus), and many others provide inexpensive tools to identify and eradicate the most common types of malicious code as they enter a computer, as well as destroy those already lurking on a hard drive. Anti-virus programs can be set up so that e-mail attachments are inspected before you click on them, and the attachments are eliminated if they contain a known virus or worm. It is not enough, however, to simply install the software once. Because new viruses are developed and released every day, daily routine updates are needed in order to prevent new threats from being loaded. Some premium-level anti-virus software is updated hourly.

Anti-virus suite packages and stand-alone programs are available to eliminate intruders such as bot programs, adware, and other security risks. Such programs work much like anti-virus software in that they look for recognized hacker tools or signature actions of known intruders.

4.4 MANAGEMENT POLICIES, BUSINESS PROCEDURES, AND PUBLIC LAWS

Worldwide, in 2019, companies were expected to spend about $124 billion on security hardware, software, and services, up about 9% from the previous year (Morgan, 2019). However, most CEOs and CIOs believe that technology is not the sole answer to managing the risk of e-commerce. The technology provides a foundation, but in the absence of intelligent management policies, even the best technology can be easily defeated. Public laws and active enforcement of cybercrime statutes also are required to both raise the costs of illegal behavior on the Internet and guard against corporate abuse of information. Let's consider briefly the development of management policy.

A SECURITY PLAN: MANAGEMENT POLICIES

In order to minimize security threats, e-commerce firms must develop a coherent corporate policy that takes into account the nature of the risks, the information assets that need protecting, and the procedures and technologies required to address the risk, as

Management Policies, Business Procedures, and Public Laws 283

FIGURE 4.12 DEVELOPING AN E-COMMERCE SECURITY PLAN

There are five steps involved in building an e-commerce security plan.

well as implementation and auditing mechanisms. **Figure 4.12** illustrates the key steps in developing a solid security plan.

A security plan begins with **risk assessment**—an assessment of the risks and points of vulnerability. The first step is to inventory the information and knowledge assets of the e-commerce site and company. What information is at risk? Is it customer information, proprietary designs, business activities, secret processes, or other internal information, such as price schedules, executive compensation, or payroll? For each type of information asset, try to estimate the dollar value to the firm if this information were compromised, and then multiply that amount by the probability of the loss occurring. Once you have done so, rank order the results. You now have a list of information assets prioritized by their value to the firm.

Based on your quantified list of risks, you can start to develop a **security policy**—a set of statements prioritizing the information risks, identifying acceptable risk targets, and identifying the mechanisms for achieving these targets. You will obviously want to start with the information assets that you determined to be the highest priority in your risk assessment. Who generates and controls this information in the firm? What existing security policies are in place to protect the information? What enhancements can you recommend to improve security of these most valuable assets? What level of risk are you willing to accept for each of these assets? Are you willing, for instance, to lose customer credit card data once every 10 years? Or will you pursue a 100-year hurricane strategy by building a security edifice for credit card data that can withstand the once-in-100-year disaster? You will need to estimate how much it will cost to achieve this level of acceptable

risk assessment
an assessment of the risks and points of vulnerability

security policy
a set of statements prioritizing the information risks, identifying acceptable risk targets, and identifying the mechanisms for achieving these targets

risk. Remember, total and complete security may require extraordinary financial resources. By answering these questions, you will have the beginnings of a security policy.

Next, consider an **implementation plan**—the steps you will take to achieve the security plan goals. Specifically, you must determine how you will translate the levels of acceptable risk into a set of tools, technologies, policies, and procedures. What new technologies will you deploy to achieve the goals, and what new employee procedures will be needed?

To implement your plan, you will need an organizational unit in charge of security, and a security officer—someone who is in charge of security on a daily basis. For a small e-commerce site, the security officer will likely be the person in charge of Internet services or the site manager, whereas for larger firms, there typically is a dedicated team with a supporting budget. The **security organization** educates and trains users, keeps management aware of security threats and breakdowns, and maintains the tools chosen to implement security.

The security organization typically administers access controls, authentication procedures, and authorization policies. **Access controls** determine which outsiders and insiders can gain legitimate access to your networks. Outsider access controls include firewalls and proxy servers, while insider access controls typically consist of login procedures (usernames, passwords, and access codes).

Authentication procedures include the use of digital signatures, certificates of authority, and PKI. Now that e-signatures have been given the same legal weight as an original pen-and-ink version, companies are in the process of devising ways to test and confirm a signer's identity. Companies frequently have signers type their full name and click on a button indicating their understanding that they have just signed a contract or document.

Biometric devices can also be used to verify physical attributes associated with an individual, such as a facial, fingerprint, or retina (eye) scan or speech recognition system. (**Biometrics** is the study of measurable biological, or physical, characteristics.) A company could require, for example, that an individual undergo a fingerprint scan before being allowed access to a website, or before being allowed to pay for merchandise with a credit card. Biometric devices make it even more difficult for hackers to break into sites or facilities, significantly reducing the opportunity for spoofing. Newer Apple iPhones (5S and later) feature a fingerprint sensor called Touch ID built into the iPhone's home button that can unlock the phone and authorize purchases without requiring users to enter a PIN or other security code. The system does not store an actual fingerprint, but rather biometric data, which is encrypted and stored only on a chip within the iPhone, and is not made available to third parties. In 2017, Apple introduced Face ID, a facial recognition system that enables users to log on to the phone using a facial scan. Using the system will be optional, and as with Touch ID, the data comprising the scan will be stored only on the chip within the phone and not in the cloud. Nonetheless, the system has raised a slew of security and privacy issues. See the *Insight on Business* case, *Are Biometrics the Solution for E-commerce Security?* for a further examination of biometrics.

Security tokens are physical devices or software that generate an identifier that can be used in addition to or in place of a password. Security tokens are used by millions of corporation and government workers to log on to corporate clients and servers. One example is RSA's SecurID token, which continuously generates six-digit passwords.

---

implementation plan
the action steps you will take to achieve the security plan goals

security organization
educates and trains users, keeps management aware of security threats and breakdowns, and maintains the tools chosen to implement security

access controls
determine who can gain legitimate access to a network

authentication procedures
include the use of digital signatures, certificates of authority, and public key infrastructure

biometrics
the study of measurable biological or physical characteristics

security token
physical device or software that generates an identifier that can be used in addition to or in place of a password

INSIGHT ON BUSINESS

ARE BIOMETRICS THE SOLUTION FOR E-COMMERCE SECURITY?

As e-commerce continues to grow and constitute an increasing share of overall commerce, cybercriminals have followed suit. Even consumers that take necessary precautions online are susceptible to identity theft and other forms of cybercrime. Malicious actors have honed techniques for bypassing traditional techniques of online verification, including stealing credit card numbers, PIN numbers, and answers to security questions. However, biometric security promises to revolutionize the way users verify themselves, potentially rendering many of the methods used by today's identity thieves obsolete.

Biometrics involves identifying individuals based on physiological characteristics that are unique to each person. These characteristics include fingerprints, the shape of each person's face, and the patterns within the irises of each person's eyes, as well as other methods such as voice recognition, analyzing heart rhythms, and even analyzing vein patterns in the palm. Whereas traditional credit card systems use physical tokens such as credit cards in tandem with private knowledge such as passwords, PIN numbers, and security questions, biometric systems use physical attributes to verify identities, which are in theory much more difficult for criminals to spoof. You can forget a password, but you can't forget your face. E-commerce companies are excited about the potential of biometrics, which could also reduce the number of abandoned shopping carts due to forgotten passwords by as much as 70%. The use of biometrics to authenticate mobile payment transactions is expected to skyrocket, with Juniper Research predicting an increase from $228 billion in 2019 to $2.5 trillion by 2024, as biometric authentication supplants traditional password-based methods as the most common method of facilitating payments.

The ideas behind biometric technologies have been around for a while, but it's only recently that widely available technology such as smartphones have become advanced enough to offer them. Not surprisingly, Apple is the leader in this area, first offering Touch ID fingerprint verification on older generations of iPhones, and later unveiling its Face ID capability with the launch of the iPhone X in late 2017. Face ID uses an advanced camera to create a 3D model of the user's face with 30,000 invisible dots. This model is then encrypted and is stored locally—it's never uploaded online, further protecting it from thieves. Face ID has replaced Touch ID as Apple's preferred method to unlock its phones and make payments, and Apple claims that its false positive rate is approximately one in a million, a significant improvement from Touch ID's 1 in 50,000.

Other smartphone manufacturers are doing their best catch up to Apple. Samsung introduced a feature called Intelligent Scan for its Galaxy S9 and S9+ phones, which combines iris and facial scanning in one system. Samsung replaced the Intelligent Scan system in its S10 phones with a system simply called Facial Recognition. However, both Samsung systems employ a 2D camera for facial recognition, rendering them vulnerable to unlocking with a simple photograph, and Samsung does not use either system for features like Samsung Pay.

Credit card companies and various banks are also working on their own biometric solutions. In 2019, Mastercard rolled out a feature it calls Mastercard Identity Check, also known

(continued)

informally as Selfie Pay—users simply take a quick selfie to confirm their identities when making credit card transactions. In China, Alibaba's Alipay system has a feature called "Smile and Pay" that works much the same way, and HSBC Bank allows Chinese customers to blink into their smartphone to confirm their identities for money transfers. The European Union's Payment Services Directive 2 requires banks to provide strong customer authentication with at least two of three elements: something the customer knows (password or PIN), something the customer has (phone or hardware token), and something the customer is (fingerprint or facial recognition).

Cybercriminals will undoubtedly be working hard to overcome the additional challenges posed by biometrics. The stakes are particularly high with biometrics because a stolen password can easily be changed, but you can't simply change your face, fingerprint, or iris. Researchers in Vietnam have claimed to be able to unlock iPhones with Face ID using masks, and although duplicating this technique is unlikely to be cost-effective, it does demonstrate proof of concept. Biometrics ensure only that the person attempting to use a service is the same person that signed up for that service—a trusted authority is still required to confirm identities when users sign up for various services. There are also privacy concerns that accompany facial recognition and other biometric technologies. In the European Union, facial recognition images may not be used to investigate a citizen's private life, and countries like China, where smartphone manufacturers Huawei, ZTE, and OnePlus were found to be secretly transmitting their Chinese users' data to the government, may abuse the technology for surveillance. Legal precedent is also mixed on whether law enforcement can compel users to unlock their phones using biometric information, whereas it clearly forbids them from compelling users to provide their passwords for more traditionally protected devices.

An emerging approach that may overcome some of these limitations to biometrics is behavioral biometrics, which measures and analyzes human activity patterns to generate a unique profile for each user. Systems using behavioral biometrics analyze patterns in keystrokes, including speed, key pressure, and finger positioning, along with geographic information such as IP address and geolocation. Once a profile is formed for a user, sufficiently large deviations from that profile trigger a warning. Companies like BioCatch are offering behavioral biometrics solutions that allow retailers and banks to form these types of profiles for their users and accurately detect instances of fraud. Behavioral biometrics do little to quell fears about the erosion of privacy, however. Smartphone users will simply have to determine whether the considerable benefits of biometrics outweigh the similarly significant privacy concerns.

SOURCES: "Juniper Research: Biometrics to Secure $2.5 Trillion in Mobile Payments by 2024, with WebAuthn Standards Driving Adoption," Businesswire.com, December 3, 2019; "PSD2: Strong Customer Authentication," Stripe.com, October 18, 2019; "Galaxy S10: Ten Features to Enable and Disable" by Adam Ismail, Tomsguide.com, March 28, 2019; "Mastercard Identity Check: Bringing Consumers a Better Digital Experience," by Chris Reid, Newsroom.mastercard.com, January 10, 2019; "Blink and You'll Miss It: The Mass-Market Adoption of Facial Verification in Business," by Husayn Kassai, Biometricupdate.com, July 2, 2018; "The Top 7 Trends For Facial Recognition in 2018," Gemalto.com, July 1, 2018; "Behavioral Biometrics and Biometrics in Payment Cards: Beyond the PIN and Password," Gemalto.com, May 6, 2018; "Biometrics Are Here: The Crazy Ways You're Going to Be Paying in the Future," by Jean Chatzky, Nbcnews.com, May 9, 2018; "Biometric Payments," Chargebacks911.com, April 16, 2018; Ben Lovejoy, "New Web Standard Would Allow Touch ID and Face ID to Be Used to Login to Websites," 9to5mac.com, April 10, 2018; "How Biometric Verification Will Revolutionize Online Checkout," by Alastair Johnson, Paymentweek.com, April 4, 2018; "Faster Delivery, Stronger Security Are 2018 Ecommerce Priorities," by Bill Marcus, Signifyd.com, March 6, 2018; "Biometric Mobile Payments the Next Disruptive Technology," Mobilepaymentconference.com, February 21, 2018; "Apple's Face ID Hacked by Vietnamese Researchers," Pymnts.com, November 28, 2017; "Decentralized Biometric Authentication Reshapes Mobile Payments," by George Avetisov, Csoonline.com, November 28, 2017; "IPhone X Review: How We Tested (and Tricked) FaceID," by Joanna Stern, *Wall Street Journal*, October 31, 2017; "BioCatch VP Touts Behavioral Biometrics as Wave of the Future," by Rawlson King, Biometricupdate.com, October 10, 2017; "HSBC Switches On Selfie Payments in China," Finextra.com, September 18, 2017; "IPhone X's Face ID Raises Security and Privacy Questions," by Natasha Lomas, Techcrunch.com, September 13, 2017; "Alibaba Debuts 'Smile to Pay' Facial Recognition Payments at KFC in China," by Jon Russell, Techcrunch.com, September 4, 2017.

Authorization policies determine differing levels of access to information assets for differing levels of users. **Authorization management systems** establish where and when a user is permitted to access certain parts of a website. Their primary function is to restrict access to private information within a company's Internet infrastructure. Although there are several authorization management products currently available, most operate in the same way: the system encrypts a user session to function like a passkey that follows the user from page to page, allowing access only to those areas that the user is permitted to enter, based on information set at the system database. By establishing entry rules up front for each user, the authorization management system knows who is permitted to go where at all times.

The last step in developing an e-commerce security plan is performing a security audit. A **security audit** involves the routine review of access logs (identifying how outsiders are using the site as well as how insiders are accessing the site's assets). A monthly report should be produced that establishes the routine and nonroutine accesses to the systems and identifies unusual patterns of activities. As previously noted, tiger teams are often used by large corporate sites to evaluate the strength of existing security procedures. Many small firms have sprung up in the last five years to provide these services to large corporate sites.

THE ROLE OF LAWS AND PUBLIC POLICY

The public policy environment today is very different from the early days of e-commerce. The net result is that the Internet is no longer an ungoverned, unsupervised, self-controlled technology juggernaut. Just as with financial markets in the last 70 years, there is a growing awareness that e-commerce markets work only when a powerful institutional set of laws and enforcement mechanisms are in place. These laws help ensure orderly, rational, and fair markets. This growing public policy environment is becoming just as global as e-commerce itself. Despite some spectacular internationally based attacks on U.S. e-commerce sites, the sources and persons involved in major harmful attacks have almost always been uncovered and, where possible, prosecuted.

Voluntary and private efforts have played a very large role in identifying criminal hackers and assisting law enforcement. Since 1995, as e-commerce has grown in significance, national and local law enforcement activities have expanded greatly. New laws have been passed that grant local and national authorities new tools and mechanisms for identifying, tracing, and prosecuting cybercriminals. For instance, a majority of states now require companies that maintain personal data on their residents to publicly disclose when a security breach affecting those residents has occurred. **Table 4.6** lists the most significant U.S. federal e-commerce security legislation and regulation. In addition, the U.S. Federal Trade Commission has asserted that it has authority over corporations' data security practices. The FTC sued the Wyndham hotel chain after hacking attacks in 2008 and 2009 resulted in a data breach that led to fraudulent credit charges of more than $10 million. According to the FTC, its investigation showed that Wyndham had failed to follow basic data security practices, while at the same time assuring customers that their data was safe. In 2015, the U.S. Court of Appeals for the Third Circuit ruled that the FTC was within the scope of its authority, opening the door for it to take a greater role, especially in light of the failure of Congress to adopt legislation governing data security. Since that time, more

---

authorization policies determine differing levels of access to information assets for differing levels of users

authorization management system establishes where and when a user is permitted to access certain parts of a website

security audit involves the routine review of access logs (identifying how outsiders are using the site as well as how insiders are accessing the site's assets)

TABLE 4.6 U.S. E-COMMERCE SECURITY LEGISLATION AND REGULATION

LEGISLATION/REGULATION	SIGNIFICANCE
Computer Fraud and Abuse Act (1986)	Primary federal statute used to combat computer crime.
Electronic Communications Privacy Act (1986)	Imposes fines and imprisonment for individuals who access, intercept, or disclose the private e-mail communications of others.
National Information Infrastructure Protection Act (1996)	Makes DoS attacks illegal; creates NIPC in the FBI.
Health Insurance Portability and Accountability Act (1996)	Requires certain health care facilities to report data breaches.
Financial Modernization Act (Gramm-Leach-Bliley Act) (1999)	Requires certain financial institutions to report data breaches.
Cyberspace Electronic Security Act (2000)	Reduces export restrictions.
Computer Security Enhancement Act (2000)	Protects federal government systems from hacking.
Electronic Signatures in Global and National Commerce Act (the "E-Sign Law") (2000)	Authorizes the use of electronic signatures in legal documents.
USA PATRIOT Act (2001)	Authorizes use of computer-based surveillance of suspected terrorists.
Homeland Security Act (2002)	Authorizes establishment of the Department of Homeland Security, which is responsible for developing a comprehensive national plan for security of the key resources and critical infrastructures of the United States; DHS becomes the central coordinator for all cyberspace security efforts.
CAN-SPAM Act (2003)	Although primarily a mechanism for civil and regulatory lawsuits against spammers, the CAN-SPAM Act also creates several new criminal offenses intended to address situations in which the perpetrator has taken steps to hide his or her identity or the source of the spam from recipients, ISPs, or law enforcement agencies. Also contains criminal sanctions for sending sexually explicit e-mail without designating it as such.
U.S. SAFE WEB Act (2006)	Enhances FTC's ability to obtain monetary redress for consumers in cases involving spyware, spam, Internet fraud, and deception; also improves FTC's ability to gather information and coordinate investigations with foreign counterparts.
Improving Critical Infrastructure Cybersecurity Executive Order (2013)	After Congress failed to pass cybersecurity legislation in 2012, this executive order issued by the Obama administration directs federal agenices to share cybersecurity threat intelligence with private sector companies that may be targets, and the development and implementation of a cybersecurity framework for private industry, incorporating best practices and voluntary standards.
Cybersharing Information Sharing Act (2015)	Encourages businesses and the federal government to share cyber threat information in the interests of national security.

than 50 companies have entered into settlements with the FTC with respect to their data security practices (Koo, 2016).

After September 11, 2001, the U.S. Congress passed the USA PATRIOT Act, which broadly expanded law enforcement's investigative and surveillance powers. The act has provisions for monitoring e-mail and Internet use. The Homeland Security Act of 2002 also attempts to fight cyberterrorism and increases the government's ability to compel information disclosure by computer and ISP sources. Recent proposed legislation that focuses on requiring firms to report data breaches to the FTC, protection of the national electric grid, and cybersecurity has all failed to pass. However, in 2015, the Cybersecurity Information Sharing Act (CISA) was signed into law. The Act, which creates a system that lets companies share evidence about attacks without the risk of being sued, had been opposed by many large technology companies and privacy advocates on the grounds that it did not do enough to protect individual privacy and could lead to increased government surveillance. However, as of 2018, only six organizations outside of the federal government were using it to share information with the government, raising serious questions about the effectiveness of the legislation, and in 2019, the U.S. Department of Homeland Security, which administers the program, indicated it would be upgrading it in an effort to encourage increased participation (Lyngaas, 2018; Johnson, 2019).

Private and Private-Public Cooperation Efforts

The good news is that e-commerce sites are not alone in their battle to achieve security on the Internet. Several organizations—some public and some private—are devoted to tracking down criminal organizations and individuals engaged in attacks against Internet and e-commerce sites. On the U.S. federal level, the Office of Cybersecurity and Communications (CS&C) within the U.S. Department of Homeland Security (DHS) is responsible for overseeing the security, resilience, and reliability of the United States' cyber and communications infrastructure. The National Cybersecurity and Communications Integration Center (NCCIC) acts as a 24/7 cyber monitoring, incident response, and management center. In addition, the DHS also operates the **United States Computer Emergency Readiness Team (US-CERT)**, which coordinates cyber incident warnings and responses across both the government and private sectors. One of the better-known private organizations is the **CERT Coordination Center** (formerly known as the Computer Emergency Response Team) at Carnegie Mellon University. CERT monitors and tracks online criminal activity reported to it by private corporations and government agencies that seek out its help. CERT is composed of full-time and part-time computer experts who can trace the origins of attacks against sites despite the complexity of the Internet. Its staff members also assist organizations in identifying security problems, developing solutions, and communicating with the public about widespread hacker threats. The CERT Coordination Center also provides product assessments, reports, and training in order to improve the public's knowledge and understanding of security threats and solutions.

Government Policies and Controls on Encryption

In the United States, both Congress and the executive branch have sought to regulate the uses of encryption and to restrict availability and export of encryption systems as a means of preventing crime and terrorism. At the international level, four organizations

US-CERT
division of the U.S. Department of Homeland Security that coordinates cyber incident warnings and responses across government and private sectors

CERT Coordination Center
monitors and tracks online criminal activity reported to it by private corporations and government agencies that seek out its help

TABLE 4.7 GOVERNMENT EFFORTS TO REGULATE AND CONTROL ENCRYPTION

REGULATORY EFFORT	IMPACT
Restricted export of strong security systems	Supported primarily by the United States. Widespread distribution of encryption schemes weakens this policy. The policy is changing to permit exports except to pariah countries.
Key escrow/key recovery schemes	France, the United Kingdom, and the United States supported this effort in the late 1990s but now have largely abandoned it. There are few trusted third parties.
Lawful access and forced disclosure	Growing support in U.S. legislation and in OECD countries.
Official hacking	All countries are rapidly expanding budgets and training for law enforcement "technical centers" aimed at monitoring and cracking computer-based encryption activities of suspected criminals.

have influenced the international traffic in encryption software: the Organization for Economic Cooperation and Development (OECD), G-7 (the heads of state of the top seven industrialized countries in the world, not including Russia, which was suspended from participation in 2014), the European Council, and the Wassenaar Arrangement (which includes 42 countries that produce sensitive industrial equipment or weapons). Various governments have proposed schemes for controlling encryption software or at least preventing criminals from obtaining strong encryption tools (see **Table 4.7**). The U.S. and U.K. governments are also devoting a large amount of resources to cryptography-related programs that will enable them to break encrypted communications collected on the Internet. Documents leaked by former NSA contractor Edward Snowden indicate that both the NSA and its U.K. counterpart, the GCHQ, may be able to break encryption schemes used by SSL/TLS, VPNs, and on 4G smartphones (Vaughan-Nichols, 2013). In recent years, the fight between the U.S. government and technology companies over encryption has shifted to the mobile platform, with Apple resisting U.S. government efforts to break Apple's iCloud and Apple iPhone encryption systems (see the Chapter 8 *Insight on Society* case, *Apple: Defender of Privacy?*) and concerns over encryption messaging apps, such as WhatsApp, Signal, and Telegram, that offer end-to-end encryption for texts, photos, and videos that makes it difficult, if not impossible, for authorities to intercept communications using such services (Isaac, 2016).

4.5 E-COMMERCE PAYMENT SYSTEMS

For the most part, existing payment mechanisms such as cash, credit cards, debit cards, checking accounts, and stored value accounts have been able to be adapted to the online environment, albeit with some significant limitations that have led to efforts to develop alternatives. In addition, new types of purchasing relationships, such as between individuals online, and new technologies, such as the development of the mobile platform,

TABLE 4.8 MAJOR TRENDS IN E-COMMERCE PAYMENTS 2019–2020

- Payment by credit and/or debit card remains the dominant form of online payment.
- Mobile retail adoption and payment volume skyrockets.
- PayPal remains the most popular alternative payment method online.
- Apple, Google, Samsung, and PayPal extend their reach in mobile payment apps.
- Large banks enter the mobile wallet and P2P payments market with apps such as Zelle.
- Square gains further traction with a smartphone app, credit card reader, and credit card processing service that permits anyone to accept credit card payments.
- Mobile P2P payment systems such as Venmo and Zelle take off. Most mobile wallets now offer P2P payments.

have also created both a need and an opportunity for the development of new payment systems. In this section, we provide an overview of the major e-commerce payment systems in use today. **Table 4.8** lists some of the major trends in e-commerce payments in 2019–2020.

Worldwide, online payments by consumers represented a market of around $4.3 trillion in 2019. Institutions and business firms that can handle this volume of transactions (mostly the large banking and credit firms) generally extract 2%–3% of the transactions in the form of fees. Given the size of the market, competition for online payments is spirited. New forms of online payment are expected to attract a substantial part of this growth.

In the United States, the primary form of online payment is still the existing credit and debit card system. Alternative payment systems includes desktop and mobile apps for payments to retail stores, online merchants, vendors, and P2P payments. Nearly all alternative payment systems rely on traditional bank and credit card institutions to store funds and credit as explained below. Providers of alternative payment systems are often involved in both online desktop payment as well as mobile wallet apps. For instance, in the United States, PayPal is the most widely used app for online payment for e-commerce transactions, as well as offering a mobile wallet app for payment to vendors and P2P payments. Mobile wallet apps are the fastest growing form of alternative payment systems, with an estimated 30% of U.S. smartphone users (64 million people) making use of such apps in 2019. **Figure 4.13** illustrates the number of consumers that use various alternative payment methods in the United States. Paypal continues to dominate the alternative payment landscape with an estimated 100 million users in the United States. However, its dominance is being challenged by faster-growing competitors such as Zelle, Apple Pay, Venmo (a P2P service now owned by PayPal), Samsung, and Google Pay.

In other countries, e-commerce payments can be very different depending on traditions and infrastructure. Credit cards are not nearly as dominant a form of online payment as they are in the United States. If you plan on operating an e-commerce site in Europe, Asia, or Latin America, you will need to develop different payment systems for each region. For instance, in Denmark and Norway, payment is primarily with debit or credit cards, while in Finland and Sweden, payment after being tendered an invoice and by mobile bank transfers are very popular in addition to credit/debit cards. In the Netherlands, the online payments service iDEAL is a popular alternative online retail payment method similar to PayPal used for almost 60% of online purchases (Ecommerce News, 2019). In Italy, consumers rely heavily

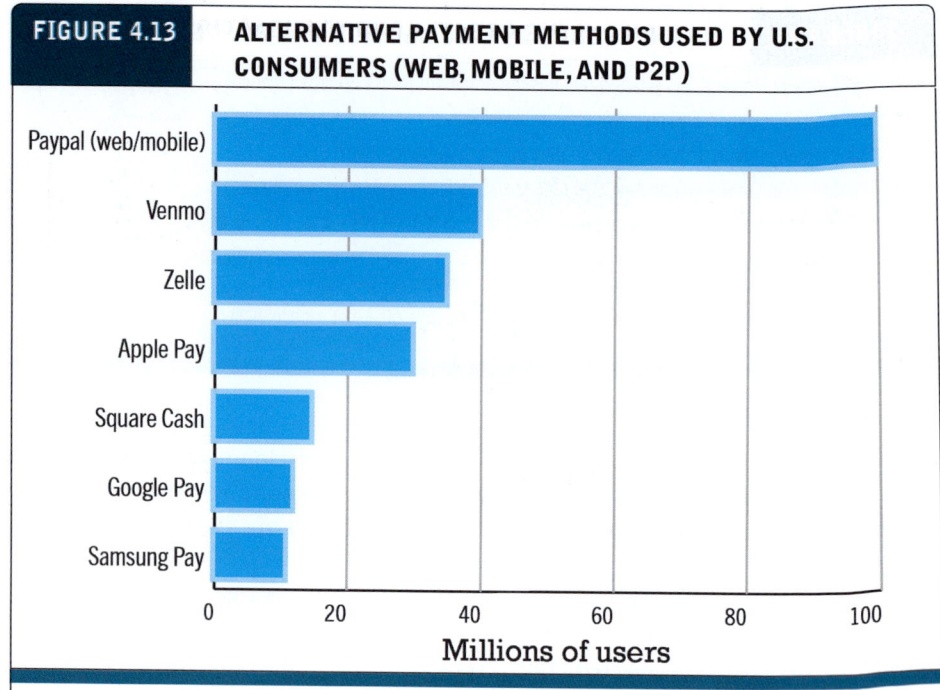

FIGURE 4.13 ALTERNATIVE PAYMENT METHODS USED BY U.S. CONSUMERS (WEB, MOBILE, AND P2P)

PayPal is still, by far, the most popular alternative payment method, but it has lost market share as rivals catch up in mobile payments.
SOURCES: Based on data from eMarketer, Inc., 2019a; PYMNTS, 2019; Grotta, 2019; authors' estimates.

on both credit cards and PayPal. In Japan, although credit cards are the primary payment method, many consumers still pick up and pay for goods using cash at local convenience stores (konbini) (eMarketer, Inc., 2017).

ONLINE CREDIT CARD TRANSACTIONS

Because credit and debit cards are the dominant form of online payment, it is important to understand how they work and to recognize the strengths and weaknesses of this payment system. Online credit card transactions are processed in much the same way that in-store purchases are, with the major differences being that online merchants never see the actual card being used, no card impression is taken, and no signature is available. Online credit card transactions most closely resemble Mail Order-Telephone Order (MOTO) transactions. These types of purchases are also called Cardholder Not Present (CNP) transactions and are the major reason that charges can be disputed later by consumers. Because the merchant never sees the credit card, nor receives a hand-signed agreement to pay from the customer, when disputes arise, the merchant faces the risk that the transaction may be disallowed and reversed, even though he has already shipped the goods or the user has downloaded a digital product.

Figure 4.14 illustrates the online credit card purchasing cycle. There are five parties involved in an online credit card purchase: consumer, merchant, clearinghouse, merchant bank (sometimes called the "acquiring bank"), and the consumer's card-issuing bank. In order to accept payments by credit card, online merchants must have a merchant account

E-commerce Payment Systems 293

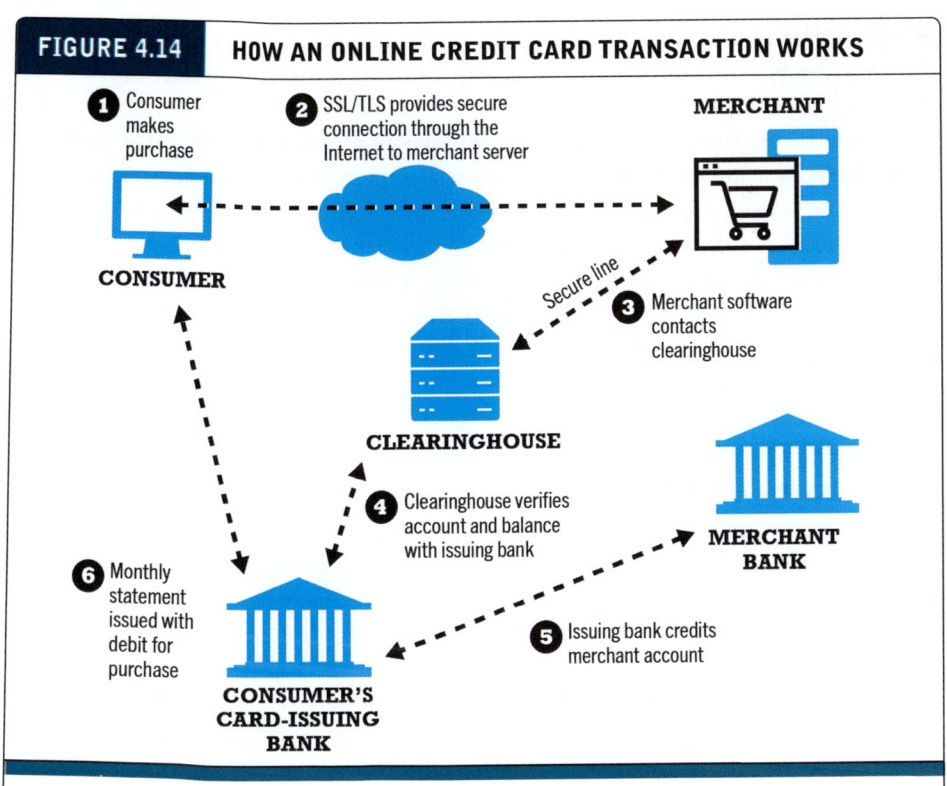

FIGURE 4.14 HOW AN ONLINE CREDIT CARD TRANSACTION WORKS

established with a bank or financial institution. A **merchant account** is simply a bank account that allows companies to process credit card payments and receive funds from those transactions.

As shown in Figure 4.14, an online credit card transaction begins with a purchase (1). When a consumer wants to make a purchase, he or she adds the item to the merchant's shopping cart. When the consumer wants to pay for the items in the shopping cart, a secure tunnel through the Internet is created using SSL/TLS. Using encryption, SSL/TLS secures the session during which credit card information will be sent to the merchant and protects the information from interlopers on the Internet (2). SSL does not authenticate either the merchant or the consumer. The transacting parties have to trust one another.

Once the consumer credit card information is received by the merchant, the merchant software contacts a clearinghouse (3). As previously noted, a clearinghouse is a financial intermediary that authenticates credit cards and verifies account balances. The clearinghouse contacts the issuing bank to verify the account information (4). Once verified, the issuing bank credits the account of the merchant at the merchant's bank (usually this occurs at night in a batch process) (5). The debit to the consumer account is transmitted to the consumer in a monthly statement (6).

Credit Card E-commerce Enablers

Companies that have a merchant account still need to buy or build a means of handling the online transaction; securing the merchant account is only step one in a two-part

merchant account
a bank account that allows companies to process credit card payments and receive funds from those transactions

process. Today, Internet payment service providers (sometimes referred to as payment gateways) can provide both a merchant account and the software tools needed to process credit card purchases online.

For instance, Authorize.net is an Internet payment service provider. The company helps a merchant secure an account with one of its merchant account provider partners and then provides payment processing software for installation on the merchant's server. The software collects the transaction information from the merchant's site and then routes it via the Authorize.net "payment gateway" to the appropriate bank, ensuring that customers are authorized to make their purchases. The funds for the transaction are then transferred to the merchant's merchant account. CyberSource is another well-known Internet payment service provider.

PCI-DSS Compliance

PCI-DSS (Payment Card Industry-Data Security Standards)
data security standards instituted by the five major credit card companies

The **PCI-DSS (Payment Card Industry-Data Security Standard)** is a global data security standard instituted by the five major credit card companies (Visa, MasterCard, American Express, Discover, and JCB). PCI-DSS is not a law or governmental regulation, but an industry-mandated standard. Every online merchant must comply with the appropriate level of PCI-DSS in order to accept credit card payments. Those that fail to comply and are involved in a credit card breach may ultimately be subjected to fines and other expenses. PCI-DSS has various levels, related to the number of credit and/or debit cards processed by the merchant each year (PCI Security Standards Council, 2016).

Limitations of Online Credit Card Payment Systems

There are a number of limitations to the existing credit card payment system. The most important limitations involve security, merchant risk, administrative and transaction costs, and social equity.

The existing system offers poor security. Neither the merchant nor the consumer can be fully authenticated. The merchant could be a criminal organization designed to collect credit card numbers, and the consumer could be a thief using stolen or fraudulent cards. The risk facing merchants is high: consumers can repudiate charges even though the goods have been shipped or the product downloaded. As you learned earlier in the chapter, credit companies have introduced EMV cards (cards with a computer chip) to reduce credit card fraud. The chip stores account data and generates a unique transaction code for each use. This has reduced credit card fraud for in-store purchases (known as card present (CP) fraud) by about 50% since introduced. But criminals have intensified their focus on card-not-present (CNP) fraud, which is expected to total $130 billion between 2018 and 2023 (Juniper Research, 2019).

The administrative costs for merchants of setting up an online credit card system and becoming authorized to accept credit cards are high. Transaction costs for merchants also are significant—roughly 3% of the purchase plus a transaction fee of 20–35 cents per transaction, plus other setup fees.

Credit cards are not very democratic, even though they seem ubiquitous. Millions of young adults do not have credit cards, along with millions of others who cannot afford cards or who are considered poor risks because of low incomes.

ALTERNATIVE ONLINE PAYMENT SYSTEMS

The limitations of the online credit card system have opened the way for the development of a number of alternative online payment systems. Chief among them is PayPal. PayPal (purchased by eBay in 2002 and then spun-off as an independent company again in 2015) enables individuals and businesses with e-mail accounts to make and receive payments up to a specified limit. Paypal is an example of an **online stored value payment system**, which permits consumers to make online payments to merchants and other individuals using their bank account or credit/debit cards. It is available in 202 countries and 25 currencies around the world. PayPal builds on the existing financial infrastructure of the countries in which it operates. You establish a PayPal account by specifying a credit, debit, or checking account you wish to have charged or paid when conducting online transactions. When you make a payment using PayPal, you e-mail the payment to the merchant's PayPal account. PayPal transfers the amount from your credit or checking account to the merchant's bank account. The beauty of PayPal is that no personal credit information has to be shared among the users, and the service can be used by individuals to pay one another even in small amounts. However, one issue with PayPal is its relatively high cost. For example, when using a credit card as the source of funds, to send or request money, the cost ranges from 2.9% to 5.99% of the amount (depending on the type of transaction) plus a small fixed fee (typically $0.30) per transaction.

Although PayPal is by far the most well-known and commonly used online credit/debit card alternative, there are a number of other alternatives as well. Amazon Pay is aimed at consumers who have concerns about entrusting their credit card information to unfamiliar online retailers. Consumers can purchase goods and services at non-Amazon websites using the payment methods stored in their Amazon accounts, without having to reenter their payment information at the merchant's site. Amazon provides the payment processing. Visa Checkout (formerly V.me) and MasterCard's MasterPass substitute a user name and password for an actual payment card number during online checkout. Both MasterPass and Visa Checkout are supported by a number of large payment processors and online retailers. However, they have not yet achieved the usage of Paypal.

PayPal Credit (formerly Bill Me Later) also appeals to consumers who do not wish to enter their credit card information online. PayPal Credit is an open-ended credit account. Users select the PayPal Credit option at checkout.

Dwolla is a payment service that transfers money from a customer's bank account to firms they want to pay without using the major credit card processing systems. Dwolla provides firms and government agencies with software that enable the transfer of funds. Dwolla's software uses the existing ACH (Automated Clearing House) system established by the Federal Reserve and banking firms to digitally transfer funds in hours, rather than three or four days. It can also verify bank accounts and balances. Credit and debit card systems charge from 1.9% to 2.9% for the amount of each transaction, whereas Dwolla charges 25 cents per transaction, irrespective of the transaction amount. Dwolla has raised more than $50 million in venture funding since its inception in 2010, and counts among its customers banks, the U.S. Treasury, several state agencies, and the Chicago Mercantile Exchange. It is currently working with the U.S. Federal Reserve's Faster Payment Task Force on developing real-time payments with very low fees (Dwolla, 2018; Lunden, 2017; Groenfeldt, 2017).

online stored value payment system
permits consumers to make instant, online payments to merchants and other individuals based on value stored in an online account

MOBILE PAYMENT SYSTEMS: YOUR SMARTPHONE WALLET

Mobile payment systems are the fastest growing component of alternative payments. The use of mobile devices as payment mechanisms is already well established in Asia and many countries in Europe, such as Denmark, Norway, Italy, and the Netherlands, and is now growing in the United States, where the infrastructure to support mobile payment is now in place. Mobile payments involve any type of payment using a mobile device, including bill pay, online purchases, in-store purchases, and P2P payments. Mobile wallets (sometimes also referred to as digital wallets) are smartphone apps that store debit cards, reward coupons, invoices, and vouchers that might be found in a traditional wallet (First Annapolis Consulting, 2017).

There are three primary types of mobile wallet apps: universal proximity wallets, branded store proximity wallets, and P2P apps. **Universal proximity mobile wallets**, such as PayPal, Apple Pay and Google Pay, that can be used at a variety of merchants for point-of-sale transactions if the merchant supports that service (e.g. has an Apple merchant app and can accept such payments), are the most-well known and common type. **Branded store proximity mobile wallets** are mobile apps that can be used only at a single merchant. For instance, Walmart, Target, Starbucks, and Dunkin Donuts all have very successful wallets for in-store purchases. **P2P mobile payment apps** are used for payments among individuals who have the same app. Apple Pay, Google Pay, and Samsung Pay are among the most popular mobile wallet apps used worldwide, although in China Alipay and WeChat Pay dominate (See **Figure 4.15**). Overall, in 2019, almost 950 million people worldwide used proximity mobile payment wallet apps (eMarketer, Inc., 2019b).

universal proximity mobile wallets

can be used at a variety of merchants for point-of-sale transactions

branded store proximity mobile wallets

can be used only at a single merchant

P2P mobile payment apps

used for payments between individuals

FIGURE 4.15 LEADING MOBILE WALLETS AROUND THE WORLD

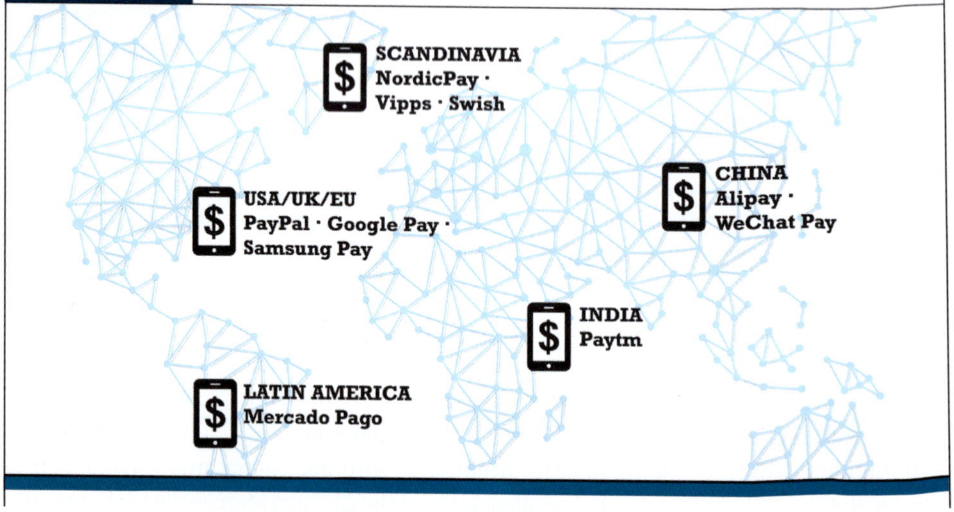

SCANDINAVIA
NordicPay · Vipps · Swish

USA/UK/EU
PayPal · Google Pay · Samsung Pay

CHINA
Alipay · WeChat Pay

INDIA
Paytm

LATIN AMERICA
Mercado Pago

Apple Pay, Google Pay, and Samsung Pay are among the top mobile wallets globally, while Alipay and WeChat Pay dominate in China.

SOURCES: Based on data from eMarketer, Inc., 2019b.

In the United States, mobile proximity apps were expected to process about $100 billion in payments in 2019, up almost 42% from 2018. U.S. P2P mobile payment app transaction value was expected to be even higher, reaching almost $310 billion in 2019 (eMarketer, Inc., 2019a).

Mobile payments continue to be the fastest growing form of payments, but constitute a tiny portion of the $50 trillion U.S. payments market, which is dominated by credit and debit cards and automated billing (called ACH payments). Consumers remain comfortable with using credit cards, although branded in-store payment apps at U.S. national retailers like Starbucks, Walmart, and Target have been very successful and are growing more rapidly in terms of adopters and especially actual usage in stores than Apple Pay, Google Pay, and Samsung Pay. In P2P payments, the leaders are Zelle, offered by over 250 U.S. banks and Venmo (owned by PayPal) (Crosman, 2018; Federal Reserve, 2018). For a closer look at mobile payments, see the case study, *Alipay and WeChat Pay Lead in Mobile Payments*, at the end of the chapter.

Near field communication (NFC) is the primary enabling technology for mobile wallets. **Near field communication (NFC)** is a set of short-range wireless technologies used to share information among devices within about 2 inches of each other (50 mm). NFC devices are either powered or passive. A connection requires one powered device (the initiator, such as a smartphone), and one target device, such as a merchant NFC reader, that can respond to requests from the initiator. NFC targets can be very simple forms such as tags, stickers, key fobs, or readers. NFC peer-to-peer communication is possible where both devices are powered. Consumers can swipe their NFC-equipped phone near a merchant's reader to pay for purchases.

near field communication (NFC)
a set of short-range wireless technologies used to share information among devices

BLOCKCHAIN AND CRYPTOCURRENCIES

Blockchain is a technology that enables organizations to create and verify transactions on a network nearly instantaneously without a central authority. Traditionally, organizations maintained their own transaction processing systems on their own databases, and used this record of transactions to keep track of orders, payments, production schedules, and shipping. For instance, when you place an order online it is entered into a transaction database as an order record. As the order works its way through the firm's factories, warehouses, shipping, and payments process, the initial record expands to record all this information about this specific order. You can think of this as a *block of information* that's created for every order and that grows over time as the firm processes the order. When the process is completed, the order fulfilled and paid for, the result is a connected *chain of blocks* (or linked records) associated with that initial order.

blockchain
technology enables organizations to create and verify transactions on a network nearly instantaneously without a central authority

Blockchain transforms this process in several ways, but the basic idea of a transaction from start to finish being composed of a chain of blocks of information remains the same. A **blockchain system** is a transaction processing system that operates on a distributed and shared database (called a peer-to-peer or P2P computer network) rather than a single organization's database. The system is composed of a distributed network of computers. Unlike traditional databases, distributed ledgers are managed through a peer-to-peer (P2P) architecture and do not have a centralized database. It is inherently decentralized and is often called a *distributed ledger*. The blockchain maintains a continuously growing list of records called blocks. Each block contains a timestamp and link to a previous block.

blockchain system
transaction processing system that operates on a distributed and shared database (a peer-to-peer (P2P) network) rather than a single organization's database.

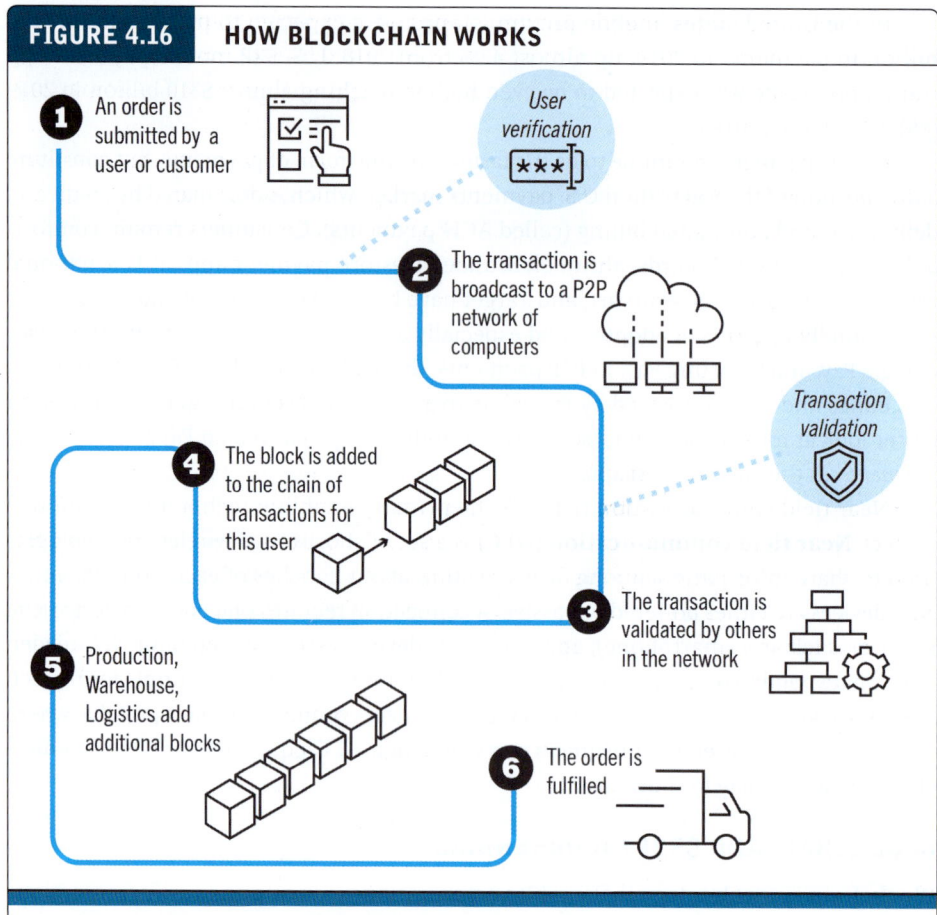

A blockchain system is a distributed database that records transactions in a P2P network of computers.

Once a block of data is recorded on the blockchain ledger, it cannot be altered retroactively. When someone wants to add a transaction, participants in the network (all of whom have copies of the existing blockchain) run algorithms to evaluate and verify the proposed transaction. Legitimate changes to the ledger are recorded across the blockchain in a matter of seconds or minutes and records are protected through cryptography. **Figure 4.16** illustrates the basic concepts of a blockchain system.

There are many risks in a distributed transaction database that shares transaction information among thousands of firms. A person or firm could enter a false transaction or change an existing transaction. Imposters could falsely claim a product has shipped when it has not. Encryption is used to avoid these risks. What makes a blockchain system possible and attractive is encryption and authentication of the participants, which ensures that only legitimate actors can enter information, and only validated transactions are accepted. Once recorded, the transaction cannot be changed.

There are many large benefits to firms using blockchain databases. Blockchain networks radically reduce the cost of verifying users, validating transactions, and the risks of storing and processing transaction information across thousands of firms. While a hurricane or earthquake can destroy a firm's private database, these events would disturb only a single node in the P2P network, while the records remain stored on all the other nodes in the network. Instead of thousands of firms building their own private transaction systems, and then integrating them with suppliers, shippers, and financial institution systems, blockchain offers a single, simple, low-cost transaction system for participating firms. Standardization of recording transactions is aided through the use of *smart contracts*. Smart contracts are computer programs that implement the rules governing transactions between firms, e.g., what is the price of products, how will they be shipped, when will the transaction be completed, who will finance the transaction, what are financing terms, and the like. All the elements of a traditional legal contract can be monitored by a smart contract to ensure the terms are being met by parties in the transaction.

The simplicity and security that blockchain offers has made it attractive for storing and securing financial transactions, medical records, and other types of data. Blockchain is a foundation technology for cryptocurrencies described below as well as supply chain management, which we discuss further in Chapter 12.

Cryptocurrencies are purely digital assets that work as a medium of exchange using blockchain technology and cryptography. **Bitcoin** is the most prominent example of cryptocurrency in use today, but many other cryptocurrencies have emerged in the last few years. Cryptocurrencies have grown meteorically from no value at all in 2008, when Bitcoin was invented, to a market capitalization in the hundreds of billions of dollars by the end of 2019. Bitcoin and other cryptocurrencies represent the intersection of complicated technology, economics, geopolitics, and social dynamics. Proponents believe that cryptocurrencies represent the future of money; skeptics believe that collectively, they are destined for narrow use at best, and complete collapse at worst.

Bitcoin was created by a mysterious figure or group known only by the pseudonym Satoshi Nakamoto in response to the worldwide financial crises that roiled world markets in the late 2000s. As opposed to traditional paper- and coin-based currencies, which are controlled by central banking systems in the countries that create them, Bitcoin is fully decentralized—no one controls Bitcoin. Instead, Bitcoin is managed through the use of blockchain, which automates the process of synchronizing the ledger. Even the most ardent skeptics of Bitcoin typically accept that blockchain technology has revolutionary potential in fields involving transactions between multiple entities.

Bitcoin's blockchain is maintained by hundreds of thousands of computers that are running specialized Bitcoin software. Each "block" represents a series of transactions that have been made and is protected with a cryptographic string known as a hash. The hash contains an encrypted timestamp and transaction data pertaining to the values of the transactions that were made, as well as a link to the previous block in the chain, but the identity of the parties to each transaction is protected. Because the blockchain and the ledger are maintained by so many individual users, if anyone attempts to alter the blockchain (for example, to make it seem like they have more Bitcoin than they really do), the discrepancy is quickly detected by thousands of other users and is subsequently corrected. In addition to being fully decentralized, Bitcoin is also nearly completely

cryptocurrency

purely digital asset that works as a medium of exchange using cryptography

Bitcoin

most prominent example of cryptocurrency in use today

anonymous. While anyone can view completed transactions on the blockchain, they cannot see who made the transactions or how many Bitcoins other users have. Executing a Bitcoin transaction does not require a name or a social security number. Instead, it merely requires a Bitcoin wallet, a simple program that allows you to store and spend Bitcoin that is protected by encryption keys.

The specialized Bitcoin software that ensures the accuracy of the blockchain is also used to "mine" new Bitcoins into circulation. Central banking systems have the ability to print money and control its circulation. Bitcoin decentralizes and widely distributes this responsibility as well. When a Bitcoin is sent from one person to another, the record of that transaction is stored within a block. When enough transactions are completed to fill one block and a new block is required, thousands of miners around the world running this specialized software compete to perform the cryptographic calculations that will protect the data contained within the new block. Whoever completes these calculations first is rewarded with a fixed amount of Bitcoin. As of the end of 2019, this amount was 12.5 Bitcoins, which was worth something in the range of $87,500 at that time. This reward is the incentive for users around the world to devote their computing power to running the Bitcoin network. There are only 21 million Bitcoins available to be mined, and as of the end of 2019, there were approximately 18 million of these in circulation already. However, Satoshi Nakamoto stipulated from the outset that the computational power required to mine Bitcoins would increase significantly over time, and that the coin reward would also decrease over time, in part to compensate for the rising value of the currency. Just as with gold, there is a fixed number of Bitcoins and they cannot be created out of thin air, but unlike gold, Bitcoin weighs nothing and costs nothing to store and move.

Bitcoin's most ardent zealots say that the blockchain provides unprecedented security, extremely cheap and fast transfer of funds across borders, limited control from central banking authorities, and the ability to reliably store money for citizens of countries with unstable currencies. However, in practice, Bitcoin has earned a reputation as a highly speculative asset whose sudden price fluctuations have prevented it from achieving widespread use for day-to-day purchases. The price of Bitcoin has fluctuated so wildly that the U.S. Department of Justice opened a criminal probe into potential price manipulation, and an academic paper published in 2018 found that Bitfinex, the biggest Bitcoin exchange in the world, was using a proprietary currency called Tether to prop up the price of Bitcoin if it started to drop at any point between March 2017 and March 2018. A whopping 40% of Bitcoin is held by only 1,000 users, and the trading patterns of these users still creates a big impact on Bitcoin's price. Bitcoin also has a reputation as the preferred method of payment for people buying illegal drugs, guns, and other illicit goods from dark web marketplace, thanks to the currency's anonymity.

Proponents of Bitcoin tout its capacity for secure, fast transactions, but Bitcoin also turns out to have major issues with theft and fraud. Although Bitcoin is very secure at the point of transaction, hackers have exploited vulnerabilities in online cryptocurrency exchanges to execute thefts of cryptocurrencies worth millions of dollars. Without a central bank in charge to address these thefts, Bitcoin holders often have no recourse to recover their funds. See **Table 4.9** for a list of some notable hacks of Bitcoin and other cryptocurrencies. Bitcoin mining worldwide has also grown to use a huge amount of

TABLE 4.9		NOTABLE BITCOIN/ALTCOIN HACKS	
TARGET	**DATE**	**SIZE**	**DESCRIPTION**
Mt. Gox	2011	750,000 BTC	Largest BTC hack to date. Mt. Gox was a Japanese-based exchange. After the hack, it quickly halted operations. Investors lost all of their funds with no refunds.
Bitfinex	2016	120,000 BTC	Second largest BTC hack. Bitfinex issued tokens and plans to refund users' missing coins.
NiceHash	2017	$70 million in BTC and altcoins	NiceHash is a marketplace for mining digital currencies. Hackers gained access to coins via a compromised company computer.
Binance	2019	$40 million in BTC	Hackers infiltrated Taiwan-based Binance, one of the world's largest cryptocurrency exchanges, and used a variety of methods, including phishing, viruses, and other attacks, to carry out a large-scale security breach.

energy, more than the entire amount consumed by Switzerland, and around 0.30% of the world's electricity consumption, according to researchers at the University of Cambridge in 2019, giving environmentalists cause for concern (Vincent, 2019).

Some world governments and financial regulatory bodies perceive Bitcoin to be a potential threat to the sovereignty of their central banking systems, and a number of countries, such as China and South Korea, have banned virtual currency exchanges. However, in general, Bitcoin is gaining acceptance in the financial world. In the United States, major investment banks initially regarded Bitcoin with intense skepticism. But the parent company for the New York Stock Exchange has developed an online trading platform for Bitcoin, and the Chicago Mercantile Exchange accepts Bitcoin trades. And while a handful of countries, including Algeria, Bangladesh, and Bolivia, have made Bitcoin fully illegal, and major banks in other countries like Canada and India have temporary bans on the currency, Bitcoin is now mostly legal worldwide.

Because Bitcoin has no centralized authority, decisions about the future of the currency are made by its community, and that often leads to disagreements. Other cryptocurrencies have been created to improve upon the model of Bitcoin or achieve slightly different goals. These are commonly referred to as "altcoins," and they can be bought and sold along with Bitcoin on all major cryptocurrency exchanges. Bitcoin currently represents about 70% of the full market for cryptocurrencies, with altcoins making up the remainder (Godbole, 2019). See **Table 4.10** for some other prominent examples of altcoins.

An increasingly common method for businesses to raise capital is via an **initial coin offering (ICO)**, where the company issues cryptocurrency tokens that are used to purchase goods and services from that company once it gets off the ground. Crowdfunding sites such as Indiegogo have begun to offer ICO funding, although many regulatory

initial coin offering (ICO)
method of raising capital involving the issuance of cryptocurrency tokens that are used to purchase goods and services from that company

TABLE 4.10　EXAMPLES OF ALTCOINS

NAME	DESCRIPTION
Ethereum/Ether	Ethereum is a decentralized software platform that allows blockchain-based apps to be built and used using Ether, the platform's currency. Lower transaction costs and faster transaction speeds than Bitcoin.
Ripple	A real-time global settlement network that allows for instant low-cost international payments. The distributed ledger of Ripple does not require coin mining to update, making Ripple unique among altcoins. Backed by major banking organizations.
Bitcoin Cash	Result of a fork in Bitcoin's currency – larger block sizes, faster transaction speeds, and lower transaction fees.
Litecoin	Lightweight coin that generates blocks and confirms transactions faster than Bitcoin.
Monero	Coin with special focus on privacy, using different hash algorithms and other techniques to anonymize all elements of a transaction.
Zcash	Coin with "shielded" transactions that hide even the amount transacted.

organizations have either issued warnings about the riskiness of ICOs or demanded that ICOs register as a security like any other financial instrument. ICO tokens are easily bought and sold on online exchanges, making them much more liquid than shares of equity in a company purchased using traditional funding methods, which can be difficult to sell. The amount raised via ICOs has grown rapidly, with over $26 billion raised between 2014 and 2019 (Popov, 2019). For more on ICOs, see the *Insight on Business* case in Chapter 5, *Crowdfunding Takes Off*.

4.6　ELECTRONIC BILLING PRESENTMENT AND PAYMENT

In 2007, for the first time, the number of bill payments made online exceeded the number of physical checks written in the United States (Fiserv, 2007). In the $21.5 trillion U.S. economy with a $14.7 trillion consumer sector for goods and services, there are billions of bills to pay. No one knows for sure, but some experts believe the life-cycle cost of a paper bill for a business, from point of issuance to point of payment, ranges from $3 to $7. This calculation does not include the value of time to consumers, who must open bills, read them, write checks, address envelopes, stamp, and then mail remittances. The billing market represents an extraordinary opportunity for using the Internet as an electronic billing and payment system that potentially could greatly reduce both the cost of paying bills and the time consumers spend paying them. Estimates vary, but online payments are believed to cost between only 20 to 30 cents to process.

Electronic billing presentment and payment (EBPP) systems are systems that enable the online delivery and payment of monthly bills. EBPP services allow consumers to view bills electronically using either their desktop PC or mobile device and pay them through electronic funds transfers from bank or credit card accounts. More and more companies are choosing to issue statements and bills electronically, rather than mailing out paper versions, especially for recurring bills such as utilities, insurance, and subscriptions.

electronic billing presentment and payment (EBPP) system
form of online payment system for monthly bills

MARKET SIZE AND GROWTH

In 2002, 61% of bill payments in the United States were made by check, and only 12% by online bill payments. In contrast, today online bill payments account for more than 55% of all bill payments, while paper checks now account for less than 20%. Among online households, almost three-quarters pay at least one bill online each month, and almost half receive at least one bill electronically each month. Mobile bill payments are surging, with 42% of U.S. households paying at least one bill on a mobile device. Most consumers cited the convenience and time saved by using mobile bill payment (Fiserv, 2017).

One major reason for the surge in EBPP usage is that companies are starting to realize how much money they can save through online billing. Not only is there the savings in postage and processing, but payments can be received more quickly (3 to 12 days faster, compared to paper bills sent via regular mail), thereby improving cash flow. Online bill payment options can also reduce the number of phone calls to a company's customer service line. In order to realize these savings, many companies are becoming more aggressive in encouraging their customers to move to EBPP by instituting a charge for the privilege of continuing to receive a paper bill.

Financials don't tell the whole story, however. Companies are discovering that a bill is both a sales opportunity and a customer retention opportunity, and that the electronic medium provides many more options when it comes to marketing and promotion. Rebates, savings offers, cross-selling, and upselling are all possible in the digital realm, and much less expensive than mailed envelopes stuffed with offers.

EBPP BUSINESS MODELS

There are four EBPP business models: online banking, biller-direct, mobile, and consolidator.

The online banking model is the most widely used today. Consumers establish an online payment service with their banks and use it to pay bills as they come due or automatically make payments for, say, rent. The payments are made directly to the seller's bank account. This model has the advantage of convenience for the consumer because the payments are deducted automatically, usually with a notice from the bank or the merchant that their account has been debited.

In the biller-direct model, consumers are sent bills by e-mail notification, and go to the merchant's website to make payments using their banking credentials. This model has the advantage of allowing the merchant to engage with the consumer by sending

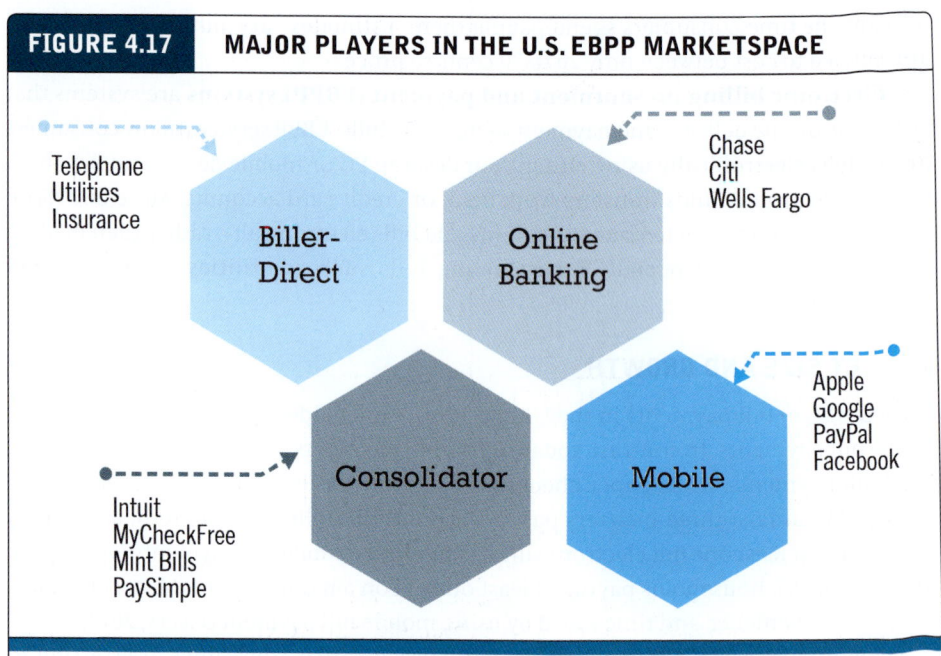

FIGURE 4.17 MAJOR PLAYERS IN THE U.S. EBPP MARKETSPACE

The main business models in the EBPP marketspace are biller-direct, online banking, consolidator, and mobile. Infrastructure providers support all of these competing models.

coupons or rewards. The biller-direct model is a two-step process, and less convenient for consumers.

The mobile model allows consumers to make payments using mobile apps, once again relying on their bank credentials as the source of funds. Consumers are notified of a bill by text message and authorize the payment. An extension of this is the social-mobile model, where social networks like Facebook integrate payment into their messaging services. The mobile model has several advantages, not least of which is the convenience for consumers of paying bills while using their phones, but also the speed with which bills can be paid in a single step. This is the fastest growing form of EBPP. In 2016, Facebook and PayPal announced a deal in which Facebook users can pay for purchases on Facebook using PayPal. Facebook Messenger can be used for P2P payments and payments to groups to pay for meals and other activities. Facebook does not charge for these transfers (Chaykowski, 2017; Wagner, 2017; Demos, 2016).

In the consolidator model, a third party, such as a financial institution or a focused portal such as Intuit's Paytrust, Fiserv's MyCheckFree, Mint Bills, and others, aggregates all bills for consumers and permits one-stop bill payment. This model has the advantage of allowing consumers to see all their bills at one website or app. However, because bills come due at different times, consumers need to check their portals often. The consolidator model faces several challenges. For billers, using the consolidator model means an increased time lag between billing and payment, and also inserts an intermediary between the company and its customer.

Supporting these primary business models are infrastructure providers such as Fiserv, Yodlee, FIS Global, ACI Worldwide, MasterCard RPPS (Remote Payment and Presentment Service), and others that provide the software to create the EBPP system or handle billing and payment collection for the biller. **Figure 4.17** categorizes the major players in the EBPP marketspace.

In the European Union, the Revised Payment Service Directive (PSD 2), which went into effect in 2018, enables bank customers to more easily use third-party providers to pay bills and manage their finances by requiring banks to give such providers access to bank customer accounts through open application program interfaces (APIs).

4.7 CAREERS IN E-COMMERCE

With cybercrime in the headlines nearly every day, positions in the cybersecurity field are growing rapidly, with many remaining unfilled for lack of candidates specifically trained in the field. Cybersecurity is an interdisciplinary field that requires knowledge in technology, human behavior, finance, risk, law, and regulation, so students with a broad range of backgrounds may be successful in obtaining entry-level cybersecurity positions. There is particular demand in industries such as financial services, healthcare, retail, and education, as well as government, all of which have recently suffered high-profile attacks. Security positions are typically also well-compensated. Position titles include incident responder, security analyst, security auditor, security engineer, penetration tester, and security software developer, among others.

THE COMPANY

The company is one of the top banking and financial services firms in the United States. It has over 5,000 branches in all 50 states, over 12,000 ATM machines, and serves over 40 million consumers and small businesses in its retail banking division. The firm has over $600 billion in assets under management. The company's online website and mobile apps provide financial services to over 10 million retail customers. The online sites and mobile apps provide nearly all the services available in local branches, including transferring funds, P2P payments, bill payments, online deposits, and payments. The firm believes that in five years more than 60% of its customers will conduct nearly all their banking transactions online, with the exception of mortgages and wealth management.

Along with other financial services firms of all sizes, the firm is a significant target for hackers and digital criminals. It has suffered through a number of security breaches in its online banking operations, including customer data breaches, credit and bank card fraud, denial of service attacks, and phishing threats to its internal systems. As a result, the firm has launched a major cyber security division that has a large budget (currently at over $350 million) to protect its customers' assets.

THE POSITION: CYBERSECURITY THREAT MANAGEMENT TEAM TRAINEE

You will be a trainee member of the Cybersecurity Threat Management Team, responsible for supporting and coordinating cybersecurity activities at the bank. Your responsibilities include:

- Responding to requests for information from business partners (internal & external).
- Providing governance, guidance, and setting priorities for risk-based threat management, mitigation, and remediation.
- Providing information to stakeholders for their meetings to illustrate and communicate the state of information security risks.
- Advising Division Managers on developing security threats and conducting a risk analysis.
- Reviewing, developing, testing, and implementing security plans, products, and control techniques.
- Coordinating the reporting of data security incidents.
- Monitoring existing and proposed security standard setting groups, including state and federal legislation and regulations.
- Researching attempted efforts to compromise security protocols.

QUALIFICATIONS/SKILLS

- Bachelor's degree in business administration, management information systems, or computer science with coursework in IT security and/or e-commerce security
- Knowledge of security research tools, products, and standards
- Ability to learn vendor and in-house security solutions
- Ability to develop and write scripts for automating security routines
- Ability to achieve SANS Institute security certifications or CISSP (Certified Information Systems Security Professional)
- Ability to develop applications/solutions for enhancing and automating daily routines
- Strong analytical, problem solving, and conceptual thinking skills
- Strong writing and presentation skills
- Ability to work with technical and non-technical business managers

PREPARING FOR THE INTERVIEW

This chapter provides much foundational information about the online security environment (Section 4.1), the different types of online security threats (Section 4.2), various technology solutions (Section 4.3), and the development of security plans (Section 4.4). To prepare for the interview, review these sections. You should be able to demonstrate familiarity with various types of threats typically aimed at firms of this type, such as the different types of malicious code, phishing, data breaches, credit card fraud and theft, identity theft, DoS and DDoS attacks, as well as the dangers posed by insiders, poorly designed software, and cloud, mobile, and IoT security issues. Review the *Insight on Society* case on Equifax so that you can talk intelligently about the issues raised by that data breach. Reread Section 4.3 to make sure that you can demonstrate basic knowledge of various technology solutions, such as encryption, security protocols such as SSL/TLS, VPNs, different types of firewalls, and IDS and IPS. Review Section 4.4 so you can speak about the development of business policies and procedures related to security as well.

POSSIBLE FIRST INTERVIEW QUESTIONS

1. What do you think are the most potentially damaging types of attacks aimed at us?

The breach of customer data is the most damaging, regardless of how it occurs, either through a hacking attack or a phishing attack. The second major threat would be a DDoS (Distributed Denial of Service) attack that prevents customers from accessing their accounts. A third major threat is an attack on the bank's networks that connect the branches to the bank's data centers. If these went down, this would severely impact bank operations.

2. What do you think should be the broad outlines of an online security policy?

To answer this question, you can refer to what you have learned in Section 4.4 about the development of security plans, and in particular Figure 4.12. Any plan needs to start with a risk assessment of the major threats and their potential costs to the bank. A basic security policy is the second step that reflects the risks the bank actually faces. A third step is to devise an implementation plan that engages managers and employees in all the divisions. Last, an ongoing threat reporting and security audit needs to be in place to measure the effectiveness of the security policies and identify areas of continued threat.

3. In terms of remedies, what do you believe are the four most important solutions to online security issues for banks?

To answer this question, you can draw on the information you have learned from Section 4.3 about various technology solutions to online security issues. This is a complex question because it depends in part on which bank products and services are being analyzed. But just considering online consumer retail banking transactions, two-factor authentication at the front end where customers log in would be one solution to identity fraud. Encryption of consumer data might also be possible as a solution to malware hacking customer databases that contain personal information. More generally, a really solid program for training employees with access to customer data in security precautions would potentially limit social engineering attacks such as spoofing and phishing. A fourth solution would be to ensure that all internal systems, especially desktops and local networks, are current with upgrades issued by the major software and hardware vendors.

4. As you probably know, social engineering, such as phishing, is a major threat for us. What would you recommend for minimizing this threat?

To answer this question, you can refer to information contained in Section 4.2 on social engineering and phishing, making reference to the growing use of business e-mail compromise phishing and W-2 phishing. You can suggest that spreading awareness of these types of attacks among the workforce may make it less likely that employees will fall prey to them. You might also note that social engineering attacks, and cybercriminals gaining access to customer accounts, will occur despite the best security policies. It is a matter of when, not if. Having plans in place to cope with these inevitable occurrences is the best policy for minimizing the impacts of these attacks.

5. Many security techniques impose costs on our customers. The more powerful our security software, hardware, and protocols, the greater the chance customers will find our online sites more difficult to use, and slower. What do you think about this dilemma?

To answer this question, you can draw on the information in Section 4.1 on the tension between security and other values, such as ease of use. You might suggest that all security policies and procedures should be analyzed for their potential impact on customer services and system performance. Based on this analysis of system performance, the delays in system performance caused by security protocols can be measured. Surveys of consumers can also produce data measuring how security measures impact perceptions of service quality. Most customers will not notice delays of a few milliseconds in system response times but would notice a five-second delay in service. A data and analytics approach could help answer this question.

4.8 CASE STUDY

Alipay and WeChat Pay

Lead in Mobile Payments

With over one billion consumers worldwide expected to use a mobile wallet to make a proximity mobile payment in 2020, it's no surprise that a slew of companies, including smartphone manufacturers and payment processing companies, are aggressively pursuing global expansion for their mobile payment products. Traditional U.S. tech giants like Google and Apple are aspiring to become the preferred mobile payment platform in as many countries as possible worldwide; however, Chinese tech companies Alibaba and Tencent have a commanding lead in this space, not Google and Apple.

China boasted 61% of the world's users of proximity mobile payments in 2019—a total of over 575 million people and an increase of 10% from 2017. Proximity mobile payments are those that take place at the point of sale, where the person paying for a good or service uses their phone in tandem with NFC, QR codes, Bluetooth, or other, similar technology to make a payment. Not every country has embraced proximity mobile payments, but China has proved to be the perfect environment for them to catch on. In

© Xinhua/Alamy Stock Photo

Western countries like the United States and Europe, credit cards are still in widespread use and have been for many years, as are other payment systems that are tied to banks, such as debit cards and checks. However, China's rapid, consistent economic growth in the past few decades has allowed it to bypass credit cards completely in favor of mobile payment apps. There are only 0.31 credit cards per capita in China, compared to 2.5 credit cards per capita in the United States.

In 2018, over 60 billion mobile payment transactions occurred in China, totaling over $41 trillion. In contrast, in the United States, consumers only paid about $70 billion via mobile payments in 2018. In nearly every metric, China has outpaced the rest of the world in mobile payments. In China, even street people accept handouts via QR codes; street musicians lift pictures of QR codes to allow passersby to provide tips with Alipay or WeChat Pay. Only now, with the Chinese mobile payments market nearly completely saturated, have other countries like India begun to grow in mobile payment adoption at a faster rate; India had about 98 million mobile payment users in 2019, a distant second to China's 575 million, but India grew at a robust rate of almost 30% in 2019, with double-digit increases expected to continue until 2023. Nevertheless, only about 38% of Indian smartphone users and 11% of the population of India currently use mobile payments. Other countries in Asia-Pacific with heavy adoption of mobile payments include South Korea (about 37% of smartphone users), Japan (about 25%), Indonesia (about 20%), and Australia (about 20%). In many countries, the advent of biometric authentication has been a major driver of mobile payment adoption, since it greatly reduces the chances of identity theft and speeds up transaction speeds at the point of sale.

Despite China's overwhelming adoption of proximity mobile payments, the country does not have a thriving marketplace of many companies jockeying for dominance; just as in the United States, a small number of tech titans have cornered most of the market. Founded in 1999 by Jack Ma and Peng Lei, Alibaba is China's largest e-commerce company, offering B2B e-commerce on its flagship Alibaba website, C2C e-commerce on its Taobao marketplace, and B2C e-commerce on its Tmall site. The company's sales dwarf those of even Amazon and Walmart thanks to the sheer size of the Chinese market in which it operates (see the Chapter 12 opening case for more information on Alibaba). In 2004, Alibaba created Alipay in response to widespread lack of trust between buyers and sellers on both the Alibaba and Taobao platforms. In 2011, Ma transferred Alipay out of Alibaba's direct ownership into Ant Financial, a financial services holding company that Ma controlled, but Alibaba continues to have a significant interest in Alipay.

Alipay is an escrow-based system, where funds moving from one party to another are held by Alipay until both sides of the transaction give their full approval. The system helped Alibaba gain the trust of Chinese consumers, and when smartphone adoption began to skyrocket in 2008, Alipay's share of China's mobile payments market also skyrocketed. Between 2008 and 2019, the number of mobile Internet users in China grew from 118 million to over 780 million, and percentage of the population that are digital buyers grew from less than 15% of Chinese consumers to almost 60% in 2019.

By 2019, Alipay had reached a milestone, with 1 billion active users worldwide. Alipay has begun to grow into other areas, including Pakistan, South Korea, Malaysia, Thailand, and Singapore, since the Chinese market has edged closer to full saturation. As the company's user base has grown, Alipay has greatly diversified its offerings beyond online and mobile payment. Alipay offers four main services beyond payments: loans, insurance, investment, and credit scores. Payments used to be Alipay's only focus; now mobile payment is the gateway to a much larger array of financial products, all of which are more profitable than the original payments business. For example, Alipay's Yu'e Bao money market fund is now easily the largest such fund in the world; Alipay users can quickly and easily invest in the fund with the same app they use to make payments at a restaurant or grocery store. Alipay also uses algorithmic assessments to offer loans both to individuals and to businesses; its AI-powered risk engine has reduced Alipay's fraud-loss rate dramatically to lower than 5 incidences in every 10 million transactions. Alipay offers three types of loans: its Ant Micro Loan, which is intended for small businesses; its JieBei loans, for individual consumers with high credit scores, who in turn typically use the money to shop on Alibaba's marketplaces; and its Huabei (or Ant Check Later) loan, which allows users to buy items on credit without paying interest. In addition to reducing fraud, Alibaba's algorithmic approach also allows the company to process loan requests incredibly fast. Alibaba uses transaction data to analyze how a business is doing and how competitive it is in its market as well as the credit ratings of the companies it partners with.

Chinese regulators have not always been happy with Alipay's growing array of financial products. Often, Alipay has had to trim down or adjust features in response to government pressure. For example, Alipay lowered its withdrawal limits and investment limits for investors in Yu'e Bao; in addition, Alipay was punished for automatically enrolling users of its other services into its Sesame Credit credit scoring system. Alipay was also forced to stop working with unlicensed financial businesses and untrustworthy online microlenders. Sesame Credit is now primarily used for non-financial purposes, such as visa approvals and background checks for bike rentals. Still, Alipay is a staple for millions of Chinese consumers, and the company has worked to ensure that Chinese citizens traveling abroad can use Alipay to pay for goods overseas. For example, taxis in New York City now offer Alipay as a payment option. Alipay can now be used in 42 different countries. China is the world's largest source of outbound tourism; Chinese travelers spent $115 billion overseas in 2018 on a combined 130 million trips, and 2018 was the first year in which mobile payments became the most common way Chinese travelers paid for goods overseas. Alipay is also working on projects involving blockchain technology, artificial intelligence (AI), security, the Internet of Things, and many more.

In China, Alipay has only one real competitor: WeChat Pay. Just as Alipay arose from Alibaba and its lineup of e-commerce sites, WeChat Pay arose from the incredibly popular text and voice messaging service WeChat, operated by tech titan Tencent Holdings. WeChat Pay also boasts over 1 billion users. Like Alipay, payment is only a small portion of WeChat's larger ecosystem of services. WeChat offers social networking features that resemble Facebook's News Feed, featuring a comment system that is more tightly limited to close friends; WeChat can also be used to pay parking tickets, call an ambulance, translate from Chinese to English, pay bills, book train and air transportation, reserve hotel rooms, make charitable donations, and perform online banking with the WeBank online bank—it can even be used as a makeshift dating service. The sheer number of features offered by the WeChat app has made it central to Chinese consumers' lives and increased the likelihood that they will use the app to make mobile payments.

WeChat stores money that can be used to pay for goods and services or to send to others; in addition, WeChat has rolled out the extremely popular "red packet" feature, based on a long-standing Chinese tradition practiced on the Chinese New Year and other significant occasions. Using this feature, users can divide a predetermined amount of money into small virtual "packets" called hongbao and send them to a group chat, allowing members of the group to race to claim each packet. In 2018, 768 million people used the red packet feature to celebrate the Chinese New Year, and 230 billion WeChat messages were sent on the eve of the new year.

WeChat has made significant inroads against Alipay's dominance in the Chinese market. One technique it has used to achieve this is partnerships with other prominent Chinese services, such as Chinese rideshare service Didi Chuxing, with whom WeChat Pay has an exclusive partnership. WeChat has a similar arrangement with the Meituan Waimai on-demand food delivery service, which no longer accepts Alipay due to its partnership with WeChat. Walmart's Chinese outlets also do not accept Alipay for these reasons. WeChat has also sought partnerships with foreign businesses, such as Japan's Line messaging service; WeChat partnered with Line Pay in 2018 to make it easier for Chinese tourists in Japan to make mobile payments. WeChat has grown rapidly worldwide; in 2019, WeChat Pay could be used in 49 countries.

To that end, WeChat has developed a cross-border payment system in partnership with payment firm Travelex to allow Chinese tourists to shop overseas. Chinese customers of U.S. retailers can use Travelex Pay to purchase goods; the money in their WeChat Pay accounts is used to generate a digital gift card in U.S. dollars, which is then immediately spent to purchase the desired items. Already, many of the biggest U.S. retailers that are popular with Chinese tourists are participating in the plan. The appeal is that it helps tourists avoid having to carry a lot of cash, and Chinese credit cards can trigger large fees for foreign transactions, which this method avoids. WeChat and Alipay have both stated that their international expansion is focused on allowing Chinese travelers abroad to use the same features they are used to in China, but industry analysts suspect that both companies have greater ambitions for the U.S. market, which still lags far behind in mobile payment adoption compared to China.

Both WeChat and Alipay are also similar in the enormous trove of data they possess on their users. Because Alibaba and WeChat are so central to Chinese consumers' lives, both companies know a great deal about what their users buy, who their friends are, what their credit scores are, and much, much more. The Chinese government has seemingly completely unfettered access to WeChat messages, even retrieving deleted messages when they deem it necessary, and has also heavily invested in and supported Alibaba. Some

SOURCES: "China's Ant Financial Has No Timetable for a Listing, but Targets 2 Billion Users in a Decade," By Saheli Choudhury, Cnbc.com, November 19, 2019; "Global Mobile Payment Users 2019," by Jasmine Enberg, eMarketer, Inc., October 24, 2019; "China Mobile Payment Users 2019," by Man-Chung Cheung, eMarketer, Inc., October 24, 2019; "Confirmed: Googe Terminated Project Dragonfly, Its Censored Chinese Search Engine," by Jeb Su, Forbes.com, July 19, 2019; "Paytm Looks to Hit 12 Trillion Transactions by End of FY20," by Shreya Nandi, Livemint.com, June 5, 2019; "The $41.5 Trillion Shopping Bill of China's Smartphone Users, " by Pooja Singh, Entrepreneur.com, March 29, 2019; "Alipay: Chinese Tourists Prefer Mobile Payments,"

analysts speculate that because privacy is simply not as significant a cultural value in China as it is in other countries, WeChat and Alipay are in a better position to monetize their trove of user data than other companies might be.

While Alipay and WeChat Pay have been big winners in China's mobile payment marketplace over the last decade, American tech companies have been left to play catchup. Apple in particular has a small fraction of users using Apple Pay compared to both Alipay and WeChat Pay; WeChat also functions similarly on the iPhone and Android, making the two operating systems mostly indistinguishable to Chinese smartphone users. For that reason, Chinese consumers often prefer the lower-cost Android, at Apple's expense. Google has had its own problems with China over the years, though, including philosophical objections to China's content censorship policy; Google seemingly reversed course in 2018 with its Dragonfly content censorship engine, undertaken jointly with cooperation from Chinese regulators, but as of 2019 China has reportedly withdrawn its support for the project and Google confirmed that the project had been terminated. It seems unlikely that Google Pay will make a dent in China's mobile payment marketplace without the ability to create a similar ecosystem of products and services to the ones that Alibaba and WeChat can offer.

Around the world, other countries and payment systems are gaining traction. For example, Alibaba-backed Paytm, India's leading mobile wallet, is capitalizing on the rapid growth in mobile payment adoption in the country; it had 350 million registered users as of mid-2019, and that number continues to grow quickly. Just like WeChat and Alipay, Paytm allows users to make payments and send money to other users as well as book travel arrangements. In Malaysia, the popular ridesharing service Grab has continued to expand, opening its platform to third-party services to develop more functionality akin to WeChat as well as launching the GrabPay mobile wallet and GrabFood food delivery service. Boost is another popular payment service in Malaysia. In Singapore, DBS PayLah and SingtelDASH are in widespread use, as is GrabPay.

Another important battleground for mobile payment providers is Hong Kong, which is unique in the region in its reliance on cash and credit cards. As a result, Western tech companies are slightly more competitive with Alipay and WeChat in the region. On the other hand, Hong Kong citizens have widely adopted the Octopus stored value card, which is accepted by convenience stores, restaurants, and public transit. Launched in 1997, there are more than 35 million Octopus cards in circulation, or approximately five per Hong Kong resident. Mobile payment companies seeking to expand into Hong Kong and tap into its lucrative consumer base will require at least as competitive an option as Octopus.

Alipay and WeChat are positioned extremely well going forward, with massive user bases in China, profitable business models thanks to their vibrant ecosystems of services, and the backing of two of the biggest tech companies in the world in Alibaba and Tencent, respectively. If Alipay and WeChat Pay are unsuccessful in growing into a particular region, they could simply opt to go the route of strategic acquisitions; Alipay and its parent Ant Financial have already begun doing this. However, both companies face challenges in their attempts to expand into Western markets, where credit cards are already in widespread

Pymnts.com, January 21, 2019; "Alipay Hits 1 Billion Global Users," by Charlotte Yang, Caixinglobal.com, January 10, 2019; "Alipay Changes Name to Hanbao (But for Users, Nothing Will Change)," by Manya Koetse, Whatsonweibo.com, January 8, 2019; "A Closer Look: Apple's Troubles in China Grow as WeChat Underlines iPhone's Appeal," by Cam MacMurchy, 9to5mac.com, January 3, 2019; "Alipay vs Wechat Pay: Mobile Payment Giants Driving China's Cashless Transformation," by Ashley Galina Dudarenok, Asiaspeakers.org, January 2, 2019; "A Surprising Number of Countries Now Accept WeChat Pay or Alipay," by Julianna Wu, Techinasia.com, December 10, 2018; "Mobile Payments in China Are Growing So Fast, Predictions Can't Keep Up," by Matthew Keegan, Jingdaily.com, November 8, 2018; "China Leads Asia-Pacific for Mobile Payment Adoption," by Danielle Long, Thedrum.com, October 28, 2018; "WeChat Pay, China's Popular Payment Tool, Expands U.S. Offering," by Evie Liu, Barrons.com, October 19, 2018; "What the Largest Global Fintech Can Teach Us About What's Next in Financial Services," Cbinsights.com, October 4, 2018; "Digital Payment Firms Fight for Hong Kong Market," Channelnewsasia.com, August 16, 2018; "Chinese Tech Giant Tencent Plans to Expand Its US Payments Footprint—Despite Ongoing Trade War," by Arjun Kharpal, Cnbc.com, July 18, 2018; "WeChat Pay to Keep Overseas Focus on Outbound Tourism Instead of Offering More Local Wallets," by Celia Chen and Iris Deng, Scmp.com, July 11, 2018; "Future of Cashless Payments in Singapore," by Quah Mei Lee, Frost.com, June 8, 2018; "One Photo Shows That China Is Already in a Cashless Future," by Harrison Jacobs, Businessinsider.com, May 29, 2018; "Why China's Payment Apps Give U.S. Bankers Nightmares," by Jennifer Surane and Christopher Cannon, Bloomberg.com, May 23, 2018; "Chinese Government Admits Collection of Deleted WeChat Messages," by

Devin Coldewey, Techcrunch.com, April 30, 2018; "Google Steps Up Global Fight for Digital Wallet as China Dominates Mobile Payments," by Zen Soo and Alice Shen, Scmp.com, February 21, 2018.

use and are trusted by consumers. Without a sufficiently compelling reason, customers in Europe and the United States are unlikely to ditch their credit cards and switch not just to Alipay or WeChat Pay, but even to U.S.-based services like Apple Pay and Google Pay. Nevertheless, this technology has emerged quickly, with China and many other countries as proof of concept, and the market might look completely different in just a few years' time.

Case Study Questions

1. Why has China been an ideal environment to support mobile payment systems?
2. How has Alipay changed from its original iteration?
3. How has WeChat grown to rival Alipay in mobile payment market share in China?
4. Why have countries like the United States been slow to adopt mobile payment systems?

4.9 REVIEW

KEY CONCEPTS

- **Understand the scope of e-commerce crime and security problems, the key dimensions of e-commerce security, and the tension between security and other values.**
- While the overall size of cybercrime is unclear, cybercrime against e-commerce sites is growing rapidly, the amount of losses is growing, and the management of e-commerce sites must prepare for a variety of criminal assaults.
- There are six key dimensions to e-commerce security: integrity, nonrepudiation, authenticity, confidentiality, privacy, and availability.
- Although computer security is considered necessary to protect e-commerce activities, it is not without a downside. Two major areas where there are tensions between security and website operations are:
    - *Ease of use*—The more security measures that are added to an e-commerce site, the more difficult it is to use and the slower the site becomes, hampering ease of use. Security is purchased at the price of slowing down processors and adding significantly to data storage demands. Too much security can harm profitability, while not enough can potentially put a company out of business.
    - *Public safety*—There is a tension between the claims of individuals to act anonymously and the needs of public officials to maintain public safety that can be threatened by criminals or terrorists.

- **Identify the key security threats in the e-commerce environment.**
- The most common and most damaging forms of security threats to e-commerce sites include:
  - *Malicious code*—viruses, worms, Trojan horses, ransomware, and bot networks are a threat to a system's integrity and continued operation, often changing how a system functions or altering documents created on the system.
  - *Potentially unwanted programs (adware, spyware, etc.)*—a kind of security threat that arises when programs are surreptitiously installed on your computer or computer network without your consent.
  - *Phishing*—any deceptive, online attempt by a third party to obtain confidential information for financial gain.
  - *Hacking and cybervandalism*—intentionally disrupting, defacing, or even destroying a site.
  - *Credit card fraud/theft*—one of the most-feared occurrences and one of the main reasons more consumers do not participate in e-commerce. The most common cause of credit card fraud is a lost or stolen card that is used by someone else, followed by employee theft of customer numbers and stolen identities (criminals applying for credit cards using false identities).
  - *Identity fraud*—involves the unauthorized use of another person's personal data, such as social security, driver's license, and/or credit card numbers, as well as user names and passwords, for illegal financial benefit.
  - *Spoofing*—occurs when hackers attempt to hide their true identities or misrepresent themselves by using fake e-mail addresses or masquerading as someone else.
  - *Pharming*—involves redirecting a web link to an address different from the intended one, with the site masquerading as the intended destination.
  - *Denial of Service (DoS) and Distributed Denial of Service (DDoS) attacks*—hackers flood a website with useless traffic to inundate and overwhelm the network, frequently causing it to shut down and damaging a site's reputation and customer relationships.
  - *Sniffing*—a type of eavesdropping program that monitors information traveling over a network, enabling hackers to steal proprietary information from anywhere on a network, including e-mail messages, company files, and confidential reports. The threat of sniffing is that confidential or personal information will be made public.
  - *Insider jobs*—although the bulk of Internet security efforts are focused on keeping outsiders out, the biggest threat is from employees who have access to sensitive information and procedures.
  - *Poorly designed server and client software*—the increase in complexity and size of software programs has contributed to an increase in software flaws or vulnerabilities that hackers can exploit.
  - *Social network security issues*—malicious code, PUPs, phishing, data breaches, identity fraud, and other e-commerce security threats have all infiltrated social networks.
  - *Mobile platform security issues*—the mobile platform presents an alluring target for hackers and cybercriminals, and faces all the same risks as other Internet devices, as well as new risks associated with wireless network security.
  - *Cloud security issues*—as devices, identities, and data become more and more intertwined in the cloud, safeguarding data in the cloud becomes a major concern.
- **Describe how technology helps secure Internet communications channels and protect networks, servers, and clients.**
- Encryption is the process of transforming plain text or data into cipher text that cannot be read by anyone other than the sender and the receiver. Encryption can provide four of the six key dimensions of e-commerce security: message integrity, nonrepudiation, authentication, and confidentiality.
- There are a variety of different forms of encryption technology currently in use. They include:

- *Symmetric key cryptography*—Both the sender and the receiver use the same key to encrypt and decrypt a message.
- *Public key cryptography*—Two mathematically related digital keys are used: a public key and a private key. The private key is kept secret by the owner, and the public key is widely disseminated. Both keys can be used to encrypt and decrypt a message. Once the keys are used to encrypt a message, the same keys cannot be used to unencrypt the message.
- *Public key cryptography using digital signatures and hash digests*—This method uses a mathematical algorithm called a hash function to produce a fixed-length number called a hash digest. The results of applying the hash function are sent by the sender to the recipient. Upon receipt, the recipient applies the hash function to the received message and checks to verify that the same result is produced. The sender then encrypts both the hash result and the original message using the recipient's public key, producing a single block of cipher text. To ensure both the authenticity of the message and nonrepudiation, the sender encrypts the entire block of cipher text one more time using the sender's private key. This produces a digital signature or "signed" cipher text that can be sent over the Internet to ensure the confidentiality of the message and authenticate the sender.
- *Digital envelope*—This method uses symmetric cryptography to encrypt and decrypt the document, but public key cryptography to encrypt and send the symmetric key.
- *Digital certificates and public key infrastructure*—This method relies on certification authorities who issue, verify, and guarantee digital certificates (a digital document that contains the name of the subject or company, the subject's public key, a digital certificate serial number, an expiration date, an issuance date, the digital signature of the certification authority, and other identifying information).
- In addition to encryption, there are several other tools that are used to secure Internet channels of communication, including: Secure Sockets Layer (SSL)/Transport Layer Security (TLS), virtual private networks (VPNs), and wireless security standards such as WPA2.
- After communications channels are secured, tools to protect networks, the servers, and clients should be implemented. These include: firewalls, proxies, intrusion detection and prevention systems (IDS/IDP), operating system controls, and anti-virus software.

■ **Appreciate the importance of policies, procedures, and laws in creating security.**

- In order to minimize security threats, e-commerce firms must develop a coherent corporate policy that takes into account the nature of the risks, the information assets that need protecting, and the procedures and technologies required to address the risk, as well as implementation and auditing mechanisms.
- Public laws and active enforcement of cybercrime statutes also are required to both raise the costs of illegal behavior on the Internet and guard against corporate abuse of information.
- The key steps in developing a security plan are:
  - *Perform a risk assessment*—an assessment of the risks and points of vulnerability.
  - *Develop a security policy*—a set of statements prioritizing the information risks, identifying acceptable risk targets, and identifying the mechanisms for achieving these targets.
  - *Create an implementation plan*—a plan that determines how you will translate the levels of acceptable risk into a set of tools, technologies, policies, and procedures.
  - *Create a security team*—the individuals who will be responsible for ongoing maintenance, audits, and improvements.
  - *Perform periodic security audits*—routine reviews of access logs and any unusual patterns of activity.

■ **Identify the major e-commerce payment systems in use today.**

- The major types of e-commerce payment systems in use today include:

- *Online credit card transactions*, which are the primary form of online payment system. There are five parties involved in an online credit card purchase: consumer, merchant, clearinghouse, merchant bank (sometimes called the "acquiring bank"), and the consumer's card-issuing bank. However, the online credit card system has a number of limitations involving security, merchant risk, cost, and social equity.
- *PayPal*, which is an example of an alternative payment system that permits consumers to make instant, online payments to merchants and other individuals based on value stored in an online account. Other examples include Amazon Pay, Visa Checkout, MasterPass, and PayPal Credit.
- *Mobile payment systems*, which use either credit card readers attached to a smartphone (Square, PayPal Here) or near field communication (NFC) chips, which enable mobile payment at point-of-sale (Apple Pay and Samsung Pay).
- *Cryptocurrencies*, such as Bitcoin and other altcoins. Cryptocurrencies are growing in importance and can be used to hide payments from authorities, as well as support the legitimate exchange of value.

- **Describe the features and functionality of electronic billing presentment and payment systems.**
- Electronic billing presentment and payment (EBPP) systems are a form of online payment systems for monthly bills. EBPP services allow consumers to view bills electronically and pay them through electronic funds transfers from bank or credit card accounts.
- Major players in the EBPP marketspace include: online banking, biller-direct systems, mobile payment systems, and consolidators.

QUESTIONS

1. What is a VPN and what is its value to an organization?
2. What features or abilities does an intrusion prevention system use to protect a network?
3. Identify and describe the five main steps in establishing a company's security plan.
4. Differentiate between the security dimension of confidentiality and the concept of online privacy.
5. Outside of the United States, what types of payments are popular for online purchases?
6. Why has card not-present (CNP) fraud increased in recent years?
7. Describe the three primary types of mobile payment apps.
8. How does blockchain work?
9. What risks do Bitcoin users face?
10. What role does ease of use play in ensuring e-commerce security?
11. How are the SSL/TLS protocols used in securing Internet communications?
12. What is nonrepudiation and why is it an important dimension of e-commerce security? What technologies are used to establish nonrepudiation?
13. In what ways is WPA3 vulnerable to hackers?
14. What does PSD2 require for customer authentication?
15. What is BEC phishing?
16. Why are botnets considered an especially important threat to e-commerce, more so than, say, an individual, destructive virus?
17. Why are security issues associated with the Internet of Things even more challenging than existing security issues related to the Internet?
18. What is the Heartbleed bug and how does it threaten security?

19. How does code signing protect a mobile app?
20. What is a next generation firewall?

PROJECTS

1. Imagine you are the owner of an e-commerce website. What are some of the signs that your site has been hacked? Discuss the major types of attacks you could expect to experience and the resulting damage to your site. Prepare a brief summary presentation.

2. Given the shift toward m-commerce, do a search on m-commerce (or mobile commerce) crime. Identify and discuss the security threats this type of technology creates. Prepare a presentation outlining your vision of the new opportunities for cybercrime that m-commerce may provide.

3. Find three certification authorities and compare the features of each company's digital certificates. Provide a brief description of each company as well, including number of clients. Prepare a brief presentation of your findings.

4. Research the challenges associated with payments across international borders and prepare a brief presentation of your findings. Do most e-commerce companies conduct business internationally? How do they protect themselves from repudiation? How do exchange rates impact online purchases? What about shipping charges? Summarize by describing the differences between a U.S. customer and an international customer who each make a purchase from a U.S. e-commerce merchant.

REFERENCES

Alert Logic. "Cloud Security Report: Research on the Evolving State of Cloud Security 2017." (2017).

Barrett, Brian. "The Next Generation of Wi-Fi Security Will Save You From Yourself." Wired.com (June 26, 2018).

Blue, Violet. "You Say Advertising, I Say Block That Malware." Engadget.com (January 8, 2016).

Chaykowski, Kathleen. "Facebook Messenger Debuts Group Payments." Forbes.com (April 11, 2017).

Check Point Research Team. "Banking Trojans Are on the Rise: Here's How to Avoid Being Robbed." Blog.checkpoint.com (April 25, 2017).

Chirgwin, Richard. "Microsoft and FBI Storm Ramparts of Citadel Botnets." *The Register* (June 6, 2013).

CIO.gov. "HTTP Strict Transport Security." (2016).

Cisco "2018 Annual Cybersecurity Report." (2018).

Cisco. "2017 Annual Cybersecurity Report." (2017).

Cody, Brian. "The Ultimate Guide to Mobile Malware and Dodgy Apps." Uk.norton.com (January 27, 2017).

Constantin, Lucian. "Police Operation Disrupts Beebone Botnet Used for Malware Distribution." Pcworld.com (April 9, 2015).

Corbett, Erin. "Google + Will Shut Down After Security Hole Exposed User Data to Outside Developers, Report Says." Fortune.com (October 8, 2018).

Crosman, Penny. "Zelle's Bumpy Ride Toward Ubiquity." *American Banker* (April 25, 2018).

Crowe, Jonathan. "Alert: New Surge in W-2 Phishing Scams Affects More than 120,000 Employees." Blog.barkly.com (March 2017).

Cybersecurity Insiders. "2020 Insider Threat Report." (2019).

Cybersecurity Insiders/Alert Logic. "2018 Cloud Security Report." (2018).

Datta, Saikat. "Security Breach in NIC Allowed Hackers to Issue Fake Digital Certificates—Hindustan Times." Medianama.com (August 14, 2014).

Demos, Telis. "PayPal Gets Friendlier with Facebook." *Wall Street Journal* (October 24, 2016).

Dwolla. "Dwolla Announces $12 million Investment." (February 12, 2018).

Ecommerce News. "iDeal Used for 59% of Dutch Purchases." Ecommercenews.edu (June 6, 2019a).

eMarketer, Inc. (Yoram Wurmser). "US Mobile Payment Users 2019: User Growth Slows, but Transaction Volume Surges." (October 2019a).

eMarketer, Inc. (Jasmine Enberg). "Global Mobile Payment Users 2019: More Than 1 Billion People Worldwide Will Make an In-Store Mobile Payment in 2020." (October 2019b).

eMarketer, Inc. (Jasmine Enberg). "Global Ecommerce Platforms 2017: A Country-by-Country Review of the Top Retail Ecommerce Sites." (July 2017).

Federal Reserve Bank of San Francisco. "Understanding Consumer Cash Use: Preliminary Findings from the 2016 Diary of Consumer Payment Choice." (November 28, 2017).

First Annapolis Consulting. "Study of Mobile Banking & Payments: Mobile Wallet Report." (March 2017).

Fiserv. "Fiserv Insights: Ninth Annual Consumer Billing Preference Survey." (March 2017).

Fiserv. "Eighth Annual Billing Household Survey." (March 2016).

Fiserv. "2007 Consumer Bill Payments Trends Survey: Volume of Electronic Payments." (2007).

Frias, Lauren. "Capital One Says It Was Hit with Data Breach, Affecting Tens of Millions of Credit Card Applications." Businessinsider.com (July 29, 2019).

Garcia-Tobar, Alexander. "Five More Myths of Email Authentication." Valimail.com (February 14, 2019).

Godbole, Omkar. "Bitcoin's Total Share of Crypto Market Now Highest Since March 2017." Coindesk.com (September 3, 2019),

Greenberg, Andy. "Hackers Remotely Kill a Jeep on the Highway—With Me In It." Wired.com (July 21, 2015).

Groenfeldt, Tom. "Dwolla Brings Real-Time Experience To Fed's Faster Payments Task Force." Forbes.com (January 25, 2017).

Grotta, Sarah. "Round Up of Recent Person-to-Person Payment Data." Paymentsjournal.com (April 25, 2019).

Hackett, Robert. "On Heartbleed's Anniversary, 3 of 4 Big Companies Are Still Vulnerable." *Fortune* (April 7, 2015).

Hasham, Salim, Chris Rezek, Maxence Vancauwenberghe, and Josh Weiner. "Is Cybersecurity Incompatible with Digital Convenience?" Mckinsey.com (August 2016).

IBM Security. "Future of Identity Study." (January 29, 2018).

IBM Security. "IBM X-Force Threat Intelligence Index 2018." (March 2018).

Identity Theft Resource Center (ITRC). "2018 Annual Data Breach Year-End Review." (2019).

Internet Society. "Policy Brief: The Internet of Things." (October 7, 2016).

Internet Society. "The Internet of Things: An Overview." (2015).

Isaac, Mike. "WhatsApp Introduces End-to-End Encryption." *New York Times* (April 5, 2016).

Isaac, Mike, and Sheera Frenkel. "Facebook Security Breach Exposes Accounts of 50 Million Users." *New York Times* (September 28, 2018).

Javelin Strategy & Research. "2019 Identity Fraud Study: Fraudsters Seek New Targets and Victims Bear the Brunt." (March 6, 2019).

Johnson, Derek. "DHS Looks to Upgrade Flagging Info Sharing Program," Fcw.com (September 6, 2019).

Johnson, N. F., M. Zheng, Y. Vorobyeva, A. Gabriel, H. Qi, N. Velasquez, P. Manrique, D. Johnson, E. Restrepo, C. Song, and S. Wuchty. "New Online Ecology of Adversarial Aggregates: ISIS and Beyond." *Science* (June 17, 2016).

Juniper Research. "Juniper Research: Retailers to Lose $130bn Globally in Card-Not-Present Fraud Over the Next Five Years." (January 2, 2019).

Kan, Michael. "Flaws in Wi-Fi's New WPA3 Protocol Can Leak a Network's Password." Pcmag.com (April 11, 2019).

Kan, Michael. "New Mirai-like Malware Targets IoT Devices." Pcmag.com (October 20, 2017).

Koo, Jimmy. "FTC Security Cases to Continue in '17 Amid Uncertainty." Bna.com (December 7, 2016).

Kujawa, Adam. "Why Is Malwarebytes Blocking Coinhive?" Malwarebytes.com (July 19, 2018).

Leger, Donna Leinwand. "Credit Card Info Sold on Hacker Sites." *USA Today* (September 4, 2014).

Loeb, Larry. "Malwarebytes Thinks Potentially Unwanted Programs Are Malware." SecurityIntelligence.com (October 13, 2016).

Lunden, Ingrid. "Payments Startup Dwolla Raises $6.85M More, Debuts Access API." Techcrunch.com (January 20, 2017).

Lyngaas, Sean. "Private Sector Isn't Sharing Data with DHS's Threat Portal." Cyberscoop.com (June 28, 2018).

Majkowski, Marek. "Mobile Ad Networks as DDoS Vectors: A Case Study." Blog.cloudfare.com (September 25, 2015)

Malwarebytes. "All About Adware." (March 5, 2018).

McAfee/Center for Strategic and International Studies (James Lewis). "Economic Impact of Cybercrime—No Slowing Down." (February 2018).

Mitnick, Kevin. *Ghost in the Wires*. Little, Brown & Co. (2011).

Morgan, Steve. "Global Cybersecurity Spending Predicted to Exceed $1 Trillion from 2017–2021." Cybersecurityventures.com (June 10, 2019).

Murphy, Mike. "A New Data Breach May Have Exposed Personal Information of Almost Every American Adult." Marketwatch.com (June 28, 2018).

Netscout. "NETSCOUT 14th Annual Worldwide Infrastructure Security Report: Cloud in the Crosshairs." (2019).

Neustar. "DDos Attacks Up 241% in Q3 2019 Compared to Same Period Last Year." (November 19, 2019).

Osborne, Charlie. "The Dark Web: How Much Is Your Bank Account Worth?" Zdnet.com (March 20, 2018).

Pagliery, Jose. "FBI Teams Up with Hackers to Bust Bank Robbing Botnet." Cnn.com (October 13, 2015).

PCI Security Standards Council. "Payment Card Industry Security Standards Council Releases PCI Data Security Standard Version 3.2." (April 28, 2016).

Perlroth, Nicole, and Vindu Goel. "Defending Against Hackers Took a Back Seat at Yahoo, Insiders Say." *New York Times* (September 28, 2016).

Ponemon Institute/Accenture. "Ninth Annual Cost of Cybercrime Study: Unlocking the Value of Improved Cybersecurity Protection." (March 6, 2019).

Ponemon Institute/IBM Security. "Cost of a Data Breach Report 2019." (July 23, 2019).

Ponemon Institute. "2018 State of Endpoint Security Risk" (2018).

Popov, Artem. "Life After the ICO Hype: What's in Store for the Collective Investment Market?" Forbes.com (October 25, 2019).

PYMTS. "Venmo and Zelle's P2P Battle Royale." PYMNTS.com (February 1, 2019).

Ricker, Thomas. "Wi-Fi Security Has Been Breached, Say Researchers." Theverge.com (October 16, 2017).

Riley, Brian. "EMV Credit Cards: Achieving Success at $10 an Hour." Paymentjournal.com (September 17, 2018).

Sanger, David, and Nicole Perlroth. "A New Era of Internet Attacks Powered by Everyday Devices." *New York Times* (October 22, 2016).

Schuman, Evan. "Starbucks Caught Storing Mobile Passwords in Clear Text." *Computerworld* (January 15, 2014).

Schwartz, John. "Fighting Crime Online: Who Is in Harm's Way?" *New York Times* (February 8, 2001).

Scmagazine.com. "Forgotten Conficker Worm Resurfaces to Aid WannaCry." (May 22, 2017).

Software Engineering Institute. "Common Sense Guide to Mitigating Insider Threats, 4th Edition." Sei.cmu.edu (December 2012).

Stack, Brian. "Here's How Much Your Personal Information Is Selling for on the Dark Web." Experian.com (April 9, 2018).

Steele, Jason. "Payment Method Statistics." Creditcards.com (May 30, 2018).

Stein, Lincoln D. *Web Security: A Step-by-Step Reference Guide*. Reading, MA: Addison-Wesley (1998).

Storm, Darlene. "MEDJACK: Hackers Hijacking Medical Devices Create Backdoors in Hospital Networks." Computerworld.com (June 8, 2015a).

Storm, Darlene. "2 More Wireless Baby Monitors Hacked: Hackers Remotely Spied on Babies and Parents." Computerworld.com (April 22, 2015b).

Sullivan, Laurie. "Google Releases Bad Ads Report: Pushes Trust, Safety." Mediapost.com (March 14, 2018).

Symantec, Inc. "Internet Security Threat Report 2019, Volume 24." (April 2019).

Symantec, Inc. "Internet Security Threat Report 2018, Volume 23." (April 2018).

Symantec, Inc. "Internet Security Threat Report 2017 Volume 22." (April 2017).

Thales/Ponemon Institute. "Protecting Data in the Cloud: 2019 Thales Cloud Security Study Global Edition." (2019).

TrendMicro. "Conficker/Downad 9 Years After: Examining Its Impact on Legacy Systems." Blog.trendmicro.com (December 7, 2017).

U.S. Department of Justice. "How to Protect Your Networks From Ransomware." (2016).

Vaughan-Nichols, Steven J. "FREAK: Another Day, Another Serious SSL Security Hole." Zdnet.com (March 3, 2015).

Vaughan-Nichols, Steven J. "Has the NSA Broken SSL? TLS? AES?" Zdnet.com (September 6, 2013).

Verizon. "2018 Data Breach Investigations Report." (2018).

Vincent, James. "Bitcoin Consumes More Energy Than Switzerland, According to New Estimate." Theverge.com (July 4, 2019).

Voreacos, David. "5 Hackers Charged in Largest Data Breach Scheme in U.S." Bloomberg.com (July 26, 2013).

Vuijsje, Eliana. "Top Five Malvertising Attacks of 2016." Blog.geoedge.com (December 19, 2016).

Wagner, Kurt. "Facebook's Business Model for Messenger Won't Be Payments and Commerce After All." Recode.net (April 11, 2017).

Wakabayashi, Daisuke. "A Contrite Sony Vows Tighter Security." *Wall Street Journal* (May 1, 2011).

Warren, Tom. "Microsoft Offers $250,000 Bounty to Prevent the Next Meltdown and Spectre CPU Flaws." Theverge.com (March 14, 2018).

Warren, Tom. "Microsoft Releases New Windows XP Security Patches, Warns of State-Sponsored Cyberattacks." Theverge.com (June 13, 2017).

Webroot. "2018 Webroot Threat Report." (2018).

Wills, Amanda. "New Snowden Leak: NSA Program Taps All You Do Online." Mashable.com (August 1, 2013).

Wingfield, Nick. "Spam Network Shut Down." *Wall Street Journal* (March 18, 2011).

Zarras, Apostolis, Alexander Kapravelos, Gianluca Stringhini, Thorsten Holz, Christopher Krugel, and Giovanni Vigna. "The Dark Alleys of Madison Avenue: Understanding Malicious Advertisements." ICM '14 Vancouver, BC, Canada (November 5–7, 2014).

Zurkus, Kacy. "Malvertising Campaign Delivers Millions of Bad Ads." Infosecurity-magazine.com (July 30, 2018).

CHAPTER 5

E-commerce Business Strategies

LEARNING OBJECTIVES

After reading this chapter, you will be able to:

- Identify the key components of e-commerce business models.
- Describe the major B2C business models.
- Describe the major B2B business models.
- Understand key business concepts and strategies applicable to e-commerce.

Australia's Canva Grows
from Startup to Super Unicorn

© dennizn/shutterstock

Creating your own business is a daunting proposition, but a host of companies have been seeking to democratize the process and make it easier for budding entrepreneurs. Social media platforms allow anyone to begin marketing themselves on a shoestring budget. Website creation services like Squarespace, Wix, and Weebly offer drag-and-drop, template-based solutions for business owners without the requisite experience in website design. Now, Australian-based Canva is seeking to do the same with graphic design, which until now has required expertise in complicated software. The user-base for Canva's drag-and-drop online platform is growing like wildfire as people with no graphic design experience at all discover that they, too, can make professional looking designs of every type, from business cards, to presentations, to high school yearbooks, and everything in between.

In 2007, Canva's founders, Melanie Perkins and her now-fiancé Cliff Obrecht, began their journey with the launch of Fusion Books, a company specifically focused on high school yearbooks in their native Australia. Headquartered in Perth, Fusion was a web-based platform that allowed schools to design yearbooks online. Perkins had been an instructor at the University of Western Australia, teaching students how to use software like Adobe InDesign and Photoshop, when she realized that there had to be a better way. She began working on the idea of a web-based design platform from her family home, and eventually she and Obrecht took out a loan to hire technical help to build it. Soon, over 400 Australian schools began to use Fusion Books to create their yearbooks. Despite the company's success, Perkins had a bigger vision for the company than her budget could support. However, acquiring venture capital as an Australian tech startup nowhere near Silicon Valley proved difficult. Perkins reported that for every time her pitches received interest, they were rejected hundreds of times more.

Fast forward to the present day, and Canva has raised over $241 million over 11 total rounds of funding, including an $85 million round in October 2019 from industry giants such as Sequoia China, General Catalyst, and Bessemer Venture Partners, and the company is now valued at $3.2 billion dollars, well beyond the elusive billion-dollar "unicorn" status that few startups ever achieve. Perkins and Obrecht's 15% stakes in the company are now worth well over $430 million. Canva has been profitable by EBITDA (earnings before interest, tax, depreciation and amortization, a metric often used for startup companies to assess their finances) since 2017, and the company's revenue, which doubled in 2019 to $200 million, is expected to double once again in 2020.

Meeting investor Bill Tai was a turning point for Perkins. Although Tai helped by introducing Canva's founders to his wide network of potential venture capitalists, he also challenged Canva to hire only the highest-level engineers they could find. He also introduced them to Lars Rasmussen, the founder of Google Maps, who vetted their potential engineering hires, finding most to be lacking, and helped advise them on how to build a strong group of engineers. The company patiently waited a full year to make any technical hires. Eventually, Perkins and Obrecht met Cameron Adams, a highly respected former Google employee who had founded another startup in Sydney. After convincing him to join Canva as a co-founder and chief product officer, both talented engineers and venture capital became much easier to acquire, and after assembling their initial engineering team in 2012, Canva officially launched in 2013.

Canva has a tiered business model, offering a freemium product to the vast majority of its users, but also a professional product with significantly more features and an enterprise version for businesses. Although converting freemium users to paying customers is a challenge for any startup, Canva has some advantages in that regard. Because customers are often used to paying premium prices for similar products from Adobe and other established software companies, Canva's user base is more apt to convert to paying customers than users of other freemium services. It's also exactly the right time for a business like Canva: businesses have never been more interested in creating and maintaining an elegant, well-designed online presence. Although Canva's 2013 launch proceeded with minimal fanfare, over 50,000 users signed up in its first month of operation, and quickly grew to 600,000 users who made a total of 3.5 million designs in 2014. In 2019, Canva has over 20 million users from 190 countries using the company's freemium version alone.

But it's not just the price that compares favorably to other offerings in this market; Canva's primary selling point is its ease of use. Gone are the days when you would need to take a class like the one Perkins once taught to achieve your graphic design goals. Canva's mission is to allow customers with no design experience at all to create material of any type that looks like it was made by a professional. For most, the freemium version is sufficient, but Canva has generated plenty of interest in its paid versions. Canva's professional version costs $10 per month, a significant saving over the cost of Adobe's product line. Canva's enterprise version is now used by 85% of Fortune 500 companies, who value the ability to maintain more consistent marketing and branding materials across the organization. Canva allows organizations to manage which approved brand assets, fonts, and colors are used by various companies. With Canva, the days when a company used several different logos because employees can't agree or locate a standard version are over.

Canva also sells access to a growing array of stock photos, which can be purchased either for one-time use for $1 or lifetime use for $20. In 2019, Canva acquired stock photo

SOURCES: "Making Money, Making History: The Biggest Capital Raises of 2019," by Priscilla Pho, Smartcompany.com.au, December 17, 2019; "Canva Uncovered: How a Young Australian Kitesurfer Built a $3.2 Billion (Profitable!) Startup Phenom," by Alex Konrad, Forbes.com, December 11, 2019; "Canva Partners with Facebook and Google," by Paige Murphy, Adnews.com.au, December 9, 2019; "Canva Co-founder on the Changing Face of Communica-

providers Pexels and Pixabay and launched a new service, Photos Unlimited, which will cost $12.95 per month or $120 per year for unlimited access to the Canva's full array of stock photos. Other features that Canva currently offers or has announced plans to launch include Canva for Education, a partnership with schools in Australia to provide versions of Canva for student use; Canva Apps, a service allowing developers to build tools that integrate with the Canva platform, which companies like Dropbox, Google Drive, and Instagram have done; and Canva Video, a video editing service expected to launch in 2020 that uses the same drag-and-drop principles that Canva hopes will revolutionize video editing the way its flagship service is poised to revolutionize static graphic design.

Although Canva is based in Australia and also boasts a large user base in the U.S., the company has grown rapidly worldwide, including in markets that have been difficult historically for many companies to find success, such as China. Canva hired the former head of LinkedIn China to build an office there, and the company developed a China-specific version of its product that uses QR codes, which are popular in China, as well as strong integration with Chinese messaging apps like WeChat. Canva also developed Arabic and Hebrew versions, which are challenging due to complex typography and an interface that reflects the right-to-left orientation of those languages. Perkins has described the company's goals to expand into India and Brazil as well.

Canva's pathway is not without challenges. Firstly, Adobe is not about to quietly allow Canva to become a powerhouse in its own market. Adobe released its own freemium product called Adobe Spark and the company reported in 2019 that it had given out 23 million Spark accounts to teachers and students worldwide. Canva has also experienced growing pains; the company that took a full year to hire an engineer has grown rapidly to over 700 employees, and each time it hires a new batch of employees, the company's back-end infrastructure is tested, and often needs to be redesigned. Canva recently rewrote the entire front-end interface of its flagship web app, for example. Lastly, in May 2019, Canva experienced a data breach that exposed 139 million usernames and e-mails. Although users' passwords were encrypted and no credit card information was accessed in the attack, the incident was a wake-up call for the company, which now uses two-factor authentication to protect user data.

Canva's user base remained supportive throughout the hacking incident, and indeed Canva's customers are devoted to the service, creating 130 million different designs each month. Canva can be used to create e-mail marketing, infographics, Instagram stories, social media posts, and much more. Perkins believes that Canva is currently achieving about 1% of what she believes the company will be in the future, and that empowering people everywhere to design anything they can imagine is a business model built to last.

tions," by Edward Pollitt, Bandt.com.au, December 9, 2019; "Canva Introduces Video Editing, Has Big Plans for 2020," by Jordan Crook, Techcrunch.com, December 6, 2019; "Profiling Canva: One of the Most Successful Female-Led Tech Companies in the World," by Chiradeep BasuMallick, Martechadvisor.com, November 27, 2019; "It Took Canva a Year to Make Its First Technical Hire. Now It's a Hiring Machine," by Kimberly Weisul, Inc.com, November 27, 2019; "Valued at $3.2 Billion, Canva is Ready to Design a New Future and End 'Death by Power-Point,'" by Alyssa Newcomber, Fortune.com, November 26, 2019; "Design from Down Under: One-on-One with the CEO of Canva," by Jonathan Kim and Jon Fortt, Cnbc.com, November 8, 2019; "Canva Has Partnered with U.S. Marketing Platform HubSpot to Make Designing and Distributing Images Easier," by Sharon Masige, Businessinsider.com.au, November 4, 2018; "Australian Unicorn Canva Targets China, India, and Brazil," by Kristie Neo, Asia.nikkei.com, August 30, 2019; "Billion Dollar Design: Canva's Melanie Perkins on How She Turned Her 'Future of Publishing' Idea into a Unicorn," by Pooja Singh, Entrepreneur.com, August 5, 2019; "Nearly 140 Million User Data Leaked in Canva Hack," Cisomag.com, May 28, 2019; "Australia's Design Unicorn, Canva, Picks up Two Free Image-Sharing Services, and Launches New Photo Product," by Jonathan Shieber, Techcrunch.com, May 17, 2019; "Canva Cofounder and CEO Melanie Perkins Leads Her Unicorn," by Kathy Caprino, Forbes.com, April 5, 2019 "Australia's Canva Has Become a Unicorn by Bringing Online Design Tools to the Masses," by Jay Kim, Forbes.com, February 14, 2019.

The opening case on Canva illustrates the process of turning a good business idea into a successful business model that produces profits.

Thousands of firms have discovered that they can spend other people's invested capital much faster than they can get customers to pay for their products or services. In most instances of failure, the business model of the firm is faulty from the beginning. In contrast, successful e-commerce firms have business models that are able to leverage the unique qualities of the Internet, the Web, and the mobile platform, provide customers real value, develop highly effective and efficient operations, avoid legal and social entanglements that can harm the firm, and produce profitable business results. In addition, successful business models must scale. The business must be able to achieve efficiencies as it grows in volume. But what is a business model, and how can you tell if a firm's business model is going to produce a profit?

In this chapter, we focus on business models and basic business concepts that you must be familiar with in order to understand e-commerce.

5.1 E-COMMERCE BUSINESS MODELS

INTRODUCTION

business model
a set of planned activities designed to result in a profit in a marketplace

business plan
a document that describes a firm's business model

e-commerce business model
a business model that aims to use and leverage the unique qualities of the Internet, the Web, and the mobile platform

A **business model** is a set of planned activities (sometimes referred to as *business processes*) designed to result in a profit in a marketplace. A business model is not always the same as a business strategy, although in some cases they are very close insofar as the business model explicitly takes into account the competitive environment (Magretta, 2002). The business model is at the center of the business plan. A **business plan** is a document that describes a firm's business model. A business plan always takes into account the competitive environment. An **e-commerce business model** aims to use and leverage the unique qualities of the Internet, the Web, and the mobile platform.

EIGHT KEY ELEMENTS OF A BUSINESS MODEL

If you hope to develop a successful business model in any arena, not just e-commerce, you must make sure that the model effectively addresses the eight elements listed in **Figure 5.1**. These elements are value proposition, revenue model, market opportunity, competitive environment, competitive advantage, market strategy, organizational development, and management team. Many writers focus on a firm's value proposition and revenue model. While these may be the most important and most easily identifiable aspects of a company's business model, the other elements are equally important when evaluating business models and plans, or when attempting to understand why a particular company has succeeded or failed (Kim and Mauborgne, 2000). In the following sections, we describe each of the key business model elements more fully.

value proposition
defines how a company's product or service fulfills the needs of customers

Value Proposition

A company's value proposition is at the very heart of its business model. A **value proposition** defines how a company's product or service fulfills the needs of customers (Kambil,

FIGURE 5.1 THE EIGHT KEY ELEMENTS OF A BUSINESS MODEL

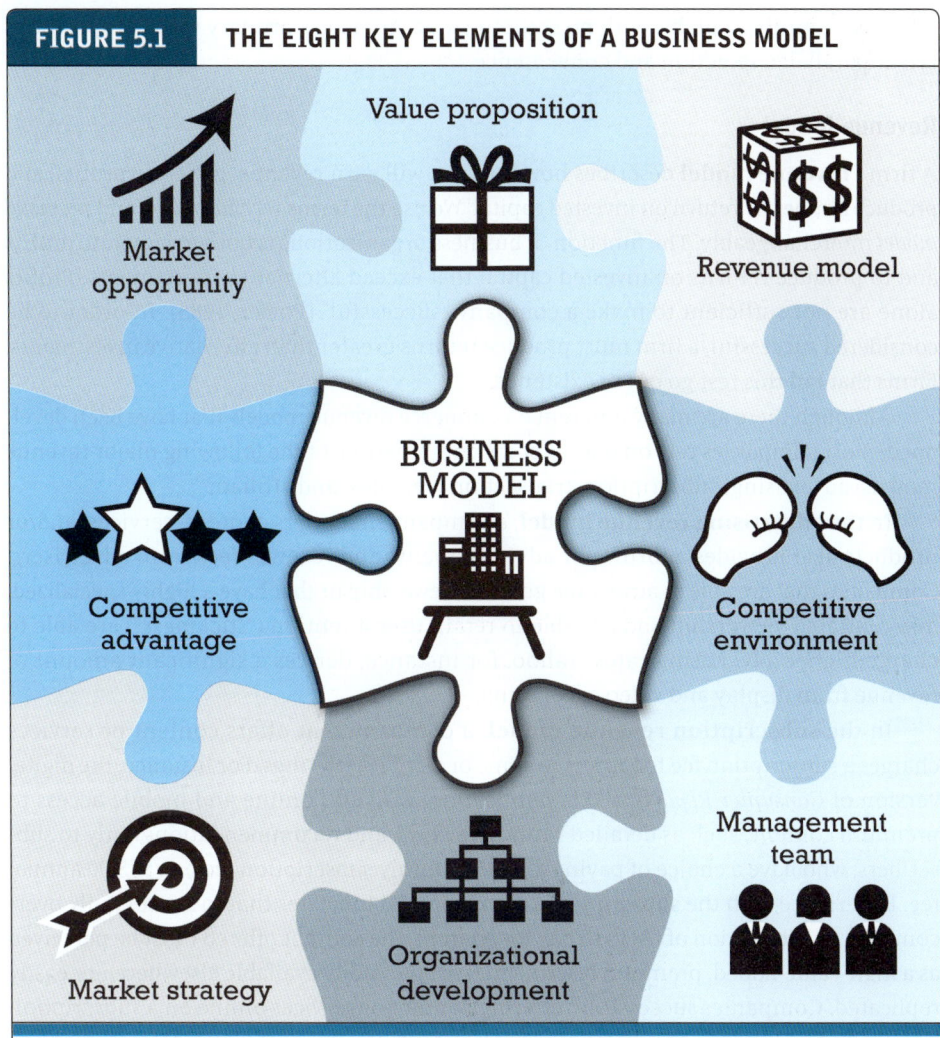

A business model has eight key elements. Each element must be addressed if you hope to be successful.

Ginsberg, and Bloch, 1998). To develop and/or analyze a firm's value proposition, you need to understand why customers will choose to do business with the firm instead of another company and what the firm provides that other firms do not and cannot. From the consumer point of view, successful e-commerce value propositions include personalization and customization of product offerings, reduction of product search costs, reduction of price discovery costs, and facilitation of transactions by managing product delivery.

For instance, before Amazon existed, most customers personally traveled to book retailers to place an order. In some cases, the desired book might not be available, and the customer would have to wait several days or weeks, and then return to the bookstore to pick it up. Amazon makes it possible for book lovers to shop for virtually any book in print from the comfort of their home or office, 24 hours a day, and to know immediately whether a book is in stock. Amazon's Kindle takes this one step further by making e-books instantly available with no shipping wait. Amazon's primary value propositions are unparalleled selection and convenience.

Revenue Model

A firm's **revenue model** describes how the firm will earn revenue, generate profits, and produce a superior return on invested capital. We use the terms *revenue model* and *financial model* interchangeably. The function of business organizations is both to generate profits and to produce returns on invested capital that exceed alternative investments. Profits alone are not sufficient to make a company "successful" (Porter, 1985). In order to be considered successful, a firm must produce returns greater than alternative investments. Firms that fail this test go out of existence.

Although there are many different e-commerce revenue models that have been developed, most companies rely on one, or some combination, of the following major revenue models: advertising, subscription, transaction fee, sales, and affiliate.

In the **advertising revenue model**, a company that offers content, services, and/or products also provides a forum for advertisements and receives fees from advertisers. Companies that are able to attract the greatest viewership or that have a highly specialized, differentiated viewership and are able to retain user attention ("stickiness") are able to charge higher advertising rates. Yahoo, for instance, derives a significant amount of revenue from display and video advertising.

In the **subscription revenue model**, a company that offers content or services charges a subscription fee for access to some or all of its offerings. For instance, the digital version of *Consumer Reports*, a U.S. publication, provides online and mobile access to premium content, such as detailed ratings, reviews, and recommendations, only to subscribers, who have a choice of paying a $6.95 monthly subscription fee or a $35.00 annual fee. Experience with the subscription revenue model indicates that to successfully overcome the disinclination of users to pay for content, the content offered must be perceived as a high-value-added, premium offering that is not readily available elsewhere nor easily replicated. Companies successfully offering content or services online on a subscription basis include eHarmony (dating services), Ancestry (genealogy research), Microsoft's Xbox Live (video games), Pandora, Spotify, and Apple Music (music), Scribd and Amazon's Kindle Unlimited program (e-books), and Netflix and Hulu (television and movies). See **Table 5.1** for examples of various subscription services.

Recently, a number of companies have been combining a subscription revenue model with a freemium strategy. In a **freemium strategy**, the companies give away a certain level of product or services for free, but then charge a subscription fee for premium levels of the product or service.

In the **transaction fee revenue model**, a company receives a fee for enabling or executing a transaction. For example, eBay provides an auction marketplace and receives a small transaction fee from a seller if the seller is successful in selling the item. E*Trade, a financial services provider, receives transaction fees each time it executes a stock transaction on behalf of a customer.

In the **sales revenue model**, companies derive revenue by selling goods, content, or services to customers. Companies such as Amazon, Asos, and Mothercare all have sales

---

revenue model
describes how the firm will earn revenue, produce profits, and produce a superior return on invested capital

advertising revenue model
a company provides a forum for advertisements and receives fees from advertisers

subscription revenue model
a company offers its users content or services and charges a subscription fee for access to some or all of its offerings

freemium strategy
companies give away a certain level of product or services for free, but then charge a subscription fee for premium levels of the product or service

transaction fee revenue model
a company receives a fee for enabling or executing a transaction

sales revenue model
a company derives revenue by selling goods, information, or services

TABLE 5.1	EXAMPLES OF SUBSCRIPTION SERVICES
NAME	DESCRIPTION
eHarmony.co.uk (dating)	• Free: Create profile and view profiles of matches • Basic (see photos, send and receive messages): £18.95 a month for 6 months; £9.95 a month for 1 year • Total Connect (Basic plus additional services): £19.95 a month for 6 months; £12.95 a month for 1 year
Ancestry.co.uk (genealogical research)	• Essentials (key UK census records only): £10.99 for 1 month; £54.99 for 6 months • Premium (all UK and Ireland records): £13.99 for 1 month; £69.99 for 6 months • Worldwide (UK, Ireland and all international records): £19.99 for 1 month; £99.99 for 6 months
Kindle Unlimited UK	• Unlimited books for £7.99/month (over 1 million books from which to choose)
Spotify (music)	• Many different permutations, depending on device (mobile, tablet, or desktop) and plan chosen (Free, Unlimited, or Premium)

revenue models. A number of companies are also using a subscription-based sales revenue model. Birchbox, which offers home delivery of beauty products for £10 per month or £110 per year plus £2.95 p&p/month, is one example. Dollar Shave Club, which sells razor blades by subscription and was acquired by Unilever for $1 billion, is another. See the case study at the end of the chapter for a further look at Dollar Shave Club.

In the **affiliate revenue model**, companies that steer business to an "affiliate" receive a referral fee or percentage of the revenue from any resulting sales. For example, MyPoints makes money by connecting companies with potential customers by offering special deals to its members. When they take advantage of an offer and make a purchase, members earn "points" they can redeem for freebies, and MyPoints receives a fee. Community feedback companies typically receive some of their revenue from steering potential customers to websites where they make a purchase.

Table 5.2 on page 332 summarizes these major revenue models. The *Insight on Society* case, *MADE.com: Furniture for the Crowd*, examines MADE.COM's use of social communities and social networks to drive its business model.

Market Opportunity

The term **market opportunity** refers to the company's intended **marketspace** (i.e., an area of actual or potential commercial value) and the overall potential financial opportunities available to the firm in that marketspace. The market opportunity is usually divided into smaller market niches. The realistic market opportunity is defined by the revenue potential in each of the market niches where you hope to compete.

affiliate revenue model
a company steers business to an affiliate and receives a referral fee or percentage of the revenue from any resulting sales

market opportunity
refers to the company's intended marketspace and the overall potential financial opportunities available to the firm in that marketspace

marketspace
the area of actual or potential commercial value in which a company intends to operate

INSIGHT ON SOCIETY

MADE.COM: FURNITURE FOR THE CROWD

In 2010, Ning Li, Brent Hoberman, and Julien Callede launched MADE.COM in the United Kingdom with a modest investment of £2.5 million. Ning's idea was to cut out the middleman in the supply chain and halve the price of contemporary designer furniture by selling directly to the customer. Entrepreneur Brent Hoberman not only saw an investment opportunity but also the potential for an innovative online brand, one that could shift the focus of retailing by putting customers in control and allowing them to influence the product design. He called this metailing—transforming shoppers into a community of designers. Even the funding for its new products came from crowdsourcing. MADE.COM has since built a network of experimental showrooms around Europe and launched MADE Unboxed, a social community with its own social network.

The company's innovative approach has been successful in disrupting the supply chain in the furniture industry across Europe. The last time the industry saw a change this significant was over 50 years ago, when IKEA transformed the way people shopped for furniture. The Swedish giant established its unique market position by selling highly functional furniture at relatively low prices, with customers making their purchases at large out-of-town warehouses. MADE.COM is now challenging this with its own innovative approach to selling online and in-store.

MADE.COM has emerged as a highly differentiated customer-centric brand that has built competitive advantage by focusing on its customers and building relationships with all of its stakeholders. Using a business model that enables collaboration with independent designers, technology startups, and customers ensures that the brand always manages to be relevant and fresh. The model has enabled the company to build innovative teams capable of being highly responsive to new trends much more rapidly than larger high-street rivals.

MADE.COM's success was based on exploiting a market opportunity: selling directly from manufacturer to consumer and involving customers in the design production processes. To accomplish this on a large scale, in 2017 the company set up TalentLAB, a digital platform that allows designers, both new and established, to upload their ideas, which are then shortlisted by the MADE.COM team. But the brand takes the principles of crowdfunding still further. When the designers share their ideas through TalentLAB, customers place a deposit on a design they like. The designs that are chosen most get manufactured, and refunds are given to customers whose choices didn't make the cut.

Through its social community of customers, MADE.COM can identify new trends, fuel continuous innovation in furniture design, as well as add value to its offer. The company regularly launches new ranges and can stop producing items as soon as it detects their popularity fading. Social commerce enables MADE's Unboxed community to build confidence and loyalty among its online shoppers, and these customers become brand advocates and influencers.

MADE.COM's social community business model may be a unique value proposition, but this is not the only factor behind its success. Another important facet of the brand's online business model is the social media community it has leveraged to reinforce that value proposition—MADE Unboxed has enabled the brand to extend its reach without having to employ an advertising agency. This online community was started when co-founder Julien Callede, who was looking for a way to display the online company's products in a physical setting, introduced the idea of asking customers to take photographs of the products in their own homes and share them online. Displaying the furniture in a natural setting proved popular and boosted enthusiasm about the furniture items; it also provided free online advertising on social media and helped to build strong relationships with customers, who liked being a part of a growing community of furniture buyers and designers. The communications team were also early adopters of shoppable Instagram stories, which allowed MADE.COM to tune into the 90 million people in the United Kingdom who click on tags in buyable posts every month.

Collaboration at MADE.COM doesn't stop at MADE Unboxed. MADE Labs, a technology innovation lab based in Shoreditch, London, provides space for innovative start-up businesses to work on creating better shopping experiences. It has reported several successful collaborations so far. Companies working in the technology labs are closely linked across the business to enable rapid decision-making over adoption and implementation. One example of a collaboration is the tech startup Hulabalook, which developed an online tool for the many customers who find it difficult to visualize how a piece of furniture might fit in their homes. Called the Sofasizer, the tool helps shoppers find the perfect-sized sofa—this not only increases customer satisfaction but also reduces the number of costly returns.

MADE.COM and French start-up Hubstairs have built a community of over 300 interior designers to offer an AI-driven tailored design service. MADE customers can upload their design ideas, colors, and room dimensions to the Hubstairs design platform, and for £89, they get a bespoke design service. Customers tell the Hubstairs team the styles they like and upload photographs of the rooms they want to change. They are provided with personalized 3D computer-generated photographic layouts to help visualize how a furnished room might turn out, and the AI recommends suitable products to fit the new design. This integration of human and AI input costs much less than more traditional face-to-face design services.

Another company that collaborates with MADE.COM is Go Instore, which helps connect customers around the world with physical showrooms using a one-way video link combined with two-way audio. Customers can thus see the products online and ask for advice in real time from in-store staff at showrooms in London, Paris, Amsterdam, Berlin, Birmingham, and Redbrick (West Yorkshire). There are plans to spread this technology further across Europe in 2020.

The online retailer is rapidly becoming a highly profitable dot.com, expanding throughout Europe and earning higher revenues year-on-year. In 2018, the revenue increased was up by 37% to £173 million, £100 million of which came from sales in the United Kingdom. But MADE.COM is still looking forward to more innovations in the online furniture industry. According to Chief Technology Officer Jonathan Howell, by 2022, the average age profile of shoppers will be younger and dominated by Millennials, a target market MADE.COM is eager to comprehend. MADE.COM is a brand tailor-made for a growing market of digital natives for whom online purchasing is entirely conventional. It must continue to find new ways to be relevant and innovative for a new generation of "me-tail" shoppers.

■ **SOURCES:** "Affordable Interior Design Service," Made.com; "MADE.COM Aims to Halve Designer Furniture Prices," by Richard Wray, Theguardian.com, March 22, 2010; "Made Launches Tech Innovation Lab," by Paul Farley, Furniturenews.net, April 17, 2019; "Instagram Stories Rolls Out In-app Shopping Globally," by Rebecca Stewart, *The Drum*, September 17, 2018; "MADE.COM Founder: We Want to Be the New Ikea," by Anne Cassidy, Theguardian.com, September 18, 2017; "MADE.COM—Unique Business Model," Consumervaluecreation.com, February 18, 2018; "MADE.COM on the Value of Social Commerce," by Ben Davis, Econsultancy.com, April 22, 2016; "Brent Hoberman Uses His Experience to Support New UK Businesses," by Andrew Cave, *The Telegraph*, March 27, 2010; "TalentLAB," Made.com; "MADE.COM Launches 'MADE Labs' Tech Innovation Team," by Fiona Briggs, *Retail News*, April 17, 2019; "MADE.COM—Carving Out a Distinctive Furniture Business Model," Abaresearch.co.uk, March 22, 2017; "Unboxed Lets You See MADE.COM Products in Real Homes," by Ruby Munson-Hirst, Wired.com, July 23, 2014; "We're Doing It Ourselves: Why MADE.COM Doesn't Need an Ad Agency," by Rebecca Stewart, *The Drum*, February 22, 2019.

Case contributed by Fiona Ellis-Chadwick, Loughborough University

TABLE 5.2 — FIVE PRIMARY REVENUE MODELS

REVENUE MODEL	EXAMPLES	REVENUE SOURCE
Advertising	Yahoo Facebook	Fees from advertisers in exchange for advertisements
Subscription	eHarmony The Economist Netflix	Fees from subscribers in exchange for access to content or services
Transaction Fee	eBay E*Trade	Fees (commissions) for enabling or executing a transaction
Sales	Amazon Asos Birchbox iTunes	Sales of goods, information, or services
Affiliate	MyPoints	Fees for business referrals

For instance, let's assume you are analyzing a software training company that creates online software-learning systems for sale to U.S. businesses. The overall size of the software training market for all market segments is approximately $70 billion. The overall market can be broken down, however, into two major market segments: instructor-led training products, which comprise about 70% of the market ($49 billion in revenue), and online training, which accounts for 30% ($21 billion). There are further market niches within each of those major market segments, such as the Fortune 500 online training market and the small business online training market. Because the firm is a start-up firm, it cannot compete effectively in the large business online training market (about $15 billion). Large brand-name training firms dominate this niche. The start-up firm's real market opportunity is to sell to the thousands of small business firms that spend about $6 billion on online software training. This is the size of the firm's realistic market opportunity (see **Figure 5.2**).

Competitive Environment

A firm's **competitive environment** refers to the other companies selling similar products and operating in the same marketspace. It also refers to the presence of substitute products and potential new entrants to the market, as well as the power of customers and suppliers over your business. We discuss the firm's environment later in the chapter. The competitive environment for a company is influenced by several factors: how many competitors are active, how large their operations are, what the market share of each competitor is, how profitable these firms are, and how they price their products.

Firms typically have both direct and indirect competitors. Direct competitors are companies that sell very similar products and services into the same market segment. For example, Priceline and Travelocity, both of whom sell discount airline tickets online, are direct competitors because both companies sell identical products—cheap tickets.

competitive environment
refers to the other companies operating in the same marketspace selling similar products

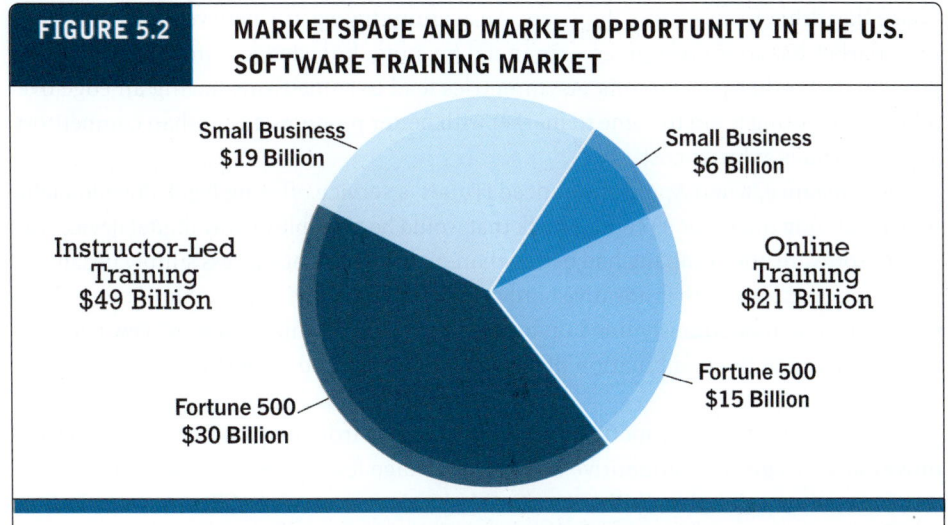

FIGURE 5.2 MARKETSPACE AND MARKET OPPORTUNITY IN THE U.S. SOFTWARE TRAINING MARKET

Marketspaces are composed of many market segments. Your realistic market opportunity will typically focus on one or a few market segments.

Indirect competitors are companies that may be in different industries but still compete indirectly because their products can substitute for one another. For instance, automobile manufacturers and airline companies operate in different industries, but they still compete indirectly because they offer consumers alternative means of transportation. CNN, a news outlet, is an indirect competitor of ESPN, not because they sell identical products, but because they both compete for consumers' time online.

The existence of a large number of competitors in any one segment may be a sign that the market is saturated and that it may be difficult to become profitable. On the other hand, a lack of competitors could signal either an untapped market niche ripe for the picking, or a market that has already been tried without success because there is no money to be made. Analysis of the competitive environment can help you decide which it is.

Competitive Advantage

Firms achieve a **competitive advantage** when they can produce a superior product and/or bring the product to market at a lower price than most, or all, of their competitors (Porter, 1985). Firms also compete on scope. Some firms can develop global markets, while other firms can develop only a national or regional market. Firms that can provide superior products at the lowest cost on a global basis are truly advantaged.

Firms achieve competitive advantages because they have somehow been able to obtain differential access to the factors of production that are denied to their competitors—at least in the short term (Barney, 1991). Perhaps the firm has been able to obtain very favorable terms from suppliers, shippers, or sources of labor. Or perhaps the firm has more experienced, knowledgeable, and loyal employees than any competitors. Maybe the firm has a patent on a product that others cannot imitate, or access to investment capital through a network of former business colleagues or a brand name and popular

competitive advantage
achieved by a firm when it can produce a superior product and/or bring the product to market at a lower price than most, or all, of its competitors

asymmetry
exists whenever one participant in a market has more resources than other participants

first-mover advantage
a competitive market advantage for a firm that results from being the first into a marketplace with a serviceable product or service

complementary resources
resources and assets not directly involved in the production of the product but required for success, such as marketing, management, financial assets, and reputation

unfair competitive advantage
occurs when one firm develops an advantage based on a factor that other firms cannot purchase

perfect market
a market in which there are no competitive advantages or asymmetries because all firms have equal access to all the factors of production

leverage
when a company uses its competitive advantages to achieve more advantage in surrounding markets

image that other firms cannot duplicate. An **asymmetry** exists whenever one participant in a market has more resources—financial backing, knowledge, information, and/or power—than other participants. Asymmetries lead to some firms having an edge over others, permitting them to come to market with better products, faster than competitors, and sometimes at lower cost.

For instance, when Apple announced iTunes, a service offering legal, downloadable individual song tracks for 99 cents a track that would be playable on any digital device with iTunes software, the company had better-than-average odds of success simply because of Apple's prior success with innovative hardware designs, and the large stable of music firms that Apple had meticulously lined up to support its online music catalog. Few competitors could match the combination of cheap, legal songs and powerful hardware to play them on.

One rather unique competitive advantage derives from being a first mover. A **first-mover advantage** is a competitive market advantage for a firm that results from being the first into a marketplace with a serviceable product or service. If first movers develop a loyal following or a unique interface that is difficult to imitate, they can sustain their first-mover advantage for long periods (Arthur, 1996). Amazon provides a good example. However, in the history of technology-driven business innovation, most first movers often lack the **complementary resources** needed to sustain their advantages, and often follower firms reap the largest rewards (Rigdon, 2000; Teece, 1986). Indeed, many of the success stories we discuss in this book are those of companies that were slow followers—businesses that gained knowledge from the failure of pioneering firms and entered into the market late.

Some competitive advantages are called "unfair." An **unfair competitive advantage** occurs when one firm develops an advantage based on a factor that other firms cannot purchase (Barney, 1991). For instance, a brand name cannot be purchased and is in that sense an "unfair" advantage. Brands are built upon loyalty, trust, reliability, and quality. Once obtained, they are difficult to copy or imitate, and they permit firms to charge premium prices for their products.

In **perfect markets**, there are no competitive advantages or asymmetries because all firms have access to all the factors of production (including information and knowledge) equally. However, real markets are imperfect, and asymmetries leading to competitive advantages do exist, at least in the short term. Most competitive advantages are short term, although some can be sustained for very long periods. But not forever. In fact, many respected brands fail every year.

Companies are said to **leverage** their competitive assets when they use their competitive advantages to achieve more advantage in surrounding markets. For instance, Amazon's move into the online grocery business leverages the company's huge customer database and years of e-commerce experience.

Market Strategy

No matter how tremendous a firm's qualities, its marketing strategy and execution are often just as important. The best business concept, or idea, will fail if it is not properly marketed to potential customers.

Everything you do to promote your company's products and services to potential customers is known as marketing. **Market strategy** is the plan you put together that details exactly how you intend to enter a new market and attract new customers.

For instance, Twitter, YouTube, and Pinterest have a social network marketing strategy that encourages users to post their content for free, build personal profile pages, contact their friends, and build a community. In these cases, the customer becomes part of the marketing staff!

market strategy
the plan you put together that details exactly how you intend to enter a new market and attract new customers

Organizational Development

Although many entrepreneurial ventures are started by one visionary individual, it is rare that one person alone can grow an idea into a multi-million dollar company. In most cases, fast-growth companies—especially e-commerce businesses—need employees and a set of business procedures. In short, all firms—new ones in particular—need an organization to efficiently implement their business plans and strategies. Many e-commerce firms and many traditional firms that attempt an e-commerce strategy have failed because they lacked the organizational structures and supportive cultural values required to support new forms of commerce (Kanter, 2001).

Companies that hope to grow and thrive need to have a plan for **organizational development** that describes how the company will organize the work that needs to be accomplished. Typically, work is divided into functional departments, such as production, shipping, marketing, customer support, and finance. Jobs within these functional areas are defined, and then recruitment begins for specific job titles and responsibilities. Typically, in the beginning, generalists who can perform multiple tasks are hired. As the company grows, recruiting becomes more specialized. For instance, at the outset, a business may have one marketing manager. But after two or three years of steady growth, that one marketing position may be broken down into seven separate jobs done by seven individuals.

organizational development
plan that describes how the company will organize the work that needs to be accomplished

For instance, according to some sources, Pierre Omidyar started eBay to help his girlfriend trade Pez dispensers with other collectors, but within a few months the volume of business had far exceeded what he alone could handle. So he began hiring people with more business experience to help out. Soon the company had many employees, departments, and managers who were responsible for overseeing the various aspects of the organization.

Management Team

Arguably, the single most important element of a business model is the **management team** responsible for making the model work. A strong management team gives a model instant credibility to outside investors, immediate market-specific knowledge, and experience in implementing business plans. A strong management team may not be able to salvage a weak business model, but the team should be able to change the model and redefine the business as it becomes necessary.

management team
employees of the company responsible for making the business model work

Eventually, most companies get to the point of having several senior executives or managers. How skilled managers are, however, can be a source of competitive advantage or disadvantage. The challenge is to find people who have both the experience and the ability to apply that experience to new situations.

To be able to identify good managers for a business start-up, first consider the kinds of experiences that would be helpful to a manager joining your company. What kind of technical background is desirable? What kind of supervisory experience is necessary? How many years in a particular function should be required? What job functions should be fulfilled first: marketing, production, finance, or operations? Especially in situations where financing will be needed to get a company off the ground, do prospective senior managers have experience and contacts for raising financing from outside investors?

Table 5.3 summarizes the eight key elements of a business model and the key questions that must be answered in order to successfully develop each element.

RAISING CAPITAL

Raising capital is one of the most important functions for a founder of a start-up business and its management team. Not having enough capital to operate effectively is a primary reason why so many start-up businesses fail. Many entrepreneurs initially "bootstrap" to get a business off the ground, using personal funds derived from savings, credit card advances, home equity loans, or from family and friends. Funds of this type are often referred to as **seed capital**. Once such funds are exhausted, if the company is not generating enough revenue to cover operating costs, additional capital will be needed. Traditional sources of capital include incubators, commercial banks, angel investors, venture capital firms, and strategic partners. One of the most important aspects of raising capital is the ability to boil down the elements of the company's business plan into an **elevator pitch**, a short two-to-three minute (about the length of an elevator ride, giving rise to its name) presentation aimed at convincing investors to invest. **Table 5.4** lists the key elements of an elevator pitch.

seed capital
typically, an entrepreneur's personal funds derived from savings, credit card advances, home equity loans, or from family and friends

elevator pitch
short two-to-three minute presentation aimed at convincing investors to invest

TABLE 5.3	KEY ELEMENTS OF A BUSINESS MODEL
COMPONENTS	KEY QUESTIONS
Value proposition	Why should the customer buy from you?
Revenue model	How will you earn money?
Market opportunity	What marketspace do you intend to serve, and what is its size?
Competitive environment	Who else occupies your intended marketspace?
Competitive advantage	What special advantages does your firm bring to the marketspace?
Market strategy	How do you plan to promote your products or services to attract your target audience?
Organizational development	What types of organizational structures within the firm are necessary to carry out the business plan?
Management team	What kinds of experiences and background are important for the company's leaders to have?

TABLE 5.4	KEY ELEMENTS OF AN ELEVATOR PITCH
ELEMENT	DESCRIPTION
Introduction	Your name and position; your company's name, and a tagline in which you compare what your company does to a well-known company. Example: "My name is X, I am the founder of Y, and we are the Uber/Amazon of Z."
Background	The origin of your idea and the problem you are trying to solve.
Industry size/market opportunity	Brief facts about the (hopefully very large) size of the market.
Revenue model/numbers/growth metrics	Insight into your company's revenue model and results thus far, how fast it is growing, and early adopters, if there are any.
Funding	The amount of funds you are seeking and what it will help you achieve.
Exit strategy	How your investors will achieve a return on their investment.

Incubators (sometimes also referred to as accelerators) such as Rocket Internet (profiled in Chapter 1's *Insight on Business* case) typically provide a small amount of funding, but more importantly, also provide an array of services to start-up companies that they select to participate in their programs, such as business, technical, and marketing assistance, as well as introductions to other sources of capital. Well-known incubator programs include INiTS (Austria), Accelerace (Denmark), Numa (France), and SeedRocket (Spain).

Obtaining a loan from a commercial bank is often difficult for a start-up company without much revenue, but it may be worthwhile to investigate programs offered by the governmental agencies. The advantage of obtaining capital in the form of a loan (debt) is that, although it must be repaid, it does not require an entrepreneur to give up any ownership of the company.

Angel investors are typically wealthy individuals (or a group of individuals) who invest their own money in an exchange for an equity share in the stock in the business. In general, angel investors make smaller investments (typically $1 million or less) than venture capital firms, are interested in helping a company grow and succeed, and invest on relatively favorable terms compared to later-stage investors. The first round of external investment in a company is sometimes referred to as Series A financing.

Venture capital investors typically become more interested in a start-up company once it has begun attracting a large audience and generating some revenue, even if it is not profitable. **Venture capital investors** invest funds they manage for other investors such as investment banks, pension funds, insurance companies, or other businesses, and usually want to obtain a larger stake in the business and exercise more control over the operation of the business. Venture capital investors also typically want a well-defined "exit strategy," such as a plan for an initial public offering (IPO) or acquisition of the company

incubators
typically provide a small amount of funding and also an array of services to start-up companies

angel investors
typically wealthy individuals or a group of individuals who invest their own money in exchange for an equity share in the stock of a business; often are the first outside investors in a start-up

venture capital investors
typically invest funds they manage for other investors; usually later-stage investors

by a more established business within a relatively short period of time (typically 3 to 7 years), that will enable them to obtain an adequate return on their investment. Venture capital investment often ultimately means that the founder(s) and initial investors will no longer control the company at some point in the future.

Crowdfunding involves using the Internet to enable individuals to collectively contribute money to support a project. The concepts behind crowdfunding have been popularized by Kickstarter and Indiegogo, but they could not be used for equity investments in for-profit companies due to various laws and regulations. However, this is changing. For example, in the United States, the JOBS Act and associated regulations issued by the U.S. Securities and Exchange Commission has enabled companies to use the Internet to solicit investors to invest in small and early-stage startups in exchange for stock. In Europe, the European Commission has indicated an intention to support crowdfunding and in 2018 presented a proposal for regulation of crowdfunding service providers, which it believes will improve access to crowdfunding, as well as provide better protections for investors, including rules on information disclosure, governance, and risk management (European Commission, 2018). A new form of fundraising, using virtual currency such as Bitcoin, has also recently started to take root. Sometimes referred to as an initial coin offering (ICO), such offerings enable startups to raise capital without having to comply with securities regulations, and as such, present significant risk to investors (Aitken, 2017). See the Insight on Business case, *Crowdfunding Takes Off*, for a further look at the issues surrounding crowdfunding.

crowdfunding
involves using the Internet to enable individuals to collectively contribute money to support a project

CATEGORIZING E-COMMERCE BUSINESS MODELS: SOME DIFFICULTIES

There are many e-commerce business models, and more are being invented every day. The number of such models is limited only by the human imagination, and our list of different business models is certainly not exhaustive. However, despite the abundance of potential models, it is possible to identify the major generic types (and subtle variations) of business models that have been developed for the e-commerce arena and describe their key features. It is important to realize, however, that there is no one correct way to categorize these business models.

Our approach is to categorize business models according to the different major e-commerce sectors—B2C and B2B—in which they are utilized. You will note, however, that fundamentally similar business models may appear in more than one sector. For example, the business models of online retailers (often called e-tailers) and e-distributors are quite similar. However, they are distinguished by the market focus of the sector in which they are used. In the case of e-tailers in the B2C sector, the business model focuses on sales to the individual consumer, while in the case of the e-distributor, the business model focuses on sales to another business. Many companies use a variety of different business models as they attempt to extend into as many areas of e-commerce as possible. We look at B2C business models in Section 5.2 and B2B business models in Section 5.3.

A business's technology platform is sometimes confused with its business model. For instance, "mobile e-commerce" refers to the use of mobile devices and cellular and

INSIGHT ON BUSINESS

CROWDFUNDING TAKES OFF

Think you have the next big idea but lack the resources to make it happen? Crowdfunding sites might be your best shot. Sites such as Kickstarter, Indiegogo, and RocketHub have led the growth of crowdfunding. A World Bank study predicts that capital raised via crowdfunding will exceed around $93 billion by 2025. The Internet is the ideal medium for crowdfunding because it allows individuals and organizations in need of funds and potential backers to find one another around the globe. For instance, Kickstarter is available for projects in 14 European countries, as well as the United States, Canada, Mexico, Australia, New Zealand, Singapore, Hong Kong, and Japan. Indiegogo is also focusing on international growth, with campaigns having been started in 235 different countries and territories to date.

How do sites like Kickstarter and Indiegogo work? The idea is simple—an inventor, artist, or activist looking to raise money for a project uses the site to create a page for that project. The sites take a small commission, usually about 5%, on completed projects. Backers often receive some type of reward, often corresponding to the size of their contribution to the project.

Crowdfunding is becoming a mainstay in the development of movies, video games, art installations, and many other types of projects. For instance, in the United Kingdom, one of the top projects funded is a 3-D game called Yooka-Laylee, created by Playtonic Games, that raised almost £2.1 million from over 73,000 backers.

Successful crowdfunding projects typically share some common elements. One of the most important is a clear and concise presentation of the idea, especially through the use of video. The crowdfunding campaign is in many ways similar to presenting a business plan and should touch on the same eight elements of a business model, such as the project's value proposition and its target market.

Not every crowdfunding project gets off the ground—Kickstarter reports that only about 37.5% of its approximately 475,000 projects thus far have reached their funding goals. Sometimes projects that do get off the ground simply flame out, disappointing their backers. For instance, Europe's biggest Kickstarter project, for the development of the Zano, an autonomous, intelligent, swarming nano drone, went bankrupt before ever completing its product despite raising over £2.34 million from over 12,000 backers. Kickstarter now requires fundraisers to disclose the risks associated with their project and now also requires photos of prototype products (instead of simply drawings, simulations, or renderings) for inventions. Both Kickstarter and Indiegogo now offer project creators access to experts in design and manufacturing to help them better understand their costs and the feasibility of their products. But backers still have no real recourse with respect to projects that never get off the ground or unresponsive founders.

A new use of crowdfunding is to provide seed capital for startup companies in return for equity (shares) in the company, known as equity crowdfunding. The United States has been a global pioneer in the development of crowdfunding. Under the JOBS Act passed by the U.S. Congress in 2012, a company can crowdfund up to $1 million over a 12-month period, and in 2016, the rules requiring potential investors to be accredited (having a net worth of at least $1 million dollars) were relaxed to allow smaller investors to purchase equity stakes of $2,000 or more. A number of states in the United States have their own crowdfunding rules that allow local businesses

(continued)

to raise money in this way, and the 2016 regulations also fixed a loophole preventing these businesses from advertising to investors from outside their respective states. However, equity crowdfunding requires extensive compliance from businesses, with steep penalties for any irregularities, and potential investors are still subject to the usual risks involved in investing.

In Europe, the situation is more complicated. Although the European Commission has indicated an intention to support crowdfunding and in 2018 presented a proposal for regulation of crowdfunding service providers, which it believes will improve access to crowdfunding, as well as provide better protections for investors, currently national laws in countries throughout Europe vary widely, with the United Kingdom, Italy, and France each taking their own unique approaches. In the United Kingdom, crowdfunding is regulated by the Financial Conduct Authority (the FCA). Unlike in the United States, where legislation specifically enabling crowdfunding has been enacted, in the United Kingdom the FCA has relied on amending rules under the Financial Services and Markets Act 2000 to facilitate the development of crowdfunding. These rules went into effect in 2014. In December 2019, after the high-profile failure of Lindy, one P2P platform, the FCA implemented more stringent regulations designed to make sure consumers are better protected and that the P2P crowdfunding market is able to operate in a sustainable fashion. The three main UK crowdfunding platforms are Seedrs (the first platform to gain FCA approval), Crowdcube, and SyndicateRoom.

Italy was one of the first European countries to regulate equity crowdfunding in 2013, and since then it has updated those regulations several times to enlarge the category of companies that can be crowdfunded, simplify the regulatory framework, reduce the costs associated with crowdfunding, and expand the number of people able to invest. In France, companies are able to raise up to €1 million via equity crowdfunding without having to notify the French financial markets authority. Australia has also enacted legislation that allows businesses to raise funds through crowdfunding with less stringent disclosure and reporting requirements than its regular securities regulation. Singapore has also eased the regulatory requirements on crowdfunding platforms.

In Europe, much of the crowdfunding still takes the form of peer-to-peer lending rather than equity investment. Some of the leading companies in this area include Zopa, Ratesetter and Funding Circle. Funding Circle has facilitated loans to small businesses in the UK, Germany, the Netherlands, and the United States totalling more than $10 billion since its launch in 2010. Auxmoney is continental Europe's largest P2P lender and in 2018, it facilitated more than €500 million in consumer loans, up almost 75% from the previous year.

SOURCES: "Funding Circle Surpasses $10 Billion Lent to Small Businesses Globally," Fundingcircle.com, August 15, 2019; "Crowdfunding UK Small Business: Everything You Need to Know," by Rob Murray Brown, Growthbusiness.co.uk, July 18, 2019; "UK Tightens Rules on P2P Lenders," by Pymnts, Payments.com, June 4, 2019; "German Lending Marketplace auxomeny Overtakes Midsize Banks in Consumer Loan Origination," by Therese Torris, Crowdfunderinsider.com, February 13, 2019; Kickstarter.com, accessed January 28, 2020; Indiegogo.com, accessed January 28, 2020; "Yook-Laylee," Playtonicgames.com, accessed January 3, 2019; "Top 10 Crowdfunding Platforms for Business in 2018, by Michael Somerville, Growthbusiness.co.uk, November 30, 2018; "The 5th UK Alternative Finance Industry Report,' by Bryan Zhang et al., Cambridge Centre for Alternative Finace, University of Cambridge Judge Business School, November 2018; "While Still Comparatively Small, Italian Crowdfunding Market Experiencing Rapid Growth," by JD Alois, Crowdfundinsider.com, July 23, 2018; "Commission Proposal for a Regulation on European Crowdfunding Service Providers. Ec.europa.eu, March 8, 2018; "The Current State of Crowdfunding in France," Crowdfundinghub.eu, accessed January 3, 2018; "Crowdfunding Platforms Crack Down on Risky Campaigns,"by Mark Harris, Backchannel.com, May 18, 2017; "Regulation of Crowdfunding in Selected Places," Research Office Legislative Council Secretariat, Legco.gov.hk, July 21, 2017;"Crowdfunding in Europe." Europarl.europa.eu, January 2017; "New Crowdfunding Rules Let the Small Fry Swim with Sharks," by Stacy Cowley, *New York Times*, May 14, 2016; "New Rules for Equity Crowdfunding in Italy," by Grow VC Group, Growvc.com, March 2016; "Zano: The Rise and Fall of Kickstarter's Mini-Drone," by Rory Cellan-Jones, BBC.com, January 20, 2016; "S.E.C. Gives Small Investors Access to Equity Crowdfunding," by Stacy Cowley, *New York Times*, October 30, 2015; "World Bank: Crowdfunding Investment Market to Hit $93 Billion by 2025," by Richard Swart, PBS.org, December 10, 2013.

wide area networks to support a variety of business models. Commentators sometimes confuse matters by referring to mobile e-commerce as a distinct business model, which it is not. All of the basic business models we discuss below can be implemented on both the traditional Internet/Web and mobile platforms. Likewise, although they are sometimes referred to as such, social e-commerce and local e-commerce are not business models in and of themselves, but rather subsectors of B2C and B2B e-commerce in which different business models can operate.

You will also note that some companies use multiple business models. For instance, Amazon has multiple business models: it is an e-retailer, content provider, market creator, e-commerce infrastructure provider, and more. eBay is a market creator in the B2C and C2C e-commerce sectors, using both the traditional Internet/Web and mobile platforms, as well as an e-commerce infrastructure provider. Firms often seek out multiple business models as a way to leverage their brands, infrastructure investments, and assets developed with one business model into new business models.

Finally, no discussion of e-commerce business models would be complete without mention of a group of companies whose business model is focused on providing the infrastructure necessary for e-commerce companies to exist, grow, and prosper. These are the e-commerce enablers. They provide the hardware, operating system software, networks and communications technology, applications software, web design, consulting services, and other tools required for e-commerce (see **Table 5.5**). While these firms may not be conducting e-commerce per se (although in many instances, e-commerce in its traditional sense is in fact one of their sales channels), as a group they have perhaps profited the most from the development of e-commerce. We discuss many of these players in the following chapters.

5.2 MAJOR BUSINESS-TO-CONSUMER (B2C) BUSINESS MODELS

Business-to-consumer (B2C) e-commerce, in which online businesses seek to reach individual consumers, is the most well known and familiar type of e-commerce. **Table 5.6** on page 343 illustrates the major business models utilized in the B2C arena.

E-TAILER

Online retail stores, often called **e-tailers**, come in all sizes, from giant Amazon to tiny local stores. E-tailers are similar to the typical bricks-and-mortar storefront, except that customers only have to connect to the Internet or use their smartphone to place an order. Some e-tailers, which are referred to as "bricks-and-clicks," are subsidiaries or divisions of existing physical stores and carry the same products. In the United States, REI, JCPenney, Barnes & Noble, Walmart, and Staples are examples of companies with complementary online stores. Others, however, operate only in the virtual world, without any ties to physical locations. Amazon, Blue Nile, and Bluefly are examples of this type of e-tailer. Several other variations of e-tailers—such as online versions of direct mail catalogs, online malls, and manufacturer-direct online sales—also exist.

e-tailer
online retail store

TABLE 5.5	E-COMMERCE ENABLERS
INFRASTRUCTURE	**PLAYERS**
Hardware: Web Servers	HP • Dell • Lenovo
Software: Web Server Software	Microsoft • IBM • Red Hat Linux (Apache) • Oracle
Cloud Providers	Amazon Web Services • Microsoft Azure • IBM Cloud • Google Cloud Platform
Hosting Services	Liquid Web • WebIntellects • 1&1 • HostGator • Hostway
Domain Name Registration	GoDaddy • Network Solutions • Dotster
Content Delivery Networks	Akamai • Limelight Networks • Amazon CloudFront
Site Design	Weebly • Wix • Squarespace • Jimdo
Small/Medium Enterprise E-commerce Platforms	Shopify • BigCommerce • YoKart
Enterprise E-commerce Platforms	Magento • IBM • Oracle • Salesforce • SAP • Intershop
M-commerce Hardware Platforms	Apple • Samsung • LG
M-commerce Software Platforms	Mobify • PredictSpring • Usablenet • GPShopper
Streaming, Rich Media, Online Video	Adobe • Apple • Webcollage
Security and Encryption	VeriSign • Check Point • GeoTrust • Entrust Datacard • Thawte • Intel Security
Payment Systems	PayPal • Authorize.net • Chase Paymentech • Cybersource
Web Performance Management	Compuware • SmartBear • Dynatrace
Comparison Engine Feeds/Marketplace Management	ChannelAdvisor • CommerceHub • CPC Strategy
Customer Relationship Management	Oracle • SAP • Salesforce • Microsoft Dynamics
Order Management	JDA Software • Jagged Peak • Monsoon
Fulfillment	JDA Software • Jagged Peak • CommerceHub
Social Marketing	Buffer • HootSuite • SocialFlow
Search Engine Marketing	iProspect • ChannelAdvisor • Merkle
E-mail Marketing	Constant Contact • Cheetah Digital • Bronto Software • MailChimp
Affiliate Marketing	CJ Affiliate • Rakuten LinkShare
Customer Reviews and Forums	Bazaarvoice • PowerReviews • BizRate
Live Chat/Click-to-Call	LivePerson • Bold360 • Oracle
Web Analytics	Google Analytics • Adobe Analytics • IBM Digital Analytics • Webtrends

Given that the overall global retail market in 2019 was estimated to be around $25 trillion, the market opportunity for e-tailers is very large. Every Internet and smartphone user is a potential customer. Customers who feel time-starved are even better prospects, because they want shopping solutions that will eliminate the need to drive to the mall or store (Bellman, Lohse, and Johnson, 1999). The e-tail revenue model is product-based, with customers paying for the purchase of a particular item.

TABLE 5.6 B2C BUSINESS MODELS

BUSINESS MODEL	VARIATIONS	EXAMPLES	DESCRIPTION	REVENUE MODELS
E-tailer	Virtual Merchant	Amazon, Blue Nile, Bluefly	Online version of retail store, where customers can shop at any hour of the day or night without leaving their home or office	Sales of goods
	Bricks-and-Clicks	Walmart, Target	Online distribution channel for a company that also has physical stores	Sales of goods
	Catalog Merchant	L.L.Bean, LillianVernon	Online version of direct mail catalog	Sales of goods
	Manufacturer-Direct	Dell, Mattel, Nike	Manufacturer uses online channel to sell direct to customer	Sales of goods
Community Provider		Facebook, LinkedIn, Twitter, Pinterest	Sites where individuals with particular interests, hobbies, common experiences, or social networks can come together and "meet" online	Advertising, subscription, affiliate referral fees
Content Provider		Wall Street Journal, Netflix, Apple Music	Offers customers newspapers, magazines, books, film, television, music, games, and other forms of online content	Advertising, subscription fees, sales of digital goods
Portal	Horizontal/General	Yahoo, AOL, MSN, Facebook	Offers an integrated package of content, search, and social network services: news, e-mail, chat, music downloads, video streaming, calendars, etc. Seeks to be a user's home base	Advertising, subscription fees, transaction fees
	Vertical/Specialized (Vortal)	Sailnet	Focuses on a particular subject matter or market segment	Advertising, subscription fees, transaction fees
	Search	Google, Bing	Focuses primarily on offering search services	Advertising, affiliate referral
Transaction Broker		E*Trade, Expedia, Monster, Travelocity, Orbitz	Processors of online transactions, such as stockbrokers and travel agents, that increase customers' productivity by helping them get things done faster and more cheaply	Transaction fees
Market Creator		eBay, Etsy, Uber, Airbnb	Businesses that use Internet technology to create markets that bring buyers and sellers together	Transaction fees
Service Provider		Envoy, Wave, RocketLawyer	Companies that make money by selling users a service, rather than a product	Sales of services

barriers to entry
the total cost of entering a new marketplace

This sector, however, is extremely competitive. Because **barriers to entry** (the total cost of entering a new marketplace) into the e-tail market are low, tens of thousands of small e-tail shops have sprung up. Becoming profitable and surviving is very difficult, however, for e-tailers with no prior brand name or experience. The e-tailer's challenge is differentiating its business from existing competitors.

Companies that try to reach every online consumer are likely to deplete their resources quickly. Those that develop a niche strategy, clearly identifying their target market and its needs, are best prepared to make a profit. Keeping expenses low, selection broad, and inventory controlled is key to success in e-tailing, with inventory being the most difficult to gauge. Online retail is covered in more depth in Chapter 11.

COMMUNITY PROVIDER

community provider
creates an online environment where people with similar interests can transact (buy and sell goods); share interests, photos, and videos; communicate with like-minded people; and receive interest-related information

Although community providers are not a new phenomenon, the Internet has made such sites for like-minded individuals to meet and converse much easier, without the limitations of geography and time to hinder participation. **Community providers** create an online environment where people with similar interests can transact (buy and sell goods); share interests, photos, videos; communicate with like-minded people; receive interest-related information; and even play out fantasies by adopting online personalities called avatars. Facebook, LinkedIn, Twitter, and Pinterest, and hundreds of other smaller, niche social networks all offer users community-building tools and services.

The basic value proposition of community providers is to create a fast, convenient, one-stop platform where users can focus on their most important concerns and interests, share the experience with friends, and learn more about their own interests. Community providers typically rely on a hybrid revenue model that includes subscription fees, sales revenues, transaction fees, affiliate fees, and advertising fees from other firms that are attracted by a tightly focused audience.

Community providers make money from advertising and through affiliate relationships with retailers. Some of the oldest online communities are The Well, which provides a forum for technology and Internet-related discussions, and The Motley Fool, which provides financial advice, news, and opinions. The Well offers various membership plans ranging from $10 to $15 a month. Motley Fool supports itself through ads and selling products that start out "free" but turn into annual subscriptions.

Consumers' interest in communities is mushroomingand participation in communities is one of the fastest growing online activities. While many community providers have had a difficult time becoming profitable, many have succeeded over time, with advertising as their main source of revenue. Both the very large social networks such as Facebook, Twitter, and LinkedIn, as well as niche social networks with smaller dedicated audiences, are ideal marketing and advertising territories. Traditional online communities such as The Motley Fool and WebMD (which provides medical information to members) find that the breadth and depth of knowledge offered is an important factor. Community members frequently request knowledge, guidance, and advice. Lack of experienced personnel can severely hamper the growth of a community, which needs facilitators and managers to keep discussions on course and relevant. For the newer community social networks, the most important ingredients of success appear to be ease and flexibility of use, and a strong customer value proposition. For instance, Facebook leapfrogged over its rival MySpace by encouraging the development of third-party revenue-producing applications.

Online communities benefit significantly from offline word-of-mouth, viral marketing. Online communities tend to reflect offline relationships. When your friends say they have a profile on Facebook, and ask you to "friend" them, you are encouraged to build your own online profile.

CONTENT PROVIDER

Content providers distribute information content, such as digital video, music, photos, text, and artwork. Content providers can make money via a variety of different revenue models, including advertising, subscription fees, and sales of digital goods. For instance, in the case of Spotify, a monthly subscription fee provides users with access to millions of music tracks. Other content providers, such as the *Financial Times* online newspaper, *Harvard Business Review*, and many others, charge customers for content downloads in addition to, or in place of, a subscription fee.

Of course, not all online content providers charge for their information: just look at the websites or mobile apps for ESPN, CIO, CNN, and the online versions of many newspapers and magazines. Users can access news and information without paying a cent, although sometimes they may be required to register as a member. These popular online content providers make money in other ways, such as through advertising and partner promotions. Increasingly, however, "free content" may be limited to headlines and text, whereas premium content—in-depth articles or videos—is sold for a fee.

Generally, the key to becoming a successful content provider is owning the content. Traditional owners of copyrighted content—publishers of books and newspapers, broadcasters of radio and television content, music publishers, and movie studios—have powerful advantages over newcomers who simply offer distribution channels and must pay for content, often at very high prices.

Some content providers, however, do not own content, but syndicate (aggregate) and then distribute content produced by others. *Syndication* is a major variation of the standard content provider model. Aggregators, who collect information from a wide variety of sources and then add value to that information through post-aggregation services, are another variation. For instance, Shopzilla collects information on the prices of thousands of goods online, analyzes the information, and presents users with tables showing the range of prices and links to the sites where the products can be purchased. Shopzilla adds value to content it aggregates, and resells this value to advertisers.

Any e-commerce start-up that intends to make money by providing content is likely to face difficulties unless it has a unique information source that others cannot access. For the most part, this business category is dominated by traditional content providers. The *Insight on Technology* case, *Connected Cars and the Future of E-commerce,* discusses how changes in Internet technology are driving the development of new business models in the online content market.

Online content is discussed in further depth in Chapter 9.

content provider
distributes information content, such as digital news, music, photos, video, and artwork

INSIGHT ON TECHNOLOGY

CONNECTED CARS AND THE FUTURE OF E-COMMERCE

Get ready! Within the next few years, your car is likely to become a major platform for e-commerce. You will be able to browse the Web, shop online, participate in social networks, and consume online content, all while commuting or simply taking an afternoon drive. And beyond that are many new services only dimly recognized now, but technically possible.

What will make this all possible is a confluence of forces and interests. Major players include automobile manufacturers, big tech companies, and telecommunications companies who are all seeking to leverage the Internet of Things (IoT), artificial intelligence software, autonomous self-driving, and other related technology development to both extend and create new markets for their services. The annual investment spent on smart cars and autonomous vehicles in 2014–2018 was estimated to be $20–$40 billion in the United States and much larger if Europe and China are included.

Currently 45% of the cars sold in the United States are connected to the Internet either by tethering mobile devices or dedicated on-board computers. Smart cars build on this connected car foundation by embedding technologies that perform some or all of the driving functions, from parking assistance and adaptive cruise control to eventually fully autonomous operation. This will free up driving time for more e-commerce marketing and services for providers.

By 2025, chances are good that you will no longer want to buy a car. Instead you may subscribe for a monthly fee to a mobility service that will provide you with a car when you need it. A recent study by Intel estimates the global value of new mobility services at $7 trillion by 2050. The largest part of this emerging market will be generated by consumer mobility services such as car subscriptions and on-demand mobility ($3.7 trillion), followed by B2B mobility services like transportation, delivery and service fleets ($3 trillion), and new emerging services in industries such as hotels, tourism, dining, healthcare, safety, and entertainment ($300 billion).

Other analysts point to four generic business models: mobility services (car pooling, on-demand ride services, and vehicle sharing or renting); customer experience (entertainment, loyalty programs, concierge service, games and other apps); car services (vehicle customized settings, predictive maintenance, usage-based insurance, mobile payments, and shopping/purchasing); and safety (driver condition monitoring, video surveillance, road side sign recognition, driver coaching, anti-theft tracing, and emergency calling).

The impact of smart cars and autonomous vehicles on e-commerce is enormous. For content distributors, connected cars provide a potentially huge market. Cars are already the main source of radio revenues in the United States, but cars will eventually become like a mobile living room, where passengers have access to all of the same types of media that they have when they're at home or using their cell phones. As cars become more and more automated and drivers are able to shift from driving to watching video content, industry analysts project that in-car entertainment revenue may increase by more than $20 billion, to a potential $36 billion by 2021. Content providers are already striking deals with automakers.

For example, advertisers are imagining ways to use smart cars to create immersive, 360-degree ad experiences. The size of the potential e-commerce impact can only be estimated at this time. For instance, the average commute time for 150 million commuting workers is 30 minutes. That works out to 30 billion hours of "wasted" time in a year, and a large opportunity for online advertisers. For instance, 150 million commuters each spend their time on Facebook while commuting; that translates into roughly 100 million hours per day, or 25 billion hours of new potential ad exposure time annually. Google and Facebook hope to be the dominant players in this expanded marketing platform.

Car manufacturers have their own plans for capturing this new e-commerce platform. The market leverage of automakers is that they make the cars and will decide with whom to share the rewards. Morgan Stanley estimates that if General Motors added a $1 a month subscription fee for in-car services, it would generate $1 billion a year in earnings, and add 20% to its stock price. Why share that with Apple, Google, Amazon, or Facebook?

Apple, Google, and Microsoft, the dominant players in mobile and desktop operating systems, believe that smart connected cars offer the opportunity of extending those platforms and expanding their influence by becoming the operating system of the car's content platform, and possibly the entire car. Apple's CarPlay and Google's Android Auto, apps that can replace the usually awful car manufacturer displays with their familiar interfaces along with voice-activated Siri and Google Assistant capabilities are already being placed in cars. E-mail, voice-activated texting, music, videos, streaming music, and social networking can easily be deployed to consumers who already know how the software interfaces look, feel, and work. For Google, the leader in search advertising, smart cars will offer an additional platform to display ads.

But car manufacturers are not about to give the user experience and revenue to Google and Apple without a fight. To that end, Ford patented a driverless car windshield entertainment system that could be the basis for this type of advertising as well as consuming traditional video content. Other forms of personalization could include the ability to find the nearest available parking place, locating nearby favorite restaurants or other attractions. As part of GM's $500 million investment in Lyft, the companies announced ambitious plans to deploy a centralized fleet of shared, electric, autonomous vehicles. Lyft envisions themed "experience pods" offering on-board beauty salons or touchscreen tables for remote collaboration alongside conventional entertainment services. One can imagine a raft of new commercial services, including dining (from fast-casual commuting to remote vending), healthcare (mobile clinic and treatments), hospitality (pod hotels), and retailing.

The future of connected smart cars is not all rosy, and many of the services offered may come with a price tag in the form of additional monthly subscriptions that many consumers will not accept. Questions about the safety, reliability, privacy, and security of smart cars abound. But if past experience is a guide, there seems to be an insatiable demand on the part of this Internet generation to stay connected and to consume content, purchase online, and socialize with their friends. The connected smart car will likely be a new venue for these activities.

SOURCES: "Apple CarPlay: The Good, The Bad, and The What Were They Thinking?," by David Gewirtz, Zdnet.com, May 3, 2018; "Automakers Are Primed to Become 'Landlords of Mobile Real Estate,' and It Could Net GM $1 Billing," by Graham Rapier, Businessinsider.com, May 2, 2018; "From Buzz to Bucks: Automotive Players on the Highway to Car Data Monetization," McKinsey Center for Future Mobility, March 2018; "The Re-imagined Car: Shared, Autonomous, and Electric," by Boston Consulting Group, December 17, 2017; "Data Driven Business Models in Connected Cars and Beyond," by Dr. Gabriel Seiberth, Accenture Digital, December 15, 2017; "Connected Cars Bring New Business Models and New Disruption," by Crystal Valentine, RTinsights.com, October 19, 2017; "Business Models Will Drive the Future of Autonomous Vehicles," by Sivaramakrishnan Somasegar and Daniel Li, Techcrunch.com, August 25, 2017; "The End of Car Ownership," by Tim Higgins, *Wall Street Journal*, June 20, 2017; "The Internet of Things for Smart Cars," by Victoria Petrock, eMarketer, Inc., June 2017.

PORTAL

portal
offers users powerful search tools as well as an integrated package of content and services all in one place

Portals such as Yahoo, MSN, and AOL offer users powerful search tools as well as an integrated package of content and services, such as news, e-mail, instant messaging, calendars, shopping, music downloads, video streaming, and more, all in one place. Initially, portals sought to be viewed as "gateways" to the Internet. Today, however, the portal business model is to be a destination. They are marketed as places where consumers will hopefully stay a long time to read news, find entertainment, and meet other people (think of destination resorts). Portals do not sell anything directly—or so it seems—and in that sense they can present themselves as unbiased. Portals generate revenue primarily by charging advertisers for ad placement, collecting referral fees for steering customers to other sites, and charging for premium services.

Although there are numerous portals/search engines, the top five in the United States (Google, Microsoft's Bing, Yahoo (Verizon Media), Ask, and AOL) gather more than 95% of search engine traffic because of their superior brand recognition. Many of the top portal/search engines were among the first to appear on the Web and therefore had first-mover advantages. Being first confers advantage because customers come to trust a reliable provider and experience switching costs if they change to late arrivals in the market. By garnering a large chunk of the marketplace, first movers—just like a single telephone network—can offer customers access to commonly shared ideas, standards, and experiences (something called *network externalities*, which we describe in later chapters). The traditional portals have company: Facebook and other social networks are now the initial start or home page (portal) for millions of Internet users in the United States.

Yahoo, AOL, and others like them are considered to be horizontal portals because they define their marketspace to include all users of the Internet. Vertical portals (sometimes called vortals) attempt to provide similar services as horizontal portals, but are focused around a particular subject matter or market segment. For instance, Sailnet focuses on the world's sailing community, and provides sailing news, articles, discussion groups, free e-mail, and a retail store. Although the total number of vortal users may be much lower than the number of portal users, if the market segment is attractive enough, advertisers are willing to pay a premium in order to reach a targeted audience. Also, visitors to specialized niche vortals spend more money than the average Yahoo visitor. Google and Ask can also be considered portals of a sort, but focus primarily on offering search and advertising services. They generate revenues primarily from search engine advertising sales and also from affiliate referral fees.

TRANSACTION BROKER

transaction broker
processes transactions for consumers that are normally handled in person, by phone, or by mail

Companies that process transactions for consumers normally handled in person, by phone, or by mail are **transaction brokers**. The largest industries using this model are financial services, travel services, and job placement services. The online transaction broker's primary value propositions are savings of money and time. In addition, most transaction brokers provide timely information and opinions. Companies such as Monster offer job searchers a global marketplace for their talents and employers a national resource for that talent. Both employers and job seekers are attracted by the convenience and currency of information. Online stock brokers charge commissions that are considerably less than traditional brokers, with many offering substantial deals, such as cash and a certain number of free trades, to lure new customers.

Given rising consumer interest in financial planning and the stock market, the market opportunity for online transaction brokers appears to be large. However, while millions of customers have shifted to online brokers, some are still wary about switching from their traditional broker who provides personal advice and a brand name. Fears of privacy invasion and the loss of control over personal financial information also contribute to market resistance. Consequently, the challenge for online brokers is to overcome consumer fears by emphasizing the security and privacy measures in place, and, like physical banks and brokerage firms, providing a broad range of financial services and not just stock trading. This industry is covered in greater depth in Chapter 11.

Transaction brokers make money each time a transaction occurs. Each stock trade, for example, nets the company a fee, based on either a flat rate or a sliding scale related to the size of the transaction. Attracting new customers and encouraging them to trade frequently are the keys to generating more revenue for these companies. Travel sites generate commissions from travel bookings and job sites generate listing fees from employers up front, rather than charging a fee when a position is filled.

MARKET CREATOR

Market creators build a digital environment in which buyers and sellers can meet, display and search for products and services, and establish prices. Prior to the Internet and the Web, market creators relied on physical places to establish a market. Beginning with the medieval marketplace and extending to today's New York Stock Exchange, a market has meant a physical space for transacting business. There were few private digital network marketplaces prior to the Web. The Web changed this by making it possible to separate markets from physical space. Prime examples are Priceline, which allows consumers to set the price they are willing to pay for various travel accommodations and other products (sometimes referred to as a reverse auction), and eBay, the online auction platform utilized by both businesses and consumers. Market creators make money by either charging a percentage of every transaction made, or charging merchants for access to the market.

market creator
builds a digital environment where buyers and sellers can meet, display products, search for products, and establish a price for products

For example, eBay's auction business model is to create a digital environment for buyers and sellers to meet, agree on a price, and transact. This is different from transaction brokers who actually carry out the transaction for their customers, acting as agents in larger markets. At eBay, the buyers and sellers are their own agents. Each sale on eBay nets the company a commission based on the percentage of the item's sales price, in addition to a listing fee. eBay is one of the few e-commerce companies that has been profitable virtually from the beginning. Why? One answer is that eBay has no inventory or production costs. It is simply a middleman.

The market opportunity for market creators is potentially vast, but only if the firm has the financial resources and marketing plan to attract sufficient sellers and buyers to the marketplace. In 2019, eBay had more than 180 million active buyers, and this makes for an efficient market (eBay Inc., 2019). There are many sellers and buyers for each type of product, sometimes for the same product, for example, laptop computer models. Many other digital auctions have sprung up in smaller, more specialized vertical market segments such as jewelry and automobiles.

Uber, Airbnb, and Lyft are another example of the market creator business model (although they could also be categorized as service providers). On-demand service companies (also sometimes called sharing economy companies) are market creators that have developed online platforms that allow people to sell services, such as transportation or spare rooms, in a marketplace that operates in the cloud and relies on the Web or smartphone apps to conduct transactions. It is important to note that, although referred to as sharing economy or mesh economy companies, these companies do not in fact share resources. Users of these services are either selling something or buying something, and the companies produce revenue by extracting fees for each transaction. However, they do unlock the economic value in spare resources (personal cars and rooms) that might otherwise have been lost. In the process they have created huge online markets. For instance, Uber (founded in 2009) currently operates in over 700 cities in 69 countries around the world. Airbnb, founded in 2008, operates in more than 220 countries and over 100,000 cities, has over 7 million listings available, and has had over 500 million people use its services.

SERVICE PROVIDER

service provider
offers services online

While e-tailers sell products online, **service providers** offer services online. There's been an explosion in online services that is often unrecognized. Photo sharing, video sharing, and user-generated content (in blogs and social networks) are all services provided to customers. Google has led the way in developing online applications such as Google Maps, Google Docs, and Gmail. Other personal services such as online medical bill management, financial and pension planning, and travel recommendation are showing strong growth.

Service providers use a variety of revenue models. Some charge a fee, or monthly subscriptions, while others generate revenue from other sources, such as through advertising and by collecting personal information that is useful in direct marketing. Many service providers employ a freemium revenue model, in which some basic services are free, but others require the payment of additional charges. Much like retailers who trade products for cash, service providers trade knowledge, expertise, and capabilities for revenue.

Obviously, some services cannot be provided online. For example, dentistry, plumbing, and car repair cannot be completed via the Internet. However, online arrangements can be made for these services. Online service providers may offer computer services, such as data storage (Dropbox and Carbonite), provide legal services (RocketLawyer), or accounting or bookkeeping services (Wave, Bench). Grocery shopping sites such as Ocado and Waitrose are also providing services.[1] To complicate matters a bit, most financial transaction brokers (described previously) provide services such as college tuition and pension planning. Travel brokers also provide vacation-planning services, not just transactions with airlines and hotels. Indeed, mixing services with your products is a powerful business strategy pursued by many hard-goods companies (for example, warranties are services).

---

[1] Ocado and other e-commerce businesses can also be classified as online retailers insofar as they warehouse commonly purchased items and make a profit based on the spread between their buy and sell prices.

The basic value proposition of service providers is that they offer consumers valuable, convenient, time-saving, and low-cost alternatives to traditional service providers or provide services that are truly unique. Where else can you search billions of web pages, or share photos with as many people instantly? Research has found, for instance, that a major factor in predicting online buying behavior is *time starvation*. Time-starved people tend to be busy professionals who work long hours and simply do not have the time to pick up packages, buy groceries, send photos, or visit with financial planners (Bellman, Lohse, and Johnson, 1999). The market opportunity for service providers is as large as the variety of services that can be provided and potentially is much larger than the market opportunity for physical goods. We live in a service-based economy and society; witness the growth of fast-food restaurants, package delivery services, and wireless cellular phone services. Consumers' increasing demand for convenience products and services bodes well for current and future online service providers.

Marketing of service providers must allay consumer fears about hiring a vendor online, as well as build confidence and familiarity among current and potential customers. Building confidence and trust is critical for service providers just as it is for retail product merchants.

5.3 MAJOR BUSINESS-TO-BUSINESS (B2B) BUSINESS MODELS

In Chapter 1, we noted that business-to-business (B2B) e-commerce, in which businesses sell to other businesses, is more than six times the size of B2C e-commerce, even though most of the public attention has focused on B2C. For instance, it is estimated that revenues for all types of B2B e-commerce worldwide totaled an estimated $27 trillion in 2019, compared to about $4.3 trillion for all types of retail and travel-related B2C e-commerce. Clearly, most of the revenues in e-commerce involve B2B e-commerce. Much of this activity is unseen and unknown to the average consumer. **Table 5.7** lists the major business models utilized in the B2B arena.

E-DISTRIBUTOR

Companies that supply products and services directly to individual businesses are **e-distributors**. W. W. Grainger, for example, is the largest distributor of maintenance, repair, and operations (MRO) supplies in the United States and also operates in Canada, Mexico, the United Kingdom, 11 countries in Europe, and Asia. In the past, Grainger relied on catalog sales and physical distribution centers in metropolitan areas. Its catalog of equipment went online in 1995. In 2018, Grainger's e-commerce platform, which includes websites and mobile apps, produced $6.9 billion in sales (62% of its total revenue) worldwide for the company.

E-distributors are owned by one company seeking to serve many customers. However, as with exchanges (described on the next page), critical mass is a factor. With e-distributors, the more products and services a company makes available, the more attractive it is to potential customers. One-stop shopping is always preferable to having to visit numerous sites to locate a particular part or product.

e-distributor

a company that supplies products and services directly to individual businesses

TABLE 5.7 — B2B BUSINESS MODELS

BUSINESS MODEL	EXAMPLES	DESCRIPTION	REVENUE MODEL
(1) NET MARKETPLACE			
E-distributor	Grainger, Amazon Business	Single-firm online version of retail and wholesale store; supply maintenance, repair, operation goods; indirect inputs	Sales of goods
E-procurement	Ariba Supplier Network, Proactis	Single firm creating digital markets where sellers and buyers transact for indirect inputs	Fees for market-making services, supply chain management, and fulfillment services
Exchange	Go2Paper	Independently owned vertical digital marketplace for direct inputs	Fees and commissions on transactions
Industry Consortium	The Seam, SupplyOn	Industry-owned vertical digital market open to select suppliers	Fees and commissions on transactions
(2) PRIVATE INDUSTRIAL NETWORK			
	Walmart, Procter & Gamble	Company-owned network that coordinates supply chains with a limited set of partners	Cost absorbed by network owner and recovered through production and distribution efficiencies

E-PROCUREMENT

e-procurement firm
creates and sells access to digital markets

Just as e-distributors provide products to other companies, **e-procurement firms** create and sell access to digital markets. Firms such as Ariba, for instance, have created software that helps large firms organize their procurement process by creating mini-digital markets for a single firm. Ariba creates custom-integrated online catalogs (where supplier firms can list their offerings) for purchasing firms. On the sell side, Ariba helps vendors sell to large purchasers by providing software to handle catalog creation, shipping, insurance, and finance. Both the buy and sell side software is referred to generically as "value chain management" software.

B2B service provider
sells business services to other firms

B2B service providers make money through transaction fees, fees based on the number of workstations using the service, or annual licensing fees. They offer purchasing firms a sophisticated set of sourcing and supply chain management tools that permit firms to reduce supply chain costs. In the software world, firms such as Ariba are sometimes also called software as a service (SaaS) or platform as a service (PaaS) providers; they are able to offer firms much lower costs of software by achieving scale economies. **Scale economies** are efficiencies that result from increasing the size of a business, for instance, when large, fixed-cost production systems (such as factories or software systems) can be operated at full capacity with no idle time. In the case of software, the marginal cost of a digital copy of a software program is nearly zero, and finding additional buyers for an expensive software program is exceptionally profitable. This is much more efficient than having every firm build its own supply chain management system, and it permits firms such as Ariba to specialize and offer their software to firms at a cost far less than the cost of developing it.

scale economies
efficiencies that arise from increasing the size of a business

EXCHANGES

Exchanges have garnered most of the B2B attention and early funding because of their potential market size even though today they are a small part of the overall B2B picture. An **exchange** is an independent digital marketplace where hundreds of suppliers meet a smaller number of very large commercial purchasers (Kaplan and Sawhney, 2000). Exchanges are owned by independent, usually entrepreneurial start-up firms whose business is making a market, and they generate revenue by charging a commission or fee based on the size of the transactions conducted among trading parties. They usually serve a single vertical industry such as steel, polymers, or aluminum, and focus on the exchange of direct inputs to production and short-term contracts or spot purchasing. For buyers, B2B exchanges make it possible to gather information, check out suppliers, collect prices, and keep up to date on the latest happenings all in one place. Sellers, on the other hand, benefit from expanded access to buyers. The greater the number of sellers and buyers, the lower the sales cost and the higher the chances of making a sale. The ease, speed, and volume of transactions are summarily referred to as *market liquidity*.

exchange
an independent digital marketplace where suppliers and commercial purchasers can conduct transactions

In theory, exchanges make it significantly less expensive and time-consuming to identify potential suppliers, customers, and partners, and to do business with each other. As a result, they can lower transaction costs—the cost of making a sale or purchase. Exchanges can also lower product costs and inventory-carrying costs—the cost of keeping a product on hand in a warehouse. In reality, as will be discussed in Chapter 12, B2B exchanges have had a difficult time convincing thousands of suppliers to move into singular digital markets where they face powerful price competition, and an equally difficult time convincing businesses to change their purchasing behavior away from trusted long-term trading partners. As a result, the number of exchanges has fallen significantly.

INDUSTRY CONSORTIA

Industry consortia are industry-owned *vertical marketplaces* that serve specific industries, such as the automobile, aerospace, chemical, floral, or logging industries. In contrast, *horizontal marketplaces* sell specific products and services to a wide range of companies. Vertical marketplaces supply a smaller number of companies with products and services of specific interest to their industry, while horizontal marketplaces supply companies in

industry consortia
industry-owned vertical marketplaces that serve specific industries

different industries with a particular type of product and service, such as marketing-related, financial, or computing services. For example, SupplyOn, founded in 2000 and owned by industrial giants Bosch (one of the world's largest suppliers of automotive components), Continental (a leading automotive manufacturing company), and Schaeffler (a global manufacturer of various types of bearings), among others, provides a shared supply chain collaboration platform for companies in various manufacturing industries. In 2018, in addition to its shareholders, its customers included Airbus, BMW, BorgWarner, Siemens, Thales, and many other major global manufacturing companies.

Industry consortia have tended to be more successful than independent exchanges in part because they are sponsored by powerful, deep-pocketed industry players, and also because they strengthen traditional purchasing behavior rather than seek to transform it.

PRIVATE INDUSTRIAL NETWORKS

private industrial network
digital network designed to coordinate the flow of communications among firms engaged in business together

A **private industrial network** (sometimes referred to as a private trading exchange or PTX) is a digital network designed to coordinate the flow of communications among firms engaged in business together. The network is owned by a single large purchasing firm. Participation is by invitation only to trusted long-term suppliers of direct inputs. These networks typically evolve out of a firm's own enterprise resource planning (ERP) system, and are an effort to include key suppliers in the firm's own business decision making. For instance, Walmart operates one of the largest private industrial networks in the world for its suppliers, who on a daily basis use Walmart's network to monitor the sales of their goods, the status of shipments, and the actual inventory level of their goods.

We discuss the nuances of B2B e-commerce in more detail in Chapter 12.

5.4 HOW E-COMMERCE CHANGES BUSINESS: STRATEGY, STRUCTURE, AND PROCESS

Now that you have a clear grasp of the variety of business models used by e-commerce firms, you also need to understand how e-commerce has changed the business environment in the last decade, including industry structures, business strategies, and industry and firm operations (business processes and value chains). We return to these concepts throughout the book as we explore the e-commerce phenomenon. In general, the Internet is an open standards system available to all players, and this fact inherently makes it easy for new competitors to enter the marketplace and offer substitute products or channels of delivery. The Internet tends to intensify competition. Because information becomes available to everyone, the Internet inherently shifts power to buyers who can quickly discover the lowest-cost provider. On the other hand, the Internet presents many new opportunities for creating value, for branding products and charging premium prices, and for enlarging an already powerful offline physical business such as Walmart or Sears.

Recall Table 1.2 in Chapter 1 that describes the truly unique features of e-commerce technology. **Table 5.8** suggests some of the implications of each unique feature for the overall business environment—industry structure, business strategies, and operations.

TABLE 5.8 EIGHT UNIQUE FEATURES OF E-COMMERCE TECHNOLOGY

FEATURE	SELECTED IMPACTS ON BUSINESS ENVIRONMENT
Ubiquity	Alters industry structure by creating new marketing channels and expanding size of overall market. Creates new efficiencies in industry operations and lowers costs of firms' sales operations. Enables new differentiation strategies.
Global reach	Changes industry structure by lowering barriers to entry, but greatly expands market at the same time. Lowers cost of industry and firm operations through production and sales efficiencies. Enables competition on a global scale.
Universal standards	Changes industry structure by lowering barriers to entry and intensifying competition within an industry. Lowers costs of industry and firm operations by lowering computing and communications costs. Enables broad scope strategies.
Richness	Alters industry structure by reducing strength of powerful distribution channels. Changes industry and firm operations costs by reducing reliance on sales forces. Enhances post-sales support strategies.
Interactivity	Alters industry structure by reducing threat of substitutes through enhanced customization. Reduces industry and firm costs by reducing reliance on sales forces. Enables differentiation strategies.
Information density	Changes industry structure by weakening powerful sales channels, shifting bargaining power to consumers. Reduces industry and firm operations costs by lowering costs of obtaining, processing, and distributing information about suppliers and consumers.
Personalization/ Customization	Alters industry structure by reducing threats of substitutes, raising barriers to entry. Reduces value chain costs in industry and firms by lessening reliance on sales forces. Enables personalized marketing strategies.
Social technologies	Changes industry structure by shifting programming and editorial decisions to consumers. Creates substitute entertainment products. Energizes a large group of new suppliers.

INDUSTRY STRUCTURE

E-commerce changes industry structure, in some industries more than others. **Industry structure** refers to the nature of the players in an industry and their relative bargaining power. An industry's structure is characterized by five forces: *rivalry among existing competitors*, the *threat of substitute products, barriers to entry into the industry*, the *bargaining power of suppliers*, and the *bargaining power of buyers* (Porter, 1985). When you describe an industry's structure, you are describing the general business environment in an industry and the overall profitability of doing business in that environment. E-commerce has the potential to change the relative strength of these competitive forces (see **Figure 5.3**).

industry structure
refers to the nature of the players in an industry and their relative bargaining power

E-commerce has many impacts on industry structure and competitive conditions. From the perspective of a single firm, these changes can have negative or positive implications depending on the situation. In some cases, an entire industry can be disrupted, while at the same time, a new industry is born. Individual firms can either prosper or be devastated.

industry structural analysis
an effort to understand and describe the nature of competition in an industry, the nature of substitute products, the barriers to entry, and the relative strength of consumers and suppliers

When you consider a business model and its potential long-term profitability, you should always perform an industry structural analysis. An **industry structural analysis** is an effort to understand and describe the nature of competition in an industry, the nature of substitute products, the barriers to entry, and the relative strength of consumers and suppliers.

E-commerce can affect the structure and dynamics of industries in very different ways. Consider the recorded music industry, an industry that has experienced significant change because of e-commerce. Historically, the major record companies owned the exclusive rights to the recorded music of various artists. With the entrance into the marketplace of substitute providers such as Napster and Kazaa, millions of consumers began to use the Internet to bypass traditional music labels and their distributors entirely. In the travel industry, entirely new middlemen such as Travelocity entered the market to compete with traditional travel agents. After Travelocity, Expedia, CheapTickets, and other travel services demonstrated the power of e-commerce marketing for airline tickets, the actual owners of the airline seats—the major airlines—banded together to form their own Internet outlet for tickets, Orbitz, for direct sales to consumers (although ultimately selling the company to a private investor group). Clearly, e-commerce creates *new industry dynamics* that can best be described as the give and take of the marketplace, the changing fortunes of competitors.

Yet, in other industries, e-commerce has strengthened existing players. In the chemical and automobile industries, e-commerce is being used effectively by manufacturers to strengthen their traditional distributors. In these industries, e-commerce technology has not fundamentally altered the competitive forces—bargaining power of suppliers, barriers to entry, bargaining power of buyers, threat of substitutes, or rivalry among competitors—within the industry. Hence, each industry is different and you need to examine each one carefully to understand the impacts of e-commerce on competition and strategy.

New forms of distribution created by new market entrants can completely change the competitive forces in an industry. For instance, consumers gladly substituted free access to Wikipedia for a $699 set of encyclopedias, or a $40 DVD, radically changing the competitive forces in the encyclopedia industry. As described in Chapter 9, the content industries of newspapers, books, movies, games, and television have been transformed by the emergence of new distribution platforms.

Inter-firm rivalry (competition) is one area of the business environment where e-commerce technologies have had an impact on most industries. In general, e-commerce has increased price competition in nearly all markets. It has been relatively easy for existing firms to adopt e-commerce technology and attempt to use it to achieve competitive advantage vis-à-vis rivals. For instance, e-commerce inherently changes the scope of competition from local and regional to national and global. Because consumers have access to global price information, e-commerce produces pressures on firms to compete by lowering prices (and lowering profits). On the other hand, e-commerce has made it possible for some firms to differentiate their products or services from others. Amazon patented one-click purchasing, for instance, while eBay created a unique, easy-to-use interface and a differentiating brand name. Therefore, although e-commerce has increased emphasis on price competition, it has also enabled businesses to create new strategies for differentiation and branding so that they can retain higher prices.

It is impossible to determine if e-commerce technologies have had an overall positive or negative impact on firm profitability in general. Each industry is unique, so it is necessary to perform a separate analysis for each one. Clearly, e-commerce has shaken the foundations of some industries, in particular, content industries (such as the music, newspaper, book, and software industries) as well as other information-intense industries such as financial services. In these industries, the power of consumers has grown relative to providers, prices have fallen, and overall profitability has been challenged. In other industries, especially manufacturing, e-commerce has not greatly changed relationships with buyers, but has changed relationships with suppliers. Increasingly, manufacturing firms in entire industries have banded together to aggregate purchases, create industry exchanges or marketplaces, and outsource industrial processes in order to obtain better prices from suppliers. Throughout this book, we document these changes in industry structure and market dynamics introduced by e-commerce.

INDUSTRY VALUE CHAINS

While an industry structural analysis helps you understand the impact of e-commerce technology on the overall business environment in an industry, a more detailed industry value chain analysis can help identify more precisely just how e-commerce may change business operations at the industry level. One of the basic tools for understanding the impact of information technology on industry and firm operations is the value chain. The concept is quite simple. A **value chain** is the set of activities performed in an industry or in a firm that transforms raw inputs into final products and services. Each of these activities adds economic value to the final product; hence, the term *value chain* as an interconnected set of value-adding activities. **Figure 5.4** illustrates the six generic players in an industry value chain: suppliers, manufacturers, transporters, distributors, retailers, and customers.

value chain
the set of activities performed in an industry or in a firm that transforms raw inputs into final products and services

By reducing the cost of information, e-commerce offers each of the key players in an industry value chain new opportunities to maximize their positions by lowering costs and/or raising prices. For instance, manufacturers can reduce the costs they pay for goods by developing Internet-based B2B exchanges with their suppliers. Manufacturers can develop direct relationships with their customers, bypassing the costs of distributors and retailers. Distributors can develop highly efficient inventory management systems to reduce their costs, and retailers can develop highly efficient customer relationship management systems to strengthen their service to customers.

FIGURE 5.4   E-COMMERCE AND INDUSTRY VALUE CHAINS

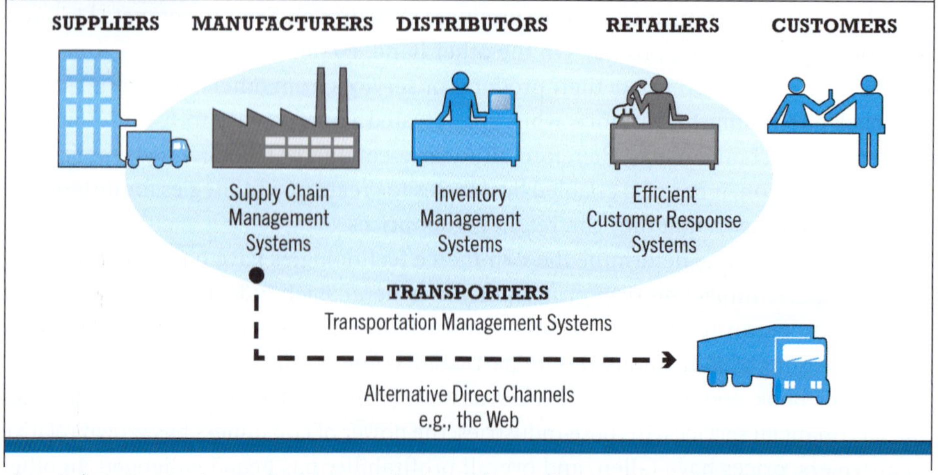

Every industry can be characterized by a set of value-adding activities performed by a variety of actors. E-commerce potentially affects the capabilities of each player as well as the overall operational efficiency of the industry.

Customers in turn can search for the best quality, fastest delivery, and lowest prices, thereby lowering their transaction costs and reducing prices they pay for final goods. Finally, the operational efficiency of the entire industry can increase, lowering prices and adding value for consumers, and helping the industry to compete with alternative industries.

FIRM VALUE CHAINS

The concept of value chain can be used to analyze a single firm's operational efficiency as well. The question here is: How does e-commerce technology potentially affect the value chains of firms within an industry? A **firm value chain** is the set of activities a firm engages in to create final products from raw inputs. Each step in the process of production adds value to the final product. In addition, firms develop support activities that coordinate the production process and contribute to overall operational efficiency. **Figure 5.5** illustrates the key steps and support activities in a firm's value chain.

firm value chain
the set of activities a firm engages in to create final products from raw inputs

E-commerce offers firms many opportunities to increase their operational efficiency and differentiate their products. For instance, firms can use the Internet's communications efficiency to outsource some primary and secondary activities to specialized, more efficient providers without such outsourcing being visible to the consumer. In addition, firms can use e-commerce to more precisely coordinate the steps in the value chains and reduce their costs. Finally, firms can use e-commerce to provide users with more differentiated and high-value products. For instance, Amazon provides consumers with a much larger inventory of books to choose from, at a lower cost, than traditional book stores. It also provides many services—such as instantly available professional and consumer reviews, and information on buying patterns of other consumers—that traditional bookstores cannot.

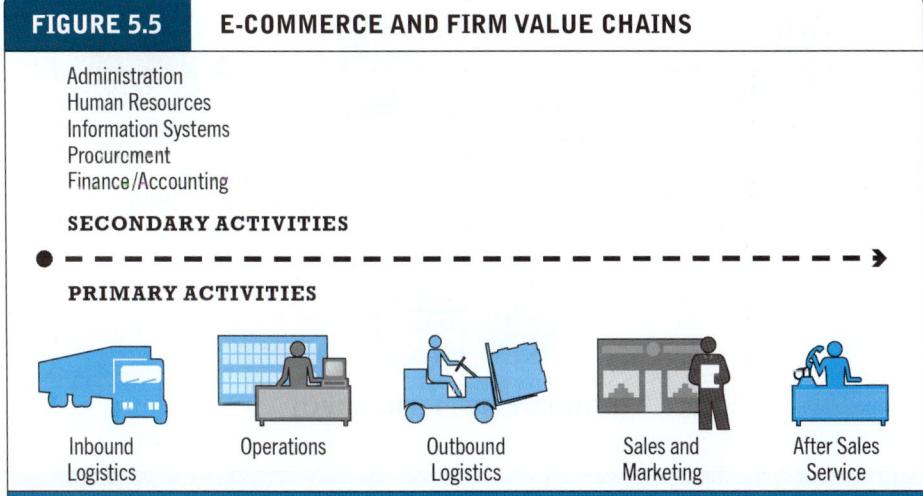

FIGURE 5.5 E-COMMERCE AND FIRM VALUE CHAINS

Every firm can be characterized by a set of value-adding primary and secondary activities performed by a variety of actors in the firm. A simple firm value chain performs five primary value-adding steps: inbound logistics, operations, outbound logistics, sales and marketing, and after sales service.

FIRM VALUE WEBS

While firms produce value through their value chains, they also rely on the value chains of their partners—their suppliers, distributors, and delivery firms. E-commerce creates new opportunities for firms to cooperate and create a value web. A **value web** is a networked business ecosystem that uses e-commerce technology to coordinate the value chains of business partners within an industry, or at the first level, to coordinate the value chains of a group of firms. **Figure 5.6** illustrates a value web.

A value web coordinates a firm's suppliers with its own production needs using an Internet-based supply chain management system. We discuss these B2B systems in Chapter 12. Firms also use the Internet to develop close relationships with their logistics partners. For instance, Amazon relies on UPS tracking systems to provide its customers with online package tracking, and it relies on the U.S. Postal Service systems to insert packages directly into the mail stream. Amazon has partnership relations with hundreds of firms to generate customers and to manage relationships with customers. In fact, when

value web

networked business ecosystem that coordinates the value chains of several firms

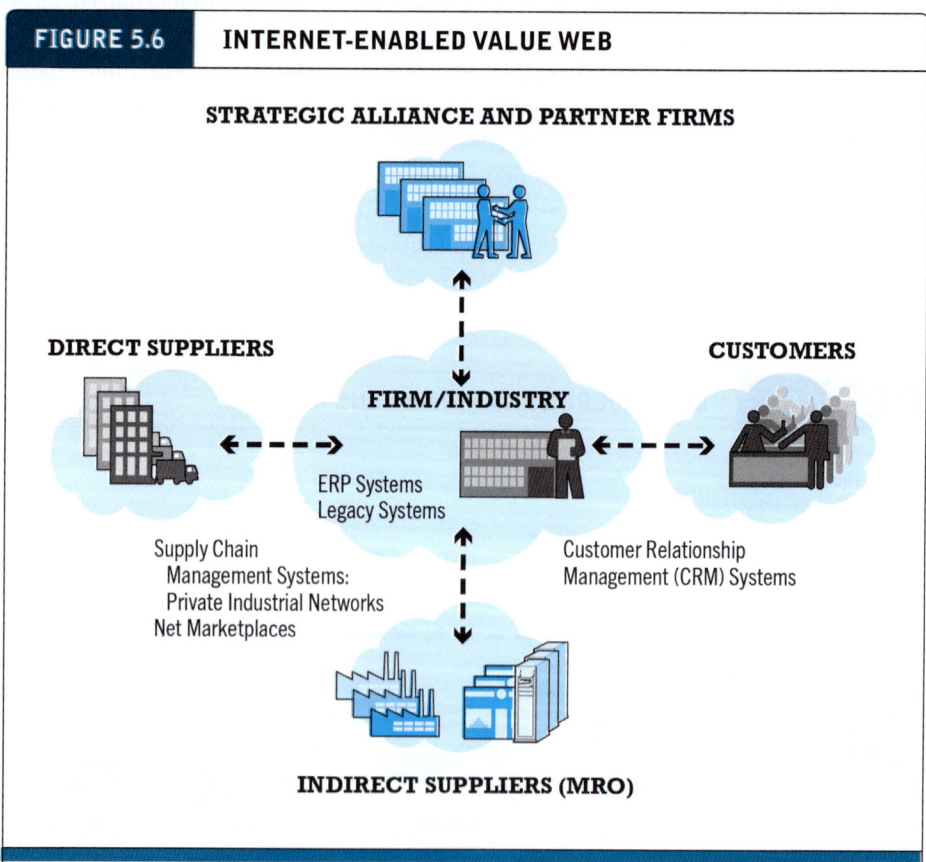

FIGURE 5.6 INTERNET-ENABLED VALUE WEB

Internet technology enables firms to create an enhanced value web in cooperation with their strategic alliance and partner firms, customers, and direct and indirect suppliers.

you examine Amazon closely, you realize that the value it delivers to customers is in large part the result of coordination with other firms and not simply the result of activities internal to Amazon. The value of Amazon is, in large part, the value delivered by its value web partners. This is difficult for other firms to imitate in the short run.

BUSINESS STRATEGY

A **business strategy** is a set of plans for achieving superior long-term returns on the capital invested in a business firm. A business strategy is therefore a plan for making profits in a competitive environment over the long term. **Profit** is simply the difference between the price a firm is able to charge for its products and the cost of producing and distributing goods. Profit represents economic value. Economic value is created anytime customers are willing to pay more for a product than it costs to produce. Why would anyone pay more for a product than it costs to produce? There are multiple answers. The product may be unique (there are no other suppliers), it may be the least costly product of its type available, consumers may be able to purchase the product anywhere in the world, or it may satisfy some unique needs that other products do not. Each of these sources of economic value defines a firm's strategy for positioning its products in the marketplace. There are four generic strategies for achieving a profitable business: differentiation, cost, scope, and focus. We describe each of these below. The specific strategies that a firm follows will depend on the product, the industry, and the marketplace where competition is encountered.

Although the Internet is a unique marketplace, the same principles of strategy and business apply. As you will see throughout the book, successful e-commerce strategies involve using the Internet and mobile platform to leverage and strengthen existing business (rather than destroy your business), and to provide products and services your competitors cannot copy (in the short term anyway). That means developing unique products, proprietary content, distinguishing processes (such as Amazon's one-click shopping), and personalized or customized services and products (Porter, 2001). There are five generic business strategies: product/service differentiation, cost competition, scope, focus, and customer intimacy. Let's examine these ideas more closely.

Differentiation refers to all the ways producers can make their products or services unique and distinguish them from those of competitors. The opposite of differentiation is **commoditization**—a situation where there are no differences among products or services, and the only basis of choosing is price. As economists tell us, when price alone becomes the basis of competition and there are many suppliers and many customers, eventually the price of the good/service falls to the cost to produce it (marginal revenues from the nth unit equal marginal costs). And then profits are zero! This is an unacceptable situation for any business person. The solution is to differentiate your product or service and to create a monopoly-like situation where you are the only supplier.

There are many ways businesses differentiate their products or services. A business may start with a core generic product or service, but then create expectations among users about the "experience" of consuming the product or using the service— "Nothing equals the experience of driving a BMW." Businesses may also augment products and services by

business strategy
a set of plans for achieving superior long-term returns on the capital invested in a business firm

profit
the difference between the price a firm is able to charge for its products and the cost of producing and distributing goods

differentiation
refers to all the ways producers can make their products or services unique and different to distinguish them from those of competitors

commoditization
a situation where there are no differences among products or services, and the only basis of choosing is price

adding features to make them different from those of competitors. And businesses can differentiate their products and services further by enhancing their abilities to solve related consumer problems. For instance, tax programs such as TurboTax can import data from spreadsheet programs, as well as be used to file tax returns online. These capabilities are enhancements to the product that solve a customer's problems. The purpose of marketing is to create these differentiation features and to make the consumer aware of the unique qualities of products and services, creating in the process a "brand" that stands for these features. We discuss marketing and branding in Chapters 6 and 7.

In their totality, the differentiation features of a product or service constitute the customer value proposition we described in earlier sections of this chapter. E-commerce offers some unique ways to differentiate products and services, such as the ability to personalize the shopping experience and to customize the product or service to the particular demands of each consumer. E-commerce businesses can also differentiate products and services by making it possible to purchase the product from home, work, or on the road (ubiquity); by making it possible to purchase anywhere in the world (global reach); by creating unique interactive content, videos, stories about users, and reviews by users (richness and interactivity); and by storing and processing information for consumers of the product or service, such as warranty information on all products purchased or income tax information online (information density).

strategy of cost competition

offering products and services at a lower cost than competitors

Adopting a **strategy of cost competition** means a business has discovered some unique set of business processes or resources that other firms cannot obtain in the marketplace. Business processes are the atomic units of the value chain. For instance, the set of value-creating activities called Inbound Logistics in Figure 5.5 is in reality composed of many different collections of activities performed by people on the loading docks and in the warehouses. These different collections of activities are called *business processes*—the set of steps or procedures required to perform the various elements of the value chain.

When a firm discovers a new, more efficient set of business processes, it can obtain a cost advantage over competitors. Then it can attract customers by charging a lower price, while still making a handsome profit. Eventually, its competitors go out of business as the market decisively tilts toward the lowest-cost provider. Or, when a business discovers a unique resource, or lower-cost supplier, it can also compete effectively on cost. For instance, switching production to low-wage-cost areas of the world is one way to lower costs.

Competing on cost can be a short-lived affair and very tricky. Competitors can also discover the same or different efficiencies in production. And competitors can also move production to low-cost areas of the world. Also, competitors may decide to lose money for a period as they compete on cost.

E-commerce offers some ways to compete on cost, at least in the short term. Firms can leverage ubiquity by lowering the costs of order entry (the customer fills out all the forms, so there is no order entry department); leverage global reach and universal standards by having a single order entry system worldwide; and leverage richness, interactivity, and personalization by creating customer profiles online and treating each individual consumer differently—without the use of an expensive sales force that performed these functions in the past. Finally, firms can leverage information intensity by providing consumers with detailed information on products, without maintaining either expensive catalogs or a sales force.

While e-commerce offers powerful capabilities for intensifying cost competition, which makes cost competition appear to be a viable strategy, the danger is that competitors have access to the same technology. The *factor markets*—where producers buy supplies—are open to all. Assuming they have the skills and organizational will to use the technology, competitors can buy many of the same cost-reducing techniques in the marketplace. Even a skilled labor force can be purchased, ultimately. However, self-knowledge, proprietary tacit knowledge (knowledge that is not published or codified), and a loyal, skilled workforce are in the short term difficult to purchase in factor markets. Therefore, cost competition remains a viable strategy.

Two other generic business strategies are scope and focus. A **scope strategy** is a strategy to compete in all markets around the globe, rather than merely in local, regional, or national markets. The Internet's global reach, universal standards, and ubiquity can certainly be leveraged to assist businesses in becoming global competitors. eBay, for instance, along with all of the other top 20 e-commerce companies, has readily attained a global presence. A **focus/market niche strategy** is a strategy to compete within a narrow market segment or product segment. This is a specialization strategy with the goal of becoming the premier provider in a narrow market. For instance, L.L.Bean uses e-commerce to continue its historic focus on outdoor sports apparel; and W. W. Grainger focuses on the narrow MRO market segment. E-commerce offers some obvious capabilities that enable a focus strategy. Firms can leverage richness and interactivity to create highly focused messages to different market segments; information intensity makes it possible to focus e-mail and other marketing campaigns on small market segments; personalization—and related customization—means the same product can be customized and personalized to fulfill the very focused needs of specific market segments and consumers.

Another generic strategy is **customer intimacy**, which focuses on developing strong ties with customers. Strong linkages with customers increase *switching costs* (the costs of switching from one product or service to a competing product or service) and thereby enhance a firm's competitive advantage. For example, Amazon's one-click shopping that retains customer details and recommendation services based on previous purchases makes it more likely that customers will return to make subsequent purchases.

Table 5.9 summarizes the five basic business strategies.

Industry structure, industry and firm value chains, value webs, and business strategy are central business concepts used throughout this book to analyze the viability of and prospects for e-commerce companies. In particular, the signature case studies found at the end of each chapter are followed by questions that may ask you to identify the competitive forces in the case, or analyze how the case illustrates changes in industry structure, industry and firm value chains, and business strategy.

E-COMMERCE TECHNOLOGY AND BUSINESS MODEL DISRUPTION

While e-commerce has changed most industries in terms of their structure, processes, and strategies, in some cases e-commerce has radically changed entire industries,

scope strategy
competing in all markets around the globe, rather than just local, regional, or national markets

focus/market niche strategy
competing within a narrow market or product segment

customer intimacy
focuses on developing strong ties with customers in order to increase switching costs

TABLE 5.9 BUSINESS STRATEGIES

STRATEGY	DESCRIPTION	EXAMPLE
Differentiation	Making products and services unique and different in order to distinguish them from those of competitors	Warby Parker (vintage-inspired prescription eyeglasses)
Cost competition	Offering products and services at a lower cost than competitors	Walmart
Scope	Competing in all markets around the globe, rather than merely in local, regional, or national markets	Apple iDevices
Focus/market niche	Competing within a narrow market or product segment	Bonobos (men's clothing)
Customer intimacy	Developing strong ties with customers	Amazon; Netflix

disruptive technologies
technologies that underpin a business model disruption

digital disruption
a business model disruption that is driven by changes in information technology

driving incumbent firms out of business, greatly altering the economics of an industry, and spawning entirely new firms and value chains (Schumpeter, 1942). When new technologies are at the core of a change in the way business is done, they are referred to as **disruptive technologies**. When the technology involved is digital, the term **digital disruption** is used. Usually it is not the technology per se that is disruptive—in fact, it can be rather ordinary and commonplace. Instead, the disruption occurs when an innovative firm applies the technology to pursue a different business model and strategy than existing firms, perhaps discovering a whole new market that existing firms did not even know existed (Bower and Christensen, 1995; Christensen and Leslie, 2000). For instance, personal computers using off-the-shelf inexpensive processors and technologies disrupted the market for mainframe and mini-computers. All the eight elements of a business model identified previously can be affected by disruptive technologies, from the business value proposition to the revenue model, market opportunity, competitive environment, competitive advantage, market strategy, organizational development, and management. In short, it's a whole new world that often confuses and surprises successful companies who tend to ignore, dismiss, and/or mock the early disruptive products. For instance, the entrepreneurs who introduced personal computers identified an entire new market of customers that had been ignored by the large computer firms, along with new price points, competitive factors, and market strategy, using new organizational, management teams, and employees with different skills. Many existing firms could not compete, and dissolved. Similar dynamics can be found in communications (disrupted by e-mail), data storage, music, photography, publishing, and transportation (Lepore, 2014). In 2019, firms like Uber and Airbnb had a significant impact on the taxi and lodging industries.

Not all technologies are disruptive (Christensen et al., 2015; King and Baatartogtokh, 2015). In fact, most successful companies use technology to sustain their current business models, industry structure, processes, and strategies. This use of technology is referred to as **sustaining technology** because it helps companies to cope with competitive pressures and improve their products, and serve their customers with less expensive, more powerful, or unique products. But the same technology can be used by innovative entrepreneurs (**disruptors**) to destroy existing business models. Here's how it works.

Successful companies use whatever technology is available to incrementally improve their products, focusing on the customer by improving quality, price, and service. The incumbent and dominant firms seek to maintain the status quo in an industry, and their firms. In the first disruptive stage, disruptors, often funded by new sources of finance, introduce new products that are less expensive, less capable, and of poorer quality. The first personal computers used relatively unsophisticated technology compared to mainframe computers of the 1970s. These early products nevertheless find a niche in a market that incumbents do not serve or are unaware of. In the second stage, disruptors improve their products at a rapid pace, taking advantage of newer technologies at a faster pace than incumbents, expanding their niche market, and eventually attracting a larger customer base from the incumbents' market. When word processors, and eventually Microsoft Office, were married to the more powerful PC of the 1980s, they attracted a new market of business managers and professionals that was not served by incumbents. The concept was entirely new at the time. The successful incumbents never thought business professionals, let alone people working at home, would like to have a computer at their desk to create documents, build spreadsheets, and make presentation slides. The people and companies that developed personal computers were outsiders to the mainframe computer industry. They were disruptors. They had the vision.

In the third stage, the new products and business model become good enough, and even superior to products offered by incumbents. In the fourth stage, incumbent companies lose market share, and either go out of business or are consolidated into other more successful firms that serve a much more limited customer base. Some incumbents survive by finding new customers for their existing product, adopting some of the newer products and business models in separate divisions of their firms, or moving into other often nearby markets. For instance, mainframe computers are still made by IBM, but they are one of the few survivors. They survived by sustaining innovation in their traditional market of large-scale computing for Fortune 500 firms, moving into computing services, data centers, enterprise software, and most recently cloud computing, business analytics, data mining, and machine learning. As for the PC industry, it is currently being disrupted by smartphones and tablet computers, created by outsiders who played a small role in the personal computer world, and who have

sustaining technologies
technologies that enable the incremental improvement of products and services

disruptors
the entrepreneurs and their business firms that lead a business model disruption

identified huge consumer markets that incumbent PC manufacturers did not realize even existed. They have the vision, for now, but they face new digital disruptors sure to follow.

Why don't the existing companies realize the changes that are coming, and take steps to compete directly with the disruptors? Successful incumbents usually have enormous capital reserves, in-depth technology and intellectual skills, and access to prestigious management consulting firms. Why didn't Kodak see the transition to digital photography? Why didn't Canon see the smartphone camera as a powerful competitor to digital cameras? Why don't firms disrupt their own business models? The answers are complex. Incumbent technologists and professionals may be trained in an *unfit fitness*, having the wrong skills for the current environment. Shareholders expect returns on investment, not destruction of a firm's historic and cherished profitable products. The existing customer base comes to expect continuous improvement in existing products—not a business disruption, but business as usual. These powerful practices, all of which make good business sense, prevent incumbent firms from meeting the challenges of business model disruption. It is unclear at this time if the two most innovative firms in the current e-commerce environment, Apple and Google, will prove any different from previous incumbents.

5.5 CAREERS IN E-COMMERCE

In this section, we'll examine a job posting by a company that uses both a B2C, as well as a B2B, e-commerce business model.

THE COMPANY

The company is a manufacturer of more than 3,500 different tools for both the do-it-yourself consumer market, as well as the electrical and telecommunications industries, where it is a leading provider. The company's products are sold through consumer retail outlets, as well as through direct sales to industry. In 2007 the company launched its first website. The company is in the process of developing a digital marketing initiative, and is hoping to greatly expand its B2C and B2B e-commerce revenues by developing a robust web presence, including apps for mobile devices and on social media.

POSITION: ASSISTANT MANAGER OF E-BUSINESS

You will work with the e-commerce team on initiatives to expand the company's e-commerce presence, including website development, search engine optimization, mobile commerce, social media, video, and e-mail. Other responsibilities include helping to:

- Develop an e-commerce road map and timeline for the development of e-commerce capabilities throughout the firm.
- Develop a B2B e-commerce presence to support the distributor network in collaboration with the sales and marketing teams.
- Develop and maintain an online and offline catalog content management system to support the consumer and distributor websites.

- Develop and maintain a search engine optimization plan.
- Develop a mobile and social marketing plan.
- Collaborate with the information technology (IT), sales, and marketing departments to ensure IT capabilities can support the e-commerce plan and that content and branding efforts are consistent across all channels and align with company's vision.
- Develop strategic plans and budgets for the e-commerce plan.

QUALIFICATIONS/SKILLS

- Bachelor's degree in business administration, management information systems, e-commerce, or digital marketing
- Basic knowledge of digital content management, social and mobile marketing, marketing automation, and/or web design and development
- Strong communication, content, presentation, and writing skills
- Problem solving and critical thinking skills
- Ability to collaborate with other members of the e-commerce team

PREPARING FOR THE INTERVIEW

When preparing for an interview, it is essential to do in-depth research on the firm and its industry. In this case, you should be familiar with the B2C and B2B tool marketplace, including major competitors. You also should be thoroughly familiar with the company's website and its social media presence on Facebook, Twitter, LinkedIn, and blogs, if any. Be prepared to discuss what you know with the interviewer at the appropriate moment. Review Section 5.1 so that you can demonstrate that you understand basic elements of a business plan, such as value propositions, different revenue models, market opportunity, market strategy, and so on. Review Sections 5.2 and 5.3 so that you can speak about the differences between B2C and B2B business models. In this case, it appears that the firm will be using both an e-tailer as well as an e-distributor business model. Finally, review Section 5.4, which provides you with an excellent overview of basic business concepts, as well as business strategies, applicable to e-commerce.

POSSIBLE FIRST INTERVIEW QUESTIONS

1. The company is launching a major effort to develop our e-commerce sales. In the past we have relied on consumer stores and direct sales to other firms. What do you think our value proposition should be in these markets? Why should customers buy on our websites and use our apps?

You could start by talking about what makes a company like Amazon such a popular online retailer. Major factors include its product search engine, its wide selection, ease of purchase, 2-day shipping, reliable fulfillment, and convenient returns. Price is less important than its service and convenience. The company should focus on developing similar capabilities. The bottom line is that people will shop on the firm's websites if they provide a winning customer experience.

2. What kinds of services could we provide our customers that would attract them to our sites?

You can suggest that many people who buy tools may not know how to use them most appropriately or effectively. One of the best ways to educate consumers is through videos, which could be delivered via an official company YouTube channel or provided on the firm's websites, with links to the YouTube channel.

3. What kinds of strategic partners should we be working with to develop our online sales?

You could point out that very successful firms rarely do everything themselves. The firm should develop relationships with key providers of services such as UPS and FedEx for logistics and shipping; online payments systems like PayPal and credit card providers; technology providers to handle the supply chain and warehousing automation; and customer relationship management firms like Salesforce to maintain a close connection with customers. Firms specializing in e-mail campaigns, search engine optimization, video production, and mobile and social media marketing are also important strategic partners.

4. In the B2B market we will initially be an e-distributor, selling our products online. What kinds of other opportunities should we explore in the B2B arena?

Other B2B business opportunities that may be relevant include participating in exchanges, establishing relationships with e-procurement firms, and/or seeking to become a preferred vendor as part of a private industrial network.

5. For many of our products we face stiff competition from low-cost imported tools. What would you recommend that the firm's strategy be in meeting this competition?

You can suggest that one way to compete on price with low-cost imports is to introduce a low-cost line of tools. Although low in price, they might have margins equal to or greater than tools made in the United States. Another strategy would be to move production to low-cost countries but maintain the same high quality. On the other hand, a differentiation strategy might be best by offering higher-quality "professional" level tools to consumers, relying on the existing brand strengths to sell at higher prices. The firm can choose to develop a focused strategy based solely on the U.S. market, or alternatively, to develop foreign sales and broaden the scope of competition. Which strategy, or combination of strategies, to pursue would take some careful analysis.

6. On the sell side, do you think we should open stores on Amazon, eBay, or other large online retailers, or should we put all our efforts into developing our own branded websites?

You might suggest that many manufacturers rely on both their own sites, as well as Amazon, to sell to consumers. Given Amazon's broad reach it would seem a good idea to use Amazon as a platform for certain very popular tools, and have links to the firm's own websites for consumers who want to see more of the company's products.

7. How do you think we can use social media to support our e-commerce initiative? Should a tools company have a social media presence?

You can suggest here that social media is an excellent platform for branding messages and consumer information. In addition to Facebook, there may be other social networks directed more specifically toward the firm's customers. Twitter should definitely be monitored routinely for customer mentions, to identify influencers to support the firm's products, and of course to obtain direct customer feedback. It would be a good idea to have a social media specialist in marketing to focus on social media marketing.

5.6 CASE STUDY

Dollar Shave Club:
From Viral Video to $1 Billion in Just Five Years

In the past decade, the disruptive influence of the Internet and the mobile platform has reshaped the music industry, newspapers and book publishing, software distribution, and data storage, just to name a few high-profile examples. Companies with business models that would have been inconceivable years ago are ruling the tech landscape today. And traditional retailers find themselves under threat from a host of unexpected startups. One of the more unexpected success stories is the rise of Dollar Shave Club from a small startup with a viral video touting low-cost razor blades to a $1 billion company in less than five years.

Modern entrepreneurs are on the hunt for markets where customers perceive unfairness or inefficiency, but can't do much about it. The U.S. market for razor blades in 2012 was exactly that type of market. Gillette held a 72% market share for razor blades and used its near-monopoly power to great advantage, charging as much as 167% markups for razor blades. Originally, Gillette, Schick, and other razor manufacturers disrupted the business model in their industry by offering razors at low cost or even a loss, and then selling replacement blades at a significant markup, allowing them to make money indefinitely. Today, Dollar Shave Club is disrupting them.

Dollar Shave Club's founder, Michael Dubin, shown below, saw an opportunity where others saw an impenetrable market controlled by an unstoppable juggernaut. Dubin's road

© ZUMA Press, Inc./Alamy Stock Photo

map for Dollar Shave Club was as follows: first, his company would use a subscription-based model that would allow customers to order razors and blades sent directly to their homes for as little as $1 a month before shipping, saving time and money while also undercutting Gillette to gain market share. The company's razors are made inexpensively in South Korea, and distribution was originally done entirely in-house. Cutting out retail outlets creates savings that the company can pass on to its customers. Next, Dubin wanted to create a lifestyle brand as opposed to a simple delivery service, illustrating its contrast with the bigger brands.

Fast forward to 2019, and Gillette's share of the U.S. razor market had dropped significantly, to 53%, due almost entirely to Dollar Shave Club and similar subscription-based companies like Harry's. By 2019, Dollar Shave Club had over 4 million subscribers, over 600 employees, and had become the third largest shaving brand in the United States, behind Gillette and Schick. In 2016, retailing giant Unilever purchased Dollar Shave Club for a whopping $1 billion. Dollar Shave Club had yet to turn a profit and earned only around $150 million in 2015, so that price tag may have seemed steep at the time, but Unilever desperately needed Dollar Shave Club's expertise in online marketing and branding, and Dollar Shave Club's sales have grown explosively in just a few years.

It's not a stretch to say that without "the video," Dollar Shave Club might not be where it is today. In 2012, Dubin himself starred in an online advertisement introducing his company to the world. In it, Dubin strolls through one of his warehouses, cracking jokes while highlighting the selling points of his service, including the surprisingly high costs of razors at supermarkets and their many needless features. The video identifies celebrity endorsements as a primary culprit for the high costs of razors. In 2018, the video had over 25 million views and is frequently cited as an example of marketing done right. The video cost just $4,500 to produce, but generated 12,000 subscriptions in the hours immediately after it went live; and while its impact on the growth of the company is impossible to fully measure, it's certainly paid for itself many times over.

The video is the highest-profile example of Dubin's commitment to turn Dollar Shave Club into a brand that inspires loyalty and engagement in its customers. The company maintains an assortment of perks for its members, including an online men's lifestyle magazine called MEL, a flyer with each delivery called "Bathroom Minutes" that resembles the comics section in the newspaper, and a company podcast that tackles quirky and amusing topics. Dollar Shave Club also employs approximately 100 "Club Pros," who offer grooming advice via e-mail, text, social media, or over the phone. Dubin was the company's first Club Pro, and he traveled the country with other Dollar Shave Club employees to talk to people about what types of features men were looking for in razors and other grooming options. The cross-country trips confirmed Dubin's suspicion that Gillette and other bigger brands had lost sight of what customers actually wanted with its increasingly complicated razors, laden with features nobody actually cared about.

Dollar Shave Club prioritizes unscripted customer service: real live people as opposed to automated systems and interfaces. The Club Pros are just one example. Even rank and file customer service representatives are trained to respond to customer queries in a playful way consistent with the company's brand. For example, one potential customer jokingly asked a customer service agent to solve a Rubik's cube in under two minutes to earn the customer's business. The very next day, the company posted a video clip of an

SOURCES: "Procter & Gamble Writes Down Gillette Business but Remains Confident in Its Future," by Amelia Lucas, Cnbc.com, July 30, 2019' "Funny Is Good Business: Dollar Shave Club Brand Review," by Daniel, Brandastic.com, July 26, 2019; "What Happens When a Business Built on Simplicty Gets Complicated? Dollar Shave Club's Founder Michael Dubin Found Out," by Barbara Booth, Cnbc.com, March 23, 2019; "Dollar Shave Club Deepens Its Executive Bench with C-Suite Hires from Target and Nike," Prnewswire.com, May 1, 2018; "Venture Funding into Subscription Startups Tapers Off," by Mary Ann Azevedo, Crunchbase.com, March 9, 2018; "Dollar Shave Club Is Entering the Cutthroat World of UK Razors: 'We Like Competition'," by Oscar Williams-Grut, Businessinsider.com, January 30, 2018; "How Storytelling Turned Dollar Shave Club into a Billion Dollar Brand," by Joe Lazauskas and Shane Snow, Convinceandconvert.com, accessed 2018; "Gillette Is Introducing Cheaper Blades to Fend Off Dollar Shave Club and Harry's," by Phil Wahba, Fortune.com, November 29, 2017; "What Dollar Shave Club Says About the Future of Subscription Services," by Daphne Howland, Retaildive.com, November 6, 2017; "What It Takes to Build a Company That You Can Sell for $1 Billion, According to a Guy Who Just Did It," by Sonya Mann, Inc.com, October 12, 2017; "How Psychographics Made Dollar Shave Club a Winner," by Ben Zifkin, Mediapost.com, September 12, 2017; "Gillette One Ups Dollar Shave Club with On-Demand Razor Ordering Service Where You Text to Order," by Lauren Thomas, Cnbc.com, May 9, 2017; "Gillette Just Made an Unprecedented Change to Be More Like its Competitors," by Dennis Green, Businessinsider.com, May 9, 2017; "How Dollar

agent doing just that on Facebook. Amused Dollar Shave Club subscribers frequently post particularly memorable interactions with customer service on online forums. For many companies, customer service is a struggle, but for Dollar Shave Club, it's a strength.

Dollar Shave Club uses member feedback to make decisions regarding its product line as well. For example, an exfoliating cloth intended for use in the shower received lukewarm reviews from customers, so the company fully redesigned it from scratch and refunded all of its members who had purchased the initial version. Today, the company uses a 500-member panel of its longest-tenured customers to test new products and offer feedback.

Dollar Shave Club's commitment to its brand and to its members has made the company's customer base extremely loyal and likely to become ambassadors for the brand of their own volition. The typical Dollar Shave Club customer is young, comfortable viewing Internet advertising, and a good fit with the company's easygoing, humorous branding. This valuable user base and impressive relationship with its customers was of major interest to Unilever, whose acquisition of Dollar Shave Club illustrates the pressure that traditional retailers are feeling to learn to sell directly to the consumer, as opposed to via traditional bricks-and-mortar shopping outlets. Companies like Unilever are also much more comfortable advertising on television and focusing on demographic groups, and while Dollar Shave Club did launch its first Super Bowl advertisement in 2016, the company rose to prominence using online-only videos to spread awareness of its brand to highly targeted demographics. Dollar Shave Club only needs to advertise to men, which they can do much more easily online than on television.

Although Dollar Shave Club is a relatively lean company, it still has had to significantly improve its IT infrastructure to keep pace with the company's rapid growth. The company's rapidly growing team of engineers have built the company's software and platforms from scratch. Because Dollar Shave Club's subscription model is relatively new, many e-commerce website vendors, such as Magento, which the company initially used for its website, don't work seamlessly with monthly billing and delivery functions, and Dollar Shave Club's workarounds for the problem frequently malfunctioned. The company realized the need for a customized platform and built one in just three months, including a CRM platform called Brain, a marketing automation platform called Voice that sends out customer e-mails, and other customized applications such as Arm for order fulfillment, Ears for telephone-based customer support, and Hypothalamus for machine learning and data science. Dollar Shave Club is one of many startups that rely fully on Amazon Web Services for its computing resources and bandwidth. AWS's scalability allowed Dollar Shave Club to handle the sudden influx in site traffic it received after its Super Bowl ad.

Dollar Shave Club's rapid growth has come in large part at the expense of Gillette, which is now aggressively seeking to protect its commanding position in the shaving market. In 2017, Gillette launched its Gillette On Demand service, which allows customers to order new razors and blades by text message, as well as receive every fourth order for free after three regular orders. Gillette On Demand orders will arrive within three business days of ordering, and Gillette claims it will offer price points that are competitive with Dollar Shave Club. Gillette also responded to criticisms that its products are overpriced by slashing prices across the board and launched a marketing campaign designed to bring back departed customers. They also sued Dollar Shave Club for patent infringement, but because Dollar Shave Club's razors are simplistic by design, they are likely to enjoy better protection from patent infringement than if they chose to make razors with distinctive features the way Gillette does. The company continued its efforts to recapture lost market share by adding new features to their razors at no extra cost to consumers, but Gillette continues to lose traction in this competitive market.

Dollar Shave Club's growth in the United States has stalled somewhat since its acquisition by Unilever, but the point of the acquisition was for Dollar Shave Club to use Unilever's size and scale to expand globally. After its acquisition, Dollar Shave Club built out its executive team with a Chief Digital Officer, Chief Technology Officer, several other technology-focused executives, and a slew of new engineers to prepare the company for its impending growth. In 2018, Dollar Shave Club officially launched in the United Kingdom, and revealed plans to continue its expansion into Europe. Dubin has noted that thanks to the backing of Unilever, he no longer has to spend multiple months each year raising more venture capital, and can instead focus on the goals of the business, which have not changed. The company rose to prominence because of its understanding of the American male, and it will need to learn how to generate the right message all over again in different countries, where culture and grooming standards are different. The global razor market is valued at approximately $17.5 billion. If Dollar Shave Club can maintain its focus on its brand and its members as it grows, it's likely to meet with similar success in other countries.

More broadly, subscription services in other areas, such as BirchBox for makeup and StitchFix and Trunk Club for clothing, have not been as successful replicating Dollar Shave Club's business model, with lower penetration rates and customer retention rates than Dollar Shave Club. Venture capital for these types of companies has fallen steeply, and only a small percentage of U.S. shoppers have signed up for a subscription service, with the majority of shoppers indicating that they're not interested in any of them. It's possible that only a small number of these companies will still be around in a few years' time, but Dollar Shave Club is well positioned to be one of them.

Shave Club's Founder Built a $1 Billion Company That Changed the Industry," by Jaclyn Trop, Entrepreneur.com, March 28, 2017; "Dollar Shave Club Wins Market Share and Customers with Back-to-Basics Approach," by Alan Livsey, *Financial Times*, March 16, 2017; "The Next Dollar Shave Club Will Need to Meet 3 Criteria," by Tory Green, Businessinsider.com, July 30, 2016; "How Companies Like Dollar Shave Club Are Reshaping the Retail Landscape," by Farhad Manjoo, *New York Times*, July 27, 2016; "$1 Billion for Dollar Shave Club: Why Every Company Should Worry," by Steven Davidoff Solomon, *New York Times*, July 26, 2016; "Manufacturers Make, Shops Sell, But Dollar Shave Club Breaks That Mould," *The Guardian*, July 24, 2016; "Dollar Shave Club Built a Billion Dollar Brand with Bizarre Videos," by Shan Li, *Los Angeles Times*, July 21, 2016; "Why Unilever Really Bought Dollar Shave Club," by Jing Cao and Melissa Mittelman, Bloomberg.com, July 20, 2016; "How Dollar Shave Club Went from Viral Marketer to Engineering Powerhouse," by Natalie Gagliordi, Zdnet.com, July 8, 2016; "Why Dollar Shave Club Invests in Unscripted Customer Service," *Los Angeles Times*, by David Pierson, September 26, 2015.

Case Study Questions

1. What is Dollar Shave Club's business model and how does it differ from its competitors?
2. What are the key elements of Dollar Shave Club's value proposition for consumers?
3. What revenue model does Dollar Shave Club use and why does it work for them?
4. How would you characterize Dollar Shave Club's online business strategy?
5. How have Dollar Shave Club's competitors responded?

5.7 REVIEW

KEY CONCEPTS

- Identify the key components of e-commerce business models.

A successful business model effectively addresses eight key elements:
- *Value proposition*—how a company's product or service fulfills the needs of customers. Typical e-commerce value propositions include personalization, customization, convenience, and reduction of product search and price delivery costs.
- *Revenue model*—how the company plans to make money from its operations. Major e-commerce revenue models include the advertising model, subscription model, transaction fee model, sales model, and affiliate model.
- *Market opportunity*—the revenue potential within a company's intended marketspace.
- *Competitive environment*—the direct and indirect competitors doing business in the same marketspace, including how many there are and how profitable they are.
- *Competitive advantage*—the factors that differentiate the business from its competition, enabling it to provide a superior product at a lower cost.
- *Market strategy*—the plan a company develops that outlines how it will enter a market and attract customers.
- *Organizational development*—the process of defining all the functions within a business and the skills necessary to perform each job, as well as the process of recruiting and hiring strong employees.
- *Management team*—the group of individuals retained to guide the company's growth and expansion.

- Describe the major B2C business models.

There are a number of different business models being used in the B2C e-commerce arena. The major models include the following:
- *Portal*—offers powerful search tools plus an integrated package of content and services; typically utilizes a combined subscription/advertising revenue/transaction fee model; may be general or specialized (vortal).
- *E-tailer*—online version of traditional retailer; includes virtual merchants (online retail store only), bricks-and-clicks e-tailers (online distribution channel for a company that also has physical stores), catalog merchants (online version of direct mail catalog), and manufacturers selling directly to the consumer.
- *Content provider*—information and entertainment companies that provide digital content; typically utilizes an advertising, subscription, or affiliate referral fee revenue model.
- *Transaction broker*—processes online sales transactions; typically utilizes a transaction fee revenue model.
- *Market creator*—uses Internet technology to create markets that bring buyers and sellers together; typically utilizes a transaction fee revenue model.
- *Service provider*—offers services online.
- *Community provider*—provides an online community of like-minded individuals for networking and information sharing; revenue is generated by advertising, referral fees, and subscriptions.

- Describe the major B2B business models.

The major business models used to date in the B2B arena include:
- *E-distributor*—supplies products directly to individual businesses.
- *E-procurement*—single firms create digital markets for thousands of sellers and buyers.
- *Exchange*—independently owned digital marketplace for direct inputs, usually for a vertical industry group.

- *Industry consortium*—industry-owned vertical digital market.
- *Private industrial network*—industry-owned private industrial network that coordinates supply chains with a limited set of partners.

■ **Understand key business concepts and strategies applicable to e-commerce.**

E-commerce has had a major impact on the business environment in the last decade, and has affected:
- *Industry structure*—the nature of players in an industry and their relative bargaining power by changing the basis of competition among rivals, the barriers to entry, the threat of new substitute products, the strength of suppliers, and the bargaining power of buyers.
- *Industry value chains*—the set of activities performed in an industry by suppliers, manufacturers, transporters, distributors, and retailers that transforms raw inputs into final products and services by reducing the cost of information and other transaction costs.
- *Firm value chains*—the set of activities performed within an individual firm to create final products from raw inputs by increasing operational efficiency.
- *Business strategy*—a set of plans for achieving superior long-term returns on the capital invested in a firm by offering unique ways to differentiate products, obtain cost advantages, compete globally, or compete in a narrow market or product segment.

QUESTIONS

1. What distinguishes an e-commerce business plan from a traditional business plan?
2. Identify and describe the business model element that specifies how the company's product will fulfill the needs of its customers.
3. How can e-commerce technologies be used to improve a firm's value web?
4. What are some of the traditional sources of capital for startups?
5. What is a disruptive technology, and how does it differ from a sustaining technology?
6. How does e-commerce enable competition based on cost?
7. What is an on-demand services company?
8. What are some of the ways a firm can pursue a differentiation strategy?
9. What are the benefits offered by incubator investor firms over other traditional sources of capital?
10. What is an unfair competitive advantage?
11. What is an industry structural analysis and what is its place in the e-commerce business plan?
12. What is the key to success for content providers?
13. Discuss the impact of e-commerce technologies on inter-firm rivalry (competition).
14. What disadvantages are faced by "first-mover" companies entering a marketspace?
15. Why is the e-tail sector so competitive?
16. Describe the feature of ubiquity as it applies to e-commerce technology and describe how it has affected the business environment over the past decade.
17. What kinds of firms are considered to be e-commerce enablers?
18. What is an initial coin offering?
19. Define market opportunity and describe how you would determine a new company's realistic market opportunity.
20. What are the main elements of an elevator pitch?

PROJECTS

1. Select an e-commerce company. Visit its website or mobile app and describe its business model based on the information you find there. Identify its customer value proposition, its revenue model, the marketspace it operates in, who its main competitors are, any comparative advantages you believe the company possesses, and what its market strategy appears to be. Also try to locate information about the company's management team and organizational structure. (Check for a page labeled "the Company," "About Us," or something similar.)

2. Examine the experience of shopping online versus shopping in a traditional environment. Imagine that you have decided to purchase a digital camera (or any other item of your choosing). First, shop for the camera in a traditional manner. Describe how you would do so (for example, how you would gather the necessary information you would need to choose a particular item, what stores you would visit, how long it would take, prices, etc.). Next, shop for the item on the Web or via a mobile app. Compare and contrast your experiences. What were the advantages and disadvantages of each? Which did you prefer and why?

3. During the early days of e-commerce, first-mover advantage was touted as one way to success. On the other hand, some suggest that being a market follower can yield rewards as well. Which approach has proven to be more successful—first mover or follower? Choose two e-commerce companies that prove your point, and prepare a brief presentation to explain your analysis and position.

4. Select an e-commerce company that has participated in an incubator program such as Y Combinator, Startupbootcamp, Seedcamp, or INiTS, or another of your choosing, and write a short report on its business model and the amount and sources of capital it has raised thus far. Include your views on the company's future prospects for success. Then create an elevator pitch for the company.

5. Select a B2C e-commerce retail industry segment such as pet products, sporting goods, or toys, and analyze its value chain and industry value chain. Prepare a short presentation that identifies the major industry participants in that business and illustrates the move from raw materials to finished product.

REFERENCES

Aitken, Roger. "EU Regulator Follows U.S. SEC with Stark 'ICO Risk" Warnings." Forbes.com (November 13, 2017). Arthur, W. Brian. "Increasing Returns and the New World of Business." *Harvard Business Review* (July–August 1996).

Barney, J. B. "Firm Resources and Sustained Competitive Advantage." *Journal of Management* Vol. 17, No. 1 (1991).

Bellman, Steven, Gerald L. Lohse, and Eric J. Johnson. "Predictors of Online Buying Behavior." *Communications of the ACM* (December 1999).

Bower, Joseph L., and Clayton Christensen. "Disruptive Technologies: Catching the Wave." *Harvard Business Review* (January–February, 1995).

Christensen, Clayton M., Michael E. Raynor, and Rory McDonald. "What Is Disruptive Innovation?" *Harvard Business Review* (December 2015).

eBay, Inc. "eBay Inc. By the Numbers," (accessed January 28, 2020).

European Commission. "Commission Proposal for a Regulation on European Crowdfunding Service Providers. Ec.europa.eu (March 8, 2018).

Johnson, Mark, and Clayton Christensen. "Reinventing Your Business Model." *Harvard Business Review* (December 2008).

Kambil, Ajit, Ari Ginsberg, and Michael Bloch. "Reinventing Value Propositions." Working Paper, NYU Center for Research on Information Systems (1998).

Kanter, Elizabeth Ross. "The Ten Deadly Mistakes of Wanna-Dots." *Harvard Business Review* (January 2001).

Kaplan, Steven, and Mohanbir Sawhney. "E-Hubs: The New B2B Marketplaces." *Harvard Business Review* (May–June 2000).

Kim, W. Chan, and Renee Mauborgne. "Knowing a Winning Business Idea When You See One." *Harvard Business Review* (September-October 2000).

King, Andrew A., and Baljir Baatartogtokh. "How Useful Is the Theory of Disruptive Innovation?" *Sloan MIT Management Review* (September 15, 2015).

Lepore, Jill. "The Disruption Machine: What the Gospel of Innovation Gets Wrong." *New Yorker* (June 23, 2014).

Magretta, Joan. "Why Business Models Matter." *Harvard Business Review* (May 2002).

Porter, Michael E. "Strategy and the Internet." *Harvard Business Review* (March 2001).

Porter, Michael E. *Competitive Advantage: Creating and Sustaining Superior Performance.* New York: Free Press (1985).

Rigdon, Joan I. "The Second-Mover Advantage." *Red Herring* (September 1, 2000).

Schumpeter, Joseph A. *Capitalism, Socialism and Democracy.* London: Routledge, 1942.

Teece, David J. "Profiting from Technological Innovation: Implications for Integration, Collaboration, Licensing and Public Policy." *Research Policy* 15 (1986).

CHAPTER 6

E-commerce Marketing and Advertising

LEARNING OBJECTIVES

After reading this chapter, you will be able to:

- Understand the key features of the Internet audience, the basic concepts of consumer behavior and purchasing, and how consumers behave online.
- Identify and describe the basic digital commerce marketing and advertising strategies and tools.
- Identify and describe the main technologies that support online marketing.
- Understand the costs and benefits of online marketing communications.

InMobi's
Global Mobile Ad Network

Watch out, tech titans! InMobi, an innovative company based in Bangalore, India, is making some serious waves in the global mobile advertising network marketplace currently dominated by Google, Facebook, and Twitter. InMobi was founded in early 2007 by four graduates of the Indian Institute of Technology, Kanpur, including current CEO Naveen Tewari. After trying out several less sucessful business models, they honed in on mobile advertising. Apple had just introduced the iPhone in early 2007, and few companies were focusing yet on the cellphone as a mobile advertising platform. This idea proved to be the company's golden ticket, and in 2008, Tewari convinced venture firms Kleiner Perkins Caufield & Byers and Sherpalo Investments to make an $8 million investment in the company. They then moved to Bangalore, deeming it a better location from which to attract talent.

© YAY Media AS/Alamy Stock Vector

InMobi bills itself as a mobile advertising platform and solutions provider. It acts as an intermediary between companies that want to advertise and content owners/publishers that offer mobile content, often in the form of apps. For instance, if you've seen the advertisements that appear when you play games on a smartphone, you've probably seen InMobi's mobile ad platform at work. InMobi serves over 200 billion mobile ads a month to over 1.64 billion consumers in over 200 countries. There are over 30,000 apps and mobile sites on the InMobi network, and the company tracks over 2.5 billion app downloads on its platform. InMobi makes money by keeping a percentage of the revenue per ad, typically 30%–40%. Increasingly, InMobi has focused on native advertising as the marketplace abandons banner ads and moves toward more creative and interactive formats. Native advertising appears seamlessly within an app and often as if it were a post from a friend. InMobi's customers include Unilever, Samsung, Microsoft, Adidas, and a rapidly growing number of other prominent companies and brands.

InMobi grew quickly using a "reverse market strategy," establishing leadership positions in Asia and Africa first and then tackling the EU and U.S. markets. Today, the company employs over 900 people and has offices around the world, including in Asia (India, China, Singapore, Malaysia, South Korea, Taiwan, and Japan), Australia, the European Union (Germany, the United Kingdom, Spain, France, and Sweden), the Middle East (the UAE), and the United States (San Francisco). Fueled in part by a $200 million investment from Japanese media and telecommunications giant Softbank, which valued InMobi at over $1

SOURCES: "WPP and inMobi Group Enter into a Multi-Year Strategic Partnership to Co-build Unique Benefits," Wpp.com, September 11, 2019; "InMobi's Glance Raises $45M to Expand Outside of India," by Manish Singh, September 10, 2019; "InMobi's Newly-Created Lock-screen Technology Business Just Raised $45 Million," by Ananya Bhattacharya, Qz.com, September 20, 2019; "Start-up Poster Boy inMobi May Hit $1-bn Revenue," by Peerzada Abrar & Yuvraj Malik, Business-standard.com, May 2, 2019; "India's InMobi Ramps Up Ad Challenge to Google and Facebook," by Prabhu Mallikarjunan, *Nikkei Asian Review*, March 4, 2019; "TruFactor, a New Business Unit of inMobi, Launches a Secure Data Platform for Telcos Powered by Microsoft Azure, Inmobi.com, February 25, 2019; "SoftBank-backed InMobi to Invest $100 Million in New Unit TruFactor," by Leslie D'Monte, Livemint.com, February 25, 2019; "Ad-fraud Shift from Desktop to Mobile Sparks Partnership," by Ginger Conlon, Thedrum.com, December 11, 2018; "Start-up Poster Boy InMobi Pivots, Eyes Enterprise Space," by Peerzada Abrar, Thehindu.com, October 28, 2018; "InMobi in Big Boys Club Thanks to Top Allies," by Raghu Krishnan, Economictimes.indiatimes.com, October 23, 2018; "Sprint Sells Mobile Advertising Unit to InMobi," by Sheila Dang, Reuters.com, October 17, 2018; "Eros Now Anounces Partnership with InMobi," Businesswire.com, August 2, 2018; "InMobi Launches Programmatic Exchange in Asia Pacific to Accelerate Mobile Spend," by Shawn Lim, Thedrum.com, July 25, 2018; "InMobi and Microsoft Partner on Cloud-based Mobile Enterprise Marketing Platform," by Dean Takahashi, Venturebeat.com, June 26, 2018; "InMobi Scoops up AerServ for $90 Million," by Ginny Marvin, Martechtoday.com, January 10, 2018; "InMobi: Is India's First Unicorn Really Profitable?" by Dearton Thomas Hector and Anand J, Vccircle.com, January 8, 2018; "InMobi Ready for Bolder Bets, Plans India Expansion," by Nishant Sharma, Bloombergquint.com,

billion, InMobi generates the majority of its revenues from the United States (55%), but revenues from China (25%) have grown quickly, since the country is an area of weakness for competitors Facebook and Google, and other emerging markets such as India and Indonesia have also shown promise. InMobi launched its programmatic exchange in Asia Pacific in late 2018.

Can InMobi truly hope to challenge Google, which is currently the dominant leader in market share? Although its revenues grew by 20% to over $500 million for its fiscal year 2018–2019, it recorded a $5 million loss for the year. However, InMobi boasts a growing number of partnerships with ad agencies such as WPP and with other tech firms, including marketing company Amobee, payment processing firm Stripe, Chinese tech firms APUS and Xiaomi, and Dell. In 2018, it added Sprint and Microsoft to this list, purchasing Sprint's mobile and data advertising company, Pinsight Media, and moving its InMobi Marketing Cloud to Microsoft Azure, combining its own data with Microsoft's in the process. Together, the two companies hope to attract large companies to use InMobi's solutions for mobile marketing in tandem with the Azure cloud. In 2019, inMobi launched TruFactor, an independent business unit derived from its Pinsight Media acquisition, aimed at telecommunications companies and using Microsoft Azure at the delivery platform. InMobi plans to invest $100 million in TruFactor. Tewari also points to InMobi's primary focus on mobile, compared to Google, which is involved in many different areas, as well as its low cost compared to Google, Facebook, and other Silicon Valley companies. InMobi also claims that its technology is superior and that its data on customers is richer and more granular. InMobi backed up its claims when it became one of the first mobile advertising companies to offer a 100% viewability guarantee, a rarity in the modern landscape of ad blockers and ad fraud. As more advertisers gravitate to the mobile platform, its emphasis on ensuring that ads are viewable should help InMobi differentiate itself from the pack.

InMobi has partnered with video advertising and tracking firm DoubleVerify to ensure that its ads are viewable and trackable by third parties. inMobi is working with DoubleVerify to curtail common forms of ad fraud, including app spoofing (apps which impersonate more popular apps to fool consumers), hidden embedded browsers (browsers that secretly take app users to advertisers' sites without permission), and apps that fully hijack mobile devices. In 2018, InMobi also purchased mobile revenue management platform AerServ, which further boosted its video ad capability and boosted InMobi's presence in the United States. AerServ runs 90 billion ad sessions each month across over 2,000 apps and has developed proprietary technology that allows real-time bidding on ad space within native apps, improving revenues for publishers. After the acquisition, InMobi achieved a 90% viewability rate and 70% video completion rate, both of which are double the industry benchmarks.

Tewari's confidence in InMobi's proprietary technology stems from InMobi's "appographic" targeting system, which uses algorithms and data on how users interact with apps to determine very precise trends and preferences of those users. To develop the system, InMobi studied over 100,000 apps and how different types of consumers used them. The result is a system so accurate that InMobi has guaranteed 2%–3% increases in engagement by app developers using InMobi's services. InMobi has continued to innovate, honing the Geo Context Targeting system used in its Smart Ads, which it says generate ten times the interaction compared to traditional ads and more than three times the conversion rate of traditional ads. SmartAds support rich media and are tailored based on users' personal details and geographic conditions in the area, such as location and nearby weather. For example, if you're strolling city streets on a hot summer afternoon, you'll be given advertisements for cold beverages from nearby food chains.

Although InMobi's revenues have grown significantly in the past few years, the company has struggled to meet the growth targets set by Tewari and other analysts in years past. Tewari boldly predicted that the company would soon be earning $1 billion in revenue, but has not yet achieved that benchmark. The company has only shown a profit in one year (2017) since its founding in 2007. This is in part because of high-profile failures such as theMiip personalized discovery tool, which was launched in 2015 with expectations that it would generate up to $1 billion in revenue, but which was discontinued almost completely soon thereafter due to its lukewarm reception. InMobi also struggled to adjust to significant attrition within its senior management and staff, with the company's chief financial officer, vice president of finance, and vice president of engineering all leaving the company. Finally, the company was hit with a $4 million fine by the U.S. Federal Trade Commission for keeping data on underage users without consent.

However, InMobi appears to have weathered these storms and is positioned to succeed going forward. The company trimmed its staff and renewed its focus on its core businesses, which have proven to be successful and stable. Perhaps most promising of all for inMobi's prospects is the continuing trend toward programmatic digital display advertising, and mobile advertising in general. Another potential area of growth for the company is selling ads via over-the-top (OTT) television services, which allow content providers to bypass traditional cable providers in favor of Internet-based streaming. In 2018, InMobi partnered with Indian OTT service Eros to allow advertisers to sell ads on the Eros Now content streaming platform. In 2019, inMobi launched a new subsidiary, Glance, which uses artificial intelligence to show media content in local languages such as Hindi, Tamil, and Telugu, as well as English, and otherwise personalize on Android smartphone lock screens. Through partnerships with various manufacturers, the platform is installed by default in 70% of all new smartphones being sold in India. In the future are plans to expand the platform to short videos as well as games, with further plans for shopping and real-time local marketing. inMobi also plans to expand Glance beyond India, raising $45 billion in venture capital for that purpose. Though profitability has been elusive for InMobi, the company has continued to narrow its losses as it scales and grows into new markets. Although InMobi has powerful competitors in Google and Facebook, there is enough room for many winners in this growing market.

November 5, 2017; "InMobi Turns Profitable, Revenue Crosses $300m in 2016," by Shilpa Phadnis and Sujit John, Timesofindia.indiatimes.com, April 5, 2017; "InMobi Partners with Xiaomi for Displaying Video Ads," by Vivek Pai, Medianama.com, January 4, 2017; "InMobi Bulks Up on Viewability Via Partnerships with Moat and DoubleVerify," by Tobi Elkin, Mediapost.com, November 1, 2016; "Mobile Adtech Co InMobi to Double Its Investment in China," by Shadma Shaikh, Economictimes.indiatimes.com, October 13, 2016; "InMobi Technologies to Discontinue Use of Mascot Function on Miip Platform," by Sadhana Chathurvedula, Livemint.com, June 17, 2016; "InMobi Vouches 100% Viewability on Mobile Ads," by Dhanya Ann Thoppil, Livemint.com, November 20, 2015; "India's Global Ad Giant Taking on Google and Facebook," by Kinjal Pandya-Wagh, Bbc.com, October 20, 2015; "With $100 Million, InMobi Raises the Banner for the Future," by Pankaj Mishra, *Economic Times*, September 29, 2015; "India's InMobi Ties Up with China's APUS to Take On Google," Cnbc.com, September 16, 2015; "Dell, InMobi Forge Alliance for E-Commerce Platform," by Anirban Sen, *Economic Times*, September 14, 2015; "Why InMobi May Be India's Most Innovative Company," by Malini Goyal, *Economic Times*, August 2, 2015; "InMobi Decoded: How Bangalore-based Firm Is Taking On Google and Facebook," by Peerzada Abrar and Krithika Krishnamurthy, *The Economic Times*, March 7, 2014; "How inMobiI Grew from a Startup to a Giant Mobile Ad Network," by Willis Wee, Techinasia.com, May 16, 2013; "Softbank Invests $200M in InMobi," by Jamie Yap, Zdnet.com, September 15, 2011.

Perhaps no area of business has been more affected by Internet and mobile platform technologies than marketing and marketing communications. As a communications tool, the Internet affords marketers new ways of contacting millions of potential customers at costs far lower than traditional media. The Internet also provides new ways—often instantaneous and spontaneous—to gather information from customers, adjust product offerings, and increase customer value. The Internet has spawned entirely new ways to identify and communicate with customers, including search engine marketing, social marketing, behavioral targeting, and targeted e-mail, among others. And the Internet was just the first transformation. Today, the mobile platform based on smartphones and tablet computers is transforming online marketing and communications yet again. **Table 6.1** summarizes some of the significant new developments in online marketing and advertising for 2019–2020.

The subject of online marketing, branding, and market communications is very broad and deep. We have created two chapters to cover the material. In this chapter, we begin by examining consumer behavior on the Web, the major types of online marketing and branding, and the technologies that support advances in online marketing. We then focus on understanding the costs and benefits of online marketing communications. In Chapter 7, we focus on the social, mobile, and local marketing phenomenon in greater depth.

6.1 CONSUMERS ONLINE: THE INTERNET AUDIENCE AND CONSUMER BEHAVIOR

Before firms can begin to sell their products online, they must first understand what kinds of people they will find online and how those people behave in the online marketplace. In this section, we focus primarily on individual consumers in the business-to-consumer (B2C) arena. However, many of the factors discussed apply to the B2B arena as well, insofar as purchasing decisions by firms are made by individuals. We cover B2B marketing in more depth in Chapter 12. For readers who have no background in marketing, we have created an online Learning Track, Learning Track 6.1, that discusses basic marketing and branding concepts.

INTERNET TRAFFIC PATTERNS: THE ONLINE CONSUMER PROFILE

We will start with an analysis of some basic background demographics of online consumers. The first principle of marketing and sales is "know thy customer." Who is online, who shops online and why, and what do they buy? In 2019, over 3.8 billion people of all ages had access to the Internet (eMarketer, Inc., 2019a).

Although the number of new online users increased at a rate of 30% a year or higher in the early 2000s, over the last several years, this growth rate has slowed. U.S. e-commerce businesses can no longer count on a double-digit growth rate in the online population to fuel their revenues. The days of rapid growth in the U.S. Internet population are over.

TABLE 6.1	WHAT'S NEW IN ONLINE MARKETING AND ADVERTISING 2019–2020
BUSINESS	
	• Online marketing and advertising spending worldwide continues to increase (by over 17% in 2019), while most forms of traditional media marketing and advertising were either flat or declined. • Mobile advertising in all formats continues to be one of the fastest growing types of digital advertising, and now is the platform for almost 75% of all digital advertising spending. • Search engine marketing and advertising maintains its importance, but its rate of growth is slowing somewhat compared to other formats. • Social and local marketing spending continue to rapidly expand. • Viewability issues and ad fraud raise increasing concerns for marketers. • Native advertising and other forms of content marketing continue to rise.
TECHNOLOGY	
	• Ad blocking software usage increases, creating concerns for both online publishers and advertisers. • Big data: online tracking produces oceans of data, challenging business analytics programs. • Cloud computing makes rich marketing content and multi-channel, cross-platform marketing a reality. • Programmatic advertising (an automated, technology-driven method of buying and selling display and video ads) takes off.
SOCIETY	
	• Targeted advertising based on behavioral tracking leads to growing privacy awareness and fears.

Intensity and Scope of Usage

The slowing rate of growth in the Internet population is compensated for, in part, by an increasing intensity and scope of use. For instance, in 2019, about 85% of the U.S. population regularly used the Internet, spending over six and a half hours a day using digital media (eMarketer, Inc., 2019a, 2019b). Internet use by U.S. teens is even more pervasive, with 95% having access to a smartphone, and with 45% reporting that they use the Internet almost constantly, while another 44% say they use it several times a day (Pew Research Center, 2018a). Today, smartphones and tablets are major access points to the Internet, particularly for teens and young adults. Almost 3.3 billion people, almost 85% of all Internet users, access the Internet using a mobile device (eMarketer, Inc., 2019c). Owners of mobile devices in the UK spend over three and a half hours a day using them for nontelephone activities such as viewing videos, visiting social networks, and playing games (eMarketer, Inc., 2019d). Engaging in such activities is widespread—for example, in the United States in 2018, around 230 million users watched videos, over 180 million visited a social network, over 140 million played games, and millions of others listened to music or shopped. As the amount of time spent using mobile devices continues to increase, it is beginning to generate somewhat of a backlash, and in 2018, Apple introduced several new features that will help users monitor, and set limits on, their smartphone usage (Reardon and Tibkin, 2018).

Demographics and Access

In the United States, demographic profile of the Internet—and e-commerce—has changed greatly since 1995. Up until 2000, single, white, young, college-educated males with high incomes dominated the Internet. This inequality in access and usage led to concerns about a possible "digital divide." However, in recent years, there has been a marked increase in Internet usage by females, minorities, seniors, and families with modest incomes, resulting in a notable decrease—but not elimination—in the earlier inequality of access and usage.

A roughly equal percentage of men (88%) and women (85%) in the United States use the Internet today. Young adults (18–24) form the age group with the highest percentage of Internet use at over 98%, followed closely by teens (12–17) at 97%. Adults in the 25–54 group are also strongly represented, all with percentages of over 90%. Another fast-growing group online is the 65 and over segment, about 70% of whom now use the Internet. The percentage of very young children (0–11 years) online has also spurted, to about 68% of that age group. Future Internet user growth in the United States will come predominantly from those aged 65 and older and from children in the 0–11 age bracket (eMarketer, Inc., 2019e, 2019f).

Variation across racial and ethnic groups is not as wide as across age groups. Ten years ago, there were significant differences among such groups in the United States, but this has receded. In 2019, 92% of whites used the Internet, compared to 88% of Hispanics, and 85% of blacks. About 98% of U.S. households with income levels above $75,000 used the Internet, compared to only 82% of households earning less than $30,000. Over time, income differences have declined but they remain significant with over a 15% gap between the highest category of household income and the lowest. Amount of education also makes a significant difference when it comes to Internet usage. Of those individuals with less than a high school education, only 71% went online in 2019, compared to 98% of individuals with a college degree or more. Even some college education boosted Internet usage, with that segment reaching 95% (Pew Research Center, 2019a).

Overall, the so-called "digital divide" has indeed moderated, but it still persists along income, education, age, and ethnic dimensions. Gender, income, education, age, and ethnicity also impact online behavior. According to the Pew Research Center, U.S. adults over the age of 65, those who have not completed high school, those who make less than $30,000 a year, and Hispanics are all less likely to purchase products online. Women are slightly more likely to purchase online than men, but not significantly so. With respect to online banking, the demographics are similar—those 65 and older are less likely than any age group to bank online, while those with at least some college are more likely than those with a high school diploma or less. Online banking is also more popular with men than women. No significant differences were found in terms of ethnicity (Pew Research Center, 2012). Other commentators have observed that children of poorer and less educated families spend considerably more time using their access devices for entertainment (movies, games, Facebook, and texting) than do children from wealthier households. For all children and teenagers, the majority of time spent on the Internet is often labeled as "wasted time" because the majority of online use is for entertainment, and not education or learning.

Type of Internet Connection: Broadband and Mobile Impacts

While a great deal of progress has been made in reducing glaring gaps in access to the Internet, there are still inequalities in access to broadband service. Research by the Pew Research Center indicates that broadband adoption levels are lower for older adults, those with low levels of education, and those with low household incomes. Rural residents, African Americans, and Latinos are also less likely to have a home broadband connection. For marketers, the broadband audience offers unique opportunities for the use of multimedia marketing campaigns and for the positioning of products especially suited for this more educated and affluent audience. It is also important to note that just because a household does not have broadband access, it does not mean that household members do not use the Internet; they just do so from another location such as a library or via a smartphone. Certain groups are particularly reliant on smartphones for online access: younger adults in the 18–29 age group, those with low household incomes and levels of education, and non-whites (Pew Research Center, 2019b). The explosive growth of smartphones and tablet computers connected to broadband cellular and Wi-Fi networks is the foundation for a truly mobile e-commerce and marketing platform, which did not exist a few years ago.

Community Effects: Social Contagion in Social Networks

For a physical retail store, the most important factor in shaping sales is location, location, location. If you are located where thousands of people pass by every day, you will tend to do well. But for Internet retailers, physical location has almost no consequence as long as customers can be served by shipping services such as UPS or the post office or their services can be downloaded to anywhere. What does make a difference for consumer purchases on the Internet is whether or not the consumer is located in "neighborhoods" where others purchase on the Internet. These neighborhoods can be either face-to-face and truly personal, or digital. These so-called neighborhood effects, and the role of social emulation in consumption decisions, are well known for goods such as personal computers. In general, there is a relationship between being a member of a social network and purchasing decisions. Yet the relationship between "connectedness" (either offline or online) and purchase decisions is not straightforward or simple. People who score in the top 10%–15% of connectedness "do their own thing" to differentiate themselves and often do not share purchase decisions with friends. In fact, highly connected users often stop purchasing what their friends purchase. One can think of them as iconoclasts. The middle 50% of connected people very often share purchase patterns of their friends. One can think of these people as "keeping up with the Joneses" (Iyengar et al., 2009). A study of 6,000 social network users found that social networks have a powerful influence on shopping and purchasing behavior. An estimated 40% of social media users have purchased an item after sharing or favoriting it on Facebook, Pinterest, or Twitter. Facebook is the network most likely to drive customers to purchase, followed by Pinterest and Twitter. Social networks increase research online, followed by purchase offline (sometimes referred to as ROPO or webrooming), driving purchase traffic into physical stores where the product can be seen, tried, and then purchased. This is the opposite of the showrooming effect where consumers shop in stores and then purchase online. The ROPO/webrooming effect has been found to be as large as the showrooming effect (eMarketer, Inc., 2018e; Vision Critical, 2013; Schleifer, 2013; Sevitt and Samuel, 2013).

Membership in social networks has a large influence on discovering new independent music, but less influence on already well known products (Garg, 2009). Membership in an online brand community like Ford's Facebook page and community has a direct effect on sales (Adjei et al., 2009). Amazon's recommender systems ("Consumers who bought this item also bought ...") create co-purchase networks where people do not know one another personally, but nevertheless triple the influence of complementary products (Oestreicher-Singer and Sundararajan, 2008). The value of social networks to marketers rests on the proposition that brand strength and purchase decisions are closely related to network membership, rank, prominence, and centrality (Guo et al., 2011).

CONSUMER BEHAVIOR MODELS

Once firms have an understanding of who is online, they need to focus on how consumers behave online. The study of **consumer behavior** is a social science discipline that attempts to model and understand the behavior of humans in a marketplace. Several social science disciplines play roles in this study, including sociology, psychology, and economics. Models of consumer behavior attempt to predict or "explain" what consumers purchase and where, when, how much, and why they buy. The expectation is that if the consumer decision-making process can be understood, firms will have a much better idea how to market and sell their products. **Figure 6.1** illustrates a general consumer behavior model that takes into account a wide range of factors that influence a consumer's marketplace decisions. Learning Track 6.2 contains further information about the cultural, social, and psychological background factors that influence consumer behavior.

Online consumer behavior parallels that of offline consumer behavior with some obvious differences. It is important to first understand why people choose to purchase online rather than in a store. While price is an important consideration, consumers also shop online because of convenience, which in turn is produced largely by saving them time. Overall transaction cost reduction appears to be a major motivator for choosing the online channel (eMarketer, Inc., 2018e).

consumer behavior
a social science discipline that attempts to model and understand the behavior of humans in a marketplace

FIGURE 6.1 A GENERAL MODEL OF CONSUMER BEHAVIOR

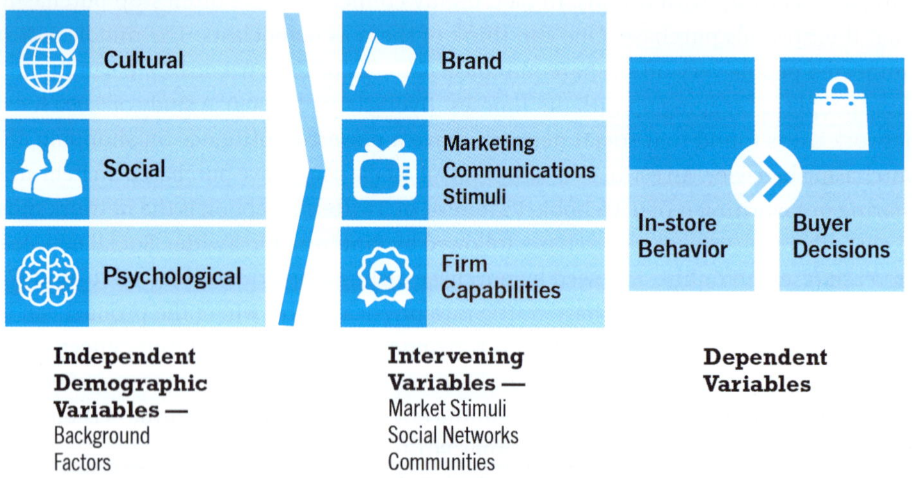

Independent Demographic Variables — Background Factors	Intervening Variables — Market Stimuli Social Networks Communities	Dependent Variables
Cultural	Brand	In-store Behavior → Buyer Decisions
Social	Marketing Communications Stimuli	
Psychological	Firm Capabilities	

Consumer behavior models try to predict the decisions that consumers make in the marketplace.
SOURCE: Adapted from Kotler and Armstrong, *Principles of Marketing*, 13e, 2009, reprinted by permission of Pearson Education, Inc.

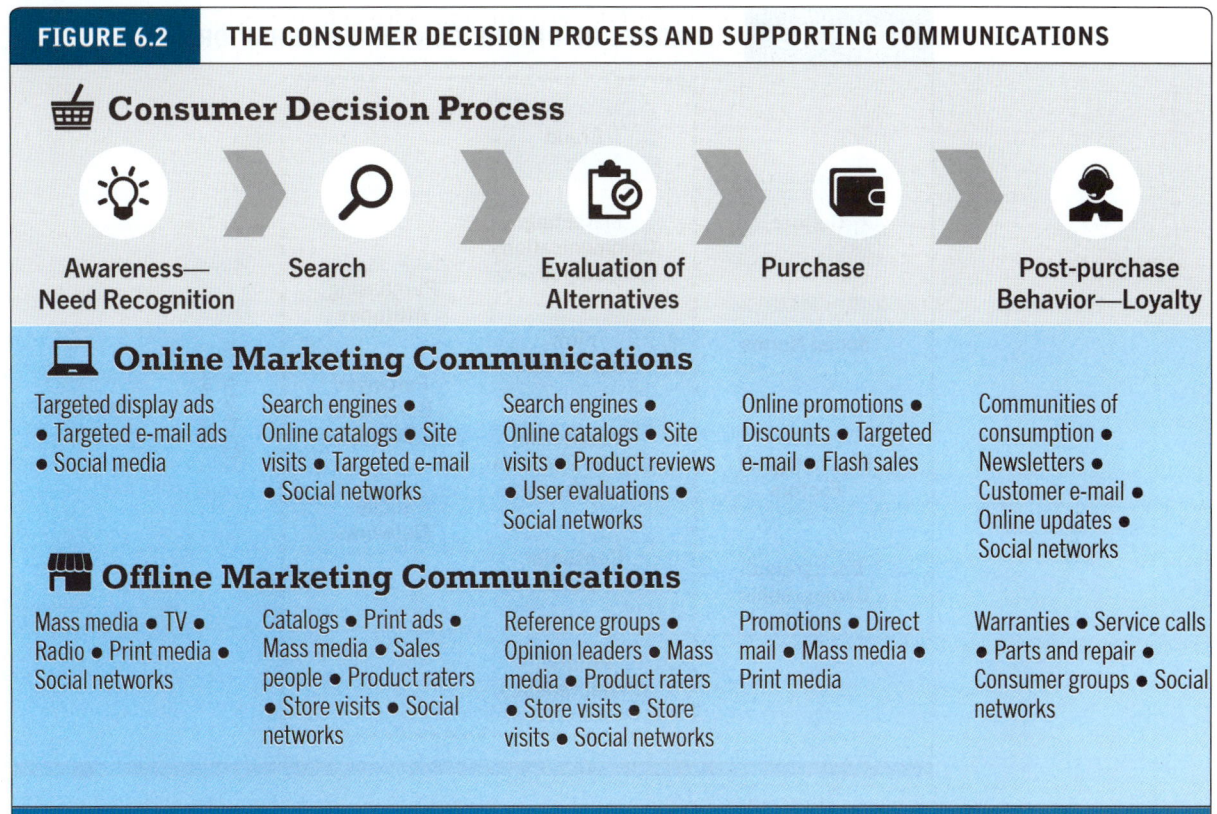

FIGURE 6.2 THE CONSUMER DECISION PROCESS AND SUPPORTING COMMUNICATIONS

THE ONLINE PURCHASING DECISION

Once online, why do consumers actually purchase a product or service at a specific site? Among the most important reasons are price and the availability of free shipping. That the seller is someone whom the purchaser trusts is also a very important factor. The ability to make a purchase without paying tax and the availability of an online coupon are also significant factors.

You also need to consider the process that buyers follow when making a purchase decision, and how the Internet environment affects consumers' decisions. There are five stages in the consumer decision process: awareness of need, search for more information, evaluation of alternatives, the actual purchase decision, and post-purchase contact with the firm. **Figure 6.2** shows the consumer decision process and the types of offline and online marketing communications that support this process and seek to influence the consumer before, during, and after the purchase decision.

The stages of the consumer decision process are basically the same whether the consumer is offline or online. On the other hand, the general model of consumer behavior requires modification to take into account new factors, and the unique features of e-commerce that allow new opportunities to interact with the customer online also need to be

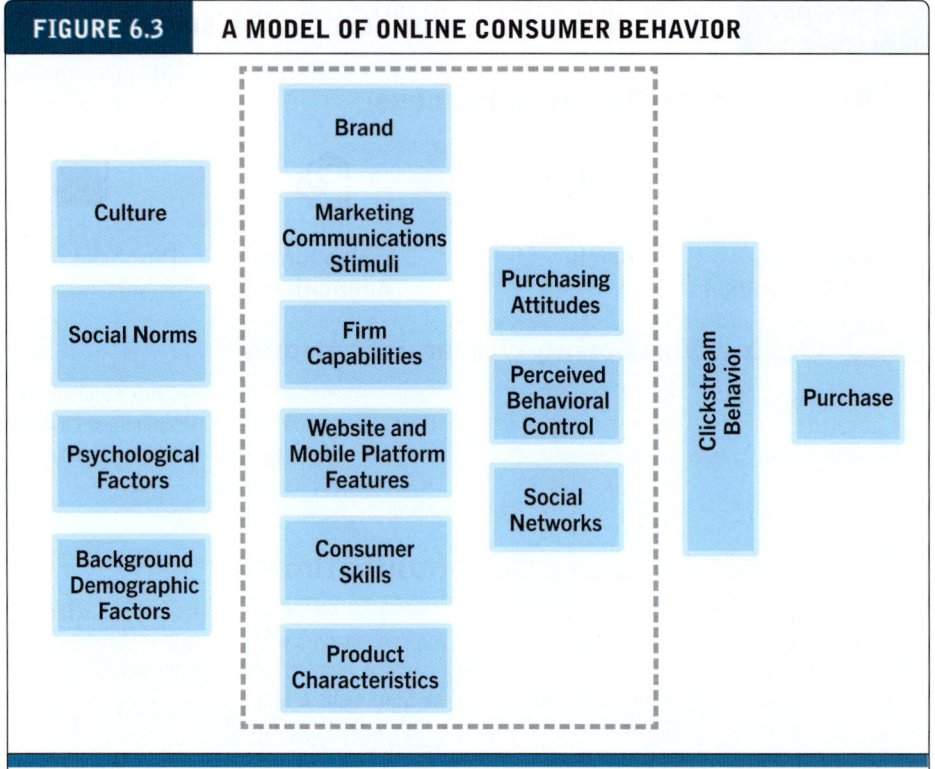

FIGURE 6.3 A MODEL OF ONLINE CONSUMER BEHAVIOR

In this general model of online consumer behavior, the decision to purchase is shaped by background demographic factors, several intervening factors, and, finally, influenced greatly by clickstream behavior very near to the precise moment of purchase.

accounted for. In **Figure 6.3**, we have modified the general model of consumer behavior to focus on user characteristics, product characteristics, and website and mobile platform features, along with traditional factors such as brand strength and specific market communications (advertising) and the influence of both online and offline social networks.

In the online model, website and mobile platform features, along with consumer skills, product characteristics, attitudes towards online purchasing, and perceptions about control over the online environment come to the fore. Website and mobile platform features include latency (delay in downloads), navigability, and confidence in online security. There are parallels in the analog world. For instance, it is well known that consumer behavior can be influenced by store design, and that understanding the precise movements of consumers through a physical store can enhance sales if goods and promotions are arranged along the most likely consumer tracks. Consumer skills refers to the knowledge that consumers have about how to conduct online transactions (which increases with experience). Product characteristics refers to the fact that some products can be easily described, packaged, and shipped online, whereas others cannot. Combined with traditional factors, such as brand, advertising, and firm capabilities, these factors lead to specific attitudes about purchasing from an e-commerce firm (trust in the firm and favorable customer experience) and a sense that the consumer can control his or her environment online.

Clickstream behavior refers to the transaction log that consumers establish as they move about the Web, from search engine to a variety of sites, then to a single site, then to a single page, and then, finally, to a decision to purchase. These precious moments are similar to "point-of-purchase" moments in traditional retail. A study of over 10,000 visits to an online wine store found that detailed and general clickstream behavior were as important as customer demographics and prior purchase behavior in predicting a current purchase (Van den Poel and Buckinx, 2005). Clickstream marketing takes maximum advantage of the Internet environment. It presupposes no prior "deep" knowledge of the customer (and in that sense is "privacy-regarding"), and can be developed dynamically as customers use the Internet. For instance, the success of search engine marketing (the display of paid advertisements by search engines) is based in large part on what the consumer is looking for at the moment and how they go about looking (detailed clickstream data). After examining the detailed data, general clickstream data is used (days since last visit, past purchases). If available, demographic data is used (region, city, and gender).

clickstream behavior
the transaction log that consumers establish as they move about the Web

SHOPPERS: BROWSERS AND BUYERS

The picture of Internet use sketched in the previous section emphasizes the complexity of behavior online. Although the Internet audience still tends to be concentrated among the well-educated, affluent, and youthful, the audience is increasingly becoming more diverse. Clickstream analysis shows us that people go online for many different reasons. Online shopping is similarly complex. Beneath the surface of the over $4.2 trillion B2C e-commerce market in 2019 are substantial differences in how users shop online.

For instance, as shown in **Figure 6.4**, over 88.8% of UK Internet users of ages 14 and older are "buyers" who actually purchase something online. Another 5.4% research

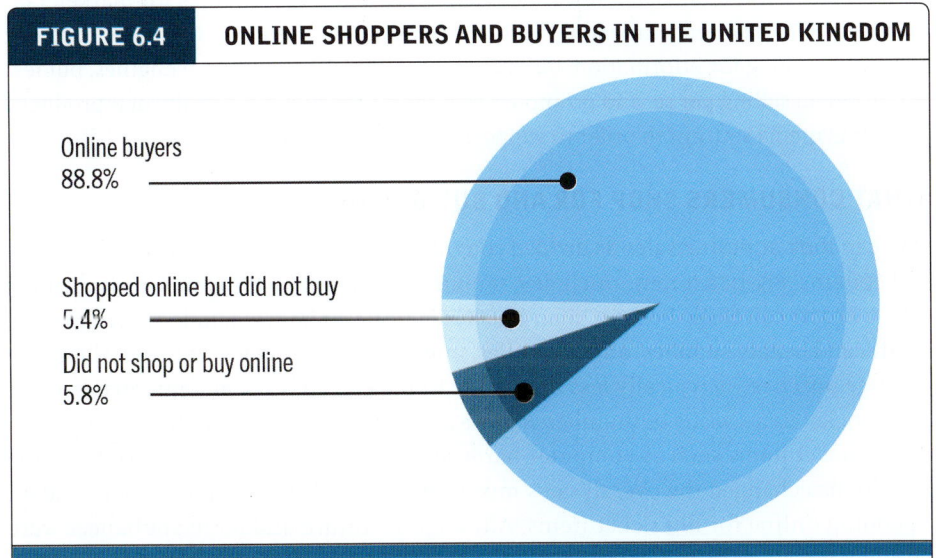

FIGURE 6.4 ONLINE SHOPPERS AND BUYERS IN THE UNITED KINGDOM

Online buyers
88.8%

Shopped online but did not buy
5.4%

Did not shop or buy online
5.8%

Over 94% of UK Internet users of ages 14 and older shop online on desktop computers and mobile devices, either by researching products or by purchasing products online. The percentage of those actually purchasing has increased to over 88%. Only 5.8% do not buy or shop online.
SOURCE: Based on data from eMarketer, Inc., 2019g.

products online ("browsers"), but purchase them offline. Worldwide, there were over 2 billion online buyers in 2019, and that number is expected to grow to almost 2.5 billion by 2023. Most marketers find this an exciting prospect. (eMarketer, Inc., 2019g, 2019h).

The significance of online browsing for offline purchasing should not be underestimated. Although it is difficult to precisely measure the amount of offline sales that occur because of online product research, Forrester Research estimates that about $2.6 trillion of U.S. in-store retail purchases in 2018 were influenced by consumers' use of digital devices prior to or during a physical shopping trip, about half of total in-store sales (Forrester Research, 2018).

E-commerce is a major conduit and generator of offline commerce. The reverse is also true: online traffic is driven by offline brands and shopping. While online research influences offline purchases, it is also the case that offline marketing media heavily influence online behavior including sales. Traditional print media (magazines and newspapers) and television are by far the most powerful media for reaching and engaging consumers with information about new products and directing them to the Web. Online communities and blogging are also very influential but not yet as powerful as traditional media. This may be surprising to many given the attention to social networks as marketing vehicles, but it reflects the diversity of influences on consumer behavior and the real-world marketing budgets of firms that are still heavily dominated by traditional media. Even more surprising in the era of Facebook, face-to-face interactions are a more powerful influence than participation in online social communities.

These considerations strongly suggest that e-commerce and traditional commerce are coupled and should be viewed by merchants (and researchers) as part of a continuum of consuming behavior and not as radical alternatives to one another. Commerce is commerce; the customers are often the same people. Customers use a wide variety of media, sometimes multiple media at once. The significance of these findings for marketers is very clear. Online merchants should build the information content of their sites to attract browsers looking for information, build content to rank high in search engines, put less attention on selling per se, and promote services and products (especially new products) in offline media settings in order to support their online stores.

WHAT CONSUMERS SHOP FOR AND BUY ONLINE

You can look at online sales as divided roughly into two groups: small-ticket and big-ticket items. Big-ticket items include computer equipment and consumer electronics, where orders can easily be more than $1,000. Small-ticket items include apparel, books, health and beauty supplies, office supplies, music, software, videos, and toys, where the average purchase is typically less than $100. In the early days of e-commerce, sales of small-ticket items vastly outnumbered those of large-ticket items. But the recent growth of big-ticket items such as computer hardware, consumer electronics, furniture, and jewelry has changed the overall sales mix. Consumers are now much more confident spending online for big-ticket items. Although furniture and large appliances were initially perceived as too bulky to sell online, these categories have rapidly expanded in the last few years. Free shipping offered by Amazon and other large retailers has also contributed to consumers buying many more expensive and large items online such as air conditioners. Refer to Figure 9.2 to see how much consumers spent online for various categories of goods in 2018.

INTENTIONAL ACTS: HOW SHOPPERS FIND VENDORS ONLINE

Given the prevalence of "click here" display ads, one might think customers are "driven" to online vendors by spur-of-the-moment decisions. In fact, only a tiny percentage of shoppers click on display ads to find vendors. E-commerce shoppers are highly intentional. Typically, they are focused browsers looking for specific products, companies, and services. Once they are online, a majority of consumers use a search engine as their preferred method of research for purchasing a product. Many will go directly to a online marketplace, such as Amazon or eBay, and some will go directly to a specific retail website (eMarketer, Inc., 2018e). Merchants can convert these "goal-oriented," intentional shoppers into buyers if the merchants can target their communications to the shoppers and design their sites in such a way as to provide easy-to-access and useful product information, full selection, and customer service, and do this at the very moment the customer is searching for the product. This is no small task.

WHY SOME PEOPLE DON'T SHOP ONLINE

About 5.8% of UK Internet users do not shop or buy online. Why not? One of the most important factors cited by those who don't shop or buy online is the "trust factor," the fear that online merchants will cheat you, lose your credit card information, or use personal information you give them to invade your personal privacy, bombarding you with unwanted e-mail and pop-up ads. Secondary factors can be summarized as "hassle factors," like shipping costs, returns, and inability to touch and feel the product.

TRUST, UTILITY, AND OPPORTUNISM IN ONLINE MARKETS

A long tradition of research shows that the two most important factors shaping the decision to purchase online are utility and trust (Brookings Institute, 2011; Kim et al., 2009; Ba and Pavlou, 2002). Consumers want good deals, bargains, convenience, and speed of delivery. In short, consumers are looking for utility. On the other hand, in any seller-buyer relationship, there is an asymmetry of information. The seller usually knows a lot more than the consumer about the quality of goods and terms of sale. This can lead to opportunistic behavior by sellers (Akerlof, 1970; Williamson, 1985; Mishra, 1998). Consumers need to trust a merchant before they make a purchase. Sellers can develop trust among online consumers by building strong reputations of honesty, fairness, and delivery of quality products—the basic elements of a brand. Online recommendations from previous purchasers and feedback forums are examples of trust-building online mechanisms (eMarketer, Inc., 2017a). Online sellers who develop trust among consumers are able to charge a premium price for their online products and services (Kim and Benbasat, 2006, 2007; Pavlou, 2002). A review of the literature suggests that the most important factors leading to a trusting online relationship are perception of website credibility, ease of use, and perceived risk (Corritore et al., 2006). An important brake on the growth of e-commerce is lack of trust. Newspaper and television ads are more trusted than online ads (eMarketer, Inc., 2017b). Personal friends and family are more powerful determinants of online purchases than membership in social networks. These attitudes have grown more positive over time, but concerns about the use of personal information by online marketers continue to raise trust issues among consumers.

6.2 DIGITAL COMMERCE MARKETING AND ADVERTISING STRATEGIES AND TOOLS

Online marketing has many similarities to, and differences from, ordinary marketing. (For more information on basic marketing concepts, see Learning Tracks 6.1 and 6.2.) The objective of online marketing—as in all marketing—is to build customer relationships so that the firm can achieve above-average returns (both by offering superior products or services and by communicating the brand's features to the consumer). These relationships are a foundation for the firm's brand. But online marketing is also very different from ordinary marketing because the nature of the medium and its capabilities are so different from anything that has come before.

There are four features of online marketing that distinguish it from traditional marketing channels. Compared to traditional print and television marketing, online marketing can be more personalized, participatory, peer-to-peer, and communal. Not all types of online marketing have these four features. For instance, there's not much difference between a marketing video splashed on your computer screen without your consent and watching a television commercial. However, the same marketing video can be targeted to your personal interests, community memberships, and allow you to share it with others. Marketers are learning that the most effective forms of online marketing have all four of these features.

STRATEGIC ISSUES AND QUESTIONS

In the past, the first step in building an online brand was to build a website, and then try to attract an audience. The most common "traditional" marketing techniques for establishing a brand and attracting customers were search engine marketing, display ads, e-mail campaigns, and affiliate programs. This is still the case: building a website is still a first step, and the "traditional" online marketing techniques are still the main powerhouses of brand creation and online sales revenue. But today, marketers need to take a much broader view of the online marketing challenge, and to consider other media channels for attracting an audience such as social media and mobile devices, in concert with traditional websites.

The five main elements of a comprehensive multi-channel marketing plan are: website, traditional online marketing, social marketing, mobile marketing, and offline marketing. **Table 6.2** illustrates these five main platforms, central elements within each type, some examples, and the primary function of marketing in each situation. Each of the main types of online marketing is discussed in this section and throughout the chapter in greater detail.

Immediately, by examining Table 6.2, you can understand the management complexity of building brands online. There are five major types of marketing, and a variety of

TABLE 6.2 THE DIGITAL MARKETING ROADMAP

TYPE OF MARKETING	PLATFORMS	EXAMPLES	FUNCTION
Website	Traditional website	Ford.com	Anchor site
Traditional Online Marketing	Search engine marketing	Google; Bing; Yahoo	Query-based intention marketing
	Display advertising	Yahoo; Google; MSN	Interest- and context-based marketing; targeted marketing
	E-mail	Major retailers	Permission marketing
	Affiliates	Amazon	Brand extension
Social Marketing	Social networks	Facebook	Conversations; sharing
	Micro blogging sites	Twitter	News, quick updates
	Blogs/forums	Tumblr	Communities of interest; sharing
	Visual marketing	Pinterest/Instagram	Branding; sharing
	Video marketing	YouTube	Engage; inform
	Game marketing	Chipotle Spot the Imposter game	Identification
Mobile Marketing	Mobile site	m.ford.com	Quick access; news; updates
	Apps	Ford Mustang Customizer app	Visual engagement
		My Ford	Visual engagement
Offline Marketing	Television	Apple/The Human Family: Shot on iPhone	Brand anchoring; inform
	Newspapers	American Airlines/The World's Greatest Flyers Fly American	Brand anchoring; inform
	Magazines	Apple Watch/Vogue Magazine	Brand anchoring; inform

different platforms that perform different functions. If you're a manager of a startup, or the website manager of an existing commercial website, you face a number of strategic questions. Where should you focus first? Build a website, develop a blog, or jump into developing a Facebook presence? If you have a successful website that already uses search engine marketing and display ads, where should you go next: develop a social network presence or use offline media? Does your firm have the resources to maintain a social media marketing campaign?

A second strategic management issue involves the integration of all these different marketing platforms into a single coherent branding message. Often, there are different groups with different skill sets involved in website design, search engine and display marketing, social media marketing, and offline marketing. Getting all these different specialties to work together and coordinate their campaigns can be very difficult. The danger is that a firm ends up with different teams managing each of the four platforms rather than a single team managing the digital online presence, or for that matter, marketing for the entire firm including retail outlets.

A third strategic management question involves resource allocation. There are actually two problems here. Each of the different major types of marketing, and each of the different platforms, has different metrics to measure its effectiveness. In some cases, for new social marketing platforms, there is no commonly accepted metric, and few that have withstood critical scrutiny or have a deep experience base providing empirical data. For instance, in Facebook marketing, an important metric is how many Likes your Facebook page produces. The connection between Likes and sales is still being explored. In search engine marketing, effectiveness is measured by how many clicks your ads are receiving; in display advertising, by how many impressions of your ads are served. Second, each of these platforms has different costs for Likes, impressions, and clicks. In order to choose where your marketing resources should be deployed, you will have to link each of these activities to sales revenue. You will need to determine how much clicks, Likes, and impressions are worth. We address these questions in greater detail in Chapter 7.

THE WEBSITE AS A MARKETING PLATFORM: ESTABLISHING THE CUSTOMER RELATIONSHIP

A firm's website is a major tool for establishing the initial relationship with the customer. The website performs four important functions: establishing the brand identity and consumer expectations, informing and educating the consumer, shaping the customer experience, and anchoring the brand in an ocean of marketing messages coming from different sources. The website is the one place the consumer can turn to find the complete story. This is not true of apps, e-mail, or search engine ads.

The first function of a website is to establish the brand's identity and to act as an anchor for the firm's other web marketing activities, thereby driving sales revenue. This involves identifying for the consumer the differentiating features of the product or service in terms of quality, price, product support, and reliability. Identifying the differentiating features of the product on the website's home page is intended to create expectations in the user of what it will be like to consume the product. For instance, Snapple's website creates the expectation that the product is a delicious, refreshing drink made from high quality, natural ingredients. Ford's website focuses on automobile technology and high miles per gallon. The expectation created by Ford's website is that if you buy a Ford, you'll be experiencing the latest automotive technology and the highest mileage. At the location-based social network website for Foursquare, the focus is on meeting friends, discovering local places, and saving money with coupons and rewards.

Websites also function to anchor the brand online, acting as a central point where all the branding messages that emanate from the firm's multiple digital presences, such as Facebook, Twitter, mobile apps, or e-mail, come together at a single online location. Aside from branding, websites also perform the typical functions of any commercial establishment by informing customers of the company's products and services. Websites, with their online catalogs and associated shopping carts, are important elements of the online customer experience. **Customer experience** refers to the totality of experiences that a

customer experience
the totality of experiences that a customer has with a firm, including the search, informing, purchase, consumption, and after-sales support for its products, services, and various retail channels

customer has with a firm, including the search, informing, purchase, consumption, and after-sales support for the product. The concept "customer experience" is broader than the traditional concept of "customer satisfaction" in that a much broader range of impacts is considered, including the customer's cognitive, affective, emotional, social, and physical relationship to the firm and its products. The totality of customer experiences will generally involve multiple retail channels. This means that, in the customer's mind, the website, mobile site and apps, Facebook page, Twitter feed, physical store, and television advertisements are all connected as part of his or her experience with the company.

TRADITIONAL ONLINE MARKETING AND ADVERTISING TOOLS

Below we describe the basic marketing and advertising tools for attracting e-commerce consumers: search engine marketing, display ad marketing (including banner ads, rich media ads, video ads, and sponsorships), e-mail and permission marketing, affiliate marketing, viral marketing, and lead generation marketing.

Companies spent over $660 billion on advertising in 2019, and an estimated $330 billion of that amount on **online advertising**, which includes display (banners, video, and rich media), search, sponsorships, classifieds, lead generation, and e-mail, on desktop and laptop computers, as well as mobile devices (see **Figure 6.5**). The top three

online advertising
a paid message on a website, online service, or other interactive medium

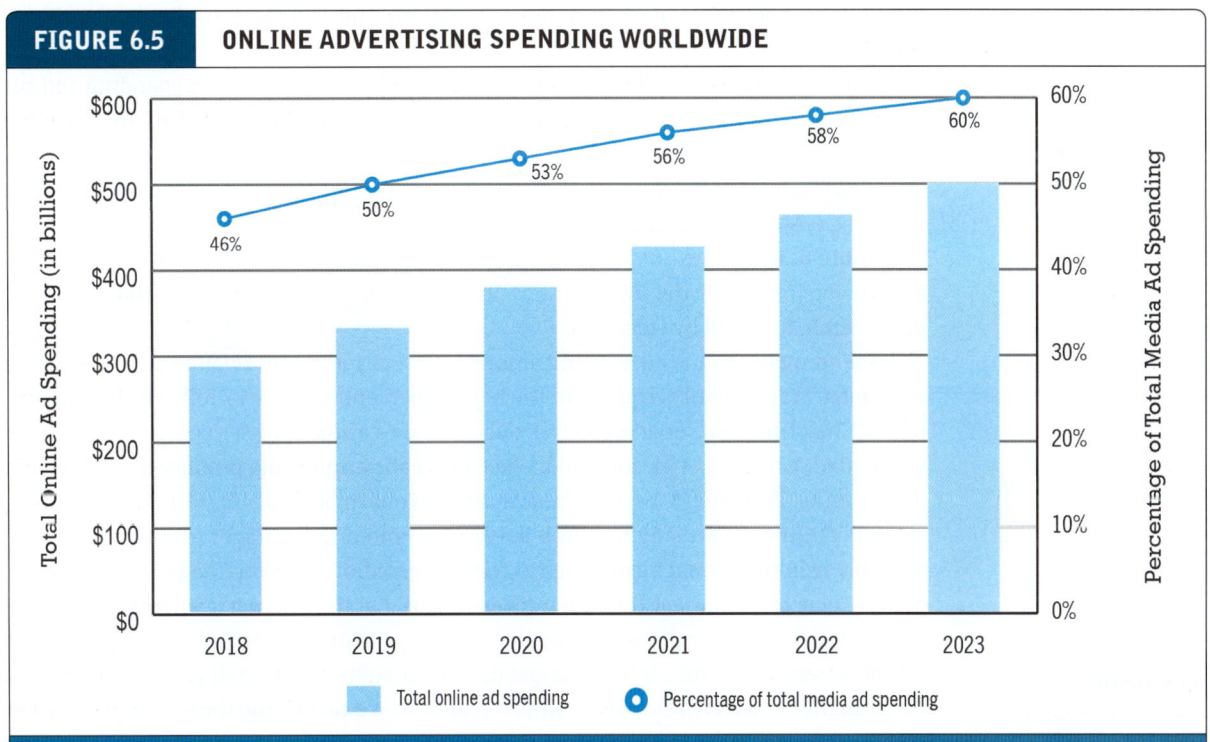

FIGURE 6.5 ONLINE ADVERTISING SPENDING WORLDWIDE

Spending on online advertising worldwide is expected to grow from around $330 billion in 2019 to over $500 billion by 2023, comprising almost 60% of total media ad spending.
SOURCE: Based on data from eMarketer, Inc., 2019i, 2019j.

TABLE 6.3 ONLINE ADVERTISING SPENDING IN THE UNITED STATES FOR SELECTED FORMATS (IN BILLIONS)

FORMAT	2019	2023	AVERAGE GROWTH RATE
Search	$55.2	$86.1	13%
Video	$34.6	$59.5	17.1%
Banner ads	$25.9	$39.7	12.7%
Rich media	$5.3	$6.1	3.9%
Sponsorships	$2.8	$3.7	8.1%
Lead generation	$2.6	$3.2	6.7%
Classifieds	$2.2	$2.6	4.9%
E-mail	$0.49	$0.68	10.5%

SOURCE: Based on data from eMarketer, Inc., 2019n, 2019o, 2019p..

digital advertising platforms in terms of estimated ad revenues in 2019 were Google ($105 billion), Facebook ($70 billion, including Instagram), and Alibaba ($30 billion) (eMarketer, Inc., 2019k).

In the last five years, advertisers have aggressively increased online spending and cut outlays on traditional channels. In 2017, for the first time, the amount spent on online advertising worldwide exceeded the amount spent on television advertising worldwide, and by 2023, television advertising is expected to account for only about 24% of total ad spending (eMarketer, Inc., 2019l).

Table 6.3 provides some comparative data on the amount of spending for certain advertising formats in the United States. In 2019, the highest amount of spending was for paid search, followed by video ads.

Spending on online advertising among different industries is somewhat skewed. In the United States, retail accounts for the highest percentage (21.9%), followed by automotive (12.3%), financial services (12.1%), telecommunications (10.4%), consumer packaged goods (8.6%), travel (8.4%), consumer electronics and computing products (7.7%), media (6.3%), entertainment (5.3%), and healthcare and pharmaceuticals (3%) (eMarketer, Inc., 2019m). Online advertising has both advantages and disadvantages when compared to advertising in traditional media, such as television, radio, and print (magazines and newspapers). One big advantage for online advertising is that the Internet is where the audience has moved, especially the very desirable 18–34 age group. A second big advantage for online advertising is the ability to target ads to individuals and small groups and to track performance of advertisements in almost real time. **Ad targeting**, the sending of market messages to specific subgroups in the population in an effort to increase the likelihood of a purchase, is as old as advertising itself, but prior to the Internet, it could only be done with much less precision, certainly not down to the level of individuals. Ad targeting is

ad targeting
the sending of market messages to specific subgroups in the population

also the foundation of price discrimination: the ability to charge different types of consumers different prices for the same product or service. With online advertising, it's theoretically possible to charge every customer a different price.

Theoretically, online advertising can personalize every ad message to precisely fit the needs, interests, and values of each consumer. In practice, as we all know from spam and constant exposure to ads that are of little interest, the reality is very different. Online advertisements also provide greater opportunities for interactivity—two-way communication between advertisers and potential customers. The primary disadvantages of online advertising are concerns about its cost versus its benefits, how to adequately measure its results, and the supply of good venues to display ads. For instance, the owners of websites who sell advertising space ("publishers") do not have agreed-upon standards or routine audits to verify their claimed numbers as do traditional media outlets. We examine the costs and benefits of online advertising as well as research on its effectiveness in Section 6.4.

Search Engine Marketing and Advertising

In 2019, companies spent about $140 billion on search engine marketing and advertising, over 42% of all spending for digital marketing (eMarketer, Inc., 2019q). Briefly, this is where the eyeballs are (at least for a few moments) and this is where advertising can be very effective by responding with ads that match the interests and intentions of the user. The click-through rate for search engine advertising is generally 1%–4% (with an average of around 2%) and has been fairly steady over the years. The top search engine throughout Western Europe is Google, with a market share of over 90%. **Search engine marketing (SEM)** refers to the use of search engines to build and sustain brands. **Search engine advertising** refers to the use of search engines to support direct sales to online consumers.

Search engines are often thought of as mostly direct sales channels focused on making sales in response to advertisements. While this is a major use of search engines, they are also used more subtly to strengthen brand awareness, drive traffic to other websites or blogs to support customer engagement, to gain deeper insight into customers' perceptions of the brand, to support other related advertising (for instance, sending consumers to local dealer sites), and to support the brand indirectly. Search engines can also provide marketers insight into customer search patterns, opinions customers hold about their products, top trending search keywords, and what their competitors are using as keywords and the customer response. For example, PepsiCo, home of mega brands like Pepsi and Doritos, does not directly sell its products online, but has several branding websites aimed at consumers, investors, and shareholders. The focus is on building, sustaining, and updating the Pepsi collection of branded consumer goods. A search on Pepsi will generate numerous search results that link to Pepsi marketing materials.

Types of Search Engine Advertising Search engine sites originally performed unbiased searches of the Web's huge collection of web pages and derived most of their revenue from banner advertisements. This form of search engine results is often called **organic search** because the inclusion and ranking of websites depends on a more or less "unbiased"

search engine marketing (SEM)
involves the use of search engines to build and sustain brands

search engine advertising
involves the use of search engines to support direct sales to online

organic search
inclusion and ranking of sites depends on a more or less unbiased application of a set of rules imposed by the search engine

application of a set of rules (an algorithm) imposed by the search engine. Since 1998, search engine sites slowly transformed themselves into digital yellow pages, where firms pay for inclusion in the search engine index, pay for keywords to show up in search results, or pay for keywords to show up in other vendors' ads.

Most search engines offer **paid inclusion** programs, which, for a fee, guarantee a website's inclusion in its list of search results, more frequent visits by its web crawler, and suggestions for improving the results of organic searching. Search engines claim that these payments—costing some merchants hundreds of thousands a year—do not influence the organic ranking of a website in search results, just inclusion in the results. However, it is the case that page inclusion ads get more hits, and the rank of the page appreciates, causing the organic search algorithm to rank it higher in the organic results.

Google claims that it does not permit firms to pay for their rank in the organic results, although it does allocate two to three sponsored links at the very top of their pages, albeit labeling them as "Sponsored Links." Merchants who refuse to pay for inclusion or for keywords typically fall far down on the list of results, and off the first page of results, which is akin to commercial death.

Pay-per-click (PPC) search ads are the primary type of search engine advertising. In **keyword advertising**, merchants purchase keywords through a bidding process at search sites, and whenever a consumer searches for that word, their advertisement shows up somewhere on the page, usually as a small text-based advertisement on the right, but also as a listing on the very top of the page. The more merchants pay, the higher the rank and greater the visibility of their ads on the page. Generally, the search engines do not exercise editorial judgment about quality or content of the ads although they do monitor the use of language. In addition, some search engines rank the ads in terms of their popularity rather than merely the money paid by the advertiser so that the rank of the ad depends on both the amount paid and the number of clicks per unit time. Google's keyword advertising program is called Google Ads (formerly AdWords).

Network keyword advertising (**context advertising**), introduced by Google as its AdSense product in 2002, differs from the ordinary keyword advertising described previously. Publishers (websites that want to show ads) join these networks and allow the search engine to place "relevant" ads on their sites. The ads are paid for by advertisers who want their messages to appear across the Web. Google-like text messages are the most common. The revenue from the resulting clicks is split between the search engine and the site publisher, although the publisher gets much more than half in some cases.

Search engine advertising is nearly an ideal targeted marketing technique: at precisely the moment that a consumer is looking for a product, an advertisement for that product is presented. Consumers benefit from search engine advertising because ads for merchants appear only when consumers are looking for a specific product. Thus, search engine advertising saves consumers cognitive energy and reduces search costs (including the cost of transportation needed to do physical searches for products).

Because search engine marketing can be very effective, companies optimize their websites for search engine recognition. The better optimized the page is, the higher a ranking it will achieve in search engine result listings, and the more likely it will appear on the top of the page in search engine results. **Search engine optimization (SEO)** is the process of improving the ranking of web pages with search engines by altering the content

paid inclusion
for a fee, guarantees a website's inclusion in its list of sites, more frequent visits by its web crawler, and suggestions for improving the results of organic searching

pay-per-click (PPC) search ad
primary type of search engine advertising

keyword advertising
merchants purchase keywords through a bidding process at search sites, and whenever a consumer searches for that word, their advertisement shows up somewhere on the page

network keyword advertising (context advertising)
publishers accept ads placed by Google on their websites, and receive a fee for any click-throughs from those ads

search engine optimization (SEO)
techniques to improve the ranking of web pages generated by search engine algorithms

and design of the web pages and site. By carefully selecting key words used on the web pages, updating content frequently, and designing the site so it can be easily read by search engine programs, marketers can improve the impact and return on investment in their web marketing programs.

Google and other search engine firms make frequent changes to their search algorithms in order to improve the search results and user experience. Google, for instance, reportedly makes over 600 search engine changes in a year. Most are small unannounced tweaks. Recent major changes have included Panda, Penguin, Hummingbird, Knowledge Graph, an unnamed algorithm that has been nicknamed Mobilegeddon, and Possum. **Panda** was introduced in 2011 in an effort to weed out low-quality sites from search results. Those sites with thin content, duplicate content, content copied from elsewhere on the Web, and content that did not attract high-quality hits from other sources were systematically pushed down in the search results. Google introduced **Penguin** in 2012 in an effort to punish websites and their SEO marketing firms who were manipulating links to their site in order to improve their rankings. The Google search engine rewards sites that have links from many other sites. What some marketers discovered is that Google could not tell the quality of these back links, and they began to manufacture links by putting their clients onto list sites, creating multiple blogs to link to their clients' sites, and paying others to link to their clients' sites. Penguin evaluates the quality of links to a site, and pushes down in the rankings those sites that have poor-quality back links. Between 2012 and 2016, Google released four major Penguin updates, and by September 2016 it had become part of the core Google algorithm.

Many search engines are attempting to capture more of what the user intended, or might like to know about a search subject. This is often referred to as semantic search. Google introduced **Hummingbird** in 2013. Rather than evaluate each word separately in a search, Google's semantically informed Hummingbird will try to evaluate an entire sentence. Semantic search more closely follows conversational search, or search as you would ordinarily speak it to another human being. RankBrain, a part of the Hummingbird algorithm introduced in 2015, is a machine learning system that helps Google understand the meaning behind queries and serves the best-matching response.

Google introduced **Knowledge Graph** in 2012 as an effort to anticipate what you might want to know more about as you search on a topic or answer questions you might not thought of asking. Since 2013, results of Knowledge Graph appear on the right of the screen and contain more information about the topic or person you are searching on. Not all search terms have a Knowledge Graph result. Google displays information based on what other users have searched for in the past, as well as its database on over 1 billion objects (people, places, and things), and more than 70 billion facts.

In 2015, Google released an algorithm update (nicknamed Mobilegeddon) that made the "mobile-friendliness" of websites a much stronger ranking factor for mobile searches. Websites that are not optimized for mobile now have a much lower ranking in mobile search results. And starting in November 2015, Google began lowering the search rank of mobile websites that display an ad that obscures the screen and asks users whether they would like to install the site's mobile app, on the grounds that such ads are less mobile-friendly. Companies that use such ads, such as Yelp, LinkedIn, Pinterest, and others, have charged that Google's new policy is in part an effort to protect its web search revenue from

Panda
change in the Google algorithm to eliminate low-quality sites from search results

Penguin
change in the Google algorithm to eliminate sites with low-quality back links

Hummingbird
semantic search component of Google's search algorithm

Knowledge Graph
function in Google's search engine that displays a selection of facts related to your search term that you may be interested in knowing more about

Possum
algorithm update that varies local results based on searcher's location

Fred
algorithm update that targets websites that violate Google guidelines

social search
effort to provide fewer, more relevant, and trustworthy results based on the social graph

mobile apps that lure users away from the Web. In 2016, Google introduced **Possum**, an algorithm update that varies search results based on the user's location; so for example, the closer a user is to a business's address, the more likely it is to appear among the local results. In 2017, Google released the **Fred** algorithm, which targets websites that violate Google's guidelines, primarily blogs with low-value, ad-centered content. Since then, Google has released a number of unnamed broad core algorithm updates, about which it has not provided many details (Moz.com, 2020).

Social Search **Social search** is an attempt to use your social contacts (and your entire social graph) to provide search results. In contrast to search engines that use a mathematical algorithm to find pages that satisfy your query, social search reviews your friends' (and their friends') recommendations, past web visits, and use of Like buttons. One problem with traditional search engines is that they are so thorough: enter a search for "smartphone" on Google and in .52 seconds you will receive 1.23 trillion results, some of which provide helpful information and others that are suspect. Social search is an effort to provide fewer, more relevant, and trustworthy results based on the social graph. Facebook's first effort to create a social search engine was Facebook Graph Search, which it launched in 2013. Graph Search produced information from within a user's network of friends supplemented with additional results provided by Bing. In 2014, Facebook introduced a series of changes to Graph Search, dropping its relationship with Bing, rebranding the product as Facebook Search, and providing keyword search functionality that enables users to find people, photos, posts, videos, and links on Facebook by searching for words within a post. Results are ranked using a personalization algorithm based in part on the user's relationship to the poster.

Search Engine Issues While search engines have provided significant benefits to merchants and customers, they also present risks and costs. For instance, search engines have the power to crush a small business by placing its ads on the back pages of search results. Merchants are at the mercy of search engines for access to the online marketplace, and this access is dominated by a single firm, Google. How Google decides to rank one company over another in search results is not known. No one really knows how to improve in its rankings (although there are hundreds of firms who claim otherwise). Google editors intervene in unknown ways to punish certain websites and reward others. Using paid sponsored listings, as opposed to relying on organic search results, eliminates some, but not all, of this uncertainty.

Other practices that degrade the results and usefulness of search engines include:

click fraud
occurs when a competitor clicks on search engine results and ads, forcing the advertiser to pay for the click even though the click is not legitimate

- **Click fraud** occurs when a competitor clicks on search engine results and ads, forcing the advertiser to pay for the click even though the click is not legitimate. Competitors can hire offshore firms to perform fraudulent clicks or hire botnets to automate the process. Click fraud can quickly run up a large bill for merchants, and not result in any growth in sales.

content farms
companies that generate large volumes of textual content for multiple websites designed to attract viewers and search engines

- **Content farms** are companies that generate large volumes of textual content for multiple websites designed to attract viewers and search engines. Content farms profit by attracting large numbers of readers to their sites and exposing them to ads. The content typically is not original but is artfully copied or summarized from legitimate content sites.

- **Link farms** are groups of websites that link to one another, thereby boosting their ranking in search engines that use a page ranking algorithm to judge the "usefulness" of a site. For instance, in the 2010 holiday season, JCPenney was found to be the highest ranked merchant for a large number of clothing products. On examination, it was discovered that this resulted from JCPenney's hiring a search engine optimization company to create thousands of websites that linked to JCPenney's website. As a result, JCPenney's website became the most popular (most linked-to) website for products like dresses, shirts, and pants. No matter what popular clothing item people searched for, JCPenney came out on top. Experts believe this was the largest search engine fraud in history. Google's Panda series of updates to its search algorithms were aimed in part at eliminating link farms (Castell, 2014).

link farms

groups of websites that link to one another, thereby boosting their ranking in search engines

Display Ad Marketing

In 2019, companies spent around $170 billion on all forms of display ad marketing, almost 52% of all spending for digital marketing. Display ads include a number of different types of ads, including banner ads, rich media ads, and video ads. Sponsorships and native advertising are also considered types of display ad marketing. More than 6 trillion display ads were estimated to have been served on desktop and mobile devices in 2018. The top three display ad companies in 2019 were Facebook, Alibaba, and Google, which together accounted for over two-thirds of total display ad revenue worldwide (eMarketer, Inc., 2018a). The Interactive Advertising Bureau (IAB), an industry organization, has established voluntary industry guidelines for display ads. Publishers are not required to use these guidelines, but many do. For many years, IAB categorized display ads based on fixed pixel sizes, such as a medium rectangle (300 x 250 pixels), large rectangle (336 x 280 pixels), leaderboard (728 x 90 pixels), and wide skyscraper (100 x 600 pixels) (the top performing sizes, according to Google) (Google, 2020). However, in 2017, the IAB released the final version of its new standard ad unit portfolio, based on aspect ratio and size range, rather than fixed pixel size, allowing for flexible sizing and delivery of a more consistent ad experience across multiple screen sizes and devices. Ad types are now identified as horizontal (typically placed at the top or bottom of the screen), vertical (typically placed on the right or left edge of the screen), tiles (typically placed in a grid layout), or full page (which cover the full screen of the device in either a portrait or landscape layout). The guidelines are based on HTML5 technology and cover all types of display ads, as well as new ad experiences such as augmented reality, virtual reality, 360-degree ads, and emoji ads, among others. Another important aspect of the new guidelines is their incorporation of LEAN principles. LEAN is an acronym that stands for lightweight, encrypted, AdChoices-supported, and non-invasive advertising. In an attempt to enhance consumer acceptance of advertising, the standard contains guidelines with respect to animations, ad expansions, close buttons, user initiation, interstitials (ads that appear before, in-between, or after the primary content), video and auto-play video and audio, as well as a list of disruptive ad experiences that are no longer permitted, such as pop-up ads (ads that overlay or cover the content after the user has started viewing the content), auto expansion (ads that expand without user initiation), auto-play video with audio, and flashing animations (IAB Technology Lab, 2017). However, despite the new IAB standards, a recent survey of U.S. Internet uses found that 71% of the respondents believed that ads were more intrusive today than they were three years ago (Kantar Millward Brown, 2018).

Banner Ads Banner ads are the oldest and most familiar form of display marketing. They are also the least-effective and the lowest-cost form of online marketing. A banner ad displays a promotional message in a rectangular box on the screen of a desktop computer or mobile device. A **banner ad** is similar to a traditional ad in a printed publication but has some added advantages. When clicked, it brings potential customers directly to the advertiser's website, and the site where the ad appears can track the user's behavior on the site. The ability to identify and track the user is a key feature of online advertising. Banner ads often feature video and other animations. It's important to note that, although the terms banner ad and display ad are often used interchangeably, banner ads are just one form of display ad.

banner ad
displays a promotional message in a rectangular box at the top or bottom of a computer screen

Rich Media Ads Ads that employ interactive features that engage the user, such as animations (moving graphics), or elements that trigger new content experiences, such as ad expansion, where the ad expands to a size bigger than its original size, or video play, are referred to as **rich media ads**. They are more effective than simple banner ads. For instance, one research report that analyzed 24,000 different rich media ads with more than 12 billion impressions served in North America over a six-month period found that exposure to rich media ads boosted advertiser site visits by nearly 300% compared to standard banner ads. Viewers of rich media ads that included video were six times more likely to visit the advertiser's website, by either directly clicking on the ad, typing the advertiser's URL, or searching (MediaMind, 2012).

rich media ad
ad employing interactive features that engage the user

Video Ads Online **video ads** are TV-like advertisements that appear as in-page video commercials or before, during, or after a variety of content. **Table 6.4** describes some of the different types of video ads. The most widely used are in-stream video advertisements that display before (pre-roll), during (mid-roll), or at the end of (post-roll) a video that a user has clicked on.

video ad
TV-like advertisement that appears as an in-page video commercial or before, during, or after content

TABLE 6.4	TYPES OF VIDEO ADS	
FORMAT	DESCRIPTION	WHEN USED
Linear video ad	Pre-roll; takeover; ad takes over video for a certain period of time	Before, between, or after video
Nonlinear video ad	Overlay; ad runs at same time as video content and does not take over full screen	During, over, or within video
In-banner video ad	Rich media; ad is triggered within banner, may expand outside banner	Within web page, generally surrounded by content
In-text video ad	Rich media; ad is delivered when user mouses over relevant text	Within web page, identified as a highlighted word within relevant content

Although from a total spending standpoint, online video ads are still small when compared to the amount spent on search engine advertising, video ads are another fast growing form of online advertisement, accounting for about $45 billion in online advertising spending worldwide in 2019, about 14% of all online advertising spending (eMarketer, Inc., 2019r). The rapid growth in video ads is due in part to the fact that video ads are far more effective than other display ad formats. For instance, according to research analyzing a variety of ad formats, in-stream video ads had click-through rates 12 times that of rich media and 27 times that of standard banner ads (MediaMind, 2012). Research by the IAB indicates that interactive digital video has even greater impact than typical, non-interactive video formats, with interaction rates three to four times higher, and brand awareness heightened by more than 50% (Interactive Advertising Bureau, 2014).

There are many specialized video advertising networks that run video advertising campaigns for national advertisers and place these videos on their respective networks of websites. Firms can also establish their own video and television sites to promote their products. Retail sites are among the largest users of advertising videos. For instance, Zappos, one of the largest online shoe retailers, has a video for every one of its over 100,000 products.

Sponsorships A **sponsorship** is a paid effort to tie an advertiser's name to particular information, an event, or a venue in a way that reinforces its brand in a positive yet not overtly commercial manner. Sponsorships typically are more about branding than immediate sales. A common form of sponsorship is targeted content (or advertorials), in which editorial content is combined with an ad message to make the message more valuable and attractive to its intended audience. For instance, WebMD, the leading medical information website in the United States, displays sponsored pages on the WebMD website from companies such as Phillips to describe its home defibrillators, and Lilly to describe its pharmaceutical solutions for attention deficit disorders among children. Social media sponsorships, in which marketers pay for mentions in social media, such as blogs, tweets, or in online video, are also a popular tactic. Sponsorships have also moved onto the mobile platform. The line between sponsorship marketing and native advertising (discussed in the next section) is somewhat blurry.

sponsorship
a paid effort to tie an advertiser's name to information, an event, or a venue in a way that reinforces its brand in a positive yet not overtly commercial manner

Native Advertising Advertising that looks similar to editorial content is known as **native advertising**. Native advertising is not new. Traditional native advertising includes television infomercials, newspaper advertorials, and entire sections of newspapers and magazines that are given over to advertisers, where the advertising looks similar to the rest of the publication. In the online world, native ads are most often found on social media, especially mobile social media, as part of a Facebook News Feed, Instagram Story, Twitter Timeline, or Pinterest Promoted Pin. Mobile social networks do not have room for ads on the right side of the screen (the sidebar or right rail), and therefore native ads in the form of posts that look like other posts are the favored option. In the United States, native advertising's share of mobile display ad revenues has skyrocketed from 14% in 2012 to almost 85% in 2019 (eMarketer, Inc., 2019s).

native advertising
advertising that looks similar to editorial content

Typically, native ads mimic the editorial content around them, and increasingly include video. They appear outside the normal or expected area for ads and are labeled to indicate they are not editorial content, although in most cases the word "ad" is not used. On the Web or mobile screens, native ads are usually distinguished by a "sponsored" tag underneath the headline, often in a different color. Online native advertising is growing rapidly, especially on social networks.

Researchers have found that 35% of online consumers cannot distinguish between editorial content and sponsored ads that look like editorial content, even if the ads are labelled as sponsored or promoted. Most consumers do not know what sponsored or promoted means. In a survey of 10,000 consumers, researchers found that consumers skip over labels like sponsored, and many do not understand the difference between paid and unpaid content (Franklyn, 2013). Yet market researchers have found that native ads are far more influential with consumers. Consumers look at native ads for about twice as long as they do banner ads, 53% more frequently than display ads; native ads raise purchase intent by 18%; and consumers are twice as likely to share a native ad with a family member as a regular ad. Marketers and advertisers are opposed to labeling native advertising with the word "ad" and instead prefer other tags.

Native advertising is controversial. Critics contend that the purpose of native ads is to deceive or fool the consumer into thinking the ad has the same validity as the editorial content in media. In 2015, the U.S. Federal Trade Commission issued an enforcement policy statement on deceptively formatted advertisements and guidelines, setting forth explicit rules for native ads. The FTC said it would examine the entire ad, including factors such as its overall appearance, its similarity of its style to editorial content on the site on which it appears, and the degree to which it is distinguishable from such content. It further advised that labels indicating the commercial nature of the content need to be prominently displayed upon the viewer's first contact with the contact (Federal Trade Commission, 2015a, 2015b). In 2016, in the first action under the new guidelines, the FTC charged that a native advertising campaign run by national retailer Lord & Taylor on Instagram deceived consumers. Lord & Taylor agreed to settle the complaint (Feil, 2016). However, compliance with the FTC's native advertising guidelines still remains problematic. A study by Media Radar that examined native ads from nearly 13,000 brands found that almost 40% of sites publishing native ads were still not compliant with FTC guidelines (Fletcher, 2017). In December 2017, the FTC issued a staff report exploring consumers' advertising recognition in the context of native advertising, and urging advertisers and publishers once again to follow its guidelines (Federal Trade Commission, 2017).

Content Marketing Native advertising is usually focused on partnering with a specific publisher. **Content marketing** creates a content campaign for a brand and then tries to secure placement on a variety of websites. Examples of content include articles, infographics, case studies, interactive graphics, white papers, and even traditional press releases. The aim of content marketing is to increase visitors to a company's website, organic search rankings, and brand engagement via social media (Libert, 2015).

content marketing
creates a content campaign for a brand and then attempts to secure placement on a variety of websites

Advertising Networks In the early years of e-commerce, firms placed ads on the few popular websites in existence, but by early 2000, there were hundreds of thousands of sites where ads could be displayed, and it became very inefficient for a single firm to purchase ads on each individual website. Most firms, even very large firms, did not have the capability by themselves to place banner ads and marketing messages on thousands of websites and monitor the results. Specialized marketing firms called **advertising networks** appeared to help firms take advantage of the powerful marketing potential of the Internet, and to make the entire process of buying and selling online ads more efficient and transparent. These ad networks have proliferated and have greatly increased the scale and liquidity of online marketing.

Advertising networks represent the most sophisticated application of Internet database capabilities to date, and illustrate just how different Internet marketing is from traditional marketing. Advertising networks sell advertising and marketing opportunities (slots) to companies who wish to buy exposure to an online audience (advertisers). Advertising networks obtain their inventory of ad opportunities from a network of participating sites that want to display ads on their sites in return for receiving a payment from advertisers everytime a visitor clicks on an ad. These sites are usually referred to as web publishers. Marketers buy audiences and publishers sell audiences by attracting an audience and capturing audience information. Ad networks are the intermediaries who make this market work efficiently.

Figure 6.6 illustrates how these systems work. Advertising networks begin with a consumer requesting a page from a member of the advertising network (1). A connection is established with the third-party ad server (2). The ad server identifies the user by reading

advertising networks
connect online marketers with publishers by displaying ads to consumers based on detailed customer information

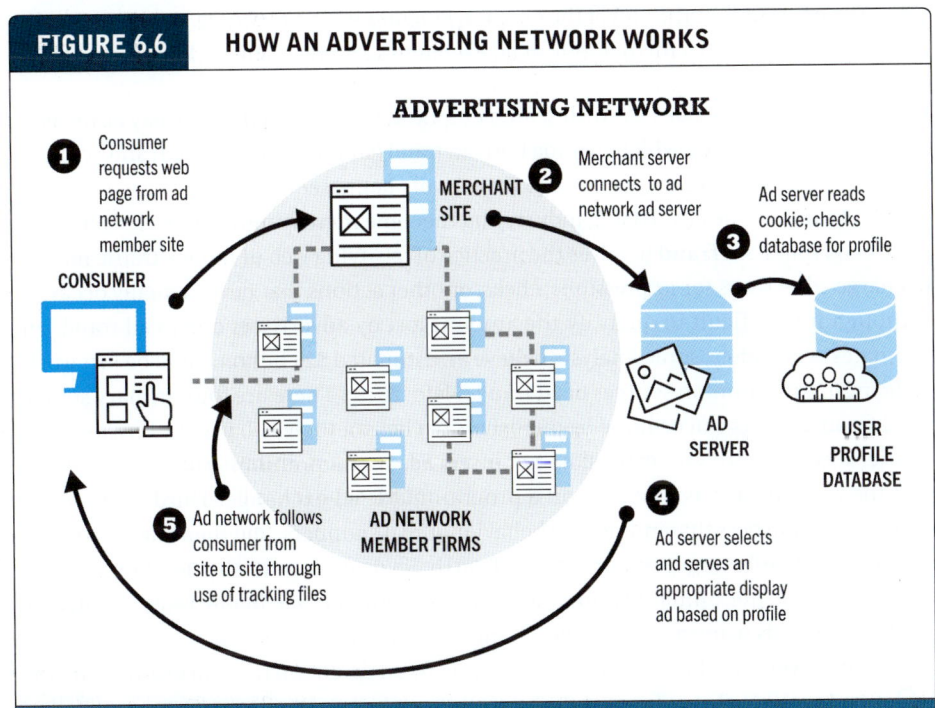

FIGURE 6.6 — HOW AN ADVERTISING NETWORK WORKS

Millions of publishers have audiences to sell, and pages to fill with ads. Thousands of advertisers are looking for audiences. Ad networks are intermediaries that connect publishers with marketers.

the cookie file on the user's hard drive and checks its user profile database for the user's profile (3). The ad server selects an appropriate banner ad based on the user's previous purchases, interests, demographics, or other data in the profile (4). Whenever the user later goes online and visits any of the network member sites, the ad server recognizes the user and serves up the same or different ads regardless of the site content. The advertising network follows users from site to site through the use of web tracking files (5).

Advertising Exchanges, Programmatic Advertising, Real-Time Bidding Today, most online display advertising is being delivered by ad exchanges that use programmatic advertising and real-time bidding. An **ad exchange** is a digital marketplace that uses an automated auction-based method known as **programmatic advertising** to match supply and demand of online display advertising. Programmatic advertising uses a **real-time bidding (RTB) process** to match advertiser demand for display ads with publisher supply of web page space. Publishers are able to sell their inventory of empty web pages, often excess inventory that could not be sold directly. Want to contact males age 18 to 34, recent visitors to a car site, unmarried, high risk-taking profile, located in New York or California, urban home, and financial service industry employment? An ad exchange will allow you to bid in real time on this audience against other advertisers, and then manage the placement of ads, accounting, and measurement for your firm. Ad exchanges offer tremendous global scale and efficiency. One of the best known is Google's Ad Manager (formerly Google DoubleClick Ad Exchange (AdX)), which includes hundreds of ad networks (the supply side), and provides a digital market for buyers to purchase audiences (the demand side). The case study at the end of the chapter, *Programmatic Advertising: Real Time Marketing*, provides you with a further look at ad exchanges and real-time bidding.

Display Advertising Issues As with search engine advertising, online display advertising is not without its issues, which include both ad fraud (similar to click fraud) and concerns about viewability (whether display ads are actually being seen).

    Ad Fraud. The advertising industry has become increasingly concerned about the issue of ad fraud. **Ad fraud** involves the practice of falsifying web or mobile traffic in order to charge advertisers for impressions, clicks, or other actions that never actually occurred. Although it is difficult to quantify the amount lost by advertisers due to ad fraud, and estimates very widely, some analysts believe an estimated $23 billion could be lost worldwide in 2020 to common sources of ad fraud (Slefo, 2019). There are four primary sources of ad fraud. Botnets can be hired by publishers to click on their web pages to create phony traffic. Second, a browser extension can insert ads into a premium publisher's website, and then list the ads as available on a programmatic ad exchange. Third, ad targeting firms can create bots that imitate the behavior of real shoppers, and then charge advertisers for successfully targeting consumers. Fourth, if you are a publisher looking to attract ads to your site, the simplest technique is simply to hire people in low-wage countries to click on your ads using a proxy server (Kantrowitz, 2014).

    Large advertisers have begun to hire online fraud detection firms (a growth industry) to determine the extent of fraud in their campaigns. Verizon Wireless, L'Oreal, and Kellogg are among the firms that found millions of dollars of ad fraud in recent campaigns, and

---

ad exchanges
auction-based digital marketplace where ad networks sell ad space to marketers

programmatic advertising
automated, auction-based method for matching demand and supply for online display ads

real-time bidding (RTB) process
used to match advertiser demand for display ads with publisher supply of web page space

ad fraud
falsifying web or mobile traffic in order to charge advertisers for impressions, clicks, or other actions that never actually occurred

have demanded advertising networks to either reimburse them or generate real web traffic in the amount of the fraud.

Viewability. A significant percentage of online ad impressions served are not actually viewed or even viewable (Scully, 2019). There are a number of reasons for this situation. First, there is no mechanism for measuring how many people actually see an online ad that has been served. The same is true of most offline print and TV advertising, although several methods and certifications have been developed over decades to accurately measure audience exposure. There are no such mechanisms for online advertising. Second, a large percentage of ads served appear lower down on the screen where users are less likely to go, or video ads on auto-play are playing in areas the user cannot see. Advertisers are still charged for ads that are served but not viewed. Unscrupulous publishers can place multiple ads on top of each other and charge multiple times for the same page space. Third, botnets can be programmed to click on ads on fraudulent websites, generating impressions and ad serves, but no one actually sees the ads. The Media Rating Council, an advertising industry group, released a very low standard for "viewability" in 2014: an ad was considered viewable if half of the ad could be viewed for at least one second. For video ads, half of the video needed to be viewable for two seconds (Hof, 2014). A revised version of the guidelines issued in 2015 addressed some additional specific issues, but did not alter the baseline standard. Unviewed ads are just as profitable as viewed ads for web publishers and advertising agencies. For advertisers, they represent the half of marketing expenditures that is wasted. The advertisers who pay for online ads began to demand guarantees of viewability, with some industry participants requiring more stringent standards. For instance, GroupM, the world's largest advertising buyer, requires that 100% of the pixels be in view for a full second in order for the ad to be considered viewable (Marvin, 2017). Several companies, including comScore, began offering tagging technology that can partially measure viewability (Vranica, 2014). In 2019, the MRC finally issued updated guidelines for mobile ads: an ad must be 100% in view for 2 seconds or more (Degtev, 2019).

Ad Blocking. Over the past several years, use of ad-blocking software, which can eliminate display ads, pre-roll video ads, retargeted ads, and some types of native ads on desktops and laptops, has been growing. Ad blockers operate in a manner very similar to a firewall, recognizing and eliminating content based on IP address. Ad blockers have become very easy to install, with programs such as Adblock Plus offered as extensions for Firefox, Chrome, and other web browsers. In 2019, about 25% of Internet users in the United States were estimated to be employing ad blockers, with their most prevalent use among the younger, more technically advanced audience (eMarketer, Inc., 2019u). Gaming, newsgroup/forums, and social network sites are the most frequently affected by ad-blocking. Although advertisers are not yet panicked about ad blocking, it is a trend that they are watching with increasing concern. Some websites, such as Wired, The Guardian, and Salon, have made a direct appeal to their users to turn off their ad blockers or to make a donation instead.

E-mail Marketing

When e-mail marketing began, unsolicited e-mail was not common. **Direct e-mail marketing** (e-mail marketing messages sent directly to interested users) was one of the first

direct e-mail marketing
e-mail marketing messages sent directly to interested users

and most effective forms of online marketing communications. Direct e-mail marketing messages are sent to an opt-in audience of Internet users who, at one time or another, have expressed an interest in receiving messages from the advertiser. By sending e-mail to an opt-in audience, advertisers are targeting interested consumers. By far, in-house e-mail lists are more effective than purchased e-mail lists. Because of the comparatively high response rates and low cost, direct e-mail marketing remains a common form of online marketing communications. Other benefits of e-mail marketing include its mass reach, the ability to track and measure response, the ability to personalize content and tailor offers, the ability to drive traffic to websites for more interaction, the ability to test and optimize content and offers, and the ability to target by region, demographic, time of day, or other criteria. In 2019, although companies spent a relatively small amount when compared to search and display ad marketing, e-mail marketing still packed a punch with solid customer response. Click-through rates for legitimate e-mail depend on the promotion (the offer), the product, and the amount of targeting, but average around 3%–4%. Despite the deluge of spam mail, e-mail remains a highly cost-effective way of communicating with existing customers, and to a lesser extent, finding new customers. Mobile devices have become the predominant method for accessing e-mail.

E-mail marketing and advertising is inexpensive and somewhat invariant to the number of mails sent. The cost of sending 1,000 e-mails is about the same as the cost to send 1 million. The primary cost of e-mail marketing is for the purchase of the list of names to which the e-mail will be sent. In the United States, this generally costs anywhere from 5 to 20 cents a name, depending on how targeted the list is. Sending the e-mail is virtually cost-free. In contrast, the cost to acquire the name, print, and mail a 5 x 7-inch direct mail post card is around 75 to 80 cents a name.

While e-mail marketing often is sales-oriented, it can also be used as an integral feature of a multi-channel marketing campaign designed to strengthen brand recognition. Relevancy in the form of behavior-based triggers, segmentation, personalization, and targeting remain major themes in e-mail marketing in 2019. For instance, Jeep created an e-mail campaign to a targeted audience who had searched on SUVs, and visited Chrysler and Jeep Facebook pages. The e-mail campaign announced a contest based on a game users could play online that involved tracking an arctic beast with a Jeep. Recipients could sign up on Facebook, Twitter, or the Jeep blog.

Although e-mail can still be an effective marketing and advertising tool, it faces three main challenges: spam, software tools used to control spam that eliminate much e-mail from user inboxes, and poorly targeted purchased e-mail lists. **Spam** is unsolicited commercial e-mail (sometimes referred to as "junk" e-mail) and *spammers* are people who send unsolicited e-mail to a mass audience that has not expressed any interest in the product. Spammers tend to market pornography, fraudulent deals and services, scams, and other products not widely approved in most civilized societies. Legitimate direct opt-in e-mail marketing is not growing as fast as behaviorally targeted display ads and search engine advertising because of the explosion in spam. Consumer response to even legitimate e-mail campaigns has become more sophisticated. In general, e-mail works well for maintaining customer relationships but poorly for acquiring new customers.

spam
unsolicited commercial e-mail

While click fraud may be the Achilles' heel of search engine advertising, spam is the nemesis of effective e-mail marketing and advertising. The percentage of all e-mail that is spam averaged around 55% in 2018 (Clement, 2019). Most spam originates from bot networks, which consist of thousands of captured PCs that can initiate and relay spam messages (see Chapter 5). Spam volume has declined somewhat since authorities took down the Rustock botnet in 2011. Spam is seasonally cyclical, and varies monthly due to the impact of new technologies (both supportive and discouraging of spammers), new prosecutions, and seasonal demand for products and services.

Legislative attempts in the United States to control spam have been mostly unsuccessful. Thirty-seven states have laws regulating or prohibiting spam (National Conference of State Legislatures, 2015). State legislation typically requires that unsolicited mail (spam) contain a label in the subject line ("ADV") indicating the message is an advertisement, requires a clear opt-out choice for consumers, and prohibits e-mail that contains false routing and domain name information (nearly all spammers hide their own domain, ISP, and IP address).

The U.S. Congress passed the first national anti-spam law ("Controlling the Assault of Non-Solicited Pornography and Marketing" or CAN-SPAM Act) in 2003, and it went into effect in January 2004. The act does not prohibit unsolicited e-mail (spam) but instead requires unsolicited commercial e-mail messages to be labeled (though not by a standard method) and to include opt-out instructions and the sender's physical address. It prohibits the use of deceptive subject lines and false headers in such messages. The FTC is authorized (but not required) to establish a "Do Not E-mail" registry. State laws that require labels on unsolicited commercial e-mail or prohibit such messages entirely are pre-empted, although provisions merely addressing falsity and deception may remain in place. The act imposes fines of $10 for each unsolicited pornographic e-mail and authorizes state attorneys general to bring lawsuits against spammers. The act obviously makes lawful legitimate bulk mailing of unsolicited e-mail messages (what most people call spam), yet seeks to prohibit certain deceptive practices and provide a small measure of consumer control by requiring opt-out notices. In this sense, critics point out, CAN-SPAM ironically legalizes spam as long as spammers follow the rules. For this reason, large spammers have been among the bill's biggest supporters, and consumer groups have been the act's most vociferous critics.

In contrast, Canada's anti-spam law is one of the toughest in the world. Unlike the CAN-SPAM Act, Canada's law is based on an opt-in model and prohibits the sending of commercial e-mail, texts, and social media messaging unless the recipient has given his or her consent. Violations of the law can lead to penalties of up to $1 million for individuals and $10 million for organizations. The first phase of the law went into effect in 2014. The law applies anytime a computer within Canada is used to send or access an electronic message, so companies located within the United States that send e-mail to Canada must comply with the law. In 2017, an additional section of the law that allows private individuals and organizations that are affected by a violation of the law to sue went into effect, broadening its impact (Fowler, 2017).

Affiliate Marketing

Affiliate marketing is a form of marketing where a firm pays a commission, typically anywhere between 4% to 20%, to other websites (including blogs) for sending customers

affiliate marketing
commissions paid by advertisers to affiliate websites for referring potential customers to their website

to their website. Affiliate marketing generally involves pay-for-performance: the affiliate or affiliate network gets paid only if users click on a link or purchase a product.

Visitors to an affiliate website typically click on ads and are taken to the advertiser's website. In return, the advertiser pays the affiliate a fee, either on a per-click basis or as a percentage of whatever the customer spends on the advertiser's site. Paying commissions for referrals or recommendations long predated the Web.

For instance, Amazon has a strong affiliate program consisting of more than 1 million participant sites, called Associates, which receive up to 10% in advertising fees on sales their referrals generate. Affiliates attract people to their blogs or websites where they can click on ads for products at Amazon. Members of eBay's Affiliates Program can earn 40% to 80% of eBay's revenue on winning bids and Buy It Now transactions as well as $20 to $35 for each active registered user sent to eBay. Amazon, eBay, and other large e-commerce companies with affiliate programs typically administer such programs themselves. Smaller e-commerce firms who wish to use affiliate marketing often decide to join an affiliate network (sometimes called an affiliate broker), such as CJ Affiliate and Rakuten Linkshare, which acts as an intermediary. Bloggers often sign up for Google's AdSense program to attract advertisers to their sites. They are paid for each click on an ad and sometimes for subsequent purchases made by visitors.

Viral Marketing

viral marketing
the process of getting customers to pass along a company's marketing message to friends, family, and colleagues

Just as affiliate marketing involves using a trusted website to encourage users to visit other sites, **viral marketing** is a form of social marketing that involves getting customers to pass along a company's marketing message to friends, family, and colleagues. It's the online version of word-of-mouth advertising, which spreads even faster and further than in the real world. In the offline world, next to television, word of mouth is the second most important means by which consumers find out about new products. And the most important factor in the decision to purchase is the face-to-face recommendations of parents, friends, and colleagues. Millions of online adults in the United States are "influencers" who share their opinions about products in a variety of online settings. In addition to increasing the size of a company's customer base, customer referrals also have other advantages: they are less expensive to acquire because existing customers do all the acquisition work, and they tend to use online support services less, preferring to turn back to the person who referred them for advice. Also, because they cost so little to acquire and keep, referred customers begin to generate profits for a company much earlier than customers acquired through other marketing methods. There are a number of online venues where viral marketing appears. E-mail used to be the primary online venue for viral marketing ("please forward this e-mail to your friends"), but venues such as Facebook, Pinterest, Instagram, Twitter, YouTube, and blogs now play a major role.

Lead Generation Marketing

lead generation marketing
uses multiple e-commerce presences to generate leads for businesses who later can be contacted and converted into customers

Lead generation marketing uses multiple e-commerce presences to generate leads for businesses who later can be contacted and converted into customers through sales calls, e-mail, or other means. In one sense, all Internet marketing campaigns attempt to develop leads. But lead generation marketing is a specialized subset of the Internet marketing industry that provides consulting services and software tools to collect and manage leads for firms, and to convert these leads to customers. Companies spent an estimated $2.6 billion on lead generation marketing in 2019 (Gutman, 2019). Sometimes called "inbound marketing," lead generation marketing firms help other firms build websites, launch e-mail campaigns, use social network sites and blogs to optimize the generation of leads, and then manage those leads by initiating further contacts, tracking interactions, and interfacing with customer relationship management systems to keep track of customer-firm interactions. One of the foremost lead generation marketing firms is Hubspot, which has developed a software suite for generating and managing leads.

SOCIAL, MOBILE, AND LOCAL MARKETING AND ADVERTISING

In this section we provide a very brief overview of the social, mobile, and local marketing and advertising landscape. Then, in Chapter 7, we provide a much more in-depth examination of social, mobile, and local marketing and advertising tools.

Social marketing and advertising involves the use of online social networks and communities to build brands and drive sales revenues. There are several kinds of social networks, from Facebook, Twitter, Pinterest, and Instagram, to social apps, social games, blogs, and forums (websites that attract people who share a community of interests or skills). In 2019, companies spent over $90 billion worldwide on social network marketing and advertising. Nevertheless, this represented only about 30% of all online marketing and is still dwarfed by the amount spent on search engine advertising and display advertising (eMarketer, Inc., 2019u).

Social networks offer advertisers all the main advertising formats, including banner ads, native advertising, short pre-roll and post-roll ads associated with videos, and sponsorship of content. Having a corporate Facebook page is in itself a marketing tool for brands just like a web page. Many firms, such as Coca-Cola, have shut down product-specific web pages and instead use Facebook pages.

Blogs can also be used for social marketing. Blogs have been around for a decade and are a part of the mainstream online culture (see Chapter 2 for a description of blogs). Around 30 million people write blogs, and around 84 million read blogs in the United States. Blogs play a vital role in online marketing. Although more firms use Twitter and Facebook, these sites have not replaced blogs, and in fact often point to blogs for long-form content. Because blog readers and creators tend to be more educated, have higher incomes, and be opinion leaders, blogs are ideal platforms for ads for many products and services that cater to this kind of audience. Because blogs are based on the personal opinions of the writers, they are also an ideal platform to start a viral marketing campaign. Advertising networks that specialize in blogs provide some efficiency in placing ads, as do blog networks, which are collections of a small number of popular blogs, coordinated by a central management team, and which can deliver a larger audience to advertisers. For more information on social marketing using blogs, see Learning Track 6.3.

Marketing on the mobile platform has exploded and constituted almost 75% of the overall $330 billion spent on online marketing in 2019. In 2019, companies spent over $240 billion worldwide on all forms of mobile marketing, and that amount is expected to almost double, to over $400 billion, by 2023 (eMarketer, Inc., 2019w). A number of factors are driving advertisers to the mobile platform, including much more powerful devices, faster networks, wireless local networks, rich media and video ads, and growing demand for local advertising by small businesses and consumers. Most importantly, mobile is where the eyeballs are now and increasingly will be in the future: almost 3.3 billion people worldwide access the Internet at least some of the time from mobile devices.

Mobile marketing includes the use of display banner ads, rich media, video, native advertising, games, e-mail, text messaging, in-store messaging, Quick Response (QR) codes, and couponing. Mobile is now a required part of the standard marketing budget. Apps on mobile devices constitute a marketing platform that did not exist a few years ago. Apps are a nonbrowser pathway for users to experience the Web and perform a number of tasks, from reading the newspaper to shopping, searching, and buying. Apps provide users much faster access to content than do multi-purpose browsers. Apps have begun to influence the design and function of traditional websites as consumers are attracted to the look and feel of apps, and their speed of operation. The opening case, *InMobi's Global Mobile Ad Network*, provides more information on mobile marketing.

Along with social marketing and mobile marketing, local marketing is the third major trend in e-commerce marketing in 2019–2020. The growth of mobile devices has accelerated the growth of local search and purchasing. New marketing tools like local advertisements on social networks and daily deal sites are also contributing to local marketing growth.

We examine social, mobile, and local marketing in much greater depth in Chapter 7.

MULTI-CHANNEL MARKETING: INTEGRATING ONLINE AND OFFLINE MARKETING

Without an audience, marketing is not possible. With the rapid growth of the Internet, media consumption patterns have changed greatly as consumers are more and more likely to engage with online media, from videos and news sites, to blogs, Twitter feeds, Facebook friends, and Pinterest posts. Increasingly, marketers are using multiple online channels to "touch" customers, from e-mail to Facebook, search ads, display ads on mobile devices, and affiliate programs. Forrester Research reports, for instance, that most customers purchased online following some web marketing influence, and nearly half of online purchases followed multiple exposures to web marketing efforts (Forrester Research, 2016).

In 2013, for the first time ever, the average UK adult spent more time with digital media per day than watching TV. In 2019, the average UK adult spent over five hours a day online and using a mobile device for something other than telephone calls, compared to about two and a half hours watching television (eMarketer, Inc., 2019d). An increasing percentage of media consumers multitask by using several media at once in order to increase the total media exposure. In this environment, marketers are increasingly developing multi-channel marketing programs that can take advantage of the strengths of various media, and reinforce branding messages across media. Online marketing is not the only way, or by itself the best way, to engage consumers. Internet campaigns can be significantly strengthened by also using e-mail, TV, print, and radio. The marketing communications campaigns most successful at driving traffic to a website have incorporated both online and offline tactics, rather than relying solely on one or the other. Several research studies have shown that the most effective online advertisements are those that use consistent imagery with campaigns

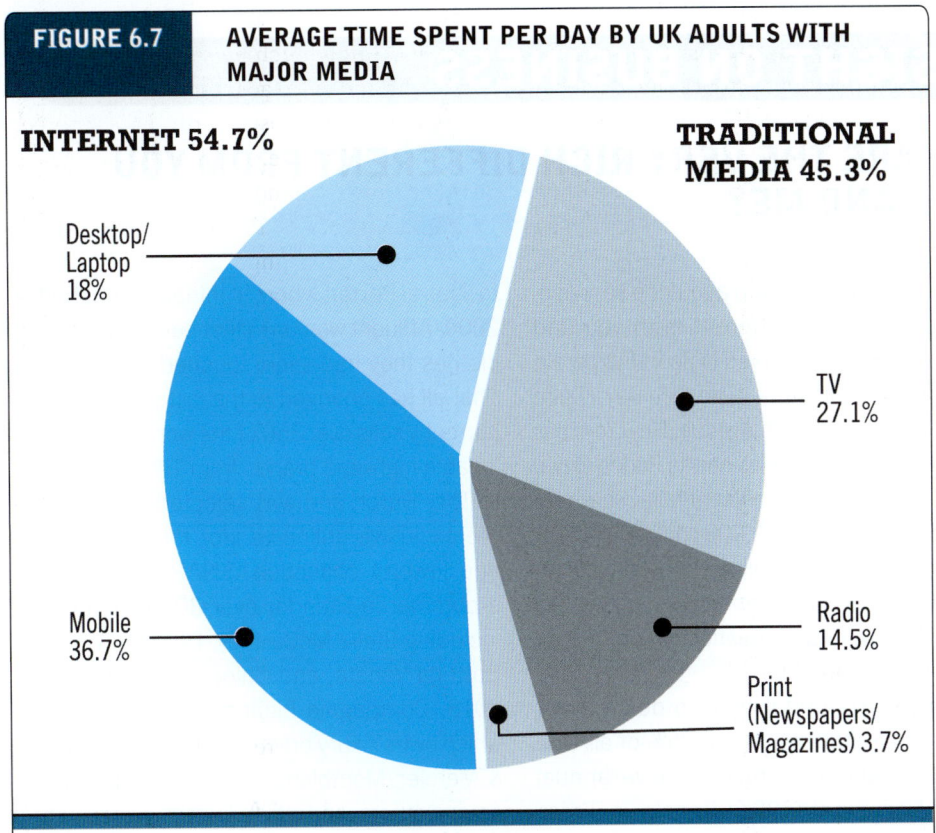

FIGURE 6.7 AVERAGE TIME SPENT PER DAY BY UK ADULTS WITH MAJOR MEDIA

Online marketing should be coupled with offline marketing to achieve optimal effectiveness.
SOURCE: Based on data from eMarketer, Inc., 2019d.

running in other media at the same time. **Figure 6.7** illustrates the amount of time UK adults spend with different types of media on an average day. *Insight on Business: Are the Very Rich Different from You and Me?* examines how luxury goods providers use online marketing in conjunction with their offline marketing efforts.

OTHER ONLINE MARKETING STRATEGIES

In addition to the "traditional" online marketing and advertising tools we have previously discussed, such as search engine, display, and e-mail marketing, and the newer social, mobile, and local marketing and advertising tools, there are also a number of other, more-focused online marketing strategies. Here we examine tools aimed at customer retention, pricing, and a strategy known as the "long tail."

Customer Retention Strategies

The Internet offers several extraordinary marketing techniques for building a strong relationship with customers and for differentiating products and services.

Personalization, One-to-One Marketing, and Interest-based Advertising (Behavioral Targeting) No Internet-based marketing technique has received more popular and

INSIGHT ON BUSINESS

ARE THE VERY RICH DIFFERENT FROM YOU AND ME?

"Let me tell you about the very rich. They are different from you and me." So observed F. Scott Fitzgerald in the short story, "The Rich Boy." Palm Beach has its Worth Avenue, New York has its Fifth Avenue, Los Angeles has its Rodeo Drive, and Chicago has the Magnificent Mile. So where do the rich go to get that $5,000 cocktail dress or that $3,000 Italian suit online? It turns out they may not be so different from the rest of us: they look for online deals and situations where quality can be had at a bargain.

Even experts find it hard to define what it means to be affluent. About 25% of all U.S. households (about 31 million) have annual household income of $100,000 or above. These are often referred to as HENRYs (High Earners, Not Yet Rich). But the really affluent (sometimes called the hyperaffluent) are those 2.5 million (the top 2% of U.S. households) that earn more than $350,000 a year. And then there are the 9 million households (0.7% of households) that earn more than $1 million a year. These are the ultra-rich.

Retail consumption in general is highly skewed: the wealthiest top 10% of households account for about 50% of all retail spending and over 35% of all e-commerce retail spending. Wealthy Americans are opening their wallets to spend on expensive clothing, accessories, jewelry, and beauty products, and increasingly, purchasing luxury products online. Online sales of personal luxury goods are expected to account for 25% of sales of such goods by 2025.

The Yoox Net-a-Porter Group (YNAP) is one of the world's leading online luxury fashion retailers, reaching over 180 countries. Luxury goods designers would not even consider selling to Net-a-Porter when it initially launched in 2000. Affluent women in that period only bought clothes they had seen, touched, and tried on. That all has changed in the last decade. YNAP currently sells over 350 of the world's most fashionable high-end brands from Tiffany, to Gucci, to Tory Burch and was selected by Chanel as the exclusive online vendor for Chanel's first fine jewelry collection. YNAP also operates e-commerce sites for over 30 luxury brands, including Stella McCartney, Dolce & Gabbana, Bottega Veneta, and Chloe, among others. In 2018, Compagnie Financiere Richemont SA, which owns luxury brands Cartier, Piaget, Baume & Mercier, Montblanc, and Van Cleef & Arpels, among others, and which already owned almost 50% of YNAP's equity, purchased its remaining shares for about $3.3 billion. According to Johann Rupert, Richemont's chairman, the purchase was aimed at strengthening Richemont's focus on the online channel, which the company recognizes has become critically important to meeting luxury consumers' needs.

YNAP also has a number of competitors, most notably Farfetch, a UK-based online marketplace similar to eBay but which specifically caters to the luxury goods industries. Farfetch offers goods from over 500 boutiques around the world, as well as a variety of major luxury retailers, such as Burberry, Stella McCartney, Jil Sanders, and Harvey Nichols.

Even the rich are not immune to the lure of a good deal. The problem is that luxury retailers are typically loath to offer sales because they believe sales detract from their reputations. To get around this problem, luxury retailers often offer "secret" discounts via flash e-mail campaigns and private online sales in which selected online customers are e-mailed alerts. Neiman Marcus calls them Midday Dash sales: two-hour online-only sales with 50% off on luxury goods that can be purchased only by clicking a link in the e-mail.

Luxury retailers have another dilemma: they need to attract not just the ultra-affluent, but also the aspirational HENRYs who are far more numerous and anxious to display their wealth. They need to be both exclusive and accessible. One solution is the so-called Mercedes Benz strategy: build luxurious but affordable cars for the HENRYs while maintaining a focus on high-end truly luxury models for the ultra-affluent. Mercedes Benz combines a dual-level product strategy with effective use of social and mobile media. The explosion of social media and the increasing investments in the online channel by luxury companies has reinforced and enlarged the community of those who explore, comment upon, and eventually purchase luxury goods. Mercedes' Facebook page is a main hub of interaction between the brand and its customers, with over 21 million followers entertained with sweepstakes, videos, images, news, and links to its blog for additional insight into why Mercedes is unique and worth all that money. Mercedes also uses Twitter, YouTube, Instagram, Pinterest, and a dozen mobile apps to engage a broader range of customers by providing personalized video tours of its cars.

Developing an online marketing approach that increases a company's access to consumers while retaining an image of exclusivity was the challenge faced by Tiffany & Co. The company is in the enviable position of being perhaps the most famous jewelry company in the United States. Tiffany's offline marketing communications seek to engender feelings of beauty, quality, and timeless style—all hallmarks of the Tiffany brand. How does Tiffany maintain its approach on the Web, a medium that often emphasizes speed and flashy graphics over grace and elegance, and low-cost bargains over high-priced exclusive fashion? The Web, for the most part, is all about low prices and great deals—concepts that are anathema to the high-fashion merchants like Tiffany. The answer is apparent in a visit to the Tiffany website. The site features limited inventory, with a focus on high-resolution images of its exclusive and original designs in jewelry and apparel. There are no sales, coupons, discounts, or other offers although visitors can choose jewelry in lower price ranges (less than $250 for instance). The website and Facebook brand page reflect custom service and design, calm, and simplicity. The prices are equally exclusive: an exquisite Atlas Hinged Bangle in 18k rose gold with round brilliant diamonds for $9,000, and sunglasses for $500.

Today, Tiffany has shifted more of its direct marketing effort from the offline catalog to the online catalog and an increasing social media presence, including Facebook (over 10 million followers), Instagram, Pinterest, Twitter, Tumblr, and YouTube. Today, Tiffany is recognized as one of the leaders in digital competence among luxury jewelry brands. For instance, in a 2018 study of 70 luxury watch and jewelry consumer brands, Tiffany and Cartier were the only two brands given the highest rating (Genius). Tiffany received particularly high marks for its performance and engagement in social media marketing, especially Instagram.

SOURCES: Yoox Net-a-Porter Group, "Who We Are," ynap.com, accessed January 24, 2020; "Farfetch's First Year as a Public Company Has Not Gone Well," by Marc Bain, Qz.com, August 20, 2019; "Global Luxury Retail in the Digital Era, Icsc.com, June 11, 2019; "Global Powers of Luxury Goods 2019," by Deloitte, April 15, 2019; "Luxury Fashion Marketplace Farfetch Closes at $28.45, up 42% on Its First Day of Trading on NYSE," by Ingrid Lundgren, Techcrunch.com, September 21, 2018; "Luxury and Technology," by Walpole and CBRE, September 2018; "Tiffany, Cartier Receive Highest Marks for Their Digital Competence," by Anthony DeMarco, Forbes.com, February 26, 2018; "U.S. Affluents 2018: Examining the Foundations of Their Consumer Behavior," by Mark Dolliver, eMarketer, Inc., February 2018; "With Online Luxury in Vogue, Richemont Snaps up Yoox Net-a-Porter," by Matthew Dalton, *Wall Street Journal,* January 22, 2018; "Bringing Conversational Commerce to Our Customers," Ynap.com, September 2017; "How Luxury Shoppers Are Changing the Face of Retail," by Cooper Smith and Nancee Halpin, Businessinsider.com, May 2, 2016; "Tiffany Outshines Luxury Competition on Social Media," by Matt Lindner, Internetretailer.com, December 28, 2015; "Net-A-Porter Unveils New Weapon in Luxury E-commerce Battle," by Phil Wahba, Fortune.com, May 12, 2015.

one-to-one marketing (personalization)
segmenting the market based on a precise and timely understanding of an individual's needs, targeting specific marketing messages to these individuals, and then positioning the product vis-à-vis competitors to be truly unique

academic comment than "one-to-one" or "personalized marketing." **One-to-one marketing (personalization)** segments the market on the basis of individuals (not groups), based on a precise and timely understanding of their needs, targeting specific marketing messages to these individuals, and then positioning the product vis-à-vis competitors to be truly unique. One-to-one marketing is the ultimate form of market segmentation, targeting, and positioning—where the segments are individuals.

The movement toward market segmentation has been ongoing since the development of systematic market research and mass media in the 1930s. However, e-commerce and the Internet are different in that they enable personalized one-to-one marketing to occur on a mass scale. A recent survey found that 85% of companies were implementing some form of personalization for online customer interactions, and of those organizations not yet doing so, over half planned to use website or in-app personalization within the next year. Of those using personalization, almost 90% reported a lift or improvement as a result (Evergage, 2016).

The Amazon website is a good example of personalization at work. The site greets registered users by name (based on cookie files), recommends purchases based on user preferences (stored in a user profile in their database) as well as what other consumers purchased, and expedites checkout procedures based on prior purchases.

behavioral targeting
involves using online and offline behavior of consumers to adjust the advertising messages delivered to them online

interest-based advertising (IBA)
another name for behavioral targeting

Behavioral targeting involves using the online and offline behavior of consumers to adjust the advertising messages delivered to them online, often in real time (milliseconds from the consumer's first URL entry). The intent is to increase the efficiency of marketing and advertising, and to increase the revenue streams of firms who are in a position to behaviorally target visitors. Because behavioral targeting as a label has somewhat unfavorable connotations, the online advertising industry, led by Google, has introduced a new name for behavioral targeting. They call it **interest-based advertising (IBA)**.

One of the original promises of the Web has been that it can deliver a marketing message tailored to each consumer based on this data, and then measure the results in terms of click-throughs and purchases. If you are visiting a jewelry site, you would be shown jewelry ads. If you entered a search query like "diamonds," you would be shown text ads for diamonds and other jewelry. This was taken one step further by advertising networks composed of several thousand sites. An advertising network could follow you across thousands of websites and come up with an idea of what you are interested in as you browse, and then display ads related to those interests. For instance, if you visit a few men's clothing sites in the course of a few hours, you will be shown ads for men's clothing on most other sites you visit subsequently, regardless of their subject content. If you search for a certain pair of shoes at Zappos, you will be shown ads for the exact same shoes at other sites, such as Facebook. Behavioral targeting combines nearly all of your online behavioral data into a collection of interest areas, and then shows you ads based on those interests, as well as the interests of your friends. What's new about today's behavioral targeting is the breadth of data collected: your e-mail content, social network page content, friends, purchases online, books read or purchased, newspaper sites visited, and many other behaviors. And finally, ad exchanges take the marketing of all this information one step further. Most popular websites have more than 100 tracking programs on their home pages that are owned by third-party data collector firms who then sell this information in real time to the highest-bidding advertiser in real-time online auctions. Ad exchanges make it possible for advertisers to retarget ads at individuals as they roam across the Internet. **Retargeting** involves showing the same or similar ads to individuals across multiple websites. Retargeting has become a popular tactic, in large part due to its perceived effectiveness. For instance, marketers often use retargeting in an attempt to reach users who have abandoned a shopping cart. Over 90% of marketers believe retargeting ads performs equal or better than search advertising or e-mail. And as more and more consumers use multiple devices, including mobile devices, for online access, the ability to retarget ads across devices is becoming a topic of great interest to marketers (AdRoll, 2017, eMarketer, Inc., 2016).

retargeting
showing the same ad to individuals across multiple websites

There are four methods that online advertisers use to behaviorally target ads: search engine queries, the collection of data on individual browsing history online (monitoring the clickstream), the collection of data from social network sites, and increasingly, the integration of this online data with offline data like income, education, address, purchase patterns, credit records, driving records, and hundreds of other personal descriptors tied to specific, identifiable persons. This level of integration of both "anonymous" as well as identifiable information is routinely engaged in by Google, Microsoft, Yahoo, Facebook, and legions of small and medium-sized marketing firms that use their data, or collect data from thousands of websites using web beacons and cookies. On average, online information bureaus maintain 2,000 data elements on each adult person in their database. The currency and accuracy of this data are never examined, and the retention periods are not known. Currently, there are no federal laws or regulations governing this data.

Earlier in the chapter we described search engine advertising in some detail. Search engine advertising has turned out to be the most effective online advertising format by several orders of magnitude, and provides more than 80% of the revenue of Google, the world's largest online advertising agency. Why is search engine advertising so effective? Most agree that when users enter a query into a search engine, it reveals a very specific intention to shop, compare, and possibly purchase. When ads are shown at these very moments of customer behavior, they are 4 to 10 times as effective as other formats. The author John Battelle coined the phrase and the notion that the Web is a database of intentions composed of the results from every search ever made and every path that searchers have followed, since the beginning of the Web. In total, this database contains the intentions of all mankind. This treasure trove of intentions, desires, likes, wants, and needs is owned by Google, Microsoft, and to a lesser extent, Yahoo (Battelle, 2003). Battelle later extended the concept of a database of intentions beyond search to include the social graph (Facebook), status updates (Twitter and Facebook), and the "check-in" (Facebook, Foursquare, and Yelp) (Battelle, 2010). The database of intentions can be exploited to track and target individuals and groups. Not only is this capability unprecedented, but it's growing exponentially into the foreseeable future. The potential for abuse is also growing exponentially.

The decline in the growth rate of search engine advertising caused the major search engine firms to seek out alternative forms of future growth, which include display, rich media, and video advertising on millions of web publisher sites. Web publishers have responded by producing billions of pages of content. In this environment, the effectiveness of display ads has been falling in terms of response rates and prices for ads. Behavioral targeting is an effective way to solve this problem and increase response rates. Behavioral targeting of both search and display advertising is currently driving the expansion in online advertising.

Behavioral targeting seeks to optimize consumer response by using information that web visitors reveal about themselves online, and if possible, to combine this with offline identity and consumption information gathered by companies such as Acxiom. Behavioral targeting is based on real-time information about visitors' use of websites, including pages visited, content viewed, search queries, ads clicked, videos watched, content shared, and products they purchased. Once this information is collected and analyzed on the fly, behavioral targeting programs attempt to develop profiles of individual users, and then show advertisements most likely to be of interest to the user.

For a variety of technical and other reasons, this vision has, thus far, not been widely achieved. The percentage of ads that are actually targeted is unknown. Many advertisers use less-expensive context ads displayed to a general audience without any targeting, or minimal demographic targeting. The quality of the data, largely owned by the online advertising networks, is quite good but hardly perfect. The ability to understand and respond—the business intelligence and real-time analytics—is still weak, preventing companies from being able to respond quickly in meaningful ways when the consumer is online. The firms who sell targeted ads to their clients claim the targeted ads are two or three times more effective than general ads. There is not very good data to support these claims from independent sources. Generally these claims confound the impact of brands on targeted audiences, and the impact of the ads placed to this targeted audience. Advertisers target groups that are most likely to buy their product even in the absence of targeting ads at them. The additional impact of a targeted ad is much smaller than ad platforms claim. A research report based on real data from 18 ad campaigns on Yahoo, involving 18.4 million users, found that brand interest is the largest single factor in determining targeted ad effectiveness, and not the targeted ad itself (Farahat and Bailey, 2012). And marketing companies are not yet prepared to accept the idea that there need to be several hundred or a thousand variations on the same display ad depending on the customer's profile. Such a move would raise costs. Last, consumer resistance to targeting continues: over 90% of Americans are opposed to having companies track their online behavior even if they receive a free service or product (Joe, 2016). Some consumers find marketing messages that are too personalized are "creepy." For example, suppose you visited the Hanes website to look at underclothing. How would you feel about receiving an unsolicited e-mail from Hanes thanking you for your visit and asking you to come back? How would you feel about getting a similar text message or telephone call, or being served a constant array of underclothing ads as you traverse the Web? What if a company mined your Pinterest pins, Facebook posts, or Twitter feed? Although some consumers might not be disturbed by this, many others find it to be "off-putting" at the very least. The public and congressional reaction to behavioral targeting is described more fully in Chapter 8.

Customization and Customer Co-Production Customization is an extension of personalization. **Customization** means changing the product—not just the marketing message—according to user preferences. **Customer co-production** means the users actually think up the innovation and help create the new product.

Many leading companies now offer "build-to-order" customized products on the Internet on a large scale, creating product differentiation and, hopefully, customer loyalty.

customization
changing the product, not just the marketing message, according to user preferences

customer co-production
in the online environment, takes customization one step further by allowing the customer to interactively create the product

Customers appear to be willing to pay a little more for a unique product. The key to making the process affordable is to build a standardized architecture that lets consumers combine a variety of options. For example, Nike offers customized sneakers through its NIKEiD program on its website. Consumers can choose the type of shoe, colors, material, and even a logo of up to eight characters. Nike transmits the orders via computers to specially equipped plants in China and Korea. At the My M&M's website, customers can get their own message printed on custom-made M&Ms.

Information goods—goods whose value is based on information content—are also ideal for this level of differentiation. For instance, the *New York Times*—and many other content distributors—allows customers to select the news they want to see on a daily basis. Many websites, particularly portal sites such as Yahoo, MSN, and AOL, allow customers to create their own customized version of the website. Such pages frequently require security measures such as usernames and passwords to ensure privacy and confidentiality.

Customer Service A website's approach to customer service can significantly help or hurt its marketing efforts. Online customer service is more than simply following through on order fulfillment; it has to do with users' ability to communicate with a company and obtain desired information in a timely manner. Customer service can help reduce consumer frustration, cut the number of abandoned shopping carts, and increase sales.

Most consumers want to, and will, serve themselves as long as the information they need to do so is relatively easy to find. Online buyers largely do not expect or desire "high-touch" service unless they have questions or problems, in which case they want relatively speedy answers that are responsive to their individual issue. Researchers have found that online consumers strongly attach to brands when they have a problem with an order. Customer loyalty increases substantially when online buyers learn that customer service representatives are available online or at an 800-number and were willing and able to resolve the situation quickly. Conversely, online buyers who do not receive satisfaction at these critical moments often terminate their relationship with the business and switch to merchants that may charge more but deliver superior customer service (Ba et al., 2010; Wolfinbarger and Gilly, 2001).

There are a number of tools that companies can use to encourage interaction with prospects and customers and provide customer service—FAQs, customer service chat systems, intelligent agents, and automated response systems—in addition to the customer relationship management systems described in the preceding section.

Frequently asked questions (**FAQs**), a text-based listing of common questions and answers, provide an inexpensive way to anticipate and address customer concerns. Adding an FAQ page on a website linked to a search engine helps users track down needed information more quickly, enabling them to help themselves resolve questions and concerns. By directing customers to the FAQs page first, websites can give customers answers to common questions. If a question and answer do not appear, it is important for sites to make contact with a live person simple and easy. Offering an e-mail link to customer service at the bottom of the FAQs page is one solution.

Real-time customer service chat systems (in which a company's customer service representatives interactively exchange text-based messages with one or more customers on a real-time basis) are an increasingly popular way for companies to assist online shoppers during a purchase. Chats with online customer service representatives can provide direction,

frequently asked questions (FAQs)
a text-based listing of common questions and answers

real-time customer service chat systems
a company's customer service representatives interactively exchange text-based messages with one or more customers on a real-time basis

answer questions, and troubleshoot technical glitches that can kill a sale. Leading vendors of customer service chat systems include LivePerson and ClickDesk. Vendors claim that chat is significantly less expensive than telephone-based customer service. However, critics point out this conclusion may be based on optimistic assumptions that chat representatives can assist three or four customers at once, and that chat sessions are shorter than phone sessions. Also, chat sessions are text sessions, and not as rich as talking with a human being over the phone. On the plus side, chat has been reported to raise per-order sales figures, providing sales assistance by allowing companies to "touch" customers during the decision-making process. Evidence suggests that chat can lower shopping cart abandonment rates, increase the number of items purchased per transaction, and increase the dollar value of transactions. "Click to call" or "live call" is another version of a real-time online customer service system, in which the customer clicks a link or accepts an invitation to have a customer service representative call them on the telephone.

Intelligent agent technology is another way customers are providing assistance to online shoppers. Intelligent agents are part of an effort to reduce costly contact with customer service representatives. **Automated response systems** send e-mail order confirmations and acknowledgments of e-mailed inquiries, in some cases letting the customer know that it may take a day or two to actually research an answer to their question. Automated shipping confirmations and order status reports are also common.

automated response system
sends e-mail order confirmations and acknowledgments of e-mailed inquiries

Pricing Strategies

As we noted in Chapter 1, during the early years of e-commerce, many academics and business consultants predicted that the Web would lead to a new world of information symmetry and "frictionless" commerce. In this world, newly empowered customers, using intelligent shopping agents and the nearly infinite product and price information available on the Internet, would shop around the world (and around the clock) with minimal effort, driving prices down to their marginal cost and driving intermediaries out of the market as customers began to deal directly with producers (Wigand and Benjamin, 1995; Rayport and Sviokla, 1995; Evans and Wurster, 1999; Sinha, 2000). The result was supposed to be an instance of the **Law of One Price**: with complete price transparency in a perfect information marketplace, one world price for every product would emerge. Frictionless commerce would, of course, mean the end of marketing based on brands.

Law of One Price
with complete price transparency in a perfect information marketplace, there will be one world price for every product

But it didn't work out this way. Firms still compete for customers through price as well as product features, scope of operations, and focus. **Pricing** (putting a value on goods and services) is an integral part of marketing strategy. Together, price and quality determine customer value. Pricing of e-commerce goods has proved very difficult for both entrepreneurs and investors to understand.

pricing
putting a value on goods and services

In traditional firms, the prices of traditional goods—such as books, drugs, and automobiles—are usually based on their fixed and variable costs as well as the market's **demand curve** (the quantity of goods that can be sold at various prices). *Fixed costs* are the costs of building the production facility. *Variable costs* are costs involved in running the production facility—mostly labor. In a competitive market, with undifferentiated goods, prices tend toward their *marginal costs* (the incremental cost of producing the next unit) once manufacturers have paid the fixed costs to enter the business.

demand curve
the quantity of goods that can be sold at various prices

Firms usually "discover" their demand curves by testing various price and volume bundles, while closely watching their cost structure. Normally, prices are set to maximize profits. A profit-maximizing company sets its prices so that the *marginal revenue* (the revenue a company receives from the next unit sold) from a product just equals its marginal costs. If a firm's marginal revenue is higher than its marginal costs, it would want to lower prices a bit and sell more product (why leave money on the table when you can sell a few more units?). If its marginal revenue for selling a product is lower than its marginal costs, then the company would want to reduce volume a bit and charge a higher price (why lose money on each additional sale?).

In the early years of e-commerce, something unusual happened. Sellers were pricing their products far below their marginal costs. Some sites were losing money on every sale. How could this be? New economics? New technology? The Internet age? No. Internet merchants could sell below their marginal costs (even giving away products for free) simply because a large number of entrepreneurs and their venture capitalist backers thought this was a worthwhile activity, at least in the short term. The idea was to attract eyeballs with free goods and services, and then later, once the consumer was part of a large, committed audience, charge advertisers enough money to make a profit, and (maybe) charge customers subscription fees for value-added services (the so-called "*piggyback*" strategy in which a small number of users can be convinced to pay for premium services that are piggybacked upon a larger audience that receives standard or reduced-value services). To a large extent, social network sites and user-generated content sites have resurrected this revenue model with a focus on the growth in audience size and not short-term profits. To understand the behavior of entrepreneurial firms, it is helpful to examine a traditional demand curve (see **Figure 6.8**).

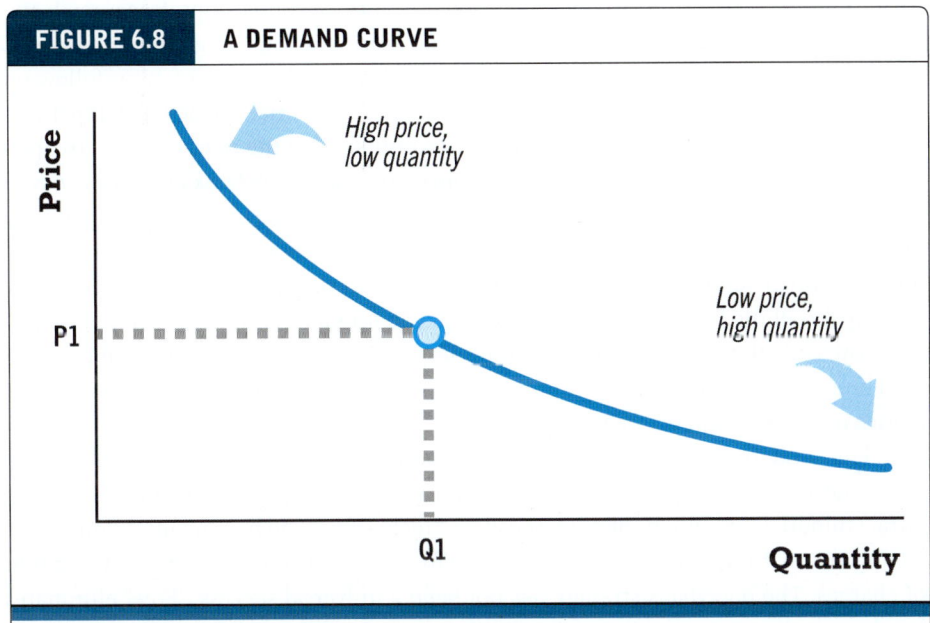

FIGURE 6.8 A DEMAND CURVE

A demand curve shows the quantity of product (Q) that could be sold at various prices (P).

A small number of customers are willing to pay a great deal for the product—far above P1. A larger number of customers would happily pay P1, and an even larger number of customers would pay less than P1. If the price were zero, the demand might approach infinity! Ideally, in order to maximize sales and profits, a firm would like to pick up all the money in the market by selling the product at the price each customer is willing to pay. This is called **price discrimination**—selling products to different people and groups based on their willingness to pay. If some people really want the product, sell it to them at a high price. But sell it to indifferent people at a much lower price; otherwise, they will not buy. This only works if the firm can (a) identify the price each individual would be willing to pay, and (b) segregate the customers from one another so they cannot find out what the others are paying. Therefore, most firms adopt a fixed price for their goods (P1), or a small number of prices for different versions of their products.

price discrimination
selling products to different people and groups based on their willingness to pay

What if the marginal cost of producing a good is zero? What should the price be for these goods? It would be impossible then to set prices based on equalizing marginal revenue and marginal cost—because marginal cost is zero. The Internet is primarily filled with information goods—from music to research reports, to stock quotes, stories, weather reports, articles, pictures, and opinions—whose marginal cost of production is zero when distributed over the Internet. Thus, another reason certain goods, such as some information goods, may be free on the Internet is that they are "selling" for what it costs to produce them—next to nothing. Content that is stolen has zero production costs. Content that is contributed by users also has zero production costs for the websites themselves.

Free and Freemium Everyone likes a bargain, and the best bargain is something for free. Businesses give away free PCs, free data storage, free music, free websites, free photo storage, and free Internet connections. Free is not new: banks used to give away "free" toasters to depositors in the 1950s. Google offers free office apps, free e-mail, and free collaboration sites. There can be a sensible economic logic to giving things away. Free content can help build market awareness and can lead to sales of other follow-on products. Finally, free products and services knock out potential and actual competitors (the free browser Internet Explorer from Microsoft spoiled the market for Netscape's browser). "Freemium," to borrow a phrase from Chris Anderson's book *Free: The Future of a Radical Price*, is another pricing strategy. The freemium pricing model is a cross-subsidy online marketing strategy where users are offered a basic service for free, but must pay for premium or add-on services. The people who pay for the premium services hopefully will pay for all the free riders on the service. Skype uses a freemium model: millions of users can call other Skype users on the Internet for free, but there's a charge for calling a land line or cell phone. Dropbox, Spotify, and a host of others offer premium services at a price in order to support free services.

"Free" and "freemium" as pricing strategies do have limits. In the past, many e-commerce businesses found it difficult to convert the eyeballs into paying customers. Free sites attract hundreds of millions of price-sensitive "freeloaders" who have no intention of ever paying for anything, and who switch from one free service to another at the very mention of charges. The piggyback strategy has not been a universal success. "Free" eliminates a rich price discrimination strategy. Clearly some of the freeloaders would indeed pay a small amount each month, and this revenue is lost to the firms who offer significant services for free. Some argue that everything digital will one day be free in part because Internet users expect it to be so. But the history of "free" includes broadcast television, which used to be "free" (it was advertising-supported), but the public eventually had no problem moving to cable television and DVDs as paid services. The exceptions to "free" are really valuable streams of information that are exclusive, expensive to produce, not widely distributed, unique, and have immediate consumption or investment value. Even in the age of the Internet, these digital streams will sell for a price greater than zero. There probably is no free lunch after all, at least not one that's worth eating.

Versioning One solution to the problem of free information goods is **versioning**—creating multiple versions of the goods and selling essentially the same product to different market segments at different prices. In this situation, the price depends on the value to the consumer. Consumers will segment themselves into groups that are willing to pay different amounts for various versions. Versioning fits well with a modified "free" strategy. A reduced-value version can be offered for free, while premium versions can be offered at higher prices. What are characteristics of a "reduced-value version"? Low-priced—or in the case of information goods, even "free"—versions might be less convenient to use, less comprehensive, slower, less powerful, and offer less support than the high-priced versions. Just as there are different General Motors car brands appealing to different market segments (Cadillac, Buick, Chevrolet, and GMC), and within these divisions, hundreds of models from the most basic to the more powerful and functional, so can information goods be "versioned" in order to segment and target the market and position the products. In the realm of information goods, online magazines, music companies, and book publishers offer sample content for free, but charge for more powerful content. The *New York Times*, for instance, allows you to read a certain number of articles a month online for free, but if you want to read more, you must have a digital subscription. Some websites offer "free services" with annoying advertising, but turn off the ads for a monthly fee.

versioning

creating multiple versions of information goods and selling essentially the same product to different market segments at different prices

Bundling "Ziggy" Ziegfeld, a vaudeville entrepreneur at the turn of the twentieth century in New York, noticed that nearly one-third of his theater seats were empty on some Friday nights, and during the week, matinee shows were often half empty. He came up with an idea for bundling tickets into "twofers": pay for one full-price ticket and get the next ticket free. Twofers are still a Broadway theater tradition in New York. They are based on the idea that (a) the marginal cost of seating another patron is zero, and (b) a great many people who would not otherwise buy a single ticket would buy a "bundle" of tickets for the same or even a slightly higher price.

Bundling of information goods online extends the concept of a twofer. **Bundling** offers consumers two or more goods for a price that is less than the goods would cost when purchased individually. The key idea behind the concept of bundling is that although consumers typically have very diverse ideas about the value of a single product, they tend to agree much more on the value of a bundle of products offered at a fixed price. In fact, the per-product price people are willing to pay for the bundle is often higher than when the products are sold separately. Bundling reduces the variance (dispersion) in market demand for goods.

bundling

offers consumers two or more goods for a reduced price

Dynamic Pricing and Flash Marketing The pricing strategies we have discussed so far are all fixed-price strategies. Versions and bundles are sold for fixed prices based on the firm's best effort at maximizing its profits. But what if there is product still left on the shelf along with the knowledge that someone, somewhere, would be willing to pay something for it? It might be better to obtain at least some revenue from the product, rather than let it sit on the shelf, or even perish. Imagine also that there are some people in every market who would pay a hefty premium for a product if they could have it right away. In other situations, such as for an antique, the value of the product has to be discovered in the marketplace (usually because there is a belief that the marketplace would value the product at a much higher price than its owner paid as a cost). In other cases, the value of a good is equal to what the market is willing to pay (and has nothing to do with its cost). Or let's say you want to build frequent visits to your site and offer some really great bargains for a few minutes each day, or the whole day with a set time limit. Here is where dynamic pricing mechanisms come to the fore, and where the strengths of the Internet can be seen. With **dynamic pricing**, the price of the product varies, depending on the demand characteristics of the customer and the supply situation of the seller.

There are a number of different kinds of dynamic pricing mechanisms. For instance, *auctions* have been used for centuries to establish the instant market price for goods. Auctions are flexible and efficient market mechanisms for pricing unique or unusual goods, as well as commonplace goods such as computers, flower bundles, and cameras.

Yield management is quite different from auctions. In auctions, thousands of consumers establish a price by bidding against one another. In *yield management*, managers set prices in different markets, appealing to different segments, in order to sell excess capacity. Airlines exemplify yield management techniques. Every few minutes during the day, they adjust prices of empty airline seats to ensure at least some of the 50,000 empty airline seats are sold at some reasonable price—even below marginal cost of production. Amazon and other large online retailers frequently use yield management techniques that involve changing prices hourly to stimulate demand and maximize revenues. Amazon can also track shopping behavior of individuals seeking a specific product, such as a laser printer. As the consumer searches for the best price, Amazon can observe the offering prices on other websites, and then adjust its prices dynamically so that when the user visits Amazon again, a lower price will be displayed than all other sites visited.

Yield management works under a limited set of conditions. Generally, the product is perishable (an empty airline seat perishes when the plane takes off without a full load); there are seasonal variations in demand; market segments are clearly defined; markets are competitive; and market conditions change rapidly (Cross, 1997). In general, only very large firms with extensive monitoring and database systems in place have been able to afford yield management techniques.

Surge pricing is a kind of dynamic pricing used by companies such as Uber. Uber uses a dynamic pricing algorithm to optimize its revenue, or as the company claims, to balance supply and demand. Prices have surged from two to ten times or higher during storms and popular holiday periods. Uber was sharply criticized for using this scheme in New York City during Hurricane Sandy. Critics claim the practice amounts to price gouging, which

dynamic pricing
the price of the product varies, depending on the demand characteristics of the customer and the supply situation of the seller

during an emergency is illegal in some states like New York. Uber counters that the higher prices bring more of its drivers onto the streets, increasing supply just when needed. But surge pricing, like most dynamic pricing schemes, is not the same as an open auction, where price movements are transparent to all. Uber does not make its data on supply and demand available to the public. Therefore it is impossible to know if Uber prices go up during holidays and storms because demand exceeds supply or because Uber wants to increase profits. In 2014, Uber reached an agreement with the New York State Attorney General to limit pricing surges during emergencies (Isaac, 2014).

A third dynamic pricing technique is *flash marketing*, which has proved extraordinarily effective for travel services, luxury clothing goods, and other goods. Using e-mail or dedicated website features to notify loyal customers (repeat purchasers), merchants offer goods and services for a limited time (usually hours) at very low prices. JetBlue has offered $14 flights between New York and Los Angeles. Deluxe hotel rooms are flash marketed at $1 a night. Companies like Rue La La, HauteLook (owned by Nordstrom), and Gilt Groupe are based on flash marketing techniques. Gilt (now owned by Rue La La) purchases overstocked items from major fashion brands and then offers them to their subscribers at discounted prices via daily e-mail and SMS flash messages. Typically, the sale of an item lasts for two hours or until the inventory is depleted. On many occasions, Gilt rises to the top of most frequently visited websites when it conducts a sale. Critics point out that these sites take advantage of compulsive shoppers and lead to overshopping for unneeded goods.

The Internet has truly revolutionized the possibilities to engage in dynamic, and even misleading, pricing strategies. With millions of consumers using a site every hour, and access to powerful databases, merchants can raise prices one minute and drop them another minute when a competitor threatens. Bait-and-switch tactics become more common: a really low price on one product is used to attract people to a site when in fact the product is not available.

Long Tail Marketing

Consider that Amazon sells a larger number of obscure books than it does of "hit" books (defined as the top 20% of books sold). Nevertheless, the hit books generate 80% of Amazon's revenues. Consumers distribute themselves in many markets according to a power curve where 80% of the demand is for the hit products, and demand for nonhits quickly recedes to a small number of units sold. In a traditional market, niche products are so obscure no one ever hears about them. One impact of the Internet and e-commerce on sales of obscure products with little demand is that obscure products become more visible to consumers through search engines, recommendation engines, and social networks. Hence, online retailers can earn substantial revenue selling products for which demand and price are low. In fact, with near zero inventory costs, and a good search engine, the sales of obscure products can become a much larger percentage of total revenue. Amazon, for instance, has millions of book titles for sale at $2.99 or less, many written by obscure authors. Because of its search and recommendation engines, Amazon is able to generate profits from the sale of this large number of obscure titles. This is called the **long tail effect**. See *Insight on Technology: The Long Tail: Big Hits and Big Misses*.

long tail effect
a colloquial name given to various statistical distributions characterized by a small number of events of high amplitude and a very large number of events with low amplitude

INSIGHT ON TECHNOLOGY

THE LONG TAIL: BIG HITS AND BIG MISSES

Coined by *Wired Magazine* writer Chris Anderson in 2004, the Long Tail describes statistical distributions characterized by a small group of events of high amplitude and a large group of events with low amplitude. The concept is straightforward. Think Hollywood movies: there are a few big hits and also thousands of films that no one ever hears about. It's the legion of misses that make up the Long Tail. Anderson claimed that the Web would change the rules: no matter how much content you put online, someone, somewhere will show up to buy it, thanks to online search, social networks, and recommendation engines.

On the Internet, where search costs are tiny and where companies aren't forced to maintain a physical store, online retailers like Amazon and Alibaba offer millions of products for sale compared to typical bricks-and-mortar retailers. Wherever you look on the Web, you can find items that only a few people are interested in buying. But with over 3.8 billion people online, even a one-in-a-million product could find almost 4,000 buyers.

One problem with the Long Tail is that people sometimes have difficulty finding niche products because they are—by definition—largely unknown. Well-designed recommender systems can combat this issue by guiding consumers to obscure results that may better answer a search query than the more popular selections. Netflix and Amazon have spent millions on improving their recommender systems, and Pandora's recommender system focuses on generating quality music without regard to popularity.

Search engine optimization is another area where marketers are trying to unlock the power of the Long Tail. Long Tail keywords are phrases that a small but significant number of people might use to find products. For instance, instead of investing in keywords such as "shoes" or "men's shoes," which are dominated by bigger retailers, marketers focused on the Long Tail might choose a keyword like "purple all-weather running shoes," where their firm is much likelier to outrank its competition. Because Long Tail searches are, by definition, more specific, marketers can achieve conversion rates over twice as high as more popular keywords and searches if they are able to match the right products with these types of searches. Long Tail searches comprise as much as 70% of all search queries according to Hitwise, and around 15%–20% of daily Google searches are search queries that have never been used before. Google has added features that improve these types of searches, including a feature called broad match, which allows a keyword to trigger an advertisement even when the search phrase is misspelled or phrased confusingly. With the advent of voice-activated speakers and other devices, more consumers are using natural language searches (searches that are phrased in the way we would speak naturally, like "Where is the nearest pizza place?") to find products and services. Because voice search is relatively new compared to traditional text-based search, these searches are likelier to belong to the Long Tail.

Anderson claimed that the Internet would revolutionize digital content by making even niche products highly profitable, and that the revenues produced by small niche products would ultimately outweigh the revenues of hit movies, songs, and books. But newer research is mixed on the revenue potential in the Long Tail. Solid best sellers have expanded and produce the overwhelming majority of online media revenues. Several recent papers looked at consumer habits on different platforms, including Netflix and music-streaming service Rhapsody, concluding that as the number of choices facing a consumer continues to grow, the likelier customers are to stick with the safer options they already know. Netflix credits its recent increase in revenue and subscribers to its growing list of original series and recently added blockbuster hits, not the thousands of titles in its Long Tail. In fact, its DVD business, where most of its Long Tail titles are available, has only about 2.4 million subscribers, compared to about 150 million worldwide subscribers of its streaming service, which consists primarily of new original series and more popular movies and TV shows. The situation is similar in the music industry. As music services compete to offer increasingly large catalogs of songs, the well-known artists do better, while each individual member of the Long Tail finds it harder to stand out. On mobile devices especially, "front end display" for music services and e-books is smaller than on desktop screens, and only the superstars get this valuable marketing real estate.

On the other hand, up-and-coming artists have fewer barriers to entry and more avenues than ever to promote themselves without the aid of major labels. Artists like violinist Lindsey Stirling started out in the Long Tail, putting up videos on YouTube, and have since become major commercial successes. Spotify has focused on improving the visibility of its Discovery Weekly and Fresh Finds features, which connect lesser-known artists with wider audiences. And although Netflix may be driven primarily by blockbusters, it uses highly specific Long Tail categories such as "Imaginative Time Travel Movies from the 1980s" to narrow down exactly what its subscribers are interested in. One group of researchers also found that algorithms can identify "idiosyncratic" users that are more likely to respond to Long Tail search results, allowing marketers to provide Long Tail products to customers who want to see them. In certain product categories, such as consumer goods, the Long Tail has found new life as consumers increasingly turn online to find specific products (in many case local or artisanal) that match exact needs. Walmart has used the Long Tail to better compete with Amazon in e-commerce, with a rapidly expanding product lineup available from its e-commerce website.

Both the Long Tail and the winner-take-all approaches have implications for marketers and product designers. In the Long Tail approach, online merchants, especially those selling digital goods such as content, should build up huge libraries of content because they can make significant revenues from niche products that have small audiences. In the winner-take-all approach, the niche products produce little revenue, and firms should concentrate on hugely popular titles and services.

▬ **SOURCES:** "Netflix Ships Milestone 5 Billionth Disc," by Steven Musil, Cnet.com, August 27, 2019, "Alexa, What Is Long-Tail Marketing and Why Does It Matter?," by Carm Lyman, Forbes.com, August 8, 2018, "Content Marketing Can Drive Long tail SEO," by Armando Roggio, Practicalecommerce.com, March 5, 2018; "The Long Tail Theory, Debunked: We Stick with What We Know," Mackinstitute.wharton.upenn.edu, February 22, 2018; "The Long Tail: When a Famous Theory Got (Almost) All Wrong," by Willy Braun, Medium.com, November 23, 2017; "Walmart Is Coming for Amazon—and Winning," by Alex Moazed, Inc.com, October 11, 2017; "Fattening the Long Tail Items in E-commerce," by Bipul Kumar and Pradip Kumar Bala, *Journal of Theoretical and Applied Electronic Commerce Research*, September 2017; "No Mercy/No Malice: The Long Tail Has New Life," by Scott Galloway, 12inc.com, April 7, 2017; "Long Tail Keywords: How to Get Tons of Traffic from 'Unpopular' Search Queries," by David McSweeney, Ahrefs.com, November 29, 2016; "What Netflix Can Teach Us About Long-Tail Keyword Research," by Ryan Shelley, Searchengineland.com, September 20, 2016; "SEO: How to Maximize the Long Tail," by Jill Kocher, Practicalecommerce.com, August 12, 2016; "The Long Tail Theory Can Be Reality for Traditional Megabrands," by Robin Lewis, *Forbes*, May 31, 2016; "Where's the Long Tail? Spotify Touts Its Artist Discovery," by Andrew Flanagan, Billboard.com, May 26, 2016; "The Hidden Value of Long Tail SEO," Hittail.com, April 21, 2016; "7 Brilliant Examples of Brands Driving Long-Tail Organic Traffic," by Neil Patel, Neilpatel.com, December 22, 2015; "Hidden in the Long Tail," *The Economist*, January 10, 2015; "Recommendation Networks and the Long Tail of Electronic Commerce," by Gail Oestreicher-Singer, New York University, 2012; "Research Commentary—Long Tails vs. Superstars: The Effect of Information Technology on Product Variety and Sales Concentration Patterns," by Erik Brynjolfsson et al., *Information Systems Research*, December 2010; "How Does Popularity Affect Choices? A Field Experiment," by Catherine Tucker and Juanjuan Zhang, *Management Science*, May 2011; "From Niches to Riches: Anatomy of the Long Tail," by Eric Brynjolfsson et al., *MIT Sloan Management Review*, Summer 2006; "The Long Tail," by Chris Anderson, *Wired Magazine*, October 2004.

6.3 INTERNET MARKETING TECHNOLOGIES

Internet marketing has many similarities to and differences from ordinary marketing. The objective of Internet marketing—as in all marketing—is to build customer relationships so that the firm can achieve above-average returns (both by offering superior products or services and by communicating the product's features to the consumer). But Internet marketing is also very different from ordinary marketing because the nature of the medium and its capabilities are so different from anything that has come before. In order to understand just how different Internet marketing can be and in what ways, you first need to become familiar with some basic Internet marketing technologies.

THE REVOLUTION IN INTERNET MARKETING TECHNOLOGIES

In Chapter 1, we listed eight unique features of e-commerce technology. **Table 6.5** describes how marketing has changed as a result of these new technical capabilities.

On balance, the Internet has had four very powerful impacts on marketing. First, the Internet, as a communications medium, has broadened the scope of marketing communications—in the sense of the number of people who can be easily reached as well as the locations where they can be reached, from desktops to mobile smartphones (in short, everywhere). Second, the Internet has increased the richness of marketing communications by combining text, video, and audio content into rich messages. Arguably, the Web is richer as a medium than even television or video because of the complexity of messages available, the enormous content accessible on a wide range of subjects, and the ability of users to interactively control the experience. Third, the Internet has greatly expanded the information intensity of the marketplace by providing marketers (and customers) with unparalleled fine-grained, detailed, real-time information about consumers as they transact in the marketplace. Fourth, the always-on, always-attached, environment created by mobile devices results in consumers being much more available to receive marketing messages. One result is an extraordinary expansion in marketing opportunities for firms.

WEB TRANSACTION LOGS

transaction log
records user activity at a website

registration forms
gather personal data on name, address, phone, zip code, e-mail address, and other optional self-confessed information on interests and tastes

shopping cart database
captures all the item selection, purchase, and payment data

How can e-commerce sites know more than a department store or the local grocery store does about consumer behavior? A primary source of consumer information on the Web is the transaction log maintained by all web servers. A **transaction log** records user activity at a website. The transaction log is built into web server software. Transaction log data becomes even more useful when combined with two other visitor-generated data trails: registration forms and the shopping cart database. Users are enticed through various means (such as free gifts or special services) to fill out registration forms. **Registration forms** gather personal data on name, address, phone, zip code, e-mail address (usually required), and other optional self-confessed information on interests and tastes. When users make a purchase, they also enter additional information into the shopping cart database. The **shopping cart database** captures all the item selection, purchase, and payment data. Other potential additional sources of data are information users submit on product forms, contribute to chat groups, or send via e-mail messages using the "Contact Us" option on most sites.

TABLE 6.5 IMPACT OF UNIQUE FEATURES OF E-COMMERCE TECHNOLOGY ON MARKETING

E-COMMERCE TECHNOLOGY DIMENSION	SIGNIFICANCE FOR MARKETING
Ubiquity	Marketing communications have been extended to the home, work, and mobile platforms; geographic limits on marketing have been reduced. The marketplace has been replaced by "marketspace" and is removed from a temporal and geographic location. Customer convenience has been enhanced, and shopping costs have been reduced.
Global reach	Worldwide customer service and marketing communications have been enabled. Potentially hundreds of millions of consumers can be reached with marketing messages.
Universal standards	The cost of delivering marketing messages and receiving feedback from users is reduced because of shared, global standards of the Internet.
Richness	Video, audio, and text marketing messages can be integrated into a single marketing message and consuming experience.
Interactivity	Consumers can be engaged in a dialog, dynamically adjusting the experience to the consumer, and making the consumer a co-producer of the goods and services being sold.
Information density	Fine-grained, highly detailed information on consumers' real-time behavior can be gathered and analyzed for the first time. "Data mining" Internet technology permits the analysis of terabytes of consumer data every day for marketing purposes.
Personalization/ Customization	This feature potentially enables product and service differentiation down to the level of the individual, thus strengthening the ability of marketers to create brands.
Social technology	User-generated content and social network sites, along with blogs, have created large new audiences online, where the content is provided by users. These audiences have greatly expanded the opportunity for marketers to reach new potential customers in a nontraditional media format. Entirely new kinds of marketing techniques are evolving. These same technologies expose marketers to the risk of falling afoul of popular opinion by providing more market power to users who now can "talk back."

For a website that has a million visitors per month, and where, on average, a visitor makes 15 page requests per visit, there will be 15 million entries in the log each month. These transaction logs, coupled with data from the registration forms and shopping cart database, represent a treasure trove of marketing information for both individual sites and the online industry as a whole. Nearly all Internet marketing capabilities are based on these data-gathering tools. For instance, here are just a few of the interesting marketing questions that can be answered by examining a site's web transaction logs, registration forms, and shopping cart database:

- What are the major patterns of interest and purchase for groups and individuals?
- After the home page, where do most users go first, and then second and third?
- What are the interests of specific individuals (those we can identify)?
- How can we make it easier for people to use our site so they can find what they want?
- How can we change the design of the site to encourage visitors to purchase our high-margin products?
- Where are visitors coming from (and how can we optimize our presence on these referral sites)?
- How can we personalize our messages, offerings, and products to individual users?

Businesses can choke on the massive quantity of information found in a typical site's log file. We describe some technologies that help firms more effectively utilize this information below.

SUPPLEMENTING THE LOGS: COOKIES AND OTHER TRACKING FILES

While transaction logs create the foundation of online data collection at a single website, marketers use tracking files to follow users across the Web as they visit other sites. There are three primary kinds of tracking files: cookies, Flash cookies, and web beacons. A **cookie** is a small text file that websites place on the hard disk of visitors' client computers every time they visit, and during the visit, as specific pages are visited. Cookies allow a website to store data on a user's computer and then later retrieve it. The cookie typically includes a name, a unique ID number for each visitor that is stored on the user's computer, the domain (which specifies the web server/domain that can access the cookie), a path (if a cookie comes from a particular part of a website instead of the main page, a path will be given), a security setting that provides whether the cookie can only be transmitted by a secure server, and an expiration date (not required). First-party cookies come from the same domain name as the page the user is visiting, while third-party cookies come from another domain, such as ad serving or adware companies, affiliate marketers, or spyware servers. On some websites, there are literally hundreds of tracking files on the main pages.

A cookie provides web marketers with a very quick means of identifying the customer and understanding his or her prior behavior at the site. Websites use cookies to determine how many people are visiting the site, whether they are new or repeat visitors, and how often they have visited, although this data may be somewhat inaccurate because people share computers, they often use more than one computer, and cookies may have been inadvertently or intentionally erased. Cookies make shopping carts and "quick checkout" options possible by allowing a site to keep track of a user as he or she adds to the shopping cart. Each item added to the shopping cart is stored in the site's database along with the visitor's unique ID value.

Ordinary cookies are easy to spot using your browser, but Flash cookies, beacons, and tracking codes are not easily visible. All common browsers allow users to see the cookies placed in their cookies file. Users can delete cookies, or adjust their settings so that third-party cookies are blocked, while first-party cookies are allowed.

With growing privacy concerns, over time the percentage of people deleting cookies has risen. The more cookies are deleted, the less accurate are web page and ad server

cookie
small text file that websites place on the hard disk of visitors' client computers that allows the website to store data about the visitor on the computer and later retrieve it

metrics, and the less likely marketers will be able to understand who is visiting their sites or where they came from. As a result, advertisers have sought other methods. One way is using Adobe Flash software, which creates its own cookie files, known as Flash cookies. Flash cookies can be set to never expire, and can store about 5 MB of information compared to the 1,024 bytes stored by regular cookies.

Although cookies are site-specific (a website can only receive the data it has stored on a client computer and cannot look at any other cookie), when combined with web beacons (also called "bugs," "clear GIFs," or "pixel tags"), they can be used to create cross-site profiles. Web beacons are tiny (1-pixel) graphic files embedded in e-mail messages and on websites. Web beacons are used to automatically transmit information about the user and the page being viewed to a monitoring server in order to collect personal browsing behavior and other personal information. For instance, when a recipient opens an e-mail in HTML format or opens a web page, a message is sent to a server calling for graphic information. This tells the marketer that the e-mail was opened, indicating that the recipient was at least interested in the subject header. Web beacons are not visible to users. They are often clear or colored white so they are not visible to the recipient. You may be able to determine if a web page is using web beacons by using the View Source option of your browser and examining the IMG (image) tags on the page. As noted above, web beacons are typically one pixel in size and contain the URL of a server that differs from the one that served the page itself.

Using cookies on mobile devices has been less effective. Regular cookies on the mobile Web are reset every time a user closes his or her mobile browser and in-app cookies can't be shared between apps, making both of limited utility. However, with the increasing numbers of people using mobile devices to access the Internet, it is not surprising that telecommunications companies have begun to use tracking files. In late 2014, it was revealed that Verizon Wireless and AT&T were inserting a tracking header called a Unique Identifier Header (UIDH) into HTTP requests issued to websites from mobile devices, enabling them to track the online activities of their subscribers. Commentators call these tracking headers zombie cookies, perma-cookies, or supercookies because they cannot be deleted the way that regular browser cookies can. Following an outcry by privacy advocates and an FCC investigation, AT&T reportedly stopped using supercookies, and in 2016, Verizon settled with the FCC, agreeing to pay a $1.35 million fine, and to obtain customer permission before sharing tracking data with other companies and even with other parts of Verizon, including sites owned by AOL. In addition, Verizon agreed to inform customers about its ad targeting practices in the first instance. The FCC also is considering whether to outlaw the use of supercookies entirely.

In an effort to more effectively track consumers across devices, other cross-device tracking methods have begun to be developed. **Deterministic cross-device tracking** relies on personally identifiable information such as e-mail address used to log into an app and website on different devices. Facebook, Google, Apple, Twitter, and other companies that have very large user bases and have both desktop and mobile properties that require logins are the most likely to be able to effectively exploit deterministic matching. **Probabilistic cross-device tracking** uses algorithms developed by vendors such as Drawbridge, BlueCava, and Tapad to analyze thousands of anonymous data points, such as device type, operating system, and IP address, to create a possible match. This type of

deterministic cross-device tracking
relies on personally identifiable information such as e-mail address used to log into an app and website on different devices

probabilistic cross-device tracking
uses algorithms to analyze thousands of anonymous data points to create a possible match

matching is, not surprisingly, less accurate than deterministic matching (Schiff, 2015; Whitener, 2015).

In 2016, the U.S. Federal Trade Commission urged the ad industry to allow consumers to opt out of cross-device tracking, noting that consumers' increased use of ad blocking indicated their displeasure with the current state of online advertising. In response, the Digital Advertising Alliance (DAA) issued guidance that makes clear that the transparency and choice obligations of its existing Self-Regulatory Principles also apply to cross-device tracking. In 2017, the Network Advertising Initiative (NAI) and the DAA introduced new versions of opt-out tools for cookie-based and non-cookie-based tracking technologies complying with their respective best practice industry codes. Apple's iOS 11 and above includes a feature called Intelligent Tracking Prevention (ITP) for its Safari browser. Safari already blocked third-party cookies by default but ITP extended that functionality by ensuring that first-party cookies would generally only be available for a 24-hour window after a user visited a site. Thereafter, the cookie cannot be used for most forms of tracking, and the cookie is deleted entirely if the user does not visit the site within 30 days (AdExchanger, 2017; Ha, 2017). In 2018, Apple announced an updated version of ITP, further limiting how advertisers can track browsing data using cookies by completely removing the 24-hour tracking window, and since then, it has continued to release updated versions that further limit the ability of advertisers to track users (Marvin, 2019; Wuerthele, 2018). Not surprisingly, the advertising industry has become quite alarmed and some major advertising alliances, including the Internet Advertising Bureau, have called upon Apple to rethink its plan, claiming that it will sabotage the economic model of the Internet. *Insight on Society: Every Move You Take, Every Click You Make, We'll Be Tracking You* further examines the use of tracking files.

DATABASES, DATA WAREHOUSES, DATA MINING, AND BIG DATA

Databases, data warehouses, data mining, and the variety of marketing decision-making techniques loosely called *profiling* are at the heart of the revolution in Internet marketing. **Profiling** uses a variety of tools to create a digital image for each consumer. This image can be quite inexact, even primitive, but it can also be as detailed as a character in a novel. The quality of a consumer profile depends on the amount of data used to create it, and the analytical power of the firm's software and hardware. Together, these techniques attempt to identify precisely who the online customer is and what they want, and then, to fulfill the customer's criteria exactly. These techniques are more powerful, far more precise, and more fine-grained than the gross levels of demographic and market segmentation techniques used in mass marketing media or by telemarketing.

In order to understand the data in transaction logs, registration forms, shopping carts, cookies, web bugs, and other unstructured data sources like e-mails, tweets, and Facebook Likes, Internet marketers need massively powerful and capacious databases, database management systems, and analytic tools.

Databases

The first step in interpreting huge transaction streams is to store the information systematically. A **database** is a software application that stores records and attributes. A telephone book is a physical database that stores records of individuals and their attributes

profiling
profiling uses a variety of tools to create a digital image for each consumer

database
a software application that stores records and attributes

INSIGHT ON SOCIETY

EVERY MOVE YOU TAKE, EVERY CLICK YOU MAKE, WE'LL BE TRACKING YOU

Most e-commerce firms want to know as much personal information about their customers as possible. One of the main ways firms discover your personal information online is by placing so-called "tracking files" on your computer's browser. There are several kinds of third-party tracking files. Cookies are the best known. These simple text files assign a unique number to your computer, which is then used to track you across the Web as you move from one site to another. Web beacons (sometimes also referred to as web bugs) are a little more pernicious. Beacons are small software files that track your clicks, choices, purchases, and even location data from mobile devices, and then send that information, often in real time, to advertisers tracking you. Beacons can also assign your computer a unique number and track you across the Web. Tracking may also occur as you visit websites equipped with HTML5 local storage and use apps on smartphones. Most Facebook apps, for instance, send personal information, including names, to dozens of advertising and Internet tracking companies. A number of telecommunications companies use supercookies, which are updated whenever a user accesses a website with a mobile device. Mobile service carriers then provide those sites with additional information about the user for a cost.

So how common is web and mobile tracking? Various researchers have found a very widespread surveillance system. According to Ghostery, a browser extension that detects and blocks third-party trackers, 90% of the top 500 websites had at least one digital tracker, while 65% had at least 10. About 20% had 50 or more, with some pulling in trackers from other sources (piggybacking). Research by Apple reached a similar conclusion, with its tests showing that some popular websites are embedded with more than 70 trackers. A previous Ghostery study conducted using anonymous statistics from 850,000 users and analyzing 144 million page loads found that over 77% of all pages loaded had at least one tracker. Google's tracking infrastructure was the most prevalent: trackers from Google Analytics were found on over 46% of all pages loaded, while trackers from Doubleclick (Google Ads) were found on 18.5%; Google Publisher, 15.1%; Google Tag Manager, 14.6%; and Google AdSense, 9.9%. Trackers from Facebook Connect were also common, with Facebook Connect trackers found on over 20% of pages loaded; Facebook Custom Audience, 7.1%; and Facebook Social Plugins, 6.7%. In 2019, a *New York Times* reporter visited 47 sites over a period of a few days and discovered that hundreds of trackers followed him, from which an extensive amount of detail could be extracted, such as exact location, including latitude, longitude, city, state, country, and zip code (all based on IP address); browser information; operating system details; as well as the content viewed.

While tracking firms claim the information they gather is anonymous, this is true in name only. Scholars have shown that with just a few pieces of information, such as age, gender, zip code, and marital status, specific individuals can be easily identified. In addition, through a technique known as browser fingerprinting, a company can identify you through your computer's characteristics, such as browser type and version, operating system and version, screen resolution, supported fonts, plugins, time zone,

(continued)

language and font preferences, and hardware configurations. When Facebook acts as a third-party tracker, it knows your identity if you have a Facebook account and are logged in. It is also possible for a tracker to de-anonymize a user by algorithmically exploiting the statistical similarity between their browsing history and their social media profile.

Although there have been several industry efforts to address users' concerns about online privacy, one roadblock involved the meaning of Do Not Track (DNT). Privacy groups pushed for DNT that is automatically enabled and requires users to turn it off to allow tracking. The advertising industry, not surprisingly, favored a form of DNT that is not automatically enabled and requires users to turn it on. Nearly all browsers now offer users the option of using a DNT feature, although users have to remember to turn it on. DNT is not mandatory, and as a result, websites often ignore DNT requests because it is more profitable for them to do so, with advertisers willing to pay up to seven times more for a highly targeted ad. In February 2019, Apple decided to disable Safari's DNT setting due to its lack of utility and because it believed the setting might make users even more vulnerable to tracking by enabling browser fingerprinting, a technique that lets ad networks defeat ad blockers by identifying unique characteristics in a user's browser configuration. Major companies such as Yahoo, AOL, and Twitter have also abandoned the DNT standard, citing the lack of traction that DNT has encountered. Although some websites like Pinterest, Medium, and Reddit still do follow DNT guidelines, these prominent defections are setbacks for the standard. The W3C also abandoned its effort to create a standard for DNT in 2019. Some users have turned instead to ad-blocking browser plug-ins such as AdBlock and Disconnect to avoid ads entirely. This has put additional pressure on websites as the pool of web users that advertisers can reach slowly shrinks.

Major websites and the online advertising industry insist their industry can self-regulate and preserve individual privacy, but evidence suggests intervention from a neutral party will be necessary. But all hope is not totally lost. At the same time as companies are using technology to track users, there are others who are using technology in an effort to thwart the trackers. As you have already read in the chapter, Apple's Intelligent Tracking Prevention system blocks third-party cookies on its Safari browser, and its newest version deletes first-party cookies as well. Apple also limits the technical details that the Safari browser provides to trackers in an effort to defeat browser fingerprinting. In a similar effort, Mozilla also protects users by blocking tracking by default and offers options to block slow-loading trackers. The Ghostery study found that sites with trackers took twice as much time to load as sites without trackers.

▬ **SOURCES:** "I Visited 47 Sites. Hundreds of Trackers Followed Me," by Farhad Manjoo, *New York Times*, August 23, 2019; "How the Tragic Death of Do Not Track Ruined the Web for Everyone," by Glenn Fleishman, Fastcompany.com, March 17, 2019; "Apple Is Withdrawing Safari's Do Not Track Feature," by Mariella Moon, Engadget.com, February 7, 2019; "Apple, Firefox Tools Aim to Thwart Facebook, Google Tracking," by Anick Jesdanun, Cnbc.com, September 14, 2018; "Firefox Will Soon Block Ad-Tracking Software by Default," by Nick Statt, Theverge.com, August 30, 2018; "The Tracker Tax: How Pervasive Web Code Steals Your Privacy and Time," by Steven Melendex, Fastcompany.com, May 1, 2018; "Web Tracking: What You Should Know About Your Privacy Online," by Princiya, Medium.freecodecamp.org, April 23, 2018; "Tracking the Trackers: Ghostery Study Reveals That 8 Out of 10 Websites Spy on You," by Ghostery Team, Ghostery.com, December 4, 2017; "Do Not Track Implementation Guide Launched," by Alan Toner and Andres Arrieta, Eff.org, November 1, 2017; "New Twitter Policy Abandons a Longstanding Privacy Pledge," by Jacob Hoffman-Andrews, Eff.org, May 22, 2017; "How 'Do Not Track' Ended Up Going Nowhere," by Dawn Chmielewski, Recode.net, January 4, 2016; "FCC Says Sites Can Ignore 'Do-Not-Track' Requests," by Bill Synder, Cio.com, November 10, 2015; "Clear Rules of the Road with the Do Not Track Policy," by Peter Eckersley, Rainey Reitman, and Alan Toner, Eff.org, August 8, 2015; "'Do Not Track Compromise' Is Pitched," by Elizabeth Dwoskin, *Wall Street Journal*, August 5, 2015; "Do Not Track—The Privacy Standard That's Melting Away," by Mark Stockley, Nakedsecurity.sophos.com, August 26, 2014.

such as names, addresses, and phone numbers. A **database management system** (**DBMS**) is a software application used by organizations to create, maintain, and access databases. The most common DBMS are DB2 from IBM and a variety of SQL databases from Oracle, Sybase, and other providers. **Structured query language (SQL)** is an industry-standard database query and manipulation language used in relational databases. **Relational databases** such as DB2 and SQL represent data as two-dimensional tables with records organized in rows, and attributes in columns, much like a spreadsheet. The tables—and all the data in them—can be flexibly related to one another as long as the tables share a common data element.

Relational databases are extraordinarily flexible and allow marketers and other managers to view and analyze data from different perspectives very quickly.

Data Warehouses and Data Mining

A **data warehouse** is a database that collects a firm's transactional and customer data in a single location for offline analysis by marketers and site managers. The data originate in many core operational areas of the firm, such as website transaction logs, shopping carts, point-of-sale terminals (product scanners) in stores, warehouse inventory levels, field sales reports, external scanner data supplied by third parties, and financial payment data. The purpose of a data warehouse is to gather all the firm's transaction and customer data into one logical repository where it can be analyzed and modeled by managers without disrupting or taxing the firm's primary transactional systems and databases. Data warehouses grow quickly into storage repositories containing terabytes (trillions of bytes) of data on consumer behavior at a firm's stores and websites. With a data warehouse, firms can answer such questions as: What products are the most profitable by region and city? What regional marketing campaigns are working? How effective is store promotion of the firm's website? Data warehouses can provide business managers with a more complete awareness of customers through data that can be accessed quickly.

Data mining is a set of analytical techniques that look for patterns in the data of a database or data warehouse, or seek to model the behavior of customers. Website data can be "mined" to develop profiles of visitors and customers. A **customer profile** is simply a set of rules that describe the typical behavior of a customer or a group of customers at a website. Customer profiles help to identify the patterns in group and individual behavior that occur online as millions of visitors use a firm's website. For example, almost every financial transaction you engage in is processed by a data mining application to detect fraud. Phone companies closely monitor your cell phone use as well to detect stolen phones and unusual calling patterns. Financial institutions and cell phone firms use data mining to develop fraud profiles. When a user's behavior conforms to a fraud profile, the transaction is not allowed or is terminated (Mobasher, 2007).

There are many different types of data mining. The simplest type is **query-driven data mining**, which is based on specific queries. For instance, based on hunches of marketers who suspect a relationship in the database or who need to answer a specific question, such as "What is the relationship between time of day and purchases of various products at the website?", marketers can easily query the data warehouse and produce a database table that rank-orders the top 10 products sold at a website by each hour of the day. Marketers can then change the content of the website to stimulate more sales by

database management system (DBMS)
a software application used by organizations to create, maintain, and access databases

structured query language (SQL)
industry-standard database query language used in relational databases

relational databases
represent data as two-dimensional tables with records organized in rows and attributes in columns; data within different tables can be flexibly related as long as the tables share a common data element

data warehouse
a database that collects a firm's transactional and customer data in a single location for offline analysis

data mining
a set of analytical techniques that look for patterns in the data of a database or data warehouse, or seek to model the behavior of customers

customer profile
a description of the typical behavior of a customer or a group of customers at a website

query-driven data mining
data mining based on specific queries

highlighting different products over time or placing particular products on the home page at certain times of day or night.

Another form of data mining is model-driven. **Model-driven data mining** involves the use of a model that analyzes the key variables of interest to decision makers. For example, marketers may want to reduce the inventory carried on the website by removing unprofitable items that do not sell well. A financial model can be built showing the profitability of each product on the site so that an informed decision can be made.

A more fine-grained behavioral approach that seeks to deal with individuals as opposed to market segments derives rules from individual consumer behavior (along with some demographic information) (Adomavicius and Tuzhilin, 2001a; Chan, 1999; Fawcett and Provost, 1996, 1997). Here, the pages actually visited by specific users are stored as a set of conjunctive rules. For example, if an individual visits a site and typically ("as a rule") moves from the home page to the financial news section to the Asian report section, and then often purchases articles from the "Recent Developments in Banking" section, this person—based on purely past behavioral patterns—might be shown an advertisement for a book on Asian money markets. These rules can be constructed to follow an individual across many different websites.

There are many drawbacks to all these techniques, not least of which is that there may be millions of rules, many of them nonsensical, and many others of short-term duration. Hence, the rules need extensive validation and culling (Adomavicius and Tuzhilin, 2001b). Also, there can be millions of affinity groups and other patterns in the data that are temporal or meaningless. The difficulty is isolating the valid, powerful (profitable) patterns in the data and then acting on the observed pattern fast enough to make a sale that otherwise would not have been made. As we see later, there are practical difficulties and trade-offs involved in achieving these levels of granularity, precision, and speed.

The Challenge of Big Data

Until recently, most data collected by organizations consisted of structured transaction data that could easily fit into rows and columns of relational database management systems. Since then, there has been an explosion of data from web traffic, e-mail messages, social media content (tweets, status messages), even music playlists, as well as machine-generated data from sensors that, due to the plummeting cost of data storage and powerful new processing capabilities, can now be stored and analyzed to draw connections and make inferences and predictions. This data may be unstructured or semi-structured and thus not suitable for relational database products that organize data in the form of columns and rows. The term **big data** refers to this avalanche of digital data that creates huge data sets, often from different sources, in the petabyte and exabyte range. The volumes of data are so large that traditional DBMS cannot capture, store, and analyze the data in a reasonable time. Some examples of big data challenges are analyzing 8 terabytes of tweets generated by Twitter each day to improve your understanding of consumer sentiment towards your products; 100 million e-mails in order to place appropriate ads alongside the e-mail messages; or 500 million call detail records to find patterns of fraud and churn. According to the IDC technology research firm, data is more than doubling every two years, so the amount of data available to organizations is skyrocketing. The next frontier will be data derived from the Internet of Things (IoT).

---

model-driven data mining

involves the use of a model that analyzes the key variables of interest to decision makers

big data

huge data sets, often from different sources, in the petabyte and exabyte range

Marketers are interested in big data because it allows them to link huge amounts of data from a variety of different sources, which in the past they were unable to do, and mine it for patterns of consumer behavior, with the potential to provide new insights into customer behavior, financial market activity, or other phenomena. For instance, Evrythng, an IoT platform company, has partnered with Trueffect, a digital ad firm, to develop ways that marketers can use data generated by connected appliances and other devices in order to directly communicate with and target advertising with consumers. However, to derive business value from this data, organizations need new technologies and analytic tools capable of managing and analyzing nontraditional data along with their traditional enterprise data. While marketers say big data is their biggest opportunity, only 14% are confident in their use of big data (Tadena, 2015).

To handle unstructured and semi-structured data in vast quantities, as well as structured data, many organizations are using Hadoop. **Hadoop** is an open source software framework managed by the Apache Software Foundation that enables distributed parallel processing of huge amounts of data across inexpensive computers. It breaks a big data problem down into subproblems, distributes them among up to thousands of inexpensive computer processing nodes, and then combines the result into a smaller data set that is easier to analyze. You've probably used Hadoop to find the best airfare on the Internet, get directions to a restaurant, search on Google, or connect with a friend on Facebook.

Hadoop
a software framework for working with various big data sets

Hadoop can process large quantities of any kind of data, including structured transactional data, loosely structured data such as Facebook and Twitter feeds, complex data such as web server log files, and unstructured audio and video data. Hadoop runs on a cluster of inexpensive servers, and processors can be added or removed as needed. Companies use Hadoop to analyze very large volumes of data as well as for a staging area for unstructured and semi-structured data before it is loaded into a data warehouse. Twitter's Hadoop clusters, which host more than 300 petabytes of data (30,000 times more information than in the Library of Congress) across tens of thousands of servers, are at the core of its data platform (Agarawal, 2018). Facebook also stores over 300 petabytes of data on Hadoop clusters. Yahoo uses Hadoop to track user behavior so it can modify its home page to fit user interests. Life sciences research firm NextBio uses Hadoop and HBase to process data for pharmaceutical companies conducting genomic research. Top database vendors such as IBM, Hewlett-Packard, Oracle, and Microsoft have their own Hadoop software distributions. Other vendors offer tools for moving data into and out of Hadoop or for analyzing data within Hadoop. In addition, there are many new tools being developed for big data analysis in addition to Hadoop. One example is Spark, an open source product being supported by IBM that can deliver results faster than Hadoop.

MARKETING AUTOMATION AND CUSTOMER RELATIONSHIP MANAGEMENT (CRM) SYSTEMS

Marketing automation systems are software tools that marketers use to track all the steps in the lead generation part of the marketing process. The marketing process begins with making the potential customer aware of the firm and product, and recognizing the need for the product. This is the beginning of a lead—someone who might buy. From there, consumers need to find you as they search for products; they will compare your products with your competitors' offerings and at some point, choose to purchase. Software

marketing automation systems
software tools that marketers use to track all the steps in the lead generation part of the marketing process

can help in each of these stages of the marketing process. A number of firms sell software packages that can visualize most of the online marketing activities of a firm and then track the progression from exposure to display ads, finding your firm on a search engine, directing follow-up e-mail and communications, and finally a purchase. Once leads become customers, customer relationship management systems take over the maintenance of the relationship.

Customer relationship management systems are another important Internet marketing technology. A **customer relationship management (CRM) system** is a repository of customer information that records all of the contacts that a customer has with a firm (including websites) and generates a customer profile available to everyone in the firm with a need to "know the customer." CRM systems also supply the analytical software required to analyze and use customer information. Customers come to firms not just over the Web but also through telephone call centers, customer service representatives, sales representatives, automated voice response systems, ATMs and kiosks, in-store point-of-sale terminals, and mobile devices (m-commerce). Collectively, these are referred to as "**customer touchpoints**." In the past, firms generally did not maintain a single repository of customer information, but instead were organized along product lines, with each product line maintaining a customer list (and often not sharing it with others in the same firm).

In general, firms did not know who their customers were, how profitable they were, or how they responded to marketing campaigns. For instance, a bank customer might see a television advertisement for a low-cost auto loan that included an 800-number to call. However, if the customer came to the bank's website instead, rather than calling the 800-number, marketers would have no idea how effective the television campaign was because this web customer contact data was not related to the 800-number call center data. **Figure 6.9** illustrates how a CRM system integrates customer contact data into a single system.

CRMs are part of the evolution of firms toward a customer-centric and marketing-segment–based business, and away from a product-line–centered business. CRMs are essentially a database technology with extraordinary capabilities for addressing the needs of each customer and differentiating the product or service on the basis of treating each customer as a unique person. Customer profiles can contain the following information:

- A map of the customer's relationship with the institution
- Product and usage summary data
- Demographic and psychographic data
- Profitability measures
- Contact history summarizing the customer's contacts with the institution across most delivery channels
- Marketing and sales information containing programs received by the customer and the customer's responses
- E-mail campaign responses
- Website visits
- Mobile app downloads

customer relationship management (CRM) system
a repository of customer information that records all of the contacts that a customer has with a firm and generates a customer profile available to everyone in the firm with a need to "know the customer"

customer touchpoints
the ways in which customers interact with the firm

FIGURE 6.9 A CUSTOMER RELATIONSHIP MANAGEMENT SYSTEM

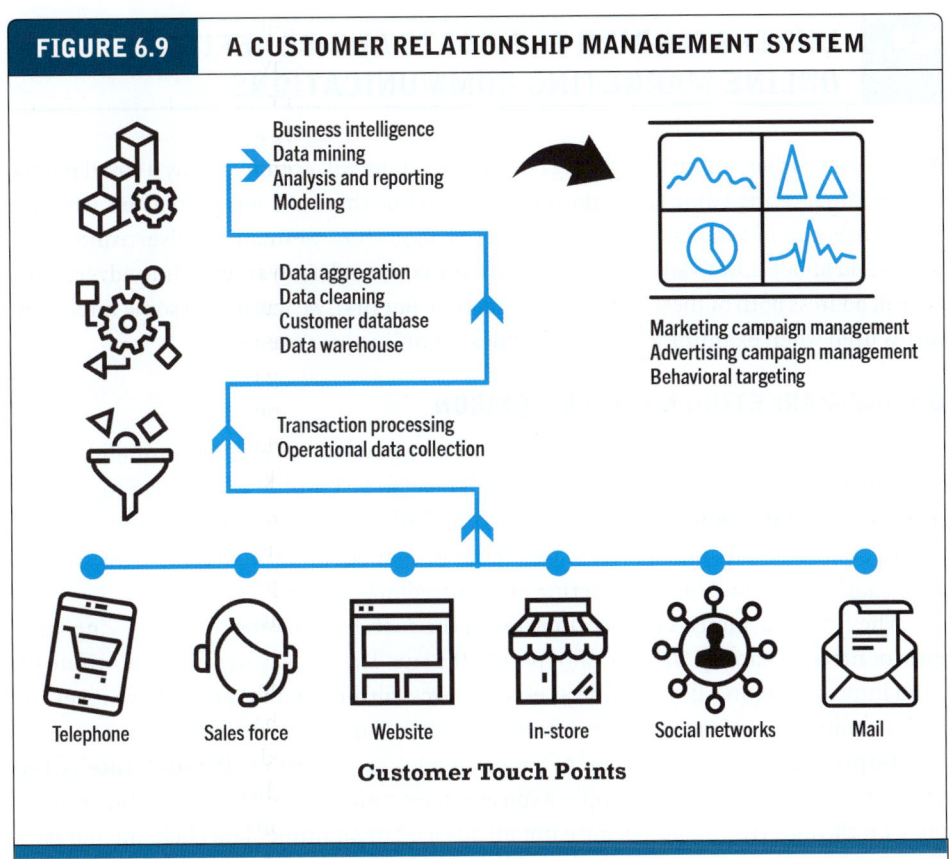

This is an example of a CRM system. The system captures customer information from all customer touchpoints as well as other data sources, merges the data, and aggregates it into a single customer data repository or data warehouse where it can be used to provide better service, as well as to construct customer profiles for marketing purposes. Online analytical processing (OLAP) allows managers to dynamically analyze customer activities to spot trends or problems involving customers. Other analytical software programs analyze aggregate customer behavior to identify profitable and unprofitable customers as well as customer activities.

With these profiles, CRMs can be used to sell additional products and services, develop new products, increase product utilization, reduce marketing costs, identify and retain profitable customers, optimize service delivery costs, retain high lifetime value customers, enable personal communications, improve customer loyalty, and increase product profitability. The goal is what is known as a "360-degree" view that enables a company to know what its customers buy, how they browse, what kinds of communications and offers will engage them, and more. Leading CRM vendors include Oracle, SAP, Microsoft, Salesforce, and SugarCRM, many of which offer cloud-based versions of their CRM products. One issue facing cloud CRM providers and global companies that use those products is European Union data regulations that will require them to reassess how they use CRM data in order to avoid violating those regulations. All the major vendors offer cloud-based SaaS CRM applications.

6.4 UNDERSTANDING THE COSTS AND BENEFITS OF ONLINE MARKETING COMMUNICATIONS

As we noted earlier, online marketing communications still comprise only a small part of the total marketing communications universe. While there are several reasons why this is the case, two of the main ones are concerns about how well online advertising really works and about how to adequately measure the costs and benefits of online advertising. We will address both of these topics in this section. But first, we will define some important terms used when examining the effectiveness of online marketing.

ONLINE MARKETING METRICS: LEXICON

In order to understand the process of attracting prospects via marketing communications and converting them into customers, you will need to be familiar with online marketing terminology. **Table 6.6** lists some terms commonly used to describe the impacts and results of "traditional" online marketing such as display ads and e-mail campaigns. Metrics for social, mobile, and local marketing are covered in Chapter 7.

The first nine metrics focus primarily on the success of a website in achieving audience or market share by "driving" shoppers to the site. These measures often substitute for solid information on sales revenue as e-commerce entrepreneurs seek to have investors and the public focus on the success of the website in "attracting eyeballs" (viewers).

Impressions are the number of times an ad is served. **Click-through rate (CTR)** measures the percentage of people exposed to an online advertisement who actually click on the advertisement. Because not all ads lead to an immediate click, the industry has invented a term for a long-term hit called **view-through rate (VTR)**, which measures the 30-day response rate to an ad. **Hits** are the number of HTTP requests received by a firm's server. Hits can be misleading as a measure of website activity because a "hit" does not equal a page. A single page may account for several hits if the page contains multiple images or graphics. A single website visitor can generate hundreds of hits. For this reason, hits are not an accurate representation of web traffic or visits, even though they are generally easy to measure; the sheer volume of hits can be huge—and sound impressive—but not be a true measure of activity. **Page views** are the number of pages requested by visitors. However, with increased usage of web frames that divide pages into separate sections, a single page that has three frames will generate three page views. Hence, page views per se are also not a very useful metric.

Viewability rate is the percentage of ads (either display or video) that are actually seen by people online. See page 407 for a further discussion of the issue of viewability.

The number of unique visitors is perhaps the most widely used measure of a website's popularity. The measurement of **unique visitors** counts the number of distinct, unique visitors to a website, regardless of how many pages they view. **Loyalty** measures the percentage of visitors who return in a year. This can be a good indicator of a site's web following, and perhaps the trust shoppers place in a site. **Reach** is typically a percentage of the total number of consumers in a market who visit a website; for example, 10% of all book purchasers in a year will visit Amazon at least once to shop for a book. This provides an idea of the power of a website to attract market share. **Recency**—like loyalty—measures

---

impressions
number of times an ad is served

click-through rate (CTR)
the percentage of people exposed to an online advertisement who actually click on the banner

view-through rate (VTR)
measures the 30-day response rate to an ad

hits
number of http requests received by a firm's server

page views
number of pages requested by visitors

viewability rate
percentage of ads that are actually seen by people online

unique visitors
the number of distinct, unique visitors to a site

loyalty
percentage of purchasers who return in a year

reach
percentage of the total number of consumers in a market who will visit a site

recency
average number of days elapsed between visits

TABLE 6.6 MARKETING METRICS LEXICON

DISPLAY AD METRICS	DESCRIPTION
Impressions	Number of times an ad is served
Click-through rate (CTR)	Percentage of times an ad is clicked
View-through rate (VTR)	Percentage of times an ad is not clicked immediately but the website is visited within 30 days
Hits	Number of HTTP requests
Page views	Number of pages viewed
Viewability rate	Percentage of ads that are actually seen online
Unique visitors	Number of unique visitors in a period
Loyalty	Measured variously as the number of page views, frequency of single-user visits to the website, or percentage of customers who return to the site in a year to make additional purchases
Reach	Percentage of website visitors who are potential buyers; or the percentage of total market buyers who buy at a site
Recency	Time elapsed since the last action taken by a buyer, such as a website visit or purchase
Stickiness (duration)	Average length of stay at a website
Acquisition rate	Percentage of visitors who indicate an interest in the website's products by registering or visiting product pages
Conversion rate	Percentage of visitors who become customers
Browse-to-buy ratio	Ratio of items purchased to product views
View-to-cart ratio	Ratio of "Add to cart" clicks to product views
Cart conversion rate	Ratio of actual orders to "Add to cart" clicks
Checkout conversion rate	Ratio of actual orders to checkouts started
Abandonment rate	Percentage of shoppers who begin a shopping cart purchase but then leave the website without completing a purchase (similar to above)
Retention rate	Percentage of existing customers who continue to buy on a regular basis (similar to loyalty)
Attrition rate	Percentage of customers who do not return during the next year after an initial purchase

VIDEO ADVERTISING METRICS	
View time	How long does the ad actually stay in view while it plays
Completion rate	How many viewers watched the complete video
Skip rate	How many viewers skipped the video

E-MAIL METRICS	
Open rate	Percentage of e-mail recipients who open the e-mail and are exposed to the message
Delivery rate	Percentage of e-mail recipients who received the e-mail
Click-through rate (e-mail)	Percentage of recipients who clicked through to offers
Bounce-back rate	Percentage of e-mails that could not be delivered
Unsubscribe rate	Percentage of recipients who click unsubscribe
Conversion rate (e-mail)	Percentage of recipients who actually buy

the power of a website to produce repeat visits and is generally measured as the average number of days elapsed between shopper or customer visits. For example, a recency value of 25 days means the average customer will return once every 25 days.

Stickiness (sometimes called *duration*) is the average length of time visitors remain at a website. Stickiness is important to marketers because the longer the amount of time a visitor spends at a website, the greater the probability of a purchase. However, equally important is what people do when they visit a website and not just how much time they spend there.

The metrics described so far do not say much about commercial activity nor help you understand the conversion from visitor to customer. Several other measures are more helpful in this regard. **Acquisition rate** measures the percentage of visitors who register or visit product pages (indicating interest in the product). **Conversion rate** measures the percentage of visitors who actually purchase something. Conversion rates can vary widely, depending on the success of the site and device used. Websites viewed on traditional desktops/laptops still remain the most effective vehicle for converting visitors into purchasers, with a global conversion rate of 3.9%, with tablet computers the second most effective (3.5%). Conversion rates on smartphones lag significantly behind, at just 1.8% (Monetate, 2019). The **browse-to-buy ratio** measures the ratio of items purchased to product views. The **view-to-cart ratio** calculates the ratio of "Add to cart" clicks to product views. **Cart conversion rate** measures the ratio of actual orders to "Add to cart" clicks. **Checkout conversion rate** calculates the ratio of actual orders to checkouts started. **Abandonment rate** measures the percentage of shoppers who begin a shopping cart form but then fail to complete the form and leave the website. Abandonment rates can signal a number of potential problems—poor form design, lack of consumer trust, or consumer purchase uncertainty caused by other factors. Recent studies on shopping cart abandonment found abandonment rates ranging from 57% to 76% (Baymard Institute, 2020). Among the reasons for abandonment were security concerns, customer just checking prices, couldn't find customer support, couldn't find preferred payment option, and the item being unavailable at checkout. Given that more than 80% of online shoppers generally have a purchase in mind when they visit a website, a high abandonment rate signals many lost sales. **Retention rate** indicates the percentage of existing customers who continue to buy on a regular basis. **Attrition rate** measures the percentage of customers who purchase once but never return within a year (the opposite of loyalty and retention rates).

Specific types of advertising have their own special metrics. For instance, for video ads, **view time** (how long the ad actually stays in view while it plays) and **completion rate** (how many viewers watch the entire video ad) are important factors. Research has shown that brand recall is significantly higher when the entire ad is watched, making the completion rate metric more meaningful to advertisers than the click-through rate (Adler, 2015).

E-mail campaigns also have their own set of metrics. **Open rate** measures the percentage of customers who open the e-mail and are exposed to the message. Generally, open rates are quite high, in the area of 50% or greater. However, some browsers open mail as soon as the mouse cursor moves over the subject line, and therefore this measure

---

stickiness (duration)
average length of time visitors remain at a site

acquisition rate
percentage of visitors who register or visit product pages

conversion rate
percentage of visitors who purchase something

browse-to-buy ratio
ratio of items purchased to product views

view-to-cart ratio
ratio of "Add to cart" clicks to product views

cart conversion rate
ratio of actual orders to "Add to cart" clicks

checkout conversion rate
ratio of actual orders to checkouts started

abandonment rate
% of shoppers who begin a shopping cart, but then fail to complete it

retention rate
% of existing customers who continue to buy

attrition rate
% of customers who purchase once, but do not return within a year

view time
how long the video ad actually stays in view while it plays

completion rate
how many viewers watch the complete video ad

open rate
% of customers who open e-mail

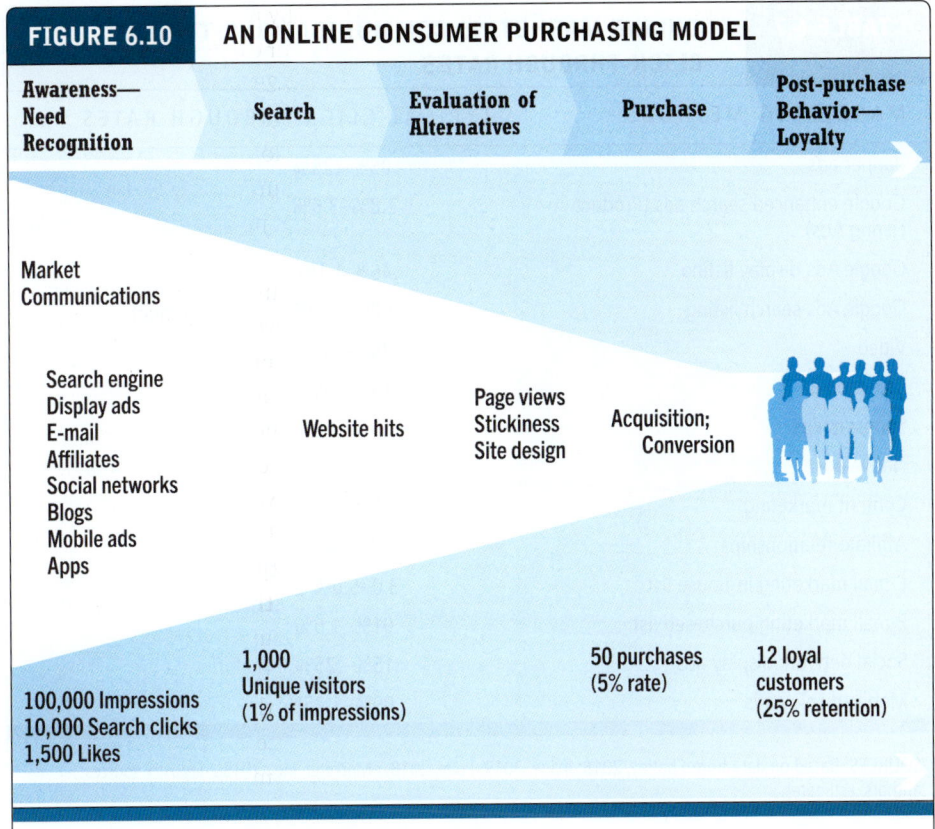

The conversion of visitors into customers, and then loyal customers, is a complex and long-term process that may take several months.

can be difficult to interpret. **Delivery rate** measures the percentage of e-mail recipients who received the e-mail. **Click-through rate (e-mail)** measures the percentage of e-mail recipients who clicked through to the offer. Finally, **bounce-back rate** measures the percentage of e-mails that could not be delivered.

There is a lengthy path from simple online ad impressions, website visits, and page views to the purchase of a product and the company making a profit (see **Figure 6.10**). You first need to make customers aware of their needs for your product and somehow drive them to your website. Once there, you need to convince them you have the best value—quality and price—when compared to alternative providers. You then must persuade them to trust your firm to handle the transaction (by providing a secure environment and fast fulfillment). Based on your success, a percentage of customers will remain loyal and purchase again or recommend your website to others.

HOW WELL DOES ONLINE ADVERTISING WORK?

What is the most effective kind of online advertising? How does online advertising compare to offline advertising? The answers depend on the goals of the campaign, the nature of the product, and the quality of the website you direct customers toward. The

delivery rate
% of e-mail recipients who received e-mail

click-through rate (e-mail)
% of e-mail recipients who clicked through to the offer

bounce-back rate
percentage of e-mails that could not be delivered

TABLE 6.7 ONLINE MARKETING COMMUNICATIONS: TYPICAL CLICK-THROUGH RATES

MARKETING METHODS	TYPICAL CLICK-THROUGH RATES
Banner ads	.05%–.25%
Google enhanced search ads (Product Listing Ads)	2.8%–3.6%
Google Ads display listing	.46%-1.1%
Google Ads search listing	2.09%–6.05% (3.2% average)
Video	.34%–.85%
Rich media	.14%–.35%
Sponsorships	1.5%–3.0%
Native ads	.80–1.8%
Content marketing	.19%–.29%
Affiliate relationships	.20%–.40%
E-mail marketing in-house list	3.0–5.0%
E-mail marketing purchased list	.01%–1.5%
Social network display ads	.15%–.25%
Mobile display ads	.09%–1.25%

SOURCES: Based on data from Chaffey, 2018; Irvine, 2019; Polar, 2018; eMarketer, Inc., 2018b; industry sources; authors' estimates.

answers also depend on what you measure. Click-through rates are interesting, but ultimately it's the return on the investment (ROI) in the ad campaign that counts. More than 70% of marketing executives said they would spend even more on digital ads if ability to measure ROI improved (Tadena, 2015). Complicating matters is the difficulty of **cross-platform attribution**, which involves understanding how to assign appropriate credit to different marketing initiatives on a variety of platforms that may have influenced a consumer along the way to an ultimate purchase. There is increasing recognition that first-click and last-click models that focus, as their names indicate, on either the first or last marketing channel or advertising format that a consumer engages with prior to a purchase, are no longer sufficient.

Table 6.7 lists the click-through rates for various types of online marketing communications tools. There is a great deal of variability within any of these types, so the figures should be viewed as general estimates. Click-through rates on all these formats are a function of personalization and other targeting techniques. For instance, several studies have found that e-mail response rates can be increased 20% or more by adding social sharing links. And while the average Google click-through rate is less than 1%, some merchants can hit 10% or more by making their ads more specific and attracting only the most interested people. Permission e-mail click-through rates have been fairly consistent over the last five years, in the 3%–5% range. Putting the recipient's name in the subject line can double the click-through rate. (For unsolicited e-mail and outright spam, response rates are much lower, even though about 20% of U.S. e-mail users report

cross-platform attribution
understanding how to assign appropriate credit to different marketing initiatives that may have influenced a consumer on the way to a purchase

clicking occasionally on an unsolicited e-mail.) The click-through rate for video ads may seem low, but it is twice as high as the rate for banner ads.

How effective is online advertising compared to offline advertising? In general, the online channels (e-mail, search engine, display ads, video, and social, mobile, and local marketing) compare very favorably with traditional channels. This explains in large part why online advertising has grown so rapidly in the last five years. Search engine advertising has grown to be one of the most cost-effective forms of marketing communications and accounts for, in large part, the growth of Google. Direct opt-in e-mail is also very cost-effective. This is, in part, because e-mail lists are so inexpensive and because opt-in e-mail is a form of targeting people who are already interested in receiving more information.

A study of the comparative impacts of offline and online marketing concluded that the most powerful marketing campaigns used multiple forms of marketing, including online, catalog, television, radio, newspapers, and retail store. Traditional media like television and print media remain the primary means for consumers to find out about new products even though advertisers have reduced their budgets for print media ads. Consumers who shop multiple channels are spending more than consumers who shop only with a single channel, in part because they have more discretionary income but also because of the combined number of "touchpoints" that marketers are making with the consumers. The fastest growing channel in consumer marketing is the multi-channel shopper.

THE COSTS OF ONLINE ADVERTISING

Effectiveness cannot be considered without an analysis of costs. Initially, most online ads were sold on a barter or **cost per thousand (CPM)** impressions basis, with advertisers purchasing impressions in 1,000-unit lots. (As viewability becomes increasingly important to advertisers, some are paying on a vCPM (viewable CPM basis); i.e, per 1,000 impressions that were in view.) Today, other pricing models have developed, including **cost per click (CPC)**, where the advertiser pays a prenegotiated fee for each click an ad receives; **cost per action (CPA)**, where the advertiser pays a prenegotiated amount only when a user performs a specific action, such as a registration or a purchase; and hybrid arrangements, combining two or more of these models (see **Table 6.8**). According to the Interactive

cost per thousand (CPM)
advertiser pays for impressions in 1,000-unit lots

cost per click (CPC)
advertiser pays prenegotiated fee for each click an ad receives

cost per action (CPA)
advertiser pays only for those users who perform a specific action

TABLE 6.8	DIFFERENT PRICING MODELS FOR ONLINE ADVERTISEMENTS
PRICING MODEL	DESCRIPTION
Barter	Exchange of ad space for something of equal value
Cost per thousand (CPM)	Advertiser pays for impressions in 1,000-unit lots
Cost per click (CPC)	Advertiser pays prenegotiated fee for each click ad received
Cost per lead (CPL)	Advertiser pays only for qualified leads or contacts
Cost per action (CPA)	Advertiser pays only for those users who perform a specific action, such as registering, purchasing, etc.
Hybrid	Two or more of the above models used together
Sponsorship	Term-based; advertiser pays fixed fee for a slot on a website

Advertising Bureau, in 2018, about 62% of digital ad spending used a performance-based pricing model, while about 35% used a CPM-based model, and 3.3% used a hybrid model (Interactive Advertising Bureau/Pricewaterhouse Coopers, 2019).

While in the early days of e-commerce, a few online sites spent as much as $400 on marketing and advertising to acquire one customer, the average cost was never that high. While the costs for offline customer acquisition are higher than online, the offline items are typically far more expensive. If you advertise in the *Wall Street Journal*, you are tapping into a wealthy demographic that may be interested in buying islands, jets, and expensive homes in France. A full-page black-and-white ad in the *Wall Street Journal* National Edition costs about $250,000, whereas other papers are in the $10,000 to $100,000 range.

One of the advantages of online marketing is that online sales can generally be directly correlated with online marketing efforts. If online merchants can obtain offline purchase data from a data broker, the merchants can measure precisely just how much revenue is generated by specific banners or e-mail messages sent to prospective customers. One way to measure the effectiveness of online marketing is by looking at the ratio of additional revenue received divided by the cost of the campaign (Revenue/Cost). Any positive whole number means the campaign was worthwhile.

A more complex situation arises when both online and offline sales revenues are affected by an online marketing effort. A large percentage of the online audience uses the Web to "shop" but not buy. These shoppers buy at physical stores. Merchants such as Sears and Walmart use e-mail to inform their registered customers of special offers available for purchase either online or at stores. Unfortunately, purchases at physical stores cannot be tied precisely with the online e-mail campaign. In these cases, merchants have to rely on less-precise measures such as customer surveys at store locations to determine the effectiveness of online campaigns.

In either case, measuring the effectiveness of online marketing communications—and specifying precisely the objective (branding versus sales)—is critical to profitability. To measure marketing effectiveness, you need to understand the costs of various marketing media and the process of converting online prospects into online customers.

In general, online marketing communications are more costly on a CPM basis than traditional mass media marketing, but are more efficient in producing sales. **Table 6.9** shows costs for typical online and offline marketing communications in the United States. For instance, the average cost for 30 seconds of commercial time during a prime-time network television broadcast is about $134,000, not including the cost to produce the advertisement. Average cost per thousand (CPM) for television ads depends in part on the market in which they are shown, and typically vary from $15 to $35. In contrast, a banner ad costs virtually nothing to produce and can be purchased for a cost of $5–$10 per thousand impressions. Direct postal mail can cost 80 cents to $1 per household drop for a post card, while e-mail can be sent for virtually nothing and costs only $5–$15 per thousand targeted names. Hence, e-mail is far less expensive than postal mail on a CPM basis. **Effective cost-per-thousand (eCPM)** is a metric that measures return on investment from an ad by dividing the total earnings from the ad by the total number of impressions in thousands.

effective cost-per-thousand (eCPM)

measures return on investment from an ad by dividing the total earnings from the ad by the total number of impressions in thousands

TABLE 6.9 TRADITIONAL AND ONLINE ADVERTISING COSTS IN THE UNITED STATES COMPARED

TRADITIONAL ADVERTISING

Local television	$1,500–$15,000 for a 30-second commercial; $45,000 for a highly rated show
Network television	$80,000–$600,000 for a 30-second spot during prime time; the average is $134,000
Cable television	$5,000–$8,000 for a 30-second ad during prime time
Radio	$100–$1,000 for a 60-second spot, depending on the time of day and program ratings
Newspaper	$120 per 1,000 circulation for a full-page ad
Magazine	$50 per 1,000 circulation for an ad in a regional edition of a national magazine, versus $120 per 1,000 for a local magazine
Direct mail	$15–$20 per 1,000 delivered for coupon mailings; $25–$40 per 1,000 for simple newspaper inserts
Billboard	$1,500–$30,000 for a large billboard for a 4-week period, with a minimum of 5–20 billboards

ONLINE ADVERTISING

Desktop banner ads	$1–$5 per 1,000 impressions, depending on size and how targeted the ad is (the more targeted, the higher the price)
Video and rich media	$20–$25 per 1,000 ads, depending on the website's demographics
E-mail	$5–$15 per 1,000 targeted e-mail addresses
Sponsorships	$30–$75 per 1,000 viewers, depending on the exclusivity of the sponsorship (the more exclusive, the higher the price)
Social network ads	$0.50–$3.00 per 1,000 impressions, with news feed ads at the high end of the range
Mobile display ads	$1.50–$3.25 per 1,000 impressions, including media costs, charges for first- or third-party data, and service fees

MARKETING ANALYTICS: SOFTWARE FOR MEASURING ONLINE MARKETING RESULTS

A number of software programs are available to automatically calculate activities at a website or on a mobile device. Tracking the viewing and behavior of consumers across myriad devices and media channels is a much more difficult task. Other software programs and services assist marketing managers in identifying exactly which marketing initiatives are paying off and which are not.

The purpose of marketing is to convert shoppers into customers who purchase what you sell. The process of converting shoppers into customers is often called a "purchasing funnel." We have characterized this as a process, rather than a funnel, that is composed of several stages: awareness, engagement, interaction, purchase, and post-purchase

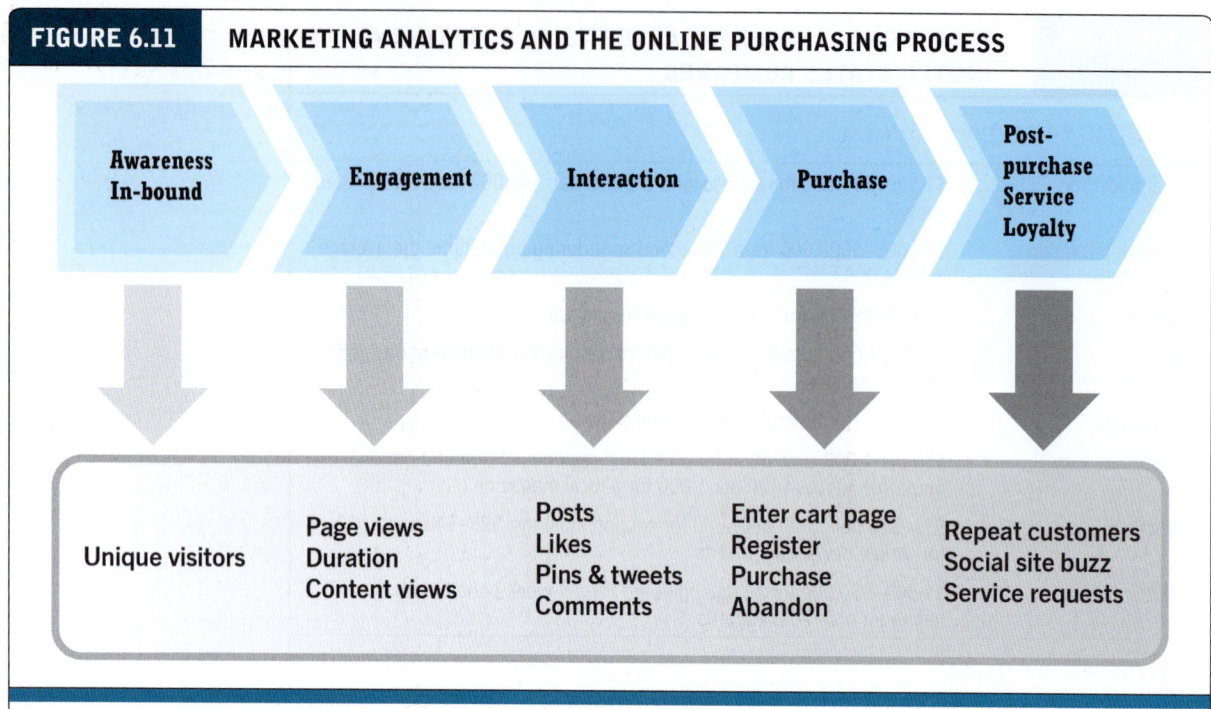

FIGURE 6.11 MARKETING ANALYTICS AND THE ONLINE PURCHASING PROCESS

Marketing analytics help e-commerce firms to better understand consumer behavior at each stage of the online purchasing process.

marketing analytics software

collects, stores, analyzes, and graphically presents data on each of the stages in the conversion of shoppers to customers process on e-commerce sites

service and loyalty. **Marketing analytics software** collects, stores, analyzes, and graphically presents data on each of the stages in the conversion of shoppers to customers (see **Figure 6.11**).

Marketing analytics packages can tell business managers how people become *aware* of their site, and where they come from (e.g., search, self-entered URL, e-mail, social campaigns, or off-line traditional print and TV ads), along with demographic, behavioral, and geographic information. Are shoppers coming from mobile devices, Facebook, or Pinterest? This information can help managers decide the best ways to drive traffic, the so-called "in-bound" links to a site. Once on the website, analytics packages can record how *engaged* visitors are with the site's content, measured in terms of pages viewed and duration on site. This information can allow managers to change the design or their sites, or change the content viewers are seeing. For instance, video testimonials from product users may be much more engaging than expert reviews or user text comments. In a social marketing world, where consumers' opinions and behavior can be harvested and broadcast to their friends, an important intermediate step in the consumer conversion process is to encourage visitors to *interact* with your content and share their experiences, opinions, preferences, and behaviors with their friends, as well as other visitors to the site. Marketing analytics packages can track visitor interaction and help managers decide what content leads to higher levels of visitor interaction with friends and other visitors. The *purchase activity* on the shopping cart page is a major focus of analytics tools not just because this is where the revenue is generated, but also because this is where the customer frequently exits the entire site and the firm loses a potential sale. The current shopping cart abandonment is 57% to 76% in the United States, with little change over the last few years, and higher in other countries (Baymard Institute, 2020). This seems like an extraordinary rate but, like most of the indicators discussed in this chapter, abandonment is a complex phenomenon and often not what it seems. Consumers use carts like a shopping list, and don't complete the transaction immediately; they use it for price comparison and to know shipping costs, or taxes; they complete transactions later on a different device, such as a mobile phone. Another measure of near-purchase activity is the add-to-cart rate. Marketing analytics software can help managers tease out the meaning of behavior on a website's shopping cart page. Finally, marketing analytics can help managers discover customer *loyalty and post-purchase* behavior. In an increasingly social marketing environment, marketing managers need to know how their products and services are being talked about on other sites, Facebook pages, Instagram Stories, or Twitter tweets, often called "buzz" or sentiment analysis. Are the comments positive or negative? What is the source of negative comments? Possible candidates are poor quality, high costs, poor warranty service, and shipping issues.

The end objective of marketing analytics packages is to help business managers optimize the return on investment on their marketing efforts, and to do this by building a detailed understanding of how their consumers behave. Marketing analytics also allows managers to measure the impact of specific marketing campaigns involving, say, discounts, loyalty points, and special offers, as well as regional, or demographic-based campaigns. Aside from its role in enhancing management decision making, and optimizing the effectiveness of building an e-commerce presence, marketing analytics packages also enable a near real-time marketing capability where managers are able to change the content of a website, respond to customer complaints and comments, and align campaigns with trending topics or news developments, all in a near real-time manner (real-time may be a matter of minutes or at most 24 hours).

While there are a great many marketing analytics firms and software packages on the market, the leaders are Google Analytics, Adobe Analytics, IBM Digital Analytics, and Webtrends. Marketing analytics software is often part of a comprehensive package sold to corporations from hardware, to web design tools, cloud services, and management expertise.

6.5 CAREERS IN E-COMMERCE

As you've learned in this chapter, the online advertising industry is one of the most robust and fastest-growing sectors of the online economy. There are positions within companies (similar to the one detailed in this section), within the online advertising industry itself, and also with companies such as Google, Facebook, Amazon, and others, that provide the platform for online advertisements.

THE COMPANY

The company is an organic food grocer based in Munich, Germany, where it started as a single grocery store selling organic and locally farmed foods in 2000. Today the firm operates 250 total retail stores throughout Germany and has over 5,000 employees.

The company provides customers with a one-stop shop for organic produce, raw dairy, humanely raised meats, gourmet items, baked goods, supplements, and household items. The firm has begun a major effort to build an online presence with a new website and social marketing efforts, and is considering online ordering and on-demand delivery of organic foods to its affluent, young customer base.

The German organic food market is the largest in Europe and the second-largest market in the world. Since 2000, sales of organic food in Germany have more than tripled, and have steeply increased over the last few years, reaching over €10 billion in 2017, almost 30% of the total organic food sales in the European Union.

THE POSITION: DIGITAL MARKETING ASSISTANT

You will work with the Marketing Team to communicate with customers and vendors using digital marketing tools to enhance brand engagement, education, and online customer service. Your role will include:

- Collaborating with Marketing Team's promotional calendar for digital, print, and in-store marketing materials.
- Creating supplemental content for Total's blog, website, e-mail newsletters, and social media accounts.
- Updating the company's website with new content, implementing SEO, and monitoring all web activity.
- Updating the company's social media accounts: Facebook, Google+, Twitter, Pinterest, and Instagram.
- Researching social media developments and trends.
- Working with Store Managers, Category Managers, and other team members to plan and facilitate store, team member, and product-specific posts.
- Responding and managing customer reviews posted online (Yelp, Google, etc.).
- Generating monthly reports to analyze the success of digital marketing efforts.

QUALIFICATIONS/SKILLS

- Undergraduate degree in the humanities or social sciences, with course work in MIS, e-commerce, digital marketing, statistics, web design, or social media
- Proficiency in WordPress, Facebook for Business, Facebook Ads Manager, Instagram, Pinterest, Twitter, Hootsuite, Sprout Social, Google MyBusiness, Google Analytics, Yelp for Businesses, and Microsoft Office
- Excellent verbal and written communication skills
- Copywriting and editing expertise
- Experience or background in customer service
- Photography and basic photo editing skills
- Understanding of search engine optimization
- Ability to multi-task and work in a fast-paced environment
- Good time management skills

- Ability to work independently and as part of a team
- Knowledge about and familiarity with food/ingredient sourcing, health and wellness, sustainable agriculture, organic foods, and current news/trends in the natural foods industry is a plus!

PREPARING FOR THE INTERVIEW

This chapter provides foundational material that you should be familiar with as you embark on interviewing for a position in the online marketing and advertising industry. Begin by reviewing Section 6.1, so that you can demonstrate that you have some knowledge of the demographics of the Internet audience and online consumer behavior, particularly the consumer decision process (Figure 6.2). Section 6.2 provides an overview for you of digital marketing and advertising strategies and tools. You should be prepared to show that you are familiar with the wide variety of online marketing and advertising tools, such as search engine marketing and advertising, display advertising in its different formats (banner ads, rich media, video ads, content marketing, and native advertising, as well as the use of programmatic advertising networks), e-mail marketing, affiliate marketing, and also social, mobile, and local marketing, as well as with various customer retention and pricing strategies. You can also impress your interviewer by indicating awareness of some of the issues associated with the different types of online advertising, such as ad fraud, viewability, and the increasing use of ad blocking software. While this particular position is not a technical one, it would also be worthwhile to review the various Internet marketing technologies discussed in Section 6.3, as well as Section 6.4, so that you can demonstrate that you have some familiarity with the costs and benefits of online marketing communications. Pay particular attention to the online marketing metrics lexicon (Table 6.6), as you will want to show that you have some basic knowledge about how the effectiveness of online advertising is measured, as well some of the issues surrounding the topic, such as the difficulties of cross-platform attribution.

POSSIBLE FIRST INTERVIEW QUESTIONS

1. What do you think are some of the advantages of developing an online channel for branding and direct sales rather than using traditional media such as print advertising or television?

You can suggest that online marketing is more effective than traditional channels because people are spending more and more time online than ever before to view content, find out information on products, and purchase. An online presence means customers can not just view an ad, but also purchase at nearly the same time. This is far more convenient for the customer than reading a newspaper ad, or watching a TV show, and then driving to a store for the actual purchase. It's all about the customer experience and making it as easy as possible to purchase products.

2. Do you think the Internet and social networks are a good way to promote organic products and generate direct sales, as well as drive more customers to our stores?

You can suggest that the largest market for organic foods is young professionals, and this demographic group is also very active on social sites, and familiar with ordering goods and food online.

3. Word of mouth is a very powerful marketing tool. How do you think we can achieve more effective word-of-mouth online marketing?

You can suggest that online marketing and advertising involves contacting customers who are already a part of social networks like Facebook, Twitter, and others. Many are members of online self-help networks as well. The online audience is highly connected to others in family, professional, and interest networks. You will be marketing to existing social networks as much as to individuals.

4. Aside from websites and social networks, what other online marketing channels should we be focusing on that would be effective for our target audience?

You can suggest that display ads and search engine ads might be effective for organic food products. Display ads would work well if you can identify what other websites your customers use for news, entertainment, and information, and then place display ads on those sites. Programmatic advertising networks could help the firm find those sites and place the ads. Search engine ads can be placed in response to queries about health issues.

5. Do you think our customers would be interested in home delivery of organic foods?

You could suggest that if the products could be ordered and delivered on the same day, and are just as fresh as in-store products, then yes, on-demand, same-day delivery would be very attractive to young families where both parents often work.

6.6 CASE STUDY

Programmatic Advertising:
Real-Time Marketing

The holy grail of advertising and marketing is to deliver the right message to the right person at the right time. If this were possible, no one would receive ads they did not want to see, and then no advertising dollars would be wasted, reducing the costs to end users and increasing the efficiency of each ad dollar. In the physical world, only a very rough approximation of this ideal is possible. Advertisers buy television and radio spots, newspaper ads, and billboards based on broad demographics, and the context in which the ad will be shown.

The Internet promised to change this traditional method of buying ad space by allowing advertisers to gather personal information on consumers through the use of cookies placed on the user's browser, which tracked behavior and purchases online and could be matched with offline information as well. Advertisers could then use this information to target ads to just the desired individuals they were seeking, based on personal characteristics, interests, and recent clickstream behavior. From the beginning, e-commerce was a trade-off for consumers between privacy and efficiency: let us know more about you, and we will show you only the advertising and products you are interested in seeing and would be likely to respond to. For brands, the promise was scale and cost: let us know who you are looking for and we will find millions of people on thousands of websites that fit your criteria. E-commerce was supposed to end the mass advertising that began in 19th-century newspapers, 20th-century radio, and exploded with the growth of television.

The latest rendition of these promises from the ad tech industry is programmatic advertising, which it touts as an automated algorithmic platform that allows large brands to bid for ad space (web pages) on hundreds of thousands, and even millions, of websites, in coordinated campaigns, measure the results, and extend brands to tens of millions of consumers with unprecedented scale. In 2019, advertisers are expected to spend about $85 billion on programmatic advertising worldwide, over two-thirds of all digital display ad spending. But in the past few years, it has become clear that the promise of programmatic advertising has not been realized and has many risks for brands. In fact, it has injured many brands, and the ad tech industry is reeling from advertiser criticism that the existing online ad ecosystem lacks transparency, fails to protect brands, is rife with fraudulent clicks by bots, and lacks metrics for judging the cost effectiveness of ads.

Contrary to the rosy promises of the online ad industry, most notably the ad giants Google, Facebook, and Twitter, most of the display ads shown to website visitors are irrelevant, sometimes hilariously so, to visitors' interests. For this reason, the click-through rate for banner advertising is stunningly low, well under 1%, and the price of generic display ads is less than $1.00 per thousand views because of their low response rate. Check this out: visit Yahoo (one of the largest display advertisers on earth) on any device, look at the prominent ads on screen, and ask yourself if you are really interested in the ad content at that moment in time. Often, it is an ad for something you have recently searched for on Google or even already purchased at Amazon or other sites. These ads will follow you for days as you are re-targeted across the web and on mobile devices. Researchers have found that only 20% of Internet users find that display ads on websites are relevant to their interests, and depending on the type of ad (sidebar, native inline, pre-roll video, or video and display ads) are viewed unfavorably by 50% to 78% of visitors. How many times a day do you click X to stop a video roll on the top of the screen?

To understand how we ended up in this situation, it's useful to review briefly how the Internet ad industry evolved. Digital display advertising has progressed through three eras. In the early 2000s, a firm with a website interested in ad revenue (a "publisher") would sell space on its site to other firms (advertisers), usually through an ad agency or via a direct relationship. These were primarily manual transactions. By 2005, ad networks emerged. These networks allowed advertisers to buy ad space on thousands of participating sites in a single purchase and allowed publishers to sell to advertisers more efficiently. Prices were negotiated among the parties. This was very similar to the manner in which ads on cable TV were sold. By 2011, even larger ad exchanges emerged and began using automated real-time bidding for ad space. This provided advertisers access to an even larger pool of publisher ad spaces that numbered up to the millions of websites. Prices and ad placement were automated by algorithms and adjusted based on real-time open auctions, in which advertising firms and brands indicated what they were willing to pay to advertise to consumers meeting specific criteria. Google, Facebook, Twitter, and others developed their own proprietary automated bidding platforms. Collectively, these are called real-time bidding (RTB) programmatic advertising platforms. The result today is an extraordinarily complex ecosystem of players, and sophisticated technologies (called the ad technology stack).

In programmatic ad platforms, scale has increased dramatically. In 2018, there are thousands of advertisers and millions of web pages where ads can be placed. The ads are chosen and generated based on the user's browser cookie history and information about the web page, so that ads can supposedly target the right consumers. The content of the web page and the ad location on the page are also important. Millions of website pages have content injurious to brands (fake news, hate language, or violence), or just very poor content, even no content. All programmatic advertising platforms use big data repositories that contain personal information on thousands to millions of online shoppers and consumers; analytic software to classify and search the database for shoppers with the desired characteristics; and machine learning techniques to test out combinations of consumer characteristics that optimize the chance of a purchase resulting from exposure to an ad. All of this technology is designed to lower the cost and increase the speed and scale of advertising in an environment where there are hundreds of millions of web pages to fill with ads, and millions of online consumers looking to buy at any given moment.

Programmatic ad platforms have since evolved into three different types: traditional auction-based real time bidding (RTB) "open exchange," a marketplace open to all advertisers and publishers of website pages; private marketplace (PMP), which also uses real time bidding, where publishers invite selected advertisers to bid on their inventory; and programmatic direct (PD), where advertisers deal directly with well-established publishers who have developed their own supply-side platforms (an automated inventory of available ad space). Currently, about 60% of programmatic advertising is programmatic direct and 19% is PMP. Open exchange RTB is no longer growing and represents only about 10% of programmatic marketing. The trend is towards publishers, especially well-known brands with large budgets, to reduce their dependence on the operators of the platforms, and exert much more control over where their ads appear, how visible they are, and what content they are associated with. To find out why, continue reading.

Currently, less than 20% of online display advertising in the United States, UK, Canada, France, and Germany is still done in a non-automated, traditional environment that involves marketers using e-mail, fax, phone, and text messaging in direct relationships with publishers. Traditional methods are often used for high-value premium ads, say, the top of the screen with a video; expanding ads seen at major newspapers, magazines, and portal sites; and native ads appearing alongside or interwoven with native content. This is the world of the traditional insertion order: if you want to advertise on a specific newspaper or magazine website, call the ad department and fill out an insertion order. For instance, if you are a brand selling biking accessories, you can tell your ad agency to place ads in biking magazine websites and on social networks, targeting the readers of those magazines. In this environment, firms who want to sell products and services online hire advertising agencies to develop a marketing plan, and the agency directly contracts with the ad department of the publishers.

This traditional environment is expensive, imprecise, and slow, in part because of the number of people involved in the decision about where to place ads. Also, the technology used is slow, and the process of learning which of several ads is optimal could take weeks or months. Real-time so-called A/B testing is difficult. The ads could be targeted to a more precise group of potential customers, and to a much larger group of potential customers. While context advertising on sites dedicated to a niche product is very effective, there are many other websites or social network pages visited by bikers that might be equally effective, and cost much less.

SOURCES: "Programmatic Digital Display Ad Spending," by Lauren Fisher, eMarketer, Inc.; November 2019; "Amazon Advertising 2018," by Nicole Perrin, eMarketer, Inc., September 18, 2018; "How Sellers Trick Amazon to Boost Sales," by Laura Stevens, *Wall Street Journal*, July 28, 2018; "Amazon—Once Again—Fights Fake Reviews, Click Fraud," by Laurie Sullivan, Mediapost.com, July 30, 2018; "Bot Baseline Report 2016–2017," by Association of National Advertisers, May 2018; "US Programmatic Ad Spending Forecast 2018," by Lauren Fisher, eMarketer, Inc., April 5, 2018; "P&G Contends Too Much Digital Ad Spending Is a Waste," by Suzanne Vranica, *Wall Street Journal*, March 1, 2018; "Programmatic Advertising Failed to Meet Expectations: It Dead-ended with Fraud and Security Threats," by Erik Huberman, Adweek.com, March 9, 2018; "YouTube Revamped Its Ad System. AT&T Still Hasn't Returned," by Sapna Maheshwari, *New York Times*, February 12, 2018; "YouTube Hiring More Humans to Train Computers to Police the Site," by Daisuke Wakabayashi, *New York Times*, December 4, 2017; "What's the Difference Between RTB, PMPs and Programmatic Direct?," by Sovrn Holdings, Sovrn.com, October 10, 2017; "Programmatic Ad Spending Worldwide, 2012–2019," eMarketer, Inc., November 20, 2017; "Consumer Favorability Towards Selected Types of Ads in the United States as of September 2017," Statista.com, October 10, 2017; "How Much Digital Ad Spend Is Lost to Fraudulent Bots?," by Ayaz Nanji, Marketingprofs.com, June 13, 2017; "Display Ad Performance Metrics," eMarketer, Inc., May 2017; "Display Ad Viewability Rates, by Device & Format," eMarketer, Inc., May 2017; "He Buys a Lot of Ads, and He's

The process is very different in a programmatic direct (PD) environment. Ad agencies have access to any of several programmatic ad platforms offered by Google, Yahoo, AOL, Facebook, Twitter, and many other pure ad platforms. Working with their clients, the ad agency more precisely defines the target audience to include men and women, ages 24–35, who live in zip codes where mountain biking is a popular activity, have mentioned biking topics on social networks, have e-mail where mountain biking is discussed, make more than $70,000 a year, and currently do not own a mountain bike. The ad agency enters a bid expressed in dollars per thousand impressions for 200,000 impressions to people who meet most or all of the characteristics being sought. The platform returns a quote for access to this population of 200,000 people who meet the characteristics required. The quote is based on what other advertisers are willing to pay for that demographic and characteristics. The quote is accepted or denied. If accepted, the ads are shown to people as they move about the Web, in real time. As people visit various websites, the automated program assesses whether they meet the desired characteristics, and displays the mountain bike ad within milliseconds to that person. The programmatic direct platforms also track the responses to the ads in real time, and can change to different ads and test for effectiveness based on the platform's experience in near real time. The programmatic direct platforms claim they use algorithms and machine learning programs that can identify over time the most effective ads on the most productive websites. At least this is the promise. Increasingly, large advertisers do not use agencies but deal directly with the ad platforms like Google, Facebook, and most recently Amazon (now the third largest display ad platform).

In private marketplace (PMP) transactions, a group of publishers invite selected advertisers to bid on ad space, often using the publishers' own customer data. Generally, the publishers know more about their customers than the ad platforms' algorithms and databases can provide. For instance, the leading online newspapers might combine their inventory of ad space (web pages) and invite premium big-budget brands to bid on the space. This gives the publishers much more control over who advertises on their pages, and gives advertisers a shot at getting premium ad space, better page placement, and better results from more precise knowledge of the consumer. This is reflected in higher costs for the advertisers. In the PMP model, a single publisher directly contracts with selected brands and advertisers for guaranteed placement of ads, and like PMP methods, offers both parties more control and precision. Brands and ad agencies bid for this space in a semi-automated environment. In some cases, prices are negotiated directly between the publisher and the brands or their ad agencies. Real-time bidding is not used.

The risks of RTB in open exchanges are that brands lose a great deal, if not all, control over the presentation of ads, including what websites they appear on, where on the screen they appear (above or below the "fold" or scroll), how long the ad is present on screen, who is doing the clicking on the ads (real interested persons or bots or fake people), and the content of the website.

For instance, up until recently JPMorgan Chase had ads appearing on an estimated 400,000 websites a month using programmatic RTB open exchange auctions. It became suspicious when only 12,000 sites produced any clicks. An intern was assigned to visit each one to see if they were appropriate for the bank. The intern discovered that 7,000 were not, leaving 5,000 for "whitelisting" acceptable as pre-approved websites. JPMorgan Chase has not experienced any fall-off in the visibility of its ads on the Internet since it eliminated

355,000 websites from its ad campaign. Going forward, JPMorgan Chase intends to winnow the list to only 1,000 whitelisted sites. One of the blacklisted sites advertising the JPMorgan Chase's private client services turned out to be a website that advocated violence.

In 2017, YouTube came under intense fire by leading brands because their YouTube ads were appearing next to offensive material, promoting racism, hate, and terrorism. As a result, JPMorgan Chase, Verizon, Gerber, AT&T, Johnson & Johnson, Lyft, and Procter & Gamble (the world's largest advertiser) all pulled ads from YouTube. Many of these firms have not returned to YouTube despite Google hiring thousands of employees to monitor websites and teach machine learning algorithms what is an acceptable website for ads.

In addition to malicious sites, there are millions of fake sites on the Web set up for the sole purpose of displaying ads and generating revenue. In 2018, Facebook shut down 1.5 billion fake accounts, and Twitter closed 70 million fake accounts in two months. No one knows the total number of fake accounts remaining. Many of the fake sites are bots that generate clicks but have no real people viewing the ads. While RTB open exchange platforms try to prevent this behavior, they can easily be defeated. The result is large ad expenditures but fewer legitimate clicks, and lower conversions. Analysts estimate that the top 50 online media publishers account for only 5% of all ads shown on the Web. This means 95% of the ads are being shown on niche websites with small audiences, or completely fake sites, with fake visitors. In general, ad platforms have little idea, if any, of where the ads are appearing, the content of the websites, or who is clicking. Top brands with large budgets no longer believe the ad platforms' claims that they use algorithms and machine learning to weed out fake sites, hate sites, and sites that feature porn.

Frustrated with Digital Advertising," by Sapna Maheswari, *New York Times*, April 9, 2017; "Advancing Programmatic Advertising: Buyers and Sellers Seek Greater Control," by eMarketer, Inc., April 2017; "Did JPMorgan Chase Just Start a Digital Advertising Revolution?," by George Slefo, Adage.com, March 31, 2017; "Chase Had Ads on 400,000 Sites. Then on Just 5,000. Same Results," by Sapna Maheswari, *New York Times*, March 29, 2017; "Consumer Attitude Towards Website Advertising Formats: A Comparative Study of Banner, Pop-up and In-line Display Advertisements," by Tri de Le, *Journal of Internet Marketing and Advertising*, January 13, 2017; "Display Ad Click-through Rates (CTR), by Device," by eMarketer, Inc., December 2016; "US Programmatic Ad Spending Forecast: Most Mobile Display and Video Ad Dollars to be Automated by 2018," by Lauren Fisher, eMarketer, Inc., September 26, 2016; "The New Display Ad Tech Stack," by Lauren Fisher, eMarketer, Inc., May 2016.

Case Study Questions

1. Pay a visit to your favorite portal and count the total ads on the opening page. Count how many of these ads are (a) immediately of interest and relevant to you, (b) sort of interesting or relevant but not now, and (c) not interesting or relevant. Do this 10 times and calculate the percentage of the three kinds of situations. Describe what you find and explain the results using this case.

2. Advertisers use different kinds of "profiles" in the decision to display ads to customers. Identify the different kinds of profiles described in this case, and explain why they are relevant to online display advertising.

3. How can display ads achieve search-engine–like results?

4. Do you think instant display ads based on your immediately prior clickstream will be as effective as search engine marketing techniques? Why or why not?

6.7 REVIEW

KEY CONCEPTS

- **Understand the key features of the Internet audience, the basic concepts of consumer behavior and purchasing, and how consumers behave online.**
  - Key features of the Internet audience include the number of users online, the intensity and scope of use, demographics and aspects, the type of Internet connection, and community effects.
  - Models of consumer behavior attempt to predict or explain what consumers purchase, and where, when, how much, and why they buy. Factors that impact buying behavior include cultural, social, and psychological factors.
  - There are five stages in the consumer decision process: awareness of need, search for more information, evaluation of alternatives, the actual purchase decision, and post-purchase contact with the firm.
  - The online consumer decision process is basically the same, with the addition of two new factors: website and mobile platform capabilities and consumer clickstream behavior.

- **Identify and describe the basic digital commerce marketing and advertising strategies and tools.**
  - A *website* is the major tool for establishing the initial relationship with the customer.
  - *Search engine marketing and advertising* allows firms to pay search engines for inclusion in the search engine index (formerly free and based on "objective" criteria), receiving a guarantee that their firm will appear in the results of relevant searches.
  - *Display ads* are promotional messages that users can respond to by clicking on the banner and following the link to a product description or offering. Display ads include banner ads, rich media, video ads, and sponsorships.
  - *E-mail marketing* sends e-mail directly to interested users, and has proven to be one of the most effective forms of marketing communications.
  - *Lead generation marketing* uses multiple e-commerce presences to generate leads for businesses who later can be contacted and converted into customers.
  - *Affiliate marketing* involves a firm putting its logo or banner ad on another firm's website from which users of that site can click through to the affiliate's site.
  - *Viral marketing* is a form of social marketing that involves getting customers to pass along a company's marketing message to friends, family, and colleagues.
  - *Social marketing and advertising* involves using the social graph to communicate brand images and directly promote sales of products and services.
  - *Mobile and local marketing and advertising* involves using display ads, search engine advertising, video ads, and mobile messaging on mobile devices such as smartphones and tablet computers, often using the geographic location of the user.
  - *Multi-channel marketing* (combining offline and online marketing efforts) is typically the most effective. Although many e-commerce ventures want to rely heavily on online communications, marketing communications campaigns most successful at driving traffic have incorporated both online and offline tactics.
  - *Customer retention techniques* for strengthening customer relationships include personalization, one-to-one marketing, and interest-based advertising, customization and customer co-production, and customer service (such as CRMs, FAQs, live chat, intelligent agents, and automated response systems).
  - *Online pricing strategies* include offering products and services for free, versioning, bundling, and dynamic pricing.

- Identify and describe the main technologies that support online marketing.
  - *Web transaction logs*—records that document user activity at a website. Coupled with data from the registration forms and shopping cart database, these represent a treasure trove of marketing information for both individual sites and the online industry as a whole.
  - *Tracking files*—various files, like cookies, web beacons, Flash cookies, and apps, that follow users and track their behavior as they visit sites across the Web.
  - *Databases, data warehouses, data mining, and profiling*—technologies that allow marketers to identify exactly who the online customer is and what they want, and then to present the customer with exactly what they want, when they want it, for the right price.
  - *CRM systems*—a repository of customer information that records all of the contacts a customer has with a firm and generates a customer profile available to everyone in the firm who has a need to "know the customer."

- Understand the costs and benefits of online marketing communications.
  - Key terms that one must know in order to understand evaluations of online marketing communications' effectiveness and its costs and benefits include:
    - Impressions, click-through rate, view-through rate, hits, page views, stickiness (duration), unique visitors, loyalty, reach, recency, acquisition rate, conversion rate, browse-to-buy ratio, view-to-cart ratio, cart conversion rate, checkout conversion rate, abandonment rate, retention rate, attrition rate, open rate, delivery rate, click-through rate (e-mail), bounce-back rate.
  - Studies have shown that low click-through rates are not indicative of a lack of commercial impact of online advertising, and that advertising communication does occur even when users do not directly respond by clicking. Online advertising in its various forms has been shown to boost brand awareness and brand recall, create positive brand perceptions, and increase intent to purchase.
  - Effectiveness cannot be considered without analysis of cost. Typical pricing models for online marketing communications include barter, cost per thousand (CPM), cost per click (CPC), cost per action (CPA), hybrid models, and sponsorships.
  - Online marketing communications are typically less costly than traditional mass media marketing. Also, online sales can generally be directly correlated with online marketing efforts, unlike traditional marketing communications tactics.

QUESTIONS

1. What are some of the ways that gender, income, education, age, and ethnicity impact online purchasing behavior?
2. What are the main reasons consumers choose the online channel?
3. What is clickstream behavior and how is it used by marketers?
4. What is native advertising, and why is it controversial?
5. Why are CRM systems an important Internet marketing technology?
6. How do the MRC's new standards address the issue of ad viewability?
7. What are the five main elements of a comprehensive marketing plan? What are some different platforms used for each?
8. Why are marketers interested in big data?
9. What are three strategic questions that online marketing managers need to address?
10. What are the primary marketing functions of a website?
11. How does the IAB's new guidelines for display ads differ from its old guidelines?
12. What are some issues associated with the use of search engine advertising?
13. Why is e-mail marketing still useful?
14. How are blogs being used for advertising and marketing?

15. Why is Apple's ITP feature controversial?
16. What are two types of cross-device tracking?
17. What is retargeting, and why has it become a popular marketing technique?
18. Shopping cart abandonment rates are typically 70% or higher. Why is this rate so high and what techniques can help improve this rate?
19. Which type of ad pricing is most common?
20. What are some of the issues associated with native advertising?

PROJECTS

1. Go to www.strategicbusinessinsights.com/vals/presurvey.shtml. Take the survey to determine which lifestyle category you fit into. Then write a two-page paper describing how your lifestyle and values impact your use of e-commerce. How is your online consumer behavior affected by your lifestyle?
2. Visit Net-a-porter.com and create an Internet marketing plan for it that includes each of the following: one-to-one marketing, affiliate marketing, viral marketing, blog marketing, and social network marketing. Describe how each plays a role in growing the business, and create a slide presentation of your marketing plan.
3. Use the Online Consumer Purchasing Model (Figure 6.10) to assess the effectiveness of an e-mail campaign at a small website devoted to the sales of apparel to the ages 18–26 young adult market in the United States. Assume a marketing campaign of 100,000 e-mails (at 25 cents per e-mail address). The expected click-through rate is 5%, the customer conversion rate is 10%, and the loyal customer retention rate is 25%. The average sale is $60, and the profit margin is 50% (the cost of the goods is $30). Does the campaign produce a profit? What would you advise doing to increase the number of purchases and loyal customers? What web design factors? What communications messages?
4. Surf the Web for at least 15 minutes. Visit at least two different e-commerce sites. Make a list describing in detail all the different marketing communication tools you see being used. Which do you believe is the most effective and why?
5. Do a search for a product of your choice on two search engines. Examine the results page carefully. Can you discern which results, if any, are a result of a paid placement? If so, how did you determine this? What other marketing communications related to your search appear on the page?
6. Examine the use of rich media and video in advertising. Find and describe at least two examples of advertising using streaming video, sound, or other rich media technologies. (Hint: Check the sites of online advertising agencies for case studies or examples of their work.) What are the advantages and/or disadvantages of this kind of advertising? Prepare a 3- to 5-page report on your findings.
7. Visit Facebook and examine the ads shown in the right margin and in your News Feed. What is being advertised and how do you believe it is relevant to your interests or online behavior? You could also search on a retail product on Google several times, and related products, then visit Yahoo or another popular site to see if your past behavior is helping advertisers track you.

REFERENCES

Adjei, Mavis, and Stephanie Noble. "The Influence of C2C Communications in Online Brand Communities On Purchase Behavior." *Journal of the Academy of Marketing Science*, Vol. 38, No. 5 (2009).

Adomavicius, Gediminas, and Alexander Tuzhilin. "Using Data Mining Methods to Build Customer Profiles." *IEEE Computer* (February 2001a).

Adomavicius, Gediminas, and Alexander Tuzhilin. "Expert-Driven Validation of Rule-Based User Models in Personalization Applications." *Data Mining and Knowledge Discovery* (January 2001b).

AdRoll. "Retargeting 101: Results That Will Get You Promoted." (May 11, 2017).

Agrawal, Parag. "A New Collaboration with Google Cloud." Blog.twitter.com (May 3, 2018).

Akerlof, G. "The Market for 'Lemons' Quality Under Uncertainty and the Market Mechanism." *Quarterly Journal of Economics* (August 1970).

Ba, Sulin, Jan Stallaert, and Zhongju Zhang. "Balancing IT with the Human Touch: Optimal Investment in IT-Based Customer Service." *Information Systems Research* (September 2010).

Ba, Sulin, and Paul Pavlou. "Evidence on the Effect of Trust Building Technology in Electronic Markets: Price Premiums and Buyer Behavior." *MIS Quarterly* (September 2002).

Bakos, J. Y., and Erik Brynjolfsson. "Bundling and Competition on the Internet: Aggregation Strategies for Information Goods." *Marketing Science* (January 2000).

Battelle, John. "The Database of Intentions Is Far Larger Than I Thought." Battellemedia.com (March 5, 2010).

Battelle, John. "Search Blog." Battellemedia.com (November 13, 2003).

Baymard Institute. "Cart Abandonment Rate Statistics." Baymard.com (accessed January 24, 2020).

Brookings Institute. "Online Identity and Consumer Trust: Assessing Online Risk." (January 2011).

Castell, John. "Google Panda Explained for Website Owners." Linkedin.com (June 12, 2014).

Chaffey, Dave. "Average Display Advertising Clickthrough Rates" (September 10, 2019).

Chan, P. K. "A Non-Invasive Learning Approach to Building Web User Profiles." In *Proceedings of ACM SIGKDD International Conference* (1999).

Clement, J. "E-mail Spam Rate Worldwide 2012–2018." (March 20, 2019).

Corritore, C. L., B. Kracher, and S. Wiedenbeck, "On-line Trust: Concepts, Evolving Themes, a Model." *International Journal of Human-Computer Studies* (2006).

Crawford, Todd. "Opinion: 5 Predictions for Affiliate Marketing in 2018." Mobilemarketingwatch.com (November 10, 2017).

Cross, Robert. "Launching the Revenue Rocket: How Revenue Management Can Work For Your Business." *Cornell Hotel and Restaurant Administration Quarterly* (April 1997).

Degtev, Ilya. "Revised MRC Viewability Guidelines: Everything You Need to Know." Brightcove.com (October 3, 2019).

eMarketer, Inc. "US Internet Users and Penetration." (April 2019a).

eMarketer, Inc. "Average Time Spent with Media in the US, 2017–2021." (April 2019b).

eMarketer, Inc. "Mobile Phone Internet Users and Penetration Worldwide." (April 2019c).

eMarketer, Inc. "Average Time Spent with Media by Users in the UK, 2017–2021." (April 2019d).

eMarketer, Inc. "Internet Users and Penetration, by Gender." (March 2019e).

eMarketer, Inc., "Internet Uers and Penetration, by Age." (March 2019f).

eMarketer, Inc. "Digital Shopper and Buyer Penetration in the UK, 2018–2023." (May 2019g)

eMarketer, Inc. "Digital Buyers, by Country" (December 2019h).

eMarketer, Inc. "Digital Ad Spending, by Country," (October 2019i).

eMarketer, Inc. "Digital Ad Spending Penetration, by Country." (October 2019j).

eMarketer, Inc. "Digital Ad Revenues, by Company, Worldwide." (October 2019k).

eMarketer, Inc. "Total Media Ad Spending Worldwide, by Media, 2018–2024." (January 10, 2019l).

eMarketer, Inc. "Digital Ad Spending in the US, by Industry, 2016–2020." (July 2019m)

eMarketer, Inc. "US Digital Ad Spending, by Format." (October 2019n).

eMarketer, Inc. "US Digital Ad Spending Growth, by Format." (October 2019o).

eMarketer, Inc. "US Display Ad Spending Growth, by Format." (October 2019p).

eMarketer, Inc."Search Ad Spending, by Country." (October 2019q).

eMarketer, inc. "Display Ad Spending, by Country" (October 2019r).

eMarketer, Inc. "US Native Display Ad Spending, by Device." (March 2019s).

eMarketer, Inc. (Amy He). "Ad Blocking Growth is Slowing Down but Not Going Away." (July 26, 2019t).

eMarketer, Inc. "Worldwide Social Network Ad Revenues, by Company." (October 2019u).

eMarketer, Inc. "Worldwide Mobile Ad Spending." (October 2019v).

eMarketer, Inc. "Net Display Ad Revenue Share Worldwide, by Company, 2016–2020." (September 2018a).

eMarketer, Inc. "Clickthrough Rates (CTR)." (2018b)

eMarketer, Inc. "Trust in Online Reviews Remains High, Survey Finds." (November 10, 2017a).

eMarketer, Inc. "Consumer Trust Is Evolving in the Digital Age." (January 3, 2017b).

eMarketer, Inc. (Lauren Fisher). "Cross-Device Targeting: A More Holistic Audience View and a More Compelling Customer Experience." (December 13, 2016).

Evans, P., and T. S. Wurster. "Getting Real About Virtual Commerce." *Harvard Business Review* (November–December 1999).

Evergage. "2016 Trends in Personalization." (June 2016).

Farahat, Ayman, and Michael Bailey. "How Effective is Targeted Advertising." International World Wide Web Conference Committee (April 26–20, 2012).

Fawcett, Tom, and Foster Provost. "Adaptive Fraud Detection." *Data Mining and Knowledge Discovery* (1997).

Fawcett, Tom, and Foster Provost. "Combining Data Mining and Machine Learning for Effective User Profiling." In *Proceedings of the Second International Conference on Knowledge Discovery and Data Mining* (1996).

Federal Trade Commission. "Blurred Lines: An Exploration of Consumers' Advertising Recognition in the Contexts of Search Engines and Native Advertising." (December 2017).

Federal Trade Commission. "Native Advertising: A Guide for Businesses." (December 2015a).

Federal Trade Commission. "Enforcement Policy Statement on Deceptively Formatted Advertisements." (December 2015b).

Feil, Jessica. "Good Lord, & Taylor! Of Course You Need to Disclose Native Ads." Ftcbeat.com (March 16, 2016).

Fletcher, Paul. "Report: Nearly 40% of Publishers Ignore FTC's Native Advertising Rules." Forbes.com (March 19, 2017).

Forrester Research (Satish Meena). "Forrester Analytics: Digital-Influenced Retail Sales Forecast, 2018 to 2023 (US)." (December 10, 2018).

Fowler, David. "Marketers: Are You ready for Canada's July 1 Spam Law?" Techcrunch.com (May 13, 2017).

Franklyn, David J. "Consumer Recognition and Understanding of Native Advertisements." Federal Trade Commission (December 4, 2013).

Garg, Rajiv. "Peer Influence and Information Difusion in Online Networks: An Empirical Analysis." Carnegie Mellon University, School of Information Systems and Management, Working Paper, 2009.

Google Inc. "Guide to Ad Sizes." (accessed January 25, 2020).

Guo, Stephen, M. Wang, and J. Leskovec. "The Role of Social Networks in Online Shopping Choice: Information Passing, Price of Trust, and Consumer Choice." Stanford University (June 2011).

Gutman, A. "Digital Lead Generation Ad Spend in the U.S. 2019–2023." Statista,com (August 27, 2019b).

Hof, Robert. "The One Second Rule: New Viewability Metrics Exposes How Low Online Advertising Standards Still Are." *Forbes* (March 3, 2014).

IAB Technology Laboratory. "IAB New Standard Ad Unit Portfolio." (July 2017).

Interactive Advertising Bureau. "Digital Video Rising Starts Added to IAB Standard Ad Portfolio, Augmenting Sight, Sound & Motion with Interactivity at Scale." (February 10, 2014).

Interactive Advertising Bureau (IAB)/PriceWaterhouseCoopers. "IAB Internet Advertising Revenue Report: 2018 Full Year Results." (May 2019).

Irvine, Mark. "Google Ads Benchmarks for Your Industry [Updated!]." Wordstream.com (August 27, 2019).

Isaac, Mike. "Uber Reaches Deal with New York on Surge Pricing in Emergencies." *New York Times* (July 8, 2014).

Iyengar, Raghuram, S. Han, and S. Gupta. "Do Friends Influence Purchases in a Social Network?" Harvard Business School. Working Paper, 2009.

Joe, Ryan. "FTC Commissioner Julie Brill: Ad Industry Must Shape Up, or Face the Wrath of Ad Blockers." Adexchanger.com (January 22, 2016).

Kanter Millward Brown. "AdReaction: The Art of Integration." (January 16, 2018).

Kantrowitz, Alex. "Inside Google's Secret War Against Ad Fraud." Adage.com (May 18, 2015).

Kantrowitz, Alex. "Digital Ad Fraud Is Rampant. Here's Why So Little Has Been Done about It." Adage.com (March 24, 2014).

Kim, D., and I. Benbasat. "The Effects of Trust-Assuring Arguments on Consumer Trust in Internet Stores." *Information Systems Research* (2006).

Kim, D., and I. Benbasat. "Designs for Effective Implementation of Trust Assurances in Internet Stores." *Communications of the ACM* (July 2007).

Kim, Dan, Donald Ferrin, and Raghav Rao. "Trust and Satisfaction, Two Stepping Stones for Successful E-Commerce Relationships: A Longitudinal Exploration." *Journal of Information Systems Research* (June 2009).

Kotler, Philip, and Gary Armstrong. *Principles of Marketing, 13th Edition*. Upper Saddle River, NJ: Prentice Hall (2009).

Libert, Kelsey. "Comparing the ROI of Content Marketing and Native Advertising." *Harvard Business Review* (July 6, 2015).

Marvin, Ginny. "Apple's Latest ITP Updates: What Marketers Need to Know." Marketingland.com (December 12, 2019).

Marvin, Ginny. "GroupM Sheds Light on Its Updated Standards for Display & Video Ads." Marketingland.com (August 30, 2017).

MediaMind Inc. "Consumers 27 Times More Likely to Click-Through Online Video Ads than Standard Banners." (September 12, 2012).

Mishra, D. P., J. B. Heide, and S. G. Cort. "Information Asymmetry and Levels of Agency Relationships." *Journal of Marketing Research* (1998).

Mobasher, Bamshad. "Data Mining for Web Personalization." Center for Web Intelligence, School of Computer Science, Telecommunication, and Information Systems, DePaul University, Chicago, Illinois. (2007).

Monetate. "E-commerce Quarterly Benchmarks: Q2 2019." (2019)

Moz.com. "Google Algorithm Update History." (accessed January 25, 2020).

National Conference of State Legislatures. "State Laws Relating to Unsolicited Commercial of Bulk E-mail (SPAM)." (December 3, 2015).

Neff, Jack. "Media Rating Council Proposes Mobile Viewability Definition That Matches Desktop." Adage.com (April 1, 2016).

Oestreicher-Singer, Gail, and Arun Sundararajan. "The Visible Hand of Social Networks." *Electronic Commerce Research* (2008).

Pavlou, Paul. "Institution-Based Trust in Interorganizational Exchange Relationships: The Role of Online B2B Marketplaces on Trust Formation." *Journal of Strategic Information Systems* (2002).

Pew Research Center. "Internet/Broadband Fact Sheet." (June 12, 2019a).

Pew Research Center. (Monica Anderson). "Mobile Technology and Home Broadband 2019." (June 13, 2019b).

Pew Research Center. (Monica Anderson and Jingjing Jiang). "Teens, Social Media & Technology 2018." (May 31, 2018).

Pew Research Center. (Kathryn Zickuhr and Aaron Smith). "Digital Differences." (April 13, 2012).

Polar. "2017 Branded Content Benchmarks: A Snapshot of Global Branded Content Performance." (2018).

Rayport, J. F., and J. J. Sviokla. "Exploiting the Virtual Value Chain." *Harvard Business Review* (November–December 1995).

Robinson, Jim. "What You Need to Know About the Changing Affiliate Landscape." Marketingprofs.com (August 8, 2014).

Schiff, Allison. "A Marketer's Guide to Cross-Device Identity." Adexhanger.com (April 9, 2015).

Schleifer, Dan. "Which Social Network Makes Your Customers Buy?" *Harvard Business Review* (April 2, 2013).

Scott, Samuel. "The $8.2 Billion Adtech Fraud Everyone Is Ignoring." Techcrunch.com (January 6, 2016).

Scully, Joey. "What Advertisers Should Know about Impressions vs. Viewable Impressions." Merkleinc.com (July 17, 2019).

Sevitt, David, and Alexandra Samuel. "Vision Statement: How Pinterest Puts People in Stores." *Harvard Business Review* (July–August, 2013).

Shapiro, Carl, and Hal Varian. *Information Rules: A Strategic Guide to the Network Economy.* Cambridge, MA: Harvard Business School Press (1999).

Sinha, Indrajit. "Cost Transparency: The Net's Real Threat to Prices and Brands." *Harvard Business Review* (March–April 2000).

Slefo, George. "Report: Ad Fraud to Hit $23 Billion, Isn't Going Down." Adage.com (June 3, 2019).

Tadena, Nathalie. "Marketers Say They Would Spend Even More on Digital Ads If Measurement Improved." *Wall Street Journal* (July 6, 2015).

Tobii/Mediative. "The Effectiveness of Display Advertising on a Desktop PC vs. a Tablet Device." (August 2012).

Van den Poel, Dirk, and Wouter Buckinx. "Predicting Online Purchasing Behavior." *European Journal of Operations Research*, Vol. 166, Issue 2 (2005).

VisionCritical Corporation. "From Social to Sale: 8 Questions to Ask Your Customers." (June 2013).

Vranica, Suzanne. "A 'Crisis' in Online Ads: One-Third of Traffic is Bogus." *Wall Street Journal* (March 23, 2014).

Whitener, Michael. "Cookies Are So Yesterday; Cross-Device Tracking Is In—Some Tips." Iapp.org (January 27, 2015).

Wigand, R. T., and R. I. Benjamin. "Electronic Commerce: Effects on Electronic Markets." *Journal of Computer Mediated Communication* (December 1995).

Williamson, O. E. *The Economic Institutions of Capitalism.* New York: Free Press (1985).

Wolfinbarger, Mary, and Mary Gilly. "Shopping Online for Freedom, Control and Fun." *California Management Review* (Winter 2001).

Wuerthele, Mike. "Here's How Apple Protects Your Privacy in Safari with Intelligent Tracking Protection 2.0." Appleinsider.com (June 20, 2018).

CHAPTER 7

Social, Mobile, and Local Marketing

LEARNING OBJECTIVES

After reading this chapter, you will be able to:

- Understand the difference between traditional online marketing and the new social-mobile-local marketing platforms and the relationships between social, mobile, and local marketing.
- Understand the social marketing process from fan acquisition to sales and the marketing capabilities of social marketing platforms such as Facebook, Twitter, and Pinterest.
- Identify the key elements of a mobile marketing campaign.
- Understand the capabilities of location-based local marketing.

Pinterest Expands
Around the Globe

Like all successful e-commerce companies, Pinterest taps into a simple truth. In Pinterest's case, the simple truth is that people love to collect things and show off their collections to others. Founded in 2009 by Ben Silbermann, Evan Sharp, and Paul Sciarra and launched in March 2010, Pinterest allows you to create virtual scrapbooks of images, video, and other content that you "pin" (save) to a virtual bulletin board or pin board. Popular categories include fashion, home décor, DIY and crafts, food and drink, and animals. Find something that you particularly like? In addition to saving and perhaps commenting on it, you can re-pin it to your own board or follow a link back to the original source. You can follow one or more of that pinner's boards to keep track of everything she or he pins. As of the end of 2019, there were 240 billion pins on Pinterest on 5 billion different boards.

© Blaize Pascall/Alamy Stock Photo

Pinterest originally positioned itself as a social network. However, it has changed its tune and now describes itself as a visual search tool for discovering and saving creative ideas (and potential purchases). Search has become the core part of its mission. It views Google, rather than Facebook, Twitter, or Instagram, as its primary competition.

Already extremely popular in the United States, Pinterest has focused its efforts on international expansion as it seeks to continue its explosive growth. As of the end of 2019, Pinterest had over 330 million monthly active members worldwide, with the number of international users increasing by 35% in 2019. About 70% of Pinterest's members are women, but men are its fastest-growing demographic: according to Pinterest, the number of male users is growing at 50% year over year. Pinterest is growing quickly—the company grew from 100 to 200 million users 2.5 times faster than it grew from zero to 100 million users, and the company expects to have 400 million users by the end of 2020.

Like Facebook, Twitter, and many other startup companies, Pinterest focused initially on refining its product and building its user base, but not surprisingly, its investors began to push it to begin generating revenue. Pinterest's first step was to offer business accounts that provided additional resources for brands. In 2013, it introduced Rich Pins, which allowed companies to embed information, such as current pricing and availability, as well as a direct

SOURCES: "Pinterest Reaches 335 Million Active Users, Surpasses $1 Billion in Revenue in 2019," by Andrew Hutchinson, Socialmediatoday.com, February 8, 2020; "Pinterest Form 10-K for the fiscal year ended December 31, 2019," filed with Securities and Exchange Commission, February 7, 2020; "Pinterest Shares Surge After Earnings Beat," by Annie Palmer, Cnbc.com, February 6, 2020; "Freshening Up the Look of Pinterest," Newsroom.pinterest.com, November 1, 2019; "Pinterest Eyes India, SE Asia for Global Expansion," by Madhav Chanchani, Economictimes.indiatimes, September 26, 2018; "Pinterest Is a Unicorn. It Just Doesn't Act Like One," by Erin Griffith, *New York Times,* September 9, 2018; "Pinterest Thinks the Future Lies in Visual Discovery—And Wants

link to a product page. In 2014, Pinterest took the official leap into the advertising arena, launching a beta version of ads it called Promoted Pins that appear in search results and category feeds. Around the same time, Pinterest also introduced a search engine, called Guided Search, which suggests related terms to refine a search. Guided Search is based on user metadata, such as gender, board titles, captions, and comments related to pins, to create different categories and subcategories.

In the last several years, Pinterest has gotten serious about monetization. The company has rolled out a wide variety of advertising formats and features, including Cinematic Pins; a variety of ad targeting options for advertisers; Search Ads; and Pinterest Shopping Ads, which automatically convert a company's product catalog into advertisements that link directly to the point of purchase. Pinterest has now turned its sights to the search advertising market. Pinterest search differs from other types of search because it is visual and typically happens in the early stages of a person's decision process. Pinterest believes search advertising revenue will drive the company to profitability and that it can challenge Google in the mobile search arena, not by outperforming Google in traditional search, but rather by outperforming it in visual search. To that end, Pinterest is making significant investments in search technology, such as deep-learning assisted visual search and its visual search engine, Lens, which can automatically isolate the different objects in an image stored on a user's camera and give users the ability to start searching for similar elements on Pinterest. Lens is used to complete 600 million searches per month and has proven so effective that Pinterest began using the underlying technology to power its text-based searches as well. Pinterest's CEO Ben Silbermann believes people increasingly are going to want to query the world around them as opposed to searching for phrases with just text, and Lens is a technology that makes that possible.

Thanks to its diverse array of advertising techniques and to the potential of Lens, analysts believe Pinterest is destined to become a significant factor in social e-commerce and e-commerce in general. Pinterest is significantly ahead of other social networks such as Facebook, Instagram, and Twitter in terms of the percentage of users who use it to find or shop for products. A whopping 98% of Pinterest users have tried new things they discovered on the platform, and 87% have bought something they found on the site. That number is only 71% on other social media platforms. Even more appealing to advertisers is that 97% of search queries on Pinterest do not specify a particular brand. Pinterest offers plenty of opportunity for companies to win the business of undecided potential customers. Pinterest has also differentiated itself in that it is upbeat and positive at a time when other social networks, such as Facebook and Twitter, have become more combative and divisive. Pinterest's purely visual nature also makes it a more natural fit for shopping than Facebook. Pinterest searches also occur completely independently of Google, making it a threat to Google's search business.

Eighty percent of Pinterest users access the site on mobile devices. Pinterest provides apps for iPhone, iPad, Android, and Windows Phone, as well as a mobile version of its website using HTML5. Pinterest Mobile runs inside the smartphone's browser rather than as a stand-alone program. Pinterest releases new versions of its mobile apps on a regular basis, and in 2016 launched a nearly completely written iOS app that allows the home page to load much more quickly, scales to the different number of iOS screens more efficiently and is readable in all 31 languages in which Pinterest is available. According to co-founder Evan Sharp, the smartphone is the platform Pinterest focuses on when it develops new features and products. In November 2019, Pinterest refreshed the look of its iOS and Android apps to make Pinterest even more visual, personalized, and search-oriented.

International expansion continues to be a major area of focus and has been the primary driver of Pinterest's rapid growth. The number of international users increased by 35% in 2019, compared to an increase of just 8% in the number of U.S. users. Pinterest introduced its first localized site for the United Kingdom in 2013 and has worked to make its platform feel more regional, focusing initially on the United Kingdom, France, Germany, Japan, and Brazil. In 2018, it turned its attention to India and Southeast Asia. Tastes vary from country to country, and Pinterest has embraced the challenge of providing the content that best resonates with users of each country, adjusting details as simple as the fonts used on each country's site and the translation of buttons, and as complicated as the differences in fashion in different parts of the world. For example, in many countries, the word "pin" doesn't make as much sense as it does in the United States, so the company renamed its Pin It button to "Save" in 2016. Pinterest began selling Promoted Pins and Promoted Videos in Canada and the United Kingdom in 2016 and launched the Pinterest UK Shop to allow users to purchase items from specially curated collections. In 2017, it extended Promoted Pins to Ireland, Australia, and New Zealand, and in 2018, began preparing to sell ads in non-English-speaking countries, starting with France. In 2019, it added Germany, Austria, Spain, and Italy. The company's performance there and in other worldwide regions will go a long way in determining its success.

To improve the experience for international users, Pinterest fully overhauled the technology behind its site to ensure that Pinterest runs smoothly for users of any device, even outdated smartphones, and in any country. First, Pinterest standardized its appearance across its Web, iOS, and Android versions as well as across all of its localized sites in different countries. Then, it scaled down its menus to emphasize the images instead of the interface. Pinterest engineers also redesigned the site's swipe function on mobile phones so that the site can prepare to load photos you are likely to scroll to next, ensuring that they appear without delay and reducing the device requirements to use the site. These changes have doubled the site's overall speed and ensured that more users can seamlessly use Pinterest. In 2018, to further unlock international growth, Pinterest revamped its domain structure, moving its international domains to country code top-level domains, for example, from pinterest.com/de to just pinterest.de. The result has been increased traffic growth, increased clicks and views, and stronger geo-targeting signals in many search engine algorithms.

At the moment, the future looks very bright for Pinterest. The company went public in April 2019, and while it has yet to turn a profit, it recorded over $1 billion in revenue in 2019, up from just $100 in 2015, and expects to top $1.5 billion in revenue in 2020. Pinterest believes it has a winning strategy to differentiate itself from other social markets and, so far, appears to be executing that strategy successfully.

February 9, 2017; "Pinterest's New 'Lens' Tool Places Real-World Objects in Digital Context," by Kathleen Chaykowski, Forbes.com, February 8, 2017; "Pinterest Expands Search Ad Offerings," by Danny Goodwin, Searchenginejournal.com, February 1, 2017; "At Pinterest, Shopping Beats Social Media," by Maghan McDowell, Wwd.com, October 24, 2016; "Promoted Video: Now Available in the UK," by Adele Cooper, Business.pinterest.com, October 3, 2016; "Launch of Pinterest UK Shop," by Kate Allchin, Blog.pinterest.com, September 16, 2016; "Interactive Pinterest Pins Let Shoppers in Brazil Bring Offline Items Online," by Saqib Shah, Digitaltrends.com, June 4, 2016; "Pinterest Renames 'Pin It' Button as 'Save' in Push for Global Growth," by Kathleen Chaykowski, Forbes.com, June 2, 2016; "Pinterest's Plans for World Domination," by Lara O'Reilly, Businessinsider.com, April 28, 2016; "Pinterest Is a Sleeping Giant—Don't Underestimate It," by Madjumita Murgia, Telegraph.co.uk, April 28, 2016; "Pinterest Announces Complete Overhaul of iOS App with Performance & Visual Improvements," by Chance Miller, 9to5mac.com, April 19, 2016; "Pinterest Launches Promoted Pins Internationally, Starting with the UK," by Paul Sawers, Venturebeat.com, April 7, 2016; "Pinterest Begins Overseas Ad Push," by Yoree Koh, *Wall Street Journal*, April 6, 2016; "Pinterest Opens Up Promoted Pins for UK Advertisers, with John Lewis and Made.com Among Launch Partners," by Rebecca Stewart, Thedrum.com, April 6, 2016; "With Buyable Pins, Pinterest Lets You Buy Stuff Right in the App," by JP Mangalindan, Mashable.com, June 2, 2015; "Can Pinterest Be Found in Translation," by Sarah Frier, Businessweek.com, May 22, 2014; "Pinterest (Officially) Jumps the Pond," by Zak Stambor, Internetretailer.com, May 10, 2013.

7.1 INTRODUCTION TO SOCIAL, MOBILE, AND LOCAL MARKETING

Social, mobile, and local marketing have transformed the online marketing landscape. Before 2007, Facebook was a fledgling company limited to college students. Apple had not yet announced the iPhone. Online marketing consisted largely of creating a corporate website, buying display ads on Yahoo, purchasing AdWords on Google, and sending e-mail. The workhorse of online marketing was the display ad that flashed brand messages to millions of users who were not expected to respond immediately, ask questions, or make observations. The primary measure of success was how many "eyeballs" (unique visitors) a website produced, and how many "impressions" a marketing campaign generated. An impression was one ad shown to one person. Both of these measures were carryovers from the world of television, which measures marketing in terms of audience size and ad views.

FROM EYEBALLS TO CONVERSATIONS

After 2007, everything began to change, with the rapid growth of Facebook and other social network sites, the explosive growth of smartphones beginning with Apple iPhone in 2007, and the growing interest in local marketing. What's different about the new world of social-mobile-local marketing and advertising are the related concepts of "conversations" and "engagement." Marketing today is based on businesses marketing themselves as partners in multiple online conversations with their customers, potential customers, and even critics. Your brand is being talked about on the Web and social media (that's the conversation part). Today, marketing your firm and brands requires you to locate, identify, and participate in these conversations. Social marketing means all things social: listening, discussing, interacting, empathizing, and engaging. Rather than bombarding your audience with fancier, louder ads, instead have a conversation with them and engage them in your brand. The emphasis in online marketing has shifted from a focus on eyeballs to a focus on participating in customer-oriented conversations. In this sense, social marketing and advertising is not simply a "new ad channel," but a collection of technology-based tools for communicating with shoppers.

In the past, businesses could tightly control their brand messaging and lead consumers down a funnel of cues that ended in a purchase. That is not true of social marketing. Consumer purchase decisions are increasingly driven by the conversations, choices, tastes, and opinions of the consumer's social network. Social marketing is all about businesses participating in and shaping this social process.

FROM THE DESKTOP TO THE SMARTPHONE AND TABLET

In 2015, for the first time, spending on mobile marketing exceeded that spent on desktop/laptops. **Figure 7.1** illustrates the rapidly changing trajectory of ad spending between 2014 and 2022. In 2013, marketers spent 83% of their worldwide online ad spending on desktops and only 17% on mobile. By 2019, that percentage had totally flipped, with 73% of ad spending devoted to mobile and only 21% to desktop/laptops. The marketing dollars are following customers and shoppers from the desktop computer

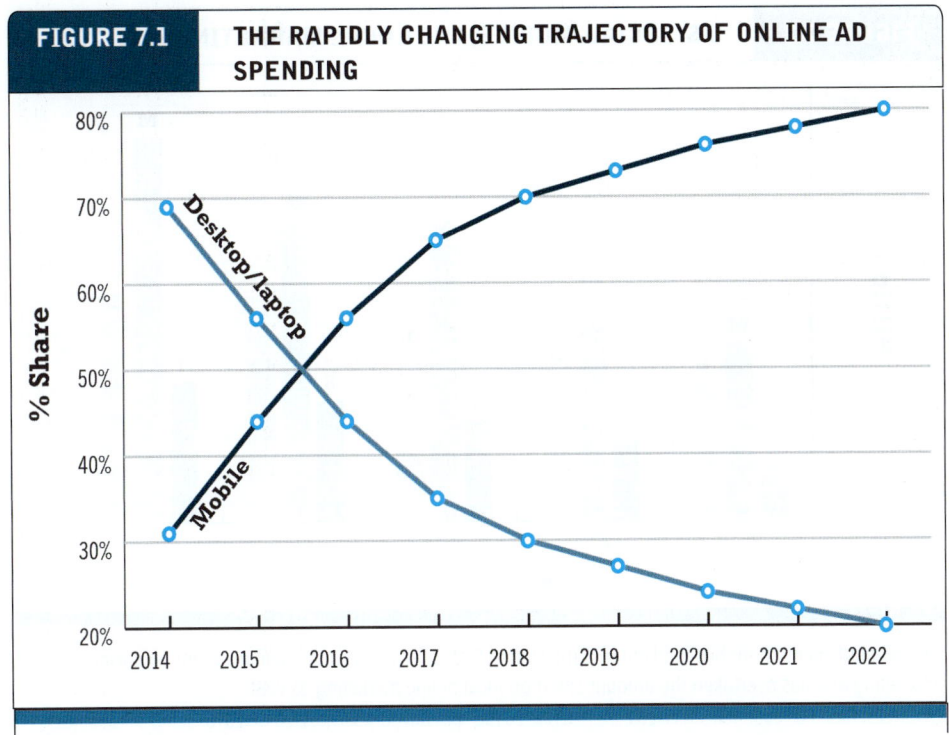

FIGURE 7.1 THE RAPIDLY CHANGING TRAJECTORY OF ONLINE AD SPENDING

By 2022, mobile marketing is expected to account for about 80% of all digital ad spending.
SOURCE: Based on data from eMarketer, Inc., 2019a.

to mobile devices. Today, social, mobile, and local marketing are the fastest growing forms of online marketing (**Figure 7.2**). In 2019, in the United States, spending on mobile marketing was almost triple the amount spent on social marketing. By 2020, it is estimated that mobile marketing spending in the United States will account for around $120 billion annually, while social marketing will be about $44 billion (eMarketer, Inc., 2019b, 2019c). However, this figure underestimates the total social marketing spending because of the high percentage of visits to social networks that originate from a mobile device. For instance, over 90% of Twitter's U.S. users access Twitter from a mobile device; almost two-thirds of Facebook's active U.S. user base are mobile-only members. A substantial part of the mobile marketing spending should also be counted as "social" marketing. Nevertheless, the figure indicates the extraordinary impact that mobile devices are having on marketing expenditures. In 2019, U.S. advertisers were expected to spend about $60 billion on local online advertising. However, as with social and mobile, there is significant overlap between local marketing and mobile and social marketing, with much of local marketing being also either social or mobile, or both.

THE SOCIAL, MOBILE, LOCAL NEXUS

Social, mobile, and local digital marketing are self-reinforcing and connected. For instance, as mobile devices become more powerful, they are more useful for accessing Facebook and other social sites. As mobile devices become more widely adopted, they can be used by customers to find local merchants, and for merchants to alert customers in

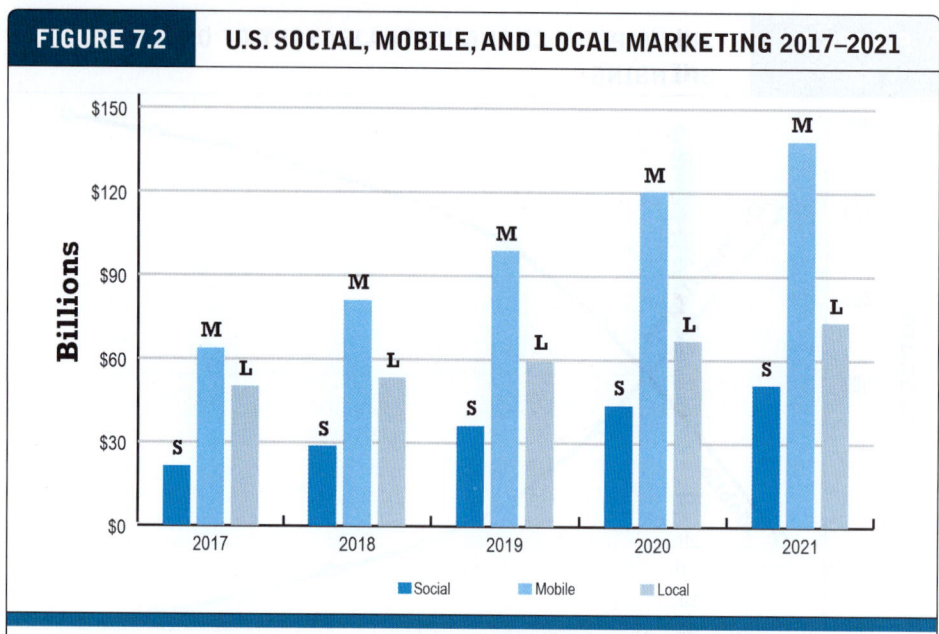

Figure 7.2 U.S. SOCIAL, MOBILE, AND LOCAL MARKETING 2017–2021

The amount spent on mobile marketing in the United States far exceeds the amount spent on social marketing and has overtaken the amount spent on local online marketing as well.
SOURCES: Based on data from eMarketer, Inc., 2019b, 2019c; BIA Advisory Services, 2019, 2018; authors' estimates.

their neighborhood to special offers. Over time, these will become more overlapped as the three platforms become more tightly coupled.

In 2019, almost 95% of Facebook's U.S. ad revenue was generated by its mobile audience. Mobile constitutes similar share (about 92%) of Twitter's ad revenues! Local marketing and mobile are highly related: local advertisers most often target mobile devices. And a considerable amount of mobile ad spending comes from local advertisers. The strong ties among social, mobile, and local marketing have significant implications for managing your own marketing campaign in this new environment. The message is that when you design a social marketing campaign, you must also consider that your customers will be accessing the campaign using mobile devices, and often they will also be looking for local content. Social-mobile-local must be seen in an integrated marketing framework. **Figure 7.3** puts social-mobile-local forms of advertising in context.

In the sections that follow we will examine social, mobile, and local marketing more closely. The focus will be on describing the primary marketing tools of each platform and how to envision and manage a marketing campaign on each platform.

7.2 SOCIAL MARKETING

Social marketing differs markedly from traditional online marketing. The objectives of traditional online marketing are to put your business's message in front of as many visitors

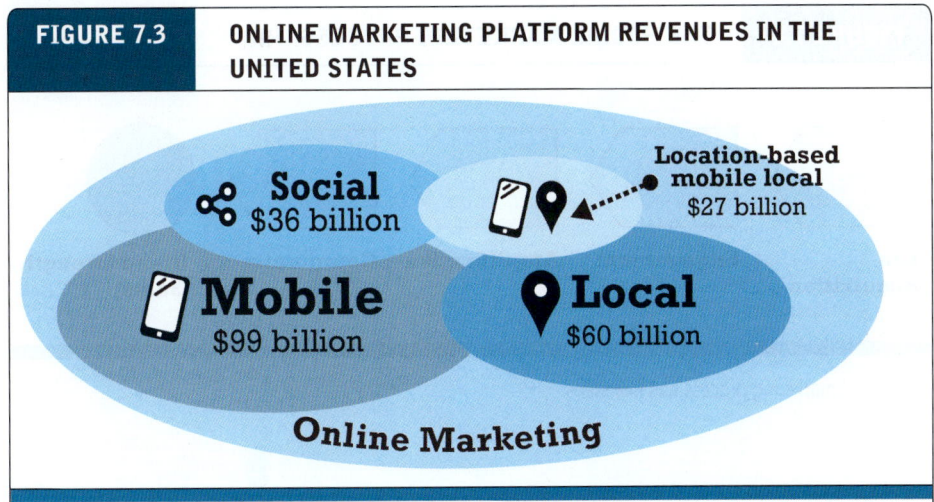

FIGURE 7.3 ONLINE MARKETING PLATFORM REVENUES IN THE UNITED STATES

Mobile marketing is aimed often at local audiences and is the fastest growing form of online marketing, followed closely by social marketing on social networks. Mobile local is in its infancy but it is also growing far faster than traditional desktop marketing.
SOURCES: Based on data from eMarketer, Inc., 2019b, 2019c; BIA Advisory Services, 2019; authors' estimates.

as possible and hopefully encourage them to come to your website to buy products and services, or to find out more information. The more "impressions" (ad views) you get, and the more unique visitors, the better. Traditional online marketing never expected to listen to customers, much less have a conversation with them, any more than TV advertisers expected to hear from viewers.

In social marketing, the objective is to encourage your potential customers to become fans of your company's products and services, and engage with your business by entering into a conversation with it. Your further objective is to encourage your business's fans to share their enthusiasm with their friends, and in so doing create a community of fans online. Ultimately, the point is to strengthen the brand and drive sales, and to do this by increasing your "share of online conversation." There is some reason to believe that social marketing is more cost effective than traditional marketing although this is still being explored.

SOCIAL MARKETING PLAYERS

There are hundreds of social networks worldwide, but the most popular (Facebook, Instagram, Twitter, LinkedIn, Pinterest, Snapchat, and Tumblr) account for over 90% of all visits. (See Chapter 10 for a full discussion of social networks.)

While the number of monthly unique visitors is a good measure of market reach, it is not helpful in understanding engagement—the amount and intensity of user involvement. One measure of engagement is the amount of time users spend on a social network. Here, Facebook once again dominates, with U.S. adults overall averaging 17 hours a month on Facebook (eMarketer, Inc., 2019d).

For a manager of a social marketing campaign, these findings suggest that in terms of reach and engagement, the place to start a social campaign is Facebook. Yet visitors to

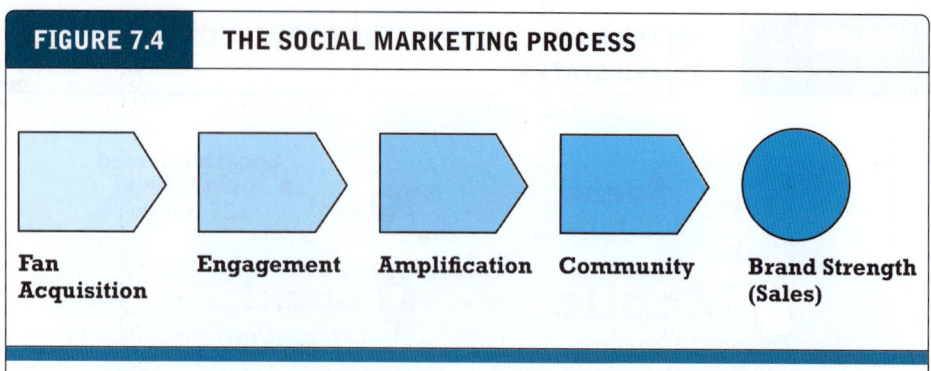

The social marketing process has five steps.

the other leading social networks collectively account for a significant amount of the social market space, and therefore, a social marketing campaign also has to include them at some point. It helps that social network users use multiple social networks. Facebook users are likely to be users at Twitter, Pinterest, LinkedIn, Instagram, and Snapchat. In addition, marketers need to be aware of what has come to be known as dark social. **Dark social** refers to those forms of social sharing that occur off the major social networks, through alternative communication tools such as interpersonal conversations, group meetings, and friendships, not to mention e-mail, instant messages, texts, and mobile messaging apps. While U.S. adults overall averaged over 26 hours a month on all networks combined, there are 720 total hours in a month. Therefore, less than 4% of all social life in a month involves online social networks, while more than 96% does not (eMarketer, Inc., 2019d).

dark social
those forms of social sharing that occur off the major social networks, through alternative communication tools such as e-mail, instant messages, texts, and mobile messaging apps

THE SOCIAL MARKETING PROCESS

At first glance the large number of different social sites is confusing, each with a unique user experience to offer, from Twitter's micro blogging text messaging service, to Tumblr's blogging capability, and to graphical social sites like Pinterest and Instagram. Yet they can all be approached with a common framework. **Figure 7.4** illustrates a social marketing framework that can be applied to all social, mobile, and local marketing efforts.

There are five steps in the social marketing process: Fan acquisition, engagement, amplification, community, and brand strength (sales). Each of these steps in the process can be measured. The metrics of social marketing are quite different from those of traditional web marketing or television marketing. This is what makes social marketing so different—the objectives and the measures. This will become more apparent as we describe marketing on specific social sites.

fan acquisition
attracting people to your marketing messages

Social marketing campaigns begin with **fan acquisition**, which involves using any of a variety of means, from display ads to News Feed and page pop-ups, to attract people to your Facebook page, Twitter feed, or other platform like a web page. It's getting your brand "out there" in the stream of social messages. Display ads on social sites have a social dimension (sometimes called "display ads with social features" or simply "social ads"). Social ads encourage visitors to interact and do something social, such as participate in a contest, obtain a coupon, or obtain free services for attracting friends.

The next step is to generate **engagement,** which involves using a variety of tools to encourage users to interact with your content and brand located on your Facebook or web pages. You can think of this as "starting the conversation" around your brand. You want your fans to talk about your content and products. You can generate engagement through attractive photos, interesting text content, and blogger reports, with plenty of opportunities for users to express opinions. You can also provide links to Pinterest photos of your products or fan comments on blog sites like Tumblr.

Once you have engaged visitors, you can begin to use social network features to amplify your messages by encouraging users to tell their friends by clicking a Like or +1 button, or by sending a message to their followers on Twitter. **Amplification** involves using the inherent strength of social networks. On Facebook, the average user has 120 "friends." This includes all people they have ever friended, including people whom they don't really know (and who don't really know them). Facebook users typically have only three to four close friends with whom they can discuss confidential matters, and a larger set of around 20 friends with whom they have two-way communications (mutual friends). Let's use 20 as a reasonable number of mutual friends for marketing purposes. For marketers, this means that if they can attract one fan and encourage that fan to share his or her approval with his or her friends, the message can be amplified twenty times: 20 friends of the one fan can be influenced. Best of all: the friends of fans are free. Marketers pay to attract only the initial fan and they are not charged by social sites (currently) for the amplification that can result.

Once you have gathered enough engaged fans, you will have created the foundation for a **community**—a more or less stable group of fans who are engaged and communicating with one another over a substantial period of time (say several months or more). Marketers have a number of tactics to nurture these communities, including inside information on new products, price breaks for loyalty, and free gifts for bringing in new members. The ultimate goal is to enlarge your firm's "share of the online conversation." The process ends with strengthening the brand and, hopefully, additional sales of products and services. Brand strength can be measured in a variety of ways both online and offline, a subject that is beyond the boundaries of this text (Ailawadi et al., 2003; Aaker, 1996; Simon and Sullivan, 1993; Keller, 1993).

Ultimately, the point of marketing is to drive sales revenue. Measuring the impact of a social marketing campaign on brand strength and sales is still being explored by marketers, social network managers, and researchers, but generally the results are positive: social marketing campaigns drive sales. Most of the top social networks, including Facebook, Pinterest, and Instagram, have added social commerce features, such as Buy buttons and other shopping functionality that makes it even easier for the targets of those social marketing campaigns to act on them and make a purchase.

FACEBOOK MARKETING

Nearly everyone reading this book has a Facebook page. There are power users who spend hours a day on Facebook, some with thousands of "friends," and there are casual users who have a small set of perhaps 20 friends and relatives. While most have a basic understanding of Facebook, it's worthwhile to review the major features of Facebook before discussing its marketing potential.

engagement
encouraging visitors to interact with your content and brand

amplification
encouraging visitors to share their Likes and comments with their friends

community
a stable group of fans engaged and communicating with one another over a substantial period of time about your brand

Basic Facebook Features

Table 7.1 describes various Facebook features that are important in terms of using Facebook as a marketing platform. Reviewing Table 7.1, it is clear that Facebook is built to encourage people to reveal as much personal information about themselves as feasible, including activities, behavior, photos, music, movies, purchases, and preferences. One result is that Facebook is the world's largest repository of deeply personal behavioral information on the Internet. Facebook knows a great deal more about its users than Google does about its users. Second, Facebook's features are built to maximize the connections among people in the form of notifications, tagging, messaging, posting, and sharing. In many instances, the movement of personal information is so widespread that it is beyond the understanding of users and outside observers. The effect of these two factors is to greatly magnify the social density of the Facebook audience. **Social density** refers to the number of interactions among members of a group and reflects the "connectedness" of a group, even if these connections are forced on users. For instance, some natural groups of people are not very "social" and few messages flow among members. Other natural groups are loquacious and chatty with many messages flowing among members. The scope, intensity, and depth of Facebook's repository of personal information and rich social network present extraordinary marketing opportunities.

social density
refers to the number of interactions among members of a group and reflects the "connectedness" of a group, even if these connections are forced on users

Facebook Marketing Tools

Facebook offers a number of marketing and advertising opportunities and tools for branding and developing community on its platform.

Reactions Buttons The Reactions and Share buttons on Facebook, and similar buttons on other social sites, are perhaps the single most important element in the rise of social marketing. "Like" is the engine of social marketing. The Like button was introduced by Facebook on its own website in 2009 and rolled out as a plug-in to other websites in 2010. In 2016, Facebook added five additional buttons (Love, laughter (Haha), surprise (Wow), sadness, and anger) and rebranded the Like button as Reactions. Unlike traditional online advertising, the **Reactions buttons** give users a chance to share their feelings about content and other objects they are viewing and websites they are visiting. For instance, the Like button communicates your support of comments, photos, activities, brands, articles, and products to your friends, and also to the Facebook social graph and third-party marketers. The Reactions buttons are available on virtually all Facebook content, including status updates, photos, comments, brands, timelines, apps, and even ads. The ubiquitous Like button also appears on external sites, mobile and social apps, and ads. These sites are utilizing Facebook's Social Plugins, and when you Like something outside of Facebook, it appears on your Timeline, where friends can comment on the activity. The Like button is one way Facebook knows what other sites you visit. According to Facebook, the Like button has over 10 billion views a day across millions of websites, with 30% of those impressions coming on mobile devices (Facebook, 2016).

Reactions buttons
give users a chance to share their feelings about content and other objects they are viewing

Brand Pages Facebook's early efforts at brand marketing focused on the development of brand pages as a means for firms to establish a direct relationship with their current

TABLE 7.1 BASIC FACEBOOK FEATURES

FEATURE	DESCRIPTION
Profile	As part of account creation, you create a profile that includes certain personal information. The profile may also include photos and other media. Establishes baseline information that will be shared with friends.
Friend search	Helps you find friends who are already using Facebook, as well as friends who are not, typically by searching your e-mail contact list. Creates your baseline social network based on prior contacts.
Timeline	A history of your actions on Facebook, including photos, history of posts, and comments to your News Feed, as well as life events that you post and want others to see as a part of your profile. Additions you make to your Timeline may appear on your friends' News Feed. Creates additional links with friends.
Tagging	Ability to tag photos, status updates, check-ins, or comments with the names of friends. Tagging links to that person's Timeline and News Feed. Your friends are notified they have been tagged, and you are linked to their Timeline. Friends of your friends may also be notified. Whenever Facebook detects the person in a new image, it notifies all those who have tagged the photo that this friend appears in a new photo that you can link to. The tagging tool is designed to create additional connections among users.
News Feed	Facebook's News Feed is a continuously updated list of stories from friends, Groups, and Pages that you have liked on Facebook. Ads running in the News Feed are a major ad revenue producer for Facebook. News Feed stories include status updates, photos, videos, links, app activity, and Likes. Provides a continual stream of messages from friends and advertisers.
Groups	Facebook Groups provide a platform for people with common interests to share content with one another. Any Facebook user can set up and manage a group. Groups may be public or private (only open by invitation) or secret (not able to be searched for).
Status update	A way to post your comments, observations, and location to all your friends.
Reactions buttons	In 2016, Facebook redesigned its Like button functionality to add five additional buttons and rebranded it as Reactions. In addition to the familiar Like button, users can now register additional reactions, such as Love, laughter (Haha), surprise (Wow), sadness, and anger.
Messenger	Facebook's instant messaging app, used by over 1.3 billion people every month. Offers a variety of marketing options, including sponsored messages from chatbots, in-box video and display ads, and broadcast messages from small and medium-sized businesses.
Third-party Apps	Third-party apps add functionality to Facebook. Apps run the gamut from games (Candy Crush Saga; FarmVille) to photos (Instagram, now part of Facebook), music (Spotify), and publications (Washington Post Social Reader). Your personal information and that of your friends is shared with apps that you install. Most apps are free, and most rely on revenues from advertising.
Open Graph	A feature used by app developers to integrate their apps into the Facebook pages of users who sign up for the app, and in that sense, it opens the Facebook social graph to the developer, who can then use all the features of Facebook in the app. For instance, this feature allows your performance on game apps to be sent to your Friend's News Feeds. Supports the development of social apps and increases links among users.
Search	In 2013, Facebook introduced Graph Search, a "social" search engine that searched your social network for answers to queries. It was a semantic search engine insofar as it provided a single answer rather than a list of links based on an algorithm's estimate of user intentions. It was also a hybrid search engine that relied on Bing to supplement results. In 2015, Facebook significantly expanded its Search functionality. It now focuses on keywords and includes everyone's public posts, Likes, photos, and interests (including posts by brands), and makes them available to all users of Facebook, friends or not. In 2016, Facebook reported that users were doing 2 billion searches a day of 2.5 trillion posts.

and potential customers. Nearly all Fortune 1000 companies, and hundreds of thousands of smaller firms, have Facebook brand pages, similar to brand websites, on Facebook as an adjunct to their main website. The purpose of a brand page is to develop fans of the brand by providing users opportunities to interact with the brand through comments, contests, and offerings. Using social calls to action, such as "Like us on Facebook" and "Share," brand pages can escape their isolation and make it more easily into users' social networks, where friends can hear the message. In 2015, Facebook began offering a new Shops tab for Facebook brand pages that features products and services, taking it further into the realm of social e-commerce.

Social brand pages have many more social opportunities for fans to like and comment than are typical of traditional web pages. However, corporate websites have, over time, adopted many social features and the two are now often indistinguishable. Brand pages on Facebook typically attract more visitors than a brand's website.

Brands can get exposure on Facebook either organically or via paid advertisements. Organic reach is free, and happens when fans see the brand's updates and posts in their News Feed, or when others who are not fans see that content because a fan liked, commented, or shared the post (viral reach). In order to ensure that they get the exposure that they want for their marketing messages, most companies choose one of the paid advertising formats discussed below.

Facebook enables you to choose from a variety of different marketing objectives, including promoting your Page posts/ads (Page Post Engagement); obtaining Likes for your Facebook page to grow your company's audience and brand (Page Likes); getting people to click through to your website (Clicks to Websites); getting people to take certain actions on your website (Website Conversions); getting people to install an app (App Installs); getting people to use an app (App Engagement); creating offers for people to redeem (Offer Claims); and getting people to watch a video (Video Views).

Once you have chosen a marketing objective, the next decision is to whom you want to target the advertisement. Facebook ads can be targeted based on location, age, interest, gender, education level, relationship status, and political views, as well as to custom audiences defined by the marketer. However, in 2018, after being sued by National Fair Housing Alliance for enabling advertisers to discriminate against legally protected groups, Facebook eliminated over 5,000 targeting options that allowed advertisers to exclude audiences based on attributes such as ethnicity or religion (Tobin and Merrill, 2018). Facebook can also create what it calls a lookalike audience based on demographics shared with the custom audience identified by the marketer. In 2018, after the Cambridge Analytica scandal (see the *Insight on Society* case, *Facebook and the Age of Privacy*, in Chapter 1), Facebook introduced a new Custom Audiences certification tool that requires marketers to guarantee that e-mail addresses used for ad targeting were obtained with user consent (Constine, 2018).

Once the marketing objectives and audience have been determined, the next decision is where to place the advertisement. Facebook has four basic locations from which to choose: the News Feed, the right-hand column or sidebar section of Facebook pages, and the mobile News Feed. Ads can also be placed within apps.

News Feed Page Post Ads The News Feed is the most prominent place for advertisements. The News Feed is the center of the action for Facebook users and where Facebook users spend most of their time because that is where posts from their friends appear. Page Post Ads appear in a user's News Feed along with all of the other posts and status updates that normally appear from friends. Page Post Ads have a tiny tag that indicates that they are sponsored (i.e., are advertisements) but otherwise look very similar to posts from friends. Sometimes the ads have a social context ("John Smith and Jane Doe like Pottery Barn") and can be liked, shared, and commented on, just like any other post. Page Post Ads can contain text, photos, video, and links. They can be used for many of the marketing objectives mentioned above, such as increasing brand engagement, obtaining Likes for the brand's Facebook page, and encouraging app installs and engagement. Advertisers can also include a Buy button in News Feed Page Post Ads that allows people to purchase items without leaving Facebook. Companies pay to promote or boost Page Post Ads in order to extend their reach. This has become increasingly important as Facebook has reduced the organic reach that brands previously enjoyed for free in an effort to increase advertising revenues.

Right-Hand Column Sidebar Ads These display ads are located in the right-hand column or sidebar of Facebook pages. They are often used to direct users to off-Facebook content such as website landing pages and content offers. Facebook has recently reduced the number of ads that appear in the right-hand column sidebar from seven to two, increased their size, and made them consistent with the format of News Feed Page Post Ads in an effort to enhance their performance.

Facebook Live Facebook introduced Facebook Live, its free video streaming service, in 2016. Since that time nearly 2 billion people have watched Facebook Live. Facebook Live can be used to stream live content that followers can interact with by commenting, liking, and sharing. The video can be saved on a brand's page and followers can continue to interact with it.

Video Ads In 2014, Facebook began showing 15-second video autoplay ads. Since that time, Facebook video ads have become an increasingly important part of Facebook advertising strategy. In order to continue to grow its advertising revenue without overloading and turning off users by having too many ads, Facebook is now focusing on video ads, which command a premium and therefore generate more revenue. One challenge has been that video ads autoplay in silent mode, requiring advertisers to adapt their video for that medium. Another challenge has been the issue of metrics. In 2016, Facebook admitted that for two years, it had been overestimating the average viewing time for video ads, possibly by 60%–80%, because it had only been including video views of more than three seconds in its metric. In 2017, Facebook agreed to undergo regular audits by the Media Rating Council, an industry group that certifies ad metrics, and to provide more detailed data to independent third-party measurement companies, such as how many ads are viewable, how long ads appear on screen, and whether audio is on for the ad. In 2018, a group of advertisers filed a fraud claim against Facebook, alleging that it knew of the issues with its video metrics for over a year before disclosing the problem (Vranica, 2018).

Facebook Watch In 2017, Facebook launched Facebook Watch, a video-on-demand service, in the United States, and rolled out the service globally in 2018. Facebook Watch includes professionally produced original short-form and long-form video, live game shows, news programming, interactive game shows, and more. Facebook Watch offers advertisers both pre-roll and mid-roll advertising options. The service offers personalized recommendations as well as categories of bundled content.

Mobile Ads Facebook introduced Facebook for Mobile in 2007. Users can also access Facebook using a mobile browser although it is slower. In 2019, almost 95% of Facebook ad revenue came from its mobile ad platform.

Because the smartphone screen is much smaller than regular computer screens, there is no room for sidebar ads on the right-hand column, so all mobile ads need to be displayed in the users' News Feed. Mobile ads can include many of the ad formats described above, including video ad. Critics complain that the number of ads in the mobile News Feed becomes distracting and annoying. Mobile ads often take up the entire screen. There also is less targeting of mobile ads, which increases the likelihood users will see irrelevant ads. So far, despite the annoyance, Facebook mobile users continue to sign up and view.

Facebook Messenger In 2016, Facebook began allowing companies to deploy chatbots on Messenger, Facebook's instant messaging app, to provide automated customer support and other e-commerce services, and introduced Sponsored Messages that allow companies to send messages to customers who had previously engaged with them. Facebook also launched a Buy Now button for the Messenger app that enables customers to make payments via Stripe or Paypal to companies advertising on Messenger without having to leave Messenger. In 2017, Facebook added display ads in Facebook Messenger in-boxes, and in 2018, introduced autoplay video ads within Messenger in-boxes, as well as Facebook Messenger Broadcasts, which allow small businesses to send text blasts.

Facebook Exchange (FBX)
a real-time bidding system that allows advertisers to target their ads based on personal information provided by Facebook

Facebook Exchange (FBX) **Facebook Exchange (FBX)** is a real-time bidding system that allows advertisers to target their ads based on personal information provided by Facebook. FBX competes with Google's display ad system Google Ads (formerly Double-Click) and other real-time exchanges. Visitors to third-party websites are marked with a cookie, and can then be shown ads related to their web browsing when they return to Facebook.

Table 7.2 summarizes the major tools used by marketers to build their brands on Facebook.

Starting a Facebook Marketing Campaign

Prior to starting a Facebook marketing campaign, there are some basic strategy questions you need to address. While every product presumably could benefit from a social marketing campaign, how is this true of your products? Who is your audience? How can you reach them? How have real-world social networks been used in the past to support sales in your industry? Can you be a "thought leader"? Once you have identified your audience, what content will get them excited and interested? Where are you going to get the content? What will it cost and what impact do you expect it to have on your brand and sales? At this point you do not need a detailed budget, but you should be able to develop estimates of the cost of such a campaign, as well as anticipated revenues.

If you're new to Facebook marketing, start simple and build on your fan base based on experience. A typical marketing campaign for Facebook might include the following elements:

- Establish a Facebook page for your brand. Content is king: have interesting, original content that visitors can be enthusiastic about. Acquire fans.

TABLE 7.2 BASIC FACEBOOK MARKETING TOOLS

MARKETING TOOL	DESCRIPTION
Reactions Buttons	Amplification. A feature that allows users to express support (and as of 2016, other reactions as well) for content on social sites to their friends and friends of friends. The one tool that marketers cannot control. Currently free.
Brand Pages	Engagement and community building. Similar to a business web page, but much more social by encouraging user interaction and response; ongoing discussions among the community of fans. Brand pages are currently free. Shops tab for brand pages allows companies to feature products and services for sale.
News Feed Page Post Ads	Fan acquisition. Paid brand messages can be inserted into the News Feed. Requires payment. Buy button can also be embedded in News Feed Page Post Ads.
Right-Hand Column Sidebar Ads	Fan acquisition. Display ads in the right-hand column (sidebar) similar to display ads elsewhere on the Web. Requires payment.
Facebook Live	Fan acquisition and engagement. Video streaming service within Facebook. Can be used to stream live content that followers can interact with by commenting, liking, and sharing. Video can be saved on a brand's page and followers can continue to interact with it. Free.
Video Ads	Fan acquisition and engagement. Video ads autoplay in silent mode on both desktop and mobile News Feeds. Requires payment.
Facebook Watch	Fan acquisition and engagement. Pre-roll and mid-roll video ads. Requires payment.
Mobile Ads	Fan acquisition. Mobile News Feed Page Post Ads are delivered to smartphones and tablets. Requires payment.
Sponsored Messages/Broadcast	Fan acquisition and engagement. Messages to customers who had previously engaged with them via Messenger chatbot or, in the case of small- and medium-sized businesses, directly from the company. Requires payment.
Facebook Exchange (FBX)	Facebook's real-time ad exchange, which sells ads and retargets ads through online bidding. Advertisers place cookies on user browsers when they visit a site, and when they return to Facebook, they are shown ads on the right side from the site they visited. Requires payment.

TABLE 7.3	SELECTED FACEBOOK MARKETING CAMPAIGNS
COMPANY	MARKETING CAMPAIGN
D+AF	Taiwan-based women's shoe company used Facebook ads to drive brand awareness in new markets, automatically showing relevant products from its catalog based on users' browsing history on and off Facebook. Also showed ads to users who had visited its site but didn't buy or add products to their online cart. The campaign resulted in 2.3% click-through rate and a 6.6X increase in daily orders.
Airbnb	Targeted people who had previously viewed listings on Airbnb's website by dynamically serving Facebook ads featuring relevant properties in those same locations. Reached over 235 million people in one month and tripled Airbnb's return on ad spending investment compared to a previous campaign.
SunButter	Used a series of Facebook video ads to target health-conscious users likely to be interested in sunflower seed butter, increasing both brand awareness and units sold.

- Use comment and feedback tools to develop fan comments. You want visitors to engage with your content. You can also encourage bloggers to develop content for your page.
- Develop a community of users. Try to encourage fans to talk with one another, and develop new (free) content for your page.
- Encourage brand involvement through videos and rich media showing products being used by real customers.
- Use contests and competitions to deepen fan involvement.
- Develop display ads for use on Facebook.
- Develop display ads for use in response to social search queries.
- Liberally display the Like button so fans share the experience with their friends.

Table 7.3 provides some examples of Facebook marketing campaigns. For more information on social marketing using Facebook, see Learning Track 7.1.

Measuring Facebook Marketing Results

There are many ways to measure the success of a Facebook marketing campaign, some very sophisticated. This is a very new field that changes daily. Making matters more complicated is that industry sources sometimes use different names to refer to the same thing! Where this occurs we try to give both the most reasonable name and alternative names you might find in trade literature.

Table 7.4 describes some of the basic metrics to use when evaluating a social marketing campaign. It uses the five steps of the social marketing process found in Figure 7.4—fan acquisition, engagement, amplification, community, and ultimately brand strengthening and sales—as an organizing schema.

While the ultimate goal of Facebook marketing is to drive sales (which typically will take place on your website), it is very important to understand what the elements of social marketing that produce these sales are, and how they can be improved.

At the most elementary level, the number of fans (or followers) generated is the beginning of all social marketing. Visitors become fans when they like your content. In the early days of social marketing, firms put a great deal of emphasis on the size of the fan base, and collecting Likes. This is less important today, as social marketing managers have become more sophisticated. Fan engagement in your content and brand is the first step toward developing a truly social experience, and arguably is more important than simply the number of impressions or the number of fans. Fans that you never hear from are not valuable. Engagement relates to how your fans are interacting with your content, how intensely, and how often. Understanding the kinds of content (videos, text, photos, or posts from fans) that create the highest levels of engagement is also very important (Unmetric, 2015).

The ability to amplify your marketing message by tapping into the social network of your fans is also at the core of social marketing. This can be measured very simply as

TABLE 7.4 MEASURING FACEBOOK MARKETING RESULTS

SOCIAL MARKETING PROCESS	MEASUREMENT
Fan acquisition (impressions)	The number of people exposed to your Facebook brand page posts and paid ads (impressions).
	The percentage of those exposed who become fans/followers.
	The ratio of impressions to fans/followers.
Engagement (conversation rate)	The number of posts, comments, and responses.
	The number of views of brand page content.
	The number of Likes generated per visitor.
	The number of users who responded to games, contests, and coupons (participation).
	The number of minutes on average that visitors stay on your page (duration).
	The rate of Likes per post or other content (applause rate).
Amplification (reach)	The percentage of Likes, shares, or posts to other sites (the rate at which fans share your content).
Community	The monthly interaction rate with your content (i.e., the monthly total of posts, comments, and actions on your Facebook brand page).
	The average monthly on-site minutes for all fans/followers.
	The ratio of positive to negative comments.
Brand Strength/Sales	The percentage (or revenue) of your online sales that is generated by Facebook links compared to other platforms, such as e-mail, search engines, and display ads.
	The percentage of Facebook-sourced customer purchases compared to other sources of customers (conversion ratio).
	The conversion ratio for friends of fans/followers.

the rate at which fans recommend your content to their friends, and how many of their friends further recommend your content to their friends.

Measuring the strength of a Facebook community is not that much different from measuring the strength of an offline community. In both cases you attempt to measure the collective activities of all in the community. Among your fans, how many actively participate? What is the total number of actions taken by fans in a month? How many minutes of involvement are generated each month? What is the percentage of favorable comments?

Finally, measuring sales that result from social campaigns is also straightforward. First, measure the percentage of sales you receive from the Facebook channel. You can easily measure the number of visits to your website that originate on Facebook, and the sales these visits generate. In addition, you can compare purchase rates (conversion rate) for fans and compare these to conversion rates for non-fans from Facebook. More important, you can compare the Facebook conversion rate to other visitors who come from different marketing channels, such as e-mail, display ads, and blogs.

Facebook marketing has entered its second generation even though it's only a few years old. The emphasis today in social marketing has gone beyond collecting Likes and more toward building engagement with high-quality content that fans want to share with their friends; nurturing stable communities of intensely involved fans and friends of fans; and ultimately turning these communities of fans into communities of purchasers.

There are a variety of Facebook analytics tools that provide valuable information about your Facebook marketing efforts. Facebook Page Insights, provided by Facebook, tracks a number of metrics. It has an Overview tab that provides a snapshot of data about a page's performance, such as the number of actions on the page views, page Likes, reach, recommendations, post engagements, videos, and page followers, as well as additional tabs (Likes, Reach, People, and Posts) that enable advertisers to drill down even further.

Social media management system HootSuite enables teams to execute marketing campaigns across multiple networks from one dashboard, and also provides custom reports. Major analytics providers, such as Google Analytics, Webtrends, and IBM Digital Analytics, also provide Facebook reporting modules. Read the *Insight on Technology* case study, *Optimizing Social Marketing with Accuracast*, for a further look at how organizations can use analytics tools to help them better understand social marketing.

TWITTER MARKETING

Twitter is a social network originally based on 140-character text messages. It now allows users to send and receive 280-character messages, as well as news articles, photos, and videos. Twitter had about 285 million active users worldwide in 2019. In 2019, Twitter generated about $3.5 billion in revenue, almost all of which came from ads that appeared in users' timelines (tweet stream).

Twitter was designed from the start as a real-time text messaging service. Twitter offers advertisers and marketers a chance to interact and engage with their customers in real time and in a fairly intimate, one-on-one manner. Advertisers can buy ads that look like organic tweets (the kind you receive from friends), and these ads can tie into and enhance marketing events like new product announcements or pricing changes.

INSIGHT ON TECHNOLOGY

OPTIMIZING SOCIAL MARKETING WITH ACCURACAST

Companies of all shapes and sizes are now tapping into the power of social media for marketing and advertising to improve their bottom lines and enrich their relationships with their customers. As social media continues to become entrenched in the business and cultural landscape, an ecosystem of companies has sprung up around it to meet the growing demand. One major area of growth is in social media analytics— tools that allow companies to track and report social media account performance and generate recommendations on how to optimize social media marketing efforts. AccuraCast is one such company.

Founded in 2004, AccuraCast is London's leading digital marketing agency and bills itself as the longest-running independent search marketing agency in the UK. AccuraCast offers a wide array of marketing services, including programmatic advertising, display advertising, search advertising, SEO, social media marketing, and mobile internet marketing, and offers these tools in all major languages to more than 200 clients worldwide, including PwC, Disney, Stella Artois, and LG. The company has steadily grown over the last 15 years, moving offices multiple times to accommodate its rising number of employees.

AccuraCast offers distinct marketing services for Facebook, Twitter, LinkedIn, and other social networks like Pinterest, Snapchat, and Instagram. AccuraCast was one of the first handful of accredited Facebook Marketing Consultants, a partner program launched by Facebook, and has expertise in every area of the Facebook platform, including Facebook Pixel and Facebook Product Catalogues as well as other Facebook services like Instagram, Messenger, and WhatsApp. The company can target users based on demographics, hobbies, interests, profession, or favorite TV show or sports teams. AccuraCast created a stroke awareness social media marketing campaign for the UK's National Health Service (NHS) spanning Facebook and YouTube that logged over two million viewers in under three months, and helped promote a marketing video for LG to acquire over a million hits.

AccuraCast is experienced in promoting unique events that fall outside the scope of normal advertising campaigns. For example, the company worked with Wimbledon and Rematch Live, a new theater company that shows live, immersive replays of classic sporting events, to promote the climactic Wimbledon finals of 1980 between John McEnroe and Bjorn Borg. AccuraCast focused not only on sports enthusiasts, but also people with an interest in 1980s fashion and culture, as well as people fitting the profile of 'adventure seekers' in the London area. The advertising for the event was primarily on Facebook, but YouTube and Google search were also involved. The result was an emphatic success, with thousands of attendees for the event and over one million users reached throughout the ad campaign. AccuraCast has also promoted similar one-off events such as the Ultimate Fighting Championship's UFC 229 event between Conor McGregor and Khabib Nurmagomedov, which was billed as the most anticipated fight in the history of the UFC.

AccuraCast also worked with celebrity chef Jamie Oliver and his publishers, Penguin Random House and Kosmos Uitgevers, to promote his recipe book *5 Ingredients*, a cookbook with simple recipes anyone can prepare

(continued)

quickly. In this case, the target demographics were busy professionals, especially younger males, even those without an observable interest in cooking. AccuraCast used the Carousel ad format on Facebook to allow users to look at a completed dish and the five ingredients required to create it. These ads contained buttons that redirected users to Amazon, where the book was available for purchase. AccuraCast also designed ads and animated GIFs for use on YouTube and other platforms. Over the course of the campaign, AccuraCast tracked which segments were responding to each advertisement and used that data to make changes and improve performance. Oliver's book was the top seller on Amazon UK for ten weeks and remained in the top five sellers for over six months after its publication in summer 2017.

While AccuraCast has had success with one-off events and product launches, they have also had success with more traditional marketing campaigns that simply spread brand awareness, such as NTT Communications' promotion of their data centers. NTT hoped to generate ten new leads from an advertising campaign that targeted different audiences across Twitter, LinkedIn, Google search, and YouTube. For example, on Twitter, Accuracast targeted certain hashtags and users who followed accounts related to data centers and enterprise software, whereas on Twitter, the company targeted users based on job titles, company size, and location. The goal was for individuals to read NTT's white papers about high density computing and its importance to data centers. The result of the campaign was over triple the number of leads that NTT had targeted, including an 11% conversion rate on LinkedIn.

Keeping up with trends in social media marketing is not easy, with existing networks all innovating different features and new networks sprouting up all the time. Artificial intelligence (AI) is one area that marketers like AccuraCast are beginning to employ with more frequency. AI allows companies to bid on advertising space using more precise algorithms that are geared toward specified goals, such as staying within budget or maximizing cost per acquisition; it allows companies to create chatbots that can process both voice and text to reduce the burden on human customer service representatives; and it allows companies to automate the process of sending marketing e-mails, keeping track of when recipients tend to check their mailboxes and using other forms of tracking to improve performance. AccuraCast has also launched its alpha version of Unyte.ai, a marketing platform that allows users to create custom AI solutions across multiple social media channels.

AccuraCast prides itself on its ethics, confidentiality, and privacy with user data. There are techniques known as "black hat SEO," such as keyword stuffing (repeating keywords in a webpage's visible content or metadata to improve its search ranking), private link networks (a group of sites that link to one another to exploit major search engine algorithms' emphasis on number of incoming and outgoing links), and cloaking (presenting content to search engine crawlers that is different than what users end up seeing), all of which are deliberate manipulations of search engine results. AccuraCast guarantees its clients 100% ethical SEO, which are the accepted, legal forms of industry marketing. In an industry where some companies push the envelope, AccuraCast's customers can trust that they are receiving strong results without compromising their values.

SOURCES: "A Week in My Life: Farhad Dlvecha, UK Managing Director of AccuraCast," by Josh Peachey, Prolificlondon.co.uk, September 16, 2019; "AI Tools Marketers Can Use Now," Accuracast.com, June 21, 2019; "Facebook Advertising Agency," Accuracast.com, accessed February 2020; "Wimbledon Rematch Live Launch," Accuracast.com, accessed February 2020; "Jamie Oliver: Marketing a Bestseller," Accuracast.com, accessed February 2020; "NTT Europe B2B Marketing," Accuracast.com, accessed February 2020; "About Us," Accuracast.com, accessed February 2020; "Statement of Ethics," Accuracast.com, accessed February 2020.

According to a survey of almost 5,500 Twitter users, 66% of those surveyed had discovered a new small or medium-sized business (SMB) on Twitter, 94% planned to purchase from the SMBs they follow, and 69% had purchased from an SMB because of something they saw on Twitter (Twitter + Research Now, 2016).

Basic Twitter Features

While most people probably know what a tweet is, Twitter offers marketers many other ways of communicating using Twitter (Newberry, 2018). In fact, Twitter has introduced a whole new vocabulary that is specific to Twitter's platform. **Table 7.5** describes the most common Twitter features.

Twitter Marketing Tools

There are many kinds of Twitter marketing products, and the firm is creating new ones every few months. The current major Twitter marketing tools include the following.

Promoted Tweets. Advertisers pay to have their tweets appear in users' search results. Promoted Tweets are Twitter's version of Google's AdWords. The tweets appear as "promoted" in the search results. Pricing typically is on a "cost-per-click" basis, based on an auction run by Twitter on the Twitter ad platform and might range from $.50 to $10 per

TABLE 7.5	TWITTER FEATURES
FEATURE	DESCRIPTION
Tweet	280-character text message. Messages can be private (to a single person or one to one), public (to everyone, one to many), or to a group of followers.
Followers	You can follow someone's tweets and receive them as soon as they are made. Others can follow your tweets.
Message (DM)	A direct private message (DM) is like an e-mail that only you and the recipient can read.
Hashtag #<word>	Like a Twitter search engine, #<word> organizes the conversations on Twitter around a specific topic. Click on a hashtag and you are taken to the search results for that term.
Mention	A public Tweet that includes another user's name "@username." You can click on mentions and link back to that person's profile. As a public tweet, your followers will be alerted as well.
Moments tab	Curated highlights of what is happening on Twitter at that moment.
Reply	A public response to a tweet using the Reply button. Replies show up on your timeline and that of the person you are responding to.
Timeline	Your timeline is your home page on Twitter listing the tweets you have received in chronological order, the most recent first. Click on a tweet in the timeline and it expands to reveal videos and photos. Place your mouse over a tweet to reply, retweet, or make it a favorite (which is passed to your followers).
Retweet	Allows you to send along a tweet to all of your followers.
Links	Twitter has a link-shortening feature that allows you to paste in a URL of any link and it will be automatically shortened.

engagement. Twitter also offers Twitter Promote Mode for a flat $99 a month, which enables an advertiser to promote its first 10 tweets a day to a selected audience. An "ad carousel" allows up to 12 ads to be shown in a single space, enabling users to swipe through the Promoted Tweets. Promoted Tweets can be geo-targeted and also offer keyword targeting that enables advertisers to send the tweets to specific users based on keywords in their recent tweets or tweets with which they have interacted. Promoted Tweets can be plain text or include a single or multiple images, or can include a website card (link to website), basic app card (link to app), or image app card (photo plus link to app). In 2016, Twitter introduced conversational ads, which enables marketers to include a call to action button with customizable hashtags to encourage consumer engagement within Promoted Tweets.

Promoted Trends. Advertisers pay to move their hashtags (# symbol used to mark keywords in a tweet) to the top of Twitter's Trends List. Otherwise, hashtags are found by the Twitter search engine, and only those that are organically popular make it to the Trends List. Promoted Trends are available for purchase in 50 different countries. There are also enhanced versions, such as Promoted Trend Spotlight, which provide additional exposure.

Promoted Accounts. Advertisers pay to have their branded account suggested to users who are likely to be interested in the account in the "Who to Follow" list, Twitter's account recommendation engine, on the Twitter home page. Promoted Accounts can be targeted by interest, geography, and gender, and are priced on a cost-per-follower basis, with advertisers paying only for new followers gained. Prices range from $.50 to $2.50.

Amplify. The Twitter Amplify program provides marketers with a real-time digital dashboard so they can see the resulting tweet activity about the show or the brand. Based on this information, marketers can send Promoted Tweets to users who tweeted about a show. They can alter the copy as well based on other information about the tweeters. For example, Jim Beam used Amplify to promote its new Jim Beam Red Stag brand of premium bourbon. The intent was to increase brand awareness, purchase intent, and user engagement. The strength of Twitter, according to Jim Beam marketers, is that it allows the brand to be a part of a real-time conversation, as opposed to Facebook, which is better at reaching a mass audience but not at engaging consumers in real time. The power of social media, including Facebook, is finding consumer advocates who will speak on behalf of the brand.

Promoted Video. In 2014, building on the Amplify program, Twitter announced a beta test of Promoted Video, which allows advertisers to distribute video on the Twitter platform. In 2015, Twitter began allowing advertisers to use Promoted Video to link directly to app installations and also added an ad purchasing feature for videos called "optimized action bidding" that enables marketers to customize ad purchases to improve return on investment. In 2018, Promoted Video was Twitter's largest ad revenue-generating format, responsible for over 50% of its ad revenues (Wagner, 2018).

Twitter Cards. Marketers can embed a "card" into a tweet. When users click on the tweet, a promotional offer appears and users are asked to sign up. Cards are different from display ads because they are used only by businesses who want to develop new leads, and they

TABLE 7.6 TWITTER MARKETING TOOLS

TWITTER MARKETING TOOLS	DESCRIPTION
Promoted Tweets	Advertisers pay to have their tweets appear in users' search results and timelines. The tweets appear as "promoted," and the pricing is on a per-click basis, based on an auction run on the Twitter ad platform. Promoted Tweets can be both keyword- and geo-targeted and can include images as well as links (cards) to websites and apps. An "ad carousel" allows up to 12 ads to be shown in a single space, enabling users to swipe through the Promoted Tweets.
Promoted Trends	Advertisers pay to move their hashtags (# symbol used to mark keywords in a tweet) to the top of Twitter's Trends List. Otherwise, hashtags are found by the Twitter search engine, and only those that are organically popular make it to the Trends List.
Promoted Accounts	Advertisers pay to have their branded account suggested to users likely to be interested in the account in the "Who to Follow" list, Twitter's account recommendation engine, available on the Twitter home page. Promoted Accounts can be specifically targeted and are priced on a cost-per-follower basis.
Amplify	A real-time digital dashboard connecting television commercials and tweet activity.
Promoted Video	Advertisers can distribute videos on the Twitter platform and use Promoted Videos to link directly to app installlations.
Twitter Card	Promotional offers that appear in users' Twitter timeline of messages with a coupon or other offer. Used for lead generation.
Mobile Ads	All of the above formats delivered on mobile devices, as well as mobile app install and app engagement ads.

always include an offer, such as 50% off your next cup of coffee. This is a one-click process. The users' e-mail and Twitter account names are automatically obtained by Twitter and sent to marketers, who can then follow up with a tweet or an e-mail.

Mobile Ads. Because over 90% of Twitter users access Twitter on a mobile device, most of the above referenced marketing tools can be considered mobile ads tools. Mobile is the primary driver of Twitter's business and the source of most of its revenue. In addition to all of the above formats, in 2014, Twitter added mobile app install and app engagement ads, which have been lucrative formats for Facebook as well.

Table 7.6 summarizes these Twitter marketing tools.

Starting a Twitter Marketing Campaign

If you're new to Twitter marketing, start simple and build on your follower base using experience as a guide for what works. A typical marketing campaign for Twitter may include the following elements:

- Establish a Twitter account. Start following others you are interested in or conversations that you might want to participate in with #<topic>. Don't expect any followers at first. Your visibility rises as you follow others, who will begin to tweet back or retweet interesting content. Then start retweeting content you think the group would be interested in, and start encouraging ongoing conversations.

- Try Promoted Tweets. Twitter has a very good online ad tool that allows you to define an ad, establish the groups you would like to target, and understand the costs. You might start with a regional or metropolitan Promoted Tweet. Test various formats. You don't have to pay for Promoted Tweets unless someone clicks on the tweet, so it is up to you to make those clicks count. Direct users to your website and offer a coupon or discount. Once you get some experience using Promoted Tweets, you can also try Twitter Promote Mode.
- Promoted Trends can be very expensive—around $200,000. If your budget will allow, and your topic is of general interest to a large audience, you can try this tool. Geo-targeting is possible.
- Twitter Cards are something that small and medium-sized businesses can use. If you sell anything locally, from pizza to stationery, make up an offer and build a Twitter Card specifying the geo-location where your business is located.

As with Facebook, the objective is to establish your brand identity online and seek out engagement with users, not immediate sales. Encourage others to retweet your content and offers to their friends.

Table 7.7 describes some selected Twitter marketing campaigns.

Measuring Twitter Marketing Results

Measuring the results of Twitter marketing is similar to measuring the results of Facebook and other social marketing platforms, with some minor changes to account for the unique qualities of Twitter. **Table 7.8** describes some basic ways to measure the results of a Twitter marketing campaign.

TABLE 7.7	SELECTED TWITTER MARKETING CAMPAIGNS
COMPANY	MARKETING CAMPAIGN
LEGO	Launched a global campaign on Twitter, using Promoted Trends and other ad formats, employing the hashtag #RebuildTheWorld, which was retweeted nearly 100,000 times within the first four days after launch.
Domino's Pizza	Allows users to order from Domino's by tweeting an emoji of a pizza or the #easyorder. Domino's Twitter chatbot then routes the order to the appropriate location and asks additional questions if necessary.
Samsung	Samsung Australia used a Twitter chatbot in Direct Messages to raise awareness of its televisions by asking users about their TV viewing preferences and providing them with personalized recommendations. Samsung then used a Direct Message Card to target people interested in TV, movies, video games, and sports. The chatbot had an 89% completion rate and over 20% longer engagement time than average visits to the Samsung website.
UNTUCKit	Season-specific as well as "evergreen" photo ad campaigns for retail company that sell shirts designed to be worn untucked. Ads included a website tag that allows UNTUCKit to track site visits and conversion and also to retarget site visitors. Built brand awareness and increased online retail sales.

TABLE 7.8	MEASURING TWITTER MARKETING RESULTS
SOCIAL MARKETING PROCESS	MEASUREMENT
Fan acquisition (impressions)	The number of people exposed to your Promoted Tweets, Promoted Trends, etc. (impressions). The number of followers and monthly growth.
Engagement (conversation rate)	The number of comments, responses to, and retweets of your tweets. The number of views of brand page content. The number of users that responded to games, contests, and coupons (participation). The number of minutes on average that followers stay on your page (duration).
Amplification (reach)	The rate at which fans retweet or otherwise share your tweets.
Community	The monthly interaction rate (i.e., the monthly total of comments and responses to, and retweets of, your content). The average monthly onsite minutes for all followers. The ratio of positive to negative tweets.
Brand Strength/Sales	The number of leads generated (people who sign up for news or content). Visitor/lead rate: the number of visitors that become leads to compare campaigns. The percentage (or revenue) of your online sales generated by Twitter links compared to other platforms, such as e-mail, search engines, and display ads. The percentage of Twitter-sourced customer purchases compared to other sources of customers (conversion ratio).

Tools provided by Twitter include a dashboard that provides real-time information on impressions, retweets, clicks, replies, and follows for Promoted Tweets and Promoted Accounts. Twitter's Tweet Activity dashboard provides data on how every tweet performs in terms of mentions, follows, and reach. Twitter's Followers dashboard enables marketers to track the growth of the follower base, as well as information about their interests, geography, and engagement. Twitter's Twitter Card dashboard provides information on how Twitter Cards drive clicks, app installs, and retweets.

Third-party tools include TweetDeck, which enables you to track mentions, people, and keywords; Twitalyzer, which provides one-click access to Twitter metrics that analyze followers, mentions, retweets, influencers, and their locations; and BackTweets, which allows you to search through a tweet archive for URLs sent via Twitter.

PINTEREST MARKETING

Pinterest provides users with an online board to which they can "pin" interesting pictures (see the opening case, *Pinterest: A Picture Is Worth a Thousand Words*). The success of Pinterest is based in part on a shift in consumer behavior enabled by new technologies: people talk about brands using pictures rather than words. Large numbers of users are pinning and instagramming about their lives using pictures.

Pinterest has been one of the fastest growing sites in online history. In 2010, Pinterest had 10,000 users in the United States, then 12 million by the end of 2011, and over 330 million by the end of 2019. Today, almost 30% of Internet users in the United States use Pinterest on a regular basis. Pinterest's visitors are overwhelmingly female: about 70% are women, but men were its fastest growing demographic, and its users cover a broad age demographic range from grandparents to teenagers, with Millennials forming the largest single segment. The hope for marketers, and Pinterest, is that its "referral capacity" (the ability to direct users to retail websites where they can purchase something) will rapidly increase as its audience grows and intensity of use grows.

You can think of Pinterest as a highly interactive and social online magazine. One difference, of course, is that users (including business firms) contribute all the photos. Pinterest currently has 36 categories of boards from gifts, animals, art, cars, and motorcycles to crafts, food, and men's and women's fashion. Users can pin to these boards, create their own boards, and follow other pinners and boards as well. Firms can create their own brand boards and product pins. By the end of 2019, there were 225 billion pins on Pinterest on 5 billion different boards.

One way to look at the billions of pictures on Pinterest is as disguised display ads—click, and off you go to a brand website for a purchase. Pinterest pins are much better than display ads because they are unobtrusive, and because they don't look like display ads. Instead, they look like sumptuous catalog or magazine photos. In the future, analysts believe, Pinterest could charge an affiliate fee for any subsequent purchases. Pinterest could also charge businesses for creating brand sites or boards, which currently are free.

Basic Pinterest Features

Marketing on Pinterest requires that you understand the basic features and capabilities of Pinterest. While all users of Pinterest understand how to pin photos to an online scrapbook, many other capabilities are less well understood or used. **Table 7.9** provides a list of various Pinterest features.

Pinterest Marketing Tools

Pinterest's first step into the marketing arena was to offer business accounts that provided additional resources for brands. In 2013, it introduced Rich Pins, which allowed companies to embed information, such as current pricing and availability, as well as a direct link to a product page. In 2014, Pinterest took the official leap into paid advertising. It launched Promoted Pins with a select group of national brands and also announced a trial of a Do It Yourself version of Promoted Pins for small and medium-sized businesses, to be paid for on a cost per click basis, similar to the Google AdWords platform. Promoted Pins appear in search results and category feeds. In 2015, Pinterest rolled out Promoted Pins to all its U.S.-based partners and added Cinematic Pins. It also added Buyable Pins for eligible merchants on select e-commerce platforms such as Shopify, BigCommerce, Magento, and Salesforce Commerce Cloud, allowing users to buy products directly on the Pinterest site, and pay with Apple Pay. In 2016, Pinterest added additional ad-targeting options, launched Promoted Video ads, and began offering

TABLE 7.9   PINTEREST FEATURES

FEATURE	DESCRIPTION
Pins	Used to post a photo to a Pinterest board.
Board	An online scrapbook where photos are organized by the user.
Repins	The ability to pin the photos of other users to your own boards and to share with your friends.
Hashtags and keywords	Use hashtags in the description of pins, e.g., #cars, #sports cars. Use keywords people are likely to use when searching for specific content.
Share	Share pinned photos with friends on Facebook, Twitter, and e-mail.
Image Hover	A widget you can add to your browser. When your mouse hovers over an online image, the Pin It button pops up and you can pin the photo automatically to your Pinterest boards.
Embed	Allows you to automatically embed pinned photos into your website or blog.
Me+ Contributors	Allows followers to contribute to your boards.
Follow	Users can choose to follow other pinners and boards and receive e-mail updates.
Number of Pins and Followers	A count of the number of pins and the number of followers visible at the top of the brand page.
Link to URL; Link to pinner	Click on the URL of the company who pinned a photo; click on a link to the person who pinned a photo.
Price display	Hover over a product and price and other information displays.
Integration with Facebook and Twitter	Login from Facebook, Twitter, and other social sites. Your personal profile (but not your photo) information from Facebook comes over to Pinterest; your pins go onto your Facebook Timeline. Twitter and Pinterest profile pages are also integrated.
Pin It browser button (bookmarklet)	Browsers' red Pin It button. Users drag the button onto their browser screen, allowing them to instantly pin photos they see on the Web.
Apps	Smartphone and tablet apps that allow users to pin photos, browse pins and boards, get ideas while shopping, and display pins.
Pinterest widget	Pin It button that makes it easy for people to pin images from your site.
Pinterest Lens	Visual search app that allows users to point their smartphone camera at an item, then tap to see related images or ideas.

its search inventory to advertisers for the first time. Products for search advertising include keyword campaigns, similar to keyword ad campaigns on Google, and shopping campaigns, which take an advertiser's product catalog and automatically match up ads to keywords associated with that catalog. Pinterest has also started exploiting its visual search engine for advertising purposes by serving up ads based on user's organic search based on the visual similarity between the products in the ads and the products in the visual search results. **Table 7.10** identifies and describes some of the primary Pinterest marketing tools.

TABLE 7.10	PINTEREST MARKETING TOOLS
MARKETING TOOL	DESCRIPTION
Rich Pins	Rich Pins enable advertisers to include extra information directly on the pin itself. There are six types of Rich Pin: Product, App, Place, Article, Movie, and Recipe. Product Pins include real-time pricing, availability, and link to where the item can be purchased. App Pins include an install button that allows a user to download an app without leaving Pinterest. Place Pins include a map, address, and phone number. Article Pins include a headline, author, and story description.
Promoted Pins	A way to promote pins to a targeted audience, and pay for click-through to your website.
Cinematic Pins	A made-for-mobile ad format that displays a short animation when the user scrolls down through the ad; only plays a full-length version when the user clicks on the ad, providing more user control over the experience.
Buyable Pins/Shop the Look Pins	Merchants can create Buyable Pins that allow users to purchase product featured in pin without leaving Pinterest. Shop the Look Pins have white dots that identify different parts of a "look" that, when tapped on, enable a user to shop for each item shown.
Promoted Video	Uses Pinterest's new native video ad player to allow marketers to run video ads.
Add Pin It or Follow button to your website (Pinterest widget)	Makes it easy for visitors to pin photos from your website, and be notified when you post new photos to your site.
Pin as display ad	Pinned photo acts as a display ad by directing users back to a firm's website.
Brand page	Allows companies to create a corporate brand page. In the past, Pinterest did not distinguish between a personal page and a corporate brand page.
Create theme-based boards to reflect your brand messaging	Pinterest recommends that business boards not be strictly sales-oriented, but lifestyle-oriented instead.
URL Link to stores	Makes it easier for consumers to click through links on brand pages and product pins so they can reliably purchase what they see. The goal is to integrate photos of inventory with Pinterest to make items more easily tracked. What this means is retailers can see a definite link between a sale and a photo they pinned. Currently, after thousands of repins, clicking on the URL sometimes leads to a broken link.
Integration with other social sites	Ask your Facebook fans and Twitter followers to pin photos of your products and tag you. Repin these photos to your brand page on Pinterest. Give a shout-out to your loyal users and fans to show potential customers how much current users like using your product.
Network with users, followers, and others	As with Facebook and Twitter, comment, mention, and communicate with others using Pinterest. Participate in the community and you will become better known, and learn more about potential customers and what they believe and to what they aspire.
Search advertising	Ad campaigns based on keyword, product catalogs, and visual search.

TABLE 7.11 SELECTED PINTEREST MARKETING CAMPAIGNS

COMPANY	CAMPAIGN
Tastemade Indonesia	Entertainment company based in Indonesia that produces online food and travel-related videos used a variety of Pinterest marketing tools, such as Rich Pins, themed boards, and short videos to expand its global reach.
Birds Eye UK	Used Promoted Pins and Video Pins to drive reach for campaign focusing on frozen peas and waffles to encourage UK families to use frozen foods. Video pins had a 50% view-through rate and 5.5 million video views.
Nordstrom	Used in-store signage depicting products with the most engagement on Pinterest. Has more followers on Pinterest than on Facebook or Twitter.
Blue Apron	Subscription-based food delivery service pins its most popular recipes to different boards. High-quality, compelling photography helps drive engagement.
UNIQLO	Clothing retailer used dozens of accounts to pin graphics in a five-column arrangement on its Pinterest page, allowing users to scroll down and animate the images.

For instance, Lands' End has several brand pages on Pinterest, one of which is Lands' End Canvas. Search for Lands' End Canvas and it takes you to the page that Lands' End Canvas created and where Lands' End has pinned some of its catalog photos. You can see the number of people who have pinned these photos elsewhere, and the total number who follow this line of clothing and have posted their own photos. When you click on a photo, you get a larger version of the photo (sometimes called a photo landing page), and the chance to link to the website (canvas.landsend.com) where you can purchase the product and find similar ones. You will also see on this photo landing page a picture of the person who pinned the photo, other boards where it was pinned, and recommendations for related photos and products in a section titled "People who pinned this also pinned…."
Table 7.11 provides a brief description of Pinterest marketing campaigns of selected other retailers.

Starting a Pinterest Marketing Campaign

Before leaping into a Pinterest campaign, ask yourself some questions about your products and services, and then identify some strategic objectives for your Pinterest presence. First, sketch out a vision of what you hope to accomplish with a Pinterest presence. Are you an established company trying to strengthen your brand? Are you the new kid on the block that no one knows and you want to start a marketing campaign? Are your products visual and can your brand be expressed in a set of pictures? Most products have a visual component, some more compelling than others. Is the consumer accustomed to seeing the products in your industry expressed through photos? For instance, food is increasingly a visual experience with the growth of food magazines and websites.

Next, consider the target demographic for your products and services, and compare it to the Pinterest demographic. Currently, about 70% of Pinterest's users are women, and while this might change over time, your offerings will have to be attractive to women. Do your products or services appeal to this demographic?

Think about strategy in your marketspace. What are your competitors doing? Are they on Pinterest? Do they have an effective presence? What types of people follow your competitors and what are the users pinning? How many followers, re-pinners, brand pages, and product pins are there? Because photos are central to a Pinterest presence, where will the photos for your brand pages come from? Are you, or a member of your team, a skilled photographer? You can pin photos from all over the Web, and from other Pinterest boards, but then you're just sharing content, not creating unique and unusual content.

Pinterest is an adjunct to a fully developed marketing plan, both online and offline. You will want to integrate your social and online marketing efforts with a Facebook and Twitter presence. You can share photos from your website, and send web photos to your brand pages. The same photos can be used on your Facebook page and on Twitter. Your customers will be using all these platforms and you will have to follow them to keep up.

Once you have envisioned your Pinterest campaign and developed a marketing plan, you can start implementing your plan. In order to implement your Pinterest plan, you should have a traditional website where your products are displayed (a catalog) and can be purchased. Second, you should also have a Facebook brand page to develop followers and a method for informing your followers of new Pins. Once these are in place, you can begin your Pinterest campaign:

- Create a Pinterest brand page and start pinning photos of your products. Continue to add more pins, and change them regularly. Be sure your photos are the same quality level or higher than those of your competitors. If necessary, hire a skilled photographer. Brand pages generally do not allow followers to pin photos but only to follow and comment. The idea here is to control the content of your brand page, and develop other boards where followers can pin pictures.

- Create multiple theme-based life style boards. Develop several theme-based boards that emphasize life styles or fashions. Pinterest is not just, or even primarily, a selling site. It is also an entertainment and branding site. You want followers to adore your photos. On theme-based boards you will want others besides yourself to be able to pin.

- Use URL links and keywords. Make sure your pins have a URL link to your store, or to vendor stores, so followers can easily buy as well as "see." Be sure to use keywords and hashtags to classify each of your photos so they show up in Pinterest searches. Remember, Pinterest cannot "see" a photo or understand its content. It only "knows" the content based on your tags.

- Use Pinterest Rich Pins. If you are in the food, retail, or movie distribution business, Product Pins are worth a try if you have a popular product at an attractive price, or if you want to use a specific product as a loss-leader to motivate people to come to your website (where you can expose them to your entire catalog of products). Once you have some experience with Rich Pins, you can also experiment with the various types of paid advertising that Pinterest offers, such as Promoted Pins, Cinematic Pins, and Video Ads.

- Use Pin It buttons. Add a Pin It button to your website and Facebook page to encourage fans and followers to pin your photos to their own boards, and to recommend them to friends.

- Use your Facebook and Twitter networks. Start using your Facebook and Twitter networks by adding a Pin It button to Facebook (also called a Pinterest tab), and start sharing your pinned photos with your followers.
- Integrate with Facebook and Twitter. Create Facebook and Twitter logins so that users can go to your pins and boards without leaving the Facebook and Twitter sites.
- Be social. Join the conversation. Follow other pinners and boards and ask to receive e-mail and Facebook updates.

Measuring Pinterest Marketing Results

As with any social marketing platform, the key dimensions to measure for a Pinterest marketing effort are fan (follower) acquisition, engagement, amplification, community, and sales. **Table 7.12** describes some basic ways to measure the results of a Pinterest marketing campaign.

TABLE 7.12 — MEASURING PINTEREST MARKETING RESULTS

SOCIAL MARKETING PROCESS	MEASUREMENT
Fan acquisition (impressions)	The number of people exposed to your pins.
	The number of followers and the rate of growth.
	The number of people that have pinned your product photos.
	The percentage of those exposed to your pins who also pin them to their own or other boards.
Engagement (conversation rate)	The number of posts, comments, and responses to your brand or pins on Pinterest.
	The number of users who are responding to games, contests, and coupons (participation).
	The number of minutes on average fans stay on your brand or product pages (duration).
	The rate of pins per post or other content (applause rate).
Amplification	The rate at which fans share your pinned photos by sharing or repinning to their own or others' boards.
Community	The monthly interaction rate with your content (i.e., the monthly total of pins, comments, and actions on your Pinterest brand page).
	The average monthly onsite minutes for all fans.
	The ratio of positive to negative comments.
Brand Strength/Sales	The percentage of your online sales that are generated by Pinterest links (referrals) compared to other platforms, such as e-mail, search engines, and display ads.
	The percentage of Pinterest-sourced customer purchases, compared to other sources of customers (conversion ratio).
	The conversion ratio for users receiving repinned photos (friends of followers).

Pinterest provides a built-in web analytics service that offers insights into how people are interacting with pins that originate from their websites. There are several firms that will help produce the metrics referred to in Table 7.12. For instance, Curalate is an online service to measure the impact of Pinterest and other visual social media. It listens and measures visual conversations by seeing what pictures users pin and repin, and also analyzes the colors in the picture. Curalate currently has over 450 brands using its platform.

MARKETING ON OTHER SOCIAL NETWORKS: INSTAGRAM, SNAPCHAT, AND LINKEDIN

There are a great many social networks where products and services can be marketed, the largest of which include Instagram, LinkedIn, and Snapchat. Instagram is a visual social network: users and advertisers post photos and videos to their friends, potential customers, and the public at large. In 2019, Instagram (owned by Facebook) had over 1 billion users worldwide, 2 million active advertisers, and 25 million business profiles. Over 70% of Instagram's audience is under 35, but its most rapidly growing demographic groups are those comprised of people over the age of 35. In 2019, Instagram generated about $15 billion in ad revenues worldwide (eMarketer, Inc, 2019e).

As with other social networks, users create a profile. There is a Feed that provides a listing of photos and videos (up to 15 seconds long) posted by friends or advertisers. Using a feature called Direct, users can send photos and videos to specific people. Using Explore, users can search for public profiles and photos. Instagram also has a powerful photo editing suite called Layout.

Similar to Facebook, advertisers have brand profiles and run marketing campaigns by sending posts to users' Feeds. Instagram ad campaigns consist of display ads and video ads of exceptional quality, similar to a printed magazine. Carousel ads can include multiple still photos or videos in a single ad. Ads can link to advertisers' websites and now can include a Buy button. For brands that want to drive mass awareness around premieres, product launches, and key moments, Instagram developed what it calls its Marquee ad product, which reaches millions of people. Marquee ads generally last a single day, promise to deliver a guaranteed number of impressions, and can be posted several times during the day to catch different audiences. In 2016, Instagram also added a Stories feature to compete with a similar feature offered by Snapchat and, in 2017, made it available as a paid advertising product. Instagram Stories typically include a montage of images and/or videos, sometimes annotated with graphics and emoticons, and disappear after 24 hours. Major brands have eagerly embraced the format and regularly include Stories in their Instagram marketing efforts. For instance, Airbnb ran a series of Instagram Stories and reported a double-digit increase in ad recall (Instagram, 2017; Shields, 2016).

Snapchat is a mobile messaging app/social network that allows its users to chat and send images and videos (snaps) that disappear after a relatively short period of time once they have been viewed. Snapchat bills itself as a method for visually capturing important moments and communicating them creatively via a variety of tools such as geofilters (which tailor an image to the user's location) and lenses (a type of augmented reality that allows users to alter their face in a variety of ways). Snapchat was initially aimed at the under-25 demographic and in 2019, Millennials represented about 40% of Snapchat's 80 million monthly active U.S. users. In addition to targeting a desirable demographic, Snapchat is also attractive to advertisers because research indicates that it is also very sticky, with over 50% of users saying that they used it many times a day and even constantly. However, in early 2018, Snapchat released a redesign of its app that was roundly criticized and which created a significant backlash among its users. Snapchat's user growth slowed as a result.

Since it was initially released, Snapchat has introduced a number of features that present advertising opportunities, including Snapchat Stories (a way for users to simultaneously share snaps, which remain live for 24 hours, with all or just some of their friends), Live Stories (a compilation of snaps from various users at events and locations around the world that are compiled by Snapchat editors into a Live Story that typically has a lifespan of 24 hours), and Discover (unique content from brands chosen by Snapchat). Snapchat offers advertisers a variety of ad types, including Snap Ads (short 10-second-or-less full-screen vertical video ads that have audio turned on by default), Sponsored Geofilters (geofilters that use brand imagery and messaging), and Sponsored Lenses (lenses that use brand imagery). Interactive versions of Snap Ads (known as Snap Ads with Attachments) are also available, and allow a user to swipe to extend the ad to view additional video content, an article, a web page, or an app install offer. Ads can be purchased on a flat fee or cost-per-thousand (CPM) impressions basis. Snapchat has also introduced a number of ad targeting capabilities, added third-party measurement partners, and a self-serve programmatic ad buying tool. Snapchat generated about $1.53 billion in ad revenue in 2019, with that number expected to increase to over $2.6 billion by 2021 (eMarketer, Inc., 2018e; comScore, Inc., 2019f, 2017).

LinkedIn, while generating far less average engagement, nevertheless attracts a highly educated, professional, and managerial audience that is intensively engaged in careers and employment. LinkedIn is a social network focused on professional networking, where users post their resumes, and potential employers hunt for new hires. See the opening case in Chapter 10 for more information on LinkedIn.

As with other social networks, users build a profile, but in this case, sharing their professional background, degrees, employment, and skill set. Companies can create a free company profile page that includes a logo, header image, an About section, and various posts. Companies can also create a showcase page to highlight a specific product or service, as well as a Career page (which requires payment) targeted at recruiting. There is a Feed that provides a listing of posts from colleagues and friends, and sponsored posts (ads) from firms. Display ads also appear on the right and bottom of the page. Advertisers can use LinkedIn's self-serve advertising platform or place ads using LinkedIn Advertising Partner Solutions, which provide more variety and ad options than self-service ads, including premium display advertising, sponsored inMail, and ads that urge users to follow a specific company or join a specific group. LinkedIn also provides a publishing platform called LinkedIn Pulse, which allows users to publish articles to expand their brand and thought leadership. Advertisers tend to use LinkedIn for branding purposes and typically are not soliciting sales.

THE DOWNSIDE OF SOCIAL MARKETING

Social marketing is not without its disadvantages. Sometimes social media campaigns backfire. One problem is that brands lose a substantial amount of control over what people say about their brands (see the *Insight on Society* case, *The Dark Side of Social Networks*, in Chapter 10 for a variety of examples) and also lose control over where their ads appear in terms of other content on social sites. Ads placed on Facebook according to an algorithm can be placed near content that does not represent the values of the brand. This is not peculiar to social marketing, as advertising using Google's advertising platform faces the same problem. This is very different, however, from TV ads where brands maintain near complete control. Social networks are unique in that disgruntled consumers, or just malicious people, can post material that is inaccurate and/or embarrassing.

TikTok is a new social marketing platform based on the sharing of short-form videos. Read the *Insight on Society* case, *Social Marketing on TikTok: Worth the Risk?* to learn more about TikTok and additional issues that can arise with respect to social marketing.

7.3 MOBILE MARKETING

Mobile marketing involves the use of mobile devices such as smartphones and tablet computers to display banner ads, rich media, video, games, e-mail, text messaging, in-store messaging, QuickResponse (QR) codes, and couponing. Mobile is now a required part of the standard marketing budget. Mobile devices represent a radical departure from previous marketing technologies simply because the devices integrate so many human and consumer activities from telephoning or texting friends, to listening to music, watching videos, tracking locations, and shopping. The more mobile devices can do, the more people rely on them in daily life. In 2019, about 3.3 billion people worldwide used a mobile device for Internet access (eMarketer, Inc., 2019g). According to Deloitte's Global Mobile Consumer Survey, consumers check their smartphones an average of 52 times a day (Deloitte, 2018). Most mobile phone users keep their phone within arm's length 24 hours a day. For many, it's the first thing they check in the morning, the last thing they check at night, and the first tool to use when there's a question of where to go, what to do, and where to meet up.

OVERVIEW: M-COMMERCE TODAY

It's a short number of steps from owning a smartphone or tablet, to searching for products and services, browsing, and then purchasing. The rate of growth of retail m-commerce has skyrocketed over the last several years, growing worldwide at over 30% annually, and in 2019, it accounted for almost 65% of all retail e-commerce revenues worldwide. **Figure 7.5** illustrates the expected growth of mobile and "traditional" retail e-commerce worldwide to 2023.

Initially, m-commerce was focused primarily on digital goods, such as music, videos, games, and e-books. Today, however, traditional retail products and travel services are the

INSIGHT ON SOCIETY

SOCIAL MARKETING ON TIKTOK: WORTH THE RISK?

In the last few years, several social networks have grown into multi-billion-dollar companies in the blink of an eye. Although Facebook remains the most dominant social network, others like Instagram, Twitter, and Snapchat are now household names with millions of users and lofty valuations. The newest company to emerge on the scene is TikTok, a Chinese short-form video sharing app launched in 2017 that has already amassed over 500 million active monthly users worldwide. In 2018, TikTok became the first Chinese social media app to be the most downloaded app in the United States and is now available in over 150 countries and 75 languages.

TikTok is the spiritual successor to Vine, a now-defunct app with a similar focus on short-form videos. Many TikTok videos feature music, with users lip-syncing, singing, and dancing; others focus on comedy and creativity within the fifteen-second window of each video. Users can 'remix' posts from other users and put their own spin on them, using the app's array of editing tools, filters, and other effects. Algorithms analyze the viewing habits of each user and provide content that is customized based on their activity. TikTok's rapid ascent is due in part to its stark contrast to other social networks. For example, Instagram has an extremely polished feel, with immaculate photographs and images of people at their very best; TikTok, by contrast, is more spontaneous, silly, and fun to use.

TikTok also skews much younger than other social networks, with 60% of its worldwide monthly users between the ages of 16 and 24. For many of these users, Facebook is the stodgy old social network their parents use, and TikTok is the place to go to be among peers. This demographic skew presents a host of opportunities and challenges for marketers. On the one hand, advertisers are desperate to gain a foothold with such a valuable set of potential customers, but on the other, the company has run afoul of regulatory agencies with lax data protections for its underage users, concerns which are compounded by the company's close relationship with the Chinese government. TikTok has also drawn criticism for failing to act decisively against malicious actors on its platform.

Brands have flocked to TikTok in spite of such concerns, with companies like Sony, Paramount, Adidas, Nike, Samsung, and Ralph Lauren all establishing strong presences on the app. Companies have sought to run TikTok advertising campaigns that blend well with its light-hearted feel; for example, luxury clothing retailer Burberry challenged its users to recreate its company logo using hand movements, prompting 30,000 video responses that generated 57 million views. Casual food chain Chipotle capitalized on a viral video of a Chipotle employee deftly flipping the tinfoil lid of a meal onto the top of its plate, promoting the hashtag #ChipotleLidFlip and soliciting user submissions; it received 111,000 submissions from 59,000 users that generated 104 million views. These are numbers that have social media marketers salivating. TikTok, like other social media platforms, has also given rise to influencers with large followings; advertising products with the aid of these influencers is another popular method for brands to reach the coveted TikTok audience. Other TikTok advertising options include branded filters and 'brand takeovers,' or full-screen ads

(continued)

that appear when users open the app for a limited duration, such as one day.

As with many rapidly growing social networks, TikTok has pursued growth above all else, leaving it open to criticism of its handling of user data and of its ability to police its platform. TikTok was fined a record-high $5.7 million by the U.S. Federal Trade Commission for violating the Children's Online Privacy Protection Act (COPPA) and is under investigation by similar regulatory agencies in the UK for knowingly hosting content from users under age 13 and failing to seek parental consent before collecting personal information from those users. TikTok lacks any system for verifying the birthdate that new users submit and keeps all user profiles public until they change their account settings, further worrying privacy advocates.

TikTok users also report that the system for reporting malicious content is severely flawed, leading to a system of vigilante justice where users take screenshots to publicly shame bad behavior. Cybersecurity firm Check Point also discovered vulnerabilities in the app's code, allowing attackers to manipulate videos, spoof direct messages that contain malicious links, delete and upload videos without user consent, and make hidden videos public. TikTok has since fixed those vulnerabilities, but users were exposed for nearly a full year.

The company also added terms to filters to block certain searches, but critics worry that the company's censorship goes beyond obviously objectionable content and veers into stifling political descent. ByteDance, TikTok's parent company, is required to provide complete access to all user data to the Chinese government, which has well-established censorship policies. For example, during the Hong Kong protests of 2019, TikTok had almost no content relating to the protests. U.S. lawmakers have voiced concerns about the safety of the app, members of the U.S. military are forbidden from using it, and many politicians stay away from TikTok due to national security concerns. In 2019, India banned the app, citing similar concerns, but it was unblocked after TikTok pledged to invest a billion dollars in India within the next three years. TikTok has 200 million users in India, solidifying the country as one of its strongest markets.

Despite all of these concerns, ByteDance has had no trouble acquiring venture capital backing, with investments that include $3 billion from SoftBank at a company valuation of a staggering $75 billion. Though the company is not currently profitable and is focusing more on growth than adding advertising revenue streams, TikTok will eventually have to deal with the challenges of adding more ads without compromising the fun, carefree feel that its user base has come to enjoy. ByteDance may eventually be forced to spin off part of the company to avoid further regulatory action from the U.S. and other countries concerned with its data management practices.

SOURCES: "TikTok 101: A Primer for Brands," by Taylor Peterson, Marketingland.com, February 3, 2020; "Tiktok Issues New Guidelines, to Remove Content That Threatens Violence Against Individuals, Groups," Financialexpress.com, January 9, 2020; "Report Details TikTok Security Vulnerabilities in 2019," by Orion Rummler, Axios.com, January 8, 2020; "TikTok Fixes 'Serious' Security Flaws," Bbc.com, January 8, 2020; "TikTok Security Issues Exposed App Users to Hackers," by Anthony Cuthbertson, Independent.co.uk, January 8, 2020; "TikTok Continues to Refine Content Policies in Response to Various Concerns," by Andrew Hutchinson, Socialmediatoday.com, December 9, 2019; "Dissecting TikTok: How Event Marketers Can Leverage the Short-Form Video App," by Kait Shea, Eventmarketer.com, December 2, 2019; "What's Going On with TikTok?", by Shona Ghosh and Clancy Morgan, Businessinsider.com, November 20, 2019; "TikTok: Should We Trust the Chinese Social-media Video App?," bbc.com, November 7, 2018; "TikTok Continues to Grow, but New Challenges Await," by Matt Barker, Marketingweek.com, November 4, 2019; "How TikTok Holds Our Attention," by Jia Tolentino, The New Yorker, September 23, 2019; "What Is TikTok, Is the App Dangerous for Children and What Should Parents Know?," by Patrick Knox, Thesun.co.uk, September 13, 2019; "'Advertisers Ask if It's Worth the Risk': Users Flock to Troubled TikTok, but Will Brands?," by John McCarthy, Thedrum.com, July 31, 2019; "Parents' Ultimate Guide to TikTok," by Frannie Ucciferri, Commonsensemedia.com, July 27, 2018; "TikTok Under Investigation over Child Data Use," by Alex Hern, The Guardian, July 2, 2019; "TikTok Has a Predator Problem. A Network of Young Women Is Fighting Back," by Ryan Broderick, Buzzfeednews.com, June 24, 2019.

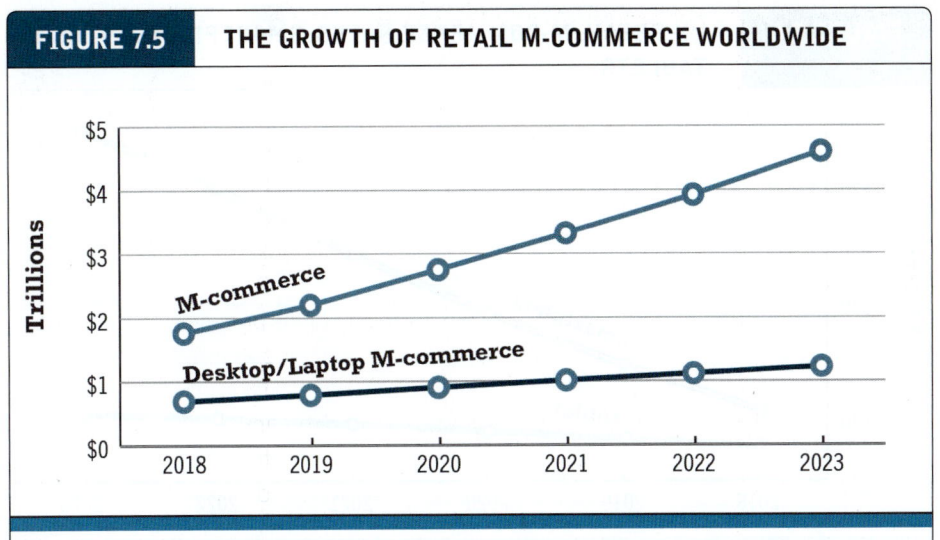

FIGURE 7.5 THE GROWTH OF RETAIL M-COMMERCE WORLDWIDE

Retail m-commerce is expected to grow to almost $4.6 trillion by 2023, accounting for almost 75% of all retail e-commerce revenues worldwide.
SOURCES: Based on data from eMarketer, Inc., 2019h, 2019i.

source of much of the growth in m-commerce. Not surprisingly, the giant in the United States is Amazon. Amazon is by far and away the leading mobile retail app, with over 180 million monthly unique visitors, reaching almost 50% of all U.S. adult smartphone users. Amazon's mobile app is the only retail e-commerce app in the top 10 most used smartphone apps. According to a recent survey, almost 60% of Amazon shoppers identified mobile devices as their primary choice for shopping on Amazon (comScore, Inc., 2019, 2018; Judge, 2017; Howland, 2017).

Increasingly, consumers are using their mobile devices to search for people, places, and things—like restaurants and deals on products they saw in a retail store. The rapid switch of consumers from desktop platforms to mobile devices is driving a surge in mobile marketing expenditures. Because search is so important for directing consumers to purchase situations, the mobile search advertising market is very important for search engines like Google. Desktop search revenues are slowing for both. Google's mobile ad business is growing rapidly, but the prices it can charge for mobile ads are far less than for desktop computer ads. The challenge facing Google and other mobile marketing firms is how to get more consumers to click on mobile ads, and how to charge marketers more for each click. And the answer lies with the consumer who decides what and when to click.

How People Actually Use Mobile Devices

If you plan a mobile marketing campaign, it's important to understand how people actually use their mobile devices (which may be different from what you do or think others do).

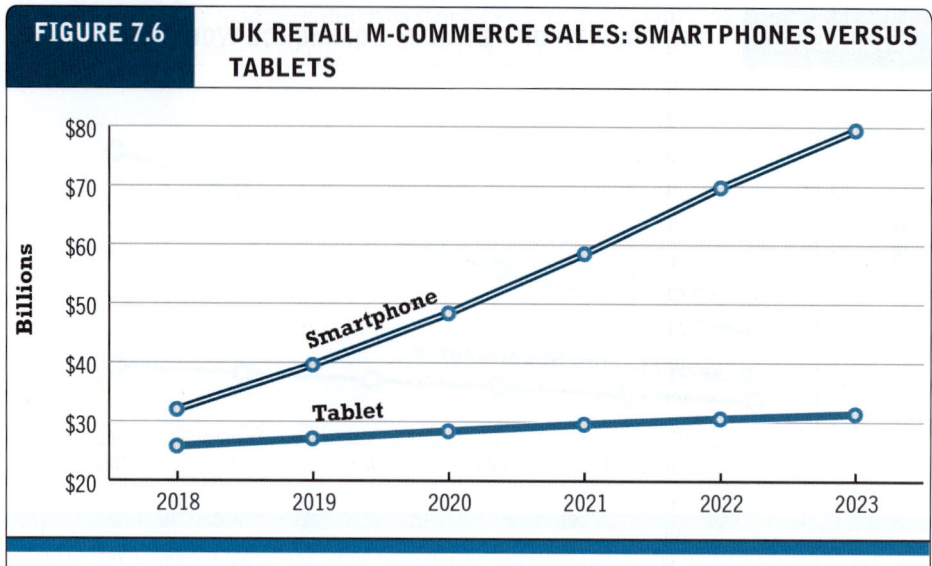

FIGURE 7.6 UK RETAIL M-COMMERCE SALES: SMARTPHONES VERSUS TABLETS

Contrary to earlier expectations, retail m-commerce sales on smartphones are increasing at a much faster rate than those on tablet computers.
SOURCES: Based on data from eMarketer, Inc., 2019j.

For instance, most of us think people use their mobile devices on the go, but according to one of the very few studies of actual mobile behavior, the majority of mobile minutes actually occur in the home. We know Americans spend over 6 and a half hours with digital media on average daily, and over three and three-quarters of these hours are spent using mobile devices—smartphones and tablets. What are they doing during that time?

Recent data show that entertainment, not shopping or buying, is the primary focus (at least in terms of time) for mobile device users. Of the over three and three-quarters hours a day that people in the United States spend using their mobile devices, over one hour is spent listening to music, almost 50 minutes on social networks, almost 40 minutes on watching video, and over 20 minutes playing mobile games (eMarketer, 2019k, 2019l).

But while mobile devices are still primarily used for entertainment, socializing, and communicating, with less time spent using them for shopping or buying, this pattern is not necessarily permanent. M-commerce is surging. Initial expectations were that tablets would provide the primary m-commerce platform, but that has not proven to be the case. As the size of smartphone screens has grown and their resolution improved, coupled with better mobile search, better location- and context-based discovery, and better mobile payment systems, the smartphone buying experience has improved, resulting in rapidly growing smartphone m-commerce sales (**Figure 7.6**).

In-App Experiences and In-App Ads

You may think that using a browser to access the Web on your smartphone or tablet is a typical mobile activity. In reality, however, mobile users in the United States spend over 85% of their total mobile time using apps and less than 15% of their time using mobile browsers. Smartphone apps in particular have been the biggest driver in the growth in digital media usage. Time spent on tablet apps is declining, in contrast, as smartphone screens increase in both size and resolution. On average, users use only about 20 apps a month on their smartphones. Almost 90% of all app time is spent on a user's top five apps. There may be millions of apps on the iOS and Android cloud servers, but just a handful are actually generating sufficient user traffic to be of interest to general advertisers. YouTube is the top smartphone app in the United States in terms of percentage of reach, followed by Facebook. Google has seven of the top 15 apps (YouTube, Google Search, Google Maps, Gmail, Google Play, Google Drive, and Google Photos), while Facebook has three (Facebook, Facebook Messenger, and Instagram) (eMarketer, Inc., 2019l, Iqbal, 2019; comScore, Inc., 2019).

The implications for marketers are quite clear: if consumers are primarily using apps rather than browsing the Web on their mobile devices, marketers need to place ads in apps where most of the action is for attracting consumers, and that means social network, game, and video apps. Second, if mobile consumers only use, on average, 20 apps, then marketers need to concentrate their marketing in these popular apps, let's say, the top 100. Niche marketers, on the other hand, can concentrate their ads in apps that support that niche. A distributor of diving equipment, for instance, could place ads in apps devoted to the diving community. There may not be many users of the app, but those who do use it are highly motivated on the topic.

Another implication for marketers is that rather than focus on mobile display ads that are difficult to read, the best ad may be an entertaining video ad that captures the viewer's attention or an ad in an app that is precisely targeted to the consumer's current activities and interests.

How the Multi-Screen Environment Changes the Marketing Funnel

Along with the growth of smartphones and tablets comes a multi-screen world: smartphones, tablets, desktops, and television. The reality, and the future, of computing devices is that consumers will be multi-platform: using desktops and laptops at work and home, and smartphones and tablets at home as well as when moving about. Television will be available all the time, both at home and on the go via tablets and smartphones. Consumer purchasing behavior changes in a multi-screen world. Consumers will often be using two or more screens at once, tweeting when watching a TV show, or moving seamlessly from a TV ad, to a mobile search for more information, to a later tablet purchase screen. Several research studies have found that 90% of multi-device users switch among screens to complete tasks, for instance, viewing an ad on TV, searching on a smartphone for the product, and then purchasing it with a tablet. Consumers move seamlessly among devices, either sequentially or simultaneously. Also, the more screens people use, the more shopping and purchasing they do. One conclusion is that the more screens consumers have, the more consumer touchpoints or marketing opportunities exist (Google, Inc., 2012).

The implications of the multi-device platform, or screen diversity environment, are that marketing needs to be designed for whatever device the consumer is using, and consistent branding across platforms will be important. Screen diversity means that one ad size, for instance, will not fit all situations, and that branding images will need to be adjusted automatically based on the device the consumer is using. From a design perspective, graphics and creative elements will appear differently depending on the screen. This is called responsive design or responsive creative design. Responsive design is a design process that allows your marketing content to resize, reformat, and reorganize itself so that it looks good on any screen. You can see responsive design in action if you look at any portal on a desktop, and then compare the screen to that same portal viewed on a smartphone or tablet. You are likely to find there are three versions of the screen, one for each platform. The requirement to find customers on multiple screens can add considerably to the cost of marketing online. Companies need to develop a presence and market not only on websites, but on mobile websites, and/or smartphone and tablet apps as well. Perhaps they may not be able to afford all three of these, and may want to choose only one. In that case, which is the best? Much depends on what the point of the marketing is. To drive sales, a website might be more effective, but to drive brand awareness and engagement, social and entertainment apps might be better.

But even beyond screen adaptability, a multi-screen world means merchants need to be on all platforms, and to be integrated across platforms, in order to send a coherent message and to create a convenient consumer platform. The marketing environment today is much more complex than placing banner ads on pages or on search engine results pages on the Web.

BASIC MOBILE MARKETING FEATURES

As billions of consumers adopt mobile devices, mobile marketing expenditures have rapidly grown and, in 2016, exceeded the amount spent on advertising on the desktop platform for the first time. This trend is expected to continue through 2023 (see **Figure 7.7**). In 2019, mobile marketing expenditures accounted for over 70% of all spending on

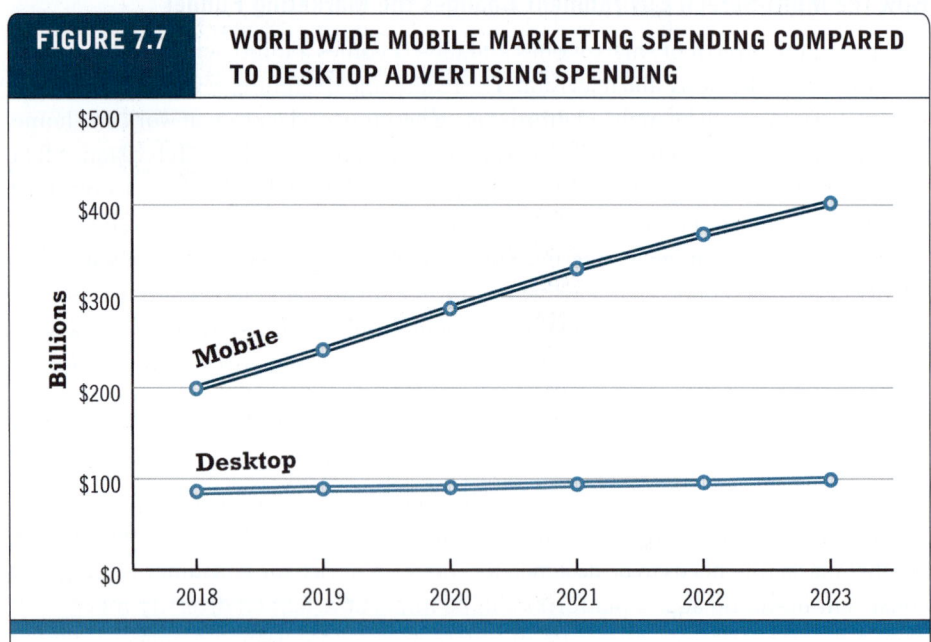

FIGURE 7.7 WORLDWIDE MOBILE MARKETING SPENDING COMPARED TO DESKTOP ADVERTISING SPENDING

Spending on mobile marketing is growing much more rapidly than spending on advertising aimed at desktop computers. By 2023, it is expected that advertisers will be spending four times as much on mobile marketing as on desktop marketing.
SOURCE: Based on data from eMarketer, Inc., 2019a, 2019m.

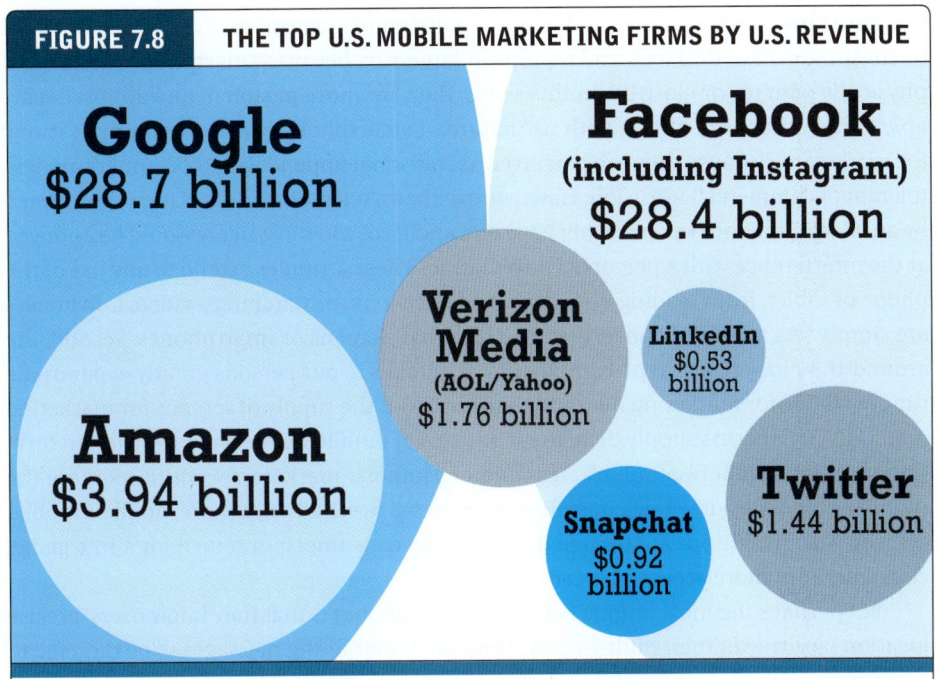

FIGURE 7.8 THE TOP U.S. MOBILE MARKETING FIRMS BY U.S. REVENUE

Mobile advertising is dominated by Google and Facebook/Instagram. Google dominates in mobile search ads, while Facebook/Instagram dominates in mobile display ads.
SOURCE: Based on data from eMarketer, Inc., 2019n.

online marketing, which is extraordinary given that smartphones appeared only 11 years ago in 2007, and tablets not until 2010. Analysts believe that if current mobile marketing growth rates continue, by 2022, spending on mobile marketing will account for over 77% of all online advertising and over three times as much spent on desktop advertising.

Mobile advertising in the United States is dominated by Google and Facebook/Instagram. Google had $28.7 billion in mobile ad revenues in 2019, constituting about 29% of the entire market, but down from 45% in 2012. On the mobile platform, Google is still the king of search, generating about $25 billion from mobile search ads in 2019, about 58% of all mobile search ad spending. Facebook is a close second in mobile ad revenue and if the ad revenues of Instagram, which is owned by Facebook, are included with Facebook's, Facebook's share of mobile ad revenue increases to over 28%. Just as Google dominates in mobile search ads, Facebook dominates in mobile display ads, accounting for over 43% of all spending on such ads if Instagram is included. Other major players in the mobile marketing marketplace include Amazon, with a 4% share, Verizon Media (Yahoo and AOL), with about a 1.8% share, and Twitter (1.5%) (eMarketer, Inc., 2019o) (see **Figure 7.8**).

The Technology: Basic Mobile Device Features

Everybody knows the capabilities of smartphones and tablets. But what is it about mobile platforms that makes them any different from desktops? What features make them especially suitable for marketing?

For starters, smartphones today play a much more central role in the personal life of consumers than desktops and laptops in large part because smartphones are always physically with us, or close by. In this sense, they are more personal, and almost "wearable." The "always on, always with us" nature of smartphones has several implications for marketers. Because they are perceived as "personal appendages," consumers are less tolerant of commercial intrusion. Have you ever had a telephone conversation interrupted by an advertisement? You probably have not, and if so, you most likely would be annoyed at the interference with a personal conversation. These attitudes extend to any use of the phone or tablet, from reading e-mail, visiting Facebook, or watching a video. Consumers are simply less tolerant of advertising on the small screens of smartphones. Second, the around-the-clock physical proximity of smartphones to our persons greatly expands the time available for marketing materials and increases the supply of screens for marketing materials. This excess supply decreases the price of mobile marketing messages. In turn, there is a tension between marketers and consumers: marketers want to increase the number of mobile ads, while consumers want to see fewer ads, not more, on their mobile devices. Ads inside apps are treated differently by consumers: in return for a free game, consumers are more accepting of ads.

But perhaps the most unique feature of smartphones is that they know users' precise location by virtue of their built-in GPS. This allows marketing messages to be targeted to consumers on the basis of their location, and supports the introduction of location-based marketing and local marketing (described in Section 7.4). While websites may know a desktop's general location, it is a very imprecise fix, and the position of the desktop does not change as the user moves about. **Table 7.13** summarizes the features of mobile devices that marketers can leverage.

TABLE 7.13	FEATURES OF MOBILE DEVICES
FEATURE	DESCRIPTION
Personal communicator and organizer	Telephone plus calendars and clocks to coordinate life on a personal scale.
Screen size and resolution	Resolution of both tablets and phones is high enough to support vibrant graphics and video.
GPS location	Self-locating GPS capability.
Web browser	Standard browsers will operate all websites and applications.
Apps	Over a million specialized applications running in native code and extending the functionality of mobile devices.
Ultraportable and personal	Fits into a pocket, or a briefcase for tablets, able to be used anywhere and on the go.
Multimedia capable: video, audio, text	Fully capable of displaying all common media from video to text and sound.
Touch/haptic technology	Enhances touch screens by providing feedback in the form of vibration, force, or motion.

FIGURE 7.9 U.S. MOBILE AD SPENDING BY FORMAT

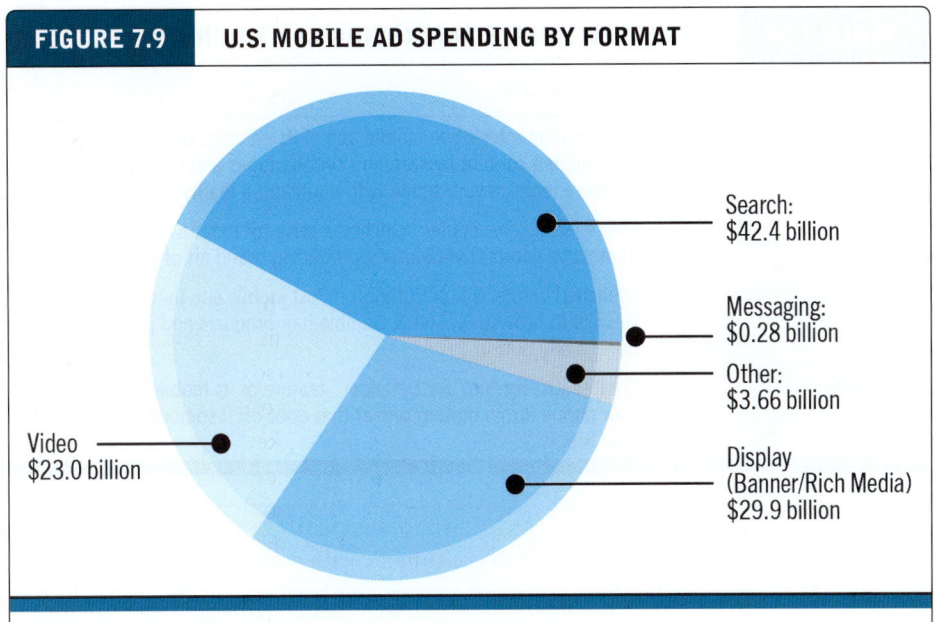

Search engine advertising is still the most popular mobile marketing format.
SOURCE: Based on data from eMarketer, Inc., 2019p.

MOBILE MARKETING TOOLS: AD FORMATS

Unlike social marketing, mobile marketing does not require much of a new marketing vocabulary. All the marketing formats available on the desktop are also available on mobile devices. With few exceptions, mobile marketing is very much like desktop marketing—except it is smaller. The major marketing opportunities in mobile marketing are search ads, display ads, videos, and rich media, messaging (SMS/MMS/PPS), and some other familiar formats like e-mail, classified, and lead generation. **Figure 7.9** illustrates the relative size of U.S. mobile marketing expenditures by format. The marketing formats on mobile devices are search ads, display (banners, rich media, and sponsorships), video, text/video messaging, and other (including e-mail, classifieds, and lead generation).

In 2019, search engine advertising continued to be the most popular mobile marketing format in the United States, accounting for 43% of all mobile ad spending, not surprising given that search is the second most common smartphone application (after voice and text communication). Search engine ads can be further optimized for the mobile platform by showing ads based on the physical location of the user. Display ads (banner ads, rich media, and sponsorships) are the second leading ad format, accounting for about 30% of mobile ad spending. Display ads can be served as a part of a mobile website or inside apps and games. Ad networks such as Google's AdMob, Facebook, Twitter's MoPub, Verizon Media, and InMobi (see the opening case in Chapter 6) are some of the largest providers of mobile display advertising. Video ads are about 23% of mobile marketing, and are a fast growing segment because of their very high click rates. Most desktop video ads can be resized for use on mobile phones and tablets. Mobile messaging

TABLE 7.14 SELECTED MOBILE MARKETING CAMPAIGNS

COMPANY	CAMPAIGN
Ikea	Launched an interactive mobile app of its catalog, allowing users to view hidden content by scanning certain pages and to test how furniture looks in your home with augmented reality.
Just for Men	Men's facial care retailer launched a series of mobile ads with interactive sports trivia quizzes, producing brand lift of 24%.
Target	Launched banner ad on Huffington Post mobile site that enabled viewers to browse Procter & Gamble hair products and purchase using a buy button.
McDonald's	Created just-for-fun "Fry Defender" feature of its mobile apps, turning your phone into a motion sensor that goes off if someone approaches your fries.

generally involves SMS text messaging to consumers, with coupons or flash marketing messages. Messaging can be effective for local advertising because consumers can be sent messages and coupons as they pass by or visit locations (see Section 7.4).

Social networks such as Facebook, Twitter, and Pinterest have generally brought desktop advertising techniques over to the mobile platform, with some alterations of the interface for use on small-screen smartphones. In the process, social networks have brought real innovation to the mobile marketing experience, including News Feed posts on Facebook and Promoted Tweets in Twitter. **Table 7.14** provides selected examples of mobile marketing campaigns and techniques used by several well-known firms.

Mobile marketing is uniquely suited for branding purposes, raising awareness through the use of video and rich interactive media such as games. Read the *Insight on Business* case, *Mobile Marketing Revs Up with 3D and Augmented Reality*, for a further look.

STARTING A MOBILE MARKETING CAMPAIGN

As with all marketing campaigns, start by identifying your objectives and understanding just how a mobile marketing campaign might help your firm. Are you a new, unknown startup seeking to develop a brand image, or an already existing brand looking to strengthen your presence and sell products? Is there something about your products that makes them especially attractive to a mobile audience? For instance, if you sell to local customers walking by your shop, then you might want to use the GPS capabilities of smartphones to target consumers who are nearby.

Next, consider the target demographic for your campaign and products. The most active purchasers on mobile devices are men, and they are more likely to buy consumer electronics equipment and digital content. Women are more likely to cash in coupons and respond to flash sales and deals. Younger consumers are more likely to research products and price on mobile devices, and more likely to share experiences using social media. Mobile shoppers and buyers are more affluent than the online population in general. These demographics are averages, and mobile marketing campaigns do not need to restrict themselves to these averages. Find out where your mobile customers are

INSIGHT ON BUSINESS

MOBILE MARKETING REVS UP WITH 3D AND AUGMENTED REALITY

The mobile platform is the dominant marketing platform today, driven by the advent of smartphones. The use of mobile devices to actually purchase products or services online (as opposed to just shopping and browsing online) has grown significantly, and local businesses are taking advantage of the passive GPS capability of smartphones to create location-based marketing for potential customers who are physically close by. But mobile marketing is also good for introducing new products and building brand recognition, with sales taking place elsewhere and offline. Newer advertising formats such as 3D ads, augmented reality (AR) ads, and virtual reality (VR) ads are redefining advertising in the smartphone era.

3D advertising, which uses video and other interactive features that take advantage of the capabilities of modern mobile devices, is one increasingly popular method of advertising for companies that have a big advertising budget. Honda's campaign for its Odyssey minivan, created in partnership with mobile advertising firm Amobee, owned by Singapore-based telecommunications firm Singtel, is a good example of 3D advertising in action. Honda's goal was to simulate the experience of seeing the car in person using a three-dimensional virtual showroom. The ad can be accessed in either 3D or VR formats. The 3D ad allows viewers to rotate the image of the vehicle using the touch screen, pick between a variety of colors, and view additional information about each vehicle by selecting on-screen icons. The VR ad allows consumers to view a virtual representation of the vehicle, simulating its actual appearance. Because these types of ad use many innate features of smartphones, they actually take up less bandwidth than similar HTML5 rich media ads.

Amobee keeps track of engagement with its advertisements in real time, ensuring that consumers remain anonymous but measuring how much time different demographics of users engage with individual elements of each ad. Amobee has an in-house data management platform with over 1 million profiles featuring customer information such as gender, age, location, and interests. This enables Amobee to accurately measure the effectiveness of its advertising campaigns. In this case, Honda saw a 84% increase in overall ad engagement rate.

AR advertising is another fast-growing field that has mobile advertisers excited. If you use Snapchat, chances are good that you've seen the Dancing Hot Dog, which has been viewed over 2 billion times by Snapchat users. The famous frankfurter is the first and most prominent example of what Snapchat calls a 3D World Lens, or an image overlaid on your phone screen while using the phone's camera. The virtual objects are nonetheless fully three-dimensional, meaning you can walk around them and view them from any angle. Advertisers are understandably excited about the possibility of using this new format to bring their products or characters to life in Snapchat users' real world environments in a way that doesn't feel like advertising.

BMW created an AR version of its X2 vehicle for Snapchat users, allowing users to walk around the car and see it in perfect detail. By the middle of 2019, Snapchat users had

(continued)

created over 400,000 Lenses, playing with them over 15 billion times. Hundreds of companies have run World Lens advertisements to date, including Nike, Foot Locker, Hershey's, and Budweiser, which released a Lens during the Super Bowl consisting of its iconic Clydesdale horse kicking a football. Snapchat also offers software called Lens Studio, which allows companies to create their own Lenses without Snapchat's involvement. Snapchat has partnered with Oracle to help it target these advertisements using third-party data. Using Oracle user profiles created using demographic information, user purchases, and other information, advertisers have the option to run World Lens ads nationally or for smaller groups targeted by age, gender, or interest. Not to be outdone, Facebook has entered the fray with its own offering, Facebook AR Studio. While Snapchat is firmly established in the AR advertising space, Michael Kors released a Facebook ad that allows users to virtually try on sunglasses, while Sephora did the same for cosmetics.

These types of ads are currently available mostly to bigger brands due to their prohibitive cost, which can reach the hundreds of thousands of dollars for a month-long campaign. However, Lens Studio and Facebook AR Studio should help to democratize the process of creating these ads, and AR advertising revenue is expected to reach almost $9 billion by 2023, up from $453 million in 2018. Retail brands with physical products are great fits for 3D and AR ads, while companies offering services such as financial institutions may never be interested. Currently, these ads offer excellent engagement rates, but some of that may be due to novelty; when they become more commonplace, they may also be slightly less effective. Still, the trend toward 3D and AR advertising is undeniable. One industry survey showed that most of consumers already say that AR is changing how and where they shop and that AR advertising makes shopping more fun. Snapchat ads now offer buttons that drive users to install apps, purchase products, or watch further media about a product. Retailers such as snack brand Takis have had success with ad campaigns consisting of 3D display ads, and 360-degree AR games. Apple and Google are also likely to enter this space shortly. The advertising industry may be in the midst of a paradigm shift. 3D and AR advertising have the potential to leave traditional advertising behind, the way mobile devices have done to the desktop.

SOURCES: "AR Advertising Revenue Worldwide, 2018 & 2023," eMarketer.com, August 22, 2019; "Snap Partner Summit/The Future of Lenses," Snap.com, April 4, 2019; "Takis Scores with 3D and 360-Degree VR Video Ad Campaign," by Robert Williams, Mobilemarketer.com, August 23, 2018; "It's Time for Ad Formats to Evolve and Keep Pace with Changing Consumer Demands," by Jeff Lucas, Adweek.com, July 24, 2018; "Introducing New Ways to Inspire Holiday Shoppers with Video," Facebook.com, July 10, 2018; "Snapchat's Programmatic Augmented Reality Ads Are Gaining Traction," by Ilyse Liffreing, Digiday.com, May 16, 2018; "Snapchat's Betting Its Future on Augmented Reality Ads—Here Are All the Different Types," by Tanya Dua, Businessinsider.com, April 27, 2018; "AR and 3D Can Help Media Publishers in Their Battle Against Facebook and Snap," by Ara Parikh, Venturebeat.com, April 12, 2018; "3D Ads: How You Can Advertise in 3D and Up Engagement," Omnivirt.com, February 25, 2018; "Snapchat's Lens Studio App Opens Augmented-Reality Format to Everyone, Including Self-Serve Advertisers," by Tim Peterson, Marketingland.com, December 14, 2017; "BMW Test Drives Snapchat Lenses in First 3D Car Ad," by Garett Sloane, Adage.com, November 22, 2017; "Honda and RPA Drive Innovation with First to Market Opportunity, Creating Industry-First Sharable and Scalable Virtual Reality Campaign," Amobee.com, accessed 2018; "Snapchat's World Lenses Are Just the Tip of the AR Advertising Iceberg," by Tommy Palladino, Next.reality.news, September 29, 2017; "Sponsored Snapchat World Lenses Bring Brand Characters to Augmented Reality," by Hillary Grigonis, Digitaltrends.com, September 29, 2017; "IronSource Launches 'World's First' AR Ads for Mobile Games," by Stewart Rogers, Venturebeat.com, September 28, 2017; "ARAD Helps Developers Get Ads in Their Augmented Reality Apps," by Matthew Lynley, Techcrunch.com, September 17, 2017; "What Snapchat's Dancing Hot Dog Means for the Future of AR," by Garett Sloane, Adage.com, July 24, 2017.

congregating. Are your mobile customers likely to be using apps, and if so, what are they? Are your customers likely to be on Facebook or use Twitter? Or are your customers most likely to find you on a Google mobile search page?

Finally, consider the marketspace where you hope to succeed. What are your competitors doing on the mobile platform? Is their presence effective? Where do they place their marketing efforts: display ads on web portals, or display ads in Google search results? Or can they be found as in-app ads? What apps are they advertising in? How are they represented on Facebook Mobile? Do they also have a Twitter and/or Pinterest brand page? Do your competitors have an app that users can easily download? You'll want to be able to meet your competitors on each of the platforms they have adopted. Once you've developed an initial vision for your marketing campaign, you can develop a timeline and an action plan of how to meet the milestones identified in your timeline.

Once you have envisioned your marketing campaign and identified your market, it is time to start implementing your mobile campaign. Here are some steps to follow:

- Develop a mobile website so mobile consumers can see and buy your products. Make your mobile website social by including links to Facebook, Twitter, Pinterest, and other social networks.
- Develop a Facebook brand page so your social and mobile marketing efforts are integrated.
- Develop a Twitter brand page so customers can follow your posts.
- If you already use a display advertising program like Google's AdWords or a Facebook display ad account, you can create a new campaign using the same ads designed specifically for mobile platforms.
- Consider opening an AdMob account, in part because ad networks can publish and track your ads on multiple platforms simultaneously.
- Develop marketing content that is aimed specifically at the mobile user, with videos and high levels of interactivity designed for the mobile screen.
- Measure and manage your campaign. Google's AdWords, along with many other ad networks, will host and manage your mobile campaigns. In addition, they can provide you with a host of campaign measures that will allow you to see which mobile ads and techniques are attracting the most followers, comments, and social activity concerning your brand. With this basic data you can start to manage the mobile marketing campaign by reducing expenditures on ads that do not work and increasing the budget of ads that do work.

MEASURING MOBILE MARKETING RESULTS

There are many different mobile marketing objectives, and therefore different types of mobile marketing campaigns. Some campaigns are sales-oriented, based on display and search ads, offering coupons or discounts, and taking users directly to a website where they can buy something. Measuring the results of these mobile campaigns follows similar campaigns launched on desktops. Other campaigns focus on branding, where the objective is to engage consumers in a conversation, acquire them as fans, and spread

512 CHAPTER 7 Social, Mobile, and Local Marketing

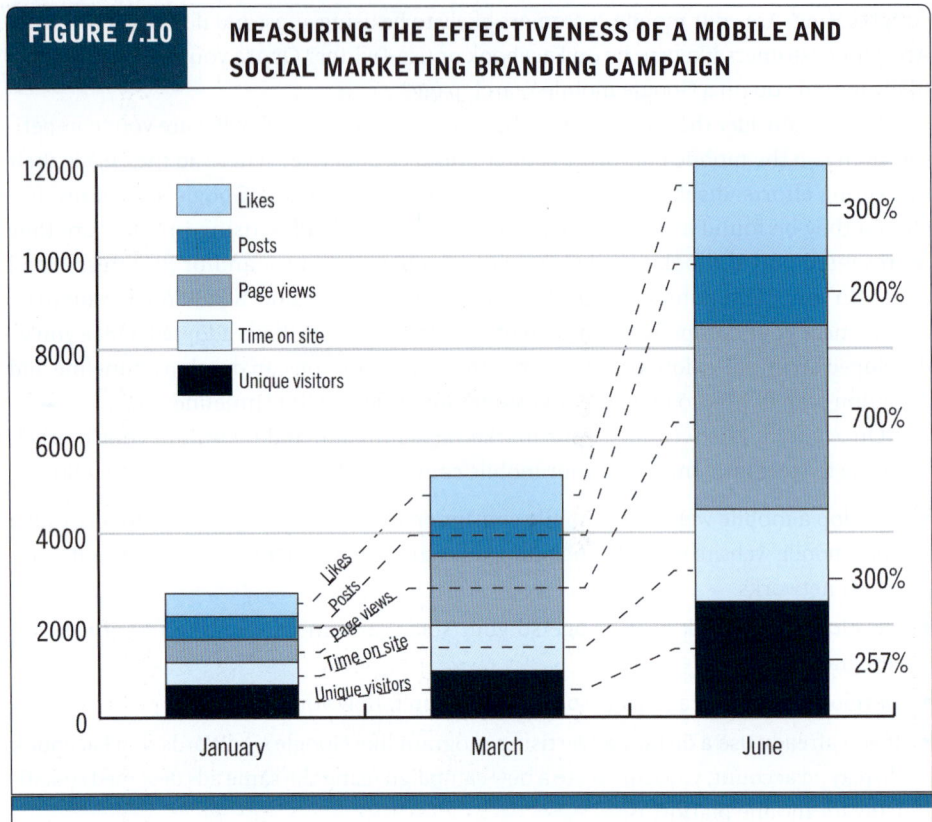

The effectiveness of a branding campaign utilizing the mobile platform and social marketing can be measured by examining the number of Likes, posts, page views, time on site, and unique visitors.

the word among their friends. You can use the framework from Figure 7.4 on page 436 to measure the results of these campaigns. The key dimensions to measure for mobile social campaigns are fan acquisition, engagement, amplification, community, brand strength (center of conversation), and sales.

Figure 7.10 illustrates how a brand-oriented marketing campaign utilizing the mobile platform and social marketing might present its effectiveness measures over a six-month period. In a branding campaign, the object is not so much sales as it is strengthening consumers' engagement with the brand. In the example provided in Figure 7.10, acquiring fans is measured by the number of unique visitors. Here you can see that over six months, visitors have more than doubled. Engagement is reflected in the time on-site (in minutes); amplification is measured by the number of Likes, and this has expanded threefold. Community is measured by the number of posts, suggesting fans are actively engaging with one another and the brand. Posts have also doubled in the period. Brand strength is best summarized in this figure as the composite picture of fan acquisition, engagement, amplification, and community measures. Measuring the impacts of this mobile campaign on ultimate sales requires going a step further and measuring which sales can be attributed to this mobile campaign.

7.4 LOCAL AND LOCATION-BASED MOBILE MARKETING

Location-based marketing is one of the fastest growing segments of the digital marketing universe. **Location-based marketing** targets marketing messages to users based on their location. Generally, location-based marketing involves marketing of location-based services. **Location-based services** involve providing services to users based on their location. Examples of location-based services are: personal navigation (How do I get there?), point-of-interest (What's that?), reviews (What's the best restaurant in the neighborhood?), friend-finder (Where are you? Where's the crowd?), and family-tracker services (Where is my child?). There is a connection, of course: the more people use their mobile devices to search for and obtain local services, the more opportunities there are for marketers to target consumers with messages at just the right moment, at just the right location, and in just the right way—not too pushy and annoying, but in a way to improve the consumer experience at the moment of local shopping and buying. This is the ideal in any event. Location-based marketing can take place on a desktop as well because browsers and marketers know your approximate location. But in this section we focus primarily on location-based mobile marketing, which is where the greatest growth and opportunities lie.

Experience and market research suggest that consumers want local ads, offers, information, and content. Consumers have a high likelihood of acting on local ads and purchasing the products and services offered. Because it has evolved so rapidly in the last five years, experience and research with respect to location-based marketing is a work in progress with many different platforms, providers, and techniques. Measures of effectiveness and returns on investment are being developed.

location-based marketing
targets marketing messages to users based on their location

location-based services
involve providing services to users based on their location

THE GROWTH OF LOCAL MARKETING

Prior to the release of Google Maps in 2005, nearly all local advertising was nondigital and provided by local newspapers, radio and television stations, local yellow pages, and billboards. Of course, some was digital, involving the websites of local merchants. In 2019, total media ad spending in the United States was about $240 billion, and approximately $149 billion of this is local media spending by both national and local brands. An estimated 40% of this local advertising (about $60 billion) involves truly local firms like restaurants, grocery stores, theaters, and shoe stores marketing to their local audience. The remaining 60% of local media marketing involves large national firms marketing to local audiences, such as an ad for Coca-Cola in a local newspaper or websites created for local auto dealers by national firms. Of the $149 billion of local media spending, about 40% ($60 billion) was spent on online marketing, and this amount is expected to grow to $67 billion by 2020 (eMarketer, Inc., 2019q; BIA Advisory Services, 2019).

After the introduction of Google Maps, online local marketing began to rapidly expand. Google Maps on desktop computers enabled the targeting of ads to users based on a general sense of their IP address and enabled merchants to display ads to users based on the general location of potential customers, usually within a several square-mile radius. IP addresses can be used to identify a city, and a neighborhood within the city, but not a zip code, street, or building. Google Maps helped users answer the question "Where can I find an Italian restaurant" in a city or section of a city from their desktop. The arrival of smartphones in 2007, and Google's mobile Maps app, took this one step further. The GPS receivers in second-generation smartphones introduced in 2008 (Apple's 3G iPhone), along with other techniques, meant that a user's location (latitude and longitude) could be fairly well known by cell phone manufacturers, marketers, service providers, and carriers like AT&T and Verizon. These developments opened an entirely new growth path for local online advertising that heretofore had been confined to the desktop. In this new world, a local food market could shout out to mobile phone users as they walked by the store, offering discounts to responders, and users in turn could search for specific retail stores nearby, even checking their inventory before walking into the store.

THE GROWTH OF LOCATION-BASED (LOCAL) MOBILE MARKETING

Location-based (local) mobile marketing is currently a small part of the online marketing environment, but it is expected to triple over the next 5 years. **Figure 7.11** helps put the location-based mobile market in perspective. In 2019, total spending on online marketing was about $129 billion and local online marketing was a healthy and surprisingly large $60 billion. The part of local online that is location-based mobile is expected to generate an estimated $27 billion.

The ad formats used in local mobile marketing are familiar—search ads, display, native/social, videos, and SMS text messages. Search ads displayed as a part of user search results comprise the largest location-based mobile ad format. The local mobile search market is dominated by Google. Social/native ads are the second largest format. Display

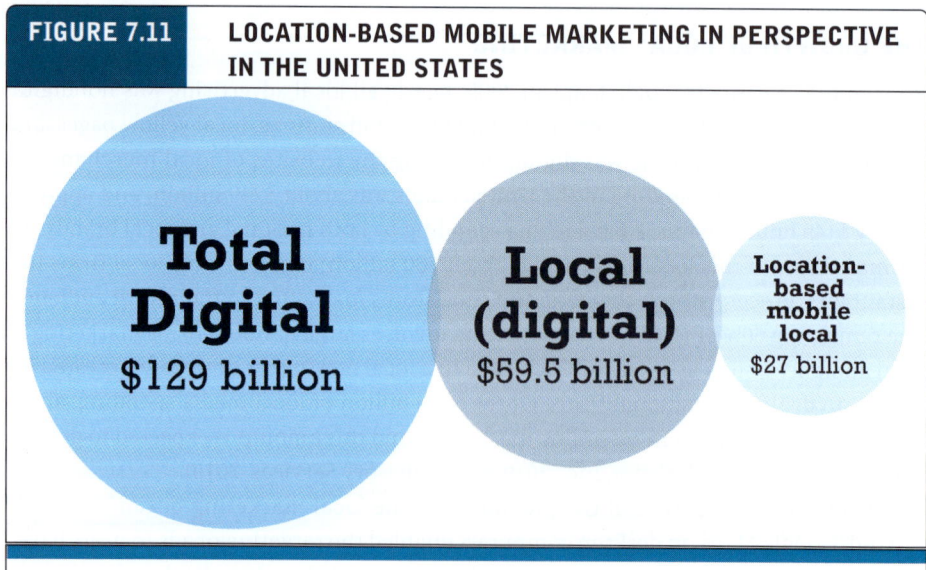

FIGURE 7.11 LOCATION-BASED MOBILE MARKETING IN PERSPECTIVE IN THE UNITED STATES

Local online marketing in the United States accounted for about $59.5 billion in marketing expenditures in 2019, with location-based mobile expected to account for about $27 billion of that amount.
SOURCES: Based on data from eMarketer, Inc., 2019r; BIA Advisory Services, 2019.

ads are the third largest format. Here the main players are Facebook and Google. Together, Google and Facebook account for the vast majority of location-based mobile marketing.

LOCATION-BASED MARKETING PLATFORMS

The key players in location-based mobile marketing are the same giants who dominate the mobile marketing environment described in a previous section, namely, Google, Facebook, Verizon Media (Yahoo/AOL) Twitter, YP (formerly Yellow Pages), and Pandora. Google is clearly the leading location-based marketer largely because of its widely used Google Maps app on smartphones. When a consumer searches for a location on Google Maps, it is an ideal marketing moment to pop an ad before the consumer's eyes. Google My Business is a simple but effective service that provides short business profiles when users search for a specific business. Google's Android operating system has location functionality built into the system, and Google apps, like Google Maps, continuously update the user's location. Google purchased a mobile advertising firm called AdMob in 2009 and claims to be the world's largest mobile advertising firm for both Android and Apple's iOS operating systems. App developers use AdMob to provide their apps with consumer and user location information. Google also sells location information to independent marketing firms. Marketing firms use AdMob to develop full-screen rich media ads. Google's main revenue stream comes from its AdWords service, where marketers bid for keywords on Google's search engine. AdWords used to be the same whether displayed on a desktop computer or a mobile device. Google has upgraded its AdWords service to optimize ads for user contexts and devices, and to provide management of campaigns across all mobile and desktop devices. For instance, if a customer searches for "pizza" on a desktop computer from work at 1 PM, he or she would be shown nearby restaurants and a quick order form. If the customer searched for "pizza" at 8 PM on a smartphone within a half-mile of a pizza restaurant, he or she might be shown a click-to-call phone number and directions to the restaurant. Pizza restaurants pay Google for the chance to show up in these searches.

Google has an advantage in the location-based market: it has developed extensive maps of Wi-Fi networks throughout the world, allowing it to develop much more precise location information than competitors.

LOCATION-BASED MOBILE MARKETING: THE TECHNOLOGIES

Location-based services and marketing require marketers and local service providers to have a fairly precise idea of where consumer mobile devices are located. There are two general types of location-based marketing techniques: geo-aware and proximity marketing. **Geo-aware** techniques identify the location of a user's device and then target marketing to the device, recommending actions within reach (which, in itself, requires the marketer to know where relevant things like stores are located). For instance, a marketer may target smartphones within several square city blocks to alert them to available offers from participating merchants. **Proximity marketing** techniques identify a perimeter around a physical location, and then target ads to users within that perimeter, recommending actions possible within the fenced-in area (geo-fencing). The perimeter can be from hundreds of feet (in urban areas) to several miles (in suburban locations). For instance, if users walk into the geo-fenced perimeter of a store, restaurant, or retail shop,

geo-aware
techniques that identify the location of a user's device and then target marketing to the device

proximity marketing
techniques that identify a perimeter around a physical location, and then target ads to users within that perimeter, recommending actions possible within the fenced-in area

they will receive ads from these businesses. Both of these techniques utilize the same locating technologies.

Ad networks, local-mobile marketing firms, providers of devices and services like Google and Apple, as well as phone companies use several methods for locating mobile devices, none of which are perfect, and all of which have varying degrees of accuracy. **Table 7.15** describes the major locating technologies used to enable location-based services and marketing.

GPS (Global Positioning System) location is the most accurate positioning method in theory. In practice, the signal can be weak in urban areas, nonexistent inside buildings, signals can be deflected, and it can take a long time (30–60 seconds) for the device to acquire the signal and calculate a position. When a clear signal is obtained, GPS can be accurate to within 3–10 meters under ideal conditions, but more frequently, a cell phone's GPS is accurate only to within 50 meters—half a football field. Also, users have to activate the feature, and many do not for privacy reasons. Assisted GPS (A-GPS) supplements GPS information with other information from the phone network to speed up acquisition. Nearly all smartphones use A-GPS. In Apple's iOS, users can decide whether to turn Location Services on or off. When turned on, the iOS uses GPS, cellular, and Wi-Fi networks to determine the user's approximate location to within 10 meters (30 feet) although in many situations accuracy can be much higher, around 15 feet. The user's iPhone continuously reports its position to Apple servers.

Cell tower location is used by wireless telephone carriers to track the location of their devices, which is required to complete phone calls as devices pass from the range of one tower into the range of another. Cell tower location is also the basis of the wireless

TABLE 7.15	MAJOR LOCATING TECHNOLOGIES
TECHNOLOGY	DESCRIPTION
GPS	The user's device downloads GPS data from a GPS satellite. First introduced with the Apple 3G iPhone in 2008. Today, cellphones are required to broadcast their GPS location for emergency assistance purposes.
Wi-Fi	Estimates user's location within a radius of a known Wi-Fi access point.
Bluetooth low energy (BLE)	Used by Apple in iBeacon. Uses less battery power than traditional Bluetooth or GPS and more accurate than targeting through Wi-Fi triangulation.
Geo-search	Uses location information based on the user's search queries.
Cell tower	AT&T, Verizon, and other carriers are in constant contact with their devices, which allows approximation of location by triangulation and refinement of the unit's GPS location. Wireless carriers use a cell phone's MAC address to identify the phone and the location.
Sign in/registration	Estimates users' location when they self-identify their location using sign-in services or social network posts.

emergency response system in the United States. The FCC's wireless Enhanced 9-1-1 (E9-1-1) rules require wireless carriers to track cellphone locations whether or not the user has turned on location services in order to assist emergency responders in locating users who make 911 calls.

Wi-Fi location is used in conjunction with GPS signals to more accurately locate a user based on the known location of Wi-Fi transmitters, which are fairly ubiquitous in urban and suburban locations. Apple, Google, and other mobile service providers have developed global databases of wireless access points simply by driving cars around urban areas in much of the world. Google uses Street View cars to build a global database of wireless access points and their geographic location. Android applications can use this database to determine the approximate location of individuals based on the Wi-Fi networks detected by their mobile devices. All Wi-Fi devices continuously monitor the presence of local Wi-Fi networks, and mobile devices report back this data to Apple and Microsoft, along with other device manufacturers, who use similar methods. The goal of these technologies is to provide consumers and marketers with "micro-location data" accurate to within a few feet to support truly real-time, accurate, local marketing at the personal level. For instance, if you are looking at a rack of dress shirts in a retail store, an accurate positioning system could detect this and direct you to appropriate accessories like socks and ties on surrounding shelves.

WHY IS LOCATION-BASED MOBILE MARKETING ATTRACTIVE TO MARKETERS?

Consumers who seek information about local businesses using mobile devices are much more active and ready to purchase than desktop users. In part this is because desktop searchers for local information are not in as close proximity to merchants as are mobile searchers. A Google survey found that over 80% of U.S. consumers use smartphones and tablet computers to conduct local searches on search engines for a variety of local information such as business hours, local store addresses and directions, and availability of products at local stores. The survey found that consumers search for local information through the purchase process, and 50% of smartphone users visited a store within a day of their local search, and 18% made a purchase within a day. The survey also found that over 60% of smartphone users wanted ads customized both to their city/zip code and to their immediate surroundings (Google, 2014). As a result, almost 80% of U.S. marketing professionals recently surveyed indicated that they planned to increase their use of location data over the next two years, with the amount spent on location-based mobile advertising expected to almost double between 2018 and 2022 (eMarketer, Inc., 2018).

LOCATION-BASED MARKETING TOOLS

Location-based digital marketing, like social marketing, presents students of digital marketing with a confusing array of new services, platforms, and firms that provide these services. While some local-based marketing techniques, like placing ads on Google's AdSense platform aimed at mobile customers, are relatively easy to establish for the small business owner, others require the help of mobile marketing provider firms.

A New Lexicon: Location-Based Digital Marketing Features

Location-based services involve providing services to users based on their location. Examples include personal navigation, point-of-interest, reviews, friend-finder, and family-tracker services. **Table 7.16** describes how some of these features can be used for marketing.

TABLE 7.16	LOCATION-BASED MARKETING TOOLS AND CAMPAIGNS
LOCATION-BASED MARKETING TOOLS	**DESCRIPTION**
Geo-social-based services marketing	Users share their location with friends. Can be used for check-in services like Foursquare; friend finders; transportation services.
Location-based services marketing	Provides services to consumers looking for local services and products.
Mobile-local social network marketing based on users' location	Facebook expands local offerings of deals by local firms, display ads using News Feed. Facebook Marketplace, which enables people to easily buy and sell within their local communities, in 2016.
	Upgraded Foursquare app Swarm focuses on social updates from specific locations and sending recommendations and deals.
	Social network monitoring: sends messages within an app based on mentions of interest in products in Facebook and Twitter posts. MomentFeed allows marketers to listen to social chatter on social networks by location, then target consumers with geo-specific ads. Used by Pizza Hut, Starbucks, and local restaurants.
	Intent marketing: scanning social networks for indications of real-time consumer interest in specific products. H&M partnered with LocalResponse to promote clothing inspired by the movie *Girl With the Dragon Tattoo*.
Proximity marketing	Send messages to consumers in the area of a store or outlet to generate sales using a virtual fence around a retail location (could also be an airport, train station, or arena). Generally opt in. Whole Foods places geofences around its stores to target ads and offers to mobile users passing by.
In-store messaging	Messaging consumers while entering or browsing in a store.
	Retailers collect, analyze, and respond to customers' real-time shopping behavior. Macy's, Lord & Taylor, and Target use beacon marketing to greet customizers and offer deals.
Location-based app messaging	PayPal's mobile app detects customers near a store that offers PayPal payment options and entices them with offers to visit.

Proximity Marketing with Beacons

While all location-based marketing is in some sense proximity marketing, Apple's introduction of iBeacon in 2013 with its iOS 7 made it possible for retail store retailers to communicate directly and quite precisely with customers as they passed within a few feet of in-store beacons. There are many close proximity technologies, such as QR codes, Wi-Fi, and NFC (Near Field Communication), but each has drawbacks in terms of precision, cost, and widespread availability. Apple's iBeacon uses a technology called Bluetooth Low Energy (BLE). Android phones also have this capability. BLE is inexpensive to implement, and uses much less power than traditional Bluetooth. Unlike QR codes, BLE has a two-way, push-pull communication capability. Using QR codes, consumers need to show the code to a QR scanner, and then they see information on a product. With iBeacon, consumers can be contacted as soon as they walk into a store and exposed to special offers, and then, when browsing the store, contacted as they pass specific areas, like the jewelry department. This all takes place automatically on the user's iPhone. Consumers can respond to these messages as well. For retailers, in-store beacon marketing is aimed at four objectives. The customer can be engaged immediately on entry to the store, and then accompanied electronically from one area to another, somewhat similar to how luxury retail stores assign a salesperson to high-end consumers. Second, beacons can be used to stimulate loyalty programs. Consumers who buy often can be noticed upon entering the store. Third, retailers can engage in flash sales, instant discounts, and other impulse marketing programs inside their physical stores. Finally, beacons can be used silently, not pushing offers or goods, but instead just gathering data directly about in-store consumer behavior.

Currently, beacon technology, essentially in-store Bluetooth devices that can communicate with user smartphones entering the store, consists of stand-alone apps, each following different standards. But several technology firms are trying to build beacon capabilities into their popular platforms. In 2015, Google announced its Eddystone open-source standard that can work with iOS or Android. Advertisers are beginning to take advantage of this technology. For example, Google has certified a proximity marketing company Proxama to provide beacon services based on Eddystone to its customers. One application involves alerting consumers to prizes, offers, and apps when they are near a beacon located near tourist attractions and transportation hubs. In 2016, Google began working on making it possible for people to use beacons without having to first download an app, and in 2017 piloted Project Beacon, sending free beacons to businesses who have used Google's advertising services and which it believed would benefit from location marketing (Haines, 2018). Facebook has rolled out Place Tips, offering free Bluetooth devices to merchants. When users are recognized as being close to a merchant, Facebook posts to their News Feed suggesting they visit the merchant or buy a product.

In 2014, after a successful test of iBeacon at its flagship stores in San Francisco and New York, Macy's rolled out 4,000 iBeacon installations to its stores nationwide. Using an app from Shopkick (a marketing firm) called shopBeacon, Macy's customers who have downloaded the app receive notifications to open the app when they enter a Macy's store. Customers receive promotions, deals, and discounts. The hope is that by using proximity marketing, retail stores will be able to attract more consumers to their stores, and increase purchases from those who come to their stores. Other adopters of beacon technology include Rite Aid, which has installed the techology at more than 4,500 of its U.S. stores, Target, Urban Outfitters, American Eagle Outfitters, Lord & Taylor, and Sephora.

However, despite the claims of proponents of beacon marketing, beacon technology has not yet revolutionized mobile marketing. Beacons require users to have Bluetooth turned on. But only 20% of smartphone users in the United States have Bluetooth turned on, and another 20% believed their smartphones did not have Bluetooth (even though they likely did have it). Consumers may also be concerned about the privacy and security implications of being tracked through a store or on the streets (Kwet, 2019). Many do not want to be bothered with in-store notifications, and may resent the intrusion. One beacon platform firm found that pushing notices to in-store consumers actually led to a decline in the use of the app, and more than one push notice caused a 300% drop in app usage (Looper, 2017; da Silva, 2017; eMarketer, Inc., 2016). Nevertheless, the beacon technology market is expected to continue growing through 2024, when it is expected that it will exceed $25 billion. Apple's iBeacon is expected to account for more than 50% of the market, while Google's Eddystone project is also projected to show growth during this time period. The retail sector is expected to be the primary generator of revenues, accounting for more than 55% (DeCode Staff, 2019; Wadhwani, 2018).

STARTING A LOCATION-BASED MARKETING CAMPAIGN

As with all marketing campaigns, start by identifying your objectives and understand just how a location-based mobile marketing campaign might help your business. Location-based marketing is generally much more action-oriented than other forms of online marketing. A person is in a given location only for a short time, measured in minutes and hours, rarely days or weeks. If you want the consumer to do something, it's now. Does your product or service have this quality? Is there something related to a person's location that fits with your product? Is there something about your products that makes them especially attractive to a mobile audience at a specific location and time? There are very few products and services that don't have a location connection.

Next, consider the target demographic for your campaign and products. Location-aware consumers (those with mobile devices and familiar with location-based services) tend to be a younger, more educated, and wealthier demographic. They have many of the same characteristics as all mobile shoppers.

A strategic analysis of your marketspace is very important. The same questions that you would seek to answer if you were doing a nonlocation-aware mobile marketing campaign apply to a location-based marketing effort, such as examining what your competitors are doing.

Once you have envisioned your marketing campaign and identified your market, it is time to start implementing your mobile campaign. The same steps that you would follow in implementing a mobile campaign apply to location-based marketing as well. Note that you can't do everything at once—mobile-centric and location-based. Start by doing something simple like local search. Then consider more sophisticated local-based marketing tactics.

TABLE 7.17 — MOBILE LOCATION-BASED MARKETING EFFECTIVENESS

SOCIAL MARKETING PROCESS	MEASUREMENT
Acquisition	Impressions; click-through; unique visitors to a mobile or desktop website; pages viewed; time on site.
Engagement	Inquire; reserve; visit a physical store; click-to-call; check maps for directions; register; request more information; posts and comments; responders to offers; Likes generated per visitor; click-to-call rate.
Amplification	SMS to friends; notify friends of location; share location or offers with friends.
Community	Content generated by visitors or responders; reviews; posts; positive comments generated.
Sales	Purchases; percentage increase in sales due to local mobile campaign; percentage of customers from local mobile.

MEASURING LOCATION-BASED MARKETING RESULTS

There are a great many ways to measure the success of a mobile location-based campaign, some very sophisticated. The measures of success will vary depending on the objective of the campaign, which might be to raise the awareness of your brand among consumers, to bring customers to your retail store, or a click-to-call campaign where you want people to make reservations for a concert.

Because mobile local campaigns use the same marketing ad formats as both traditional and mobile web marketing, the basic measures of effectiveness are similar. For instance, the number of impressions (people who see an ad), click-through rate, and unique visitors are basic measures for a mobile local campaign. But mobile location-based marketing is much more personal and social than traditional web marketing or even simple mobile marketing: it's a marketing message directed to a consumer's personal mobile device based on that person's location. Local mobile marketers hope consumers will take follow-on action almost immediately—inquire, reserve, click-to-call, friend, and ultimately purchase. **Table 7.17** describes some of the basic dimensions and metrics to use when evaluating a mobile marketing campaign. The nature of the location-based campaign makes a difference for how you measure success. For instance, in a click-to-call campaign, you want to measure the volume of calls, duration of call, new versus existing customers, and the number of accidental or hostile calls.

7.5 CAREERS IN E-COMMERCE

Social marketing is one of the fastest growing segments of online marketing (the other being mobile marketing), generating over $21 billion annually. If you love using social media, a position in social marketing may be an excellent fit. Possible job titles include social media associate, social media analyst, social media coordinator, social media planner, social community manager, and social media strategist, among others.

THE COMPANY

The company is a marketing and public relations company. Founded in 2005 as a traditional media platform agency, it has changed the focus of its business to social media platforms such as Facebook, Pinterest, and Twitter. The firm designs, develops, and manages websites, social network pages, blogs, and long form research reports for a variety of clients in financial services, publishing, and educational institutions. The company has 550 employees with a diverse range of skills from content creators to graphic artists, web designers, researchers, and digital marketing specialists with a focus on social and mobile campaigns.

THE POSITION: SOCIAL MEDIA ASSOCIATE

You will work with the Digital Marketing Department. The Social Media Marketing Associate role is an entry-level position. Social Media Marketing Associates create content and manage specific projects for nonprofit and corporate clients involving social media marketing. Responsibilities include:

- Creating various types of content for social media marketing campaigns for multiple clients.
- Writing and editing blog posts.
- Creating and editing long-form content (e-books, reports, infographics, slide decks, etc.).
- Creating landing pages, forms, and ad content using marketing software tools.
- Managing paid promotions on various social networks.
- Conducting A/B testing programs for social media ad campaigns.
- Creating and editing reports.
- Proofreading print and digital content for grammar and typographical errors.
- Brainstorming strategies for social media marketing efforts.

QUALIFICATIONS/SKILLS

- College degree in humanities, social sciences, or marketing, with course work in digital marketing, e-commerce, and/or graphics design
- Experience with personal or business social networks and blogs
- Excellent writing and communication skills
- Propensity for technology and creative thinking
- Basic understanding of website design, digital media, and content marketing
- Interest in the causes/business goals of our clients
- Willingness to engage in problem-solving in a collaborative environment
- Strong organization skills and attention to detail
- Desire to grow in learning and professional development

PREPARING FOR THE INTERVIEW

This chapter provides you with the foundational material that you should be familiar with when interviewing for a position in social marketing. Begin by reviewing Section 7.1 so you can demonstrate your knowledge of the broad trends in social marketing, especially the idea of conversations with consumers as opposed to simply displaying ads. The rapid growth in mobile marketing and the connection to local marketing are also important (Figures 7.1 and 7.2). Review Section 7.2 to demonstrate your understanding of the key players in social marketing and the basic process of social marketing (Figure 7.4). The concepts of amplification and community are key to the success of social marketing. Chances are good your new position will utilize one or several of the major social platforms, but certainly Facebook, Twitter, Pinterest, and most likely, Instagram. Review the parts of Section 7.2 that describe the marketing tools for each of these social networks. Also pay attention to how the results of campaigns on each social network can be measured. You can impress your interviewer by describing some of the successful social campaigns listed in Tables 7.3, 7.7, and 7.11, and probably will earn some extra points by showing that you are aware of some of the issues involved in social marketing discussed in the *Insight on Society* case, *Social Marketing on TikTok: Worth the Risk?* Although the job description does not mention mobile marketing explicitly, the subject will no doubt come up, as social and mobile are inextricably intertwined. Review Section 7.3 on the growth of mobile marketing and how much mobile time is spent on social networks. Location-based marketing is not mentioned in the job description, but some of the firm's clients may be interested in geo-marketing, and it would be advisable to review the location-based marketing tools in Table 7.16.

POSSIBLE FIRST INTERVIEW QUESTIONS

1. What kinds of experiences have you had creating social media content?

If you have not had previous experience creating social media content for a business, think about the types of content you have posted on your own social network profiles, your purpose in posting the content, and the impact your content had on the target audience. If you have had experience working on a social media marketing campaign, describe your role, the challenges you faced, and how you solved these challenges.

2. One of our clients is a media firm that focuses on health and exercise. Currently, its primary market is adults over the age of 55. The client would like to target 24-to-36-year-olds. How do you think a firm like this could use Facebook or other social networks to promote its products?

You might suggest that younger Millennials are very attracted to video, and that YouTube, Facebook, and Instagram videos are a good way to reach this younger market. Also, Facebook News Feed display ads are effective and inexpensive if they are targeted to the correct groups, such as to people who have expressed an interest in exercise, or who belong to networks that have a health and exercise theme. You might also mention that Millennials are much more likely to use their mobile devices on social networks, and therefore the emphasis for this client should be on reaching the younger mobile audience.

3. One of our clients is a regional retail bank. They report that more and more of their customers are using mobile phones to access their services. How would you recommend they use social marketing?

You might suggest that because this bank has a built in mobile-aware customer base, it seems an ideal audience to reach through social networks such as Facebook and Twitter, and also LinkedIn, which attracts affluent professionals, just the kind of new customer the bank will be seeking to attract. Also, the bank's own mobile app is an ideal place to display new products and services.

4. Many of our clients are small businesses like health food stores, restaurants, and specialty retailers. What would you suggest is a good way to reach these local customers via social media?

Local businesses are ideally suited to use social mobile marketing to reach their audience. Google is one of the largest local marketing firms, providing location, contact, and product and service descriptions. Also, location-based marketing is readily available on Facebook and other social networks. Local businesses could use the firm's help in setting up Google ads, Facebook pages, and implementing a geo-marketing program that might include proximity marketing and in-store messaging.

5. The online marketing process has changed for most of our clients in part because people are using multiple screens, from TV, to desktops, to mobile phones. How should we advise our clients about which platforms to use, and how to build a consistent brand over all these channels?

You can impress your interviewer by agreeing that screen diversity means that a single ad cannot be used on all platforms and needs to be adjusted to fit different devices and screen sizes. The graphics and creative elements will need to be adjusted for each platform in what is called responsive design. In some cases, firms may have to develop very different ads for different platforms. This will add to costs. But firms generally will need to appear on both desktop and mobile devices.

7.6 CASE STUDY

ExchangeHunterJumper.com:
Building an International Brand with Social Marketing

The Internet and Web have enabled thousands of business ideas to become online realities. The Internet has reduced the costs of starting a small business, and allowed small players to effectively use the same marketing and selling tools as major corporations. Small businesses usually occupy a market niche not occupied by big players or corporations. One such market niche in America, comprising about 10,000 to 30,000 players, is the high-end horse show circuit. These are people who are willing to drop $200,000 on a horse that can jump a five-foot fence with ease. This may be a very small market, but its members are highly motivated to both buy and sell horses, and they are willing to spend in the process. ExchangeHunterJumper.com is one example of how a small business focusing on a tiny niche market was able to successfully build an online brand.

According to Dagny Amber Aslin, founder and owner of ExchangeHunterJumper.com (The Exchange), a website created to help owners and professional trainers sell high-end competition horses, it's hard to "get rich" or even make money on the Internet. She adds, "There are a lot of preconceived notions … I beat down a path previously unplowed. It cost

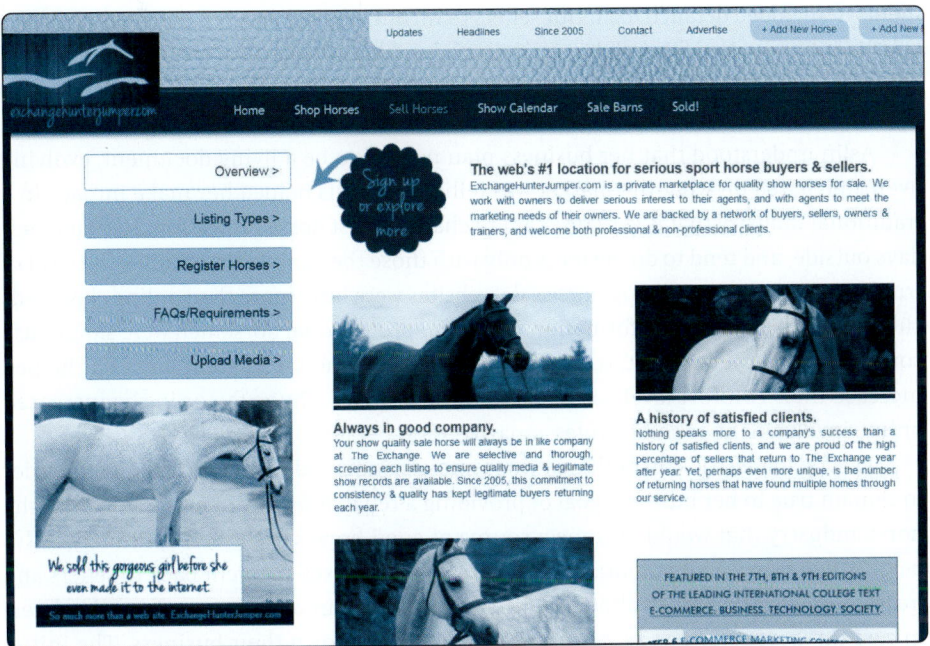

Copyright©2014, ExchangeHunterJumper.com, Equinnovus LLC

us a lot of money and we suffered many setbacks from our mistakes." Yet the site is still growing and has succeeded where others failed. How did Aslin break through and develop a site that works for professionals buying and selling alike? How did she build trust? How did she market her services?

Experience helped. Aslin started with applicable experience—in the horse world and in the world of Internet marketing. In addition to riding and competing as a child, Aslin spent several years working as a professional trainer. Working six-day weeks, including weekends, and spending most of her time outdoors riding, teaching, and competing, she saw first-hand the challenges facing professional horsemen, and she gained valuable credibility with those who would become her audience.

While working in the horse business, and learning how difficult it was to make a living, she took a part-time job as an assistant to a top California real estate agent, helping him market and sell high-end real estate in the Santa Barbara area. Among other activities, she helped him develop and expand his website. Through that experience, she realized that "selling six-figure horses and seven-figure houses are ridiculously similar—both tend to be overpriced, have emotional strings attached, require vettings and exhaustive negotiations, involve agents, and the list goes on." In 2005, when she moved from California back to the Midwest, where she had spent her childhood, The Exchange was born. Thirteen years later, the equine marketing model she has built is a customized version of the real estate program she assisted with in Santa Barbara.

Aslin knew that busy horse professionals needed a high-quality, reliable source of suitable mounts for their clients, but their day-to-day business lives left them little time to thoroughly search the market, and they often lacked a good grasp of modern media technology. The same dilemma applied when it came to selling high-end horses. In response, she created an organized, professional process for preparing online horse sale advertisements. It included detailed forms for sellers to fill out, and she insisted that quality photos and video be provided for each horse advertised, enabling her to turn the descriptions into accurate portrayals of each animal and its capabilities. She created a fee structure that was reasonable and affordable, and she developed a multi-channel marketing program.

Aslin understood that her business plan needed to be a living document, evolving over time based on what the market was telling her. This helped her make inroads in a traditional industry that is very resistant to change. Most horse professionals spend their days outside, and tend to do business only with those they know personally—the level of trust is very low. Most existing horse sale websites were little more than online classifieds cluttered with unreliable information. Although professional horsemen were slow to use computers and the Internet, the rise of smartphones and tablet computers has helped increase their comfort level with technology and been a huge factor in the increased online involvement of horse professionals.

The Exchange took all of these things into account, and Aslin went further. In order to remain true to her business goal of providing a reliable service to professionals in the horse industry that would become a source of good horses described accurately, Aslin personally reviewed all potential advertisers. In some cases she went back to sellers and insisted on higher-quality photographs and video, and in other cases where she determined the horse was not as represented, she turned down their business. The initial business plan process involved strict screening, and it meant turning away money and valuing quality over quantity in every area—horses, buyers, traffic, and ads. It was a hard and expensive premise to adhere to when building a reputation from scratch, but through persistence and dedication it has worked, and today, The Exchange's reputation and "brand" has become one of its most valuable assets.

In discussing some of the obstacles she faced in getting The Exchange up and running, Aslin starts with education—her own or lack thereof, specifically in the areas of graphic design and web technology. While she knew what professional horsemen needed, she did not know how to translate that into graphic design or onto the Web. She says that looking back on the original logo and print designs is "a painful exercise," but she is happy with the current direction.

The budget was also an initial obstacle, as there wasn't a lot of money to spend up front. However, in hindsight, she believes that gave her an advantage because she had to learn what her market wanted and was able to do so without breaking the bank. Conversely, her main competitor took an opposite track, spent big up front, missed the mark with customers, and is now defunct.

In addition, she faced the negative perception among industry professionals and prospective buyers that equine Internet advertising was "worthless." Further, much of her target audience barely knew how to use a computer, didn't have e-mail addresses, and had been doing business in the same old-school manner for decades. For a few key players this worked very well, but it left a void for those outside that inner circle to move horses. Through a combination of knowledge of the marketplace, on-the-job training, perseverance, and listening to what the market was telling her, The Exchange has successfully begun to fill that void. Today, The Exchange typically manages the marketing for 160–180 horses at any given time, and anticipates that this number will likely increase to over 200 in the near future.

Here's how it works. The Exchange handles advertising for sellers and trainers across the country. In 2019, the prices of show horses advertised on The Exchange ranged from $25,000 to $250,000. The Exchange specializes strictly in hunter-jumper show horses, and specifically those suited for high-level competition.

Trainers/sellers who sign up for a premium listing pay a flat $250 fee for the initial advertisement and a subscription fee of $35/month (less for multiple horses), which includes a listing on The Exchange's website featuring the horse's details, photos, show record, lineage, and videos. The Exchange provides copy-writing services and professionally edits all videos supplied by sellers, hosting them on its private server and making them available to download, embed, and share. Each listing typically takes 8–10 hours to prepare. In 2012, The Exchange added a second listing alternative—a Sale Barn listing for $300 a month that allows for listing of up to 10 horses. A three-month commitment is required, but there are no initial or other fees. Once the commitment is fulfilled, sellers can deactivate and then reactivate their Sale Barn page as needed at any time without any further charge. Aimed at high-volume operations with frequent turnover, the Sale Barn page can link to the seller's website, YouTube, Facebook, and Twitter feeds, if available, with the goal of increasing overall brand awareness for the seller's business. Aslin designed the Sale Barn as an affordable option for professionals who might otherwise be reluctant to spend on marketing. The Sale Barn page provides sellers with a mini website and social media advertising, including three sidebar Facebook ads each week. These have the advantage of promoting not only the sellers but also have proved to be a useful promotional tool for the Sale Barn package itself, since those who click on the ad end up on the ExchangeHunterJumper website and are able to see its services first-hand and in depth. International sellers are given a slight additional discount. The Sale Barn program has proven to be a major success, with 19 different sale barns listed, including one in Germany and two in Canada.

Statistics show that a horse's first month online is most successful in terms of the number of web page visits. With the addition of monthly campaign management, The Exchange helps keep each horse's marketing fresh and up to date. Updates can immediately escalate a horse's popularity as much as 30% and attract new potential buyers. Sellers are encouraged to provide updates as frequently as possible. Online videos add to the brand of the horse for sale and are especially important for young horses or those "growing into" their price tags. Updates are added to the website and promoted through various media outlets including Facebook and e-mail campaigns.

Sellers currently fill out two separate forms: a credit card registration form and an equine fact sheet. The fact sheet includes a long series of checkboxes from which sellers select preworded traits, coupled with space for additional written descriptions. This saves some production time, although writing the actual copy is still a major part of the value that The Exchange provides. To implement this option, Aslin spent time investigating form-building tools. Custom-built form solutions were likely to be too expensive, so she played with numerous online form generators and ultimately was able to find some that offered great functionality at a relatively low cost. So, for example, a seller can indicate that the horse is a "jumper" and questions specific to jumpers will be displayed.

The Exchange develops a specific marketing strategy for each horse listed. This includes reviewing information submitted, combing through a horse's official show record, considering impartial impressions, and identifying the most likely buyers. If The Exchange thinks that the photos or videos don't help to sell the horse, they advise the seller on how to improve them. This advice stems from experience in marketing all types of horses from coast to coast, and an understanding of varied buyer profiles and geographic trends that exist in the market.

Social marketing forms the core of the Exchange's marketing efforts. Starting in 2009, The Exchange began experimenting with social media including RSS feeds, YouTube, Facebook, Twitter, and Instagram. Aslin notes that when she began The Exchange, social media was not yet the phenomenon that it is today, but when its significance started to become apparent, she had no choice but to jump in and begin using it, learning as she went. The Exchange has experienced varying success with social media. For instance, The Exchange runs multiple RSS feeds through the free service, FeedBurner, although thus far, the equestrian set does not appear to be particularly interested in RSS feed subscriptions. Initially, the Exchange used a professional video management system from Vzaar to host its videos, but also maintained a YouTube channel to increase exposure and appear on YouTube "Horse for Sale" searches. In 2018, it decided to switch solely to YouTube, in part because YouTube provides the ability for companies to limit the advertising shown with videos. Facebook has been the most resounding social media success. The Exchange now has over 24,000 followers on Facebook. In addition, Aslin's personal Facebook friends, which number almost 2,700, extend her cumulative Facebook reach to almost 27,000 friends and followers, and make her online marketing efforts even more personal. The Exchange's Twitter account has about 2,000 followers, and links with both The Exchange's Facebook page and its YouTube channel. The YouTube channel has over 70,000 views. The Exchange's Instagram feed has over 7,500 followers. Because every business is different, The Exchange's experience suggests it's important for e-commerce sites to experiment with social media to determine which outlets are most effective in reaching their specific target audiences. Currently, The Exchange spends what it characterizes as a "fair amount of money" boosting posts and promotion content on Facebook each month, which Aslin has found has become increasingly necessary in order for her social media marketing on the platform to have any effect. Aslin has also found that posting in various Facebook Groups focused on sales of the types of horses marketed on the Exchange (currently free) often results in good "click-bait" and some increased website traffic.

To track the effectiveness of her social marketing efforts, Aslin uses various tracking systems. For instance, Google Analytics allows her to track exactly how many people are on the ExchangeHunterJumper site in real time and how they got there. Aslin has found that focusing solely on Likes is not sufficient. For example, she notes that a photo she posted advertising a horse on Facebook generated only 10 Likes, but that actually almost 150 people followed the link associated with the photo to the ExchangeHunterJumper website. She also uses a short URL service, Bitly, to create unique URLs associated with Facebook and other social media posts that have built-in click trackers. This enables her to quickly see the collective success of her social marketing efforts; in a good month, bit.ly stats show around 8,000 click-throughs to the ExchangeHunterJumper site.

Another challenge is developing the actual social media content, which needs to be presented in such as way as to attract attention, and determining the optimal amount and timing of new content to post each day. Aslin notes that if she posts too many times a day, or posts too much content too close together, the reach of her posts seems to drop off.

Although Facebook is currently the primary social marketing platform for ExchangeHunterJumper, the firm also has loyal followers on Instagram and Twitter. Although Aslin doubts that many of these followers are actual buyers or sellers at this time, she notes that in the future they probably will be. Her site has grown up along with her clientele, and children who once drooled over ponies on her site are now, 13 years later, soon-to-be adults and, possibly, young professionals.

The firm's website is also a key element of its e-commerce presence. Aslin continually reviews the design of the website with an eye to making it the most effective marketing tool possible. She built the original site herself in 2005 and updated it almost yearly in response to her target market's needs. In 2012, Aslin relaunched the site for a fifth time, and for the first time ever hired a professional web development team to convert the static HTML site into a dynamically driven content management system on the Expression Engine platform. While she was able to keep costs low by designing and developing the site's CSS layout, the advanced functionality that was desired, such as the sale horse filter that enables shoppers to sort horses based on price, location, gender, type, and size, still

SOURCES: Exchangehunterjumper.com, accessed February 19, 2020; Interview with Amber Aslin, founder of ExchangeHunterJumper, November 2018, October 2017, November 2016, September 2014, September 2013, and September 2012.

required a hefty five-figure investment. Aslin believes the ability to get to know the market and update the site accordingly has kept The Exchange fresh and innovative. Every iteration of the website has been focused on meeting the target market's needs. For instance, she has also spent considerable time and expense to make sure The Exchange's website, including video, works just as well on mobile devices as it does on a traditional laptop or desktop computer. However, given changes in Google's search algorithms with respect to mobile sites, which has had the effect of pushing the Exchange down in search results, Aslin is once again considering a redesign.

In addition to the website, The Exchange uses a variety of other marketing strategies, including e-mail campaigns, magazine advertising, and word of mouth. It ceased distributing its four-color, printed National Sales List booklet due to its high cost, and now relies almost totally on various types of online marketing. Aslin has found it has been extremely helpful to have the web development experience she has honed over the years. Here are some of her words of wisdom: She feels that entrepreneurs don't necessarily have to know how to build sites, but do need to be familiar with what is and what is not possible in site construction. It is important to understand which functions are complicated and which are not, so that overly complicated add-ons that don't really add to the user experience can be eliminated from tight budgets. It's also important to know what technology is popular now and what technology is just around the corner. Even if you think you are proficient in all the tasks you will need to launch your business, with the rapid pace of technology, you inevitably spend much of your time learning something totally new, whether you want to or not.

By paying attention to these words of wisdom, as well as to detail at every step of the marketing process, The Exchange has managed to build a successful brand, one the horse community has come to rely upon.

Case Study Questions

1. Find a site on the Web that offers classified ads for horses. Compare this site to exchangehunterjumper.com in terms of the services offered (the customer value proposition). What does The Exchange offer that other sites do not?

2. In what ways were social media effective in promoting The Exchange brand? Which media led to the highest increase in sales and inquiries? Why?

3. Make a list of all the ways The Exchange attempts to personalize its services to both buyers and sellers.

7.7 REVIEW

KEY CONCEPTS

- **Understand the difference between traditional online marketing and the new social-mobile-local marketing platforms and the relationships between social, mobile, and local marketing.**
  - Social, mobile, and local marketing have transformed the online marketing landscape. The major trends and concepts include:
    - The emphasis in online marketing has shifted from exposing consumers to messages toward engaging them in conversations about your brand.
    - Social marketing means all things social: listening, discussing, interacting, empathizing, and engaging the consumer.
    - Social marketing and advertising is not simply a "new ad channel," but a collection of technology-based tools for communicating with shoppers.
    - In the past, businesses could tightly control their brand messaging and lead consumers down a funnel of cues that ended in a purchase. This is no longer the case. Instead, consumer purchase decisions are increasingly driven by the conversations, choices, tastes, and opinions of the consumer's social network.
    - Social, mobile, and local marketing are the fastest growing forms of online marketing.
  - Social, mobile, and local digital marketing are self-reinforcing and connected.
  - Local and mobile marketing are highly related: local advertisers most often target mobile devices.
  - The strong ties among social, mobile, and local marketing have significant implications for managing a marketing campaign in this new environment. When you design a social marketing campaign, you must also consider that your customers will be accessing the campaign using mobile devices, and often they will also be looking for local content.

- **Understand the social marketing process from fan acquisition to sales and the marketing capabilities of social marketing platforms such as Facebook, Twitter, and Pinterest.**
  - In social marketing, the objective is to encourage your potential customers to become fans of your company's products and services and engage with your business by entering into a conversation with it.
  - There are five steps in the social marketing process model: fan acquisition, engagement, amplification, community, and brand strength and sales.
  - Facebook is a social network that is designed to encourage people to reveal as much personal information about themselves as feasible, including activities, behavior, photos, music, movies, and purchases.
  - Facebook's features are built to maximize the connections among people in the form of notifications, tagging, messaging, posting, and sharing. In many instances, the movement of personal information is so widespread that it is beyond the understanding of users.
  - Social density refers to the number of interactions among members of a group and reflects the "connectedness" of a group, even if these connections are forced on users.
  - Facebook has many marketing tools, including Reactions buttons, Brand Pages, News Feed ads, Right-hand sidebar ads, mobile ads, video ads, and Facebook Exchange.
  - The effectiveness of Facebook ads can be measured using five stages of the social marketing model: fan acquisition, engagement, amplification, community, and ultimately brand strengthening and sales.
  - Twitter is a micro-blogging social network that allows users to send and receive 280-character messages as well as videos, photos, and article previews.
  - Twitter marketing tools include Promoted Tweets, Promoted Trends, Promoted Accounts, Enhanced Profile Pages, the Twitter Amplify program, Twitter Cards, and app install and app engagement ads.

- Measuring the results of Twitter marketing is similar to measuring the results of Facebook and other social marketing platforms, with some minor changes to account for the unique qualities of Twitter.
- Pinterest is a social network that provides users with an online board to which they can "pin" interesting pictures. The success of Pinterest is based in part on a shift in consumer behavior enabled by new technologies: people talk about brands using pictures rather than words.
- Pinterest marketing tools include Promoted Pins; adding a Pin It logo to your website; pinning photos to Pinterest and directing users to your website; creating theme-based Pin It boards; placing URLs to stores that you support and receive lead generation fees from; integrating your pins and boards with other social sites; networking with users and followers.
- Pinterest campaigns can be measured using the same procedures as for Facebook and Twitter. The key dimensions to measure are fan (follower) acquisition, engagement, amplification, community, and sales.
- Other social networks, such as Instagram, Snapchat, and LinkedIn, provide similar advertising opportunities to marketers.
- One downside of social marketing is that brands lose a substantial amount of control over where their ads appear in terms of other content and what people say about their brands on social sites.

■ **Identify the key elements of a mobile marketing campaign.**
- Although still in its infancy, mobile marketing involves the use of mobile devices such as smartphones and tablet computers to display banner ads, rich media, video, games, e-mail, text messaging, in-store messaging, QuickResponse (QR) codes, and couponing.
- Mobile devices represent a radical departure from previous marketing technologies simply because the devices integrate so many human and consumer activities from telephoning or texting friends, to listening to music, watching videos, and using the Web to shop and purchase goods.
- The mobile platform has changed over the past few years, and there are now almost as many tablet users as smartphone users in the United States.
- Mobile users spend the vast majority of their time using mobile apps as opposed to mobile web browsers. Marketers need to place ads in apps where consumers spend most of their time.
- Mobile devices create a multi-screen world: smartphones, tablets, desktops, and television. The reality, and the future, of computing devices is that consumers will be multi-platform: using desktops and laptops at work and home, and smartphones and tablets at home as well as when moving about.
- The implications of the multi-device platform, or screen diversity, environment are that marketing needs to be designed for whatever device the consumer is using, and consistent branding across platforms will be important.
- Unlike social marketing, mobile marketing does not require a great deal of new marketing vocabulary. All the marketing formats available on the desktop are also available on mobile devices. With few exceptions, mobile marketing is very much like desktop marketing—except it is smaller, mobile, and with the user all the time.
- The major marketing opportunities in mobile marketing are search ads, display ads, videos and rich media, messaging (SMS/MMS/PPS), and other familiar formats like e-mail, classified, and lead generation.
- The effectiveness of mobile marketing can be measured using the dimensions of the social marketing process model: fan acquisition, engagement, amplification, community, brand strength, and sales. Traditional web-browser-based metrics also can be used when measuring mobile campaigns.

■ **Understand the capabilities of location-based local marketing.**
- Location-based marketing is the targeting of marketing messages to users based on their location. Generally, location-based marketing involves marketing of location-based services.
- Examples of location-based services are personal navigation, point-of-interest, reviews, friend-finder, and family-tracker services.

- Location-based marketing is dependent on two technologies: accurate mapping software and mobile device geo-positioning technologies like GPS, Wi-Fi network location data, and Bluetooth low energy (BLE) technology.
- Location-based mobile marketing is currently a small part of the online marketing environment, but is expected to double over the next two years, and is growing far faster than any other form of digital advertising.
- The ad formats used in local mobile marketing are familiar—search ads, display, social/native advertising, video, and SMS text messages. A very large percentage of these local mobile ads will be delivered by search engines such as Google, and social sites such as Facebook.
- The key players in location-based mobile marketing are the same giants of advertising who dominate the mobile marketing environment: Google, Facebook, Apple, Twitter, YP (formerly Yellow Pages), Pandora, and Millennial Media.
- Geo-aware techniques identify the location of a user's device and then target marketing to the device, recommending actions within reach.
- Geo-targeting of ads involves sending ads based on the user's location.
- Proximity marketing techniques identify a perimeter around a physical location, and then target ads to users within that perimeter, recommending actions possible within the fenced-in area.
- In-store messaging involves messaging consumers while entering and browsing in a retail store. This requires a very precise calculation of location.
- Consumers who seek information about local businesses using mobile devices are much more active and ready to purchase than desktop users.
- Measuring the effectiveness of location-based mobile campaigns involves using the same techniques used for browser-based search and display ads (impressions), but also should include the dimensions of the social marketing process model such as acquisition, engagement, amplification, community, and brand strength and sales.

QUESTIONS

1. How and why has online marketing changed since 2007?
2. What are the difficulties in differentiating the social, local, and mobile marketing channels?
3. What is meant by the social marketing term amplification, and how is it created and measured?
4. What is meant by the term conversation as it applies to online marketing and how do businesses engage in a conversation?
5. What does the term dark social refer to?
6. Identify and describe the first step in a social marketing campaign.
7. How would you measure the brand strength of a Facebook marketing campaign?
8. What is the downside of social marketing?
9. Why did Facebook agree to undergo regular audits by the Media Rating Council?
10. How would you measure engagement for your Twitter marketing campaign?
11. From a business perspective, what are the disadvantages or challenges in social marketing?
12. How can marketers use Snapchat for advertising?
13. How is Pinterest blurring the lines between social marketing and social e-commerce?
14. What challenges do Google and other mobile marketing firms face?
15. What kind of social marketing platform is TikTok?
16. How does marketing on LinkedIn differ from marketing on other social networks?
17. Why are retail m-commerce sales on smartphones increasing at a faster rate than on tablet computers?
18. What is social density and why is it important to social marketing?
19. Discuss Amazon's impact on m-commerce.
20. What are some of the issues with respect to using beacon technology for marketing?

PROJECTS

1. Choose two different online companies and for each, try to identify the social, mobile, and local marketing efforts the company has implemented. Do they use social plug-ins on their websites? Do they have a Facebook page? If so, visit those pages to see how they are using them. How is the Facebook page different from the company's website? Can you identify how the firms use mobile marketing? Use your smartphone or tablet to access their apps, if they have one, and websites. Are their websites designed specifically for each platform? In conclusion, compare and critically contrast these firms, and make recommendations for how you, as a marketing manager, would improve their effectiveness.

2. Visit your Facebook profile page and examine the ads shown in the right margin. What is being advertised and how do you believe it is relevant to your interests or online behavior? Make a list of ads appearing in your News Feed. Are these ads appropriately targeted to you in terms of your demographics, interests, and past purchases? Surf the web, visiting at least two retail websites. In the next 24 hours, do you see advertising on Facebook related to your surfing behavior?

3. Visit two websites of your choice and apply the social marketing process model to both. Critically compare and contrast the effectiveness of these sites in terms of the dimensions of the social marketing process. How well do these sites acquire fans, generate engagement, amplify responses, create a community, and strengthen their brands? What recommendations can you make for these sites to improve their effectiveness?

4. Identify two Pinterest brand pages. Identify how they use Pinterest marketing tools described in this chapter. Are there some tools they are not using? What recommendations can you make for these companies to improve their Pinterest marketing campaigns?

REFERENCES

Aaker, D. A. "Measuring Brand Equity Across Products and Markets." *California Management Review*, Vol 38, No. 3, pp. 102–20. (1996).

Ailawadi, Kusum L., Donald R. Lehmann, and Scott A. Neslin. "Revenue Premium as an Outcome Measure of Brand Equity." *Journal of Marketing*, 67 (October), 1–17 (October 2003).

BIA Advisory Services. "U.S. Local Advertising Revenue to Exceed $161B in 2020, According to BIA Advisory Services' Forecast." (November 6, 2019).

BIA Advisory Services. "BIA/Kelsey Sees Significant Growth in Local Spending in 2018 and Beyond, as Advertisers Embrace Location-Targeted, Social and Web Platforms." Biakelsey.com (February 1, 2018).

comScore, Inc. "2019 Global State of Mobile." (December 2019).

comScore, Inc. "The 2017 U.S. Mobile App Report." (August 2017).

Constine, Josh. "Facebook Plans Crackdown on Ad Targeting by Email Without Consent." Techcrunch.com (April 1, 2018).

da Silva, Michelle. "Proximity Marketing: How to Attact More Shoppers with Beacon Technology. Shopify.com (April 12, 2017).

Decode Staff. "This is the Future: Beacon Technology!" Medium.com (May 29, 2019).

Deloitte. "Global Mobile Consumer Survey." (2018).

eMarketer, Inc. "Worldwide Mobile Ad Spending." (October 2019a).

eMarketer, Inc., "U.S. Mobile Ad Spending." (October 2019b).

eMarketer, Inc. "U.S. Social Network Ad Spending." (October 2019c).

eMarketer, Inc. "Average Time Spent per Day with Social Networks." (November 2019d).

eMarketer, Inc. "Worldwide Instagram Ad Revenues." (October 2019e).

eMarketer, Inc. "Worldwide Snapchat Ad Revenues." (October 2019f).

eMarketer, Inc. "Mobile Phone Internet Users and Penetration Worldwide." (April 2019g).

eMarketer, Inc. "Retail Mcommerce Sales." (December 2019h).
eMarketer, Inc. "Retail Mcommerce Sales Penetration by Country, % of Total Retail Ecommerce Sales." (December 2019i).
eMarketer, Inc. "UK Retail Mcommerce Sales, by Device." (December 2019j).
eMarketer, Inc. (Mark Dolliver). "U.S. Time Spent with Media 2019." (May 30, 2019k).
eMarketer, Inc. (Yoram Wormser). "U.S. Time Spent with Mobile 2019." (May 30, 2019l).
eMarketer, Inc. "Digital Ad Spending Worldwide, by Region." (October 2019m).
eMarketer, Inc. "U.S. Mobile Ad Revenues, by Company." (October 2019n).
eMarketer, Inc. "U.S. Mobile Ad Revenue Share, by Company." (October 2019o).
eMarketer, Inc. "U.S. Mobile Ad Spending by Format." (October 2019p).
eMarketer chart, "U.S. Total Media Ad Spending." (October 2019q).
eMarketer, Inc. "U.S. Digital Ad Spending." (October 2019r).
eMarketer, Inc. (Jennifer King). "Many Marketers Look to Location Data to Plan Their Efforts." (June 21, 2018).
eMarketer, Inc. "What's Going On with Beacons?" (July 15, 2016).
Facebook. "Developer News: New Ways to Share, Save, and Engage." Developers.facebook.com (June 28, 2016).
Google, Inc. "Understanding Consumers' Local Search Behavior." (May 2014).
Google, Inc. "The New Multiscreen World." (August 2012).
Haines, Elliot. "5 Things You Need to Know About Beacon Technology." Wordstream.com (October 4, 2018).
Howland, Daphne. "Report: Amazon Leapfrogs Rivals in Mobile Commerce." Retaildive.com (January 19, 2017).
Iqbal, Soor. "App Download and Usage Statistics (2019)." Businessofapps.com (November 19, 2019).
Instagram. "Instagram Stories Ads—Now Available for All Businesses Globally." Business.instagram.com (March 1, 2017).
Judge, Alison. "Survey: Amazon Weaknesses Are Opportunities for Retailers." Blog.brandingbrand.com (March 6, 2017).
Keller, K. L. "Conceptualizing, Measuring and Managing Customer-Based Brand Equity." *Journal of Marketing*, Vol. 57 (January 1993).
Kwet, Michael. "In Stores, Secret Surveillance Tracks Your Every Move." *New York Times* (June 14, 2019).
Looper, Jen. "Beacons in the Internet of Things (IoT)." Data-informed.com (April 3, 2017).
Newberry, Christina. "How to Use Twitter Ads Like a Pro and Get the Most Out of Your Budget." Blog.hootsuite.com (August 20, 2018).
Shields, Mike. "Publishers Flock to New Instagram Stories." *Wall Street Journal* (August 12, 2016).
Simon, C. J., and M. J. Sullivan. "The Measurement and Determinants of Brand Equity: A Financial Approach." *Marketing Science*, Vol. 12, No 1, pp. 28–52. (1993).
Tobin, Arianna, and Jeremy B. Merrill. "Besieged Facebook Says New Ad Limits Aren't a Response to Lawsuits." Propublica.org (August 23, 2018).
Twitter + Research Now. "Customer Insights 2016: The Value of a Follower." (2016).
UnMetric. "29 Must-Know Terms for Every Social Media Analyst." (2015).
Vranica, Suzanne. "Advertisers Allege Facebook Failed to Disclose Key Metric Error for More Than a Year." *Wall Street Journal* (October 16, 2018).
Wadhwani, Preeti. "Beacon Technology Market Set to Surpass $25 Billion by 2024." Rfidjournal.com (February 28, 2018).
Wagner, Kurt. "Twitter Says Half of Its Business is Video—What Does That Mean?" Recode.net (April 30, 2018).

CHAPTER 8

Ethics, Law, and E-commerce

LEARNING OBJECTIVES

After reading this chapter, you will be able to:

- Understand why e-commerce raises ethical, social, and political issues.
- Understand basic concepts related to privacy and information rights, the practices of e-commerce companies that threaten privacy, and the different methods that can be used to protect online privacy.
- Understand the various forms of intellectual property and the challenges involved in protecting it.
- Understand how the Internet is governed and why taxation of e-commerce raises governance and jurisdiction issues.
- Identify major public safety and welfare issues raised by e-commerce.

The Right to Be Forgotten:
Europe Leads on Internet Privacy

In 2014, Google was forced to begin removing search engine query results in Europe after a ruling by the Court of Justice of the European Union (CJEU), Europe's highest court. The ruling gave individuals the right to request that certain links to personal information found through a search of their names be removed. The CJEU's ruling has come to be known as the "right to be forgotten" (sometimes given the acronym RTBF or referred to as the "right to delist"). The CJEU's ruling marked the beginning of a new era of digital privacy in the European Union, based on the simple idea that individuals have a right to manage their online personal information and public image. Google, Facebook, Twitter, and many other U.S. Internet-based firms whose business models depend on virtually no limitations on the collection and use of personal information have lobbied strongly against the idea that individuals have a right to manage their personal online information. However, the CJEU's decision is final, and Google and other major search engines are implementing the ruling. While simple in concept, the right to be forgotten can be devilishly difficult and expensive to implement in practice.

© Lee Avison/Alamy Stock Photo

The CJEU's decision was based on a 2010 lawsuit brought by Spanish citizen Mario Costeja Gonzalez against a Spanish newspaper, Google Spain, and Google Inc. (the American parent firm), which had linked his name with an auction notice in a newspaper that his house had been repossessed and was being sold in order to pay off debts. A Google search on Gonzalez's name returned a link to the newspaper notice as the most prominent link. Gonzalez's suit said that issues of his debt and foreclosure had been resolved years ago, and that the reference to this event was irrelevant and an invasion of his privacy as defined in the European Union Data Protection Directive—Europe's digital-era privacy legislation that governed personal information in the 28 countries that make up the European Union. Gonzalez requested that the newspaper remove or alter the pages it posted online and that Google Spain and Google Inc. be required to remove the link between his name and the auction notice in the newspaper. Gonzalez said he was not worried about his online image as much as the impact on his work and reputation as a lawyer, and the potential of the notice to injure his law business.

Google and the newspaper argued that because the server providing the results for Google searches in Spain was located outside Europe, the EU rules and privacy legislation did not apply. Google also argued that it was a search engine that simply provided links to information stored by others, not a data repository, and that it was not responsible for the accuracy or relevance of information stored by other organizations. Consequently, Google claimed that it should not be subject to the EU Data Protection Directive because it pertained only to data repositories. Finally, Google argued that under European law, individuals did not have the right to request that their personal data be removed from accessibility via a search engine. In public statements, Google also said it would be difficult or impossible to respond to thousands or millions of requests to eliminate links; granting these rights would allow criminals, fraudsters, sexual predators, and corrupt public officials to rewrite history; and that it would be very expensive to respond to requests and would potentially limit innovation in the future.

In 2014, the CJEU ruled that EU data protection policies were not limited by territory and that they applied to search engines no matter where the servers were located. Second, the CJEU found that search engines are "controllers" of individual personal data within the European Union and therefore must comply with EU rules. Prior to this ruling, search engines like Google had been considered merely processors of online data, and therefore exempt from data protection rules in Europe. Finally the CJEU found that Europeans did indeed have a right to ask search engines to remove links to personal information about them (the "right to be forgotten") when that information was inaccurate, inadequate, irrelevant, or excessive. The economic interests of the search engine to provide unfettered access to personal information did not justify interfering with the individual's right to be forgotten and personal privacy.

The CJEU also clarified that the right to be forgotten was not absolute, but would have to be balanced against other rights and obligations such as freedom of expression, freedom of the press, and the broader public interest. For instance, the CJEU's ruling did not require the newspaper to change any of the pages in its archives. Gonzalez' original auction notice remains. Rather than a blanket right granted to whoever applies to have information removed from search engines, instead the CJEU required a case-by-case assessment that examines the type of information, its potential for harm to the individual's private life, and the interest of the public in having access to that information. Also, for "public figures," those who have thrust themselves into public roles, such as politicians, celebrities, or business leaders, the public interest in knowing may trump the private interest in being forgotten.

As of January 2020, Google said it had received almost 900,000 requests from people who wanted, in aggregate, over 3.49 million links to online information about them removed, and that it had removed about 46% of those links based on internal guidelines that it has developed. France, Germany, and the United Kingdom have generated more than half of all delisting requests. Over 50% of requests relate to links on social media, and another 19% of requests pertain to news reports with respect to individuals. The top 1% of requesters generate 20% of all requests. While Google points to its 46% removal rate as a sign that it is even-handed in its judgments about what content to remove, critics complain that the decisions should not be left in the hands of private companies.

Regulators in France have demanded that Google remove delisted search results globally, not just from European servers. This level of compliance was not required by the original ruling or by EU regulations. In 2016, France fined Google for failing to remove delisted

SOURCES: "Google Transparency Report," Transparencyreport.google.com, accessed February 19, 2020; "California 'Right to Be Forgotten Law,'" by Emilie Elliott, Carnaclaw.com, October 28, 2019; "'Right to Be Forgotten' Privacy Rule Is Limited by Europe's Top Court," by Adam Satariano, *New York Times*, September 24, 2019; "Finnish Court Issues Precedent 'Right to Be Forgotten' Decision for Google to Remove Data," Yle.fi, August 7, 2018; "Google Warns Against Possible Expansion of 'Right to Be Forgotten,'" by Wendy Davis, Mediapost.com, July 26, 2018; "The Right to Be Forgotten Risks Becoming a Tool to Curb Free Press," by Michael J. Oghia, Opendemocracy.net, July 9, 2018; "When 2 + 2 Might Equal 5," by Floyd Abrams, *New York Times*,

materials from American servers. Google appealed the decision to the CJEU, arguing that rulings by European courts could affect the experience of Internet users in the United States. The reactions to the CJEU's rulings and France's efforts to extend the right to forget beyond the boundaries of Europe reflect a deep digital divide between Europe and the United States when it comes to privacy and the balance between managing personal information (privacy) and freedom of expression and the press. In Europe, many nations celebrated the original ruling on the right to be forgotten as a victory over arrogant U.S. Internet companies and their cavalier attitudes towards user privacy. In the United States, the right to be forgotten does not exist—U.S. newspapers and technologists emphasize the importance of a free press and warn against making it possible for individuals to hide their past misdoings. However, surveys indicate that nearly 90% of Americans supports some form of the right to be forgotten. In September 2019, the CJEU ruled in Google's favor, declaring that the right to be forgotten was not an absolute right, and only applies within the European Union. Notwithstanding the ruling, regulators in France have stated that they might still request a global delisting of search results in cases where it is deemed necessary to guarantee the privacy rights of the individuals involved.

When individuals in the European Union and United Kingdom have been dissatisfied with Google's decisions, they have taken to local courts to appeal them, with mixed results. In Finland, a high court ruled in 2018 that the request of a man convicted of murder to remove related links was justified, and that Google would have to eliminate those links from its search results. The man had been found in court to have had a health condition that absolved him of much of the responsibility in the case, and while his crime was very serious, the court ruled that his right to privacy outweighed the public's right to the information. In England, two claimants convicted of white-collar crimes in the 1990s sued for the right to be forgotten, and the case was heard by a British high court. In the case of one claimant, who was convicted of accounting fraud, the court ruled that the crime was relevant to the public interest, and therefore should not be deleted; but in the case of the other, who had been convicted of conspiracy to carry out surveillance and intercept communications, the court ruled that the case had no interest to the public, and therefore upheld his right to be forgotten. Perhaps the most important element of the court's rulings was the fact that the court rejected Google's claim that it should be protected by provisions that support journalists. The judge ruled that Google should not be considered a journalist merely due to the fact that it provides access to journalistic content, since it is entirely dependent upon external sites for this content. In another 2018 ruling, a German court refused to force Google to remove links pertaining to a murder committed by two claimants.

In 2018, the European Union's General Data Protection Regulation (GDPR) codified many of the regulations pertaining to the right to be forgotten, including listing the criteria that would justify an individual's request to remove links from search results. In the United States, the California Consumer Privacy Act (CCPA), which went into effect on January 1, 2020, provides California residents with the right to request deletion of personal information collected by certain businesses. Although not as broad as the GDPR, the CCPA is the first law in the United States to codify a right similar to the right to be forgotten and may be a harbinger of similar laws to come in other states.

May 7, 2018; "How Does California's Erasure Law Stack Up Against the EU's Right to Be Forgotten," by Shaudee Dehghan, Iapp.org, April 17, 2018; "High Court Establishes 'Right to Be Forgotten' in English Law," by Abigail Healey and David Engel, Lexology.com, April 16, 2018; "Google Seeks to Limit 'Right to Be Forgotten' By Claiming It's Journalistic," by Chava Gourarie, Cjr.org, April 6, 2018; "GDPR: Look Out for 'Right to Be Forgotten Storms' Ahead," by Jon Oltsik, Csoonline.com, March 15, 2018; "Google Has Received 650,000 'Right To Be Forgotten' Requests Since 2014," Npr.org, February 28, 2018; "The Right to Erasure of Right to Be Forgotten Under the GDPR Explained and Visualized," I-scoop.eu, accessed 2018; "The Right to Be Forgotten Is the Right to Have an Imperfect Past," by Susan Moore, *The Guardian*, August 7, 2017; "UK Citizens to Get More Rights Over Personal Data Under New Laws," by Rowena Mason, *The Guardian*, August 6, 2017; "Google's Right to Be Forgotten Appeal Heading to Europe's Top Court," by Natasha Lomas, Techcrunch.com, July 19, 2017; "The Right to Be Forgotten," by Martin von Haller, Digitalbusiness.law, June 16, 2016; "Google Takes Right to Be Forgotten Battle to France's Highest Court," by Alex Hern, *The Guardian,* May 19, 2016; "Google to Extend 'Right to Be Forgotten' to All Its Domains Accessed in EU," *The Guardian*, February 11, 2016; "Google Will Further Block Some European Search Results," by Mark Scott, *New York Times,* February 11, 2016; "Right to Be Forgotten? Not That Easy," by Danny Hakim, *New York Times*, May 29, 2014; "EU Court Ruling a Victory for Privacy," *Der Spiegel*, May 20, 2014; "After European Court Order, Google Works on a Tool to Remove Links," by Mark Scott, *New York Times*, May 15, 2014; "Factsheet on the 'Right to Be Forgotten' Ruling," Court of Justice of the European Union, May 14, 2014; "European Court Lets Users Erase Records on Web," by David Streitfield, *New York Times*, May 13, 2014; "Daily Report: Europe Moves to Reform Rules Protecting Privacy," *New York Times*, March 13, 2014.

Determining how or whether personal information should be retained or deleted on the Internet is just one of many ethical, social, and political issues raised by the rapid evolution of the Internet and e-commerce. For instance, as discussed in the opening case, whether individuals lose control over all personal information once it is placed on the Internet is still up for debate in the United States. In Europe, in contrast, individuals do retain rights to their personal information. These questions are not just ethical questions that we as individuals have to answer; they also involve social institutions such as family, schools, business firms, and in some cases, entire nation-states. And these questions have obvious political dimensions because they involve collective choices about how we should live and what laws we would like to live under.

In this chapter, we discuss the ethical, social, and political issues raised in e-commerce, provide a framework for organizing the issues, and make recommendations for managers who are given the responsibility of operating e-commerce companies within commonly accepted standards of appropriateness.

8.1 UNDERSTANDING ETHICAL, SOCIAL, AND POLITICAL ISSUES IN E-COMMERCE

The Internet and its use in e-commerce have raised pervasive ethical, social, and political issues on a scale unprecedented for computer technology. Entire sections of daily newspapers and weekly magazines are devoted to the social impact of the Internet. But why is this so? Why is the Internet at the root of so many contemporary controversies? Part of the answer lies in the underlying features of Internet technology itself, and the ways in which it has been exploited by business firms. Internet technology and its use in e-commerce disrupt existing social and business relationships and understandings.

Consider, for instance, Table 1.2 (in Chapter 1), which lists the unique features of Internet technology. Instead of considering the business consequences of each unique feature, **Table 8.1** examines the actual or potential ethical, social, and/or political consequences of the technology.

We live in an "information society," where power and wealth increasingly depend on information and knowledge as central assets. Controversies over information are often disagreements over power, wealth, influence, and other things thought to be valuable. Like other technologies, such as steam, electricity, telephones, and television, the Internet and e-commerce can be used to achieve social progress, and for the most part, this has occurred. However, the same technologies can be used to commit crimes, attack innocent people, despoil the environment, and threaten cherished social values. Before automobiles, there was very little interstate crime and very little federal jurisdiction over crime. Likewise with the Internet: before the Internet, there was very little "cybercrime."

Many business firms and individuals are benefiting from the commercial development of the Internet, but this development also exacts a price from individuals, organizations, and societies. These costs and benefits must be carefully considered by those

TABLE 8.1 — UNIQUE FEATURES OF E-COMMERCE TECHNOLOGY AND THEIR POTENTIAL ETHICAL, SOCIAL, AND/OR POLITICAL IMPLICATIONS

E-COMMERCE TECHNOLOGY DIMENSION	POTENTIAL ETHICAL, SOCIAL, AND POLITICAL SIGNIFICANCE
Ubiquity—Internet/web technology is available everywhere: at work, at home, and elsewhere via mobile devices, anytime.	Work and shopping can invade family life; shopping can distract workers at work, lowering productivity; use of mobile devices can lead to automobile and industrial accidents. Presents confusing issues of "nexus" to taxation authorities.
Global reach—The technology reaches across national boundaries, around the Earth.	Reduces cultural diversity in products; weakens local small firms while strengthening large global firms; moves manufacturing production to low-wage areas of the world; weakens the ability of all nations—large and small—to control their information destiny.
Universal standards—There is one set of technology standards, namely Internet standards.	Increases vulnerability to viruses and hacking attacks worldwide, affecting millions of people at once. Increases the likelihood of "information" crime, crimes against systems, and deception.
Richness—Video, audio, and text messages are possible.	A "screen technology" that reduces use of text and potentially the ability to read by focusing instead on video and audio messages. Potentially very persuasive messages that may reduce reliance on multiple independent sources of information.
Interactivity—The technology works through interaction with the user.	The nature of interactivity at commercial sites can be shallow and meaningless. Customer e-mails are frequently not read by human beings. Customers do not really "co-produce" the product as much as they "co-produce" the sale. The amount of "customization" of products that occurs is minimal, occurring within predefined platforms and plug-in options.
Information density—The technology reduces information costs, and raises quality.	While the total amount of information available to all parties increases, so does the possibility of false and misleading information, unwanted information, and invasion of solitude. Trust, authenticity, accuracy, completeness, and other quality features of information can be degraded. The ability of individuals and organizations to make sense out of this plethora of information is limited.
Personalization/Customization—The technology allows personalized messages to be delivered to individuals as well as groups.	Opens up the possibility of intensive invasion of privacy for commercial and governmental purposes that is unprecedented.
Social technology—The technology enables user content generation and social networking.	Creates opportunities for cyberbullying, abusive language, and predation; challenges concepts of privacy, fair use, and consent to use posted information; creates new opportunities for surveillance by authorities and corporations into private lives.

seeking to make ethical and socially responsible decisions in this new environment. The question is: How can you as a manager make reasoned judgments about what your firm should do in a number of e-commerce areas—from securing the privacy of your customer's clickstream to ensuring the integrity of your company's domain name?

A MODEL FOR ORGANIZING THE ISSUES

E-commerce—and the Internet—have raised so many ethical, social, and political issues that it is difficult to classify them all, and hence, complicated to see their relationship to one another. Clearly, ethical, social, and political issues are interrelated. One way to organize the ethical, social, and political dimensions surrounding e-commerce is shown in **Figure 8.1**. At the individual level, what appears as an ethical issue—"What should I do?"—is reflected at the social and political levels—"What should we as a society and government do?" The ethical dilemmas you face as a manager of a business using the Web reverberate and are reflected in social and political debates. The major ethical, social, and political issues that have developed around e-commerce over the past 10 years can be loosely categorized into four major dimensions: information rights, property rights, governance, and public safety and welfare.

Some of the ethical, social, and political issues raised in each of these areas include the following:

- **Information rights:** What rights to their own personal information do individuals have in a public marketplace, or in their private homes, when Internet technologies make information collection so pervasive and efficient? What rights do individuals have to access information about business firms and other organizations?
- **Property rights:** How can traditional intellectual property rights be enforced in an Internet world where perfect copies of protected works can be made and easily distributed worldwide in seconds?

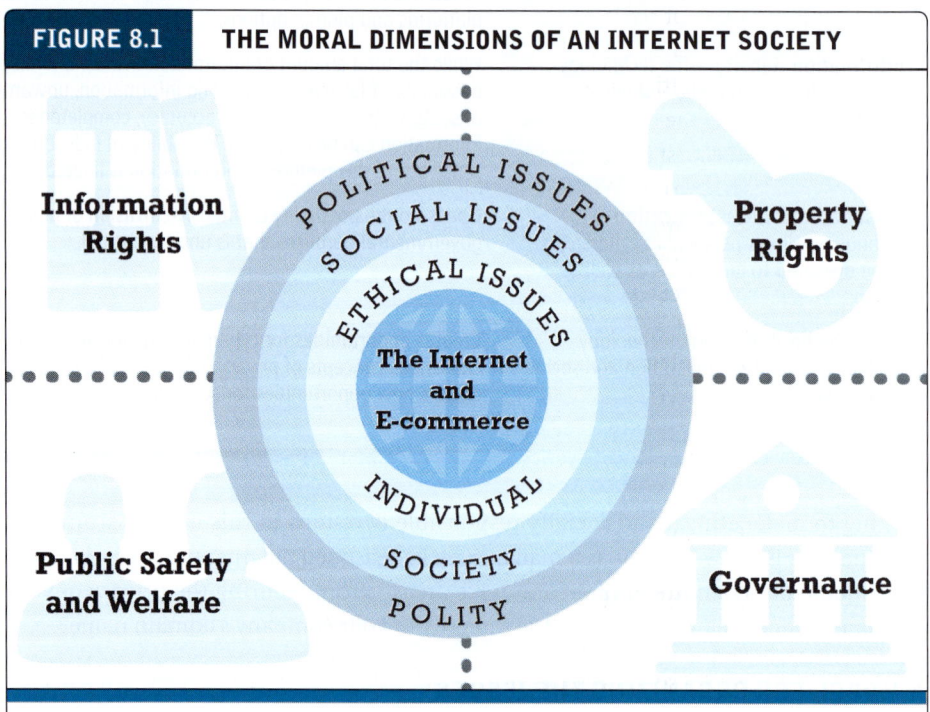

FIGURE 8.1 THE MORAL DIMENSIONS OF AN INTERNET SOCIETY

The introduction of the Internet and e-commerce impacts individuals, societies, and political institutions. These impacts can be classified into four moral dimensions: property rights, information rights, governance, and public safety and welfare.

- **Governance:** Should the Internet and e-commerce be subject to public laws? And if so, what law-making bodies have jurisdiction—state, federal, and/or international?
- **Public safety and welfare:** What efforts should be undertaken to ensure equitable access to the Internet and e-commerce channels? Should governments be responsible for ensuring that schools and colleges have access to the Internet? Are certain online content and activities—such as fake news, pornography, gambling, or anonymous tweeting of hateful language—a threat to public safety and welfare? What about connected cars? Should mobile commerce be allowed from moving vehicles?

To illustrate, imagine that at any given moment, society and individuals are more or less in an ethical equilibrium brought about by a delicate balancing of individuals, social organizations, and political institutions. Individuals know what is expected of them, social organizations such as business firms know their limits, capabilities, and roles, and political institutions provide a supportive framework of market regulation, banking, and commercial law that provides sanctions against violators.

Now, imagine we drop into the middle of this calm setting a powerful new technology such as the Internet and e-commerce. Suddenly, individuals, business firms, and political institutions are confronted by new possibilities of behavior. For instance, individuals discover that they can download perfect digital copies of music tracks from websites without paying anyone, something that, under the old technology of CDs, would have been impossible. This can be done, despite the fact that these music tracks still legally belong to the owners of the copyright—musicians and record label companies. Then, business firms discover that they can make a business out of aggregating these digital musical tracks—or creating a mechanism for sharing musical tracks—even though they do not "own" them in the traditional sense. The record companies, courts, and legislatures were not prepared at first to cope with the onslaught of online digital copying. Courts and legislative bodies had to create new laws and reach new judgments about who owns digital copies of copyrighted works and under what conditions such works can be "shared." It may take years to develop new understandings, laws, and acceptable behavior in just this one area of social impact. In the meantime, as an individual and a manager, you will have to decide what you and your firm should do in legal "gray" areas, where there is conflict between ethical principles but no clear-cut legal or cultural guidelines. How can you make good decisions in this type of situation?

Before examining the four moral dimensions of e-commerce in greater depth, we will briefly review some basic concepts of ethical reasoning that you can use as a guide to ethical decision making, and provide general reasoning principles about the social and political issues of the Internet that you will face in the future.

BASIC ETHICAL CONCEPTS: RESPONSIBILITY, ACCOUNTABILITY, AND LIABILITY

Ethics is at the heart of social and political debates about the Internet. **Ethics** is the study of principles that individuals and organizations can use to determine right and wrong courses of action. It is assumed in ethics that individuals are free moral agents who are in a position to make choices. When faced with alternative courses of action, what is the

ethics
the study of principles that individuals and organizations can use to determine right and wrong courses of action

responsibility

as free moral agents, individuals, organizations, and societies are responsible for the actions they take

accountability

individuals, organizations, and societies should be held accountable to others for the consequences of their actions

liability

a feature of political systems in which a body of law is in place that permits individuals to recover the damages done to them by other actors, systems, or organizations

due process

a process in which laws are known and understood and there is an ability to appeal to higher authorities to ensure that the laws have been correctly applied

correct moral choice? Extending ethics from individuals to business firms and even entire societies can be difficult, but it is not impossible. As long as there is a decision-making body or individual (such as a board of directors or CEO in a business firm, or a governmental body in a society), their decisions can be judged against a variety of ethical principles.

If you understand some basic ethical principles, your ability to reason about larger social and political debates will be improved. In western culture, there are four basic principles that all ethical schools of thought share: responsibility, accountability, liability, and due process. **Responsibility** means that as free moral agents, individuals, organizations, and societies are responsible for the actions they take. **Accountability** means that individuals, organizations, and societies should be held accountable to others for the consequences of their actions. The third principle—liability—extends the concepts of responsibility and accountability to the area of law. **Liability** is a feature of political systems in which a body of law is in place that permits individuals to recover the damages done to them by other actors, systems, or organizations. **Due process** is a feature of law-governed societies and refers to a process in which laws are known and understood, and there is an ability to appeal to higher authorities to ensure that the laws have been correctly applied.

You can use these concepts immediately to understand some contemporary Internet debates. For instance, consider the 2005 U.S. Supreme Court decision in the case of *Metro-Goldwyn-Mayer Studios v. Grokster, et al.* MGM had sued Grokster and other P2P networks for copyright infringement. The court decided that because the primary and intended use of Internet P2P file-sharing services such as Grokster, StreamCast, and Kazaa was the swapping of copyright-protected music and video files, the file-sharing services should be held accountable and shut down. Although Grokster and the other networks acknowledged that the most common use of the software was for illegal digital music file-swapping, they argued that there were substantial, nontrivial uses of the same networks for legally sharing files. They also argued they should not be held accountable for what individuals do with their software, any more than Sony could be held accountable for how people use VCRs, or Xerox for how people use copying machines. Ultimately, the Supreme Court ruled that Grokster and other P2P networks could be held accountable for the illegal actions of their users if it could be shown that they intended their software to be used for illegal downloading and sharing, and had marketed the software for that purpose. The court relied on copyright laws to arrive at its decisions, but these laws reflect some basic underlying ethical principles of responsibility, accountability, and liability.

Underlying the *Grokster* Supreme Court decision is a fundamental rejection of the notion that the Internet is an ungoverned "Wild West" environment that cannot be controlled. Under certain defined circumstances, the courts will intervene into the uses of the Internet. No organized civilized society has ever accepted in the long term the proposition that technology can flaunt basic underlying social and cultural values. Through all of the industrial and technological developments that have taken place, societies have intervened by means of legal and political decisions to ensure that the technology serves socially acceptable ends without stifling the positive consequences of innovation and wealth creation. The Internet in this sense is no different, and we can expect societies around the world to exercise more regulatory control over the Internet and e-commerce in an effort to arrive at a new balance between innovation and wealth creation, on the one hand, and other socially desirable objectives on the other. This is a difficult balancing act, and reasonable people will arrive at different conclusions.

ANALYZING ETHICAL DILEMMAS

Ethical, social, and political controversies usually present themselves as dilemmas. A **dilemma** is a situation in which there are at least two diametrically opposed actions, each of which supports a desirable outcome. When confronted with a situation that seems to present an ethical dilemma, how can you analyze and reason about the situation? The following is a five-step process that should help:

dilemma

a situation in which there are at least two diametrically opposed actions, each of which supports a desirable outcome

1. **Identify and clearly describe the facts.** Find out who did what to whom, and where, when, and how. In many instances, you will be surprised at the errors in the initially reported facts, and often you will find that simply getting the facts straight helps define the solution. It also helps to get the opposing parties involved in an ethical dilemma to agree on the facts.

2. **Define the conflict or dilemma and identify the higher-order values involved.** Ethical, social, and political issues always reference higher values. Otherwise, there would be no debate. The parties to a dispute all claim to be pursuing higher values (e.g., freedom, privacy, protection of property, and the free enterprise system). For example, supporters of the use of advertising networks such as Google Ads (formerly DoubleClick) argue that the tracking of consumer movements on the Web increases market efficiency and the wealth of the entire society. Opponents argue this claimed efficiency comes at the expense of individual privacy, and advertising networks should cease their activities or offer web users the option of not participating in such tracking.

3. **Identify the stakeholders.** Every ethical, social, and political issue has stakeholders: players in the game who have an interest in the outcome, have invested in the situation, and usually have vocal opinions. Find out the identity of these groups and what they want. This will be useful later when designing a solution.

4. **Identify the options that you can reasonably take.** You may find that none of the options satisfies all the interests involved, but that some options do a better job than others. Sometimes, arriving at a "good" or ethical solution may not always be a balancing of consequences to stakeholders.

5. **Identify the potential consequences of your options.** Some options may be ethically correct but disastrous from other points of view. Other options may work in this one instance but not in other similar instances. Always ask yourself, "What if I choose this option consistently over time?"

Once your analysis is complete, you can refer to the following well-established ethical principles to help decide the matter.

CANDIDATE ETHICAL PRINCIPLES

Although you are the only one who can decide which ethical principles you will follow and how you will prioritize them, it is helpful to consider some ethical principles with deep roots in many cultures that have survived throughout recorded history:

- **The Golden Rule:** Do unto others as you would have them do unto you. Putting yourself into the place of others and thinking of yourself as the object of the decision can help you think about fairness in decision making.

- **Universalism:** If an action is not right for all situations, then it is not right for any specific situation (Immanuel Kant's categorical imperative). Ask yourself, "If we adopted this rule in every case, could the organization, or society, survive?"

- **Slippery Slope:** If an action cannot be taken repeatedly, then it is not right to take at all. An action may appear to work in one instance to solve a problem, but if repeated, would result in a negative outcome. In plain English, this rule can be stated as "once started down a slippery path, you may not be able to stop."

- **Collective Utilitarian Principle:** Take the action that achieves the greater value for all of society. This rule assumes you can prioritize values in a rank order and understand the consequences of various courses of action.

- **Risk Aversion:** Take the action that produces the least harm, or the least potential cost. Some actions have extremely high failure costs of very low probability (e.g., building a nuclear generating facility in an urban area) or extremely high failure costs of moderate probability (speeding and automobile accidents). Avoid the high-failure cost actions and choose those actions whose consequences would not be catastrophic, even if there were a failure.

- **No Free Lunch:** Assume that virtually all tangible and intangible objects are owned by someone else unless there is a specific declaration otherwise. (This is the ethical "no free lunch" rule.) If something someone else has created is useful to you, it has value and you should assume the creator wants compensation for this work.

- **The New York Times Test (Perfect Information Rule):** Assume that the results of your decision on a matter will be the subject of the lead article in the *New York Times* the next day. Will the reaction of readers be positive or negative? Would your parents, friends, and children be proud of your decision? Most criminals and unethical actors assume imperfect information, and therefore they assume their decisions and actions will never be revealed. When making decisions involving ethical dilemmas, it is wise to assume perfect information markets.

- **The Social Contract Rule:** Would you like to live in a society where the principle you are supporting would become an organizing principle of the entire society? For instance, you might think it is wonderful to download illegal copies of Hollywood movies, but you might not want to live in a society that does not respect property rights, such as your property rights to the car in your driveway, or your rights to a term paper or original art.

None of these rules is an absolute guide, and there are exceptions and logical difficulties with all of them. Nevertheless, actions that do not easily pass these guidelines deserve some very close attention and a great deal of caution because the appearance of unethical behavior may do as much harm to you and your company as the actual behavior.

Now that you have an understanding of some basic ethical reasoning concepts, let's take a closer look at each of the major types of ethical, social, and political debates that have arisen in e-commerce.

8.2 PRIVACY AND INFORMATION RIGHTS

Privacy is arguably the most complex ethical issue raised by e-commerce, as well as the changing technology of human communications brought on by the Internet and mobile devices. It may be the most delicate and vexing issue of our digital age, one that will continue to evolve through this century. How can we square the ever-growing power of digital technologies to gather personal information by businesses and government with the notion that individuals have the right to be left alone, free to think what they want without fear, and control how their information used?

In ways not anticipated by technologists or politicians, these digital technologies and devices have become the primary means of personal interaction with other people and firms. The smartphone and Internet are now at the center of social, political, and business life. In the fast-growing online marketplace for goods and services, these technologies efficiently and faithfully record human market behavior in ways never imagined. The resulting trove of personal private information gathered by online merchants has no precedent in history. Laws and regulations to govern the use of this information are weak and poorly defined. As a result, consumers often feel they have lost control over their personal information online. And, indeed, they have.

WHAT IS PRIVACY?

The claim to **privacy** rests on the moral right of individuals to be left alone, free from surveillance or interference from other individuals or organizations, including the state. Privacy is one girder supporting freedom: without the privacy required to think, write, plan, and associate independently and without fear, social and political freedom, particularly freedom of expression, is weakened, and perhaps destroyed. You cannot have a democratic society without privacy.

Information privacy is a subset of privacy that rests on four central premises. First, individuals have a moral right to be able to control the use of whatever information is collected about them, whether or not they consented to the gathering of information in the first place. Individuals should be able to edit, delete, and shape the use of their online personal information by governments and business firms. In this view, individuals even have the "**right to be forgotten**," as discussed in the opening case (Rosen, 2012).

Second, individuals have a moral right to know when information is being collected about them, and must give their consent prior to collecting their personal information. This is the principle of "informed consent," that people are rational actors who are informed, and who will make their own choices in the marketplace, including the decision whether to give their information in return for some benefit.

privacy
the moral right of individuals to be left alone, free from surveillance or interference from other individuals or organizations, including the state

information privacy
subset of privacy that rests on four central premises, including the moral rights to control use of information collected and to know whether information is being collected, the right to personal information due process, and the right to have personal information stored in a secure manner

right to be forgotten
the claim of individuals to be able to edit and delete personal information

Third, individuals have a right to personal information due process. The process of collecting, sharing, and disseminating personal information must be "fair" and transparent to everyone. Systems of personal information—whether public or private—must be publicly known (no secret systems), operate according to a published set of rules (terms of use policies) describing how governments and firms will use personal information, and define ways in which people can edit, correct, and shape their personal information in a system of records.

Fourth, individuals have a right to have their personal information stored in a secure manner. Personal record systems must have procedures in place to protect personal information from intrusion, hacking, and unauthorized uses. It is important to note that while privacy and security are not the same, they are linked. Without security of personal information, there obviously cannot be privacy. For example, the 2017 data breach at Equifax involving the loss of detailed information on over 145 million people was not only a security breach, but also an invasion of privacy (Andriotis and Minaya, 2017).

These principles of personal information privacy are reflected in a doctrine called Fair Information Practices (FIP), established by the U.S. Federal Trade Commission (FTC) in 2000 (see **Table 8.2**). We discuss the role of the FTC in protecting personal private information further later in the chapter.

PRIVACY IN THE PUBLIC SECTOR: PRIVACY RIGHTS OF CITIZENS

The concept and practice of privacy, and its legal foundation, are very different in the public versus the private sector. In the public sector, concepts of privacy have a long

TABLE 8.2	THE FTC'S FAIR INFORMATION PRACTICE PRINCIPLES
Notice/Awareness (core principle)	Sites must disclose their information practices before collecting data. Includes identification of collector, uses of data, other recipients of data, nature of collection (active/inactive), voluntary or required, consequences of refusal, and steps taken to protect confidentiality, integrity, and quality of the data.
Choice/Consent (core principle)	There must be a process in place allowing consumers to choose how their information will be used for secondary purposes other than supporting the transaction, including internal use and transfer to third parties. Opt-in/opt-out must be available.
Access/Participation	Consumers should be able to review and contest the accuracy and completeness of data collected about them in a timely, inexpensive process.
Security	Data collectors must take reasonable steps to assure that consumer information is accurate and secure from unauthorized use.
Enforcement	There must be a mechanism to enforce FIP principles in place. This can involve self-regulation, legislation giving consumers legal remedies for violations, or federal statutes and regulation.

SOURCES: Based on data from Federal Trade Commission, 1998, 2000.

history that has evolved over two centuries of court rulings, laws, and regulations in the United States and Europe. In the private sector, concepts of privacy are much more recent, and in the age of the Internet, in a state of flux, debate, and argument.

The claim to individual privacy in the public sector, the arena of politics, power, and authority, is largely a European and American phenomenon that started as an attempt to limit the power of political executive leaders—kings, despots, and presidents, and to establish an acceptable relationship between citizens and their leaders.

In the United States, these claims were written into the U.S. Constitution and the Bill of Rights. The First Amendment guarantees citizens freedom of speech, association, and religion, and prohibits Congress from passing any laws that challenge these rights. The Fourth Amendment prohibits government agents from unreasonable searches and seizures of a citizen's premises, and requires a court-sanctioned warrant based on probable cause prior to any search of a person's premises. Much later, the Fourth Amendment was extended beyond the home to a very limited set of physical places. Warrants are not required when consent is given, for most motor vehicle searches, or when evidence is in plain view. The Fourteenth Amendment prohibits states from passing laws that deprive persons of life, liberty, or property, which the courts have interpreted as protecting the privacy of personal behavior in the home.

The word privacy is not mentioned in these founding documents, but it is considered to be necessary (implicit) for these amendments to mean anything. If privacy is denied, then freedom of speech, association, and religion is not possible. If one's premises cannot be protected against unreasonable searches by government, then there is no privacy.

However, relying on court decisions involving the Constitution to protect individuals has turned out to be inadequate in modern times. The founding documents of the 18th century did not define the rights of individuals to their personal information collected by government agencies in the routine course of administration, or the rights of citizens to obtain documents created by government agencies. There were no systems of records containing personal information in the 18th and 19th centuries, and government documents were routinely denied to inquisitive reporters and ordinary citizens by executive fiat and convenience. In 1974, the U.S. Congress passed an omnibus Privacy Act, which for the first time defined the privacy rights of a citizen vis-à-vis federal government record systems. The Privacy Act regulates the collection and use of data collected by federal agencies and defines fair information practices applicable to federal government systems such as those created by the Internal Revenue Service and the Social Security Administration. It's important to remember that Privacy Act protections apply only to government intrusions on privacy, not private firms' collection and use of personal information.

In addition to the Privacy Act, there are also a host of other U.S. federal laws (and state laws) that protect individuals against unreasonable government intrusions (see **Table 8.3** for a list of federal privacy laws that apply to the U.S. government). These statutes attempt to implement Fair Information Practices in a wide variety of public systems of personal information.

PRIVACY IN THE PRIVATE SECTOR: PRIVACY RIGHTS OF CONSUMERS

When the first large-scale, nationwide computerized systems began to appear in the United States in the 1960s, privacy issues and claims rose. For instance, credit card systems

TABLE 8.3 FEDERAL PRIVACY LAWS APPLICABLE TO THE U.S. GOVERNMENT

NAME	DESCRIPTION
Freedom of Information Act of 1966	Gives people the right to inspect information about themselves held in government files; also allows other individuals and organizations the right to request disclosure of government records based on the public's right to know.
Privacy Act of 1974, as amended	Regulates the federal government's collection, use, and disclosure of data collected by federal agencies. Gives individuals a right to inspect and correct records.
Privacy Protection Act of 1980	Prohibits government agents from conducting unannounced searches of press offices and files if no one in the office is suspected of committing a crime.
Electronic Communications Privacy Act of 1986	Makes conduct that would infringe on the security of electronic communications illegal.
Computer Security Act of 1987	Makes conduct that would infringe on the security of computer-based files illegal.
Computer Matching and Privacy Protection Act of 1988	Regulates computerized matching of files held by different government agencies.
Driver's Privacy Protection Act of 1994	Limits access to personal information maintained by state motor vehicle departments to those with legitimate business purposes. Also gives drivers the option to prevent disclosure of driver's license information to marketers and the general public.
E-Government Act of 2002	Regulates the collection and use of personal information by federal agencies.
USA Freedom Act of 2015	Imposes limits on the bulk collection by federal agencies of U.S. citizens' telecommunication metadata.

for the first time gave retail merchants and financial institutions the ability to systematically collect digital information on consumer behavior. For the first time there were very large private national databases that contained a history of whatever people purchased, from whom, and where. Large national private credit rating agencies appeared and began developing consumer credit histories, with details on personal finances from credit card to loan payments. These developments led to the first efforts to claim a right to consumer privacy. Other institutions within the education, health, and financial services sectors also began creating very large-scale databases involving millions of citizens. There followed a host of U.S. federal and state laws that applied to specific industries from credit reporting, finance, and health, to video stores (see **Table 8.4**). The pattern of protecting privacy in the United States is not with a general privacy statute covering all record systems, but instead to develop privacy statutes piecemeal, one industry at a time, as abuses become known. For instance, all states have legislation requiring firms to report data breaches to the public but there is no federal legislation. Despite a growing number of very large data breaches at a variety of retail, health, financial firms, and portals like Yahoo, the U.S. Congress has thus far failed to pass data breach notification legislation.

TABLE 8.4   PRIVACY LAWS AFFECTING PRIVATE INSTITUTIONS

NAME	DESCRIPTION
SELECTED FEDERAL PRIVACY LAWS	
Fair Credit Reporting Act of 1970	Regulates the credit investigating and reporting industry. Gives people the right to inspect credit records if they have been denied credit and provides procedures for correcting information.
Family Educational Rights and Privacy Act of 1974	Requires schools and colleges to give students and their parents access to student records and to allow them to challenge and correct information; limits disclosure of such records to third parties.
Right to Financial Privacy Act of 1978	Regulates the financial industry's use of personal financial records; establishes procedures that federal agencies must follow to gain access to such records.
Cable Communications Policy Act of 1984	Regulates the cable industry's collection and disclosure of information concerning subscribers.
Video Privacy Protection Act of 1988	Prevents disclosure of a person's video rental records without court order or consent.
Children's Online Privacy Protection Act (1998)	Prohibits deceptive practices in connection with the collection, use, and/or disclosure of personal information from and about children on the Internet.
Telephone Consumer Protection Act of 1991	Regulates telemarketing messages. FCC amended regulations to also apply to such messages delivered via text, mobile app, or other forms of wireless communication to a mobile device. Requires consumers' prior express consent for such messages.
Health Insurance Portability and Accountability Act of 1996 (HIPAA)	Requires healthcare providers and insurers and other third parties to promulgate privacy policies to consumers and establishes due process procedures.
Financial Modernization Act (Gramm-Leach-Bliley Act) (1999)	Requires financial institutions to inform consumers of their privacy policies and permits consumers some control over their records.
SELECTED STATE PRIVACY LAWS	
Privacy of personal information	The California Consumer Privacy Act of 2018 gives residents new privacy rights to be informed about the kind of personal information collected by personal data companies of any kind, and the rights to delete information, opt out of the sale of their information, and to access their information in a usable format so they can transfer their information to another service.
Online privacy policies	The California Online Privacy Protection Act of 2003 was the first state law in the United States requiring owners of commercial websites or online services to post a privacy policy. The policy must, among other things, identify the categories of personally identifiable information (PII) collected about site visitors and categories of third parties with whom the information may be shared. A number of states require government websites to establish privacy policies or procedures or incorporate machine-readable privacy policies into their websites.
Digital device privacy	The California Electronic Communications Privacy Act requires law enforcement to obtain a search warrant, wiretap order, or similar authority in order to obtain information from smartphones and other electronic devices without the owner's consent. Thus far, there are no state or federal laws defining privacy for Internet of Things (IoT) devices, such as Amazon's Alexa.
Spyware legislation	A number of states, including California, Utah, Arizona, Arkansas, and Virginia, among others, have passed laws that outlaw the installation of spyware on a user's computer without consent.
Disclosure of security breaches	Every state has enacted legislation requiring private or governmental entities to notify individuals of security breaches of information involving PII. There is no comprehensive federal law regulating data breaches, data privacy, and cybersecurity matters.
Data encryption	Many states require health, financial, and insurance firms to encrypt some personal information that flows over the Internet.

Another issue that has arisen associated with using legislation to address privacy violations is the question of the harm that must be shown in order to give rise to the right to sue. For instance, a California man named Thomas Robins sued Spokeo, a company that sells personal data online to employers and individuals looking for information on prospective partners. Robins sued based on a section of the Fair Credit Reporting Act that provides damages of up to $1,000 against data-gathering firms if these reports are false and cause concrete harm, even if the harm cannot be quantified. Robins claimed the profile about him distributed by Spokeo was substantially erroneous. Robins claims this false data potentially caused him to lose employment and other opportunities although he had no evidence he had experienced any real-world harm. Robins also claimed the right to organize a class action group composed of people similarly harmed. A lower court agreed with Robins and his right to organize a class action suit for others similarly harmed. In 2016, the U.S. Supreme Court opted not to decide the case, but remanded it back to the lower court with instructions to more precisely define "concrete" harm, suggesting it must actually exist and be a real harm (*Spokeo v. Robins, 136 S.Ct. 1540* (2016)). However, real harm, the Court agreed, could include intangible harms as well as the risk of real harm in the future. On the other hand, the majority also stated that mere procedural errors, like misreporting a person's zip code, or minor errors, would not constitute a real harm. In 2017, the lower court once again agreed with Robins and held that his alleged injuries were concrete enough to provide a basis upon which to sue Spokeo (*Robins v. Spokeo, Inc., 867 F.3d 1108* (2017)). In 2018, the Supreme Court declined to review the decision, leaving it to the lower courts to decide how to apply the ruling, creating continuing uncertainty (Foley & Lardner LLP, 2018; Liptak, 2016; Werner and Poell, 2017).

While there is a very long history to the discussion of privacy in the public sector in Europe and the United States, and a more recent history of applying these ideas to very large-scale private institutions (such as banks, medical providers, and insurance companies), the same is not true of consumer privacy in public markets. E-commerce is based on online markets and transactions. Since village markets appeared in ancient villages, to the present day, there rarely has been a claim to privacy in public, open markets. Think about the local farmers markets today: few, if any, people claim that what they purchase is private, or that others should not see what they are buying or the prices they pay. Merchants in public markets collected personal information in the course of commerce. "Knowing your customer" meant knowing the name, personal preferences, interests, purchases, and background of consumers. Consumer behavior in public markets was not protected by common law or our founding documents like the Constitution.

Yet no one anticipated the rise of Google, Facebook, Amazon, Netflix, and other e-commerce companies that collect personal information on nearly the entire population of the United States (and the world). No one anticipated that e-commerce would involve over 225 million people in the United States; that a single company would dominate online retail (Amazon); that a single company would dominate the online search market and gather very detailed data on consumer intentions and interests (Google); or that a single firm would become a repository of the social life of billions of people (Facebook). The emergence of the Internet, the Web, and smartphones, and their use in truly huge online markets involving most of the American population, has greatly enlarged the ability of merchants, financial institutions, and marketing firms to gather digital consumer data,

TABLE 8.5	PERSONAL INFORMATION COLLECTED BY E-COMMERCE SITES	
Name	Gender	Education
Address	Age	Preference data
Phone number	Occupation	Transaction data
E-mail address	Location	Clickstream data
Social security number	Location history	Device used for access
Bank account numbers	Likes	Browser type
Credit card numbers	Photograph	

use it for their own commercial purposes, and potentially abuse that information. These same forces have also spurred the growth of demands for the protection of consumer personal privacy in the digital era.

As it turns out, the Internet, the Web, and the mobile platform provide an ideal environment for both business and government to invade the personal privacy of millions of consumers on a scale unprecedented in history. Perhaps no other recent issue has raised as much widespread social and political concern as protecting the privacy of Internet users.

Information Collected by E-commerce Companies

As you have learned in previous chapters, e-commerce companies routinely collect a variety of information from or about consumers who visit and/or make purchases at their websites or mobile apps. Some of this data constitutes **personally identifiable information (PII)**, which is defined as any data that can be used to identify, locate, or contact an individual (Federal Trade Commission, 2000). Other data is **anonymous information**, where the identity of the person is not a name but an assigned code. This anonymous information includes demographic and behavioral information, such as age, occupation, income, zip code, ethnicity, and browsing behavior without identifying who you are. **Table 8.5** lists some of the personal identifiers that may be collected by e-commerce companies. This is not an exhaustive list, and in fact, many online companies collect hundreds of different data points on visitors. For instance, a study of nine data brokers identified twelve broad categories of information collected by brokers, and 240 data elements from address history, to liens and political leanings, to vehicle and travel data (Federal Trade Commission, 2014). Facebook collects over 500 data elements on its users and their friends. Although anonymous, this detailed information is still "personal," and a name identifier can be attached to the information quite easily.

Advertising networks and search engines also track the behavior of consumers across thousands of popular sites, not just at one site, via cookies, web beacons, tracking software, spyware, and other techniques. For instance, simply clicking a Like button on a website enables Facebook to track your movements across the entire Web.

Table 8.6 identifies some of the major ways online firms gather information about consumers.

personally identifiable information (PII)
Any data that can be used to identify, locate, or contact an individual

anonymous information
Demographic and behavioral information that doesn't include any personal identifiers

TABLE 8.6 THE INTERNET'S MAJOR INFORMATION-GATHERING TOOLS AND THEIR IMPACT ON PRIVACY

INTERNET CAPABILITY	IMPACT ON PRIVACY
Smartphones and apps	Used to track location and share photos, addresses, phone numbers, search, and other behavior to marketers.
Advertising networks	Used to track individuals as they move among thousands of websites.
Social networks	Used to gather information on user-provided content such as books, music, friends, and other interests, preferences, and lifestyles.
First-party cookies	Used to track individuals at a single site. Store user activity while on the website and enable login, shopping carts, understanding user behavior, and navigation features.
Third-party cookies (beacons)/HTML5 storage cookies	Placed by advertising networks and data collection firms with the permission of the website being visited. Used to track online behavior, searches, and sites visited across thousands of sites for the purpose of displaying "relevant" advertising. HTML5 storage cookies are placed in HTML5 storage or device storage, which has a much larger capacity than cookie files (0.5 Mb versus 4 k).
Persistent cookies	Remain active after a browsing session and stay active for a set period of time; useful in retargeting ads and cross-site tracking.
Device fingerprinting	Programs based on third-party servers that uniquely identify a device based on the operating system, local network, browser, graphics chip, graphics driver, installed fonts, and other features.
Search engine behavioral targeting	Uses prior search history, demographics, expressed interests, geographic, or other user-entered data to target advertising.
Deep packet inspection	Uses software installed at the ISP level to track all user clickstream behavior.
Shopping carts	Used to collect detailed payment and purchase information.
Forms	Online forms that users voluntarily fill out in return for a promised benefit or reward that are linked with clickstream or other behavioral data to create a personal profile.
Site transaction logs	Used to collect and analyze detailed information on page content viewed by users.
Search engines	Used to trace user statements and views on newsgroups, chat groups, and other public forums on the Web, and profile users' social and political views. Google returns name, address, and links to a map with directions to the address when a phone number is entered.
IP address	The unique number assigned to every device on the Internet, revealed by users when they use the Internet. Used to identify the ISP provider, region, local area network IP, and potentially the individual device. With a few other pieces of information, individuals are easily identified. Used by law enforcement, telecommunications companies, and ad firms to trace communications and user behavior across the Internet.
Cross-device tracking	Integrates the login information on smartphones with browser tracking from websites to create an integrated file on specific users; shared with ad network firms.

TABLE 8.7	INTERNET USERS' EFFORTS TO PRESERVE PRIVACY
ACTION	PERCENTAGE WHO HAVE DONE THIS
Cleared web browser history or cookies.	59%
Refused to provide information if felt wasn't relevant.	57%
Used web browser settings to disable or turn off cookies.	34%
Deleted or edited something previously posted online.	29%
Used a temporary e-mail address or user name.	25%
Provided inaccurate or false information about self.	24%
Refused to use website that required real name.	23%
Used public computer in order to browse anonymously.	12%
Attempted to get something posted online about them removed.	11%
Encrypted phone calls, text messages, or e-mail.	10%
Used proxy server, Tor, or VPN to browse Web anonymously.	9%

SOURCE: Based on data from Pew Research, 2018a, 2016a; 2015.

Key Issues in Online Privacy of Consumers

In recent polls, 90% of Americans are concerned about their online privacy, and 91% believe they have lost control over their online information. High on the list of public concerns are profiling (and the use of profiles to target ads), social network privacy, sharing of information by marketers, mobile device privacy, and privacy issues associated with digital assistant devices such as the Amazon Echo. By large majorities, most Americans do not trust private firms or governments to protect their information. According to Pew Research Center, 86% of American Internet users surveyed have taken steps to remove or mask information about themselves online, while many (over 60%) say they would like to do more (Pew Research Center, 2018a, 2016a, 2016b). **Table 8.7** describes some of the ways Internet users attempt to protect their privacy.

Marketing: Profiling, Behavioral Targeting, and Retargeting

Billions of people around the world go online on an average day. Marketers would like to know who these people are, what they are interested in, where they are, what they are doing, and what they buy. The more precise and complete the information, the more valuable it is as a predictive and marketing tool. Armed with this information, marketers can make their ad campaigns more efficient by targeting specific ads at specific groups or individuals, and they can even adjust the ads for specific groups.

profiling
the creation of digital images that characterize online individual and group behavior

data image
collection of data records used to create a behavioral profile of consumers

anonymous profiles
identify people as belonging to highly specific and targeted groups

personal profiles
add a personal e-mail address, postal address, and/or phone number to behavioral data

Most popular websites allow third parties—including online advertising networks such as Google Ads (formerly DoubleClick), Microsoft Advertising, and others—to place "third-party" cookies and web tracking software on a visitor's computer in order to engage in profiling the user's behavior across thousands of other websites that are also members of the advertising network. **Profiling** is the creation of **data images** (a collection of data records used to create behavioral profiles of consumers) that characterize online individual and group behavior. **Anonymous profiles** identify people as belonging to highly specific and targeted groups, for example, 20- to 30-year-old males, with college degrees and incomes greater than $30,000 a year, and interested in high-fashion clothing (based on recent search engine use). **Personal profiles** add a personal e-mail address, postal address, and/or phone number to behavioral data. Increasingly, online firms are linking their online profiles to personal offline consumer data collected by database firms tracking credit card purchases, as well as established retail and catalog firms. As you learned in Chapter 6, behavioral targeting is the use of personal profile information to determine which ads a consumer will see online. Retargeting is the practice of showing consumers the same ad on many different websites they visit. For instance, if you use Google to search for a new kitchen clock, ads for kitchen clocks will follow you to Yahoo, Facebook, and thousands of other sites you browse.

The online advertising networks have added several new dimensions to established offline marketing techniques. First, they have the ability to precisely track not just consumer purchases, but all online browsing behavior at thousands of websites, including browsing book lists, filling out preference forms, and viewing content pages. Second, they can dynamically adjust what the shopper sees on screen—including prices. Third, they can build and continually refresh high-resolution data images. Most computers have hundreds of these programs installed without consumer consent or understanding.

Both American and European regulators have objected to Google's policy of integrating personal information from all of its services into a single personal profile, and failing to adequately inform users about what it is doing with their personal information. In 2016, Google issued a new privacy policy, which it characterized as providing users with more control over the data it collects and how it is used while allowing Google to show the user more relevant ads. The change enabled Google to combine third-party browsing data generated by Google Ads with the user's individual Google search and e-mail data, enabling the creation of what some have referred to as a super profile (Drozdiak and Nicas, 2017). Privacy groups expressed concerns when Google purchased Nest, the maker of digital home thermostats and smoke detection devices that are connected to the Internet. Although Nest said that Nest accounts were not cross-linked with Google accounts, it admitted that it did share personal information with Google when connected to Google's "Works with Nest integration" system (Gibbs, 2015a). Even the effort to protect the security of such devices runs the risk of invading consumer privacy. A group of researchers at Cornell University found that while encryption can protect the contents of data generated by smart devices, even the act of generating and transmitting encrypted data can be enough to allow inferences about personal information to be conveyed (Baird, 2017).

Facial recognition adds a new dimension to profiling and behavioral targeting. Originally developed as a tool to recognize terrorists, local police departments have widely adopted the technology to identify wanted persons, finding it much faster than fingerprint databases (Teicher, 2018). The technology is evolving rapidly and has now spread into the commercial arena. A number of uses of facial recognition are already commonplace. Facebook and Google use the software to automatically suggest name tags for members or their friends in photographs and both are currently facing lawsuits that this practice violates the Illinois Biometric Information Privacy Act, one of a growing number of state laws that address this issue and which require firms to have user consent to collecting biometric and facial information (Marotti, 2018). Unlike credit cards, digital facial images cannot be changed or renewed. This has not deterred Facebook and others from continuing to work on advanced facial recognition technology, which is unsurprising given that the global market for such technologies is forecast to grow to $12 billion by 2020 (Adroit Market Research, 2020). Facebook's 2.5 billion users, who upload over 350 million photos every day, many of them tagged to specific individuals, provide companies with a massive potential database of faces. Although Facebook says it doesn't have any plans to directly sell its database, it is likely at some point that it will want to mine it for commercial exploitation, for instance, by using it to better target ads to its users. For instance, Facebook has filed for patents on technology allowing it to tailor ads based on users' facial expressions (Korta, 2017; Bennett, 2017).

Apple is another company investing heavily in facial recognition technology. Apple's Face ID uses a 3D scan of the user's face as an authenticating mechanism. The biometric data is stored on the phone itself, but even so Face ID has raised a number of privacy concerns. For instance, in order for Face ID to function, at least some of the iPhone's sensors must always be on, scanning for potential faces, potentially gathering data without users being aware, and raising the possibility that this functionality could be exploited by third-party app developers. Privacy advocates are concerned that Apple's championing of facial recognition technology positions it to become the new norm. For instance, Facebook reportedly has its own version of Face ID that it is testing as a means of verifying identity when a user is located out of his or her account. But many are still leery of the technology, with several surveys finding that about 70% of those surveyed felt it was "creepy" (Fingas, 2019; eMarketer, Inc., 2017; Lomas, 2017).

Network advertising firms argue that online profiling and targeting ads benefits both consumers and businesses. Profiling permits targeting of ads, ensuring that consumers see advertisements mostly for products and services in which they are actually interested. Businesses benefit by not paying for wasted advertising sent to consumers who have no interest in their product or service. The industry argues that by increasing the effectiveness of advertising, more advertising revenues go to the Internet, which in turn subsidizes free content on the Internet. Last, product designers and entrepreneurs benefit by sensing demand for new products and services by examining user searches and profiles. Yet contemporary research has found that most Americans (65%) do not accept the trade-off between the loss of their privacy in return for market efficiency or other benefits (Pew Research Center, 2018a, 2016a).

Critics argue that profiling undermines the expectation of anonymity and privacy that most people have when using the Internet, and changes what should be a private experience into one where an individual's every move is recorded. As people become aware that their every move is being watched, they will be far less likely to explore sensitive topics, browse pages, or read about controversial issues. How can people experience freedom if they believe their every move on the Internet is being watched? In most cases, the profiling is invisible to users, and even hidden. Consumers are not notified that profiling is occurring. Profiling permits data aggregation on hundreds or even thousands of unrelated sites on the Web (Zhe, 2017).

Critics debate the economic benefits of profiling because it allows firms to engage in price discrimination, charging more for goods based on, for instance, zip code, gender, and ethnicity (Singer, 2015). The cookies placed by ad networks are persistent, and they can be set to last days, months, years, or even forever. Their tracking occurs over an extended period of time and resumes each time the individual logs on to the Internet. This clickstream data is used to create profiles that can include hundreds of distinct data fields for each consumer. Associating so-called anonymous profiles with personal information is fairly easy, and companies can change policies quickly without informing the consumer. Although the information gathered by network advertisers is often anonymous (non-PII data), in many cases, the profiles derived from tracking consumers' activities are linked or merged with personally identifiable information. Anonymous behavioral data is far more valuable if it can be linked with names, offline consumer behavior, e-mail addresses, and postal addresses.

Social Networks: Privacy and Self Revelation

Social networks pose a unique challenge for the maintenance of personal privacy because they encourage people to reveal details about their personal lives (passions, loves, favorites, photos, videos, and personal interests), and to share them with their friends. In return, users get access to a free social network service. Social networks have greatly enlarged the depth, scope, and richness of information collected by private corporations. While Google's search engine is a massive database of personal intentions, Facebook has created a massive database of friends, preferences, Likes, posts, photos, and videos. An Austrian researcher was able to obtain his Facebook file (possible under European laws) and received a 1,222-page document of messages, photos, posts, and friends (Sengupta, 2012). Some social networkers share these personal details with everyone on the social network. On the face of it, this would seem to indicate that people who participate in social networks voluntarily give up their rights to personal privacy. How could they claim an expectation of privacy? When everything is shared, what's private?

But the reality is that many participants in social networks have a very keen sense of their personal privacy. Facebook is a prime example of senior management pushing the envelope of privacy, and experiencing a number of public relations reversals, intense critical reaction, and growing government concern. For a review of Facebook's various positions on online privacy over the years, and public and governmental reaction to these issues, refer to the *Insight on Society* case, *Facebook and the Age of Privacy*, in Chapter 1.

The result of these public conflicts suggests that social network participants do indeed have a strong expectation of privacy in the sense that they want to control how "their" information is used. People who contribute user-generated content have a strong sense of ownership over the content that is not diminished by posting the information on a social network for one's friends. As for members who post information to everyone, not just friends, these should be seen as "public performances" where the contributors voluntarily publish their performances, just as writers or other artists. In these situations, the claim to privacy is not credible.

Mobile Devices: Privacy Issues

As the mobile platform becomes more and more important, mobile and location-based privacy issues are also becoming a major concern. In addition to being able to track and store user location, mobile devices and associated apps are storehouses of personal information that can be shared with third parties such as advertisers and app developers, often without the awareness of the user. For instance, in 2017 analysts discovered that Facebook was using a software app it owned called Onavo that enabled it to track how millions of individuals were using their mobile phones, especially to track the success of rivals like Snapchat (Seetharaman and Morris, 2017). Onavo was removed from the Apple App Store in 2018.

Let's consider smartphone cross-device tracking and its marriage to cross-site web data. Smartphones are tracking devices by design: telecommunications companies and smartphone operating systems need to know where you are, and your phone is continually connecting to nearby cell towers. No cookies are needed to track your moves or clicks, simply because you can't use a cell phone without identifying yourself, even with the SIM card removed or the phone turned off in some devices. Apple's iOS keeps cell location information encrypted on the user's phone while Android reports this information to its servers. Users usually share this information with apps, such as Uber or Facebook, when they sign up for the app. Smartphone operating systems (Apple and Android) assign an anonymized ad tracking numbers to all users, and these can be used to target specific users. Apple's iOS allows users to reset this number, but doing so is not easy or well-known. Smartphones do not use cookies but apps and services are able to positively identify users through their phone logins whenever they use a service such as social networks, email, or shopping sites. These apps share this information with partner advertising platforms, which correlate the positive ID of the user with browser information collected from the same user at web sites. The result is a **cross-device graph** (digital dossier) for each user that identifies all the devices used by any individual, and tracks that individual's behavior regardless of the device used (Federal Trade Commission, 2017). Cross-device graphs will increasingly include user data collected from all Internet devices (IoT) such as car, home, and business sensing devices.

Smartphone and app technology also enables **persistent location tracking**, or the ability to track the geo-location of phone users whether they are using location tracking apps or not. For instance, Facebook, along with many others, is able to track any visits by users of third-party websites that contain a Like button, as well as their physical location, whether or not the user is logged in to Facebook. Even when apps are not activated, they can be sending location data to a variety of servers, including, of course, the wireless service providers (Goldman, 2017). Apps are major enablers of location tracking data, which is then sold to advertisers. Users can use options in the cell phone's operating system to not share location information (location services) with apps, but whatever information apps collect from their users is subject only to their own privacy policies (Nield, 2018; Bonnington, 2017). Some apps, like Google Maps, will not operate without location services turned on. The default option for most apps is to permit location reporting, and most users accept this option when signing up for the app.

cross-device graph
a data file that combines web and smartphone tracking data, as well as IoT devices, into a single comprehensive user profile

persistent location tracking
the ability to track the geo-location of phone users whether they are using location tracking apps or not

Consumer Privacy Regulation and Enforcement: The U.S. Federal Trade Commission

In the United States, the FTC has taken the lead in conducting research on online privacy, recommending legislation to Congress, and enforcing privacy regulations. The FTC is a cabinet-level agency charged with promoting the efficient functioning of the marketplace by protecting consumers from unfair or deceptive practices and increasing consumer choice by promoting competition. In addition to reports and recommendations, the FTC enforces existing legislation by filing complaints, and levying fines, and filing lawsuits against corporations it believes are in violation of federal trade laws. The FTC can also impose a federal monitor or reporting system to ensure the firm complies with agency rulings. In addition, the FTC also makes recommendations to Congress for new consumer privacy legislation.

Earlier in this section we described the FTC's Fair Information Practice (FIP) principles (see Table 8.2), on which it bases its assessments of how well firms are protecting consumer privacy. The FTC's FIP principles set the ground rules for what constitutes due process privacy protection procedures at e-commerce and all other websites—including government and nonprofit websites—in the United States. Embedded within FIP principles is the concept of **informed consent** (defined as consent given with knowledge of all material facts needed to make a rational decision). There are traditionally two models for informed consent: opt-in and opt-out. The **opt-in model** requires an affirmative action by the consumer to allow collection and use of information. For instance, using opt-in, consumers would first be asked if they approved of the collection and use of information, and then directed to check a selection box if they agreed. Otherwise, the default is not to approve the collection of data. In the **opt-out model**, the default is to collect information unless the consumer takes an affirmative action to prevent the collection of data by checking a box or by filling out a form. In the United States, most e-commerce companies that offer informed consent use the opt-out model. Unless the consumer checks a box to specifically decline, information is collected. Often, the selection box is at the very bottom of the web page, where the consumer is unlikely to see it, or located within complex menus.

The FTC's FIP principles are guidelines, not laws. In the United States, for example, business firms can gather transaction information generated in the marketplace and then use that information for other purposes, without obtaining the explicit affirmative informed consent of the individual. In Europe, this would be illegal. A business in Europe cannot use marketplace transaction information for any purpose other than supporting the current transaction, unless it obtains the individual's consent in writing or by filling out an on-screen form.

However, the FTC's FIP guidelines are often used as the basis of legislation. The most important online privacy legislation to date that has been directly influenced by the FTC's FIP principles is the Children's Online Privacy Protection Act (COPPA) (1998), which requires websites to obtain parental permission before collecting information on children under 13 years of age.

In the last decade, the FTC has broadened its approach to privacy beyond notice, informed consent, and opt-in/opt-out choice requirements to include a harm-based

informed consent
consent given with knowledge of all material facts needed to make a rational decision

opt-in model
requires an affirmative action by the consumer to allow collection and use of consumer information

opt-out model
the default is to collect information unless the consumer takes an affirmative action to prevent the collection of data

approach, focusing on practices that are likely to cause harm or unwarranted intrusion in consumers' daily lives. In several reports the FTC has recognized the limitations of its earlier FIP approach. It has found that "informed consent" is not effective when consumers do not know about, or understand, online firms' data collection practices. Consumers do not understand, and often fear, bring tracked from one website to another. Online firms often change their privacy policies without notice, and these policies are written in obscure language that confuses consumers. The FTC has also found the distinction between personal information and anonymous information to be invalid because it is easy for firms to identify consumers personally by name, email, and address based on so-called anonymous data. As a result the FTC developed a new framework to address consumer privacy. **Table 8.8** summarizes the important aspects of this framework.

TABLE 8.8 THE FTC'S CURRENT PRIVACY FRAMEWORK

PRINCIPLE	APPLICATION
Scope	Applies to all commercial entities that collect or use consumer data; not limited to those that just collect PII.
Privacy by Design	Companies should promote consumer privacy throughout the organization and at every stage of development of products and services: • Data security • Reasonable collection limits • Reasonable and appropriate data retention policies • Data accuracy • Comprehensive data management procedures
Simplified Choice	Companies should simplify consumer choice. Need not provide choice before collecting and using data for commonly accepted practices: • Product and fulfillment • Internal operations, fraud prevention • Legal compliance • First-party marketing For all other commercial data collection and use, choice is required, and should be clearly and conspicuously offered at a time and in a context in which consumer is providing data. Some types of information or practices (children, financial and medical information, deep packet inspection) may require additional protection through enhanced consent. Special choice mechanism for online behavioral advertising: "Do Not Track."
Greater Transparency	Increase transparency of data practices by: • Making privacy notices clearer, shorter, and more standardized to enable better comprehension and comparison • Providing consumers with reasonable access to data about themselves • Providing prominent disclosures and obtaining express affirmative consent before using consumer data in a materially different manner than claimed when data was collected • Educating consumers about commercial data privacy practices

SOURCE: Based on data from Federal Trade Commission, 2010.

The FTC also supports a Do Not Track mechanism for online behavioral advertising. The mechanism would involve placing a persistent cookie on a consumer's browser and conveying its setting to sites that the browser visits to signal whether or not the consumer wants to be tracked or receive targeted advertisements. A number of bills have been introduced in Congress to implement Do Not Track, but as yet none have been passed due to the opposition of the online advertising industry. Refer to the *Insight on Technology* case, *Every Move You Take, Every Click You Make, We'll Be Tracking You*, in Chapter 6 for a discussion of the difficulties that have developed in implementing Do Not Track.

A common perception is that no one is doing anything about online invasion of privacy. Yet over the last decade the FTC has brought over 170 enforcement actions against firms involving privacy issues, including spam, social networking, behavioral advertising, pretexting, spyware, peer-to-peer file sharing, and mobile devices (Federal Trade Commission, 2018a). **Table 8.9** describes a small sample of these enforcement actions.

Through periodic reports, the FTC also exerts influence on the online arena by acting as the lead federal agency in developing privacy policy, updating privacy principles and policies as new technologies and business practices emerge. For instance, in 2012, the FTC released a report describing industry best practices for protecting the privacy of Americans and focuses on five areas: Do Not Track, mobile privacy, data brokers, large platform providers (advertising networks, operating systems, browsers, and social media companies), and the development of self-regulatory codes. The report called for implementation of an easy-to-use, persistent, and effective Do Not Track system; improved disclosures for use of mobile data; making it easier for people to see the files about themselves compiled by data brokers; development of a central website where data brokers identify themselves; development of a privacy policy by large platform providers to regulate comprehensive tracking across the Internet; and enforcement of self-regulatory rules to ensure firms adhere to industry codes of conduct (Federal Trade Commission, 2012).

In 2014, the FTC issued a report on the data broker industry, which is at the heart of the online and offline privacy debate in the United States. The report found that data brokers operate without transparency, and most users have no idea how their information is being used. The report found that data brokers collect and store billions of data elements covering nearly every U.S. consumer. One of the nine data brokers studied had information on more than 1.4 billion consumer transactions and 700 billion data elements. Another broker adds more than 3 billion new data points to its database each month. The report called for legislation giving consumers more control over their personal information by creating a centralized portal where data brokers would identify themselves, describe their information collection and use practices, and provide links to access tools and opt-outs; require brokers to give consumers access to their data; provide opportunities to opt-out of data collection; describe where they get information and what inferences they make from the data; and require retailers to notify customers when they share information with data brokers (Federal Trade Commission, 2014).

In 2017, the FTC released a report on cross-device tracking where platforms, publishers, and advertisers connect consumer activity across smartphones, computers, and other digital devices, which enables them to link consumers' behavior across devices, and also to link that behavior to off-line purchase databases (Federal Trade Commission, 2017). The FTC's most recent emphasis is not on restricting the collection of information (as in

TABLE 8.9	FTC PRIVACY ENFORCEMENT ACTIONS
COMPANY	COMPLAINTS AND SETTLEMENTS
PayPal	FTC charged that PayPal misled consumers about the extent to which they could control the privacy of their transactions on Venmo, which is owned by PayPal. The FTC also charged that Venmo violated the Gramm-Leach Bliley Act's privacy rule, which requires financial institutions to deliver privacy notices to their customers. PayPal settled the charges with the FTC, agreeing to stop misrepresenting the extent of control provided by Venmo's privacy settings and submitting to a biennial third-party audit of its compliance for 10 years (2018).
Uber	Uber allowed employees unmonitored access to driver and rider personal information despite public statements to the contrary. The FTC required Uber to stop misrepresenting its information practices, implement a privacy policy, and submit to audits for 20 years (2017).
Ashley Madison	Ashley Madison lured 19 million customers with fake profiles of women designed to convert them into paid members and failed to protect personal information on 36 million users, which hackers then released. The FTC required it to implement a comprehensive data-security program, third-party audits, and fined it $1.6 million (2016).
Snapchat	Snapchat deceived consumers with promises about the disappearing nature of messages sent through the service (despite marketing claims, there were several simple ways that recipients could save snaps) and failed to provide security for personal information. The FTC required Snapchat to cease misrepresenting claims of protecting the privacy, security, or confidentiality of users' information, and to implement a comprehensive privacy program and implement a monitoring program for the next 20 years (2014).
Epic Marketplace	Online ad firm used "history sniffing" cookies to secretly gather browsing data from millions of consumers on 45,000 websites about their interest in sensitive medical and financial issues ranging from fertility and incontinence to debt relief and personal bankruptcy, and then send targeted emails. Required to stop using history sniffing and delete and destroy all data collected using the technology (2013).
Facebook	Facebook deceived users by allowing personal information to be shared and made public. The FTC required Facebook to provide clear notice to consumers how it would share information, and submit to privacy audits for 20 years (2012).
Google	Google violated the privacy settings in Apple's Safari browser. The FTC fined Google $22.5 million (2012).
Google	Deceptive tactics, violating its own privacy policies in Google Buzz social network. The FTC required Google to start a privacy program and permit an audit for 20 years (2011).

previous eras of privacy regulation), but instead on giving consumers rights with respect to the information collected about them in large databases and its use by various businesses and agencies. This is called a "consumer rights-based" privacy policy and represents a change in the meaning of privacy from "leave me alone" to "I want to know and control how my personal information is being used." The FTC has also recently held workshops on connected cars, student privacy and education technology, the changing nature of identity theft, and informational injury.

Consumer Privacy Regulation: The U.S. Federal Communications Commission (FCC)

In 2015, in the context of the controversy over net neutrality (discussed further later in this chapter), broadband Internet service providers (ISPs) such as Verizon, Comcast, and AT&T, which own the networks that are the foundation of the Internet, were classified as being like public utility services similar to telephone companies and hence subject to regulation by the FCC. In 2016, the FCC approved new privacy rules applicable to these companies. Up until this time, the focus on Internet privacy issues had centered on how websites and apps use personal information. However, broadband ISPs have also had access to much of the same information, such as data on transactions, location, browsing and app usage, and even social security numbers, which they collected without user consent. The broadband ISPs have been selling this information or using it for targeted advertising, just as Google, Facebook, and hundreds of other websites and apps do. The FCC's regulations required broadband ISPs to notify users of their new privacy options by e-mail or on their websites and to obtain user consent to collect this information. ISPs would not be allowed to offer service contingent on consumers surrendering their privacy and could not deny service to consumers who did not permit them to collect personal information (as is typical under Terms of Service policies for websites). For the first time in the decades-long debate over Internet privacy, a regulatory agency declared that personal information gathered by Internet firms belonged to consumers, not the owners of the networks. This was the first time in the United States that a federal agency recognized a property right to personal information (as opposed to a moral or constitutional right). The new rules did not apply to websites, which are not under FCC regulation (FCC, 2016; Kang, 2016). These new rules were strongly opposed by the Internet industry, arguing that they unfairly punished telecommunications providers for behavior that was permitted for Facebook, Google, and other online platforms. In early 2017, Congress voted to repeal the new rules, and currently, broadband ISPs can continue tracking and selling people's browsing and app utilization without notifying them (Kang, 2017).

Privacy and Terms of Use Policies

As noted previously, one conceptual basis of American privacy law is notification and consent. It is assumed that consumers can read Terms of Use notices (or privacy policies) concerning how a website will use their personal information, and then make a rational choice to either consent to the terms of use, opt out of the data collection (if that is an option), or stop using the site. Until recently, many U.S. e-commerce companies rejected the concept of informed consent and instead simply published their information use policy on their site. Nearly all websites have Terms of Use policies that users can find if they look carefully. These Terms of Use policies are sometimes called privacy policies, and they describe how the firms will use information collected on their sites. These policies are notices, and as noted above, it is assumed that anyone who uses the site has implicitly agreed to the Terms of Use policy. A study reviewed 30 popular social network and community sites and found that it would take the average reader about eight hours to simply read the policy. The longest policy was SoundCloud's, with 7,961 words. Obviously

TABLE 8.10	CRITERIA TO USE WHEN EXAMINING PRIVACY POLICIES

- Can the privacy policy be easily found, reviewed, and understood by users?
- Does the privacy policy fully disclose how personal information will and will not be used by the organization? Is information about users ever shared or sold without users' explicit permission?
- Can users decide if they want to participate?
- Can users decide and actively indicate that they agree to be profiled, tracked, or targeted?
- Can users decide how and if their sensitive information is shared?
- Are users able to change any information that they input about themselves?
- Can users decide who can access their information?
- Are users notified promptly if their information is lost, stolen, or improperly accessed?
- Can users easily report concerns and get answers?
- Do users receive a copy of all disclosures of their information?

a critical flaw with informed consent as the basis of privacy protections is that it assumes the average user can understand what privacy they may be giving up by using a site (Singer, 2014; Fiesler et al., 2014). For instance, Yahoo's privacy policy begins by stating that Yahoo takes the user's privacy seriously and Yahoo does not rent, sell, or share personal information about users with others or non-affiliated companies. However, there are a number of exceptions that significantly weaken this statement. For instance, Yahoo may share the information with "trusted partners," which could be anyone that Yahoo does business with, although perhaps not a company that the user might choose to do business with. In its privacy policy, Yahoo also says it uses cookies, device identifiers, and web beacons in order to track user clickstream behavior across the Web. Advertisers are sold access to this information. U.S. businesses argue that informing consumers by publishing a terms of use policy is sufficient to establish the users' informed consent. Privacy advocates argue that many terms of use/privacy policy statements on U.S. websites are obscure and difficult to read, and legitimate just about any use of personal information.

While politicians, privacy advocates, and the Internet industry wrangle over what the rules for privacy should be, very little attention has been paid to actually measuring the strength of privacy policies for individual companies, comparing them to other companies, and understanding how privacy policies have changed over time at a specific company. Is Facebook's privacy policy worse than, better than, or about the same as Apple's, or Google's? Have privacy policies improved after ten years of debate, or have they deteriorated?

A research project provides some preliminary answers to these questions. The researchers developed a measure of privacy policies by applying 10 privacy policy principles when reviewing policies (see **Table 8.10**) (Shore and Steinman, 2015). You will recognize these principles because they derive in primary part from the FTC and Fair Information Practices doctrines previously described. The dimensions themselves were measured on a four-point scale from 0 to 4 (0 meaning the privacy policy fails to meet the criterion and 4 indicating the criterion was fully achieved).

You can use the principles in Table 8.10 as a way to measure the privacy policy of your own online business or another firm. You can measure a single firm at two points in time to see how its policies changed, or compare two or more firms at a single point in time. Shore and Steinman chose to look at Facebook's privacy policies over a ten-year period from 2005 to 2015. They found that Facebook's privacy policies improved from 2005 to 2009, at one point reaching 90% implementation of the criterion, and then steadily declined to 25% in 2015. The areas of notable decline were the amount of information gathered and monitored, informing users about what is shared, clearly identifying data used for profiling, giving users choices in privacy settings, providing information on how Facebook uses cookies, beacons, and weblogs to gather data, and providing an easily understood privacy policy document. The researchers noted that Facebook's privacy policy started out in 2005 with 1,000 words, and by 2015 had ballooned to over 12,000 words! Facebook has since revised its privacy policies several times. It is now 4,200 words, and reportedly is rarely read by users (Hautala, 2018).

Privacy Protection in Europe: The General Data Protection Regulation (GDPR)

In May 2018 the European Commission implemented the EU **General Data Protection Regulation (GDPR)**, arguably the most important privacy legislation since the FTC's Fair Information Practices Principles of 1998. The GDPR applies to all firms and organizations that collect, store, or process personal information of EU citizens, and its protections apply worldwide, regardless of where the processing of the information takes place (European Commission, 2018; Satariano, 2018).

General Data Protection Regulation (GDPR)
Updated framework governing data protection in EU member countries that replaces Data Protection Directive

The GDPR is an updated framework for protecting PII (personally identifiable information) and replaces the Data Protection Directive of 1998. In Europe, privacy protection is historically much stronger than it is in the United States. In the United States, there is no federal agency charged with enforcing privacy laws. And there is no single privacy statute governing private use of PII. Instead, privacy laws are piecemeal, sector by sector, e.g., medical privacy, educational privacy, and financial privacy laws. These are enforced by the FTC, through self-regulation by businesses, and by individuals who must sue agencies or companies in court to recover damages. This is expensive and rarely done.

In the European Union, data protection laws are comprehensive, applying to all organizations, and enforced by data protection agencies in each country that pursue complaints brought by citizens and actively enforce privacy laws. The GDPR protects a wide variety of PII: basic identity information such as name, address, and ID numbers; web data such as location, IP address, cookie data, and RFID tags; health and genetic data; mobile phone number; driver's license and passport number; biometric and facial data; racial and ethnic data; political opinions; and sexual orientation.

Table 8.11 describes the most important provisions of the GDPR. The main objective of this new framework is to strengthen the rights of citizens to their own personal information and to strengthen oversight of firms to ensure they implement these individual rights. A second thrust was to harmonize conflicting data protection standards among the 28 European nations that are members of the European Union and create a single EU agency to implement and enforce the regulation. The third goal was the ability to enforce the framework worldwide, applying it to all organizations that operate in the European Union or process data pertaining to EU citizens, regardless of where the organization is located.

For individuals, the GDPR requires organizations to allow consumers to access all their personal information without charge within one month; delete personal data (the right to be forgotten); ensure data portability so consumers are not locked into a particular

TABLE 8.11	THE GENERAL DATA PROTECTION REGULATION (GDPR)
Purpose	• Harmonize data privacy laws across Europe • Reshape the way organizations across the region approach data privacy. • Protect and empower EU citizens' data privacy
Scope	• Applies to all firms and organizations worldwide that collect, process, or use personal information of EU citizens
Administration and enforcement	• Creates a new EU-wide Information Commissioners Office to enforce the regulation in the European Union. Each country also has its own Data Protection Agency
Individual rights	• Easier access to all personal data without charge within one month • Right to be forgotten (power to erase data) • Data portability: allow people to move their data to other providers • Give users more control over the use of their data by third parties and partners • Right to seek damages for abuse, including class action suits
Organizational requirements	• Enterprise-level data governance • Data protection officer in all firms with more than 250 employees, reporting to senior management • Requires explicit consent before collecting data on people (positive opt-in) • Published rationale for data collection and how long it will be held • Requires firms to report breaches, hacks, and unauthorized disclosure within 72 hours • Third-party risk management. Firms are liable for data shared with partners and must maintain a list of all sharing firms • Requires firms to maintain a record of all EU personal data • Privacy by design of all new systems • Targeting limits: allows anonymized data for audience targeting, but targeting based on social media or other personal profiles remains a grey area • New schedule of fines: up to $20 million or 4% of global revenue • Privacy shield: agreements with non-EU countries to ensure any data processed outside the European Union meets EU GDPR standards

service (data portability); and the right to sue providers for damages or abuse of PII, including class action law suits.

Organizational requirements have been strengthened to include requiring organizations to have a data protection officer that reports to senior management; requiring explicit consent before collecting data (positive opt-in) and eliminating default op-in processes; publishing the rationale for data collection and the length of retention; reporting of beaches and hacks within 72 hours; liability for data shared with partners or other firms and a listing of all firms data is shared with; requiring privacy protections to be built into all new systems (privacy by design); and limiting the targeting and retargeting of individuals to audience-level, anonymized data, rather than targeting based on intimate, personal profiles. Organizations are required to limit the collection of personal data to only that which is needed to support a task, or a transaction, and then delete it shortly thereafter (Schechner, 2018). Abuse of PII is subject to fines of up to $20 million or 4% of the organization's global revenue, whichever is greater. Finally, the European Union has

privacy shield agreements

designed to ensure that EU data processed in non-EU nations meets GDPR standards

safe harbor agreements

private self-regulating policy and enforcement mechanism that meets the objectives of government regulators and legislation but does not involve government regulation or enforcement

the ability to enforce the GDPR's requirements with non-EU countries like the United States via the use of inter-governmental **privacy shield agreements**, which are designed to ensure that EU data processed in non-EU nations meets GDPR standards. Privacy shield agreements are a more enforceable version of earlier **safe harbor agreements**, which provide a private self-regulating policy and enforcement mechanism that meets the objectives of government regulators and legislation but does not involve government regulation or enforcement (Lomas, 2018).

The GDPR is clearly aimed at Facebook, Google, Twitter, and other ad-based online businesses that build collections of personal data by tracking individuals across the Web, merging that data with data from firms and data brokers in order to build comprehensive digital images (profiles) and to target these persons with ads. Google and Facebook are both extremely popular in Europe, and dominate their markets, but at the same time are widely criticized for invading privacy and not protecting PII. European regulators and politicians point to Facebook allowing Cambridge Analytica, a political consulting firm, to gain access to over 100 million user accounts in 2016 and a 2018 data breach of 50 million Facebook accounts as evidence that Facebook is unable to protect the privacy of Europeans. Google is also in the cross-hairs of EU regulators for its monopoly on search in the European Union, abuse of that monopoly by ranking Google services above others on its search pages, and abuse of its ownership of the Android operating system by requiring smartphone manufacturers to pre-install Google apps on Android phones, as well as evading taxes on revenues earned in EU countries. Both firms, along with Microsoft's Windows 10 operating system, have been accused of "deceit by design" through the use of threats against users who choose strong privacy protections on their services, and screen designs that encourage users to give up as much personal information as possible (Pop and Schechner, 2018; Meyer, 2018).

At this time, it is unclear exactly how GDPR will be applied to profiling on websites and targeting at the personal level. The regulation gives a green light to using anonymized data aimed at specific audiences, e.g., all persons interested in purchasing a new car, or searching for concert tickets, also called context advertising.

Although global firms have been aware of the GDPR requirements since 2016 and had two years to plan for its implementation, there are still many ambiguities in language and uncertainties about its impact that will need to be worked out (Deloitte, 2018; Stupp, 2018). For instance, it is unclear if GDPR will allow tracking of individuals across the Internet and the collection of tertiary information not directly related to a transaction.

Industry Self-Regulation

Federal and state government regulation alone is insufficient to protect consumer privacy. The technology evolves quickly, and provides marketers more tools to collect and use consumer private information before legislatures and government agencies can respond. The online industry in the United States has historically opposed online privacy legislation, arguing that industry can do a better job of protecting privacy than government.

The primary focus of industry efforts has been the development of online "seals" that attest to a company's privacy policies. A number of non-profit organizations, such as the Better Business Bureau (BBB), TrustArc (formerly TRUSTe), and WebTrust, have established this sort of online seal program. However, such programs have had a limited impact on online privacy practices, and critics argue that they are not particularly effective in safeguarding privacy. In 2015, for instance, the FTC finalized a settlement in which it fined TRUSTe for failing to annually recertify privacy programs in more than 1,000 instances although claiming that it did so on its website (Davis, 2015). Since that time, TrustArc has morphed its seal into a Privacy Feedback button, which it says provides companies a visible way to show customers they care about privacy and let users know about the option to ask questions or provide feedback to the companies regarding their privacy practices through TRUSTe's Dispute Resolution System, which is an online tool that lets users report alleged violations of posted privacy statements and specific privacy issues. TrustArc no longer verifies company privacy policies.

The advertising network industry has also formed an industry association, the Network Advertising Initiative (NAI), to develop privacy policies. The NAI policies have two objectives: to offer consumers a chance to opt out of advertising network programs (including e-mail campaigns), and to provide consumers redress from abuses. In order to opt out, the NAI has created a website—Networkadvertising.org—where consumers can use a global opt-out feature to prevent network advertising agencies from placing their cookies on a user's computer. If a consumer has a complaint, the NAI has a link where complaints can be filed (Network Advertising Initiative, 2018).

The AdChoices program is another industry-sponsored initiative to encourage websites to be more transparent about how they use personal information and to make it more likely that appropriate ads are shown to users by asking users themselves. An AdChoices icon appears next to ads, and clicking on this icon provides more information and the opportunity to provide feedback to the advertiser. There is no data available yet to indicate how well this program is working.

A powerful form of corporate self-regulation is market and public pressure. When firms engage in behavior that is repugnant to consumers, the resulting firestorm of tweets, blogs, and postings on social media is often enough to encourage them to take corrective action, albeit often under the pressure of FTC and FCC investigations. For instance, Facebook, Google, and other companies have developed a number of tools that allow users to set their privacy preferences and restrict the use of their information for interest-based advertising. Google, Apple, and most browser firms have also developed tools for individuals to use in order to limit the uses of their information. Millions of users do take advantage of these tools. Yet the larger majority does not because they are hard to find and even harder to understand (Fowler, 2018; Stern, 2016).

In general, industry efforts at self-regulation in online privacy have not succeeded in reducing American fears of privacy invasion during online transactions, or in reducing the level of privacy invasion. At best, self-regulation has offered consumers notice about whether a privacy policy exists, but usually says little about the actual use of the information, does not offer consumers a chance to see and correct the information or control its use in any significant way, offers no enforceable promises for the security of that information, and offers no enforcement mechanism (Hoofnagle, 2005).

Technological Solutions

A number of technological solutions have been developed to deal with the invasion of privacy on the Web and mobile platform. As described earlier in this chapter and in

cross-site tracking
uses various types of cookies to track users across the web

cross-device tracking
uses cell phone login and other user-supplied data, combined with cross-site tracking data, to develop a comprehensive picture of user behavior across all devices

device fingerprinting
collects unique information from a user's browser or smartphone that can be combined with other data files to identify specific devices and users

Chapter 6, the essential threat to privacy is the tracking of users and recording their behavior on multiple sites (**cross-site tracking**) and multiple devices (**cross-device tracking**) in order to sell ads to firms who wish to show advertising to those users. There are other threats as well, such as **device fingerprinting** where the unique features of a user's computer or smartphone can be used to identify the device and the user and correlated with tracking data for future use. As cookies are increasingly blocked by users or browsers, inhibiting behavioral tracking, device fingerprinting, which does not require cookies to uniquely identify users and track them across the Web, is becoming increasingly popular.

Third-party cookies that communicate with external servers to report activities online are the foundation of online surveillance and tracking on the Web, regardless of where they are stored. Privacy is further threatened by IP trackers that log IP address, which, when combined with other information, are able to identify users as they browse the Internet. Effective technological solutions to prevent tracking must prevent the operation of third-party cookies and hide the identity (IP address) of users. **Table 8.12** lists some common tools for reducing or eliminating online tracking, and other online and mobile privacy threats.

TABLE 8.12	TECHNOLOGICAL PROTECTIONS FOR ONLINE PRIVACY	
TECHNOLOGY	**PRODUCTS**	**PROTECTION**
Intelligent Tracking Prevention (ITP)	Apple Safari, Privacy Badger	Monitors and disables tracking cookies
Differential privacy software	Apple	Reduces the ability to merge different files and de-anonymize consumer data
Privacy default browsers	Epic, Ghostery, Cliqz	Eliminates tracking cookies and prevents IP tracking using a VPN
Message encryption	Signal, Gdata, Whisper, Telegram, Ceerus	Apps that encrypt text and other data transferred using smartphones
Spyware blockers	Spyware Doctor, ZoneAlarm, Ad-Aware, and Spybot	Detects and removes spyware, adware, keyloggers, and other malware
Pop-up and Ad blockers	Most browsers; add-on programs: Adblock Plus, PopupMaster	Prevents calls to ad servers; restricts downloading of images at user request
Secure e-mail	ZL Technologies, SafeMess, Hushmail, Pretty Good Privacy (PGP)	E-mail and document encryption
Anonymous remailers	Jack B. Nymble, Java Anonymous Proxy, Mixmaster	Send e-mail without trace
Anonymous surfing	Freedom Websecure, Anonymizer.com, Tor, GhostSurf	Surf without a trace using VPN networks
Cookie managers	Cookie Monster and most browsers	Blocks third-party cookies
Public key encryption	PGP Desktop	Program that encrypts your mail and documents

Ad blockers (described in Chapter 6) can be useful in blocking obnoxious ads, but they typically do not address the problem of cross-site tracking, and they allow ad servers that meet certain requirements to use tracking cookies to operate in the background. Most browsers allow users to block all cookies, or all third-party cookies, but researchers have found that advertisers have found ways around these tools, and this action often interferes with web page operation (Wagenseil, 2018; Chaikivsky, 2018). Using built-in browser tools to manage cookies and eliminate all cookies is fruitless because the next site you visit will load cookies again, and many are the same ones you had eliminated earlier.

Beginning in 2010, responding to pressure from a growing number of Internet users who objected to being tracked, and encouraged by the FTC, browser manufacturers, began installing Do Not Track (DNT) settings in their browsers. Virtually all browsers today have a DNT function that sends a user's request to websites that they not install tracking cookies in users' browser. Unfortunately, most websites do not honor these requests, and they do not inform users they are being tracked despite their browser settings. (See the Chapter 6 *Insight on Society* case, *Every Move You Take, Every Click You Make, We'll Be Tracking You*, for more information about DNT.) Likewise with private session options in most browsers: they eliminate local browsing history, but tracking cookies continue to operate in the background sending data to third-party servers.

In 2017, as previously discussed in Chapter 6, Apple responded to consumer complaints about cross-site tracking and began implementing **Intelligent Tracking Prevention (ITP)** for its Safari browser. ITP uses machine learning techniques in the browser (not on a central server) to identify which cookies represent a tracking threat and prevents them from communicating with their servers, disarming them. Safari notifies the user when a cookie attempts to connect to a third-party server, asking users if they want to allow it. If tracking cookies make three attempts to communicate with external servers in 24 hours despite user choices, they are eliminated from the browser (Toner, 2017). Similar capabilities to prevent tracking are available with an application called Privacy Badger developed by the Electronic Frontier Foundation (Miagkov, 2018). Intelligent tracking prevention essentially eliminates cross-site tracking and user surveillance, and is a direct threat to the online advertising industry (Nichols, 2017). In 2018, Apple began to implement **differential privacy software** that inhibits the ability of advertisers to merge anonymized consumer data files with other tracking files in order to precisely identify consumers despite efforts to anonymize their data (Greif, 2018; Zawadziński and Wlosik, 2016).

In 2018, Google implemented an ad-blocking tool in Chrome that blocks ads from sites that do not conform to the Better Ads Standard of the Coalition for Better Ads (CBA). These standards ban obnoxious ad formats such as pop-ups, auto-play videos, and interstitial ads that obscure the whole page. Similar ad blocking tools are widely available, and in 2019, more than 25% of U.S. Internet users had installed them (eMarketer, Inc., 2019). While this approach may reduce the number and effectiveness of some tracking cookies, it does not prevent cross site tracking for advertisers that comply with CBA standards.

The most effective tools to reduce or eliminate tracking are **privacy default browsers** such as Epic, Cliqz Browser, and Ghostery. These browsers identify tracking cookies as they are loaded onto browsers and eliminate them from the browser. They also have

Intelligent Tracking Prevention (ITP)
Apple machine-based learning tool that monitors tracking cookies and eliminates those not desired by the user

differential privacy software
inhibits the ability of advertisers to merge anonymized consumer data files with other tracking files

privacy default browsers
identify tracking cookies as they are loaded onto browsers and eliminate them from the browser.

built-in VPN (virtual private network) software that prevents websites from identifying a device's IP address. These features operate in the background without user intervention or requests for the user to approve, eliminating third-party cookies at the outset of a browsing session. In these browsers, privacy is the default option (Keizer, 2018).

Encryption is also potentially an important technology to preserving privacy of messages and documents. As noted above, Apple implemented encryption of its devices and iMessage text messaging, and there are many popular apps to encrypt communications among digital devices. Private browsing is another privacy tool available in most browsers that disables browsing history and cookies. This can be useful for protecting a consumer's computer in a shared environment where several users have access to the same computer. Browsing history is still retained on the web server. Some technologies address the security aspects of privacy, especially the threat of man-in-the-middle attacks. Specialized browsers like Epic and Ice Dragon encrypt users' browsing and other data entirely, even at the server level. A very common security protocol is HTTPS, which encrypts the messages between a computer and the computer server and verifies that users are communicating with an authentic website and not an imposter site.

PRIVACY PROTECTION AS A BUSINESS

As websites have become more invasive and aggressive in their use of personal information in the last five years, public concerns have grown, and a small number of startup firms have sprung up that enable users to reclaim control over their personal information and monetize their information by selling it to third-party firms, mostly advertising firms. Suppose you could get control of all the personal information you share with Facebook, Google, banks, credit card companies, and even e-mail, deposit that information in a personal data account in a hosted secure digital vault, and sell access to that information to interested parties, without identifying yourself? Potentially, this flips the traditional ad-based Internet on its head: instead of giving up control of your personal information in return for a service, like a social network, you can sell that information yourself to third parties. These ideas have several names: Personal Data Economy (PDE), the Internet of Me, and Life Management tools.

The idea of individuals claiming ownership of their personal data, depositing it in a trusted data store, and then selling that information to third parties is not new, but with the development of supportive digital technologies, it can be considered today a technically feasible approach to some contemporary privacy issues such as control over personal information and transparency (Laudon, 1986; Elvy, 2017). Firms such as Datacoup, Digi.me, Meeco, and the Hub of All Things are raising venture funding to test these ideas.

For instance, Datacoup is a New York startup that pays subscribers $8 a month in return for access to their social media, search, financial, and purchase information. After anonymizing the data, it sells access to companies who can analyze it for trends in online behavior (Datacoup, 2020; Mitchell, 2018; Simonite, 2017). Meeco.me, an Australian startup, has developed a blockchain approach to personal data, which it calls a life management tool that allows individuals to see precisely what information about themselves is being shared online and with whom, to control the information they want to share, and then seek compensation from third-party users (Meeco.me, 2018; Leigh,

2016). Digi.me, a UK-based startup, has developed an app that allows users to aggregate all their personal information from any source and stores it on a cloud storage service like Dropbox or iCloud. From there, users control what information they will share and can choose a variety of tools to analyze their data. Digi.me received a $6 million investment from a founder of eBay in 2016 (Sherriff, 2019; Newman, 2018). The Hub of All Things (HAT) is a UK-based open source project that enables users to decide what information to store in their own cloud-based micro-server, establishing an intellectual property right in their own data, and then controlling their information through a personal data exchange (Hub of All Things, 2020; Sterling, 2018).

An entirely different non-technological method for reducing tracking is **pay-for-privacy (PFP)**. In this method, some broadband providers, such as AT&T's GigaPower service, offer two different levels of service: ad-supported and privacy-supporting-service. Ad-supported service is $30–$50 less than privacy-supporting service. Essentially, users who want to be free from ads and tracking by telecommunications companies will be asked to pay for their privacy. So far, companies such as Google, Facebook, and Twitter do not offer this functionality, but may in the future as ad-blocking and cookie-blocking software becomes more powerful (Elvy, 2017; Chen, 2017). It is well known that users will not pay much, if anything, to preserve their privacy, and therefore most users will choose to accept tracking as the low-cost alternative (Acquisti et al., 2013).

All of these efforts have shortcomings and risks, but they are useful examples of how technology might be used to address privacy issues in the near future. The PFP model might result in only affluent users having privacy. The PDE model might result in only wealthy consumers selling their personal information because it is more valuable to advertisers (Mobile Ecosystem Forum, 2017). Either model could result in online privacy for some, but not all.

pay-for-privacy (PFP)
method for allowing users to pay a fee to experience ad-free or tracking-free web experiences

PRIVACY ADVOCACY GROUPS

There are a number of privacy advocacy groups that monitor developments in privacy. Some of these sites are industry-supported, while others rely on private foundations and contributions. Some of the better-known sites are listed in **Table 8.13**. There are also a number of privacy policy institutes at universities throughout the United States.

TABLE 8.13	PRIVACY ADVOCACY GROUPS
ADVOCACY GROUP	FOCUS
Electronic Privacy Information Center (EPIC)	Washington, DC-based public interest research center focused on privacy and civil liberties issues
Privacy International	International watchdog organization focused on privacy intrusions by government and businesses
Center for Democracy and Technology (CDT)	Foundation- and business-supported group with a legislative focus
Electronic Frontier Foundation (EFF)	Nonprofit organization focused on defending user privacy, free expression, and other civil liberties
Privacy Rights Clearinghouse	Educational clearinghouse

LIMITATIONS ON THE RIGHT TO PRIVACY: LAW ENFORCEMENT AND SURVEILLANCE

We've emphasized that privacy in the public sector, freedom from government restrictions and searches, is very different from privacy in the private, consumer market sector. But increasingly these different realms of personal information are coming together.

Today, the online and mobile behavior, profiles, and transactions of consumers are routinely available to a wide range of government agencies and law enforcement authorities, contributing to rising fears among online consumers, and in some cases, their withdrawal from the online marketplace. The last few years have not been good for advocates of privacy, with revelations that federal government agencies have been routinely gathering cell phone call data on Americans and foreigners in the United States for a period of several years with scant judicial oversight. In 2013, Edward Snowden, a security contractor for the U.S. National Security Agency (NSA), began releasing NSA documents to *The Guardian*, a UK newspaper, providing a detailed description of NSA surveillance programs of both U.S. and foreign citizens. These programs were unprecedented in scope and involved wholesale collection of cell phone metadata around the world, tapping communications lines of Google, Yahoo, and other Internet services, and tapping cell phones of foreign leaders. The program did not target U.S. citizens. The NSA enlisted the support of the major telecommunications carriers to give it information about Americans' phone calls and e-mail in a program called PRISM. These programs were conceived in the aftermath of the terrorist attack on the United States on September 11, 2001, and were envisaged as necessary to protect the country. The programs were authorized by the USA PATRIOT Act of 2001, and subsequent amendments, authorized and supervised by the U.S. Foreign Intelligence Surveillance Act Court (FISA Court, or FISC) pursuant to the Foreign Intelligence Surveillance Act (FISA), were reviewed by relevant legislative committees. The PRISM program was therefore lawful. Many in the computer science academic community were aware of these programs, in part because they participated in the development of techniques for discovering patterns in large data sets, as well as machine learning programs. Nevertheless, the revelations alarmed average citizens who previously believed that if they did nothing wrong, surely the government would not be collecting information about them. The revelations also heightened public awareness and criticism of Internet firms like Google and Facebook, and others engaging in extensive tracking and consumer surveillance (Pew Research Center, 2018b). Google, Facebook, Microsoft, and others have since tried to resist or prevent warrantless government access to their consumer data (Apuzzo et al., 2015).

Advances in technology for storing, processing, and analyzing unimaginable quantities of personal data, referred to as big data and business analytics (data mining and representation software), have further heightened perceptions that privacy is increasingly difficult to define and protect in the age of e-commerce and social networks (Kakutani, 2013; Mayer-Schonberger and Cukier, 2013).

Striking a balance between security and liberty is at the center of the privacy debate (Ford, 2013). While the Internet used to be thought of as impossible for governments to control or monitor, nothing could be actually further from the truth. Law enforcement authorities have long claimed the right under numerous statutes to monitor any form of electronic communication pursuant to a court order and judicial review and based on the reasonable belief that a crime is being committed. This includes the surveillance of consumers engaged in e-commerce. The Communications Assistance for Law Enforcement Act (CALEA), the USA PATRIOT Act, the Cyber Security Enhancement Act, and the Homeland Security Act all strengthen the ability of law enforcement agencies to monitor Internet users without their knowledge and, under certain circumstances when life is purportedly at stake, without judicial oversight. The USA PATRIOT Act, designed to combat terrorism inside the borders of the United States, permitted nearly unlimited government surveillance without court oversight, according to several senators (Savage, 2012). However, in general, requests to conduct surveillance by government agencies require the approval of a FISA court. In 2015, several provisions of the USA PATRIOT Act expired. In response, Congress passed the USA Freedom Act, which imposes some limits on the bulk collection by the National Security Agency and other U.S. intelligence agencies of U.S. citizens' telecommunications metadata, but continues to allow surveillance of individuals pursuant to a FISA court order.

There are many Congressional privacy initiatives including the Email Privacy Act, which regulates email providers; the Preserving American Privacy Act, which regulates the collection of information by drones; and the Online Communications and Geolocation Protection Act, which regulates the uses of personal geo-location data. However, at this time, it is not likely that any of these proposed bills will be enacted by Congress.

Taking matters into its own hands, in 2014, Apple introduced the iPhone 6, which offers the ability to encrypt e-mail, photos, and contacts stored on the phone using a strong end-to-end encryption algorithm (E2EE) designed to prevent third parties from reading the messages while in transit. Apple also encrypted data stored on the physical iPhone device. The device data can only be decrypted by using a passcode that only the user possesses, and Apple does not retain the key to the code. As a result, the NSA potentially could not force Apple or Google to reveal such user data. In September 2015, Apple said it could not comply with a court order to turn over text messages in real time involving an investigation of drug and gun runners (Apuzzo et al., 2015). Not surprisingly, the NSA, Federal Bureau of Investigation, and other law enforcement officials are not happy with this prospect and fear that it will enable criminals and terrorists to evade surveillance. Apple and Google contend that in order for them to compete globally, they must be able to convince consumers that their data is secure, a task made more difficult as a result of the Snowden revelations (Sanger and Chen, 2014). In March 2016, the FBI announced it had cracked the iPhone device encryption without Apple's support, and in April 2016, said it would be helping local law enforcement agencies decrypt smartphone and other devices using encryption. With sufficient computing power, common encryption methods can be cracked. Read the *Insight on Technology* case: *Apple: Defender of Privacy?* for a further discussion of this issue.

Law enforcement's ability to obtain data from mobile phones without a warrant has been the subject of a number of court cases. In 2014, the U.S. Supreme Court, in a path-breaking unanimous decision, ruled that police needed a warrant prior to searching a person's cell phone for information (*Riley v. California*, 134 S. Ct. 2473 (2014)). All mobile devices will likely receive this protection against general, warrantless police searches (Savage, 2014). An earlier decision in 2012 requires police to obtain a warrant prior to attaching GPS tracking devices to a suspect's car (*United States v. Jones*, 565 U.S. 400 (2012)). In both cases, the Supreme Court found that cell phones held extensive detailed personal information, retained information

INSIGHT ON TECHNOLOGY

APPLE: DEFENDER OF PRIVACY?

It's rare, in fact unprecedented, that an Internet giant would take a public stand to support the privacy of individuals from government surveillance, and then back it up by making it impossible for law enforcement agencies hunting criminals and terrorists to gain access to the personal information of these persons. But that's the position that Apple and its CEO, Tim Cook, have taken with respect to data stored on iPhones. Equally unprecedented is the support being given to Apple by Google, Facebook, Microsoft, and others whose very business models are based on the largely unregulated collection of personal information that is then sold to advertisers.

The conflict between law enforcement and Apple rose to national attention when, on December 3, 2015, two terrorists attacked county employees in San Bernardino, California killing 14 people. The terrorists owned an Apple iPhone 5c, which has an operating system that encrypts the contents of the locked phone. Only someone who knows the phone's four-digit passcode can access the data on the phone. After 10 unsuccessful tries at unlocking the phone, the phone's operating system permanently encrypts the data on the phone. In this case, the owner was deceased and the passcode was unknown. The FBI asked Apple to unlock the phone so it could examine it for possible evidence. Apple refused, stating that it does not maintain a record of the unlock keys to its encrypted phones. The FBI ordered Apple to update the phone's operating system to enable it to bypass the permanent lock function, which would allow the FBI to try every four-digit combination until the passcode was found. Apple does update user operating systems routinely, and this is technically feasible.

However, Apple refused to do this, because it had not built such an operating system and did not have the computer code. Apple claimed computer code is like speech, and forcing a person or firm to write code was a violation of the First Amendment guarantees of freedom of speech. In the past, Apple has provided information from its cloud storage service, which has so far remained unencrypted, to law enforcement officials pursuant to a court order. But in this instance, it claimed breaking the encryption on the terrorist's phone would set a precedent that would threaten everyone's civil liberties worldwide.

The FBI filed a law suit against Apple demanding Apple provide the assistance needed to access the phone. Using the All Writs Act of 1789, the FBI argued it had a court order requiring Apple to provide assistance. In February 2016, a federal court agreed with the FBI, and ordered Apple to provide the FBI reasonable assistance to bypass the auto-erase function of phone. Apple appealed, but just prior to the hearing, the FBI said it had found a third party who could access the data on the phone. The appeal hearing was delayed, and to date, the question has not been definitively decided.

The firm that the FBI hired used the iPhone's charging port to break its security. Two firms (Cellebrite and Greyshift) began to market this technology to law enforcement agencies. In response, Apple closed this security hole in 2018 by disabling the power port an hour after the phone is locked. Apple also announced a portal for law enforcement agencies where they could request unencrypted information about suspects from iCloud's database. Meanwhile, federal officials began urging Congress to pass legislation requiring smartphone manufacturers to provide access to law enforcement supported by a court order.

Going forward, it is clear that the government and Apple and other tech companies will clash again over the right of government investigators to access encrypted information in pursuit of a lawful investigation. For instance, in 2016, the FBI and Apple clashed over the FBI's desire to access the iPhone data of a terrorist who stabbed 10 people at Minnesota's Mall of America. In 2017, the Justice Department debated how to deal with Facebook's WhatsApp, a very popular messaging application that provides a means of encrypted communication, which is not accessible even when a judge has approved a wiretap. Facebook and WhatsApp have thus far refused to provide assistance. Yet federal case and statute law have determined that law enforcement wiretaps are an essential and constitutional law enforcement tool.

How common is this problem? In New York City, police officials say they have hundreds of iPhones used by criminals that cannot be unlocked. In an earlier 1977 U.S. Supreme Court case, the court determined that the All Writs Act could be used to compel the New York Telephone Company to install a device on a rotary phone to track the dial numbers of criminals. The Communications Assistance for Law Enforcement Act (CALEA), and other legislation passed in the post–9-11 era contain provisions requiring telecommunications carriers to design and build their systems in such a way that law enforcement can gain access to communications of suspected criminals and terrorists. CALEA has been extended to include VoIP and Internet broadband traffic, but is limited, for now, to telecommunications carriers, and does not apply to manufacturers of digital devices like iPhones or their associated operating systems, like iOS and Android. This is not new on the American scene: government tapping into wire communications among criminals and terrorists was initiated by Abraham Lincoln during the Civil War in 1862 when telegraph lines were tapped to access troop movement and logistics communications. Whether electrical, electronic, or digital, the federal government has always claimed the right to monitor and record private conversations pursuant to court orders and a legitimate law enforcement action. Nearly all goverments, whether democratic or autocratic, claim similar rights.

Throughout the controversy Tim Cook, Apple's CEO, has maintained that unlocking its iPhones and providing extraordinary access or backdoors to law enforcement or others could unleash a torrent of requests from governments around the world, including China and other totalitarian regimes, seeking access to the phones of their citizens. Millions of iPhone users, some in totalitarian countries, would be susceptible to government hacking of their personal information, messages, and transactions. These dangers, Cook believes, weigh more heavily than dangers brought about by terrorists using iPhones or WhatsApp to communicate with impunity. An independent panel of computer scientists in 2015 reported that building a backdoor for U.S. law enforcement would be technically difficult, and would also quickly become available on the Internet and used by hackers. Communications privacy would be terminally lost.

There are risks in granting law enforcement a backdoor to Apple's encryption. But there is also the real and present risk that should the iPhone become the preferred and protected communication tool for criminals and terrorists, beyond government surveillance and monitoring, millions of Apple customers, not to mention millions of others, would become more vulnerable to actual crimes and real terrorist attacks.

This is not the first time that Tim Cook has taken Apple in the direction of strong privacy protection. In 2015, Cook gave a most unusual speech, rejecting the idea that customers have

(continued)

to make a trade-off between privacy and security. Cook believes people have a fundamental right to privacy. Some of the most prominent firms in Silicon Valley, Cook argued, lull their customers into giving up a treasure of personal information in order to receive some service, like cloud storage, social networking, or photo services for "free." In fact, Cook argued, the trade-off comes at a high cost to the consumer in the form of loss of privacy and fear about what might become of their personal information. In the end, he said, consumers will regret the trade. These companies, he noted, are gobbling up everything they can learn about consumers and trying to monetize it by selling it to advertisers. Cook famously noted that for firms like Facebook, Google, and others, the customer is the product.

Critics point to the irony in Apple's position. Smartphones like Apple's iPhone provide the technical platform for Google's mobile search engine and Facebook's mobile social network. Both of these firms derive most of their revenue from mobile advertising targeted to individuals based on their personal information. The commercial invasion of privacy may annoy Cook, but even if Apple does not itself advertise, Apple benefits because it helps Apple sell iPhones where privacy-invading apps proliferate.

In 2017, Apple took a different privacy path in China, which had passed a strict new set of laws requiring operators of online app stores to remove nearly all virtual private network (VPN) apps from their stores. VPN apps are used by Chinese citizens to prevent the Chinese government from intercepting their browsing and messaging behavior, and are an important way for dissidents to express their views and to get outside the great firewall of China. Apple, Google, Microsoft, and cloud operators like Amazon all complied quickly. Apple derives 25% of its revenue from sales of iPhones in China and its app store, which is its second largest market after the United States. Critics wondered why Apple responded without protest if it is so concerned about privacy and customer perception. Apple claims that it has not provided a backdoor into its encryption. The situations are not entirely analogous, but observers believe that it is just a matter of time before the Chinese government demands that Apple provide a backdoor to its encryption as well. What will Apple do then? Leaving the country is not an option from a business perspective.

Most observers believe the dispute between U.S. law enforcement and Apple will ultimately go before the Supreme Court, which will have to balance the interests of government gaining access to private information for law enforcement purposes, the interests of consumers to privacy, and the interests of firms like Facebook, Apple and Google, whose business models are based on consumers committing more and more of their personal information to digital devices.

SOURCES: "Apple Is Creating an Online Tool for Police to Request Information About Users," by Stephen Nellis, Cnbc.com, September 6, 2018; "Apple to Close iPhone Security Hole That Law Enforcement Uses to Crack Devices," by Jack Nicas, *New York Times*, June 13, 2018; "Justice Dept. Revives Push to Mandate a Way to Unlock Phones," by Charlie Savage, *New York Times*, March 24, 2018; "Reports That 'Privacy Is Dead' Have Been Greatly Exaggerated," by Lawrence Cappello, *Wall Street Journal*, September 4, 2017; "Apple's Silence in China Sets a Dangerous Precedent," by Farhad Manjoo, *New York Times*, July 31, 2017; "Apple Is Pulling VPNs from the Chinese App Store. Here's What That Means," by Brian Fung, *Washington Post*, July 31, 2017; "Apple's Capitulation to China's VPN Crack-down Will Return to Haunt It at Home," by Mike Butcher, Techcrunch.com, July 30, 2017; "Security Backdoor Found in End-to-End Encryption System Used in WhatsApp," by Ben Lovejoy, 9to5mac.com, January 13, 2017; "FBI v. Apple: One Year Later, It Hasn't Settled Much," by Taylor Armerding, CSOonline.com, January 30, 2017; "Why the FBI Breach of the iPhone Is a Win for Users," by Christopher Mims, *Wall Street Journal*, April 4, 2016; "U.S. Says Outside Party Could Unlock Terrorists iPhone," by Daisuke Wakabayashi, *New York Times*, March 22, 2016; "WhatsApp Encryption Said to Stymie Wiretap Order," by Matt Apuzzo, *New York Times*, March 12, 2016; "Explaining Apple's Fight with the F.B.I.," by Mike Isaac, *New York Times*, February 17, 2016; "Judge Tells Apple to Help Unlock iPhone Used by San Bernardino Gunman," by Eric Lichtblau, *New York Times*, February 16, 2016; *United States v. New York Telephone Co.* 434 U.S. 159 (1977); "What Your iPhone Doesn't Tell Apple," by Geoffrey Fowler, *Wall Street Journal*, September 15, 2015; "The Tradeoff Fallacy: How Marketers Are Misrepresenting American Consumers and Opening Them Up to Exploitation," by Joseph Turow, et al., Annenberg School of Communications, University of Pennsylvania, September 2015; "What Apple's Tim Cook Overlooked in His Defense of Privacy," by Farhad Manjoo, *New York Times*, June 10, 2015; "Tim Cook Says Apple 'Doesn't Want Your Data.' Let's Not Say Things We Can't Take Back," by Lily Hay Newman, Slate.com, June 3, 2015.

for many years, and stored many different types of information. Much of a person's intimate and personal life can be stored on cell phones, or cloud servers, making them the modern equivalent of personal papers, which are protected under the Fourth Amendment to the U.S. Constitution ("right of the people to be secure in their persons, houses, papers, and effects, against unreasonable searches and seizures"). In 2018, the Supreme Court ruled in a landmark decision (*Carpenter v. United States*) that the government needed to obtain a warrant based on probable cause to obtain and use mobile phone location histories held by cell phone companies and potentially all firms that collect this data. The Court concluded that cell phones had become so powerful, ubiquitous, and necessary to daily life that they can achieve near perfect surveillance of users, like an ankle monitor. The Court ruled that unlimited law enforcement access to this information was a violation of the Fourth Amendment that prohibits unreasonable searches (Liptak, 2018, 2017).

Government agencies are among the largest users of private sector commercial data brokers, such as Acxiom, Experian, and TransUnion Corporation, that collect a vast amount of information about consumers from various offline and online public sources, such as public records and the telephone directory, and non-public sources, such as "credit header" information from credit bureaus (which typically contains name, aliases, birth date, social security number, current and prior addresses, and phone numbers). Acxiom is one of the largest private personal databases in the world with an estimated 1,500 data points on 200 million Americans (Boutain, 2016; Singer, 2012). Information contained in individual reference services' databases ranges from purely identifying information (e.g., name and phone number) to much more extensive data (e.g., driving records, criminal and civil court records, property records, and licensing records). This information can be linked to online behavior information collected from other commercial sources to compile an extensive profile of an individual's online and offline behavior. The growing link between private and public sector personal information, creating a dossier society, had been predicted even before the Internet (Laudon, 1986). Now a growing reality, some critics and authors have forecast the end of privacy in the 20th century sense, and the dawning of a new 21st century era where people need to accept the pervasive monitoring of their behavior while at the same time protecting their privacy more vigorously using available tools (Weigend, 2017; Rose, 2017).

8.3 INTELLECTUAL PROPERTY RIGHTS

> Congress shall have the power to "promote the progress of science and useful arts, by securing for limited times to authors and inventors the exclusive right to their respective writings and discoveries."
> —Article I, Section 8, Constitution of the United States, 1788

Next to privacy, the most controversial ethical, social, and political issue related to e-commerce is the fate of intellectual property rights. Intellectual property encompasses all the tangible and intangible products of the human mind. As a general rule, in the United

States, the creator of intellectual property owns it. For instance, if you personally create an e-commerce site, it belongs entirely to you, and you have exclusive rights to use this "property" in any lawful way you see fit. But the Internet potentially changes things. Once intellectual works become digital, it becomes difficult to control access, use, distribution, and copying. These are precisely the areas that intellectual property seeks to control.

Digital media differ from books, periodicals, and other media in terms of ease of replication, transmission, and alteration; difficulty in classifying a software work as a program, book, or even music; compactness—making theft easy; and difficulty in establishing uniqueness. Before widespread use of the Internet, copies of software, books, magazine articles, or films had to be stored on physical media, such as paper, computer disks, or videotape, creating hurdles to distribution, and raising the costs of illegal copies.

The Internet technically permits millions of people to make perfect digital copies of various works—from music to plays, poems, and journal articles—and then to distribute them nearly cost-free to hundreds of millions of online users. The proliferation of innovation has occurred so rapidly that few entrepreneurs have stopped to consider who owns the patent on a business technique or method that they are using on their site. The spirit of the Web has been so free-wheeling that many entrepreneurs ignored trademark law and registered domain names that could easily be confused with another company's registered trademarks. In short, the Internet has demonstrated the potential to disrupt traditional conceptions and implementations of intellectual property law developed over the last two centuries.

The major ethical issue related to e-commerce and intellectual property concerns how we (both as individuals and as business professionals) should treat property that belongs to others. From a social point of view, the main questions are: Is there continued value in protecting intellectual property in the Internet age? In what ways is society better off, or worse off, for having the concept of property apply to intangible ideas, including music, books, and movies? Should society make certain technology illegal or restrict the use of the Internet just because it has an adverse impact on some intellectual property owners? From a political perspective, we need to ask how the Internet and e-commerce can be regulated or governed to protect the institution of intellectual property while at the same time encouraging the growth of e-commerce and the Internet.

TYPES OF INTELLECTUAL PROPERTY PROTECTION

There are four main types of intellectual property protection: copyright, patent, trademark law, and trade secrets law. In the United States, the development of intellectual property law begins with the U.S. Constitution, which mandated Congress to devise a system of laws to promote "the progress of science and the useful arts." Congress passed the first copyright law in 1790 to protect original written works for a period of 14 years, with a 14-year renewal if the author was still alive. Since then, the idea of copyright has been extended to include music, films, translations, photographs, and most recently the designs of vessels under 200 feet (Fisher, 1999). The copyright law has been amended (mostly extended) 11 times in the last 40 years.

The goal of intellectual property law is to balance two competing interests—the public and the private. The public interest is served by the creation and distribution of inventions, works of art, music, literature, and other forms of intellectual expression. The private interest is served by rewarding people for creating these works through the creation of a time-limited monopoly granting exclusive use to the creator.

Maintaining this balance of interests is always challenged by the invention of new technologies. In general, the information technologies of the last century—from radio and television to CD-ROMs, DVDs, and the Internet—have at first tended to weaken the protections afforded by intellectual property law. Owners of intellectual property have often, but not always, been successful in pressuring legislatures and the courts to strengthen the intellectual property laws to compensate for any technological threat, and even to extend protection for longer periods of time and to entirely new areas of expression. In the case of the Internet and e-commerce technologies, once again, intellectual property rights are severely challenged. In the next few sections, we discuss the significant developments in each area: copyright, patent, and trademark.

COPYRIGHT: THE PROBLEM OF PERFECT COPIES AND ENCRYPTION

In the United States, **copyright law** protects original forms of expression such as writings (books, periodicals, lecture notes), art, drawings, photographs, music, motion pictures, performances, and computer programs from being copied by others for a period of time. Up until 1998, the copyright law protected works of individuals for their lifetime plus 50 years beyond their life, and works created for hire and owned by corporations, such as Mickey Mouse of the Disney Corporation, for 75 years after initial creation. Copyright does not protect ideas—just their expression in a tangible medium such as paper, cassette tape, or handwritten notes.

In 1998, Congress extended the period of copyright protection for an additional 20 years, for a total of 95 years for corporate-owned works, and life plus 70 years of protection for works created by individuals (the Copyright Term Extension Act, also known as the CTEA). In *Eldred v. Ashcroft*, the Supreme Court ruled that the CTEA was constitutional, over the objections of groups arguing that Congress had given copyright holders a permanent monopoly over the expression of ideas, which ultimately would work to inhibit the flow of ideas and creation of new works by making existing works too expensive (*Eldred v. Ashcroft*, 2003; Greenhouse, 2003a). Librarians, academics, and others who depend on inexpensive access to copyrighted material opposed the legislation.

In the mid-1960s, the U.S. Copyright Office began registering software programs, and in 1980, Congress passed the Computer Software Copyright Act, which clearly provides protection for source and object code and for copies of the original sold in commerce, and sets forth the rights of the purchaser to use the software while the creator retains legal title. For instance, the HTML code for a web page—even though easily available to every browser—cannot be lawfully copied and used for a commercial purpose, say, to create a new website that looks identical.

Copyright protection is clear-cut: it protects against copying of entire programs or their parts. Damages and relief are readily obtained for infringement. The drawback to copyright protection is that the underlying ideas behind a work are not protected, only their expression in a work. A competitor can view the source code on your website to see how various effects were created and then reuse those techniques to create a different website without infringing on your copyright.

copyright law

protects original forms of expression such as writings, art, drawings, photographs, music, motion pictures, performances, and computer programs from being copied by others for a minimum of 70 years

TABLE 8.14	FAIR USE CONSIDERATIONS TO COPYRIGHT PROTECTIONS
FAIR USE FACTOR	INTERPRETATION
Character of use	Nonprofit or educational use versus for-profit use.
Nature of the work	Creative works such as plays or novels receive greater protection than factual accounts, e.g., newspaper accounts.
Amount of work used	A stanza from a poem or a single page from a book would be allowed, but not the entire poem or a book chapter.
Market effect of use	Will the use harm the marketability of the original product? Has it already harmed the product in the marketplace?
Context of use	A last-minute, unplanned use in a classroom versus a planned infringement.

Fair Use Doctrine

Copyrights, like all rights, are not absolute. There are situations where strict copyright observance could be harmful to society, potentially inhibiting other rights such as the right to freedom of expression and thought. As a result, , in the United States, the doctrine of fair use has been created. The **doctrine of fair use** permits teachers, writers, and others to use copyrighted materials without permission under certain circumstances. **Table 8.14** describes the five factors that courts consider when assessing what constitutes fair use.

The fair use doctrine draws upon the First Amendment's protection of freedom of speech (and writing). Journalists, writers, and academics must be able to refer to, and cite from, copyrighted works in order to criticize, or even discuss them. Professors are allowed to clip a contemporary article just before class, copy it, and hand it out to students as an example of a topic under discussion. However, they are not permitted to add this article to the class syllabus for the next semester without compensating the copyright holder.

What constitutes fair use has been at issue in a number of cases. In *Kelly v. Arriba Soft* (2003) and *Perfect 10, Inc. v. Amazon.com, Inc. et al.,* (2007), the U.S. Federal Circuit Court of Appeals for the 9th Circuit held that the display of thumbnail images in response to search requests constituted fair use. A similar result was reached by the U.S. District Court for the District of Nevada with respect to Google's storage and display of websites from cache memory, in *Field v. Google, Inc.* (2006). In all of these cases, the courts accepted the argument that caching the material and displaying it in response to a search request was not only a public benefit, but also a form of marketing of the material on behalf of its copyright owner, thereby enhancing the material's commercial value. In what's known as the "dancing baby case," a mother uploaded a 30-second video to YouTube of her baby dancing to a song by Prince called Let's Go Crazy. Universal Music Group, the owner of the copyright to the song, objected and issued a DMCA takedown notice to YouTube. The mother sued, claiming that Universal failed to consider whether use of the song in the video was fair use before issuing the takedown notice. The 9th Circuit U.S. Court of Appeals

doctrine of fair use
under certain circumstances, permits use of copyrighted material without permission

agreed that a copyright owner must consider fair use before sending a takedown notice. In 2017, the U.S. Supreme Court declined to review the case, leaving the ruling of the 9th Circuit Court of Appeals in force (Hurley, 2017; Morran, 2016; Bergen, 2015).

Fair use was also at issue in a lawsuit filed by the Authors Guild and five major publishing companies against Google. In 2004, Google announced a book project with two parts. A Partner Program would scan books with the permission of publishers, index the books, post snippets of the books on line, and make bibliographic information available on Google's search engine. In the second project, called the Library Project, Google aimed to scan all the books in several university and public libraries, and then make snippets and parts of the book available online without receiving permission from the publishers or paying royalties. Google said it would never show a full page, just relevant portions of a page in response to searches. In 2005, the Authors Guild and the large book publishers filed a lawsuit seeking to prevent Google from implementing the Library Project.

Google argued that the Library Project constituted fair use of publishers' copyrighted works because it only published snippets. Moreover, Google claimed that it was simply helping libraries do what they are intended to do, namely, lend books. Library lending is considered a fair use following an agreement in the late 1930s with publishers, and such lending was codified into the Copyright Act of 1976. Google claimed that helping libraries make books more available to the public was in the broader public interest, and extended existing rights of libraries to encourage book availability.

In 2013, eight years later, a U.S. federal court finally found in favor of Google without reservation by ruling that Google's scanning and making snippets of text available to the public was "fair use" under U.S. copyright law. The judge believed the project had a broad public purpose of making it easier for students, researchers, teachers, and the general public to find books, while also preserving consideration for author and publisher rights. The Google project was "transformative" in the court's view, giving books a new character and purpose, making it easier to discover old books, and leading to increased sales. After a decade of litigation, the U.S. Supreme Court ruled in 2016 that Google's Library Project was fair use, and the matter is settled from a legal perspective (Liptak and Alter, 2016). In the meantime, the project itself stalled, and efforts to scan so-called orphan books in libraries where the copyright holder could not be identified have ended. Google now appears less than enthusiastic about pursuing the project, in part, analysts believe, because the project offered no hope of ever making a return on the investment, and created a rift with the author and publishing community upon which it depends for content against which to show ads.

The Digital Millennium Copyright Act of 1998

The **Digital Millennium Copyright Act (DMCA)** of 1998 was the first major effort to adjust the copyright laws of the United States to the Internet age, and remains to this day, the primary statute that defines the relationship between copyright owners, Internet service providers (which in this context also includes website publishers as well as firms that provide Internet service), and end-users of copyrighted material. The law implements two international treaties of the World Intellectual Property Organization (WIPO), a worldwide body formed by the major nations in North America and Europe, as well as Japan.

Digital Millennium Copyright Act (DMCA)
the first major effort to adjust the copyright laws to the Internet age

TABLE 8.15	THE DIGITAL MILLENNIUM COPYRIGHT ACT
SECTION	IMPORTANCE
Title I, WIPO Copyright and Performances and Phonograms Treaties Implementation	Makes it illegal to circumvent technological measures to protect works for either access or copying or to circumvent any electronic rights management information.
Title II, Online Copyright Infringement Liability Limitation	Limits liability of ISPs and search engines for copyright infringement if they comply with safe harbors. Requires ISPs to "take down" sites they host if they are infringing copyrights, and requires search engines to block access to infringing sites if they receive proper notice of infringement from the copyright owner.
Title III, Computer Maintenance Competition Assurance	Permits users to make a copy of a computer program for maintenance or repair of the computer.
Title IV, Miscellaneous Provisions	Requires the Copyright Office to report to Congress on the use of copyright materials for distance education; allows libraries to make digital copies of works for internal use only; extends musical copyrights to include "webcasting."

SOURCE: Based on data from United States Copyright Office, 1998.

This is one case where law preceded or at least was contemporaneous with digital technology. **Table 8.15** summarizes the major provisions of the DMCA.

There are a number of different actors and conflicting interests involved in the process of delivering content on the Internet. Obviously, copyright owners do not want their work copied and distributed without their consent (and probably compensation), and they do not want their digital rights management software programs broken, compromised, or made ineffectual. ISPs want the freedom to use content within the provisions of "fair use" and do not want to be held liable for content that users may post to their websites. ISPs argue that they are similar to telephone transmission lines, merely providing a method of communication, and they should not be required to monitor their users' activities to see if they are posting copyrighted material. Such surveillance, ISPs and civil libertarians argue, would constitute a restriction on freedom of expression. In addition, the economics of the Internet could be compromised if ISPs were unnecessarily restricted and pay the costs of vetting all content posted by users. The business model of many Internet firms depends on creating large, even huge, audiences, and the more content that can be displayed, the larger the audience, and the more ads can be sold. ISPs also generate revenue from selling bandwidth, so the greater the bandwidth required to support large audiences, the better it is for them. Restricting content is bad for business.

Finally, consumers of Internet content want as much content as possible, at the lowest cost possible, or even free. The more content for users to consume, the more they benefit from the Internet.

The DMCA tries to balance these different interests. Title I of the DMCA implements the WIPO Copyright Treaty of 1996, which makes it illegal to make, distribute, or use devices that circumvent technology-based protections of copyrighted materials, and attaches stiff fines and prison sentences for violations. This makes it illegal, for instance, to break the security software typically found on DVDs, Amazon's Kindle books, and similar devices. There are a number of exceptions to the strong prohibitions against defeating a copyright protection scheme, however, including exceptions for libraries to examine works for adoption, for reverse engineering to achieve interoperability with other software, for encryption research, and for privacy protection purposes.

Title II of the DMCA creates two safe harbors for ISPs. The first safe harbor (the Online Copyright Infringement Liability Limitation Act) provides that ISPs will not be held liable for infringing material that users post to blogs, web pages, or forums, as long as the ISP did not have knowledge that the content was infringing, did not receive any financial benefit attributable to the infringing activity (assuming they can control this activity), and acts expeditiously to remove infringing content when notified by a notice of infringement. This means that users of, say, YouTube, can post material that infringes a copyright and YouTube cannot be held liable (safe harbor) as long as it does not know the material is infringing, and if it demonstrates that it has in place procedures to take down infringing content once it becomes aware of the matter or receives a proper notice from the copyright owner. Such a notice is called a takedown notice, a claim by the copyright owner that the ISP is hosting infringing content. Copyright owners can also subpoena the personal identities of any infringers using an ISP.

The second safe harbor relates to links to infringing material: ISPs will not be held liable for referring or linking users to a site that contains infringing material or infringing activity. So, for example, a search engine that directs users to a website that contains pirated songs or movies cannot be held liable. This safe harbor is applicable as long as ISPs did not have knowledge they were linking users to sites containing infringing content, did not receive any financial benefit attributable to the infringing activity (assuming they can control this activity), and acts expeditiously to remove or disable any such link after receiving a proper notice from the copyright owner.

There are a number of administrative requirements for ISPs to be protected by the safe harbor provisions. ISPs must designate an agent to receive takedown notices; adopt and publish a copyright infringement policy (this can be part of a terms of use policy); and comply with takedown notices by removing the content, and/or links to the content. The penalties for willfully violating the DMCA include restitution to the injured parties of any losses due to infringement. Criminal remedies may include fines up to $500,000 or five years imprisonment for a first offense, and up to $1 million in fines and 10 years in prison for repeat offenders. These are serious penalties, but they have rarely been imposed.

The DMCA relieves ISPs of any liability for posting or linking to copyrighted material, if they can meet the safe harbors' conditions. This means users of YouTube can post what they want, and YouTube will not be held liable for infringing content even if it violates YouTube's terms of use policy, which states that users shall not post infringing content.

However, it does require YouTube to remove content or links that are infringing once it receives a valid takedown notice. With respect to receiving financial benefits, ISPs may indeed receive financial benefits from posting infringing content if they can show that they can't control the behavior of their users, or that there is no way of knowing prior to the posting that the material is infringing. For instance, how can YouTube be held responsible for users who post copyrighted songs or movies? How could YouTube know, at the time of posting, that the content is infringing?

ISPs and individuals who post content are also protected from frivolous takedown notices. For instance, the ruling in the "dancing baby" case discussed on page 546 put copyright owners on notice that they needed to be careful issuing takedown notices if use of the copyrighted material might constitute fair use and that the DMCA does not supersede the doctrine of fair use.

Safe harbor provisions of the DMCA were also at the heart of a $1 billion lawsuit originally brought by Viacom in 2007 against Google and YouTube for willful copyright infringement. In the Viacom case, Viacom alleged that YouTube and Google engaged in massive copyright infringement by deliberately and knowingly building up a library of infringing works to draw traffic to the YouTube site and enhance its commercial value. Entire episodes of shows like SpongeBob SquarePants and The Daily Show were appearing on YouTube without permission or payment. In response, Google and YouTube claimed that they are protected by the DMCA's safe harbor provisions and that it is impossible to know whether a video is infringing or not. YouTube also does not display ads on pages where consumers can view videos unless it has an agreement with the content owner. In 2007, Google announced a filtering system (Content ID) aimed at addressing the problem. It requires content owners to give Google a copy of their content so Google can load it into an auto-identification system. Then, after a video is uploaded to YouTube, the system attempts to match it with its database of copyrighted material and removes any unauthorized material. The copyright owner has several options: it can mute the audio; block a whole video; monetize the video by running ads against it; and track the video's viewer statistics. Since YouTube launched Content ID in 2008, copyright holders have received over $2 billion from the system (Awal, 2018). In 2014, seven years after the billion dollar suit was filed, and multiple court room appearances, Google and Viacom settled out of court. Google's ability to take down copyrighted material using Content ID had become very effective, and Google agreed to rent hundreds of Viacom shows (Kaufman, 2014). Both parties recognized in a joint statement that they could achieve their objectives by collaborating rather than continuing the lawsuit. In 2018, YouTube rolled out Copyright Match, which uses matching technology similar to Content ID's to notify creators if their videos have been stolen and posted by another party on Youtube (Liao, 2018).

The DMCA continues to be a source of litigation. In 2017, a U.S. federal circuit court ruled that blogging platform LiveJournal could be liable for infringing content posted with the approval of community moderators, who had broad discretion over the user-generated content that appears on the site, and that the use of such moderators might lead to the forfeiture of a DMCA's safe harbor that normally protects such websites (*Mavrix Photographs, LLC v. LiveJournal, Inc.* (2017)) (Roberts, 2017).

In another important case that has also chipped away at DMCA safe harbor protection, *BMG Rights Management v. Cox Communications*, a U.S. federal judge let stand a $25 million jury award against Cox Cable in favor of BMG, a rights management firm, for willful contributory infringement. BMG argued that Cox, an ISP, was allowing subscribers to use BitTorrent to upload copyrighted songs to various websites without an effective policy for preventing this activity, and failing to remove repeat offenders from its service. Cox argued that it was just a pipeline to the Internet and could not be held liable for what its users posted or what software they used. The court left the jury award against Cox in place, but but it refused to shut Cox down, as BMG had requested, noting that while there is a public benefit to reducing copyright infringement, because Cox provides access to the Internet and enables freedom of speech, these interests trumped BMG's interest in copyright protection. However, the judge also ordered Cox to pay an additional $8 million in legal fees to BMG on the grounds that Cox had willfully violated the DMCA. On appeal, the 5th Circuit U.S. Federal Court of Appeals affirmed that Cox was not entitled to a DMCA safe harbor, but sent the case back to be re-tried due to other errors by the district court judge. In August 2018, BMG reported that it had settled the case for a substantial payment by Cox (Farrell, 2018; Mullin, 2017; Gardner, 2016).

Copyright owners from the film and music industry are lobbying Congress for changes in the DMCA that would require websites and ISPs to take more effective actions in removing infringing content (Raymond, 2016). Musicians and film makers have begun to protest the compensation they receive from streaming services (see Chapter 10).

While there has been some progress in limiting infringing content on the Internet, apps such as Periscope, as well as live streaming functionality on Facebook, YouTube, Vimeo, Twitch, and other sites, make it easy for people to capture live video and stream it. This makes it it extremely difficult for content owners to protect the value of their live products. Periscope is owned by Twitter and users can post live videos to Twitter. Periscope received over 26,000 DMCA takedown requests in the period from January to June 2019, and Twitter removed material in response to 84% of those requests (Twitter, 2020). But the DMCA takedown notices do not help a unique live event such as a championship boxing match retain its value. The value of the event is largely in attracting viewers willing to pay to see it live, and once a free alternative is available, that value is diminished.

Copyright Protection in the European Union

The European Union is taking a far more proactive view of copyright protection on the Internet, as it has with privacy with the GDPR. In the past, the European Union had adopted legislation very similar to the DMCA in the United States where the burden of protecting copyright fell to the content creators and publishers. This situation has dramatically changed.

In June 2019, the EU's Directive on Copyright in the Digital Single Market became effective. Countries that are part of the EU have two years to pass legislation to implement the Directive. The UK government has already stated that it will not adopt the directive. The Directive is intended to force firms like Google and Facebook to pay creators and publishers of content such as music, news, and art, which Internet firms often use without fair compensation (Vincent, 2020; European Commission, 2019; EU Parliament, 2018; Schechner and Pop, 2018; Brown, 2018; Michaels 2018).

The legislation was strongly opposed by aggregators of content, such as Google, Facebook, Amazon, Wikipedia, and others, as a costly effort that would restrict Internet freedom of expression, but was strongly supported by news organizations, music companies, and artists who believe they are not fairly compensated for their work (Brown, 2018).

The legislation gives publishers the right to negotiate payment for digital use of their content, and requires online video sites to pay for copyrighted content and develop screen software to prevent uploads of content by users that is not licensed by the owners. Currently, platforms like Google and Facebook aggregate headlines and music on their sites with links to the content creators, and receive ad revenue on these pages that they do not share with the publishers. There is also a halo effect: Facebook and Google became the primary place where users go to find content. While this drives users to publisher sites, the publishers do not receive any of the ad revenue generated by their content shown on aggregator sites, which makes it difficult for publishers to attract subscribers independently. Currently, copyrighted material can be uploaded by users and can only be taken down at the owners/publisher's request, which is costly and time consuming for publishers. YouTube tools that help publishers identify stolen videos such as Content ID and Copyright Match are considered inadequate by publishers. Ultimately, this legislation is an effort by publishers and artists to obtain compensation for their content, which is indexed and aggregated by tech firms. The new copyright legislation also reflects European objections to the dominance of American Internet firms like Google and Facebook, and like the GDPR, is part of a longer-term EU strategy called Single Digital Market, which aims to integrate digital policies involving privacy and intellectual property across the entire European Union rather than have each country make policy in these areas (European Commission, 2015).

PATENTS: BUSINESS METHODS AND PROCESSES

> "Whoever invents or discovers any new and useful process, machine, manufacture, or composition of matter, or any new and useful improvement thereof, may obtain a patent therefore, subject to the conditions and requirements of this title."
>
> —Section 101, U.S. Patent Act

patent

grants the owner an exclusive monopoly on the ideas behind an invention for 20 years

A **patent** grants the owner a 20-year exclusive monopoly on the ideas behind an invention. The congressional intent behind patent law was to ensure that inventors of new machines, devices, or industrial methods would receive the full financial and other rewards of their labor and still make widespread use of the invention possible by providing detailed diagrams for those wishing to use the idea under license from the patent's owner. Patents are obtained from the United States Patent and Trademark Office (USPTO), which was created in 1812. Obtaining a patent is much more difficult and time-consuming than obtaining copyright protection (which is automatic with the creation of the work). Patents must be formally applied for, and the granting of a patent is determined by Patent Office examiners who follow a set of rigorous rules. Ultimately, federal courts decide when patents are valid and when infringement occurs.

Patents are very different from copyrights because patents protect the ideas themselves and not merely the expression of ideas. There are four types of inventions for which patents are granted under patent law: machines, man-made products, compositions of matter, and processing methods. The U.S. Supreme Court has determined that patents extend to "anything under the sun that is made by man" (*Diamond v. Chakrabarty*, 1980) as long as the other requirements of the Patent Act are met. There are three things that cannot be patented: laws of nature, natural phenomena, and abstract ideas. For instance, a mathematical algorithm cannot be patented unless it is realized in a tangible machine or process that has a "useful" result (the mathematical algorithm exception).

In order to be granted a patent, the applicant must show that the invention is new, original, novel, nonobvious, and not evident in prior arts and practice. As with copyrights, the granting of patents has moved far beyond the original intent of Congress's first patent statute, which sought to protect industrial designs and machines. Patent protection has been extended to articles of manufacture (1842), plants (1930), surgical and medical procedures (1950), and software (1981). The Patent Office did not accept applications for software patents until a 1981 U.S. Supreme Court decision that held that computer programs could be a part of a patentable process. Since that time, thousands of software patents have been granted. Virtually any software program can be patented as long as it is novel and not obvious.

Essentially, as technology and industrial arts progress, patents have been extended to both encourage entrepreneurs to invent useful devices and promote widespread dissemination of the new techniques through licensing and artful imitation of the published patents (the creation of devices that provide the same functionality as the invention but use different methods) (Winston, 1998). Patents encourage inventors to come up with unique ways of achieving the same functionality as existing patents. For instance, Amazon's patent on one-click purchasing caused Barnesandnoble.com to invent a simplified two-click method of purchasing.

The danger of patents is that they stifle competition by raising barriers to entry into an industry. Patents force new entrants to pay licensing fees to incumbents, and thus slow down the development of technical applications of new ideas by creating lengthy licensing applications and delays.

E-commerce Patents

Much of the Internet's infrastructure and software was developed under the auspices of publicly funded scientific and military programs in the United States and Europe. Unlike Samuel F. B. Morse, who patented the idea of Morse code and made the telegraph useful, most of the inventions that make the Internet and e-commerce possible were not patented by their inventors. The early Internet was characterized by a spirit of worldwide community development and sharing of ideas without consideration of personal wealth (Winston, 1998). This early Internet spirit changed in the mid-1990s with the commercial development of the Web.

In 1998, a landmark legal decision, *State Street Bank & Trust v. Signature Financial Group, Inc.*, paved the way for business firms to begin applying for "business methods" patents. In this case, a U.S. Federal Circuit Court of Appeals upheld the claims of Signature Financial to a valid patent for a business method that allows managers to monitor and record financial information flows generated by a partner fund. Previously, it was thought business methods could not be patented. However, the court ruled there was no reason to disallow business methods from patent protection, or any "step by step process, be it electronic or chemical or mechanical, [that] involves an algorithm in the broad sense of the term" (*State Street Bank & Trust Co. v. Signature Financial Group*, 1998). The State Street decision led to an explosion in applications for e-commerce "business methods" patents. In 2010, the U.S. Supreme Court issued a divided opinion on business methods patents in the *Bilski et al. v. Kappos* case (*Bilski et al. v. Kappos*, 2010). The majority argued that business methods patents were allowable even though they did not meet the traditional "machine or transformation test," in which patents are granted to devices that are tied to a particular machine, are a machine, or transform articles from one state to another. The minority wanted to flatly declare that business methods are not patentable in part because any series of steps could be considered a business method (Schwartz, 2010). The Supreme Court struck another blow against business method patents in 2014, with its decision in *Alice Corporation vs. CLS Bank International*. The Court ruled that basic business methods cannot be patented and that while software can be patented, implementing an abstract idea that otherwise could not be patented by using software does not transform the idea into a patentable innovation (*Alice Corporation Pty. Ltd. v. CLS Bank International*, 2014).

Table 8.16 lists some of the better-known e-commerce patents. Some are controversial. Reviewing these, you can understand the concerns of commentators and corporations. Some of the patent claims are very broad (for example, "name your price" sales methods), have historical precedents in the pre-Internet era (shopping carts), and seem "obvious" (one-click purchasing). Critics of online business methods patents argue that the Patent Office has been too lenient in granting such patents, and that in most instances, the supposed inventions merely copy pre-Internet business methods and thus do not constitute "inventions" (Harmon, 2003; Thurm, 2000; Chiappetta, 2001). The Patent Office argues, on the contrary, that its Internet inventions staff is composed of engineers, lawyers, and specialists with many years of experience with Internet and network technologies, and that it consults with outside technology experts before granting patents. To complicate matters, the European Patent Convention and the patent laws of most European countries do not recognize business methods per se unless the method is implemented through some technology (Takenaka, 2001).

TRADEMARKS: ONLINE INFRINGEMENT AND DILUTION

> A trademark is "any word, name, symbol, or device, or any combination thereof ... used in commerce ... to identify and distinguish ... goods ... from those manufactured or sold by others and to indicate the source of the goods."
> —The Trademark Act, 1946

trademark
a mark used to identify and distinguish goods and indicate their source

Trademark law is a form of intellectual property protection for **trademarks**—a mark used to identify and distinguish goods and indicate their source. Trademark protections exist at both the federal and state levels in the United States. The purpose of trademark law is twofold. First, trademark law protects the public in the marketplace by ensuring that it gets what it pays for and wants to receive. Second, trademark law protects the owner—who has spent time, money, and energy bringing the product to the marketplace—against piracy and misappropriation. Trademarks have been extended from single words to pictures, shapes, packaging, and colors. Some things may not be trademarked such as common words that are merely descriptive ("clock"). Federal trademarks are obtained, first, by use in interstate commerce, and second, by registration with the U.S. Patent and

TABLE 8.16 SELECTED E-COMMERCE PATENTS

COMPANY	SUBJECT	UPDATE
Amazon	One-click purchasing	Considered to be one of the most contentious e-commerce patents. Amazon attempted to use patent originally granted to it in 1997 to force changes to Barnes & Noble's website, but a federal court overturned a previously issued injunction. Eventually settled out of court. In 2007, a USPTO panel rejected some of the patent because of evidence another patent predated it. Amazon amended the patent, and the revised version was confirmed in 2010. Patent expired on September 11, 2017.
Priceline	Buyer-driven "name your price" sales	Originally filed by Walker Digital, an intellectual property laboratory, and then assigned to Priceline. Granted by the USPTO in 1999. Shortly thereafter, Priceline sued Microsoft and Expedia for copying its patented business method.
Akamai	Internet content delivery global hosting system	A broad patent granted in 2000 covering techniques for expediting the flow of information over the Internet. Akamai sued Digital Island for violating the patent and, in 2001, a jury found in its favor.
DoubleClick	Dynamic delivery of online advertising	The patent underlying DoubleClick's business of online banner ad delivery, originally granted in 2000. DoubleClick sued competitors 24/7 Media and L90 for violating the patent and ultimately reached a settlement with them.
Overture	Pay for performance search	System and method for influencing position on search result list generated by computer search engine, granted in 2001. Competitor FindWhat sued Overture, charging that patent was obtained illegally; Overture countered by suing both FindWhat and Google for violating patent. Google agreed to pay a license fee to Overture in 2004 to settle.
Acacia Technologies	Streaming video media transmission	Patents for the receipt and transmission of streaming digital audio and/or video content originally granted to founders of Greenwich Information Technologies in 1990s. Patents were purchased by Acacia, a firm founded solely to enforce the patents, in 2001.
Soverain Software	Purchase technology	The so-called "shopping cart" patent for network-based systems, which involves any transaction over a network involving a seller, buyer, and payment system. In other words, e-commerce! Soverain filed suit against Amazon for patent infringement, which Amazon paid $40 million to settle. In 2013 a federal district court ruled Soverain's claims against Newegg in part invalid.
MercExchange (Thomas Woolston)	Auction technology	Patents on person-to-person auctions and database search, originally granted in 1995. eBay ordered to pay $25 million in 2003 for infringing on patent. In 2007, a motion for permanent patent injunction against eBay was denied. MercExchange and eBay settled the dispute in 2008 on confidential terms.
Google	Search technology	Google PageRank patent filed in 1998 and granted in 2001. Became non-exclusive in 2011 and expired in 2017.
Google	Location technology	Patent for a method of using location information in an advertising system issued to Google in 2010.
Apple	Social technology	Apple applied for a patent in 2010 that allows groups of friends attending events to stay in communication with each other and share reactions to live events as they are occurring.
Facebook	Social technology	A 2010 patent on an algorithm for developing personalized stories and newsfeeds on a social network.

Trademark Office (USPTO). Federal trademarks are granted for a period of 10 years and can be renewed indefinitely.

Disputes over federal trademarks involve establishing infringement. The test for infringement is twofold: market confusion and bad faith. Use of a trademark that creates confusion with existing trademarks, causes consumers to make market mistakes, or misrepresents the origins of goods is an infringement. For instance, in 2015, Multi Time Machine (MTM) sued Amazon for violation of its trademarks and confusing consumers looking to buy MTM watches. MTM makes military-style watches that are not sold on Amazon. If a user searches on Amazon for an MTM watch, the search results shows watches being offered by MTM competitors that are similar in style to MTM's. MTM argued that this could confuse customers. The court ultimately ruled for Amazon, based on the grounds that the products that appeared on the page in response to the search were clearly labeled (Smith, 2017). In addition, the intentional misuse of words and symbols in the marketplace to extort revenue from legitimate trademark owners ("bad faith") is proscribed.

In 1995, the U.S. Congress passed the Federal Trademark Dilution Act (FTDA), which created a federal cause of action for dilution of famous marks. This legislation dispenses with the test of market confusion (although that is still required to claim infringement), and extends protection to owners of famous trademarks against **dilution**, which is defined as any behavior that would weaken the connection between the trademark and the product. In 2006, the FTDA was amended by the Trademark Dilution Revision Act (TDRA), which allows a trademark owner to file a claim based on a "likelihood of dilution" standard, rather than having to provide evidence of actual dilution. The TDRA also expressly provides that dilution may occur through blurring (weakening the connection between the trademark and the goods) and tarnishment (using the trademark in a way that makes the underlying products appear unsavory or unwholesome). Internationally, WIPO handles many cybersquatting cases under its Uniform Dispute Resolution Procedures. In 2014, WIPO warned that the expansion of generic top-level domains authorized by ICANN is likely to be very disruptive in terms of trademark protection (New, 2014). Although the cost of obtaining a new gTLD is not unsubstantial (it is estimated to be more than $180,000), by early 2020, over 1,230 new generic top-level domain (gTLDs) had been approved (Sadowsky, 2020). Successful applicants become owners of these gTLDs, and can create and sell new domains with the gTLD suffix, such as Avenger.movie. Many of these new domains may potentially conflict with the established trademarks of others.

To deal with these trademark conflicts, ICANN developed a set of procedures to rapidly resolve disputes called the Uniform Rapid Suspension System (URS), a domain name dispute procedure that allows a trademark owner to seek suspension of a domain name in a new gTLD. ICANN also established a Trademark Clearing house as a repository of data on registered, court-validated, or statute-protected trademarks. Trademark owners register their marks for a fee.

One successful applicant for a new gTLD was Vox Populi Registry Ltd. Vox purchased the gTLD .sucks, and began selling domains such as Apple.sucks and CitiGroup.sucks exclusively to corporations who did not want their brand name associated with .sucks. (Bloomberg News, 2015). In 2017, Vox temporarily dropped the price of .sucks domains, which typically cost much more, to $1.99 in an effort to stimulate consumer and advertising markets for the domain (Allemann, 2016).

dilution

any behavior that would weaken the connection between the trademark and the product

Trademarks and the Internet

The rapid growth and commercialization of the Internet have provided unusual opportunities for existing firms with distinctive and famous trademarks to extend their brands to the Internet. These same developments have provided malicious individuals and firms the opportunity to squat on Internet domain names built upon famous marks, as well as attempt to confuse consumers and dilute famous or distinctive marks (including your personal name or a movie star's name). The conflict between legitimate trademark owners and malicious firms was allowed to fester and grow because Network Solutions Inc. (NSI), originally the Internet's sole agency for domain name registration for many years, had a policy of "first come, first served." This meant anyone could register any domain name that had not already been registered, regardless of the trademark status of the domain name. NSI was not authorized to decide trademark issues (Nash, 1997).

In response to a growing number of complaints from owners of famous trademarks who found their trademark names being appropriated by web entrepreneurs, the U.S. Congress passed the **Anticybersquatting Consumer Protection Act (ACPA)** in 1999. The ACPA creates civil liabilities for anyone who attempts in bad faith to profit from an existing famous or distinctive trademark by registering an Internet domain name that is identical or confusingly similar to, or "dilutive" of, that trademark. The act does not establish criminal sanctions. It proscribes using "bad-faith" domain names to extort money from the owners of the existing trademark (**cybersquatting**), or using the bad-faith domain to divert web traffic to the bad-faith domain that could harm the good will represented by the trademark, create market confusion, or tarnish or disparage the mark (**cyberpiracy**). It is conceivable that domains such as the previously described Apple.sucks might be seen as a kind of cybersquatting and a violation of the ACPA. The act also proscribes the use of a domain name that consists of the name of a living person, or a name confusingly similar to an existing personal name, without that person's consent, if the registrant is registering the name with the intent to profit by selling the domain name to that person.

Trademark abuse can take many forms on the Web. **Table 8.17** lists the major behaviors on the Internet that have run afoul of trademark law and some of the court cases that resulted.

Cybersquatting and Brandjacking

In one of the first cases involving the ACPA, E. & J. Gallo Winery, owner of the registered mark "Ernest and Julio Gallo" for alcoholic beverages, sued Spider Webs Ltd. for using the domain name Ernestandjuliogallo.com. Spider Webs Ltd. was a domain name speculator that owned numerous domain names consisting of famous company names. The Ernestandjuliogallo.com website contained information on the risks of alcohol use, anti-corporate articles about E. & J. Gallo Winery, and was poorly constructed. The court concluded that Spider Webs Ltd. was in violation of the ACPA and that its actions constituted dilution by blurring because the Ernestandjuliogallo.com domain name appeared on every page printed off the website accessed by that name, and that Spider Webs Ltd. was not free to use this particular mark as a domain name (*E. & J. Gallo Winery v. Spider Webs Ltd.*, 2001). In 2009, a court upheld the largest cybersquatting judgment to date: a $33 million verdict in favor of Verizon against OnlineNIC, an Internet domain registration company that had used over 660 names that could easily be confused with legitimate

Anticybersquatting Consumer Protection Act (ACPA)
creates civil liabilities for anyone who attempts in bad faith to profit from an existing famous or distinctive trademark by registering an Internet domain name that is identical or confusingly similar to, or "dilutive" of, that trademark

cybersquatting
involves the registration of an infringing domain name, or other Internet use of an existing trademark, for the purpose of extorting payments from the legitimate owners

cyberpiracy
involves the same behavior as cybersquatting, but with the intent of diverting traffic from the legitimate site to an infringing site

TABLE 8.17 INTERNET AND TRADEMARK LAW EXAMPLES

ACTIVITY	DESCRIPTION	EXAMPLE CASE
Cybersquatting	Registering domain names similar or identical to trademarks of others to extort profits from legitimate holders	*E. & J. Gallo Winery v. Spider Webs Ltd.*, 129 F. Supp. 2d 1033 (S.D. Tex., 2001) aff'd 286 F. 3d 270 (5th Cir., 2002)
Cyberpiracy	Registering domain names similar or identical to trademarks of others to divert web traffic to their own sites	*Ford Motor Co. v. Lapertosa*, 2001 U.S. Dist. LEXIS 253 (E.D. Mich., 2001); *PaineWebber Inc. v. Fortuny*, Civ. A. No. 99-0456-A (E.D. Va., 1999); *Playboy Enterprises, Inc. v. Global Site Designs, Inc.*, 1999 WL 311707 (S.D. Fla., 1999); *Audi AG and Volkswagen of America Inc. v. Bob D'Amato* (No. 05-2359; 6th Cir., November 27, 2006)
Metatagging	Using trademarked words in a site's metatags	*Bernina of America, Inc. v. Fashion Fabrics Int'l, Inc.*, 2001 U.S. Dist. LEXIS 1211 (N.D. Ill., 2001); *Nissan Motor Co., Ltd. v. Nissan Computer Corp.*, 289 F. Supp. 2d 1154 (C.D. Cal., 2000), aff'd, 246 F. 3rd 675 (9th Cir., 2000)
Keywording	Placing trademarked keywords on web pages, either visible or invisible	*Playboy Enterprises, Inc. v. Netscape Communications, Inc.*, 354 F. 3rd 1020 (9th Cir., 2004); *Nettis Environment Ltd. v. IWI, Inc.*, 46 F. Supp. 2d 722 (N.D. Ohio, 1999); *Government Employees Insurance Company v. Google, Inc.*, Civ. Action No. 1:04cv507 (E.D. VA, 2004); *Google, Inc. v. American Blind & Wallpaper Factory, Inc.*, Case No. 03-5340 JF (RS) (N.D. Cal., April 18, 2007)
Linking	Linking to content pages on other sites, bypassing the home page	*Ticketmaster Corp. v. Tickets.com*, 2000 U.S. Dist. Lexis 4553 (C.D. Cal., 2000)
Framing	Placing the content of other sites in a frame on the infringer's site	*The Washington Post, et al. v. TotalNews, Inc., et al.* (S.D.N.Y., Civil Action Number 97-1190)

Verizon domain names. Although there have not been many cases decided under the ACPA, that does not mean the problem has gone away. Impersonation of individuals and brands on social network sites adds another dimension to the problem. Both Twitter and Facebook make cybersquatting and impersonation a violation of their terms of service.

However, it is not always easy for a firm to prevent trademark infringement by cybersquatters, or to prevent squatters from profiting from their infringing activities. In 2015, for instance, the Academy of Motion Picture Arts and Sciences (AMPAS) accused domain registrar GoDaddy of cybersquatting (*Academy of Motion Picture Arts and Sciences v. GoDaddy.com Inc et al.*, 2015). AMPAS claimed GoDaddy acted in bad faith by allowing customers to purchase 293 domain names such as Academyawards.net, Oscarsredacademyawards.net, Oscarsredcarpet.com, Billycrystal2012oscars.com, and Theoscargoestothehangover.com, and then sharing in the advertising revenues those pages generated. The court ruled that GoDaddy relied on representations of their users that their domain registrations did not infringe any trademarks, and that it took down domains after receiving takedown requests. AMPAS failed to prove intent to profit from AMPAS marks, according to the court. This suit demonstrates that trademark owners need to be vigilant in detecting infringement, sending takedown notices immediately, and following up to make sure the infringing sites are taken down. The burden is clearly on the trademark owner. The suit also demonstrates that cybersquatters have little incentive to stop trying to defraud and confuse consumers. If they are caught, their sites are taken down, but there is no penalty for trying (Stempel, 2015).

Cyberpiracy

Cyberpiracy involves the same behavior as cybersquatting, but with the intent of diverting traffic from the legitimate site to an infringing site. In *Ford Motor Co. v. Lapertosa*, Lapertosa had registered and used a website called Fordrecalls.com as an adult entertainment website. The court ruled that Fordrecalls.com was in violation of the ACPA in that it was a bad-faith attempt to divert traffic to the Lapertosa site and diluted Ford's wholesome trademark (*Ford Motor Co. v. Lapertosa*, 2001).

The Ford decision reflects two other famous cases of cyberpiracy. In the *Paine Webber Inc. v. Fortuny* case, the court enjoined Fortuny from using the domain name www.painewebber.com—a site that specialized in pornographic materials—because it diluted and tarnished Paine Webber's trademark and diverted web traffic from Paine Webber's legitimate site—Painewebber.com (*Paine Webber Inc. v. Fortuny*, 1999). In the *Playboy Enterprises, Inc. v. Global Site Designs, Inc.* case, the court enjoined the defendants from using the Playboy and Playmate marks in their domain names Playboyonline.net and Playmatesearch.net and from including the Playboy trademark in their metatags. In these cases, the defendants' intention was diversion for financial gain (*Playboy Enterprises, Inc. v. Global Site Designs, Inc.*, 1999).

Typosquatting is a form of cyberpiracy in which a domain name contains a common misspelling of another site's name. These domains are sometimes referred to as "doppelganger" domains. Often the user ends up at a site very different from one they intended to visit. For instance, John Zuccarini is an infamous typosquatter who was jailed in 2002 for setting up pornographic websites with URLs based on misspellings of popular children's brands, such as Bob the Builder and Teletubbies. The FTC fined him again in 2007 for engaging in similar practices (McMillan, 2007). Harvard Business School professor Ben Edelman conducted a study that found that there were at least 938,000 domains typosquatting on the top 3,264 ".com" websites, and that 57% of these domains included Google pay-per-click ads. In 2011, Facebook filed a lawsuit against 25 typosquatters who established websites with such domain names as Faceboook, Facemook, Faceboik, and Facebooki. In 2013, Facebook was awarded $2.8 million in damages.

Metatagging

The legal status of using famous or distinctive marks as metatags is more complex and subtle. The use of trademarks in metatags is permitted if the use does not mislead or confuse consumers. Usually this depends on the content of the site. A car dealer would be permitted to use a famous automobile trademark in its metatags if the dealer sold this brand of automobiles, but a pornography site could not use the same trademark, nor a dealer for a rival manufacturer. A Ford dealer would most likely be infringing if it used "Honda" in its metatags, but would not be infringing if it used "Ford" in its metatags. (Ford Motor Company would be unlikely to seek an injunction against one of its dealers.)

In the *Bernina of America, Inc. v. Fashion Fabrics Int'l, Inc.* case, the court enjoined Fashion Fabrics, an independent dealer of sewing machines, from using the trademarks "Bernina" and "Bernette," which belonged to the manufacturer Bernina, as metatags. The court found the defendant's site contained misleading claims about Fashion Fabrics' knowledge of Bernina products that were likely to confuse customers. The use of the Bernina trademarks as metatags per se was not a violation of ACPA, according to the court, but in combination with the misleading claims on the site would cause confusion and hence infringement (*Bernina of America, Inc. v. Fashion Fabrics Int'l, Inc.*, 2001).

In the *Nissan Motor Co., Ltd. v. Nissan Computer Corp.* case, Uzi Nissan had used his surname "Nissan" as a trade name for various businesses since 1980, including Nissan Computer Corp. Nissan.com had no relationship with Nissan Motor, but over the years began selling auto parts that competed with Nissan Motor. The court ruled that Nissan Computer's behavior did indeed infringe on Nissan Motor's trademarks, but it refused to shut the site down. Instead, the court ruled Nissan Computer could continue to use the Nissan name and metatags, but must post notices on its site that it was not affiliated with Nissan Motor (*Nissan Motor Co., Ltd. v. Nissan Computer Corp.*, 2000).

Keywording

The permissibility of using trademarks as keywords on search engines is also subtle and depends (1) on the extent to which such use is considered to be a "use in commerce" and causes "initial customer confusion" and (2) on the content of the search results.

In *Playboy Enterprises, Inc. v. Netscape Communications, Inc.*, Playboy objected to the practice of Netscape's and Excite's search engines displaying banner ads unrelated to *Playboy Magazine* when users entered search arguments such as "playboy," "playmate," and "playgirl." The Ninth Circuit Court of Appeals denied the defendant's motion for a summary judgment and held that when an advertiser's banner ad is not labeled so as to identify its source, the practice could result in trademark infringement due to consumer confusion (*Playboy Enterprises, Inc. v. Netscape Communications, Inc.*, 2004).

Google has also faced lawsuits alleging that its advertising network illegally exploits others' trademarks. For instance, insurance company GEICO challenged Google's practice of allowing competitors' ads to appear when a searcher types "Geico" as the search query. A U.S. district court ruled that this practice did not violate federal trademark laws as long as the word "Geico" was not used in the ads' text (*Government Employees Insurance Company v. Google, Inc.*, 2004). Google quickly discontinued allowing the latter, and settled the case (Associated Press, 2005). In 2009, Rosetta Stone, the language-learning software firm, filed a lawsuit against Google for trademark infringement, alleging its AdWords program allowed other companies to use Rosetta Stone's trademarks for online advertisements without permission. In 2012, the 4th Circuit Court of Appeals held that a jury might hold Google liable for trademark infringement, pointing to evidence that an internal Google study found that even sophisticated users were sometimes unaware that sponsored links were advertisements. In 2012, Rosetta Stone and Google settled, which was seen as a strategic win for Google because it eliminated one of the last major cases challenging the legitimacy of its AdWords program. Currently Google allows anyone to buy anyone else's trademark as a keyword. In 2011, Microsoft decided to follow this practice as well with Bing and Yahoo Search.

Linking

Linking refers to building hypertext links from one site to another site. This is obviously a major design feature and benefit of the Web. **Deep linking** involves bypassing the target site's home page and going directly to a content page. In *Ticketmaster Corp. v. Tickets.com*, Tickets.com—owned by Microsoft—competed directly against Ticketmaster in the events ticket market. When Tickets.com did not have tickets for an event, it would direct users to Ticketmaster's internal pages, bypassing the Ticketmaster home page. Even though its logo was displayed on the internal pages, Ticketmaster objected on the grounds that such "deep linking" violated the terms and conditions of use for its site (stated on a separate page altogether and construed by Ticketmaster as equivalent to a shrink-wrap license), and constituted false advertising, as well as the violation of copyright. The court found, however, that deep linking per se is not illegal, no violation of copyright occurred because no copies were made, the terms and conditions of use were not obvious to users, and users were not required to read the page on which the terms and conditions of use appeared in any event. The court refused to rule in favor of Ticketmaster, but left open further argument on the licensing issue. In an out-of-court settlement, Tickets.com nevertheless agreed to stop the practice of deep linking (*Ticketmaster v. Tickets.com*, 2000).

linking
building hypertext links from one site to another site

deep linking
involves bypassing the target site's home page, and going directly to a content page

Framing

Framing involves displaying the content of another website inside your own website within a frame or window. The user never leaves the framer's site and can be exposed to advertising while the target site's advertising is distorted or eliminated. Framers may or may not acknowledge the source of the content. In *The Washington Post, et al. v. TotalNews, Inc.*, The Washington Post Company, CNN, Reuters, and several other news organizations filed suit against TotalNews, Inc., claiming that TotalNews's use of frames on its website, TotalNews.com, infringed upon the respective plaintiffs' copyrights and trademarks, and diluted the content of their individual websites. The plaintiffs claimed additionally that TotalNews's framing practice effectively deprived the plaintiffs' websites of advertising revenue.

TotalNews's website employed four frames. The TotalNews logo appeared in the lower left frame, various links were located in a vertical frame on the left side of the screen, TotalNews's advertising was framed across the screen bottom, and the "news frame," the largest frame, appeared in the center and right. Clicking on a specific news organization's link allowed the reader to view the content of that particular organization's website, including any related advertising, within the context of the "news frame." In some instances, the framing distorted or modified the appearance of the linked website, including the advertisements, while the appearance of TotalNews's advertisements, in a separate frame, remained unchanged. In addition, the URL remained fixed on the TotalNews address, even though the content in the largest frame on the website was from the linked website. The "news frame" did not, however, eliminate the linked website's identifying features.

framing
involves displaying the content of another website inside your own website within a frame or window

The case was settled out of court. The news organizations allowed TotalNews to link to their websites, but prohibited framing and any attempt to imply affiliation with the news organizations (*The Washington Post, et al. v. TotalNews, Inc.*, 1997).

TRADE SECRETS

Much of the value created by a firm lies not in copyrights, patents, or even trademarks. There is a kind of intellectual property that has to do with business procedures, formulas, and methods of manufacture and service delivery, from which the firm derives value and which it does not want to share with others in the form of a patent application or copyright application. This type of intellectual property is referred to as **trade secrets.** Most famously, the formula for Coca Cola is considered a trade secret, as are the manufacturing techniques for producing General Electric's jet engine turbine blades. Trade secrets differ from other copyright and patent protections because they may not be unique or novel. Information in a firm can be considered a trade secret if (a) it is a secret (something that others do not know), (b) has commercial value to its owner, and (c) the owner has taken steps to protect the secret. U.S. corporations are believed to own trillions of dollars of trade secrets (Gershman, 2016).

Until recently, trade secrets were defined and enforced mostly in state laws because historically businesses were local, as was theft of business trade secrets. In the digital age, when business is national and global, a new level of protection is needed that would make it easier to enforce trade secret laws. In 2016, the Defend Trade Secrets Act (DTSA), which creates a federal private right of action for trade secret protection, was enacted. DTSA is a response to the large-scale theft of trade secrets (also known as economic sabotage) by hackers and foreign nations from American corporate and government information systems. The European Union has a similar Trade Secrets Directive to protect European firms and nations (Winston & Strawn, 2019). According to the U.S. Patent and Trade Office, the theft of trade secrets is one of the largest transfers of wealth in history, costing U.S. firms $300 billion a year (Lee, 2016). However, it is unclear if the new Act actually will be capable of protecting firms from theft of trade secrets.

CHALLENGE: BALANCING THE PROTECTION OF PROPERTY WITH OTHER VALUES

The challenge in intellectual property ethics and law is to ensure that creators of intellectual property can receive the benefits of their inventions and works, while also making it possible for their works and designs to be disseminated and used by the widest possible audience (with the exception of trade secret law where the object is not to share or distribute for the common good). Protections from rampant theft of intellectual property inevitably lead to restrictions on distribution, which then restricts payments to creators for the use of their works—which in itself can slow down the distribution process. Without these protections, however, and without the benefits that flow to creators of intellectual property, the pace of innovation could decline. In the early years of e-commerce, up to 2005, the balance has been struck more toward Internet distributors and their claim to be free from restrictions on intellectual content, particularly music. Since the development of the iTunes store, smartphones, and tablets, after 2005, the balance has swung back toward content owners, largely because Internet distributors depend on high-quality content to

trade secret

information that is secret, has commercial value, and has been protected by its owner attract audiences, but also partly due to the effectiveness of lawsuits in raising the costs to Internet firms that fail to protect intellectual property.

8.4 GOVERNANCE

Governance has to do with social control: Who will control the Internet? Who will control the processes of e-commerce, the content, and the activities? What elements will be controlled, and how will the controls be implemented? A natural question arises and needs to be answered: Why do we as a society need to "control" e-commerce? Because e-commerce and the Internet are so closely intertwined (though not identical), controlling e-commerce also involves regulating the Internet.

governance

has to do with social control: who will control e-commerce, what elements will be controlled, and how will the controls be implemented

CAN THE INTERNET BE CONTROLLED?

Early Internet advocates argued that the Internet was different from all previous technologies. They contended that the Internet could not be controlled, given its inherent decentralized design, its ability to cross borders, and its underlying packet-switching technology that made monitoring and controlling message content impossible. Many still believe this to be true today. The implication is that the content and behavior of e-commerce sites—indeed Internet sites of any kind—cannot be "controlled" in the same way. Content issues such as pornography, gambling, and offensive written expressions and graphics, along with commercial issue of intellectual property protection, ushered in the current era of growing governmental regulation of the Internet and e-commerce throughout the world. Currently, we are in a mixed-mode policy environment where self-regulation through a variety of Internet policy and technical bodies co-exists with limited government regulation (Stone, 2010). See Chapter 2 for a review of the different governing bodies involved in overseeing the Internet, including ICANN and IANA, and changes in the United States' authority over IANA.

In fact, as you learned in the Chapter 2 *Insight on Society* case, *Government Regulation and Surveillance of the Internet*, the Internet is technically very easily controlled, monitored, and regulated from central locations (such as network access points, telecommunication firm or agency fiber trunk lines, as well as servers and routers throughout the network). For instance, in China, Saudi Arabia, Iran, North Korea, Thailand, Singapore, and many other countries, access to the Web is controlled from government-owned centralized routers that direct traffic across their borders and within the country (such as China's "Great Firewall of China," which permits the government to block access to certain U.S. or European websites), or via tightly regulated ISPs operating within the countries. In China, for instance, all ISPs need a license from the Ministry of Information Industry (MII), and are prohibited from disseminating any information that may harm the state or permit pornography, gambling, or the advocacy of cults. In addition, ISPs and search engines such as Google, Yahoo, and Bing typically self-censor their Asian content by using only government-approved news sources or, in the case of Google, exit the country altogether. Twitter is not planning any Chinese presence. China has also instituted regulations that require cafes, restaurants, hotels, and bookstores to install web monitoring software that identifies those using wireless services and monitors web activity. Because of the design of the Internet, a substantial part of global Internet traffic flows through U.S. telecommunication facilities.

Following the outbreak of street demonstrations in 2009 protesting a rigged election, the Iranian government unleashed one of the world's most sophisticated mechanisms for controlling and censoring the Web. Built with the assistance of Western companies like Siemens and Nokia, the system uses deep packet inspection to open every packet, look for keywords, reseal it, and send it on the network.

In the United States, as we have seen in our discussion of intellectual property, e-commerce sites can be put out of business for violating existing laws, and ISPs can be forced to "take down" offending or stolen content. Government security agencies such as the NSA and the FBI can obtain court orders to monitor ISP traffic and engage in widespread monitoring of millions of e-mail messages. Under the USA PATRIOT Act, American intelligence authorities are permitted to tap into whatever Internet traffic they believe is relevant to the campaign against terrorism, in some limited circumstances without judicial review. Working with the large ISP firms such as AT&T, Verizon, and others, U.S. security agencies have access to nearly all Internet communications throughout the country. And many American corporations are developing restrictions on their employees' at-work use of the Web to prevent gambling, shopping, and other activities not related to a business purpose.

In the United States, efforts to control media content on the Web have run up against equally powerful social and political values, and commercial interests, that protect freedom of expression, including several rulings by the Supreme Court that have struck down laws attempting to limit online content in the United States. The online industry leaders have strongly opposed restrictions on what their users post, or the notion that they should exercise editorial control over user content. However, both regulators and online firms are struggling to define the limits of free speech in the wake of the growth of online bullying, phony news sites, and hate groups. These concerns were heightened in the 2016 presidential election where hackers associated with the Russian government were alleged to have exploited the open nature of sites like Facebook, Google, and Twitter to spread fake news, provide links to hate group sites, and target ads to susceptible people. The U.S. Constitution's First Amendment says, "Congress shall make no law . . . abridging the freedom of speech, or of the press." As it turns out, the 200-year-old Bill of Rights has been a powerful brake on efforts to control 21st century online content.

TAXATION

Few questions illustrate the complexity of governance and jurisdiction more potently than taxation of e-commerce sales. In both Europe and the United States, governments rely on sales taxes based on the type and value of goods sold. In Europe, these taxes are collected along the entire value chain, including the final sale to the consumer, and are called "value-added taxes" (VAT), whereas in the United States, taxes are collected by states and localities on final sales to consumers and are called consumption and use taxes. In the United States, there are 50 states, 3,000 counties, and 12,000 municipalities, each with unique tax rates and policies. Cheese may be taxable in one state as a "snack food" but not taxable in another state (such as Wisconsin), where it is considered a basic food. Consumption taxes are generally recognized to be regressive because they disproportionately tax poorer people, for whom consumption is a larger part of their total income. Nevertheless, state and local sales taxes are a major source of revenue, especially in states where there are no income taxes.

Sales taxes were first implemented in the United States in the late 1930s as a Depression-era method of raising money for localities. Ostensibly, the money was to be used to build infrastructure such as roads, schools, and utilities to support business development, but over the years the funds have been used for general government purposes of the states and localities. In most states, there is a state-based sales tax, and a smaller local sales tax. The total sales tax ranges from zero in some states (North Dakota) to as much as 13% in New York City for the combined state and city sales taxes.

The development of "remote sales" such as mail order/telephone order (MOTO) retail in the United States in the 1970s broke the relationship between physical presence and commerce, complicating the plans of state and local tax authorities to tax all retail commerce. States sought to force MOTO retailers to collect sales taxes for them based on the address of the recipient, but Supreme Court decisions in 1967 and 1992 established that states had no authority to force MOTO retailers to collect state taxes unless the businesses had a "nexus" of operations (physical presence) in the state.

The explosive growth of e-commerce, the latest type of "remote sales," once again raised the issue of how—and if—to tax remote sales. For many years, e-commerce benefited from a tax subsidy of up to 13% for goods shipped to high sales-tax areas. Local retail merchants complained bitterly about the e-commerce tax subsidy. E-commerce merchants argued that this form of commerce needed to be nurtured and encouraged, and that in any event, the crazy quilt of sales and use tax regimes would be difficult to administer for Internet merchants. Online giants like Amazon argued that they should not have to pay taxes in states where they had no operations because they do not benefit from local schools, police, fire, and other governmental services. State and local governments meanwhile see billions of tax dollars slipping from their reach. But as Amazon's business model has changed with its building of large distribution centers close to urban areas to enable next-day delivery, so has its opposition to paying sales taxes softened. In 2015, the Supreme Court upheld a challenge to a Colorado law that would have required firms to report online sales to state residents as one step to ensure the residents paid taxes on such sales in Colorado, which is required by state law. In 2018, in the landmark *South Dakota v. Wayfair* case, the Supreme Court reversed its earlier position and ruled that states can levy sales taxes on online sales. The *Insight on Business* case, *New Rules Extend EU Taxation of E-commerce*, provides further insight into the fight over e-commerce sales taxes.

In 1998, the U.S. Congress passed the Internet Tax Freedom Act, which placed a moratorium on "multiple or discriminatory taxes on electronic commerce," as well as on taxes on Internet access, for three years until 2001. Since that time, the moratorium has been extended several times, and in 2016, Congress made the ban permanent.

NET NEUTRALITY

Net neutrality refers to the idea that ISPs, including cable Internet and wireless carriers, should treat all data on the Internet in the same manner, and not discriminate or price differentially by content, protocol, platform, hardware, or application. Prior to 2015, ISPs could discriminate against certain users on the basis of protocol or amount of usage. For instance, users of illegal downloading sites that utilize the BitTorrent

net neutrality
the concept that Internet service providers should treat all Internet traffic equally (or "neutrally")

INSIGHT ON BUSINESS

NEW RULES EXTEND EU TAXATION OF E-COMMERCE

Most people are happy when they discover they don't have to pay any sales tax on a purchase they make online. However, few stop to consider the implications that this may have. Governments in the last few years have been suffering a persistent budget crunch. Many countries that levy sales taxes have been eyeing the lost revenue from e-commerce sales, estimated to be in the billions. As e-commerce establishes itself as an ever-increasing percentage of the retail economy, governments worldwide are putting their collective feet down and demanding tax revenue from all online transactions.

The European Union and the United States have a combined population of more than 800 million people. In both areas, the tax code is changing to reflect the new online landscape, where goods and services are sold without a physical presence or local representative in the countries where they are purchased. In 2013, the European Union standardized its tax collection practices for e-businesses, bringing them more in line with businesses that are not situated in the EU.

In 2014, new EU regulations were implemented that compelled companies providing online services to EU customers to collect a value-added tax, or VAT, regardless of whether the company has a physical presence in that area or not. The customer's location is the determinant of whether the new EU rules apply. VAT was formerly due at the location of the sellers, but is now due at the location of the buyer. In the past, companies would save money by incorporating in countries with low VAT rates, such as Ireland or Luxembourg. The 2014 regulations were intended to combat this trend. Companies outside the European Union already had to submit VAT based on its customers' locations when selling to EU B2C customers, but starting in 2015, it became policy for EU companies selling to EU B2C customers as well.

Having VAT due at the location of customers as opposed to the sellers' location requires that EU-based businesses register in every EU country where their customers reside and charge VAT at local rates. Registration can cost upwards of €8,000 per country, representing a major roadblock for smaller firms. Many small business owners were unhappy with the system and demanded change. In 2016, the European Commission responded to these concerns and proposed rules that would dramatically simplify the VAT requirements for online retailers. The new rules were adopted by the European Council in December 2017 and will go into effect over time, beginning initially in 2019 and then with additional new rules following in 2021. The new rules require EU companies to register with a "One Stop Shop" online portal controlled by their own national tax authorities instead of with each individual country in the European Union. Smaller businesses making sales of €10,000 or less can treat sales as domestic sales using the VAT rates in their own countries. The requirements for larger businesses to verify the location of their customers were also reduced from two pieces of evidence to one. Many of these rules are already in place for online companies selling services, but not goods; in 2021, the new rules will extend to companies selling goods online as well. In 2021, online marketplaces will also become responsible for ensuring that VAT is collected on sales of goods on their platforms by non-EU companies to EU consumers.

Although EU businesses welcome the new rules and expect savings in the billions of euros, they still have significant regulatory burdens. They must distinguish between B2C and B2B customers, classify them by residence and store that information, and maintain systems that charge variable tax rates depending on whether customers are within the European Union or outside it.

The United States is one of the rare countries around the world that does not levy a VAT. With the adjustments to the EU's tax collection procedures, it's possible that the United States will follow suit at some point, perhaps as the result of pressure from retailers forced to navigate the confusing patchwork of local regulations. In 2020, Britain exited the European Union, putting its e-commerce future in limbo. It, too, may need to update its rules and regulations to keep pace with the pro-business changes to the VAT or risk its online retailers falling behind the rest of the EU.

VAT standard percentages in EU countries vary from the high teens, such as in Germany, Luxembourg, and Malta, to the mid-twenties, such as in Sweden, Denmark, and Romania, though the reduced percentages are closer to 10% and below for certain goods and services. The majority of countries have at least a 20% VAT, and the highest rate is Hungary's 27%. The European Union has also stipulated that wherever the Internet is used solely as a means of communication, this does not necessarily create a taxable good. However, whereas it was once the case in the United States that e-commerce businesses received special protections against taxation, the European Union is considering adjusting its rate reductions to reflect the fact that digital information services may in some cases actually be more valuable than the direct equivalent of traditional products. For example, e-books have search facilities, hyperlinks, and archives, and should perhaps not be sold with a steeply reduced VAT rate. In 2016, along with the changes mentioned previously, the European Commission announced that it would begin applying the same VAT tax rates to e-books and online newspapers, arguing that they no longer need legal protection given the shift from physical to digital media platforms.

Other countries outside the European Union and the United States are also grappling with the issue of e-commerce taxes. A number of countries have implemented VAT or goods and services (GST) taxes on foreign e-commerce sales, including Russia, Japan, South Korea, New Zealand, and South Africa. In Australia, new rules took effect in 2017 requiring foreign providers to register and collect GST on digital goods and services supplied to Australian consumers. Australia also eliminated the exemption from tax for low-value imports beginning in July 2018. Taiwan has also implemented rules applying to B2C providers of online streaming services, music downloads, and gaming subscriptions. Foreign e-commerce companies with annual sales to the Taiwanese consumer market that exceed TWD 480,000 (about €13,500) are required to register, charge, and collect VAT and file bi-monthly VAT returns. Similar actions in other countries can be expected as governments worldwide seek to maximize tax revenues from e-commerce.

▬ **SOURCES:** "Commission Welcomes Agreement on New Rules Paving the Way for Better VAT Collection on Online Sales," European Commission, March 12, 2019; "Modernising VAT for Cross-border E-commerce," European Commission, accessed January 7, 2019; "VAT: New Details on Rules for E-commerce Presented, Including a New Role for Online Marketplaces in the Fight Against Tax Fraud," European Commission, December 11, 2018; "VAT on Electronic Commerce: New Rules Adopted," Consilium.europa.eu, December 5, 2017; "GST on Low Value Imported Goods," Ato.gov.au, July 19, 2017; "VAT Changes Continue to Hit Global E-commerce," by Nick Hart, Radiusworldwide.com, June 7, 2017; "Commission Proposes New Tax Rules to Support E-commerce and Online Businesses in the EU," Europa.eu, December 1, 2016; "Modernising VAT for E-commerce: Questions and Answers," Europa.eu, December 1, 2016; "EU Proposes Simplifying VAT Rules to Boost Online Trade," by Philip Blenkinsop, Reuters.com, December 1, 2016; "EU Online Sellers Hail VAT Reform as 'Game Changer,'" by Joe Kirwin, Bna.com, December 2, 2016; "Single Vat Return: Is It Back to the Drawing Board?" by Jacek Szufan, Tmf group.com, December 3, 2015; "#VATMESS Is About to Get Much Messier," by Hugo Grimston, Techcrunch.com, October 10, 2015; "EU Targets Single VAT Registration on B2C E-Commerce 2017," Vatlive.com, May 7, 2015; "How the New Value-Added Tax Guidelines for Selling Digital Goods Affect Your Online Store," by Kathy Bricaud, Ecwid.com, January 23, 2015; "How New VAT Regulations Will Affect SMEs—and How to Prepare," by Carol Tricks, *The Guardian*, December 8, 2014; "#VAT-Mess: UK's Army of Start-Up Firms Protest over New European VAT Rules Aimed at Curbing Tax Dodging by Web Giants," by Vicki Owen, Thisismoney.co.uk, November 29, 2014; "New EU VAT Regulations Could Threaten Micro-businesses, by Kitty Dann and Eleanor Ross, *The Guardian*, November 25, 2014; "European VAT: 10 Things Online Sellers Need to Know About Taxes on Digital Goods and Services," by Rick Minor, Forbes.com, May 15, 2014.

protocol were blocked or throttled back (Internet speeds were slowed). Users who watched large volumes of movies on Netflix or other services were occasionally throttled back; wireless cellphone carriers choked off data speeds for heavy users when their networks became clogged; and large Internet services like Netflix and YouTube, which together consume an estimated 50% of the Internet's bandwidth in the United States, were encouraged to strike deals with ISPs and pay a higher fee than ordinary business or home users (Gryta, 2015a).

ISPs had long opposed the idea of net neutrality. ISPs claimed they needed to be able to manage the loads on their networks to ensure stable service, without blackouts or slowdowns. Throttling back heavy users was necessary to manage network load. They also argued that heavy individual or business users should pay more than the average user at home who uses the Web for e-mail, web surfing, and e-commerce, all of which do not require a lot of bandwidth. They also argued that preventing them from charging more for higher speeds would discourage them from investing in additional infrastructure. More to the point, the ISPs claimed the FCC did not have the authority to regulate ISPs because ISPs were not defined by the FCC as common carriers like traditional telephone companies. ISPs instead were classified in FCC regulations of the 1990s as information services in large part because the Internet, at that time, was considered to be a innovative provider of information that should be nurtured and not interfered with or regulated by the FCC. The Internet then was just not that important to the operation of society.

In 2015, the FCC ruled that Internet broadband service providers should be viewed as public utilities similar to telephone companies, and therefore should be regulated by the FCC in order to ensure fair access to all, deployment of acceptable broadband service levels, and competition among providers. This change reflected the fact that the Internet had evolved by 2015 into one of the primary telecommunications services in the country, and world, necessary to the everyday life of millions of people, businesses, and governments, and therefore a common carrier vital to the operation of society (just like a telephone or railroad service). The FCC was created by the Communications Act of 1934 to regulate telegraph and radio, and then later added regulation of television, satellite, and cable in all states. The FCC also overruled state laws that made it difficult for cities to operate their own broadband networks. In this way, a decades-long debate over net neutrality moved a step towards resolution. The ruling did not provide for regulation of ISP pricing, which remained in the hands of the ISPs (Gryta, 2015b). In 2016, a federal appeals court upheld the FCC view that ISPs were utilities that act as neutral platforms for transmission of speech.

However, the debate over net neutrality is not yet over. In 2017 the Trump administration reversed the FCC's 2015 net neutrality ruling, and in 2018, returned to the previous regulatory framework, in which ISPs would be regarded as information services, and not regulated utilities subject to FCC regulations (FCC, 2017). In October 2019, a federal appeals court upheld the repeal of the FCC's net neutrality regulations, but also ruled that the FCC did not have the power to prohibit states from enacting their own regulations. California had previously adopted such regulations in 2018, but had frozen them pending the outcome of the lawsuit. The new ruling leaves the door open for California, as well as other states (Hussain, 2019).

ANTITRUST, MONOPOLY, AND MARKET COMPETITION IN THE INTERNET ERA

For the first time in the history of the Internet and e-commerce, a broad swath of opinion makers, including economists, politicians, regulators, civic groups, and journalists, are saying that some e-commerce firms have become powerful monopolies that are restricting competition by snuffing out or buying smaller innovative firms, and engaging in restraint of trade. Alphabet (Google), Amazon, and Facebook, in particular, are in the cross-hairs of critics because they not only dominate their markets, but also dominate our daily lives. These firms have grown rapidly, in part by scooping up smaller innovative firms, adding to their already large market share in their respective industries. The tech giants have not helped themselves in this debate by invading privacy on an unprecedented level, failing to secure their users' personal information, allowing their platforms to be used by foreign powers, enabling the dissemination of fake and misleading stories, and driving small retailers out of business. These firms also use their financial resources to prevent legislation that might constrain them: big tech firms are now spending more money on lobbying in Washington D.C. than all other industries with the exception of the financial services and pharmaceutical industries. Critics are proposing that these firms be broken up or regulated. The cultural and regulatory honeymoon for big tech firms is coming to an end. Are these firms too big, too powerful, and too injurious to the public good?

These questions are not new in the United States or elsewhere in free market economies. They have to do with defining what constitutes unfair "monopolistic" competition, restraint of trade, and monopolistic behavior of firms, as well as assessing the consequences of monopoly for consumer prices, quality, variety, and innovation. Additional political and social issues include the interests of small businesses being able to compete with very large businesses and how to ensure concentrations of economic power lead to socially desirable outcomes rather than a concentration of political power that might overwhelm the voices of small business and individuals in the political process. See the end of chapter case *Are Big Tech Firms Getting "Too Big"?* for a more detailed examination of these issues.

8.5 PUBLIC SAFETY AND WELFARE

Governments everywhere claim to pursue public safety, health, and welfare. This effort produces laws governing everything from weights and measures to national highways, to the content of radio and television programs. Electronic media of all kinds (telegraph, telephone, radio, and television) have historically been regulated by governments seeking to develop a rational commercial telecommunications environment and to control the content of the media—which may be critical of government or offensive to powerful groups in a society. Historically, in the United States, newspapers and print media have been beyond government controls because of constitutional guarantees of freedom of speech. Electronic media such as radio and television, on the other hand, have always been subject to content regulation because they use the publicly owned frequency spectrum and hence come under a variety of federal laws and regulatory agencies, primarily the FCC. Telephones have also been regulated as public utilities and "common carriers," with special social burdens to provide service and access, but with no limitations on content.

In the United States, critical issues in e-commerce center around the protection of children, strong sentiments against pornography in any public media, efforts to control gambling, and the protection of public health through restricting sales of drugs and cigarettes.

PROTECTING CHILDREN

Pornography is an immensely successful Internet business. Statistics with respect to revenues generated by online pornography range widely. A sample of the million most-visited sites in the world found that 4% of the websites contained pornographic material, and 14% of web searches involved sexual content. Others have estimated that 20% of online searches involve pornography (Webroot, 2017; Ward, 2013). Online pornography is estimated to generate $10 to $12 billion annually in the United States, and the global revenue is estimated to be $97 billion. Traditional DVD porn revenues have fallen off by 80% as so-called tube sites (YouTube for porn) have rapidly expanded with free and freemium content online. Piracy is rampant as with traditional video content. Revenues are now primarily derived from premium subscriptions and advertising.

To control the Web as a distribution medium for pornography, in 1996, the U.S. Congress passed the Communications Decency Act (CDA). This act made it a felony criminal offense to use any telecommunications device to transmit "any comment, request, suggestion, proposal, image, or other communications which is obscene, lewd, lascivious, filthy, or indecent" to anyone, and in particular, to persons under 18 years of age (Section 502, Communications Decency Act of 1996). In 1997, the the U.S. Supreme Court struck down most of the CDA as an unconstitutional abridgement of freedom of speech protected by the First Amendment. While the government argued the CDA was like a zoning ordinance designed to allow "adult" websites for people 18 years of age or over, the Court found the CDA was a blanket proscription on content and rejected the "cyberzoning" argument as impossible to administer. One section of the CDA that did survive scrutiny, Section 230, provides immunity for providers and users of interactive computer services (such as ISPs and websites) from being considered a publisher that might be liable for harmful content posted by others. This is the law that allows social networks, blogs, and online bulletin boards to operate without fear of being held liable for online defamation or libel. In 2002, the Supreme Court struck down another law, the Child Pornography Prevention Act of 1996, which made it a crime to create, distribute, or possess "virtual" child pornography that uses computer-generated images or young adults rather than real children, as overly broad (*Ashcroft v. Free Speech Coalition*). The Children's Online Protection Act (COPA) of 1998 met with a similar fate.

In 2001, Congress passed the Children's Internet Protection Act (CIPA), which requires schools and libraries in the United States to install "technology protection measures" (filtering software) in an effort to shield children from pornography. In 2003, the Supreme Court upheld CIPA, overturning a federal district court that found the law interfered with the First Amendment guarantee of freedom of expression. The Supreme Court, in a 6–3 opinion, held that the law's limitations on access to the Internet posed no more a threat to freedom of expression than limitations on access to books that librarians choose for whatever reason not to acquire. The dissenting justices found this analogy inappropriate and instead argued the proper analogy was if librarians were to purchase encyclopedias and then rip out pages they thought were or might be offensive to patrons. All the justices agreed that existing blocking software was overly blunt, unable to distinguish child pornography from sexually explicit material (which is protected by the First Amendment), and generally unreliable (Greenhouse, 2003b). The difficulty of identifying and removing pornography from the Internet is exemplified by Facebook's experience. Posting pornography is a violation of Facebook's Terms of Service, and it has removed thousands of pornographic postings and deleted the accounts of posters. Nudity is prohibited as well as suggestive images (which are undefined). But even with its advanced algorithms, assisted by human editors, Facebook routinely has eliminated museum-quality legitimate works of art. For instance, in 2016 it eliminated an iconic Pulitzer Prize-winning photo of a nude 9-year old girl fleeing napalm bombs during the Vietnam War, and pictures of women who were breast feeding. Both works were restored after a public outcry (Scott and Isaac, 2016). Critics pointed out that Facebook is surely a tech company as its CEO often argues, but it surely is also a global media company that controls what articles, videos, and photos that people will be allowed to see.

Other legislation such as the 2002 Domain Names Act seeks to prevent unscrupulous website operators from luring children to pornography using misleading domain names or characters known to children. A plan to create an .xxx domain for adult website content was approved by ICANN in 2010, and in 2011, limited registration for .xxx domains began. Trademark holders who do not wish their brand to be associated with an .xxx domain can block requests by other companies for domain names that include their brand name. The 2003 Protect Act is an omnibus law intended to prevent child abuse that includes prohibitions against computer-generated child pornography. Part of that statute was previously held to be unconstitutional by the Eleventh Circuit Court of Appeals, but in 2008, the Supreme Court reversed the circuit court and upheld the provision (Greenhouse, 2008).

The Children's Online Privacy Protection Act (COPPA) (1998) prohibits websites from collecting information on children under the age of 13. It does permit such data collection if parental consent is obtained. Because COPPA does not interfere with speech or expression, it has not been challenged in the courts. However, since 1998, entirely new technologies like social networks, online tracking, advertising networks, online gaming, and mobile apps have appeared that are now being used to gather data on children and which were not specifically addressed in COPPA or FTC regulations. Responding to these changes in technology and public pressure, the FTC announced a new set of rules that are now in effect. The new rules prohibit online tracking of children across the Web with cookies or any other technology such as persistent identifiers; prohibit ad networks from following children across the Web and advertising to them without parental consent; make clear that mobile devices are subject to COPPA, including games and software apps; and make clear that third-party data collection firms that collect data on websites are responsible for any unlawful data collection.

Search engines and ISPs also have a role to play in eliminating child pornography from the Web. The Internet Watch Foundation is a private non-profit organization based in the United Kingdom whose mission is to eliminate child pornography from the Web, and has over 200 corporate members from the Internet technology community (Internet Watch Foundation, 2020). In 2015, Google, Facebook, Microsoft, and Twitter joined together and are using the Internet Watch Foundation's hash list to remove abusive child images from their services. Other companies working with the Internet Watch Foundation include Cisco, Blackberry, Dropbox, and PayPal (Lien, 2015).

CIGARETTES, GAMBLING, AND DRUGS: IS THE WEB REALLY BORDERLESS?

In the United States, both the states and the federal government have adopted legislation to control certain activities and products in order to protect public health and welfare. Cigarettes, gambling, medical drugs, and of course addictive recreational drugs are either banned or tightly regulated by federal and state laws (see *Insight on Society: The Internet Drug Bazaar*). Yet these products and services are ideal for distribution over the Internet through e-commerce sites. Because the sites can be located offshore, they can operate beyond the jurisdiction of state and federal prosecutors. Or so it seemed until recently. In the case of cigarettes, state and federal authorities have been quite successful in shutting down tax-free cigarette websites within the United States by pressuring PayPal and credit card firms to drop cigarette merchants from their systems. The major shipping companies—UPS, FedEx, and DHL—have been pressured into refusing shipment of untaxed cigarettes. Philip Morris has also agreed not to ship cigarettes to any resellers that have been found to be engaging in illegal Internet and mail order sales. However, a few offshore websites continue to operate using checks and money orders as payments and the postal system as a logistics partner, but their level of business has plummeted as consumers fear state tax authorities will present them with huge tax bills if they are discovered using these sites. The Prevent All Cigarette Trafficking Act, passed in 2010, restricts the sale of untaxed cigarettes and other tobacco products over the Internet and bans the delivery of tobacco products through the U.S. mail.

Gambling also provides an interesting example of the clash between traditional jurisdictional boundaries and claims to a borderless, uncontrollable Web. In the United States, gambling of all kinds is largely a matter of state and local laws, but in 2006 Congress passed the Unlawful Internet Gambling Enforcement Act of 2006 (UIGEA), which prohibited financial institutions from transferring funds to or from Internet gambling sites, but did not remove from the states the ability to regulate gambling of all kinds. While online gambling per se is not prohibited by this act, and no person has ever been arrested for online gambling, this legislation initially crippled the online gambling industry within the United States. The U.S. Department of Justice enforced the law vigorously, denying offshore operators access to American payment systems, seizing assets, crippling their U.S. business, and arresting several executives. However, the mood has changed in the last five years. online gambling sites moved to alternative currencies, such as cryptocurrencies, which are not regulated by the UIGEA, enabling them sidestep the law (Legalsportsbetting.com, 2019). State revenue needs have grown, and many in the casino gambling industry have switched sides and now support online

INSIGHT ON SOCIETY

THE INTERNET DRUG BAZAAR OPERATES AROUND THE GLOBE

Every year since 2008, Interpol has conducted Operation Pangea, an international effort involving over 150 countries to combat the sales of illegal drugs online. Between 2008 and 2019, Operation Pangea has resulted in the shutting down of 82,000 websites, more than 3,000 arrests, and the removal of more than 105 million doses of illegal drugs from circulation.

A Google search for drugs "no prescription" in 2020 returns more than 5.5 million results. In many countries, trafficking in illegal prescription drugs now equals or exceeds the sale of heroin, cocaine, and amphetamines. While properly regulated Internet pharmacies offer a valuable service by increasing competition and access to treatments in underserved regions, industry researchers have found that 98% of online pharmacies don't require a prescription, and 40% of online pharmacies were selling dangerous synthetic opioids such as fentanyl.

The sale of drugs without a prescription is not the only danger posed by the Internet drug bazaar. Rogue online pharmacy sites may be selling counterfeit drugs or unapproved drugs. For instance, Interpol found that over 10% of all medical products sold online are counterfeit, affecting all regions of the world. The U.S. Food and Drug Administration (FDA) has issued past warnings that consumers who had purchased Ambien, Xanax, and Lexapro online had instead received a product containing haloperial, a powerful antipsychotic drug. In recent years, synthetic opioids, most of which originate in China and India, have grown in popularity. According to the European Monitoring Centre for Drugs and Drug Addiction (EMCDDA), drug overdose deaths in Europe have continued to rise, driven by the increasing use of synthetic opioids such as fentanyl.

Despite these dangers, online pharmacies remain alluring and are one of the fastest growing business models, with, oddly, senior citizens—usually some of the most law-abiding citizens—leading the charge for cheaper drugs. Typically, online pharmacies are located in countries where prescription drugs are price-controlled, or where the price structure is much lower, such as Canada, the United Kingdom, and European countries, as well as India and Mexico. U.S. citizens can often save 50%–75% by purchasing from online pharmacies located in other countries.

Another haven for online purveyors of illegal drugs is the "darknet," which consists of sites that are not accessible by search engines and often feature security measures designed to promote anonymity or to mask illegal activity. Known as darknet marketplaces, these sites require users to run special software to mask users' IP addresses and only accept cryptocurrencies like Bitcoin to further protect user privacy. Fentanyl is particularly popular among darknet buyers, even though some marketplaces have banned its sale because even small doses can be fatal. According to the EMCDDA, most sales on darknets are related to drugs, and such sales are responsible for more than 90% of the total economic revenue of darknets worldwide. In addition, almost half of all darknet drug sales originate from vendors based in Europe.

Several years ago, the most prominent darknet marketplace was the Silk Road, which, in its heydey, was estimated to attract as much as $45 million a year in illegal drug purchases and $1.2 billion worth of total transactions.

(continued)

But in 2013, the Silk Road's founder and chief operator, Ross Ulbricht, was arrested, charged with drug trafficking and money laundering, and eventually sentenced to life in prison in 2015.

Although the arrest was seen as a major blow to illegal drug trafficking at the time, as one market closes, others pop up to take its place. There are fewer risks to personal safety and violence when buying drugs online compared to in-person from drug dealers, and as governments attempt to crack down on popular opioids, many users have flocked to darknet marketplaces to compensate. In 2017, multiple law enforcement agencies working together took major steps to break this cycle when they shut down the two most prominent darknet marketplaces, AlphaBay and Hansa. First, the FBI took over AlphaBay, a two-year-old marketplace that had 200,000 users and 40,000 vendors combining to produce over ten times the volume of the Silk Road. They also oversaw the detention of the marketplace's founder, Alexandre Cazes, and seized $18 million in assets from him. Cazes took his own life in a jail cell in Thailand shortly thereafter. At approximately the same time, Dutch law enforcement arrested the website administrators for the second largest darknet marketplace, Hansa, confiscating $2.6 million worth of cryptocurrency. However, Dutch police had coordinated with the FBI and other organizations to keep this secret for a full month, collecting thousands of addresses for buyers, many of whom had just signed up after the closure of AlphaBay, and more information on over 50,000 transactions. They eventually shared that information with Europol and other law enforcement organizations. The combined takedowns of these two marketplaces initially curtailed activity on other darknet sites, as users feared that law enforcement might be lurking there as well, but the downtick in illegal activity was only temporary and revenues and trade volume associated with drug sales on the darknet returned to its previous levels within a year.

The EMCDDA issues an annual in-depth analysis of the illegal drug market within the European Union. The 2019 report found that EU citizens spend around €30 billion on illegal drugs. Citing globalization, technology advances, and the Internet as primary causes, the reports note that the illicit drug market has become increasingly dynamic and innovative, and that Europe has become a major drug production hub. The reports further note that the Internet has expanded the possibilities for drug supply and trafficking, allowing drug markets to become hybrid markets that combine traditional social and economic opportunity structures with new opportunities provided by the Internet. In addition, the Internet has not only opened the way for new criminal actors, but has also reconfigured relations among suppliers, intermediaries, and buyers. These reports suggest that drug regulation enforcement needs to adapt with the times. As e-commerce brings down global borders, the need for a global strategy, as opposed to individual countries and a patchwork of enforcement strategies, has grown.

SOURCES: "EU Drug Markets Report 2019," EMCDDA and Europol, November 26, 2019; "Operation Pangea—Shining a Light on Pharmaceutical Crime," by Interpol, Interpol.int, November 21, 2019; "Europe Drug Report: Trends and Developments 2019," EMCDDA, June 2019; "A New Map of the 'Darknet' Suggests Your Local Drug Pusher Now Works Online," Technologyreview.com, January 12, 2018; "On the Darknet, Drug Buyers Aren't Looking for Bargains," Phys.org, August 12, 2017; "What China's Growing Role in Illegal Drug Production Tells Us About the Future of the Drug War," by Mike Riggs, Newsweek.com, August 10, 2017; "2 Leading Online Black Markets Are Shut Down by Authorities," by Nathaniel Popper and Rebecca R. Ruiz, *New York Times*, July 20, 2017; "Opioid Dealers Embrace the Dark Web to Send Deadly Drugs by Mail," by Nathaniel Popper, *New York Times*, June 10, 2017; "Online Sales of Illicit Drugs Triple Since Silk Road Closure," by Steven Musil, Cnet.com, August 10, 2016; "Shedding Light on the Dark Web," *The Economist*, July 16, 2016; "Seniors Most Vulnerable to Illegal Online Drug Sales, Says ASOP," by Loren Bonner, Pharmacist.com, June 24, 2016; "The Internet and Drug Markets," EMCDDA, February 2016; "Ross Ulbricht, Creator of Silk Road Website, Is Sentenced to Life in Prison," by Benjamin Weiser, *New York Times*, May 29, 2015.

gambling, seeing it as a revenue growth opportunity. The ethical issues surrounding online gambling may have less influence on the public debate than the need for new tax revenues, and for firms, the hope for additional revenues.

In 2012, Delaware became the first U.S. state to legalize online gambling, and three others have followed: Nevada (online poker only), New Jersey, and Pennsylvania. Online gambling is also legal in the U.S. Virgin Islands. A number of states including Michigan, Colorado, and Montana are considering bills that would legalize online gambling in 2020 (PlayUSA.com, 2020).

Until 2018, real-world sports betting outside of authorized venues such as horse race tracks, was illegal in the United States. States were specifically prohibited from authorizing sports betting by the Professional and Amateur Sports Protection Act (PASPA), and therefore could not garner tax revenues from what became a $150 billion illegal industry, an estimated 66% of which was taking place online in 2017. In 2018 the Supreme Court found that the PASPA was unconstitutional and for the first time allowed states to authorize and tax sports betting, including online sports betting. New Jersey was the first state to legalize online sports betting and has since been joined by eight other states (Nevada, West Virginia, Indiana, Pennsylvania, Iowa, New Hamphire, Oregon, and Rhode Island (PlayUSA.com, 2020; Liptak and Draper, 2018; D'Andrea, 2018). Fantasy sports and betting is also exploding. Two firms dominate the online fantasy sports market: DraftKings and FanDuel. Both firms advertise heavily during college and professional sports games. In fantasy sports, players assemble their ideal fantasy teams, drafting real-life athletes to their team, and then, based on the performance of those players in real games, they can win significant prizes. The most popular sports are college football and basketball, and professional football and baseball. Players are given a budget that they can use to draft players, and some of the combined fees for each game make up the pool for which players compete. Entry fees range widely from less than a dollar, to over $1,000 (Belson, 2015). DraftKings claims that several winner prizes have exceeded $1 million although none of the sites publish a list of winners.

Fantasy sports were exempted from the Unlawful Internet Gambling Enforcement Act of 2006 (UIGEA) under industry pressure from the then much smaller fantasy sports business. The industry argued that fantasy sports are not gambling, but instead games of skill like chess or Scrabble. As the industry has grown to billion-dollar venture capital valuations, however, and with allegations of cheating customers, deceptive practices, lack of transparency, and insider irregularities, state and federal legislators are holding hearings and considering regulations (Russo, 2015; Drape and Williams, 2015). In 2015, the New York State attorney general told both DraftKings and FanDuel to stop taking entries from New York State residents because, in the state's opinion, their operations constituted illegal gambling and the sites engaged in false and misleading advertising. Citibank cut off credit card processing for both sites (Bogdanish and Glanz, 2016). After lengthy legislative hearings and strong support from sports fans, New York reversed its position, agreeing that when played fairly, fantasy sports was a game of skill, not gambling. The governor signed legislation legalizing fantasy sports as a state-regulated industry, claiming it would add $4 billion to the state's education fund (Gouker, 2016). The sites also agreed to pay $12 million in fines (Drape, 2016). In February 2020, however, a New York State appeals court ruled that the law legalizing fantasy sports violated the

New York State Constitution's ban on gambling, throwing its future in New York into doubt (Campbell, 2020).

In November 2016, DraftKings and FanDuel proposed to merge. Together the two companies control more than 90% of the U.S. market. In June 2017, the FTC, along with the attorneys general of California and the District of Columbia, sued to block the merger and in July 2017 the companies decided to abandon the plan.

8.6 CAREERS IN E-COMMERCE

This chapter provides you with an overview of the major ethical, social, and political issues involving the Internet and e-commerce. Companies are becoming increasingly aware that such issues can have a significant impact on their bottom line. Jobs that specifically deal with these issues can typically be found in a company's compliance department, but awareness of these issues is also necessary for all employees of a company.

THE COMPANY

The company operates a global online advertising exchange platform that connects online sites that have inventory (web publishers who have space on their websites where ads can be displayed, also called "ad opportunities") with buyers—firms that want to advertise. Consumer behavior data is collected by the online sites, and made available to buyers, who may add their own consumer information into the mix. The platform allows buyers to choose specific market segments (e.g., Millennial parents interested in purchasing a house). The platform's analytics helps buyers decide how much to pay for the inventory, make bids for the inventory, and tracks the performance of the resulting online ads. The company has 20 offices in the United States and in four other countries. The firm has 700 employees, serves 4,000 advertisers, analyzes 500 billion online ad opportunities daily, and serves over 150 million ads for its marketing customers each day. The company manages this complex process of finding and selling ad opportunities using machine learning that looks for patterns in the data and tries to identify the most likely consumers who will click on a specific ad. All of this takes place in milliseconds.

Advertising exchanges or platforms are the basis for programmatic advertising where marketing firms sell or match ad opportunities on publisher websites or social networks to firms seeking to display ads targeted to very specific segments. Programmatic advertising is now the most widely used method of buying and selling digital display ads on both desktop and mobile devices, accounting for $38 billion in revenue, over 70% of all online ad display dollars. The growth in this market is a product of convenience, speed, and precision in finding the best opportunities for firms.

POSITION: E-COMMERCE PRIVACY RESEARCH ASSOCIATE

You will be working in the Compliance department to ensure privacy and data protection compliance while enabling business innovation. The position involves research on privacy, domestic, and international regulations and policies, and industry best practices. Your responsibilities include:

- Monitoring, digesting, and developing written summaries of proposed and enacted legislation, regulations, court decisions, industry guidelines, trade journals, and other relevant publications in privacy, cybersecurity, information security, and technology.
- Researching federal, state, and international laws and regulations related to data security, information security, and privacy, including laws related to compromised data and security breach incidents. Additional areas may include laws and regulations related to online marketing, social media, e-commerce, and technology.
- Researching global data protection and privacy compliance in the online advertising market, drawing on knowledge and experience of specific government/industry requirements and best practices.
- Analyzing existing and developing products and solutions to ensure they comply with applicable privacy and data protection laws and industry best practices.
- Guiding and supporting lines of business on legal and regulatory requirements related to compromised data incidents, privacy, and cybersecurity.
- Reviewing contracts with vendor and customer firms to ensure compliance with privacy regulations and industry best practices.
- Developing educational and training materials for business client groups and other divisions of the firm.

QUALIFICATIONS/SKILLS

- B.A. in the humanities, business, information systems, business, marketing, or political science, with course work in e-commerce, statistics, business strategy, and digital marketing
- Basic understanding of privacy and privacy law in the United States, and how it relates to online digital advertising
- Interest in international business and data protection laws in the E.U., Latin America, and Asia/Pacific
- Knowledge of the digital marketing industry, software service platforms, and programmatic advertising platforms
- Excellent written and oral communication skills, including a clear and concise drafting style
- Strong research skills
- Excellent customer service and interpersonal skills
- Exceptional analytical and problem solving skills with the ability to think strategically and provide business advice
- Advanced Microsoft Office (Word, Excel, Outlook, and PowerPoint) skills
- Strong organizational skills, including ability to manage timelines and balance multiple deadlines
- Comfortable with desktop and mobile technology and an active user of online or mobile applications and social networks

PREPARING FOR THE INTERVIEW

To prepare for this interview, re-read the sections of this chapter that address the responsibilities listed by the employer. In this case, the position requires familiarity with privacy legislation and regulation in both the United States and the European Union, which is covered in Section 8.2. Also review the opening case and the Insight on Technology case. It will also be worthwhile to do some background research on the firm and the industry where it operates (see the closing case study in Chapter 6, which discusses the programmatic advertising industry).

POSSIBLE FIRST INTERVIEW QUESTIONS

1. We're looking at candidates who have an interest in the protection of consumer privacy, but who also understand the need for our clients to communicate with online consumers. What's your experience with your own sense of your privacy when online, and why do you think consumers are concerned about their online privacy?

You can start with the last question: consumers are concerned about their privacy because they are concerned they do not know or understand what happens to their personal information online, and they feel they have no control over how it is used. Second, you could discuss how you feel about protecting your privacy on sites like Facebook. Facebook does provide a number of tools for limiting the personal information that other users can see, and it is really up to individuals to use those tools. On the other hand, Facebook's tools can be confusing to understand, and many users still feel they do not really control who sees their postings, or how the information is being used by Facebook or advertisers.

2. Aside from social network tools provided by various sites, what are some of the software and tools that consumers are using to protect their privacy online? Do you think any of these tools interfere with our programmatic marketing business?

You could describe some of the tools you or your friends may have used, or considered, to protect your privacy while browsing or messaging. You could discuss tools such as anonymous browsing software, Do Not Track options in web browsers, password managers, encrypted email, digital file shredders, anti-tracking tools, and ad-blockers. Anonymous browsing software, anti-tracking tools, and ad-blocker tools are becoming more popular among sophisticated users, and, yes, these tools probably do interfere somewhat with online marketing campaigns.

3. How do you think our industry and firm should respond to the growing use of these tools, and the public's concerns about online privacy?

You could answer this by programs developed by the online advertising industry, such as Network Advertising Initiative (NAI), which certify that firms have adopted industry privacy standards and best practices. Two practices stand out: the NAI's global opt-out website that allows consumers to avoid tracking and cookies from specific sites, and the AdChoice program that gives users a better sense of how their information is being used, and the ability to turn off certain ads that are inappropriate. These efforts give users some degree of control over what is collected, and how it is used. In addition, there are several new startups that offer privacy management software that helps firms understand how they are meeting industry best practices, such as the OneTrust Privacy Management Platform.

4. Our firm receives large quantities of consumer online behavioral data that we use to display ads for our clients. We do not know the personal names of these consumers, or their specific addresses, and they are identified only by an assigned number, and of course their online behavior and basic demographic information. Is this an invasion of their privacy?

You could suggest that many online consumers do believe they are personally identifiable online by name, address, and geo-location, even if this is not always true. For instance, online tracking of consumers from one web site to another gives many the impression they are personally being watched as they browse. They do not understand they are known only as a cookie number, or customer number. Facial recognition technology, however, is very personal, and raises new concerns.

5. We have many clients that operate in the European Union, which has very different privacy laws and data protection regulations from those in the United States. What do you think are some of the key differences between European and American privacy regulations and laws?

You can suggest that one major difference is that the European Union has privacy laws that require a default opt-out option from tracking or placing cookies, and requires users to explicitly agree to opt-in to tracking, cookies, and other ways of following people online. European countries have data protection agencies that enforce privacy laws, but the United States does not. EU countries have also adopted right to be forgotten regulations that give users the ability to have certain information removed from search engines.

8.7 CASE STUDY

Are Big Tech Firms Getting "Too Big"?

Want to connect with friends? It's Facebook (or its subsidiary Instagram). Search for something online? Google, what else. Shop online? It's Amazon. Critics argue that Amazon, Google, and Facebook have built impregnable digital platforms that restrict entrance to competitors, reduce competition, and provide extraordinary pricing power, enough to crush competitors. Critics claim that Big Tech will do anything, including paying absurd acquisition prices, to stifle competition and to preserve their monopoly positions. In the United States, critics say antitrust regulators and politicians don't get it: it's not about consumer welfare or prices. The strategy of Big Tech firms is to aggregate huge user numbers by eliminating competitors, especially smaller startups.

In order to understand the current situation, first you must understand a little bit about the history of antitrust regulation in the United States. Beginning with the Sherman

Antitrust Act of 1890 through the 1950s, Congress passed multiple pieces of legislation to restrain, and if necessary, break up the industrial giants of the 19th and 20th centuries. The purpose of this legislation was to ensure that small firms and entrepreneurs could enter markets; to define and prevent anti-competitive practices; to protect consumers and other firms from exorbitant prices, in short, any behavior that resulted in *a restraint of free trade*. Legislators believed that restraint of trade would ultimately lead to lower product quality, reduced or restricted production and supply, and less innovation. While this legislation did not precisely define "monopoly," it referred to a situation where a single firm, or group of firms, dominated an entire industry, and, importantly, engaged in behaviors intended to restrict competition and free trade and to maintain their dominance. Dispersion of both economic and political power was a central aim of early antitrust legislation.

Sheer size and market power (market share) were considerations in determining what exactly a monopoly was. "Bigness" was in general suspicious, although "bigness" per se was not by itself a criterion for monopoly. More important were concrete actions taken by powerful companies to harm the market environment for competitors, as well as the structure of the industry, in particular the vertical integration of the supply chain that prevents competitors from even starting a new business in the industry.

The classic antitrust case is *Standard Oil Co. of New Jersey v. United States* (1911). John D. Rockefeller was a co-founder of the Standard Oil Trust. Over a period of 30 years, the Trust grew to control oil exploration, transportation (pipelines and railroads), refining, and distribution down to the retail level, dominating the marketing of oil products. This is called *vertical integration* or taking control of the supply chain for an entire industry. One result of Standard Oil's behavior was complete control of pricing oil products, enabling it to charge below cost prices in some markets to bankrupt their competitors, and simultaneously charging monopoly high prices in markets where it faced no competition (called *predatory* or *discriminatory pricing*).

In 1911, the Supreme Court ruled that Standard Oil was in violation of the Sherman Antitrust Act, and chose to change the structure of Standard Oil by breaking it up into 34 separate firms that hopefully would compete with one another and remain independent, as well as proscribing the firm from other practices with the intent of establishing new monopolies. Several of these firms have recombined with one another over the last hundred years and today form a large part of the ExxonMobil Corporation, the largest oil company in the United States.

Antitrust laws and court decisions recognized that some monopolies, when they resulted from simply being the most efficient producer of high-quality products sold at competitive prices, were "innocent" and legal. In other cases, where the very nature of the product and market required very large initial capital investments with few rewards in the short term until a large scale was attained, dominant firms were considered *natural monopolies*. Electrical and gas utilities, telephone and cable systems, and railroads have very high initial investments that can only be justified by capturing a large share of a market. Often these firms are the first to develop a technology and achieve a *first-mover advantage*. Natural monopolies create barriers to entry into a market simply by virtue of the investment size required for new entrants, as well as other nearly insurmountable advantages in efficiency, brand, and patents.

Both innocent and natural monopolies may engage in anti-competitive behaviors that are not in the public interest because they control, as do all monopolies, the market, including pricing, quality, supply of product or service, and reduced innovation. In these cases, legislatures have turned to regulation to control pricing and service levels in the public interest, in addition to structural changes. For instance, in the early 20th century, the federal government nationalized the entire telephone and telecommunications industry, with the intent of creating a single national system operated by a single firm, AT&T. The following year, states took over regulation of the industry, including prohibiting new companies from competing and introducing new standards and competing telephone lines to avoid duplication, and higher prices. Even telephone handsets had to be produced solely by AT&T's equipment firm, Western Electric. The theory was that national telephone service required a single provider that could provide efficient service to the entire country. Later in 1980s, with the evolution of new devices and new technology such as microwave communications, which did not require huge capital investments, courts broke up AT&T into seven regional Bell operating companies, allowing competitors to provide telephone service and equipment to the market.

Antitrust thinking changed markedly during the 1960s due to changes in economic thinking, and interpretation by courts, as well as changes in the economy and politics. In this period, concentration of economic power was not seen as anti-competitive, but instead was believed to lead to greater efficiency and lower prices for consumers. During this time period, courts viewed the practice of dropping prices as an example of "price competition," not "predation," and therefore not an illegal restraint of trade. In this view, the only criterion that should be used when assessing the behavior of large firms, or considering mergers of large firms into truly giant firms, was economic efficiency and consumer prices.

Similarly, buying up key firms in the supply chain was re-thought as leading to greater efficiency for firms, not evidence of restraint of trade or preventing new players from entering a market. Firms that "integrated" their production through vertical integration were more efficient than firms that did not integrate. Moreover, as firms gained efficiency it was believed that they would pass these benefits onto consumers in the form of lower prices. After the 1960s, the major constructs of classical antitrust thinking and legislation—predatory pricing, discriminatory pricing, and vertical integration—were no longer viewed as problematic, but rather seen as advancing consumer interests by lowering prices. This new thinking was directly opposite of earlier antitrust thinking and laws.

Fast forward to the 21st century. Amazon is an example of a firm that does not fit the rational model of 1960s antitrust thinking. Amazon's strategy has been to focus on maximizing market share, not profits, and therefore it is willing to price retail products at or below cost for long periods of time, not just holiday sales. It is able to do this in part because private capital and public markets have been willing to provide low-cost financing in the form of extraordinarily high stock prices despite Amazon's failure for many years to show a profit. Amazon operates the largest online retail platform, with over 500,000 different products, from shoes, dresses, batteries, books, to computers and wrenches. It is the largest third-party online market platform in the United States, with almost 3 million third-party merchants, including over 1 million in Europe. As a result, it has an unprecedented trove of information on consumer behavior and the pricing of goods sold by merchants on the platform. Amazon has at least ten lines of business aside from retailing, including web services (Amazon Web Services (AWS)), movie and TV production, fashion design, book publishing, and hardware manufacturing. With multiple lines of business, Amazon is able to drop prices below cost in one line of business, such as books, in order to support another line of business, like its sales of Kindle readers and tablet computers. It is willing to run its retail operation at a loss, or break-even, as other lines such as AWS make the lion's share of its profits. Amazon uses its pricing algorithms to change prices on thousands of goods several times a day. For the most part, neither the public nor government regulators can track these price changes, or their impact on competitors and merchants.

For instance, in 2007, Amazon began selling e-books at $9.99, below their cost to Amazon, rather than at the traditional publisher price of $14.99, in part to subsidize its Kindle readers. Amazon used its platform power to delist books from the publisher Hachette in 2014 after Hachette objected to Amazon selling its e-books for less than the publisher wanted, and below its cost. In other product lines, such as batteries, cables, and hundreds of other products, Amazon has developed its own house brand called Amazon Basics, based on its platform knowledge of sales volumes, revenue, and estimated profitability. In 2019, Amazon was forced to admit during testimony before the U.S. Congress that it uses aggregated data drawn from third-party sellers to develop and promote its own branded products. In Europe, the European Commission announced a similar investigation into whether Amazon is abusing its role as a seller of its own products while at the same time operating a third-party marketplace. Amazon's familiar recommender system ("people who bought this also bought this") highlights Amazon's private-label brands when available. One of the worst fears of Amazon's merchants is that Amazon may decide to develop its own competing products. For instance, in Amazon created a new meal delivery kit to compete against a tiny, but fast growing rival, Blue Apron. As of 2019, Amazon offered almost 160,000 different private brand products.

Facebook faces similar criticism of using its platform to destroy or buy its competitors. In 2012, Facebook saw two companies growing faster than it was: Instagram and WhatsApp. After failing in its efforts to build effective competing services, it bought Instagram for $1 billion, and in 2014 bought WhatsApp for an astounding $21.8 billion. When HouseParty, a private hangout app for friends, refused a Facebook purchase offer in 2015, Facebook built its own competing app called Bonfire.

In 2016, Facebook developed a live video app and put popular Meerkat, the market leader startup, out of business. The rise of Snapchat provides another example. Snapchat's key feature is that it allows users to easily send photos and videos, with a focus on the camera instead of a keyboard. In 2013 Facebook's offer to buy the firm was rejected. Shortly thereafter Facebook created a copycat service called Instagram Stories that mimicked Snapchat's features. Since that time, the use of Instagram Stories has been growing at a significantly higher rate than that of Snapchat's. Over time, Facebook has developed copies of Snapchat features in its other related services, Messenger and WhatsApp. The share price of Snap, Snapchat's parent company, has sunk to less than half at which the company went public in 2017. Investors fear Facebook will overwhelm the firm. In February 2020, the European Commission announced an investigation into Facebook's alleged attempts to identify and eliminate potential rivals.

Critics identify Google as a monopoly not simply based on its market size, but because of its horizontal integration behavior, and its search engine's favoritism to its own services, which results in competitors' organic search results being placed lower on the first page, or buried on back pages, or delisted. Critics consider both of these behaviors to be a restraint of trade by eliminating Google's competitors with the intent to preserve its search and advertising dominance. Google's horizontal strategy follows the Big Tech play book: buy up competitors or degrade their access to the Google search platform. Google purchased YouTube in 2006 for $1.6 billion after its own effort to create an online video hub called Google Videos failed to gain an audience. In 2008, Google bought DoubleClick, one of the online advertising network pioneers, for $3.1 billion. Google bought Waze in 2013 for $1 billion because it was a popular rival to Google Maps due to its graphical mapping interface. Apple is the only remaining competitor in online mapping, a distant second, but still a threat.

When vertical search engines directing users to lowest-price websites grew in popularity, and competed with Google's plans for a shopping service, it reduced their availability on the Google search engine. This happened with Foundem, a UK-based vertical search engine that steered users to the lowest prices on the Web; Foundem.com competed well with Google's Froogle (now called Google Shopping). When Foundem started catching on in 2012, Google changed its search algorithm so Foundem did not show up on the first page, but was buried in later pages, or disappeared altogether. A similar fate happened to TradeComet, KinderStart NexTag, and other vertical search engines, all of whom have complained to the European Commission and the FTC. In 2017, after a seven-year investigation, the European Union fined Google $2.7 billion for abusing its market dominant search engine by demoting competing vertical shopping services to, on average, the fourth page, while showing its own Google Shopping images at the top of the first page.

Google defended its actions by arguing these sites are link farms, aggregators of other content on the Web, and therefore a violation of its recently changed search algorithm rules, which punish sites without original content that just link to other sites. But the court responded that Google Shopping's results also are mostly content provided by other sites, usually advertisers who paid for the top listing. The European Commission was aware of this similarity and considered Google to be operating its own vertical search engine.

Similarly, in the United States, the review site Yelp, with a following in the millions, suddenly found its local reviews were no longer listed as first or second on Google, but down the page, while Google's paid ads came up first even when they did not contain any reviews or original content other than ads for restaurants. If users enter "Italian restaurants nearby", the first listings are for advertisers. In 2009, Google tried to buy Yelp but was rejected. Later it started pulling Yelp content into its own results so users did not have to visit Yelp at all. Getty Images had a similar experience: in 2013 Getty Images lost 85% of its traffic when Google started directing searches for images directly to its own search engine, rather than to Getty Images. When Getty complained, it was told it could always not list anything on Google. Both firms experienced reduced revenues from Google's actions.

Amazon, Facebook, and Google are among the most popular Web and mobile services. People love them and use them daily. Because Google and Facebook do not charge users for their services, they cannot be accused of reducing consumer welfare by increasing prices. Therefore they cannot be accused of predatory pricing or discriminatory pricing. If anything, for the same zero cost to consumers, these firms have increased their usefulness to consumers, and substantially increased consumer welfare. Amazon is often a price-leader in both online and offline retail, is extraordinarily easy to use, provides unprecedented variety and choice, and has attracted 50% of the Internet audience to its loyalty program, Amazon Prime. As long as consumer welfare (price) is the single criterion of regulating monopolies, then these firms are acceptable on antitrust grounds.

However, if the core principle behind antitrust legislation is to protect and encourage competition by limiting the ability of dominant corporations to damage their smaller competitors, and to reduce consumer choice, then Big Tech firms may be liable on grounds of limiting competition, denying opportunities for new entrants, discouraging new innovative companies from even trying to enter markets, and, as a result, creating an anti-competitive market environment, and restraining trade. However, new concepts and new laws and regulations would be needed to make these behaviors of Big Tech explicitly illegal.

One conceptual change would be to view these firms as platforms providing access to audiences and capturing consumer time on site, rather than traditional businesses selling products and services. These are not traditional businesses of the 19th and 20th centuries. These firms are fine examples of network effects: the larger the number of users, the greater the value. The market value of Facebook, Google, and Amazon lies in their online audience size and dominance of user online time. This leaves open the question of what is "too much" mindshare. Is it 30%, 50%, or 90%? Congress, federal regulators, and jurists will have to decide this.

In this line of reasoning, one possible solution to Big Tech dominance is to increase the review of proposed mergers with a view to protecting innovative small firms from purchase if they result simply in the dominant firm gaining larger audiences, and capturing more of the consumers' time, denying this mindshare to competitors. Mergers that are not truly horizontal mergers, such as Facebook buying WhatsApp, which was not in the social network market per se, could be prevented on grounds the merger would simply increase market mindshare for Facebook and hinder the ability of innovative startups to enter.

A second solution regarding existing monopolies would be to split them up into stand-alone independent companies. Amazon could be split into ten stand-alone companies such as a retail company, a web services company, a media company, a logistics firm, and others. Facebook could be split into social network, messaging, and photo-sharing companies. Google could be split into a search advertising network, a computer hardware company, and a video-sharing company. Instead of three oligopolies, numerous independent companies would be created. The merger policy described above would be used to prevent these firms from combining again into monopolies or oligopolies.

A third solution follows the European example of dealing with Big Tech mega-firms. The European Union is pursuing a regulatory model for Big Tech firms in a number of

SOURCES: "EU Deepens Antitrust Inquiry Into Facebook's Data Practices," by Sam Schechner, Emily Glazer, and Valentina Pop, *Wall Street Journal*, February 6, 2020; "Amazon Has 1.1 Million Active Sellers in Europe," Ecommercenews.eu, November 26, 2019; "Amazon Admits to Congress that It Uses 'Aggregated' Data from Third-Party Sellers to Come Up with Its Own Products," by Lauren Feiner, Cnbc.com, November 19, 2019; "Amazon Faces Probe in Europe Over Use of Merchant Data," by Sam Schechner, *Wall Street Journal*, July 17, 2019; "Google Fined $1.7 Billion in EU for Restricting Rivals' Ads," by Sam Schechner and Valentina Pop, *Wall Street Journal*, March 20, 2019; "Why Do the Biggest Companies Keep Getting Bigger?", by Christopher Mims, *Wall Street Journal*, July 26, 2018; "Google Fined $5.1 Billion by E.U. in Android Antitrust Ruling," by Adam Satariano, July 18, 2018; "The Case Against Google," by Charles Duhigg, *New York Times*, February 25, 2018; "How to Curb Silicon Valley Power Even with Weak Antitrust Laws," by Nitasha Tiku, Wired.com, January 5, 2018; "The Antitrust Case Against Facebook, Google and Amazon," by Greg Ip, *Wall Street Journal*, January 16, 2018; "Herfindahl-Hirshman Index of Market Market Concentration," United States Department of Justice, 2018; "Horizontal Merger Guidelines," United States Department of Justice, 2018; "The New Copycats: How Facebook Squashes Competition from Startups," by Betsy Morris and Deepa Seetharaman, *Wall Street Journal*, August 9, 2017; *The Four: The Hidden DNA of Amazon, Apple, Facebook, and Google*, by Scott Galloway, Random Books, 2017; "Antitrust in a Time of Populism," by Carl Shapiro, Haas School of Business at the University

areas such as antitrust, privacy, and taxation. In antitrust the focus is on the anti-competitive behavior of big firms, and the use of meaningful fines for violations of competitive laws and regulations. For instance, the European Union fined Google a record $5.1 billion in 2018 for forcing Samsung, Huawei, and other smartphone makers to prioritize Google search, its Chrome browser, and other apps in return for allowing them to use the Android operating system. The regulators believe Google did this in order to retain the dominance of its search engine advertising business, denying rivals the chance to compete and consumers the benefits of a competitive market. In addition to the fine, the largest in history against Big Tech, Google was required to separate its Android system from its other apps, including Google Docs, the search engine bar, browser, and potentially Google Store, Google Play, and Google Shopping. The penalty for violating this order can reach as high as 5% of Google's average daily global income, which could amount to billions of dollars. This decision followed the same playbook as the 2017 decision to fine Google $2.7 billion for pushing its own products and services to the top of search engine results. In 2019, the European Commission fined Google yet again, this time for $1.7 billion, for abusing its dominance in search to limit competition with respect to a service called AdSense for Search, which involves the sale of text ads on search results that appear on third party websites.

It is unclear which of these three kinds of remedies might succeed in the U.S. context. For the last 30 years, the federal government has taken a hands-off attitude towards regulating the Internet and the growing concentration of Internet markets, in the name of innovation and economic growth of a nascent industry. The Internet industry is no longer nascent, but ascendant, and increasingly accused of abusing its economic and political power. Conservative and liberal populist groups, some calling for the break-up of Big Tech firms, are forcing the debate on Big Tech abuse of power in the areas of privacy and antitrust. The European model rejects the contemporary U.S. notion that price and efficiency are the only criteria to judge monopolistic behavior, and instead focuses on the impacts on market entry by new innovative firms, and whether or not there is true competition in a market as indicated by many competitors. The European model is a much broader view of antitrust, similar to that of the earlier period of American antitrust legislation, which looked at the structure of markets and competition, not just consumer prices.

Case Study Questions

1. How does the first era of antitrust thinking (1890–1950s) differ from the second era?

2. What is a "natural monopoly" and how has the United States dealt with natural monopolies?

3. What are three possible solutions to the market dominance and anti-competitive behavior of Facebook, Google, and Amazon?

4. How does the European model of antitrust differ from the American model?

8.8 REVIEW

KEY CONCEPTS

- **Understand why e-commerce raises ethical, social, and political issues.**
  - Internet technology and its use in e-commerce disrupts existing social and business relationships and understandings. Suddenly, individuals, business firms, and political institutions are confronted by new possibilities of behavior for which understandings, laws, and rules of acceptable behavior have not yet been developed. Many business firms and individuals are benefiting from the commercial development of the Internet, but this development also has costs for individuals, organizations, and societies. These costs and benefits must be carefully considered by those seeking to make ethical and socially responsible decisions in this new environment, particularly where there are as yet no clear-cut legal or cultural guidelines.
  - The major issues raised by e-commerce can be loosely categorized into four major dimensions:
    - *Information rights*—What rights do individuals have to control their own personal information when Internet technologies make information collection so pervasive and efficient?
    - *Property rights*—How can traditional intellectual property rights be enforced when perfect copies of protected works can be made and easily distributed worldwide via the Internet?
    - *Governance*—Should the Internet and e-commerce be subject to public laws? If so, what law-making bodies have jurisdiction—state, federal, and/or international?
    - *Public safety and welfare*—What efforts should be undertaken to ensure equitable access to the Internet and e-commerce channels? Do certain online content and activities pose a threat to public safety and welfare?
  - Ethical, social, and political controversies usually present themselves as dilemmas. Ethical dilemmas can be analyzed via the following process:
    - Identify and clearly describe the facts.
    - Define the conflict or dilemma and identify the higher-order values involved.
    - Identify the stakeholders.
    - Identify the options that you can reasonably take.
    - Identify the potential consequences of your options.
    - Refer to well-established ethical principles, such as the Golden Rule, Universalism, the Slippery Slope, the Collective Utilitarian Principle, Risk Aversion, the No Free Lunch Rule, the *New York Times* Test, and the Social Contract Rule, to help you decide the matter.

- **Understand basic concepts related to privacy and information rights, the practices of e-commerce companies that threaten privacy, and the different methods that can be used to protect online privacy.**
  - To understand the issues concerning online privacy, you must first understand some basic concepts:
    - *Privacy* is the moral right of individuals to be left alone, free from surveillance or interference from others.
    - *Information privacy* includes the right to control personal information, to know what is being collected, the right to due process, and the right to have personal information stored securely.
    - *Due process* as embodied by the Fair Information Practices doctrine, informed consent, and opt-in/opt-out policies also plays an important role in privacy.
  - Concepts of privacy are different in the public versus the private sector. In the public sector, privacy is protected by founding documents. In the private sector, privacy is less well defined, and only emerging.
  - Almost all e-commerce companies collect some personally identifiable information in addition to anonymous information and use cookies to track clickstream behavior of visitors. Advertising networks and search

engines also track the behavior of consumers across thousands of popular sites, not just at one site, via cookies, spyware, search engine behavioral targeting, and other techniques.
- There are a number of different methods used to protect online privacy. They include:
  - Legal protections deriving from constitutions, common law, federal law, state laws, and government regulations. In the United States, rights to online privacy may be derived from the U.S. Constitution, tort law, federal laws such as the Children's Online Privacy Protection Act (COPPA), the FTC's Fair Information Practice principles, and a variety of state laws. In Europe, the European Commission's General Data Protection Regulation (GDPR) has standardized and broadened privacy protection in the European Union nations.
  - Industry self-regulation via industry alliances, which seek to gain voluntary adherence to industry privacy guidelines and safe harbors. Some firms also hire chief privacy officers.
  - Privacy-enhancing technological solutions include spyware and pop-up blockers, secure e-mail, anonymous remailers, anonymous surfing, cookie managers, disk file-erasing programs, policy generators, and public key encryption programs.

■ **Understand the various forms of intellectual property and the challenges involved in protecting it.**

- *Copyright law* protects original forms of expression such as writings, drawings, and computer programs from being copied by others for a minimum of 70 years. It does not protect ideas—just their expression in a tangible medium. Copyrights, like all rights, are not absolute. The doctrine of fair use permits certain parties under certain circumstances to use copyrighted material without permission. The Digital Millennium Copyright Act (DMCA) was the first major effort to adjust copyright law to the Internet age. The DMCA implements a World Intellectual Property Organization treaty, which declares it illegal to make, distribute, or use devices that circumvent technology-based protections of copyrighted materials, and attaches stiff fines and prison sentences for violations.
- *Patent law* grants the owner of a patent an exclusive monopoly to the ideas behind an invention for 20 years. Patents are very different from copyrights in that they protect the ideas themselves and not merely the expression of ideas. There are four types of inventions for which patents are granted under patent law: machines, man-made products, compositions of matter, and processing methods. In order to be granted a patent, the applicant must show that the invention is new, original, novel, nonobvious, and not evident in prior arts and practice. Most of the inventions that make the Internet and e-commerce possible were not patented by their inventors. This changed in the mid-1990s with the commercial development of the Web. Business firms began applying for "business methods" and software patents.
- *Trademark protections* exist at both the federal and state levels in the United States. Trademark law protects the public in the marketplace by ensuring that it gets what it pays for and wants to receive and also protects the owner who has spent time, money, and energy bringing the product to market against piracy and misappropriation. Federal trademarks are obtained, first, by use in interstate commerce, and second, by registration with the U.S. Patent and Trademark Office (USPTO). Trademarks are granted for a period of 10 years and can be renewed indefinitely. Use of a trademark that creates confusion with existing trademarks, causes consumers to make market mistakes, or misrepresents the origins of goods is an infringement. In addition, the intentional misuse of words and symbols in the marketplace to extort revenue from legitimate trademark owners ("bad faith") is proscribed. The Anticybersquatting Consumer Protection Act (ACPA) creates civil liabilities for anyone who attempts in bad faith to profit from an existing famous or distinctive trademark by registering an Internet domain name that is identical or confusingly similar to, or "dilutive" of, that trademark. The major behaviors on the Internet that have run afoul of trademark law include cybersquatting, cyberpiracy, metatagging, keywording, linking, and framing.
- *Trade secret laws* protect intellectual property having to do with business procedures, processes, formulas, and methods of manufacture.

- **Understand how the Internet is governed and why taxation of e-commerce raises governance and jurisdiction issues.**
  - Governance has to do with social control: who will control e-commerce, what elements will be controlled, and how will those controls be implemented. We are currently in a mixed-mode policy environment where self-regulation, through a variety of Internet policy and technical bodies, co-exists with limited government regulation.
  - E-commerce raises the issue of how—and if—to tax remote sales. In 1998, Congress passed the Internet Tax Freedom Act, which placed a moratorium on multiple or discriminatory taxes on electronic commerce, and any taxation of Internet access, and in 2016 made it permanent. In 2018, the Supreme Court ruled that states could tax e-commerce sales even if the company making the sale did not have a physical connection to the state. Net neutrality refers to the idea that Internet service providers (ISPs), including cable Internet and wireless carriers, should treat all data on the Internet in the same manner, and not discriminate or price differentially by content, protocol, platform, hardware, or application. Net neutrality remains an area of controversy in 2018.

- **Identify major public safety and welfare issues raised by e-commerce.**
  - Critical public safety and welfare issues in e-commerce include:
    - The protection of children and strong sentiments against pornography. Several attempts by the U.S. Congress to legislate in this area have been struck down as unconstitutional. The Children's Internet Protection Act (CIPA), which requires schools and libraries in the United States to install "technology protection measures" (filtering software) in an effort to shield children from pornography, has, however, been upheld by the U.S. Supreme Court.
    - Efforts to control gambling and restrict sales of cigarettes and drugs. In the United States, cigarettes, gambling, medical drugs, and addictive recreational drugs are either banned or tightly regulated by federal and state laws. Many offshore sites for these products and services have been shut down following government pressure. Online gambling is growing, but slower than anticipated. Online fantasy sports betting is growing rapidly, and the U.S. Supreme Court has ruled that states can authorize and regulate online sports betting.

QUESTIONS

1. Identify the four main dimensions that e-commerce ethical, political, and social issues fall into and provide an example of how each dimension might apply to an individual.
2. Define the ethical principle of accountability and describe two ways in which Internet technologies have raised accountability issues.
3. What concerns does the use of mobile devices bring to the issue of information privacy?
4. What is an ethical dilemma? Describe the two tactics you can use to resolve or reach a greater understanding of the dilemma.
5. How can the effectiveness of privacy policies be measured?
6. Why has the development of the Internet brought about so many ethical, political, and social issues?
7. Why does a mobile app such as Periscope raise copyright concerns?
8. What are some of the ethical, social, or political issues raised by the information density created by e-commerce technology?
9. Define information privacy. What are its central premises?
10. What are the three main objectives of the GDPR?
11. Why do social networks pose a unique problem to the issue of information privacy, and how might sharing personal information on a social site adversely affect a user?

12. Why is the European Directive on Copyright supported by news organizations, music companies, and artists?
13. What is the current legal status of net neutrality regulation in the United States?
14. Identify the five steps outlined in the text you can use to analyze ethical conflicts.
15. What are some of the potential ethical, social, or political implications raised by the global reach of e-commerce technologies?
16. How do privacy default browsers work?
17. Why are the Defend Trade Secrets Act and its European equivalent, the Trade Secrets Directive, necessary?
18. Define cybersquatting. How is it different from cyberpiracy? What type of intellectual property violation does cybersquatting entail?
19. What is the "right to be forgotten"? What are some of the risks and benefits of establishing this right?
20. How does the U.S. Digital Millennium Copyright Act implement the WIPO Copyright Treaty of 1996?

PROJECTS

1. Go to Google and find the Advanced Search link. Examine its SafeSearch filtering options. Surf the Web in search of content that could be considered objectionable for children using each of the options. What are the pros and cons of such restrictions? Are there terms that could be considered inappropriate to the filtering software but be approved by parents? Name five questionable terms. Prepare a brief presentation to report on your experiences and to explain the positive and negative aspects of such filtering software.

2. Develop a list of privacy protection features that should be present if a website is serious about protecting privacy. Then, visit at least four well-known websites and examine their privacy policies. Write a report that rates each of the websites on the criteria you have developed.

3. Review the provisions of the Digital Millennium Copyright Act of 1998. Examine each of the major sections of the legislation and make a list of the protections afforded property owners and users of copyrighted materials. Do you believe this legislation balances the interests of owners and users appropriately? Do you have suggestions for strengthening "fair use" provisions in this legislation?

4. Review the section on net neutrality and search for two articles that take a position on the topic. Summarize each article and then write an essay describing your own position on net neutrality.

REFERENCES

Academy of Motion Picture Arts and Sciences v. GoDaddy.com Inc et al. U.S. District Court, Central District of California, No. 10-03738 (2015).

Acquisti, Alessandro, Leslie K. John, & George Loewenstein. "What Is Privacy Worth?" *Journal of Legal Studies* (2013).

Adroit Market Research. "Facial Recognition Market to Hit $12 Billion by 2020." Globenewswire.com (January 27, 2020).

Alice Corporation Pty. Ltd. v. CLS Bank International, et al., Supreme Court of the United States, No. 13-298. June 19, 2014.

Allemann, Andrew. ".Sucks Domain to Drop Its Price 99% in January." (December 12, 2016).

Andriotis, Anna, and Ezequiel Minaya. "Equifax Reports Data Breach Possibly Affecting 143 Million U.S. Consumers." *Wall Street Journal* (September 8, 2017).

Apuzzo, Matt, David Sanger, and Michael Schmidt. "Apple and Other Tech Companies Tangle with U.S. Over Data Access." *New York Times* (September 7, 2015).

Ashcroft v. Free Speech Coalition, 535 U.S. 234 (2002).

Associated Press. "Google Settles Final Piece of Geico Case." BizReport.com (September 8, 2005).

Awal. "Decoding Content ID: How Artists Make Money on YouTube." Awal.com (August 7, 2018).

Baird, Nikki. "If Consumer Privacy Isn't Already Dead, IoT Could Kill It." Forbes.com (August 31, 2017).

Belson, Ken. "A Primer on Daily Fantasy Football Sites." *New York Times* (October 6, 2015).

Bennett, Jared. "Facebook: Your Face Belongs to Us." Thedailybeast.com (July 31, 2017).

Bergen, Mark. "'Dancing Baby' Copyright Ruling Hands Temporary Win to YouTube, Facebook." Recode.net (September 14, 2015).

Bernina of America, Inc. v. Fashion Fabrics Int'l., Inc. 2001 U. S. Dist. LEXIS 1211 (N. D. Ill., Feb. 8, 2001).

Bilski et al. v. Kappos, 177 L. Ed. 2d 792, 130 S. Ct. 3218, 561 U.S. 593 (2010).

Bloomberg News. "Master of Your Domain? Maybe in .Com But Not in .Sucks." (May 13, 2015).

Bogdanish, Walt, and James Glanz. "Fantasy Sites Are Dealt New Rebuff by Citigroup." *New York Times* (February 5, 2016).

Bonnington, Christina. "Your Phone Is Always Tracking Your Location." Slate.com (November 25, 2017).

Boutin, Paul. "The Secretive World of Selling Data About You." *Newsweek* (May 30, 2016).

Brown, Ryan. "'Catastrophic': EU Passes Controversial Copyright Law That Could Hit the Likes of Google and Facebook." Cnbc.com (September 18, 2018).

Campbell, Jon. "Q & A: Can I Still Play DraftKings, FanDuel in New York?," Democrateandchronicle.com (February 7, 2020).

Capitol Records LLC et al. v. Vimeo LLC et al. 2nd U.S. Circuit Court of Appeals, No. 14-1048 (2016).

Carpenter v. United States. No. 16-402, 585 U.S. ____ (2018).

Chaikivsky, Andrew. "Want to Protect Against Websites That Spy on You? Get an Ad Blocker." *Consumer Reports* (February 2018).

Chen, Caleb. "AT&T GigaPower Plans to Charge Extra Per Month Again If You Want Privacy, No Ads." Privateinternetaccess.com (June 27, 2017).

Chiappetta, Vincent. "Defining the Proper Scope of Internet Patents: If We Don't Know Where We Want to Go, We're Unlikely to Get There." *Michigan Telecommunications Technology Law Review* (May 2001).

D'Andrea, Christian. "Supreme Court Ruling Allows States to Legalize and Regulate Sports Betting." SBnation.com (May 14, 2018).

Datacoup. "How It Works." Datacoup.com (accessed February 19, 2020).

Deloitte, "Are You Ready for GDPR?" *Wall Street Journal* (May 25, 2018).

Diamond v. Chakrabarty, 447 US 303 (1980).

Drape, Joe. "DraftKings and FanDuel to Pay $6 Million Each to Settle New York Claims." *New York Times* (October 25, 2016).

Drape, Joe, and Jacqueline Williams. "FanDuel Makes Changes." *New York Times* (October 8, 2015).

Drozdiak, Natalia, and Jack Nicas. "Google Privacy-Policy Change Faces New Scrutiny in EU." *Wall Street Journal* (January 24, 2017).

E. & J. Gallo Winery v. Spider Webs Ltd. 129 F. Supp. 2d 1033 (S.D. Tex., 2001) aff'd 286 F. 3d 270 (5th Cir., 2002).

Eldred v. Ashcroft, 537 U.S. 186 (2003).

Elvy, Stacy-Ann. "Paying for Privacy and the Personal Data Economy." *Columbia Law Review* Vol. 117, No. 6 (October 2017).

eMarketer, Inc. (Ross Benes). "US Ad Blocking Users and Penetration." (July 2019).

eMarketer, Inc. (Monica Melton). "Some Technology Creeps Consumers Out. Facial Recognition, AI Are the Creepiest." (July 5, 2017).

European Commission. "Modernisation of the EU Copyright Rules." Ec.europa.eu (July 8, 2019).

European Commission. "2018 Reform of EU Data Protection Rules." Europa.eu (2018).

European Commission. "Commission Proposes New Tax Rules to Support E-commerce and Online Businesses in the EU." Europa.eu (December 1, 2016).

European Commission. "A Digital Single Market Strategy for Europe." Europa.eu (June 5, 2015).

European Parliament. "Amendments Adopted by the European Parliament on 12 September 2018 on the Proposal for a Directive of the European Parliament and of the Council on Copyright in the Digital Single Market." Europa.eu (September 12, 2018).

Federal Communications Commission. "Restoring Internet Freedom Notice of Proposed Rulemaking." (May 23, 2017).

Federal Communications Commission. "Protecting the Privacy of Customers of Broadband and Other Telecommunications Services." (October 27, 2016).

Federal Trade Commission. "FTC Releases Annual Privacy and Data Security Update 2018." (January 18, 2018a).

Federal Trade Commission. "Cross Device Tracking." (August 15, 2017).

Federal Trade Commission. "Data Brokers: A Call for Transparency and Accountability." (May 27, 2014).

Federal Trade Commission. "Protecting Consumer Privacy in an Era of Rapid Change." (March 26, 2012).

Federal Trade Commission. "Protecting Consumer Privacy in an Era of Rapid Change." (December 2010).

Federal Trade Commission. "Privacy Online: Fair Information Practices in the Electronic Marketplace." (May 2000).

Federal Trade Commission. "Privacy Online: A Report to Congress." (June 1998).

Field v. Google, Inc. 412 F.Supp. 2nd 1106 (D. Nev., 2006).

Fiesler, Casey, Jessica L. Feuston, and Amy Bruckman. "Copyright Terms in Online Creative Communities." Georgia Institute of Technology, Working Paper (April 26, 2014).

Fingas, Jon. "Facebook Is Testing a Face Detection Tool to Verify Your Identity (Updated)." Engadget.com (November 5, 2019).

Fisher, William W. III. "The Growth of Intellectual Property: A History of the Ownership of Ideas in the United States." Law.harvard.edu/Academic_Affairs/coursepages/tfisher/iphistory.html (1999).

Foley & Lardner LLP. "Supreme Court Will Not Look at Spokeo Again, Leaving Lower Courts to Grapple with Article III Uncertainties." Foley.com (February 8, 2018).

Ford, Paul. "Balancing Security and Liberty in the Age of Big Data." Businessweek.com (June 13, 2013).

Ford Motor Co. v. Lapertosa. 2001 U.S. Dist. LEXIS 253 (E. D. Mich. Jan. 3, 2001).

Fowler, Geoffrey. "Hands Off My Data! 15 Default Privacy Settings You Should Change Right Now." *Washington Post* (June 1, 2018).

Fung, Brian. "The Group That Created '.sucks' Now Wants Government to Keep It from Spinning Out of Control." *Washington Post* (April 9, 2015).

Gardner, Eriq. "Judge Upholds $25 Million Judgment Against ISP Over User Piracy." *Hollywood Reporter* (August 9, 2016).

Gershman, Jacob. "Congress May Be About to Shake Up Trade Secret Law: Is That a Good Thing?" *Wall Street Journal* (April 27, 2016).

Gibbs, Samuel. "Google's New Nest Cam Is Always Watching, If You Let It into Your Home." *The Guardian* (June 18, 2015).

Goldman, Eric. "Facebook Persistent Tracking Lawsuit Crashes Again." Ericgoldman.org (July 13, 2017).

Gouker, Dustin. "Daily Fantasy Sports Is Back In Business In New York: Gov. Cuomo Signs Bill." Legalsportsreport.com (August 3, 2016).

Government Employees Insurance Company v. Google, Inc. Civ. Action No. 1:04cv507 (E.D. VA, December 15, 2004).

Greenhouse, Linda. "Supreme Court Upholds Child Pornography Law." *New York Times* (May 20, 2008).

Greenhouse, Linda. "20 Year Extension of Existing Copyrights Is Upheld." *New York Times* (January 16, 2003a).

Greenhouse, Linda. "Justices Back Law to Make Libraries Use Internet Filters." *New York Times* (June 24, 2003b).

Greif, Bjorn. "Cookies, Fingerprinting, and Co. Tracking Methods Clearly Explained." Cliqz.com (January 3, 2018).

Gryta, Thomas. "An Early Net-Neutrality Win: Rules Prompt Sprint to Stop Throttling." *Wall Street Journal* (June 17, 2015a).

Gryta, Thomas. "FCC Approves Net Neutrality Rules, Setting Stage for Legal Battle." *Wall Street Journal* (February 26, 2015b).

Harmon, Amy. "Pondering Value of Copyright vs. Innovation." *New York Times* (March 3, 2003).

Hautala, Laura. "Facebook's New Data Policy: Answers to Your Privacy Questions." Cnet.com (April 21, 2018).

Hoofnagle, Chris Jay. "Privacy Self-Regulation: A Decade of Disappointment." Electronic Privacy Information Center (Epic.org) (March 4, 2005).

Hub of All Things. "The Hub of All Things: Own Your Personal Data." Hubofallthings.com (accessed February 19, 2020).

Hurley, Lawrence. "U.S. Top Court Turns Away 'Dancing Baby' Copyright Case." Reuters.com (June 19, 2017).

Hussain, Suhauna. "Upholding FCC's Repeal of Net Neutrality Rules, Court Opens Door for California to Enforce Its Own." Latimes.com (October 3, 2019).

Internet Watch Foundation. "Our Mission." IWF.org (accessed February 20, 2020).

Jin, Ginger Zhe. "Artificial Intelligence and Consumer Privacy." National Bureau of Economic Research (December 18, 2017).

Kakutani, Michiko. "Watched by the Web: Surveillance Is Reborn." *New York Times* (June 10, 2013).

Kang, Cecilia. "California Lawmakers Pass Nation's Toughest Net Neutrality Law." *New York Times* (August 31, 2018a).

Kang, Cecilia. "Justice Department Sues to Stop California Net Neutrality Law." *New York Times* (September 30, 2018b).

Kang, Cecilia. "Broadband Providers Will Need Permission to Collect Private Data." *New York Times*, (October 27, 2016).

Kaufman, Leslie. "Viacom and YouTube Settle Suit Over Copyright Violations." *New York Times* (March 18, 2014).

Keizer, Gregg. "What Is the Epic Browser (and What Makes It Different)?" Computerworld.com (July 3, 2018).

Kelly v. ArribaSoft. 336 F3rd 811 (CA 9th, 2003).

Kendall, Brent. "Supreme Court Hears Apple-Samsung Patent Case." *Wall Street Journal* (October 12, 2016).

Kendall, Brent, and Daisuke Wakabayashi, "Apple Wins Ruling in Patent Case Against Samsung." *Wall Street Journal* (September 17, 2015).

Korte, Amy. "Federal Court in Illinois Rules Biometric Privacy Lawsuit Against Google Can Proceed." Illinoispolicy.org (March 8, 2017).

Kravets, David. "Supreme Court's New Term: Surveillance, Hacking, Sports Betting—and Cake, Too." Arstechnica.com (October 2, 2017).

Laudon, Ken. "Markets and Privacy." *Communications of the Association of Computing Machinery* (September 1996).

Laudon, Kenneth C. Dossier Society. Columbia University Press, 1986.

Lee, Michelle. "Protecting America's Secret Sauce: The Defend Trade Secrets Act Signed Into Law." Huffingtonpost.com (May 11, 2016).

Legalsportsbetting.com "What Is the UIGEA." (October 23, 2019).

Leigh, Liz. "Meeco Is a Life Management Platform that Gives Users Total Control of Their Data." Startupdaily.net (Apr. 13, 2016).

Liao, Shannon. "YouTube Will Now Notify Some Creators When Their Videos Are Stolen." Theverge.com (July 11, 2018).

Lien, Tracy. "Google, Facebook, Twitter Join Crackdown On Child Porn." *Los Angeles Times* (August 10, 2015).

Liptak, Adam. "In Ruling on Cellphone Location Data, Supreme Court Makes Statement on Digital Privacy." *New York Times* (June 22, 2018).

Liptak, Adam. "Supreme Court to Hear Cellphone Tracking Case." *New York Times* (June 5, 2017).

Liptak, Adam. "Supreme Court Returns False-Data Case to Appeals Panel." *New York Times* (May 16, 2016).

Liptak, Adam, and Alexandra Alter. "Challenge to Google Books Is Declined by Supreme Court." *New York Times* (April 18, 2016).

Liptak, Adam, and Kevin Draper. "Supreme Court Ruling Favors Sports Betting." *New York Times* (May 14, 2018).

Lomas, Natasha. "EU Parliament Calls for Privacy Shield to Be Pulled until US Complies." Techcrunch.com (July 5, 2018).

Lomas, Natasha. "iPhone X's Face ID Raises Security and Privacy Questions." Techcrunch.com (September 13, 2017).

Marotti, Ally. "Facebook Could Be Forced to Pay Billions of Dollars Over Alleged Violations of Illinois Biometrics Law." *Chicago Tribune* (April 17, 2018).

Mavrix Photographs, LLC v. LiveJournal, Inc, 873 F.3d 1045 (2017).

Mayer-Schonberger, Viktor, and Kenneth Cukier. *Big Data: A Revolution That Will Transform How We Live, Work, and Think*. Eamon Dolan/Houghton Mifflin Harcourt (2013).

McMillan, Robert. "Porn Typosquatter Fined Again by FTC." *InfoWorld* (October 16, 2007).

Meeco.me. "Zero Knowledge Proofs of the Modern Digital Life for Access, Control, Delegation and Consent of Identity and Personal Data." Technical Whitepaper Version 1.0, Meeco.me, (May 13th, 2018).

Meyer, David. "'Deceived by Design:' Google and Facebook Accused of Manipulating Users Into Giving Up Their Data." *Fortune* (June 27, 2018).

Miagkov, Alexei, et. al. "Giving Privacy Badger a Jump Start." Electronic Frontier Foundation (EFF) (August 22, 2018).

Michaels, Daniel. "Copyright Battle in Europe Pits Media Companies Against Tech Giants." *Wall Street Journal* (September 10, 2018).

Mitchell, Vincent. "What If the Companies That Profit from Your Data Had to Pay You?" Phys.org (July 30, 2018).

Mobile Ecosystem Forum. "Understanding the Personal Data Economy: The Emergence of a New Data Value-Exchange." (July 28, 2017).

Morran, Chris. "'Dancing Baby' YouTube Lawsuit May Go Before Supreme Court." Consumerist.com (August 12, 2016).

Mullin, Joe. "Cox Must Pay $8M in Fees on Top of Jury Verdict for Violating DMCA." Arstechnica.com (February 2, 2017).

Nash, David B. "Orderly Expansion of the International Top-Level Domains: Concurrent Trademark Users Need a Way Out of the Internet Trademark Quagmire." *The John Marshall Journal of Computer and Information Law*, Vol. 15, No. 3 (1997).

Network Advertising Initiative. "NAI Consumer Opt Out." Optout.networkadvertising.org (accessed October 24, 2018).

New, William. "WIPO: Internet Domain Expansion Disruptive to Trademark Strategies." Ip-watch.com (March 17, 2014).

Newman, Jared. "Digi.me Wants to Put You Back in Charge of Your Personal Data." *Fast Company* (August 29, 2018).

Nichols, James. "Is This The Way The Tracking Cookie Crumbles?" *Forbes* (December 22, 2017).

Nield, David. "All the Ways Your Smartphone and Its Apps Can Track You." Gizmodo.com (January 4, 2018).

Nissan Motor Co., Ltd. v. Nissan Computer Corp. 289 F. Supp. 2d 1154 (C. D. Cal.), aff'd, 2000 U. S. App. LEXIS 33937 (9th Cir. Dec. 26, 2000).

PaineWebber Inc. v. Fortuny, Civ. A. No. 99-0456-A (E. D. Va. Apr. 9, 1999).

Perfect 10, Inc. v. Amazon.com, Inc. 487 F3rd 701 (CA 9th, 2007).

Pew Research Center (Lee Rainie) "Americans' Complicated Feelings About Social Media in an Era of Privacy Concerns." (March 27, 2018a).

Pew Research Center (Abigail Geiger). "How Americans Have Viewed Government Surveillance and Privacy Since Snowden Leaks." (June 4, 2018b).

Pew Research Center. (Lee Rainie). "The State of Privacy in Post-Snowden America." (September 21, 2016a).

Pew Research Center. (Lee Rainie and Maeve Duggan). "The State of Privacy: Privacy and Information Sharing." (January 14, 2016b).

Pew Research Center. (Mary Madden and Lee Rainie). "Americans' Attitudes About Privacy, Security, and Surveillance." (May 20, 2015).

Playboy Enterprises, Inc. v. Global Site Designs, Inc. 1999 WL 311707 (S. D. Fla. May 15, 1999).

Playboy Enterprises, Inc. v. Netscape Communications, Inc. 354 F. 3rd 1020 (9th Cir., 2004).

Pop, Valentina, and Sam Schechner. "EU Demands Facebook Update 'Misleading' Fine Print." *Wall Street Journal* (September 20, 2018).

Povich, Elaine. "How Casinos, States Are Winning Big from Online Gambling." Huffingtonpost.com (June 6, 2017).

Riley v. California, 134 S. Ct. 2473 (2014).

Roberts, Jeff. "Court Ruling on Celebrity Photos Raises New Copyright Risk for Websites." Fortune.com (April 10, 2017).

Robins v. Spokeo, Inc., 867 F.3d 1108 (9th Cir. 2017).

Rose, Frank. "Confronting the End of Privacy." *Wall Street Journal* (February 3, 2017).

Rosen, Jeffrey. "The Right to be Forgotten." *Stanford Law Review*, 64. Stan. L. Rev. Online 88 (February 13, 2012).

Rubin Brown LLP. "Gaming Statistics 2017." (2017).

Russo, Ralph. "Daily Fantasy Football Draws Attention, Ire of NCAA." *Associated Press* (October 8, 2015).

Sadowsky, George. "ICANN: Do Not Allow Closed New gTLDs with Generic Strings." Circleid.com (February 16, 2020).

Sanger, David, and Brian Chen. "Signaling Post-Snowden Era, New iPhone Locks Out N.S.A." *New York Times* (September 26, 2014).

Satariano, Adam. "The European Union on Friday Enacts the World's Toughest Rules to Protect People's Online Data." *New York Times* (May 24, 2018).

Savage, Charlie. "Between the Lines of the Cellphone Privacy Ruling." *New York Times* (June 25, 2014).

Savage, Charlie. "Democratic Senators Issue Strong Warning About Use of the Patriot Act." *New York Times* (March 16, 2012).

Schechner, Sam. "GDPR Takes Effect on Friday—Here's What to Expect." *Wall Street Journal* (May 24, 2018).

Schechner, Sam, and Valentina Pop. "EU Advances on Copyright Bill Opposed by Silicon Valley." *Wall Street Journal* (September 12, 2018).

Schwartz, John. "Justices Take Broad View of Business Methods Patents." *New York Times* (June 28, 2010).

Scott, Mark, and Mike Isaac. "Facebook Restores Iconic Vietnam War Photo It Censored for Nudity." *New York Times* (September 9, 2016).

Seetharaman, Deepa, and Betsy Morris. "Facebook's Onavo Gives Social-Media Firm Inside Peek at Rivals' Users Information." *Wall Street Journal* (August 13, 2017).

Selyukh, Alina. "Internet Companies Plan Online Campaign to Keep Net Neutrality Rules." Npr.org (July 11, 2017).

Sengupta, Somini. "Europe Weighs Tough Law on Online Privacy." *New York Times* (January 23, 2012).

Sherriff, Lucy. "This App Enables You to Make Money Off Your Own Personal Data." Forbes.com (March 29, 2019).

Shore, Jennifer, and Jill Steinman. "Did You Really Agree to That? The Evolution of Facebook's Privacy Policy." Harvard Dataverse. http://dx.doi.org/10.7910/DVN/JROUKG. (August 6, 2011).

Simonite, Tom. "One Startup's Vision to Reinvent the Web for Better Privacy." *MIT Technology Review* (January 13, 2017).

Singer, Natasha. "The Government's Consumer Data Watchdog." *New York Times* (May 23, 2015).

Singer, Natasha. "Didn't Read Those Terms of Service? Here's What You Agreed to Give Up." *New York Times* (April 28, 2014).

Singer, Natasha. "Consumer Data, But Not For Consumers." *New York Times* (July 21, 2012).

Smith, Chris Silver. "Initial Interest Confusion Rears Its Ugly Head Once More in Trademark Infringement." Searchengineland.com (May 26, 2017).

Spokeo, Inc. v. Robins. 136 S.Ct. 1540 (2016).

State Street Bank & Trust Co. v. Signature Financial Group, 149 F. 3d 1368 (1998).

Stempel, Jonathan. "GoDaddy Prevails in Lawsuit over Oscar Trademarks." Reuters, September 11, 2015.

Sterling, Bruce. "It's Tech-Lash Season, Part II." Wired.com (January 30, 2018).

Stern, Joanna. "Stop Ads That Follow You on Facebook, Google, and the Web." *Wall Street Journal* (November 4, 2016).

Stone, Brad. "Scaling the Digital Wall in China." *New York Times* (January 15, 2010).

Stupp, Catherine. "Companies Grapple with Shifting International Data Rules." *Wall Street Journal* (August 3, 2018).

Takenaka, Toshiko. "International and Comparative Law Perspective on Internet Patents." *Michigan Telecommunications Technology Law Review* (May 15, 2001).

Teicher, Jordan. "What Do Facial Recognition Technologies Mean for Our Privacy?" *New York Times* (July 18, 2018).

Thurm, Scott. "The Ultimate Weapon: It's the Patent." *Wall Street Journal* (April 17, 2000).

Ticketmaster v. Tickets.com. 2000 U.S. Dist. Lexis 4553 (C.D. Cal., August 2000).

Toner, Alan. "With New Browser Tech, Apple Preserves Privacy and Google Preserves Trackers." Electronic Frontier Foundation (EFF) (June 7, 2017).

Twitter. "Twitter Transparency Report." (accessed February 20, 2020).

United States v. Jones, 565 U.S. 400 (2012).

United States Copyright Office. "Digital Millennium Copyright Act of 1998: U.S. Copyright Office Summary." (December 1998).

Vincent, James. "The UK Won't Implement EU's Controversial Copyright Directive After Brexit." Theverge.com (January 27, 2020).

Wagenseil, Paul. "Guess What: Ad Blockers Don't Block Ads That Well." Tomsguide.com (August 16, 2018).

Washington Post Co., et al. v. TotalNews, Inc., et al., S.D.N.Y., Civil Action Number 97-1190 (February 1997).

Webroot. "Internet Pornography by the Numbers; A Significant Threat to Society." (September 15, 2017).

Weigend, Andreas. *Data for the People*, Basic Books, 2017.

Werner, Paul, and Davie Poell. "Spokeo-Round 3: The Ninth Circuit Finds Alleged Statutory Violation Sufficiently 'Concrete' to Satisfy Article III Standing." Lexology.com (August 29, 2017).

Winston, Brian. *Media Technology and Society: A History From the Telegraph to the Internet.* Routledge (1998).

Winston & Strawn. "EU Trade Secrets Directive: What Are Reasonable Steps?." Winston.com (February 7, 2019).

Zawadziński, Maciej, and Michal Wlosik. "What Is Device Fingerprinting and How Does It Work?" Clearcode.com (September 22, 2016).

CHAPTER 9

Online Media

LEARNING OBJECTIVES

After reading this chapter, you will be able to:

- Understand the major trends in the consumption of media and online content, the major revenue models for digital content delivery, digital rights management, and the concept of media convergence.
- Understand the key factors affecting the online publishing industry.
- Understand the key factors affecting the online entertainment industry.

Spotify and Deezer:
European Streaming Music Services Spread Around the Globe

Today, streaming music is one of the fastest growing types of online media services. Spotify and Deezer are two prime examples of this type of service.

Spotify, founded in Sweden by Daniel Ek and Martin Lorentzon, allows users to stream the music they want on the platform of their choice. Spotify launched in Europe in 2008 and soon became the leading streaming music service in Europe. Spotify uses a freemium business model: consumers can listen to up to a certain number of hours of advertising-supported free music each month or pay for an ad-free premium subscription. However, Spotify has struggled to show a profit, with a loss of $186 million in 2019. Many analysts are skeptical that Spotify's business model can work over the long term, but Spotify believes that as it grows, its margins will improve. Its 2019 loss represented a significant improvement over the company's financial results in the previous three years, and Spotify continues to grow rapidly while some of its rivals stagnate. To that end, Spotify has continued to slash prices for new users, offering three months of streaming for only $0.99. It now has almost 125 million paid subscribers and over 270 million monthly overall users worldwide. Spotify launched an initial public offering in 2018 that used the rarely-seen technique of a direct listing, as opposed to selling shares to institutional investors first. In early 2020, Spotify's shares were trading in roughly the same price range as its initial public office share price ($147/share) and it was valued at a whopping $27 billion.

Spotify faces strong competition: In addition to long-time competitors such as Deezer (discussed below) and Pandora, Apple, Google, and Amazon all now have streaming music services. Spotify has also had to deal with some prominent artists withholding their music from the service to protest what they believe to be inadequate compensation. Spotify has countered that as its platform continues to grow, payouts to artists will improve. Many record labels report satisfaction with the royalties their artists receive, but some disputes have continued over the percentage of streaming revenues Spotify pays. Spotify was the target of a series of lawsuits alleging that the company unlawfully streamed as many as 21% of its 30 million songs without a license. Spotify settled one such suit from prominent music label Wixen Music in 2018, which followed a similar suit previously settled for $43 million in 2016. Typically, when the rightsholder of a piece of music is unclear, Spotify streamed

© Felix Choo/Alamy Stock Photo

SOURCES: "How Many Users Do Spotify, Apple Music, and Other Big Music Streaming Services Have?," Musically.com, February 19, 2020; "Spotify Technology S.A. Announces Financial Results for Fourth Quarter 2019," Businesswire.com, February 5, 2020; "Spotify Increases Paid User Base to 124M, Reports $7.44B Revenue in 2019," by Marc Schneider, Billboard.com, February 5, 2020; "Spotify in Early Talks to Buy Sports and Pop-Culture Outlet The Ringer," by Anne Steele and Benjamin Mullin, *Wall Street Journal*, January 17, 2020; Tim Ingham, "Spotify Overtakes Deezer's Subscriber Base in France—But, Says Deezer, Spot Can't Match Its Payouts," Music-it anyway while it worked to determine where it should pay royalties. This policy helped it quickly boost its catalog of music and gain market share, but the company has paid a steep price in settlement fees. In the United States, the recently enacted Music Modernization Act (discussed further in the chapter) will provide a process to deal with this issue in the future.

Spotify has also seen one of its key metrics, average revenue per paying user (ARPU), drop for many consecutive years as it seeks to continue its rapid growth in emerging markets. Average Spotify subscribers now pay $20 less per year than they did four years ago. The advent of "family plans" that allow several listeners to share a subscription has also contributed to the drop in ARPU. Record labels have been unhappy about this trend as they patiently wait for Spotify to become profitable. Record labels have also expressed displeasure over Spotify's decision to offer emerging artists licensing deals that bypass the usual channels of signing with a label. Spotify has offered musicians agreements that allow them to keep much higher percentages of streaming revenues on their platform and retain ownership of their music. This type of deal threatens the heart of the big record labels' business model, and the "Big Three" (Universal, Sony, and Warner) responded in kind, threatening to block Spotify's launch in India by withholding licensing to their music catalogs.

In pursuit of the profitability that both record labels and investors demand, Spotify has begun to more aggressively pursue new advertising formats. Subscriptions account for 90% of Spotify's revenue, so there is room for advertising to grow significantly as a share of Spotify's overall business. Spotify began selling brands the ability to sponsor its highly-regarded Discover Weekly custom playlist in 2018, and Spotify also began to sell ad space on its own original podcasts. In 2018, Spotify profited hugely when Chinese-based Tencent Music went public, and Spotify's 9% stake in the company nearly doubled in value, giving Spotify its first ever profitable quarter, but investors know that nothing about Spotify's underlying fundamentals have changed—at least for now.

Deezer is a French-based firm grappling with many of the same challenges as Spotify. Deezer is the second-largest streaming music service in Europe behind Spotify, also offering unlimited access to a catalog of 44 million songs, an advanced recommendation engine, and a lively social community. Deezer was founded by Jonathan Benassaya and Daniel Marhely in 2007. In 2008, it received an $8.5 million angel investment and rapidly expanded to dominate the French streaming music market, where it maintained an edge over Spotify until 2019, when Spotify finally surpassed Deezer in French subscribers. However, Deezer still accounts for the most streaming revenues in France, with a 37.5% market share to Spotify's 25.3%. Deezer has 7 million paying subscribers and 14 million monthly active users. Using a freemium business model similar to other streaming services, Deezer offers free unlimited access for a limited time for registered users, who thereafter can continue to listen for free for 10 hours a month.

Deezer stands out in a crowded music streaming marketplace in several ways. In 2019, Deezer operated in 185 countries, more than any of its competitors. Deezer has targeted markets such as Paraguay, Bolivia, Nigeria, South Africa, Japan, Israel, and other non-English speaking markets that lack a strong alternative to the established giants, and the company announced its expansion into India in 2019. Deezer has shown strong growth in the Middle East/North Africa (MENA) region in particular, where only 2% of the public regularly streams music, compared to figures as high as 40% in Scandinavia. Deezer's success in areas with the potential for rapid growth has caused the company to revisit its previously-stalled plans to launch an IPO, with the company now saying that it is weighing its options to go public in 2020 or 2021.

Both Deezer and Spotify have seen very strong growth in podcast usage, with Deezer showing 250% increases in podcast usage on its platform from 2018 to 2020 and Spotify logging 200% growth over that same span. Deezer purchased the Stitcher podcast network in 2014 and has continued to add podcast publishers via acquisition, with its latest round of 5 prominent podcast publishers acquired in 2019; Spotify is devoting even more resources to podcasts, completing a deal to buy The Ringer and its stable of 30 sports and pop-culture themed podcasts in 2020 and spending a total of $400 million on podcasts in 2019, spanning more than two dozen deals for original and exclusive podcast content.

Google and Amazon have not stood by idly, using their deep pockets to try to capture more market share. Google offers Google Play Music as well as its YouTube Music Premium subscription service. Some analysts speculate that one of these companies will eventually acquire Spotify, and that music streaming works better as a smaller, less profitable component of a very large company. Spotify and Deezer still have faith in their long-term prospects, and with the music streaming market expected to grow to $28 billion in annual revenue by 2030, there's ample room for many winners in the near future.

Deezer Puts the Focus on Difference," by Trevor Clawson, Forbes.com, November 30, 2017; "Deezer: The French Music Streaming Service Taking on Spotify, Apple and Amazon," by Sophie Sassard, September 20, 2017; "Will Spotify Kill the Music Download?," by Charles Arthur, *The Guardian*, December 26, 2016; "Here's Deezer's Grand Plan to Take Over the Music-Streaming World," by Nick Pino, Techradar.com, December 21, 2016; "Race to the Bottom? Spotify Launches a 99-cent Premium Subscription Trial," by Charlotte Hassan, Digitalmusicnews.com, November 30, 2015; "Music Streaming Service Deezer Abandons IPO Plans," by Stuart Dredge, *The Guardian*, October 28, 2015; "Deezer Buys Stitcher, Adds 35K Talk Radio Shows and Podcasts to Its Music Platform," by Ingrid Lunden, Techcrunch.com, October 24, 2014.

The opening case illustrates how online content distributors like Spotify and Deezer are challenging both traditional and newer digital music distribution channels. If consumers can stream any song whenever they want to on whatever device they want, the demand for physical CDs as well as iTunes downloads is reduced. On the other hand, it is not clear that Spotify or Deezer have viable business models. The case also illustrates how a traditional content business like recorded music has survived the initial digital disruption of its business and begun to develop new innovative digital distribution channels that replace revenues from earlier products like CDs. As Internet users increasingly change their habits, spurred on by the growth of mobile devices, they are challenging existing business models that worked for decades to support newspapers, books, magazines, television, Hollywood movies, and the music industry. Clearly, the future of content—news, music, and video—is online. Today, the print industry, including newspapers, books, and magazines, is having a difficult time coping with the movement of their readership to digital alternatives. Broadcast and cable television, along with Hollywood and the music industry, are also wrestling with outdated business models based on physical media. Established media giants are continuing to make extraordinary investments in unique online content, new technology, new digital distribution channels, and entirely new business models in order to stay relevant to the Internet audience. Internet giants like Apple, Google, Amazon, and Facebook are competing with the established firms for dominance in online content creation and distribution.

9.1 ONLINE CONTENT

No other sector has been so challenged by the Internet and the Web than the content industries. The online content industries are organized into two major categories: the print industries (newspapers, magazines, and books), and the entertainment industries, which includes television, movies, music (including radio), and games.

In this chapter, we will look closely at publishing (newspapers, magazines, and books) and entertainment (television and movies, music and radio, and games) as they attempt to transform their traditional media into digitally deliverable forms and experiences for consumers, while at the same time earning profits. These industries make up the largest share of the commercial content marketplace, both offline and online. In each of these industries, there are powerful offline brands, significant new pure-play online providers and distributors, consumer constraints and opportunities, a variety of legal issues, and mobile technology platforms that offer an additional content distribution system in the form of smartphones and tablet computers.

Table 9.1 describes the most recent trends in online content and media for 2019–2020.

CONTENT AUDIENCE: WHERE ARE THE EYEBALLS?

In 2018, the average American adult spends around 4,500 hours each year consuming various media, more than twice the amount of time spent at work (2,000 hours/year) (see

TABLE 9.1 WHAT'S NEW IN ONLINE CONTENT AND MEDIA, 2019–2020

BUSINESS

- Explosive growth of the mobile platform accelerates the transition to digital content.
- Amazon, Google (YouTube), Hulu, Netflix, and Apple become significant players in the content production business.
- The cable industry continues to be challenged by the growth of Internet content producers and distributors, with additional new competition from big Internet technology companies, such as Google and Apple.
- The number of Americans who watch digital video continues to increase, to over 235 million people, over 80% of all U.S. Internet users, and over 70% of the U.S. population.
- The number of Americans subscribing to subscription-based OTT television continues to grow, to over 180 million (about 55% of the U.S. population).
- E-book sales growth slows but audio book revenues increase.
- Americans continue to spend more on online movies than on DVDs.
- Americans continue to spend more on digital music than on physical units, and more on streaming music than downloaded music.
- Online readership of newspapers exceeds print readership. Online ad revenues and subscriptions grow but not enough to offset declining print ad revenues.
- Console game sales flatten as mobile gaming soars.
- The four Internet Titans compete: Apple, Google, Amazon, and Facebook vie for ownership of the online entertainment and content ecosystem, selling experiences as well as content.
- Industry convergence continues, with technology and telecommunications companies purchasing media content companies.

TECHNOLOGY

- Smartphones, tablet computers, and e-readers together create a rich mobile entertainment environment.
- Netflix remains the largest consumer of Internet bandwidth, while Amazon, Facebook, Apple, and Google are ramping up their bandwidth consumption.
- Apps become the foundation individual for an app economy as they morph into content-distribution platforms that are proprietary, where users can be charged for content.
- Cloud services grow to serve the huge market for mobile content.

SOCIETY

- Media consumption: Americans spend around 4,500 hours a year consuming various types of media, more than twice as many hours as they work.
- Time spent using digital media exceeds time spent with television; time spent on mobile devices exceeds time spent on desktops.
- Conflict continues over net neutrality rules that prohibit broadband providers from blocking, slowing down, or speeding up access to specific websites. Although federal rules have been repealed, various states have imposed similar restrictions, which are being challenged in court.

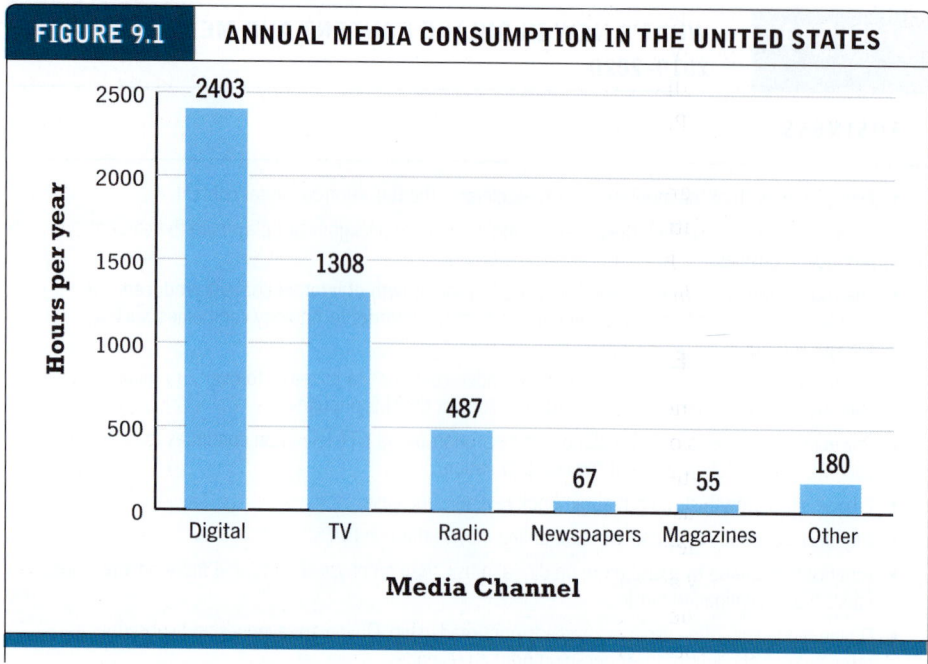

Americans spend around 4,500 hours annually on various types of media, with the majority of those hours consuming various forms of digital media online.
SOURCES: Based on data from eMarketer, Inc., 2019a; authors' estimates.

Figure 9.1). The proliferation of mobile devices—tablets and smartphones—has led to an increase in the total amount of time spent listening to radio, watching TV and movies, and reading books, newspapers, and even magazines. In 2019, time spent with digital media accounted for over 50% of total media time spent. In the past, the number of hours of TV viewing was far larger than the time spent with digital media, but since the development of the mobile platform, time spent on desktops plus mobile devices now consumes over six and a half hours per day compared to three and a half hours spent watching television on a TV (eMarketer, Inc., 2019a). On the other hand, a great deal of Internet usage involves watching digital video, including television shows and movies. In 2019, around 235 million Americans (over 70% of the U.S. population) watched digital video and over 180 million Americans (almost 55% of the population) subscribe to over-the-top television subscription services (eMarketer, Inc., 2019b, 2018). The distinction between Internet usage and television usage is not easy to make. Only the method of transmission is different: cable and satellite TV versus the Internet.

Initially, researchers believed that time spent on the Internet would reduce consumer time available for other media. This is referred to as cannibalization. The alternative argument was that the Internet and traditional media are complementary and mutually supportive rather than substitutive. The most recent data reveals a complex picture. Television viewing remains strong, video viewing on all devices has increased, and the reading of all kinds of books, including e-books and physical books, has increased. "Smart" television sets are Internet-enabled, allowing consumers to use the Internet to view TV shows on their traditional TVs. Total music consumption measured in hours a day listening to music has increased even as sales of CDs have drastically declined; likewise, movie consumption has increased even as DVD sales have also declined markedly. Nevertheless, the bottom line is that physical media are declining relative to the rapidly expanding digital media for all kinds of content. Print media and music have been severely impacted, as described below.

Millennials, the generation of people born between 1980 and 2000 (sometimes referred to as Digital Natives), are often thought to consume media very differently from their parents and Baby Boomers. For a discussion of how Millennials differ in media consumption, see *Insight on Society: Are Millennials Really All That Different?*

CONTENT MARKET: ENTERTAINMENT AND MEDIA INDUSTRY REVENUES

In 2018, U.S. entertainment and media industry revenues (both traditional and digital, and including all forms of revenue, such as advertising, subscription fees, and consumer purchases) were estimated to be about $353 billion. The various entertainment industries (television, movies, music, and games) together accounted for about 78% of total revenues, with the print media industries (books, newspapers, and magazine, both physical and digital) collectively accounting for about 22%. Within the entertainment industries, the television and movie industries (including broadcast and traditional pay TV, home entertainment subscription and download services, and box office movies) accounted for the lion's share of revenues, together representing about 58% of total revenues. The video game industry accounted for about 12%. The music industry, in the form of recorded music (both physical and digital) and radio, accounted for about 8% (see **Figure 9.2**). Smartphones and tablet computers have created new revenue streams for entertainment

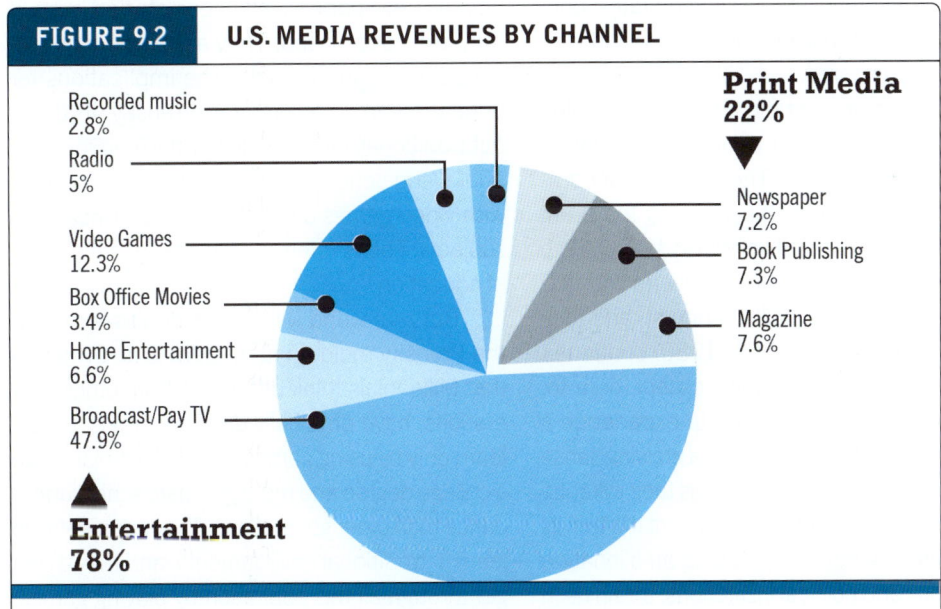

FIGURE 9.2 U.S. MEDIA REVENUES BY CHANNEL

The various entertainment industries generate over three-quarters of U.S. media revenues.
SOURCES: Based on data from industry sources; authors' estimates.

INSIGHT ON SOCIETY

ARE MILLENNIALS REALLY ALL THAT DIFFERENT?

If you were born between 1981 and 2000, congratulations! You are a Millennial and the subject of Millennial mania, which is now gripping the advertising, retailing, educational, and journalistic worlds. Not since the Baby Boomers has so much coverage been given to a single generation.

Some people believe that Millennials are so different from previous generations that they require new kinds of products, new types of marketing and advertising techniques to persuade them to buy, and entirely new educational techniques. Millennials drink more specialty coffee, so coffee makers are responding with multiple new specialty coffee drinks. How about an orange-pineapple latte? There's a lot of money at stake getting the pulse of Millennials and figuring out how to market to them. Millennials now make up the largest generation in the United States, constituting about 80 million consumers, and over 30% of the labor force.

Millennials are just the latest in a long line of generalizations about people who grew up in specific time periods. The Greatest Generation (1901–1924) came of age during the Great Depression and served in World War II. The Baby Boomers (1946–1964) grew up with the civil rights movement, political unrest, and rock and roll. Generation X (1965–1980) continued the trends of the Baby Boomers except more so. Generation Xers were the first to experience a slowdown in living standards and a growing sense that they might not earn as much as their parents. The Millennials are continuing many of the trends of previous generations, including an alienation from cultural and political institutions, a decline in religious belief and marriage rates, higher levels of student loan debt, poverty, and unemployment, and the reality—not just the fear—that they will earn less than their parents at a similar age. The Millennials are much more ethnically diverse as well: nearly half of the Millennial generation were not born in the United States compared to 25% of the previous generations.

But perhaps most important according to some is that Millennials are digital natives: they are the first generation to be born into the digital revolution of the 20th century. They grew up with the commercial Internet. According to Marc Prensky, an author and promoter of educational games, Millennials' brains are physically different because of long-term exposure to interactive video games, console controllers (the "twitch" effect), graphical interfaces, and non-linear hypertext experiences on the Internet. Today's digital natives, in this view, cannot learn from books, newspapers, or linear stories even if they are video-based. They are bored by these old-school learning tools. The implications for education are, according to Prensky, to throw out traditional, old-style, linear thinking found in books and school curricula, and replace these with video games and link-clicking for nearly all subjects. This is referred to as the "gamification" of education.

But real-world Millennials don't seem to fit the Prensky mold. In fact, there is no evidence that Millennials think differently from other generations, have physically different brains, or can learn only by using games. More Millennials have a college degree and more graduate school attendance than other generations. They apparently do learn in traditional environments, and they didn't get through all this education by playing games! Academic researchers have dismissed much of the digital native thesis, finding little support for claims that Millennials have adopted learning styles that are radically different from those of their parents.

But clearly Millennials have had a very different experience growing up with technology than their parents, given the incredible advancement of digital technologies in the last three decades that have created entirely new platforms like smartphones, tablets, digital photography, and highly interactive console and PC games, all of which have changed how content—books, newspapers, magazines, TV, and Hollywood movies—is created, distributed, and consumed. Millennials probably think like everyone else, but they do have different patterns of content consumption. Let's look at the data.

Given their intense use of the Internet, and absorption in digital experiences, including games, one would think Millennials would read few books (too boring and not twitchy or interactive enough), and that they would believe the Internet contained just about all the content and knowledge worth knowing about. Not so, according to a large study by Pew Research: Millennials are more likely to have read a book in the past 12 months than older adults, 88% versus 79%. Almost 40% report having read an e-book in the past year, about the same as older adults. They are more likely to use a smartphone to read e-books than a Kindle. And they are more likely to think that there's a lot of useful information that is not on the Internet, more so than older adults. They are more likely to have used a library in the past twelve months, and more likely to have used a library website. Even more unexpected: a study of 2,000 American and U.K. Millennials found this group overwhelmingly preferred printed books to e-books, and preferred buying them at bookstores rather than online stores like Amazon. Apparently, 600 years of reading printed books has created a print habit that might survive the Internet!

Millennials are only half as likely to subscribe to a print newspaper, but they are more likely to read news on digital news sites or get news (or links to news stories) from social sites, and to use their cell phones to follow news stories. Millennials are not news-less: 69% read news stories every day, some in print and even more online.

Given Millennials' intense exposure to high-speed, interactive, "twitch"-oriented video and video games, surely they are not about to watch passive, linear TV series online or offline, like regular cable television, or stream feature-length movies that require concentration. Surely they would not sit for 30 hours to binge watch a TV series already ten years old. Here too, the evidence does not fit the stereotype, although there are some differences. Contrary to the stereotype, Millennials watch 100–130 hours of regular cable TV per month, about the same as older adults. Marketers believe Millennial interest in TV is greater than any generation. Over 70% watch television live, without digital delays or streaming, slightly less than older adults. They like comedy and sitcoms more than older adults, and are more likely to watch TV on a smartphone or tablet. They also adore older TV series that they may have watched as children. In fact, they seem to have transformed the Internet from a media that involves reading to one that involves viewing. About 55% of binge viewers are Millennials.

Millennials are more involved with online video: they watch 200 more videos per month than older adults, mostly on YouTube, in large part because they are more likely to have and use smartphones. Millennials are nearly twice as likely to use streaming services like Netflix, Hulu, and Amazon, and are less likely to have cable or satellite TV service than older adults. About 21% of Millennials have no pay TV service, almost twice as many as older adults. Millennials are not cutting the cord in large numbers, although they are more likely to have never had cable TV ("cord nevers"). Some of this results from Millennials having lower incomes than older adults. They are using their smartphones and tablets as TV substitutes, viewing TV shows wherever and whenever they want. Millennials are driving a surge in YouTube action sports videos (surfing, skateboarding, and snowboarding). Finally, Millennials play a more active role in creating video content than older adults by posting photos and videos to social sites.

Millennials really do consume content differently than older adults of previous generations, although the differences appear to be far less and more commonsensical than journalists portray. For instance, Millennials take more advantage of the latest technologies from smartphones to streaming music and TV services than, say, Baby Boomers, although Baby Boomers, the generation that created the digital revolution, have adopted the new technologies nearly as much. Millennials have not lost interest in society or news about society, they just access it online somewhat more than older adults. Millennials do indeed create and share more content than elders, and control their TV schedules more often, including binge watching, even though they are watching hundreds of hours of traditional cable TV every month.

Reaching Millennials can be a problem for marketers. They are more likely to visit content sites such as Vice and Vox than traditional print sources, but their most frequent news sites include CNN and the New York Times websites. They are more likely to use ad blockers and tune out any kind of online ad. They are more visual and are more likely to use Tumblr, Pinterest, and Instagram. And they are much more likely to use mobile payment methods than Boomers.

As with all gross characterizations of entire generations, it's a mistake to think of Millennials as a single group. Millennials have both a higher percentage with college degrees and a higher percentage of people with only high school degrees; they are both richer and poorer than previous generations, more ethnically diverse, much more likely to be recent immigrants, have higher levels of unemployment, are less likely to marry early, and more likely to live with their parents to later ages and to delay child bearing. Contrary to marketers' assumptions, the Millennial population is actually many different communities, with different tastes and consumption patterns.

Millennials are different, but not so different that we don't recognize them. They are inheritors of very powerful digital technologies, to be sure, but inheritors also of several thousand years of literature, history, and culture, which they continue to find of enduring value.

SOURCES: "Millennials on Millennials: In the Know, On the Go," Nielsen.com, September 10, 2018; "Netflix Is Trouncing the Competition and It Should Stay on Top—Younger Viewers Love It," by Sarah Toy, Marketwatch.com, July 8, 2018; "State of OTT," comScore.com., June 26, 2018; "Millennials Stand Out for Their Technology Use, but Older Generations Also Embrace Digital Life," by Jingjing Jiang, Pewresearch.org, May 2, 2018; "Millennials Favor Smartphones for Second-Screening," by Rahul Chadha, eMarketer, Inc.. January 12, 2018; "Why Newspaper Subscriptions Are on the Rise," by Tien Tzuo, Techcrunch.com, March 4, 2017; "The Changing Economics and Demographics of Young Adulthood: 1975–2016," by Jonathan Vespa, U.S. Census Bureau, April 2017; "For First Time in Modern Era, Living With Parents Edges Out Other Living Arrangements for 18- to 34-Year-Olds," by Richard Fry, Pew Research Center, May, 2016; "Millennials Are the Most Likely Generation of Americans to Use Public Libraries," by Abigail Geiger, Pew Research Center, June 21, 2017; "The Majority of Millennials Actively Ignore Ads," eMarketer, Inc., August 25, 2016; "Which Media Companies Are Winning the Battle for Millennials?," by Ken Doctor, Politico.com, August 9, 2016; "Marketing to Millennials: Visual Buyers," by Curalate, Inc., July 2016; "Younger vs. Older US Adult Millennials as Digital Users," by eMarketer, Inc., January 2016; "For Online Sports Videos, the Action Is Off the Field," by Conor Dougherty, *New York Times*, September 11, 2015; "The Rise of Phone Reading," by Jennifer Maloney, *Wall Street Journal*, August 14, 2015; "Millennials: Seven Insights into Their Evolving Screen Choices and Viewing Habits," by Jeremy Kressman, eMarketer, Inc., August 2015; "State of the News Media 2015," by Amy Mitchell, Pew Research Center, Journalism and Media, April 29, 2015; "Millennials' Media Usage," by Mark Doliver, eMarketer, Inc., April 2015; "New Research Reveals Print Habits Die Hard With Millennial Readers," Publishingtechnology.com, March 26, 2015; "How Millennials Get News: Inside the Habits of America's First Digital Generation," by The Media Insight Project, American Press Institute, March 16, 2015; "15 Economic Facts About Millennials," by The Council of Economic Advisers, The White House, October 2014; "Are Digital Natives a Myth or Reality? University Students' Use of Digital Technologies," by Anoush Margaryan, Allison Littlejohn, and Gabrielle Vojt, *Computers & Education*, Volume 56, Issue 2, February 2011; "Digital Natives, Digital Immigrants," by Marc Prensky, in *On the Horizon* (MCB University Press, Vol. 9, No. 5, October 2001); "Digital Natives, Digital Immigrants, Part II," by Marc Prensky, in *On the Horizon* (MCB University Press, Vol. 9, No. 6, October 2001); "Millennials Rising: The Next Great Generation," by Neil Howe, William Strauss, and R. J. Matson, *Vintage*, September 2000.

and media firms. Content is no longer tied to physical products and can be delivered over the Internet from cloud servers to multiple mobile devices, reducing costs for consumers.

ONLINE CONTENT: CONSUMPTION, REVENUE MODELS, AND REVENUE

Now let's look at what kinds of online content U.S. Internet users consumed online in 2019 (**Figure 9.3**). It's not a surprise that 83% of Internet users watched online video of various kinds, but it may be a surprise that over 60% of Internet users visited online news sites such as Yahoo News. Playing digital games was also very popular. The percentage of Internet users that read e-books initially grew at triple-digit rates when the Kindle was introduced in 2007 and the iPad in 2010, but has since slowed. What this reveals is that Internet users retain their affinity to traditional formats—TV shows and movies, music, games, news, and books—and bring these tastes to the Internet and their mobile devices.

In the early years, multiple surveys found that a large percentage of the Internet audience expected to pay nothing for online content although equally large percentages were willing to accept advertising in return for free content. In reality, on the early Web, there wasn't much high-quality content. Few initially thought the pay model could compete with the "free" model, and many Internet analysts believed that information on the Internet needed to be free. The movie industry and cable TV systems and cable content providers had a totally different history: they always charged for services and content, and their executives and investors never thought information should be free. The culture of the Internet began to change when Apple introduced iTunes in 2003 as a source of relatively inexpensive, high-quality music, and firms such as YouTube (and its parent Google), which

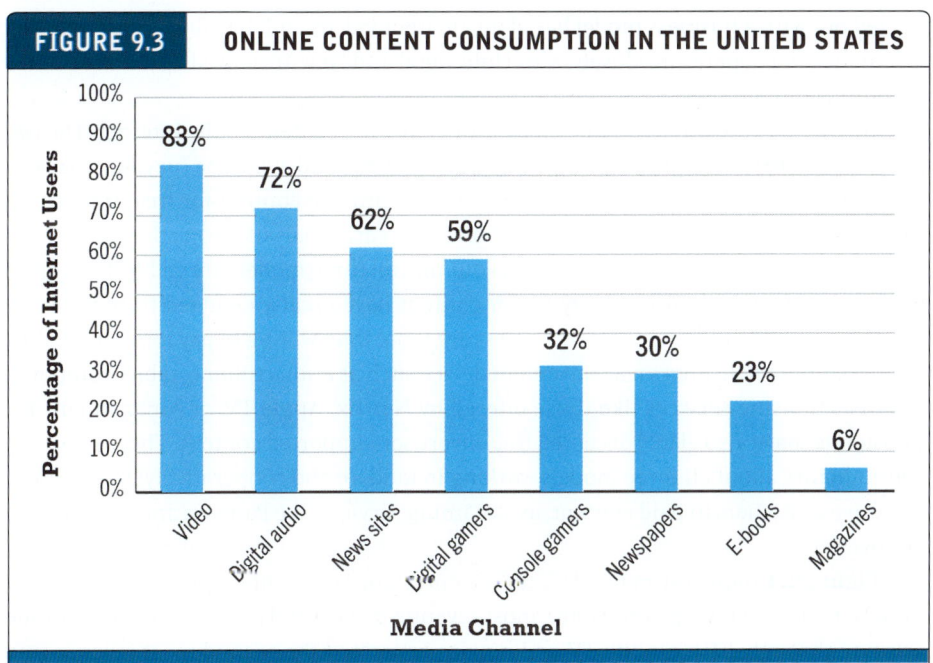

FIGURE 9.3 ONLINE CONTENT CONSUMPTION IN THE UNITED STATES

SOURCES: Based on data from eMarketer, Inc., 2019b, 2019c, 2019d, 2019e; Pew Research Center, 2019a; Washington Post, 2019; Ebizmba.com, 2020; industry sources; authors' estimates.

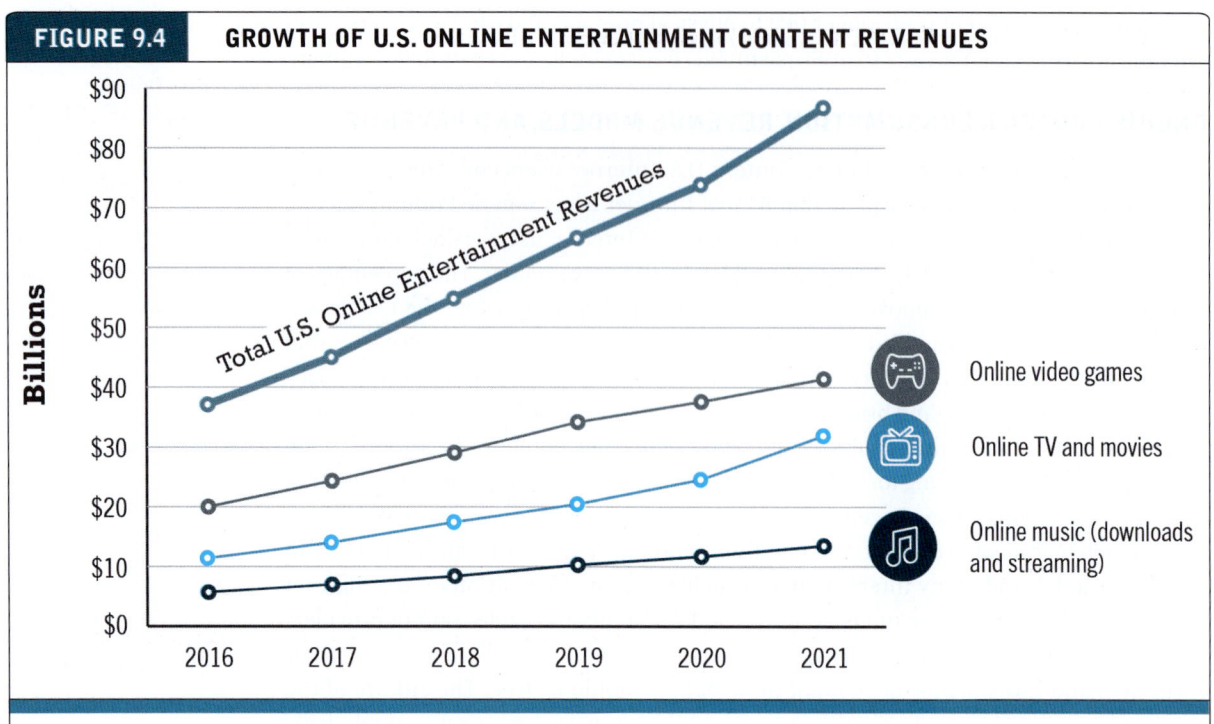

FIGURE 9.4 GROWTH OF U.S. ONLINE ENTERTAINMENT CONTENT REVENUES

SOURCES: Based on data from industry sources; authors' estimates.

started out with a business model based on amateur videos and illegally uploaded music videos, began cooperating closely with Hollywood and New York production studios for premium content.

Today, there are three revenue models for delivering content on the Internet. The two pay models are subscriptions (usually "all you can eat") and a la carte (pay for what you use). The third model uses advertising revenue to provide content for free, sometimes with a freemium (higher price) option. Contrary to early analysts' projections that "free" would drive "paid" out of business, it turns out that all three models are viable. Consumer behavior and attitudes toward paying for content have greatly changed from the early years and in 2018, millions of Internet users are more than willing to pay for high-quality, unique content delivered on a convenient device such as a smartphone, tablet computer, or e-reader, using services like those offered by Netflix, Apple TV, or Amazon Fire TV. Consumers have also gladly accepted free advertiser-supported content. There's nothing contradictory about all three models working in tandem and cooperatively: free content can drive customers to paid content, as streaming services like Pandora and Spotify have discovered.

Figure 9.4 shows estimated U.S. online entertainment content revenues, projected to 2021. Online games generated the most revenue in 2019 and are expected to continue growing through 2021. Online TV and movies generated the second most revenue and are expected to grow by nearly 30% over the next three years. While revenue from online music sales in the form of downloads has declined significantly, music streaming revenues have offset the decline in downloads.

DIGITAL RIGHTS MANAGEMENT (DRM) AND WALLED GARDENS

Digital rights management (DRM) refers to a combination of technical (both hardware and software) and legal means for protecting digital content from unlimited reproduction and distribution without permission. DRM hardware and software encrypts content so that it cannot be used without some form of authorization typically based on a payment. The objective is to control the uses of content after it has been sold or rented to consumers. Essentially, DRM can prevent users from purchasing and making copies for widespread distribution over the Internet without compensating the content owners. While music tracks in the iTunes Store were originally protected by DRM, in 2009, Apple abandoned the practice because of user objections, and because Amazon had opened an online music store in 2007 without any DRM protections, with the support of music label firms, who came to realize that DRM prevented them from exploiting the opportunities of the Internet and perhaps even encouraged an illegal market. Streaming content services are inherently difficult to copy and re-distribute. Movies streamed from Netflix are technically difficult for the average user to capture and share, although apps like Periscope (Twitter) make live re-streaming very easy even if the quality is low. Likewise, music streamed from Pandora is cumbersome to record and share. Streaming services, including both Apple and Amazon, use a kind of DRM called a **walled garden** to restrict the widespread sharing of content. They do this by tying the content to the hardware, operating system, or streaming environment. E-books purchased from Amazon can only be read on Kindles or Kindle apps, and Kindle books cannot be converted to other formats. By locking the content to a physical device, or a digital stream with no local storage, the appliance makers derive additional revenues and profits by locking customers into their service or device and satisfy the demands of content producers to be fairly compensated for their work. Google's YouTube identifies and tracks copyrighted music and removes it if music labels have not granted permission, and offers owners the revenue from advertising if they choose to let the music remain on the site. These efforts have not eliminated pirated content, but they have greatly reduced its prevalence in the U.S.

digital rights management (DRM)
refers to the combination of technical and legal means for protecting digital content from unlimited reproduction without permission

walled garden
refers to a kind of DRM that uses proprietary file formats, operating systems, and hardware to control the use of content after initial sale

MEDIA INDUSTRY STRUCTURE

The U.S. media industry prior to 1990 was composed of many smaller independent corporations specializing in content creation and distribution in the separate industries of film, music, television, book and magazine publishing, and newspaper publishing. During the 1990s and into this century, after an extensive period of consolidation, huge entertainment and publishing media conglomerates emerged.

The U.S. media content industry is still organized largely into three separate vertical stovepipes: print, movies, and music. Each segment is dominated by a few key players, and generally there is very little crossover from one segment to another. For example, newspapers typically do not also produce Hollywood films, and publishing firms do not own newspapers or film production studios. The purchase of the *Washington Post* in 2013 by Jeff Bezos, the founder of Amazon, and an Internet mogul in his own right, was an anomaly. Even within media conglomerates that span several different media segments, separate divisions generally control each media segment.

In the past, we have not included the delivery platform firms, such as Comcast, Altice, AT&T, Verizon, Sprint, and Dish Network, in this analysis because in general they did not focus on the creation of content but instead just moved content produced by others across cable, satellite, and telephone networks. However, within the last several years, this has begun to change. Comcast led the way with the acquisition of a majority interest in NBC Universal. AT&T's merger with Time Warner and Verizon's purchase of Yahoo, along with its previous acquisition of AOL, are signs that the telecommunications companies are moving into the content creation and distribution market, as well as the Internet advertising industry, in a major way as revenues from its traditional cable Internet and wireless business slow. Content attracts viewers who pay subscription fees and attract advertisers as well.

MEDIA CONVERGENCE: TECHNOLOGY, CONTENT, AND INDUSTRY STRUCTURE

Media convergence is a much used but poorly defined term. There are at least three dimensions of media where the term convergence has been applied: technology, content (artistic design, production, and distribution), and the industry's structure as a whole. Ultimately for the consumer, convergence means being able to get any content you want, when you want it, on whatever platform you want it—from an iPod to an iPad, Android phone, or home PC, or a set-top device like Apple TV and Amazon Fire TV.

Technological Convergence

Convergence from a technology perspective **(technological convergence)** has to do with the development of hybrid devices that can combine the functionality of two or more existing media platforms, such as books, newspapers, television, movies, radio, and games, into a single device. Examples of technological convergence include the iPad, iPhone, and Android ("smartphones") that combine telephone, print, music, photos, and video in a single device.

technological convergence
development of hybrid devices that can combine the functionality of two or more existing media platforms into a single device

Content Convergence

A second dimension of convergence is **content convergence**. There are three aspects to content convergence: design, production, and distribution.

There is a historical pattern in which content created in an older media technology migrates to the new technology largely intact, with little artistic change. Slowly, the different media are integrated so that consumers can move seamlessly back and forth among them, and artists (and producers) learn more about how to deliver content in the new media. Later, the content itself is transformed by the new media as artists learn how to fully exploit the capabilities in the creation process. At this point, content convergence and transformation has occurred—the art is different because of the new capabilities inherent to new tools. For instance, European master painters of the fifteenth century in Italy, France, and the Netherlands (such as van Eyck, Caravaggio, Lotto, and Vermeer) quickly adopted new optical devices such as lenses, mirrors, and early projectors called *camera obscura* that could cast near-photographic quality images on canvases, and in the process they developed new theories of perspective and new techniques of painting landscapes and portraits. Suddenly, paintings took on the qualities of precision, detail, and realism found later in photographs (Boxer, 2001). A similar process is occurring

content convergence
convergence in the design, production, and distribution of content

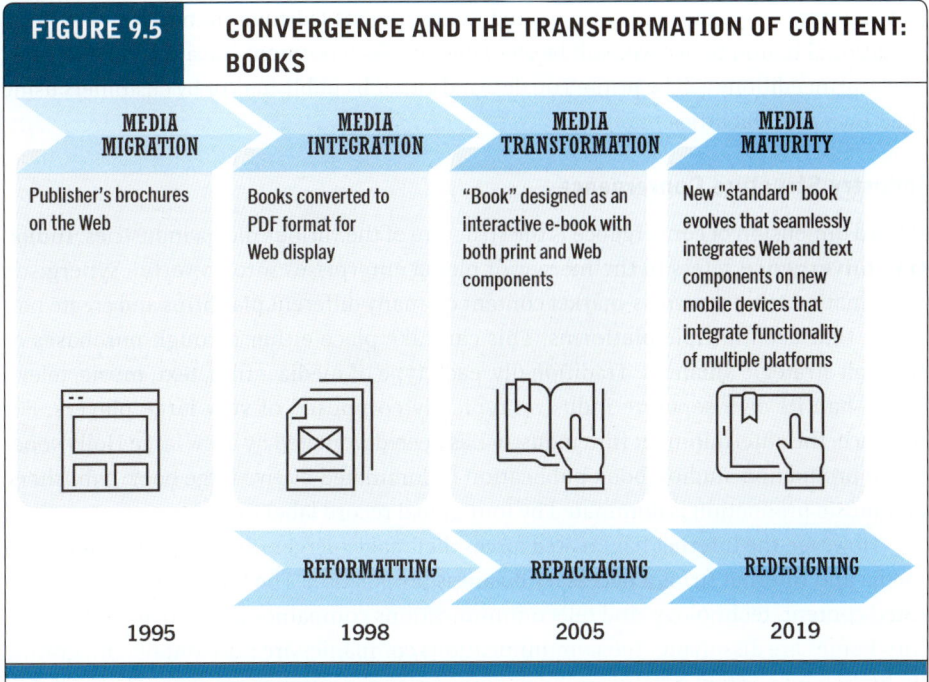

The Internet is making it possible for publishers and writers to transform the standard "book" into a new form that integrates features of both text and the Internet, and also transforms the content of the book itself.

today as artists and writers assimilate new digital and Internet tools into their toolkits. For instance, GarageBand from Apple enables low-budget independent bands (literally working in garages) to mix and control eight different digital music tracks to produce near-professional sounding recordings on a shoestring budget. Writers of books and their publishers are turning to digital video and simulations to heighten the user experience. Online newspapers are changing the news cycle to a 24-hour stream, producing their own video channels, and expanding user comment opportunities on their websites.

On the production side, tools for digital editing and processing (for film and television) are driving content convergence. Given that the most significant cost of content is its creation, if there is a wide diversity of target delivery platforms, then it is wise to develop and produce only once using digital technology that can deliver to multiple platforms. Generally, this means creating content on digital devices (hardware and software) so that it can be delivered on multiple digital platforms.

Figure 9.5 depicts the process of media convergence and transformation using the example of books. For example, consider this book. Today, this book is written with a view to appearing online, as well as in e-book form, and it is now moving closer to the media maturity stage, in which the book is available mostly as a purely digital product with substantial visual and audio content that can be displayed on many different digital devices. By that time, the learning experience will be transformed by greater use of interactive graphics, videos, simulations, as well as an integrated testing system that monitors student performance during the semester. Even the number of pages read by students, and the time on page, will be monitored by this digital learning management system. Traditional bound books will still be available (books have many advantages), but most likely, print editions will be printed on demand either by publishers or by customers using their own print facilities.

Industry Structure Convergence

A third dimension of convergence is the structure of the various media industries. **Industry convergence** refers to the merger of media enterprises into powerful, synergistic combinations that can cross-market content on many different platforms and create new works that use multiple platforms. This can take place either through purchases or through strategic alliances. Traditionally, each type of media—film, text, music, television—had its own separate industry, typically composed of very large players. For instance, the entertainment film industry has been dominated by a few large Hollywood-based production studios, book publication is dominated by five large book publishers, and music production is dominated by four global record label firms.

However, the Internet has created forces that make mergers and partnerships among media and Internet firms a necessary business proposition. The borders that once separated content, technology, and telecommunications companies that provided the pipes into homes are dissolving. Telecommunications companies are horizontally integrating by buying up content producers. Tech companies are purchasing content companies as well. Distributors like Netflix are integrating vertically by buying content producers (PriceWaterhouseCoopers (PWC), 2018). Media industry convergence may be necessary to finance the substantial changes in both the technology platform and the content. Traditional media firms who create the content generally do not possess the core competencies or financial heft to distribute it on the Internet. Technology companies that dominate the Internet (Google, Apple, Amazon, and Facebook) have the competency and wealth to pursue Internet channel strategies, but until recently did not have the competencies needed to create content. Business combinations, licensing deals, and partnerships are made to solve these issues.

While traditional media companies have not done well in purchases of Internet platform companies, the technology owners such as Apple, Amazon, Facebook, Microsoft, and Google have generally avoided merging with media companies, and instead rely on contractual arrangements with media companies to protect intellectual property rights and to create a business pricing model that both parties can accept. However, this pattern is changing. For instance, CBS Inc., a movie and television content producer, produces television shows for Netflix; Netflix, Hulu, and Amazon produce and distribute their own original TV series; Google is producing original content designed for Internet distribution on YouTube. Amazon created its own book imprint, Amazon Books Publishing, and entered the book publishing business. And as noted previously, telecommunications companies have joined the fray, with Verizon acquiring Yahoo and AT&T acquiring Time Warner. In this sense, the Internet is changing the media industry from what it was in the recent past.

In the end, consumers' demands for content anywhere, anytime, and on any device are pushing the technology and content companies toward both strategic alliances and strategic conflicts in their search for advantage.

industry convergence
merger of media enterprises into synergistic combinations that create and cross-market content on different platforms

9.2 THE ONLINE PUBLISHING INDUSTRY

Nothing is quite so fundamental to a civilized society as reading text. Text is the way we record our history, current events, thoughts, and aspirations, and transmit them to all others in the civilization who can read. Even television shows and movies require scripts. Today, the U.S. publishing industry (composed of books, newspapers, magazines, and periodicals) is an $80 billion media sector based originally on print, and it is now moving rapidly to the Internet and mobile delivery. The Internet offers the text publishing industry an opportunity to move toward a new generation of newspapers, magazines, and books that are produced, processed, stored, distributed, and sold over the Web, available anytime, anywhere, and on any device. The same Internet offers the possibility of destroying many existing print-based publishing businesses that may not be able to make this transition and remain profitable.

ONLINE NEWSPAPERS

Newspapers 2019 remained the most troubled segment of the print publishing industry. U.S. newspaper industry revenues have shrunk from their high of almost $60 billion in 2000 to only about $25.3 billion in 2018 (see **Figure 9.6**). The newspaper labor force has roughly been cut in half over this period. The newspaper industry has been in an extended period of digital disruption since the rise of the Web in 2000 and the emergence of powerful search engines like Google, which allow consumers to search for and read news articles on

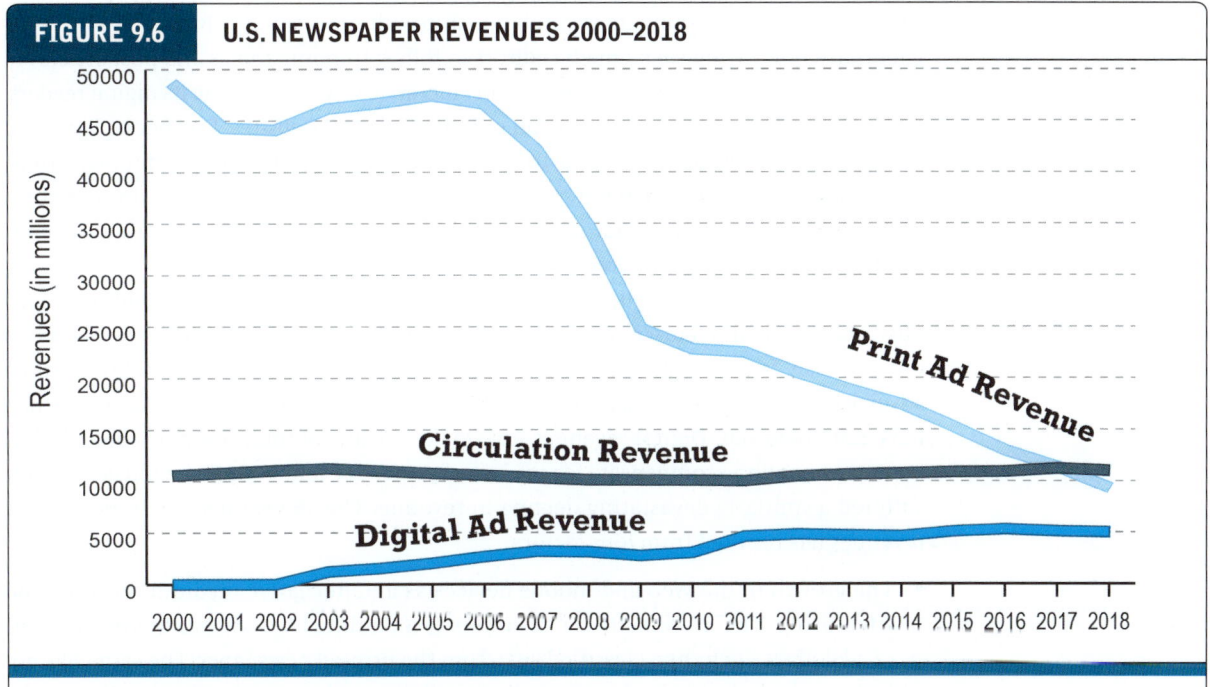

FIGURE 9.6 U.S. NEWSPAPER REVENUES 2000–2018

U.S. newspaper ad revenues have declined by 50% since 1980. As a percentage of total revenues, circulation subscription revenues have become more important. Digital advertising revenue is a small but growing source of revenue, hitting around $5 billion in 2018.
SOURCES: Based on data from Pew Research Center, 2019b; Newspaper Association of America, 2017, 2016.

any subject without having to browse a physical newspaper or an online edition. Social media sites have become a major source of unique visitors to online newspapers, who, unfortunately, do not browse for news and usually stay on the newspaper's site for only a few moments to read a single article. These fleeting visitors typically do not engage with the newspaper as a whole or with its online ads. Even before the Internet and Web, newspaper revenue was falling due to the influence of earlier technologies like broadcast and cable television. In 2014, three of the largest newspaper organizations (Gannett, Tribune Company, and E.W. Scripps) spun off their newspaper operations as independent firms so they could focus on television and other media assets, including in some cases, successful digital properties. Newspapers will now be pure-play print and online enterprises and will have to make it on their own without the protection of television or other media assets (Carr, 2014).

The striking growth of alternative pure digital news sources in the last five years, from Twitter and Facebook, to Vox, Vice, BuzzFeed, and Huffington Post, poses additional challenges. Online news sources are attracting millions of consumers everyday and steer potential newspaper readers—both online and offline—away from the most valuable front page of print and digital edition newspapers. In 2015, the *New York Times*, along with nine other news media outlets, agreed as an experiment to embed a few of its articles directly into Facebook's News Feed as a way to attract millions of new readers, and hopefully convert them from free readers to paid digital subscribers. Facebook called these news stories Instant Articles. What started as an experiment became a significant source of readers for newspaper articles, but not the entire newspaper. By 2018 the major newspapers had withdrawn from the program because Facebook was draining newspaper sites of visitors, and strengthening its own relationship with news readers (Brown, 2018). Newspapers are now hiring social media editors to follow trending topics and post articles to newsfeeds. Newspaper websites are the most lucrative way to monetize its digital readers. Major newspapers are now focusing on redesigning their websites, Facebook pages, and using push notifications of curated articles in topic areas of interest to their power users. Newspaper survival will depend on how fast newspaper organizations can transform themselves from print to digital, and how fast they can monetize the expanding audience for news all the time, anywhere, on all devices.

As can be seen from Figure 9.6, while newspaper circulation revenues (subscriptions plus newsstand sales) have remained basically flat since 2000, print advertising has fallen precipitously from a high of $48 billion in 2000 to just around $9 billion in 2018. Online advertising in newspapers increased gradually from 2011 through 2016, but since then have remained flat. Digital revenues now make up 20% of total revenues, but this has not been enough to compensate for the loss of print ad revenue. Only the music industry suffered a similarly devastating decline in revenue. The 15-year decline in newspaper revenues has resulted from four factors:

- The growth of the Web and mobile devices as an alternative medium for news and advertising. The movement of consumers to an online life style has drained billions of ad dollars (including classified ads) from the printed newspaper. The same has not been true of television advertising as we will discuss later in the chapter. Even radio advertising has stood up well to the digital revolution.

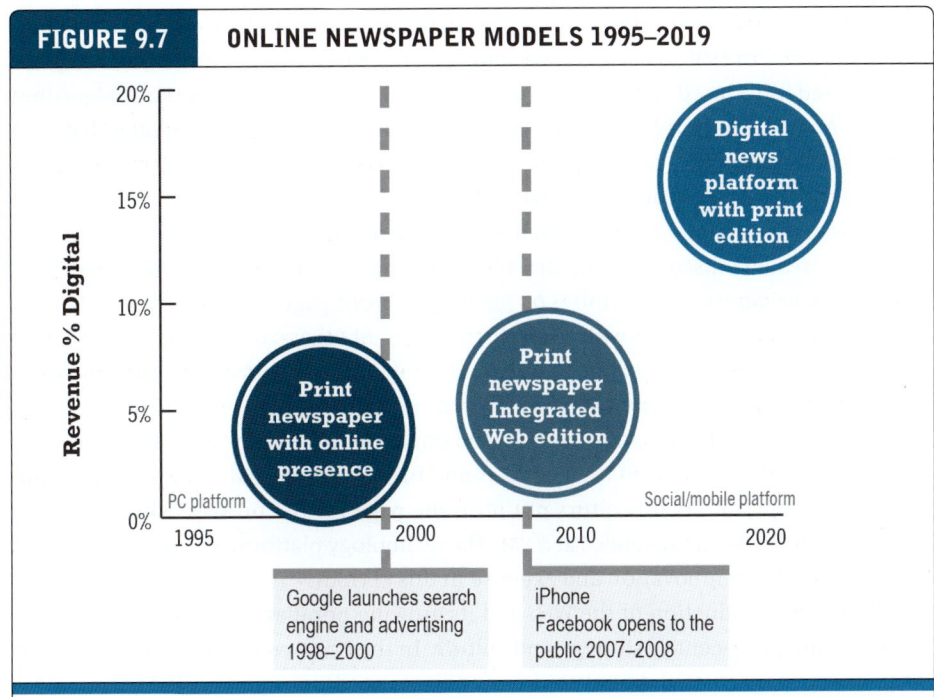

FIGURE 9.7 ONLINE NEWSPAPER MODELS 1995–2019

Newspapers have gone through three different business models as they adapt to the Internet.

- The rise of alternative digital sources for news, commentary, feature stories, and articles.
- The difficulty that traditional newspaper firms and their managers experience in developing suitable business and revenue models that could survive and even prosper on the Internet, and the mobile/social platform.
- The rise of social media and search engines, primarily Google, that have directed users to news sites for single articles rather than to the newspapers' websites.

From Print-centric to Digital First: The Evolution of Newspaper Online Business Models

Since 1995, when e-commerce and digital advertising began, through to the present, newspapers have developed three distinct business models in an effort to adapt to the Internet, and more recently, the mobile and social platform (see **Figure 9.7**). The three models are: Print-centric (1995–2000), Integrated Print/Web (2000–2010), and the current model, Digital First (2010–present). You can compare these models on four dimensions:

- **Search and discovery:** How do readers find the news?
- **Awareness:** How are potential readers made aware of news?
- **Engagement:** How are readers engaged with the news and journalists?
- **Technology platform:** How, when, and where is the news delivered to readers? (New York Times, 2017).

The milestones reflect important dates in the evolution of the Web and the mobile-social platform. In 1998 to 2000, Google launched its search engine with 60 million pages indexed, and introduced search engine paid advertising based on its Page Rank algorithm. In 2007, Apple introduced its iPhone, creating a truly mobile and universal web device, and Facebook opened its site to the public, and in 2008 signed up over 100 million users, creating the first large-scale, online social network.

Prior to the development of the Web, search engines, mobile devices, and social media platforms, readers discovered the news by browsing (a form of searching) the printed paper. They became aware of stories by reading the front page, section pages, and article titles. Readers did not engage with journalists, editors, or other contributors, except for the few who wrote letters to the editor (less than 1% of all readers). Journalism was considered a profession, and readers were not expected to do much more than read and be fascinated, enlightened, and entertained by people who obviously were more informed than they. Journalists worked all day on their articles and filed them at 5 PM; professional editors revised the copy, and compositors put it on the page for the presses, which ran after midnight. The news stream ended at 5 PM. The technology platform was print, sometimes with color (a major innovation and expense in this period).

With the introduction of the Web and its growing popularity, newspapers retained their existing print-centric strategy and culture. In the Print-centric period from 1995 to 2000, newspapers created digital copies of their print editions and posted them online. Readers discovered stories as they did before, by reading the front page online, following links to stories, and clicking on topic areas or sections (e.g., Sports or Technology). Stories were promoted by a business department that sought to enlarge the print audience and to attract advertisers based on readership and online visitors. Digital advertising was very limited, in part because advertisers did not believe it was effective. Readers were not engaged with journalists except insofar as they read the stories and could identify with the subjects of stories. The business process of creating journalism did not change: articles were filed at 5 PM and went to print editors, and then were sent to the web team and the print group. There was little difference, if any, between the print and online versions. The technology platform for the digital edition was the desktop or laptop, and news was consumed at home and work.

In the Integrated Print/Web period, from 2000 to 2010, newspapers adopted multimedia elements such as video, added more interactive elements like crossword puzzles and contests, and provided more reader feedback opportunities, especially on opinion and editorial pages. There were opportunities to personalize the news using RSS feeds and push news to the reader. Nevertheless, news was discovered by the reader visiting the website; promoting content online was limited, primarily to RSS feeds. Readers were somewhat more engaged. The technology platform remained the desktop or laptop platform.

In the Digital First period, from 2010 to the present, three developments in the technology and popular audience platform occurred: the rapid adoption of smartphones and tablets, and the equally astounding growth of social media sites like Facebook and Twitter, which have come to dominate consumer time on the Web and mobile devices. In addition, the rise of startup news sites specifically focused on using the new technology and platforms has spurred newspapers to radically transform their business—or go out of business. The new platform is not based on personal computers using a browser, but on mobile devices and apps, with desktops and laptops now just one pillar of the delivery platform. In this new environment, the news does not stop at 5 PM, but goes on 24×7. Stories start with an initial short article that is updated through the day, followed by thousands of tweets, then millions of shares on multiple social sites and on Google. Often amateurs on scene know more about the news in the first hours of a story than any collection of journalists in their offices. Amateurs provide video feeds and commentary to the editors and journalists.

The Digital First business model inverts previous models: the top priority is producing the most engaging, continually updated digital edition, and then producing a print product based on the news developed in the digital edition. In the case of pure digital startups, there is no print edition, and the news is just a continuous stream of updates, blogs, tweets, and posts, rather than a fixed article. News articles are time-stamped, indicating an update is on the way and the reader should return to follow the story. Instead of waiting for readers to discover the news, or search for the news on a search engine, the news is pushed to readers on any of a variety of venues where they happen to be—social media sites, mobile news feeds, e-mail, Twitter, or Yahoo or Google News. Journalists remain paid professionals, but they follow Twitter feeds and social media sites, and promote their stories and personas on social media sites and TV news shows. Their job is no longer simply reporting and writing, and getting the facts right, but promoting and engaging readers on a personal level through their own efforts. Superior reporting and writing is no longer the sole criterion for hiring and advancement. More emphasis is put on reporters' abilities to attract audiences on their own social media pages and Twitter feeds.

The Digital First business model is not yet a reality for traditional newspapers. The largest print newspaper organizations, such as the *Wall Street Journal, New York Times, Washington Post*, and others, have begun the journey towards becoming Digital First news organizations. In 2014 the *Wall Street Journal* launched its Real-Time news desk, a headquarters group of 60 editors aiming to produce a continuous and lively flow of digital news and commentary to social media sites, mobile followers, and its online sites (Romenesko, 2014). The *New York Times* also initiated a Digital First model in 2014 and has driven its digital-only news subscribers to 3.5 million, over two-thirds of its total 5.25 million subscriber base. The *Times* is continuing to become more digital by becoming more visual, creating more original video and graphics, and audio tracks. It is also using more digital native journalistic forms like the Daily Briefing feature, which gives digital readers a synopsis of the articles they should read, and Watching, a feature that curates streaming movies and videos viewers might find interesting. In 2019, the Times exceeded $800 million in annual digital revenue for the first time, a goal it had pledged to meet by the end of 2020 (Benton, 2020; Tracy, 2020; New York Times, 2017). The *Wall Street Journal* has also launched a digital first website, with redesigned web and video pages, iPad and Android apps, and a greater emphasis on breaking news stories that are refined in the course of a 24-hour news cycle. The *Financial Times*, the *Washington Post, USA Today,* and Bloomberg News have all made similar changes to succeed in a mobile-tablet-desktop digital marketplace.

Online Newspaper Industry: Strengths and Challenges

The newspaper industry still has some major strengths, which it will need to draw upon as it faces the challenges of the future. In the following section, we review those strengths and challenges.

Strength: Newspaper Audience Size and Growth. Online readership of newspapers is growing at more than 15% a year. Over 80% of U.S. adults surveyed by the Pew Research Center get news online at least some of the time (Pew Research Center, 2019b, 2019d). See **Figure 9.8** for a list of various newspapers in the United States and the UK, in terms of unique monthly visitors online. The online newspaper is one of the most successful of all online media in terms of audience size. Mobile newspaper readership is especially strong among young persons due to their greater usage of smartphones and tablet computers. Young people (age 18–34) are more likely to read news online than older people.

Newspapers have responded to the changing audience by providing access to their content on all digital platforms. With almost 80% of Americans accessing the Internet with a mobile device, in a few short years newspapers have become truly multi-platform by developing apps and websites optimized for mobile devices, and an integral part of many social network users, with 35% of readers using social networks to access articles (see **Figure 9.9**). Only 51% of newspaper readers are exclusively print readers, while 49% use a combination of the Web, print, and/or mobile (Pew Research Center, 2017). Mobile traffic is continuing to grow for most newspapers, while the number of desktop visitors is declining. In 2019, almost 60% of Americans surveyed reported that they often read the

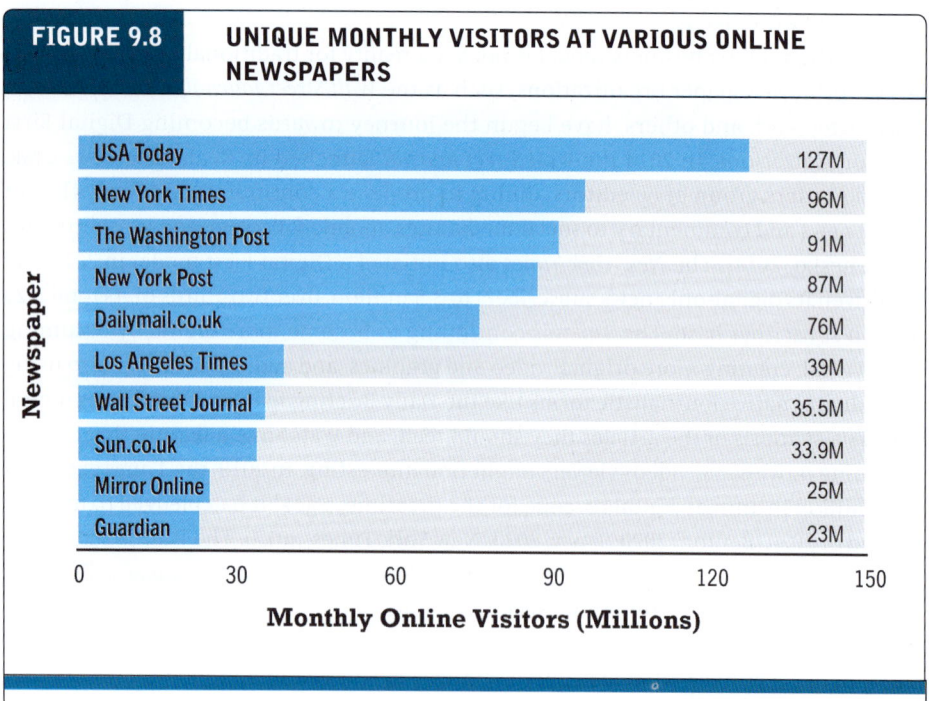

FIGURE 9.8 UNIQUE MONTHLY VISITORS AT VARIOUS ONLINE NEWSPAPERS

Newspaper	Monthly Online Visitors (Millions)
USA Today	127M
New York Times	96M
The Washington Post	91M
New York Post	87M
Dailymail.co.uk	76M
Los Angeles Times	39M
Wall Street Journal	35.5M
Sun.co.uk	33.9M
Mirror Online	25M
Guardian	23M

Online newspaper readership at leading national newspaper websites is expanding rapidly.
SOURCES: Based on data from comScore, Inc., 2020; newspaper media kits; authors' estimates.

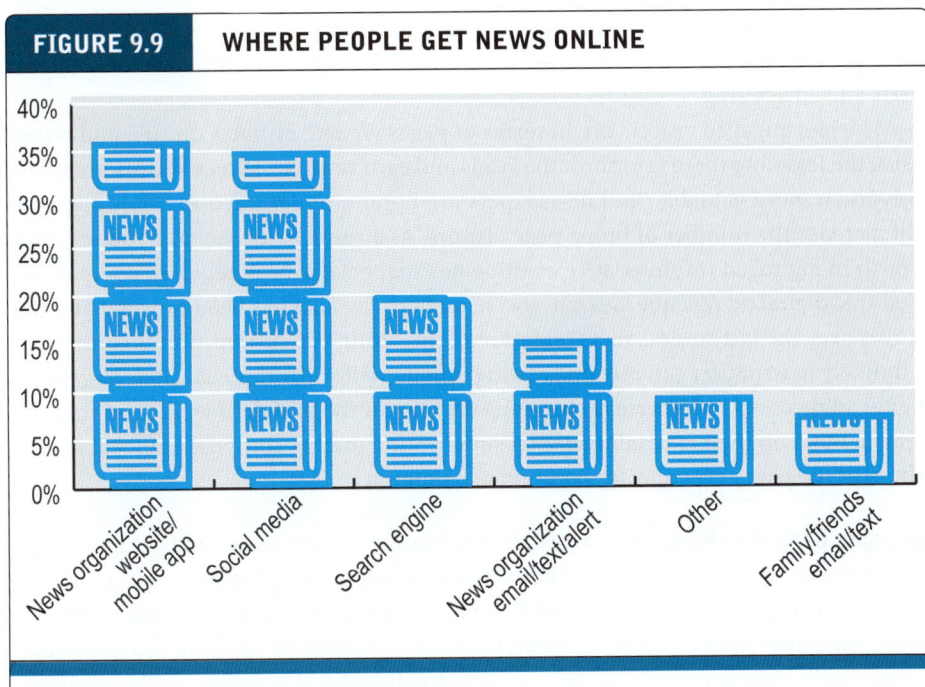

The most common platforms for consuming news online are news organization websites and social media.
Source: Based on data from Pew Research Center, 2017.

news on a mobile device. In contrast, only 30% of those surveyed reported that they often used a desktop or laptop computer. Newspapers in particular have a trust advantage over social media. About 60% of social media news viewers believe the news there is mostly inaccurate, while 67% of news organization news viewers expect the news to be largely accurate (Pew Research Center, 2019d, 2018; Kearny, 2018; Newspaper Association of America, 2017; Pew Research Center, 2017).

Online newspapers also attract a wealthy, educated, and consumer-intense demographic, reaching 64% of 25- to 34-year-olds, and 75% of individuals in households earning more than $100,000 a year on average. Given the large online newspaper audience, it is clear that the future of newspapers lies in the online and mobile market even as readership and subscriptions to the traditional print newspapers continue to decline at a steady pace.

Challenge: Digital Ad Revenue. Newspapers hope that the digital ad revolution and revenue will hit their shores, and lift total ad revenues. But here's the problem: while unique visitors to newspaper websites are expanding, increasingly this traffic is less valuable for two reasons. First, the audience is increasingly coming from social media sites and search engines in order to find specific articles, rather than coming directly to the newspaper's home page (so-called side-door entry). Second, these visitors from social sites are less engaged, and less valuable. People who come directly to a newspaper's website view, on average, 24 pages of content. If they use a search engine or social site they view around 5 pages of content. For this reason, major news organizations including newspapers have avoided posting content to social media sites and have reduced social media alerts and advertising.

The less engaged visitors are in terms of pages viewed, minutes on site, and return visits, the less time there is to show them ads and earn revenue. Direct visitors are therefore much more valuable, and newspapers are hoping re-designed websites and apps will increase the number of home page visitors. As a result, with the exception of 2016, growth in digital ad revenues at U.S. online newspapers has been tepid. In comparison, total U.S. digital ad revenue (search, social, and display ads) has been growing at a rate of 20% over the last several years (eMarketer, Inc., 2019f). If current trends continue, it is unlikely newspapers can rely on growing unique visitors from social sites, or growing digital ad revenues, to reverse the revenue declines of the past decade. Instead they will need to build on their expanding digital subscription market composed of loyal readers who visit the paper everyday for curation and opinion.

Strength: Content Is King. Why do people continue to buy newspapers and pay for newspaper content online? The oft-repeated bon mot that "content is king" appears to be true in the case of print as well as online content of all kinds, including news and pure digital news sites. As in competitive sports, in general, quality counts. The reason why online newspapers attract exceptionally large and loyal audiences who are deeply engaged is simple: quality of content. Compared to other media, newspapers are the most trusted source of news and commentary on local, national, and international stories. A recent survey of over 8,000 Americans found that newspapers were the most trusted source of news by far, followed by television news, with social media sites being the least trustworthy (Kearney, 2018). Local newspapers produce the highest levels of ad engagement: 35% of consumers report making purchases on the basis of local newspaper ads. Online display ads, e-mail campaigns, and fleeting mobile ads do not even come close to these engagement levels. Newspapers employ about 38,000 reporters, editors, photographers and film or video editors, down from almost 75,000 in 2006, but still many more than television, radio, or native digital news sources (Pew Research, 2019b).

Challenge: Finding a Revenue Model. In 1995, when the first newspaper websites appeared, newspapers offered their content for free, with registration. The hope was that advertising would support the website's operation and provide a new revenue stream for the print edition content. In some cases, free content was limited to the most popular articles and did not include the classified ads, a lucrative newspaper franchise. At that time, print advertising provided over 75% of revenues and subscription revenue generated about 25%.

Charging for general newspaper content was an obvious answer, but publications that tried this during the 1995–2005 period were punished by an Internet culture that expected online content such as music and news to be free. Public willingness to pay for digital content of all kinds has changed greatly for reasons described earlier.

Newspapers (and online magazines as well) have benefited from the changes in public perception. Today, 78% of U.S. newspapers with circulations of over 50,000 have some sort of charge for online access. Of these, 64% use a **metered subscription** model (which provides access to a limited number of articles for free, but requires payment of a

metered subscription provides access to a limited number of articles for free, but requires payment of a subscription fee once that limit is exceeded

subscription fee once that limit is exceeded), 12% provide most content for free, but charge a subscription fee to access premium content, and 3% use a **paywall** (paid subscription service) model (American Press Insitute, 2018; Williams, 2016).

paywall
paid subscription service

Meanwhile, the News Media Alliance, a leading trade industry group of 2,000 news organizations, whose members include the *New York Times*, the *Wall Street Journal*, the *Washington Post*, local newspapers, and major television news organizations, has proposed federal legislation in the United States that would allow newspapers to bargain as a group with Internet distributors, creating, as it were, its own news collective bargaining entity, to negotiate with the Internet duopoly of Google and Facebook. This legislation would require an exemption for the newspaper industry from the Sherman Antitrust Act, which prohibits such industry collaboration. The Alliance argues that Google and Facebook have monopolized the online advertising industry with over a 60% market share, and nearly all new online ad business, strangling the news organizations that produce the content (reporting, editing, headlines, and stories) used or posted on Google and Facebook without compensation. For instance, if you search on Google for a recent story, headlines and article summaries from the major news organizations will appear with links to the story. The news organizations receive no compensation for this link, and while they can show ads once people arrive at their sites, they are not paid for the headlines and summaries that fill Google's pages (Travis, 2018; Chavern, 2017). The outlook for this legislation becoming law is slim, but it is another pressure point on the Internet titans to pay more for use of content from legitimate news sites (Isaac and Ember, 2017; Rutenberg, 2017).

Challenge: Growth of Pure Digital Competitors. The Web has provided an opportunity for newspapers to extend their print brands, but at the same time it has given digital entrepreneurs the opportunity to disaggregate newspaper content by creating specialized websites for popular content such as weather, classified ads (Craigslist), restaurant and product reviews (Yelp), as well as topical national and international news sites and apps that compete with online newspapers. Despite the declining revenues of the traditional print newspaper industry, entrepreneurs have poured money into news sites, and even print newspapers. For instance, Warren Buffett purchased 28 newspapers for an estimated $344 million in a belief that newspapers delivering comprehensive and reliable information to small, tightly bound communities, and that have a reasonable Internet strategy, will be viable for a long time (Berkshire Hathaway, 2013). In 2013, Jeffrey Bezos purchased the iconic *Washington Post* for $250 million in the belief that newspapers are not just papers but news-gathering and distribution businesses independent of any technology or platform (Hagey and Bensinger, 2013). Mexican billionaire Carlos Slim Helú, a Latin American telecommunications tycoon, owns 15% of the *New York Times*. In 2018, Marc Benioff, billionaire co-founder and CEO of Salesforce.com, purchased the iconic 93-year-old *Time Magazine* for $190 million. He was following in the footsteps of Laurene Powell Jobs, Steven Jobs' wife, who in 2017 purchased a majority interest in *The Atlantic Magazine*. These investments by wealthy Big Tech executives are largely made in the belief that independent news and journalism are national treasures to be preserved in the Internet age (Lee, 2018).

TABLE 9.2	NATIVE DIGITAL NEWS SITES
COMPANY	DESCRIPTION
Huffington Post	Founded in 2005, sold to AOL for $350 million in 2011. Aggregates content from traditional news outlets, invited paid bloggers, legions of unpaid bloggers, and original reporting.
BuzzFeed	Founded in 2006. Focus on using social media to generate viral stories, shareable content like quizzes and listicles ("The five most important people"), and photos. Also includes more traditional news topics like politics, business, and technology. Originally a news aggregator but now hires journalists for traditional news reporting.
Vox	Founded in 2014. Covers politics and general news. Hired Ezra Klein (ex-*Washington Post* writer) to be editor-in-chief. Eschews banner ads for sponsored videos and stories.
Reddit	Founded in 2005. Purchased by Condé Nast in 2006 and operated as an independent company. Refers to itself as the front page of the Internet and operates a bulletin board of user-generated posts made up of thousands of forums including science trivia, politics, videogames, humor, and photos, broken up into over a million communities monitored by moderators and referred to as subreddits. Registered community members can submit content, such as text posts or direct links. Mostly male, college-educated members contribute content. Limited advertising on the main pages.
Vice	Founded as a magazine in 1994 and moved on to websites in 2000 as Vice Media. A bulletin board of user-generated articles, aggregated content, and photos. Focuses on irreverent content appealing to young readers and reporting from dangerous locations. Vice's YouTube channel is a video-based news site.

While print newspapers are attracting wealthy individual investors, venture capital investors have poured over over $10 billion into purely digital online news sites. **Table 9.2** describes some leading native digital news sites and their investment profile. Native digital news companies grew rapidly in the period 2014–2017, but their growth has slowed since then. The top ten native digital sites have audiences comparable or exceeding nationally known online newspapers. **Figure 9.10** lists the top native digital news sites in terms of their unique monthly visitors.

Not all digital news services succeed, and few, if any, are profitable so far. Many of the native digital sites in Figure 9.10 have announced reductions in staff. As it turns out, native digital news sites face the same problems as traditional newspapers, namely, few loyal readers, lack of advertising revenues, and competition from Google and Facebook. Even the disruptors are being disrupted (Stack, 2017).

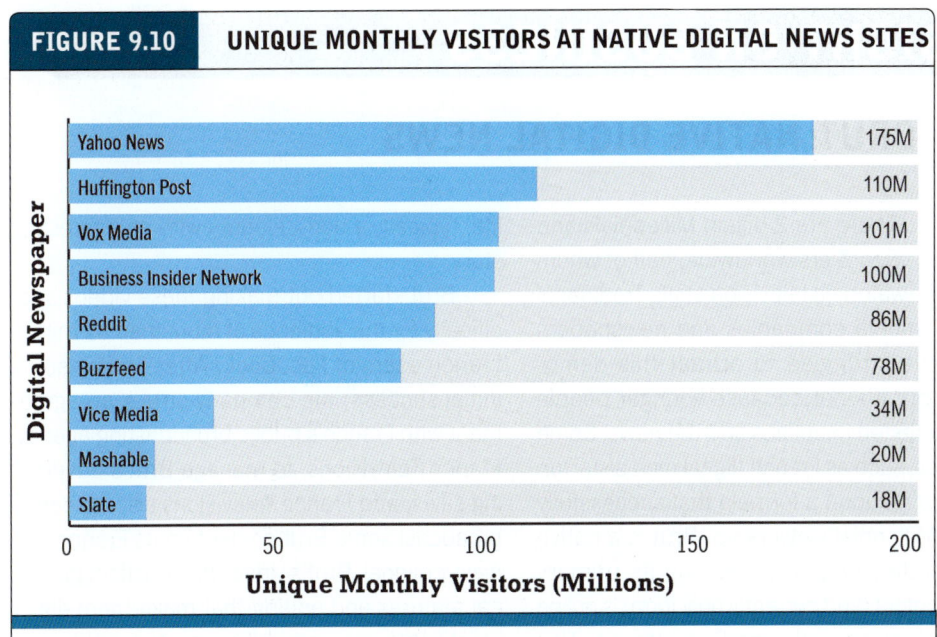

FIGURE 9.10 UNIQUE MONTHLY VISITORS AT NATIVE DIGITAL NEWS SITES

Native digital news sites have greatly expanded their unique visitor count and are direct competitors of established newspapers and their online editions.
Sources: Based on data from comScore, Inc., 2020; industry sources; authors' estimates.

Challenge: Surviving Digital Disruption. The newspaper industry would appear at first glance to be a classic case of a disruptive technology—the Internet, mobile devices, and apps—destroying a traditional business model based on physical products and physical distribution. Incumbents (the existing print newspapers) slowly and incrementally improve their products over time. New firms—disruptors—introduce new products (Huffington Post, BuzzFeed, Vox), which are not as good as the incumbents' products, but are based on newer and more powerful technologies. The new products are less expensive, or free, and target underserved or entirely new markets. They often are founded and promoted by people new to the industry. Eventually the disruptor's products are improved and become more acceptable, or good enough. At this point, the new products and the disruptors start draining significant market share from the incumbents who eventually fail. Incumbents fail for a variety of reasons, from an expensive legacy production process, large human capital investments, a contrary culture, and an inability to perceive rapid changes in the business and technology environment. For a description of a news industry startup that may have a disruptive impact on traditional newspapers, see the *Insight on Business* case, *Brut: Native Digital News*.

Pure digital news sites have many advantages over print newspapers. They don't have the cost of printing papers; they can create new work flows and business processes that are more efficient and timely; they have a lower cost structure, often relying on user generated content and minimal payments to reporters and bloggers, with lower

INSIGHT ON BUSINESS

BRUT: NATIVE DIGITAL NEWS

There are 2 billion Millennials and Gen Z-ers worldwide, half of whom watch no television at all. Traditional media companies and newspapers have struggled to attract this demographic, but it's not because younger people are uninterested in politics and the news. Some companies, such as French digital media startup Brut, have hit upon a formula that successfully attracts Millennial viewership. Brut is a native digital media company, meaning its primary form of content (and currently only form) is online video content via social media platforms. This business model has spurred Brut's growth from a nascent startup in 2017 to a media powerhouse that boasts 300 million monthly viewers worldwide as of 2020.

Brut's founders all have backgrounds in French television, including two former employees of the French version of *Saturday Night Live* and an editorial producer who had worked on the French equivalent of *The Daily Show*, *Le Petit Journal*. They shared a dissatisfaction with the way television news introduces an issue and then moves onto the next topic without in-depth discussion. Brut's goal was to cover trending topics in culture and politics with a different point of view from more traditional mainstream media sources. The company's founders describe its point of view as irreverent and iconoclastic. Brut's videos are intended to not just spark interest and viewership, but spark conversation. At launch, Brut's goal was to create five to six videos per day with a clear focus, including videos with a fresh approach to topics everyone was talking about, videos that make viewers laugh, and videos that take an in-depth view of someone's life, typically a non-celebrity with an interesting story.

Brut started out making these videos specifically for the audience of more than 31 million French users of Facebook. After finding some initial success, the company struck an agreement with France's public broadcasting agency, France Televisions, to manage Brut's advertising sales, and France Televisions also agreed to broadcast some Brut content on its France Info news channel. Brut's videos have distinct graphical features and editing that make them easily identifiable, even amid the crowded video landscape on Facebook. Brut's competitors include Refinery28, NowThis, Business Insider, Mic, Mashable, and other French media companies, in addition to traditional news media outlets.

In just a few short years, Brut has managed to outperform all of these digital competitors. Three-fourths of Brut's audience is between the ages 18 and 34, with a nearly even gender split (just under half are female). This demographic spurred Brut to explosive early growth; the company amassed 80 million video views within six months of the company's launch. The company has become a strong player in markets outside its native France; for example, the company ranked second in total video views on Facebook in the United States in 2019. While Brut is still most active on Facebook, it also redistributes its content on Twitter, YouTube, and Dailymotion, and creates some platform-specific content for Instagram and Snapchat as well.

Brut has had success with Facebook Live video as well. With mistrust in traditional media on the rise, especially among younger viewers, live video offers viewers the exact view that journalists are seeing at the time and is considered more trustworthy and engaging. For example, Brut reporters on the scene for the 2018 Yellow Vest protests in Paris recorded as many as 17 million viewers in a single day. These numbers disprove the idea that young people are uninterested in the news; they are just consuming it differently from prior generations. Brut viewers are also more apt to engage in debate and conversation through comments. The company's founders boast that as much as one-third of Brut content is inspired by careful analysis of viewer comments on prior videos. That responsiveness stands in contrast to traditional media networks as well.

Investors have taken notice of Brut's rapidly growing user base. Brut raised a round of funding worth €10 million in 2018 and raised an additional $40 million in 2019 after it announced it would officially launch in the United States. While Brut was already technically operational in the United States prior to 2019, the announcement indicated that the company would begin hiring sales staff to monetize its U.S. viewership, which grew from 30 million to 110 million monthly views per month in 2018. Advertisers have noticed Brut too; Brut has formed partnerships with Netflix, Airbnb, Ralph Lauren, Nike, and many other premier worldwide brands. Brut carefully monitors its sponsored advertising content for overall quality, knowing that its Millennial user base is amenable to branded content but strongly dislikes anything with the overt feel of advertising.

Brut plans on using this funding to continue its rapid growth. Brut already creates country-specific content for France, America, India, China, Mexico, the UK, Japan, and Spain. It also has ambitions to build out its company's website, which is currently a bare-bones collection of links to all of the company's social media accounts. The company plans to invest heavily in natural language analysis tools to better understand what its viewers want to see based on user comments. To that end, the company has already partnered with social media monitoring company CrowdTangle to develop metrics for identifying potential sources of popular content. Brut has also partnered with Google Cloud to quickly deliver its video content to any part of the world in which it operates, as well as to handle spikes in site traffic resulting from videos going unexpectedly viral. While Brut carefully analyzes user comments to inform its future content decisions, the company's leadership insists that they do not want to be a "data-driven company," providing content they already know viewers will like; instead, Brut hopes to provide engaging, smart content that people had no idea they would like as much as they do.

SOURCES: "Brut: Anticipating Traffic Peaks by Using Google Kubernetes Engine for Platform Automation," Cloud.google.com/customers/brut, accessed February 2020; "Tech Startup Brut Is Betting on Native Social Video for Millennials and Gen Zers with $40M in New Funding; Expands with Launch in the U.S.," Techstartups.com, October 31, 2019 "Brut CEO on the 'Super Polarized' U.S. Media Landscape, Wanting to Be the Netflix of News," by Georg Szalai, Hollywoodreporter.com, October 31, 2019; "Video News Startup Brut Raises $40M, Officially Launches in the U.S.," by Anthony Ha, Techcrunch.com, October 30, 2019; "Millennial, Gen Z-Focused Brut Launches in U.S., Raises $40 Million," by Melynda Fuller, Mediapost.com, October 31, 2019; "Brut and C40 Cities Announce Long-term Partnership to Showcase How Cities Are Building a Future We Can Trust," c40.org, February 20, 2019; "How a Video Team Reached 25 Million People in One Month," by Chris Miles, Facebook.com, January 28, 2019; "BRUT Raises 10 Million Euros in Funding," Myfrenchstartup.com, July 4, 2018; "Brut Is Seeing Phenomenal Growth—They Say It's Because of CrowdTangle," Medium.com/@crowdtangle, April 11, 2018; "Brut Shares How They Went From 0 to 80 Million Monthly Video Views in Just Six Months," Facebook.com/facebookmedia/blog, June 5, 2017; "This French Startup Is Betting on Native Social Video and Is Now Eyeing Expansion to the U.S.," by Ingrid Cobben, Niemanlab.org, April 12, 2017.

or no pension costs; and they can take advantage of newer technologies for producing the news. While the quality of journalism on these pure digital sites is not as good as traditional print newspapers, this situation is changing as the pure digital sites hire talented journalists and editors from print newspapers that are experiencing financial difficulties.

What online news sites often do not have is credibility and trust. For instance, BuzzFeed has been the subject of many lawsuits accusing it of copying content from competing newspapers and sites without attribution, claiming the content as its own. Without trust and quality, native digital news sites can become distractions filled with celebrity photos, click-bait headlines, and virtually no original reporting.

If the newspaper industry has a future, it will be online and multiplatform. The challenge for newspapers is to create value by focusing on differentiated, timely, and exclusive content available nowhere else; to transform its culture of journalism to provide a continuous news stream just as its pure digital competitors; and to make this content available anywhere, anytime, anyplace, on any device. In short, newspapers will have to become Digital First publications, while maintaining their historic quality edge, and meeting the challenge from their pure digital competitors. Major print newspapers are making this transition and growing digital subscriptions, and ad revenues.

MAGAZINES REBOUND ON THE DIGITAL PLATFORM

The Internet and the Web did not have much impact on magazine sales at first, in part because the PC was no match for the high-resolution, large-format pictures found in, say, *Life* or *Time*. However, as screens improved, as video on the Web became common, and the economics of color publishing changed, print magazine circulation began to plummet and advertisers turned their attention to the digital platform on the Web, where readers were increasingly getting their news, general-interest journalism, and photographic accounts of events. Magazine newsstand sales have declined significantly since 2001. News magazines like *Time*, *Newsweek*, and *U.S. News and World Report* have been the hardest hit. In contrast, special-interest, celebrity, fashion, lifestyle, and automobile magazines have remained relatively stable (Sutcliffe, 2016; Castillo, 2016).

Despite the shrinkage of print subscription and newsstand sales in the past few years, the total magazine audience size (print and digital) increased by 25% from 2014 to 2018, due entirely to growth of digital magazines, especially mobile web editions, and the percentage of adults who read digital edition magazines has more than quadrupled since 2011 (Magazine Publishers Association, 2019, 2018a, 2018b, 2017). An estimated 225 million people read print or digital magazines each year. More than one-third of tablet computer owners read magazine content once a week, and there are an estimated 1,200 magazine apps for mobile readers. Total U.S. revenues from subscriptions and newsstand sales of magazines were around $27 billion in 2018, slightly less than they were in 2017 (Statista, 2018). Ad revenues constituted about $15 billion of the total, the rest being subscription and newstand sales (Watson, 2019a, 2019b). The bad news is that magazine digital ad revenues are expected to be flat for the next few years. Digital ad revenue is only making up for some of the decline in print revenue. One possible solution is to begin charging a subscription fee for access to the digital editions, which currently are often free. Magazine publishers (and increasingly newspaper publishers) also rely on aggregators like Apple News+ (built upon the foundation of Texture, an early magazine aggregator app, which Apple acquired in 2018), Zinio, Magzter, and Flipboard who make it possible for customers to find their favorite magazines using a single app. A **magazine/newspaper aggregator** is a website or app that offers users online subscriptions and sales of many digital magazines and magazines. Magazines have been effective users of social media, in part because of their stunning photos and images. In 2019, magazines had 525 million Likes and followers on Facebook alone, with significant traffic on Instagram, Twitter, and Pinterest (MPA, 2019).

To survive, magazines must create a uniquely digital online and mobile version of their print magazine, without at the same time losing their unique brand and quality, and still maintaining a print presence. For instance, *The New Yorker*, founded in 1925, publishes a mix of news, culture, short stories, and the arts written by some of America's finest and best known authors, along with cartoons and movie reviews. Thoroughly grounded in print ink and paper, the magazine underwent a digital remaking following its introduction of a metered paywall in 2014 (Bilton, 2014). *The New Yorker* established a forty-person digital staff to bring its print authors and new full-time journalists to the online audience. The digital edition of *The New Yorker* is in continuous production 24x7, producing upwards of 18 original posts a day, while the print edition continues its deadline-driven 47 annual issues (Mullin, 2017). *The New Yorker* has aggressively pursued an online presence on Facebook (around 4.3 million Likes and followers), Twitter (almost 9 million), and Instagram (4 million), along with other social media sites. *The New Yorker*'s mobile audience has swelled. Contrary to initial expectations, mobile readers are more likely to read and complete long stories on their phones than on their desktops. The digital makeover has worked: *The New Yorker* routinely has around 12 million unique visitors a month, with 34 million video views, growing its print-digital edition to $1.3 million subscribers paying $149 a year. Subscription revenue is now more than 70% of total revenue, and far less fickle than ad revenue. The magazine is hoping to expand digital subscriptions to 2 million in the next five years through unique content and international editions. The future of magazines as with newspapers is tied to digital subscription growth. (Wiedeman, 2019; Moses, 2018; 2017).

magazine/newspaper aggregator

a website or app that provides subscriptions and sales of many digital magazines and newspapers

E-BOOKS AND ONLINE BOOK PUBLISHING

The book publishing industry's experience with the Internet is very different from that of the newspaper and magazine industries. Despite the extraordinarily rapid growth of U.S. e-book sales (25% or more annually in the early years), sales of print books have until recently been steady and book publishing revenues have been fairly stable over the last five years. In 2018, U.S. book sales were flat, bringing in $25.8 billion in revenue, about the same as the previous year. Bright spots were the almost 30% growth in audio books (following a similar 30% increase the previous), and strong growth in non-fiction books across all categories (adult, children's and young adult). E-book sales (including indie e-books) remained stable, with the highest percentage of publisher revenue in adult fiction coming from e-books, with a 28% share of the adult fiction market (AAP, 2019; Anderson, 2019). (see **Figure 9.11**).

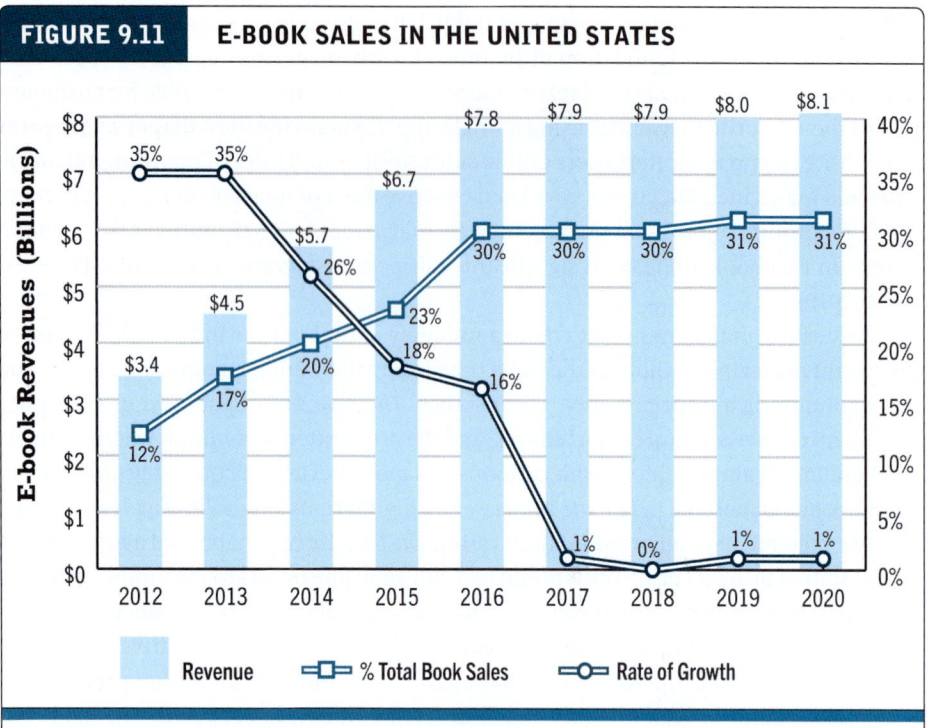

FIGURE 9.11 E-BOOK SALES IN THE UNITED STATES

This figure shows the total revenues and the percentage that e-book sales constitute of total trade book sales revenues in the United States, as well as the change in the growth of revenues. As the graph shows, growth in e-book revenues has slowed significantly since 2013.
Sources: Based on data from AAP, 2019, 2018; Authorearnings.com, 2018; industry sources; authors' estimates.

The first commercially successful e-book was Stephen King's *Riding the Bullet*, a 66-page novella that King made available on Amazon in 2000. At first it was free, and there were 400,000 downloads on the first day, crashing Amazon's servers. When the price was raised to $2.50, demand remained brisk. Ten years later, Amanda Hocking, an unknown writer from Austin, Minnesota, uploaded one of her vampire novels, *My Blood Approves*, to Amazon's self-publishing site, and later to the Barnes & Noble e-book store. Her novels had been rejected by many of the publishing houses in New York. Within a year, she had sold more than 1 million copies of her e-books, which generally sell for 99 cents to $2.99, and earned more than $2 million.

In the space of a decade, e-books have gone from an unusual experiment by a major author, to an everyday experience for millions of Americans, and an exciting new market for authors, changing the process of writing, selling, and distributing books. An entire new channel for self-published authors now exists, a channel not controlled by the major publishing companies and their professional editors. Over 44% of Amazon's top 100 selling e-books are now self-published, selling for less than $2.50, generating around 14% of e-book revenue for Amazon. The Big Five traditional publishers, in contrast, sell 48% of Amazon's e-books although they generate over 40% of Amazon's e-book revenue with prices around $16/per e-book. (Authorearnings, 2018). However, only around 100 indie authors have sold more than 1 million copies of their books, according to Amazon. The vast majority of indie authors are unable to make a living solely from e-book sales.

Accounting for independent e-book sales in the mix of total book sales is difficult because most self-published e-books sold on Amazon do not have ISBNs (International Standard Book Numbers), and, therefore, are not counted by the publishing industry, whose books always have ISBNs. Industry-based reports on e-book sales only include those published with ISBNs. The book distribution market has been greatly changed, and yet it is apparent that the major publishing firms still maintain their positions as the dominant source of book content in terms of revenue. In addition, while bookstore chains like Borders and Waldenbooks have disappeared and Barnes & Noble faces significant challenges, the number of small independent bookstores has grown by almost 50% since 2009. Independent bookstores initially declined from about 4,000 in 2002 to about 1,650 in 2009, largely because of the growth of national bookstore chains like Barnes & Noble, and the growth of Amazon's online book sales. But from 2009 to 2018, about 820 independent stores opened, a 49% increase. Independent stores are still growing at a rapid pace, and many have successfully transformed their legacy business models and technology to compete with Amazon by sponsoring community events, curating and displaying books, and creating a supportive culture for book lovers. In some cases, legacy business models and technologies can adapt to new digital models and technologies (Raffaelli, 2020, 2018, 2017). Since 2015 even Amazon has opened seventeen physical bookstores in major cities, with plans to expand to additional locations.

Amazon and Apple: The New Digital Media Ecosystems

Although precursors of e-books and e-book readers were introduced in the early 2000s, it was not until 2007 that the future of e-books was firmly established. In that year, Amazon introduced the Kindle, which allowed users to download books from the Kindle store using AT&T's cell network. E-books received another boost in 2009 when Barnes & Noble introduced its Nook e-reader, and in 2010 when Apple introduced its first iPad tablet computer. With its large, high-resolution screen, the iPad was an even better e-book reader than the Kindle, albeit not as easily slipped into a purse. Amazon greatly improved its Kindle, and in 2020 its Fire HD 10 tablet with a high resolution 10" color screen sells for $110, while its paper-white Kindle dedicated reader is $129. Apple, in an effort to increase its e-book market share, introduced a new Book app to replace its iBooks app. The new app has a tab for audio books.

Today, Amazon and Apple together account for 92% of the e-book market, with Amazon the leader with a 83% market share and Apple in second at 9% (Barnes & Noble's Nook has experienced declining market share, but still accounts for about 4%) (Gurman, 2018). Amazon's Kindle Store contains millions of e-book titles, while Apple's Books (formerly iBooks) Store has over 2.5 million. The result of the Amazon and Apple ecosystems, combining hardware, software, and online mega stores, was an explosion in online book content, readership, authorship, marketing, and at least a partial upending of the traditional book publishing and marketing channels.

The process of writing and publishing a book has similarly been changed. In the traditional process, authors worked with agents, who sold book manuscripts to editors and publishers, who sold books through bookstores, at prices determined largely by the publishers. Because bookstores had a vested interest in selling books at a profit, there was only limited discounting during clearance sales. In the new publishing model, unknown authors still write books, but then bypass traditional agent and publisher channels and instead self-publish digital books that are sold on Amazon or by Apple. Prices are determined by the author, usually much lower than traditional books depending on the popularity of the author. The digital distributor takes a percentage of the sale (usually 30%). New self-published authors often give away their early works to develop an audience, and then, when an audience appears, charge a small amount for their books, typically 99 cents to $2.99. Marketing occurs by word of mouth on social networks, author blogs, and public readings. Although only a very few self-published authors have thus far struck it rich like Amanda Hocking, the possibility has been enough to arouse the passions of thousands of potential writers of the great American novel, as well as lesser genres from police procedurals to paranormal romance novels.

E-book Business Models

The e-book industry is composed of intermediary retailers (both bricks-and-mortar stores and online merchants), traditional publishers, technology developers, device makers (e-readers), and vanity presses (self-publishing service companies). Together, these players have pursued a wide variety of business models and developed many alliances in an effort to move text onto desktop and increasingly mobile screens.

There are five large publishers that dominate trade book, education, and religious book publishing. These traditional publishers have the largest content libraries for conversion to e-books and they produce over 80% of new book titles in a year. In the e-book marketplace, the large publishers started out using a **wholesale model** of distribution and pricing, in part because this is the same model they used with hard cover books. In this model, the retail store pays a wholesale price for the book and then decides at what price to sell it to the consumer. The retailer sets the price with, of course, some kind of understanding with the publisher that the book will not be given away for free. In the past, the wholesale price was 50% of the retail price. With e-books, publishers discovered that some online retailers like Amazon and Apple began to sell books below their cost in order to encourage customers to purchase their e-book reader devices or to sell them other goods. The real value in e-books for Amazon and Apple is selling digital devices. While the publishers were expecting e-books to sell for $14, Amazon began selling them for $5, reducing the publishers' revenue by at least half. Amazon not only sold millions of Kindles but also sold 90% of all e-book titles on the Web in 2011. Amazon had a de facto monopoly on e-books.

In response, the top five publishers, along with Apple, introduced an **agency model** of distribution in which the distributor is an agent of the publisher, and can be directed to sell e-books at a price determined by the publisher, around $14.99 and higher for certain titles. In return for a 30% commission, Apple agreed to support this model, as did Google, neither of whom were comfortable watching as Amazon dominated one of the hottest areas of web content sales. Amazon's prices rose to this level, and its market share fell to 60%.

wholesale model
prices are determined by retailer

agency model
the retailer is an agent and prices are set by the publisher

The Justice Department was not delighted: it sued the five publishers and Apple for price fixing in violation of antitrust laws. The case was settled and Apple paid a fine of $450 million. The settlement created a public relations storm for Amazon as writers, journalists, politicians, and publishers decried Amazon's use of its market power to sell books that would bankrupt the established publishing industry. Since 2016 Amazon and publishers have reached an informal detente: publishers now set their e-book prices, generally at the same or higher prices as their print editions. Amazon discounts print books but not below their wholesale cost. Today, each publisher (and not an industry consortium) makes an agreement with Amazon about the price of their books (agency model). Today, e-book prices from major publishers are variable, but generally sell for around $15. For instance, in January 2020, John Grisham's novel *The Guardians*, published by Doubleday in October 2019, sells at $14.99 for a Kindle e-book, and $17.97 for a hardcover edition.

Interactive Books: Converging Technologies

The future of e-books may depend in part on changes in the concept and design of a book just as with online newspapers and magazines. The modern e-book is not really very different from the first two-facing page, bound books that began to appear in seventeenth-century Europe and had already appeared in the fourth century BCE in ancient China. The traditional Western book has a very simple, nondigital operating system: text appears left to right, pages are numbered, there is a front and a back cover, and text pages are bound together by stitching or glue. In educational and reference books, there is an alphabetical index in the back of the book that permits direct access to the book's content. While these traditional books will be with us for many years given their portability, ease of use, and flexibility, a parallel new world of interactive e-books is often predicted to emerge in the next five years. Digital interactive books combine audio, video, and photography with text, providing the reader with a multimedia experience thought to be more powerful than simply reading a book. Apple offers iBooks Author, an app to help authors create interactive books. Several start-up firms have attempted to create digital video trade books that combine text with supporting video and photo materials. These efforts have not succeeded for a variety of reasons, and most have morphed into self-publishing platforms for independent authors. Major textbook publishing firms are creating digital products that combine e-text with video, simulations, testing, and course management for faculty. These digital media products are gaining market acceptance, and are less expensive than traditional printed books. Some experts believe that traditional print books will be curiosities by 2025, while other experts predict the future will be a blend of print and digital media products.

9.3 THE ONLINE ENTERTAINMENT INDUSTRY

In this section, we will first take an overall look at the online entertainment industry in general and drill down and look more closely at each of the major sectors: television, movies, music, and games. Together, these entertainment industries generated around

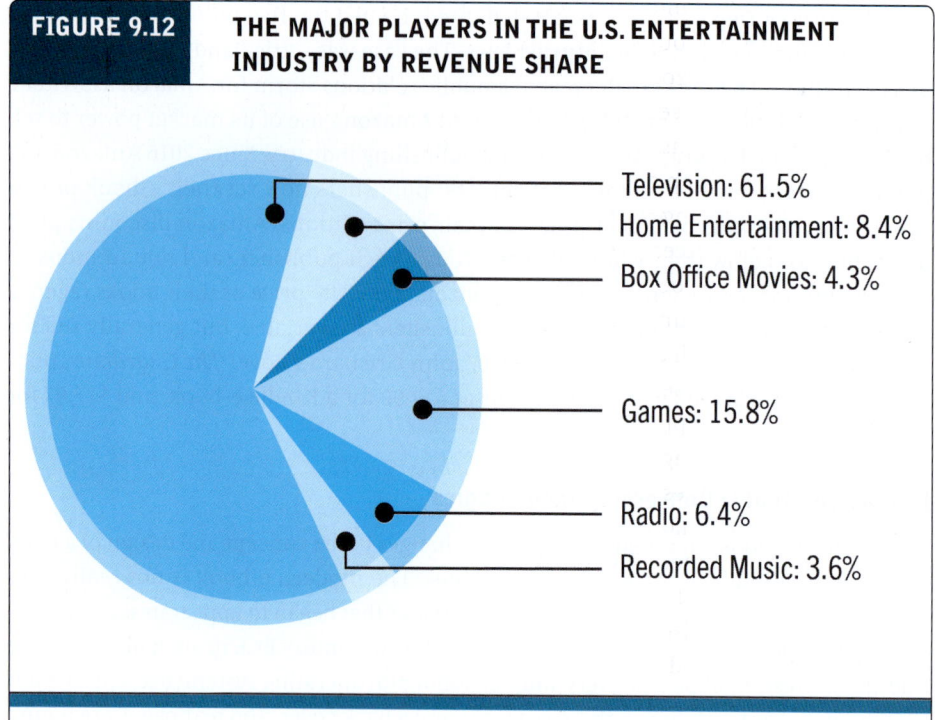

FIGURE 9.12 THE MAJOR PLAYERS IN THE U.S. ENTERTAINMENT INDUSTRY BY REVENUE SHARE

Television: 61.5%
Home Entertainment: 8.4%
Box Office Movies: 4.3%
Games: 15.8%
Radio: 6.4%
Recorded Music: 3.6%

Sources: Based on data from industry sources; authors' estimates.

$275 billion in U.S. revenue in 2018, including both digital and traditional format revenues. In recent years, the lines dividing these various industries have begun to blur, particularly in the area of home entertainment, which involves both television and movies. **Figure 9.12** illustrates the relative sizes of the various entertainment industry sectors. The broadcast, cable, and satellite television industry is, by far, the largest, with about $170 billion in revenues generated by advertising and cable and satellite pay TV fees. Both the television and movie industry share in home entertainment revenues involving the physical and digital a la carte sale or rental of television episodes and feature-length movies, as well as subscription services (about $23 billion). Box office movies generate another $12 billion. The game industry generates about $43 billion from sales of game hardware, software, and online games. The music industry is composed of radio and recorded music, which together generate about $27 billion. Radio remains a strong revenue producer, generating about $17.5 billion, primarily from advertising revenues from FM and AM broadcast technologies. Recorded music generates about $9.8 billion, about half of its size ten years ago, but has been gaining revenue for the last several years as a result of streaming revenues.

Along with the other content industries, the entertainment industry is undergoing a transformation brought about by the Internet, the extraordinary growth of mobile devices, and very large investments by big technology firms in video on demand subscription services and the development of original content. Several forces are at work. Mobile devices, coupled with the easy availability of entertainment content now offered by Apple, Amazon, Netflix, Hulu, and many others, have changed consumer preferences and increased demand for such content, whether in subscription or a la carte pay-per-view forms. Social networks are also spurring the delivery of entertainment content to desktop and mobile devices. Social networks are rapidly adding video and live video-streaming to their services, as well as providing a platform for sharing TV and movie experiences. Facebook executives in 2017 announced that they wanted to become a "video first" social network and in 2018 launched Facebook Watch, a YouTube competitor. Amazon launched Prime Video Channels in 2018 as well. Both are competitors for cable TV as well as YouTube. The iTunes Store and Amazon provide download music services where users pay for tracks and albums. Music subscription services like Pandora, Spotify, and Apple Music have millions of subscribers. Both kinds of services—download and streaming—have demonstrated that millions of consumers are willing to pay reasonable prices for high-quality content, portability, and convenience. The growth in broadband has obviously made possible both wired and wireless delivery of all forms of entertainment over the Internet, potentially displacing cable and broadcast television networks. Closed platforms, like the Kindle, Apple Music, and streaming services, like Netflix, also work to reduce the need for DRM. Streaming music and video are inherently protected because in the past the content has been difficult to download to a computer (similar to cable TV). All of these forces have combined to bring about a transformation in the entertainment industries.

In an ideal world, consumers would be able to watch any movie, listen to any music, watch any TV show, and play any game, when they want, and where they want, using whatever Internet-connected device is convenient. This idealized version of a convergent media world has not yet arrived, but clearly this is the direction of the Internet-enabled entertainment industry, in part because technology will enable this outcome, but also because of the emergence of very large-scal e, integrated technology media companies like Amazon, Google, Apple, and Netflix. Many analysts believe the large entertainment media giants of the future will be technology companies that have moved into the production of content and not content producers becoming Internet titans. This transition is already beginning.

When we think of the producers of entertainment in the offline world, we tend to think about television networks such as CBS, NBC, ABC, Fox, HBO, or Showtime; Hollywood film studios such as MGM, Disney, Paramount, and 21st Century Fox; and music labels such as Sony BMG, Atlantic Records, Columbia Records, and Warner Records. Interestingly, many of these brand names are moving to have significant entertainment presence on the Internet with their own streaming and on-demand services. Although traditional forms of entertainment such as television shows and Hollywood movies are now commonplace online, neither the television nor film industries have built an industry-wide delivery system. Instead, they are building relationships with tech-based Internet distributors like Netflix, Google, Amazon, Facebook, and Apple, all of which have become significant players in media distribution and content similar to cable TV networks. The Internet is the new distribution channel.

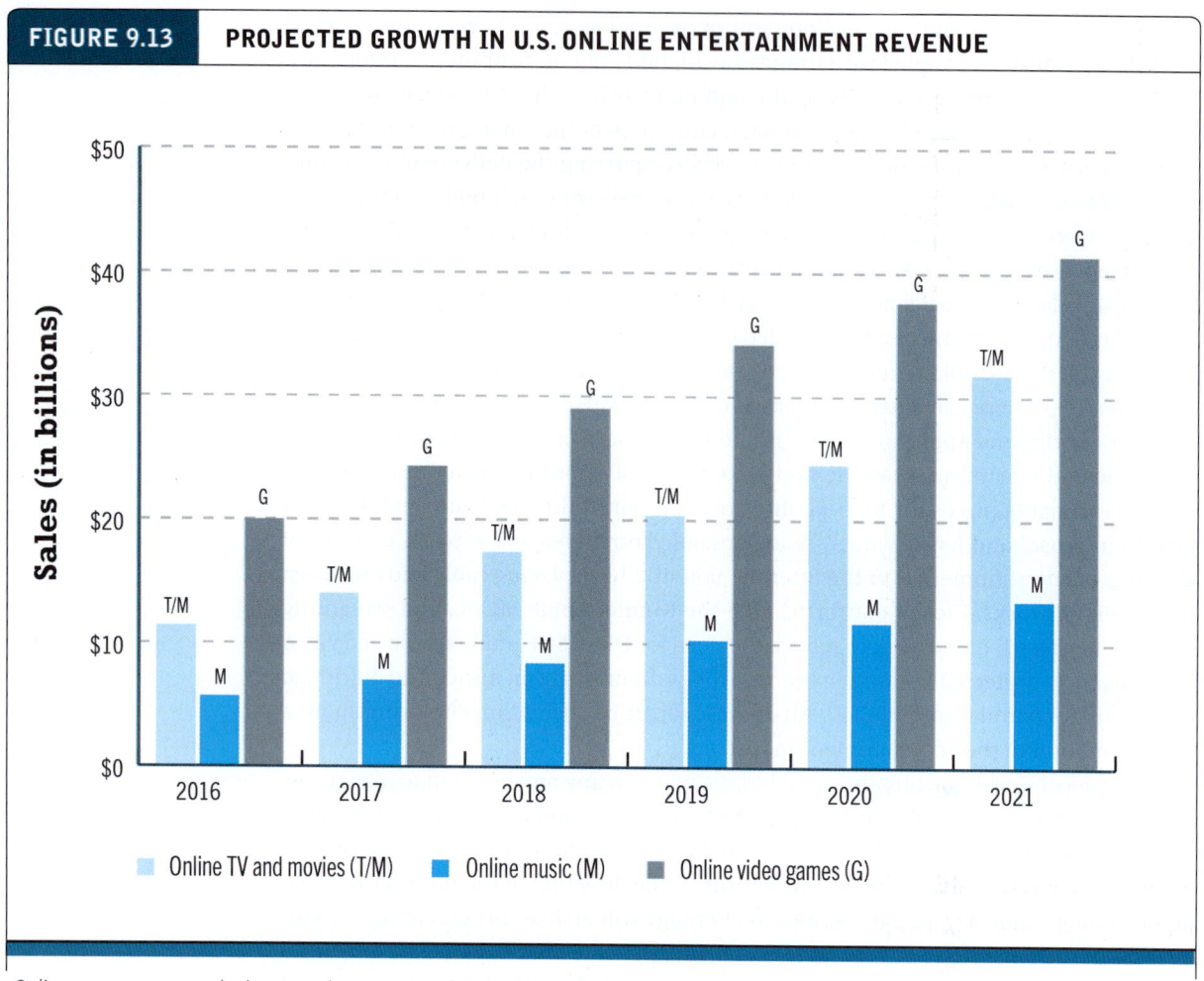

FIGURE 9.13 PROJECTED GROWTH IN U.S. ONLINE ENTERTAINMENT REVENUE

Online games generate the largest online revenues, followed by online TV and movies.
SOURCES: Based on data from industry sources; authors' estimates.

Figure 9.13 shows the growth for U.S. online entertainment revenues from 2016 to 2021 for the major players: online TV and movies, online games, and online music. Revenues from online TV and movies are expected to almost triple between 2016 and 2021. Online game revenues are also expected to grow rapidly, doubling from 2016 to 2021. Online music revenues from all formats, although much smaller on an absolute basis than online television and movie and game revenue, are also expected to more than double during this time period. Overall, the strong growth in online entertainment revenues during this time period, from about $37 billion in 2016 to an estimated $87 billion in 2021—more than doubling over the five-year period—explains why so many firms are focused on the online entertainment market.

TABLE 9.3	DIGITAL MEDIA DEVICES
DEVICE	DESCRIPTION
Apple TV	Provides content from Apple's Apple TV app plus thousands of other channels/apps, including Amazon Prime Video, Netflix, Hulu, HBO, Showtime, etc. Does not provide access to Google Play. Includes touchpad remote control and Siri voice recognition.
Google Chromecast	Streams content from Google Play store as well as from other providers such as Amazon Prime, Netflix, Hulu, HBO, ESPN, YouTube, and thousands of others. Must have account that provides access to these services. Does not provide direct access to Apple TV. Unlike other devices with on-screen interfaces that display channels/apps that can be selected and played via use of a remote controller, with Chromecast you find the content you want on the Chrome browser or mobile device and then "cast" it to TV through the Chromecast player. Lowest cost device.
Amazon Fire TV	Tightly integrated with Amazon Prime, provides access to Amazon's original content and thousands of other content providers, now also including Apple TV. Google Play content can be accessed via YouTube app. Comes in two basic models: set top box (Fire TV) and Fire TV stick.
Roku	Stream content from 2500+ channels/apps, including Netflix, Amazon Prime Video, Apple TV, Google Play, HBO, etc. Must have account that provides access to these services. Various models available, differentiated by performance, features, and price, ranging from set top box to streaming stick.

HOME ENTERTAINMENT: TELEVISION AND MOVIES

The television and movie home entertainment industry in 2019 remained in the midst of a transition to a new delivery platform—the Internet via smartphones and tablet computers, as well as dedicated digital media devices such as Apple TV, Google Chromecast, Amazon Fire TV, and Roku (see **Table 9.3**).

In the past, the dominant way consumers obtained a TV signal was from over-the-air broadcasters, cable TV, and satellite distributors. Today, alternative **"over-the-top" (OTT) services**, which offer consumers access to television shows and full-length feature movies using Internet service rather than cable or satellite TV service, have been developed led by powerful technology companies such as Apple, Google, Amazon, Hulu, Netflix, and others. OTT services include the ability to download content after purchase or rental, as well as subscription streaming and "live" TV services (see **Table 9.4**).

The cable/satellite TV distribution model is being challenged. This transition follows an earlier but related transition to DVRs and time-shifting by consumers, who no longer want to be constrained by television executives' programming and scheduling decisions. The ability to conveniently download television programming and feature-length movies from distributors such as Apple TV and Amazon Prime Video, as well as streaming subscription services provided by Netflix, Amazon, Apple TV, Hulu, and others, provide a powerful alternative to traditional cable/satellite television delivery systems. OTT

over-the-top (OTT) services

offer consumers access to television shows and full-length feature movies using Internet service rather than cable or satellite TV service

TABLE 9.4 MAJOR OVER-THE-TOP (OTT) SERVICES

TYPE OF SERVICE	DESCRIPTION
PURCHASE/RENT AND DOWNLOAD	
Apple TV (formerly Apple iTunes)	Over 100,000 TV shows and movies available for purchase /rent. Purchase options for television shows include single episode, season, season pass, and multi-pass.
Amazon Prime Video	In addition to SVOD service, also offers option to purchase or rent thousands of movies and TV episodes, a la carte or with a season pass.
SUBSCRIPTION VIDEO ON DEMAND (SVOD) SERVICES	
Amazon Prime Video	Thousands of movies and TV episodes, original programming; $8.99/month (free for Amazon Prime subscribers), includes some ads for original content; over 100 premium channels (HBO, Showtime, Starz) also available for additional charge. Not available on Google Chromecast devices.
Netflix	Thousands of movies and TV series along with original programming; $8.99–$15.99/month, no ads.
Hulu	TV series from broadcasting and cable networks; new and classic movies; original programming; $5.99–$11.99/month; $5.99 plan includes some ads.
Apple TV+	Launched in November 2019. Original movies and TV series. $4.99/month. No ads.
BROADCAST/CABLE SVOD SERVICES	
CBS All Access	Live CBS TV channels (news, sports, events) plus over 10,000 episodes of CBS programming on demand; $5.99–$9.99/month; live TV and $5.99 plan have ads.
HBO Now	TV series, movies, documentaries, and other original programming; $14.99/month, no ads.
Showtime Anytime	Live and on-demand access to Showtime programming, $10.99/month, no ads.
Disney+	Launched in November 2019. Movies and TV series, including original content, from Disney-owned brands, such as Pixar, Marvel, Lucasfilm and National Geographic. $6.99/month. No ads.
"LIVE"/ON-DEMAND OTT SERVICES	
Sling TV	Offered by Dish Network (satellite provider). 25–50 live TV channels (from national, regional, and local broadcast and cable networks), $20–$40/month, includes ads.
AT&T TV Now (DirecTV Now)	Offered by AT&T. Over 120 live TV channels, plus over 25,000 on-demand titles and original programming. Additional programming from HBO, etc., available for extra cost, $50–$135/month, includes ads.
Hulu with Live TV	Over 60 channels of live content, including sports, news, current episodes of TV shows, as well as on-demand movies, TV, and original programming, $54.99/month, includes ads.
YouTube TV	Over 70 live TV channels, including regional sports and cable networks; some original programming, also available on-demand, $50/month, includes ads.

services offer unbundled, a la carte access: consumers do not have to purchase a bundle of channels, most of which they never watch. Nor must TV watching be linear. Watching a TV series in linear fashion as it is aired over an entire season is increasingly being supplanted by binge watching, where all available episodes of a series are viewed over a relatively short period of time. OTT distributors like Netflix, Amazon, Hulu, and Apple are gaining market power vis-à-vis TV and movie production firms, and cable/satellite television delivery systems are losing ground.

Although the number of U.S. adults watching pay TV via cable/satellite systems is declining (down by over 4% in 2019, with an estimated 40 million U.S. households reducing or eliminating cable/satellite TV), the big TV screen in the home is still as popular as ever, supported by social networks that buzz with chat about what's on TV right now and Internet-connected smart TVs. In 2019, almost 55% of the U.S. population (over 180 million people) uses an OTT subscription service in addition to or instead of cable/satellite TV, and this percentage is expected to increase to almost 60% (over 195 million people) by 2022 (eMarketer, Inc., 2019g, 2018).

The new platform is changing how, when, and where consumers watch TV. The term "home entertainment" has become somewhat of a misnomer, as viewing has extended far beyond the home. The best screen when commuting or traveling is the smartphone and tablet. Cloud computing has shifted the focus away from ownership of content to access to content anywhere, anytime, from any device as a streaming service. Streaming has replaced downloading as the preferred consumer viewing platform, with subscription streaming services expanding more rapidly than the purchase and downloading of content. Netflix is the market leader in streaming TV and movies, with revenue of $20.15 billion in 2019, up from $11.7 billion in 2017.

The Internet and the mobile platform have also changed the viewing experience. In the past, television was often a social event involving family and friends in the same room watching a single TV show. Today, the social circle has expanded to include friends in different locations, co-viewing shows and texting, commenting, and chatting online while the show unfolds, changing television from a "lean back and enjoy" experience into a "lean forward and engage" experience. The most important activity in today's television household may not be what's on screen, but instead what's being said about what's on screen.

In Hollywood, the transition to a digital delivery platform is well underway, with the industry poised to maintain its revenue stream. As consumers have become fully connected to broadband networks on mobile, desktop, and home TVs, Hollywood has responded with a host of alternative viewing options. As a result, consumer spending on movie entertainment has been stable, with significant growth on digital platforms.

The key to the success of Hollywood studios in the digital era is their control over original, full-length feature production, and control over who will distribute their movies, when, and how. As Big Tech firms pour billions into content creation, Hollywood and New York studios are reaping a windfall in production money. Distributors—whether Internet providers or cable systems—need to meet the terms of Hollywood studios.

Aside from box office theater revenues, the movie industry derives revenue from both physical formats (DVDs) and digital formats like selling movies for download (called

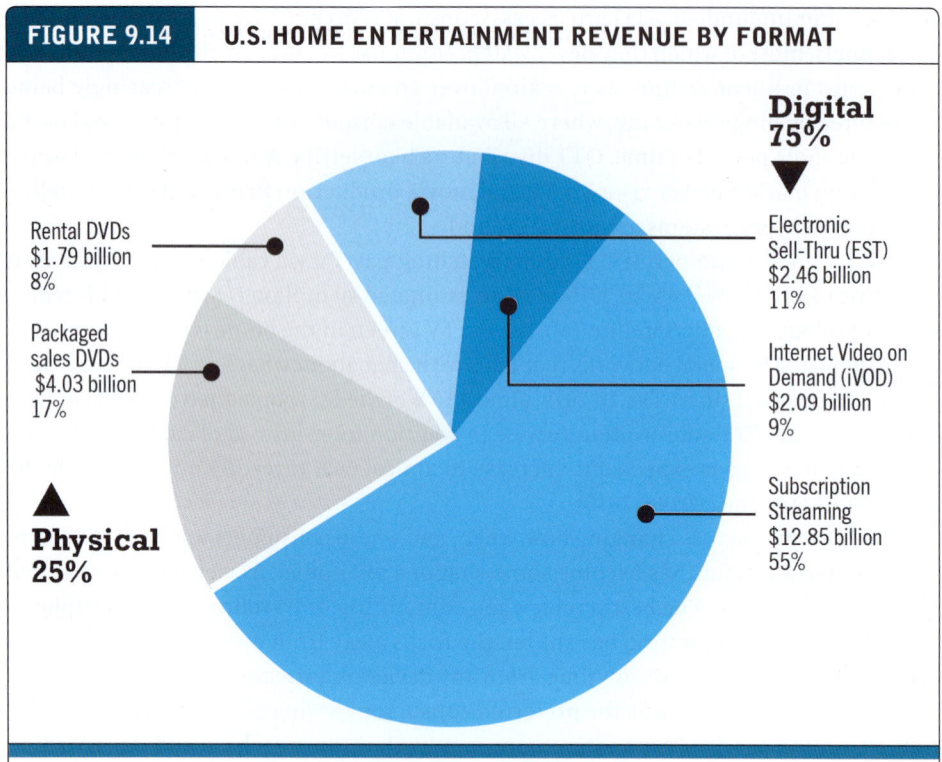

Physical formats (sales and rentals of DVDs) now only constitute 25% of home entertainment revenue, and this percentage is rapidly shrinking. Revenue from digital formats, particularly subscription streaming, is growing at a much higher rate and now accounts for 75% of the home entertainment market.
Source: Based on data from eMarketer, Inc. 2019h.

Electronic Sell-Through (EST)
selling movies online for download and ownership

Internet Video on Demand (iVOD)
selling access to specific movies a la carte on cable TV and over the Internet

Electronic Sell-Through or **EST**), selling access on cable or the Internet to specific movies a la carte (called **Internet Video on Demand (iVOD)**), and subscription streaming over the Internet (see **Figure 9.14**).

Each of these digital formats has a leading player. The EST download leader is Apple's iTunes Store. Consumers purchase and own the downloaded movie. Apple is also the leader in iVOD a la carte rentals, but other major players include Amazon, Hulu, and cable systems, which also rent movies on demand. Netflix is, of course, the leading subscription streaming service, both in terms of the number of subscribers and the time spent using the service. Subscription streaming has grown faster and larger than iVOD, and this is reflected in the market share of Netflix, Amazon, and Hulu (see **Figure 9.15**). New entrants of significant size include Apple TV+, launched in November 2019, and premium cable television networks such as HBO and Showtime. More new competitors are on the way: to compete with Netflix and other tech companies, some major Hollywood studios, such as Disney, have built their own streaming services and cut ties with Netflix and the other major streaming services.

Revenue from sale and rental of DVDs in the United States has been declining since 2006, sometimes at double-digit rates. In 2018, revenue from sales and rentals of DVDs

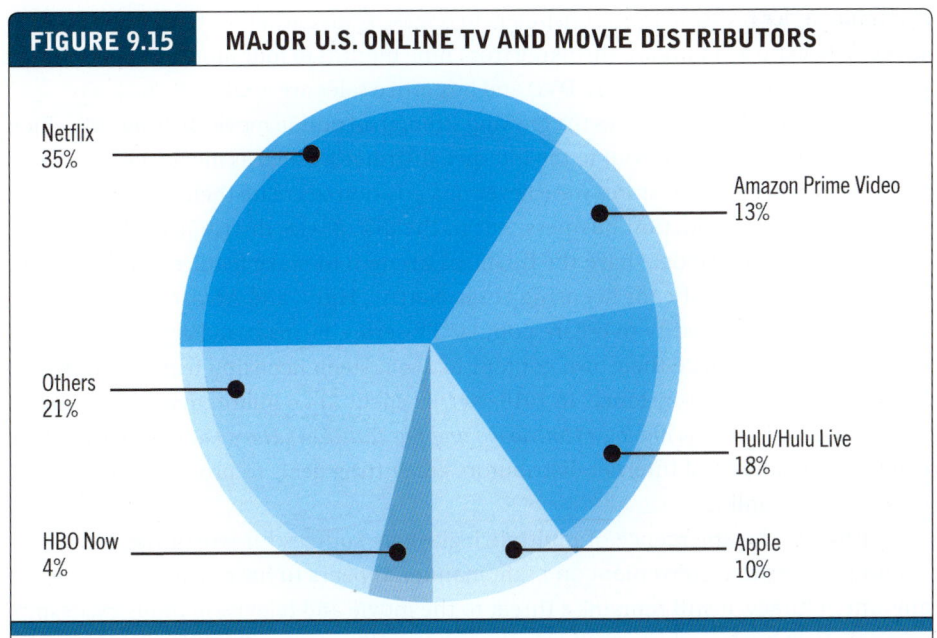

FIGURE 9.15 MAJOR U.S. ONLINE TV AND MOVIE DISTRIBUTORS

Netflix is the leading online television and movie distributor, with its revenues deriving from subscriptions. Amazon Prime garners revenues from subscriptions, EST and iVOD. Apple's revenues currently primarily come from EST and iVOD, although that is likely to change now that Apple's Apple TV+ subscription streaming service has been launched.
Sources: Based on data from eMarketer, 2019i; industry sources, authors' estimates.

was $5.8 billion, down by over 15% compared to 2017. Sales and rentals of physical DVDs are now only 25% of total home movie revenues. The decline in DVD revenues is offset by the stunning growth of digital formats, especially subscription streaming, which grew in 2018 to almost $13 billion, up 30% in a year! Of all the content industries, the movie industry has been best able to maintain its revenue stream and not be digitally destroyed by new technologies, at least for now.

Hollywood faces a number of challenges as it tries to keep up with a rapidly changing distribution platform, increasingly digital, streaming, and even mobile. The fastest growing digital streaming format does not produce much revenue on a per unit basis. Studios make about $4.50 on each DVD, but only $2.00 for each VOD downloaded movie sale, and only 50 cents for each streamed movie. This means the studios are under pressure to keep their new movies in the physical format of DVDs, digital theater display, or video downloads, and use the streaming channel (such as Netflix) for older movies that have already been seen by millions of customers or might not sell at any price without the Internet (i.e., as part of the Long Tail, as discussed in Chapter 6). Hollywood achieves this market segmentation by controlling the **release window** of movies, staggering market release. This is a form of price discrimination: those who really want to see the movie as soon as possible are willing to pay a higher price. The first tier is the theater box office, followed by DVDs, cable video-on-demand, then Internet video-on-demand, and finally subscription streaming services. Of course, the longer the studios hold a first-rate movie off the Internet, the greater the likelihood it will be pirated. The release window is

release window
staging the release of new movies across different distribution channels with different prices

changing under pressure from consumers to release films earlier to streaming and VOD services. Release windows are shrinking from nine months to four months, especially for poorly performing movies where DVD and box office sales are weak.

A second challenge involves the growing strength of online movie distributors, which may become competitors. Prior to the Internet, distributors such as movie theater chains and DVD rental and sales stores were never in a position to create their own movies and enter the movie production business. But in the digital era, distributors like Netflix, Amazon, Hulu, and Google have the financial strength to make feature-length movies, and reduce their significant licensing costs. Netflix, Hulu, and Amazon have already demonstrated their ability to create popular TV series. Firms based on streaming are incentivized to produce their own content to avoid steep licensing fees demanded by Hollywood studios. For instance, in 2019, Netflix spent $14.6 billion to acquire content worldwide. *Insight on Technology: Hollywood and Big Tech: Let's Have Lunch* describes how Hollywood studios and Internet distributors are cutting deals to provide more TV and movie content online.

Although the emergence of multiple legitimate sources for streaming and downloading movies in a convenient and safe manner appears to have reduced the overall amount of piracy, it still remains a threat to the movie and television industry, despite years of effort by the industry and government to reduce piracy. In the past, bit torrents and cyberlockers/file hosting sites (like Megaupload) were the most common methods of piracy, but today, sites that offer streaming of pirated content have become much more popular. For instance, one study found that out of a total of almost 80 billion visits worldwide to 14,000 different film and TV piracy sites, almost 75% were to streaming sites, while only 17% were to bit torrent-based sites where pirated movies are downloaded (Spangler, 2016).

The monetary amount the movie industry loses as a result of piracy is unknown. In the past, the industry estimated that it lost over $30 billion worldwide in 2017 in pirated movies and television shows distributed over the Internet, copied from DVDs, early production copies, and in-theater videoing. Independent analysts doubt the figure is this high, but measurement is very difficult (Bialik, 2003). A Google research paper found that searches for pirated movies have been dropping steadily, while searches for online rentals and streaming are up. As Google has moved into a closer relationship with TV and movie studios, and has its own ambitions to create original content, it has strengthened its efforts to reduce access to pirate sites. Google has changed its search algorithm to push pirated movie sites far down in search results, or removed sites altogether, making it difficult to find movies through its search engine. Insofar as searches are an indicator of consumer interest and intent, the public interest in pirated movies in the United States is declining, although in the rest of the world piracy remains a significant factor. Services like Netflix and iTunes that permit access to streams of movies for a small monthly fee, or download rentals for a few dollars, have arguably reduced the motivation to pirate movies for many potential pirates.

In countries like France, which has passed strong laws to protect artists and discourage illegal downloading (the HADOPI laws), once the laws were implemented, sales of movies on DVDs and legitimate downloading sites increased by 25% in the following twelve months (Danaher et al., 2013).

INSIGHT ON TECHNOLOGY

HOLLYWOOD AND BIG TECH: LET'S HAVE LUNCH

All things considered, 2018 was a mixed year for the movie industry. Box office receipts were $11.9 billion in North America, up from the previous year. However, global box office sales were flat, up only 1% to $41 billion. Sales in China and Asia Pacific grew, offsetting declines in global box office receipts. Admissions in North America were up by 5%, with around 1.3 billion tickets sold, and the average ticket price and number of films released were both relatively stable. Online home entertainment revenues from downloading and streaming continued to increase, to $17.5 billion, an increase of almost 25% from 2017.

So far, the movie business has avoided the kind of disruption that has occurred in the print and music business. People still crowd into theaters to see the latest movies (in 2018, *Black Panther* and *Avengers: Infinity War* both had North American box office revenues of over $675 million), many still rent or purchase DVDs, and many are willing to pay for streamed movies even if they are older than what they can see in the theater. But the traditional Hollywood studios are facing new challenges from the tech industry titans who own the online distribution channels.

The reasons why Hollywood has survived the disruptive potential of the Internet are complex. The Internet has made older movies more valuable simply because they can be inexpensively stored on cloud servers, are easily discovered by consumers, and can be streamed for nearly zero cost, producing a new revenue stream. The revenues lost by the relentless fall in sales of DVDs are being made up by revenues from online streaming services and download sales. Older movies are especially benefitting from streaming.

But all is not totally well in Tinseltown. Once movies are shown in theaters, where Hollywood generates almost 35% of its revenue, they move on to less-profitable venues, from DVDs (which are very profitable) to cable television video-on-demand services, and then to Internet distributors like Netflix, Amazon, Hulu, and Apple for either purchase, rental download, or streaming. Internet streaming services are low on the Hollywood food chain in part because they don't have the revenues to pay for the latest movies. Eventually, movies end up with cable networks and broadcast television stations years after they were released. This "release window" differs for various films based on the studio's estimate of the revenue potential for each film. A very popular film will be delayed all along the release window.

Hollywood is facing several problems moving forward to a world where most people will be watching movies on the Internet, either at home, or on the go, using tablet computers and smartphones. One problem is that the fastest growing segment of its business, the Internet, is also the least profitable. A second problem is that Hollywood does not control its own Internet distribution network, but instead is forced to rely on the likes of Netflix, Apple, Amazon, and Google, all of which attract large online audiences and possess the technology to distribute at scale over the Internet. Likewise, the big Internet distributors face a content problem: they cannot attract large audiences unless they can access recently made movies. Old movies

(continued)

and movie libraries on Netflix have limited appeal; consumers are looking for the latest releases. But Hollywood charges a very high premium for recent movies and demands to retain ownership of movies.

Initially, Hollywood was highly dependent on Amazon's sales of DVDs as rental revenue from physical stores declined. Apple TV (formerly iTunes) and Amazon Prime are the largest downloading services of movies a la carte (so-called electronic sell-through, or EST). But the market dynamics have changed, in large part because of Netflix's success with its streaming video model. Why download to own when you can subscribe to a steady stream of movies and TV shows (where Netflix makes most of its revenues through subscription fees)? Hollywood is in the enviable position of being pursued by Internet distributors who are short of high-quality video content. This is very different from what happened in the music business over the last decade. Multiple buyers of movies have appeared, not just Amazon or Apple. Google has developed its own streaming media device and service (like Apple TV) that is a platform for movie streaming. Hulu is also ramping up its own distribution platform.

Netflix continues to dominate online home entertainment revenues, with a 35% market share. At one time, Apple had a 70% share, and Hollywood studios feared Apple would be able to dominate Internet distribution and dictate prices. Now with Netflix dominating the streaming market, Hollywood fears it will be forced to sell its product for a pittance compared to DVD prices. For this reason, Hollywood restricts the release of movies to Netflix and other streaming services, doling out access to recent movies very carefully. Hollywood would much prefer that fans download movies rather than wait to rent or stream them. To encourage this, Hollywood has created Digital HD and 4K Digital Ultra HD (UHD) that allows fans to download high-definition copies of movies prior to their release on DVD or video-on-demand services. There are different versions of Digital HD. For example, Disney Movies Anywhere allows consumers to pay for recent HD movies stored on a cloud server, and play them anywhere, anytime. Vudu (owned by Walmart but reportedly in talks to be acquired by Comcast subsidiary NBCUniversal) enables downloading of HD movies and digital locker storage for play later. Amazon's Digital Copy service enables the purchase of a digital-only movie, as well as a DVD with digital copy access. In these ways Hollywood can afford to release new movies into digital distribution channels because consumers are willing to pay a premium, or buy the DVD for full price and receive a digital cloud copy for "free." It's called discriminatory pricing: charging some customers more for the same product based on demand.

Digital HD movies are priced so that they produce as much revenue as traditional DVDs. This is the first time Hollywood has changed its release window strategy in order to drive digital download sales. The studios can charge a premium price for new movie digital downloads, making this outlet more valuable than either the DVD channel or the video-on-demand channel offered by cable networks. In some cases, movie producers such as Disney and Sony have opened up their own online stores for selling recent releases directly to consumers. This opens the possibility that Hollywood studios can circumvent Internet distributors entirely.

More and more large firms are entering the premium video downloading and streaming market, competing with one another and driving up prices. For instance, Netflix purchased the exclusive right to stream Disney, Marvel, Pixar, and Lucasfilm titles during the first pay TV window, blocking their release on HBO or

Starz, and keeping them off of Amazon Prime, Hulu, and other streaming services as well. But Amazon and Hulu remain major competitors with Netflix for movies. In 2018 Disney removed its content from Netflix and in November 2019 launched its own streaming service.

Facebook, late to the fast-growing streaming market, reportedly spent $2.5 billion in 2019. Apple announced it was actively shopping for TV and movie talent for its new Apple TV+ streaming service with a $6 billion checkbook. This is still a pittance compared to the $14.6 billion Netflix spent acquiring content in 2019. Meanwhile, Amazon spent a reported $6 billion for content in 2019. And Google is transforming YouTube from a video free-for-all into a streaming service of high-quality content by spending an estimated $900 million on original content in 2019. Several of these tech players are vying to display ads on their new video screens, while others like Amazon, Hulu, Netflix, and Apple TV+ rely on subscriptions.

The competition for original quality content by the tech giants is driving up prices in Hollywood, with soaring demand for acting and directorial talent. There are over 340,000 jobs in the core business of producing, marketing, manufacturing, and distributing movies and TV shows, and this number has been expanding at around 5% annually in the last few years. Average salaries have increased to $90,000, 68% higher than the average pay nationwide.

Future job growth is expected to be nearly twice the 7% growth rate for all jobs in the 2016–2026 period. This is good news for Hollywood and young people in search of a career in TV and movies, but the outcome is not clear. The tech companies have the resources to buy the studios outright. While unlikely, Hollywood studios can develop their own Internet streaming services. As mentioned before, Disney, the largest Hollywood studio, launched its own streaming service in November 2019. Consumers may find that all these competing services balkanize their viewing universe, requiring them to sign up to multiple services to view what they want, and pay subscription fees for each one.

In the end, Hollywood and the Internet need each other, and the only question is how to find the price, define the terms of trade, and cut a deal where both parties come out winners. It's time to have lunch. The flurry of deals bodes well for consumers, and probably for Internet distributors and Hollywood studios as well. Given the shift of eyeballs to online entertainment, Hollywood is expanding its audience, maintaining and even enhancing its prices. With lots of Internet distributors competing, Hollywood gains in power from the competition among alternative distributors. Netflix will not have a stranglehold over the Hollywood studios. How all these calculations and deals will work out remains to be seen. Tune in next year on the same channel.

SOURCES: "Comcast Seeks to Buy Vudu from Walmart," by Rich Smith, Fool.com, February 21, 2020; "U.S. Subscription Video Landscape 2020," by Ross Benes, eMarketer.com, February 20, 2020; "Who Are the Biggest Spenders in Entertainment," by Brandon Katz, Observer.com, January 7, 2020; "How Much Are the Streaming Giants Spending on Content?", by Stephen Lovely, Fool.com, September 8, 2019; "2018 Theme Report," MPPA, March 2019; "Facing Historic Labor Shortages, Companies Snap Up Teenagers," by Jennifer Levitz and Eric Morath, *Wall Street Journal*, April 16, 2018; "So You Want to Be in Pictures: Jobs in Video Production," by Alan Zilberman, Bureau of Labor Statistics, 2018; "Movie Theaters Have a Bigger Problem Than This Summer of Duds," by Erich Schwartzel, *Wall Street Journal*, August 11, 2017; "TV Production Is Soaring in L.A. but That Means More Competition for Soundstages," *Los Angeles Times*, June 6, 2017; "Netflix's Big Exclusivity Deal for Disney's Latest Movies Starts in September," by Chris Welch, Theverge.com, May 23, 2016.

MUSIC

In 1999, the recorded music industry hit a high point with an estimated $14 billion in revenue, but then slid precipitously down through the years to a low of $6.7 billion in 2015. The fall was caused by the decline in CD sales and the growth of much less costly digital downloads (EST), both legal (Apple's iTunes) and illegal (piracy). The situation began to change in 2016 with the explosion in streaming music subscription services. Revenues began to grow for the first time in more than a decade. In 2018, the industry generated about $9.8 billion in U.S. revenues, up 11% from 2017, and marking three consecutive years of growth (RIAA, 2020, 2019). While illegal pirated file sharing and downloads of music were the leading edge of a digital tide that initially deeply disrupted the music industry, first legal digital download and then streaming services have put a damper on illegal music piracy. Legal digital music sources have saved the recorded music industry by generating solid revenues and profits, albeit not as generous as in the heyday of CDs.

In 2018, digital revenues constituted over 85% of all U.S. music revenues (about $8.4 billion) (see **Figure 9.16**). Revenues from physical sources (about $1.15 billion) continued to decline and only accounted for 12% of the industry's revenue. Streaming music sales from ad-supported streaming and subscription streaming sites totaled $7.4 billion, or about 75% of industry revenue, while revenue from digital downloads constituted 11%. Industry revenues are still only about two-thirds of what they were in 1999, but what started as digital destruction is starting to look like a digital resuscitation (RIAA, 2020, 2019).

For most of its history, the music industry depended on a variety of physical media to distribute music—acetate records, vinyl recordings, cassette tapes, and finally CD-ROMs.

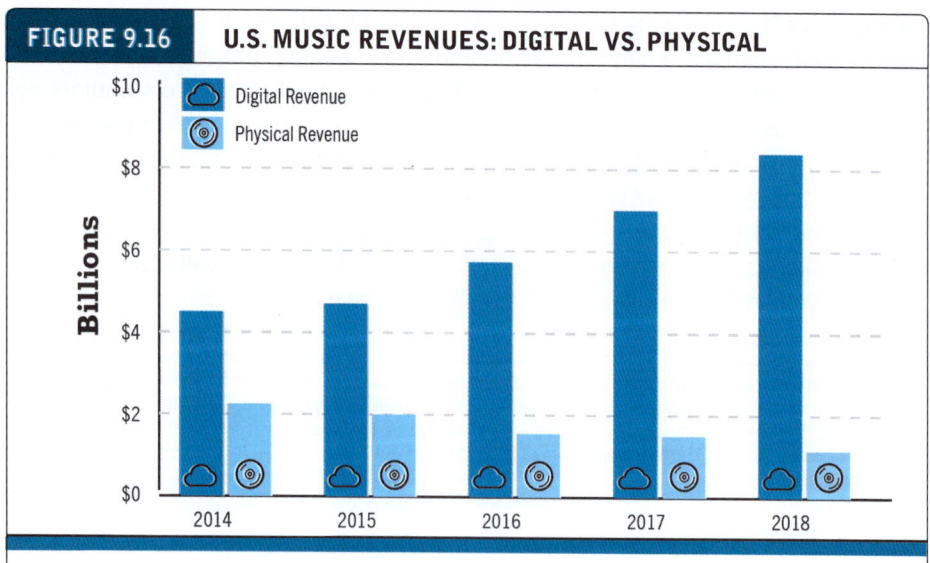

Music industry revenues have fallen by 50% since 2000. Revenues began to grow again in 2016, due to the rise of streaming services. Revenue from digital sources now constitutes over 85% of all U.S. music revenues.

Sources: Based on data from RIAA, 2020, 2019, 2018.

At the core of its revenue was a physical product. Since the 1950s, that physical product was an album—a collection of bundled songs that sold for a much higher price than singles. The Internet changed all that when, in 2000, a music service called Napster begin distributing pirated music tracks over the Internet to consumers using their PCs as record players. Despite the collapse of Napster due to legal challenges, hundreds of other illegal sites showed up, resulting in music industry revenues falling from $14 billion in 1999 to around $7 billion in 2015. The appearance of powerful mobile media players beginning in 2001 that could be connected to the Internet, like Apple's iPod, and later, the iPhone and iPad, and then the stunning growth of music streaming sites, further eroded sales of CD albums. Streaming has fundamentally altered the sale of physical music formats as well as digital downloads, because it is no longer necessary to "own" a physical or digital unit in order for consumers to hear the music they want.

The music industry initially resisted the development of legal digital channels of distribution, but ultimately and reluctantly struck deals with Apple's new iTunes Store in 2003, as well as with several small subscription music services, for online distribution. By the time streaming music services appeared on the scene in 2006, the music industry had dropped its opposition to digital formats, and quickly reached agreements with Pandora, Spotify, and others to stream music on their subscription and "free" ad-supported services in return for fees. At that time, digital downloads of tracks and albums and fees from streaming music services were widely perceived as the savior of the music industry, which was losing sales to piracy and file sharing. Nevertheless, revenues from these sources pale in comparison to revenues that used to be produced by CD albums. **Figure 9.17** shows consumer spending on digital music in three different formats: singles, albums, and streaming music.

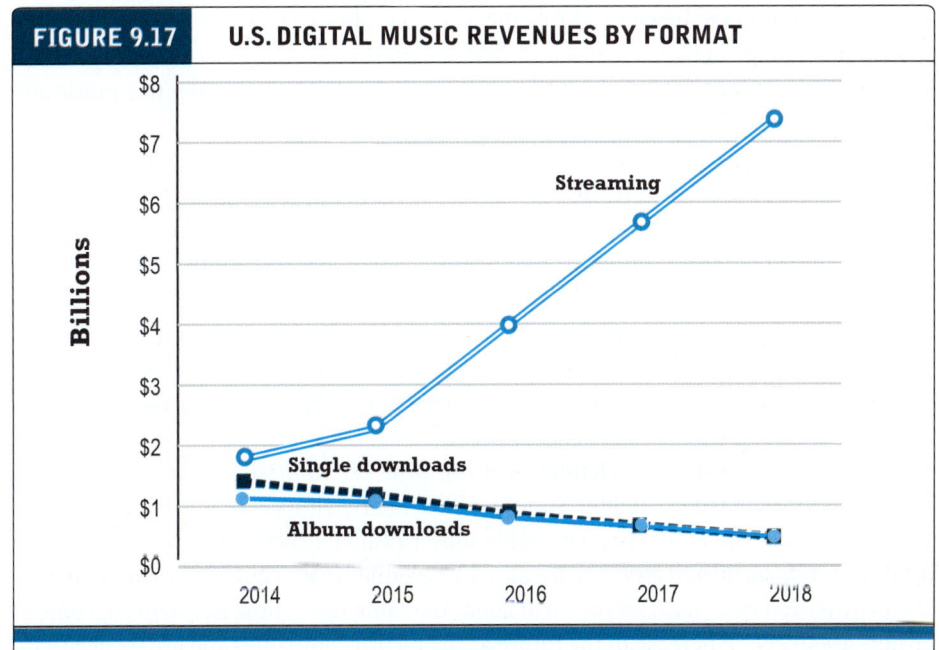

FIGURE 9.17 U.S. DIGITAL MUSIC REVENUES BY FORMAT

Streaming music has grown to be the largest source of digital music revenues, as downloads of singles and albums have declined.
Sources: Based on data from RIAA, 2020, 2019, 2018.

There are two primary kinds of digital music services, each with a different business model: digital download and streaming music services. Digital download services (also known as download to own) are provided by Apple iTunes, Amazon, and Google Play, and enable users to download tracks and albums a la carte and pay a fee for each song. Increasingly, the songs are stored on a cloud server so users can listen to the music from any of several personal devices. All revenue derives from the sale of albums or single tracks. Digital downloads only generated about $1 billion in 2018, declining by over 25% from 2017, and representing only about 11% of the industry's revenue. Digital downloads were eclipsed by the sale of physical units in 2017 for the first time since 2011. Instead, streaming music services is the fastest growing segment.

Streaming music services (sometimes also known as Internet radio) like Pandora now owned by Sirius XM), Spotify, Apple Music, Amazon Music Unlimited, Google Play Music (which merged with YouTube Music in 2019), and Tidal shift the concept of owning music to the ability to access music from any device, anywhere, at any time. Music is typically not stored on user devices but is instead delivered to listeners from cloud servers (although some services also offer download/digital locker service). Pandora offers a curated service that allows users to select an artist they want to listen to, and then the site uses an algorithm to build a list of artists similar to the artist selected by the user. Users do not control what they hear and cannot repeat a selection. Spotify allows users to specify artists and songs.

Streaming music services have two revenue streams: ad-supported and subscription service. Ad-supported streaming is a freemium model that allows users access to free streamed music for a limited number of hours per month and relies on advertising to generate revenue. Streaming music services also typically offer a subscription option, which enables users to listen to ad-free music for a monthly fee. However, typically only a small percentage of listeners pay a subscription fee, and ad revenues typically exceed subscription revenues by a substantial margin. Apple Music does not offer free music and requires a monthly subscription fee of $10 for ad-free streaming.

Worldwide, over 300 million people subscribed to music streaming services in 2019 (Mulligan, 2019). However, while music streaming services are growing listeners at a torrid pace, few have managed to earn a profit because of infrastructure costs, the costs of acquiring music content from the music labels, and freemium revenue models supported by advertising revenues. Streaming services offered by Big Tech companies like Apple, Amazon, and Google can afford to run these services at a loss because they create new customers for their physical devices, operating systems, and other services. As a result, it is unclear if independent streaming music services have a viable business model.

Spotify, discussed in the chapter opening case, exemplifies the difficulties of the music streaming business model. Spotify makes nearly all its revenue from its almost 125 million subscribers who pay a monthly subscription fee. While its revenue increased by almost 30% in 2019 to about €6.8 billion, its payments to record companies, artists, and distribution costs have increased at about the same rate. These payments to content owners are likely to increase in the future as the record companies and artists negotiate better distribution agreements and as a result of the Music Modernization Act passed in 2018, which is further described below. In 2019, although Spotify was able to record an operating profit in the third quarter, it still ended the year with an overall loss. The company claims that its business will eventually scale and become consistently profitable with a larger audience, but this seems to defy business logic. Nevertheless, investors see upside opportunity in Spotify because of its audience of millions of young Millennials, its large research budget, and its petabyte-size database on user behavior. Despite its overall losses over the last three years, its stock price has remained relatively close to its April 2018 IPO price of $165 (Spotify Technology, S.A., 2020).

One of the issues surrounding streaming music is the compensation of artists and music labels for content. While music labels might receive 32 cents for every iTunes track they sell, they receive only .63 of a penny on a streamed version of the same song. This revenue is split with the artists, who receive .32 of a penny. *Rolling Stone* calculated that a very popular song selling 1 million streams would produce revenue of $3,166 for the artist and a similar amount for the music label. For artists, ad-supported streaming pays considerably less than subscription streaming. For this reason, many artists and groups refuse to allow free ad-supported streaming of their music. In 2014, Taylor Swift, one of the world's most popular singers, pulled her music from Spotify's free service because it paid such a low royalty rate. In 2015, she similarly pulled her album *1989* from Apple's newly announced Apple Music service because Apple was planning to not charge for the first three months of the service. Many other singers have withdrawn their performances from free streaming services, and there is a growing movement among musicians toward seeking higher compensation from streaming sites. Streaming services have responded by increasing their payouts to musicians for subscription-based streaming and in 2018, Congress passed the Music Modernization Act (MMA), aimed specifically at these issues. The MMA enables songwriters and artists to receive royalties on older songs recorded before 1972, create a legal process for music professionals to obtain unclaimed royalties due to them (previously these were held onto by the streaming services), and create a licensing database paid for by the streaming services but overseen by music publishers and songwriters that should streamline how songwriters are paid, all of which should help ensure that artists are paid more and have an easier time collecting royalties they are owed (Deahl, 2018).

GAMES

The online game industry is an astounding success story, growing from $6 billion in U.S. revenues in 2012 to over $43 billion in 2018. Smartphones have driven most of this growth in the last five years because they enable games to be played anywhere, anytime, and do not require bulky equipment, consoles, or extended engagement of time (Entertainment Software Association (ESA), 2019). In 2016, augmented reality game developer Niantic released its free augmented reality game, *Pokemon GO*, for Apple iOS and Android phones (see **Figure 9.18**). *Pokemon GO* is a GPS-based application that overlays exotic monsters on the phone's screen. The aim is to locate, capture, and train these characters. Users are rewarded with stardust (virtual currency). The game identifies PokeStops, points of interest or historic locations, where users can pick up Poke Balls used to capture Pokemon, and Pokemon gyms, where users can train their

FIGURE 9.18 POKEMON GO

The augmented reality game *Pokemon GO* took the world by storm.
© Anna Stowe/Alamy Stock Photo.

monsters, capture others, and receive rewards. There are plenty of opportunities to buy virtual tools to speed up the capture of Pokemon (Poke Balls cost $1 in the store but are free at PokeStops), and advertisers can pay to have their streets or businesses become a PokeStop, attracting huge crowds of players and potential customers. In one month *Pokemon GO* became the most popular app download from iTunes and Google Play. In two months, *Pokemon GO* had 200 million players worldwide and generated over $300 million in revenue. Since its release, Pokemon Go has been downloaded over 540 million times worldwide and has generated over $3 billion in revenue (SensorTower, 2019). Although the fascination with Pokemon has faded somewhat, especially among Millennials who have moved on to other games, many adult users have remained active. *Pokemon GO* provides an example of how the online gaming world is changing from its initial focus on console and PC desktop gaming to mobile phone gaming and professional e-sport gaming as a stadium and spectator sport.

There are different types of digital gamers, who often overlap the various categories. PC gamers play games on a desktop or laptop computer. They are often called casual gamers because they play games for a few minutes at a time, stop and start games, and are not intensively involved. Social gamers are those who play games using a web browser or app on a social network like Facebook, often with friends. Mobile gamers play games using their smartphones or tablet computers. Mobile gamers are casual gamers as well, with fleeting involvement. Massively multiplayer online (MMO) gamers use their computers to play with a large number of players around the globe. Console gamers play games online (or offline) using a dedicated console like Xbox, PlayStation, or Wii. Often, console gamers are connected over the Internet to enable group play and conversations.

Console gaming used to be the heart of the digital gaming industry, and still is from a revenue perspective. But this changed rapidly with the introduction of smartphones and tablets, as well as social and casual gaming, which do not require users to purchase an expensive console or packaged software. Smartphones and tablets have ushered in an era of free-to-play and $1.99 game apps and much simpler game scenarios that do not require millions of investment dollars to develop. Over 165 million Internet users play some kind of game online in the United States. In 2019, over 125 million Americans played games on smartphones and over 100 million played on tablets, more than those who played games on game consoles (about 90 million). PC gamers (about 95 million) are more common than console gamers. In reality, gamers often use all of these platforms at different times (see **Figure 9.19**).

In the United States, revenue from digital games (not including hardware) in all formats (mobile, PC based, massive multiplayer, social, and console) in 2018 was estimated

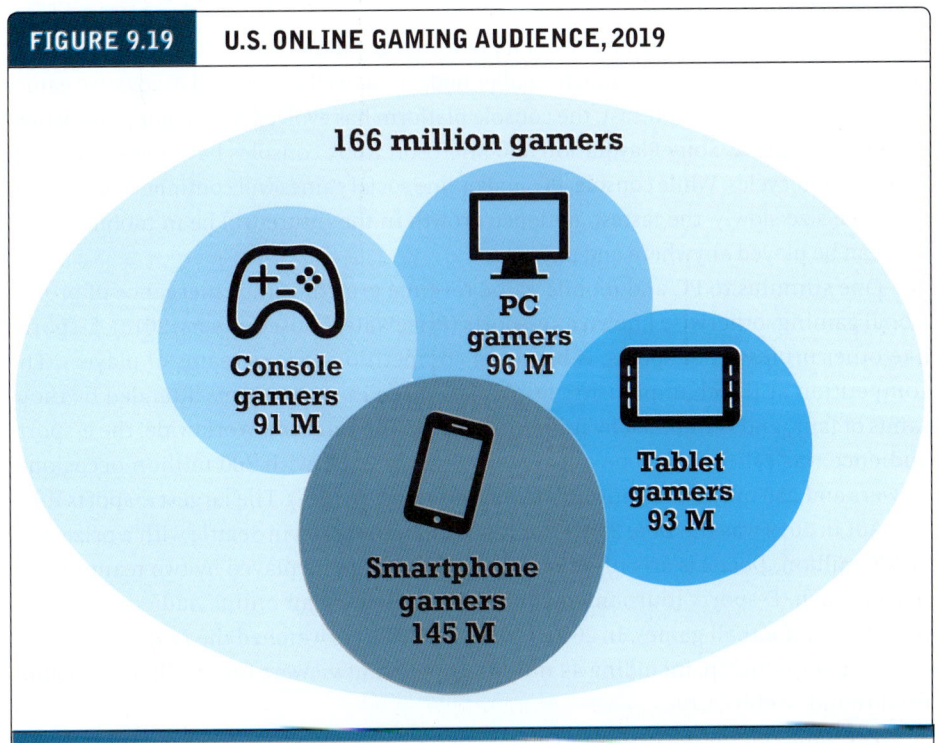

FIGURE 9.19   U.S. ONLINE GAMING AUDIENCE, 2019

166 million gamers

Console gamers 91 M

PC gamers 96 M

Tablet gamers 93 M

Smartphone gamers 145 M

The mobile platform (smartphone and tablets) has become the preferred platform for the majority of gamers.
Sources: Based on data from eMarketer, Inc., 2019d, 2019e, 2019j, 2019k, 2019l.

at $36 billion (not including the sale of hardware) (ESA, 2019). To put this in perspective, the $36 billion game sector is more than three times the size of all digital music revenue in 2018.

While many more people play mobile and desktop games online, about half of online gaming revenue (including hardware) is generated by console gamers, largely through the purchase of physical games on DVDs or online digital downloads of the games. PC and games generate the other half (eMarketer, 2017). In terms of the future, online game revenues are expected to continue to grow through 2021, reaching over $40 billion.

The rapid growth in the number of people playing mobile games based on tablets and smartphones is a sea change for the gaming industry that was previously dominated by closed-platform console games and hardware firms like Microsoft, Nintendo, and Sony, and software firms like Activision and Electronic Arts. The growth of smartphones, tablets, and mobile games has catapulted Apple's App Store and the Google Play store into the leading merchants of digital games, which, of course, use Apple and Google Android hardware and software. Apple and Google take 30% of game sales and also benefit from the sales of the hardware and software needed to play the games. Mobile games appeal to a younger demographic, offer lower prices, and initially are often free. You can play mobile games anywhere you can use a phone, which is nearly everywhere. Console games take much longer to develop, have very large budgets, and are expensive to purchase.

The mobile platform is a more open platform that allows thousands of developers to create entertaining games on much smaller budgets, as well as new and innovative games on a faster schedule. In contrast, the console platform has evolved much more slowly than mobile computing. Sony PlayStation and Microsoft Xbox consoles have five- to six-year development cycles. While console, PC, and online social games will continue to grow their audience size slowly, the fastest audience growth in the future will be in mobile games that can be played anywhere and anytime.

One stimulus to PC and mobile game revenue growth is the emergence of professional gaming, otherwise known as e-sports (PriceWaterhouseCoopers, 2018). E-sports, like other professional sports, is based on competition among teams of players. The competition at the championship level takes place in auditoriums attended by thousands of fans, and is watched by millions more on the Internet. Worldwide, the e-sports audience was estimated to be over 550 million in 2019, with 300 million occasional viewers and 250 million enthusiasts (eMarketer, Inc, 2019m). The largest e-sports tournament in 2019 was the *Dota 2* International Championship in Seattle with a prize pool of $30 million. *Dota 2* is an online multiplayer battle game played by two teams of five players each. E-sports tournaments now routinely draw an online audience equal to professional football games. In 2019, 100 million viewers watched the *League of Legends* World championship, including 44 million concurrent viewers for the championship's final round (Webb, 2019).

The games are broadcast over cable television channels, but more commonly over Internet channels like Twitch.tv. Twitch was purchased by Amazon in 2015 for $1.1 billion. Twitch.tv draws peak-time audiences of over 2 million viewers, as many as MTV, TruTV, and MSNBC, to name a few cable networks. Other broadcasters include YouTube and Dailymotion (PriceWaterhouseCoopers, 2018).

The organization of the tournaments, and the prize money for the players, is provided by the games' publishers and advertisers. The leading publisher of PC games played at professional levels is Riot Games, publisher of *League of Legends* (LoL), a multiplayer online battle game. There are twenty *League of Legends* professional teams that compete with one another. The league requires teams to hire professional video game coaches. Other multiplayer games suited to arena play include *StarCraft II* and *Call of Duty*. These games are all multiplayer online battle arena games (MOBA).

Advertisers are attracted to e-sports because the audience is predominantly composed of young males between the ages of 21 and 34, who are difficult to reach using traditional media. Coca-Cola, Nissan, Ford, and Google are among the largest sponsors of e-sports. College teams have sprung up across the country, including Harvard and Princeton, and many colleges now offer scholarships for students to play on the school's video game team. NBA basketball teams are building complexes to support both regular games and e-sport teams. At current rates of growth, e-sports will approach Hollywood in terms of global revenues, and eclipse console game revenue by 2021, transforming online gaming into a popular sport similar to fantasy football but with a much larger audience.

9.4 CAREERS IN E-COMMERCE

A wide array of jobs is available in the set of related, yet diverse, industries that comprise online content and media. Jobs may involve the creation of content and/or the production of content, with the type of content ranging from newspapers to magazines to books, to television, movies, videos, music, and games, all in a variety of different forms and formats. In addition to e-commerce and other digital technology courses, coursework in communications, journalism, English and humanities, as well as courses in the creative fields, all provide relevant background for careers in online content and media. In addition to creative ability and skills, technical skills in digital media production, as well as business skills in product management, program management will also prove useful.

THE COMPANY

The company is a publishing and digital media company that started out as a single newspaper. The firm began using the Web to support its content distribution in 2006. Today, the company's operations include four daily newspapers, more than a dozen non-daily publications, and more than 100 digital sites that focus on niche audiences in sports, news, and finance.

POSITION: DIGITAL AUDIENCE DEVELOPMENT SPECIALIST

You will be working in the Media Division to develop and launch several new websites that focus on regional cuisines, entertainment, products, and life styles. The digital content of these sites includes articles, photos, video, and audio. Content will be distributed on the websites, as well as via e-mail and social networks. The main objective is to build an audience and create an engaged community of followers. Your responsibilities will include:

- Managing distribution of content across Web, social, and mobile platforms.
- Working with team members to develop a strategy that grows audience size.
- Developing experiments to test alternative media effectiveness.
- Extracting and analyzing data from a number of tools to develop an understanding of the relationship between strategy and performance.
- Developing recommendations to help drive content and audience.
- Developing new digital content and ideas that will drive audience growth.
- Rewriting, repackaging, and optimizing content from other company sites.
- Identifying new audiences and content expansion opportunities.
- Measuring performance to achieve revenue targets.
- Producing short and long-form video, photo, and text content.

QUALIFICATIONS/SKILLS

- Bachelor's degree in journalism, communications, marketing, public relations, advertising, e-commerce, social media, or a related media field
- Experience using the major social networks (Facebook, Twitter, Instagram, and Pinterest), as well as familiarity with alternative social media platforms such as Snapchat and Reddit
- Knowledge of digital journalism, video, and photo content
- Demonstrated ability to collaborate with individuals and groups
- Experience creating content for a website
- Informed on the latest digital and industry trends
- Video production skills and experience
- Understanding of the audience behavior of each major social platform
- Familiarity with project management tools

PREPARING FOR THE INTERVIEW

Begin by doing background research on the firm's services, markets, and business strategy. What makes this firm unique, who are its competitors, and what is its position in the marketplace? Then review Section 9.2 on the online publishing industry, especially the material on the emergence of native digital news and content sites. Also review the *Insight on Society* case on Millennials, and the *Insight on Business* case on Vox. All of this material will help make you conversant about trends in digital publishing industry. Also make sure you understand what a position involving digital audience development involves. You should also familiarize yourself with the capabilities of Google Analytics and research Moz (SEO training and tools), CrowdTangle (web publishing content management and social media monitoring), and Skyword (content marketing software and services). Finally, be prepared to talk about how you use social networks, and your experiences creating content for websites or blogs, including photo and video production.

POSSIBLE FIRST INTERVIEW QUESTIONS

1. Tell us about some of the industry trends that you think will have an impact on our digital publishing business within the next few years.

To answer this question, you can draw on the material in Section 9.2. First you might suggest that digital publishing and print publishing are merging into a single business model producing news articles and features like videos and rich media continuously 24x7. The major industry trends are the decline of print advertising, the rapid growth of digital advertising, the growth of social media as one of the major sources of readers, the movement of the audience to mobile devices, the need to refocus the publishing team so that it works in both digital and print media, and the growth of a digital first business model. The key to survival is for newspapers to have a large audience that is growing online and quality content that draws readers to the paper's sites and for which readers are willing to pay.

2. What can we do to attract Millennials to our content?

You want to point out that Millennials are both different and similar to older adults. Millennials have grown up in a technology-rich digital environment and use technology to consume content in different ways than members of older demographics. They are attracted to social media, to video content, lifestyle content, interactive products online, and are more likely to consume content on mobile devices. Millennials like to share content with friends on social networks. That said, Millennials read as much or more news articles and books as their parents and are typically more educated. The firm would do well to develop content for both print and digital distribution, and in the online editions, increase the use of videos, rich media, and interactive content that can be easily accessed.

3. How can we use social media to get users to engage with our content?

You can start by noting that the firm needs to place a major emphasis on reaching the connected social network audience on Facebook, Twitter, Tumblr, and subject niche social sites that focus on specific areas of life, from sports, to crafts, to television shows where engagement is very high. You can point out that social media is nearly equal to news organizations as a source of online news (see Figure 9.9). The firm should also be making use of the marketing tools available on social sites like newsfeeds, promoted posts, videos, and very precise marketing to targeted groups. Think about the features you particularly like on social sites as one way to demonstrate your social media interests and activities that the firm might learn from.

4. What can we learn from the experience of Vox Media?

You can answer this question by talking about the many new "native" digital publishers like Buzzfeed, Huffington Post, and of course, Vox. Collectively these sites garner well over 100 million monthly visitors, nearly as many as traditional online newspapers. You should have researched these sites prior to the interview, and based on your research, talk about what makes the content and presentation of these sites different from traditional online and offline newspapers. Native digital publishers have some unique ways of presenting news and articles: there are more short stories, catchy headlines, user-generated content, videos, and photos. You should also point out that many, if not all, of these native digital sites have had difficulty securing high-quality content, paying for staff, and generating enough advertising revenue to be self-sustaining.

5. What tools would you suggest we use to enhance the effectiveness of our content?

To answer this question, you can draw on research on various tools that you should have done prior to the interview. For instance, CrowdTangle is a tool that publishers can use to track how their content spreads around the Web. Skywood is a content marketing software and services tool that provides access to a community of thousands of creative freelancers. Moz is a content marketing tool, focused on search engine optimization.

9.5 CASE STUDY

Netflix:
How Does This Movie End?

The Emmys are the television industry's annual awards, the equivalent of the movie industry's Academy Awards. The Emmys provide insight into who's winning and losing in TV land and who will likely be around for the next few years. Netflix is the come-from-behind kid that started as a DVD rental company, and beginning in 2014, began to move into the ranks of original award-winning TV shows. In 2018, Netflix garnered 112 Emmy nominations, beating its content rival HBO's 108 nominations, the first time in 17 years that HBO was not first. HBO has been king of the hill in award-winning TV shows, known best for *The Sopranos* and *Sex and the City*, while Netflix is best known for *House of Cards* and *Orange Is the New Black*. In the final awards contest, HBO and Netflix tied, with each winning 23 Emmys. HBO won Best Drama with *Game of Thrones*, and Netflix won five Emmys for *The Crown*, including best historical drama. Amazon won for the first time with *The Marvelous Mrs. Maisel* for Best Comedy. In 2019, Netflix received 117 nominations and racked up 27 wins.

Netflix is quickly becoming the non-cable alternative to cable TV. By producing its own content, Netflix is able to differentiate itself from cable TV shows and attract subscribers looking for new shows, not retreads from the cable networks. However, original productions are much more expensive to produce than licensing existing content. And there are plenty of other streaming services with very large budgets, among them Amazon, Google, Apple, Facebook, and Hulu, not to mention AT&T (which purchased 21st Century

© Digitallife/Alamy Stock Photo

Fox's movie library and production facilities) and Verizon (which purchased AOL and Yahoo), both of which have TV content ambitions.

While Netflix does not release the number of viewers for any of its original series, executives credit these shows with driving Netflix to a record 167 million worldwide subscribers in 2019 (with about 61 million in the United States, accounting for about 36% of its subscribers). In 2019, Netflix operated in all foreign markets except China. Its subscriber growth rate in the United States has slowed considerably in the last few years because its market penetration is so high. Netflix's shares have increased from $15 since it first went public in 2002 to over $380 in early 2020. Netflix is still perceived as an extraordinary growth company with significant upside potential. Revenues in 2019 were $20.15 billion, up 28% from 2018, and profits were almost $1.9 billion.

Founded by two Silicon Valley entrepreneurs, Marc Randolph and Reed Hastings, in 1997, Netflix got its start as a mail order company renting DVDs of older Hollywood movie titles, delivering them to customers by postal mail. In 2000, it switched to a subscription model where customers could receive DVDs on a regular basis for a monthly fee. By 2006, it had delivered its billionth DVD and became the largest subscription provider of DVDs. In 2007, Netflix began a video-on-demand streaming service of movies although it still retains a DVD subscription business. In 2019, Netflix was the largest player in the subscription streaming market.

Netflix is one of those Silicon Valley stories that might make a good movie, or even a television series, because of its potential for disrupting the American television (or what's called premium video) market. It's a dream-come-true story of accomplishment, pluck, innovation, and Internet technology. In a few short years Netflix created the largest DVD rental business in the country, then created the largest streaming video service. Today Netflix accounts for 35% of digital TV streaming subscribers. Netflix has created the largest database on consumer video preferences and built a recommendation system that encourages consumers to see more movies. Netflix is as much a technology company as a content company: it has developed its own proprietary video encoding system and distributes its video using over 1,000 servers in the United States located close to its customers to ensure high speed and quality delivery. Netflix discovered that older TV series had strong niche followings and built a new model of "binge watching," where consumers could watch all the episodes of a series in several sittings. Netflix has entered the content creation business by developing original TV series. For this reason, Netflix is an example of convergence in the media industry, where an Internet company becomes a media content producer. Other pure media companies have taken notice and begun to develop their own streaming services, but what they lack is a database of viewer preferences that Netflix has developed over a twenty-year period and which helps Netflix make recommendations to subscribers. For this they will have to be in the market for several years, giving Netflix an advantage now.

In the movie and TV business, there are only two ways to make money: either own the content or own the pipes that deliver the content. It is even better if you can do both. Netflix has become recognized as an important pipeline to a very large audience. For instance, Netflix has struck deals with some Hollywood movie producers to become the exclusive subscription TV home studio for their content. This puts Netflix into the same league as premium channel distributors and in direct competition with other cable networks like HBO, Starz, Showtime, and A&E for the rights to show movies about eight months after their theater run is complete.

In one possible ending scenario for the Netflix movie, the company challenges the much larger cable television industry, which is based on an entirely different technology and business model, namely, selling expensive bundles of hundreds of TV channels that few people watch, then raising monthly fees faster than the rate of inflation. In 2018 for the first time the number of people using OTT streaming services exceeded those using cable TV streaming services. Given Netflix's large national audience of streamers, in this scenario, the company will find it relatively easy to make new "friends" in Hollywood and New York who are looking for ways to distribute their shows to a new online, mobile, and social world, and Hollywood will stretch the distribution window so that Internet distributors like Netflix get the same treatment as cable systems by allowing them to show the latest movies and shows at about the same time as cable systems. And the cable television industry will be forced to retreat from its bundling practices and offer customers the ability to select just those channels they actually watch. As a result, cable industry revenues would plunge while Netflix's would increase. This would be a dream scenario with a happy ending for Netflix! But happy endings happen mostly in Hollywood.

The outcome of this movie depends on how well Netflix can deal with some considerable challenges. For instance, one source of Netflix's poor profitability is that the costs of content are very high, both purchased older series as well as new content, which is far more risky. The owners of older cable TV series and Hollywood movies charge Netflix for the privilege of distributing their content as much as they do established cable TV networks. Netflix has streaming content obligations to content producers of $18 billion in the next five years. Netflix barely makes any profit on the content it must purchase. Netflix is, after all, mostly a database and delivery platform, and the company is in a constant bidding war with both cable and Internet giants all looking for the same thing—popular TV series with a built-in or potential audience. But content owners have wised up to the value of their backlist TV series and have raised their prices accordingly. Series just a year old are very expensive or not available. Netflix is paying hundreds of millions to license hit shows and movies. As a result of content owners charging more for older cable shows, Netflix has taken the more risky option of developing its own original series. But this is very expensive as well. The critically acclaimed *House of Cards* cost Netflix $100 million for 26 episodes, $4 million an episode. Newer shows like *The Crown* cost an estimated $130 million for the first two seasons, and will run about $1 billion for seven seasons. In 2019 Netflix spent over $14 billion on content alone. Content is very costly and is becoming more so as new entrants compete for the same talent. It's possible that Netflix does not scale, and that the more subscribers it has and the more it attracts them with expensive content, the less profit it will make because the cost of doing business will rise as fast or faster than revenue. This portends low profit margins for an extended period.

A second challenge Netflix faces is the risk of creating new original content. It's not as if wealthy Silicon Valley entrepreneurs can fly to Hollywood or New York with lots of cash and simply purchase new content. As one pundit noted, this might lead to a mugging, but not a successful TV series or movie. Silicon Valley is generally not the place to go if you're looking for storytellers, writers, producers, directors, talent agents, and cinematographers. Algorithms don't come up with new ideas for novels, plays, movies, or TV series, and they have not proven to be good at guessing what series will succeed in the future. Older series are proven series, and Netflix can identify which of its customers watched the series in previous years, and estimate the audience size, and whether new subscribers will be attracted by the replays. But when it comes to new TV series, Netflix has tried to use its algorithms to predict what new series its customers might be interested in with mixed results. Netflix has produced some real winners according to critics, but it has also produced some losers that did not get critical acclaim, like *Lillyhammer*, *Hemlock Grove*, *Bad Samaritans*, *Richie Rich*, and *Mitt*. The only technology company previously that has been successful with content production for movies or television is Pixar, which pioneered computer-generated animated feature-length movies. It is impossible to know how well Netflix's original content is performing because the company refuses to release this data. Nielsen has begun a rating service for Netflix shows. This service is paid for by the content producers, who will base their charges in part on how many Netflix subscribers stream their shows. This information is not public.

While Netflix stands out as a powerful Internet brand today, Netflix has many powerful competitors. Netflix does not have unique technology. In fact, streaming technology is widespread. The success of Netflix's streaming model has attracted Amazon, Disney, Apple, Google, and content producers like Hulu and HBO to the fray. In 2017 Disney announced it was starting its own streaming service and removing its content from Netflix. Verizon is planning a free, ad-supported mobile streaming service aimed at smartphone TV viewers. Some of these firms are tech firms with very large Internet audiences, strong brand names, and a good understanding of what their millions of online customers want.

Apple is the leader in downloaded movies where customers purchase or rent movies, and of course, it owns iTunes (now rebranded as Apple TV), the world's largest online media store for the purchase of music, videos, and TV series. HBO, founded in 1972, is the oldest and most successful pay television service in the United States, and the originator of a long list of highly successful original TV series and movies such as *Sex and the City*, *The Sopranos*, *The Wire*, *Game of Thrones*, and *True Blood*. If Netflix has a direct competitor on the creative front, it is HBO, a more traditional programmer that does not use computer algorithms to design its content, but instead relies on the hunches and gifts of producers and directors to produce its content.

Netflix's competitors have very deep pockets. This means Netflix also has competitors for talent and the production of new content, and perhaps price pressure as well. Along with Hulu, Amazon has emerged as the biggest competitor to Netflix's streaming services. For instance, Amazon offers free streaming to its 124 million U.S. Amazon Prime customers, and has taken on HBO TV series to stream to Prime customers without additional fees. Amazon has also moved into original series production with *The Man in the High Castle*, *Transparent*, *Mozart in the Jungle*, *The Marvelous Mrs. Maisel*, *Fleabag*, and many others, also winning many Emmy awards. Apple and Amazon have far larger databases of subscribers

SOURCES: "Netflix Form 10-K for the fiscal year ended December 31, 2019," filed with the Securities and Exchange Commission, January 29, 2020; "5 Metrics from Netflix's Record Year," by Demitrios Kalogeropoulos, Nasdaq.com, January 26, 2020; "Emmy Nominations 2019: HBO Ascendant," by Sophie Gilbert, Theatlantic.com, July 16, 2019; "Netflix Now Expects to Burn Through $3.5 Billion in Cash This Year," by Troy Wolverton, Businessinsider.com, April 16, 2019; "Emmys 2018: 'Game of Thrones' and 'Marvelous Mrs. Maisel' Win Big Awards," by John Koblin, *New York Times*, September 17, 2018; "Netflix Topples HBO in Emmy Nominations," by John Jurgensen, *Wall Street Journal*, July 12, 2018; "Verizon's Streaming TV Service Might Have Standalone App 'Channels'," by Chaim Gartenberg, Theverge.com, January 16, 2018; "Disney Unveils New Streaming Services, to End Netflix Deal," by Erich Schwartzel and Joe Flint, *Wall Street Journal*, August 8, 2017; "Netflix Is Winning the Streaming Race—But for How Long?," by Mathew Ingram, *Fortune*, March 10, 2017; "How YouTube TV Will Stack Up In The OTT Market," by Trefis Team, *Forbes*, March 7,

and their preferences. Google is actively pursuing long-form content creators for its video channel program. There is no cost to Google users because the service is ad supported.

So another possible ending for the Netflix movie is that ultimately it can't compete with Amazon, Apple, Google, Hulu, or the content producers like HBO, Disney, and CBS, all of which have started their own streaming services. Generating a negative cash flow of $3.5 billion a year to purchase content, Netflix may run out of investors who make up the difference. How can the company show a profit if cash flow is negative? It finances the purchase of content over many years, and its liabilities grow. The decline in subscriber growth in the U.S. market is causing analysts to wonder if the business model will work. Netflix's profitability may be reduced to less than shareholders can tolerate. Netflix may have created a new world of streaming, bingeing, and content production, but it may not be able to survive the world it created. This show is not over until the last episode is finished. Stay tuned.

2017; "Netflix Fuels a Surge in Scripted TV Shows. Some See a Glut," by John Koblin, *New York Times,* August 9, 2016; "Netflix and 20th Century Fox Television Distribution Announce First Global Agreement," Netflix Media Center, July 25, 2016; "Netflix Stock History: What You Need to Know," by Dan Caplinger, Fool.com, July 11, 2016; "Netflix to Be Exclusive Global Streaming Home of FX's American Crime Story Franchise in 2017," Netflix Media Center, July 25, 2016; "Can Netflix Survive the New World It Created?," by Joe Nocera, *New York Times,* June 16, 2016.

Case Study Questions

1. What are three challenges that Netflix faces?
2. What are the key elements of Netflix's strategy today?
3. Why is Netflix in competition with Apple, Amazon, HBO, and Google, and what strengths does Netflix bring to the market?

9.6 REVIEW

KEY CONCEPTS

- **Understand the major trends in the consumption of media and online content, the major revenue models for digital content delivery, digital rights management, and the concept of media convergence.**
- Major trends in the consumption of media and online content include the following:
  - The average American adult spends around 4,500 hours per year consuming various media. The most hours are spent online, using a desktop or mobile device, followed by watching television and listening to the radio.
  - Although several studies indicate that time spent on the Internet reduces consumer time available for other media, recent data reveals a more complex picture, as Internet users multitask and consume more media of all types than do non-Internet users.
  - In terms of all media revenue, television and movies accounted for about 60% of media revenues, print media (books, newspapers, and magazines) for about 24%, video games, about 10%, and music (radio and recorded music), about 7%.
  - The three major revenue models for digital content delivery are the subscription, a la carte, and advertising-supported (free and freemium) models.
  - In terms of paid online content, online games generate the most revenue, followed by online TV and movies.
  - Digital rights management (DRM) refers to the combination of technical and legal means for protecting digital content from reproduction without permission. Walled gardens are a kind of DRM that restrict the widespread sharing of content.

- The concept of media convergence has three dimensions:
  - Technological convergence, which refers to the development of hybrid devices that can combine the functionality of two or more media platforms, such as books, newspapers, television, radio, and stereo equipment, into a single device.
  - Content convergence, with respect to content design, production, and distribution.
  - Industry convergence, which refers to the merger of media enterprises into powerful, synergistic combinations that can cross-market content on many different platforms and create works that use multiple platforms.
  - In the early years of e-commerce, many believed that media convergence would occur quickly. However, many early efforts failed, and new efforts are just now appearing.

■ **Understand the key factors affecting the online publishing industry.**
- Key factors affecting online newspapers include:
  - *Audience size and growth.* Although the newspaper industry as a whole is the most troubled part of the publishing industry, online readership of newspapers is growing, fueled by smartphones, e-readers, and tablet computers.
  - *Revenue models and results.* Online newspapers predominantly rely on both advertising and subscription revenues. Digital ad revenues are not sufficient to cover losses in print advertising.
- Key factors affecting online magazines include:
  - *Online audience and growth:* Digital magazine sales have soared, with almost a third of the Internet population now reading magazines online.
  - *Magazine aggregation:* Magazine aggregators (websites or apps) offer users online subscriptions and sales of many digital magazines.
- Key factors affecting e-books and online book publishing include:
  - *Audience size and growth.* E-book sales growth has leveled off following an explosive growth period. Growth today is fueled by the Amazon Kindle, Apple iPad, and smartphones. The mobile platform of smartphones and tablets has made millions of books available online at a lower price than print books. The future of the book will be digital, although printed books are unlikely to disappear in the foreseeable future.
  - *Competing business models.* E-book business models include the wholesale model and the agency model.
  - *Convergence.* The publishing industry is making steady progress toward media convergence. Newly authored e-books are appearing with interactive rich media, which allow the user to click on icons for videos or other material, and take notes.

■ **Understand the key factors affecting the online entertainment industry.**
- The main players in the entertainment sector are the television, movie, music, and game industries. The entertainment segment is currently undergoing great change, brought about by the Internet and the mobile platform. Consumers have begun to accept paying for content and also to expect to be able to access online entertainment from any device at any time.
- Key factors include the following:
  - *Audience size and growth.* The audience for all types of online entertainment is growing dramatically.
  - *The emergence of streaming services and the mobile platform.* The major trend in the television, movie, and music industries is the move to streaming services.
  - The greatest growth is anticipated in online gaming, particularly mobile gaming and e-sports.

QUESTIONS

1. Does time spent on the Internet cannibalize or complement traditional media?
2. What are the basic revenue models for online content?

3. How have attitudes about paying for content changed since the early years of the Web?
4. What is DRM?
5. Describe the structure of the media content industry.
6. What factors are needed to support successfully charging the consumer for online content?
7. How have Internet distributors responded to the challenges that digital disruption have created for traditional newspapers?
8. Today, Amazon and Apple dominate the e-book marketplace. What impact has this had on the book publishing industry?
9. How have music streaming services impacted music industry revenue?
10. How has the Internet transformed television viewing?
11. Discuss the impact of *Pokemon GO* on the online gaming industry.
12. What is a release window and what impact does it have on the sales of online entertainment?
13. What are OTT entertainment services?
14. What are the two kinds of online movie sales and business models? Give an example of each type.
15. Why are advertisers attracted to e-sports?
16. What type of convergence does the Kindle Fire represent?
17. How is the *New York Times* attempting to deal with digital disruption?
18. How has the book publishing industry's experience with the Internet differed from the newspaper and magazine industries' experience?
19. What are some of the challenges currently facing the book publishing industry?
20. What are the four factors that have caused the decline of newspaper revenues over the past 15 years?

PROJECTS

1. Research the issue of media convergence in the newspaper industry. Do you believe that convergence will be good for the practice of journalism? Develop a reasoned argument on either side of the issue and write a 3- to 5-page report on the topic. Include in your discussion the barriers to convergence and whether these restrictions should be eased.

2. Go to Amazon and explore the different digital media products that are available. For each kind of digital media product, describe how Amazon's presence has altered the industry that creates, produces, and distributes this content. Prepare a presentation to convey your findings to the class.

3. Identify three online sources of content that exemplify one of the three digital content revenue models (subscription, a la carte, and advertising-supported) discussed in the chapter. Describe how each site works, and how it generates revenue. Describe how each site provides value to the consumer. Which type of revenue model do you prefer, and why?

4. Identify a popular online magazine that also has an offline subscription or newsstand edition. What advantages (and disadvantages) does the online edition have when compared to the offline physical edition? Has technology platform, content design, or industry structure convergence occurred in the online magazine industry? Prepare a short report discussing this issue.

5. In 2014, Amazon purchased Twitch, which lets users stream their video game sessions, for almost $1 billion. Why would Amazon spend so much money on Twitch? Create a short presentation either defending the purchase or explaining why you think it was a bad idea.

REFERENCES

American Press Institute. "Paths to Subscription: Why Recent Subscribers Chose to Pay for News." Media Insight Project (February 27, 2018).

Anderson, Porter. ""AAP Issues Its Annual 2018 StatShot Look at the US Publishing Industry," Publishingperspectives.com (June 23, 2019).

Association of American Publishers (AAP). "StatShot Annual Report." (June 21, 2019).

Association of American Publishers (AAP). "StatShot Annual Report." (July 20, 2018).

Authorearnings.com. "January 2018 Report: US Online Book Sales, Q2–Q4 2017." (January 2018).

Berkshire Hathaway Corporation. "Annual Report 2013." (March 1, 2013).

Bialik, Carl. "Studios Struggle for Focus on Film Pirates Booty." *Wall Street Journal* (April 5, 2013).

Benton, Joshua. "The Wall Street Journal Joins The New York Times in the 2 Million Digital Subscriber Club." Neimanlab.org (February 10, 2020).

Bilton, Ricardo. "Inside The New Yorker's Digital Strategy." Digiday.com (April 10, 2014).

Boxer, Sarah. "Paintings Too Perfect? The Great Optics Debate." *New York Times* (December 4, 2001).

Brown, Pete. "More Than Half of Facebook Instant Articles Partners May Have Abandoned It." *Columbia Journalism Review* (February 2, 2018).

Carr, David. "Print Is Down, and Now Out." *New York Times* (August 10, 2014).

Castillo, Michelle. "Why Some Magazines Are Going Back to Print." CNBC.com (December 23, 2016).

Chavern, David. "How Antitrust Undermines Press Freedom." *Wall Street Journal* (July 9, 2018).

Clark, Katie. "Apple's iBooks Revamp, Apple Books, Is Here." Techcrunch.com (September 17, 2018).

comScore, Inc. "Top 50 Multi-Platform Properties (Desktop and Mobile)." (January 2020).

Condenast.com. "Condé Nast Breaks Digital and Video Audience Records in November." (December 19, 2016).

Danaher, Brett, and Michael D. Smith. "Gone in 60 Seconds: The Impact of the Megaupload Shutdown on Movie Sales." *International Journal of Industrial Organization* (March 2014).

Deahl, Dani. "The Music Modernization Act Has Been Passed into Law." Theverge.com (October 11, 2018).

Digital Entertainment Group. "DEG 2018 Year End Home Entertainment Report." (January 2019).

eMarketer, Inc. "Average Time Spent per Day with Media in the US, 2017–2021 (April 2019a).

eMarketer, Inc. (Corey McNair). "US Digital Video Viewers and Penetration." (August 2019b).

eMarketer, US Digital Audio Listeners and Penetration (March 2019c).

eMarketer, Inc. "US Digital Gamers and Penetration." (March 2019d).

eMarketer, Inc. "US Digital Console Gamers and Penetration."(March 2019e).

eMarketer, Inc. "US Digital Ad Spending." (October 2019f).

eMarketer, Inc. (Ross Benes). "US Digital Video 2019." (September 19, 2019g).

eMarketer, Inc. "US Home Entertainment Rental and Sales Revenue, by Format, 2017 & 2018." (January 8, 2019h).

eMarketer, Inc. "US Subscription Video Services Revenues Estimates, 2019 (May 2019i).

eMarketer, Inc. "US Smartphone Gamers and Penetration." (March 2019j).

eMarketer, Inc. "US Tablet Gamers and Penetration." (March 2019k).

eMarketer, Inc., "US Desktop/Laptop Gamers and Penetration." (March 2019l).

eMarketer, Inc. (Lucy Koch). "Esports Playing in the Big Leagues Now." (February 5, 2019m).

eMarketer, Inc. (Jasmine Enberg). "Bundle Up! Traditional TV Providers Offer OTT Packages to Head Off Subscriber Freeze." (August 16, 2018).

eMarketer, Inc. "US Video Game Revenue by Device." (November 6, 2017).

Entertainment Software Association (ESA). "Annual Report 2018." (2019).

Gurman, Mark. "Apple's Getting Back Into the E-Books Fight Against Amazon." Bloomberg.com (January 25, 2018).

Hagey, Keach, and Greg Bensinger. "Jeff Bezos's Tool Kit for the Post." *Wall Street Journal* (August 6, 2013).

Isaac, Mark, and Sydney Ember. "Facebook, Seeking to Satisfy Publishers, May Let Them Charge for Articles." *New York Times* (July 19, 2017).

Kearny, Michael. "Trusting News Project Report 2017," Reynolds Journalism Institute, University of Missouri, 2018.

Lee, Edmund. "Laurene Powell Jobs Is Buying the Atlantic Magazine." Recode.net (July 28, 2018).

Martin, Brittany. "Los Angeles Times Among the First Partners for Apple's 'Netflix for News,'" Lamag.com (March 25, 2019).

Moses, Lucia. "How The New Yorker Plans to Double Its Paid Circulation to 2 Million." *New York Times* (March 9, 2018).

Moses, Lucia. "How The New Yorker Is Capitalizing on Its Trump Bump." Digiday.com (March 10, 2017).

MPA—The Association of Magazine Media. "Magazine Media Factbook 2019." (2019).

MPA—The Association of Magazine Media. "Magazine Media Factbook 2018/2019." (2018a).

MPA—The Association of Magazine Publishers. "The Top Technologies Magazine Publishers Will Buy in 2018." (2018b).

MPA—The Association of Magazine Media. "Magazine Media Factbook 2017/2018." (2017).

Mulligan, Mark. "Music Subscriber Market Shares H1 2019." Midiaresearch.com (December 5, 2019).

Mullin, Benjamin. "How The New Yorker Brought the Soul of the Magazine to the Web." Poynter.com (January 31, 2017).

Newspaper Association of America. "Newspaper Digital Audience Snapshot." (January 2017).

Newspaper Association of America. "Newspaper Digital Audience." (July 2016).

New York Times. " Journalism That Stands Apart. Report of the 2020 Group." (January 2017).

New York Times. "Innovation." (May 2014).

Pew Research Center (Andrew Perrin). "One in Five Americans Now Listen to Audio Books." Pewresearch.org (September 25, 2019a).

Pew Research Center. "Newspapers Fact Sheet." Journalism.org (July 9, 2019b).

Pew Research Center. "Digital News Fact Sheet." Journalism.org (July 23, 2019c).

Pew Research Center (Mason Walker). "Americans Favor Mobile Devices Over Desktops and Laptops for Getting News." Pewresearch.org (November 19, 2019d).

Pew Research Center (Katerina Eva Matsa and Elisa Shearer). "News Use Across Social Media Platforms 2018." Journalism.org (September 17, 2018).

Pew Research Center. "Social Media and News Websites are the Most Common Pathways to Online News." (February 2017).

PriceWaterhouseCoopers (PWC). "Global Entertainment and Media Outlook 2018–2022." (2018).

Raffaelli, Ryan. "Reinventing Retail: The Novel Resurgence of Independent Bookstores." Working Paper 20-068 Harvard Business School (January 2020).

Raffaelli, Ryan. "Technology Reemergence: Creating New Value for Old Technologies in Swiss Mechanical Watchmaking, 1970–2008." Harvard Business School (2018).

Raffaelli, Ryan. "How Independent Bookstores Have Thrived in Spite of Amazon.com." Harvard Business School (November 20, 2017).

Recording Industry Association of America (RIAA). "U.S. Sales Database." (accessed February 8, 2020).

Recording Industry Association of America (RIAA). "RIAA 2018 Year-End Music Industry Revenue Report." (February 28, 2019).

Recording Industry Association of America (RIAA). " News and Notes on 2017 RIAA Revenue Statistics." (2018).

Romenesko, Jim. "Wall Street Journal Memo: Newsroom Changes Mean a Faster-moving, Digital First News Operation." Jimromenesko.com. (January 21, 2014.)

Rutenberg, Jim. "News Outlets to Seek Bargaining Rights Against Google and Facebook." *New York Times* (July 9, 2017).

SensorTower. "Pokemon Go Catches $3 Billion in Lifetime Gross Revenue." Sensortower.com (October 29, 2019).

Sisario, Ben. "Spotify Is Growing, But So Are Its Losses." *New York Times* (June 15, 2017).

Spangler, Todd. "Piracy: Streaming Video Accounts for 74% of Illegal Film and TV Activity, Study Finds." Variety.com (July 28, 2016).

Spotify Technology, S.A. "Form 20-F for the fiscal year ended December 31, 2019." filed with the Securities and Exchange Commission (February 12, 2020).

Stack, Liam. "Medium Lays Off a Third of Its Staff in Pursuit of Its Vision." *New York Times* (January 4, 2017).

Statista. "Estimated Aggregate Revenue of U.S. Periodical Publishers from 2005 to 2017." (2018).

Sutcliffe, Chris. "Are Niche Publications the Future of Print? Part One." The Media Briefing. (January 8, 2016).

Tracy, Marc. "The New York Times Tops 5 Million Subscriptions as Ads Decline." New York Times (February 6, 2020).

Travis, Hannibal. *Copyright Class Struggle: Creative Economies in a Social Media Age.* Cambridge University Press (2018).

Watson, Amy. "Revenue of U.S. Periodical Publishers 2005-2018." Statista.com (November 27, 2019a).

Watson, Amy. "U.S. Magazine Industry--Statistics & Facts." Statista.com (August 27, 2019).

Webb, Kevin. "More Than 100 Million People Watched 'League of Legends' World Championship, Cementing Its Place as the Most Popular Esport." Businessinsider.com (December 18, 2019).

Wiedman, Reeves. "What's Left of Conde Nast." Nymag.com (October 28, 2019).

Williams, Alex. "Paying for Digital News: The Rapid Adoption and Current Landscape of Digital Subscriptions at U.S. Newspapers." Americanpressinstitute.org (February 29, 2016).

CHAPTER 10

Online Communities

LEARNING OBJECTIVES

After reading this chapter, you will be able to:

- Describe the different types of social networks and online communities and their business models.
- Describe the major types of auctions, their benefits and costs, how they operate, when to use them, and the potential for auction abuse and fraud.
- Describe the major types of Internet portals and their business models.

LinkedIn:
A Tale of Two Countries

LinkedIn bills itself as the world's largest professional network, allowing prospective employees to connect with people and businesses who can help their careers and giving employers tools to find talented prospective hires. As more businesses have sought to expand globally, so too has LinkedIn. However, LinkedIn is learning a lesson that many businesses have encountered before: the cultural and regulatory landscape can vary greatly from country to country. The company's experiences in China and Russia exemplify this phenomenon.

© Kristoffer Tripplaar/Alamy Stock Photo

In 2014, LinkedIn launched a fully localized version of its site in China. Companies often look to expand into China to dramatically grow their user bases, but many Western technology giants have struggled to succeed there. For instance, companies often fail to adjust their products to meet the preferences of Chinese users. LinkedIn, on the other hand, attempted to cultivate a look and feel appealing to Chinese users by forming partnerships with popular Chinese services such as messaging service WeChat, Twitter-like microblogging service Weibo, and instant messaging service QQ. LinkedIn uses these services to encourage people to sign up for its network. The company used offline advertising featuring Chinese celebrities to promote its brand and quickly established partnerships with large Chinese corporations to recruit employees.

However, for many companies, China's regulatory policies have been a significant stumbling block. LinkedIn's success in China thus far has been at least partially contingent on the company's willingness to adhere to the Chinese government's policies regarding content censorship. China targets and blocks any content viewed as unfavorable to the country's political leadership. Any company that is interested in entering the Chinese market, no matter how powerful, must remove this type of content or risk being blocked by the government. For instance, Facebook, Twitter, and YouTube are all blocked in China. Microsoft, which purchased LinkedIn for $26 billion in 2016, has also battled with China over piracy of its products and regulatory penalties that favor domestic Chinese brands.

Critics suggest that China's restrictions force companies to become accomplices in the Chinese government's censorship. Many companies have balked at this prospect. For example, Google has withdrawn many of its services from China because it is unwilling to comply with the Chinese government's regulatory demands. However, LinkedIn has had a more conciliatory attitude, partnering with Chinese Internet companies Sequoia China and China Broadband Capital to ensure a smooth transition into the Chinese market. While LinkedIn CEO Jeff Weiner has publicly stated that he opposes Chinese censorship policies, the company has complied with them to deepen the company's global penetration. Despite

SOURCES: "Statistics," News.linkedin.com, accessed February 11, 2020; "MaiMai Goes After LinkedIn, Liepin," Aimgroup.com, August 13, 2019' "MaiMai, LinkedIn China Trade Barb," Aimgroup.com, August 8, 2019;"LinkedIn Now Requires Phone Number Verification for All Users in China," by Rita Liao, Techcrunch.com, January 9, 2019; "LinkedIn's China Compromise Shows the Price of Market Access," by Erin Dunne, Washingtonexaminer.com, January 3, 2019, "LinkedIn's China Rival MaiMai Raises $200M Ahead of Planned US IPO," by Emma Lee, Techcrunch.com, August 21, 2018; "Learning from Failure: LinkedIn China," by Christopher Chen, Medium.com, July 16, 2018; "Russian Data Localization Laws: Enriching 'Security' & the Economy," by Matthew Newton and Julia Summers, Jsis.washington.edu, February 28, 2018; "60% Users from Russia Remain on LinkedIn After Year of Blocking," Crimerussia.com, November 16, 2017; "LinkedIn Faces Setback in China as It Runs Afoul of New Rules," by Paul Mozur and Carolyn Zhang, *New York Times*, November 10, 2017; "Russia Says 'Nyet,' Continues LinkedIn Block After It Refuses to Store Data in Russia," by Ingrid Lunden, Techcrunch.com, May 27, 2017; "Why LinkedIn Was Banned in Russia," by Maria Elterman, Iapp.org, January 23, 2017; "Russia Requires Apple and Google to Remove LinkedIn from Local App Stores," by Cecilia Kang and Katie Benner, *New York Times*, January 6, 2017; "LinkedIn Blocked in Russia: A Welcome Warning for Global Players?" by Adrien Henni, Venturebeat.com, November 29, 2016; "LinkedIn Is Now Officially Blocked in Russia," by Ingrid Lunden, Techcrunch.com, November 17, 2016; "Facebook, Microsoft, LinkedIn and Others Must Resist China's Orwellian Vision of the Internet," by Roseann Rife, Amnesty.org, November 16, 2016; "Can Foreign Tech Companies Win in China?" by Edward Tse, Techcrunch.com, August 28, 2016; "LinkedIn's China Strategy—When Localization Isn't Enough," by Xunshu Li, Blog.btrax.com, August 3, 2016; "For LinkedIn China, Microsoft Deal Is a Complicated Connection," by Alyssa Abkowitz, *Wall Street Journal*, June 23, 2016; "Censorship Is LinkedIn's China Friend as It Boasts User Milestone," Chinatechnews.com, April 25, 2016; "Why Some Social Networks Still Aren't Blocked in China," by Erik Crouch, Techinasia.com, April 15, 2016; "How LinkedIn China Learnt How to Win Friends and Influence People," by Li Hui, CKGSB Knowledge, July 14, 2015; "Microsoft Faces New Scrutiny in China," by Paul Mozur and Nick Wingfield, *New York Times*, January 5, 2016; "LinkedIn Goes After China with a New Joint Venture and a Localized Chinese-Language Site," by Josh Ong, Thenextweb.com, February 24, 2014.

this, LinkedIn has sometimes still run into resistance from the Chinese government, including in 2017 when China demanded that LinkedIn stop accepting new individual profiles until it added the ability to verify individual job posters. In 2019, in response to Chinese regulations, LinkedIn began to require all new and existing users with a Chinese IP address to link a mobile phone number to their account. It also reportedly employs information auditors that monitor what users in China post and regularly removes posts and profile pages based on political content.

Since the launch of its localized Chinese site, LinkedIn's Chinese membership has grown to over 49 million and is one of the company's fastest growing markets. However, LinkedIn's biggest competitor in China, Maimai, has raised almost $1 billion in funding and MaiMai's announced goal is to have an initial public offering valuing it at $10 billion or more. Maimai has over 50 million users, slightly more than LinkedIn's Chinese user base.

China may be the most high-profile country with heavy-handed requirements for foreign companies, but it is far from alone. LinkedIn discovered this first-hand in 2016 when it became the first site to be blocked in Russia under a new law that revamped the country's data storage policies, and which provides, among other requirements, that the personal data of Russian users be stored on databases located within Russia's physical borders. Russia also required that Apple and Google remove LinkedIn from their respective app stores for users in Russia.

The law meant that global companies operating in Russia without a physical presence had to quickly establish one or run the risk of being blocked. Many companies, such as Apple, Google, Uber, and Alibaba, had already complied with the demands of the new law and moved data on Russian users to their existing servers located within the country, but other companies without servers there simply took a wait-and-see approach. LinkedIn was the Russian government's first target despite the fact that only 6 million of the site's 530 million users were registered in Russia. Some analysts have suggested that Russia's decision to block LinkedIn may also have been motivated by the Russian government's desire to better control international employment opportunities for talented Russians and make it more difficult for them to find employment with firms outside of Russia.

Though LinkedIn has had an ongoing dialogue with the Russian government, as of February 2020 the site was still banned for users with Russian IP addresses. While Russian traffic to LinkedIn has declined since the ban, over 1 million Russian users still visit the site each month. Given LinkedIn's willingness to work with regulatory requirements in China, it is possible that the company will eventually develop a solution that it and Russian regulators find mutually acceptable. Many other countries have adopted laws that restrict the storage of their citizens' personal data, and as more countries seek to establish borders on the Internet, companies with global ambitions like LinkedIn may have to remain flexible.

In this chapter, we discuss social networks, auctions, and portals. What do social networks, auctions, and portals have in common? They are all based on feelings of shared interest and self-identification—in short, a sense of community. Social networks and online communities explicitly attract people with shared affinities, such as ethnicity, gender, religion, and political views, or shared interests, such as hobbies, sports, and vacations. eBay started as a community of people interested in unwanted but functional items for which there was no ready commercial market. That community turned out to be huge—much larger than anyone expected. Portals also contain strong elements of community by providing access to community-fostering technologies such as e-mail, chat groups, bulletin boards, and discussion forums.

10.1 SOCIAL NETWORKS AND ONLINE COMMUNITIES

The Internet was designed originally as a communications medium to connect scientists in computer science departments around the continental United States. From the beginning, the Internet was intended, in part, as a community-building technology that would allow scientists to share data, knowledge, and opinions in a real-time online environment (see Chapter 2) (Hiltzik, 1999). The result of this early Internet was the first "virtual communities" (Rheingold, 1993). As the Internet grew in the late 1980s to include scientists from many disciplines and university campuses, thousands of virtual communities sprang up among small groups of scientists in very different disciplines that communicated regularly using Internet e-mail, listservs, and bulletin boards. The first articles and books on the new electronic communities began appearing in the mid- to late 1980s (Kiesler et al., 1984; Kiesler, 1986). One of the earliest online communities, The Well (originally Whole Earth 'Lectronic Link), was formed in San Francisco in 1985 by a small group of people who once shared an 1,800-acre commune in Tennessee. The Well continues to have thousands of members devoted to discussion, debate, advice, and help (Well.com, 2018; Hafner, 1997; Rheingold, 1998). With the development of the Web in the early 1990s, millions of people began obtaining Internet accounts and e-mail, and the community-building impact of the Internet strengthened. By the late 1990s, the commercial value of online communities was recognized as a potential new business model (Hagel and Armstrong, 1997).

The early online communities involved a relatively small number of web aficionados, and users with intense interests in technology, politics, literature, and ideas. The technology was largely limited to posting text messages on bulletin boards sponsored by the community, and one-to-one or one-to-many e-mails. In addition to The Well, early networks included GeoCities, a website hosting service based on neighborhoods. By 2002, however, the nature of online communities had begun to change. User-created websites called blogs became inexpensive and easy to set up without any technical expertise. Photo sites enabled convenient sharing of photos. Beginning in 2007, the growth of mobile devices like smartphones, tablet computers, digital cameras, and portable media devices enabled sharing of rich media such as photos, music, and videos. Suddenly there was a much wider audience for sharing interests and activities, and much more to share.

A new culture emerged as well. The broad democratization of the technology and its spread to the larger population meant that online social networks were no longer limited to a small group but instead broadened to include a much wider set of people and tastes, especially pre-teens, teens, and college students, who were the fastest to adopt many of these new technologies. Entire families and friendship networks soon joined. The new social network culture is very personal and "me" centered, displaying photos and broadcasting personal activities, interests, hobbies, and relationships on social network profiles. Today's social networks are as much a sociological phenomenon as they are a technology phenomenon.

Currently, social network participation is one of the most common usages of the Internet, accounting for over 14.5% of total time spent with digital media (eMarketer, Inc., 2019a). The growth in social network engagement since 2014 has been driven almost entirely by smartphone usage (comScore, Inc., 2017). About 72% of all U.S. Internet users and over 60% of the total U.S. population—almost 205 million Americans—use social networks (eMarketer, Inc., 2019b). According to Facebook, it had 2.5 billion monthly active users worldwide as of December 2019. Although Facebook no longer releases statistics on the number of mobile usrs, it reports that substantially all of its daily and monthly active users access Facebook on mobile devices (Facebook, 2019). Other large social networks include LinkedIn (profiled in the opening case), Twitter, Pinterest, Instagram, Snapchat, and TikTok. While Facebook is the most popular social network, it appears to have hit a plateau in the United States, and most of its growth is offshore, where it is pushing to create basic Internet access so more people will join the network. Other social networks, such as Instagram (owned by Facebook), Pinterest, Snapchat, and TikTok are growing more quickly.

Worldwide, the social network phenomenon is even stronger with around 2.95 billion users worldwide (77% of all Internet users and over 38% of the world's total population). The number of social network users worldwide is expected to continue growing at a cumulative average rate of over 4% over the next five years. Social networks are a top online destination in every country. Asia-Pacific has the largest social network audience, followed by Latin America, but Latin America has the highest penetration of social network usage among the general population (eMarketer, Inc., 2019c). Although Facebook dominates the global social network marketspace, in some countries, localized social networks are signficant, such as Taringa! in Argentina, KakaoStory and Band in South Korea, Mixi and social messaging app Line in Japan, Qzone, WeChat, and QQ (all owned by Tencent), and Weibo in China, Xing in Germany, and VK in Russia (eMarketer, Inc, 2017). There is an online social network for you to join almost anywhere you go!

WHAT IS AN ONLINE SOCIAL NETWORK?

So exactly how do we define an online social network, and how is it any different from, say, an offline social network? Sociologists, who frequently criticize modern society for having destroyed traditional communities, unfortunately have not given us very good definitions of social networks and community. One study examined 94 different sociological definitions of community and found four areas of agreement. **Social networks** involve (a) a group of people, (b) shared social interaction, (c) common ties among members, and (d) people who share an area for some period of time (Hillery, 1955). This will be our

social network
involves a group of people, shared social interaction, common ties among members, and people who share an area for some period of time

working definition of a social network. Social networks do not necessarily have shared goals, purposes, or intentions. Indeed, social networks can be places where people just "hang out," share space, and communicate.

It's a short step to defining an **online social network** as an online location where people who share common ties can interact with one another. This definition is very close to that of Howard Rheingold—one of The Well's early participants—who coined the term *virtual communities* as "cultural aggregations that emerge when enough people bump into each other often enough in cyberspace." It is a group of people who may or may not meet one another face to face, and who exchange words, photos, videos, and ideas through the mediation of an online social meeting space. The Internet removes the geographic and time limitations of offline social networks. To be in an online network, you don't need to meet face to face, in a common room, at a common time.

online social network
an area online, where people who share common ties can interact with one another

THE GROWTH OF SOCIAL NETWORKS AND ONLINE COMMUNITIES

Figure 10.1 shows the top social networks in the United States, which together account for well over 90% of the Internet's U.S. social network activity.

Over half of the U.S. population uses Facebook. The largest group of Facebook users in the United States are 25 to 34 years old (almost 40 million), followed by 35- to 45-year-olds (32 million). About 40% of U.S. Facebook users (around 68 million) are older than 44. Adults over 65 constitute the fastest growing group on Facebook (eMarketer, Inc., 2019d). Similar patterns are observed worldwide as older populations use social networks to stay in touch with children and relatives. Instagram is the most popular social network among teens

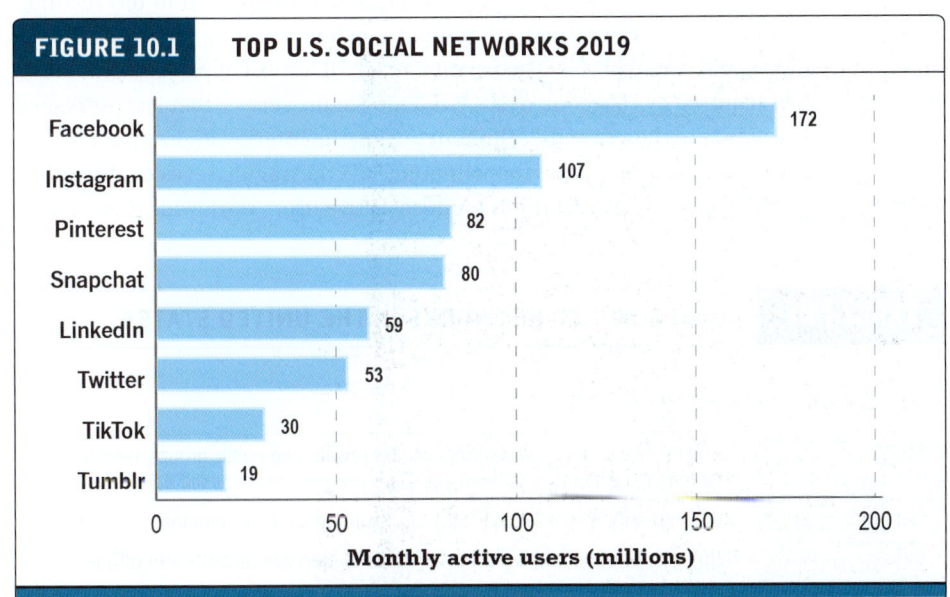

FIGURE 10.1 TOP U.S. SOCIAL NETWORKS 2019

Facebook is by far and away the dominant social network in the United States in terms of adult Internet users who visit a social network at least once a month.
Sources: Based on data from eMarketer, 2020, 2019e, 2019f.

and young adults, with Snapchat not far behind. Newer social networks tend to follow this same pattern, with young people being the first adopters.

While Facebook and Twitter still tend to dominate the news, other social networks are growing much faster than Facebook with respect to unique visitors and subscribers and are attracting marketers and advertisers as well. For instance, Pinterest, described in the opening case in Chapter 7, is a visually oriented social network that allows users to curate their tastes and preferences, expressed in visual arts. One way to think of Pinterest is as a visual blog. Users post images to an online "pinboard." The images can come from any source. Users can also "re-pin" images they see on Pinterest. Pinterest's membership has skyrocketed since its launch, accumulating over 330 million active members worldwide as of the end of 2019. Instagram is another social network that focuses on video and photo sharing. A mobile app that enables a user to easily share images to social networks, Instagram was acquired by Facebook for $1 billion in 2012 and has over 1 billion users.

Other social networks are not necessarily competing with Facebook, but adding to the social network mix and enlarging the total social network audience. **Table 10.1** describes some other popular social networks.

Contributing to the continued growth and commercial success of networks is the rapid adoption and intense use of mobile devices. Over 90% of Facebook's users worldwide are mobile social media users, although not exclusively. According to comScore, in 2019, Facebook's flagship Facebook app had the highest number of U.S. unique visitors (185 million) of all mobile apps and was the second-most popular smartphone app (behind YouTube) among U.S. smartphone users, with a reach of almost 70% (Clement, 2020). Some social networks, such as Instagram, Snapchat and TikTok, are almost entirely mobile.

A number of social networks launched since 2008 focus on messaging. Snapchat (2009) lets users send photos and videos to friends that self-extinguish in ten seconds. Snapchat Stories have a longer lifespan: 24 hours. Snapchat is among the top 12 smartphone apps among U.S. smartphone users, with a reach of almost 40% (Clement, 2020). WhatsApp (2009; acquired by Facebook in 2014) is a messaging service that lets users send text, photos, and videos to their friends' cellphones using the Internet and without having to pay telecommunications companies for cellphone SMS messaging services. According to Facebook, WhatsApp has over 1.5 billion monthly active users worldwide (Levy, 2020).

TABLE 10.1	OTHER SOCIAL NETWORKS IN THE UNITED STATES
SOCIAL NETWORK	DESCRIPTION
MeWe	Facebook-like social network that includes private and public groups, newsfeeds, chat features, and more, without ads. Does not track users or sell data.
Nextdoor	Social network focused specifically on neighbors and surrounding community.
Meetup	Helps groups of people with shared interests plan events and meet offline.
Tagged	A network aimed at introducing members to one another through games, shared interests, friend suggestions, and browsing profiles.
Vero	Social network aimed sharing recommendations and photos with friends.
Mastadon	Open-source alternative to Twitter.

TABLE 10.2	TIME SPENT BY U.S. USERS ON TOP SOCIAL NETWORKS
SOCIAL NETWORK	HOURS/MONTH
Facebook	17
Instagram	13.5
Twitter	13.5
Pinterest	13.5
Snapchat	13.3
TikTok	8.3
Tumblr	2

SOURCES: Based on data from eMarketer, Inc., 2019g, 2019h; Clement, 2019; authors' estimates.

The number of unique visitors is just one way to measure the influence of a site or app. Time is another important metric. The more time people spend on a site or app, called engagement, the more time to display ads and generate revenue. In this sense, Facebook is much more addictive and immersive than the other top social networks. Over time, Facebook has tweaked its content and algorithms in order to keep users on its site and app longer. In 2014, Facebook added videos (both ads and user-contributed), and in 2016 added live streaming video with its Facebook Live service. It tries to show videos that reflect the user's interests and friends and also plays them automatically in the News Feed, forcing users to turn them off but also ensuring that they are seen for at least a few moments. Facebook has also made changes to its News Feed algorithm to capture more user attention: increasing content from users' favorite friends; decreasing content from friends of users' friends; and showing multiple posts in a row from the same source for users with few friends. **Table 10.2** illustrates the different levels of engagement by U.S. users with the top social networks.

The amount of revenue generated is the ultimate metric for measuring a company's business potential. The top two search engine companies (Google and Baidu) together generated almost $115 billion in search and display advertising revenue worldwide in 2019. In contrast, social networks were expected to generate about $62 billion in advertising revenue (eMarketer, Inc., 2019h). Social networks are a fast growing form of Internet usage and advertising revenue, but they are not yet as lucrative as traditional search engines/portals in terms of ad dollars generated. A part of the problem is that subscribers do not go to social networks to seek ads for relevant products, nor do they pay attention to the ads that are flashed before their eyes (see Chapters 6 and 7). In addition, the small screen of the smartphone, the dominant social network platform, is not ideal for display advertising of retail goods.

TURNING SOCIAL NETWORKS INTO BUSINESSES

While the early social networks had a difficult time raising capital and revenues, today's top social networks are now monetizing their huge audiences. Early social networks relied on subscriptions, but today, most social networks rely on advertising or the investments of venture capitalists. Users of portals and search engines have come to accept advertising

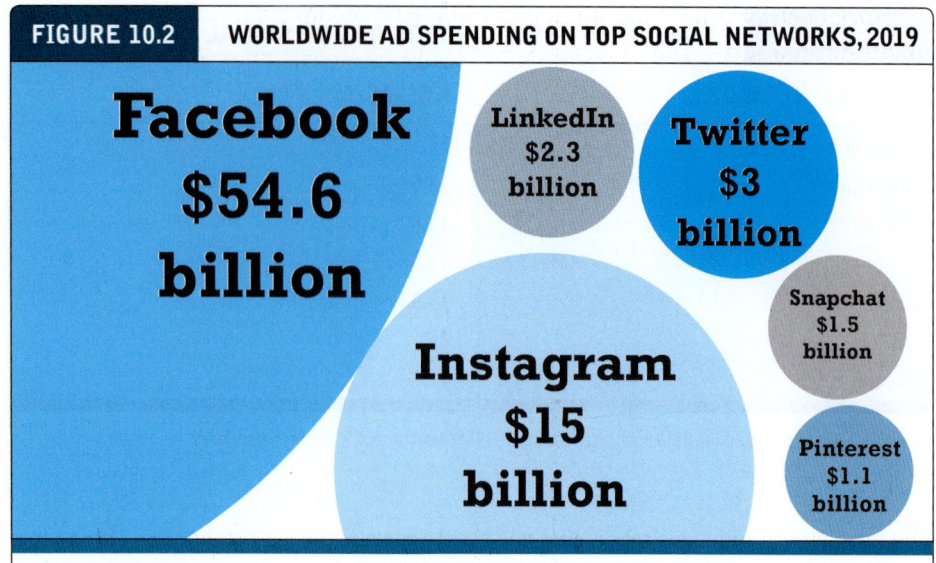

Sources: Based on data from eMarketer, Inc. 2019i; McKenna, 2020.

as the preferred means of supporting web experiences rather than paying for it. One important exception is LinkedIn, which offers basic free memberships for individuals but charges for premium services. **Figure 10.2** shows the comparative amount of ad spending on various social networks. Facebook, with over $54 billion in ad revenues, towers over the other social networks.

Social networks do not always succeed as businesses. For instance, Twitter began as a social messaging service on which users could communicate with followers. It quickly turned into an Internet broadcasting network for millions of on-scene observers acting as citizen reporters, as well as political organizers, celebrities, and politicians. In 2019, it had about 285 million users worldwide (about 53 million in the United States). Twitter's user growth, particularly in the United States, has stagnated. However, its recent financial results have been encouraging, as revenue in 2019 grew by 14% to $3.46 billion, and net income also grew to $1.47 billion, up from $1.2 billion in 2018 (Twitter, 2020.)

The rapid adoption of mobile devices initially posed a challenge to social networks like Facebook, as well as to Google's search engine, because they were largely based on the desktop platform. Google dominated mobile ad revenues up until 2013 because its search engine and Google Maps were among the most popular apps. Facebook quickly developed its own mobile app, and purchased others such as Instagram, and within the space of a few years was able to capture about 50% of the mobile display ad market, using its mobile News Feed to provide users a continual stream of ads. The top seven apps, and nine of the top eleven, are owned by either Google or Facebook (Amazon Mobile, ranked 8th, and Snapchat, ranked 11th, are the only ones that are not). For Facebook, that includes the main Facebook app (2nd), Facebook Messenger (6th), and Instagram (9th) (Clement, 2020). In 2019, around $65 billion (93%) of Facebook's revenue (including Instagram's revenue) came from mobile advertising (eMarketer, Inc., 2019j).

Social networks have had an important impact on how businesses operate, communicate, and serve their customers. A 2018 survey of Fortune 500 firms found that 98% used LinkedIn, 91% used Twitter, 89% used Facebook, and 63% used Instagram (Unboxsocial.com, 2019). The most visible business firm use of social networks is as a marketing and branding tool. A less visible marketing use of networks is as a powerful listening tool that has strengthened the role of customers and customer feedback systems inside a business. Public social networks like Facebook have not been used extensively in firms as collaboration tools thus far. However, in 2016, Facebook launched its Workplace app, designed to spur collaboration and networking inside large firms. The app faces stiff competition from a wide array of collaboration tools provided by Slack, Cisco, Microsoft, and IBM, along with other technologies like instant messaging and teleconferencing.

Social networks are where corporate brands and reputations are formed, and firms today take very seriously the topic of "online reputation," as evidenced by social network posts, commentary, chat sessions, and Likes. In this sense, social networks become an extension of corporate customer relationship management systems and extend existing market research programs. Beyond branding, social networks are being used increasingly as advertising platforms to contact a younger audience and as customers increasingly shift their eyeballs to social networks. Rosetta Stone, for instance, uses its Facebook page to display videos of its learning technology, encourage discussions and reviews, and post changes in its learning tools. Yet the business use of social networks does not always go well. The *Insight on Society* case, *The Dark Side of Social Networks*, discusses some of the risks associated with social networks.

TYPES OF SOCIAL NETWORKS AND THEIR BUSINESS MODELS

There are many types and many ways of classifying social networks and online communities. While the most popular general social networks have adopted an advertising model, other kinds of networks have different revenue sources. Social networks have different types of sponsors and different kinds of members. For instance, some are created by firms such as IBM for the exclusive use of their sales force or other employees (intra-firm communities or B2E [business-to-employee] communities); others are built for suppliers and resellers (inter-organizational or B2B communities); and others are built by dedicated individuals for other similar persons with shared interests (P2P [people-to-people] communities). In this chapter, we will discuss B2C communities for the most part, although we also discuss briefly P2P communities of practice.

Table 10.3 describes in greater detail the five generic types of social networks and online communities: general, practice, interest, affinity, and sponsored. Each type of community can have a commercial intent or commercial consequence. We use this schema to explore the business models of commercial communities.

General communities offer members opportunities to interact with a general audience organized into general topics. Within the topics, members can find hundreds of specific discussion groups attended by thousands of like-minded members who share an interest in that topic. The purpose of the general community is to attract enough members to populate a wide range of topics and discussion groups. The business model of general communities is typically advertising supported by selling ad space on pages and videos.

general communities offer members opportunities to interact with a general audience organized into general topics

INSIGHT ON SOCIETY

THE DARK SIDE OF SOCIAL NETWORKS

Almost all major companies use various types of social media marketing. Although it can be a productive method of connecting and engaging with customers, this form of marketing can also go very wrong. For instance, during the World Cup in Russia, Burger King Russia launched an ill-advised social media campaign on VK, the Russian equivalent of Facebook, offering customers a lifetime supply of Whoppers and 3 million rubles to any woman who conceived a child with a player from the Russian team. The post was quickly removed after customers objected to the inappropriateness of the promotion. Even Coca-Cola, a company renowned for its effective advertising, ran into trouble with a series of social media posts wishing its customers in different countries a Happy New Year. The company drew the ire of its Russian customers when it failed to include the territory of Crimea on the map it posted; when it tried to correct the map, its Ukrainian customers were even angrier, as they believe Crimea was annexed by Russia unlawfully.

Social media platforms that run advertisements must also be careful that they do not allow third-party advertisements to tarnish their reputations. For example, Snapchat's advertising review process failed to detect a third-party advertisement that asked users whether they would prefer to "slap Rihanna" or "punch Chris Brown." Rihanna is a survivor of domestic violence (Brown has admitted that he assaulted her) and the advertisement was instantly decried for making light of her experiences and of domestic violence in general. Rihanna herself took to Instagram to harshly criticize Snapchat, encouraging her 64 million followers to stop using the service. In response, the company's stock dropped 4%, eliminating $800 million from Snapchat's market capitalization. As a service that depends on social media influencers to enhance its popularity, Snapchat is also vulnerable to those same influencers turning against them, taking thousands of devoted followers with them. In 2018, Kylie Jenner took to Twitter to express her displeasure with Snapchat's recent app redesign, and the company's shares plunged once again, with the company losing over $1 billion this time as a result of the subsequent drop in stock price.

Customer service is another area where social media can lead to unforeseen complications. Once again, Snapchat struggled in this area. A Snapchat feature called Snapstreaks had been malfunctioning, causing users to take to Twitter to voice their issues to Snapchat's customer support account. Users found that the Twitter account was being operated by an automated bot that replied to any message with the word "streak" in it in the same manner. Users started to have fun at Snapchat's expense, asking the bot whether they should go "streaking" outside or whether different sports teams would continue their "streaks" of wins and losses. Snapchat's already damaged reputation took another hit from the fiasco. British Airways also was criticized for its customer service on Twitter in 2018, as the company frequently asked customers seeking help with flights to post confidential personal information as part of public conversations on the Twitter platform. Ironically, the company's customer service agents often stated that the information was necessary to comply with Europe's new General Data Protection Regulation (GDPR), which is intended to safeguard user information—the exact opposite of what was happening in British Airways' customer service interactions with users. British Airways was also later found to be leaking its customers' personal data improperly to third-party advertisers, likely earning them penalties under the very same GDPR they were supposed to be complying with.

Marketing and customer service are not the only social media hazards. For employees, privacy protection for Facebook posts is still being determined in the courts. For example, when Danielle Mailhoit, the manager of a Home Depot store in Burbank, California, was fired, she filed suit claiming gender and disability discrimination due to her vertigo. The defense attorney filed a broad request for all of Mailhoit's social media activity. The court ruled that Home Depot was not entitled to request the plaintiff's entire social media account, but it would allow a limited right to review specific content, in this case any communications between the plaintiff and current or former co-workers.

Employers must be careful with personal information gleaned from social networks. According to both Facebook and the American Civil Liberties Union (ACLU), some companies have been asking new hires either to friend the hiring manager or to submit their password. Facebook's Privacy Page condemns this practice, stating that it violates both individual users' and their friends' expectations of privacy, jeopardizes security, and could reveal a user's membership in a protected group. If it can be proven that membership in a protected group was discovered during the hiring process and used to reject a candidate or later used to terminate an employee, a claim can be filed under one of the Federal Equal Employment Opportunity (EEO) laws.

Legislators in a growing number of states have decided to be proactive. In 2012, California banned employers from asking prospective employees for their social media user names and passwords. Today, over half of U.S. states have laws of this nature that prevent employers from accessing potential employees' social media accounts. Additionally, at least 16 states have enacted laws that forbid educational institutions from doing so for their prospective students.

Carefully crafted policies can help companies to avoid the dark side of social networking. Companies must also develop policies regarding employee use of social networks and teach employees which infractions can be grounds for disciplinary action. IT departments must develop stringent policies to protect proprietary data and defend company networks from online fraud. Social media is an exciting tool, but one that requires safeguards.

SOURCES: "The Worst Social Media for Business Mistakes of 2019 (and What You Can Learn From Them)," by Raelene Morey, Revive.social, January 29, 2020; "State Social Media Privacy Laws," Ncsl.org, May 22, 2019; "British Airways Shows Everyone How Not to GDPR," by Natasha Lomas, Techcrunch.com, July 19, 2018; "Branding Fails That Made History," by Louisa Rochford, Ceotodaymagazine.com, April 9, 2018; "Snapchat Stock Loses $1.3 Billion After Kylie Jenner Tweet," by Kaya Yurieff, Money.cnn.com, February 23, 2018; "Posting with Caution: The DO's and DON'Ts of Social Media and HIPAA Compliance," Healthcarecompliancepros.com, February 11, 2018; "7 Ways Employee Privacy Laws Impact Social Media in the Workplace," Allpryme.com, January 25, 2018; "Why Googling Candidates Before You Decide to Interview Them Is Against the Law," by Diane Faulkner, Adp.com, February 4, 2016; "Judge Says Facebook Tagging Violates Protective Orders," by Mariella Moon, Engadget.com, January 17, 2016; "Facebook's Facing a Losing Battle to Protect Users' Privacy," by Lisa Vaas, Nakedsecurity.sophos.com, June 30, 2014; "The Dangers of Using Social Media Data in Hiring," by Gregg Skall, *Radio Business Report*, June 6, 2011; "Stored Communications Act Protects Facebook and MySpace Users' Private Communication," by Kathryn Freund, Jolt.law.harvard.edu, June 11, 2010.

TABLE 10.3	TYPES OF SOCIAL NETWORKS AND ONLINE COMMUNITIES
TYPE OF SOCIAL NETWORK / COMMUNITY	DESCRIPTION
General	Online social gathering place to meet and socialize with friends, share content, schedules, and interests. Examples: Facebook, Pinterest, Instagram, Tumblr, and Twitter.
Practice	Social network of professionals and practitioners, creators of artifacts such as computer code or music. Examples: Just Plain Folks (musicians' community), LinkedIn (business), and Doximity (physicians and health care professionals).
Interest	Community built around a common interest, such as games, sports, music, stock markets, politics, health, finance, foreign affairs, or lifestyle. Examples: Debatepolitics (political discussion group) and PredictWallStreet (stock market).
Affinity	Community of members who self-identify with a demographic or geographic category, such as women, African Americans, or Arab Americans. Examples: BlackPlanet (African American community and social network) and Marilyn's Secret, a woman-only social network.
Sponsored	Network created by commercial, government, and nonprofit organizations for a variety of purposes. Examples: Nike, IBM, Cisco, and political candidates.

practice networks
offer members focused discussion groups, help, information, and knowledge relating to an area of shared practice

interest-based social networks
offer members focused discussion groups based on a shared interest in some specific topic

affinity communities
offer members focused discussions and interaction with other people who share the same affinity

sponsored communities
online communities created for the purpose of pursuing organizational (and often commercial) goals

Practice networks offer members focused discussion groups, help, information, and knowledge relating to an area of shared practice. For instance, Linux.org is a nonprofit community for the open source movement, a worldwide global effort involving thousands of programmers who develop computer code for the Linux operating system and share the results freely with all. Other online communities involve artists, educators, art dealers, photographers, and nurses. Practice networks can be either profit-based or nonprofit, and support themselves by advertising or user donations.

Interest-based social networks offer members focused discussion groups based on a shared interest in some specific subject, such as business careers, boats, horses, health, skiing, and thousands of other topics. Because the audience for interest communities is necessarily much smaller and more targeted, these communities have usually relied on advertising and tenancy/sponsorship deals. Social networks such as College Confidential (college admissions), Ravelry (knitting and crocheting), Sailing Anarchy (sailing), and Chronicle Forums (horse enthusiasts) all are examples of social networks that attract people who share a common pursuit. Job markets and forums such as LinkedIn can be considered interest-based social networks as well.

Affinity communities offer members focused discussions and interaction with other people who share the same affinity. "Affinity" refers to self- and group identification. For instance, people can self-identify themselves on the basis of religion, ethnicity, gender, sexual orientation, political beliefs, geographical location, and hundreds of other categories. These social networks are supported by advertising along with revenues from sales of products.

Sponsored communities are online communities created by government, nonprofit, or for-profit organizations for the purpose of pursuing organizational goals. These goals can be diverse, from increasing the information available to citizens; for instance, such as Westchestergov.com, the website for Westchester County (New York) government; to an online auction such as eBay; to Tide.com, which focuses on uses of Tide detergent and is sponsored by its manufacturer (Procter & Gamble). Cisco, IBM, HP, and hundreds of other companies have developed their internal corporate social networks as a way of sharing knowledge.

SOCIAL NETWORK TECHNOLOGIES AND FEATURES

Algorithms are one of the most important technologies used by social networks. **Algorithms** are sets of step-by-step instructions, similar to a recipe, for producing a desired output from required inputs. **Computer algorithms** are computer programs that carry out step-by-step instructions to produce desired outputs (Cormen et al., 2009). Algorithms are an ancient concept, but are fundamental to how computers are used today to do everything from calculating pay checks, the amount you owe when purchasing online, selecting movies on Netflix that you are likely to watch, or recommending products you may be interested in based on your prior purchases. How, for instance, does Facebook decide which of your posts to post on your friends' News Feeds, and which Instant Articles to make available on your mobile News Feed?

The problem Facebook and other social networks need to solve is how to select content (actions of their friends and news stories) for display on users' pages that they will find interesting, and likely click on. Also, Facebook needs to prevent information that is irrelevant from appearing on user pages. **Figure 10.3** illustrates the generic algorithm Facebook uses to produce what it calls relationship-based content personalized for members of a social network based on a patent it filed in 2010. It shows the generic eight steps in the algorithm (left column), and a translation of each step (right column). Facebook users organize themselves into affinity groups by selecting and accepting one another as friends. **Affinity groups** are a key concept here and in all social networks: they are generally composed of like-minded people who share views, attitudes, purchase patterns, and tastes in music and videos. Facebook attempts to discover exactly what those views, attitudes, purchase patterns, and tastes in music and videos are, as well as demographic and other personal information. Once these are identified, Facebook attempts to find out what content is being consumed by each affinity group and matches the content to each group (relation-base content). Facebook creates a database of this relationship-based content, and serves it to other members of the group, as well as other affinity groups that share similar features.

In the end, you will be informed of what your friends are doing, liking, viewing and listening to. You will find this interesting and engaging. You will be spared hearing about other affinity groups who are very dissimilar to your affinity groups. New content (news, music, videos) that is similar to what your affinity group has liked in the past will also be served to you. For instance, if you are a staunch conservative or liberal, and you choose to click on articles that confirm your views, other members of your affinity group who share your views will have the content and your behavior displayed on their pages. They in turn may share this content with other Facebook friends, and other affinity groups of which they are a part.

While the generic algorithm appears simple, each step in the algorithm is implemented by computer programs involving tens of thousands of lines of computer code, and

algorithms
sets of step-by-step instructions, similar to a recipe, for producing a desired output from required inputs

computer algorithms
computer programs that carry out step-by-step instructions to produce desired outputs

affinity groups
generally composed of like-minded people who share views, attitudes, purchase patterns, and tastes in music and videos

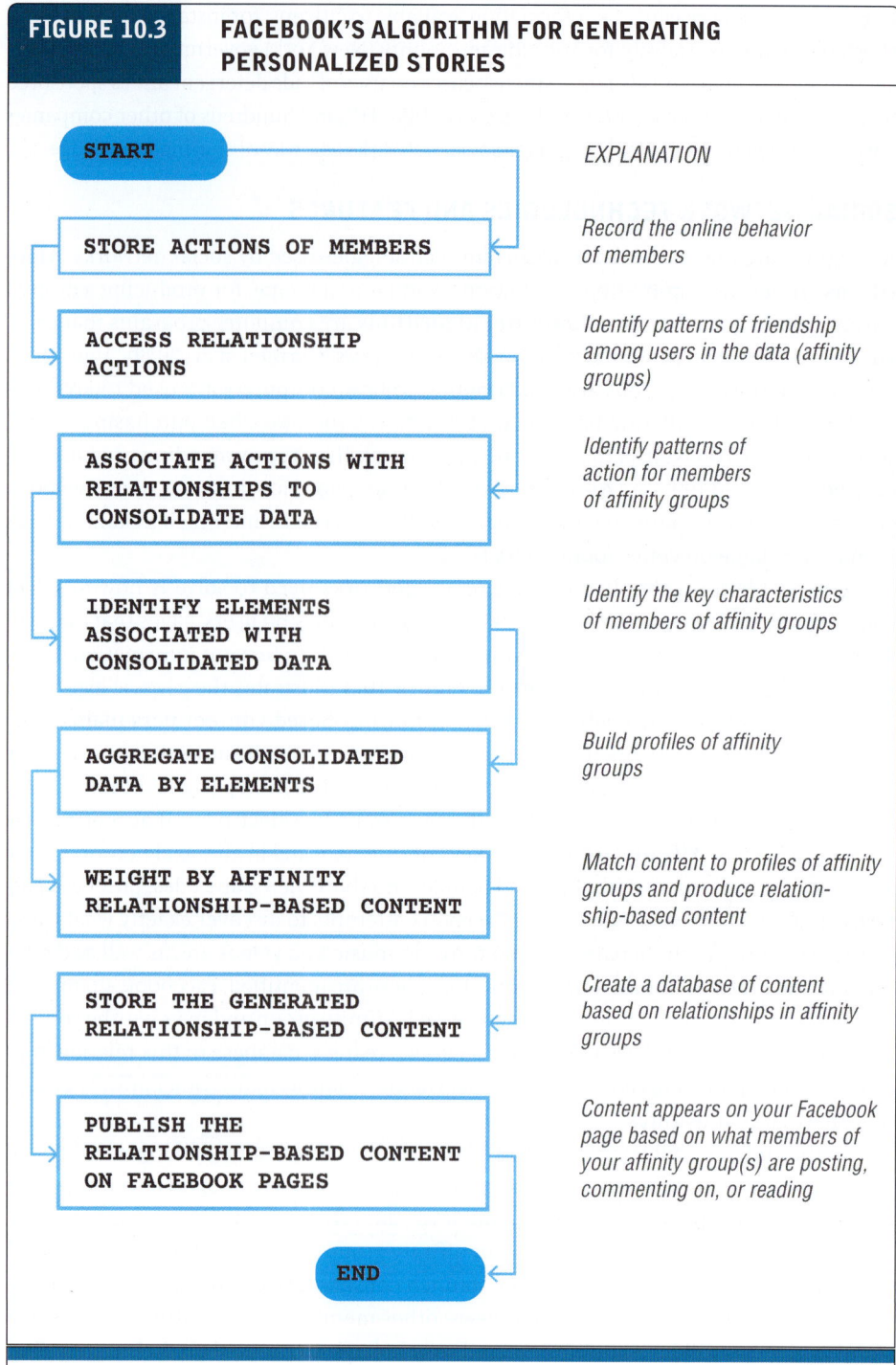

FIGURE 10.3 FACEBOOK'S ALGORITHM FOR GENERATING PERSONALIZED STORIES

Facebook uses a very complex algorithm to identify content that users are likely to click on. Each step in the algorithm is implemented by computer programs involving tens of thousands of lines of computer code and thousands of hours of software engineering and system development.

SOURCE: Based on data from U.S. Patent and Trademark Office, 2010.

TABLE 10.4 SOCIAL NETWORK FEATURES

FEATURE	DESCRIPTION
Profiles	User-created web pages that describe the owner on a variety of dimensions
Newsfeed	A listing of updates from friends, advertisements, and notifications in chronological order
Timeline	A history of updates, posts from friends, photos, and other objects in chronological order
Stories	Collection of photos and videos that capture a user's experience
Friends networks	Ability to create a linked group of friends, a social community
Network discovery	Ability to find other social networks, find new groups and friends, and discover friends of friends
Favorites (Like)	Ability to communicate favorite sites, bookmarks, content, and destinations
Games and apps	Games developed for the social network, and apps that extend its functionality
Instant messaging	Instant messaging, chat
Storage	Storage for photos, videos, text
Message boards	Ability to post updates to friends, e.g., Wall
Groups	Discussion groups, forums, and consumer groups organized by interest, e.g., For Sale Groups

thousands of hours of software engineering and system development. The data produced by over 2 billion other users worldwide currently requires nine data centers in the United States and three in international locations, a total of 15 million square feet containing tens of thousands of servers, all connected by fiber optic networks (Miller, 2018). According to Facebook, loading a user's home page involves hundreds of servers, processing tens of thousands of individual pieces of data, and delivering the information selected in less than one second. The *Insight on Technology* case, *Trapped Inside the Facebook Bubble?*, examines the social and political impact of algorithms in further depth.

Social networks also have developed a number of other software applications that allow users to engage in a number of activities. **Table 10.4** describes several additional social network functionalities.

10.2 ONLINE AUCTIONS

Auctions are used throughout the e-commerce landscape. The most widely known auctions are **consumer-to-consumer (C2C) auctions**, in which the auction house is simply an intermediary market maker, providing a forum where consumers—buyers and sellers—can discover prices and trade. The market leader in C2C auctions is eBay, which, as of the end of 2019, had over 180 million active buyers and over 1 billion items listed on any given day within thousands of different categories. In 2019, eBay had about $7.6 billion in net revenues

consumer-to-consumer (C2C) auctions
auction house acts as an intermediary market maker, providing a forum where consumers can discover prices and trade

INSIGHT ON TECHNOLOGY

TRAPPED INSIDE THE FACEBOOK BUBBLE?

During the past several years, Facebook has come under intense scrutiny in connection with the spread of false news stories (fake news) on its platform during the 2016 U.S. presidential election and thereafter. Facebook has acknowledged that hundreds of thousands of fake accounts were opened, some of them allegedly by parties associated with Russian authorities. Taking advantage of Facebook's open advertising platform, which enables just about anyone to purchase ads targeted to various groups of Facebook users, these parties were able to turn Facebook into a megaphone of misinformation by manipulating Facebook's algorithms and ad system. First, the manipulators opened fake company accounts on Facebook. Then they purchased advertising aimed at their targets' News Feeds. Facebook's advertising system enabled the manipulators to to target people they believed would be receptive to their message and likely to like it, post it, and forward it to their network of friends. Often the ads included links to a website, which had even more false news. If 1,000 people respond to a post and each of those people has 10 friends, then the message could potentially make its way to 1 million people or more in a matter of hours, influencing what Facebook's algorithms notice, which will result in even more people getting the message. These same groups also deployed thousands of bots to click on the ads, making them seem much more popular than they really were. One result of this process is the creation of a "bubble world" where messages—both true and fake—rocket through the network in hours. Researchers have found that fake news travels faster and further than real news from reputable sources because it is more alarming, emotional, and unusual.

Critics fear that Facebook is helping to create a highly polarized society: users see only the social and political views of their friends on controversial topics, creating a self-reinforcing, bubble world. Sometimes referred to as the Facebook filter trap, echo chamber, or bubble, critics believe this results in groups who never share news or interact with people who have differing views and who therefore cannot find a middle ground to share. Worse, extremist groups proliferate based on their own unchallenged facts and theories, which are never subjected to accuracy checking. It's called homophily: given a choice, people tend to associate with people like themselves. In the social network world, this translates to only being exposed to views of people who share your views, creating an echo chamber. Contrary views will rarely make it to your News Feed. Every click, Like, and keystroke creates a reality for users that may or may not be a fiction.

From Facebook's point of view, its algorithms solve an important problem for today's users of social networks: there is so much information online that users may become inundated with information that does not interest them, and makes it difficult for them to find information that does interest them. The resulting frustration could turn users away from social networks that increasingly are their main source of news and opinion. Therefore there is a need for what Facebook refers to, in its patent applications for both algorithms, as "a system to generate dynamic, relationship-based content personalized for members of a Social Network." Translated, this means the algorithms are set up to engage you and keep you on Facebook, exposing you to more ads.

Facebook's Trending algorithm, in use from 2014 to mid-2018, was a complex chunk of code that operated in real time. The algorithm monitored the behavior of over 2.2 billion users worldwide, and posted the results on the top right of users' News Feed pages, changing periodically through the day. The algorithm used keywords to process mentions and other activities of users (such as Super Bowl, skiing, baseball, etc.) and grouped them into topics. Each topic was given a trending score based on the geographic location of users posting about the topic, the number of mentions, and the rate of increase in activity. Then the trending topics were matched to the personal interests of each user, as well as other factors like gender, race, national origin, religion, age, marital status, disability, sexual orientation, educational level, and socioeconomic status. The algorithm was also sensitive to rates of change: if mentions spiked in a short period of time, the topic got boosted in ranking. The impression conveyed was that Trending was a computer-driven process that accurately and objectively reflected what users were reacting to Facebook.

But the reality was really quite different, according to former employees. The process of selecting trends evolved over several years, but from the beginning news curators (journalists) intervened and had the last say about what was, or was not, included in Trending. This was necessary because the algorithm could not distinguish between a real event (a SpaceX rocket explodes on the pad) versus a phony event (spacecraft land in New Mexico). The algorithm was also not allowed to include stories about Facebook itself. Editors also removed topics involving sex, pornography, nudity, or graphic violence. If the algorithm missed important news events for some reason, curators injected these events as Trending topics. Humans therefore played an important editorial role in creating the Trending topics, and like journalists and editors everywhere, could exercise their discretion, and perhaps insert their views, in the process.

One of the vulnerabilities of the Trending algorithm was its sensitivity to the number of mentions (which could be Likes, posts, clicks, or other behavior), and the rate of increase over short periods of time. Social scientists established a long time ago that on most controversial issues, 90% of the population appears near the middle of opinion, or close by. The other 10% of the population has views that are significantly further away from the average opinion. Sometimes called "fringe groups" or "extremists," people in these groups frequently engage in concerted short-term bursts of online posting in the hope of influencing a very large online audience by encouraging a viral sharing of their posts. Fringe groups try to take advantage of the viral nature of social networks. Facebook's algorithm tries to counter this tendency by demoting content posted by very frequent contributors.

In response to the public concern about human bias in the Trending section, and the difficulty Facebook encountered in trying to clearly explain how its Trending section works, Facebook fired its staff of 26 Trending editors in 2016, and promised to rely only on the Trending algorithm in order to eliminate human bias and be more objective. The results suggested that more false news or hoax stories, conspiracy theories, and offensive material were appearing in Trending than before. In June 2018, Facebook announced its decision to eliminate the Trending section.

The News Feed also faces similar criticism. To illustrate the strength of the News Feed echo chamber, and how reality differs for different Facebook users, the *Wall Street Journal* published a graphical representation of how very liberal and very conservative users of Facebook reacted to news articles drawn from over 500

(continued)

sources, from bloggers to reputable news organizations. The data was originally produced in a large study of user behavior funded by Facebook, conducted by Facebook researchers, and reported in the magazine *Science*. The News Feeds of 10 million users were examined. The results of the *Journal's* online data was that very liberal and very conservative Facebook users create for themselves, through their selection of news articles enabled by the News Feed algorithm, two highly divergent world views on most topics, from guns, to abortion, ISIS, political candidates, and so forth. For instance, on guns, very liberal users linked to posts critical of the National Rifle Association, school shootings, and the ready availability of guns, among others. Very conservative users linked to posts critical of gun control legislation, invasions of homes by armed criminals, and the use of guns for self-defense, among others. Facebook's researchers concluded in the *Science* article that Facebook's users do get some contrary views in their News Feeds sections, and that any bias is not caused by its algorithms, but rather by users selecting as friends people who share their views. The algorithms simply reflect what users have chosen in terms of friends and the articles they click on.

On the other hand, is Facebook any different from a traditional newspaper or cable news channel, both of which select the news and views that they believe their readers and viewers find engaging? One difference is that for traditional news producers, human beings are doing the selection of news, and responsible news organizations hire fact checkers to vet stories. At Facebook, algorithms, written by humans, automate this process of determining what is news.

In 2017, addressing critics who claimed Facebook was contributing to the erosion of democracy both in the United States and elsewhere, Facebook reversed course in an effort to reduce the exploitation of its algorithms by hiring a corps of internal employees to remove bot accounts, and hiring outside firms to check facts in posts and ads. Facebook promises to refine its algorithms using artificial intelligence and machine learning in order to detect bot accounts or content that violates its terms of service. Critics have not been impressed. Facebook algorithms created the problem in the first place. Facebook, the largest source of news in the United States, is back in the editorial business deciding what's fit and not fit to post using human editors.

SOURCES: "What Stays on Facebook and What Goes? The Social Network Cannot Answer," by Farhad Manjoo, *New York Times*, July 19, 2018; "Facebook's 'Trending' Section Is Dead as Company Offers New Approach to Breaking News," by Alyssa Newcomb, Nbcnews.com, June 1, 2018; "Facebook's 10,000 New Editors," by James Freeman, *Wall Street Journal*, May 16, 2018; "The Spread of True and False News Online," by Soroush Vosoughi, Deb Roy, and Sinan Aral, *Science*, March 9, 2018; "Facebook Wins, Democracy Loses," by Siva Vaidhyanathan, *New York Times*, September 8, 2017; "The Fake Americans Russia Created to Influence the Election," by Scott Shane, *New York Times*, September 7, 2017; "How Hate Groups Forced Online Platforms to Reveal Their True Nature," by John Herrman, *New York Times*, August 21, 2017; "Facebook Drowns Out Fake News With More Information," by Deepa Seetharaman, *Wall Street Journal*, August 3, 2017; "How Social Media Filter Bubbles and Algorithms Influence the Election," *The Guardian*, May 22, 2017; "In Race Against Fake News, Google and Facebook Stroll to the Starting Line," by Daisuke Wakabayashi and Mike Isaac, *New York Times*, January 26, 2017; "Blue Feed, Red Feed: See Liberal Facebook and Conservative Facebook, Side by Side," *Wall Street Journal*, May 18, 2016; "The Algorithm Is an Editor," by Jeffrey Herbst, *Wall Street Journal*, April 13, 2016; "Facebook's 'Trending' Feature Exhibits Flaws Under New Algorithm," by Georgia Wells, *Wall Street Journal*, September 6, 2016; "Almost No One Really Knows How Facebook's Trending Algorithm Works, But Here's An Idea," by Joseph Lichterman, NiemanLab.org, September 1, 2016; "Inside Facebook's (Totally Insane, Unintentionally Gigantic, Hyperpartisan) Political-Media Machine," by John Herrman, *New York Times*, August 24, 2016; "The Reason Your Feed Became An Echo Chamber—And What to Do About It," NPR.com, July 24, 2016; "Your Facebook Echo Chamber Just Got a Whole Lot Louder," by Brian Barrett, Wired.com, June 29, 2016; "Exposure to Ideologically Diverse News and Opinion on Facebook," by E. Bakshy, S. Messing, and L. Adamic, *Science*, June 5, 2016; "How Facebook Warps Our Worlds," by Frank Bruni, *New York Times*, May 21, 2016; "The Wall Street Journal's New Tool Gives a Side-by-Side Look at the Facebook Political News Filter Bubble," by Ricardo Bilton, *Wall Street Journal*, May 18, 2016; "Facebook Study Finds People Only Click on Links That They Agree With, Site Is an 'Echo Chamber'," by Andrew Griffin, Independent.co.uk, May 8, 2015; *The Filter Bubble*, by Eli Pariser. Penguin Books; Reprint edition (April 24, 2012); Facebook, "Generating a Feed of Stories Personalized for Members of a Social Network," US Patent 7827208 B2, United States Patent Office, published November 2, 2010.

from its Marketplaces segment, a 2% increase from 2018, and the total worth of goods sold or auctioned (Gross Merchandise Value—GMV) was around $85.5 billion (eBay, 2020). eBay continues to expand in emerging markets, which are now its fastest growing markets. While eBay started as an auction site for mostly used goods, today, almost 90% of eBay's listings are for products sold with either fixed or best offer pricing. eBay is a direct competitor of Amazon in online retail. eBay is further discussed in the case study at the end of this chapter. There are hundreds of online auctions, some specializing in unique collectible products such as stamps and coins, others adopting a more generalist approach in which almost any good can be found for sale.

Less well known are **business-to-consumer (B2C) auctions**, where a business owns or controls assets and uses dynamic pricing to establish the price. One example is Sam's Club, owned by Walmart, which offers auctions of a variety of goods. Auctions also constitute a significant part of B2B e-commerce, and more than a third of procurement officers use auctions to procure goods.

Some leading online auctions are listed in **Table 10.5**. Auctions are not limited to goods and services. They can also be used to allocate resources, and bundles of resources, among any group of bidders. For instance, if you wanted to establish an optimal schedule for assigned tasks in an office among a group of clerical workers, an auction in which workers bid for assignments would come close to producing a nearly optimal solution in a short amount of time (Parkes and Ungar, 2000). In short, auctions—like all markets—are ways of allocating resources among independent agents (bidders).

business-to-consumer (B2C) auctions
business sells goods it owns, or controls, using various dynamic pricing models

TABLE 10.5	LEADING ONLINE AUCTIONS
GENERAL	
eBay	The world market leader in auctions: over 180 million active buyers and 1 billion products.
eBid	In business since 1998. Operates in 23 countries, including the United States. Currently, one of the top competitors to eBay. Offers much lower fees.
uBid	Marketplace for excess inventory from pre-approved merchants.
SPECIALIZED	
Stacks Bowers	America's largest fully automated auction company of certified coins including ancient gold, silver, and copper coins. Also offers sports cards.
Bid4Assets	Liquidation of distressed real estate assets from government and the public sector, corporations, restructurings, and bankruptcies.
Old and Sold Antiques Auction	Online auction service specializing in quality antiques. Dealers pay a 3% commission on merchandise sold.
B2C AUCTIONS	
Samsclub.com Auctions	Merchandise from Sam's Club in a variety of categories.
Shopgoodwill	Goodwill's online auction. Offers a wide variety of collectibles, books, and antiques chosen from the goods donated to Goodwill.

BENEFITS AND COSTS OF AUCTIONS

The Internet is primarily responsible for the resurgence in auctions. The Internet provides a global environment and very low fixed and operational costs for the aggregation of huge buyer audiences, composed of millions of consumers worldwide, who can use a universally available technology (Internet browsers) to shop for goods.

Benefits of Auctions

Aside from the sheer game-like fun of participating in auctions, consumers, merchants, and society as a whole derive a number of economic benefits from participating in Internet auctions. These benefits include:

- **Liquidity:** Sellers can find willing buyers, and buyers can find sellers. Sellers and buyers can be located anywhere around the globe. Just as important, buyers and sellers can find a global market for rare items that would not have existed before the Internet.
- **Price discovery:** Buyers and sellers can quickly and efficiently develop prices for items that are difficult to assess, where the price depends on demand and supply, and where the product is rare.
- **Price transparency:** Public Internet auctions allow everyone in the world to see the asking and bidding prices for items.
- **Market efficiency:** Auctions can, and often do, lead to reduced prices, and hence reduced profits for merchants, leading to an increase in consumer welfare—one measure of market efficiency.
- **Lower transaction costs:** Online auctions can lower the cost of selling and purchasing products, benefiting both merchants and consumers. Like other Internet markets, such as retail markets, Internet auctions have very low (but not zero) transaction costs.
- **Consumer aggregation:** Sellers benefit from large online auctions' ability to aggregate a large number of consumers who are motivated to purchase something in one marketspace.
- **Network effects:** The larger an online auction becomes in terms of visitors and products for sale, the more valuable it becomes as a marketplace for everyone by providing liquidity and several other benefits listed previously, such as lower transaction costs, higher efficiency, and better price transparency.

Risks and Costs of Auctions

There are a number of risks and costs involved in participating in auctions. In some cases, auction markets can fail—like all markets at times. (We describe auction market failure in more detail later.) Some of the more important risks and costs to keep in mind are:

- **Delayed consumption costs:** Internet auctions can go on for days, and shipping will take additional time.
- **Monitoring costs:** Participation in auctions requires your time to monitor bidding.
- **Equipment costs:** Internet auctions require you to purchase a computer system and pay for Internet access.
- **Trust risks:** Online auctions are a significant source of Internet fraud. Using auctions increases the risk of experiencing a loss.

- **Fulfillment costs:** Typically, the buyer pays fulfillment costs of packing, shipping, and insurance, whereas at a physical store these costs are included in the retail price.

Online auctions such as eBay have taken a number of steps to reduce consumer participation costs and trust risk. For instance, online auctions attempt to solve the trust problem by providing a rating system in which previous customers rate sellers based on their overall experience with the merchant. Although helpful, this solution does not always work. Auction fraud is a leading source of e-commerce complaints to federal law enforcement officials. Another partial solution to high monitoring costs is, ironically, fixed pricing. At eBay, consumers can reduce the cost of monitoring and waiting for auctions to end by simply clicking on the Buy It Now button and paying a premium price. The difference between the Buy It Now price and the auction price is the cost of monitoring.

Nevertheless, given the costs of participating in online auctions, the generally lower cost of goods on Internet auctions is in part a compensation for the other additional costs consumers experience. On the other hand, consumers experience lower search costs and transaction costs because there usually are no intermediaries (unless, of course, the seller is an online business operating on an auction site, in which case there is a middleman cost), and usually there are no local or state taxes.

Merchants face considerable risks and costs as well. At auctions, merchants may end up selling goods for prices far below what they might have achieved in conventional markets. Merchants also face risks of nonpayment, false bidding, bid rigging, monitoring, transaction fees charged by the auction company, credit card transaction processing fees, and the administration costs of entering price and product information.

AUCTIONS AS AN E-COMMERCE BUSINESS MODEL

Online auctions have been among the most successful business models in retail and B2B commerce. eBay, the Internet's most lucrative auction company, has been profitable nearly since its inception. The strategy for eBay has been to make money off every stage in the auction cycle. eBay earns revenue from auctions in several ways: transaction fees based on the amount of the sale, listing fees for display of goods, financial service fees from payment systems, and advertising or placement fees where sellers pay extra for special services such as particular display or listing services.

However, it is on the cost side that online auctions have extraordinary advantages over ordinary online retailers. Online auction companies carry no inventory and do not perform any fulfillment activities—they need no warehouses, shipping, or logistical facilities. Sellers and consumers provide these services and bear these costs. In this sense, online auctions are an ideal digital business because they involve simply the transfer of information.

Even though eBay has been extraordinarily successful, the success of online auctions is qualified by the fact that the marketplace for online auctions is highly concentrated. eBay dominates the online auction market, followed by eBid and uBid. In the last several years eBay's growth has slowed considerably as consumers shift toward Buy It Now purchases rather than auctions. Many of the smaller online auction companies are not profitable because they lack sufficient sellers and buyers to achieve liquidity. In auctions, network effects are highly influential, and the tendency is for one or two very large online auctions to dominate, with hundreds of smaller specialty auctions (which sell specialized goods such as stamps) being barely profitable.

TYPES AND EXAMPLES OF AUCTIONS

The primary types of auctions found on the Internet are English auctions, Dutch Internet auctions, Name Your Own Price auctions, and so-called penny auctions.

The **English auction** is the easiest to understand and the most common form of auction on eBay. Typically, there is a single item up for sale from a single seller. There is a time limit when the auction ends, a reserve price below which the seller will not sell (usually secret), and a minimum incremental bid set. Multiple buyers bid against one another until the auction time limit is reached. The highest bidder wins the item (if the reserve price of the seller has been met or exceeded). English auctions are considered to be seller-biased because multiple buyers compete against one another—usually anonymously.

The **Dutch Internet auction** format is perfect for sellers that have many identical items to sell. Sellers start by listing a minimum price, or a starting bid for one item, and the number of items for sale. Bidders specify both a bid price and the quantity they want to buy. The uniform price reigns. Winning bidders pay the same price per item, which is the lowest successful bid. This market clearing price can be less than some bids. If there are more buyers than items, the earliest successful bids get the goods. In general, high bidders get the quantity they want at the lowest successful price, whereas low successful bidders might not get the quantity they want (but they will get something).

The **Name Your Own Price auction** was pioneered by Priceline, and is the second most-popular online auction format. Although Priceline also acts as an intermediary, buying blocks of airline tickets, hotel rooms, and vacation packages at a discount and selling them at a reduced retail price or matching its inventory to bidders, it is best known for its Name Your Own Price auctions, in which users specify what they are willing to pay for goods or services, and multiple providers bid for their business. Prices do not descend and are fixed: the initial consumer offer is a commitment to purchase at that price.

But how can Priceline offer such steep discounts off prices for services provided by major brand-name providers? There are several answers. First, Priceline "shields the brand" by not publicizing the prices at which major brands sell. This reduces conflict with traditional channels, including direct sales. Second, the services being sold are perishable: if a Priceline customer did not pay something for the empty airline seat, rental car, or hotel room, sellers would not receive any revenue. Hence, sellers are highly motivated to at least cover the costs of their services by selling in a spot market at very low prices. The strategy for sellers is to sell as much as possible through more profitable channels and then unload excess capacity on spot markets such as Priceline. This works to the advantage of consumers, sellers, and Priceline, which charges a transaction fee to sellers.

So-called penny auctions are really anything but. To participate in a **penny auction** (also known as a **bidding fee auction**), you typically must pay the penny auction company for bids ahead of time, typically 50 cents to $1 dollar, usually in packs costing $25–$50. Once you have purchased the bids, you can use them to bid on items listed by the penny auction (unlike traditional auctions, items are owned by the auction company, not third parties). Items typically start at or near $0 and each bid raises the price by a fixed amount, usually just a penny. Auctions are timed, and when the time runs out, the last and highest bidder wins the item. Although the price of the item itself may not be that high, the successful bidder will typically have spent much more than that. Unlike a traditional auction, it costs money to bid, and that money is gone even if the bidder does not win the auction. The bidder's cumulative cost of

---

English auction
most common form of auction; the highest bidder wins

Dutch Internet auction
public ascending price, multiple unit auction. Final price is lowest successful bid, which sets price for all higher bidders

Name Your Own Price auction
auction where users specify what they are willing to pay for goods or services

penny (bidding fee) auction
bidder must pay a non-refundable fee to purchase bids

bidding must be added to the final price of a successful bid to determine the true cost of the item. The Federal Trade Commission has issued an alert about penny auctions, warning that bidders may find that they spend far more than they intended (Consumer Reports.org, 2013). Examples of penny auction companies include QuiBids and DealDash.

WHEN TO USE AUCTIONS (AND FOR WHAT) IN BUSINESS

There are many different situations in which auctions are an appropriate channel for businesses to consider. For much of this chapter, we have looked at auctions from a consumer point of view. The objective of consumers is to receive the greatest value for the lowest cost. Now, switch your perspective to that of a business. Remember that the objective of businesses using auctions is to maximize their revenue (their share of consumer surplus) by finding the true market value of products and services, a market value that hopefully is higher in the auction channel than in fixed-price channels. **Table 10.6** provides an overview of factors to consider.

The factors are described as follows:

- **Type of product:** Online auctions are most commonly used for rare and unique products for which prices are difficult to discover, and there may have been no market for the goods. However, Priceline has succeeded in developing auctions for perishable commodities (such as airline seats) for which retail prices have already been established, and some B2B auctions involve commodities such as steel (often sold at distress prices). New clothing items, new digital cameras, and new computers are generally not sold at auction because their prices are easy to discover, catalog prices are high, sustainable, and profitable, they are not perishable, and there exists an efficient market channel in the form of retail stores (online and offline).

- **Product life cycle:** For the most part, businesses have traditionally used auctions for goods at the end of their product life cycle and for products where auctions yield a higher price than fixed-price liquidation sales. However, products at the beginning of their life cycle are increasingly being sold at auction. Early releases of music, books,

TABLE 10.6 FACTORS TO CONSIDER WHEN CHOOSING AUCTIONS

CONSIDERATIONS	DESCRIPTION
Type of product	Rare, unique, commodity, perishable
Stage of product life cycle	Early, mature, late
Channel-management issues	Conflict with retail distributors; differentiation
Type of auction	Seller vs. buyer bias
Initial pricing	Low vs. high
Bid increment amounts	Low vs. high
Auction length	Short vs. long
Number of items	Single vs. multiple
Price-allocation rule	Uniform vs. discriminatory
Information sharing	Closed vs. open bidding

videos, games, and electronics can be sold to highly motivated early adopters who want to be the first in their neighborhood with new products.

- **Channel management:** Manufacturers and retailers must be careful not to allow their auction activity to interfere with their existing profitable channels. For this reason, items offered by manufacturers and established retailers tend to be late in their product life cycle or have quantity purchase requirements.

- **Type of auction:** Sellers obviously should choose auctions where there are many buyers and only a few, or even one, seller. English ascending-price auctions such as those at eBay are best for sellers because as the number of bidders increases, the price tends to move higher.

- **Initial pricing:** Research suggests that auction items should start out with low initial bid prices in order to encourage more bidders to bid (see "Bid increments" below). The lower the price, the larger the number of bidders will appear. The larger the number of bidders, the higher the prices move.

- **Bid increments:** It is generally safest to keep bid increments low so as to increase the number of bidders and the frequency of their bids. If bidders can be convinced that, for just a few more dollars, they can win the auction, then they will tend to make the higher bid and forget about the total amount they are bidding.

- **Auction length:** In general, the longer auctions are scheduled, the larger the number of bidders and the higher the prices can go. However, once the new bid arrival rate drops off and approaches zero, bid prices stabilize. Most eBay auctions are scheduled for seven days.

- **Number of items:** When a business has a number of items to sell, buyers usually expect a "volume discount," and this expectation can cause lower bids in return. Therefore, sellers should consider breaking up very large bundles into smaller bundles auctioned at different times.

- **Price allocation rule:** Most buyers believe it is "fair" that everyone pay the same price in a multi-unit auction, and a uniform pricing rule is recommended. eBay Dutch Internet auctions encourage this expectation. The idea that some buyers should pay more based on their differential need for the product is not widely supported. Therefore, sellers who want to price discriminate should do so by holding auctions for the same goods on different auction markets, or at different times, to prevent direct price comparison.

- **Closed vs. open bidding:** Closed bidding has many advantages for the seller, and sellers should use this approach whenever possible because it permits price discrimination without offending buyers. However, open bidding carries the advantage of "herd effects" and "winning effects" (described later in the chapter) in which consumers' competitive instincts to "win" drive prices higher than even secret bidding would achieve.

AUCTION PRICES: ARE THEY THE LOWEST?

It is widely assumed that auction prices are lower than prices in other fixed-price markets. Empirical evidence is mixed on this assumption. There are many reasons why auction prices might be higher than those in fixed-price markets for items of identical quality, and why auction prices in one auction market may be higher than those in other auction markets.

Consumers are not driven solely by value maximization but instead are influenced by many situational factors, irrelevant and wrong information, and misperceptions when they make market decisions (Simonson and Tversky, 1992). Auctions are social events—shared social environments, in which bidders adjust to one another (Hanson and Putler, 1996). Briefly, bidders base their bids on what others have previously bid, and this can lead to an upward cascading effect (Arkes and Hutzel, 2000). In a study of hundreds of eBay auctions for Sony PlayStations, CD players, Mexican pottery, and Italian silk ties, Dholakia and Soltysinski (2001) found that bidders exhibited **herd behavior** (the tendency to gravitate toward, and bid for, auction listings with one or more existing bids) by making multiple bids on some auctions (coveted comparables), and making no bids at auctions for comparable items (overlooked comparables). Herd behavior resulted in consumers paying higher prices than necessary for reasons having no foundation in economic reality (Liu and Sutanto, 2012).

The behavioral reality of participating in auctions can produce many unintended results. Winners can suffer **winner's regret**, the feeling after winning an auction that they paid too much for an item, which indicates that their winning bid does not reflect what they thought the item was worth but rather what the second bidder thought the item was worth. Sellers can experience **seller's lament**, reflecting the fact that they sold an item at a price just above the second place bidder, never knowing how much the ultimate winner might have paid or the true value to the final winner. Auction losers can experience **loser's lament**, the feeling of having been too cheap in bidding and failing to win. In summary, auctions can lead to both winners paying too much and sellers receiving too little. Both of these outcomes can be minimized when sellers and buyers have a very clear understanding of the prices for items in a variety of different online and offline markets.

CONSUMER TRUST IN AUCTIONS

Online auction companies have the same difficulties creating a sense of consumer trust as all other e-commerce companies, although in the case of auction companies, the operators of the marketplace do not directly control the quality of goods being offered and cannot directly vouch for the integrity of the buyers or the sellers. This opens the possibility for criminal or unreliable actors to appear as either sellers or buyers. Several studies have found that trust and credibility increase as users gain more experience, if trusted third-party seals are present, and if the auction company has a wide variety of consumer services for tracking purchases (or fraud), thus giving the user a sense of control (Krishnamurthy, 2001; Stanford-Makovsky, 2002; Nikander and Karvonen, 2002; Bailey et al., 2002; Kollock, 1999). Because of the powerful role that trust plays in online consumer behavior, eBay and most online auctions make considerable efforts to develop automated trust-enhancing mechanisms such as seller and buyer ratings, escrow services, buyer and seller insurance, guaranteed money back features, and authenticity guarantees (see the next section).

WHEN AUCTION MARKETS FAIL: FRAUD AND ABUSE IN AUCTIONS

Online and offline auction markets can be prone to fraud, which produces information asymmetries between sellers and buyers and among buyers, which in turn causes auction markets to fail. Some of the possible abuses and frauds include:

- **Bid rigging:** Agreeing offline to limit bids or using shills to submit false bids that drive prices up.

herd behavior
the tendency to gravitate toward, and bid for, auction listings with one or more existing bids

winner's regret
the winner's feeling after an auction that he or she paid too much for an item

seller's lament
concern that one will never know how much the ultimate winner might have paid, or the true value to the final winner

loser's lament
the feeling of having been too cheap in bidding and failing to win

- **Price matching:** Agreeing informally or formally to set floor prices on auction items below which sellers will not sell in open markets.
- **Shill feedback, defensive:** Using secondary IDs or other auction members to inflate seller ratings.
- **Shill feedback, offensive:** Using secondary IDs or other auction members to deflate ratings for another user (feedback bombs).
- **Feedback extortion:** Threatening negative feedback in return for a benefit.
- **Transaction interference:** E-mailing buyers to warn them away from a seller.
- **Bid manipulation:** Using the retraction option to make high bids, discovering the maximum bid of the current high bidder, and then retracting the bid.
- **Non-payment after winning:** Blocking legitimate buyers by bidding high, then not paying.
- **Shill bidding:** Using secondary user IDs or other auction members to artificially raise the price of an item.
- **Transaction non-performance:** Accepting payment and failing to deliver.
- **Non-selling seller:** Refusing payment or failing to deliver after a successful auction.
- **Bid siphoning:** E-mailing another seller's bidders and offering the same product for less.

Online auctions have sought to reduce these risks through various methods including:

- **Rating systems:** Previous customers rate sellers based on their experience with them and post them for other buyers to see.
- **Watch lists:** These allow buyers to monitor specific auctions as they proceed over a number of days and only pay close attention in the last few minutes of bidding.
- **Proxy bidding:** Buyers can enter a maximum price they are willing to pay, and the auction software will automatically place incremental bids as their original bid is surpassed.

eBay and many other online auctions have investigation units that receive complaints from consumers and investigate reported abuses. Nevertheless, with millions of visitors per week and hundreds of thousands of auctions to monitor, eBay is highly dependent on the good faith of sellers and consumers to follow the rules.

10.3 E-COMMERCE PORTALS

Port: From the Latin porta, an entrance or gateway to a locality.

Portals are among the most frequently visited websites if only because they often are a user's homepage: the page to which a user points his or her web browser on startup. The top portals such as Yahoo, MSN, and AOL have hundreds of millions of unique visitors worldwide each month. Portals are gateways to the billions of web pages available on the Internet. Facebook also acts as a home page portal to the Web. Millions of users have set Facebook as their home page, choosing to start their sessions with news from their friends, and many stay on Facebook for several hours a day. We have already discussed

Facebook in Section 10.1. Perhaps the most important service provided by portals is to help people find the information they are looking for and, like newspapers, to expose people to information they were not looking for but which they nonetheless may find entertaining or interesting. The original portals in the early days of e-commerce were search engines. Consumers would pass through search engine portals on their way to rich, detailed, in-depth content on the Web. But portals evolved into much more complex websites that provide news, entertainment, images, social networks, in-depth information, and education on a growing variety of topics. Portals today seek to be a sticky destination, not merely a gateway through which visitors pass. In this respect, portals are very much like television networks: destinations for content supported by advertising revenues. Portals today want visitors to stay a long time—the longer, the better to expose visitors to ads. For the most part they succeed: portals are places where people linger for a long time.

Portals also serve important functions within a business or organization. Most corporations, universities, churches, and other formal organizations have **enterprise portals** that help employees or members navigate to important content, such as human resources information, corporate news, or organizational announcements. For instance, your university has a portal through which you can register for courses, find classroom assignments, and perform a host of other important student activities. Increasingly, these enterprise portals also provide general-purpose news and real-time financial feeds provided by content providers outside the organization. Corporate portals and intranets are the subject of other textbooks focused on the corporate uses of web technology and are beyond the scope of this book (see Laudon and Laudon, 2020). Our focus here is on e-commerce portals.

enterprise portals
help employees navigate to the enterprise's human resource and corporate content

THE GROWTH AND EVOLUTION OF PORTALS

Portals have changed a great deal from their initial function and role. As noted above, most of today's well-known portals, such as Yahoo, MSN, and AOL, began as search engines. The initial function provided by portals was to index web page content and make this content available to users in a convenient form. Early portals expected visitors to stay only a few minutes. As millions of people signed on to the Internet in the early 2000s, the number of visitors to basic search engines exploded commensurately. At first, few people understood how a web search site could make money by passing customers on to other destinations. But search engines attracted huge audiences, and therein lay the foundation for their success as vehicles for marketing and advertising. Search engines, recognizing the potential for commerce, expanded their offerings from simple navigation to include commerce (the sale of items directly from the website as well as advertising for other online retailers), content (in the form of news at first, and later in the form of weather, investments, games, health, and other subject matter), communications (e-mail, chat, and texting), and distribution of others' content. These four characteristics have become the basic definition of a portal, namely, sites that provide four functions: navigation of the Web (search), communications, commerce, and content.

Because the value of portals to advertisers and content owners is largely a function of the size of the audience each portal reaches and the length of time visitors stay on site or app, portals compete with one another on reach and unique visitors. *Reach* is defined as the percentage of the audience that visits the site or app in a month (or some other time period), and *unique visitors* is defined as the number of uniquely identified individuals who visit a website or use an app in a month. Portals are inevitably subject to network effects: The value of the portal to advertisers and consumers increases geometrically as reach increases, which, in turn, attracts still more customers. These effects have resulted in the differentiation of the portal marketspace into three tiers: a few general-purpose mega portals that garner 60%–80% of the audience, second-tier general-purpose portals that hover around 20%–30% reach, and third-tier specialized vertical market portals that attract 2%–10% of the audience. As described in Chapter 2, the top portals/search engines (Google, Yahoo, MSN/Bing, and AOL) account for more than 95% of online searches. A similar pattern of concentration is observed when considering the audience share of portals/search engines (including both desktop and mobile) as illustrated in **Figure 10.4**. However, this picture is changing as large audiences move to social networks, and millions of users make those networks their opening or home pages and the place where they spend most of their digital time. Social networks like Facebook are broadening their content with videos, movies, and news, transforming themselves into a hybrid social network and portal.

For more insight into the nature of the competition and change among portals, read *Insight on Business: Yahoo Japan Merges with Line to Create Mega Portal.*

TYPES OF PORTALS: GENERAL-PURPOSE AND VERTICAL MARKET

There are two primary types of portals: general-purpose portals and vertical market portals. **General-purpose portals** attempt to attract a very large general audience and then retain the audience by providing in-depth vertical content channels, such as

general-purpose portals
attempt to attract a very large general audience and then retain the audience by providing in-depth vertical content

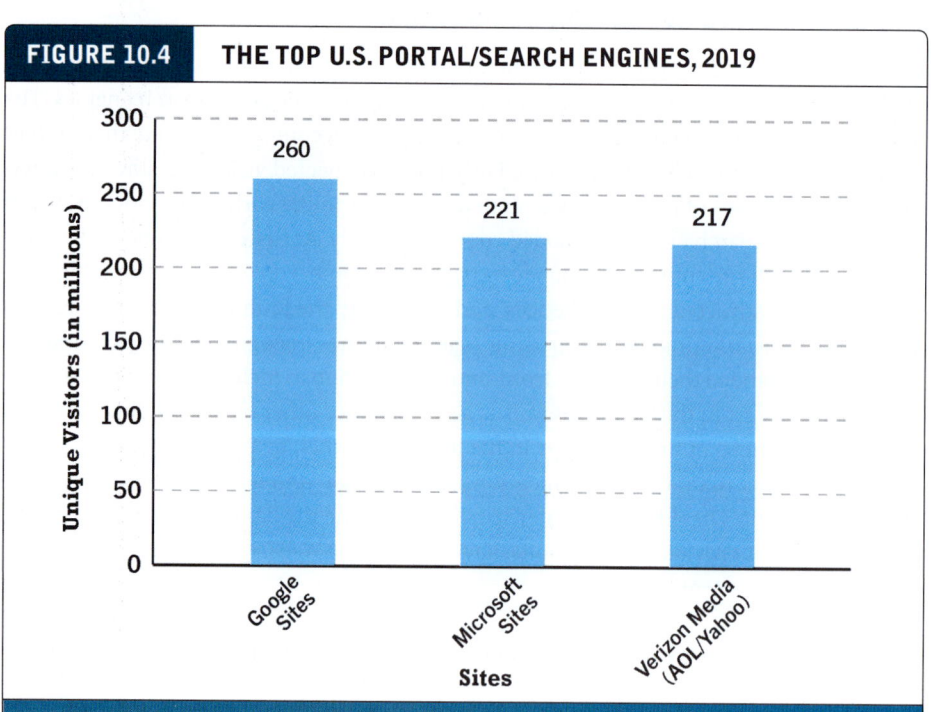

FIGURE 10.4 THE TOP U.S. PORTAL/SEARCH ENGINES, 2019

SOURCE: Based on data from comScore, 2020.

INSIGHT ON BUSINESS

YAHOO JAPAN MERGES WITH LINE TO CREATE MEGA PORTAL

Not long ago, companies like AOL, eBay, and Yahoo were dominant players in e-commerce and the tech industry more broadly. Today, they've been supplanted by Google, Apple, Facebook, and Amazon. However, Yahoo, which was purchased by Verizon in 2017 (joining AOL, which Verizon also purchased in 2015), remains surprisingly robust in one country and one country only: Japan. Yahoo's general-interest portal website remains extremely popular there, and Yahoo is pivotal to successful online search advertising campaigns in the country. In 2019, Yahoo Japan's parent company, Japanese investment conglomerate SoftBank, announced plans to merge it with Line, Japan's most popular instant messaging app, to create a company large enough both to fend off American and Chinese companies from seizing Japanese market share while competing with those same companies abroad.

In 2016, Yahoo maintained a single-digit percentage of market share for search in every market worldwide, except for Japan, where it held a shockingly large 31% of the search market. Although the company Americans remember as Yahoo now exists under Verizon rebranded as Verizon Media, Yahoo Japan has long been an independent entity and was unaffected by that acquisition. In 1996, Yahoo and SoftBank created Yahoo Japan with the goal of developing the first Japanese web portal. The site was developed with Japanese customers specifically in mind, with search functions in Japanese and other features designed to appeal to the Japanese audience. The concept of a general-purpose portal was new to Japanese Internet users and the concept became popular quickly. Yahoo has held onto its first mover advantage in the country; today, Yahoo Japan has 50 million regular users and boasts a network of 20,000 advertisers, 900 million devices, and 200 million users IDs to offer to advertisers, who can match their own lists of customers to Yahoo's and tailor customized advertising to Japanese users.

Japan has unique challenges relative to other countries, including an aging population and increased likelihood of natural disasters like earthquakes and tsunamis. Japanese tech companies lag behind their counterparts in research and development and user base. In an effort to create a company big enough to overcome these factors, SoftBank reached an agreement to acquire Line from its parent company, South Korean–based Naver, for $3.1 billion, and merge it with Yahoo Japan, creating a company with a market capitalization of $30 billion. The merger, which analysts expect the companies to complete by October 2020, will result in a company with many millions of active monthly users worldwide (67 million for Yahoo Japan and 160 million from Line). The hope is that the combined company will be Japan's first app portal, akin to WeChat in China, that performs a wide variety of every-day functions.

Line is a messaging app that is extremely popular in Japan, Thailand, Taiwan, and Indonesia. The company was first conceived in the Tokyo office of Naver by a three-person team seeking to create a smartphone app useful for peer-to-peer communication. The team then

(continued)

hastily launched the Line as a disaster response app in the wake of the 2011 Tohoku earthquake and resulting tsunami, which leveled much of the Japanese mainland and destroyed much of the country's telecommunications infrastructure. The Internet remained robust, however, and with phone networks down, Japanese citizens turned to Line to reach out to family and friends. The company quickly became popular and has since grown its user base to 82 million Japanese users and 160 million users worldwide. In Thailand, Line is used by 84% of the 70 million residents of the country in 2019.

Line offers its basic chat functionality, in-app games, a ride hailing service akin to Uber (Line Taxi), a payment service (Line Pay), and a food delivery service (Line Wow), among other features. Line has also monetized its chat service better than many of its larger competitors, offering packs of 'stickers' (large emojis) to users for a fee. Users send billions of sticks every day, and companies like Disney, Marvel, and Pixar strike deals with Line to offer packs of stickers featuring their characters. However, Line has stagnated in recent years, with losses in six of the last eight quarters and nearly nonexistent revenue growth prior to its takeover by SoftBank.

SoftBank and Naver hope that the combination of all of these services combined with Yahoo Japan's search and currently existing web portal will create a combined company capable of challenging overseas tech giants. Yahoo Japan also purchased Zozo, Japan's largest online fashion retailer, for $3.7 billion, with plans to integrate it with Yahoo Japan and Line more closely, and partnered with SBI Holdings, Japan's biggest online brokerage, with an eye toward potentially offering investment services through Line the way that WeChat offers banking services in China. The moves are a risk for SoftBank, which took a $4.6 billion loss on the failed tech real estate company WeWork in 2019, but unless Yahoo Japan and Line take bold risks, their fates may be to cede market share to foreign tech giants anyway.

SOURCES: Richard Kastelein, "Fastest Growing and Highest Revenue Mobile Messenger App in the World, Japan's LINE to Launch LINK Cryptocurrency," The-blockchain.com, February 3, 2020; "Signal's Platform Powers Yahoo! Japan's Next-Gen DMP," Signal.com, accessed February 2020; Takafumi Hotta, Masaaki Kudo, and Yoshina Sakurai, "Yahoo Japan and Line Aim for Southeast Asia Dominance," Asia.nikkei.com, November 24, 2019; Masumi Koizumi and Kazuaki Nagata, "SoftBank's Yahoo Japan-Line Merger Aims to Take On U.S. and China Online Behemoths," Japantimes.co.jp, November 18, 2019; Takashi Mochizuki, "Yahoo Japan and Chat App Line Agree to Merge," *Wall Street Journal*, November 18, 2019; Catherine Shu, "Yahoo Japan and Line Corp. Confirm Merger Agreement," Techcrunch.com, November 18, 2019; Takashi Mochizuki, "Yahoo-Line Merger Plan Raises Hopes for Japanese 'Super App,'" *Wall Street Journal*, November 14, 2019; Tim Culpan, "Line Would Be Lucky to Find a Suitor, Even Yahoo," Bloomberg.com, November 13, 2019; Alex Cattle, "Yahoo! Japan Builds Their IaaS Environment with Canonical," Ubuntu.com, November 6, 2019; Sam Nussey, "SoftBank Corp to Spend $4 Billion to Up Yahoo Japan Stake, Sees Profit Rising 24 Percent," Reuters.com, May 8, 2019; Wendy Lee, "Yahoo Japan's Future Still Looks Bright—Unlike Its U.S. Counterpart," *San Francisco Chronicle*, May 13, 2016; Harry McCracken, "How Japan's Line App Became a Culture-Changing, Revenue-Generating Phenomenon," Fastcompany.com, February 19, 2015.

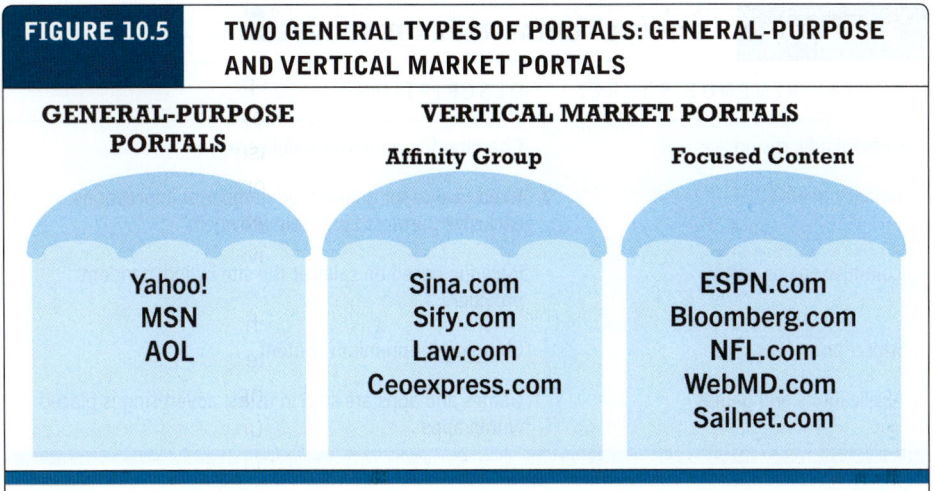

There are two general types of portals: general-purpose and vertical market. Vertical market portals may be based on affinity groups or on focused content.

information on news, finance, autos, movies, and weather. General-purpose portals typically offer search engines, free e-mail, personal home pages, chat rooms, community-building software, and bulletin boards. Vertical content channels on general-purpose portals offer content such as sports scores, stock tickers, health tips, instant messaging, automobile information, and auctions.

Vertical market portals (sometimes also referred to as vortals) attempt to attract highly focused, loyal audiences with a deep interest in either community (affinity group portals) or specialized content—from sports to the weather. In addition to their focused content, vertical market portals have recently begun adding many of the features found in general-purpose portals.

The concentration of audience share in the portal market reflects (in addition to network effects) the limited time budget of consumers. This limited time budget works to the advantage of general-purpose portals. Consumers have a finite amount of time to spend online. Facing limited time, consumers concentrate their visits at sites and apps that can satisfy a broad range of interests, from weather and travel information, to stocks, sports, retail shopping, and entertainment content.

General-purpose portals such as Yahoo try to be all things to all people and attract a broad audience with both generalized navigation services and in-depth content and community efforts. For instance, Yahoo has become one of the Web's largest sources of news. Yet changes in online consumer behavior mean that consumers are spending less time "surfing the Web" and browsing, and more time doing focused searches, research, and participating in social networks. These trends will advantage special-purpose, vertical market portals that can provide focused, in-depth community and content.

As a general matter, the general-purpose portals are very well-known brands, while the vertical content and affinity group portals tend to have less well-known brands. **Figure 10.5** lists examples of general-purpose portals and the two main types of vertical market portals.

vertical market portals
attempt to attract highly focused, loyal audiences with a deep interest in either community or specialized content

TABLE 10.7	TYPICAL PORTAL REVENUE SOURCES
PORTAL REVENUE SOURCE	DESCRIPTION
General advertising	Charging for impressions delivered
Tenancy deals	Fixed charge for guaranteed number of impressions, exclusive partnerships, "sole providers"
Commissions on sales	Revenue based on sales at the site by independent providers
Subscription fees	Charging for premium content
Applications and games	Games and apps are sold to users; advertising is placed within apps

PORTAL BUSINESS MODELS

Portals receive income from a number of different sources. The revenue base of portals is changing and dynamic, with some of the largest sources of revenue declining. **Table 10.7** summarizes the major portal revenue sources.

The business strategies of both general-purpose and vertical portals have changed greatly because of the rapid growth in search engine advertising and intelligent ad placement networks such as Google's AdSense, which can place ads on thousands of websites based on content. General portals such as AOL and Yahoo did not have well-developed search engines, and hence did not grow as fast as Google, which had a powerful search engine. Microsoft, for instance, invested billions of dollars in its Bing search engine to catch up with Google. On the other hand, general portals had content, which Google did not originally have, although it added to its content by purchasing YouTube and adding Google sites devoted to news, financial information, images, and maps. Facebook users stay and linger on Facebook three times as long as visitors to traditional portals like Yahoo. For this reason social networks, Facebook in particular, are direct competitors of Yahoo, Google, and the other portals. Yahoo struggled to grow revenues and earnings. One part of the problem was the falling price of display ads, which are the mainstay of Yahoo's ad platform. Another key issue was declining user engagement and the amount of time spent on the site and apps. To attempt to address these issues, Yahoo made a number of acquisitions including Aviate, Tumblr, and Flickr, and launched digital magazines like Yahoo Food and Yahoo Tech to curate content from around the Web. The key to display ad revenue is content and engagement: the more you can show users, the longer they stay on your site or app, the more ad revenue can be generated. So far, Yahoo and the other general portals have not been able to compete with social networks on these dimensions of engagement and time on site. After several years of pursuing unsuccessful new strategies, Yahoo agreed to sell itself to Verizon in 2016.

The survival strategy for general-purpose portals in the future is to develop deep, rich vertical content in order to reach and engage customers. The strategy for smaller vertical market portals is to put together a collection of vertical portals to form a vertical portal network. The strategy for search engines such as Google is to obtain more content to attract users for a long time and expose them to more ads.

10.4 CAREERS IN E-COMMERCE

This chapter covers three somewhat different types of e-commerce business models: social networks, auctions, and portals. Of the three, social networks (and associated social marketing) currently offer the most career opportunities, both working for companies that provide social network platforms, and working for companies that interact with those platforms. The auction marketspace is dominated by eBay, and there are also job positions available with merchants who sell on eBay. The portal business model currently faces a number of challenges, so career opportunities in that arena are somewhat limited.

In this section, we will take a closer look at a social marketing specialist position for an online retailer. Other job titles in this space might include the terms social marketing or social media in the title, as well as terms such as community/content/digital media/engagement strategist/analyst/manager.

THE COMPANY

The company is an online retailer offering unusual, creatively designed jewelry, art, kitchen goods, and unique foods that cannot be found in traditional department stores. The firm offers artisans and creators of unique goods an online marketplace. In this online craft fair, the company offers customers and creators of unique goods convenience and security: a marketplace where they can find customers without traveling to craft fairs, and a secure payment environment. The company is in the early stages of building a social marketing program in order to grow its existing online business.

POSITION: SOCIAL MARKETING SPECIALIST

You will be working with the E-commerce Marketing team, and reporting to the Director of the E-commerce Team to grow social commerce across multiple channels, primarily Facebook, Instagram, and Pinterest. Responsibilities include:
- Testing hypotheses and creating actionable insights based on creative social network campaigns
- Reporting the results of these experiments to the Team and recommending new strategies to reach our customers
- Authoring weekly social media reports on the results of social marketing for sales
- Working with other departments (e.g., product development, creative and merchandising) to ensure goal and strategy alignment, as well as to maintain brand identity
- Structuring in-depth, ad hoc analyses to uncover trends and patterns in social media
- Auditing social network measurement and listening tools
- Providing recommendations on necessary tool sets to measure advertising effectiveness and to drive insights
- Analyzing competitor performance and results to inform in-house strategy

QUALIFICATIONS/SKILLS

- BA/BS in behavioral science, management information systems, e-commerce, or business
- Course work in social network/digital marketing, and/or statistics
- Experience with e-commerce and some form of social marketing
- Experience using social networks
- Graphics, digital video, and photography a plus but not required
- Moderate to advanced Excel experience
- Excellent writing, communication, and collaboration skills
- An eye for good design
- A passion for marketing and social advertising
- Familiarity with Facebook Ads Manager, Google Analytics, or Pinterest Analytics or their equivalent

PREPARING FOR THE INTERVIEW

To prepare for the interview, do background research on the company and in particular, the niche retail space of artisanal goods, antiques, and collectables. What are the challenges posed by this marketplace? Visit the website of the firm, and its social media postings, to identify the major branding themes the firm uses to attract customers and suppliers of unique goods. Do searches on social media to discover what others are saying about the firm and its products.

Then review Section 10.1 of this chapter. This will help you to demonstrate that you are familiar with the major social networks and different ways to measure their relative influence (such as number of unique visitors, time spent, and advertising revenue). You should be familiar with the fact that most social network users access them via mobile devices. Also review the section on social network technologies and features and Table 10.4 so that you can speak about these topics in an informed manner.

Before the interview, you should also think about where your background, such as courses taken, outside experience with social networks, and your own personal interests, can be useful to the firm.

POSSIBLE FIRST INTERVIEW QUESTIONS

1. How would you compare Facebook with Pinterest as social networks where we could build an online audience for our products?

You could describe the differences among the major social networks and talk how each can be used for somewhat different purposes. For instance, Pinterest is an ideal location for pictures of the firm's offerings. Facebook would score high as a place to recruit new artists as well as display items for sale, and garner feedback from customers.

2. Given the nature of our products and customers, what other kinds of social networks should our firm be using besides Facebook, Instagram, and Pinterest?

Here you could describe interest and affinity-based networks such as deviantArt and Worthpoint to reach out to small but highly engaged interest and affinity communities.

3. What kind of experience have you had with tools for measuring the effectiveness of social marketing?

You can prepare for this question by reviewing material on ways to measure user engagement. If you have some experience in social network marketing, be prepared to discuss what role you played in measuring the success of social marketing campaigns.

4. Have you used a statistical analysis package to do research on quantitative data?

You can prepare for questions like this by taking courses in marketing or other statistics courses, and learning how to use statistical packages like SAS or SPSS for analyzing data. You may have used Google Analytics software to track campaigns. You may also have experience using simple Excel spreadsheets to track impressions and responses to marketing campaigns.

5. Are you familiar with Facebook's Ad Manager? Have you ever used Ad Manager to create ads and measure their success?

You can prepare for questions like this by doing research on Facebooks' Ad Manager, Pinterest Analytics, and Google Analytics. Virtually all ad platforms make available online packages for tracking the responses to online campaigns on their platform.

6. What kinds of projects have you worked on that involve photo and video editing, and graphics? Have you created online ads?

You can start by reviewing the firm's use of photos and videos (if any), and point out the growing use of videos to market products on virtually all the large social network platforms. Given the nature of this firm and its products, you can prepare for this by assembling a portfolio of photos, videos, and graphics that you have created, and describe how your interests will fit into the firm's social network marketing.

10.5 CASE STUDY

eBay Evolves

Founded in 1995 as an offbeat, quirky place to buy and sell almost anything via online auctions, eBay now derives the majority of its revenue from traditional e-commerce. Over the past ten years, the company has steadily transformed its business model away from its initial auction-based model and towards the fixed-price model popularized by Amazon.

After rapid early growth, eBay struggled from 2007 to 2009. For many buyers, the novelty of online auctions had worn off, and they began to prefer the simplicity of buying goods from Amazon and other fixed-price retailers, which, by comparison, had steady growth during the same time period. Search engines and comparison shopping sites were also taking away some of eBay's auction business by making items easier to find on the Web.

Former CEO John Donahoe instituted an ambitious revival plan that moved eBay away from its origins as an online flea market, partnering with retail chains to serve as another channel for current merchandise. Today, 80% of eBay's listings are new items, and eBay has over 1 billion live listings and 25 million marketplace sellers.

The small sellers who had driven eBay's early growth were encouraged to shift away from the auction format and move toward the fixed-price sales model. eBay adjusted its fees and revamped its search engine to incentivize fixed-price sales, and rather than

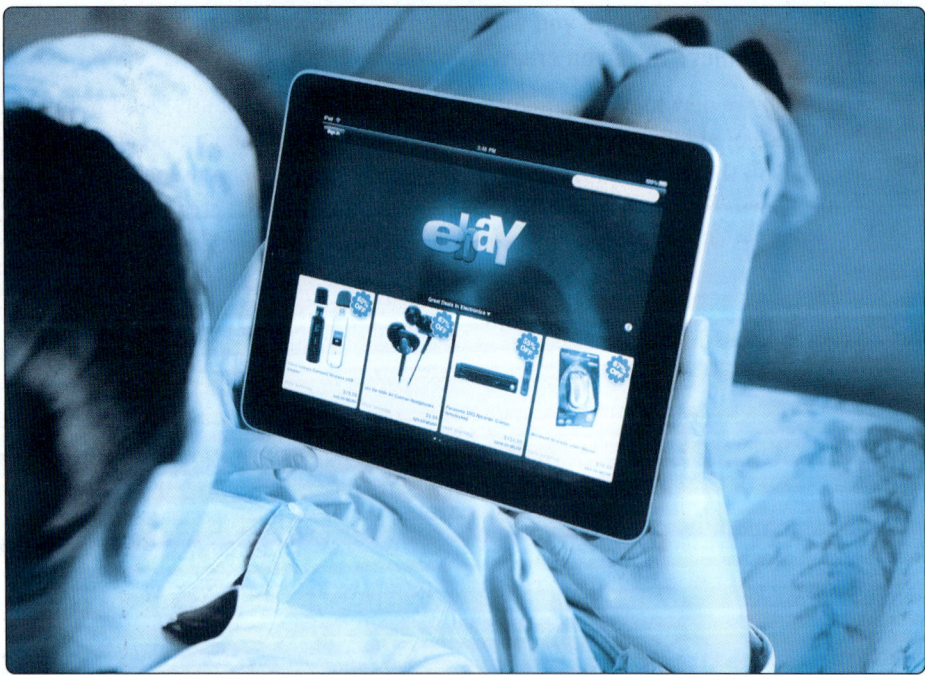

© Iain Masterton / Alamy Stock Photo

displaying auctions close to finishing at the top of search results, eBay tweaked its search tool to account for price and seller reputation so that highly rated merchants appeared first and received more exposure. The hundreds of thousands of people who supported themselves by selling on eBay and many millions more who used eBay to supplement their income were unhappy with the change, and analysts' faith in eBay's transition dwindled as its stock continued to drop.

However, eBay's purchase of PayPal in 2002 helped it survive these lean years, with PayPal accounting for as much as 40% of eBay's revenues in some years. eBay also positioned itself well for the future with its early embrace of the mobile platform, even before the iPhone hit the market. This prescience resulted in eBay achieving its 100 millionth app download and 100 millionth mobile listing very early, in 2012. eBay has also been quick to develop apps for wearable devices, including an app for the Apple Watch that allows users to see an overview of their notifications and bid statuses and a version of its Marketplace app for Android Wear devices. Over 60% of eBay's business now involves a mobile device, and the company continues to make improvements to the mobile experience on many platforms and across all of its different services. In 2018, eBay integrated "progressive app" features into its existing mobile infrastructure, which makes it function more like a native app, requiring less data to operate and allowing users to access many features even while offline. In 2019, eBay launched an all-new native app for eBay Motors, built with cutting-edge technology, including artificial intelligence, machine learning, and Flutter, an open source, cross-platform development platform.

In 2018, the company also continued the process of modernizing its platform with analytical tools. Beginning in 2016, eBay began to convert its catalog of items from its traditional unstructured "listing" format, where two identical items can appear totally different to shoppers, to a structured data format. This allows eBay to more easily gain information about different items and about purchasing trends, and also helps its product pages perform better in Google searches. eBay is also using machine learning to customize, update, and generally improve its product pages, as well as to fine-tune its search capability beyond simply matching search terms with keywords and tags. To support these efforts, the company purchased machine-learning startup SalesPredict, whose technology helps businesses predict consumer buying behavior and sales conversion. The company's revamped Seller Hub also offers many of these analytical tools and metrics to individual sellers, including inventory, order, and listing management, performance insights, and streamlined business process management.

In 2018, eBay launched its Interests feature, which allows customers to answer a quick questionnaire about their passions and hobbies, resulting in the complete transformation of the eBay home page. Shoppers can build a home page that reflects their eclectic interests in different areas, including gaming, technology, particular movie and TV series, music genres, sports teams, fashion, and outdoor activities. eBay has also redesigned its website's interface to emphasize images over text and to allow users to perform visual searches for the items they are interested in. eBay offers two types of image search, one where you can take a picture or upload a picture from a smartphone to find items that match those seen in the photo, and the other, called Find it on eBay, which allows users to do the same type of search with images found online. Machine learning powers and improves both forms of visual search, and eBay expects that its image search capability will become more and more accurate as more shoppers use the service to find products.

SOURCES: eBay, Inc. "10-K for the Fiscal Year Ended December 31, 2019," filed with the Securities and Exchange Commission, January 31, 2020; "eBay Marketplace Q4 2019 Fast Facts," Ebayinc.com, January 2019; "Buy or Sell a Car via Mobile with the New eBay Motors App," by eBay News Team, Ebayinc.com, December 12, 2019; "eBay's Buy APIs Hit $1B in GMB," by Gail Frederick, tech.ebayinc.com, December 10, 2019; "Ayden Says It's Ready to Take on the Majority of eBay's Volume Next Year," by John Stewart, Digitaltransactions.com, August 23, 2019; "eBay to Launch Fulfillment Service for Sellers," by Fareeha Ali, Digitalcommerce360.com, July 24, 2019; "Artificial Intelligence and Marketplaces: Who's Doing It, Why, and How" by AIM Group, Aimgroup.com, July 9, 2019; "How eBay Plans to Nearly Triple Its Active User Base," by Zak Stambor, Digitalcommerce360.com, August 24, 2018; "eBay Ramps up Developer Strategy with Series of API Updates," by Natalie Gagliordi, Zdnet.com, August 14, 2018; "EBay Selects Apple Pay As Its First Post-PayPal Payment Option," by Jake Krol, Mashable.com, July 24,

2018; April Berthene, "EBay Counters Prime Day with Its Own Sale," Digitalcommerce360.com, July 6, 2018; "EBay Amps Up Its Price-Match Guarantee Program," by Stephanie Crets, Digitalcommerce360.com, June 27, 2018; "Want to Understand What Ails the Modern Internet? Look at eBay," by John Herrman, *New York Times,* June 20, 2018; "We Tried Out eBay's Newest Personalization Feature—and It Should Have Amazon Terrified," by Emily Rella, Aol.com, May 24, 2018; "EBay Wants to Know Shoppers' Interests with New Personalization Tool," by Stephanie Crets, Digitalcommerce360.com, May 17, 2018; "EBay Is Exploring Offline Access with a Progressive Web App," by Paul Sawers, Venturebeat.com, May 10, 2018; "EBay Looks to Drive Shopper Engagement with Augmented Reality Tools," Digitalcommerce360.com, February 13, 2018; "EBay is Dropping PayPal; If You're a Customer, Here's What You Need to Know," by Brett Molina, *USA Today,* February 1, 2018; Jason Del Rey, "After 15 Years, eBay Plans to Cut Off PayPal as Its Main Payments Processor," Recode.net, January 31, 2018; "How eBay Offers a Personalized Mobile Experience with AI," by Daniela Forte, Multichannelmerchant.com, August 22, 2017; "eBay to Launch Visual Search Tools for Finding Products Using Photos from Your Phone or Web," by Sarah Perez, Techcrunch.com, July 26, 2017; "For eBay, AI Is Ride or Die," Venturebeat.com, July 8, 2017; "Ebay's Homepage Is for Everyone," Ebayinc.com, June 28, 2017; "Ebay Accused of Failing Its Sellers As Fraudulent Buyers Manipulate the System," by Anna Tims, *The Guardian,* May 21, 2017; "eBay's New High-End Furniture Shop, eBay Collective, Includes a Visual Search Engine," by Sarah Perez, Techcrunch.com, October 17, 2016; "eBay Acquires Visual Search Engine Corrigon for Less Than $30M," by Ingrid Lunden, Techcrunch.com, October 5, 2016; "What eBay's Machine Learning Advances Can Teach IT Professionals," by Charles Babcock, *Information Week,* September 6, 2016; "At eBay, Machine Learning Is Driving Innovative New

In 2018, eBay reported that improvements to both traditional and visual search spurred by machine learning were responsible for $1 billion in sales.

eBay has also incorporated similar AI and machine learning techniques in other areas of its business, including its ShopBot, a personalized shopping assistant that allows customers to text, talk, or provide a picture of a desired item. ShopBot asks users questions and then generates what eBay hopes will be highly accurate recommendations. Prospective buyers of an item can also ask questions that other purchasers of that item can answer, similarly to Amazon. eBay uses machine learning to algorithmically identify experienced buyers who are best able to answer the question, and as more questions are asked, the system will improve at prioritizing good questions and finding appropriate people to answer them. eBay has also dramatically improved the accessibility of its website, which can now be navigated without a mouse and is far easier to use with screen-reading software used by visually impaired shoppers. It has also added augmented reality features that allow customers to see how variations to a product would look, such as new wheels on a car, as well as to visualize the correct box size to package a product, by overlaying a graphic of the box over the image of an item. eBay has also opened up its API to developers so that they can better use eBay's back-end technology, including providing better access to its Image Search and Machine Translation tools. By the end of 2019, usage by third-party developers of eBay's APIs had driven over $1 billion in gross merchandise bought.

eBay has cracked down on fraud on the part of both buyers and sellers, one of the most common concerns about using eBay. To limit seller fraud, eBay is now authenticating items that are commonly counterfeited, such as handbags, footwear, and jewelry. Sellers can pay for the authentication service to increase their appeal to buyers, and buyers can pay to guarantee that their purchase will be voided if the product turns out to be counterfeit. Sellers are also hoping that the company will do more to prevent buyer fraud in the near future.

In 2015, eBay elected to spin off PayPal as its own separate company, leaving eBay with its Marketplaces segment, its StubHub ticket sales segment, and a handful of other business units. Although eBay's leadership had resisted a spinoff for years, the move was prompted by PayPal's desire to become more agile within the rapidly developing marketplace of online payments. As part of the split, eBay agreed to initially route 80% of its sales through PayPal, and continue to use PayPal as its back-end payment provider. However, eBay announced in 2018 that it would end that agreement, instead using Dutch payments company Adyen for its back-end payment service. While PayPal will still be a payment option for eBay customers, eBay will now have far more control over the checkout process, the way Amazon and Chinese e-commerce giant Alibaba do, and eBay will be able to charge seller fees that have traditionally been collected by PayPal, which is expected to add $2 billion in revenue to eBay's bottom line. eBay also added Apple Pay as a payment option for its customers in 2018, its first new payment service since spinning off PayPal, and in 2019, added Google Pay as an option.

eBay's international operations are an important part of its business. In 2019, international operations delivered 60% (almost $6.5 billion) of its $10.8 billion in net revenues. During 2019, eBay acquired Motors.co.uk, a UK-classifieds site, adding it to stable of international online classifieds platforms, including Gumtree UK, mobile.de, Kijiji, Marktplaats, eBay Kleinanzeigen and others, which offer online classifieds in more than 1,500 cities around the world. eBay also invested $160 million in Paytm Mall, an e-commerce marketplace in India. Paytm Mall uses eBay's Buy APIs to give its 130 million active users and 12 million registered merchants access to a wide selection of global inventory.

Although Amazon is the dominant force in online retail, eBay remains one of the most trusted online brands and e-commerce leaders, and it has worked hard to offer services that compete with Amazon, such as its eBay Plus program in Germany, which functions similarly to Amazon Prime, as well as its Guaranteed Delivery program, which ensures that 20 million of its top selling products will be delivered in 3 days or less or the buyer will receive coupons or full refunds. In 2019, in an effort to better compete with Amazon, eBay announced Managed Delivery, which will enable sellers to work with eBay to store, pack, and ship their products. eBay also has its own version of Amazon's Prime Day, a weeklong sale in July advertised as being available to all customers without needing to sign up for a subscription like Amazon Prime, and instituted a price match guarantee program for 100,000 products that will allow shoppers to receive a refund equal to the difference between eBay's price and a competitor's price, plus an additional 10%, if they can find a better price offered by Amazon, Walmart, Target, or other leading e-commerce retailers. While eBay is very unlikely to measure up to Amazon in sheer size, the company continues to market itself as a quirky alternative to Amazon, and despite some ups and downs, the company appears to have found its niche.

Approaches to Search Experiences," by Sebastian Rupley, Ebayinc.com, August 22, 2016; "EBay Completes the Acquisition of SalesPredict," Ebayinc.com, July 22, 2016; "One Year In, Building eBay for the Future," by Devin Wenig, Ebayinc.com, July 20, 2016; "Replatforming eBay: How We Are Delivering the Shopping Destination of Choice," by Steve Fisher, Ebayinc.com, July 14, 2015; "Here's Why eBay Is Acquiring SalesPredict," *Forbes*, July 14, 2016; "How eBay is Advancing New Shopping, Browsing Models," by Sebastian Rupley, Ebayinc.com, March 28, 2016; "eBay Hits 100m Mobile App Download Mark," by Dervedia Thomas, Dailydealmedia.com, September 29, 2012; "eBay: We Need to Behave More Like a Retailer," by Sarah Shearman, Tamebay.com, September 25, 2012; "Behind eBay's Comeback," by James B. Stewart, *New York Times*, July 27, 2012.

Case Study Questions

1. Contrast eBay's original business model with its current business model.

2. What are the problems that eBay is currently facing? How is eBay trying to solve these problems?

3. Are the solutions eBay is seeking to implement good solutions? Why or why not? Are there any other solutions that eBay should consider?

4. Who are eBay's top competitors online, and how will eBay's strategy help it compete?

10.6 REVIEW

KEY CONCEPTS

- **Describe the different types of social networks and online communities and their business models.**
- Social networks involve a group of people, shared social interaction, common ties among members, and a shared area for some period of time. An online social network is one where people who share common ties can interact with one another online.
- The different types of social networks and communities and their business models include:
  - *General communities:* Members can interact with a general audience segmented into numerous different groups. Most general communities began as non-commercial subscription-based endeavors, but many have been purchased by larger community portals.
  - *Practice networks:* Members can participate in discussion groups and get help or information relating to an area of shared practice, such as art, education, or medicine. These generally have a nonprofit business model in which they simply attempt to collect enough in subscription fees, sales commissions, and limited advertising to cover the cost of operations.
  - *Interest-based communities:* Members can participate in focused discussion groups on a shared interest. The advertising business model has worked because the targeted audience is attractive to marketers. Tenancy and sponsorship deals provide another similar revenue stream.
  - *Affinity communities:* Members can participate in focused discussions with others who share the same affinity or group identification. The business model is a mixture of subscription revenue from premium content and services, advertising, tenancy/sponsorships, and distribution agreements.
  - *Sponsored communities:* Members can participate in online communities created by government, non-profit, or for-profit organizations for the purpose of pursuing organizational goals. They use community technologies and techniques to distribute information or extend brand influence.

- **Describe the major types of auctions, their benefits and costs, how they operate, when to use them, and the potential for auction abuse and fraud.**
- Online auctions are markets where prices vary (dynamic pricing) depending on the competition among the participants who are buying or selling products or services. They can be classified broadly as C2C or B2C, although generally the term *C2C auction* refers to the venue in which the sale takes place, for example, a consumer-oriented auction, such as eBay, which also auctions items from established merchants. A *B2C auction* refers to an established online merchant that offers its own auctions. There are also numerous B2B online auctions for buyers of industrial parts, raw materials, commodities, and services. Within these three broad categories of auctions are several major auction types classified based upon how the bidding mechanisms work in each system:
  - *English auctions:* A single item is up for sale from a single seller. Multiple buyers bid against one another within a specific time frame with the highest bidder winning the object as long as the high bid has exceeded the reserve bid set by the seller, below which he or she refuses to sell.
  - *Dutch Internet auctions:* Sellers with many identical items for sale list a minimum price or starting bid, and buyers indicate both a bid price and a quantity desired. The lowest winning bid that clears the available quantity is paid by all winning bidders. Those with the highest bid are assured of receiving the quantity they desire but only pay the amount of the lowest successful bid (uniform pricing rule).
  - *Name Your Own Price* or *reverse auctions:* Buyers specify the price they are willing to pay for an item, and multiple sellers bid for their business. This is one example of discriminatory pricing in which winners may pay different amounts for the same product or service depending on how much they have bid.
  - *Penny (bidding fee) auctions:* Bidders pay a non-refundable fee to purchase bids.

- Benefits of auctions include: liquidity, price discovery, price transparency, market efficiency, lower transaction costs, consumer aggregation, network effects, and market-maker benefits.
- Costs of auctions include: delayed consumption, monitoring costs, equipment costs, trust risks, and fulfillment costs.
- Auction sites have sought to reduce these risks through various methods including rating systems, watch lists, and proxy bidding.
- Auctions can be an appropriate channel for businesses to sell items in a variety of situations. The factors for businesses to consider include the type of product, the product life cycle, channel management, the type of auction, initial pricing, bid increments, auction length, number of items, price allocation, and closed versus open bidding.
- Auctions are particularly prone to fraud, which produces information asymmetries between buyers and sellers. Some of the possible abuses and frauds include bid rigging, price matching, defensive shill feedback, offensive shill feedback, feedback extortion, transaction interference, bid manipulation, non-payment after winning, shill bidding, transaction non-performance, non-selling sellers, and bid siphoning.

■ **Describe the major types of Internet portals and their business models.**

- Portals are gateways to billions of web pages available on the Internet. Originally, their primary purpose was to help users find information on the Web, but they evolved into destinations that provided a myriad of content from news to entertainment. Today, portals serve four main purposes: navigation of the Web (search), content, commerce, and communication.
- Among the major portal types are:
  - *Enterprise portals:* Corporations, universities, churches, and other organizations create these to help employees or members navigate to important content such as corporate news or organizational announcements.
  - *General-purpose portals:* Examples include AOL, Yahoo, and MSN, which try to attract a very large general audience by providing many in-depth vertical content channels. Some also offer search engines, e-mail, chat, bulletin boards, and personal home pages.
  - *Vertical market portals:* Also called vortals, they attempt to attract a highly focused, loyal audience with an intense interest in either a community they belong to or an interest they hold. Vertical market portals can be divided into two main classifications, affinity group portals and focused content portals, although hybrids that overlap the two classifications also exist.
- Portals receive revenue from a number of different sources including general advertising, tenancy deals, subscription fees, and commissions on sales.
- The survival strategy for general-purpose portals is to develop deep, rich vertical content in order to attract advertisers to various niche groups that they can target with focused ads. The strategy for the vertical market portals is to build a collection of vertical portals, thereby creating a network of deep, rich content sites for the same reason.

QUESTIONS

1. What is an online social network?
2. How does a social network differ from a portal? How are the two similar?
3. What are some ways to measure the business potential and influence of a social network site?
4. List and describe the five generic types of social networks and online communities.
5. Discuss the evolution of online social networks.
6. How have social networks impacted how businesses operate, communicate, and serve their customers?
7. Are auction prices always lower than fixed prices? Why or why not?
8. What is trigger pricing and how is it used?
9. How does a Name Your Own Price auction work?

10. What role do algorithms play in social networks?
11. What risks do merchants face when they use auctions?
12. How is the portal marketspace differentiated?
13. How is the value of a portal to advertisers and content owners defined?
14. List and briefly explain the main revenue sources for the portal business model.
15. Why are mobile social networks growing so fast?
16. What is a sponsored community?
17. What are some of the unintended results of participating in auctions?
18. What are the dangers of a penny (bidding fee) auction?
19. What is herd behavior and how does it impact auctions?
20. In what way are portals like television networks?

PROJECTS

1. Find two examples of an affinity portal and two examples of a focused-content portal. Prepare a presentation explaining why each of your examples should be categorized as an affinity portal or a focused-content portal. For each example, surf the portal and describe the services each provides. Try to determine what revenue model each of your examples is using and, if possible, how many members or registered users the portal has attracted.

2. Examine the use of auctions by businesses. Go to any online auction of your choosing and look for outlet auctions or auctions directly from merchants. Research at least three products for sale. What stage in the product life cycle do these products fall into? Are there quantity purchasing requirements? What was the opening bid price? What are the bid increments? What is the auction duration? Analyze why these firms have used the auction channel to sell these goods and prepare a short report on your findings.

3. Visit one for-profit and one nonprofit sponsored social network. Create a presentation to describe and demonstrate the offering at each social network. What organizational objectives is each pursuing? How is the for-profit company using community-building technologies as a customer relations management tool?

4. Visit one of the social networks listed in Table 10.1 and compare it to Facebook. In what ways is it similar to Facebook, and in what ways is it different? Which do you prefer, and why?

REFERENCES

Arkes, H. R., and L. Hutzel. "The Role of Probability of Success Estimates in the Sunk Cost Effect." *Journal of Behavioral Decisionmaking* (2000).

Bailey, Brian P., Laura J. Gurak, and Joseph Konstan. "Do You Trust Me? An Examination of Trust in Computer-Mediated Exchange," *Human Factors and Web Development*, 2nd Edition. Mahwah, NJ: Lawrence Erlbaum (2002).

Clement, J. "Reach of Most Popular U.S. Smartphone Apps 2020," Statista.com (February 27, 2020).

Clement, J. "Most Popular Social Media Apps in the U.S. 2019, by Engagement." Statisa.com (November 25, 2019).

comScore, Inc. "Top 50 Multi-Platform Properties (Desktop and Mobile) December 2019." (accessed February 11, 2020).

comScore, Inc. "Mobile Now Accounts for Nearly 70% of Digital Media Time." (March 29, 2017).

Consumerreports.org. "With Penny Auctions, You Can Spend a Bundle But Still Leave Empty-Handed." (June 30, 2014).

Cormen, Thomas H., Charles E. Leiserson, Ronald L. Rivest, and Clifford Stein. *Introduction to Algorithms, 3rd Edition* (MIT Press) 3rd Edition. MIT Press, 2009.

Dholakia, Utpal, and Kerry Soltysinski. "Coveted or Overlooked? The Psychology of Bidding for Comparable Listings in Digital Auctions." *Marketing Letters* (2001).

eBay, Inc. "Form 10-K for the Fiscal Year Ended December 31, 2019." Filed with the Securities and Exchange Commission. (January 31, 2020).

eMarketer, Inc. (Debra Aho Williamson) "US Social Trends for 2020." (January 15, 2020).

eMarketer, Inc. "US Average Time Spent per Day with Social Networks." (November 2019a).

eMarketer, Inc. "US Social Network Users and Penetration." (November 2019b).

eMarketer, Inc. (Karin von Abrams). "Global Social Network Users." (December 12, 2019c).

eMarketer, Inc. "US Facebook Users, by Age." (November 2019d).

eMarketer, Inc. "US Social Network Users, by Platform." (November 2019e).

eMarketer, Inc. "LinkedIn Users in the US, 2018–2022." (November 2019f).

eMarketer, Inc. Facebook, Instagram and Snapchat: Average Time Spent by Users in the US, 2016–2021." (December 2019g).

eMarketer, Inc. "Average Daily Time Spent on Select Social Media According to US Social Media Users, Q1 2017–Q1 2019." (March 11, 2019h).

eMarketer, Inc. "Worldwide Digital Ad Revenues, by Company." (October 2019i).

eMarketer, Inc. "Worldwide Mobile Facebook Ad Revenues." (October 2019j).

eMarketer, Inc. (Dustin Sodano)."Global Social Media Stat-Pack: Platforms, Users and Devices." (October 2017a).

Facebook, Inc. "Form 10-K for the Fiscal Year Ended December 31, 2019." Filed with the Securities and Exchange Commission. (January 31, 2020).

Hafner, Katie. "The Epic Saga of The Well: The World's Most Influential Online Community (and It's Not AOL)." Wired (May 1997).

Hagel, John III, and Arthur G. Armstrong. *Net Gain: Expanding Markets Through Virtual Communities*. Cambridge, MA: Harvard Business School Press (1997).

Hanson, Ward, and D. S. Putler. "Hits and Misses: Herd Behavior and Online Product Popularity." *Marketing Letters* (1996).

Hillery, George A. "Definitions of Community: Areas of Agreement." *Rural Sociology* (1955).

Hiltzik, Michael. *Dealers of Lightning: Xerox PARC and the Dawn of the Computer Age*. New York: Harper Collins (1999).

Kiesler, Sara. "The Hidden Messages in Computer Networks." *Harvard Business Review* (January–February 1986).

Kiesler, Sara, Jane Siegel, and Timothy W. McGuire. "Social Psychological Aspects of Computer-Mediated Communication." *American Psychologist* (October 1984).

Kollock, Peter. "The Production of Trust in Online Markets." In *Advances in Group Processes* (Vol 16), edited by E. J. Lawler, M. Macy, S. Thyne, and H. A. Walker. Greenwich, CT: JAI Press (1999).

Krishnamurthy, Sandeep. "An Empirical Study of the Causal Antecedents of Customer Confidence in E-tailers." *First Monday* (January 2001).

Laudon, Kenneth C., and Jane P. Laudon. *Management Information Systems: Managing the Digital Firm*, 16th edition. New York, Pearson (2020).

Levy, Adam. "Facebook's Making a Big Change to Its Plans to Monetize WhatsApp." Fool.com (January 19, 2020).

Liu, Yi, and Juliana Sutanto. "Buyers' Purchasing Time and Herd Behavior on Deal-of-the-Day Group-buying Websites." *Electronic Markets* (June 2012).

McKenna, Beth. "Pinterest Stock Soars 17% on Earnings Beat and Rosy Outlook." Fool.com (February 7, 2020).

Miller, Rich. "Facebook Accelerates Its Data Center Expansion." Datacenterfrontier.com (March 10, 2018).

Nikander, Pekka, and Kristina Karvonen. "Users and Trust in Cyberspace." In the Proceedings of Cambridge Security Protocols Workshop 2000, April 3–5, 2000, Cambridge University (2002).

Parkes, David C., and Lyle Ungar. "Iterative Combinatorial Auctions: Theory and Practice." *Proceedings of the 17th National Conference on Artificial Intelligence* (AAAI-00) (2000).

Rheingold, Howard. *Hosting Web Communities*. New York: John Wiley and Sons (1998). Also see Rheingold.com for more recent articles by Rheingold.

Rheingold, Howard. *The Virtual Community*. Cambridge, MA: MIT Press (1993).

Rosenbloom, Stephanie. "For the Plugged-In, Too Many Choices." *New York Times* (August 10, 2011).

Simonson, Itamar, and Amos Tversky. "Choice in Context: Tradeoff Contrast and Extremeness Aversion." *Journal of Marketing Research*, Vol. 20, 281–287 (1992).

Stanford Persuasive Technology Lab and Makovsky & Company. "Stanford-Makovsky Web Credibility Study 2002." Stanford Persuasive Technology Lab. (Spring 2002).

Twitter, Inc. "Twitter Announces Fourth Quarter and Fiscal Year 2019 Results. Finance.yahoo.com (February 6, 2020).

Unboxsocial.com "How Fortune 500 Companies Leverage Social Media to Grow Their Business." (October 21, 2019).

United States Patent and Trademark Office. "U.S. Patent 7,827,208 B2." (November 2, 2010).

Well.com. "What is the Well." Well.com (accessed February 16, 2020).

CHAPTER 11

E-commerce Retail and Services

LEARNING OBJECTIVES

After reading this chapter, you will be able to:

- Understand the environment in which the online retail sector operates today.
- Explain how to analyze the economic viability of an online firm.
- Identify the challenges faced by the different types of online retailers.
- Describe the major features of the online service sector.
- Discuss the trends taking place in the online financial services industry.
- Describe the major trends in the online travel services industry today.
- Identify current trends in the online career services industry.
- Understand the business models of on-demand service companies.

Souq.com:

The Amazon of the Middle East Gets Acquired by Amazon

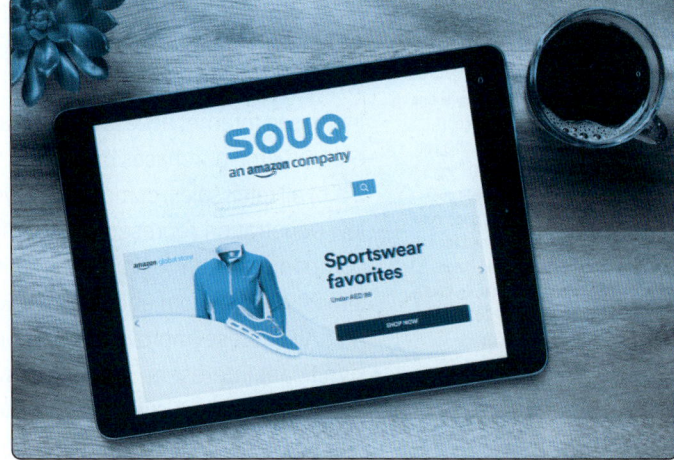

© M4OS Photos/Alamy Stock Photo

When Souq.com was launched in 2005, e-commerce in the Middle East and North Africa (MENA) region was in its infancy. With no local roadmap to follow, its original parent company Maktoob, a 1998 Internet pioneer that provided the first free Arabic-supported e-mail service, chat, greeting cards, and content channels, opted to follow the successful auction format forged ten years earlier in the West by eBay. A souq, or souk, is a traditional Arab marketplace at which a wide range of products from wood carvings and rugs to spices and food are exchanged through a bargaining process between buyer and seller. In spite of the apropos name, Dubai-based Souq struggled to thrive, especially after Maktoob was purchased by Yahoo in 2009 and Souq was left to fend for itself.

A number of problems plagued the development of e-commerce in the MENA region. For instance, different currencies, laws, and regulations complicated shipping for transactions made across different Gulf states, often necessitating bank accounts in each country and requiring local business partners. Customers were also reluctant to use online payment systems, preferring cash on delivery (COD) to entering credit card details online. However, as the years have passed, and the population in the region has grown younger (in 2019, an unprecedented 65% of the population in the region was younger than 30 years of age), MENA consumers have become more familiar with smartphones and more willing to use online payment methods.

Although Souq initially pursued a model akin to eBay, forming relationships with small local businesses and encouraging them to begin selling online, it soon discovered that the B2C model popularized by Amazon was superior to the auction format in nations where auctions were not culturally accepted. After switching to a fixed-price model in 2011, Souq has outperformed its peers. Souq also added fulfillment centers and warehouses, hired delivery and warehouse personnel trained in modernized logistics systems, and updated its data storage systems to bolster security. In 2017, Souq purchased delivery logistics company Wing.ae to help it deliver goods more efficiently, which can be difficult in MENA countries without a robust postal address system. When Souq was first founded, delivery often took 3 to 5 days, but now same-day delivery is available in some areas.

Souq also developed its payment service, Payfort, which helped standardize payments across many MENA countries and is now the leading online payment provider in the region. Though Payfort was once Souq's proprietary system, the company is now a separate

SOURCES: "Noon Founder Alabbar Says Amazon 'Should Go Back to Seattle.'" Gulfbusiness.com, December 19, 2019; "Amazon Rebrands Souq," by Daphne Howland, Retaildive.com, May 2, 2019; "Souq Users in the UAE Are Now Automatically Redirected to a New Amazon Site," by Sherisse Pham, Cnn.com, May 1, 2019; "Amazon Launches New Middle East Marketplace, and Rebrands Souq, the Company It Bought for $580 Million," by Eugene Kim, Cnbc.com, April 30, 2019; "SOUQ Launches 'Amazon Global Store' Bringing Over One Million Global Products to KSA Customers," Press.aboutamazon.

entity, and in 2019, Souq transactions were approximately half of Payfort's business. The company also partnered with MasterCard in 2016 to provide improved payment options for its customers. By 2018, various forms of e-payments in the UAE and surrounding region finally surpassed COD.

E-commerce in the MENA region is still dominated by men, and Souq has made attracting female customers a priority. To that end, Souq purchased Sukar.com, a high-fashion flash sales site, in 2012 to bolster its burgeoning fashion division. Sukar benefitted from the use of Souq's logistics and delivery systems while Souq gained customer service and fashion expertise and reinforced its position as the leading e-commerce site in the region. While women have lagged behind men as e-commerce consumers in the MENA region, increased Internet access at home and increased mobile device usage has led to a growth in e-commerce purchases by women. In Souq's current markets, online sales account for only 2% of all retail sales, compared to over 10% across Europe and over 20% in Asia-Pacific. That low penetration represents a potential huge future profit for Souq and other e-commerce companies in the region. eMarketer projects that retail e-commerce sales in MENA will almost double, from about $35 billion in 2019 to over $65 billion by 2023.

All of these improving conditions, investments, acquisitions, and upgrades generated significant interest in Souq from investors. In 2016, Souq raised more than $275 million, the largest amount ever raised in the Middle East, giving Souq a valuation of over $1 billion, making it the first company from the MENA region to achieve the "unicorn" designation for companies worth $1 billion or more. In 2016, Souq was rumored to be selling a stake in the company to Amazon at a valuation of over $1 billion. This did not come to fruition, but in 2017, after a bidding war between Amazon and Saudi-based Emaar Malls PJSC and its billionaire owner, Mohamed Alabbar, Amazon ultimately purchased the entirety of Souq for a price variously reported as either $650 million or $580 million. The deal gave Amazon access to emerging new e-commerce markets and has allowed Souq to integrate with Amazon's global seller and customer base.

Wasting little time after the merger, Souq announced the UAE launch of Amazon Global Store, which offered over 1 million Amazon products to Souq customers. Souq expanded Amazon Global Store to the Kingdom of Saudi Arabia and Egypt in 2018. In April 2019, Amazon announced the rebranding of Souq to Amazon.ae in the UAE and several of the countries in which it operates, although it has retained the Souq.com URL in Egypt and Saudia Arabia (which together provided two-thirds of the traffic to Souq.com). The new Middle East marketplace will sell over 30 million products, including products sold by Amazon in the United States, and offer the option of shopping in Arabic on both the website and Amazon app.

Souq has embraced mobile technology and social media as it attempts to increase its worldwide visibility and bolster its branding and marketing efforts. Souq's Facebook page has over 11 million Likes and followers, and the company maintains multiple active Twitter accounts focused on different areas of operation, like the UAE and Egypt, with flash deals and other useful information. In From April 2018 to March 2019, mobile customers represented more than half of all traffic on Souq.com and made 70% of purchases across all of Souq's markets of operation, justifying Souq's emphasis on strengthening its mobile platform. Souq's mobile app enabled customers to view detailed product information along with product ratings and reviews. Souq also conducted regional advertising campaigns that displayed interesting characters interrupted by Souq deliveries, and the company launched Egypt's first Internet-based youth commerce training academy to capitalize on the wave of young people in the MENA region. Souq even developed its own hardware, including the QTAB tablet computer, aimed at Arabic consumers. Souq also used its "White Friday" sale to promote itself similarly to "Black Friday" on Amazon and other American e-commerce sites.

Despite the now rebranded Souq's predominant position in the MENA region (it reportedly has over 70% share of the e-commerce retail market in Egypt and almost 50% in the UAE), competition remains intense. Other competitors include Noon.com, a startup that announced its arrival with initial funding of $1 billion in 2017. The company is backed by Mohamed Alabbar and the Saudi Arabia Public Investment Fund. After being rebuffed in their attempts to purchase Souq, they decided to try to beat Souq at its own game. Noon went live in the UAE in September 2017 and in Saudi Arabia in December 2017. In addition to the deep pockets of its founders, Noon also has One Click Delivery Services, which it purchased to connect drivers with sellers needing delivery. In addition, Noon has extensively used daily flash sales during the holiday season to build market share. It offers 20 million products in many of the same areas as Souq, including beauty, fashion, electronics, home, and kitchen, many under its own brand name. Noon uses Alabbar's extensive infrastructure of Emaar Malls to help deliver and store goods, and integrates with the Alabbar-owned Aramex delivery service as well as smaller e-commerce marketplaces Namshi and JadoPado. Noon has positioned itself as a homegrown, Arabic-first marketplace, and in December 2019, Alabbar took a jab at Amazon, reportedly saying that it should go back to Seattle. However, in mid-2018, it partnered with eBay to offer its customers a way to more easily purchase products from the United States and elsewhere. In July 2018, Noon also announced that it was opening an office in China in an effort to build relationships with Chinese brands and in 2019 signed an agreement with China's Neolix to pilot the use of autonomous delivery vehicles in Saudia Arabia and the UAE. Still, the MENA region is a fast-growing market with room for many winners, and with Amazon's support, Souq is positioned to be a force despite competition from Noon and other regional competitors.

Customers," Mastercard.com, April 11, 2016; "The Middle East's First Unicorn: Souq.com's CEO on Leadership, Timing, and Coping with Rejection," by Elizabeth MacBride, *Forbes*, March 25, 2016; "Souq, Amazon of the Middle East, Raises $275M From Tiger and More at a $1B Valuation," by Ingrid Lunden, Techcrunch.com, February 29, 2016; "Souq, Online Retailer in Middle East, Gets a $275 Million Boost," by Sara Hamdan, *New York Times*, February 29, 2016; "Souq.com: Riding High on the E-Commerce Wave," by Dina al-Wakeel, Venturemagazine.me, January 28, 2016; "Souq.com Chief Explains One of Dubai's Biggest Online Success Stories," by Jessica Hill, Thenational.ae, October 7, 2015; "Ronaldo Mouchawar: How I Created Souq.com," by Ed Attwood, Arabianbusiness.com, April 5, 2014; "Souq.com Launches Low-cost QTAB Tablet in UAE," Telecompaper.com, September 30, 2013; "After Many Slip-Ups, Mideast E-Commerce Gains Its Footing," by Sara Hamdan, *New York Times*, November 7, 2012; "Souq in Egypt: Not Relinquishing Its Crown Anytime Soon," by Omar Aysha, Wamda.com, October 18, 2012; "Why Middle East E-Commerce Site Souq.com Acquired Sister Site Sukar.com," by Nina Curley, Wamda.com, April 29, 2012; "Refocus of Souq.com Will End Auction Service," by David George-Cosh, Thenational.ae, January 2, 2011.

The opening case illustrates some of the difficulties that a pure-play startup retail company such as Souq faced, particularly when starting out in a part of the world, such as North Africa and the Middle East, that did not initally embrace e-commerce. Pure-play start-up companies often have razor-thin profit margins, lack a physical store network to bolster sales to the non-Internet audience, and often are based on unproven business assumptions that, in the long term, may not bear out. In contrast, large offline retailers have established brand names, a huge real estate investment, a loyal customer base, and established inventory control and fulfillment systems. In Souq's case, it originally adopted a business model based on the assumption that C2C auctions would find ready acceptance in its marketspace, when in fact they did not. Luckily for Souq, it was able to successfully transition to a B2C model, and take advantage of some of the benefits that this model offers. For instance, a pure-play B2C company can simplify the existing industry supply chain and instead develop a Web-based distribution system that may be more efficient than traditional retail outlets.

As with retail goods, the promise of online service providers is that they can deliver superior-quality service and greater convenience to millions of consumers at a lower cost than established bricks-and-mortar service providers and still make a respectable return on invested capital. The service sector is one of the most natural avenues for e-commerce because so much of the value in services is based on collecting, storing, and exchanging information—something for which the Web is ideally suited. And, in fact, online services have been extraordinarily successful in attracting banking, brokerage, travel, and job-hunting customers. The quality and amount of information online to support consumer decisions in finance, travel, and career placement is extraordinary, especially when compared to what was available to consumers before e-commerce. The online service sector—like online retail—has established a significant beachhead and now plays a large role in consumer time on the Internet. In areas such as brokerage, banking, and travel, online services are an extraordinary success story and have transformed their industries. In Sections 11.5–11.7 of this chapter, we take a close look at three of the most successful online services: financial services (including insurance and real estate), travel services, and career services. In Section 11.8, we examine the new on-demand services companies, such as Uber, Airbnb, and a whole host of others, that have rocketed to prominence in the last several years. Using a business model that is both local and mobile, this new type of service company provides a platform for consumers to connect with providers who can provide on-demand services, such as transportation, short-term room rental, grocery shopping, and more.

11.1 THE ONLINE RETAIL SECTOR

Table 11.1 summarizes some of these leading trends in online retailing for 2019–2020. Perhaps the most important theme in online retailing is the effort by retailers—both offline and online—to integrate their operations so they can serve customers in the various ways they want to be served.

TABLE 11.1	WHAT'S NEW IN ONLINE RETAIL 2019–2020

- Retail mobile e-commerce is exploding, increasing from around $1.3 trillion in 2018 to $2.2 trillion in 2019.
- Social networks such as Facebook, Pinterest, Instagram, together with online retailers, continue to try to understand how best to facilitate social e-commerce.
- Local e-commerce, headlined by new local on-demand service companies such as Uber, skyrockets.
- The number of online buyers continues to increase, to over 2 billion in 2019.
- Online retailers remain generally profitable by focusing on revenue growth, increasing the size of average purchase amounts, and improving efficiency of operations.
- Online retail remains the fastest growing retail channel.
- Shopping and buying online has become a normal, mainstream, everyday experience. Almost all Internet users worldwide are now online shoppers.
- The selection of goods for purchase online continues to increase to include luxury goods, such as jewelry, gourmet groceries, furniture, and wine, as customer trust and experience increase.
- Informational shopping for big-ticket items such as cars and appliances continues to expand rapidly to include nearly all retail goods (both durables and non-durables).
- Specialty retail sites show rapid growth in online retail as they develop customized retail goods and customer online configuration of goods.
- Online retailers place an increased emphasis on providing an improved "shopping experience," including ease of navigation and use, online inventory updates, interactive tools, customer feedback and ratings, and social shopping opportunities.
- Online retailers increase the use of interactive marketing technologies and techniques such as blogs, user-generated content, and video that exploit the dominance of broadband connections and offer features such as zoom, color switch, product configuration, and virtual simulations of households and businesses.
- Retailers are increasingly becoming omni-channel retailers, integrating the multiple retail channels provided by physical stores, the Web, and the mobile platform.
- Virtual merchants such as Birchbox, Naturebox, and others emerge that are using a new subscription-based revenue model for retail.
- Big data and powerful analytic programs begin to be used for predictive marketing by both large and small retailers.

By any measure, the size of the global retail market is huge: around $25 trillion in 2019. Retail sales in Asia-Pacific account for about 41% of that total, with North America accounting for about 23.5%, and Europe, 22% (eMarketer, Inc., 2019a).

THE RETAIL INDUSTRY

The retail industry is composed of many different types of firms. **Figure 11.1** illustrates the major segments: durable goods, general merchandise, food and beverage, specialty stores, gasoline and fuel, mail order/telephone order (MOTO), and online retail firms. Each of these segments offers opportunities for online retail, and yet in each segment, the uses of the Internet may differ. Some eating and drinking establishments use the Web and mobile apps to inform people of their physical locations and menus, while others offer delivery via online orders. Retailers of durable goods typically use the online channel

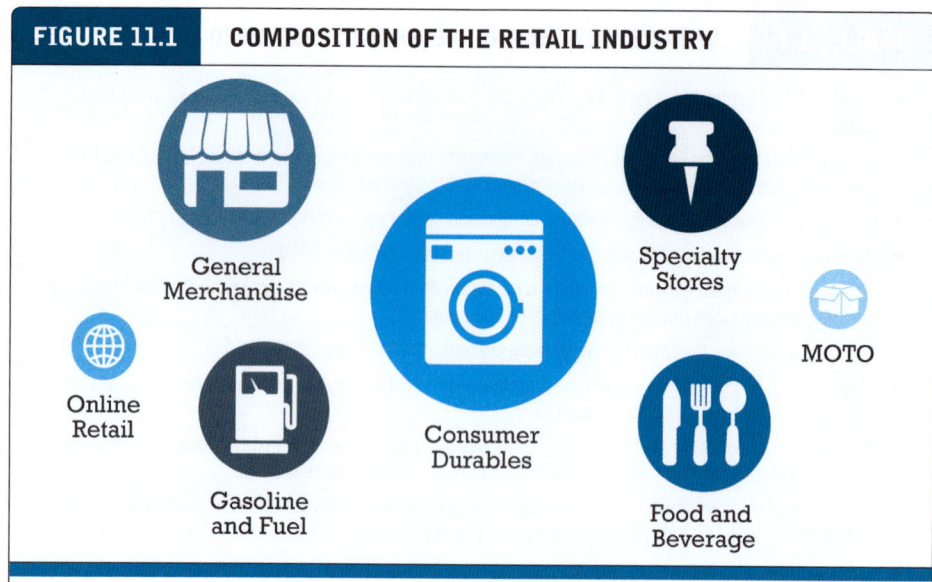

FIGURE 11.1 COMPOSITION OF THE RETAIL INDUSTRY

The retail industry can be grouped into seven major segments.
SOURCE: Based on data from U.S. Census Bureau, 2012.

primarily as an informational tool rather than as a direct purchasing tool, although this has begun to change.

The MOTO sector is the most similar to the online retail sales sector. In the absence of physical stores, MOTO retailers distribute millions of physical catalogs (their largest expense) and operate large telephone call centers to accept orders. They have developed extraordinarily efficient order fulfillment centers that generally ship customer orders within 24 hours of receipt. MOTO was the fastest growing retail segment throughout the 1970s and 1980s. It grew as a direct result of improvements in the national toll-free call system, the implementation of digital switching in telephone systems, falling long distance telecommunications prices, and of course, the expansion of the credit card industry and associated technologies, without which neither MOTO nor e-commerce would be possible on a large national scale. MOTO was the last "technological" retailing revolution that preceded e-commerce. Because of their experience in fulfilling small orders rapidly, the transition to e-commerce was not difficult for these firms.

ONLINE RETAILING

Online retail is perhaps the most high-profile e-commerce sector. Over the past decade, this sector has experienced both explosive growth and spectacular failures. Many of the early pure-play online-only firms that pioneered the retail marketspace failed. Entrepreneurs and their investors seriously misjudged the factors needed to succeed in this market. But the survivors of this early period emerged much stronger, and along with traditional offline general and specialty merchants, as well as new startups, the e-tail space is growing very rapidly and is increasing its reach and size.

E-commerce Retail: The Vision

In the early years of e-commerce, literally thousands of entrepreneurial web-based retailers were drawn to the marketplace for retail goods, simply because it was one of the largest market opportunities in the U.S. economy. Many entrepreneurs initially believed it was easy to enter the retail market. Early writers predicted that the retail industry would be revolutionized, literally "blown to bits"—as prophesied by two consultants in a famous Harvard Business School book (Evans and Wurster, 2000). The basis of this revolution would be fourfold. First, because the Internet greatly reduced both search costs and transaction costs, consumers would use the Web to find the lowest-cost products. Several results would follow. Consumers would increasingly drift to the Web for shopping and purchasing, and only low-cost, high-service, quality online retail merchants would survive. Economists assumed that the online consumer was rational and cost-driven—not driven by perceived value or brand, both of which are nonrational factors.

Second, it was assumed that the entry costs to the online retail market were much less than those needed to establish physical storefronts, and that online merchants were inherently more efficient at marketing and order fulfillment than offline stores. The costs of establishing a powerful website were thought to be minuscule compared to the costs of warehouses, fulfillment centers, and physical stores. There would be no difficulty building sophisticated order entry, shopping cart, and fulfillment systems because this technology was well known, and the cost of technology was falling by 50% each year. Even the cost of acquiring consumers was thought to be much lower because of search engines that could almost instantly connect customers to online vendors.

Third, as prices fell, traditional offline physical store merchants would be forced out of business. New entrepreneurial companies—such as Amazon—would replace the traditional stores. It was thought that if online merchants grew very quickly, they would have first-mover advantages and lock out the older traditional firms that were too slow to enter the online market.

Fourth, in some industries—such as electronics, apparel, and digital content—the market would be disintermediated as manufacturers or their distributors entered to build a direct relationship with the consumer, destroying the retail intermediaries or middlemen. In this scenario, traditional retail channels—such as physical stores, sales clerks, and sales forces—would be replaced by a single dominant channel: the Web.

Many predicted, on the other hand, a kind of hypermediation based on the concept of a virtual firm in which online retailers would gain advantage over established offline merchants by building an online brand name that attracted millions of customers, and outsourcing the expensive warehousing and order fulfillment functions—the original concept of Amazon.

As it turned out, few of these assumptions and visions were correct, and the structure of the retail marketplace in the United States, with some notable exceptions, has not been blown to bits, disintermediated, or revolutionized in the traditional meaning of the word "revolution." With several notable exceptions, online retail has often not been successful as an independent platform on which to build a successful "pure-play" online-only business. As it turns out, the consumer is not primarily price-driven when shopping on the Internet but instead considers brand name, trust, reliability, delivery time, convenience, ease of use, and above all "the experience," as at least as important as price (Brynjolfsson,

omni-channel

retailers that sell products through a variety of channels and integrate their physical stores with their website and mobile platform

Dick, and Smith, 2004). In 2019, after over two decades of e-commerce expansion, global retail e-commerce (about $3.5 billion) only accounts for about 14% of all global retail commerce ($25 trillion).

However, the Internet has created an entirely new venue for **omni-channel** firms (those that sell products through a variety of channels and integrate their physical stores with their websites and mobile platform), and in many cases, the Internet has supported the development of pure-play online-only merchants, both general merchandisers as well as specialty retailers. As predicted, online retail has indeed become the fastest growing and most dynamic retail channel in the sense of channel innovation. The Web has created a new marketplace for millions of consumers to conveniently shop. The Internet and the Web have continued to provide new opportunities for entirely new firms using new business models and new online products—such as Blue Nile, as previously described. The online channel can conflict with a merchant's other channels, such as direct sales forces, physical stores, and mail order, but this multi-channel conflict can be managed and turned into a strength.

The Online Retail Sector Today

Although online retailing is one of the smallest segments of the retail industry, constituting only about 14% of the total global retail market today, it is growing at a faster rate than its offline counterparts, with new functionality and product lines being added every day. In the United States, the computers and consumer electronics category generates the highest percentage of revenue, around $131 billion in 2019 (See **Figure 11.2**). Online shopping options for this category include Amazon, direct-manufacturers such as Apple, Dell, HP, and Lenovo, omni-channel chains such as Best Buy, and catalog merchants such as CDW and PC Connection.

The apparel and accessories category generates the second-highest percentage of revenue, around $118 billion in 2019. Consumers have a wide choice of online shopping options in this category, such as omni-channel department store chains like Macy's, Nordstrom, Target, and Walmart and specialty retailers like Gap, J.Crew, Urban Outfitters, Abercrombie & Fitch, and Ralph Lauren. This is one category where Amazon does not dominate, in part because clothing shoppers tend to identify more strongly with a specific brand than they do with products that are more of a commodity, such as consumer electronics.

The furniture and home furnishing category is third place, generating about $66.5 billion in 2019. In the past, the expense of shipping large items such as furniture, mattresses, and rugs was a deterrent to online sales, but that is beginning to change. In addition to Amazon, leading online retailers in this category include other purely online companies such as Wayfair and Overstock, as well as omni-channel retailers such as Williams-Sonoma, Restoration Hardware, Bed Bath & Beyond, and Crate and Barrel.

The health and personal care (drugs, health, and beauty supplies) category has also enjoyed steady growth, with about $53 billion in revenue in 2019 (eMarketer, Inc., 2019b).

The automobile and automobile parts and accessories category generated around $48 billion in 2019, primarily from auto parts and accessories. Currently, U.S. franchising law prohibits automobile manufacturers from selling cars directly to consumers,

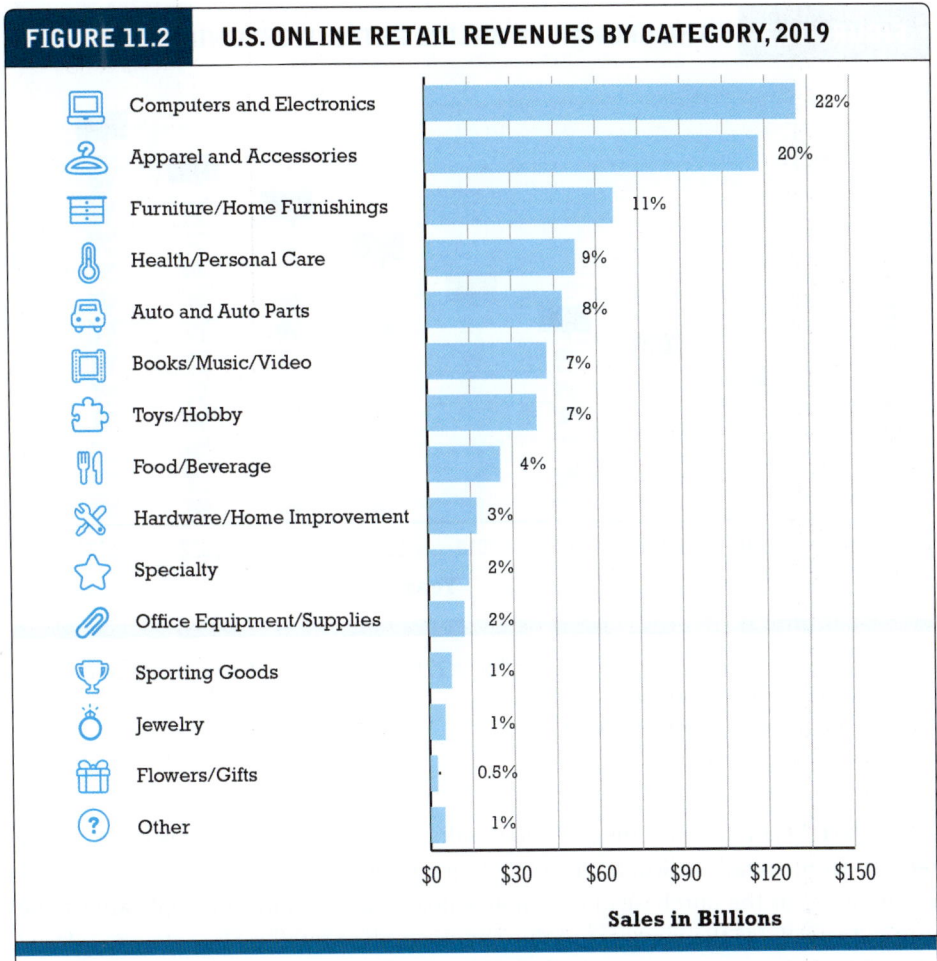

Computers and electronics is the leading online purchase category, accounting for 22% of all online retail revenues.
SOURCES: Based on data from eMarketer, Inc., 2019b, 2019c; Berthene, 2019; Cassidy, 2019; authors' estimates.

so automobile retailing is dominated by dealership networks. Automobile manufacturers use the Internet to deliver branding advertising, while dealers focus on generating leads. Consumers typically focus on product and pricing research, which they then use to negotiate with dealers. Direct online automobile sales are currently not common due to the complexity of the vehicle purchasing process, but they are likely to become more commonplace in the future. For example, Vroom is an online direct used car dealer that has raised over $720 million in venture capital. It offers a mobile app that allows users to easily filter their searches and offers delivery of purchased cars to buyers' doorsteps.

Books, music, and video are among the original items sold successfully online. This still popular online category generated about $42.5 billion in 2019. Leading retailers in this category include Amazon, Apple, Netflix, Google Play, Barnes & Noble, and Hulu.

FIGURE 11.3   THE GROWTH OF ONLINE RETAIL WORLDWIDE

Online retail revenues worldwide reached $3.5 trillion in 2019, and are expected to increase to $6.25 trillion by 2023, almost doubling from 2019.
SOURCES: Based on data from eMarketer, Inc., 2019d.

Figure 11.3 illustrates the growth of online retail revenues worldwide. When we refer to online retail, we will not be including online services revenues such as travel, job-hunting, or the purchase of digital downloads such as software applications and music. Instead, for the purposes of this chapter, online retail refers solely to sales of physical goods over the Internet. The Internet provides a number of unique advantages and challenges to online retailers. **Table 11.2** summarizes these advantages and challenges.

Despite the high failure rate of online retailers in the early years, more consumers than ever are shopping online. For most consumers, the advantages of online shopping overcome the disadvantages. In 2019, almost 55% of all Internet users over the age of 14 (over 2 billion) bought at an online retail store, generating around $3.5 trillion in online retail sales. While the number of new Internet users is not growing as rapidly at it was, this slowdown will not necessarily reduce the growth in online retail e-commerce because the average shopper is spending more on the Internet each year and finding many new categories of items to buy. For instance, in 2003, the average annual amount spent online by U.S. consumers was $675, but by 2019, it had jumped to an estimated $3,030 (eMarketer, Inc., 2019d, 2005). Also, as noted in Chapter 6, millions of additional consumers research products online and are influenced in their purchase decisions at offline stores.

The primary beneficiaries of this growing consumer support are not only the pure online companies but also the established offline retailers who have the brand-name recognition, supportive infrastructure, and financial resources to enter the online

TABLE 11.2   ONLINE RETAIL: ADVANTAGES AND CHALLENGES

ADVANTAGES	CHALLENGES
Lower supply chain costs by aggregating demand at a single site and increasing purchasing power	Consumer concerns about the security of transactions
Lower cost of distribution using websites rather than physical stores	Consumer concerns about the privacy of personal information given to websites
Ability to reach and serve a much larger geographically distributed group of customers	Delays in delivery of goods when compared to store shopping
Ability to react quickly to customer tastes and demand	Inconvenience associated with return of damaged or exchange goods
Ability to change prices nearly instantly	Overcoming lack of consumer trust in online brand names
Ability to rapidly change visual presentation of goods	Added expenses for online photography, video, and animated presentations
Avoidance of direct marketing costs of catalogs and physical mail	Online marketing costs for search, e-mail, and displays
Increased opportunities for personalization, customization	Added complexity to product offerings and customer service
Ability to greatly improve information and knowledge delivered to consumer	Greater customer information can translate into price competition and lower profits
Ability to lower consumers' overall market transaction costs	

marketplace successfully. Apart from Amazon (the leader by far), the top online retail firms in terms of online sales are all primarily omni-channel firms that have established brand names and for whom e-commerce still plays a relatively small role when compared to their offline physical store channels, such as Walmart, Macy's, Staples, Home Depot, Best Buy, Costco, Nordstrom, Target, and Kohl's. For instance, the 215 retail chains ranked in the 2019 Internet Retailer Top 1000 increased their online sales by over 16% in 2018. Many of the fastest growing firms are smaller and medium-sized merchants, particularly newcomers that focus on a particular niche. For instance, retailers ranked between 401 and 600 in the 2019 Internet Retailer Top 1000 increased their online sales by over 22%, significantly higher than the overall rate of growth (Davis, 2019a; Cassidy, 2019). Conversely, companies that can't show consumers that they can offer them something of value not available elsewhere are likely to have a difficult time surviving. For pure-play firms, the challenge is to turn visitors into customers, and to develop efficient operations that permit them to achieve long-term profitability. Profitability remains a key issue for online-only retailers. Not many of these companies are public and therefore required to report their financial results, but of the few that are, only a handful were profitable in 2018. For traditional firms that are less dependent on e-commerce sales, the challenge is to integrate the offline and online channels so customers can move seamlessly from one environment to another.

Clearly one of the most important e-commerce retail themes of 2019–2020, and into the future, is the ability of offline traditional firms such as Walmart, Target, Macy's, and others to continue to integrate their web and mobile operations with their physical store operations in order to provide an "integrated shopping customer experience" and leverage the value of their physical stores. **Table 11.3** illustrates some of the various ways in which traditional retailers have integrated the Web, the mobile platform, and store operations to develop nearly seamless omni-channel shopping. This list is not exclusive, and retailers continue to develop new links between channels, especially the mobile channel. The early results of large physical store retailers attempting to develop online channels that can compete with Amazon is difficult, expensive, and requires lengthy development times. Retail chain stores' websites have struggled to match the growth of Amazon, and many have declared bankruptcy or shut down, including Sears, Limited Stores, Gander Mountain, and Sports Authority. Many omni-channel players are attempting to acquire online capabilities via acquisition: i.e., Walmart's acquisition of Jet.com, Flipkart (one of India's largest online retailers), Hayneedle, ShoeBuy, Moosejaw, ModCloth, Bonobos and Art.com), PetSmart's acquistion of Chewy; and Bed Bath & Beyond's acquisition of One Kings Lane and PearsonalizationMall.

Likewise, pure-play online retailers like Amazon are seeking to build a physical store presence, and they are finding that this effort is difficult and will take many years to implement. Amazon purchased the Whole Foods chain of stores in 2017 as a way to quickly acquire physical presence in the retail food sector. Other acquisitions of existing retail stores by online retailers are likely.

Rather than demonstrate disintermediation, online retailing provides an example of the powerful role that intermediaries continue to play in retail trade. Established offline retailers have rapidly gained online market share. Increasingly, consumers are attracted to stable, well-known, trusted retail brands and retailers. The online audience is very sensitive to brand names and is not primarily cost-driven. Other factors such as reliability, trust, fulfillment, and customer service are equally important.

Other significant changes in retail e-commerce in 2019 were the continuing growth in social e-commerce, the growing ability of firms to market local services and products through the use of location-based marketing, and not least, the rapidly growing mobile platform composed of smartphones and tablet computers. In retail circles, smartphones have become a leading shopping tool, while tablets are increasingly both shopping and purchase platforms.

Social e-commerce refers to marketing and purchasing on social network sites like Facebook, Twitter, Pinterest, Instagram, Snapchat, and others. All of these sites have developed into major marketing and advertising platforms that help direct consumers to external websites to purchase products. Facebook, Pinterest, and Instagram have all introduced their own versions of "buy" buttons that allow consumers to more easily purchase goods on a large scale. According to Policy Factory, a series produced by Think-Tanks+, a Paris-based news agency dedicated to think-thanks, social e-commerce in the United States generated about $16.5 billion in 2018 (Policy Factory, 2019).

Whereas in the past only large firms could afford to run online marketing and ad campaigns, this has changed with the development of local marketing firms like Groupon, LivingSocial, and dozens of others, which make it possible for consumers to receive discount

TABLE 11.3 RETAIL E-COMMERCE: OMNI-CHANNEL INTEGRATION METHODS

INTEGRATION TYPE	DESCRIPTION
Online catalog	Online catalog supplements offline physical catalog and often the online catalog has substantially more product on display.
Online order, in-store pickup (BOPIS)	One of the first and now one of the most common types of integration. Also known as BOPIS (buy online, pickup in-store).
Online order, in-store returns and adjustments	Defective or rejected products ordered online can be returned to any store location. Most major omni-channel firms now offer this option.
Online order, store directory, and inventory	When items are out of stock online, customer is directed to physical store network inventory and store location.
In-store kiosk online order, home delivery	When retail store is out of stock, customer orders in store and receives at home.
In-store retail clerk online order, home delivery	Similar to above, but the retail clerk searches online inventory if local store is out of stock as a normal part of the in-store checkout process.
Manufacturers use online promotions to drive customers to their distributors' retail stores	Consumer product manufacturers such as Colgate-Palmolive and Procter & Gamble use online channels to design new products and promote existing product retail sales.
Gift card, loyalty program points can be used in any channel	Recipient of gift card, loyalty program points can use them to purchase in-store, online, or via catalog, if offered by merchant.
Mobile order, website and physical store sales	Apps take users directly to specially formatted website for ordering, or to in-store bargains.
Geo-fencing mobile notification, in-store sales	Use of smartphone geo-location technology to target ads for nearby stores and restaurants.

deals and coupons from local merchants based on their geographic location. Using billions of daily e-mails, these so-called daily deal sites have sold millions of coupons to purchase local goods and services at steep discounts. For the first time, local merchants can advertise their products and services online at a relatively inexpensive cost.

Social and local e-commerce are enabled by the tremendous growth in mobile Internet devices, both smartphones and tablet computers. In 2019, retail m-commerce worldwide generated over $2.2 trillion. In the United States, over 80% of online buyers made a purchase using a mobile device, and it is estimated that this percentage will grow to over 86% by 2023 (eMarketer, Inc., 2019e, 2019f).

11.2 ANALYZING THE VIABILITY OF ONLINE FIRMS

In this and the following chapters, we analyze the viability of a number of online companies that exemplify specific e-commerce models. We are primarily interested in understanding the near-to-medium term (1–3 years) economic viability of these firms and their business models. **Economic viability** refers to the ability of firms to survive as profitable

economic viability
refers to the ability of firms to survive as profitable business firms during a specified period

business firms during the specified period. To answer the question of economic viability, we take two business analysis approaches: strategic analysis and financial analysis.

STRATEGIC ANALYSIS

Strategic approaches to economic viability focus on both the industry in which a firm operates and the firm itself (see Chapter 5, Sections 5.2 and 5.5). The key industry strategic factors are:

- *Barriers to entry*: Can new entrants be barred from entering the industry through high capital costs or intellectual property barriers (such as patents and copyrights)?
- *Power of suppliers*: Can suppliers dictate high prices to the industry or can vendors choose from among many suppliers? Have firms achieved sufficient scale to bargain effectively for lower prices from suppliers?
- *Power of customers*: Can customers choose from many competing suppliers and hence challenge high prices and high margins?
- *Existence of substitute products*: Can the functionality of the product or service be obtained from alternative channels or competing products in different industries? Are substitute products and services likely to emerge in the near future?
- *Industry value chain*: Is the chain of production and distribution in the industry changing in ways that benefit or harm the firm?
- *Nature of intra-industry competition*: Is the basis of competition within the industry based on differentiated products and services, price, scope of offerings, or focus of offerings? How is the nature of competition changing? Will these changes benefit the firm?

The strategic factors that pertain specifically to the firm and its related businesses include:

- *Firm value chain*: Has the firm adopted business processes and methods of operation that allow it to achieve the most efficient operations in its industry? Will changes in technology force the firm to realign its business processes?
- *Core competencies*: Does the firm have unique competencies and skills that cannot be easily duplicated by other firms? Will changes in technology invalidate the firm's competencies or strengthen them?
- *Synergies*: Does the firm have access to the competencies and assets of related firms either owned outright or through strategic partnerships and alliances?
- *Technology*: Has the firm developed proprietary technologies that allow it to scale with demand? Has the firm developed the operational technologies (e.g., customer relationship management, fulfillment, supply chain management, inventory control, and human resource systems) to survive?
- *Social and legal challenges*: Has the firm put in place policies to address consumer trust issues (privacy and security of personal information)? Is the firm the subject of lawsuits challenging its business model, such as intellectual property ownership issues? Will the firm be affected by changes in Internet taxation laws or other foreseeable statutory developments?

FINANCIAL ANALYSIS

Strategic analysis helps us comprehend the competitive situation of the firm. Financial analysis helps us understand how in fact the firm is performing. There are two parts to a financial analysis: the statement of operations and the balance sheet. The statement of operations tells us how much money (or loss) the firm is achieving based on current sales and costs. The balance sheet tells us how many assets the firm has to support its current and future operations.

Here are some of the key factors to look for in a firm's statement of operations:

- *Revenues*: Are revenues growing and at what rate? Many e-commerce companies have experienced impressive, even explosive, revenue growth as an entirely new channel is created.

- *Cost of sales*: What is the cost of sales compared to revenues? Cost of sales typically includes the cost of the products sold and related costs. The lower the cost of sales compared to revenue, the higher the gross profit.

- *Gross margin*: What is the firm's gross margin, and is it increasing or decreasing? **Gross margin** is calculated by dividing gross profit by net sales revenues. Gross margin can tell you if the firm is gaining or losing market power vis-à-vis its key suppliers.

- *Operating expenses*: What are the firm's operating expenses, and are they increasing or decreasing? Operating expenses typically include the cost of marketing, technology, and administrative overhead. They also include, in accordance with professional accounting standards (see below), stock-based compensation to employees and executives, amortization of goodwill and other intangibles, and impairment of investments. In e-commerce companies, these turn out to be very important expenses. Many e-commerce firms compensated their employees with stock shares (or options), and many e-commerce firms purchased other e-commerce firms as a part of their growth strategy. Many of the companies were purchased at extremely high values using company stock rather than cash; in numerous instances, the purchased companies fell dramatically in market value. All these items are counted as normal operating expenses.

- *Operating margin*: What did the firm earn from its current operations? **Operating margin** is calculated by dividing operating income or loss by net sales revenue. Operating margin is an indication of a company's ability to turn sales into pre-tax profit after operating expenses have been deducted. Operating margin tells us if the firm's current operations are covering its operating expenses, not including interest expenses and other non-operating expenses.

- *Net margin*: **Net margin** tells us the percentage of its gross sales revenue the firm was able to retain after all expenses are deducted. Net margin is calculated by dividing net income or loss by net sales revenue. Net margin sums up in one number how successful a company has been at the business of making a profit on each dollar of sales revenues. Net margin also tells us something about the efficiency of the firm by measuring the percentage of sales revenue it is able to retain after all expenses are deducted from gross revenues, and, within a single industry, it can be used to measure the relative efficiency of competing firms. Net margin takes into account many non-operating expenses such as interest and stock compensation plans.

gross margin
gross profit divided by net sales

operating margin
calculated by dividing operating income or loss by net sales revenue

net margin
the percentage of its gross sales revenue the firm is able to retain after all expenses are deducted; calculated by dividing net income or loss by net sales revenue

When examining the financial announcements of e-commerce companies, it is important to realize that online firms often choose not to announce their net income according to generally accepted accounting principles (GAAP). These principles have been promulgated by the Financial Accounting Standards Board (FASB), a board of professional accountants that establishes accounting rules for the profession, and which has played a vital role since the 1934 Securities Act, which sought to improve financial accounting during the Great Depression. Many e-commerce firms in the early years instead reported an entirely new calculation called *pro forma earnings* (also called EBITDA—earnings before income taxes, depreciation, and amortization). Pro forma earnings generally do not deduct stock-based compensation, depreciation, or amortization. The result is that pro forma earnings are always better than GAAP earnings. The firms that report in this manner typically claim these expenses are non-recurring and special and "unusual." In 2002 and 2003, the SEC issued new guidelines (Regulation G) that prohibit firms from reporting pro forma earnings in official reports to the SEC, but still allow firms to announce pro forma earnings in public statements (Weil, 2003). Throughout this book, we consider a firm's income or loss based on GAAP accounting standards only.

A **balance sheet** provides a financial snapshot of a company's assets and liabilities (debts) on a given date. **Assets** refer to stored value. **Current assets** are those assets such as cash, securities, accounts receivable, inventory, or other investments that are likely to be able to be converted to cash within one year. **Liabilities** are outstanding obligations of the firm. **Current liabilities** are debts of the firm that will be due within one year. Liabilities that are not due until the passage of a year or more are characterized as **long-term debt**. For a quick check of a firm's short-term financial health, examine its **working capital** (the firm's current assets minus current liabilities). If working capital is only marginally positive, or negative, the firm will likely have trouble meeting its short-term obligations. Alternatively, if a firm has a large amount of current assets, it can sustain operational losses for a period of time.

11.3 E-COMMERCE IN ACTION: E-TAILING BUSINESS MODELS

So far, we have been discussing online retail as if it were a single entity. In fact, as we briefly discussed in Chapter 5, there are four main types of online retail business models: virtual merchants, omni-channel merchandisers (sometimes referred to as bricks-and-clicks or clicks-and-bricks), catalog merchants, and manufacturer-direct firms. **Figure 11.4** illustrates the respective shares of 2018 U.S. online retail sales for each of these categories of firms. In addition, there are thousands of small retailers that use the eBay and Amazon sales platforms, as well as affiliate merchants whose primary revenue derives from sending traffic to their "mother" sites. Each of these different types of online retailers faces a different strategic environment, as well as different industry and firm economics.

VIRTUAL MERCHANTS

Virtual merchants are single-channel e-commerce firms that generate almost all their revenue from online sales. Virtual merchants face extraordinary strategic challenges. They

---

balance sheet
provides a financial snapshot of a company on a given date and shows its financial assets and liabilities

assets
refers to stored value

current assets
assets such as cash, securities, accounts receivable, inventory, or other investments that are likely to be able to be converted to cash within one year

liabilities
outstanding obligations of the firm

current liabilities
debts of the firm that will be due within one year

long-term debt
liabilities that are not due until the passage of a year or more

working capital
firm's current assets minus current liabilities

virtual merchants
single-channel e-commerce firms that generate almost all of their revenue from online sales

must build a business and brand name from scratch, quickly, in an entirely new channel and confront many virtual merchant competitors (especially in smaller niche areas). Because these firms typically do not have any physical stores, they do not have to bear the costs associated with developing and maintaining physical stores but they face large costs in building and maintaining an e-commerce presence, building an order fulfillment infrastructure, and developing a brand name. Customer acquisition costs are high, and the learning curve is steep. Like all retail firms, their gross margins (the difference between the retail price of goods sold and the cost of goods to the retailer) are low. Therefore, virtual merchants must achieve highly efficient operations in order to preserve a profit, while building a brand name as quickly as possible in order to attract sufficient customers to cover their costs of operations. Most merchants in this category adopt low-cost and convenience strategies, coupled with extremely effective and efficient fulfillment processes to ensure customers receive what they ordered as fast as possible. In the following *E-commerce in Action* section, we take an in-depth look at the strategic and financial situation of Amazon, the leading online virtual merchant. In addition to Amazon, other successful virtual merchants include Wayfair, Newegg, Overstock, Zulily, Rue La La, Blue Nile, Yoox Net-a-Porter, and Shoes.com (formerly Shoebuy). Recently, a new group of virtual merchants have emerged that use a subscription revenue model. Examples include Birchbox (personalized beauty samples delivered monthly), Stitch Fix (clothing selected by a personal stylist), Barkbox (pet supplies), Naturebox (healthy snacks), Bulu Box (supplements and vitamins), and hundreds more. Virtual merchants (including Amazon) accounted for about 45% of online retail sales by the Internet Retailer Top 1000 merchants in 2019 (Davis, 2019; 2018a, 2018b; eMarketer, Inc., 2016).

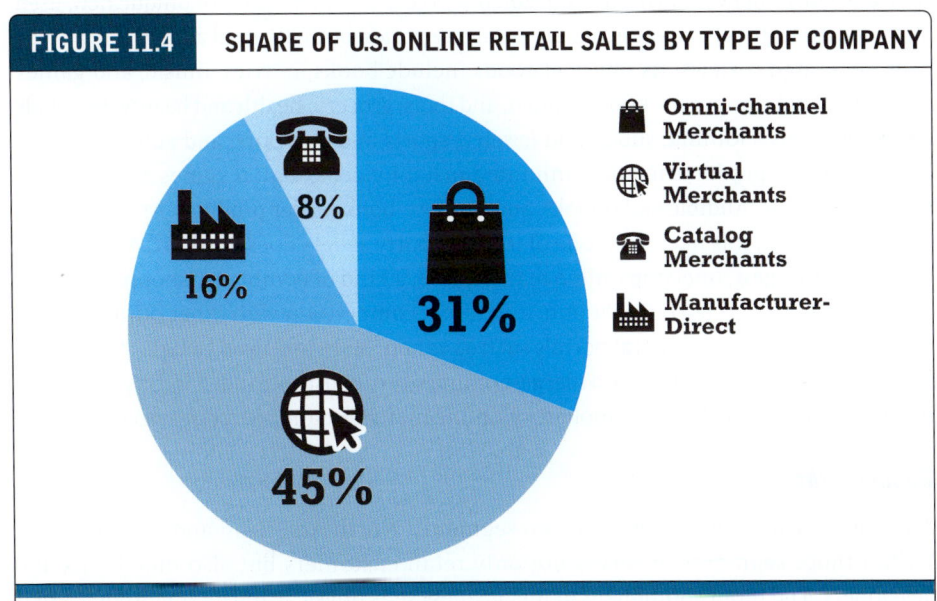

FIGURE 11.4 SHARE OF U.S. ONLINE RETAIL SALES BY TYPE OF COMPANY

Virtual merchants account for about 45% of U.S. online retail sales, although this percentage is heavily skewed by the dominance of Amazon, which by itself accounts for about 40% of all online retail.
SOURCES: Based on data from Davis, 2019, 2018a, 2018b; eMarketer, Inc., 2016; authors' estimates.

E-COMMERCE IN ACTION

AMAZON

Amazon, the Seattle-based virtual merchant, is one of the largest and most well-known companies in the world. Amazon's objective is to be Earth's most customer-centric company. In pursuing this goal, Jeff Bezos and his team have built the world's most successful and innovative online retailer.

Few business enterprises have experienced the roller-coaster ride from explosive early growth, to huge losses, and then on to profitability that Amazon has. No Internet business has been both so widely reviled and so hotly praised throughout its development. Its stock reflects these changing fortunes, fluctuating from an early high of $106 in 1999, to a low of $6 a share in 2001, then bouncing back and forth between $50–$90 in 2003–2009, and then steadily climbing over the last ten years to over $2000 a share in early 2020, making founder and CEO Jeff Bezos the richest man in the world, surpassing Bill Gates. While controversial, Amazon has also been one of the most innovative online retailing stories in the history of e-commerce. From the earliest days of e-commerce, Amazon has continuously adapted its business model based on both its market experience and its insight into the online consumer.

The Vision

The original vision shared by Jeff Bezos and other successful e-commerce pioneers was that the Internet was a revolutionary new form of commerce and that only companies that became really big early on (ignoring profitability) would survive. The path to success, according to Bezos, was to offer consumers three things: the lowest prices, the best selection, and convenience. Currently, Amazon offers consumers millions of unique new, used, and collectible items in a variety of different categories, both physical and digital, all with user-generated reviews. Its physical goods include books, movies, music, and games; electronics and computers; home, garden, and tools; grocery; health and beauty; toys, kids, and baby items; clothing, shoes, and jewelry; sports and outdoors; and auto and industrial. Its digital products include unlimited instant videos, digital games and software, streaming music, Audible audiobooks, and Kindle e-book reader products. And if Amazon does not carry it, it is likely that one of its third-party sellers does. In short, Amazon has become the largest, one-stop online marketplace, a kind of combined "shopping portal" and "product search portal" that puts it in direct competition with other omni-channel retail chains, eBay, and general portals such as Yahoo, MSN, and even Google. As Amazon succeeded in becoming the world's largest online store, it also expanded its original vision to become one of the largest suppliers of online merchant and search services.

Business Model

Amazon's business is divided into two segments: North American and International. Within those segments, it serves not only retail customers but also merchants and developers. The retail component of the business sells physical and digital products that Amazon has purchased and then resells to consumers just like a traditional retailer. It also manufactures and sells a variety of versions of its Kindle e-reader, Kindle Fire, and Amazon Echo series of devices. The company also sells products under its own private labels, including AmazonBasics, which sells common items like USB cords and batteries. While the Kindle Fire smartphone proved unsuccessful, the Echo voice-activated speaker with intelligent assistant Alexa has garnered a commanding position in a rapidly growing market for these devices, with over 70% market share, and could be Amazon's next must-have device.

Another major component of Amazon's business is its third-party merchant segment. Amazon Services enables third parties to integrate their products into Amazon's website, and use Amazon's customer technologies. In the early years of its business, Amazon entered into partnerships with large merchants such as Toys"R"Us, Borders, and Target, and created storefronts for these companies within the larger Amazon site. However, many of these businesses turned to Amazon as a last resort, hoping that if they couldn't beat Amazon, they could join them instead, with underwhelming results. For example, Toys"R"Us and Borders are now bankrupt, and Target has long since ended its partnership with Amazon, although some analysts suspect that Amazon could look to acquire Target to improve its mixture of online and offline retailing capability. Amazon has increasingly left the enterprise-level business to competitors and instead focused its efforts on small and medium-sized retail merchants.

Thousands of these types of merchants have signed on with Amazon, offering products that in some instances even compete with those that Amazon itself sells. For instance, a single product on the Amazon website may be listed for sale simultaneously by Amazon, by a large branded merchant participant such as Target, and by a business or individual selling a new, used, or collectible version of the product through Amazon Marketplace. For these types of merchants, Amazon is not the seller of record, does not own these products, and the shipping of products is usually handled by the third party (although in some instances, Amazon provides fulfillment services as well). Amazon collects a monthly fixed fee, sales commission (generally estimated to be between 10% and 20% of the sale), per-unit activity fee, or some combination thereof from the third party. In this segment, Amazon acts as an online shopping mall, collecting "rents" from other merchants and providing "site" services such as order entry and payment.

Another major part of Amazon's business is Amazon Web Services (AWS). Through this segment, Amazon offers scalable computing power and storage space for businesses without their own hardware infrastructure and provides developers with direct access to Amazon's technology platform, allowing them to build their own applications based on that platform. In 2019, AWS accounted for over $35 billion in revenues, a 37% increase over the previous year. AWS delivers more profits than Amazon's entire retail business. Refer to Chapter 2 for a more detailed examination of AWS.

Despite the profitability of AWS, Amazon still generates the bulk of its overall revenue by selling products. While Amazon started out as an online merchant of books, CDs, and DVDs, since 2002, it has diversified into becoming a general merchandiser of millions of other products. Amazon has turned itself into a major online media and content firm and, following its success with Kindle e-books, has also made a strong move into the music and streaming video business, with Amazon Music and Amazon Instant Video. In addition to Amazon.com in the United States, Amazon also operates a number of localized sites in Europe, Asia, and Canada. Amazon derived 27% of its gross revenue offshore in 2019, generating almost $75 billion, but a $1.7 billion operating loss, indicating that, true to form, the company is focusing on international growth and worrying about profits later.

Financial Analysis

Amazon's revenues have increased from about $600 million in 1998 to an astounding $280 billion in 2019 (see **Table 11.4**). This is very impressive, explosive revenue growth. However, Amazon's aggressive pursuit of growth has made it difficult for the company to maintain consistent profits in the past. From 2011 and 2014, Amazon boomeranged from losses to profitability on a yearly basis. Amazon finally strung together a series of profitable quarters in 2015, continuing through to 2019. However, Amazon continues to spend huge amounts on fulfillment centers, international expansion, and streaming video.

At the end of December 2019, Amazon had about $36 billion in cash and marketable securities. These liquid assets were obtained from sales, sales of stock and notes to the public, venture capital investors, and institutional investors in return for equity (shares) in the company or debt securities. Total assets are over $225 billion. The company emphasizes the strength of its "free cash flow" as a sign of financial strength, suggesting it has more than enough cash available to cover short-term liabilities (such as financing holiday season purchasing and major acquisitions such as the company's $13 billion purchase of Whole Foods supermarkets). Amazon's current assets should certainly be enough to cover future short-term deficits should they occur.

Strategic Analysis—Business Strategy

Amazon engages in a number of business strategies that seek to maximize growth in sales volume, while cutting prices to the bare minimum. Its revenue growth strategies include driving the growth of e-book sales by offering continuing enhancements of its Kindle e-reader and Kindle Fire tablet computer, both in the United States and internationally, as well as new e-book publishing initiatives; expanding further into the device manufacturing business, with Amazon Fire TV and Amazon Echo; expanding its music and streaming video business, with its Amazon Music and Instant Video services; expanding its AWS offerings and extending their geographic reach; moving toward a broader trading platform by expanding the third-party seller segment; continuing to grow its Amazon Business B2B marketplace segment; and moving toward greater product focus by grouping its offerings into major categories it calls "stores"; and special events that drive overall sales, such as Prime Day, an online version of Black Friday that generated over $7 billion in gross merchandise sales in 2019, compared to $4 billion in 2018. Amazon is still following Walmart's and eBay's examples by attempting to be a mass-market, low-price, high-volume online supermarket where you can get just about anything.

Specific programs to increase retail revenues are the continuation of free shipping from Amazon Retail (a strategy that has increased order sizes by 25%), Amazon Prime (which for $119 a year provides free two-day and in some instances one-day shipping, as well as free access to Prime Music and Prime Video), greater product selection, and shorter order fulfillment times. Amazon Prime membership is steadily increasing, with an estimated 150 million members globally in 2019. Amazon offers customers same-day

TABLE 11.4 AMAZON'S CONSOLIDATED STATEMENTS OF OPERATIONS AND SUMMARY BALANCE SHEET DATA 2017–2019

CONSOLIDATED STATEMENTS OF OPERATIONS (in millions)

For the fiscal year ended December 31,	2017	2018	2019
Revenue			
Net sales/products	$118,573	$141,915	$160,408
Net sales/services	59,293	90,972	120,114
Cost of sales	111,934	139,156	165,536
Gross profit	65,932	93,731	114,986
Gross margin	37.1%	40.2%	41%
Operating expenses			
Marketing	10,069	13,814	18,878
Fulfillment	25,249	34,027	40,232
Technology and content	22,620	28,837	35,931
General and administrative	3,674	4,336	5,203
Other operating expense (income), net	214	296	201
Total operating expenses	61,826	81,310	100,445
Income from operations	4,106	12,421	14,541
Operating margin	2.3%	5.3%	5.2%
Total non-operating income (expense)	(300)	(1,160)	(565)
Income before income taxes	3,806	11,261	13,976
Provision for income taxes	(769)	(1,197)	(2,374)
Equity-method investment activity, net of tax	(4)	9	(14)
Net income (loss)	3,033	10,073	11,588
Net margin	1.7%	4.3%	4.1%

SUMMARY BALANCE SHEET DATA (in millions)

At December 31,	2017	2018	2019
Assets			
Cash, cash equivalents, and marketable securities	30,986	31,750	36,092
Total current assets	60,197	75,101	96,334
Total assets	131,310	162,648	225,248
Liabilities			
Total current liabilities	57,883	68,391	87,812
Long-term liabilities	45,718	50,708	75,376
Working capital	2,314	6,710	8,522
Stockholders' Equity	27,709	43,549	62,060

SOURCE: Amazon.com, Inc., 2020a.

shipping in over 10,000 cities and towns in the United States and its Prime Now one- or two-hour delivery service in most major U.S. cities and metropolitan areas. A ticking clock can be seen next to some Amazon sale items indicating the hours remaining for an order to make it to the customer by the next day.

Amazon has moved decisively into the mobile shopping space as well, with shopping apps for the iPhone, Android, Windows Phone, and iPad. Amazon maintained a dominant position in m-commerce in 2019, with an amazing 93% of smartphone shoppers reporting that they shop on Amazon, with most of those shoppers making the majority of their mobile purchases on Amazon. Amazon has not been as successful in developing its own smartphone, however. In 2015, it withdrew its resources from the continued development of the Amazon Fire phone, which had opened to underwhelming sales in 2014 and never developed an audience.

Amazon has continued to build on the rousing success of its Kindle e-book reader platform, which it has touted as the best-selling product in its history. It has continued to release iterations of the Kindle e-book reader and Fire. According to Amazon, it now sells more Kindle books than all print books combined.

Amazon has partnered with NBC Universal, CBS, Viacom, PBS, A&E, FX, HBO, and nearly every major Hollywood studio to add content to its Instant Video library. It has also developed a number of original series to keep pace with competitors such as Netflix, Hulu and others. In 2015, Amazon's content creation arm, Amazon Studios, began to develop original movies for theatrical release, several of which have been critical successes, such as *Manchester by the Sea*, which became the first movie produced by a streaming service to win an Academy Award. Amazon Prime Video is available in over 200 countries.

On the cost side, Amazon increasingly uses "postal injection" for shipping, in which Amazon trucks deliver pre-posted packages to U.S. Postal System centers. In 2012, Amazon began an aggressive strategy to build warehouses all across the country to improve its delivery speeds. This has continued through 2019, with the opening of several new fulfillment centers. Amazon is also focusing on beating its competitors in delivery speed with same-day delivery in many areas of the country.

To that end, Amazon has taken steps to expand its delivery capability in several ways, including drone delivery and cargo jets. Amazon Prime Air is Amazon's drone delivery project, which would be capable of delivering packages up to 5 pounds in weight—upwards of 80% of all shipments. Until recently, this type of delivery method seemed closer to science fiction than reality, but Amazon appears closer than ever to making it work, despite the engineering and legal hurdles. In 2016, Amazon also agreed to lease 40 Boeing 767 jets to help manage its ever-increasing shipping demands. The company has also purchased a fleet of its own trucks and investigated the development self-driving delivery vehicles. Though it may look like Amazon is trying to take full control of its delivery operations, Amazon isn't likely to end its relationships with FedEx or UPS—the overall volume of its orders has become too high for that. However, these moves could dramatically improve per-order profit margins for the majority of Amazon orders, making life even more difficult for Amazon's traditional bricks-and-mortar competitors.

Amazon has begun to make inroads in several areas that were once thought to be impervious to e-commerce, including groceries and fashion. Although shoppers may always feel more comfortable with looking at fresh produce in person and trying on clothes before buying them, Amazon is undeterred. In 2017, Amazon purchased Whole Foods for a whopping $13.7 billion, immediately giving them 460 supermarkets to support Amazon's grocery services, such as Amazon Fresh. Amazon plans to use the stores as distribution points where customers can pick up items that they've ordered online, or pay extra to have groceries delivered. Amazon is also experimenting with a prototype checkout system called Amazon Go, which will allow grocery shoppers to grab their food and simply leave the store without stopping to pay or have items scanned by a cashier.

Amazon also launched Amazon Prime Wardrobe, a feature bundled into Amazon Prime that will allow customers to order clothing without actually buying any items, eventually charging only for the items each customer keeps. The company has also received a patent for an automated system that could custom-build garments of precise sizes for individual buyers. Even beyond fashion, Amazon is relentlessly pursuing market share in markets where it has had lower penetration, such as home appliances and cosmetics, which many customers prefer to view or try in person before buying.

Strategic Analysis—Competition

Amazon has both offline and online competition. Major competitors include eBay (its primary online competitor) and omni-channel retailers such as Walmart, Sears, and JCPenney. In 2016, Walmart purchased discount Amazon competitor Jet.com for $3.3 billion as it continued to suffer at the hands of Amazon, both falling behind in overall market capitalization and stalling in e-commerce growth as Amazon booms. Since then, Walmart has made a host of acquisitions to improve its e-commerce capability, including online clothing retailers Bonobos, Shoebuy, Moosejaw, and ModCloth and Flipkart, one of India's largest online retailers. Walmart has also begun offering free two-day shipping, the ability to quickly reorder items frequently purchased, and online grocery service, where its 4,700 stores dwarf Amazon's 460 acquired from Whole Foods, giving it a much more robust network for delivering goods. Walmart and Amazon are each trying to become more like the other—Walmart already has the physical infrastructure that Amazon is racing to build, whereas Amazon's e-commerce capability is far more advanced than Walmart's. However, Walmart also undertook a complete website redesign in 2018, dramatically simplifying its website with a minimalist, image-heavy design that stands in sharp contrast to Amazon's front page (for more on Walmart's website redesign, see the Chapter 4 opening case). Amazon still firmly has the upper hand in this battle of the titans, but Walmart has improved its e-commerce operations enough to secure its place as Amazon's biggest threat going forward. The biggest threat to Amazon's international expansion efforts is China-based Alibaba, which handles more business worldwide than eBay and Amazon combined. Amazon continues to pursue an aggressive strategy internationally, both with the launch of localized versions of its site, and acquisitions such as its purchase of Souq.com, perhaps the most prominent e-commerce company in the Middle East.

Amazon has also fully engaged in competition in the music, movie, and television industries. Amazon Music Unlimited allows users to stream music online as well as download for offline use, offers over 50 million DRM-free MP3 songs from both major music labels and thousands of independent labels, and can be played on virtually any hardware device and managed with any music software. Amazon Prime Music, launched in 2014, offers over 2 million tracks that users can stream for free. Amazon Prime Video provides access to streaming-video content including over 12,000 movies and tens of thousands of television show episodes for free to Amazon Prime members, as well as additional content that can be rented or purchased a la carte.

Strategic Analysis—Technology

Anyone who believes that information technology doesn't make a difference clearly does not know much about Amazon. Amazon arguably has the largest and most sophisticated collection of online retailing technologies available at any single online site. It has implemented numerous website management, search, customer interaction, recommendation, transaction processing, and fulfillment services and systems using a combination of its own proprietary technologies and commercially available, licensed technologies. Amazon's transaction-processing systems handle millions of items, numerous status inquiries, gift-wrapping requests, and multiple shipment methods. Customers can receive orders in single or multiple shipments, based on availability, and track the progress of each order. On the fulfillment side, every warehouse employee carries a shoehorn-sized device that combines a bar code scanner, a display screen, and a two-way data transmitter. The sheer size and scope of Amazon's technological capability was the motivation for the launch of AWS, which controlled about 33% of the cloud computing marketplace worldwide in 2019, compared to 17% for Microsoft Azure and 6% for Google Cloud Platform. Amazon also continues to invest in new versions of the Kindle e-reader, and consumer electronics such as the Kindle Fire devices, as well as projects like drone delivery and the Amazon Echo home assistant. Powered by its state-of-the-art speech recognition and cloud connectivity, the Echo has a diverse range of features that range from streaming music, doing math, updating to-do lists, getting the weather, playing games, and much more. Echo users can already manage many household appliances with the device, and as more appliances are built with Internet connectivity, this feature will only become more useful. Amazon freely released its software to third-party developers, allowing them to more easily embed the Alexa artificial intelligence technology that powers the Echo into smartphones and other products. Amazon has continued to create new iterations of the Echo, including the second generation baseline Echo device, the Echo Plus, which has a built-in hub for controlling smart home devices that the default Echo currently lacks, the Echo Show, which features a small touchscreen and camera for video chatting and web browsing, the Echo Dot, a cheaper, puck-sized device with basic Echo functionality, and the Echo Spot, a small sphere with a miniature video screen that bridges the gap between the Dot and the Show.

Strategic Analysis—Social and Legal Challenges

Amazon continually faces lawsuits concerning various aspects of its business. Most common are patent infringement suits, largely settled out of court. Currently, there are several pending patent suits, including some involving the Kindle.

In recent years, Amazon has faced increased challenges from states eager to begin collecting sales taxes from online purchases. Until 2011, only customers in five states were required to pay sales taxes. Between distribution center expansion and state legislation requiring large online sellers to collect sales tax even in the absence of a physical presence, that number has ballooned to all 45 states with sales tax. Early on, many states had offered Amazon tax break deals to lure its business, perhaps not expecting that untaxed sales would become billions of dollars in lost tax revenue. As many of those deals expire, Amazon has already begun an aggressive (and costly) expansion of its warehousing infrastructure across the United States to support same-day delivery. The rising cost of shipping represents one of the biggest threats to Amazon's long-term profitability, which explains the company's renewed efforts to explore shipping alternatives.

Future Prospects

In 2016, Amazon finally began to show investors and analysts what they had been waiting years to see—sustainable profitability. The profitability of its AWS unit is a major positive for Amazon, with revenues from AWS continuing to rapidly grow in 2019. Subscription revenue from Amazon Prime memberships is also a key component of the company's strong performance. However, Amazon has reached its current position of dominance in e-commerce by defying analysts' expectations, and the company continues to spend prodigiously to grow even larger in 2020 and beyond, potentially compromising profitability in the process. It's anyone's guess what Amazon may look like in a few years' time (Amazon.com, Inc., 2020; Levy, 2020; Bishop, 2020; Cohen and Woodard, 2020; Anderson, 2020; Ali, 2019; Marvin 2019; Kramer, 2018; Thomas, 2018; Kinsella, 2018; Cheng, 2018; Kim, 2018; McKay, 2017; Thomas, 2017; Russell and Seshagiri, 2017; Wharton, 2017).

OMNI-CHANNEL MERCHANTS: BRICKS-AND-CLICKS

Also called omni-channel merchants, **bricks-and-clicks** companies have a network of physical stores as their primary retail channel, but also have online offerings. U.S.-based omni-channel firms include Walmart, Macy's, Sears, JCPenney, Staples, OfficeMax, Costco, Target, and other brand-name merchants. While bricks-and-clicks merchants face high costs of physical buildings and large sales staffs, they also have many advantages such as a brand name, a national customer base, warehouses, large scale (giving them leverage with suppliers), and a trained staff. Acquiring customers is less expensive because of their brand names, but these firms face challenges in coordinating prices across channels and handling returns of online purchases at their retail outlets. However, these retail players are used to operating on very thin margins and have invested heavily in purchasing and inventory control systems to control costs, and in coordinating returns from multiple locations. Bricks-and-clicks companies face the challenge of leveraging their strengths and assets to the Web, building a credible website, hiring new skilled staff, and building rapid-response order entry and fulfillment systems. In 2018, omni-channel bricks-and-clicks retailers accounted for around 31% of all the Internet Retailer Top 1000's online retail sales (Davis, 2019, 2018a, 2018b; eMarketer, Inc., 2016).

bricks-and-clicks
companies that have a network of physical stores as their primary retail channel, but have also introduced online offerings

Macy's is a prime example of a traditional merchant based on physical stores moving successfully to become an omni-channel retailer. Rowland H. Macy opened the first R.H. Macy & Co. store in New York City in 1858, and moved the flagship store (now the site of the famous Macy's Thanksgiving parade) to Herald Square at 34th Street and Broadway in 1902. Today, Macy's is one of the largest national department store chains, with around 525 Macy's department stores throughout the United States.

Like many traditional retailers, Macy's has had to change its business model to accommodate the Internet. Macy's (then called Federated Department Stores Inc.) jumped into e-commerce in 1995 with the creation of the Macys.com website. In 1999, Federated bought Fingerhut, at that time a leading catalog and direct marketer, in part for its expertise in e-commerce fulfillment and database management. Although the Fingerhut acquisition did not prove to be a financial success, Macy's e-commerce efforts benefitted from the acquisition.

Macy's ranked 5th on Internet Retailer's 2019 list of the top 1000 online retailers, with an estimated $7.2 billion in online sales in 2019, representing around 30% of total sales. Macy's online sales have grown by double digits for 40 straight quarters through June 2019. Growth of its physical store sales has paled by comparison, and Macy's has closed a number of stores as it focuses more and more on its e-commerce operations. It is also expanding its e-commerce efforts in China, where it is already one of the most popular sellers on Alibaba's Tmall Global website.

The Macy's website includes an interactive catalog, enlarged product views, and ability to see products in different colors and from alternate views, including via zoom and videos. It also offers product comparisons, product ratings, and product recommendations, as well as a real-time inventory check system. Macy's website attracts around 50 million unique visitors a month.

Macy's has jumped into social media as well, with a Facebook page that has over 14 million Likes and followers, a Twitter feed with almost 950,000 followers, an Instagram with about 1.9 million followers, a Pinterest page with 20 different boards and almost 800,000 followers, and a YouTube channel with over 90,000 subscribers and about 8 million views. Macy's was also an early adopter of Buyable Pins introduced by Pinterest.

M-commerce is an important part of Macy's online success. It has iPhone and Android apps and an HMTL5 mobile website powered by Usablenet. It has redesigned both its mobile app and website in order to more closely integrate them with their physical stores. In 2019, Macy's continued to focus on refining its omni-channel approach, encompassing its physical stores, its website, and the mobile platform. Macy's offers 8 of the 9 key omnichannel features identified by Internet Retailer: buy online, pickup in store (BOPIS); curbside pickup; customer assistance services; making an in-store appointment online; shipping from store, a store locator on its website and store returns of items purchased online. Macy's is also continuing to focus on integrating its in-store and mobile experience. Shoppers in a store can scan a product with Macy's mobile app to find out the price, make the purchase through the app, and then have the item delivered to their homes. Macy rolled out enhanced mobile checkout through all of its stores in 2018. It was among the first retailers to support Apple Pay, Apple's mobile payment system, offering it in addition to Macy's own mobile wallet that allows shoppers to virtually store and access offers and coupons. In 2018, Macy's also tested virtual reality for in-store furniture departments at 69 stores and launched an augmented reality experience in furniture shopping for its iOS app (Risley, 2019; Cassidy, 2019b; Evans, 2018; Bloomberg News, 2018; Berthene, 2018; Lindner, 2017; Tong, 2016).

CATALOG MERCHANTS

U.S.-based **catalog merchants** such as Lands' End, L.L.Bean, CDW Corp., PC Connection, and Cabela's are established companies that have a national offline catalog operation, but who have also developed online capabilities. Catalog merchants face very high costs for printing and mailing millions of catalogs each year—many of which have a half-life of 30 seconds after the customer receives them. Catalog merchants typically have developed centralized fulfillment and call centers, extraordinary service, and excellent fulfillment in partnership with package delivery firms such as FedEx and UPS. Catalog firms have suffered in recent years as catalog sales growth rates have fallen. As a result, catalog merchants have had to diversify their channels either by building stores (L.L.Bean), being bought by store-based firms (Sears purchased Lands' End in 2003 before spinning it off again as an independent company in 2014), or by building a strong online presence.

catalog merchants
established companies that have a national offline catalog operation that is their largest retail channel, but who have recently developed online capabilities

Catalog firms are uniquely advantaged because they already possess very efficient order entry and fulfillment systems. However, they face many of the same challenges as bricks-and-mortar stores—they must leverage their existing assets and competencies to a new technology environment, build a credible online presence, and hire new staff. Nevertheless, in 2018, catalog merchants generated about 8% of the Internet Retailer Top 1000's online revenues (Davis, 2019, 2018a, 2018b, eMarketer, Inc., 2016).

Arguably one of the most well-known online catalog merchants is LandsEnd.com. Lands' End started out in 1963 in a basement of Chicago's tannery district selling sailboat equipment and clothing, handling 15 orders on a good day. Since then it expanded into a direct catalog merchant, distributing over 200 million catalogs annually and selling a much expanded line of "traditionally" styled sport clothing, soft luggage, and products for the home. Lands' End was one of the first apparel retailers to have an e-commerce-enabled website, launching in 1995 with 100 products and travelogue essays. In 2015, it launched a significantly redesigned website featuring a new online catalog with more brands, improved search and navigation, streamlined checkout, and new payment types such as Visa Pay. In 2016, it launched a new mobile app and made further improvements to its website (Lands' End, Inc., 2020; Maple, 2016). In 2017, it announced that it would invest even more in the e-commerce sales channel in an effort to make online shopping even more convenient for its customers, and to make it easy for customers to easily share social feedback on its products.

Lands' End has always been on the leading edge of online retailing technologies, most of which emphasize personal marketing and customized products. Lands' End was the first e-commerce website to allow customers to create a 3-D model of themselves to "try on" clothing. Lands' End "Get Live Help" enables customers to chat online with customer service representatives; Lands' End Custom allows customers to create custom-crafted clothing built for their personal measurements. While customized clothing built online was thought to be a gimmick in the early years of online retailing, today, 40% of Lands'

End clothing sold online is customized. Lands' End was 60th on Internet Retailer's list of the 2019 Top 1000 online retailers. Features that garner praise include live video chat, product recommendations that reflect a shopper's preferences, content display based on the shopper's location and referral source, and iPhone and iPad apps that deliver Lands' End catalogs to mobile users. The digital catalogs contain exclusive content, including stories written by Lands' End employees. Shoppers can also visit Lands' End on Facebook, where it has over 1.3 million Likes. Lands' End also has a Twitter presence, where it has about 220,000 followers, an Instagram account with over 80,000 followers, and 20 different Pinterest boards with almost 25,000 followers.

MANUFACTURER-DIRECT

manufacturer-direct
single- or multi-channel manufacturers who sell directly online to consumers without the intervention of retailers

Manufacturer-direct (also sometimes referred to as DTC (direct-to-consumer)) firms are either single- or multi-channel manufacturers that sell directly online to consumers without the intervention of retailers. Manufacturer-direct firms were predicted to play a very large role in e-commerce, but this has generally not happened. The primary exceptions are computer hardware, such as Apple, Dell, and Hewlett-Packard, and apparel manufacturers, such as Ralph Lauren, Nike, Under Armour, Carter's, Tory Burch, Deckers, Kate Spade, Jones Retail, and Vera Bradley. Most consumer products manufacturers do not sell directly online, although this has started to change. For instance, Procter & Gamble offers Pgshop, which carries over 50 different Procter & Gamble brands. Overall, manufacturer-direct firms accounted for about 16% of the Internet Retailer's Top 1000's online retail sales (Davis, 2019, 2018a, 2018b, eMarketer, Inc., 2016). A new breed of manufacturer-direct firms are sometimes referred to as digital native verticals. These are online companies focused on direct sourcing of materials, control of their distribution channel, and direct connection to the consumer. Examples include eyeglasses (Warby Parker), apparel (Everlane, MM. LaFleur, and Draper James), mattresses (Caspar, Endy, Saatva, and Leesa Sleep), bedding products (Parachute and Brooklinen), beauty products (Glossier and Morphe Comestics), and luggage (Away Travel), among many others.

channel conflict
occurs when retailers of products must compete on price and currency of inventory directly against the manufacturers

supply-push model
products are made prior to orders received based on estimated demand

demand-pull model
products are not built until an order is received

Manufacturer-direct firms sometimes face channel conflict challenges. **Channel conflict** occurs when retailers of products must compete on price and currency of inventory directly against the manufacturer, who does not face the cost of maintaining inventory, physical stores, or sales staffs. Firms with no prior direct marketing experience face the additional challenges of developing a fast-response online order and fulfillment system, acquiring customers, and coordinating their supply chains with market demand. Switching from a **supply-push model** (where products are made prior to orders received based on estimated demand and then stored in warehouses awaiting sale) to a **demand-pull model** (where products are not built until an order is received) has proved extremely difficult for traditional manufacturers. Yet for many products, manufacturer-direct firms have the advantage of an established national brand name, an existing large customer base, and a lower cost structure than even catalog merchants because they are the manufacturer of the goods and thus do not pay profits to anyone else. Therefore, manufacturer-direct firms should have higher margins.

Dell Technologies is one of the most frequently cited manufacturer-direct retailers. Dell operates in both the B2C and B2B arenas and is the world's largest direct computer systems supplier, providing corporations, government agencies, small-to-medium businesses, and individuals with computer products and services ordered straight from the manufacturer's headquarters in Austin, Texas. Although sales representatives support corporate customers, individuals and smaller businesses buy direct from Dell by phone, fax, and via the Internet.

When Michael Dell started the company in 1984 in his college dorm room, his idea was to custom-build computers for customers, to eliminate the middleman, and more effectively meet the technology needs of his customers. Today, the company sells much more than individual computer systems; it also offers enterprise systems, desktop, and laptop computers, as well as installation, financing, repair, and management services. By relying on a build-to-order manufacturing process, the company achieves faster inventory turnover (five days), and reduced component and finished goods inventory levels; this strategy virtually eliminates the chance of product obsolescence.

The direct model simplifies the company's operations, eliminating the need to support a wholesale and retail sales network, as well as cutting out the costly associated markup, and gives Dell complete control over its customer database. In addition, Dell can build and ship custom computers nearly as fast as a mail-order supplier can pull a computer out of inventory and ship it to the customer.

To extend the benefits of its direct sales model, Dell has aggressively moved sales, service, and support online. Dell's e-commerce website serves customers in 190 countries around the world and typically has about 16 million unique visitors per month. Dell's Premier service enables companies to investigate product offerings, complete order forms and purchase orders, track orders in real time, and review order histories all online. For its small business customers, it has created an online virtual account executive, as well as a spare-parts ordering system and virtual help desk with direct access to technical support data. Dell has also continued to broaden its offerings beyond pure hardware product sales, adding warranty services, product integration and installation services, Internet access, software, and technology consulting, referring to them as "beyond the box" offerings. These include nearly 30,000 software and peripheral products from leading manufacturers that can be bundled with Dell products. Dell has also embraced social media. It has a corporate blog, called Direct2Dell, and a presence on Facebook (with over 12 million followers), Pinterest (with 6 boards), and Twitter (with over 725,000 followers). It posts Twitter-exclusive sales for those who follow Dell Outlet. It also has a channel on YouTube with over 160,000 subscribers and 38 million views. It has mobile apps for the iPhone and Android that feature in-app purchasing, customer ratings and reviews, product comparison, order tracking, a Shopping Advisor, and easy access to various customer support options. Its mobile website uses responsive design, allowing the site to automatically adapt to consumers' devices, driving a 50% increase in conversion rate and a 70% increase in consumer satisfaction (Elastic.co, 2017).

COMMON THEMES IN ONLINE RETAILING

We have looked at some very different companies in the preceding section, from entrepreneurial virtual merchants to established offline giants. Online retail is the fastest growing channel in retail commerce, has the fastest growing consumer base, and has growing penetration across many categories of goods. On the other hand, profits for many startup ventures have been difficult to achieve, and it took even Amazon eight years to show its first profit.

The reasons for the difficulties experienced by many online retailers in achieving profits are also now clear. The path to success in any form of retail involves having a central location in order to attract a larger number of shoppers, charging high enough prices to cover the costs of goods as well as marketing, and developing highly efficient inventory and fulfillment systems so that the company can offer goods at lower costs than competitors and still make a profit. Many online merchants failed to follow these fundamental ideas, lowering prices below the total costs of goods and operations, failing to develop efficient business processes, failing to attract a large enough audience to their websites, and spending far too much on customer acquisition and marketing. Today, the lessons of the past have been learned, and far fewer online merchants are selling below cost, especially if they are startup companies. There's also been a change in consumer culture and attitudes. Whereas in the past consumers looked online for really cheap prices, they now look to online purchasing for convenience, time savings, and time shifting (buying retail goods at night from the sofa). Consumers have been willing to accept higher prices in return for the convenience of shopping online and avoiding the inconvenience of shopping at stores and malls. This allows online merchants more pricing freedom.

A second common theme in retail e-commerce is that, for the most part, disintermediation has not occurred and the retail middleman has not disappeared. Indeed, virtual merchants, along with powerful offline merchants who moved online, have maintained their powerful grip on the retail customer, with some notable exceptions in electronics and software. Manufacturers—with the exception of electronic goods—have used the Web primarily as an informational resource, driving consumers to the traditional retail channels for transactions. Leaving Amazon aside, the most significant online growth has been that of offline general merchandiser giant intermediaries such as Walmart, Costco, JCPenney, Macy's, Target, and Nordstrom. Many of the first-mover, online pure-play merchants (online intermediaries) failed to achieve profitability and closed their doors en masse as their venture capital funds were depleted. Traditional retailers have been the fast followers (although many of them cannot be characterized as particularly "fast") and are most likely to succeed online by extending their traditional brands, competencies, and assets. In this sense, e-commerce technological innovation is following the historical pattern of other technology-driven commercial changes, from automobiles to radio and television, where an explosion of startup firms attracts significant investment, but the firms quickly fail and are consolidated into larger existing firms.

A third theme is that in order to succeed online, established merchants need to create an integrated shopping environment that combines their catalog, store, and online experiences into one. Customers want to shop wherever they want, using any device, and at any time. Established retailers have significant fulfillment, inventory management, supply chain management, and other competencies that apply directly to the online channel. To succeed online, established retailers need to extend their brands, provide incentives to consumers to use the online channel (which given the same prices for goods is more efficient to operate than a physical store), avoid channel conflict, and build advertising campaigns using online search engines such as Google, Yahoo, and Bing, and shopping comparison sites.

A fourth theme is the growth of online specialty merchants selling high-end, fashionable, and luxury goods such as diamonds (Blue Nile), jewelry (Tiffany), and high fashion (Emporio Armani and Gilt Groupe) or selling discounted electronics (Best Buy), apparel (Gap), or office products (Office Depot). These firms are demonstrating the vitality and openness of the Internet for innovation and extending the range of products available online. Many virtual merchants have developed large, online customer bases, as well as the online tools required to market to their customer base. These online brands can be strengthened further through alliances and partnerships that add the required competencies in inventory management and fulfillment services. Virtual merchants need to build operational strength and efficiency before they can become profitable.

Another theme is the continuing extraordinary growth in social e-commerce, local e-commerce, and m-commerce. In the space of ten years since the first iPhone appeared, the mobile platform has emerged as a retail marketing and shopping tool, which will greatly expand e-commerce, potentially driving e-commerce to 20% of all commerce in the next five years. Local merchants will be a major benefactor of the growing m-commerce platform. In an equally short time, people have begun to spend an increasing amount of their Internet time on social networks where they share attitudes and experiences about business firms, products, and services. In a few years, social networks may turn into large purchasing platforms. For instance, in 2016, building on the increasing popularity of Facebook groups created to buy and sell merchandise, Facebook introduced Facebook Marketplace, accessed from a Shop icon at the bottom of the Facebook app. Facebook Marketplace is a blend of social, mobile, and local C2C e-commerce intended to make it easy to find, buy, and sell items offered by people in your local community (Facebook, 2016).

A final theme is the increasing use by retailers, large and small, of big data in their marketing efforts. The *Insight on Technology* case, *ASOS Uses Big Data to Find Its Most Valuable Customers*, examines this development.

11.4 THE SERVICE SECTOR: OFFLINE AND ONLINE

The service sector is typically the largest and most rapidly expanding part of the economies in advanced industrial nations such as the United States, and many European and some Asian countries. In the United States, for instance, the service sector (broadly defined) employs about four out of every five workers and accounts for about 80% of the United States' gross domestic product (GDP) (Buckley and Majumdar, 2018). E-commerce in the service sector offers extraordinary opportunities to deliver information, knowledge, and transaction efficiencies.

The major service industry groups are finance, insurance, real estate, travel, professional services such as legal and accounting, business services, health services, and educational services. Business services include activities such as consulting, advertising and marketing, and information processing. Within these service industry groups, companies can be further categorized into those that involve **transaction brokering** (acting as an intermediary to facilitate a transaction) and those that involve providing a "hands-on"

transaction brokering
acting as an intermediary to facilitate a transaction

INSIGHT ON TECHNOLOGY

ASOS USES BIG DATA TO FIND ITS MOST VALUABLE CUSTOMERS

Retailers need data. It is essential for understanding customers' needs and wants, for decision-making, and for accurately supplying the right goods to the right place and at the right time. Point-of-sale (POS) systems have come a long way since 1973, when they were first launched to help retailers and their suppliers gather accurate data on product sales and to keep track of stock, prices, etc. Access to detailed and accurate customer and product data ballooned with the introduction of technology such as bar-code scanners and payment and loyalty cards, but it was the Internet in the early 1990s that gave rise to the explosion of accessible data sources that collectively became big data.

The use of big data in retailing and other consumer-facing industries has become synonymous with predictive analytics and predictive marketing, which involves the application of statistical techniques, data mining, and machine learning to make predictions about future customer behavior. By analyzing customers' purchasing habits in relation to the touchpoints across a single customer journey as well as throughout the customer lifecycle, the behavior of millions of shoppers can be predicted, simultaneously and in real-time. Additionally, such data can be used by marketers to send very precise and personalized messages and offers to individual customers.

ASOS, which originally stood for AsSeenOnScreen, is a successful online British retailer that has used predictive marketing techniques extensively to build and grow. It was founded in 2000 by Nick Robertson and Quentin Griffiths, both of whom had retailing experience, but in physical stores. In 2004, they launched the own-label ASOS fashion to target customers in their twenties, and their online sales operation began to grow quickly. In the early days, sales were boosted by high-profile customers like Michelle Obama and Rihanna, but the brand began to analyze the likes and preferences of their customers, which soon figured strongly in shaping the direction of the corporate business model.

Over the last 20 years, ASOS has refined that model to keep pace with changing demands of twenty-something shoppers. The company realized that continued success in this market meant that it had to really focus its product ranges on the emerging search-savvy web generation, who had grown up using the Internet to find the things they were interested in and wanted to purchase. The ASOS analytics team looked at their vast data stores with a focus on product-purchasing behavior and soon identified many pages on the ASOS website that were rarely visited. The problem was often a fundamental mismatch between product and target customers; for example, less than 1% of the 21-year-old visitors to the site could afford £400 handbags. Items like these were removed and replaced with other products that were better aligned with the customers' preferences.

This product consolidation proved to be highly successful, and the brand has continued to grow since then—it is now valued at over £2.3 billion. The company has a product inventory of over 87,000 items and manages the online publication of 80,000 pieces of fashion and lifestyle content every year. Their very considered aim is to continuously meet customer expectations as well as anticipate what they will be looking for next while generating 20%–25% annual sales growth and maintaining profitability at 4%.

Like other successful online retailers, the customer is all-important, but delivering its strong commercial priorities means ASOS must recognize that not all customers are equal. ASOS uses machine learning to understand the lifetime value of a customer and predictive marketing techniques to recommend the right product to the right customer. This is a complex process that involves classifying customers by how valuable they are; understanding their likes and dislikes; analyzing their purchasing history; tracking their product returns; and engaging through social media, the Web, and apps. The customer data analysis teams at ASOS can then assign a value to each customer: high-value customers are those who regularly spend on full-price items, while low-value customers are those who spend on discounted items and frequently return products without making a purchase that sticks.

This type of classification makes it possible to plan marketing interventions aimed at driving customer retention and extending the lifetime value of high-value customers. For example, with free delivery and returns becoming standard practice across the retail industry, ASOS decided to limit the number of customers who regularly return rather than buy items, as these customers could actually cost the company more in postage costs than the customer actually spends. ASOS analysts can segment customers using machine learning, after which the company's proprietary software can produce models that show rich patterns of customer behavior. Customers can then be ranked according to how valuable they are using customer demographics, purchase and returns history, engagement with web and social media, etc.

ASOS's data scientists must be able to interpret signals from the data patterns to inform its marketing strategy and to give insights into how to extend the customer lifetime value (CLTV). The signals considered important for categorizing customers are based on their behavior when visiting the ASOS websites and social media platforms. Analyzing the time spent by a shopper and the sequence of pages they view can reveal whether they are likely to be a high- or low-value shopper; for example, high-value customers look at higher-cost, full-price new items, which are often products that also tend to be less popular, whereas lower-value customers browse during sales and when certain product ranges are offered at lower prices than competing retailers. Using ASOS's proprietary software and machine learning framework, the company's data scientists then assign customers into CLTV categories.

ASOS aims to become the world's number one destination for twenty-somethings. To the retailer, this means pushing the boundaries in the fashion retailing industry through greater investment in the use of big data, analytics, and predictive marketing techniques. ASOS has invested £600 million in developing a platform that can strengthen organizational capabilities, reduce operational costs, ensure product choice, and optimize customer engagement and retention. So far, the company has been reaping the rewards of their investments; in 2018–2019, the number of active customers grew by 10% to 20.3 million and sales grew by 13% to £2.65 billion.

Having fallen behind in the race to develop and use new predictive marketing techniques to analyze demand, the more traditional high-street retailers have found themselves being squeezed by online retailers like ASOS and Amazon. They are, however, beginning to realize the importance of these powerful digital tools. As the rest of the retail sector catches on to the value of machine learning and predictive marketing, the number one destination for twenty-somethings is likely to soon have more challengers to contend with.

SOURCES: "ASOS: The Seesaw History of a Global Online Fashion Giant," by Sarah Butler, Theguardian.com, December 17, 2018; "Annual Report and Accounts 2018," ASOSplc.com; "ASOS Uses Machine Learning To Understand Customer Value," by Ryan Skinner, Go.forrester.com, February 8, 2018; "How ASOS Founder Nick Robertson Built a £1.4 Bn Business," by Kirsty McGregor, drapersonline.com, December 20, 2017; "Predictive Analytics: Extending the Value of Your Data Warehousing Investment," by Wayne Eckerson, The Data Warehouse Institute, TDWI.org, May 10, 2007.

Case contributed by Fiona Ellis-Chadwick, Loughborough University

service. For instance, one type of financial service involves stockbrokers who act as the middle person in a transaction between buyers and sellers. Online mortgage companies such as LendingTree refer customers to mortgage companies that actually issue the mortgage. Employment agencies put a seller of labor in contact with a buyer of labor. The service involved in all these examples is brokering a transaction.

In contrast, some industries perform specific hands-on activities for consumers. In order to provide their service, these professionals need to interact directly and personally with the "client." For these service industries, the opportunities for e-commerce are somewhat different. Currently, doctors and dentists cannot treat patients over the Internet. However, the Internet can assist their services by providing consumers with information, knowledge, and communication.

With some exceptions (for example, providers of physical services, such as cleaning, gardening, and so on), perhaps the most important feature of service industries (and occupations) is that they are knowledge- and information-intense. In order to provide value, service industries process a great deal of information and employ a highly skilled, educated workforce. For instance, to provide legal services, you need lawyers with law degrees. Law firms are required to process enormous amounts of textual information. Likewise with medical services. Financial services are not so knowledge-intensive, but require much larger investments in information processing just to keep track of transactions and investments. In fact, the financial services sector is the largest investor in information technology, with over 80% of invested capital going to information technology equipment and services.

Services differ in the amount of personalization and customization required, although just about all services entail some personalization or customization. Some services, such as legal, medical, and accounting services, require extensive personalization—the adjustment of a service to the precise needs of a single individual or object. Others, such as financial services, benefit from customization by allowing individuals to choose from a restricted menu. The ability of Internet and e-commerce technology to personalize and customize service, or components of service, is a major factor undergirding the extremely rapid growth of e-commerce services. Future expansion of e-services will depend in part on the ability of e-commerce firms to transform their customized services—choosing from a list—into truly personalized services, such as providing unique advice and consultation based on a digital yet intimate understanding of the client (at least as intimate as professional service providers).

11.5 ONLINE FINANCIAL SERVICES

The online financial services sector is a shining example of an e-commerce success story, but one with many twists and turns. While the innovative online firms such as E*Trade have been instrumental in transforming the brokerage industry, the impacts of e-commerce on the large, powerful banking, insurance, and real estate firms were delayed somewhat by initial consumer resistance and the lack of industry innovation. Even today, online-only banks have not displaced traditional banks. But e-commerce has nevertheless transformed the banking and financial industries, as the major institutions have deployed their own online applications to service an increasingly connected online customer base. Insurance has become more standardized and easier to purchase online. Although security is still a concern, consumers are much more willing to trust online sites with their financial information than in the past. Firms such as Mint (now owned by Intuit), SmartyPig, Credit Karma, Moven, and Simple (now owned by Spanish banking giant BBVA) continue to show growth. Multi-channel, established financial services firms—the slow followers—also continue to show gains in online transactions.

FINTECH

In the last few years, increasing investments have been made in startup companies in the financial services industries. These companies are often referred to as fintech (short for financial technology) companies and have attracted a lot of attention in the popular press. The term fintech is poorly defined and has been applied to a wide variety of companies. The use of information technology is the financial services arena is not new: financial services companies have long made very large investments in information technology. What distinguishes many fintech companies from these earlier iterations is that they are tech companies outside the traditional financial services industries that are seeking to use technology to unbundle traditional institutional financial services and instead deliver targeted solutions, often via mobile devices and app. That said, the term fintech is also being applied to traditional financial services firm who are developing and implementing innovative technologies.

ONLINE BANKING AND BROKERAGE

NetBank and Wingspan Bank pioneered online banking in the United States in 1996 and 1997, respectively. Although late by a year or two, the established brand-name national banks have taken a substantial lead in market share as the percentage of their customers who bank online has grown rapidly. The U.S. top banks are all large, national banks that also offer online banking: Bank of America, JPMorgan Chase, Citigroup, and Wells Fargo. Major direct banks (those that operate without a network of branches or branded ATMs) in the United States include Ally Bank, TIAA Bank, Discover Bank, Capital One 360, Axos Bank, State Farm Bank, and USAA. These direct banks have seen customer deposits grow faster than regular banks, indicating their growing popularity, particularly with younger customers. Several startups have also moved into the online banking and financial services spaces. For instance, Moven offers debit account services linked with online and mobile financial management tools, along with a network of over 40,000 ATMs where users can withdraw cash. Simple, owned by Spanish bank BBVA, provides checking accounts linked to debit cards in addition to financial management tools.

In 2019, in France, for instance, over two-thirds of the adult population used online banking, and this percentage is expected to rise to over 70% by 2023. Over a third of the population used a mobile device for online banking (eMarketer, Inc, 2018a, 2018b). While online banking has become a primary banking channel for all age groups, Millennials (those in the 18- to 34-year-old group) are adopting mobile banking at a much higher rate than those who are older. Top mobile banking activities include checking balances and bank statements, transferring money from one account to another, paying bills, making bill payments, and depositing checks using smartphone apps that snap a photo of the check. Security issues still deter some. A survey by Javelin Strategy &

Research found that about 45% of those surveyed cited security concerns as the reason why they did not use mobile banking services.

From the bank's perspective, online and mobile banking can provide significant cost savings. According to PriceWaterhouseCoopers, the average in-person transaction at a bank branch costs $4.00, while an online or mobile transaction just 19 cents (Marous, 2017).

The history of online brokerage has been similar to that of online banking. Early U.S. innovators such as E*Trade have been displaced from their leadership positions in terms of numbers of online accounts by discount broker pioneer Charles Schwab and financial industry giant Fidelity (which has more mutual fund customers and more funds under management than any other U.S. firm).

According to one survey, about 25% of U.S. Internet users interact digitally with online brokerage firms. The use of mobile devices and apps for this purpose is increasing, particularly among Millennials. According to a recent E*Trade survey, almost two-thirds of Millennials use investing and trading apps on their smartphones more than once a week. The most frequent activities conducted on mobile devices include monitoring one's portfolio and the market, getting stock quotes, placing and checking on orders, and doing general financial research (E*Trade Financial Corporation, 2019). Top U.S. online brokerage firms include Fidelity, E*Trade, Charles Schwab, TD Ameritrade, and Merrill Edge (Reinkensmeyer, 2020). The major online brokerage firms are investing significantly in search engine marketing, and are among the biggest spenders in the paid search market. They are also increasingly using social media to engage with customers, although they must be careful to comply with all regulations and rules as they do so. For instance, some brokerage firms use Twitter to deliver commentary, company information, marketing, and customer service. A new wave of online financial advisors, sometimes referred to as robo-advisors, offer inexpensive automated investment management tools and advice. Examples of fintech companies that have attracted venture capital interest include Betterment (valued at over $800 million, and managing over $16 billion assets for over 300,000 customers as of 2019), Wealthfront, and Personal Capital Corp. Similar services are also offered by major U.S. online brokerage firms such as Vanguard and Schwab.

Multi-Channel vs. Pure Online Financial Services Firms

Online consumers prefer to visit financial services sites that have physical outlets or branches. In general, multi-channel financial services firms that have both physical branches or offices and solid online offerings are growing faster than pure-online firms that have no physical presence, and they are assuming market leadership as well. Traditional banking firms have literally thousands of branches where customers can open accounts, deposit money, take out loans, find home mortgages, and rent a safety deposit box. Top online brokerage firms do not have the same physical footprint as the banks do, but each has a strong physical presence or telephone presence to strengthen its online presence. Fidelity has walk-in service center branches, but it relies primarily on the telephone for interacting with investors. Charles Schwab has investment centers around the United States as an integral part of its online strategy. Pure-online banks and brokerages cannot provide customers with some services that still require a face-to-face interaction.

Financial Portals and Account Aggregators

Financial portals are sites that provide consumers with comparison shopping services, independent financial advice, and financial planning. Independent portals do not themselves offer financial services, but act as steering mechanisms to online providers. They generate revenue from advertising, referral fees, and subscription fees. For example, Yahoo's financial portal, Yahoo Finance, offers consumers the ability to track their stock portfolio, market overviews, real-time stock quotes, news, financial advice, and streaming video interviews with financial leaders. Other independent financial portals include Intuit's Quicken, MSN's MSN Money, and CNNMoney. A host of financial portal sites have sprung up to help consumers with financial management and planning such as Mint (owned by Intuit), SmartyPig, and Credit Karma.

Account aggregation is the process of pulling together all of a customer's financial (and even nonfinancial) data at a single personalized website, including brokerage, banking, insurance, loans, frequent flyer miles, personalized news, and much more. For example, a consumer can see his or her TD Ameritrade brokerage account, Fidelity 401(k) account, Travelers Insurance annuity account, and American Airlines frequent flyer miles all displayed on a single site. The idea is to provide consumers with a holistic view of their entire portfolio of assets, no matter what financial institution actually holds those assets.

The leading provider of account aggregation technology is Envestnet Yodlee. It uses screen-scraping and other techniques to pull information from 15,000 different global data sources. A smart-mapping technology is also used so that if the underlying websites change, the scraping software can adapt and still find the relevant information. Today, Envestnet Yodlee is used by over 1,200 leading financial institutions and companies, including 15 of the 20 largest U.S. banks, and this network reaches more than 100 million end users (Envestnet Yodlee, 2020).

ONLINE MORTGAGE AND LENDING SERVICES

During the early days of e-commerce, hundreds of firms launched pure-play online mortgage sites to capture the U.S. home mortgage market. Early entrants hoped to radically simplify and transform the traditional mortgage value chain process, dramatically speed up the loan closing process, and share the economies with consumers by offering lower rates.

By 2003, over half of these early-entry, pure-online firms had failed. Early pure-play online mortgage institutions had difficulties developing a brand name at an affordable price and failed to simplify the mortgage generation process. They ended up suffering from high start-up and administrative costs, high customer acquisition costs, rising interest rates, and poor execution of their strategies.

Despite this rocky start, the online mortgage market is slowly growing; it is dominated by established online banks and other online financial services firms, traditional mortgage vendors, and a few successful online mortgage firms.

Many mortgage shoppers research mortgages online, but few actually apply online because of the complexity of mortgages. Most mortgages today are written by intermediary mortgage brokers, with banks still playing an important origination role but generally not servicing mortgages they originate.

financial portals
sites that provide consumers with comparison shopping services, independent financial advice, and financial planning

account aggregation
the process of pulling together all of a customer's financial (and even nonfinancial) data at a single personalized website

Although online mortgage originations currently represent a small percentage of all mortgages, their number is expected to continue to grow slowly but surely over the next several years. In 2015, Intuit's Quicken Loans introduced Rocket Mortgage, which allows borrowers to be fully approved for a mortgage in under ten minutes. The applicant only needs to provide a few details, such as birth date, social security number, and home address, and then Rocket Mortgage uses that data to automatically obtain various types of information without the need for the borrower to manually provide any further documentation. The system then displays various loan options, and once the borrower selects one, all necessary documents (except for final closing documents) can be signed online using a secure portal. In 2019, Quicken Loans was America's largest mortgage lender by volume, and in the third quarter of 2019, closed $40 billion in home loans, the highest quarterly volume in the company's history (Quickenloans.com, 2019).

Consumer benefits from online mortgages include reduced application times, market interest rate intelligence, and process simplification that occurs when participants in the mortgage process (title, insurance, and lending companies) share a common information base. Mortgage lenders benefit from the cost reduction involved in online processing of applications, while charging rates marginally lower than traditional bricks-and-mortar institutions.

Nevertheless, the online mortgage industry has not transformed the process of obtaining a mortgage. A significant brake on market expansion is the complexity of the mortgage process, which requires physical signatures and documents, multiple institutions, and complex financing details—such as closing costs and points—that are difficult for shoppers to compare across vendors. Nevertheless, as in other areas, the ability of shoppers to find low mortgage rates online has helped reduce the fees and interest rates charged by traditional mortgage lenders.

Online lending services have also become popular. Examples of fintech companies in this area include Lending Club, which went public in 2014; Prosper (a peer-to-peer loan marketplace); Social Finance Inc. (SoFi), which focuses primarily on student loans; Avant, which uses machine learning and analytics as well as consumer data to determine how much credit it will offer to potential customers; Kreditech, which provides credit ratings and loans to people without a credit history; and Kabbage, a small business lender that also uses machine learning, public data, and other information to determine the credit of small businesses.

ONLINE INSURANCE SERVICES

Term life insurance stands out as one product group supporting the conventional wisdom that the Internet lowers search costs, increases price comparison, and decreases prices to consumers. Term life insurance is a commodity product, however, and in other insurance product lines, the Web offers insurance companies opportunities for product and service differentiation and price discrimination.

The insurance industry forms a major part of the financial services sector. It has four major segments: automobile, life, health, and property and casualty. Insurance products can be very complex. For example, there are many different types of non-automotive property and casualty insurance: liability, fire, homeowners, commercial, workers' compensation, marine, accident, and other lines such as vacation insurance. Writing an insurance policy in any of these areas is very information-intense, often necessitating personal inspection of the properties, and it requires considerable actuarial experience and data. The life insurance industry has also developed life insurance policies that defy easy comparison and can only be explained and sold by an experienced sales agent. Historically, the insurance industry has relied on thousands of local insurance offices and agents to sell complex products uniquely suited to the circumstances of the insured person and the property. Complicating the insurance marketplace is the fact that the insurance industry is not federally regulated, but rather is regulated by 50 different state insurance commissions that are strongly influenced by local insurance agents. Before a website can offer quotations on insurance, it must obtain a license to enter the insurance business in all the states where it provides quotation services or sells insurance.

Like the online mortgage industry, the online insurance industry has been very successful in attracting visitors who are looking to obtain prices and terms of insurance policies. While many national insurance underwriting companies initially did not offer competitive products directly online because it might injure the business operations of their traditional local agents, the websites of almost all of the major firms now provide the ability to obtain an online quote. There are also numerous online sites that provide comparative insurance quoting services, such as Insure.com, Esurance, Insurance.com, Selectquote, QuickQuote, and NetQuote. Even if consumers do not actually purchase insurance policies online, the Internet has proven to have a powerful influence on consumer insurance decisions by dramatically reducing search costs and changing the price discovery process. According to a recent study, for the life insurance sector, shoppers found the most useful sources of information were the websites of life insurance companies and insurance comparison/quoting sites (LL Global, Inc., 2019). However, consumers also continue to rely on financial advisors as well for advice, with many still seeking information from both sources (Insurance Information Institute, 2018). In the auto insurance arena, a recent study conducted by Facebook and comScore found that, while mobile devices play a major role in how consumers research insurance, they are still more likely to purchase offline rather than online (Sassian, 2018). Insurance companies are also making increased use of social media. For instance, a recent survey found that over a third of consumers surveyed were likely to ask for recommendations of insurance agents or financial advisors on social media and that more than half of Millennials and over 30% of Gen Xers check an agent or advsior's social media presence on LinkedIn, Facebook, and Twitter (LL Global, Inc., 2019). All of the major U.S. insurers, such as GEICO, Allstate, State Farm, Progressive, and Travelers, have a significant online presence, both on the Web and via mobile apps that allow consumers to file claims, make changes to their policy, and make payments.

The wave of interest in fintech companies previously discussed is also starting to filter into the insurance industry, with a subset labeled "insurtech" companies, who are seeking to use technologies such as big data, machine learning, and artificial intelligence to disrupt the traditional insurance industry. For example, a company named Lemonade, founded in 2015, is attempting to reinvent the homeowners and renters insurance market by cutting out agents, offering competitive rates, and using a mobile app featuring a chatbot and powered by artificial intelligence. Lemonade is initially focused on the Millennial market, with 75% of its users under the age of 35. Lemonade has raised over $480 million and is now valued at more than $2 billion (Kauflin and Stoller, 2019; Stoller, 2019).

ONLINE REAL ESTATE SERVICES

During the early days of e-commerce, real estate seemed ripe for an Internet revolution that would rationalize this historically local, complex, and local agent-driven industry that monopolized the flow of consumer information. Potentially, the Internet and e-commerce might have disintermediated this huge marketspace, allowing buyers and sellers, renters and owners, to transact directly, lower search costs to near zero, and dramatically reduce prices. However, this did not happen. What did happen is extremely beneficial to buyers and sellers, as well as to real estate agents. At one point, there were an estimated 100,000 real estate sites on the Internet worldwide. Many of these sites have disappeared and today there are only about 10,000 (Federal Trade Commission, 2018). The remaining online sites have started to make headway toward transforming the industry. In addition, most local real estate brokers in the United States have their own agency websites to deal with clients, in addition to participating with thousands of other agencies in multiple listing services that list homes online. Some of the major online real estate sites are Realtor.com (now owned by global media giant News Corp), Zillow and Trulia (now owned by the same company), Redfin, and Homes.com. In 2019, Zillow and Trulia together attracted almost 60 million unique visitors, while Realtor.com had about 18 million (Rudden, 2019).

Thus far, the major impact of Internet real estate sites has been in influencing offline decisions. The Internet has become a compelling method for real estate professionals, homebuilders, property managers and owners, and ancillary service providers to communicate with and provide information to consumers. According to the National Association of Realtors, the first step in the home buying process for nearly all ages of home buyers was to look online, often on a mobile device. Websites were the most common information source, used by over 95%, while mobile sites and apps and mobile search were each also used by almost 75%. At the same time, almost 90% also used the services of a real estate agent (National Association of Realtors, 2019).

The primary service offered by real estate sites is a listing of houses available. Realtor.com, the official site of the National Association of Realtors, lists over 3 million homes and had around 18 million unique U.S. users across desktop and mobile devices in 2019. Listings typically feature detailed property descriptions, multiple photographs, and virtual 360-degree tours. Consumers can link to mortgage lenders, credit reporting agencies, house inspectors, and surveyors. There are also online loan calculators, appraisal reports, sales price histories by neighborhood, school district data, crime reports, and social and historical information on neighborhoods. Some online real estate brokers now charge substantially less than traditional offline brokers, who typically charge 5%–6% of the sale price. They can do this because the buyers (and in some cases, the sellers) do much of the work of traditional real estate agents, such as prospecting, choosing neighborhoods, and identifying houses of interest prior to contacting an online agent. For instance, Move (the parent company of Realtor.com) also offers a "Find a Neighborhood" feature that allows users to choose the type of neighborhood they want to live in by weighing factors such as the quality (and tax costs) of schools, age of the population, number of families with children nearby, and available social and recreational services. Move also offers mobile apps for the iPad and iPhone, Android, and Windows phones.

Although there has not yet been a revolution in the industry value chain, the fintech movement is beginning to reach into the real estate industry as well. For instance, online real estate firm Opendoor, founded in 2014, purchases homes directly from sellers, enabling them to skip the step of hiring a real estate agent, and then sells them directly to buyers. OpenDoor has raised $1.3 billion in equity and $3 billion in debt and is valued at $3.8 billion. It currently operates in 20 markets, with plans to expand to 50 (Lunden, 2019).

11.6 ONLINE TRAVEL SERVICES

Online travel is one of the most successful B2C e-commerce segments. The Internet has become the most common channel used by consumers to research travel options, seek the best possible prices, and book reservations for airline tickets, hotel rooms, rental cars, cruises, and tours. Today, more travel is booked online than offline. For instance, in the United Kingdom in 2019, over 60% of the adult population used the Internet to research travel and 55% booked travel online. Online travel services revenues reached over $765 billion in 2019, and are expected to continue growing to over $1 trillion by 2023 (see **Figure 11.5**) (eMarketer, Inc., 2019g, 2019h, 2019i).

WHY ARE ONLINE TRAVEL SERVICES SO POPULAR?

Online travel sites offer consumers a one-stop, convenient, leisure and business travel experience where travelers can find content (descriptions of vacations and facilities), community (chat groups and bulletin boards), commerce (purchase of all travel elements), and customer service (usually through call centers). Online sites offer much more information and many more travel options than traditional travel agents. For suppliers—the owners of hotels, rental cars, and airlines—the online sites aggregate millions of consumers into

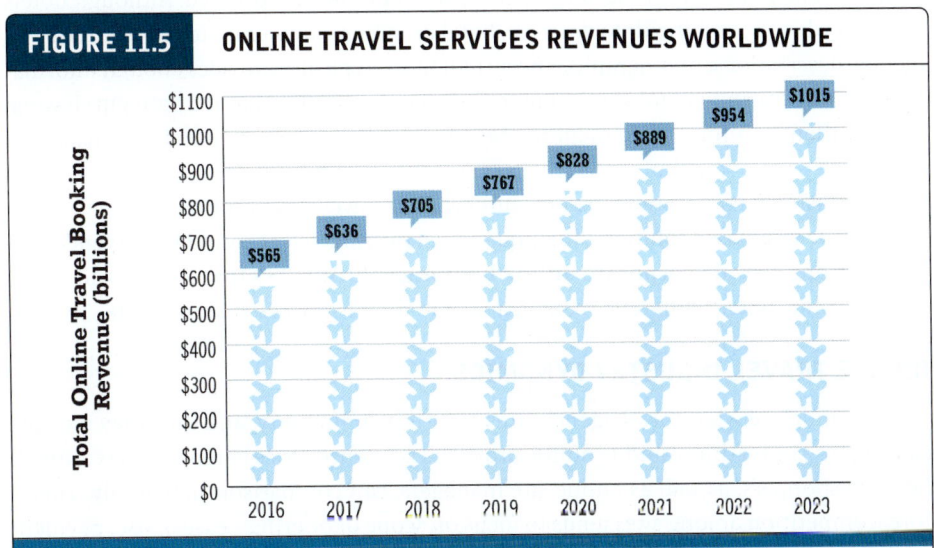

FIGURE 11.5 ONLINE TRAVEL SERVICES REVENUES WORLDWIDE

Online leisure/unmanaged business travel service revenues are expected to reach over $1 trillion worldwide by 2023.
SOURCE: Based on data from eMarketer, Inc., 2019i.

singular, focused customer pools that can be efficiently reached through on-site advertising and promotions. Online sites create a much more efficient marketplace, bringing consumers and suppliers together in a low-transaction cost environment.

Travel services are an ideal service for the Internet, and therefore e-commerce business models work well for this product. Travel is an information-intensive product requiring significant consumer research. It is a digital product in the sense that travel requirements—planning, researching, comparison shopping, reserving, and payment—can be accomplished for the most part online in a digital environment. On the travel reservation side, travel does not require any "inventory": there are no physical assets. And the suppliers of the product—owners of hotels, airlines, rental cars, vacation rooms, and tour guides—are highly fragmented and often have excess capacity. Always looking for customers to fill vacant rooms and rent idle cars, suppliers will be anxious to lower prices and willing to advertise on websites that can attract millions of consumers. The online intermediaries—such as Travelocity, Expedia, and others—do not have to deploy thousands of travel agents in physical offices across the country but can instead concentrate on a single interface with a national consumer audience. Travel services do not require the kind of expensive multi-channel "physical presence" strategy required of financial services (although they generally operate centralized call centers to provide personal customer service). Therefore, travel services "scale" better, permitting earnings to grow faster than costs. But these efficiencies also make it hard for reservation sites to make a profit.

THE ONLINE TRAVEL MARKET

There are four major sectors in the travel market: airline tickets, hotel reservations, car rentals, and travel packages. Airline tickets are the source of the greatest amount of revenue in online travel. Airline reservations are largely a commodity. They can be easily described online. The same is true with car rentals; most people can reliably rent a car over the phone or online and expect to obtain what they ordered. Although hotels are somewhat more difficult to describe, hotel branding, supplemented by websites that include descriptions, photographs, and virtual tours, typically provides enough information to most consumers to allow them to feel as if they know what they are purchasing, making them comfortable enough to make hotel reservations online. Travel packages purchased online constituted the smallest percentage of travel sales.

Increasingly, corporations are outsourcing their travel offices entirely to vendors who can provide web-based solutions, high-quality service, and lower costs. Online vendors to corporations provide **corporate online booking solutions (COBS)** that provide integrated airline, hotel, conference center, and auto rental services at a single site.

corporate online booking solutions (COBS)

provide integrated airline, hotel, conference center, and auto rental services at a single site

ONLINE TRAVEL INDUSTRY DYNAMICS

Because much of what travel agency sites offer is a commodity, and thus they face the same costs, competition among online providers is intense. Price competition is difficult because shoppers, as well as online site managers, can comparison shop easily. Therefore, competition among sites tends to focus on scope of offerings, ease of use, payment options, and personalization. Some well-known travel sites are listed in **Table 11.5**.

The online travel services industry has gone through a period of intense consolidation. Expedia now owns Travelocity, Orbitz, CheapTickets, Hotels.com, Hotwire,

TABLE 11.5	MAJOR ONLINE TRAVEL SITES
NAME	DESCRIPTION
LEISURE/UNMANAGED BUSINESS TRAVEL	
eDreams OdigO	One of Europe's largest online travel groups, formed by the merger of eDreams, Go Voyages, Opodo, and Travelink.
Expedia	Largest online travel service; leisure focus. Now also owns Orbitz, Travelocity, CheapTickets, Hotels.com, HomeAway, and Hotwire.
Orbitz	Began as supplier-owned reservation system; now owned by Expedia.
Travelocity	Leisure focus. Owned by Expedia.
Bookings Holdings	Formerly Priceline Group. Owns Priceline, Booking.com, Lowestfare.com, and Kayak. Expedia's primary competitor. Leisure focus.
TripAdvisor	Travel review site that also allows you to compare prices and book reservations.
CheapTickets	Discount airline tickets, hotel reservations, and auto rentals. Acquired by Expedia when it purchased Orbitz.
Hotels.com	Hotel reservation network; leisure and corporate focus. Owned by Expedia.
TUI AG	German multinational travel and tourism company
MANAGED BUSINESS TRAVEL	
GetThere	Corporate online booking solution (COBS). Owned by Sabre Corporation.
BCD Travel	Full-service corporate travel agency.

HomeAway, and meta-search engine Trivago. Its primary competition consists of Bookings Holdings, which owns Priceline, Booking.com, Lowestfare.com, and Kayak. Together, Expedia and Bookings Holdings control a whopping 95% of the U.S. online travel agency booking market. However, Google is also poised to become a player in the market, with its Google Flights that also provides booking functionality. The U.S. Department of Justice also cited TripAdvisor's Instant Booking service as a factor in its approval of Expedia's acquisition of Orbitz.

In addition to industry consolidation, the online travel industry has been roiled by meta-search engines that scour the Web for the best prices on travel and lodging, and then collect finder or affiliate fees for sending consumers to the lowest-price sites. Travel aggregator sites include Trivago, Kayak, Fly.com, and Mobissimo. These sites, in the eyes of many industry leaders, commoditize the online travel industry even further, cause excessive price competition, and divert revenues from the leading, branded firms who have made extensive investments in inventory and systems.

Mobile devices and apps used for pre-trip planning, booking, check-in, and context- and location-based destination information are also transforming the online travel industry. For instance, in 2019, in the United States, over 125 million people were expected to use a mobile device to research travel and over 80 million were expected to actually book travel using a mobile device, accounting for about 37% of all digital travel sales revenue. Smartphones are used much more frequently than tablets to both research and book travel (eMarketer, Inc., 2019j, 2019k, 2019l). All of the major airlines now have apps for a variety of mobile platforms to enable flight research, booking, and management. Apps from hotels and car rental companies are available from all of the major players such as Hertz and Avis for car rentals, and Marriott, Choice Hotels, Hilton, and Wyndham for hotels. Apps may sometimes target specific consumer behavior. For instance, Expedia reports that 25% of its mobile hotel sales are made at properties within 10 miles of the user's current location, indicating that they are searching for and booking rooms on-the-go, as they travel. Mobile devices are also proving to be quite popular for booking at the last minute. Marriott says that 35% of its smartphone bookings are for same-day travel (eMarketer, Inc., 2017).

Social media is also having a big impact on the online travel industry. User-generated content and online reviews are having an increasing influence on travel-buying decisions. The *Insight on Society* case, *Phony Reviews,* examines some of the issues this presents for the industry.

11.7 ONLINE CAREER SERVICES

Next to travel services, one of the Internet's most successful online services has been job services (recruitment sites) that provide a free posting of individual resumes, plus many other related career services; for a fee, they also list job openings posted by companies. Career services sites collect revenue from other sources as well, by providing value-added services to users and collecting fees from related service providers.

Although there are over 10,000 job posting sites in the United States, the online job market is dominated by two large players: Monster and CareerBuilder. Job listing aggregators, such as Indeed and SimplyHired, both owned by a Japanese-based human resources company, and Glassdoor, which also posts anonymous online reviews of companies by their employees, are also very popular. LinkedIn has also become an increasingly important player in this market (see the opening case in Chapter 10).

Traditionally, companies have relied on five employee recruitment tools: classified and print advertising, career expos (or trade shows), on-campus recruiting, private employment agencies (now called "staffing firms"), and internal referral programs. In comparison to online recruiting, these tools have severe limitations. Print advertising usually includes a per-word charge that limits the amount of detail employers provide about a job opening, as well as a limited time period within which the job is posted. Career expos do not allow for pre-screening of attendees and are limited by the amount of time a recruiter can spend with each candidate. Staffing firms charge high fees and have a limited, usually local, selection of job hunters. On-campus recruiting also restricts the number of candidates a recruiter can speak with during a normal visit and requires that employers visit numerous campuses. And internal referral programs may encourage employees to propose unqualified candidates for openings in order to qualify for rewards or incentives offered.

Online recruiting overcomes these limitations, providing a more efficient and cost-effective means of linking employers and potential employees, while reducing the total time to hire. Online recruiting enables job hunters to more easily build, update, and distribute their resumes while gathering information about prospective employers and conducting job searches.

INSIGHT ON SOCIETY

PHONY REVIEWS

People used to rely on travel agents for recommendations about travel destinations, hotels, and restaurants. Today, however, sites like TripAdvisor and Yelp have taken over that function. TripAdvisor has been a smashing success, with more than 660 million user-generated reviews, over $1.5 billion in revenue in 2017, and over 455 million monthly unique visitors worldwide. Yelp has 135 million reviews of restaurants and other services, and a market capitalization of $3.5 billion. The sites have become trusted sources for travelers as they try to decide where to travel, what hotels to book, and where to eat. A good rating can be worth thousands of dollars in bookings. But can all these reviews be trusted?

As a case in point, in 2018, a British man named Oobah Butler conducted an experiment that illustrated how easily online review sites can be manipulated. A former writer of phony reviews himself, Butler had the idea to pretend that the shed outside his house was an exclusive new restaurant using fake pictures of meals and phony reviews from his friends. As buzz built around the non-existent restaurant, which he had titled The Shed at Dulwich, Butler had to turn down hundreds of eager would-be diners, and eventually the Shed became the top-rated restaurant in London without ever serving a single customer.

Although very few businesses on TripAdvisor, Yelp, and other sites are fake like The Shed, many of the reviews on these platforms are fraudulent. Hotels pay people to create false identities and post favorable reviews on their properties and to slam competing venues. For example, prior to the 2018 World Cup in Russia, TripAdvisor closed 1,300 suspicious accounts, deleted 1,500 suspicious reviews, and flagged 250 restaurants that it suspected of purchasing fraudulent reviews. Businesses can also tarnish their reputations by mishandling bad reviews, phony or otherwise. In Australia, hotels run by the country's wealthiest man, Harry Triguboff, submitted fake e-mail addresses to TripAdvisor for guests who complained to hotel staff, ensuring that TripAdvisor could not contact them to ask for a review. In 2018, his company was fined $3 million.

Reviewers received some legal help in 2016, when Congress passed a law preventing companies from suing customers that give an honest negative review of a business. Many businesses had quietly altered their customer agreements to forbid negative customer reviews and give them legal recourse in the event of such reviews, but the new law will curtail that practice. One New York hotel attempted to add a clause in its contract that it would fine any customer $500 for writing a negative review. When customers discovered this, the hotel was eventually forced to close due to an avalanche of defiant negative reviews and bad publicity. U.S. courts are still split on the question of whether or not platforms like TripAdvisor and Yelp are themselves liable for the reviews on their sites. However, the FTC announced that it had opened an investigation into TripAdvisor's business practices with respect to its handling of potentially fraudulent reviews, and other big tech companies like Facebook have begun to take more responsibility for fraud and other misconduct that takes place on their platforms, suggesting that TripAdvisor may face more liability going forward. Elsewhere, England has passed a series of consumer protections to prevent phony reviews and other misleading practices by businesses, and an Italian court

(continued)

passed down a nine-month prison sentence and a $9,300 fine for the proprietor of a company selling fake reviews.

The authenticity of reviews is critically important to the success of Yelp and TripAdvisor, but garnering a high review score is equally important to the businesses listed on the site. Approximately 85% of customers rely on reviews when planning travel or dining, and studies have found that if a business can increase its Yelp rating by one star, its revenues will increase anywhere from 5% to 9%. Another industry study found that small businesses using Yelp experienced annual revenue increases of $8,000. This gives businesses ample incentive to post phony reviews praising their own business and slamming their competitors. A 2015 study found that 25% of Yelp reviews were labeled "suspicious," and in 2018 the data analytics company Fakespot released a tool that suggested as many as 33% of TripAdvisor reviews may be fake. TripAdvisor refuted these claims, stating that it uses information such as IP address and system settings of the reviewer's computer that Fakespot could not have accessed in order to detect fakes.

Both Yelp and TripAdvisor use their own algorithms to automate the identification and removal of phony reviews. Yelp generates notices called Consumer Alerts to inform readers when a review is likely fraudulent, while TripAdvisor employs a team of 300 experts to analyze the integrity of reviews. Nevertheless, these sites have plenty of incentive to downplay the extent of their phony review problems, since customers are more apt to visit a business if it is highly rated, and the sites receive a commission any time it generates business for a restaurant, hotel, or other destination. TripAdvisor has been fined multiple times in the past by regulatory agencies for misrepresenting the authenticity of its reviews, even changing its slogan so that it no longer referred to trustworthy reviews.

A 2017 study conducted by researchers at the University of Chicago pioneered a technique that could automate the creation of fraudulent reviews that can evade algorithms intended to detect fraud. The researchers' goal was to show that this type of technique may soon become commonplace, and they called for TripAdvisor, Yelp, and other sites to begin developing solutions to phony reviews of unprecedented effectiveness. In 2018, a Swedish group of researchers built upon this work, reverse-engineering the algorithm to better detect fake reviews.

Despite all of the uncertainty surrounding phony and negative reviews, it might be the case that TripAdvisor and Yelp are actually improving service at hotels and restaurants, providing valuable feedback on areas where a business can improve and increasing their incentive to do so. The vast majority of consumers seek out both negative and positive feedback from their prospective destinations, expecting the truth to be somewhere in between.

SOURCES: "TripAdvisor Rejects Claims that 'One in Three Reviews Is Fake'," Travelmole.com, September 24, 2018; "'One in Three TripAdvisor Reviews Are Fake, With Venues Buying Glowing Reviews,' Investigation Finds," by Guy Birchall, Foxnews.com, September 23, 2018; "Does That Yelp Review Look Too Good to Be True? This Tool May Tell You If It's Fake," by Andrew Sheeler, Sacbee.com, September 18, 2018; "A Peddler of Fake Reviews on TripAdvisor Gets Jail Time," by Sean O'Neill, Skift.com, September 12, 2018; "How TripAdvisor Changed Travel," by Linda Kinstler, *The Guardian*, August 17, 2018; "Meriton Fined $3 Million for Interfering With Negative TripAdvisor Reviews," by David Chau and Stephen Letts, Abc.net.au, July 31, 2018; "The Never-Ending War on Fake Reviews," by Simon Parkin, *The New Yorker*, May 31, 2018; "Russian Restaurants Buy Fake TripAdvisor Reviews for $570 to Impress World Cup Fans," by Brendan Cole, Newsweek.com, May 21, 2018; "Why We Need to Fight Fake Reviews," by Wesley Young, Searchengineland.com, March 26, 2018; "I Made My Shed the Top-Rated Restaurant on TripAdvisor," by Oobah Butler, Vice.com, December 6, 2017; "AI Trained on Yelp Data Writes Fake Restaurant Reviews 'Indistinguishable' from Real Deal," by James Vincent, Theverge.com, August 31, 2017; "Researchers Taught AI to Write Totally Believable Fake Reviews, and the Implications are Terrifying," by Rob Price, Businessinsider.com, August 29, 2017; "Why It's About to Get Harder to Post Fake Reviews Online," by Sophie Christie, Telegraph.co.uk, July 31, 2017; "Consumer Review Fairness Act: What Businesses Need to Know," Ftc.gov, February 2017; "Companies Will No Longer Be Able to Fine You for Negative Online Reviews," by Bruce Brown, Digitaltrends.com, November 30, 2016; "Harry Triguboff's Meriton Accused of TripAdvisor Censorship," by David Lewis,Thenewdaily.com.au, November 24, 2016; "Online Reviews Are Changing the Nature of Travel," by Elizabeth Matsangou, Businessdestinations.com, July 13, 2016; "Fake Online Reviews Trip Travelers," by Christopher Elliott, *USA Today*, December 27, 2015; "Fake It Till You Make It: Reputation, Competition, and Yelp Review Fraud," by Michael Luca and Georgios Zervas, Harvard Business School, July 2015.

IT'S JUST INFORMATION: THE IDEAL WEB BUSINESS?

Online recruitment is ideally suited for the Web. The hiring process is an information-intense business process that involves discovering the skills and salary requirements of individuals and matching them with available jobs. In order to accomplish this matchup, there does not initially need to be face-to-face interaction, or a great deal of personalization. Prior to the Internet, this information sharing was accomplished locally by human networks of friends, acquaintances, former employers, and relatives, in addition to employment agencies that developed paper files on job hunters. The Internet can clearly automate this flow of information, reducing search time and costs for all parties.

Table 11.6 lists some of the most popular U.S. recruitment sites.

Why are so many job hunters and employers using Internet job sites? Recruitment sites are popular largely because they save time and money for both job hunters and

TABLE 11.6 POPULAR ONLINE RECRUITMENT SITES

RECRUITMENT SITE	BRIEF DESCRIPTION
GENERAL RECRUITMENT SITES	
Monster	One of the first commercial online sites in 1994. Today, a public company offering general job searches in 50 countries.
CareerBuilder	Now primarily owned by Apollo Global Management, a private investor group.
Indeed	Job site aggregator
SimplyHired	Job site aggregator
Craigslist	Popular classified listing service focused on local recruiting
Glassdoor	Best known for anonymous reviews of companies and management posted by current and former employees, but also has listings for millions of jobs.
EXECUTIVE SEARCH SITES	
Korn Ferry Futurestep	Low-end executive recruiting
Spencerstuart	Middle-level executive recruiting
ExecuNet	Executive search firm
NICHE JOB SITES	
SnagAJob	Part-time and hourly jobs
USAJobs	Federal government jobs
HigherEdJobs	Education industry
EngineerJobs	Engineering jobs
Medzilla	Biotechnology, pharmaceutical, medical, and healthcare industry
Showbizjobs	Entertainment industry
Salesjobs	Sales and marketing
Dice	Information technology jobs
MBAGlobalNet	MBA-oriented community site

employers seeking recruits. For employers, the job boards expand the geographical reach of their searches, lower costs, and result in faster hiring decisions.

For job seekers, online sites are popular not only because their resumes can be made widely available to recruiters but also because of a variety of other related job-hunting services. The services delivered by online recruitment sites have greatly expanded since their emergence. Originally, online recruitment sites just provided a digital version of newspaper classified ads. Today's sites offer many other services, including skills assessment, personality assessment questionnaires, personalized account management for job hunters, organizational culture assessments, job search tools, employer blocking (prevents your employer from seeing your posting), employee blocking (prevents your employees from seeing your listings if you are their employer), and e-mail notification. Online sites also provide a number of educational services such as resume writing advice, software skills preparation, and interview tips.

For the most part, online recruitment sites work, in the sense of linking job hunters with jobs, but they are just one of many ways people actually find jobs. A survey by The Conference Board found that the majority (70%) of job seekers rely equally on both the Internet and newspapers to look for jobs, with about half relying on word-of-mouth leads, and about a quarter on employment agencies. Given that the cost of posting a resume online is zero, the marginal returns are very high.

The ease with which resumes can be posted online has also raised new issues for both job recruiters and job seekers. If you are an employer, how do you sort through the thousands of resumes you may receive when posting an open job? If you are a job seeker, how do you stand out among the thousands or even millions of others? Perhaps one way is to post a video resume. In a survey by Vault, nearly nine in 10 employers said they would watch a video resume if it were submitted to them, in part because it would help them better assess a candidate's professional presentation and demeanor, and over half said they believed video would become a common addition to future job applications. CareerBuilder became the first major online job site to implement a video resume tool for job candidates, following a previous launch for an online video brand-building tool for employers.

Perhaps one of the most important functions of online recruitment sites is not so much their capacity to actually match employers with job hunters but their ability to establish market prices and terms, as well as trends in the labor market. Online recruitment sites identify salary levels for both employers and job hunters and categorize the skill sets required to achieve those salary levels. In this sense, online recruitment sites are online national marketplaces that establish the terms of trade in labor markets. The existence of online national job sites should lead to a rationalization of wages, greater labor mobility, and higher efficiency in recruitment and operations because employers will be able to quickly find the people they need.

ONLINE RECRUITMENT INDUSTRY TRENDS

Trends for 2019–2020 in the online recruitment services industry include the following:

- **Social recruiting:** According to a recent survey of 850 hiring professionals, 77% use LinkedIn as a primary resource and 73% of people between the ages of 18 to 34 report finding a job via social channels (Hudson, 2019; Jobvite, 2018). LinkedIn, probably the most well-known business-oriented social network, has grown significantly to over 675 million members representing over 170 different industries in over 200 countries, with more than 70% of its members from outside the United States. LinkedIn's corporate hiring solutions are used by over 90 of the Fortune 100 companies, and more than 20 million open jobs are listed on LinkedIn. Consumers are using sites such as LinkedIn to establish business contacts and networks. For instance, according to LinkedIn, its members do almost 6 billion professionally-oriented searches on LinkedIn a year. Employers are also using LinkedIn to conduct searches to find potential job candidates that may not be actively job hunting. For instance, LinkedIn offers companies a feature called LinkedIn Talent Solutions that includes tools that help corporate recruiters find "passive talent" (people who are not actively looking for a new job), as well as custom company profiles that are specifically designed for recruitment. According to LinkedIn Talent Solutions, reliance on social recruiting to find quality employees has increased by over 50% since 2011, with 40% of those surveyed indicating that social professional networks were the most important source for key positions (LinkedIn Talent Solutions, 2017). Social network sites are also being used by employers to "check up" on the background of job candidates. A recent study of over 2,300 managers and human resource employees found that 70% are using social networks to screen job candidates, and 57% have rejected candidates because of content on a social site. Employers typically search Facebook, Twitter, and LinkedIn. Provocative or inappropriate photos were the biggest negative factor followed by drinking and drug references. However, on the flip side, recruiters also noted that not having any online presence at all also hurts candidates, with 47% indicating that they would be less likely to interview a job candidate if they cannot find information about that person online (Careerbuilder, 2018).

- **Mobile:** As with other forms of services, career services firms have also moved onto the mobile platform. A recent survey found that over 70% of Millennials and Gen X use mobile devices to search for jobs (Indeed.com, 2017). To reach this audience, CareerBuilder, Monster, LinkedIn, and most of the other major sites all have a mobile website, as well as apps that allow job seekers to create and upload resumes, search jobs by keyword, location, and company, e-mail jobs, browse and apply, and more. LinkedIn's app, for instance, can also recommend jobs based on data you provide on your profile page. In 2018, more than 70% of CareerBuilder's consumer audience used mobile devices, and mobile accounted for about 60% of the unique members visiting LinkedIn.

- **Job search engines/aggregators:** As with travel services, search engines that focus specifically on jobs are posing a new threat to established online career sites. For instance, Indeed, SimplyHired, and Us.jobs "scrape" listings from thousands of online job sites such as Monster, CareerBuilder, specialty recruiting services, and the sites of individual employers to provide a free, searchable index of thousands of job listings in one spot. Because these firms do not charge employers a listing fee, they are currently using a pay-per-click or other advertising revenue model.

- **Data analytics and algorithms:** Companies are increasingly using big data technologies in the hiring process, as well as adaptive algorithms that help them match job seekers to job openings.

- **Hiring by algorithm:** Companies are increasingly using algorithms to sift online job applications, focusing on key words to match job seekers with jobs.

11.8 ON-DEMAND SERVICE COMPANIES

On-demand service companies provide a platform that enables the on-demand delivery of various services, by connecting providers ("sellers") who wish to exploit their "spare" resources, such as cars, rooms with beds, and ability to perform various services via their personal labor, with consumers ("buyers") who would like to utilize those resources and services. Other common phrases sometimes used to describe these online businesses are "sharing economy," "collaborative commerce," "peer to peer consumption," "mesh economy," and "we-commerce." However, unlike traditional sharing where there is no fee charged in the transaction, these firms collect a fee from both sellers and buyers for using their platforms. In the last few years, hundreds of startups have created a plethora of such platforms that allow owners of resources that are underutilized to sell access to those resources to consumers who would prefer not to, or are unable to, buy those resources themselves.

A number of these on-demand service firms have grown exponentially over the last five years. **Table 11.7** describes just a few of the hundreds of firms whose business model is to provide transaction platforms that enable the on-demand delivery of various services. See the *Insight on Business* case, *Food Delivery on Demand in the Middle East,* for a look at two of these companies focused on the delivery of food on demand.

Collaborative commerce, trading platforms, and peer-to-peer commerce are not new. While eBay involves the sale of items at auction or for fixed prices, on-demand service firms provide sell access to cars, room, spaces, and even skilled people. What is new about these firms is their use of mobile and Internet technology to enable transactions on their platforms. This is especially true of the car and lodging services where transactions are local and mobile. Second, the growth of these firms is supported by the use of online reputation systems based on peer review, to establish a trusted environment where sellers and consumers can feel confident transacting with one another. Online peer review of both the providers and the consumers helps to ensure that both parties have acceptable reputations, and that a high quality of service is provided. These firms have learned from

TABLE 11.7	EXAMPLES OF ON-DEMAND SERVICE FIRMS
FIRM	SERVICES ENABLED
Airbnb	Lodging
Uber	Transportation
Lyft	Transportation
TaskRabbit	Errand and household tasks
Movinga	Movers
Deliveroo	Restaurant food delivery
Postmates	Courier
Zipjet	Laundry service

INSIGHT ON BUSINESS

FOOD DELIVERY ON DEMAND IN THE MIDDLE EAST

On-demand service companies have long since transitioned from fledgling startups into some of the biggest companies in all of tech. Some of the biggest examples, such as Uber and Airbnb, got their start in the United States and have since been aggressively seeking to expand into more markets worldwide. One market that has become a major focus is the Middle East (ME) region, which has burst onto the scene in the last few years as a viable opportunity for international growth thanks to rapidly rising rates of smartphone adoption and usage. However, the region already has some very strong locally based competitors in food delivery, including Bawiq and rideshare app platform Careem, both based in the United Arab Emirates (UAE).

The Middle East is particularly well suited to online food delivery, with weather conditions that incentivize staying in over going out (summers in the UAE can reach temperatures as high as 122 degrees Fahrenheit). Middle Eastern consumers already spend over a third of their incomes on transportation and food delivery, and a whopping 60% of UAE consumers now use apps to order food regularly, compared to just 18% in the United States. Despite this, Bawiq's founder, Raj Lee, felt that individual supermarket delivery services in the area were very difficult to navigate, and that his home market was ready for an app-based solution. Bawiq launched in 2018, offering supermarket food delivery from 900 supermarkets across Abu Dhabi and Dubai.

Bawiq's app was designed to minimize the number of steps required to complete an order from start to finish. The app uses geolocation to identify the location of its customers, algorithmically calculating product availability to minimize the appearance of out-of-stock items and incorrect deliveries. Bawiq also provided all of its participating supermarkets with a tablet computer that runs inventory management software, allowing for more accurate results for customers shopping on the app. Bawiq offers credit and debit card payments, an in-app wallet, and cash-on-delivery (COD) payment options. The Middle East is a region where COD is still in widespread use, as a relatively low percentage of residents have bank accounts or credit cards. U.S.-based apps, which assume that their users all have credit cards, have often found this to be a difficult transition when expanding into the ME region.

Many food delivery app platforms struggle with returns of unwanted or defective goods, which put downward pressure on already thin margins. Bawiq acknowledges the issue, hoping that over time its algorithms will improve and reduce the number of returns required. Other features of the app include a favorites list of frequently purchased items, family accounts for multiple users to share, and the ability to save preferred delivery locations within the app itself. Bawiq's deliveries also all come in reusable and recycled bags. Bawiq established an office in Malaysia in August 2019 as a gateway to the Southeast Asian market.

Careem has operated a successful rideshare service in the Middle East for years with a user base of 33 million customers in 120 cities across 15 countries and 1 million drivers. In 2018, Careem began a push into restaurant food delivery with the acquisition of RoundMenu, a delivery service active in 18 cities across 9 Middle Eastern and North African countries, rebranding it Careem NOW. Careem NOW

(continued)

also benefitted from Careem's stored payment details and addresses on file for all of its existing customers. Careem raised $700 million in 2018, with investors including carmaker Daimler and Chinese-based ride sharing service Didi Chuxing, and announced plans to invest $150 million in the Careem NOW service. In 2019, Careem Now expanded to Amman, Jordan, and Karachi, Pakistan.

Careem's success in the Middle East has come mainly at the expense of Uber. Uber has met with regulatory resistance and lukewarm customer reception in Russia, China, and Southeast Asia, and the Middle East has followed that trend. While Uber has a reputation for ignoring regulators in the markets in which it operates, Careem has worked hard with local regulators to find mutually beneficial solutions. For example, Palestinian authorities banned Careem when it attempted to expand to that area, but Careem worked behind the scenes to come to an agreement, and the ban was lifted in 2018.

Part of Careem's local appeal is that the company has adjusted its business model to better adhere to the differences in its market. For example, women were only recently permitted to drive in Saudi Arabia, and women comprise over 70% of all Careem riders. Careem has worked hard to mitigate the concerns of these riders, allowing passengers to mask their phone numbers from drivers and providing an emergency hotline to allow passengers to call for help instantly. These safeguards, along with mandatory harassment training for drivers, minimize incidents of harassment before they occur. Like Bawiq, Careem also accepts COD payments, and the company refers to its drivers as "captains," since the term "driver" carries the connotation of servitude.

On-demand service companies like Bawiq and Careem have a number of other challenges, including sustaining profitability while also keeping supermarkets and restaurants happy by minimizing transaction fees. Some individual restaurants in the area have worked to improve their own proprietary delivery systems, unhappy with the idea of paying the transaction fees required to work with app-based delivery platforms. They also face a host of competitors that are hoping for a piece of the $25 billion potential market for food delivery in the ME region by 2022. For example, UberEats' revenues are doubling every six months in Dubai, and other companies such as Dubai-based Spoonfed and Rocket Internet–owned Talabat are also growing fast. Worldwide, the market for food delivery was $105.9 billion in 2018, with 42% of all delivery orders made online. In 2020, that percentage is expected to grow to 58%, and the worldwide market is projected to grow at 3.5% each year. The ME region is showcasing particularly rapid growth; Bawiq and Careem are well positioned to take advantage. In early 2020, Uber, tired of fighting a losing battle against Careem in the Middle East, acquired its rival for $3.1 billion. Careem will continue to operate both its riding sharing service and Careem Now independently under the Careem brand.

SOURCES: "About," Bawiq.com, accessed February 9, 2020; "Uber Completes Acquisition of Careem," Businesswire.com, Januuary 2, 2020; "Careem Now Official Launches Its Food Delivery Service in Karachi, Pakistan," by MB Staff, Menabytes.com, October 1, 2019; "Careem Launches Its Delivery App Careem Now, to Invest $150 Million in the New Vertical, Available Initially in Dubai and Jeddah for Food Deliveries," by Zubair Naeem Paracha, Menabytes.com, December 17, 2018; "Careem to Launch Food Delivery Service, Complete $500M Funding Round," Pymnts.com, December 17, 2018; "Dubai's Careem to Invest $150M in New Food Delivery Service," by Sam Bridge, Arabianbusiness.com, December 17, 2018; "Uber Eats Doubles Its Dubai Business Every Six Months, Says GCC Exec," by Shayan SHakeel, Arabianbusiness.com, November 21, 2018; "How a Middle East Startup Took on Uber—and Won," by E.B. Boyd, Fastcompany.com, October 11, 2018; "Can This Startup CEO 'Uberise' Grocery Shopping in the UAE?" by Shayan Shakeel, Arabianbusiness.com, September 17, 2018; "Online Food Delivery in Dubai: A Remarkable Growth Opportunity for Burgeoning Entrepreneurs," by Yousuf Rafi, Dubaimonsters.com, August 9, 2018; "Desert Heat Lights a Fire Under Dubai's Delivery Market," by Nell Lewis, Cnn.com, May 1, 2018; "Dubai-Made Delivery App Takes Tasty Meals to Great Distances," by Adelle Geronimo, Tahawultech.com, April 9, 2018; "Careem Acquires Middle East Online Restaurant Listing Platform, to Trial Food Delivery," Reuters.com, February 18, 2018; "Dealing with the Challenge of Third-party Food Delivery Services in the UAE," by Ian Ohan, Arabianbusiness.com, February 12, 2018.

eBay and Netflix the importance of peer reviews and ratings. A third factor is that successful firms lower the cost of services like urban transportation, lodging, office space, and personal errand services. Firms that can do this are highly disruptive of existing firms and business models.

Uber and Airbnb are among the most successful and well-known on-demand service companies. See the opening case in Chapter 1 for a description of Uber and an in-depth discussion of the issues that this business model raises.

Airbnb was founded in 2008 as a way to find lodging for attendees at a business convention. Since then, Airbnb has expanded to the entire lodging marketplace, and has grown exponentially. Airbnb now operates in over 100,000 cities in more than 220 countries, and lists over 7 million properties for rent, including more than 1,400 castles and dozens of yurts in Mongolia. Since its founding, Airbnb has grown to be larger than the Intercontinental, the world's largest private hotel chain, which has about 5,656 hotels, and about 842,759 rooms around the world.

Through January 2020, Airbnb had raised around $4.4 billion in equity and debt funding and has a current valuation of $31 billion, although some analysts believe it could be worth in the neighborhood of $53 billion to $65 billion if it goes public in 2020, surpassing the valuation of Marriott International, the world's most valuable hotel company (Clark, 2019; Ting, 2018). People with spaces to rent, which can range from a single sofa to an entire apartment or house, create an account and a profile, and then list their properties on the site. The amount charged depends on the host and is usually based on the host's assessment of similar listings nearby and market demand. Travelers seeking to rent spaces register and create an account, which includes a profile. They then consult the website listings, read reviews of the host, and contact the host to arrange for the rental. After the rental period, hosts rate their renters, and vice versa. Renters pay through their Airbnb account, which must be funded by a credit card. Airbnb charges guests a sliding fee of 6% to 12%, depending on the price of the booking, and charges the host 3%. The hosts are issued an IRS 1099 form at the end of the year to report taxes due on the income.

Uber and Airbnb stand out not only as the most successful of on-demand service firms, but also as the most disruptive and controversial. For instance, with Airbnb, property renters do not have the regulatory or tax burdens that hotel owners have. It is possible that the success of Airbnb could greatly reduce the demand for regulated hotels. There is little research on this topic, but an early paper found that Airbnb had a small impact on rental income at lower-end tourist hotels, but little empirical impact on business traveler hotels (Zervas et al., 2015). The possibility of negative outcomes from transactions on these on-demand service sites (e.g., a driver robs or harms a passenger, or an apartment is destroyed by renters) is leading both firms to require liability insurance, or to offer such insurance for free. Like Uber, Airbnb faces significant legal challenges. For instance, in 2018, the European Union advised Airbnb that its terms and conditions violated a number of the EU's consumer rules, including the EU's directives on commercial practice and unfair contract terms and its regulation on jurisdiction in civil and commercial matters, forcing Airbnb to adjust them, with the changes going into effect at the end of 2018. On the flip side, the European Holiday Home Association, of which Airbnb is a leading member, has filed a complaint against a number of European cities, such as Barcelona, Berlin, Paris, and Brussels, that strictly regulate short-term rentals such as that offered by Airbnb, on the grounds that those regulations violate EU law. A recent report from UBS suggests that regulations such as these are having a negative impact on Airbnb's business, with listings and bookings growing at a slower pace than in the previous year (Ting, 2017a, 2017b).

11.9 CAREERS IN E-COMMERCE

This chapter provides you with an overview about how e-commerce is being used today in the retail and services industries.

As you've learned in this chapter, the traditional store-based retail business is in trouble as more shoppers buy online. While some retailers such as Sainsbury's Home Retail Group and Tesco have bucked the trend, many retail chains are in the process of closing stores. But while retail store sales have flattened or declined, online retail is growing at over 20%. To cope with online competitors, stored-based retailers are turning to omni-channel strategies by investing heavily in new websites, mobile apps, and social media, encouraging in-store shopping and online buying and same-day local pickup of online orders. As a result, there are an increasing number of jobs involved in retail e-commerce. For example, from 2007 to 2017 almost 400,000 new jobs in the United States were created in retail e-commerce, compared to an overall loss of 76,000 in traditional store-based retail. E-commerce jobs in the United States also have higher wages, paying about 30% more than traditional retail jobs (Sorkin, 2017).

THE COMPANY

The company is a luxury fashion retailer and department store that operates over 260 stores throughout Western Europe. The company sells apparel, shoes, jewelry, handbags, and home furnishings. The firm has several websites, including a clearance site, and a focused luxury site for designer fashions, as well as a Facebook, Instagram, and Pinterest presence. While sales at its stores have languished along with other retailers, its website sales are growing at 10% annually, and currently account for about 20% of its retail sales. The company is planning a major expansion of its online digital operations to compete with pure online retailers and to develop a more robust omni-channel presence.

POSITION: ASSOCIATE, E-COMMERCE INITIATIVES

You will be working on the E-commerce Initiatives Team with a number of internal departments to ensure the delivery of an effective online customer experience and driving e-commerce revenues. Responsibilities include:

- Gathering and analyzing web metric information and making recommendations to further improve the customer experience and sales to adjust strategies and programs.
- Recommending and managing the development of supplemental website content/sections.
- Advocating for best practices and new industry trends and opportunities for increased web sales and online branding.

- Working with internal teams to identify and implement commerce-related opportunities.
- Analyzing consumer journeys.
- Working with site designers to enhance the customer experience and optimize the digital platforms to push customers through the sales funnel, drive conversion, and increase repeat visitors.
- Supporting the business by using qualitative and quantative analytical insights to help drive on-site optimization.
- Leveraging website analytics to support customer experience optimization, including but not limited to product page, navigation, and SEO/SEM search across various digital platforms.
- Collaborating with the e-commerce and marketing teams to identify opportunities around mobile and social network features such as recommendations, reviews, and algorithms.

QUALIFICATIONS/SKILLS

- Bachelor's degree in business or marketing with course work in e-commerce, statistics, and information systems.
- Experience or knowledge of consumer online marketing strategies
- Knowledge of social and mobile marketing tools
- Understanding of site navigation, consumer pathways, and user interface design
- Knowledge of e-commerce site reporting tools and the metrics of e-commerce performance
- Ability to work well across multiple departments and independently
- Excellent analytical skills and problem solving ability
- Strong planning and organizational skills
- Excellent written and verbal communication
- Strong team player and leadership qualities

PREPARING FOR THE INTERVIEW

Do background research on the firm and the industry in which it operates. How does it compare to competitors? Re-read Sections 11.1 and 11.3 (with a particular focus on the sections that cover omni-channel retail). Also review Section 11.2 so that you can demonstrate some basic knowledge of strategic and financial analysis. It would also be worthwhile to closely review the *E-commerce in Action* case on Amazon, as understanding Amazon and the impact it has is imperative for anyone working in online retail. Finally, re-read the *Insight on Business* case in Chapter 6, *Are the Very Rich Different From You and Me?*, on marketing to the luxury audience to understand the success factors, and challenges, of online marketing to an affluent audience. Do background research on the luxury goods marketplace, and marketing to the affluent.

POSSIBLE FIRST INTERVIEW QUESTIONS

1. Why do you think sites like Amazon have been so successful with consumers?

Here, you could draw on the information that you have learned about Amazon from the *E-commerce in Action* case study in the chapter, as well as from your own experience using Amazon. Amazon stands out for its product search engine prowess and easy journey for consumers from search to purchase. Prime "free" two-day delivery and very liberal return policies are also critical to Amazon's success.

2. We're planning on developing a powerful omni-channel capability that would allow consumers to combine online and in-store shopping and purchasing, including same-day pickups at our stores. What do you think are the key success factors for this effort? What are some of the challenges?

Here, you can draw on information you have learned from the chapter (particularly Table 11.3) as well as your own experience with omni-channel retail firms like Tesco, Sainsbury's Home Retail Group, or others. Some keys to success are consistent branding of stores and websites, in-store kiosks for consumers to view inventory in the local store or online, and the need for local store employees to be re-trained as pickers for online orders and local pick-ups by consumers.

3. How can we best use social networks and mobile platforms to drive sales?

Selling luxury goods online involves creating impressive images that reflect the brands and products being sold to a very upscale audience. Visual platforms such as Instagram and Pinterest are ideal.

4. Our focus is on luxury products that are differentiated from other mass market retailers, online and offline. How should this influence our m-commerce efforts?

Real estate on mobile screens is very limited, so the emphasis should be on photos and design images that can be clicked to take mobile users to either a website or a more complete collection of photos and descriptions of apparel and accessories.

5. What experience have you had developing website content?

You can talk here about your experience developing any kind of blog or website content, including photos, videos, and text. Be sure to mention what worked, and what did not, and what you learned from the experience. You can also describe what you find to be really impressive website content, and also unattractive content.

11.10 CASE STUDY

OpenTable:
Your Reservation Is Waiting

OpenTable is the leading supplier of reservation, table management, and guest management software for restaurants. In addition, the company operates the world's most popular platform for making restaurant reservations online.

More than 54,000 restaurants in the United States, and more than 20 other countries, use OpenTable's system, and 31 million diners per month book restaurant reservations via OpenTable's website and mobile app. This system automates the reservation-taking and table management process, while allowing restaurants to build diner databases for improved guest recognition and targeted e-mail marketing. OpenTable's website and app connect directly to the thousands of computerized reservation systems at participating restaurants, and reservations are immediately recorded in a restaurant's electronic reservation book.

Restaurants purchase monthly subscriptions to the OpenTable Electronic Reservation Book (ERB), the company's proprietary software, which is installed on a touch-screen computer system and supported by asset-protection and security tools. The ERB software provides a real-time map of the restaurant floor and enables the restaurant to retain meal patterns of all parties, serving as a customer relationship management (CRM) system for restaurants. The software is upgraded periodically, and the latest version is designed to provide increased ease of use and a more thorough view of table availability to help turn more tables, enhance guest service, personalize responses to diners, coordinate the

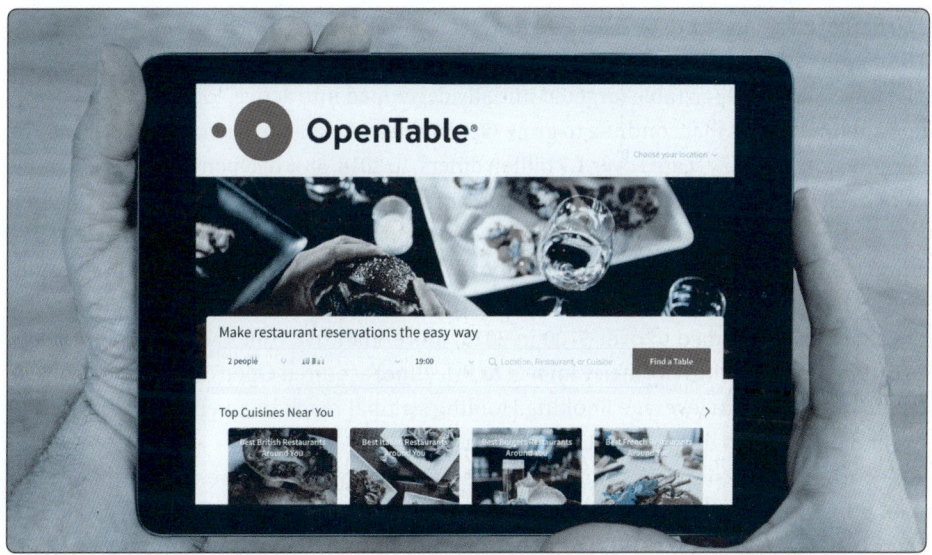

© M4OS Photos/Alamy Stock Photo

seating process, and maximize guest seating. Guest Center is a cloud-based version of the ERB that runs on iOS and Android mobile devices and the Web.

OpenTable's revenue comes primarily from subscriptions. Restaurants used to pay a one-time fee for on-site installation and training, but OpenTable has eliminated these fees to respond to competitors offering cheaper products. However, OpenTable's main subscription model is a $249 monthly charge for the use of its software and hardware in addition to a $1 transaction fee for each restaurant guest seated through online reservations. There is also a more basic version of its software called OpenTable Connect, which costs nothing per month to use, but increases the transaction fee to $2.50 per guest. The online reservation service is free to diners. When an individual makes a reservation, the site "suggests" that they send invites to their dinner companions directly from OpenTable that include a link back to the OpenTable site.

The restaurant industry was slow to leverage the power of the Internet. This was in part because the industry was, and continues to be, highly fragmented and local. The founders of OpenTable knew that dealing with these restaurants as a single market would be difficult. They also realized that the Internet would give diners instant access to reviews, menus, and other information about restaurants. And there was no method for making reservations online—we all know reserving by phone is time-consuming, inefficient, and prone to errors. To induce diners to start using an online reservation system, OpenTable would need real-time access to a number of local restaurants, and the ability to instantly book confirmed reservations around the clock.

When OpenTable was founded, most restaurants did not have computers, let alone systems that would allow online reservations made through a central website. OpenTable's initial strategy was to pay online restaurant reviewers for links to its website and to target national chains in order to quickly expand its reach. This got the company into 50 cities, but it was spending $1 million a month and bringing in only $100,000 in revenue. Not exactly a formula for success. OpenTable halted its marketing efforts and narrowed its focus to four cities: Chicago, New York, San Francisco, and Washington, D.C.

The company retooled its hardware and software to create the user-friendly ERB system and deployed a door-to-door sales force to solicit subscriptions from high-end restaurants. The combination of e-commerce, user-friendly technology, and the personal touch worked. The four markets OpenTable targeted initially developed into active, local networks of restaurants and diners that continue to grow. OpenTable has expanded across the country, and the company has now seated over 1.7 billion diners. In 2018, 58% of OpenTable's reservations were made via a mobile device, and that percentage continues to grow.

As the company grew, investors began making plans for it to go public. In 2009, the company proceeded with an initial public offering (IPO) despite poor economic conditions. The gamble paid off. On its first day of trading, OpenTable's shares climbed 59% and the share price climbed to over $100 in 2013, more than five times the $20 IPO price. In 2014, Booking Holdings (formerly known as Priceline) acquired OpenTable for $2.6 billion. OpenTable hoped to leverage Booking Holding's global reach in an effort to continue to expand its business beyond the United States.

In the past, restaurants that purchased OpenTable's software package were less likely to switch to a different service and abandon their investment. Many restaurants report that they and their staff members find the software easy to use and beneficial to their bottom line. Specifically, it streamlines operations, helps fill additional seats, and improves quality of service, providing a concrete return on investment. This has led to both high customer satisfaction and high retention rates. By creating an online network of restaurants and diners that transact with each other through real-time reservations, OpenTable has figured out how to successfully address the needs of restaurants and diners.

OpenTable's market also exhibits network effects: the more people use it, the more utility the system delivers. More diners discover the benefits of using the online reservation system, which in turn delivers value to restaurant customers, and helps attract more restaurants to the network.

However, after years of dominating the market for online reservations and guest management software, the company has ceded some ground to newer challengers. In late 2016, Booking Holdings reduced the value of OpenTable on its books by $941 million, after increased investments in its international offerings failed to produce increased profits. In 2018, Booking Holdings announced that it would combine the teams behind OpenTable and Kayak, an online booking site that has grown internationally with much more success. Restaurants have increasingly complained about OpenTable's pricing, arguing that once they have attracted and retained loyal customers, paying a $1 charge to OpenTable after each repeat booking doesn't make sense. Some restaurants also have concerns about the fact that OpenTable inserts itself in the middle of the relationship with the customer, capturing valuable marketing data.

A number of competitors have sprung up that hope to take advantage of these issues. Resy, a reservation startup that has won over some high-end restaurants by allowing restaurants to ask for a credit card to reserve, which helps reduce the number of no-shows, now serves 2.6 million diners per week and was acquired by American Express in 2019. Many restaurants that have switched to Resy report that it is far cheaper than OpenTable, sometimes reducing their monthly expenses on booking software by hundreds of dollars. Reserve, a startup with significant venture capital backing, has undercut OpenTable on price, with just a $99 subscription fee.

Yelp was formerly a partner of OpenTable's, but in 2015 it canceled that partnership and announced that it would begin using its online reviews platform to provide reservation services, directly competing with OpenTable.

Perhaps feeling the pressure from its growing list of competitors, OpenTable has focused on improving its user experience across all of its platforms. In 2018, OpenTable released a new version of GuestCenter with a full set of analytics to help restaurant owners improve efficiency. The company also released a new version of its app, simplifying its home screen to feature two main tabs, Book and Discover. The Book tab shows nearby dining options based on the user's location, while the Discover tab offers recommendations based on a user's history and preferences in a wider radius. The app allows users to fully pay for meals with a variety of popular payment services and integrates with over 600 other services, including Alexa, which allows diners to make reservations by voice.

However, at least one OpenTable employee responded to the pressures of increasing competition in a counterproductive way. In 2018, an investigation revealed that an OpenTable employee had made over 300 reservations at 45 different Chicago restaurants using Reserve with the intent of skyrocketing Reserve's rate of no-show reservations. OpenTable fully disavowed the action, firing the employee and describing it as one individual acting

SOURCES: "Global Fast Facts," Press, opentable.com, accessed February 9, 2020; "American Express Has Acquired Reservation Platform Resy," by Cale Weissman, Fastcompany.com, May 15, 2019; "OpenTable Pilots Centralized Reservations for Hospitality Groups on GuestCenter," Press.opentable.com, October 17, 2018; "The Power of OpenTable Is More Accessible Than Ever," Restaurant.opentable.com, accessed October 2018; "The Quest to Topple OpenTable," by Whitney Filloon, Eater.com, September 24, 2018; "OpenTable Now Lets Diners Choose Where They Will Be Seated," by Nancy Trejos, Usatoday.com, August 16, 2018; "OpenTable Reorganizes Its Marketing, Product and People Teams," by Kristin Hawley, Table.skift.com, June 4, 2018; "OpenTable Unveils Business Intelligence Suite for GuestCenter," Press.opentable.com, May 15, 2018; "OpenTable Caters to the On-the-Go, Last-Minute Diner with App Redesign," Press.opentable.com, May 1, 2018; "OpenTable Updates App to Make Booking Faster," by Robert Williams, Mobilemarketer.com, May 1, 2018 "Why OpenTable's Reservation Scandal is a Big Deal for Restaurants," by Nick Kindelsperger, *Chicago Tribune*, March 15, 2018; "OpenTable Says Employee Used Rival Service to Book Hundreds of Fake Restaurant Reservations," by Daniel Victor, *New York Times*, March 6, 2018; "Inside the Restaurant-Reservations Start-up Race," by Marissa Conrad, Grubstreet.com, March 2018; "OpenTable Began a Revolution. Now It's a Power Under Siege," by Stephanie Strom, *New York Times*, August 29, 2017; "OpenTable Introduces Owners and Managers iPhone App for

alone. However, with buzz building around Reserve and Resy, the latter of which scored some key defections from OpenTable such as the highly regarded Union Square Hospitality Group, this type of publicity was the last thing OpenTable needed.

However, OpenTable is still poised for success in the future. Restaurants report that being on OpenTable is better than traditional forms of advertising and remains cost-effective because of the much larger size of its user network. The company continues to focus on global expansion and has released a multi-language global app that allows diners to search for restaurants all over the globe in their native language. OpenTable remains the dominant online reservation service; Resy's 2.6 million weekly diners pales in comparison to OpenTable's 31 million. Still, OpenTable must continue to focus on providing a cost-effective experience for restaurants and a seamless experience for users to maintain its position in this growing market.

Guest Center," Opentable.com, April 26, 2017; "Online Reservation Battle Heats Up for Open Table," by Ronald Holden, Forbes.com, March 5, 2017; "OpenTable Rolls Separate Country Apps into Single App with Global Booking," by Natasha Lomas, Techcrunch.com, October 18, 2016; "OpenTable for iOS 10: New Ways to Book, Connect, and Pay," by Jonathan Grubb, Blog.opentable.com, September 13, 2016; "OpenTable Challenger Reserve Realizes It's Hard to Charge Diners, Shifts Focus to Restaurants," by Alex Konrad, Forbes, May 10, 2016; "Restaurant App Challenges Industry Giant OpenTable," by Matthew Flamm, Crainsnewyork.com, May 10, 2016; "Yelp and OpenTable End Partnership, As Allies Become Competitors," by Riley McDermid, Bizjournals.com, December 18, 2015; "OpenTable App for Apple Watch Now Available," Opentable.com, April 24, 2015; "Priceline Agrees to Buy OpenTable for $2.6 Billion," by Drew FitzGerald, Wall Street Journal, June 13, 2014.

Case Study Questions

1. What characteristics of the restaurant market made it difficult for a reservation system to work?
2. How did OpenTable change its marketing strategy to succeed?
3. Why would restaurants find the SaaS model very attractive?
4. What challenges does OpenTable face?

11.11 REVIEW

KEY CONCEPTS

- **Understand the environment in which the online retail sector operates today.**
- The retail industry can be divided into seven major firm types: general merchandise, durable goods, specialty stores, food and beverage, gasoline and fuel, MOTO, and online retail firms. Each type offers opportunities for online retail. The MOTO sector is the most similar to the online retail sales sector.
- During the early days of e-commerce, some predicted that the retail industry would be revolutionized, based on reduced search costs, lower marketing entry costs, the replacement of physical store merchants by online companies, elimination of middlemen (disintermediation), and hypermediation.
- Today, it has become clear that few of the initial assumptions about the future of online retail were correct. Also, the structure of the retail marketplace in the United States has not been revolutionized. The reality is that:
    - Online consumers are not primarily cost-driven—instead, they are as brand-driven and influenced by perceived value as their offline counterparts.
    - Online market entry costs were underestimated, as was the cost of acquiring new customers.
    - Older traditional firms, such as the general merchandising giants and the established catalog-based retailers, are taking over as the top online retail sites.

- Disintermediation did not occur. On the contrary, online retailing has become an example of the powerful role that intermediaries play in retail trade.

■ Explain how to analyze the economic viability of an online firm.

- The economic viability, or ability of a firm to survive during a specified time period, can be analyzed by examining the key industry strategic factors, the strategic factors that pertain specifically to the firm, and the financial statements for the firm.
- The key industry strategic factors include barriers to entry, the power of suppliers, the power of customers, the existence of substitute products, the industry value chain, and the nature of intra-industry competition.
- The key firm strategic factors include the firm value chain, core competencies, synergies, the firm's current technology, and the social and legal challenges facing the firm.
- The key financial factors include revenues, cost of sales, gross margin, operating expenses, operating margin, net margin, and the firm's balance sheet.

■ Identify the challenges faced by the different types of online retailers.

- *Virtual merchants* are single-channel e-commerce firms that generate all of their revenues from online sales. Their challenges include building a business and a brand name quickly, many competitors in the virtual marketplace, substantial costs to build and maintain an e-commerce presence, considerable marketing expenses, large customer acquisition costs, a steep learning curve, and the need to quickly achieve operating efficiencies in order to preserve a profit. Amazon is the most well-known example of a virtual merchant.
- *Omni-channel merchants* (bricks-and-clicks) have a network of physical stores as their primary retail channel, but also have online operations. Their challenges include high cost of physical buildings, high cost of large sales staffs, the need to coordinate prices across channels, the need to develop methods of handling cross-channel returns from multiple locations, building a credible e-commerce presence, hiring new skilled staff, and building rapid-response order entry and fulfillment systems. In the United States, Macy's is an example of a bricks-and-clicks company.
- *Catalog merchants* are established companies that have a national offline catalog operation as their largest retail channel, but who also have online capabilities. Their challenges include high costs for printing and mailing, the need to leverage their existing assets and competencies to the new technology environment, the need to develop methods of handling cross-channel returns, building a e-commerce presence, and hiring new skilled staff. Lands' End is an example of a catalog merchant in the United States.
- *Manufacturer-direct merchants* are either single- or multi-channel manufacturers who sell to consumers directly online without the intervention of retailers. Their challenges include channel conflict, quickly developing a rapid-response online order and fulfillment system; switching from a supply-push (products are made prior to orders being received based on estimated demand) to a demand-pull model (products are not built until an order is received); and creating sales, service, and support operations online. Dell is an example of a U.S.-based manufacturer-direct merchant.

■ Describe the major features of the online service sector.

- The service sector is the largest and most rapidly expanding part of the economy of advanced industrial nations.
- The major service industry groups are financial services, insurance, real estate, business services, and health services.
- Within these service industry groups, companies can be further categorized into those that involve transaction brokering and those that involve providing a "hands-on" service.
- With some exceptions, the service sector is by and large a knowledge- and information-intense industry. For this reason, many services are uniquely suited to e-commerce and the strengths of the Internet.
- E-commerce offers extraordinary opportunities to improve transaction efficiencies and thus productivity in a sector where productivity has so far not been markedly affected by the explosion in information technology.

- **Discuss the trends taking place in the online financial services industry.**
  - The online financial services sector is a good example of an e-commerce success story, but the success is somewhat different than what had been predicted in the early days of e-commerce. Today, the multi-channel established financial firms are growing the most rapidly and have the best prospects for long-term viability.
  - Multi-channel firms that have both physical branches and solid online offerings have assumed market leadership over pure-online firms.
  - Financial portals provide comparison shopping services and steer consumers to online providers for independent financial advice and financial planning.
  - Account aggregation is another rapidly growing online financial service, which pulls together all of a customer's financial data on a single personalized website.
  - Despite a rocky start, the online mortgage market is slowly growing; it is dominated by established online banks and other online financial services firms, traditional mortgage vendors, and a few successful online mortgage firms.
  - Term life insurance stands out as one product group supporting the early visions of lower search costs, increased price transparency, and the resulting consumer savings. However, in other insurance product lines, the Web offers insurance companies new opportunities for product and service differentiation and price discrimination.
  - The early vision that the historically local, complex, and agent-driven real estate industry would be transformed into a disintermediated marketplace where buyers and sellers could transact directly has not been realized.
  - The major impact of the online real estate industry is in influencing offline purchases and the primary service is a listing of available houses, with secondary links to mortgage lenders, credit reporting agencies, neighborhood information, loan calculators, appraisal reports, sales price histories by neighborhood, school district data, and crime reports.

- **Describe the major trends in the online travel services industry today.**
  - The Internet has become the most common channel used by consumers to research travel options and book reservations for airline tickets, rental cars, hotel rooms, and tours.
  - The major trends in online travel services include consolidation, the rise of meta-search engines, mobile devices, and social media.

- **Identify current trends in the online career services industry.**
  - Next to travel services, job-hunting services have been one of the Internet's most successful online services because they save money for both job hunters and employers.
  - Online recruiting can also serve to establish market prices and terms, thereby identifying both the salary levels for specific jobs and the skill sets required to achieve those salary levels.
  - The major trends in the online career services industry are social networking, mobile, job search engines, consolidation, diversification, and localization.

- **Understand the business models of on-demand service companies.**
  - On-demand service companies provide a platform that enables the on-demand delivery of various services, by connecting providers ("sellers") who wish to exploit their "spare" resources, such as cars, rooms with beds, and ability to perform various services via their personal labor, with consumers ("buyers") who would like to utilize those resources and services. The companies collect a fee from both sellers and buyers for using the platform.
  - Uber, a car rental service, and Airbnb, a room rental service, are the most well-known on-demand services companies. They are also among the most disruptive and controversial.

QUESTIONS

1. Why is the slowdown in new Internet users not causing a slowdown in the growth of online retail sales?
2. What is an omni-channel merchant? What advantages do they have? What challenges do they face?
3. What enabled firms in the MOTO retail sector to transition more easily to e-commerce than other sectors?
4. Describe three techniques retail merchants use to integrate their online and offline sales channels, beyond having an online retail store.
5. Discuss the use of online banking in France.
6. What is an intermediary? Provide an example of one. What effect has e-commerce had on retail intermediaries?
7. What is Amazon's chief business strategy, and what tactics does it use to achieve these strategies?
8. What is a digital native vertical?
9. Identify two key industry strategic factors and describe how they impact the viability of firms operating within an industry.
10. In analyzing the viability of a firm, what questions would you ask to determine how the firm may be affected by social and legal issues?
11. Describe three unique challenges that online retailers face compared to offline retailers.
12. Why is the service sector one of the most natural avenues for e-commerce?
13. What is account aggregation?
14. Why are online travel services such an ideal service for the Internet?
15. How has the insurance industry been impacted by the Internet?
16. What are two major trends currently affecting the online travel industry?
17. Describe three ways that social networking has affected the online recruitment industry.
18. What is fintech?
19. How is the company OpenDoor hoping to disrupt the real estate industry?
20. Why are on-demand service companies viewed as being disruptive and controversial?

PROJECTS

1. Access the archives at Sec.gov, where you can review annual report (10-K) filings for all public companies. Search for the 10-K report for the most recent completed fiscal year for two online retail companies of your choice (preferably ones operating in the same industry, such as Staples Inc. and Office Depot Inc., Amazon and Walmart, etc.). Prepare a presentation that compares the financial stability and prospects of the two businesses, focusing specifically on the performance of their respective e-commerce operations.
2. Find an example not mentioned in the text of each of the four types of online retailing business models. Prepare a short report describing each firm and why it is an example of the particular business model.
3. Drawing on material in the chapter and your own research, prepare a short paper describing your views on the major social and legal issues facing online retailers.
4. Choose a services industry not discussed in the chapter (such as legal services, medical services, accounting services, or another of your choosing). Prepare a 3- to 5-page report discussing recent trends affecting online provision of these services.
5. Together with a teammate, investigate the use of mobile apps in the online retail or financial services industries. Prepare a short joint presentation on your findings.

REFERENCES

Ali, Fareeha. "Amazon Prime Day 2019 Analysis in 8 Charts." Digitalcommerce360.com (July 2019).

Amazon.com, Inc. Form 10-K for the fiscal year ended December 31, 2020, filed with the Securities and Exchange Commission (January 31, 2020).

Anderson, Tim. "The Winners and Losers of Infrastructure Clouds Revealed: AWS, Microsoft, Google, and Alibaba Get Fatter." Theregisterco.uk (February 4, 2020).

Bardhan, Ashok. "The US Economy Grows, But Jobs Don't." Yale Global Online (March 13, 2014).

Benner, Katie. "Airbnb Sues Over New York Law Regulating New York Rentals." *New York Times* (October 22, 2016).

Berthene, April. "Virtual Reality Increases Furniture AOV by 60% at Macy's." Digitalcommerce360.com (September 19, 2018a).

Bishop, Todd. "Amazon Tops 150 M Paid Prime Subscribers Globally after Record Quarter for Membership Program." Geekwire.com (January 30, 2020).

Brown, Jeffrey, and Austan Goolsbee. "Does the Internet Make Markets More Competitive? Evidence from the Life Insurance Industry." John F. Kennedy School of Government, Harvard University. Research Working Paper RWP00-007 (2000).

Brynjolfsson, Erik, Astrid Andrea Dick, and Michael D. Smith. "Search and Product Differentiation at an Internet Shopbot," Center for eBusiness@MIT (December, 2004).

Buckley, Patricia and Rumki Majumdar. "The Services Powerhouse: Increasingly Vital to World Economic Growth." Deloitte.com (July 2018).

Careerbuilder. "More Than Half of Employers Have Found Content on Social Media That Caused Them NOT to Hire a Candidate, According to Recent CareerBuilder Survey." (August 9, 2018).

Cassidy, Tabitha. "2019 Ecommerce in Review: Top 10 Data Trends in Charts." Digitalcommerce360.com (December 26, 2019a).

Cassidy, Tabitha. "Top Omnichannel Retail Chains See Most Web Sales Growth." Digitalcommerce360.com (August 13, 2019b).

Cheng, Andria. "5 Key Takeaways From Amazon's Earnings." Forbes.com (February 2, 2018).

Clark, Kate. "Airbnb's WeWork Problem." Techcrunch.com (October 17, 2019).

Cohen, Simon and Nick Woodard. "Netflix vs. Amazon Prime Video: Which Streaming Service Wins Out." Digitaltrends.com (January 29, 2020).

Davis, Don. "It's Not Just Amazon: Many Top Retailers Are Growing Their Online Sales." Digitalcommerce360.com (April 18, 2019).

Davis, Don. "How the Top 1000 Online Retailers Performed in 2017." Digitalcommerce360.com (April 27, 2018a).

Davis, Don. "2018 Top 500 Movers: Retail Chains and E-commerce Startups." Digitalcommerce360.com (May 21, 2019a).

Elastic.co. "Dell: Powering the Search to Put the Customer First." (February 7, 2017).

eMarketer, Inc. "Total Retail Sales, by Country." (December 2019a).

eMarketer, Inc. "Retail Ecommerce Sales, by Product Category." (October 2019b).

eMarketer, Inc. "Retail E-commerce Sales Share, by Product Category." (October 2019c).

eMarketer, Inc. "Retail Ecommerce Sales, by Country." (December 2019d).

eMarketer, Inc. "Retail Mcommerce Sales, by Country." (December 2019e).

eMarketer, Inc. "US Mobile Buyers and Penetration, by Device." (October 2019f).

eMarketer, Inc. "UK Digital Travel Researchers and Penetration." (July 2019g).

eMarketer, Inc. "UK Digital Travel Bookers and Penetration." (July 2019h).

eMarketer, Inc. "Digital Travel Sales, by Country." (July 2019i).

eMarketer, Inc. "US Mobile Travel Researchers and Penetration, by Device." (July 2019j).

eMarketer, Inc. "US Mobile Travel Bookers and Penetration, by Device." (July 2019k).

eMarketer, Inc. "US Digital Travel Sales, by Device." (July 2019l).

eMarketer, Inc. "Digital Banking Users and Penetration in France." (July 2018a).

eMarketer, Inc. "Mobile Device Banking Users and Penetration in France." (July 2018b).

eMarketer, Inc. "Mobile Drives Growth of Online Travel." (June 21, 2017).

eMarketer, Inc. "Retail Ecommerce Sales for Internet Retailer Top 500 Retailers in North America, by Merchant Type, 2015." (April 13, 2016).

eMarketer, Inc. (Jeffrey Grau). "E-commerce in the US: Retail Trends." (May 2005).

Envestnet Yodlee. "Company." Yodlee.com (accessed February 5, 2020).

E*Trade Financial Corporation. "E*Trade Financial Q2 2019 StreetWise Report." (April 11, 2019)

Evans, Katie. "Macy's CEO Has Big Plans for Growth." Digitalcommerce360.com (March 19, 2018).

Evans, Philip, and Thomas S. Wurster. *Blown to Bits: How the New Economics of Information Transforms Strategy*. Cambridge, MA: Harvard Business School Press (2000).

Facebook. "Introducing Marketplace: Buy and Sell With Your Local Community." Newsroom.fb.com (October 3, 2016).

Federal Trade Commission. "The FTC/DOJ Workshop Current State of Real Estate Data." (June 2018).

Hirsch, Lauren, and Kate Rogers. "Walmart Beats on Earnings and Revenues as US E-commerce Push Pays Off." Cnbc.com (May 17, 2018).

Hudson, Kristen. "Why You Need to Invest in a Social Recruiting Strategy." Jobvite.com (March 29, 2019).

Indeed.com. "The Unstoppable Rise of Mobile Search: What Employers Need to Know." (July 27, 2017).

Jobvite. "2018 Jobvite Recruiter Nation Survey." (2018).

Kauflin, Jeff and Kristin Stoller. "First, Fire All the Brokers: How Lemonade, a Millennial-Loved Fintech Unicorn Is Disrupting the Insurance Business." Forbes.com (May 2, 2019).

Kinsella, Bret. "Amazon Echo Maintains Large Market Share Lead in U.S. Smart Speaker User Base." Voicebot.ai (March 8, 2018).

Kramer, Becky. "Amazon Roll-out in Spokane Follows Growth in Prime Subscriptions; Among 7 Fulfillment Centers Announced this Year." Spokesman.com (July 29, 2018).

Lands' End, Inc. "About Lands' End." Landsend.com (accessed February 5, 2020).

Levy, Nat. "Google Discloses Cloud Revenue for the First Time—Here's How It Compares to Amazon and Microsoft." Geekwire.com (February 4, 2020).

LinkedIn Talent Solutions. "U.S. and Canada Recruiting Trends 2017." (2017).

LL Global, Inc. "2019 Insurance Barometer Study." (April 1, 2019).

Lunden, Ingrid. "Opendoor Raises $300 Million on a $3.8 Billion Valuation for Its Home Marketplace." Techcrunch.com (March 20, 2019).

Marous, Jim. "The Rise of the Digital Customer." Thefinancialbrand.com (June 6, 2017).

Marvin, Rob. "How Amazon Makes Its Money." Pcmag.com (December 25, 2019).

McKay, Peter. "Walmart Is Trying to Out-Amazon Amazon." Vice.com (August 17, 2017).

National Association of Realtors. "2019 Home Buyers and Sellers Generational Trends Report." (March 14, 2018).

Policy Factory. "Social Commerce—China Ahead of the Game." Ceoworld.biz (September 2, 2019).

Quickenloans.com. "Quicken Loans Keeps Its Foot on the Gas: Nation's Largest Lender Completes Another Record-Breaking Quarter." (October 24, 2019).

Reinkensmeyer, Blain. "Barron's Broker Survey 2019 Ranking." Stockbrokers.com (January 17, 2020).

Risley, James. "Roundup: Macy's Reports Double-Digit Ecommerce Growth." Digitalcommerce360.com (August 15, 2019).

Rudden. Jennifer. "Leading Real Estate Websites in the U.S. 2019, by Monthly Visits." Statista.com (July 17, 2019).

Russell, Karl, and Ashwin Seshagiri. "Amazon Is Trying to Do (and Sell) Everything." *New York Times* (June 16, 2017).

Sorkin, Andrew. "E-commerce as a Jobs Engine? One Economist's Unorthodox View." *New York Times* (July 10, 2017).

Stoller, Kristen. "Fintech Insurer Lemonade Valued at More than $2 Billion after $300 Million Funding Deal." Forbes.com (April 11, 2019).

Thomas, Lauren. "Amazon Be Warned, The Online 'War' Is On With Wal-Mart, Analyst Says," Cnbc.com (August 17, 2017).

Ting, Deanna. "Airbnb Could Be Worth More Than Any Hotel Company." Skift.com (July 18, 2018).

Ting, Deanna. "USB Report Says Regulation Slows Airbnb Growth in Popular Markets." Skift.com (April 14, 2017a).

Ting, Deanna. "Airbnb Tries to Clear Away Political and Legal Challenges in New York and San Francisco." (May 1, 2017b).

Tong, Frank. "Macy's Plans to Launch an E-commerce Site in China in 2017." Internetretailer.com (October 7, 2016).

Weil, Jonathon. "Securities Rules Help to Close the Earning Reports GAAP." *Wall Street Journal* (April 24, 2003).

Wharton. "Amazon vs. Walmart; Which One Will Prevail." Knowledge.wharton.upenn.edu (June 27, 2017).

Zervas, Georgios, Davide Proserpio, and John W. Byers. "The Rise of the Sharing Economy: Estimating the Impact of Airbnb on the Hotel Industry." Working Paper. SSRN (May 7, 2015).

CHAPTER 12

B2B E-commerce

LEARNING OBJECTIVES

After reading this chapter, you will be able to:

- Discuss the evolution and growth of B2B e-commerce, as well as its potential benefits and challenges.
- Understand how procurement and supply chains relate to B2B e-commerce.
- Identify major trends in supply chain management and collaborative commerce.
- Understand the different characteristics and types of Net marketplaces.
- Understand the objectives of private industrial networks, their role in supporting collaborative commerce, and the barriers to their implementation.

Alibaba:
China's E-commerce King

Alibaba is China's undisputed B2C and B2B ecommerce king. Founded in 1999 by Jack Ma, it began as a B2B exchange, enabling Chinese manufacturers to sell products such as circuit breakers and hydraulic cylinders to international traders and retailers. In the next decade, the Alibaba Group branched out, first into the C2C sector and then into the B2C sector, both of which also proved lucrative.

Today, Alibaba has grown to a size that dwarfs many of the world's established tech giants. In 2014, the company made a splashy initial public offering (IPO) on the New York Stock Exchange, raising $21.8 billion. Since then, Alibaba has continued to post rapid revenue gains, growing its revenues by over 50% from 2018 to 2019, to a staggering RMB376,844 million (over $56 billion).

Alibaba operates eBay-like and Amazon-like businesses, and records more trade volume than those two companies combined. Alibaba does not hold inventory, manage warehouses, or perform fulfillment, nor does it charge its users. Instead, Alibaba runs platforms that connect sellers and buyers, and earns revenue from commissions and advertising. Alibaba dominates both the B2C and B2B e-commerce markets in China. The success of the company's IPO propelled Ma's net worth to well over $20 billion, and Ma is worth an estimated $44 billion as of January 2020. Internet penetration in China lags behind that of many Western countries but is rapidly increasing, and Chinese e-commerce is projected to grow by over 20% a year over the next five years. This offers Alibaba much room for domestic growth in addition to its international expansion efforts.

Like many early players, Alibaba used an "aggregation of supply" model to connect buyers in North America and Europe to many SME suppliers in China. It created a platform to which sellers would upload their products, businesses would upload their requirements, and supplier–buyer matches would be made. When demand for Chinese goods faltered during the global recession of 2009, Alibaba.com transitioned to recruiting sellers interested in marketing their goods to China, to Japan through its Japanese-language site (Alibaba.co.jp), and to India, where it had opened a branch.

Alibaba has three main B2B divisions. The company's English-language Alibaba.com site handles sales between importers and exporters from over 190 countries. The Chinese language site, 1688.com, focuses on domestic B2B transactions, featuring 10 million

SOURCES: "Alibaba and Amazon Are on a Collision Course in Europe," by Leo Sun, Fool.com, January 14, 2020; "The Government of Ethiopia and Alibaba Group Sign Agreements to Establish wWTP Ethiopia Hub, Businesswire.com, November 25, 2019; "Avnet Expands E-commerce Strategy in China with Alibaba," Bloomberg.com, September 24, 2019; "Alibaba.com Opens Platform to US Sellers," by Tom Brennan, Alizila.com, July 23, 2019; "Opinion: D.C. Is Finally Paying Attention to Scary Chinese Stocks, but Wall Street May Pay the Consequences," by Therese Poletti, Marketwatch.com, June 26, 2019; "Alibaba Group Announces March Quarter and Full Fiscal Year 2019 Results," Alibabagroup.com, May 15, 2019; "Alibaba's Taobao.com Still a 'Notorious Market' Despite Improvements, U.S. Says," by William Mauldin, Wsj.com, April 25, 2019 "Interview: How

storefronts and 150 million daily site visitors. AliExpress.com primarily serves small businesses, offering wholesale pricing without bulk buying requirements.

Alibaba has invested heavily in global expansion. The company has aggressively moved to expand in the United States, purchasing the U.S.-based online B2B marketplace OpenSky in 2018; Alibaba already owned a significant stake in the company and elected to purchase the rest as it prepared to make inroads in the U.S. market. Alibaba also partnered with small business lender Kabbage to provide U.S. businesses the ability to purchase goods on Alibaba using six-month loans at low interest rates, greatly improving transaction speeds and allowing businesses to increase their purchase sizes. In 2019, Alibaba launched a new program aimed at U.S.-based manufacturers, wholesalers, and distributors, enabling them to sell on its platform as well. Alibaba has also launched B2B platforms in Belgium and emerging markets such as Ethiopia, Rwanda, Malaysia, Pakistan, Brazil, and India, where the company pledged to spend $1 billion over four years to improve its B2B platform. The company has also bought stakes in a variety of delivery companies, including Cainiao, which handles 70% of mainland China's deliveries; YTO Express, which handles an average of 8 million packages a day; and Singapore's postal service, SingPost. In 2017, Alibaba pledged to invest RMB100 billion ($15 billion) over five years to create a global logistics network. The company is also developing its previously non-existent physical presence for the first time via acquisitions, including a $2.6 billion takeover of Intime Retailer, a Chinese store and mall operator, and improved its ability to process cross-border payments with its acquisition of payment provider Banking Circle. In 2019, Alibaba expanded its global ambitions for AliExpress, building on its already successful presence in Brazil and Russia by launching the platform in Spain, Italy, and Turkey.

Alibaba's site design emphasizes its robust search function, ease of use, and consumer-friendliness. However, the site has dealt with accusations of widespread counterfeiting for years. In 2016, when Alibaba joined an anti-counterfeiting group, retailers such as Michael Kors, Gucci, and Tiffany left the group in protest, and Alibaba was eventually suspended from the group after the outcry. Jack Ma has publicly stated that the problem is not that the items are fake but that the quality of fake items is as good as or better than legitimate ones, and buyers of fake items often found that while Alibaba readily refunded customers reporting counterfeit items, sellers were not punished. In 2017, Alibaba filed its first lawsuit against counterfeit sellers and announced partnerships with major brands like Samsung and Louis Vuitton to crack down on counterfeiting, and Ma attempted to backtrack on some of his earlier remarks, saying instead that counterfeiting was one of the "cancers" of Alibaba's business and pledging to take all efforts necessary to eradicate it. In 2018, Alibaba reported drastic improvements in its speed in taking down items reported as counterfeit, with 97% of items removed before a single sale had been made, and that overall takedown requests had declined 44% from 2017 to 2018. Alibaba also added over 75 brands to the anti-counterfeiting alliance it launched in 2017. However, Alibaba continues to struggle with the problem of counterfeiting, and its Taobao marketplace was included on the U.S.'s list of notorious markets in both 2018 and 2019.

Alibaba has also been accused of manipulating its sales figures via fraudulent transactions on its platforms, especially on Singles Day, China's Black Friday equivalent, and remains

---

Alibaba's North America B2B Business Streamlines the Retail Experience," by Penn Whaling, Psfk.com, January 15, 2019; "Alibaba Taps Kabbage to Loan up to $150k to SMBs After It Quietly Acquired OpenSky to Ramp in North America," by Ingrid Lunden, Techcrunch.com, January 14, 2019; "Alibaba Acquires Parent of Its Former US Marketplace," by Ina Steiner, Ecommercebytes.com, January 14, 2019; "Alibaba Inks Deal with Belgium to Create Trading Hub," Pymnts.com, December 5, 2018; "Alibaba's B2B Venture in India Sees 89% Dip in Profit," by Priyanka Pani, Thehindubusinessline.com, October 31, 2018; "Alibaba Signs up with Banking Circle for Cross-border Payments," Pymnts.com, September 27, 2018; "Alibaba Grows Its Wholesale Business with International Sellers," by Paul Demery, Digitalcommerce360.com, August 29, 2018; "Alibaba's Anti-Counterfeiting Efforts Appear to Pay Off," by Yiling Pan, Jingdaily.com, May 21, 2018; "Alibaba Adds 75 Big Names to Its Anti-counterfeiting Initiative," Thefashionlaw.com, May 7, 2018; "Alibaba to Invest $1 bn to Help Its India-based Cross-border Business Soar," by Sunny Sen, Factordaily.com, February 28, 2018, "Alibaba Takes Control of Logistics Business, Pledging $15 Billion to Expand Network," by Kane Wu and Cate Cadell, Reuters.com, September 26, 2017; "In Detroit, Jack Ma Called Counterfeit Goods the 'Cancer' of Alibaba," by Josh Horwitz, Qz.com, June 21, 2017; "Alibaba Teams Up with Samsung, Louis Vuitton and Other Brands to Fight Counterfeit Goods," by Jon Russell, Techcrunch.com, January 17, 2017; "Alibaba's Jack Ma Grabs Unusual Spotlight," by Li Yuan, *Wall Street Journal*, January 11, 2017; "Alibaba Breaks New Legal Ground in China, Sues Alleged Counterfeit Sellers," by Adam Najberg, Alizila.com, January 4, 2016; "Maersk, Alibaba Team Up to Offer Booking of Ship Places," Reuters.com, January 4, 2017; "Alibaba Will Sell You Anything, Including a Spot on a Container Ship," by Joon Ian Wong, Qz.com, January 4, 2017; "Alibaba's Jack Ma: The Problem with Counterfeits Is They're 'Better

the target of an ongoing U.S. Securities and Exchange Commission probe commenced in 2016. These concerns have failed to shake the confidence of most investors, and the company's stock price in early January 2020 was more than three times its low in 2015. Although fears due to the coronavirus outbreak in China in January 2020 are likely to impact its stock price in the short term, Alibaba is still growing extremely quickly and is extremely profitable overall.

As you'll learn in this chapter, the first wave of B2B exchanges fell short when the dotcom bubble of the early 2000s deflated. This latest wave, headlined by Alibaba, has succeeded where its predecessors failed by focusing on cost savings and affordability to meet the needs of small and medium-sized enterprises (SMEs), who aren't able to build their own marketplaces the way large companies can. As the rest of the world hatches new B2B start-ups to serve the SME market, they will have to play catch-up with Alibaba, which has been providing procurement and supply chain efficiencies to such companies for 20 years and now dominates this market. Like Alibaba, they must lower transaction costs and identify unique suppliers and products for their buyers by providing a robust store of suppliers and by using matching algorithms, personalization, and big data analytics to help buyers find the supplier with the best product to meet their needs.

Quality' Than Authentic Luxury Goods," by Marc Bain, Qz.com, June 14, 2016; "Alibaba Suspended from Anticounterfeiting Group," by Kathy Chu, *Wall Street Journal*, May 13, 2016; "Brands Are Revolting over Alibaba's Membership in an Anti-Counterfeiting Group," by Scott Cendrowski, *Fortune*, May 13, 2016; "Alibaba Is Positioning Itself as Europe's Sales Gateway to China," by Saabira Chaudhuri, *Wall Street Journal*, October 20, 2015; "China's Alibaba Plans to Introduce B2B Platform in Brazil," Macauhub.com, August 4, 2015; "Alibaba Opens B2B Platform in India," Pymnts.com, June 29, 2015; "Alibaba's B2B Plan Could Change the World of Cross-Border Commerce," Pymnts.com, May 7, 2015; "A Soaring Debut for Alibaba," by Michael J. De La Merced, *New York Times*, September 19, 2014.

The Alibaba case illustrates the exciting potential for e-commerce technologies and customer experience to move from the consumer sphere to the business-to-business (B2B) world, where companies buy from hundreds or even thousands of suppliers and in turn, sell to hundreds or potentially thousands of distributors and retailers.

This case frames the two sides of B2B e-commerce: the supply (buy) side and the sell side. On the supply side, firms have developed elaborate systems and techniques over many decades in order to manage their supply chains and the procurement process. Large firms can easily have hundreds or even thousands of suppliers of parts and materials. These are referred to as supply chain systems, which are described further in this chapter. These supply chain systems lower production costs, increase collaboration among firms, speed up new product development, and ultimately have revolutionized the way products are designed and manufactured. For instance, in the fashion industry, the combination of high-speed Internet-enabled supply chains coupled with equally high-speed trendy design not only clears shelves (and reduces the likelihood of clearance sales), but increases profits by increasing value to consumers (Zarroli, 2013; Cachon and Swinney, 2011).

The success of Alibaba provides insight into the sell side of B2B e-commerce. All the techniques of marketing, branding, and fulfillment developed in the retail e-commerce marketplace come into play when businesses sell to other businesses. Online websites, display advertising, search engine advertising, e-mail, and social media are just as relevant in B2B e-commerce as they are in B2C e-commerce, and the technologies involved are the same. For example, as consumers have moved to mobile devices to purchase retail goods, so have business procurement and purchasing agents begun to move towards mobile purchasing, inventory management, and marketing.

Alibaba is one kind of B2B Net marketplace, where thousands of suppliers can interact with thousands of business buyers on an Internet-enabled platform. There are many kinds of Net marketplaces described later in the chapter, from simple websites where a single company markets to other businesses, to more complex Net marketplaces where suppliers, producers, and distributors work collaboratively in a digital environment to produce, manufacture, and distribute their products and services.

As you'll learn in Section 12.1, Net marketplaces such as Alibaba have resulted from a decades-long evolution. In the early years of e-commerce, business firms tended to stick with direct purchases from manufacturers who were trusted, long-term trading partners rather than participate in public B2B markets. Sellers, in turn, were reluctant to participate for fear of extreme price competition and brand dilution. As a result, B2B e-commerce has evolved much more slowly than B2C e-commerce. Many of the early B2B Net marketplaces that emerged in the late 1990s and 2000s imploded within a few years. But today, following years of consolidation, some very large Net marketplaces are flourishing. We discuss the reasons for these early failures and describe how the new Net marketplaces have learned how to succeed.

In this chapter, we examine some major B2B e-commerce themes: procurement, supply chain management, and collaborative commerce. Each of these business processes has changed greatly with the evolution of B2B e-commerce systems. In Section

12.1, we provide an overview of B2B e-commerce. In Section 12.2, we look more closely at the procurement process and supply chains. In Section 12.3, we place B2B e-commerce in the context of trends in procurement, supply chain management, and collaborative commerce, and describe changes in B2B marketing environment due to e-commerce. The final two sections of this chapter describe the two fundamental types of B2B e-commerce: Net marketplaces and private industrial networks.

Table 12.1 summarizes the leading trends in B2B e-commerce in 2019–2020. Among the most important trends are growing industry concern with supply chain risk and environmental impact, along with a growing public concern with the accountability of supply chains—in particular, violations of developed-world expectations of working conditions in third-world factories that play a key role in the production of goods sold in more developed countries. What many businesses have learned in the last decade is that supply chains can strengthen or weaken a company depending on a number of factors related to supply chain efficiency such as community engagement, labor relations, environmental protection, and sustainability. Many believe that all of these related factors are important to a firm's long-term profitability (Beard and Hornik, 2011). Nearly all of the companies included in the FT Global 500 stock index now use B2B e-commerce systems. Half of all revenues of these firms are produced offshore, in part due to the globalization of supply chains. Thousands of smaller firms are also now able to employ B2B e-commerce systems as low-cost cloud computing and software-as-a-service (SaaS) versions have become widely available. Taking advantage of the mobile platform, more and more companies are using smartphones and tablet computers to run their businesses from any location. There are thousands of mobile apps available from enterprise B2B vendors such as SAP, IBM, Oracle, and others that link to supply chain management systems. Social network tools are pushing into the B2B world as well as the consumer world. B2B managers are increasingly using public and private social networks and technologies to enable long-term conversations with their customers and suppliers. Executives at firms large and small are coming to realize that they are competing not just with other firms but with those firms' supply chains as well. **Supply chain competition** refers to the fact that in some industries firms are able to differentiate their product or pricing, and achieve a competitive advantage, due to superior supply chain management. Arguably, firms with superior supply chains can produce better products, more quickly, and at a lower cost than those with simply adequate supply chains (Antai, 2011).

supply chain competition

differentiating a firm's products or prices on the basis of superior supply chain management

12.1 AN OVERVIEW OF B2B E-COMMERCE

The trade between business firms represents a huge marketplace. The total amount of B2B trade in the United States in 2019 was about $14 trillion, with B2B e-commerce contributing about $6.5 trillion of that amount (U.S. Census Bureau, 2019; authors' estimates). By 2023, B2B e-commerce is expected to grow to about $7.6 trillion in the United States. Worldwide, revenues from B2B e-commerce were estimated to be about $27 trillion in 2019 (UNCTAD, 2019).

TABLE 12.1   MAJOR TRENDS IN B2B E-COMMERCE 2019–2020

BUSINESS

- B2B e-commerce growth continues to accelerate.
- B2B e-distributors adopt the same marketing and sales techniques as successful consumer e-commerce companies such as Amazon.
- Resurgence in Net marketplaces bringing together hundreds of suppliers and thousands of buying firms. SAP Ariba, one of the largest Net marketplaces, now has over 4.6 million connected businesses, including two-thirds of the Forbes Global 2000 largest companies, operating in over 190 countries, that participate in transactions with a value of over $3 trillion a year.
- Risk management: companies heighten their focus on risks in supply chains after being blindsided in recent years by a number of natural and man-made disasters.
- Regional manufacturing: risks of far-flung global networks lead to an increase in regional manufacturing and supply chains, moving production closer to market demand.
- Flexibility: growing emphasis on rapid-response and adaptive supply chains rather than lowest cost supply chains, which typically carry great risks.
- Supply chain visibility: growing use of real-time data that allows managers to see not only across their production, but also into the production and financial condition of key suppliers.
- Social and mobile commerce and customer intimacy: B2B buyers, like consumers, are tapping into tablets, smartphones, and social networks for purchasing, scheduling, exception handling, and coordinating with their suppliers in order to manage supply chain risk.

TECHNOLOGY

- Big data: global trade and logistics systems are generating huge repositories of B2B data, swamping management understanding and controls.
- Business analytics: growing emphasis on use of business analytics software (business intelligence) to understand very large data sets and predictive analytics tools to identify the most profitable customers.
- Cloud: migration of B2B hardware and software to cloud computing and cloud apps, away from individual corporate data centers, as a means of slowing rising technology costs. B2B systems move to cloud computing providers like Amazon, Microsoft, Google, IBM, Oracle, and HP as their core technology.
- Mobile platform: growing use of mobile platform for B2B systems (CRM, SCM, and enterprise), putting B2B commerce into managers' palms.
- Social networks: increasing use of social network platforms for feedback from customers, strengthening customer and supplier relationships, adjusting prices and orders, and enhancing decision making.
- Internet of Things: The number of Internet-connected sensors and other intelligent devices that measure and monitor data continues to grow exponentially and begins to impact how supply chains operate.
- Blockchain: moves from a concept to practical applications for B2B e-commerce with potential to transform supply chains and logistics.

SOCIETY

- Accountability: growing demands for supply chain accountability and monitoring in developed countries driven by reports of poor working conditions in Asian factories.
- Sustainable supply chains: growing public demand for businesses to mitigate their environmental impact leads to reconsideration of the entire supply chain from design, production, customer service, to post-use disposal.

The process of conducting trade among business firms is complex and requires significant human intervention, and therefore, consumes significant resources. Some firms estimate that each corporate purchase order for support products costs them, on average, at least $100 in administrative overhead. Analysts estimate that the cost of a single manual order entry is about $10.50 when handled by a sales rep on the telephone. A digital order cost is estimated to be 25 to 50 cents. Administrative overhead includes processing paper, approving purchase decisions, spending time using the telephone and fax machines to search for products and arrange for purchases, arranging for shipping, and receiving the goods. Across the economy, this adds up to trillions of dollars annually being spent for procurement processes that could potentially be automated. If even just a portion of inter-firm trade were automated, and parts of the entire procurement and sales process assisted by the Internet, then literally trillions of dollars might be released for more productive uses, consumer prices potentially would fall, productivity would increase, and the economic wealth of the nation would expand. This is the promise of B2B e-commerce. The challenge of B2B e-commerce is changing existing patterns and systems of procurement on the supply chain side, and designing and implementing new marketing and distribution systems on the B2B sell side.

SOME BASIC DEFINITIONS

Before the Internet, business-to-business transactions were referred to simply as *inter-firm trade* or the *procurement process*. We use the term **B2B commerce** to describe all types of inter-firm trade to exchange value across organizational boundaries, involving both the purchase of inputs and the distribution of products and services. B2B commerce includes the following business processes: customer relationship management, demand management, order fulfillment, manufacturing management, procurement, product development, returns, logistics/transportation, and inventory management (Barlow, 2011). This definition of B2B commerce does not include transactions that occur within the boundaries of a single firm—for instance, the transfer of goods and value from one subsidiary to another, or the use of corporate intranets to manage the firm. We use the term **B2B e-commerce** (or **B2B digital commerce**) to describe specifically that portion of B2B commerce that is enabled by the Internet (including mobile apps) (Fauska et al., 2013). The links that connect business firms in the production of goods and services are referred to as the supply chain. **Supply chains** are a complex system of organizations, people, business processes, technology, and information, all of which need to work together to produce products efficiently. Today's supply chains are often global, connecting the smartphones in New York to the shipyards in Los Angeles and Qingdao, and to the Foxconn factories that produce the phones. They are also local and national in scope.

B2B commerce
all types of inter-firm trade

B2B e-commerce (B2B digital commerce)
that portion of B2B commerce that is enabled by the Internet and mobile apps

supply chain
the links that connect business firms with one another to coordinate production

automated order entry systems
involve the use of telephone modems to send digital orders

THE EVOLUTION OF B2B E-COMMERCE

B2B e-commerce has evolved over a 45-year period through several technology-driven stages (see **Figure 12.1**). The first step in the development of B2B e-commerce in the mid-1970s was **automated order entry systems** that involved the use of telephone modems to send digital orders to health care products companies such as Baxter

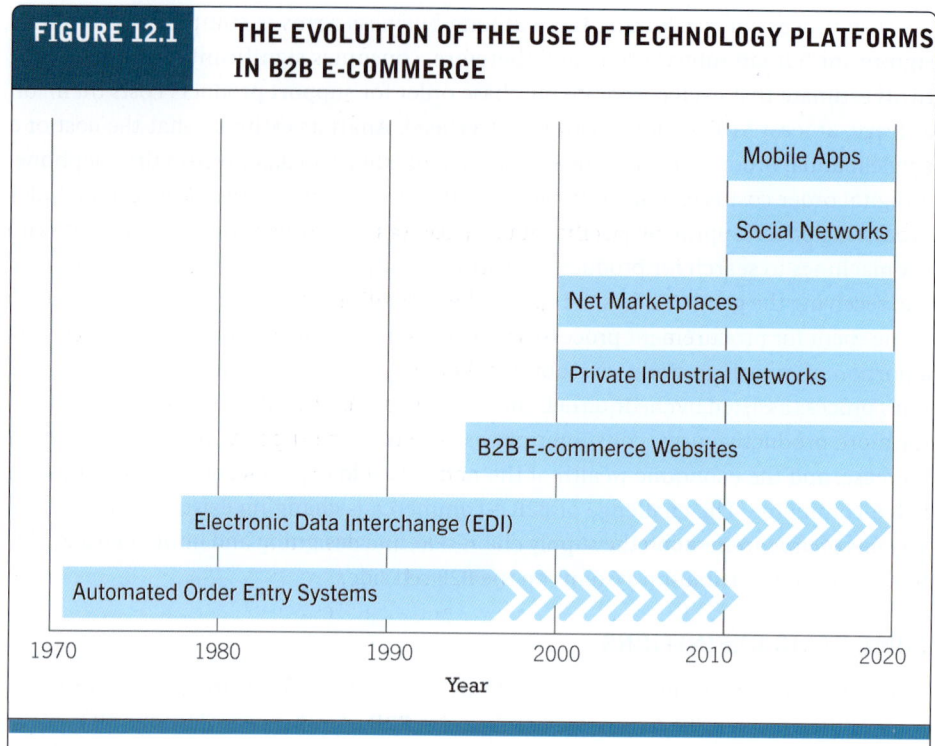

FIGURE 12.1 THE EVOLUTION OF THE USE OF TECHNOLOGY PLATFORMS IN B2B E-COMMERCE

B2B e-commerce has gone through many stages of development since the 1970s. Each stage reflects a major change in technology platforms from mainframes to private dedicated networks, and finally to the Internet, mobile apps, and social networks.

Healthcare. Baxter, a diversified supplier of hospital supplies, placed telephone modems in its customers' procurement offices to automate reordering from Baxter's computerized inventory database (and to discourage reordering from competitors). This early technology was replaced by personal computers using private networks in the late 1980s, and by Internet-connected desktop personal computers accessing online catalogs in the late 1990s. Automated order entry systems are **seller-side solutions**. They are owned by the suppliers and are seller-biased markets—they show only goods from a single seller. Customers benefited from these systems because they reduced the costs of inventory replenishment and were paid for largely by the suppliers. Automated order entry systems continue to play an important role in B2B commerce.

By the late 1970s, a new form of computer-to-computer communication called **electronic data interchange (EDI)** emerged. We describe EDI in greater detail later in this chapter, but at this point, it is necessary only to know that EDI is a communications standard for sharing business documents such as invoices, purchase orders, shipping bills, product stocking numbers (SKUs), and settlement information among a small number of firms. Virtually all large firms have EDI systems, and most industry groups have industry standards for defining documents in that industry. EDI systems are owned by the

seller-side solutions
seller-biased markets that are owned by, and show only goods from, a single seller

electronic data interchange (EDI)
a communications standard for sharing business documents and settlement information among a small number of firms

buyers, hence they are **buyer-side solutions** and buyer-biased because they aim to reduce the procurement costs of supplies for the buyer. Of course, by automating the transaction, EDI systems also benefit the sellers through customer cost reduction. The topology of EDI systems is often referred to as a **hub-and-spoke system**, with the buyers in the center and the suppliers connected to the central hub via private dedicated networks.

EDI systems generally serve vertical markets. A **vertical market** is one that provides expertise and products for a specific industry, such as automobiles. In contrast, **horizontal markets** serve many different industries.

B2B e-commerce websites emerged in the mid-1990s along with the commercialization of the Internet. **B2B e-commerce websites** are perhaps the simplest and easiest form of B2B e-commerce to understand, because they are just online catalogs of products made available to the public marketplace by a single supplier. In this sense, they mimic the functionality of B2C e-commerce websites. Owned by the supplier, they are seller-side solutions and seller-biased because they show only the products offered by a single supplier.

B2B e-commerce websites are a natural descendant of automated order entry systems, but there are two important differences: (1) the far less expensive and more universal Internet becomes the communication media and displaces private networks, and (2) B2B e-commerce websites tend to serve horizontal markets—they carry products that serve a wide variety of industries. Although B2B e-commerce websites emerged prior to Net marketplaces (described next), they are usually considered a type of Net marketplace. Today, more and more B2B manufacturers, distributors, and suppliers are using B2B e-commerce websites to sell directly to business customers, who most often are procurement/purchasing agents, as discussed in Section 12.2.

Net marketplaces emerged in the late 1990s as a natural extension and scaling-up of B2B e-commerce websites. There are many different kinds of Net marketplaces, which we describe in detail in Section 12.4, but the essential characteristic of a Net marketplace is that it brings hundreds or even thousands of suppliers into a single Internet-based environment to conduct trade with business customers. We also use the term Net marketplace to refer to Internet-enabled marketing, distribution, and sales systems.

Private industrial networks also emerged in the last decade as natural extensions of EDI systems and the existing close relationships that developed between large industrial firms and their trusted suppliers. Described in more detail in Section 12.5, **private industrial networks** (sometimes also referred to as a *private trading exchange*, or *PTX*) are Internet-based communication environments that extend far beyond procurement to encompass supply chain efficiency enhancements and truly collaborative commerce where the buyers work with the sellers to develop and design new products.

THE GROWTH OF B2B E-COMMERCE

Figure 12.2 illustrates the growth of B2B e-commerce in the United States over a 20-year period, from 2003 to 2023. From 2003 to 2019, B2B e-commerce grew from $1.8 trillion (accounting for 22% of total B2B commerce in the United States) to $6.5 trillion (46% of all B2B commerce). In the next five years, B2B e-commerce will continue to grow, and by

buyer-side solutions
buyer-biased markets that are owned by buyers and that aim to reduce the procurement costs of supplies for buyers

hub-and-spoke system
suppliers connected to a central hub of buyers via private dedicated networks

vertical market
one that provides expertise and products for a specific industry

horizontal market
market that serves many different industries

B2B e-commerce website
online catalog of products made available to the public marketplace by a single supplier

Net marketplace
brings hundreds to thousands of suppliers and buyers into a sell-side, Internet-based environment to conduct trade

private industrial networks (private trading exchange, PTX)
Internet-based communication environments that extend far beyond procurement to encompass truly collaborative commerce

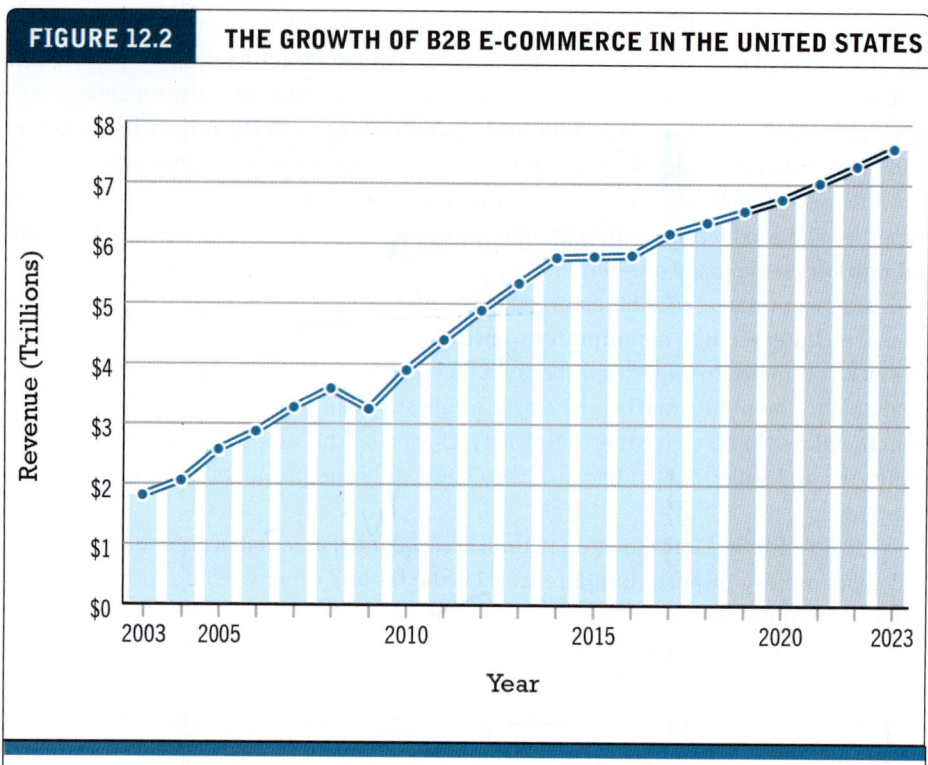

FIGURE 12.2 THE GROWTH OF B2B E-COMMERCE IN THE UNITED STATES

B2B e-commerce in the United States is more than six times the size of B2C e-commerce. In 2023, B2B e-commerce is projected to be reach around $7.6 trillion. (Note: Does not include EDI transactions.)
SOURCES: Based on data from U.S. Census Bureau, 2019; authors' estimates.

2023 is expected to reach about $7.6 trillion. **Figure 12.3** illustrates the share that each of the types of B2B commerce (traditional B2B, EDI, Net marketplaces, and private industrial networks) had of total U.S. B2B commerce in 2019. Several observations are important to note with respect to Figure 12.3. First, it shows that the initial belief that online marketplaces would become the dominant form of B2B e-commerce is not supported even though their growth rate has increased as firms like Amazon and eBay establish Net marketplaces. Second, private industrial networks play a more important role than widely assumed in B2B e-commerce. Third, EDI remains quite common and continues to be a workhorse of B2B commerce even though its growth is expected to be relatively flat in the next four years.

Not all industries will be similarly affected by B2B e-commerce, nor will all industries similarly benefit from B2B. Several factors influence the speed with which industries migrate to B2B e-commerce and the volume of transactions. Those industries in which there is already significant utilization of EDI (indicating concentration of buyers and suppliers) and large investments in information technology and Internet infrastructure can be expected to move first and fastest to B2B e-commerce utilization. The aerospace and defense, computer, and industrial equipment industries meet these criteria. Where the marketplace is highly concentrated on either the purchasing or selling side, or both,

FIGURE 12.3 U.S. B2B COMMERCE 2019

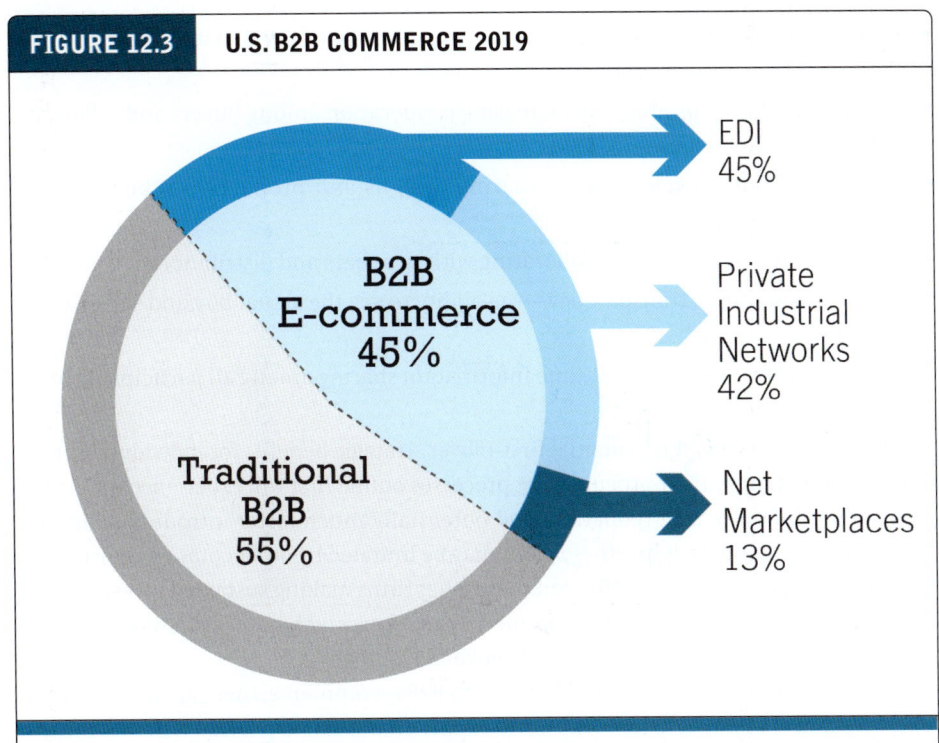

Today B2B e-commerce accounts for about slightly less than half (45%) of all B2B commerce in the United States. Within B2B e-commerce, EDI accounts for 45%, while private industrial networks account for 42%. Contrary to initial expectations, Net marketplaces only account for 13%.
SOURCES: Based on data from U.S. Census Bureau, 2019; authors' estimates

conditions are also ripe for rapid B2B e-commerce growth, as in the energy and chemical industries. In the case of health care, the federal government, health care providers (doctors and hospitals), and major insurance companies are moving toward a national medical record system and the use of the Internet for managing medical payments. Coordinating the various players in the health care system is an extraordinary B2B challenge. Firms like IBM and Microsoft, and B2B service firms like SAP Ariba, are expanding the use of information ecosystems where health providers and insurers can share information.

POTENTIAL BENEFITS AND CHALLENGES OF B2B E-COMMERCE

Regardless of the specific type, B2B commerce as a whole promises many strategic benefits to firms—both buyers and sellers—and impressive gains for the economy. B2B e-commerce can:

- Lower administrative costs
- Lower search costs for buyers
- Reduce inventory costs by increasing competition among suppliers (increasing price transparency) and reducing inventory to the bare minimum
- Lower transaction costs by eliminating paperwork and automating parts of the procurement process

- Increase production flexibility by ensuring delivery of parts just at the right time (known as just-in-time production)
- Improve quality of products by increasing cooperation among buyers and sellers and reducing quality issues
- Decrease product cycle time by sharing designs and production schedules with suppliers
- Increase opportunities for collaborating with suppliers and distributors
- Create greater price transparency—the ability to see the actual buy and sell prices in a market
- Increase the visibility and real-time information sharing among all participants in the supply chain network.

B2B e-commerce offers potential first-mover strategic benefits for individual firms as well. Firms that move their procurement processes online first will experience impressive gains in productivity, cost reduction, and potentially much faster introduction of new, higher-quality products. While these gains may be imitated by other competing firms, it is also clear from the history of B2B e-commerce that firms making sustained investments in information technology and B2B e-commerce can adapt much faster to new technologies as they emerge, creating a string of first-mover advantages.

While there are many potential benefits to B2B e-commerce, there are also considerable risks and challenges. Often real-world supply chains fail to provide visibility into the supply chain because they lack real-time demand, production, and logistics data, and have inadequate financial data on suppliers. The result is unexpected supplier failure and disruption to the supply chain. Builders of B2B supply chains often had little concern for the environmental impacts of supply chains, the sensitivity of supply chains to natural events, fluctuating fuel and labor costs, or the impact of public values involving labor and environmental policies. The result is that many Fortune 1000 supply chains are risky, vulnerable, and socially and environmentally unsustainable. Read *Insight on Society: Where's My iPad? Supply Chain Risk and Vulnerability* for a look at the impact the Tohoku earthquake in Fukushima, Japan had on global supply chains, as well as the reputational risk posed by supply chains.

12.2 THE PROCUREMENT PROCESS AND SUPPLY CHAINS

The subject of B2B e-commerce can be complex because there are so many ways the Internet can be used to support the exchange of goods and payments among organizations, efficient supply chains, and collaboration. At the most basic level, B2B e-commerce is about changing the **procurement process** (how business firms purchase goods they need to produce goods they will ultimately sell to consumers) of thousands of firms across the world. In the procurement process, firms purchase goods from a set of suppliers, and they in turn purchase their inputs from a set of suppliers. The supply chain includes not just the firms themselves, but also the relationships among them and the processes that connect them.

procurement process
how firms purchase goods they need to produce goods for consumers

INSIGHT ON SOCIETY

WHERE'S MY IPAD? GLOBAL SUPPLY CHAIN RISK AND VULNERABILITY

In 2011, a magnitude 9.0 earthquake occurred offshore of northern Japan. The Tohoku earthquake created a number of tsunami waves, some of which exceeded 100 feet in height and penetrated up to six miles inland. In their path were six nuclear reactors in the Fukushima Prefecture, the largest nuclear power site in the world. Several of the nuclear reactors exploded and began leaking dangerous levels of radiation as fuel rods melted at temperatures exceeding 5,000 degrees.

The Tohoku earthquake exposed significant weaknesses and vulnerabilities in today's modern B2B supply chains. Technology, globalization of trade, and high levels of wage disparity between the developed and undeveloped worlds have led to a massive outsourcing of manufacturing around the world. Today, every component of every manufactured product is carefully examined with an eye to finding the lowest cost and highest quality manufacturer. Production tends to concentrate at single firms. Large orders make lower prices easier to provide because of scale economies. However, when you concentrate production globally, you also concentrate risk.

As a result, the world's manufacturing base has become less redundant, flexible, and adaptive than older traditional supply chains. Interdependencies have grown into a tightly coupled machine that is quite fragile. Risk assessment in supply chains has been weak or nonexistent.

Computers, cell phones, tractors, airplanes, and automobiles are just a few of the complex manufactured goods that rely on parts and subassemblies made thousands of miles away from their final assembly plants. Most of these manufacturers know who their first-tier suppliers are but may be less aware about who supplies their suppliers, and so on down the line of the industrial spider's web that constitutes the real world of supply chains. At the time, few firms had considered the impact of an earthquake on their supply chains, let alone a nuclear meltdown.

Take Apple, for instance. In a teardown of an Apple iPad after the earthquake, IHS iSuppli (now IHS Markit), a market research firm, identified at least five major components sourced from Japanese suppliers. Not all of these suppliers were directly impacted by the earthquake, but some were, and many had sub-suppliers that were directly impacted. For instance, the iPad and iPhone's unusually shaped lithium batteries used a crucial polymer made by Kureha, a Japanese firm in the nuclear contamination zone. Kureha controlled 70% of the global production of this polymer. Apple was not the only consumer product manufacturer hit hard: computer chips are built on silicon wafers, and 25% of the world's supply at the time was made by two Japanese manufacturers, both of which had to shut down wafer production. A few years later, a tear-down of the iPhone 6 Plus found that Apple had learned its lesson and diversified its supply chain by often having two manufacturers for the same components sourced from different countries, and also having various components manufactured in different parts of the globe. Apple has followed the same practice with subsequent versions of the iPhone.

Apple was not the only manufacturer that learned a lesson in supply chain risk from the Japanese earthquake: Boeing was without carbon fiber airframe assemblies made in Japan;

(continued)

Ford and GM closed factories for lack of Japanese transmissions; and Caterpillar reduced production at its factories worldwide as it attempted to secure alternative suppliers.

Supply chain risk also involves more than disruptions in production, as Apple and many other companies have discovered. Supply chains can create reputational risks when key suppliers engage in labor and environmental practices that are unacceptable to developed world audiences. For instance, Apple was attacked in the United States and Europe after an audit by the Fair Labor Association found that workers at several assembly plants operated by Apple contractor Foxconn were exposed to toxic chemicals and forced to work over 60 hours a week under dangerous work conditions.

Similarly, a string of disasters, ranging from factory fires to building collapses, involving garment factories in South Asia revealed the brutal conditions under which garment workers toiled. Worldwide protest erupted after a fire in a clothing factory in Dhaka, Bangladesh, killed 117 workers, mostly women and children. Well-known brands from Europe and the United States, among them Walmart and Spanish giant Inditex, were producing clothing in this factory. The fire led to government and industry efforts to certify factory safety in Bangladesh and hold firms responsible for working conditions although progress in implementing safeguards has been slow.

It also isn't just natural disasters and fires that can disrupt supply lines. A strike by longshoremen on the East Coast and Gulf Coast loomed in 2018, raising significant concern from retailers who were in the midst of bringing in holiday season merchandise, but was averted when the longshoremen agreed to the terms of a new contract. In 2020, the emergence of the coronavirus epidemic in China raised widespread fears about global supply chains, particularly in the electronics industry, that rely heavily on Chinese manufacturing.

Cybercrime presents another type of supply chain risk. With hundreds of suppliers, it is very difficult for any single purchasing firm to assess the security of its suppliers' systems. Reducing the number of suppliers is one method. Working only with trusted partners is another. Yet there remains a large opportunity for cybercriminals and rogue governments to disrupt global supply chains.

One might think that in the so-called global and Internet economy, digital supply chains could quickly and effortlessly adjust to find new suppliers for just about any component or industrial material in a matter of minutes. Think again. New supply chains will need to be built that optimize not just cost but also survivability in the event of disasters, as well as meet the ethical demands of the major consuming countries in Europe and the United States.

SOURCES: "Coronavirus and the iPhone: How the Pandemic Could Disrupt China's Supply Chain," by Jason Perlow, Zdnet, January 31, 2020; "Supplier Responsibility 2019 Progress Report," by Apple Inc., March 6, 2019; "ILA Reaches Contract Agreement with East Coast, Gulf Coast Ports," by Marex, Maritime-executive.com, June 7, 2018; "Five Years After Deadly Factory Fire, Bangladesh's Garment Workers Are Still Vulnerable," Theconversation.com, November 23, 2017; "Little-Known Supplier Poised to Benefit from Apple iPhone," Mhlnews.com, August 18, 2017; "Apple's iPhone Supply Chain Begins Ramp-up for the Big Release," by Bob Ferrari, Theferrarigroup.com, May 16, 2017; "Another Apple iPhone Product Introduction and Added Supply Chain Challenges and Concerns," by Bob Ferrari, Theferrarigroup.com, September 9, 2016; "Financial Firms Grapple with Cyber Risk in the Supply Chain," by Rachael King, *Wall Street Journal*, May 25, 2015; "Apple Is Once Again Practicing Supply Chain Segmentation and Risk Mitigation," by Bob Ferrari, Theferrarigroup.com, April 23, 2015; "Supply Chain Slavery Comes Into Focus for Companies," by Ben DiPietro, *Wall Street Journal*, March 30, 2015; "Asian Supply Lines Hit by West Coast Ports," *Reuters*, February 16, 2015; "Teardown Shows Apple's iPhone 6 Cost at Least $200 to Build," by Arik Hesseldahl, Recode.net, September 23, 2014; "Infographic Breaks Down Apple's iPhone Supply Chain," by Bryan Chaffin, MacObserver.com, August 6, 2013; "Bangladesh Factory, Site of Fire That Trapped and Killed 7, Made European Brands," by Julfikar Ali Manik and Jim Yardley, *New York Times*, January 27, 2013; "Audit Faults Apple Supplier," by Jessica Vascellaro, *Wall Street Journal*, March 30, 2012; "Under the Hood of Apple's Tablet," by Don Clark, *Wall Street Journal*, March 16, 2012; "In China, Human Costs Are Built Into an iPad," by Charles Duhigg and David Barboza, *New York Times*, January 25, 2012; "Japan: The Business After Shocks," by Andrew Dowell, *Wall Street Journal*, March 25, 2011; "Some Worry the Success of Apple Is Tied to Japan," by Miguel Helft, *New York Times*, March 22, 2011; "Crisis Tests Supply Chain's Weak Links," by James Hookway and Aries Poon, *Wall Street Journal*, March 18, 2011; "Caterpillar Warns of Supply Problems from Quake," by Bob Tita, *Wall Street Journal*, March 18, 2011; "Lacking Parts, G.M. Will Close Plant," by Nick Bunkley, *New York Times*, March 17, 2011.

FIGURE 12.4 — THE PROCUREMENT PROCESS

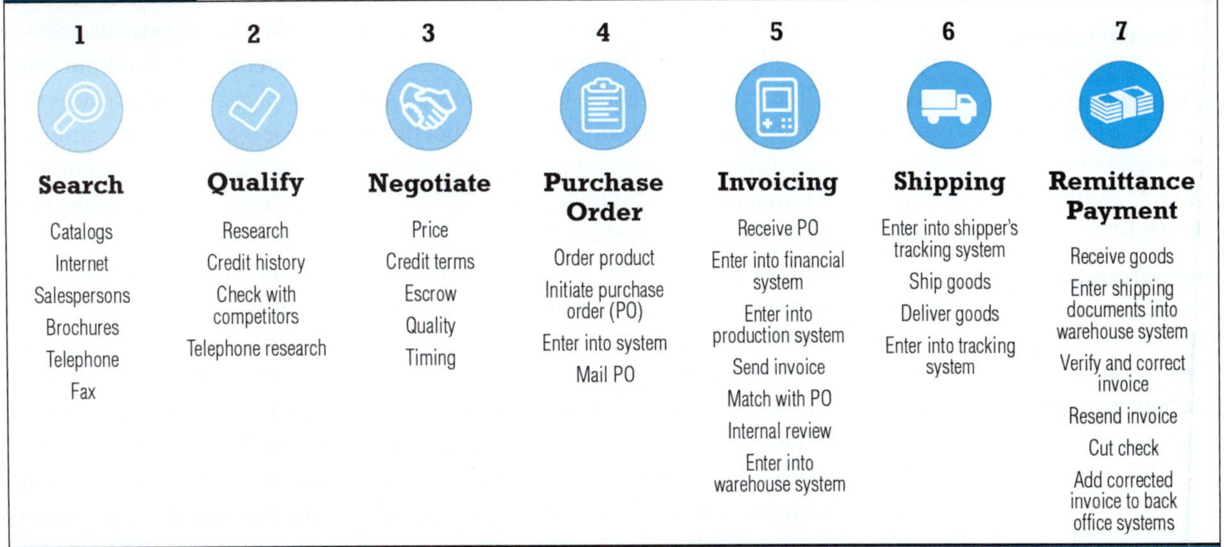

1 Search	2 Qualify	3 Negotiate	4 Purchase Order	5 Invoicing	6 Shipping	7 Remittance Payment
Catalogs	Research	Price	Order product	Receive PO	Enter into shipper's tracking system	Receive goods
Internet	Credit history	Credit terms	Initiate purchase order (PO)	Enter into financial system	Ship goods	Enter shipping documents into warehouse system
Salespersons	Check with competitors	Escrow	Enter into system	Enter into production system	Deliver goods	Verify and correct invoice
Brochures	Telephone research	Quality	Mail PO	Send invoice	Enter into tracking system	Resend invoice
Telephone		Timing		Match with PO		Cut check
Fax				Internal review		Add corrected invoice to back office systems
				Enter into warehouse system		

The procurement process is a lengthy and complicated series of steps that involves the seller, buyer, and shipping companies in a series of connected transactions.

STEPS IN THE PROCUREMENT PROCESS

There are seven separate steps in the procurement process (see **Figure 12.4**). The first three steps involve the decision of who to buy from and what to pay: searching for suppliers of specific products; qualifying both sellers and the products they sell; and negotiating prices, credit terms, escrow requirements, quality, and scheduling of delivery. Once a supplier is identified, purchase orders are issued, the buyer is sent an invoice, the goods are shipped, and the buyer sends a payment. Each of these steps in the procurement process is composed of many separate business processes and subactivities. Each of these activities must be recorded in the information systems of the seller, buyer, and shipper. Often, this data entry is not automatic and involves a great deal of manual labor, telephone calls, faxes, and e-mails.

TYPES OF PROCUREMENT

Two distinctions are important for understanding how B2B e-commerce can improve the procurement process. First, firms make purchases of two kinds of goods from suppliers: direct goods and indirect goods. **Direct goods** are goods integrally involved in the production process; for instance, when an automobile manufacturer purchases sheet steel for auto body production. **Indirect goods** are all other goods not directly involved in the production process, such as office supplies and maintenance products. Often these goods are called **MRO goods**—products for maintenance, repair, and operations.

direct goods
goods directly involved in the production process

indirect goods
all other goods not directly involved in the production process

MRO goods
products for maintenance, repair, and operations

Second, firms use two different methods for purchasing goods: contract purchasing and spot purchasing. **Contract purchasing** involves long-term written agreements to purchase specified products, with agreed-upon terms and quality, for an extended period of time. Generally, firms purchase direct goods using long-term contracts. **Spot purchasing** involves the purchase of goods based on immediate needs in larger marketplaces that involve many suppliers. Generally, firms use spot purchasing for indirect goods, although in some cases, firms also use spot purchasing for direct goods. According to some estimates, spot purchases account for at least 15%–20% of total procurement spending (The Hackett Group, Inc., 2016, Gardner, 2014).

Although the procurement process involves the purchasing of goods, it is extraordinarily information-intense, involving the movement of information among many existing corporate systems. The procurement process today is also very labor-intensive, directly involving millions of employees around the world, not including those engaged in transportation, finance, insurance, or general office administration related to the process. The key players in the procurement process are the purchasing managers. They ultimately decide who to buy from, what to buy, and on what terms. Purchasing managers ("procurement managers" in the business press) are also the key decision makers for the adoption of B2B e-commerce solutions. As purchasing managers have become more familiar and comfortable with B2C e-commerce in their personal lives, they are increasingly coming to expect the same type of purchasing experience in the B2B arena (eMarketer, Inc., 2019a). As a result, B2B manufacturers, suppliers, and distributors are finding that in order to effectively compete, they must pay more attention to the online customer experience, just as their B2C counterparts do. Features that B2B customers now expect include enhanced search functionality, up-to-date product pricing and availability information, product configurators, mobile support, apps along with websites, online support forums, live customer service reps, and a database that contains their corporate purchasing history, shipping preferences, and payment data, and provides support for repeat orders.

MULTI-TIER SUPPLY CHAINS

Although Figure 12.4 captures some of the complexity of the procurement process, it is important to realize that firms purchase thousands of goods from thousands of suppliers. The suppliers, in turn, must purchase their inputs from their suppliers. Large manufacturers such as Ford Motor Company have over 20,000 suppliers of parts, packaging, and technology. The number of secondary and tertiary suppliers is at least as large. Together, this extended **multi-tier supply chain** (the chain of primary, secondary, and tertiary suppliers) constitutes a crucial aspect of the industrial infrastructure of the economy. **Figure 12.5** depicts a firm's multi-tier supply chain.

The supply chain depicted in Figure 12.4 is a three-tier chain simplified for the sake of illustration. In fact, large Fortune 1000 firms have thousands of suppliers, who in turn have thousands of smaller suppliers. The real-world supply chain is often many layers deep. The complexity of the supply chain suggests a combinatorial explosion. Assuming a manufacturer has four primary suppliers and each one has three primary suppliers, and each of these has three primary suppliers, then the total number of suppliers in the

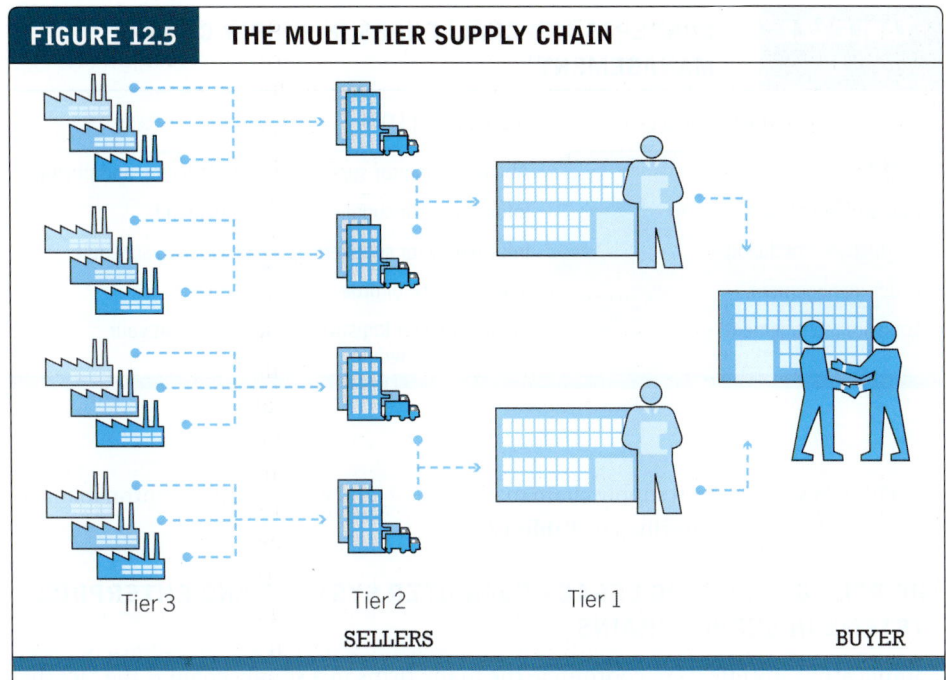

FIGURE 12.5 THE MULTI-TIER SUPPLY CHAIN

Tier 3 — Tier 2 — Tier 1
SELLERS — BUYER

The supply chain for every firm is composed of multiple tiers of suppliers.

chain (including the buying firm) rises to 53. This figure does not include the shippers, insurers, and financiers involved in the transactions.

Immediately, you can see from Figure 12.5 that the procurement process involves a very large number of suppliers, each of whom must be coordinated with the production needs of the ultimate purchaser—the buying firm. You can also understand how difficult it is to manage the supply chain, or obtain visibility into the supply chain simply because of its size and scope.

VISIBILITY AND OTHER CONCEPTS IN SUPPLY CHAIN MANAGEMENT

The global, multi-tier nature of supply chains produces a number of challenges for supply chain managers. A central concept of supply chains is **supply chain visibility**, which refers to the ability of a firm to monitor the output and pricing of its first- and second-tier suppliers, track and manage supplier orders, and manage transportation and logistics providers who are moving the products. A supply chain is visible when you know exactly what you have ordered from your suppliers and what their production schedule is, and when you can track the goods through shipping and trucking firms to your in-bound warehouse. With this knowledge, the firm's internal enterprise systems can produce production schedules and develop financial forecasts (Long, 2014; Cecere, 2014; Cecere, 2013). Generally, the more firms invest in digitally enabled supply chains, the greater the visibility managers have into the process (Caridia et al., 2010).

supply chain visibility
the extent to which purchasing firms can monitor second- and third-tier suppliers' activities

TABLE 12.2	CONCEPTS AND CHALLENGES IN SUPPLY CHAIN MANAGEMENT
CONCEPT/CHALLENGE	DESCRIPTION
Visibility	Ability to monitor suppliers, orders, logistics, and pricing
Demand forecasting	Informing your suppliers of future demand
Production scheduling	Informing your suppliers of the production schedule
Order management	Keeping track of orders to your suppliers
Logistics management	Managing your logistics partners based on your production schedule

Other key concepts in supply chain management, and which are also central management challenges, are described in **Table 12.2**.

THE ROLE OF EXISTING LEGACY COMPUTER SYSTEMS AND ENTERPRISE SYSTEMS IN SUPPLY CHAINS

Complicating any efforts to coordinate the many firms in a supply chain is the fact that each firm generally has its own set of legacy computer systems, sometimes homegrown or customized, that cannot easily pass information to other systems. **Legacy computer systems** generally are older enterprise systems used to manage key business processes within a firm in a variety of functional areas from manufacturing, logistics, finance, and human resources. **Enterprise systems** are corporate-wide systems that relate to all aspects of production, including finance, human resources, and procurement. Many large Fortune 500 global firms have implemented global enterprise-wide systems from major vendors such as IBM, SAP, Oracle, and others. Generally enterprise systems have an inward focus on the firm's internal production processes, and only tangentially are concerned with suppliers. More contemporary cloud-based dedicated B2B software that can be integrated with existing enterprise systems is growing in importance. Companies such as IBM, Oracle, SAP, and many smaller firms have developed SaaS (software as a service) or on-demand cloud-based supply chain management systems that can work seamlessly with their legacy offerings. Cloud-based supply chain management revenues are expected to continue growing at about 10% annually through 2023, although many firms prefer to maintain their own supply chain management systems on their private clouds rather than use shared public cloud services (Allied Market Research, 2019; Chao, 2015; Accenture, 2014).

legacy computer systems
older mainframe systems used to manage key business processes within a firm in a variety of functional areas

enterprise systems
corporate-wide systems that relate to all aspects of production, including finance, human resources, and procurement

12.3 TRENDS IN SUPPLY CHAIN MANAGEMENT AND COLLABORATIVE COMMERCE

It is impossible to comprehend the actual and potential contribution of B2B e-commerce, or the successes and failures of B2B e-commerce vendors and markets, without understanding ongoing efforts to improve the procurement process through a variety of supply chain management programs that long preceded the development of e-commerce.

Supply chain management (SCM) refers to a wide variety of activities that firms and industries use to coordinate the key players in their procurement process. For the most part, today's procurement managers still work with telephones, e-mail, fax machines, face-to-face conversations, and instinct, relying on trusted long-term suppliers for their strategic purchases of goods directly involved in the production process.

There have been a number of major developments in supply chain management over the last two decades that set the ground rules for understanding how B2B e-commerce works (or fails to work). These developments include just-in-time and lean production, supply chain simplification, adaptive supply chains, sustainable supply chains, electronic data interchange (EDI), supply chain management systems, and collaborative commerce.

supply chain management (SCM)
refers to a wide variety of activities that firms and industries use to coordinate the key players in their procurement process

JUST-IN-TIME AND LEAN PRODUCTION

One of the significant costs in any production process is the cost of in-process inventory: the parts and supplies needed to produce a product or service. **Just-in-time production** is a method of inventory cost management that seeks to reduce excess inventory to a bare minimum. In just-in-time production, the parts needed for, say, an automobile, arrive at the assembly factory a few hours or even minutes before they are attached to a car. Payment for the parts does not occur until the parts are attached to a vehicle on the production line. In the past, producers used to order enough parts for a week or even a month's worth of production, creating huge, costly buffers in the production process. These buffers assured that parts would almost always be available, but at a large cost. **Lean production** is a set of production methods and tools that focuses on the elimination of waste throughout the customer value chain. It is an extension of just-in-time beyond inventory management to the full range of activities that create customer value. Originally, just-in-time and lean methods were implemented with phones, faxes, and paper documents to coordinate the flow of parts in inventory. Supply chain management systems now have largely automated the process of acquiring inventory from suppliers, and made possible significant savings on a global basis. Arguably, contemporary supply chain systems are the foundation of today's global B2B production system.

just-in-time production
a method of inventory cost management that seeks to reduce excess inventory to a bare minimum

lean production
a set of production methods and tools that focuses on the elimination of waste throughout the customer value chain

SUPPLY CHAIN SIMPLIFICATION

Many manufacturing firms have spent the past two decades reducing the size of their supply chains and working more closely with a smaller group of strategic supplier firms to reduce both product costs and administrative costs, while improving quality, a trend known as **supply chain simplification**. Following the lead of Japanese industry, for instance, the automobile industry has systematically reduced the number of its suppliers by over 50%. Instead of open bidding for orders, large manufacturers have chosen to work with strategic partner supply firms under long-term contracts that guarantee the supplier business and also establish quality, cost, and timing goals. These strategic partnership programs are essential for just-in-time production models, and often involve joint product development and design, integration of computer systems, and tight coupling of the production processes of two or more companies. **Tight coupling** is a method for ensuring

supply chain simplification
involves reducing the size of the supply chain and working more closely with a smaller group of strategic supplier firms to reduce both product costs and administrative costs, while improving quality

tight coupling
a method for ensuring that suppliers precisely deliver the ordered parts, at a specific time and particular location, to ensure the production process is not interrupted for lack of parts

that suppliers precisely deliver the ordered parts at a specific time and to a particular location, ensuring the production process is not interrupted for lack of parts.

SUPPLY CHAIN BLACK SWANS: ADAPTIVE SUPPLY CHAINS

While firms have greatly simplified their supply chains in the last decade, they have also sought to centralize them by adopting a single, global supply chain system that integrates all the firm's vendor and logistics information into a single enterprise-wide system. Large software firms such as Oracle, IBM, and SAP encourage firms to adopt a "one world, one firm, one database" enterprise-wide view of the world in order to achieve scale economies, simplicity, and to optimize global cost and value.

Beginning in earnest in 2000, managers in developed countries used these new technological capabilities to push manufacturing and production to the lowest-cost labor regions of the world, specifically China and South East Asia. This movement of production to Asia was also enabled by the entrance of China into the World Trade Organization in 2001. Suddenly, it was both technologically and politically possible to concentrate production wherever possible in the lowest-cost region of the world. These developments were also supported by low-cost fuel, which made both transoceanic shipping and production inexpensive, and by relative political stability in the region. By 2005, many economists believed a new world economic order had emerged based on cheap labor in Asia capable of producing inexpensive products for Western consumers, profits for global firms, and the opening of Asian markets to sophisticated Western goods and financial products.

As it turns out, there were many risks and costs to this strategy of concentrating production in a world of economic, financial, political, and even geological instability. Today, managers need to be more careful in balancing gains in efficiency from a highly centralized supply chain, with the risks inherent to such a strategy (Long, 2014). For instance, in the global financial crisis of 2007–2009, relying on suppliers in parts of Europe where currencies and interest rates fluctuated greatly exposed many firms to higher costs than anticipated. Suddenly, key suppliers could not obtain financing for their production or shipments. As you learned in the *Insight on Society* case, the 2011 earthquake and tsunami in Japan had a significant impact on supply chains in a number of industries around the world. In 2016, another earthquake, this time in southern Taiwan, had a similar impact. Taiwan is the global manufacturing center of integrated circuit wafers, accounting for 70% of the world's production of processor chips used by Apple, IBM, Microsoft, and hundreds of other firms (Resilinc, 2016; DHL, 2016). Throughout 2018 and 2019, the imposition of tariffs on the importation of various goods by the Trump administration and the specter of a "trade war" raised supply chain disruption fears (Brown, 2018; Schomberg, 2018). In early 2020, industries braced for significant supply chain disruptions due to the coronavirus epidemic that emerged in China, while at the same time, the United Kingdom left the European Union (commonly referred to as Brexit), also rattling European supply chains (Jorgenson, 2020). In recent years, technology has also become a significant source of supply chain disruptions, with major disruptions due to failure of cloud-based services and cyberattacks (Allianz, 2019; All National Cyber Security Center, 2018; Resilinc, 2016; Rossi, 2015).

The risks and costs of extended and concentrated supply chains have begun to change corporate strategies (Chopra and Sodhi, 2014). To cope with unpredictable world events, firms are taking steps to create **adaptive supply chains** that allow them to react to disruptions in the supply chain in a particular region by moving production to a different region. Many companies are breaking up single global supply chain systems into regional or product-based supply chains and reducing the level of centralization. Using adaptive supply chains, firms can decide to locate some production of parts in Latin America, for instance, rather than having all their production or suppliers in a single country such as Japan or China. They will be able to move production around the world to temporary safe harbors. This may result in higher short-term costs, but provide substantial, longer-term risk protection in the event any single region is disrupted. Increasingly, supply chains are being built based on the assumption that global disruptions in supply are inevitable, but not predictable. The focus today is on optimal-cost, not low-cost, supply chains, and more distributed manufacturing along with more flexible supply chains that can shift reliably from high-risk to low-risk areas. Regional manufacturing means shorter supply chains that can respond rapidly to changing consumer tastes and demand levels (PriceWaterhouseCoopers and the MIT Forum for Supply Chain Innovation, 2015; Cachon and Swinney, 2011).

adaptive supply chain
allows companies to react to disruptions in the supply chain in a particular region by moving production to a different region

ACCOUNTABLE SUPPLY CHAINS: LABOR STANDARDS

Accountable supply chains are those where the labor conditions in low-wage, underdeveloped producer countries are visible and morally acceptable to ultimate consumers in more developed industrial societies. For much of the last century, American and European manufacturers with global supply chains with large offshore production facilities sought to hide the realities of their offshore factories from Western reporters and ordinary citizens. For global firms with long supply chains, visibility did not mean their consumers could understand how their products were made.

Beginning in 2000, and in part because of the growing power of the Internet to empower citizen reporters around the world, the realities of global supply chains have slowly become more transparent to the public. For instance, Nike, the world's largest manufacturer of sporting goods, came under intense criticism for exploiting foreign workers, operating sweat shops, employing children, and allowing dangerous conditions in its subcontractor factories. As a result, Nike has introduced significant changes to its global supply chain. Bangladesh is a continuing source of apparel factory fires beginning with the Dhakka fire of 2010, the Rena Plaza factory building collapse of 2013, and the second Dhakka fire in 2015, all of which resulted in deaths and injuries to workers. Around 80% of Bangladesh's export revenue comes from apparel manufacturing for global brands such as Walmart, H&M, JCPenney, Zara, and others.

accountable supply chain
one where the labor conditions in low-wage, underdeveloped producer countries are visible and morally acceptable to ultimate consumers in more developed industrial societies

With the emergence of truly global supply chains, and political changes at the World Trade Organization, which opened up European and American markets to Asian goods and services, many—if not most—of the electronics, toys, cosmetics, industrial supplies, footwear, apparel, and other goods consumed in the developed world are made by workers in factories in the less developed world, primarily in Asia and Latin America. Unfortunately, but quite understandably, the labor conditions in these factories in most cases do not meet the minimal labor standards of Europe or America even though these factories pay higher wages and offer better working conditions than other local jobs in the host country. In many cases, the cost for a worker of not having a job in what—to Western standards—are horrible working conditions is to sink deeper into poverty and even worse conditions. Many point out that labor conditions were brutal in the United States and Europe in the nineteenth and early twentieth centuries when these countries were building industrial economies, and therefore, whatever conditions exist in offshore factories today are no worse than those in developed countries in their early years of rapid industrialization.

The argument results in a painful ethical dilemma, a terrible trade-off: cheap manufactured goods that increase consumer welfare in developed countries seem to require human misery in less developed countries. Indeed, these jobs would never have been moved to less developed parts of world without exceptionally low, even survival level, wages.

Notwithstanding the argument that having a job is better than being unemployed in low-wage countries, or any country, there are some working conditions that are completely unacceptable to consumers and therefore to firms in developed countries. Among these unacceptable working conditions are slave or forced labor, child employment, routine exposure to toxic substances, more than 48 hours of work per week, harassment and abuse, sexual exploitation, and compensation beneath the minimal standard of living leaving no disposable income. These practices were, and are, in some cases typical in many low-wage countries.

A number of groups in the last decade have contributed to efforts to make global supply chains transparent to reporters and citizens, and to develop minimal standards of accountability. Among these groups are the National Consumers League, Human Rights First, the Maquila Solidarity Network, the Global Fairness Initiative, the Clean Clothes Campaign, the International Labor Organization (UN), and the Fair Labor Association (FLA). The FLA is a coalition of business firms with offshore production and global supply chains, universities, and private organizations. For member firms, the FLA conducts interviews with workers, makes unannounced visits to factories to track progress, and investigates complaints. They are also one of the major international labor standard-setting organizations (Fair Labor Association, 2017).

In 2012, the FLA released its investigation of Hon Hai Precision Industry Company (a Taiwan-based company known as Foxconn), which is the assembler of nearly all iPhones and iPads in the world. Foxconn operates what is alleged to be the largest factory in the world in Longhua, Shenzhen, where over 250,000 workers assemble electronics goods. The audit of working conditions at Foxconn was authorized by Apple, a member of the FLA, and was based on 35,000 surveys of workers at the Longhua factory. The report found over 50 legal and code violations (sometimes in violation of Chinese laws) including requiring too many hours of work a week (over 60), failing to pay workers for overtime, and hazardous conditions that injured workers (Fair Labor Association, 2012). Similar violations of labor standards continue to be found in the Middle East and Asia (Fair Labor Association, 2017).

SUSTAINABLE SUPPLY CHAINS: LEAN, MEAN, AND GREEN

Sustainable business is a call for business to take social and ecological interests, and not just corporate profits, into account in all their decision-making throughout the firm (UN

Global Compact, 2018). No small request. Since the United Nations World Commission on Environment and Development (WCED) published the first comprehensive report on sustainable business in 1987, firms around the globe have struggled with these concepts and in some cases ignored or resisted them as simply a threat to sustained profitability. The commission's report (*Our Common Future*) argued for a balance of profits, social community development, and minimal impact on the world environment, including, of course, the carbon footprint of business. Today, the consensus among major firms in Europe, Asia, and the United States has become that in the long term, and through careful planning, sustainable business and **sustainable supply chains** are just good business because it means using the most efficient environment-regarding means of production, distribution, and logistics. These efficient methods create value for consumers, investors, and communities (Suering and Muller, 2008).

sustainable supply chain
involves using the most efficient environment-regarding means of production, distribution, and logistics

Notions of sustainable business have had a powerful impact on supply chain thinking. In part, these efforts are good risk management: all advanced countries have substantially strengthened their environmental regulations. It makes good business sense for firms to prepare methods and operations suitable to this new environment.

For instance, all the major textiles brands and retailers have announced plans for a more sustainable supply chain in textiles. One of the world's truly ancient industries, textiles, supports millions of workers while consuming extraordinary resources: it takes 1,000 gallons of water to make one pound of finished cotton (your jeans, for instance). While growing cotton has its issues (fertilizer), the subsequent dyeing, finishing, and cleaning of cotton makes it the number one industrial polluter on Earth. It's not a small matter, then, that Walmart, Gap, Levi's, Nike, and other large players in the industry are taking steps to reduce the environmental impact of their operations by improving the efficiency of the entire supply and distribution chains.

With the help of IBM, SAP, and Oracle, other firms and entire industries are working to develop sustainable supply chains (Inter IKEA Group, 2019; Lopez, 2018). McKesson, North America's largest distributor of drugs, uses IBM's Supply Chain Sustainability Management Solution (SCSM) to minimize carbon dioxide emissions throughout its supply chain, while lowering its distribution costs. SCSM (a business analytics package that works with IBM's B2B software) can determine low-cost refrigeration alternatives for certain medicines (such as insulin and vaccines), identify the environmentally least harmful way to bring new products into its distribution network, and determine the best way to transport pharmaceuticals to customers.

ELECTRONIC DATA INTERCHANGE (EDI)

As noted in the previous section, B2B e-commerce did not originate with the Internet, but in fact has its roots in technologies such as EDI that were first developed in the mid-1970s and 1980s. EDI is a broadly defined communications protocol for exchanging documents among computers using technical standards developed by the American National Standards Institute (ANSI X12 standards) and international bodies such as the United Nations (EDIFACT standards).

EDI was developed to reduce the cost, delays, and errors inherent in the manual exchanges of documents such as purchase orders, shipping documents, price lists, payments, and customer data. EDI differs from an unstructured message because its messages are organized with distinct fields for each of the important pieces of information in a commercial transaction such as transaction date, product purchased, amount, sender's name, address, and recipient's name.

Each major industry in the United States and throughout much of the industrial world has EDI industry committees that define the structure and information fields of electronic documents for that industry. Estimates indicate that B2B e-commerce EDI transactions totaled about $2.8 trillion in 2019, about 45% of all B2B e-commerce (U.S. Census Bureau, 2019; authors' estimates). In this sense, EDI remains very important in the development of B2B e-commerce (Cecere, 2014).

EDI has evolved significantly since the 1980s (see **Figure 12.6**). Initially, EDI focused on document automation (Stage 1). Procurement agents created purchase orders electronically and sent them to trading partners, who in turn shipped order fulfillment and shipping notices electronically back to the purchaser. Invoices, payments, and other documents followed. These early implementations replaced the postal system for document

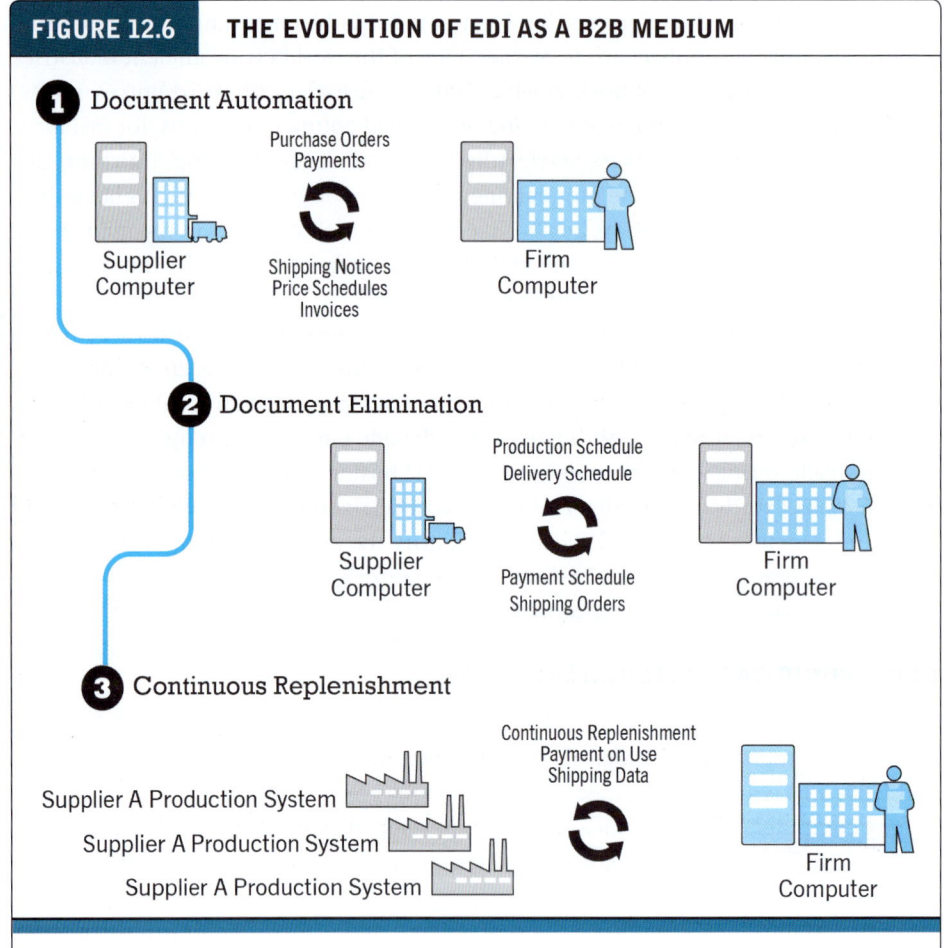

FIGURE 12.6 THE EVOLUTION OF EDI AS A B2B MEDIUM

EDI has evolved from a simple point-to-point digital communications medium to a many-to-one enabling tool for continuous inventory replenishment.

transmission, and resulted in same-day shipping of orders (rather than a week's delay caused by the postal system), reduced errors, and lower costs. The second stage of EDI development began in the early 1990s, driven largely by the automation of internal industrial processes and movement toward just-in-time production and continuous production. New methods of production called for greater flexibility in scheduling, shipping, and financing of supplies. EDI evolved to become a tool for continuous inventory replenishment. EDI was used to eliminate purchase orders and other documents entirely, replacing them with production schedules and inventory balances. Supplier firms were sent monthly statements of production requirements and precise scheduled delivery times, and the orders would be fulfilled continuously, with inventory and payments being adjusted at the end of each month.

In the third stage of EDI, beginning in the mid-1990s, suppliers were given online access to selected parts of the purchasing firm's production and delivery schedules, and, under long-term contracts, were required to meet those schedules on their own without intervention by firm purchasing agents. Movement toward this continuous real-time access model of EDI was spurred in the 1990s by large manufacturing and process firms (such as oil and chemical companies) that were implementing enterprise systems. These systems required standardization of business processes and resulted in the automation of production, logistics, and many financial processes. These new processes required much closer relationships with suppliers and logistics partners (shipping and ground transporters), who were required to be more precise in delivery scheduling and more flexible in inventory management. This level of supplier precision could never be achieved economically by human purchasing agents. This third stage of EDI enabled the era of continuous replenishment. For instance, Walmart and Toys"R"Us provide their suppliers with access to their store inventories, and the suppliers are expected to keep the stock of items on the shelf within prespecified targets. Similar developments occurred in the grocery industry.

Today, EDI must be viewed as a general enabling technology that provides for the exchange of critical business information between computer applications supporting a wide variety of business processes. EDI is an important industrial network technology, suited to support communications among a small set of strategic partners in direct, long-term trading relationships. The technical platform of EDI has changed from mainframes to personal computers, from corporate data centers to cloud-based software-as-a-service (SaaS) platforms (described below). EDI is not well suited for the development of Net marketplaces, where thousands of suppliers and purchasers meet in a digital arena to negotiate prices. EDI supports direct bilateral communications among a small set of firms and does not permit the multilateral, dynamic relationships of a true marketplace. EDI does not provide for price transparency among a large number of suppliers, does not scale easily to include new participants, and is not a real-time communications environment. EDI does not have a rich communications environment that can simultaneously support e-mail messaging, video conferencing, sharing of graphic documents, network meetings, or user-friendly flexible database creation and management.

MOBILE B2B

Just as with B2C commerce, mobile devices have become increasingly important in all aspects of B2B e-commerce, through all steps of the procurement process and throughout

Bring Your Own Device (BYOD) policy
employees use their personal smartphone, tablet, or laptop computer on the company's network

the supply chain. Many companies have adopted a **Bring Your Own Device (BYOD) policy**, in which employees use their personal smartphone, tablet, or laptop computer on the company's network, which has helped contribute to their growing importance in B2B.

On the procurement front, B2B buyers are increasingly using mobile devices for all phases of the purchase process, from discovery to decision-making, to actual purchase. A majority of B2B buyers worldwide now believe their mobile device is essential to their work, with 84% of Millennials (ages 18–35, 76% of Gen-Xers (ages 36–51), and 60% of Baby Boomers (ages 52 and over) all stating that mobile is vital (eMarketer, Inc., 2017a). B2B buyers want to be able to place orders using mobile devices just as they do in the B2C arena, and increasingly expect B2B e-commerce sites to be readily accessible from such devices, to be able to start an order from a device and finish it on their desktop and vice versa, and to be able to get online customer service on their mobile devices.

On the supply chain front, many supply chain network and software providers are enhancing their offerings by providing support for mobile devices and applications. For instance, Elementum provides a variety of mobile apps running on a cloud platform to track various aspects of the supply chain and enable supply chain visibility. For instance, Elementum's Source app enables companies to identify and respond to risks in their supply chain, providing real-time alerts on events that may impact the supply, manufacture, or distribution of components of their products. Elementum's Situation Room app helps companies monitor the health of their supply chain by providing a dashboard that provides real-time tracking of key performance indicators (KPIs) in the supply chain.

B2B IN THE CLOUD

In the traditional approach to B2B enterprise systems, firms build on their existing on-premise, enterprise production systems that keep track of their manufacturing and distribution processes to include new functionality connecting them to their suppliers' systems. This is a very expensive process that involves connecting suppliers one at a time, establishing the telecommunications channels, and managing the data quality issues, not to mention the cost of building the infrastructure of computers and telecommunications to support coordination of suppliers and B2B transactions. Cloud computing (described in Chapter 2) is increasingly being used to greatly reduce the cost of building and maintaining B2B systems.

cloud-based B2B system
shifts much of the expense of B2B systems from the firm to a B2B network provider, sometimes called a data hub or B2B platform

In **cloud-based B2B systems**, much of the expense of B2B systems is shifted from the firm to a B2B network provider, sometimes called a data hub or B2B platform (see **Figure 12.7**). The cloud platform owner provides the computing and telecommunications capability; establishes connections with the firm's partners; provides software on-demand (software-as-a-service or SaaS) to connect the firm's systems to its partners' systems; performs data coordination and cleaning; and manages data quality for all members. Network effects apply here: the cost of these tasks and capabilities is spread over all members, reducing costs for all. B2B network providers also provide communication environments and file storage services that allow partners to work together more closely, and to collaborate on improving the flow of goods and transactions. B2B network providers charge customers on a demand basis, rather than on a percentage of their transactions'

FIGURE 12.7 CLOUD-BASED B2B PLATFORMS

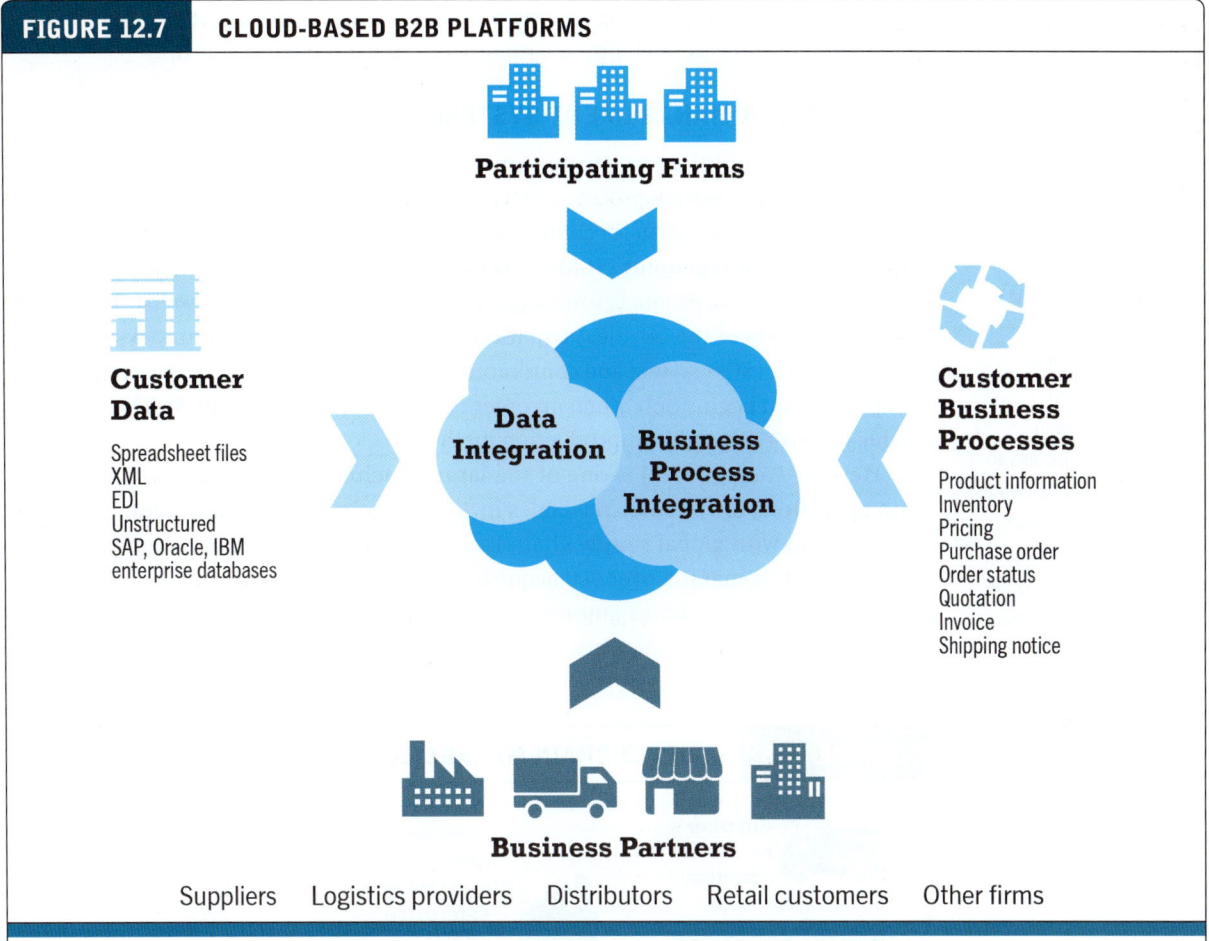

Cloud-based B2B platforms integrate a firm's customer data, business processes, and business partners into a cloud-based software system. Businesses are charged for the hardware and software platform on a utilization basis, reducing their costs significantly.

value, depending on their utilization of the network. Suppliers of traditional on-premise B2B and supply chain management systems have responded by purchasing cloud-based B2B networks in the last few years. For instance, SAP purchased Ariba, one of the first and largest cloud-based B2B transaction networks, in 2012 for $4.6 billion. SAP Ariba's Ariba Network automates over $3 trillion in commercial transactions, collaborations, and business intelligence among a wide range of suppliers, and shipping and logistics firms. SAP, the largest supplier of firm enterprise systems, supplies software that supports internal business processes. Other B2B network providers include E2Open, GT Nexus, and Elementum. Unlike traditional firm-based B2B systems, cloud-based B2B can be implemented in short periods of time to respond to corporate mergers and rapidly changing markets. In 2018, Salesforce, known for its cloud CRM systems, announced its B2B Commerce platform, which enables firms to quickly deploy websites with features unique to B2B commerce, such as complex pricing and product configurations, customized catalogs, payment and shipping options; to match commerce transactions with CRM data; and to link multiple sales channels with orders and firms (Demery, 2018).

SUPPLY CHAIN MANAGEMENT SYSTEMS

Supply chain simplification, just in time, and lean production, focusing on strategic partners in the production process, enterprise systems, and continuous inventory replenishment, are the foundation for contemporary supply chain management (SCM) systems. **Supply chain management (SCM) systems** continuously link the activities of buying, making, and moving products from suppliers to purchasing firms, as well as integrating the demand side of the business equation by including the order entry system in the process. With an SCM system and continuous replenishment, inventory is greatly reduced and production begins only when an order is received (see **Figure 12.8**). These systems enable just-in-time and lean-production methods.

Hewlett-Packard (HP) is one of the largest technology companies in the world. With operations in 170 countries, sales in 43 currencies, and 15 languages, HP is truly a global firm with global supply chain issues that became even more complicated as HP expanded by making over 200 acquisitions in the last decade. In 2019, HP has one of the largest supply chains among information technology manufacturers. HP ships 35 personal computers, 26 printers, and 280 ink and toner cartridges into more than

supply chain management (SCM) systems

continuously link the activities of buying, making, and moving products from suppliers to purchasing firms, as well as integrating the demand side of the business equation by including the order entry system in the process

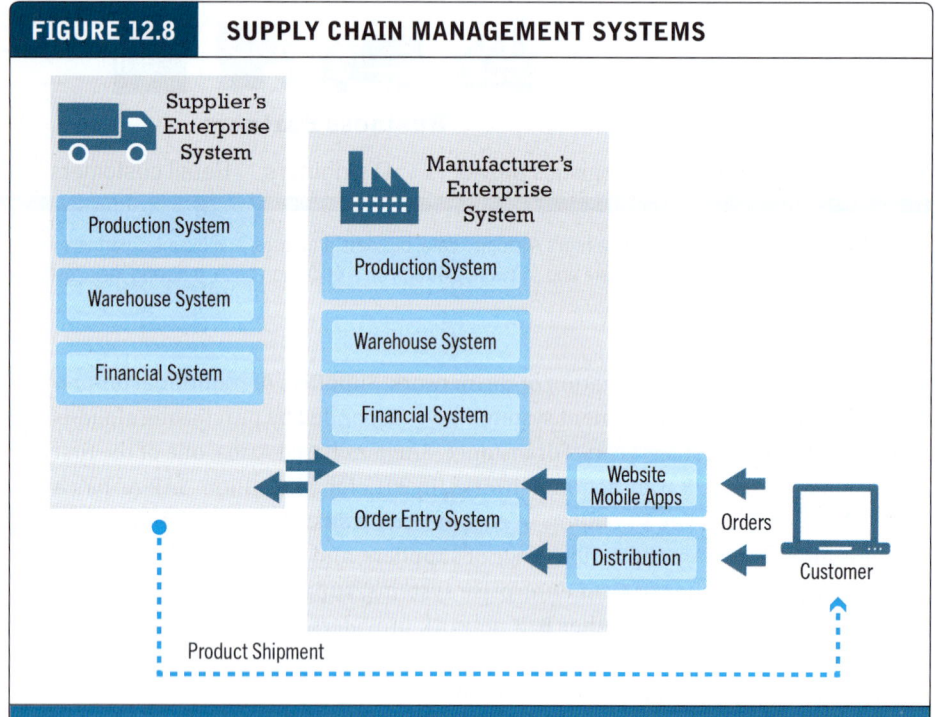

FIGURE 12.8 SUPPLY CHAIN MANAGEMENT SYSTEMS

SCM systems coordinate the activities of suppliers, shippers, and order entry systems to automate order entry through production, payment, and shipping business processes. Increasingly customers, as well as employees working throughout the supply chain, are using smartphones, tablets, and mobile apps to place and coordinate orders.

100 countries every second! In a year, HP ships 52 million computers. Its supply chain needs to operate 24/7 to coordinate a network of factories, hundreds of suppliers, and distribution and logistics partner firms. To cope with one of the most complex supply chains in the world, HP developed a web-based, order-driven supply chain management system that begins with either a customer placing an order online or the receipt of an order from a dealer. The order is forwarded from the order entry system to HP's production and delivery system. From there, the order is routed to one of several HP contractor supplier firms. The supplier's system then verifies the order with HP and validates the ordered configuration to ensure the PC can be manufactured (e.g., will not have missing parts or fail a design specification set by HP). The order is then forwarded to a production control system that issues a bar-coded production ticket to factory assemblers. Simultaneously, a parts order is forwarded to the supplier's warehouse and inventory management system. A worker assembles the computer, and then the computer is boxed, tagged, and shipped to the customer. The delivery is monitored and tracked by HP's supply chain management system, which links directly to one of several overnight delivery systems. The elapsed time from order entry to shipping is 48 hours. With this system, HP has eliminated the need to hold PCs in inventory, reduced cycle time from one week to less than 48 hours, and reduced errors. HP has extended this system to become a global B2B order tracking, reporting, and support system for HP B2B customers (HP Inc., 2019; Wadlow, 2018).

It isn't just huge technology companies that use supply chain software. There's nothing quite so perishable as fashionable underwear given the rate of fashion change. Under Armour, a leading performance athletic brand, first implemented an enterprise resource planning system in 2005, when it was a $250 million domestic wholesale apparel company. By 2015, it had grown to a $4 billion global omni-channel retail company, which was often missing sales because it did not produce enough popular items or over-produced items that were not selling well. To deal with this issue, Under Armour decided to replatform the entire company with software from SAP to predict sales, plan inventory, and coordinate suppliers (Heller, 2019; Loten and Germano, 2017).

BLOCKCHAIN AND SUPPLY CHAIN MANAGEMENT

Blockchain hardware and software promises to bring about a transformation in supply chain management. In the process, it is expected to replace the now 60-year old EDI with a near zero-cost alternative. In 2019, firms were expected to spend $2.7 billion on blockchain hardware, software, and services, an increase of over 80% from 2018 (IDC, 2019). As discussed in Chapter 5, blockchain is a transaction database that operates on a distributed P2P network that connects all the participant members in a single database that is highly secure, reliable, resilient, and inexpensive. A blockchain ledger enables all parties to a transaction to add blocks of information to the shared ledger after a validation algorithm approves the transaction. If the parties to a transaction agree it is valid, then it is added to the chain of blocks pertaining to the transaction. The identities of the originators of the transaction are digitally encrypted, and the transaction itself is encrypted, cannot be changed, and is always up-to-date and available to all parties in near real time.

Blockchain solves a number of problems with current transaction databases that firms use to keep track of orders, payments, shipment, customs requirements, and visibility into the supply chain. Currently, firms that are a party to a transaction have their own separate transaction systems which can frequently be out of sync and do not communication with one another. For instance, a mango grown in Mexico and bound for a Whole Foods' distribution center involves the grower, a Mexican trucking company, customs officials, a warehouse in the United States, and ultimately a U.S. trucking company to deliver the goods to retail outlets, as well as a retail inventory system and a shelf management system that tracks where the mango is placed in the store. Each of the firms involved in this supply chain have separate transaction processing systems. Innumberable documents are created in the process. Tracing a shipment of mangos through this maze of systems is extremely difficult, inefficient, unreliable, and costly. EDI transactions currently cost $5 to $7 each.

Blockchain offers a simpler solution to this complex traditional system by creating a single database and a single instance of all the information needed to track the movement of mangos through the supply chain. Blockchain also offers the ability of all the parties involved in a transaction to access all this information in what is called a "master ledger" that solves the visibility problem that plagues traditional supply chains (Mearian, 2018).

While the technology for blockchain is widely available, implementing blockchain supply chains is in its infancy, but growing rapidly. Financial institutions are planning to use it to track home deeds and mortgages; the music industry is planning to track songs from writers, to producers and record companies, to their play by streaming services. Shipping companies are testing blockchain for keeping track of containers, while pharmaceutical companies are exploring the use of blockchain in the drug supply chain (Norton, 2018). The *Insight on Technology* case illustrates how several firms in the food supply industry are using blockchain today.

COLLABORATIVE COMMERCE

collaborative commerce

the use of digital technologies to permit organizations to collaboratively design, develop, build, and manage products through their life cycles

Collaborative commerce is a direct extension of supply chain management systems, as well as supply chain simplification. **Collaborative commerce** is defined as the use of digital technologies to permit firms to collaboratively design, develop, build, market, and manage products through their life cycles. This is a much broader mission than EDI or simply managing the flow of information among organizations. Collaborative commerce involves a definitive move from a transaction focus to a relationship focus among the supply chain participants. Rather than having an arm's-length adversarial relationship with suppliers, collaborative commerce fosters sharing of sensitive internal information with suppliers and purchasers. Managing collaborative commerce requires knowing exactly what information to share with whom. Collaborative commerce extends beyond supply chain management activities to include the collaborative development of new products and services by multiple cooperating firms.

A good example of collaborative commerce is the long-term effort of Procter & Gamble (P&G), the world's largest manufacturer of personal and health care products, from Crest toothpaste to Tide soap, to work with suppliers and even customers to develop 50% of its product line over time. In the past, for instance, P&G would design a bottle or product package in-house, and then turn to over 100 suppliers of packaging to find out what it would cost and try to bargain that down. Using SAP Ariba's procurement network, P&G asks its suppliers to come up with innovative ideas for packaging and pricing. Taking it a step further, P&G's website, Pgconnectdevelop.com, solicits new product ideas from

INSIGHT ON TECHNOLOGY

BLOCKCHAIN IMPROVES THE FOOD SUPPLY INDUSTRY

On January 15, 2013, a news report in the Irish Independent revealed that horse meat had been found in food products sold by five different supermarket chains. The scandal quickly spread across Europe, with several companies in the food supply industry being implicated. In London, three men were charged with fraudulently selling horsemeat as though it were other meat meant for human consumption.

Food scandals are nothing new. In 2013, China's Ministry of Public Security announced its findings that the meat of rats, foxes, and mink was being sold as lamb, a practice that may have begun in 2009. Furthermore, back in 1900, 6,000 people were poisoned in Manchester after drinks were contaminated by arsenic in an attempt to cut production costs.

One of the critical issues for the food supply chain is ensuring that there is no contamination and that products are exactly what they claim to be. In addition, it is essential for the sector to know precisely where food items originated and what route they took to the consumer. Should health issues arise, tracing the item back through the supply chain means that interventions can take place to prevent subsequent problems and reduce health risks. However, this is more complex than it seems. Food supply is a complex, global business with many production processes undertaken in a variety of settings before the food reaches our table.

Blockchain is widely being recognized as a secure means of ensuring the integrity of the food supply chain. One of the companies that has been leading the use of this technology is the Vietnamese–Hungarian joint venture company TE-Food. The company was founded in 2015 and quickly established itself as leader in this field. It is now working with 6,000 companies in the food production sector and deals with 400,000 transactions every day that use blockchain technology to provide verifiable information about each step in the food production process.

Through blockchain, problems that may arise in food production can be tracked down more easily. Knowing where an animal was grazing, for instance, could be a valuable clue for identifying the source of contamination. Similarly, establishing which factory packed certain foodstuffs can help determine levels of food security. Blockchain allows TE-Foods to give access to such information to everyone in the supply chain. Indeed, the company has even released a consumer app that allows supermarket purchasers to scan the barcodes on food items and see all of the verified information about the product, such as the specific animal profile from which the product was derived, what the animal was fed, what vaccinations it had, and how it was transported.

TE-Food started offering food supply chain traceability with meat production at the end of 2016, and this was quickly followed by chicken and egg production. One issue in ensuring that everything was recorded accurately was people: the initial rollout of the company's traceability technology solely in Vietnam required the training of 10,000 workers in the food production sector.

It was at the start of 2018 that the company introduced blockchain into their traceability system. The TE-Food solution requires everyone in the supply chain to have an electronic license token based on the Ethereum blockchain system. Once each element of the food production supply

(continued)

chain has an appropriate license token, every transaction is recorded within the system as it takes place. This provides completely verified information about what occurred at each stage in the supply chain. Should any point in the food supply chain provide data that is not agreed to by all the other nodes in the network, it is not verified, and the company is alerted to a potential problem. In addition, unlike in other traceability systems, the TE-Food system's use of established Ethereum blockchain technology means that no data can be edited or altered once it is agreed upon by all nodes and recorded. This eliminates the scope for fraudulently covering up past mistakes or errors in the food supply chain. This type of system is valuable in several situations besides human health; for example, establishing that food is halal is an important requirement for many Muslims. Furthermore, blockchain food supply monitoring can also help to highlight important ethical issues, such as the use of child labor in the production process.

Of course, TE-Food is not the only player providing blockchain assurance in the food supply chain sector. IBM has its own methodology, which is based on a collaborative blockchain system run by The Linux Foundation and its partners, including IBM and Microsoft. The project provides blockchain for enterprises who may be put off by more open systems like Ethereum; there have been discussions among the financial community, for instance, that the economic model used by Ethereum may not provide long-term sustainability.

Walmart initially used IBM's blockchain system to trace sliced mangoes, which can deteriorate quickly due to a variety of factors. Walmart has since extended its use of IBM's blockchain system to meat production as well as salad foods. Having a multitude of suppliers as well as large numbers of businesses in the supply chain adds a much higher level of complexity for supermarkets. Though blockchain does appear to provide a technical solution to food supply traceability, several logistical hurdles remain. To begin with, every participant in the food supply chain, from individual farmers right through to large corporations, must use the appropriate token technology, or the blockchain is broken and rendered worthless. Walmart has started to alert its suppliers to the need to be "blockchain ready" and has given them deadlines for particular food items.

The potential for blockchain to benefit the food supply industry is demonstrated by the rapid rise in companies entering this arena. TE-Foods went from nothing to 6,000 companies signing up to use their technology within little more than a year. Major food traceability firms who have been working with older technology in this sector are now starting to use blockchain. One such example is FoodLogiQ, which was established in 2006 and is now using blockchain in its work with the fast-food company Subway. Chinese companies such as Alibaba and JD are also using blockchain in their food supply chain. TE-Foods may have been one of the pioneers in the use of blockchain in food supply, but it is clear that this is going to become a highly competitive and increasingly important sector.

▬ **SOURCES:** "About IBM Food Trust," Ibm.com, 2019; "TE-Food (TFD): Food Traceability on the Blockchain," Gem Report, Cryptogems.com, June 13, 2019; "TE-FOOD, Islah Venture, and PIHH Enter into a Tripartite Partnership to Build the First Halal Food Blockchain Hub," Medium.com, April 5, 2019; "Research: Ethereum's New Economic Model Not 'Lucrative Enough' to Keep It Secure," by David Canellis, Thenextweb.com, March 7, 2019; "The 1900 Arsenic Poisoning Epidemic," by Peter Dyer, *Journal of the Brewery History Society*, Brewery History Number 130; "The Challenges of Tracking the Food Supply Chain," by Izza PS, Medium.com, November 13, 2018; "Walmart Is Betting on the Blockchain to Improve Food Safety," by Ron Miller, Techcrunch.com, September 25, 2018; "Food Traceability on Blockchain: Walmart's Pork and Mango Pilots with IBM," *The Journal of the British Blockchain Association* Vol. 1, No. 1 (2018); "Three Men Charged over UK Horsemeat Scandal," Theguardian.com, August 26, 2016; "Rodents Sold as Lamb in Shanghai," by Chen Xiaoru, Globaltimes.cn, May 5, 2013; "Horse and Pig DNA Found in Some Supermarket Burgers," by Ed Carty, Independent.ie, January 15, 2013.

Case contributed by Graham Jones, University of Buckingham.

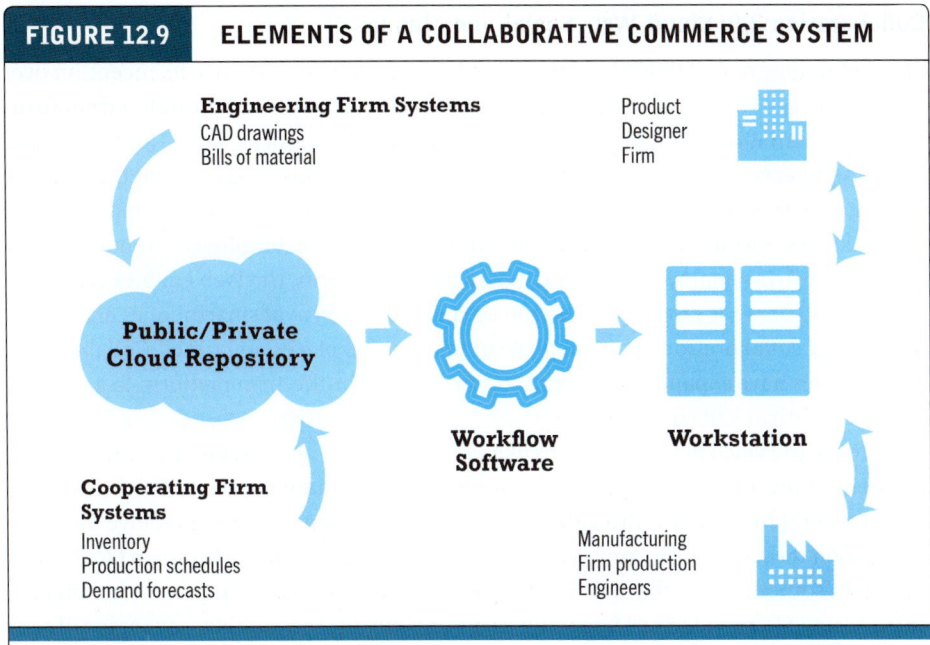

FIGURE 12.9 ELEMENTS OF A COLLABORATIVE COMMERCE SYSTEM

A collaborative commerce application includes a cloud repository where employees at several different firms can store engineering drawings and other documents. Workflow software determines who can see this data and what rules will apply for displaying the data on individual workstations.

suppliers and customers. Over 50% of P&G's new products originate with substantial input from its suppliers and customers. P&G is also collaborating with its biggest online customer, Amazon, by co-locating their operations. P&G sets aside warehouse space for P&G products purchased by Amazon customers. Amazon ships the products to its customers directly from the P&G warehouses rather than shipping them first to Amazon warehouses, and then to the consumer. This collaboration results in Amazon reducing its costs of shipping and storing goods, becoming more competitive on price compared to Walmart and Costco, and reducing the time it takes to arrive at consumers' homes. For P&G, collaboration means savings on transportation costs incurred trucking products to Amazon warehouses, and Amazon's help in boosting online sales of P&G products. Other well-known companies using collaboration to develop and deliver products include Harley Davidson, Starbucks, and GE's Ecomagination program (Hitachi Consulting, 2017; Bowman, 2017; GE Sustainability, 2018).

Although collaborative commerce can involve customers as well as suppliers in the development of products, for the most part, it is concerned with the development of a rich communications environment to enable inter-firm sharing of designs, production plans, inventory levels, delivery schedules, and the development of shared products (see **Figure 12.9**).

Collaborative commerce is very different from EDI, which is a technology for structured communications among firms. Collaborative commerce is more like an interactive teleconference among members of the supply chain. EDI and collaborative commerce share one characteristic: they are not open, competitive marketplaces, but instead are, technically, private industrial networks that connect strategic partners in a supply chain.

Collaboration 2.0: Cloud, Web, Social, and Mobile

The technology of collaborative commerce has changed greatly since its inception over thirty years ago with tools like Lotus Notes, which was used almost entirely within firms to establish an environment where employees could share ideas, notes, and ideas, and work on projects together. What's new about collaboration tools today is that the software and data are stored on cloud servers where it is less expensive, and easy to update; social networks like Facebook and Twitter are commonly used by employees in many firms, while other firms deploy their own social network platform; the Web enables very inexpensive collaborative environments; and the mobile platform of smartphones and tablets means that collaboration can take place in many more places and times. Collaboration technologies have expanded collaboration from a within-the-firm platform to a primary tool of inter-firm B2B collaboration.

Broadband video network systems like Cisco's TelePresence also play a role in enabling frequent, long-distance, collaboration among supply chain partners. TelePresence is one of several high-bandwidth video systems from different vendors that give users the impression they are sharing physical space with other participants who are in fact located remotely, sometimes on the other side of the globe (Cisco Systems, Inc. and Vital Images, 2016). Using Skype video conferencing, even tiny businesses can take advantage of very inexpensive collaborative platforms over the Web or mobile platforms.

In Section 12.5, we discuss collaborative commerce in greater depth as a technology that enables private industrial networks.

SOCIAL NETWORKS AND B2B: THE EXTENDED SOCIAL ENTERPRISE

It's a short step from collaboration with vendors, suppliers, and customers, to a more personal relationship based on conversations with participants in the supply chain using social networks—both private and public. Here, the conversations and sharing of ideas are more unstructured, situational, and personal. Procurement officers, managers of supply chains, and logistics managers are people too, and they participate in the same social network culture provided by LinkedIn, Facebook, Twitter, Instagram, and a host of other public social networks as we all do. Being able to respond to fast moving developments that affect supply chains requires something more than a website, e-mail, or telephone calls. Social networks can provide the intimate connections among customers, suppliers, and logistics partners that are needed to keep the supply chain functioning, and to make decisions based on current conditions.

Participants in the supply chain network are tapping into their tablet computers, smartphones, and social network sites for purchasing, scheduling, exception handling, and deciding with their B2B customers and suppliers. In many cases, supply chain social networks are private—owned by the largest firm in the supply chain network. In other cases, firms develop Facebook pages to organize conversations among supply chain network members.

Social networks are beginning to be common tools for managers engaged in B2B e-commerce. Public social network sites like LinkedIn, Facebook, and Twitter can be excellent for coordinating the flow of information among business partners through the supply chain. Cisco is using its website, Twitter, and Facebook to run new product campaigns for its business customers using social networks exclusively. Dell, like many businesses, uses its YouTube channel to engage suppliers and customers in conversations about existing products, and ideas for new products (eMarketer, Inc., 2019b, 2017b; Cargill, 2015).

B2B MARKETING

Despite the size of B2B e-commerce, spending on B2B digital marketing and advertising (around $6 billion in 2019) still accounted for only about 4.5% of the total amount spent on digital marketing and advertising. However, the amount of spending is growing at almost 20% annually and has doubled in the last five years. About 60% of B2B ad spending is aimed at desktops, and 40% at mobile devices. The amount spent on mobile B2B advertising is growing at over 25% annually (eMarketer, Inc., 2019b). B2B firms are increasingly going digital and mobile.

Nevertheless, B2B digital marketing and advertising clearly has not grown nearly as fast as its B2C counterpart, partly due to the slow pace of technological change in supply chain and procurement management but mostly because the B2B marketplace is fundamentally different from the B2C marketplace. In B2C marketing, firms aim at a large mass audience in the millions (one-to-many) with comparatively simple products with relatively low value, whereas many B2B firm sell low volumes of very valuable and complex products to a much small number of purchasers (one-to-one, or one to a few). In these B2B markets, face-to-face traditional salesforce marketing continues to play a large role. In addition, commercial relationships in the B2B space often involve large purchases and relationships that can span several years or longer. The sellers and buyers may have known about each other for years, even decades; the capabilities and financial situation of the firms are known. Both parties share an understanding of the price and quality of what is being exchanged in the market. In these situations, B2C retail marketing tactics are not appropriate. Instead, interpersonal relationships, networking, brand, and informative content marketing using white papers, videos, podcasts, webinars, blogs, e-books, conferences, and professional associations are the primary and most effective marketing tools. Content marketing refers to using informative media to promote sales rather than advertising the availability and price typical of display and search advertising in B2C markets (see Chapter 6). E-mail and social media play a role in content marketing by making potential customers aware of new content. A recent survey reported that almost 90% of B2B marketers use content marketing, almost 80% use e-mail marketing, almost 70% use social media as a way to reach and acquire customers. LinkedIn is the most common social network used for B2B marketing (eMarketer, Inc., 2019b, 2019c).

However, in spot purchase markets for MRO or other commodity products, B2B marketing uses many of the same marketing tactics and tools found in B2C marketing: display ads, search engine marketing, websites, social network channels, videos, and mobile ads.

B2B firms are increasingly using multiple digital channels to connect with and service their customers. A survey by eMarketer found that over 50% of B2B companies had their own website, 33% used a distributor website, 32% had a social media presence, 31% had a mobile app, 29% used e-mail marketing with buy buttons, and 23% used a B2B marketplace. Traditional tools like mail order and fax now only play a minimal role (eMarketer, Inc., 2017c).

Mobile apps are growing in importance but are not as central as they are for B2C marketing, in part because the small screen is not a good environment to describe complex products, and B2B purchasers, while they may be spending 3 hours a day or more on their mobile devices, are mostly engaged in socializing and consuming, not B2B activities.

Nevertheless, the use of mobile advertising in B2B marketing has grown as mobile devices play a larger role in workplaces and social life, especially among Millennials. According to an eMarketer report, 90% of B2B marketers surveyed used at least some mobile marketing technologies, with over 70% characterizing their usage as either advanced or intermediate. Mobile-friendly websites and apps have become important priorities for B2B marketers. However, while mobile B2B marketing is growing, it still consumes only about 37% of B2B digital marketing budgets (eMarketer, Inc., 2019b; 2017a).

Other trends in B2B marketing include sales enablement systems, the use of predictive analytics, and personalized marketing techniques. Sales enablement systems keep track of leads developed from websites, e-mail, and mobile apps, and help the salesforce track these prospective customers through the point of purchase. Predictive analytics help B2B marketers estimate the lifetime value of leads based on past marketing data. A recent survey of B2B marketers found that almost 95% were using web analytics, almost 85% were using CRM systems, and over 70% were using content management systems to improve their marketing effectiveness, enabling them to better know and understand their target customers, and provide more accurate and precise personalization (eMarketer, Inc., 2019b, 2019c).

12.4 NET MARKETPLACES: THE SELLING SIDE OF B2B

One of the most compelling visions of B2B e-commerce is that of an online marketplace that would bring thousands of fragmented suppliers into contact with hundreds of major purchasers of industrial goods for the purpose of conducting frictionless commerce. The hope was that these suppliers would compete with one another on price, transactions would be automated and low cost, and as a result, the price of industrial supplies would fall. By extracting fees from buyers and sellers on each transaction, third-party intermediary market makers could earn significant revenues. We refer to these online markets as Net marketplaces. Net marketplaces are sell-side digital environments that bring suppliers and buyers together. These Net marketplaces could scale easily as volume increased by simply adding more computers and communications equipment.

In pursuit of this vision, well over 1,500 Net marketplaces sprang up in the early days of e-commerce. Unfortunately, many of them have since disappeared but some still survive, and they are joined by other types of Net marketplaces—some private and some public—based on different assumptions and business models that are quite successful.

CHARACTERISTICS OF NET MARKETPLACES

There is a confusing variety of Net marketplaces today, and several different ways to classify them. For instance, some classify Net marketplaces on the basis of their pricing mechanisms—fixed prices or more dynamic pricing, such as negotiation, auction, or bid/ask—while others classify markets based on characteristics of the markets they serve (vertical versus horizontal, or sell-side versus buy-side), or ownership-independent third-party intermediaries (which is most common) or industry-owned consortia. Although the primary benefits and biases of Net marketplaces have to be determined on a case-by-case

TABLE 12.3 — CHARACTERISTICS OF NET MARKETPLACES: A B2B VOCABULARY

CHARACTERISTIC	MEANING
Bias	Sell-side vs. buy-side vs. neutral. Whose interests are advantaged: buyers, sellers, or no bias?
Ownership	Industry vs. third party. Who owns the marketplace?
Pricing mechanism	Fixed-price catalogs, auctions, bid/ask, and RFPs/RFQs.
Scope/Focus	Horizontal vs. vertical markets.
Value creation	What benefits do they offer customers or suppliers?
Access to market	In public markets, any firm can enter, but in private markets, entry is by invitation only.

basis depending on ownership and pricing mechanisms, it is often the case that Net marketplaces are biased against suppliers because they can force suppliers to reveal their prices and terms to other suppliers in the marketplace. **Table 12.3** describes some of the important characteristics of Net marketplaces.

TYPES OF NET MARKETPLACES

Although each of these distinctions helps describe the phenomenon of Net marketplaces, they do not focus on the central business functionality provided, nor are they capable by themselves of describing the variety of Net marketplaces.

In **Figure 12.10**, we present a classification of Net marketplaces that focuses on their business functionality; that is, what these Net marketplaces provide for businesses seeking solutions. We use two dimensions of Net marketplaces to create a four-cell classification table. We differentiate Net marketplaces as providing either indirect goods (goods used to support production) or direct goods (goods used in production), and we distinguish markets as providing either contractual purchasing (where purchases take place over many years according to a contract between the firm and its vendor) or spot purchasing (where purchases are episodic and anonymous—vendors and buyers do not have an ongoing relationship and may not know one another). The intersection of these dimensions produces four main types of Net marketplaces that are relatively straightforward: e-distributors, e-procurement networks, exchanges, and industry consortia. Note, however, that in the real world, some Net marketplaces can be found in multiple parts of this figure as business models change and opportunities appear and disappear. Nevertheless, the discussion of "pure types" of Net marketplaces is a useful starting point.

Each of these Net marketplaces seeks to provide value to customers in different ways. We discuss each type of Net marketplace in more detail in the following sections.

E-distributors

E-distributors are the most common and most easily understood type of Net marketplace. An **e-distributor** provides an online catalog that represents the products of thousands of direct

e-distributor
provides an online catalog that represents the products of thousands of direct manufacturers

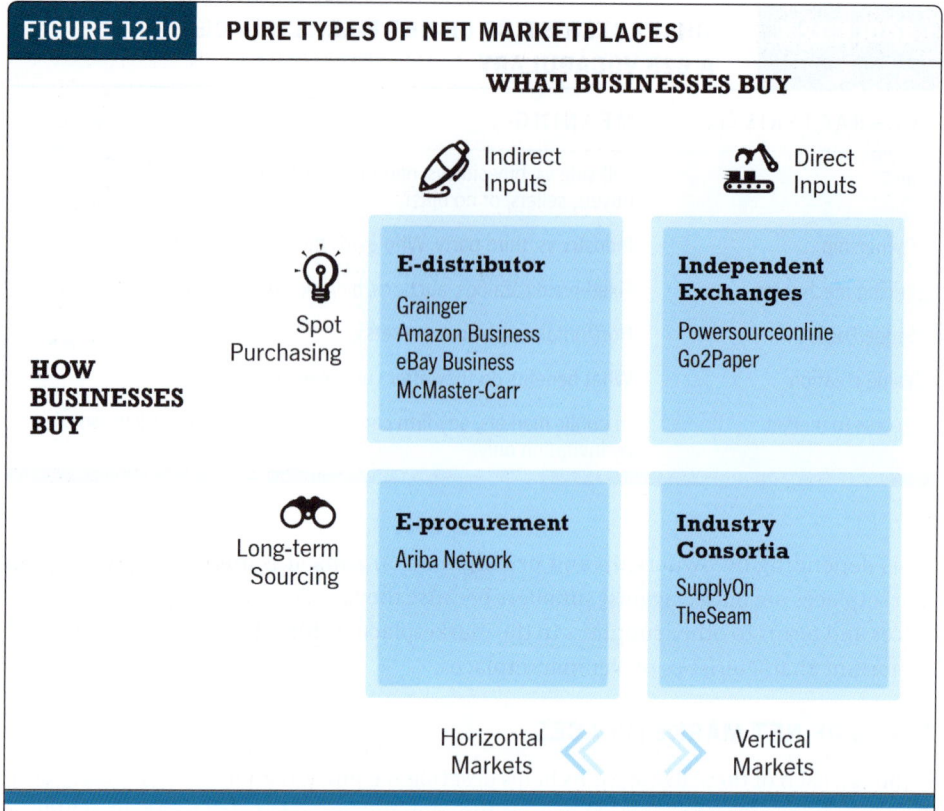

FIGURE 12.10 PURE TYPES OF NET MARKETPLACES

There are four main types of Net marketplaces based on the intersection of two dimensions: how businesses buy and what they buy. A third dimension—horizontal versus vertical markets—also distinguishes the different types of Net marketplaces.

manufacturers (see **Figure 12.11**). E-distributors are independently owned intermediaries that offer industrial customers a single source from which to order indirect goods (often referred to as MRO) on a spot, as-needed basis. A significant percentage of corporate purchases cannot be satisfied under a company's existing contracts, and must be purchased on a spot basis. E-distributors make money by charging a markup on products they distribute.

Organizations and firms in all industries require MRO supplies. The MRO function maintains, repairs, and operates commercial buildings and maintains all the machinery of these buildings from heating, ventilating, and air conditioning systems to lighting fixtures.

E-distributors operate in horizontal markets because they serve many different industries with products from many different suppliers. E-distributors usually operate public markets in the sense that any firm can order from the catalog, as opposed to private markets, where membership is restricted to selected firms.

E-distributor prices are usually fixed, but large customers receive discounts and other incentives to purchase, such as credit, reporting on account activity, and limited forms of business purchasing rules (for instance, no purchases greater than $500 for a single

FIGURE 12.11 E-DISTRIBUTORS

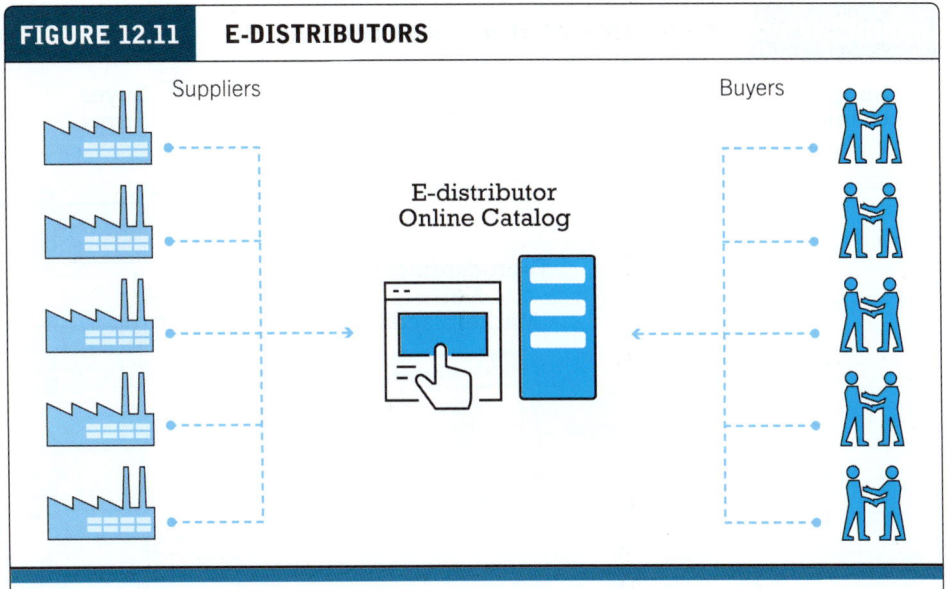

E-distributors are firms that bring the products of thousands of suppliers into a single online catalog for sale to thousands of buyer firms. E-distributors are sometimes referred to as one-to-many markets, one seller serving many firms.

item without a purchase order). The primary benefits offered to industrial customers are lower search costs, lower transaction costs, wide selection, rapid delivery, and low prices.

W.W. Grainger is one of the most frequently cited examples of an e-distributor. Grainger is involved in long-term systematic sourcing as well as spot sourcing, but its emphasis is on spot sourcing. Grainger is the largest distributor of maintenance, repair, and operations (MRO) supplies in the United States and also operates in Canada, Mexico, the United Kingdom, 11 countries in Europe, and Asia. Its revenue model is that of a typical retailer: it owns the products and takes a markup on the products it sells to customers. Grainger's website and mobile apps provide users with a digital version of Grainger's famous seven-pound catalog, plus other parts not available in the catalog (adding up to around 1.7 million parts), as well as a complete ordering and payment system. In 2018, Grainger recorded $6.9 billion in e-commerce revenues (62% of its total sales (Grainger, 2019). McMaster-Carr, a New Jersey-based industrial parts mecca for machinists and manufacturers around the world, is a similar e-distributor. NeweggBusiness is another example of an e-distributor, focused on IT and office products. Amazon entered the B2B distributor market with AmazonSupply, aiming to leverage its global B2C fulfillment infrastructure into the B2B arena, and in 2015, rebranded it as Amazon Business. Amazon Business primarily engages in spot sales of business products and provides a trading platform for multiple sellers. eBay entered the B2B e-distributors fray in 2016.

E-procurement

An **e-procurement Net marketplace** is an independently owned intermediary that connects hundreds of online suppliers offering millions of maintenance and repair parts to

e-procurement Net marketplace
independently owned intermediary that connects hundreds of online suppliers offering millions of maintenance and repair parts to business firms who pay fees to join the market

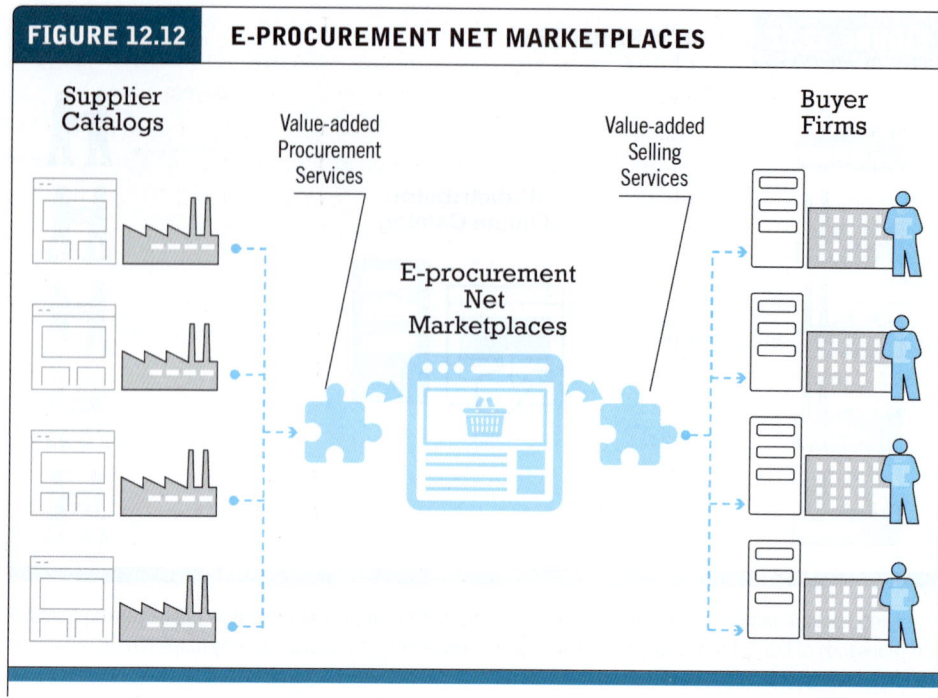

FIGURE 12.12 E-PROCUREMENT NET MARKETPLACES

E-procurement Net marketplaces aggregate hundreds of catalogs in a single marketplace and make them available to firms, often on a custom basis that reflects only the suppliers desired by the participating firms.

business firms who pay fees to join the market (see **Figure 12.12**). E-procurement Net marketplaces are typically used for long-term contractual purchasing of indirect goods (MRO); they create online horizontal markets, but they also provide for members' spot sourcing of MRO supplies. E-procurement companies make money by charging a percentage of each transaction, licensing consulting services and software, and assessing network use fees.

E-procurement companies expand on the business model of simpler e-distributors by including the online catalogs of hundreds of suppliers and offering value chain management services to both buyers and sellers. **Value chain management (VCM) services** provided by e-procurement companies include automation of a firm's entire procurement process on the buyer side and automation of the selling business processes on the seller side. For purchasers, e-procurement companies automate purchase orders, requisitions, sourcing, business rules enforcement, invoicing, and payment. For suppliers, e-procurement companies provide catalog creation and content management, order management, fulfillment, invoicing, shipment, and settlement.

E-procurement Net marketplaces are sometimes referred to as many-to-many markets. They are mediated by an independent third party that purports to represent both buyers and sellers, and hence claim to be neutral. On the other hand, because they may include the catalogs of both competing suppliers and competing e-distributors, they likely have a bias in favor of the buyers. Nevertheless, by aggregating huge buyer firms into their networks, they provide distinct marketing benefits for suppliers and reduce customer acquisition costs.

value chain management (VCM) services
include automation of a firm's entire procurement process on the buyer side and automation of the selling business processes on the seller side

Ariba stands out as one of the poster children of the B2B age, a firm born before its time. Promising to revolutionize inter-firm trade, Ariba started out in 1996 hoping to build a global business network linking buyers and sellers—sort of an eBay for business. With little revenue, the stock shot past $1,000 a share by 2000. But sellers and buyers did not join the network in large part because they did not understand the opportunity, were too wedded to their traditional procurement processes, and did not trust outsiders to control their purchasing and vendor relationship. In 2001, Ariba's share price tanked to $2.20. Ariba survived largely by selling software that helped large firms understand their procurement processes and costs. Finally, by 2008, large and small firms had become more sophisticated in their purchasing and supply change management practices, and Ariba's original idea of a global network of suppliers and purchasers of a wide variety of industrial goods came back to life. In 2012, SAP, the largest enterprise software firm, purchased Ariba for $4.3 billion in an effort to strengthen its B2B e-commerce suite. Today, SAP Ariba is a leading provider of collaborative business commerce solutions that includes an e-procurement Net marketplace called the Ariba Network, with more than 4.6 million connected companies in 190 countries and over $3 trillion in B2B e-commerce transactions annually (SAP Ariba, 2019). Other players in this market segment include Perfect Commerce, BravoSolution, A.T. Kearney Procurement & Analytic Solutions, and IBM Emptoris Sourcing.

Exchanges

An **exchange** is an independently owned online marketplace that connects hundreds to potentially thousands of suppliers and buyers in a dynamic, real-time environment (see **Figure 12.13**). Although there are exceptions, exchanges generally create vertical markets

exchange
independently owned online marketplace that connects hundreds to potentially thousands of suppliers and buyers in a dynamic, real-time environment

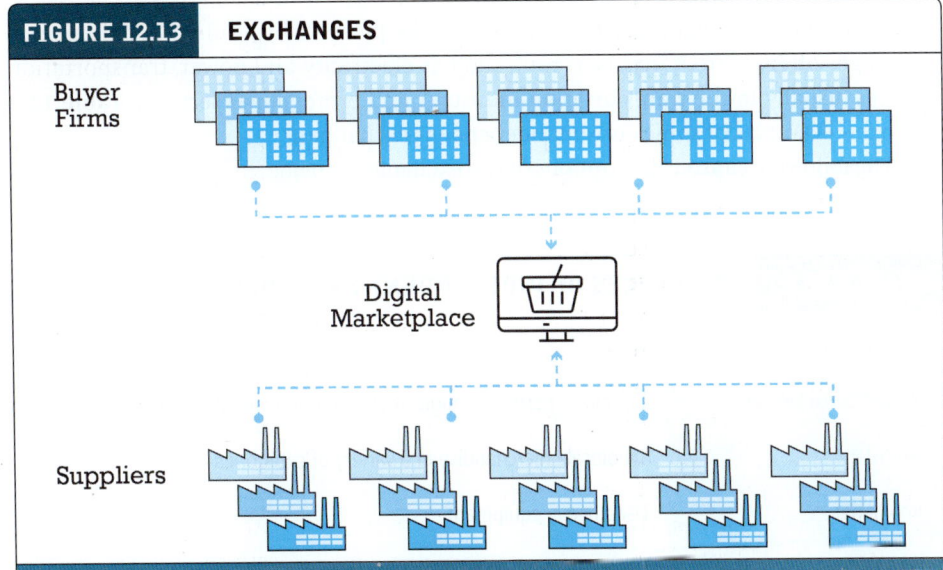

Independent exchanges bring potentially thousands of suppliers to a vertical (industry-specific) marketplace to sell their goods to potentially thousands of buyer firms. Exchanges are sometimes referred to as many-to-many markets because they have many suppliers serving many buyer firms.

that focus on the spot-purchasing requirements of large firms in a single industry, such as computers and telecommunications, electronics, food, and industrial equipment. Exchanges were the prototype Internet-based marketplace in the early days of e-commerce; as noted previously, over 1,500 were created in this period, but most have failed.

Exchanges make money by charging a commission on the transaction. The pricing model can be through an online negotiation, auction, RFQ, or fixed buy-and-sell prices. The benefits offered to customers of exchanges include reduced search cost for parts and spare capacity. Other benefits include lower prices created by a global marketplace driven by competition among suppliers who would, presumably, sell goods at very low profit margins at one world-market price. The benefits offered suppliers are access to a global purchasing environment and the opportunity to unload production overruns (although at very competitive prices and low profit margins). Even though they are private intermediaries, exchanges are public in the sense of permitting any bona fide buyer or seller to participate.

Exchanges tend to be biased toward the buyer even though they are independently owned and presumably neutral. Suppliers are disadvantaged by the fact that exchanges put them in direct price competition with other similar suppliers around the globe, driving profit margins down. Exchanges have failed in the past primarily because suppliers have refused to join them, and hence, the existing markets have very low liquidity, defeating the very purpose and benefits of an exchange. **Liquidity** is typically measured by the number of buyers and sellers in a market, the volume of transactions, and the size of transactions. You know a market is liquid when you can buy or sell just about any size order at just about any time you want. On all of these measures, many exchanges failed, resulting in a very small number of participants, few trades, and small trade value per transaction. The most common reason for not using exchanges is the absence of traditional, trusted suppliers.

While most exchanges tend to be vertical marketplaces offering direct supplies, some exchanges offer indirect inputs as well, such as electricity and power, transportation services (usually to the transportation industry), and professional services. **Table 12.4** lists a few examples of some current independent exchanges.

The following capsule descriptions of two exchanges provide insight into their origins and current functions.

liquidity

typically measured by the number of buyers and sellers in a market, the volume of transactions, and the size of transactions

TABLE 12.4	EXAMPLES OF INDEPENDENT EXCHANGES
EXCHANGE	FOCUS
PowerSource Online	Computer parts exchange, new and used computer equipment
NuOrder	Wholesale merchandise in a variety of categories
IronPlanet	Used heavy equipment
EquipNet	Used industrial equipment and online auctions
Molbase	Marketplace for chemical compounds and custom chemicals

Inventory Locator Service (ILS) has its roots as an offline intermediary, serving as a listing service for aftermarket parts in the aerospace industry. Upon opening in 1979, ILS initially provided a telephone- and fax-based directory of aftermarket parts to airplane owners and mechanics, along with government procurement professionals. As early as 1984, ILS incorporated e-mail capabilities as part of its RFQ services, and by 1998, it had begun to conduct online auctions for hard-to-find parts. ILS maintains an Internet-accessible database of over 85 million aerospace and marine industry parts, and has also developed an eRFQ feature that helps users streamline their sourcing processes. The network's 26,000+ subscribers in 93 different countries access the site over 75,000 times a day to search 85 million items in inventory (Inventory Locator Service, 2020).

JOOR is a New York-based digital wholesale exchange that connects 8,600 fashion brands, with over 200,000 retailers in 144 countries in a multi-channel digital trading platform. Founded in 2010 as an online wholesale fashion order-entry site, it has since expanded into a full-service website and app for retailers that displays manufacturer brands, tracks orders, visualizes the assortment of fashions ordered, and coordinates looks for the coming season. Fashions and colors need to be planned by retailers and manufacturers two years in advance of their sale, and making sure the colors and look are appropriate is a difficult task that requires an overview of what has been purchased. JOOR allows retailers to browse fashions by trend and exposes them to a wide range of brands they may not have discovered in the past. JOOR has increased the speed of buying and the quality of the purchaser decisions. In the past, buying agents and fashion planners had to visit manufacturer websites or read fashion journals that could be months behind fast-changing fashions, to discover the latest offerings, and place orders. With JOOR's digital platform, purchasing agents can quickly get a sense of the latest trends in fashion and place orders using a single web platform. For brands and designers, JOOR simplifies marketing efforts with a built-in customer base of retailers. JOOR transacts over $1 billion in gross merchandise volume on its platform every month and handles over 2,300 daily interactions between brands and retailers on the platform (JOOR, 2020; eMarketer, Inc., 2019a; Loeb, 2018; Chernova, 2015).

Industry Consortia

An **industry consortium** is an industry-owned vertical market that enables buyers in the industry to purchase direct inputs (both goods and services) (see **Figure 12.14**). Industry consortia emphasize long-term contractual purchasing, the development of stable relationships (as opposed to merely an anonymous transaction emphasis), and the creation of industry-wide data standards and synchronization efforts. Industry consortia are more focused on optimizing long-term supply relationships than independent exchanges, which tend to focus more on short-term transactions. The ultimate objective of industry consortia is the unification of supply chains within entire industries, across many tiers, through common data definitions, network standards, and computing platforms.

Industry consortia sprang up in part as a reaction to the development of independently owned exchanges, which were viewed by large industries (such as the automotive and chemical industries) as market interlopers that would not directly serve the interests

industry consortium
industry-owned vertical market that enables buyers to purchase direct inputs (both goods and services) from a limited set of invited participants

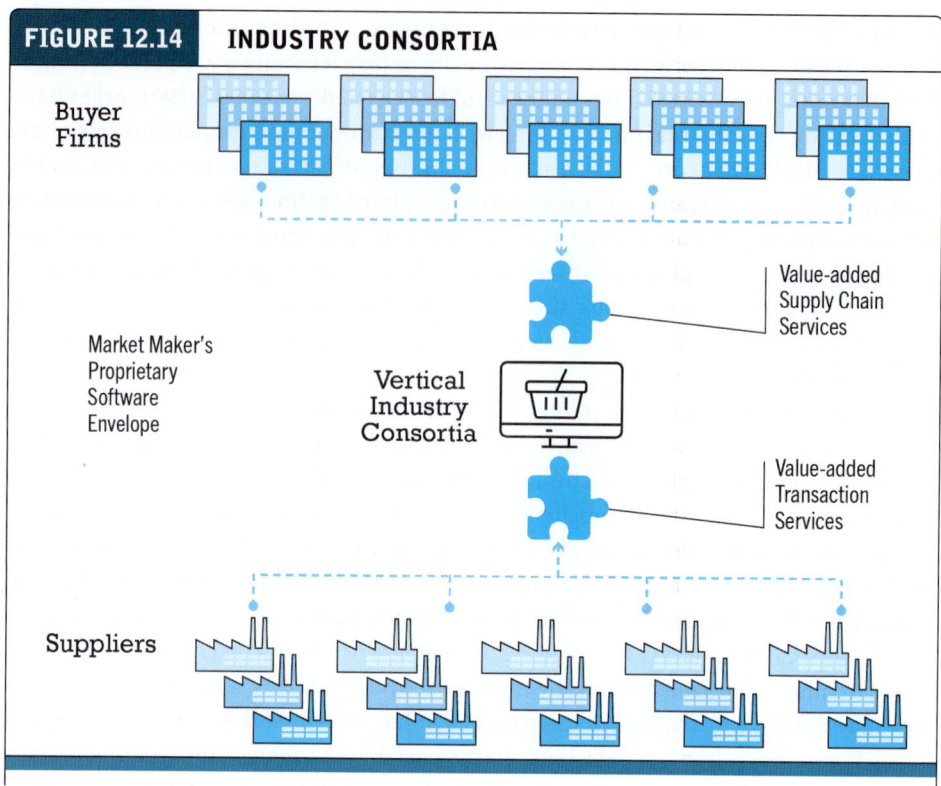

FIGURE 12.14 INDUSTRY CONSORTIA

Industry consortia bring thousands of suppliers into direct contact with a smaller number of very large buyers. The market makers provide value-added software services for procurement, transaction management, shipping, and payment for both buyers and suppliers. Industry consortia are sometimes referred to as many-to-few markets, where many suppliers (albeit selected by the buyers) serve a few very large buyers, mediated by a variety of value-added services.

of large buyers, but would instead line their own pockets and those of their venture capital investors. Rather than "pay-to-play," large firms decided to "pay-to-own" their markets. Another concern of large firms was that Net marketplaces would work only if large suppliers and buyers participated, and only if there was liquidity. Independent exchanges were not attracting enough players to achieve liquidity. In addition, exchanges often failed to provide additional value-added services that would transform the value chain for the entire industry, including linking the new marketplaces to firms' ERP systems.

Industry consortia make money in a number of ways. Industry members usually pay for the creation of the consortia's capabilities and contribute initial operating capital. Then industry consortia charge buyer and seller firms transaction and subscription fees. Industry members—both buyers and sellers—are expected to reap benefits far greater than their contributions through the rationalization of the procurement process, competition among vendors, and closer relationships with vendors.

Industry consortia offer many different pricing mechanisms, ranging from auctions to fixed prices to RFQs, depending on the products and the situation. Prices can also be negotiated, and the environment, while competitive, is nevertheless restricted to a smaller number of buyers—selected, reliable, and long-term suppliers who are often viewed as strategic industry partners. The bias of industry consortia is clearly toward the large buyers who control access to this lucrative market channel and can benefit from competitive pricing offered by alternative suppliers. Benefits to suppliers come from access to large buyer firm procurement systems, long-term stable relationships, and large order sizes.

Industry consortia can force suppliers to use the consortia's networks and proprietary software as a condition of selling to the industry's members. Although exchanges failed for a lack of suppliers and liquidity, the market power of consortia members ensures suppliers will participate, so consortia may be able to avoid the fate of voluntary exchanges. Clearly, industry consortia are at an advantage when compared to independent exchanges because, unlike the venture-capital-backed exchanges, they have deep-pocket financial backing from the very start and guaranteed liquidity based on a steady flow of large firm orders. Yet industry consortia are a relatively new phenomenon, and the long-term profitability of these consortia, especially when several consortia exist for a single industry, has yet to be demonstrated. In fact, the number of firms that can be defined as purely industry consortia has declined since the early 2000s, with many firms broadening their mission to encompass more than one industry, or more commonly, being sold by the original industry founders to private investors. For example, GHX, originally founded in 2000 by companies in the pharmaceutical and medical supply industry, is now owned by a private equity firm. E2open, originally founded by IBM, Seagate, and Hitachi as an industry consortium for companies in the high technology industries, has since become a public company and now provides a cloud-based B2B platform and services for a wide variety of industries.

However, a number of industry consortia do remain. One example is The Seam, which was founded in 2000 by leading global agribusiness companies such as Cargill, Louis Dreyfus, and others. The Seam focused initially on creating a cotton trading exchange, and has since added peanuts, grains, and excess USDA farm commodities. The Seam has handled over $8 billion in transactions since inception, and more than 90% of the cotton buyers in the United States are active participants in its Cotton Trading system. The Seam also has a Peanut Commodity Management Platform and in 2017 processed 1 million tons of farmer stock peanuts through the platform (Agritechtalk.com, 2020). **Table 12.5** lists some additional examples.

TABLE 12.5	INDUSTRY CONSORTIA BY INDUSTRY
INDUSTRY	NAME OF INDUSTRY CONSORTIUM
Agribusiness	The Seam
Automotive	SupplyOn
Chemical	Elemica
Food	Dairy.com
Hospitality	Avendra

12.5 PRIVATE INDUSTRIAL NETWORKS

Private industrial networks are the most prevalent form of B2B e-commerce in terms of transaction volume, and are expected to continue to be so into the foreseeable future. Private industrial networks can be considered the foundation of the extended enterprise, allowing firms to extend their boundaries and their business processes to include supply chain and logistics partners.

As noted at the beginning of this chapter, private industrial networks are direct descendants of existing EDI networks and are closely tied to existing ERP systems used by large firms. Like EDI, private industrial networks are owned by the buyers and are buyer-side solutions with buyer biases, but they offer significant benefits for suppliers as well. Inclusion in the direct supply chain for a major industrial purchasing company can allow a supplier to increase both revenue and margins because the environment is not competitive—only a few suppliers are included in the private industrial network. A private industrial network is a web-enabled network for the coordination of trans-organizational business processes (sometimes also called collaborative commerce). A **trans-organizational business process** requires at least two independent firms to perform (Laudon and Laudon, 2020). For the most part, these networks originate in and closely involve the manufacturing and related support industries, and therefore we refer to them as industrial networks, although in the future they could just as easily apply to some services. Private industrial networks can be viewed as extended enterprises in the sense that they often begin as ERP systems in a single firm, and are then expanded to include the firm's major suppliers. **Figure 12.15** illustrates a private industrial network originally built by Procter & Gamble (P&G) in the United States to coordinate supply chains among its suppliers, distributors, truckers, and retailers.

trans-organizational business process
process that requires at least two independent firms to perform

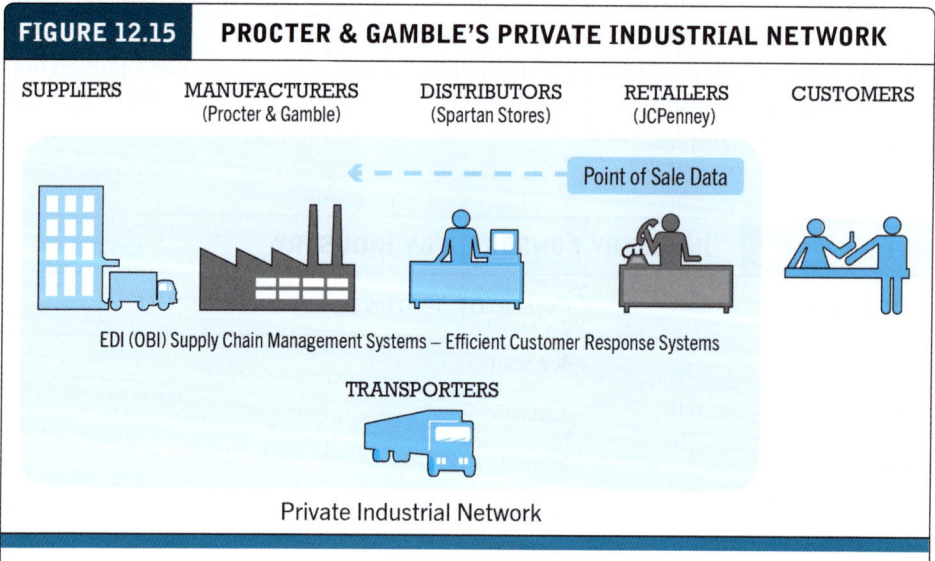

Procter & Gamble's private industrial network attempts to coordinate the trans-organizational business processes of the many firms it deals with in the consumer products industry.

In P&G's private industrial network, shown in Figure 12.15, customer sales are captured at the cash register, which then initiates a flow of information back to distributors, P&G, and its suppliers. This tells P&G and its over 70,000 suppliers the exact level of demand for thousands of products. This information is then used to initiate production, supply, and transportation to replenish products at the distributors and retailers. This process is called an efficient customer response system (a demand-pull production model), and it relies on an equally efficient supply chain management system to coordinate the supply side (Gartner, Inc., 2015). In 2015 P&G began the process of transforming its supply chain system into a fully integrated, end-to-end supply base that enables the creation of joint business plans with its suppliers. Coordinating this supply base is a control tower environment, replete with wrap-around room monitors, where real-time supply data is continuously analyzed by teams of analysts. P&G's distribution goal is to deliver products within one day of shipping to 80% of its retailers. P&G is the world's largest consumer goods manufacturer, and for many years has been ranked as the leading supply chain manager (Gartner, 2018).

GE, Dell, Cisco, Volkswagen, Microsoft, IBM, Nike, Coca-Cola, Walmart, Nokia, and Hewlett-Packard are among the firms operating successful private industrial networks.

OBJECTIVES OF PRIVATE INDUSTRIAL NETWORKS

The specific objectives of a private industrial network include:

- Developing efficient purchasing and selling business processes industry-wide
- Developing industry-wide resource planning to supplement enterprise-wide resource planning
- Increasing supply chain visibility—knowing the inventory levels of buyers and suppliers
- Achieving closer buyer-supplier relationships, including demand forecasting, communications, and conflict resolution
- Operating on a global scale—globalization
- Reducing risk by preventing imbalances of supply and demand, including developing financial derivatives, insurance, and futures markets

Private industrial networks serve different goals from Net marketplaces. Net marketplaces are primarily transaction-oriented, whereas private industrial networks focus on continuous business process coordination between companies. This can include much more than just supply chain management, such as product design, sourcing, demand forecasting, asset management, sales, and marketing. Private industrial networks do support transactions, but that is not their primary focus.

Private industrial networks usually focus on a single sponsoring company that "owns" the network, sets the rules, establishes governance (a structure of authority, rule enforcement, and control), and invites firms to participate at its sole discretion. Therefore, these networks are private. This sets them apart from industry consortia, which are usually owned by major firms collectively through equity participation. Whereas Net marketplaces have a strong focus on indirect goods and services, private industrial networks focus on strategic, direct goods and services.

For instance, True Value supplies over 4,500 independent hardware stores in the United States and around the world. The logistics are staggering to consider: they routinely process over 60,000 domestic inbound loads, and over 600 million pounds of freight. True Value imports roughly 3,500 containers through 20 international ports and 10 domestic ports. The existing inbound supply chain system was fragmented, did not permit real-time tracking of packages, and, when shipments were short or damaged, could not alert stores. The supply chain was "invisible": suppliers could not see store inventory levels, and stores could not see supplier shipments. Using a web-based solution from Sterling Commerce (an IBM company), True Value created its own private industrial network to which all suppliers, shippers, and stores have exclusive access. The network focuses on three processes: domestic prepaid shipping, domestic collect, and international direct shipping. For each process the network tracks in real time the movement of goods from suppliers to shippers, warehouses, and stores. The system has led to a 57% reduction in lead time needed for orders, a 10% increase in the fill rate of orders, and an 85% reduction in back orders. If goods are delayed, damaged, or unavailable, the system alerts all parties automatically. In 2019, it added new software from JDA Software to improve how it manages inventory and forecasts demand (True Value Company, 2020; Smith, 2019; Amato, 2018).

Perhaps no single firm better illustrates the benefits of developing private industrial networks than Walmart, described in *Insight on Business: Walmart's Private Industrial Network Supports Omni-channel Growth*.

PRIVATE INDUSTRIAL NETWORKS AND COLLABORATIVE COMMERCE

Private industrial networks can do much more than just serve a supply chain and efficient customer response system. They can also include other activities of a single large manufacturing firm, such as design of products and engineering diagrams, as well as marketing plans and demand forecasting. Collaboration among businesses can take many forms and involve a wide range of activities—from simple supply chain management to coordinating market feedback to designers at supply firms (see **Figure 12.16**).

One form of collaboration—and perhaps the most profound—is industry-wide **collaborative resource planning, forecasting, and replenishment (CPFR)**, which involves working with network members to forecast demand, develop production plans, and coordinate shipping, warehousing, and stocking activities to ensure that retail and wholesale shelf space is replenished with just the right amount of goods. If this goal is achieved, hundreds of millions of dollars of excess inventory and capacity could be wrung out of an industry. This activity alone is likely to produce the largest benefits and justify the cost of developing private industrial networks.

A second area of collaboration is *demand chain visibility*. In the past, it was impossible to know where excess capacity or supplies existed in the supply and distribution chains. For instance, retailers might have significantly overstocked shelves, but suppliers and manufacturers—not knowing this—might be building excess capacity or supplies for even more production. These excess inventories would raise costs for the entire industry and create extraordinary pressures to discount merchandise, reducing profits for everyone.

A third area of collaboration is *marketing coordination and product design*. Manufacturers that use or produce highly engineered parts use private industrial networks to coordinate both their internal design and marketing activities, as well as related activities of their supply and distribution chain partners. By involving their suppliers in product

collaborative resource planning, forecasting, and replenishment (CPFR)

involves working with network members to forecast demand, develop production plans, and coordinate shipping, warehousing, and stocking activities to ensure that retail and wholesale shelf space is replenished with just the right amount of goods

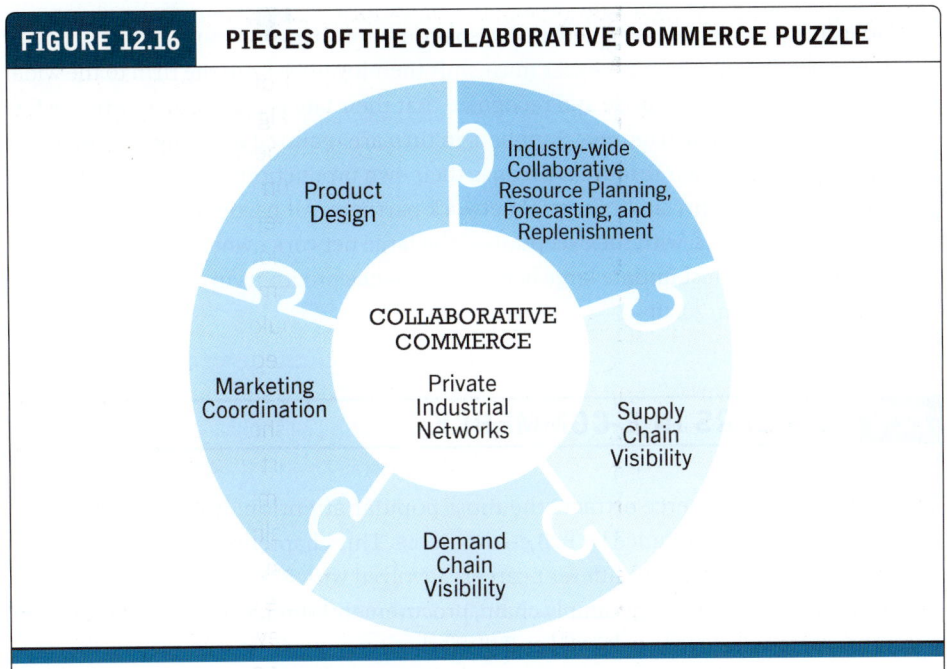

FIGURE 12.16 PIECES OF THE COLLABORATIVE COMMERCE PUZZLE

Collaborative commerce involves many cooperative activities among supply and sales firms closely interacting with a single large firm through a private industrial network.

design and marketing initiatives, manufacturing firms can ensure that the parts produced actually fulfill the claims of marketers. On the reverse flow, feedback from customers can be used by marketers to speak directly to product designers at the firm and its suppliers. For the first time, closed loop marketing (customer feedback directly impacting design and production) can become a reality.

IMPLEMENTATION BARRIERS

Although private industrial networks represent a large part of the future of B2B, there are many barriers to its complete implementation. Participating firms are required to share sensitive data with their business partners, up and down the supply chain. What in the past was considered proprietary and secret must now be shared. In a digital environment, it can be difficult to control the limits of information sharing. Information a firm freely gives to its largest customer may end up being shared with its closest competitor.

Integrating private industrial networks into existing enterprise systems and EDI networks poses a significant investment of time and money. The leading providers of enterprise systems to Fortune 500 companies (Oracle, IBM, and SAP) do offer B2B modules, and supply chain management capabilities, that can be added to their existing software suites. Nevertheless, implementing these modules is a very expensive proposition in part because the procurement side of many Fortune 500 firms is so fragmented and out-of-date. For smaller firms, cloud computing and software as a service (SaaS) alternatives are appearing on the market, which offer far less-expensive supply chain management capabilities.

Adopting private industrial networks also requires a change in mindset and behavior for employees. Essentially, employees must shift their loyalties from the firm to the wider trans-organizational enterprise and recognize that their fate is intertwined with the fate of their suppliers and distributors. Suppliers in turn are required to change the way they manage and allocate their resources because their own production is tightly coupled with the demands of their private industrial network partners. All participants in the supply and distribution chains, with the exception of the large network owner, lose some of their independence, and must initiate large behavioral change programs in order to participate (Laudon and Laudon, 2020).

12.6 CAREERS IN E-COMMERCE

Although B2C e-commerce attracts the most popular attention, it is dwarfed in both dollar volume and importance by B2B e-commerce. This chapter provides foundational information for a number of different careers involved with B2B e-commerce. Job titles include positions involving the supply chain, procurement/purchasing/sourcing, demand planning, materials, logistics, as well as B2B marketing.

THE COMPANY

The company is a leading manufacturer and wholesale distributor of musical instruments, amplifiers, speakers, and accessories. The firm supplies over 20,000 products to 6,000 dealers located throughout Europe. The company does not sell to retail customers; it only sells wholesale to music stores, retail chains, and online retailers.

POSITION: JUNIOR SUPPLY CHAIN ANALYST

The company is seeking a Junior Supply Chain Analyst who will be responsible for planning and managing production schedules to meet customer delivery requirements and to best utilize the company's productive capacity, as well as managing raw material and finished goods. The company is in the process of transitioning from a legacy SCM system to a cloud-based SCM system. Specific responsibilities include:
- Analyzing inventory and purchasing additional materials
- Creating, maintaining, and processing purchase orders.
- Account reconciliations and processing of invoicing.
- Facilitating return shipments and credit payments with national accounts.
- Communicating with national accounts to validate suggested order quantities and pricing.
- Compiling reports within Excel.
- Creating promotional and seasonal plans to maximize sales and increase Average Order Value (AOV).
- Implementing and managing mail-in rebates, instant rebates, and promotions.
- Utilizing reports and analytical tools and updating required databases on an as-needed basis.

QUALIFICATIONS/SKILLS

- Bachelor's degree or equivalent work experience required (concentration in Management Information Systems, Business, E-commerce, Accounting, Economics, Purchasing, or Supply Chain is preferred)
- Analytical skills and attention to detail
- Ability to understand and analyze complex data in order to make informed decisions
- A sharp mind with an ability to grasp concepts quickly and work out solutions to complex logic problems
- Experience in MS Office Suite, especially Excel is preferred
- Excellent communication skills, both verbal and written
- Positive attitude, strong work ethic, and ability to multi-task is a must
- Ability to work well under the stress of deadline pressure

HOW TO PREPARE FOR THE INTERVIEW

To prepare for this interview, make sure that you are familiar with the basic vocabulary of B2B e-commerce covered in Section 12.1 as well as have an understanding of the evolution of various technology platforms used in B2B e-commerce (Figure 12.1). Next, drill-down and focus on the material in Section 12.2 that covers the procurement process and supply chain. Make sure that you can talk about the various steps in the procurement process (Figure 12.4) and the different types of procurement. Be ready to show that you are knowledgeable about some of the basic concepts, challenges, and trends of supply chain management, such as supply chain visibility, just-in-time and lean production, supply chain management, adaptive supply chains, accountable supply chains, and sustainable supply chains, covered in Section 12.3. Since the company is in the process of transitioning to a cloud-based SCM system, also review the section of the text entitled "B2B in the Cloud." The case study on Elemica, although a very different industry, can also provide some potentially useful parallels that you could discuss, as it focuses on cloud-based order management and supply chain applications and services. Finally, since the position also involves a purchasing component, it would be useful to understand the different types of marketplaces in which such purchases could be made, such as from e-distributors, e-procurement companies, and exchanges, covered in Section 12.4.

POSSIBLE FIRST INTERVIEW QUESTIONS

1. Have you had any experience in purchasing supplies from vendors and managing purchase orders? Can you give an example? What were some of the challenges you faced dealing with vendors, and how did you solve them?

If you have any kind of business or volunteer experience ordering supplies, keeping track of supply inventory, invoicing, and payment tracking, then describe what you did, and talk about the challenges you faced such as vetting the supplier's credit, pricing, purchase order tracking, and delivery issues. Otherwise, do Internet research to obtain a basic understanding of vendor relations and purchase order management.

2. A key to our success is matching the stream of orders to our production and purchasing schedules. We try to avoid excess inventory of parts, and yet we need to have enough parts on hand to fulfill orders. We need to link the demand for our products to the purchasing of parts and supplies. Do you have any ideas on how we can match our purchasing of supplies to the stream of incoming orders?

You can suggest here that most supply chain management systems are linked to the order entry system. Based on incoming orders, SCMs will produce data that is fed into the production system, which, in turn, results in a list of parts needed and schedule requirements. Because this position is closely linked to SCM, you should do research on SCM systems to understand their functionality.

3. We'd like to use social media as a way to enhance communications with our suppliers. Do you have any suggestions about how we might build a social network to support our supply chain?

Here you can talk about your experience with Facebook and Twitter, especially about how business firms can use these platforms to build a social community of vendors and manufacturers. The process of building a social network for vendors is very similar to building a social network of customers. Use of video, blogs, comments, newsfeeds, and posts can be very valuable in creating a community of vendors.

4. We are trying to reduce costs of our supplies by participating in a number of Net marketplaces where vendors compete with one another on price and quality to become one of our suppliers. What do you know about B2B Net marketplaces and how they might be helpful for us?

You might point out here the four different kinds of Net marketplaces. The firm should use e-distributors to obtain the lowest cost for indirect supplies, such as Amazon Business or eBay Business. The firm could also participate in an e-procurement network such as SAP Ariba to obtain competitive quotations for supplies and direct inputs.

5. We are trying to integrate our vendors more closely into our business planning and even the design of new products. We're looking for a collaborative effort from our suppliers and greater visibility into our supply chain both for our purposes and our vendors. What do you know about collaborative commerce? What have you learned about supply chain visibility?

You could refer to private industrial networks composed of a single manufacturing firm that owns the network, and the group of suppliers that work with the manufacturer to design and build component parts, similar to that created by Procter & Gamble. In this kind of collaborative effort, both the vendors and the ultimate buyer of components work together to create and design inputs, and both benefit from the results.

12.7 CASE STUDY

Elemica:
Cooperation, Collaboration, and Community

It may seem unusual to refer to an entire industry as a community, a word reserved typically for collections of people who more or less know one another. Trade associations are one example of an industrial community. Trade associations form in an effort to pursue the interests of all members in the community although usually they do not include customers in the community. Elemica is a B2B cloud-based, digital supply chain platform aiming to revolutionize the entire supply chain of the chemical, tire and rubber, energy, and other process industries worldwide. Elemica's purpose is not just to foster cooperation on a one-to-one inter-firm basis, or just to foster collaboration on multi-firm projects, but instead to lift all boats on an industry tide by providing an inter-firm platform for communicating B2B information, and thereby making all firms more efficient. Elemica is one of the few survivors of the early B2B e-commerce years. Elemica today processes over $600 billion in annual transactions across more than 7,500 process industry trading partners, 10,000 network participants around the world, including over 100 of the largest global process manufacturers, thousands of their direct material suppliers, over 500 logistics service suppliers, as well as thousands of end customers. Clients

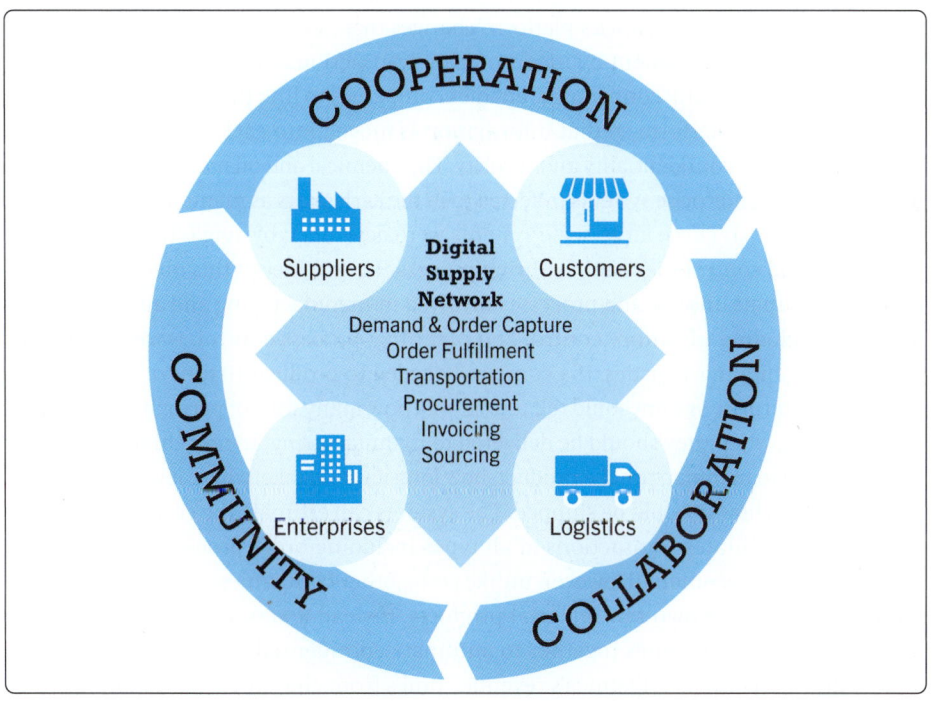

include BASF, BP, Continental, The Dow Chemical Company, DuPont, The Goodyear Tire & Rubber Company, Lanxess, Michelin, Shell, Solvay, Sumitomo Chemical, and Wacker.

Elemica was an early example of a B2B e-commerce industry consortium. It was founded by 22 leading corporations in the chemical industry (including oil and industrial gases) to provide cloud-based order management and supply chain applications and services. A single platform provides one-stop shopping so that companies can buy and sell products to one another through their own enterprise systems or using a web alternative. It also helps companies automate all of their business processes, creating efficiencies and economies of scale that lead to an improved bottom line. In 2016 Elemica was purchased by Thoma Bravo, a private equity firm, reportedly for more than $1 billion. In 2019, Eurazeo Capital, a leading global investment company listed in France, acquired a majority interest in Elemica from Thomas Bravo.

How does Elemica achieve community among a diverse, global collection of firms where firms are often both customers and vendors to one another? It unites community members by linking together their enterprise systems. This is the "social glue" that sets Elemica apart. This "super platform" permits companies to communicate with one another and to conduct transactions, handle logistics, and keep the books. The Elemica commerce platform has effectively standardized industry business transactions for all network members regardless of the type of enterprise system they have, and it has leveled the playing field for trade partners who are less technically sophisticated. This neutral platform facilitates millions of transactions for industry suppliers, customers, and third-party providers. In this sense, Elemica is one of the most sophisticated technology platforms in the B2B space.

One of the largest investments for a company is its enterprise system. Despite these investments, intercompany relationships—the backbone of its supply chain—are often left to outdated and unreliable processes. These shortcomings cost billions in lost productivity, revenue, and profit. Elemica's platform changes that. It helps its clients leverage their enterprise system investment by incorporating transactions to external trade partners. Elemica's QuickLink ERP connectivity enables companies to link their internal IT systems through a neutral platform so that information is moved into each company's database while maintaining confidentiality and security. The chemical and oil industries were among the first users of enterprise systems (referred to in the early years as manufacturing resource planning systems). These large-scale systems were developed by single firms in order to rationalize and control the manufacturing process. They achieved this objective by identifying the outputs, inputs, and processes involved in manufacturing and automating key elements including inventory control and planning, process control, warehousing and storage, and shipping/logistics. If a company needed to produce 10 tons of polyethylene plastic, its enterprise system could tell it precisely how many tons of petrochemical inputs were required, when they should be delivered to manufacturing, the machinery and labor force required to manufacture the product, how long it would take, where it would be stored, and sometimes how it would be shipped. The systems can estimate the cost at any stage.

Elemica facilitates transactions of all types including order processing and billing, and logistics management. However, unlike some other companies in the field, Elemica does not buy, sell, or own raw material products. Instead it acts as an intermediary, or network, linking companies together to automate confidential transactions. Like eBay or a credit card company, Elemica's revenue comes from charging transaction fees on a per-transaction basis. Its network of clients opens the door for companies to do business with all other connected buyers and sellers.

Elemica offers a variety of services for suppliers, customers, and logistic partners, enabling them to automate both their business processes and internal purchasing. A modular, cloud-based solution simplifies sales, procurement, and financial processes; integrates supply chain partners to diminish communication barriers; and reduces overhead and errors.

Elemica integrates information flow among global trading partners using a cloud-based business process network called the QuickLink network. This is often referred to as platform as a service (PaaS). Each client needs only a single connection to Elemica, and Elemica manages the connections to that company's external trade partners. That means a company needs only maintain one connection to Elemica (important when it's time for enterprise system maintenance or upgrade) rather than maintain a variable number of connections and infrastructure to all its trade partners. Once a company connects to Elemica, it can have access to thousands of other trading partners, including suppliers, customers, and logistics firms. Clients are charged for the service based on volume of usage. This is much more efficient than older EDI solutions to inter-company transactions. Elemica provides the platform for collaborative commerce through a fully automated integrated network of suppliers, customers, and third-party providers.

Elemica offers cloud-based solutions (SmartLink Applications) for four primary areas: Logistics Management, Customer Management, Supplier Management, and Sourcing Management. Using these solutions, companies can automate ordering, invoicing, shipment tracking, and day-to-day business operations. Companies can sign up for one or more solutions depending on their needs. The software applications are software as a service (SaaS) applications residing on Elemica cloud servers, and therefore do not require participating firms to buy any hardware or software. Firms are charged on the basis of how much of the service they use, on a demand basis.

Here's an example of how Elemica works. Let's say you need to order vinyl acetate from one of your suppliers. You put the order into your internal enterprise system, the order is automatically routed to Elemica's QuickLink network, Elemica routes the order to your supplier's internal enterprise system, and you get a confirmed receipt of the order. Elemica's QuickLink Network ensures the accuracy of the item number and purchase order number and sends an alert if there's an issue. Once an order is confirmed, Elemica's platform can be leveraged to plan and coordinate delivery and automatically send an invoice and submit payment. For small or medium firms that may not have an enterprise system, Elemica has a web portal with online software that allows firms to participate in the community with suppliers and customers. The platform offers a closed-loop process, end to end, from the purchase order, to acknowledgments, load tenders and responses, carrier status updates, and dock scheduling. All of this takes place in a few seconds with little or no human intervention. The customer can send the purchase order via e-mail or e-fax, which is then routed to Elemica. Elemica then routes it to the supplier in its preferred format, integrated with its enterprise system as though it were a true electronic order. This holistic approach to order management allows suppliers to automate the process with both strategic and core customers, without asking its customers to change their processes. It's a win-win situation for suppliers and customers. Elemica's QuickLink

Network is sometimes referred to as "Come As You Are" network because it allows firms to use whatever communication tools they currently use, such as EDI, XML, and even e-mail, or formats associated with their enterprise systems.

Unlike the automobile industry or the airline industry, where a few companies dominate, the $5+ trillion global chemical industry is made up of many companies of all sizes. In addition, unlike many other industries, chemical companies often buy the output from other chemical companies to use as raw materials for their products. Thus, chemical companies are often customers of one another as well as competitors.

In the late 1990s, senior leaders at some of the larger chemical companies began to focus on changes in technology that made the adoption of information technology and the tools of e-commerce more appealing. The questions were how to best use these advances to benefit their businesses and how to establish industry standards for electronic transactions to make them accessible and attainable for all. Leaders from companies such as Dow Chemical and DuPont determined that a cooperative alliance would be the most efficient way to move forward. They were met with initial skepticism by marketing and sales staff, worried that online procurement would negatively affect relationships. Further, senior corporate leadership wasn't sure that e-commerce would have any use in the chemical industry at all. And companies were cautious about the expense of investing in the infrastructure necessary for e-commerce.

However, there were compelling opportunities that were impossible to dismiss, including lowering costs, creating closer connections with customers and suppliers, and differentiating companies on something other than price. At the same time, new startups like e-Chemicals and PlasticsNet were making traditional chemical companies nervous. What would happen if their efforts to use information technology to streamline an inefficient supply chain helped them capture market share? In other words, if the more traditional companies didn't move forward, they might end up losing the revenue race.

When Dow began looking at startups that were using e-commerce and talking to their customers, they found that customers were concerned about making an investment to establish online connections with multiple firms. Dow and DuPont decided that the best and most economically efficient option was to offer customers the choice of a neutral one-to-one link. This would remove the obstacle of multiple connections. A strong, third-party network addressed the community concern about loss of control. The two companies decided to create and invest in a neutral e-commerce company, partnering with other companies to create the critical mass needed to make it viable.

In 1999, the corporate boards of Dow and DuPont agreed that there were major advantages to online transaction processing and additional online connections among buyers and sellers. Because time and cost considerations made multiple connections unattractive to customers, a hub concept was adopted. It was also decided that a neutral community was the best approach.

All participants shared the common goal of creating a neutral platform to facilitate inter-company transactions and enhance business processes. Dow and DuPont also reviewed the concept with the relevant regulatory agencies and received up-front approval. Ultimately, 22 global chemical companies were involved in the launch of Elemica in 2000.

When Elemica opened its doors, there were around 50 startup B2B e-commerce companies in the chemical industry. Nearly all of these B2B companies were third-party-owned Net marketplaces suitable at best for short-term sourcing of some direct inputs. Today, only a handful of these Net marketplaces for the chemical industry remain, although there is renewed interested in the space, particularly in Europe, where there are 22,500 chemical companies alone. For instance, recently, Evonik Industries launched OneTwoChem, a platform intended for use by multiple buyers and sellers.. Elemica focuses on building longer-term business relationships by creating committed and contractual supply chains. The company acts only as a facilitator of business transactions and does not directly buy and sell chemical products.

Elemica's business model has been successful primarily because it addresses the needs of chemical, tire and rubber, energy, and selected process companies of all sizes. It does this by offering multiple options for connecting to its hub system, multiple products that can be used alone or in combination, and by ensuring that only one connection integrated with a client's enterprise system is needed for all transactions. Customers can use Elemica, and take advantage of the technology it offers, without purchasing an additional internal system.

With Elemica, companies benefit from improved operational efficiency, reduced costs due to elimination of redundant systems and excess inventory, and a much higher percentage of safe and reliable deliveries. The flexibility of Elemica's solutions and network combines simplification, standardization, and efficiency. And clients have increased their profitability and improved cash flow through faster payment.

A number of very large companies use Elemica's platform. In Europe, Shell Oil started using Elemica after recognizing that it had ongoing problems with the coordination of paperwork processing and deliveries. Truck drivers would arrive at delivery sites and wait up to two hours while paperwork was filled out. These delays were costing Shell money. Once Shell began using Elemica, things improved. Today, paperwork is processed 24 hours a day, and truck waiting time has been cut from an average of two hours to an average of 15 minutes. Given this success, Shell continues to expand its relationship with Elemica.

AkzoNobel, headquartered in the Netherlands and a major producer of specialty chemicals as well as a leading global paints and coating company is another example. AkzoNobel decided to replace its legacy Vendor Managed Inventory System, which it had developed internally, with an Elemica solution. Under the Elemica system, AkzoNobel no longer has to place orders with suppliers. Instead, suppliers decide when to deliver materials to AkzoNobel based on inventory consumption levels, production forecast, and agreed levels of safety stock. Suppliers benefit because with enhanced visibility into AkzoNobel's inventory consumption and forecast, they can optimize production scheduling and transportation costs by delivering full loads of raw materials. Another long-time Elemica client, Wacker Chemie, deployed Elemica's QuickLink Email solution to automate customer orders that might have up to 30 separate line items. Previously, each line item had to be manually entered by customer support as an individual order, but QuickLink Email automated the process, saving time and reducing errors.

Through the years, Elemica has continued to innovate, developing new products to address new chains in supply chain management, including supply chain visibility, supply chain risk management, supply chain sustainability, and social collaboration tools. For instance, in 2017, Elemica introduced Elemica Pulse, a supply chain visibility tool that provides end-to-end visibility, allowing all parties to a transaction to track orders and status

SOURCES: Elemica.com, accessed February 4, 2020; "Elemica Celebrates Its 20th Anniversary as a Supply Chain Network Pioneer," by Elemica, Globenewswire.com, January 22, 2020; "Optimising the Supply Chain: The Visible Effect of Elemica's Digital Supply Network," Europeanbusinessreview.com, January 22, 2019; "Elemica Wins 2019 Supply & Demand Chain Executive Green Supply Chain Award," by Elemica, Globenewswire.com, December 11, 2019; "Elemica Named to Top 10 Procurement Solution Provider for 2019 in Europe," Elemica.com, October 14, 2019; "Elemica Closes on Eurazeo Partnership," by Elemica, Globenewswire.com, September 19, 2019; "It's Back: Chemical E-commerce Tries for an Act 2," by Rick Mullin, Cen.acs.org, March 25, 2019; "Elemica Reports Double Digit Network Growth and Announces New Product Innovations in First Quarter 2018," by Elemica, Globalnewswire.com, May 24, 2018; "Creating a True Digital Procurement Supply Chain," by Patrick Burnson, Supplychain247.com, May 15, 2018; "Elemica Gains Significant Network Growth and Software Growth in 2017 Across the Chemical and Process Industry Markets," by Elemica, Globalnewswire.com, February 13, 2018; "Elemica Customer Management Solution," by David Cahn, Resources.elemica.com, January 8, 2018; "Mapping the B2B Vertical Marketplace Ecosystem," Bowerycap.com, December 5, 2017; "When Visibile Supply Chains Yield Predictable Cash Flow," Pymnts.com, November 16, 2017; "Elemica Delivers Supply Chain Visibility with Elemica Pulse," Thepaypers.com, November 8, 2017; "Elemica Partners with DHL Resilience360 to Better Mitigate Supply Chain Risk," by Elemica, Globalnewswire.com, October 4, 2017; "Customer Success Stories: AkzoNobel," by David Cahn, Elemica.com, October 30, 2017; "Customer Success Stories: Wacker Chemie," by David Cahn, Elemica.com, October 25,

2017; "Thoma Bravo Completes Acquisition of Elemica," Elemica, July 7, 2016; "Elemica Shell Global," Royal Dutch Shell, PLC, June 2015; "Building Effective Business Networks in Process Industries Improving Supply Chain Value Networks," by Lora Cecere, Supply Chain Insights, LLC, January 2015; "Elemica: Shifting from a Shared Services Bazaar to Platform 'PaaS' Standard," by Jason Busch, Spendmatters.com, November 18, 2013; "The Social Side of Supply Chain Management," by Adrian Gonzalez, *Supply Chain Management Review*, August 2013; "Next Generation Supply Chain Networks Enable More Robust Collaborative Workflows Across Trading Partners to Increase Value," Becky Boyd, Market Wired, July 2, 2013; "Case Study: Elemica," Ebusinesswatch.org, August 25, 2009; "Once Elemica Tackled the Hard Part, the Rest Was Easy," SupplyChainBrain.com, August 5, 2009.

through the entire cycle, from order capture to shipment to receipt, invoice, and payment. Elemica Pulse uses machine learning and artificial intelligence to provide more accurate predictions of shipping and delivery dates, using a feature called the Elemica Reality Check, which analyzes data generated across Elemica's entire digital supply network with proprietary algorithms. Elemica also partnered with DHL Resilience360, a leading supply chain risk management platform to offer Elemica Risk, a supply chain risk tool to provide risk incident data to help global business identify risks within their supply chains and create strategies to mitigate risk. Elemica Trace, another new tool, provides real-time shipment and risk visibility to allow companies to monitor and proactively manage the movement of products to customers and inbound to manufacturing centers.

Elemica has also developed a sustainability program. In 2019, Elemica received its 11th consecutive SDCE Green Supply Chain award for its efforts in promoting sustainable supply chains. Elemica was chosen for helping clients automate all inbound and outbound invoices and other manual processes, as well as helping them optimize freight through collaboration on shipments, enabling shippers and carriers to lower emissions and fuel consumption. A new software tool, Elemica Quality, aids in this effort.

Elemica has also added social tools to its portfolio. The idea is to give clients the ability to discover, create, and build social business networks—just as Facebook provides its users the ability to build online social networks.

Case Study Questions

1. If you were a small chemical company, what concerns would you have about joining Elemica?

2. Elemica provides a community for participants where they can transact, coordinate, and cooperate to produce products for less. Yet these firms also compete with one another when they sell chemicals to end-user firms in the automobile, airline, and manufacturing industries. How is this possible?

3. How did the purchase of Elemica by Thoma Bravo, a private equity firm, change how Elemica fits into the B2B framework illustrated in Figure 12.10?

12.8 REVIEW

KEY CONCEPTS

- Discuss the evolution and growth of B2B e-commerce, as well as its potential benefits and challenges.
- Before the Internet, business-to-business transactions were referred to simply as *inter-firm trade* or the *procurement process*. Today, we use the term *B2B commerce* to describe all types of inter-firm trade to exchange value across organizational boundaries, involving both the buying of inputs and the marketing, selling, and

distribution of products and services, and the term *B2B e-commerce* to describe specifically that portion of B2B commerce that is enabled by the Internet and mobile apps.
- In order to understand the evolution of B2B e-commerce, you must understand several key stages:
  - *Automated order entry systems*, developed in the 1970s, involved the use of telephone modems to send digital orders.
  - *EDI* or *electronic data interchange*, developed in the late 1970s, is a communications standard for sharing various procurement documents including invoices, purchase orders, shipping bills, product stocking numbers (SKUs), and settlement information for an industry.
  - *B2B e-commerce websites* emerged in the 1990s along with the commercialization of the Internet. They are online catalogs containing the products that are made available to the general public by a single vendor.
  - *Net marketplaces* emerged in the late 1990s as a natural extension and scaling-up of the electronic storefront. Net marketplaces involve the marketing, selling, and distribution side of B2B e-commerce. The essential characteristic of all Net marketplaces is that they bring hundreds of suppliers, each with its own online catalog, together with potentially thousands of purchasing firms to form a single Internet-based marketplace.
  - *Private industrial networks* also emerged in the late 1990s with the commercialization of the Internet as a natural extension of EDI systems and the existing close relationships that developed between large industrial firms and their suppliers.
- Potential benefits of B2B e-commerce include lower administrative costs; lower search costs for buyers; reduced inventory costs; lower transaction costs; improved quality of products; decreased product cycle time; increased opportunities for collaborating with suppliers and distributors; greater price transparency; and increased visibility and real-time information sharing among all participants in the supply chain network.
- Potential risks and challenges include lack of real-time data, environmental impacts, natural disasters, labor concerns, and the impacts of economic, financial, and political instability.

■ **Understand how procurement and supply chains relate to B2B e-commerce.**
- The *procurement process* refers to the way business firms purchase the goods they need in order to produce the goods they will ultimately sell to consumers. Firms purchase goods from a set of suppliers who in turn purchase their inputs from a set of suppliers. These firms are linked in a series of connected transactions. The *supply chain* is the series of transactions that links sets of firms that do business with each other. It includes not only the firms themselves but also the relationships between them and the processes that connect them.
- There are two different types of procurements (purchases of direct goods and purchases of indirect goods) and two different methods of purchasing goods (contract purchases and spot purchases).
- The term *multi-tier supply chain* is used to describe the complex series of transactions that exists between a single firm with multiple primary suppliers, the secondary suppliers who do business with those primary suppliers, and the tertiary suppliers who do business with the secondary suppliers.

■ **Identify major trends in supply chain management and collaborative commerce.**
- *Supply chain management (SCM)* refers to a wide variety of activities that firms and industries use to coordinate the key players in their procurement process.
- *Just in time production* is a method of inventory cost management that seeks to eliminate excess inventory to a bare minimum.
- *Lean production* is a set of production methods and tools that focuses on the elimination of waste throughout the customer value chain.
- *Supply chain simplification* involves reducing the size of the supply chain and working more closely with a smaller group of strategic supplier firms to reduce both product costs and administrative costs, while improving quality.

- *Adaptive supply chains* allow companies to react to disruptions in the supply chain in a particular region by moving production to a different region.
- *Accountable supply chains* are those where the labor conditions in low-wage, underdeveloped producer countries are visible and morally acceptable to ultimate consumers in more developed industrial societies.
- *Sustainable supply chains* involve using the most efficient environment-regarding means of production, distribution, and logistics.
- EDI remains very important in B2B e-commerce.
- Mobile B2B has become increasingly important in all aspects of B2B e-commerce, through all steps of the procurement process and throughout the supply chain.
- *Cloud-based B2B systems* shift much of the expense of B2B systems from the firm to a B2B network provider, sometimes called a data hub or B2B platform.
- Contemporary *supply chain management (SCM) systems* are based on supply chain simplification, just-in-time and lean production, focusing on strategic partners in the production process, enterprise systems, and continuous inventory replenishment.
- *Collaborative commerce* involves the use of digital technologies to permit firms to collaboratively design, develop, build, market, and manage products through their life cycles, and is a direct extension of supply chain management systems, as well as supply chain simplification. Collaborative commerce today involves cloud servers, social business tools, and mobile devices.
- Social networks are providing intimate connections among customers, suppliers, and logistics partners.
- Despite the size of the B2B e-commerce, B2B marketing still accounts for only a relatively small slice of the total amount spent on digital marketing and advertising, in part due to the slow pace of technological change in supply chain and procurement management and in part due to the very different nature of B2B e-commerce compared to B2C e-commerce. For long-term sourcing, interpersonal relationships, networking, brand, and informative content marketing using white papers, videos, podcasts, webinars, blogs, e-books, conferences, and professional associations are the primary and most effective marketing tools. However, in spot purchasing markets, B2B marketing uses many of the same marketing tactics and tools found in B2C marketing: display ads, search engine marketing, websites, social network channels, videos, and mobile ads.

■ Understand the different characteristics and types of Net marketplaces.
- Net marketplaces are sell-side digital environments where sellers and buyers are brought together.
- Characteristics of Net marketplaces include their bias (seller-side vs. buy-side vs. neutral), ownership (industry vs. third party), pricing mechanism (fixed priced catalogs, auctions, and RFPs/RFQs), scope/focus (horizontal vs. vertical), value creation (customers/suppliers), and access to markets (public vs. private).
- There are four main types of "pure" Net marketplaces:
  - *E-distributors* are independently owned intermediaries that offer industrial customers a single source from which to make spot purchases of indirect or MRO goods. E-distributors operate in a horizontal market that serves many different industries with products from many different suppliers.
  - *E-procurement Net marketplaces* are independently owned intermediaries connecting hundreds of online suppliers offering millions of MRO goods to business firms who pay a fee to join the market. E-procurement Net marketplaces operate in a horizontal market in which long-term contractual purchasing agreements are used to buy indirect goods.
  - *Exchanges* are independently owned online marketplaces that connect hundreds to thousands of suppliers and buyers in a dynamic real-time environment. They are typically vertical markets in which spot purchases can be made for direct inputs (both goods and services). Exchanges make money by charging a commission on each transaction.
  - *Industry consortia* are industry-owned vertical markets where long-term contractual purchases of direct inputs can be made from a limited set of invited participants. Consortia serve to reduce supply chain inefficiencies by unifying the supply chain for an industry through a common network and computing platform.

- **Understand the objectives of private industrial networks, their role in supporting collaborative commerce, and the barriers to their implementation.**
  - Objectives of private industrial networks include developing efficient purchasing and selling business processes industry-wide; developing industry-wide resource planning to supplement enterprise-wide resource planning; increasing supply chain visibility; achieving closer buyer-supplier relationships; operating on a global scale; and reducing industry risk by preventing imbalances of supply and demand.
  - Private industrial networks are transforming the supply chain by focusing on continuous business process coordination between companies. This coordination includes much more than just transaction support and supply chain management. Product design, demand forecasting, asset management, and sales and marketing plans can all be coordinated among network members. Some of the forms of collaboration used by private industrial networks include the following:
    - *CPFR* or *industry-wide collaborative resource planning, forecasting, and replenishment* involves working with network members to forecast demand, develop production plans, and coordinate shipping, warehousing, and stocking activities.
    - *Supply chain and distribution chain visibility* refers to the fact that, in the past, it was impossible to know where excess capacity existed in a supply or distribution chain. Eliminating excess inventories by halting the production of overstocked goods can raise the profit margins for all network members because products will no longer need to be discounted in order to move them off the shelves.
    - *Marketing and product design collaboration* can be used to involve a firm's suppliers in product design and marketing activities as well as in the related activities of their supply and distribution chain partners. This can ensure that the parts used to build a product live up to the claims of the marketers. Collaborative commerce applications used in a private industrial network can also make possible closed-loop marketing in which customer feedback will directly impact product design.

QUESTIONS

1. What factors influence the speed with which industries migrate to B2B e-commerce?
2. Describe the stages of evolution of EDI.
3. What is supply chain visibility and why is it important?
4. What types of ownership models and revenue models do Net marketplaces use?
5. Describe the steps in the procurement process. Which steps are least likely to benefit from automation and e-commerce technologies?
6. What is an accountable supply chain? Why are companies now moving to establish such supply chains?
7. What is an adaptive supply chain?
8. Why do firms typically use spot purchasing for indirect goods and contractual purchasing for direct goods?
9. Explain the difference between just-in-time and lean production.
10. What two challenges to global supply chains emerged in early 2020?
11. Define sustainable business. What is the business value of a sustainable supply chain?
12. Describe three types of B2B collaboration enabled through private industrial networks.
13. What are the benefits for suppliers in a private industrial network?
14. What are some of the recent trends in B2B marketing?
15. How does JOOR differ from a private industrial network?
16. How does a cloud-based B2B platform differ from a traditional approach to B2B enterprise systems?
17. What are the advantages and disadvantages of participating in exchanges for buyers and sellers?
18. How does collaborative commerce differ from EDI? How is it similar?
19. What problems does blockchain solve with current transaction databases?
20. How have social networks impacted B2B?

PROJECTS

1. Choose an industry and a B2B vertical market maker that interests you. Investigate the site and prepare a report that describes the size of the industry served, the type of Net marketplace provided, the benefits promised by the site for both suppliers and purchasers, and the history of the company. You might also investigate the bias (buyer versus seller), ownership (suppliers, buyers, independents), pricing mechanism(s), scope and focus, and access (public versus private) of the Net marketplace.

2. Examine the website of one of the e-distributors listed in Figure 12.10, and compare and contrast it to one of the websites listed for e-procurement Net marketplaces. If you were a business manager of a medium-sized firm, how would you decide where to purchase your indirect inputs—from an e-distributor or an e-procurement Net marketplace? Write a short report detailing your analysis.

3. Assume you are a procurement officer for an office furniture manufacturer of steel office equipment. You have a single factory located in the Midwest with 2,000 employees. You sell about 40% of your office furniture to retail-oriented catalog outlets such as Quill in response to specific customer orders, and the remainder of your output is sold to resellers under long-term contracts. You have a choice of purchasing raw steel inputs—mostly cold-rolled sheet steel—from an exchange and/or from an industry consortium. Which alternative would you choose and why? Prepare a presentation for management supporting your position.

4. You are involved in logistics management for your company, a retailer of home furnishings. In the last year the company has experienced a number of disruptions in its supply chain as vendors failed to deliver products on time, and the business has lost customers as a result. Your firm only has a limited IT department, and you would like to propose a cloud-based solution. Go to the website of GT Nexus. Explore the Why GT Nexus tab, and the Industries/Retail tab. Review the various resoucves available. Write a report to senior management why you believe that a cloud-based B2B solution is best for your firm.

REFERENCES

Accenture, Inc. "Supply Chain Management in the Cloud." (June 25, 2014).

Agritechtalk.com "About The Seam." (accessed February 2, 2020).

Allianz. "Allianz Risk Barometer: 2019: Cyber Joins Business Interruption as a Leading Global Risk for Companies for the First Time." (January 15, 2019).

Allied Market Research. "Supply Chain Management Software Market." (September 2019).

Amato, Denna. "New Software Drives 'True Value' for Hardware Store Giant, Including Inventory Reductions." Chainstoreage.com (July 9, 2018).

Antai, Imoh. "A Theory of the Competing Supply Chain: Alternatives for Development." *International Business Research* Vol 4, No. 1 (January 2011).

Barlow, Alexis. "Web Technologies and Supply Chains." Glasgow Calendonian University, Scotland. In *Supply Chain Management: New Perspectives*, edited by S. Renko. (2011).

Beard, Alison and Richard Hornik, "It's Hard to Be Good," *Harvard Business Review Magazine* (November 2011).

Bowman, Robert. "Should CPG Brands Let Amazon Lure Them Away from Traditional Retailers." Supplychainbrain.com (June 12, 2017).

Brown, Randy. "Trade Wars Will Disrupt Supply Chains, Slow Global Growth." Forbes.com (July 19, 2018).

Cachon, Gerard, and Robert Swinney, "The Value of Fast Fashion: Quick Response, Enhanced Design, and Strategic Consumer Behavior." *Management Science* Vol. 57 778–795 (April 2011).

Caridia, Maria, Luca Crippa, Alessandro Perego, Andrea Sianesi, and Angela Tumino. "Supply Chain Planning and Configuration in the Global Arena." *International Journal of Production Economics* Volume 127, Issue 2, (October 2010).

Cecere, Lora. "Supply Chain Visibility in Business Networks." Supply Chain Insights, LLC (March 11, 2014).

Cecere, Lora. "EDI Workhorse of the Value Chain." Supply Chain Insights, LLC (November 20, 2013).

Chao, Loretta. "Supply Chain Management in the Cloud." *Wall Street Journal* (May 22, 2015).

Chernova, Yuliya. "Joor Hunts for Growth While Cash-Flow Positive." *Wall Street Journal* (July 6, 2015).

Chopra, Sunil, and MamMohan Sodhi. "Reducing the Risk of Supply Chain Disruptions." *MIT Sloan Management Review* (Spring 2014).

Cisco Systems, Inc. and Vital Images. "Video Conferencing Shrinks the Globe." (July 2016).

Daniels, Jennifer K. "Supply Chain Is the Star of New SAP Ad." Apics.org (September 7, 2016).

Demery, Paul. "Salesforce Launches B2B Commerce Software." Digitalcommerce360.com (June 14, 2018).

DHL, Inc. "A Look Back at 2015: The Top Ten Supply Chain Disruptions." (February 2016).

eMarketer, Inc. (Jillian Ryan). "Marketplaces 2019: B2B Ecommerce Strategies for Amazon, Alibaba, and Others." (August 6, 2019a).

eMarketer, Inc. (Jillian Ryan). "US B2B Digital Advertising Trends." (January 17, 2019b).

eMarketer, Inc. (Jillian Ryan). "Creating and Distributing Content for the Customer Journey: How B2B Marketers Can Influence Audience Behavior Through Strategic Content." (May 1, 2019c).

eMarketer, Inc. (Jillian Ryan). "B2B Mobile Marketing and Advertising: Chasing the Ever-More Mobile Buyer." (January 10, 2017a).

eMarketer, Inc. (Jillian Ryan). "B2B Social Media 2017: Tying Efforts Back to Larger Business Goals." (February 2017b).

eMarketer, Inc. "Components That Make Up Their Ominichannel Strategy According to Senior B2B Executives Worldwide*, Q2 2017." (October 2017c).

Fair Labor Association. "2017 Annual Public Report." (November 27, 2017).

Fair Labor Association. "Independent Investigation of Apple Supplier, Foxconn Report Highlights." Fairlabor.org (March 30, 2012).

Fauska, Polina, Natalia Kryvinska, and Christine Strauss. "E-commerce and B2B Services Enterprises." 2013 International Conference on Advanced Information Networking and Application Workshops, IEEE (2013).

Gardner, Dana. "SAP's Ariba Teams with eBay to Improve Rogue B2B Procurement for Buyers, Sellers, and Enterprises." It.toolbox.com (June 3, 2014).

Gartner, Inc. "Gartner Announces Rankings of Its 2015 Supply Chain Top 25: Amazon Takes the Top Spot in Top 25 Rankings; Apple and P&G Move into New Masters Category." (May 14, 2015).

GE Sustainability. "Ecomagination Progress." (2018).

Grainger. "2019 Fact Book." (April 24, 2019).

Heller, Martha. "Running with Data: Under Armour Creates Immersive, Digital Customer Experience." Cio.com (May 15, 2019).

HP Inc. "Annual Report on Form 10-K for the fiscal year ended October 31, 2019 filed with Securities and Exchange Commission."

Hitachi Consulting. "Co-creating the Future." (2017).

IDC. "New IDC Spending Guide Sees Strong Growth in Blockchain Solutions Leading to $15.9 Billion Market in 2023." (August 8, 2019).

Inter IKEA Group. "Sustainability. Summary Report FY18." (March 27, 2019).

Inventory Locator Service LLC. "About Us." ILSmart.com (accessed February 2, 2020).

JOOR. "About." Joor.com (accessed February 4, 2020).

Laudon, Kenneth C., and Jane P. Laudon. *Management Information Systems: Managing the Digital Firm*. 16th edition. Hoboken, NJ, Pearson Education, Inc. (2020).

Loeb, Walter. "JOOR Saves Retailers Time And Expense Through Digitized Wholesale Transactions." Forbes.com (April 14, 2018).

Long, Gene, Jr. "Supply Chain Resiliency: From Insight to Foresight: Sustaining Shareholder Value by Hardening the Enterprise Against External Risks." *IHS Quarterly* (March 2014).

Lopez, Edwin. "To Build 'Circular' Operations, IKEA Takes Aim at Its Supply Chain." Supplychaindive.com (March 20, 2018).

Loten, Angus, and Sara Germano. "Under Armour Links Sales Decline to Software Upgrade." *Wall Street Journal* (October 31, 2017).

Mearian, Lucas. "Blockchain Will Be the Killer App for Supply Chain Management in 2018," Computerworld.com (May 8, 2018).

National Cyber Security Center. "Example Supply Chain Attacks," (January 28, 2018).

Norton, Steven. "FedEx CIO Says Blockchain a 'Game Changer' for Supply Chain Visibility." *Wall Street Journal* (May 14, 2018).

PriceWaterhouseCoopers and the MIT Forum for Supply Chain Innovation. "Making the Right Risk Decisions to Strengthen Operations Performance." (2015).

Resilinc Inc. "Resilinc Special Supply Chain Event Case Study: 2016 Taiwan Earthquake, Assessing the Foreseeable Supply Chain Impact." (February 2016).

Rossi, Ben. "How to Protect the IT Supply Chain from Cyber Attacks." Information Age (March 24, 2015).

SAP Ariba. "SAP Ariba and SAP Fieldglass Corporate Fact Sheet." Ariba.com (May 8, 2019).

Schomberg, William. "Brexit Edges UK Companies out of EU Supply Chain." Reuters.com (May 13, 2018).

Smith, Jennifer. "True Value Retools Hardware Supply Chain." Wsj.com (July 16, 2019).

Suering, Stefan, and Martin Muller. "From a Literature Review to a Conceptual Framework for Sustainable

Supply Chain Management." *Journal of Cleaner Production* (June 12, 2008).

The Hackett Group, Inc. (Patrick Connaughton and Kurt Albertson). "Spot Buy Software: A Modern Approach to Managing Tail Spend." *Procurement Executive Insight* (April 2016).

True Value Company. "About Us." (Accessed February 2, 2020).

UN Global Compact. "Integrating the Sustainable Development Goals into Corporate Reporting: A Practical Guide." (2018).

UNCTAD (United Nations Conference on Trade and Development.) "Digital Economy Report 2019: Value Creation and Capture: Implications for Developing Countries." (2019).

U.S. Census Bureau. "E-Stats 2017: Measuring the Electronic Economy." (September 23, 2019).

Wadlow, Tom. "Hewlett Packard: Supply Chain, The Great Enabler." Techcrunch.com (April 5, 2018).

Zarroli, Jim. "In Trendy World of Fast Fashion, Styles Aren't Made to Last." Npr.org (March 11, 2013).

Index

A bolded page number indicates that the term is defined on that page.

A

a la carte revenue model, 644
A&E, 693
A.T. Kearney Procurement & Analytic Solutions, 851
A/B testing (split testing), **187**, 455
abandonment rate, 441, **442**
ABC, 669
Abu Dhabi, 795
Acacia Technologies, 591
Academy of Motion Picture Arts and Sciences v. GoDaddy.com, 594–595
Accelerace, 337
accelerator(s). *See* incubator(s)
acceptance testing, **187**
access controls, **284**
accessibility, 212–213, 738
accessibility rules, **211**
account aggregation, **781**
accountability, **544**
accountable supply chains, **831**–832
Accuracast, 482, 483–484
AceDeceiver, 264
ACH (Automated Clearing House), 295, 297
ACI Worldwide, 305
ACLU (American Civil Liberties Union), 712
Acquia, 195
acquisition rate, 441, **442**
Active Server Pages. *See* ASP
ActiveX, **209**
Activision, 686
Acxiom, 418, 579
ad blocking software, 407, 570, 571, 642
ad exchanges, **406**. *See also* advertising networks
ad fraud, 380, 406–407, 457
ad server, **141**, 196
ad targeting, 380, **396**
ad technology stack, 454
ad viewability, 380, 383, 406, 407, 440, 441, 445
Adams, Cameron, 324
adaptive delivery. *See* AWD
adaptive supply chains, 830–**831**
adaptive web delivery. *See* AWD
adaptive web design. *See* AWD
AdBlock, 434
Adblock Plus, 407, 570
AdChoices, 569
Adidas, 83, 379, 499
Adobe, 195, 342
Adobe Analytics, 342, 449
Adobe Dreamweaver CC, 137, 182, 183
Adobe Flash, 137, 139, 148, 245, 246, 431
Adobe InDesign, 323
Adobe Photoshop, 323
Adobe Sign, 257, 273
Adobe Spark, 325
Advanced Encryption Standard. *See* AES
advertisements, first banner ads, 98
advertising. *See* marketing; online advertising; online marketing; specific types
advertising networks, **405**
  privacy and, 545, 553, 554, 556, 562, 569, 607
advertising revenue model, **328**, 332, 644
advertising, traditional, 53, 447
advertorial, 403
adware, **250**
Adyen, 738
AerServ, 380
AES (Advanced Encryption Standard), **270**, 279
affiliate marketing, 342, **409**
affiliate revenue model, **329**, 332
affinity communities, **712**
affinity groups, **713**
Africa, 69, 93, 113–114, 119, 120, 379. *See also* specific countries
agency model, **666**
aggregators, 345
agile development, **190**
AgoraCart, 198
AIM (AOL Instant Messenger), 143
Airbnb, 39, 41, 49, 51, 52, 60, 63, 68, 210, 350, 365, 480, 748, 794, 797–798
Airbus, 354
airline industry, 402
Ajax (asynchronous JavaScript and XML), 209, 210
Akamai, 103, 158–161, 189, 201, 342, 591
Alabbar, Mohamed, 746, 747
Alando, 70
Alert Logic, 263
Alexa. *See* Amazon Alexa
Algeria, 301
algorithms, **713**–718, 790, 793
Alibaba, 70, 132, 286, 309, 401, 426, 702, 738, 767, 770, 811–813, 814, 842
Alice Corporation Pty. Ltd. V. CLS Bank International, 590
Alipay, 286, 296, 309–314
All Writs Act, 576, 577
AllSeen Alliance, 126, 129
Allstate, 783
Ally Bank, 779
AlphaBay, 235, 610
Alphabet, 92, 125, 152, 605. *See also* Google
Alphabet X, 92
AltaVista, 145, 146
altcoins, 301–302
Altice (Optimum Online), 645
Amazon, 39, 51, 63, 72, 93, 98, 146, 160, 246, 328, 332, 334, 341, 343, 364, 501
  affiliate program, 410
  Apple Watch app, 127, 128
  big tech, 605, 616–622
  business strategy, 764, 767
  case study, 762–769
  collaborative commerce, 843
  copyright, 52
  e-books, 664–667
  first-mover advantage, 72, 334
  long tail, 425, 426
  mission, 170
  music services, 682
  online content distribution, 636, 637, 644, 645, 648, 668–679, 682, 686, 691, 694, 695
  patents, 357, 361, 363, 591
  personalization, 416

877

Index

recommender systems, 385–386
Souq.com, 745–747
taxation, 601
trademarks, 592
Twitch.tv, 686
value chain, 359
value proposition, 327
value web, 360
VR and AR, 152
Walmart, 860
Whole Foods, 756, 764, 767
Amazon Alexa, 153, 221, 551, 763, 768, 803
Amazon Appstore, 155
Amazon Business, 352, 764, 848, 849
Amazon CloudFront, 109, 160, 342
Amazon Echo, 51, 55, 763, 764, 768
    privacy issues, 555
Amazon Fire TV, 644, 646, 671, 763, 764
Amazon Fresh, 767
Amazon Global Store, 746
Amazon Go, 767
Amazon Instant Video, 763
Amazon Kindle, 327–328, 641, 643, 645, 665, 666, 667, 669, 762, 763, 764, 766, 768
Amazon Kindle Unlimited, 328, 329
Amazon Music, 633, 635, 763, 764, 767
Amazon Pay, 295
Amazon Prime, 621, 671, 672, 675, 679, 694, 764, 761, 767, 768, 769
Amazon Prime Air, 766
Amazon Prime Music, 148, 768
Amazon Prime Video, 671, 672, 678, 766, 768
Amazon Prime Wardrobe, 767
Amazon Studios, 766
Amazon Supply, 849
Amazon UK, 484
Amazon Web Services (AWS), 108, 109–110, 111, 132, 152, 184, 185, 372, 619, 763, 764, 768, 769
Amazon Widgets, 210
America Online. *See* AOL
American Civil Liberties Union. *See* ACLU
American Eagle Outfitters, 520
American National Standards Institute (ANSI), 833
Americans with Disabilities Act (ADA), 213
Amobee, 380, 509
amplification, **473**, 480–482, 489, 495, 521
analytics, 51, 482, 483–484. *See also* web analytics; marketing analytics
analytics software, 198, 447–449
Ancestry, 328, 329
Andariel, 235
Anderson, Chris, 422, 426
Andreessen, Marc, 98, 134, 135
Android (Google), operating system, 107, 129, 148, 153, 154, 208, 218, 515, 519, 559, 568, 577, 622, 802
    apps, 154, 347, 517, 653, 684, 766, 770, 773, 784. *See also* specific apps
    malware, 261, 262–263, 264–265
Android Auto, 126, 347
Android Automotive, 126
Android Market, 154
Android Wear, 128
angel investor(s), **337**
AngularJS, 209
anonymity vs public safety, e-commerce security, 242–243

Anonymous, 252
anonymous data, 553, 556, 558, 561
anonymous information, **553**
anonymous profiles, **556**
anonymous remailers, 570
Ant Financial, 310, 311, 313. *See also* Alipay
Anticybersquatting Consumer Protection Act (ACPA), **593**, 594
antitrust laws, 605, 616–622
anti-virus software, 282
Any2Exchange, 118
AOL (America Online), 343, 348, 434, 646, 658, 692, 726–728, 732
Apache, 140, 193, 198, 207, 210
Apache Cordova, 218
Apache ServiceMix, 227
Apache Software Foundation, 437
Apache Struts, 261
App Store. *See* Apple App Store
apparel and accessories, online retail, 752, 753
Appery.io, 218
Apple, 39, 43, 51, 132, 342, 433
    app malware, 264
    biometrics, 284, 285–286
    case study, 576–578
    China, 577–578
    connected cars, 126, 347
    copyright, 52
    e-book price fixing, 666–667
    facial recognition technology, 557
    intelligent digital assistant, 153
    Intelligent Tracking Prevention (ITP), 432, 570
    mobile payments, 291, 296, 297, 310, 312, 313
    patents, 591
    privacy, 574, 576–578
    smart houses, 126
    VR and AR, 152
    Wi-Fi services, 124
Apple AirPlay, 129
Apple App Store, 49, 50, 128, 153, 154, 220
Apple ARKit, 151, 152
Apple Books, 665
Apple CarPlay, 126, 347
Apple Computer HyperCard, 97
Apple Dashboard Widgets, 210
Apple Face ID, 284, 285–286
Apple FaceTime, 144
Apple GarageBand, 647
Apple HomeKit, 126
Apple HomePod, 126
Apple iBeacon, 519–520
Apple iBooks. *See* Apple Books
Apple iBooks Author, 667
Apple iCloud, 110, 263, 290, 573
Apple iDevices, 364
Apple Intelligent Tracking Prevention (ITP), 434
Apple iOS, 107, 126, 148, 152, 154, 208, 218, 503, 515, 516, 519, 683, 771, 802
    security, 264
    privacy, 432, 559, 577
Apple iPad, 48, 107, 124, 153, 154, 643, 665, 681, 823–824, 832
    apps, 466–467, 653, 766, 772, 784
Apple iPhone, 43, 48, 67, 99, 124, 126, 137, 153–154, 468, 514, 516, 519, 652, 681, 737, 775, 823–824, 832
    Apple Watch, 127–128
    apps, 466–467, 766, 770, 771, 772, 773, 784

encryption, 290, 575, 576–578
    security, 262–265, 284–286 , 557
Apple iPod, 127, 148, 153, 681
Apple iTunes, 148, 334, 643, 645, 669, 671, 672, 674, 676, 678, 680–683, 684, 694
Apple Macintosh, 97, 134, 141, 142, 144
Apple Music, 128, 148, 328, 343, 669, 682, 683
Apple News+, 663
Apple Pay, 99, 126, 128, 291, 292, 296, 297, 313, 314, 490, 738
Apple QuickTime, 148
Apple Safari, 142, 214, 246, 276, 432, 434, 563, 570, 571
Apple Siri, 126, 128, 153, 221, 347, 671
Apple Touch ID, 284, 285
Apple TV, 644, 646, 671, 672, 678, 768
Apple Watch, 99, 126, 127–128
application gateways, 280
Application Layer, of TCP/IP, **102**, 103, 112, 113
application servers, 196–197
Applications layer, 114, **115**
app(s), 45. *See* mobile app(s); specific apps
Aquila, 93, 125
Aramex, 747
Argentina, 704
Ariba. *See* SAP Ariba
Ariba Network, 352, 837, 848, 851
ARPANET, 96, 97, 98
Art.com, 756
artificial intelligence, 153, 221, 331, 484, 738
Ascenta, 125
Ashcroft v. Free Speech Coalition, 606
Ashley Madison, 563
Asia, 117, 185, 351, 379. *See also* specific countries
Asia-Pacific, 51, 58, 84, 114, 309–314, 380, 677, 704, 746, 749. *See also* specific countries
Ask, 343, 348
Aslin, Dagny Amber, 525–530
ASOS, 328, 332, 776–777
ASP (Active Server Pages), 194, 203, 204, **207**
ASP.NET, **207**, 210
AspDotNetStorefront, 198
Assange, Julian, 252
assets, **760**
asymmetric cryptography. *See* public key cryptography
asymmetry, **334**
asynchronous JavaScript and XML. *See* Ajax
AT&T, 63, 98, 116, 126, 129, 152, 431, 457, 514, 516, 564, 600, 618, 645, 646, 648, 665, 672, 691
AT&T GigaPower, 573
AT&T Wi-Fi Services, 124
Atlantic Records, 669
attachment, e-mail, **143**
attachments, malicious, 245
attrition rate, 441, **442**
auction server, 196
auctions. *See* online auctions
AuctionWeb. *See* eBay
Audacy, 93
Audi AG and Volkswagen of America Inc., v. Bob D'Amato, 594
audio/video server, 196
augmented reality (AR), 85, 95, **150**, 151–152, 496–497, 509–510, 738
Australia, 69, 92, 132, 167–169, 185, 220, 213, 310, 313, 323, 325, 339, 340, 379, 467, 572, 603, 789
Austria, 337, 558
authentication, 268

authentication procedures, **284**
authenticity, **241**
authorization management systems, **287**
authorization policies, **287**
Authorize.net, 294, 342
Authors Guild, 583
Automated Clearing House. *See* ACH
automated order entry systems, **817**
automated response systems, **420**
automobile industry, 357, 752–753
autonomous cars, 126
AutoStore, 83
Auxmoney, 340
availability, **242**
Avant, 782
Avendra, 855
Aviate, 732
Away Travel, 772
AWD (adaptive Web design),137, **217**
AwesomenessTV, 720
AWS. *See* Amazon Web Services
Axos Bank, 779
Axway Appcelerator, 218

B

B2B (business-to-business) e-commerce, **59**, 63, **817**
    business models, 59–60, 351–354
    cloud-based, 815, 816, 828, 830, 835, 836–838, 843, 844, 855, 861, 865–870
    evolution of, 817–819
    growth, 51, 52, 60, 819–821
    marketing, 845–846
    major trends, 815, 816
    mobile, 835–836
    overview, 815–822
    potential benefits and challenges, 821–822
    sell side, 814
    social, 844–845
    supply (buy) side, 814
B2B commerce, **817**
B2B digital commerce. *See* B2B e-commerce
B2B e-commerce website, **819**
B2B server, 196
B2B service provider, **352**
B2B trade, 815
B2C (business-to-consumer) e-commerce, **58**
    business model(s), 58–59, 341–351
    growth, worldwide, 58
Baby Boomers, 639, 640, 642
backbone, **115**–116
backdoor, **248** , 577, 578
backend databases, 191
BackTweets, 489
BadB. *See* Vladislav Horohorin
Baidu, 126, 132, 145, 707
bait and switch, 72
balance sheet, **760**
Band, 704
bandwidth, **116**, 117, 119
bandwidth capacity, 95
Bangladesh, 301, 824, 831
Banking Circle, 812
bankruptcies, retail chains, 756
banner ad(s), 63, **402**

bargaining power, 355, 356
Barkbox, 761
Barnes & Noble, 341, 664, 665
barriers to entry, **344**, 355, 356
barter, 445
BASF, 866
BashBug. *See* ShellShock
Battelle, John, 417
Baxter Healthcare, 63, 817–818
Bazaarvoice, 342
BBN Technologies, 97
BBVA, 779
BCD Travel, 787
beauty products, digital native verticals, 772
BEC (business e-mail compromise) phishing, **250**
bedding products, digital native verticals, 772
Beebone botnet, 248
behavioral targeting, 413, **416**–418, 553, 554, 555–558, 562, 563, 570
Belgium, 812
Benassaya, Jonathan, 634
Bench, 350
benchmarking, **188**
Benioff, Marc, 657
Bentley Walker, 120
Berners-Lee, Tim, 50, 98, 134
Bernina of America, Inc. v. Fashion Fabrics Int'l, Inc., 594, 596
Bessemer Venture Partners, 323
Better Business Bureau (BBB), 568
Betterment, 780
Bezos, Jeff, 98, 645, 657, 762
bid rigging, 725
bid siphoning, 726
Bid4Assets, 719
bidding fee auction. *See* penny auction
big data, 51, 52, 95, **436**, 749, 775, 776–777, 783, 793
    IoT, 125
    online career services, 793
    online marketing, 436–437
    privacy issues, 574
big tech, 43, 51, 605, 616–622
Bigcommerce, 160, 198, 342, 490
Bill Me Later. *See* PayPal Credit
Bill of Rights, U.S. Constitution, 571, 600
biller-direct EBPP business model, 303–304
Bilski et al. v. Kappos, 590
Binance, 301
Bing, 145, 146, 343, 348, 393, 400, 475, 597, 599, 728, 732, 774
binge-watching, 641, 642, 673, 692, 695
BioCatch, 286
biometrics, **284**, 285–286
Birchbox, 329, 332, 373, 749, 761
Birds Eye UK, 493
bit, 101
Bitcoin(s), 239, 247, **299**–302, 338, 609
Bitcoin Cash, 302
Bitfinex, 300, 301
Bitly, 529
bits per second (Bps), 116
BitTorrent, 587, 601, 676
BizRate, 342
black hats, **253**
BlackPlanet, 712
BLE (Bluetooth low energy), 516, 519–520

blockchain, **297**–299, 573, 839–842
blockchain system, **297**
blog(s) (weblog), **149**, 411, 703
Blogger, 149
blogging, 149
blogroll, 149
Blue Apron, 493, 619
Blue Coat, 131
Blue Nile, 341, 343
BlueCava, 431
Bluefly, 341, 343, 752, 761, 775
BlueJeans Network, 165
Bluenoroff, 235
Bluetooth, 122, 123, **124**, 125, 309, 516, 519–520
Bluetooth low energy. *See* BLE
BMG Rights Management, 587
BMG Rights Management v. Cox Communications, 586–5555
BMI Baby, 213
BMW, 126, 354, 509–510
Boeing, 93, 120, 823
Boingo Wireless, 124
Bold360, 342
Bolivia, 301, 634
Bonobos, 364, 756, 767
book industry, 636, 649, 663–667. *See also* publishing industry
Booking.com, 787
Booking Holdings, 787, 802, 803
books. *See also* e-books
    music, and video, online retail, 753
    traditional, sales, 663
bookstores, physical, 665
Boost, 313
Border Gateway Protocol (BGP), **102**
Borders, 665, 763
Borg, Bjorn, 483
BorgWarner, 354
Bosch, 354
Boston Internet Exchange (BOSIX), 118
bot, **248**
bot-herder, 248
bot networks, DoS attacks, 259
botnet, **248**, 249
bounce-back rate, 441, **443**
Bouyges Telecom, 117
Box, 110
BP (British Petroleum), 866
brand(s), 72, 334
brand jacking, 593
brand strength, measuring, 480–482, 489, 495
branded store proximity mobile wallets, **296**, 297
BravoSolution, 851
Brazil, 70, 116, 325, 467, 812
bricks-and-clicks, **769**
Brin, Sergey, 145–146
Bring Your Own Device (BYOD) policy, **836**
British Airways, 710–711
broadband, 99, **117**, 119, 120, 121–124, 384–385, 637, 639, 673
broadband households, 117
broadband ISPs, FCC privacy regulation, 564
broadcast TV providers, 639, 650, 668, 669, 671, 672, 677. *See also* specific providers
Broadcom, 129
Bronto Software, 342

Brooklinen, 772
Brown, Chris, 710
browser(s). *See also* mobile browser
    mobile, 45, 49, 50
    web, 43, 45, 48, 50, 95, 98, 104, 108, 112, 134–135, 137, 142, 145
browser parasite, **250**
browse-to-buy ratio, 441, **442**
Brut, 660–661
BT Italia, 117
Buffer, 342
Buffett, Warren, 657
bug bounty programs, 253
bulletin board. *See* message board
Bulu Box, 761
Bumble, 168
bundling, **423**
Burberry, 499
Burger King Russia, 710
Bush, Vannevar, 134
business analytics, 51
business
    basic concepts, 75
    how e-commerce changes, 354–366
    impact of Internet, 354–355
    major e-commerce trends, 51, 52, 95, 816
Business Insider, 659, 660
business methods patents, 589–590
business model(s), **326**
    B2B, 59–60, 351–354
    B2C, 58–59, 341–351
    choosing, 170–171
    competitive advantage, 333–334, 336
    competitive environment, 332–333, 336
    difference from technology platform, 338, 341
    disruption, e-commerce technology, 363–366
    e-commerce, **326**–354
    elevator pitch, 337
    key elements, 326–329, 332–336
    management team, 335–336
    market opportunity, 329, 332, 333, 336
    market strategy, 334–335, 336
    multiple, 341
    organizational development, 335, 336
    raising capital, 336–338
    revenue model(s), 328–329, 332, 336
    value proposition, 326–328, 336
business model(s), B2B, 351–354, 846–862
    e-distributor, 351–352, 848–849
    e-procurement, 352, 849–851
    exchange(s), 352, 353, 851–853
    industry consortia, 352, 353–354, 853–855
    private industrial network, 352, 354, 856–862
business model(s), B2C, 58–59, 341–351, 744–743
    community provider, 343, 344–345, 701–733
    content provider, 343, 345, 649–687, 633–695
    e-tailer, 341–343, 760–779
    market creator, 343, 349–350, 715, 719–726
    on-demand service, 39–42, 43, 52, 68, 794–798
    online auction, 715, 719–726, 721
    portal, 343, 348, 732–731
    service provider, 343, 350–351, 778–793, 800–804
    transaction broker, 343, 348–349, 350, 775
business model(s), B2C e-tailer, 341–343, 760–779
    catalog merchant, 343, 771–772
    manufacturer-direct, 72, 343, 772–773
    omni-channel merchants, 341, 343, 769–771
    virtual merchant, 341–343, 760–769
business objectives, **179**
business plan, **326**
business processes, 326, 354, 362
business strategies, **361**–364
    cost competition, 361, 362–363, 364
    customer intimacy, 361, 363, 364
    differentiation, 361–362, 364
    focus/market niche, 361, 363, 364
    scope, 361, 363, 364
business-to-business (B2B) e-commerce. *See* B2B e-commerce
business-to-consumer (B2C) auctions, **719**
business-to-consumer (B2C) e-commerce. *See* B2C e-commerce
Butler, Oobah, 789
Buy buttons, 473, 477, 479, 496, 508, 756
buyer-side solutions, **743**
BuzzFeed, 650, 658, 659, 662
byte, 101
ByteDance, 500

C

C programming language, 154, 195
C++, programming language, 154
C2C (consumer-to-consumer) e-commerce, **60**
CA (certification authority), **274**
Cabela's, 771
Cabir, 262
Cable Communications Policy Act, 551
cable Internet, **119**
cable TV providers, 637, 638, 643, 646, 668–675, 677, 678. *See also* specific providers
Cable.co.uk, 117
Cainiao, 812
CakePHP, 210
California Consumer Privacy Act (CCPA), 539, 551
California Electronic Communications Privacy Act, 551
California Online Privacy Protection Act, 551
Cambridge Analytica, 76–77, 476, 568
Camp, Garrett, 39
campus/corporate area networks. *See* CANs
Canada, 83, 301, 339, 351, 409, 467, 528, 609, 764, 849
cannibalization, 638
Canon, 366
CANs (campus/corporate area network(s)), 120
CAN-SPAM Act, 288, 409
Canva, 323–325, 326
capital, raising, 336–338
Capital One, 253, 396, 779
Carbonite, 350
card-not-present (CNP)
    fraud, 238, 294
    transactions, 292
carder forums, 239
Carderplanet, 243
Cardersmarket, 243
Careem, 795–796
career services, 788, 791–793
CareerBuilder, 788, 791, 792, 793
careers, e-commerce, 79–81, 155–157, 219, 222–224, 305–308, 366–369, 449–452, 521–524, 612–615, 687–690, 733–735, 798–800,

862–864
Carnegie Mellon University, 260, 289
Carpenter v. United States, 579
cars
    autonomous (self-driving), 346–347
    connected (smart), 346–347
cart conversion ratio, 441, **442**
Cartier, 414, 415
Cascading Style Sheets. *See* CSS3
Casper, 772
catalog merchants, **771**–772
Categorical Imperative, Kant's, 546
Caterpillar, 824
Cazes, Alexandre, 610
CBS, 648, 669, 672, 695
CBS All Access, 672
CCMP, 279
ccTLDs (country-code top-level domains), 135, 137
CDN (content delivery network) industry, 159, 160, 190, 201, 342
CDs, 639, 680, 681
CDW, 752, 771
cell phone(s). *See* mobile phone(s); smartphone(s)
cell towers, 516
Cellebrite, 576
Center for Democracy and Technology (CDT), 573
Center for Strategic and International Studies, 237
CenturyLink, 116, 184
Cerf, Vint, 97
CERN, 98, 134
CERT Coordination Center, **289**
certification authority. *See* CA
CGI (Common Gateway Interface), 194, **207**
Changeup, 248
channel conflict, **772**
channel management, 723, 724
ChannelAdvisor, 342
Charles Schwab, 780
Charter Spectrum, 126
Chase Paymentech, 342
chat server, 196
chatbot, 61
CheapTickets, 357, 786, 787
Check Point, 235, 342, 500
checkout conversion rate, 441, **442**
Cheetah Digital, 342
chemical industry, 357, 865–870
Chewy, 756
Chicago Mercantile Exchange, 295, 301
Child Pornography Prevention Act, 606
children
    marketing to, 499–500
    protecting, 132, 606–608
Children's Internet Protection Act (CIPA), 606–607
Children's Online Privacy Protection Act (COPPA), 500, 551, 560, 607
Children's Online Protection Act, 606
China, 234, 325, 379, 380, 677, 692, 747, 830
    Alibaba, 811–184
    Apple, 577–578
    Bitcoin, 301
    control of Internet, 130, 599–600
    DDoS attacks, 260
    government regulation and surveillance of Internet, 131–132
    Great Firewall, 131, 599
    Internet access, 91
    LinkedIn, 701–702
    mobile malware, 264
    mobile payments, 296, 309–314
    Puma, 83, 85
    search engines, 145
    social networks, 704
    TikTok, 499–500
    Uber, 40
    VPN regulation, 578
    World Trade Organization, 830
China Broadband Capital, 701
China Unicom, 161
China Rail, 221
chip cards. *See* EMV credit cards
Chipotle, 499
Chronicle Forums, 712
cigarettes, online sales of, 608
CIO, 345
cipher. *See* key
cipher text, **268**
circuit-switching, 100
Cisco, 126, 131, 145, 238, 608, 712, 713, 844, 857
Cisco Telepresence Studios, 844
Citadel botnet, 248, 249
citizens, privacy rights of, 548–549
Citrix RightSignature, 257
CJ Affiliate, 342, 410
Clark, Jim, 98, 135
Clean Clothes Campaign, 832
clearinghouse, 293, 294
click fraud, **400**
click to call, 420
Clickability (Upland), 195
ClickDesk, 420
clickstream analysis, 389
clickstream behavior, **389**
clickstream data, 541, 553, 554, 558, 565
clickstream marketing, 389
click-through rate. *See* CTR
Cliqz, 570, 571–572
client, **105**
client/server computing, 97, 104, **105**, 106
Clinton, Hillary, 252
cloud computing, 43, 51, 52, 67, 73, 74, 75, 95, 99, **107**–111, 149, 152, 160, 185–186, 342
    models, compared, 111
    music industry and, 682
    NIST standards, 108
    online content and media, 637, 643
    security issues, 263, 266
    television and movie industry and, 673, 677–678
cloud service providers (CSP), 108, 110, 111, 184, 185–186
cloud-based B2B, 815, 816, 828, 830, 835, **836**–838, 843, 844, 855, 861, 865–870
Cloudflare, 160
CMS (content management system), **182**, 195
CNN, 333, 345, 597, 642
CNNMoney, 781
Coalition for Better Ads (CBA), 571
Coca-Cola, 411, 598, 687, 710, 857
code signing, 276
CodeIgniter, 210

Codiqa, 218
Cogent Communications, 116
cognitive energy, 54
coin/cryptocurrency miners, **250**
Coinhive, 250
ColdFusion, **209**, 210
collaborative commerce, **840**
    compared to EDI, 843
    Elemica and, 865–870
    private industrial networks and, 858, 861
    social networks and, 844–845
    technology for, 844
    trends in, 840, 843–844
collaborative resource planning, forecasting, and replenishment. *See* CPFR
Collective Utilitarian principle, 546
College Confidential, 712
co-location, **184**
Columbia Records, 669
Comcast, 126, 160, 564, 645, 646, 678
Commerce Hub, 342
commerce
    Internet-influenced, 71
    traditional compared to e-commerce, 53–57
commercial transactions, 45, 54, 63
commoditization, **361**
Common Gateway Interface. *See* CGI
Communications Act, 604
Communications Assistance for Law Enforcement Act (CALEA), 258, 575, 577
Communications Decency Act (CDA), 606
Communications Intelligence Gathering Act, Germany, 133
communities of consumption, 66
community provider, 343, **344**–345
community, **473**
    measuring, 480–482, 489, 495, 521
Compagnie Financiere Richemont SA, 414
comparison engine feed/marketplace management, 342
competition (inter-firm rivalry), 357
competitive advantage, 65, **333**–334, 336, 357
competitive environment, 172, **332**–333, 336
competitors, in marketplace, 172
completion rate, 441, **442**
Complex Media, 720
component-based development, **190**
computer algorithms, **713**
Computer Fraud and Abuse Act, 288
Computer Matching and Privacy Protection Act, 550
Computer Security Act, 550
Computer Security Enhancement Act, 288
Computer Software Copyright Act, 581
computer(s). *See* specific types
computers and consumer electronics, online retail, 752, 753
Compuware, 342
Conde Nast, 658
Conference Board, The, 792
Conficker, 246, 249
confidentiality, **241** 268
connected cars, 125–126, 346-347
connected things, 125–126
console gaming, 685, 686
consolidator EBPP business model, 304
Constant Contact, 342

Constitution. *See* U.S Constitution.
consumer(s)
    how shoppers find vendors online, 391
    key issues in online privacy, 555
    privacy rights of, 549–572
    trust, online auctions, 725
    what they shop for and buy online, 390–391
consumer aggregation, 720
consumer behavior, **386**
Consumer Reports, 328
consumer-to-consumer (C2C) auctions, **715**
consumer-to-consumer (C2C) e-commerce. *See* C2C e-commerce
content convergence, **646**–647
content delivery network. *See* CDN
content farms, **400**
content industries, impact of e-commerce on, 357
content management system. *See* CMS
content marketing, **404**, 845
content provider, 343, **345**
content. *See also* online content; online media
    consumption of, 637, 638–639, 643
    dynamic, 173, 194–196, 203, 207, 208, 209, 210
    static, 172, 194, 200, 204
    user-generated, 51, 57, 67, 149, 173
    websites, 172–173
context advertising. *See* network keyword advertising
Continental, 354, 866
contract purchasing, **826**
conversational commerce, 61
conversion rate, 441, **442**, 476, 482, 488
conversion rate (e-mail), 442
Cook, Tim, 576–578
cookie(s), 211, **430**–432, 433–434
    first-party, 430, 432, 434, 554
    HTML5 storage, 554
    persistant, 554
    third-party, 416, 432, 433–434, 554, 556, 559, 570, 571, 572, 607
cookie managers, 570
copyright(s), 75, 581–588. *See also* intellectual property
    Apple, Amazon, Google, 52
    conflict over, 51, 52
    European Union, 587–588
    P2P file sharing, 544
    Viacom lawsuit against Google and YouTube, 586
copyright law, **581**
Copyright Term Extension Act (CTEA), 581
cord cutters, 641
cord nevers, 641
CoreSite, 118
coronavirus, impact, 813, 824, 830
corporate online booking solutions (COBS), 786
cost competition, strategy of, **362**
cost per action. *See* CPA
cost per click. *See* CPC
cost per lead. *See* CPL
cost per thousand. *See* CPM
cost transparency, 56
Costco, 843
costs
    customer acquisition, 72–73
    customizing e-commerce software packages, 183
    developing e-commerce presence, 175–176, 183
    developing mobile presence, 218–219

doing business online, 72–73
maintenance of e-commerce site, 188
online advertising, 445–447
online credit card system, 294
online payment of bills, 302–303
paper bills, 302–303
retention, 72–73
search, 71, 72
startup, 72–73
transaction, 72
country-code top-level domains. *See* ccTLDs
Court of Justice of the European Union (CJEU), 537–539
Cox Cable, 587
CPA (cost per action), **445**
CPC (cost per click), **445**, 485
CPC Strategy, 342
CPFR (collaborative resource planning, forecasting, and replenishment), 858, **861**
CPL (cost per lead), 445
CPM (cost per thousand), **445**
cracker, **252**
Craigslist, 60, 791
crawlers, 145
CrawlTrack, 198
credential stuffing, 248
credit card(s), 197, 198, 292–294, 310
    CVV2, 239
    dump data, 239, 256
    e-commerce enablers, 293–294
    EMV, 256, 294
    fraud/theft, 253, 256–256, 294
    limitations, 294
    PCI-DSS compliance, 294
Credit Karma, 779, 781
CRM (customer relationship management) systems, 372, **438**
cross-device graph, 559
cross-device tracking, 431–432, 554, 559, 562, **570**
cross-platform attribution, **444**
cross-site tracking, **570**
Crowdcube, 340
crowdfunding, 330–331, **338**, 339–340
CrowdTangle, 661
Crownpeak, 194
Cruz, Senator Ted, 76
cryptocurrencies, 236, **299**–302
CryptoDefense, 247
CryptoLocker, 247, 249
cryptomining, 236
Cryptowall, 247
CSNET, 97
CSP. *See* cloud service providers
CSS, 190, 194
CSS3 (Cascading Style Sheets), **137**, 215, 217
CTR (click-through rate), 397, 398, 403, 408, 416, **440**–**443**, 444, 445, 454
Curalate, 496
current assets, **760**
current liabilities, **760**
customer co-production, **418**
customer experience, **394**
customer forums, 342
customer intimacy, **363**
customer profile, **435**

customer relationship management (CRM) software, 342
customer relationship management systems. *See* CRM systems
customer reviews, 342
customer service, 419–420
customer touchpoints, **438**
customization, **56**, 57, 211, **418**, 541. *See also* personalization
CVV, 239
Cyber Security Enhancement Act, 575
cyberattacks, global, 233–235
cybercrime, 237–240. *See also* e-commerce security
cyberlockers, 676
cyberpiracy, **593**, 594, 595
Cybersecurity Information Sharing Act, 288, 289
cybersecurity threat management team trainee, careers, 305–308
Cybersource, 294, 342
Cyberspace Electronic Security Act, 288
cybersquatting, **593**–595
cybervandalism, **252**–253

D

D+AF, 480
D3 (Data Driven Documents), 209
Dailymotion, 660, 687
Dairy.com, 855
dancing baby case, 582–583
Daraz, 69
Dark Caracal, 264–265
dark social, **472**
dark Web. *See* deep Web
darknet, 609–610
data breach(es), 236, 237, 238, 243, 247, 252, **253**, 254–255, 256, 257, 260, 261, 266, 287, 288, 289, 325
    Equifax, 253
    estimated cost to US corporations, 237
    Marriott, 253, 254–255
    Yahoo, 253
data brokers, 553, 562, 568, 579
Data Driven Documents. *See* D3
Data Encryption Standard. *See* DES
data. *See* big data
data encryption, state legislation, 551
data flow diagram, 180, 181
data image, **556**
data mining, **435**
Data Protection Directive (Europe), 537–538, 566
data warehouse, **435**
database, 198, **432**, 435
database management system. *See* DBMS
database of intentions, 417
database server, **141**, 196
Datacoup, 573
DBMS (database management system), **435**
DBS PayLah, 313
DDoS (Distributed Denial of Service) attack, 160, **259**–260, 263, 267
DDoS smokescreening, 260
DealDash, 723
Debatepolitics, 712
deep linking, **597**
deep packet inspection, 131, 132, 554, 599
deep Web, 47
Deezer, 633–635, 636
Defend Trade Secrets Act (DTSA), 598
Deliveroo, 68

Delivery Hero, 69, 70
delivery rate, 441, **443**
Dell, 108, 129, 342, 343, 752, 772–773, 844, 858
Dell, Michael, 773
demand chain visibility, 858
demand curve, **420**, 421
demand-pull model, **772**
Democratic National Committee, 252
demographic information, 171, 172
Denial of Service attack. *See* DoS attack
Denmark, 291, 296, 337, 603
Depop, 60
DES (Data Encryption Standard), **270**
desktop computer(s), 43, 48, 49, 50, 51, 52, 73. *See also* specific types
desktop marketing expenditures, versus mobile, 504–505
DESX, 270
deterministic cross-device tracking, **431**
Deutsche Bahn, 234
Deutsche Telekom, 119
device fingerprinting, 554, **570**
DevOps, **190**
DHL, 608
Diamond v. Chakrabarty, 588–588
Dice, 791
Dick's Sporting Goods, 225–228
Didi Chuxing, 312, 796
differential privacy software, 570, **571**
differentiation, **361**
differentiation strategies, 355, 357, 361–362
Diffie, Whitfield, 270
Digi.me, 573
Digital Advertising Alliance (DAA), 432
digital audience development specialist, careers, 687–690
digital certificate(s), 273, **274**–277
digital commerce advertising strategies and tools. *See* online advertising
digital commerce marketing strategies and tools. *See* online marketing
digital commerce. *See* e-commerce
digital content. *See* online content
digital disruption, 40–41, **364**, 649–662
digital divide, 384–385
digital envelope, **273**
digital gamers. *See* online gamers
Digital HD, 678
Digital Library Initiative, 145
digital marketing assistant, careers, 449–452
digital marketing. *See* online marketing
digital media, streaming devices, 671
Digital Millennium Copyright Act. *See* DMCA
digital native verticals, 772
digital natives. *See* Millennials
Digital Realty Trust, 184
digital rights management. *See* DRM
digital signature(s), 256–257, 270–**273**, 275, 276, 284,
Digital Subscriber Line. *See* DSL
digital wallets. *See* mobile wallets
digitally enabled transaction(s), 45
dilemma, **545**
dilution, **592**
direct banks, 779
direct competitors, 332
direct e-mail marketing, **407**

direct goods, **825**, 826, 847, 857
Directive on Copyright (EU), 587–588
DirecTV Now, 672
Discover Bank, 779
discriminatory pricing, 616–622
discussion board. *See* online message board
Dish Network, 645, 672
disintermediation, **65**, 756, 774
Disney, 669, 674, 678, 679, 694
Disney+, 672, 679
display advertising, 401–407
    issues, 406–407
    metrics, 440–442
    mobile, 507
disruptive technologies, 107, **364**
disruptors, **365**
Distributed Denial of Service attack. *See* DDoS attack
distributed ledger, blockchain, 297
Django, 198, **210**
DMARC, 252
DMCA (Digital Millennium Copyright Act), **583**, 584–587
DNS (Domain Name System), 98, **104**, 105
DNS namespace, 46
DNS servers, 105
Do Not Track (DNT), 434, 562, 571
doctrine of fair use, **582**
Document Object Model. *See* DOM
DocuSign, 257, 273
Dollar Shave Club, 329, 371, 373
DOM (Document Object Model), 194
domain name(s), 98, 99, **104**, 105, 135, 136, 137, 141, 592
domain name registration, 342
Domain Name System. *See* DNS
Domain Names Act, 607
Domino's Pizza, 488
DoS (Denial of Service) attack, **259**
dossier society, 579
dot-com companies, failures of, 71
dot-com crash, 64
Dotster, 342
DoubleClick, 591. *See also* Google Ads
DoubleVerify, 380
Dow Chemical Company, 866, 868
Downadup, 248
download, **146**
downloadable media, 146, 148
downloading, of movies. *See* EST
Doximity, 712
doxing, 252
DPI (Deep Packet Inspection) software, 131
DraftKings, 611–612
Draper James, 772
Drawbridge, 431
drive-by download, **246**
Driver's Privacy Protection Act, 550
DRM (digital rights management), **645**, 669
Droga5, 82
drones, Internet access, 124–125
Dropbox, 110, 263, 325, 350, 422, 608
drugs, illegal, online, 608, 609–610
Drupal, 194
DSL (Digital Subscriber Line), **119**
DTC (direct-to-consumer). *See* manufacturer-direct

dual-home systems, 280
Dubai, 70, 635, 745, 795, 796
Dubin, Michael, 370, 371, 373
due process, **544**, 547, 548, 551, 560
dump data, credit card, 239, 256
Dunkin Donuts, 296
DuPont, 866, 868,
duration. *See* stickiness
Dutch Internet auction, **722**
DVDs, 676, 677–678, 686, 691, 692
Dwolla, 295
Dyn, DDoS attack, 259, 263, 267
dynamic content, 173, 194–196, 203, 207, 208, 209, 210
Dynamic HTML (DHTML), **194**
dynamic page generation, **194**–196
dynamic pricing, 41, 53, 65, **424**–425
Dynatrace, 342

E

E & J Gallo Winery v. Spider Webs Ltd., 593, 594
E*Trade, 72, 328, 6511, 780
E.W. Scripps, 650
E2Open, 837, 855
Earnestandjuliogallo.com, 593
eBay, 51, 60, 63, 72, 98, 197, 251, 295, 341, 343, 349–350, 357, 703, 713, 715, 719, 721, 724, 725, 726, 747
    Affiliates Program, 410
    Apple Watch app, 127, 128, 737
    case study, 736–739
    competition with Amazon, 719, 736, 738, 739
    Dick's Sporting Goods and, 226
eBay Business, 848, 849
eBay Kleinanzeigen, 738
eBay ShopBot, 738
eBid, 719
EBITA (earnings before income taxes, depreciation, and amortization). *See* pro forma earnings
e-books, 663–667
EBPP (electronic billing presentment and payment), **303**–304
e-business, **45**, 46
e-business, assistant manager, careers, 366–369
e-Chemicals, 868
e-commerce, **45**
    academic disciplines, 78–79
    assessment of, 68, 71–73
    behavioral approaches to, 78–79
    big-ticket/small ticket items, 390–391
    brief history, 63–68
    demographics, 383–384
    difference from e-business, 45, 46
    entrepreneurs, 51
    ethical, social and political issues, 536–622
    evolution of, 63–68
    future opportunities, 44
    global nature, 75
    government surveillance and, 574–575, 576–578, 579
    growth, 43, 44, 51, 52
    history, 43–44, 63–68
    iconic examples, 39
    infrastructure enablers, list, 342
    introduction to, 43, 44–52
    major trends, 48, 51, 52
    mobile platform, 43, 51, 52
    organizing themes of, 73–75, 78
    periods in development of, 63–67, 68
    platforms, providers, 342
    reasons to study, 44
    relative size of different types of, 62
    small business, 51
    social networks, 43, 51, 52, 55, 57, 61–62, 63, 67
    taxation of, 600–601, 602–603
    technical approaches to, 78
    types, 58–63
    typical transaction, 244
    vulnerable points in typical transaction, 245
e-commerce business model(s). *See* business model(s)
e-commerce enablers, 341, 342
e-commerce infrastructure, trends in, 95
e-commerce initiatives associate, careers, 798–800
e-commerce merchant server software, **197**. *See also* merchant server software package
e-commerce payment systems, 290–302
    alternative payments used by U.S. consumers., 292
    alternative systems, 295
    cryptocurrencies, 299–302
    limitations of online credit cards, 294
    major trends, 291
    mobile, 296–297, 309–314
    online credit card transactions, 292–294
    other countries, 291
e-commerce platform
    choosing hardware, 200–204
    choosing software, 191–200
    costs of customizing, 183
e-commerce presence
    building, 176–189
    business and revenue models, 170–171
    costs of developing, 175–176, 183
    developing map for, 174–175
    different types, 174
    factors to consider in developing, 177
    planning, 170–176
    timelines for, 175
    visioning process, 170
e-commerce privacy research associate, careers, 612–615
e-commerce retail category specialist, careers, 79–81
e-commerce security
    anonymity vs public safety, 242–243
    cloud security issues, 263, 266
    credit card fraud/theft, 256–256
    customer and merchant perspectives, 242
    cybervandalism, 252–253
    data breaches, 253, 254–255
    DDoS attacks, 259–260
    dimensions, 241–242
    DoS attacks, 259
    encryption, 268–277
    environment, 236–243
    government policies and controls on encryption software, 289–290
    hacking, 252–253
    hacktivism, 252–253
    identity fraud, 257
    insider attacks, 260
    IoT security issues, 266–267
    legislation, list, 288

malicious code, 244–250
management policies, 282–287
MiTM attacks, 258–259
mobile platform security issues, 262–263, 264–265
networks, protecting, 279–281
pharming, 257
phishing, 250–252
plan, developing, 283
poorly designed software, 260–261
protecting clients, 281–282
protecting Internet communications, 267–281
public safety and criminal uses of the Internet, 243
public-private efforts, 289–290
PUPs, 248–249
role of law and public policy, 287–290
scope of problem, 237–238
security vs. ease of use, 242–243
sniffing, 258
social network security issues, 261–262
spam (junk) Web sites, 257–258
spoofing, 257
technology solutions, 267–282
tension with other values, 242–243
terrorism, 243
threats, 244–267
tools available to achieve, 268
trends, 236
what is good, 240–241
e-commerce site. *See also* website
    cost to maintain, 188
    information collected by, 553
    overview of tools, 204–211
e-commerce software platform. *See also* merchant server software package
    choosing, 199–200
    high-end enterprise, 199
    midrange, 199
e-commerce technology. *See also* technology, e-commerce
    ethical, social and/or political implications, 540, 541
    impact of unique features on business environment, 355
    impact on marketing, 428–429
economic viability, **757**
Economist, The, 332
eCPM (effective cost-per-thousand), **446**
Eddystone, 519, 520
Edelman, Ben, 595
EDI (Electronic Data Interchange), 63, **818**, 833–835, 843, 859
e-distributor(s), **351**, **847**–849
eDreams OdigO, 787
education, gamification of, 640
effective cost-per-thousand. *See* eCPM
E-Government Act, 550
Egypt, 746, 747
eHarmony, 328, 329, 332
Ek, Daniel, 633
Eldred v. Ashcroft, 581
Electronic Arts, 686
Electronic Communications Privacy Act, 288
electronic data interchange. *See* EDI
Electronic Frontier Foundation (EFF), 571, 573
electronic mail. *See* e-mail
Electronic Privacy Information Center (EPIC), 573
Electronic Signatures in Global and National Commerce Act (E-Sign Law), 256, 289
Elementum, 836, 837
Elemica, 855, 865–870
elevator pitch, **336**, 337
Emaar Malls PJSC, 746, 747
e-mail (electronic mail), 97, **143**, 252, 570
e-mail attachments, **143**
e-mail marketing, 342, 407–409, 441, 442–443
e-mail wiretaps, 258
eMarketer, 49, 121, 149, 150, 845, 846
Emotet, 247–248, 249
EMV credit cards, 256, 294
encryption, **268**–277, 570, 572. *See also* public key cryptography, symmetric key cryptography
end-to-end encryption (E2EE) algorithm, 575
Endy, 772
engagement, **473**
    measuring, 480–482, 489, 495, 521
EngineerJobs, 785
England, 101, 234, 539, 789. *See also* Great Britain, United Kingdom
English auction, **722**
Enhanced 45-1-1 (E9-37-1), 517
ENISA (European Union Agency for Network and Information Security), 235
enterprise portals, **727**
enterprise systems, **828**, 865–870
entertainment industry, 636, 667–687. *See also* online entertainment industry, specific industries
    revenues, 639, 643, 644, 668–670
entrepreneur(s), 51, 69–70, 336–338. *See also* start-ups; venture capital
Entrust Datacard, 342
Envestnet Yodlee, 305, 781
Envoy, 343
Epic, 570, 571–572
Epic Marketplace, 563
EPiServer, CMS, 195
e-procurement, 352–353, 849–851
e-procurement firm, **352**
e-procurement Net marketplace, **849**
Equifax data breach, 253, 548
Equinix, 118
EquipNet, 852
equity crowdfunding, 339, 340
Ericsson, 92
E-Sign Law. *See* Electronic Signatures in Global and National Commerce Act
e-signature. *See* digital signature
ESPN, 333, 671
eSports, 686–687
EST (electronic sell through), **674**, 675, 678, 681
Esurance, 783
e-tailer, **341**–344, 760–773
EternalBlue, 233, 234, 235
Ether, 302
Ethereum, 302, 841–842
Ethernet, 97
ethics, **543**–547
Ethiopia, 131
eToys, 72
Etsy, 60, 63, 344
Europasat, 120
Europe. *See also* specific countries

broadband, 117, 119
cable Internet providers, 119
cloud service providers, 185–186
government regulation and surveillance of Internet, 132
privacy protections, 566–568
retail sales, 749
satellite Internet providers, 120
taxation, 600
Western, growth in Internet usage, 113
European Commission, 213, 338, 340, 566, 602, 603, 620, 622
European Council, 213, 290, 602
European Monitoring Centre for Drugs and Drug Addiction (EMCDDA), 609, 610
European Parliament, 213, 587
European Union (EU), 51, 235, 305, 379, 797. *See also* specific countries
    big tech, 619–622
    CAs, 275
    copyright protection, 587–588
    crowdfunding, 338, 340
    Cybersecurity Act, 235
    Data Protection Directive, 537–538, 566
    European Accessibility Act (EAA), 213
    General Data Protection Regulation (GDPR), 51, 539, 566–568
    Payment Services Directive, 286, 305
    privacy issues, 537–539, 566–568
    Revised Payment Service Directive (PSD 2), 305
    Single Digital Market, 589
    taxation, 602–603
    Trade Secrets Directive, 598
European Union Agency for Network and Information Security. *See* ENISA
Europol, 233, 610
Eve.com, 72
Everlane, 772
Evonik Industries, 869
Evrythng, 437
exabyte, 158
Exceda, 161
exchange(s), **353**, **851**–853
ExchangeHunterJumper.com, 525–530
ExecuNet, 791
Exede. *See* Viasat
exit strategy, 337–338
Expedia, 72, 343, 357, 786, 787, 788
Experian, 579
exploit, 245
exploit kit, **245**
eXtensible Markup Language. *See* XML
eyeballs, 66, 468
eyeglasses, digital native verticals, 772

F

Facebook, 39, 43, 51, 67, 68, 71, 83, 92, 148, 149, 343, 344, 345, 457, 483, 484, 503, 712. *See also* social networks
    advertising revenue, 332, 470
    algorithms, 713–718
    analytics tools, 482
    as portal, 343, 348, 727–728, 732
    Ascenta purchase, 125
    basic features, 474, 475
    big tech, 605, 616–622
    brand pages, 474, 476, 479, 481
    Cambridge Analytica scandal, 568
    child pornography and, 608
    cybersquatting and, 594
    dangers of social media, 710–711
    data centers, 715
    demographics, 705–706
    echo chamber phenomenon, 716–718
    engagement, 473
    facial recognition technology, 557
    fake news controversy, 716
    fiber-optic network, 116
    first-mover advantage, 72
    friend search, 475
    FTC privacy enforcement action, 563
    Hadoop and, 437
    Internet access, India, 91–93
    live streaming, 587
    marketing campaigns, 478–480
    marketing tools, 474, 476–478
    measuring marketing results, 480–482
    mission, 170
    mobile marketing, 478, 479, 505
    mobile privacy issues, 559
    mobile users, 469, 704
    news media, 716–718
    patents, 591, 713, 716
    privacy, 76–77, 537, 552, 553, 556–559, 563–566, 568, 569, 572, 574, 576–578
    profile, 475
    purchase of WhatsApp, 143
    satellite Internet access, 120
    social e-commerce, 52, 61, 62, 63
    social marketing, 473–482
    status update, 475
    tagging, 475
    third-party apps, 475
    U.S. ad spending, 708
    U.S. presidential election 2016, 716
    user engagement, 707
    video ads, 477, 479
    VR and AR, 152
Facebook AR Studio, 510
Facebook Connect, 433
Facebook Connectivity Lab, 93, 125
Facebook Custom Audiences, 433, 476
Facebook Exchange. *See* FBX
Facebook for Mobile, 478
Facebook Graph Search, 400, 475
Facebook Groups, 475
Facebook Instant Articles, 650
Facebook Lead Ads, 456
Facebook Like button, 474, 475, 476, 477, 480, 481
Facebook Live, 477, 479, 660
Facebook Lookalike Audiences, 476
Facebook Marketplace, 60
Facebook Messenger, 51, 52, 61, 143, 144, 169, 304, 475, 478, 479, 483, 503, 708
Facebook News Feed, 475, 716–718
Facebook News Feed Page Post ads, 476–477, 479
Facebook Open Graph, 475
Facebook Place Tips, 519
Facebook Project Athena, 93
Facebook Reactions button, **474**, 475, 479
Facebook Right-Hand Column Sidebar ads, 476, 477, 478, 479, 528

Facebook Search, 400, 475
Facebook Share button, 474
Facebook Social Plugins, 433, 474
Facebook Spark AR Studio, 152
Facebook Timeline, 475
Facebook Trending algorithm, 717
Facebook Watch, 477–478
Facebook Workplace, 709
facial recognition technology, 556–557
factor markets, 363
Fair Credit Reporting Act, 551, 552
Fair Information Practices (FIP), 548, 549, 565, 566
Fair Labor Association, 824, 832
fair use, 582–583
fake accounts, 457
fake news, 600
Fakespot, 790
Family Educational Rights and Privacy Act, 551
fan acquisition, **472**
    measuring, 480–482, 489, 495
FanDuel, 611–612
fantasy sports, online gambling, 611–612
FAQs (frequently asked questions), **419**
Farfetch, 414
fast followers, 72
FastCGI, 207
Fastly, 160
Fastweb, 117
fax server, 196
FBI (Federal Bureau of Investigation), 251, 575, 576–578, 610
FBX (Facebook Exchange), 478
FCC (Federal Communications Commission), 99, 117, 431, 564, 604
FDA (Food and Drug Administration), 609
Federal Bureau of Investigation. *See* FBI
Federal Communications Commission. *See* FCC
Federal Intelligence Surveillance Act, 574
Federal Intelligence Surveillance Act (FISA) Court, 574, 575
Federal Networking Council. *See* FNC
Federal Trade Commission. *See* FTC
Federal Trademark Dilution Act, 592
FedEx, 234, 235, 608
feedback extortion, 726
FeedBurner, 528
Feedly, 140
Fiat Chrysler, 267
fiber-optic cable, **116**
fiber-optic service. *See* FiOS
Fidelity, 780
Field v. Google, Inc., 582
File Transfer Protocol. *See* FTP
Filo, David, 145
Financial Accounting Standards Board (FASB), 760
financial analysis, 759–760
financial model, 328. *See also* revenue model
Financial Modernization Act (Gramm-Leach Bliley Act), 288, 551
financial portals, **781**
financial services industries, 357
Financial Times, 56, 345
Finland, 291, 539
fintech, 779, 780, 782, 783, 785
FIOS (fiber-optic service), **119**
Firesheep, 278
firewalls, **279**–280, 281

firm value chain, **359**
firm value webs, 360–361
First Amendment. *See* U.S. Constitution, First Amendment
First Internet Bank of Indiana, 98
first mover(s), **65–66**, 72
first-mover advantage, 66, 68, 72, **334**, 348, 618–619
FIS Global, 305
FISA Amendments Reauthorization Act, 258
Fiserv, 304, 305
FitBit, 126, 128
Fitzgerald, F. Scott, 414
5G (Fifth Generation), **121,** 151
5MinMedia, 720
fixed costs, 420
Flash cookies, 430, 431
flash marketing, 415, 424–425
flash memory chips, 107
flash pricing, 72
Flickr, 732
Flipboard, 663
Flipkart, 85
Fly.com, 787
FNC (Federal Networking Council), resolution, 100
focus/market niche strategy, **363**
FogDog, 72
Food and Drug Administration. *See* FDA
FoodLogiQ, 842
Ford, 126, 347, 687, 824
Ford Motor Co. v. Lapertosa, 594, 595
Foreign Intelligence Surveillance Act, 258
formjacking, 238
Forrester Research, 71, 390, 412
Fortune 500, 709, 828
Fortune 1000, 476
Fossil, 126, 128
Foundem, 620
Foursquare, 518
4G (Fourth Generation), 122
Fox, 669
Foxconn, 824, 832
framing, **597**
France, 63, 83, 117, 132, 145, 185, 186, 213, 337, 340, 379, 467, 538–539, 660–661, 676, 779
France Televisions, 660
Franklin e-book reader, 172
FREAK, 261
Fred algorithm, 400
free, as pricing strategy, 422–423
Free Mobile, 117
Freedom of Information Act, 550
Freedom Scientific, 212
freemium strategy, 324, 325, **328**, 422–423, 634, 644
frequently asked questions. *See* FAQs
friction-free commerce, **65**, 71
frictionless commerce, 420
front end design, 190
FSOC (free space optical communications), 92
FTC, 287, 381, 403–404, 409, 548, 611, 789
    consumer rights-based privacy, 563
    COPPA, 607
    current privacy framework, 561
    Fair Information Practices (FIP) principles, 548
    Facebook settlement order, 77

marketing to children, 500
penny auctions, 723
privacy, 560–564
privacy enforcement actions, 563
privacy reports, 564–565
private industry self-regulation, 569
TRUSTe fine, 569
FTP (File Transfer Protocol), 102, **112**, 141
Fukushima nuclear reactor explosion, impact on supply chains 823
fulfillment, providers, 342
Fullz, 239
Fullzinfo, 239
Funding Circle, 340
funnel test, 187–188
furniture and home furnishings, online retail, 752
Fusion Books, 323

G

G Suite, 108
G-7/G-8, 289–290
GAAP (generally accepted accounting principles), 760
game industry, 636, 637, 639, 644, 667, 668, 670, 683–687
gamification, of education, 640
Gander Mountain, 756
Gannett, 650
Garmin, 126
Gartner, 110, 126, 186
gateway, 280
Gbps, 101
GCHQ, 290
GDES, 270
GDPR, 539, **566**–568, 684
GE (General Electric), 129, 857
GE Ecomagination, 843
Gear VR, Samsung, 95
GEICO, 596, 783
General Catalyst, 323
general communities, **709**
General Data Protection Regulation. *See* GDPR
General Electric. *See* GE
General Motors. *See* GM
general top-level domains. *See* GTLDs
Generalized Markup Language. *See* GML
general-purpose portals, 728, 731–733
Generation X, 640
GENI (Global Environment for Network Innovations), 98
geo-aware, **515**
GeoCities, 703
geo-search, 516
geo-social-based services marketing, 518
geo-targeting, Twitter Promoted Tweets, 486
GeoTrust, 342
Gerber, 457
Germany, 69, 70, 83, 132, 145, 185, 213, 234, 247, 379, 467, 538–539, 704, 739
GetThere, 787
Getty Images, 620
Ghostery, 433, 434, 570, 571–572
GHX, 855
gigabits per second (Gbps), 116
Gillette, 370, 371, 372, 373
Gilt Groupe, 425, 775
GitHub, 259

Glassdoor, 788, 791
Global Environment for Network Innovations. *See* GENI
Global Fairness Initiative, 832
global reach, 54, 57, 355, 429, 541
GlobalSign, 275
Glossier, 772
Glossybox, 70
GM (General Motors), 126, 347, 824
Gmail, 350, 503
GML (Generalized Markup Language), 137
Go Instore, 331
Go2Paper, 352, 848
go90, 720
GoDaddy, 342, 594–595
Golden Rule, 546
Golden Shield. *See* Great Firewall of China
Goldman Sachs, 220
GolfSmith, 227
Gomez, Selena, 84
Gonzalez, Mario Costeja, 537, 538
Goodyear Tire & Rubber Company, 866
Google, 39, 43, 47, 49, 50, 51, 71, 636, 637, 648, 666, 669, 671, 676, 677–679, 682, 686, 691, 694, 695, 732–733
  advertising revenue, 707
  big tech, 616–622
  child pornography and, 608
  China, 131–132
  connected cars, 126, 347
  copyright, 52
  e-sports, 687
  EU, 568, 622
  fiber-optic network, 116
  first-mover advantage, 72
  FTC privacy enforcement actions, 563
  history, 145–146
  how search engine works, 145–146, 147
  illegal drug advertising, 609
  intelligent digital assistant, 153
  Internet access, 91–93, 124–125
  Iran, 132
  local mobile search, 4515
  malvertising, 246
  mission, 170
  mobile ads, 379, 380, 501, 505, 708
  mobile payments, 291, 296, 297, 314
  Nest Labs purchase, 126, 556
  newspaper industry, 649, 651, 652, 657, 658
  patents, 591
  piracy, 676
  privacy policy, 556
  Project Loon, 92, 124–125
  Project Wing, 124
  right to be forgotten, 537–539, 568
  search portal, 343, 348
  smart houses, 126
  Titan Aerospace purchase, 124
  trademarks, 596
  YouTube. *See* YouTube
Google AdMob, 507, 511, 515
Google Ads, 398, 433, 444, 478, 545, 556
Google AdSense, 398, 410, 433, 732
Google AdWords, 146, 468, 485, 490, 511, 515, 596
Google Analytics, 198, 342, 433, 449, 482, 529

Google Android. *See* Android (Google)
Google ARCore, 152
Google Assistant, 126, 153, 221, 347
Google Cardboard, 95, 150
Google Chrome, 142, 209, 246, 276, 277, 407, 571, 622
Google Chromecast, 671, 672
Google Cloud, 132, 184, 185, 342, 661, 768
Google DayDream View, 150
Google Docs, 350, 622
Google Drive, 110, 325, 503
Google Flights, 787
Google Glass, 152
Google Hangouts, 143
Google Home, 51, 126, 153, 635
Google Library Project, 583
Google Maps, 210–211, 324, 350, 503, 513, 515, 620, 708
Google News, 653
Google Now, 153
Google PageRank, 146, 591
Google Pay, 291, 292, 296, 297, 313, 314, 738
Google Photos, 503
Google Pixel smartphone, 153
Google Play, 50, 148, 154, 220, 264, 503, 622, 671, 682, 684, 686, 753
Google Play Music, 635, 682
Google Play Protect, 265
Google Project Beacon, 519
Google Project Loon, 91–93, 124–125
Google Project Treble, 265
Google Publisher, 433
Google Reader, 140
Google Search, 92, 145–147, 398–400, 503
Google Shopping, 620, 622
Google Sites, 182, 183
Google Spain, 537
Google Street View, 124, 517
Google Tag Manager, 433
Google Wear OS, 128
Google+, 261
Google, Inc. v. American Blind & Wallpaper Factory, Inc., 594
Goto.com (Overture), 146, 591
governance, 542, **599**–605
Government Employees Insurance Company v. Google, Inc., 594, 596–597
GPS (Global Positioning System), 506, 508, 509, 514, 516, 517
  surveillance, 575, 568
GPShopper, 342
Grab, 313
GrabPay, 313
Gramm-Leach Bliley Act. *See* Health Insurance Portability and Accountability Act
Great Britain, 132, 233, 603. *See also* England, United Kingdom
Great Firewall of China, 131, 578, 599
grey hats, **253**
Greyball, Uber, 42
Greyshift, 576
Griffiths, Quentin, 776
grocery industry, Middle East, 795–796
Grokster, 544
gross margin, **759**
GroupM, 407
Groupon, 63, 210, 756
groupware server, 196
GT Nexus, 837

GTE, 98
gTLDs (general top-level domains), 135, 136, 137, 592
GTT Communications, 116
Guizhou-Cloud Big Data, 132
Gulden, Bjorn, 85
Gumtree, 60, 63, 738

H
H&M, 518, 831
Hachette, 619
hacker, **252**
hacking, 252–253
hacktivism, 236, **252**–253
hacktivists, 236, 252–253
Hadoop, **437**
Halligan, Mike, 167–169
HaLow. *See* IEEE 802.11ah
Hansa, 610
haptic technology, Taptic Engine, 127, 506
hardware. *See* specific types
hardware platform, **200**–204
Harley-Davidson, 171, 843
Harry's, 371
Harvard Business Review, 345
hash digests, 271–273
hash function, **271**–273
hashtag, 485
Hastings, Reed, 692
HauteLook, 425
Hayneedle, 756
HBase, 437
HBO, 669, 671, 672, 674, 679, 691, 693, 694, 695
HBO Now, 672, 695
health and personal care, online retail, 751
Health Insurance Portability and Accountability Act, 288, 551
Heartbleed bug, 236, **261**
Hellman, Martin, 270
HelloFresh, 69
Helu, Carlos Slim, 657
HENRYs (High Earnings, Not Yet Rich), 414, 415
herd behavior, **725**
Hewlett-Packard (HP), 838–839, 857
HigherEdJobs, 791
Hitachi, 234, 855
hit and run pricing, 72
hits, **440**, 441
Hoberman, 330
Hocking, Amanda, 664, 666
Hollywood. *See* movie industry
Home Depot, 711, 755
home entertainment, 674, 680–676. *See also* specific industries
Home24, 69
Homeland Security Act, 288, 289, 575
Homer, 247
Homes.com, 704
Hon Hai Precision Industry Company. *See* Foxconn
Honda, 509
Hong Kong, 220, 221, 313, 339, 500
HootSuite, 342, 482
horizontal market, **819**
horizontal marketplace, 354
horizontal scaling, **203**
Horohorin, Vladislav, 238

horse sales, social marketing and, 525–530
host, 94
host computer. *See* host
HostGator, 342
hosting services, 184, 342
Hostway, 342
hot spot (wireless access point), 122, 124
hotel industry. *See* travel industry
Hotels.com, 786, 787
Hotwire, 786
Hotwired, 63, 98
Houston Astros, 227
How, Ruth, 82
Howell, Jonathan, 331
HP, 108, 342
HSBC Bank, 286
HSTS, 278
HTC Exodus, 265
HTML (HyperText Markup Language), 47, 65, 94, 98, 122, 130, 134, 135, **137**–139, 140, 141, 150, 190. *See also* HTML5
HTML5, 50, 75, 95, **137**, 148, 209, 214, 215, 217, 218, 401, 466. *See also* HTML (HyperText Markup Language)
HTML5 Canvas, 137
HTTP (HyperText Transfer Protocol), 102, **112**, 134, 135, 140, 141. *See also* HTTPS
HTTP Strict Transport Security (HSTS), 278
HTTP/2, 112
HTTPS, 261, 275, 277, 278, 572
Huawei, 128, 133, 286
Hub of All Things (HAT), 573
hub-and-spoke system, **819**
Hubspot, 411
Hubstairs, 331
Huffington Post, 650, 658, 659
Hughes, 120
Hullabalook, 331
Hulu, 328, 637, 641, 648, 668, 671–674, 676, 677–679, 691, 694
Human Rights First, 832
Hummingbird, **399**
Hungary, 603
Hutchins, Marcus, 234–235, 247
hybrid advertisement pricing model, 445, 446
hybrid app, **215**
hybrid cloud, **110–111**
hyperlinks, 95, 97, 98, 106, 134, 135
HyperText Markup Language. *See* HTML
HyperText Transfer Protocol (HTTP). *See* HTTP
hypertext, **135**, 137

I

I/O intensive, **200**
IaaS (infrastructure as a service), 108
IAB (Internet Advertising Bureau), 246, 401, 403
IAB (Internet Architecture Board), 130
IANA (Internet Assigned Numbers Authority), 95, 129, 130, 599
IBA (interest-based advertising), **416**. *See also* behavioral targeting
IBM, 108, 129, 195, 342, 365, 437, 712, 713, 815, 816, 821, 828, 830, 833, 842, 855, 857, 861
IBM Bluemix, 184
IBM Cloud, 108, 342
IBM Commerce on Cloud, 199
IBM Digital Analytics, 342, 449, 482
IBM Emptoris Sourcing, 851

IBM personal computer, 97
IBM Security, 260
IBM Supply Chain Sustainability Management Solutions, 833
IBM Websphere, 183, 198, 227
ICANN (Internet Corporation for Assigned Names and Numbers), 98, 99, 129–130, 135–136, 592, 599, 607
Ice Dragon, 572
ICO (initial coin offering), **301**–302, 338
IDEA encryption algorithm, 270
IDEAL, 291
identity fraud, **257**
Identity Theft Resource Center, 253
IDS (intrusion detection system), **281**
IEEE 802.11 standards, 122–124
IESG (Internet Engineering Steering Group), 130
IETF (Internet Engineering Task Force), 112, 129, 130
IGF (Internet Governance Forum), 130
IHS Suppli. *See* IHS Markit
IHS Markit, 823
Ikea, 151, 330, 508
iKee.B worm, 263
Iliad, Trojan Horse in, 247
Illinois Biometric Information Privacy Act, 557
IM (instant messaging), **143**
IMAP (Internet Message Access Protocol), **112**
Imperial College, 235
implementation plan, **284**
impressions, **440**, 441, 468
Improving Critical Infrastructure Cybersecurity Executive Order, 288
In-addr.arpa domain, 46
incubator(s), 69–70, **337**
Indeed, 788, 791, 793
India, 40, 69, 83, 85, 91–93, 103, 277, 296, 301, 310, 313, 325, 379, 380, 381, 467, 500, 609, 634, 811, 812
Indiegogo, 338, 339
indirect competitors, 333
indirect goods, **825**, 847, 848, 850, 852, 857. *See also* MRO goods
Inditex, 824
Indonesia, 310, 380, 493
Industrial Internet Consortium, IoT standards, 129
Industrial Internet. *See* IoT (Internet of Things)
industry consortia, **353**, **853**–855
industry convergence, **648**
industry dynamics, 357
industry structural analysis, **356**
industry structure, **355**–358
industry value chains, 358–359
information asymmetry, **53**, 56, 65, 72
information density, **56**, 57, 355, 429, 541
information goods, 419
information policy set, 211
information privacy, **547**. *See also* privacy
information requirements, **179**
information rights, 542, 547–579
information society, 540
information-gathering tools, 553, 554
informed consent, 547, **560**, 561, 564, 565
Infoseek, 63
infrastructure as a service. *See* IaaS
INiTs, 337
initial coin offering. *See* ICO
initial public offering(s). *See* IPO(s)
InMobi, 379–381

insider attacks, 260
Instacart, 68
Instagram, 43, 52, 62, 67, 83, 127, 148, 149, 169, 210, 325, 471, 472, 473, 475, 483, 496, 499, 503, 505, 704–708, 710, 712
Instagram Marquee ads, 496
Instagram Stories, 496, 619
instant messaging. *See* IM
insurance industry, 782–783
Insurance.com, 783
Insure.com, 783
insurtech, 783
integrity, **241**
Intel, 107, 126, 129, 346
Intel Security, 342
intellectual property, 75, 579–599. *See also* specific types
intelligent agent technology, 420
intelligent digital assistants, 153, 221
Intelligent Tracking Prevention (ITP), 432, 570, **571**
Intelsat, 93
Interactive Advertising Bureau. *See* IAB (Interactive Advertising Bureau)
interactivity, **55**, 57, 355, 429, 541
Intercom, 169
interest-based advertising. *See* IBA
interest-based social networks, **712**
inter-firm rivalry (competition), 357
intermediaries, 72
International Labor Organization, 832
Internet, 45, **46, 94**
    architecture, 114, 115
    audience, 382–392
    backbone, 115–116
    backbone providers, 95
    broadband connections, 384–385
    communication tools, 142–145
    communications, protecting, 267–281
    community effects, 385–386
    control of, 599–600
    defined by FNC, 100
    demographics, 383–384
    ethical, social, and political issues, 540–547
    evolution, 96–99
    evolution of corporate computing and, 74
    example of client/server computing, 105–106
    features and services, 142–153
    governance of, 129–130
    government regulation and surveillance of, 131–133, 701–702
    growth, 46
    hourglass model, 114, 115
    impact on business, 354–355
    impact on marketing, 428–429
    infrastructure and access, 113–133
    intensity of use, 383
    key technology concepts, 100–113
    layers of, 114–115
    major information-gathering tools, 554
    map of physical structure in U.S., 116
    mobile impacts, 385
    scope of use, 383
    technology background, 94–113
    trademarks and, 593, 594
    traffic, 148, 158
    users' efforts to preserve privacy, 555

Internet access, 48, 383–384
    balloons, 91–93
    costs, 119
    download speeds, 119
    drones, 93, 124–125
    India, 91–93
    ISPs, 116–120
    mobile, 49, 121–124, 107, 214
    satellites, 93
    service levels and bandwidth choices, 119
    white spaces, 93, 125
    WLAN, 122–124
Internet Advertising Bureau. *See* IAB
Internet Architecture Board. *See* IAB
Internet Assigned Numbers Authority. *See* IANA
Internet Corporation for Assigned Names and Numbers. *See* ICANN
Internet Engineering Steering Group. *See* IESG
Internet Engineering Task Force. *See* IETF
Internet Exchange Points (IXPs). *See* IXPs
Internet Explorer, **135**, 142, 209
Internet Governance Forum. *See* IGF
Internet host, 46
Internet Layer, of TCP/IP, **102**
Internet marketing. *See* online marketing
Internet Message Access Protocol. *See* IMAP
Internet Network Operators Groups. *See* NOGs
Internet of Me, 572
Internet of Things. *See* IoT
Internet payment service providers, 294
Internet Protocol. *See* IP
Internet radio. *See* music, streaming
Internet Research Task Force. *See* IRTF
Internet Retailer, 71, 755, 761, 769, 770, 771, 772
Internet Service Provider(s). *See* ISP
Internet society, moral dimensions of, 542
Internet Society. *See* ISOC
Internet Systems Consortium, 46
Internet Tax Freedom Act, 601
Internet telephony, 144
Internet utility program, 111–113
Internet Watch Foundation, 608
Internet.org, 92
Internet2, 98
internetwork, 94
Interpol, 609
Intershop, 342
Intime Retailer, 812
intrusion detection system. *See* IDS
intrusion prevention system. *See* IPS
Intuit, 304, 779, 781, 782
Inventory Locator Service (ILS), 853
Investigatory Powers Act 2016, Great Britain, 133
io.js, 209
iOS. *See* Apple iOS
IoT (Internet of Things), 51, 52, 85, 95, 99, **125**–129
    Apple Watch and, 127–128
    business models, 346–347
    DDoS attacks, 259
    interoperability issues, 126, 129
    privacy, 129, 551
    security, 128, 129, 259, 266–267
IoTroop botnet. *See* Reaper
IP (Internet Protocol), **102**. *See also* IP (Internet Protocol) addresses

IP (Internet Protocol) addresses, 46, 95, 98, 100, 102–104, 105, 129, 141
    privacy issues, 554, 568
IP spoofing, 257
IP telephony, **144**
iPad (Apple). *See* Apple iPad
iPhone (Apple). *See* Apple iPhone
IPO(s) (initial public offerings(s))
    Alibaba, 811
    Deezer, 635
    Delivery Hero, 69
    HelloFresh, 69
    Home24, 69
    OpenTable, 802
    Pinterest, 467
    Rocket Internet, 69
    Spotify, 633
    Uber, 42
iProspect, 342
IPS (intrusion prevention system), **281**
IPv4, 95, 103
IPv4 Internet address, **103**
IPv6, 95, 99, 103, 125
IPv6 Internet address, **103**
Iran, 132, 599, 600
Ireland, 467, 602
IronPlanet, 852
IRTF (Internet Research Task Force), 129
ISOC (Internet Society), 112, 130, 267
ISP (Internet Service Provider), 116–120. *See also* Tier 1, Tier 2 and Tier 3 Internet Service Provider (ISP)
    FCC privacy regulation, 564
    net neutrality, 601, 604
Israel, 634
Italy, 70, 117, 291–292, 296, 340, 789–790, 812
iVOD (Internet Video ON Demand), **674**, 675
IXPs (Internet Exchange Points), **117**, 118

J

Jabong, 69
JadoPado, 747
Jagged Peak, 342
Japan, 116, 144, 221, 234, 237, 247, 292, 301, 310, 312, 339, 379, 467, 583, 603, 634, 704, 729, 811, 823–824, 829, 830
Java Database Connectivity. *See* JDBC
Java Server Pages. *See* JSP
Java, 154, 195, **208**–209, 210, 214, 217
JavaScript, 137, 190, 194, 198, **208**
Javelin Strategy & Research, 257, 779–780
JCPenney, 127, 341, 401
JDA Software Group, 227, 342
JDBC (Java Database Connectivity), 195
Jeep, 267, 408
Jenner, Kylie, 710
Jet.com, 72, 756, 767
Jim Beam, 486
Jimdo, 342
job search engines/aggregators, 793
JOBS Act. *See* Jumpstart Our Business Startups (JOBS) Act
Jobs, Laurene Powell, 657
Jobs, Steve, 153, 657
Johnson & Johnson, 457
Joomla, 196
JOOR, 853

JPMorgan Chase, 456–457
jQuery, 209, 218
JSP (Java Server Pages), 194, **208**
Jumia, 69
Jumpstart Our Business Startups (JOBS) Act, 338, 339
junior supply chain analyst, careers, 862–864
Juniper Networks, 131
Juniper Research, 238, 285
Just for Men, 508
Just Plain Folks, 712
JustEat, 39
just-in-time production, **829**

K

Kabbage, 782, 812
Kahn, Bob, 97
KakaoStory, 704
KakaoTalk, 144
Kalanick, Travis, 39, 42
Kant, Immanuel, 546
Karousel LLC, 93
Kayak, 787, 803
Kazaa, 357, 544
Kelly v. Arriba Soft, 582
Kenya, 92, 93, 125
key, **268**
keyword advertising, **398**
keywording, 596–597
Khosrowshahi, Dara, 42
Kickstarter, 210, 338, 339–340
Kijiji, 738
Kik, 143
kilobits per second (Kbps), 116
Kiloo, 472
KinderStart NexTag, 620
Kindle. *See* Amazon Kindle
King, Stephen, 664
Klaba, Octave, 185
Klein, Ezra, 658
Kleiner Perkins Caufield & Byers, 379
Kleinrock, Leonard, 97, 101
Klook Travel Technology Ltd., 220–221
Knowledge Graph, **399**
Kodak, 366
Kohl's, 127, 755
Korn Ferry Futurestep, 791
Kosmos Uitgevers, 483
Kreditech, 782
Kronos, 235, 247, 248
Kureha, 823

L

L.L.Bean, 159, 343, 363, 771
Lamoda, 69
LAMP, 210
Lands' End, 493, 771–772
Landweber, Lawrence, 97
Lanxess, 866
laptop computer(s), 43, 47, 48
latency, 101, 159
Latin America, 40, 92, 93, 103, 161, 291, 296, 634, 704, 831
Law of One Price, **420**
Lawrence, Jennifer, 263

laws, e-commerce security and, 287–289
Lazada, 70
Lazarus Group, 235
lead generation marketing, **410**
League of Legends, 687
LEAN principles, 401
lean production, **829**
Lee, Raj, 795
Leesa Sleep, 772
legacy computer systems, **828**
legacy databases, 191
legislation, European Union
    Cybersecurity Act, 235
    Data Protection Directive, 537–538, 566
    Directive on Copyright, 587–588
    European Accessibility Act (EAA), 213
    General Data Protection Regulation (GDPR), 539, 566–568
    Revised Payment Service Directive (PSD 2), 305
    Trade Secrets Directive, 598
legislation, U.S. federal
    All Writs Act, 576, 577
    Anticybersquatting Consumer Protection Act (ACPA), 593, 594
    Cable Communications Policy Act, 551
    CAN-SPAM Act, 288, 409
    Child Pornography Prevention Act, 606
    Children's Internet Protection Act, 606–607
    Children's Online Privacy Protection Act (COPPA), 500, 551, 560, 607
    Children's Online Protection Act, 606
    Communications Act, 604
    Communications Assistance for Law Enforcement Act (CALEA), 258, 575, 577
    Communications Decency Act (CDA), 606
    Computer Fraud and Abuse Act, 288
    Computer Matching and Privacy Protection Act, 550
    Computer Security Act, 550
    Computer Security Enhancement Act, 288
    Computer Software Copyright Act, 581
    Copyright Term Extension Act (CTEA), 581
    Cyber Security Enhancement Act, 575
    Cybersecurity Information Sharing Act (CISA), 288, 289
    Cyberspace Electronic Security Act (CESA), 288
    Defend Trade Secrets Act (DTSA), 598
    Digital Millennium Copyright Act (DMCA), 583–587
    Domain Names Act, 607
    Driver's Privacy Protection Act, 550
    E-Government Act, 550
    Electronic Communications Privacy Act, 288, 550
    Electronic Signatures in Global and National Commerce Act (E-Sign Law), 256, 288
    Fair Credit Reporting Act (FRCA), 551, 552
    Family Educational Rights and Privacy Act (FERPA), 551
    Federal Intelligence Surveillance Act (FISA), 258, 574
    Federal Trademark Dilution Act (FTDA), 5600
    Financial Modernization Act (Gramm-Leach Bliley Act), 288, 551
    FISA Amendments Reauthorization Act, 258
    Freedom of Information Act, 550
    Health Insurance Portability and Accountability Act, 288, 551
    Homeland Security Act, 288, 289, 575
    Internet Tax Freedom Act, 601
    Jumpstart Our Business Startups (JOBS) Act, 338, 339
    Music Modernization Act (MMA), 634, 683–684
    National Information Infrastructure Protection Act, 288
    Online Copyright Infringement Liability Limitation Act, 584
    Patent Act, 589
    Prevent All Cigarette Trafficking Act, 608
    Privacy Act, 549, 550
    Privacy Protection Act, 550
    Professional and Amateur Sports Protection Act (PASPA), 611
    Protect Act, 607
    Protect America Act, 258
    Rehabilitation Act (Section 508), 213
    Right to Financial Privacy Act, 551
    Securities Act, 760
    Telephone Consumer Protection Act (TCPA), 551
    Trademark Dilution Revision Act, 592
    21st Century Communications and Video Accessibility Act, 213
    U.S. SAFE WEB Act, 288
    Unlawful Internet Gambling Enforcement Act, 608
    USA Freedom Act, 550, 575
    USA Patriot Act, 258, 288, 289, 574, 575, 600
    Video Privacy Protection Act, 551
legislation, U.S. state,
    California Consumer Privacy Act (CCPA), 539, 551
    California Electronic Communications Privacy Act, 551
    California Online Privacy Protection Act, 551
    data encryption, 551
    employee privacy on social networks, 712
    Illinois Biometric Information Privacy Act, 557
    security breach disclosure, 551
    spyware, 551
LEGO, 488
Lei, Peng, 310
Leighton, Tom, 159
Lemonade, 783
Lending Club, 782
Lenovo, 141, 250, 342, 752
Leosat, 93
leverage, **334**
Lewin, Daniel, 159
LG, 128, 153, 342
Li, Ning, 330
liabilities, **760**
liability, **544**
Liberty Global, 119
Licklider, J.C.R., 97
Life Management tools, 572
LifeSize, 145
Like button. *See* Facebook Like button
LillianVernon, 343
Limelight Networks, 342
Limited Stores, 756
Lindy, 340
Line, 144, 312, 704, 729–730
Line Pay, 312, 730
linear TV, 641, 673
link farms, **401**
LinkedIn, 148, 343, 344, 471, 472, 483, 497, 701–702, 704, 708–709, 712, 783, 788, 792, 793
linking, **597**
Linux, 120, 140, 142, 193, 197, 207, 210, 214
Linux Foundation, 842
Linux.org, 712
Liquid Web, 342
liquidity, 720, **852**

list server, 196
listserv, 144
Litecoin, 302
live call, 420
live chat/click-to-call software, 342
live streaming, 587
LiveJournal, 149
LivePerson, 342, 420
LivingSocial, 756
local advertising, 412. *See also* location-based mobile marketing
local area networks, 97, 106
local e-commerce, 51, 52, **62**, 63, 749, 757, 775
local marketing, 412, 513–521
local mobile marketing. *See* location-based mobile marketing
local mobile search, Google, 515
local online marketing, 468–470, 513–521
LocalResponse, 518
location-based marketing, **513**
location-based mobile marketing, 469, 471, 514–521
location-based services, **513**, 518
      privacy issues, 559
logical design, **180**, 181
long tail effect, **425**
long tail marketing, 425, 426–427
long-term debt, **760**
long-term sourcing, 826, 829, 835, 849, 850, 853, 854
Lord & Taylor, 404, 518, 520
Lorentzon, Martin, 633
Los Angeles International Internet Exchange (LAIIX), 118
loser's lament, **725**
Lotus Notes, 844
Lowe's, 151
Lowestfare.com, 787
loyalty, **440**, 441
Lufthansa, 217
luggage, digital native verticals, 772
Lukaku, Romelu, 84
LulzSec, 252
Luxembourg, 602, 603
luxury marketing, 414–415
Lyft, 41, 347, 350, 457, 794

M

M-Lab, 117
Ma, Jack, 310, 811, 812
MacForTheBlind, 112
machine learning, 221, 372, 737–738, 777
Macromedia, 209
macro-virus, 249
Macy's, 518, 520, 520, 769–771
MADE.COM, 329, 330–331
madware, 263
Maersk, 235
MAEs (Metropolitan Area Exchanges), 117
magazine aggregator, **663**
magazine industry, 636, 649, 662–663. *See also* publishing industry
Magento, 199, 342, 372, 491
Magic Leap, 151, 152
Magzter, 663
mail server, **141**, 196, 280
MailChimp, 342
Mailhoit, Danielle, 712
Maimai, 702

mainframe computing, 106
Maktoob, 745
Malaysia, 311, 313, 379
malicious code (malware), 238, **244**–250
malicious mobile apps. *See* MMAs
malvertising, **245**, 246
malware. *See* malicious code
Malwarebytes, 250, 282
management policies, e-commerce security, 282–287
management team, **335**–336
Manhattan Associates, 227
man-in-the-middle attack. *See* MiTM attack
manufacturer-direct, 72, 167–168, 343, **772**–773
manufacturing industries, 357–358
many-to-few markets, 854
many-to-many markets, 850
many-to-one markets, 834
Maquila Solidarity Network, 832
marginal costs, 420, 421, 422, 423, 424
marginal revenue, 421
Marhely, Daniel, 634
Marilyn's Secret, 712
market competition, big tech, 605
market creator, 343, **349**–350
market efficiency, 720
market entry costs, 55
market liquidity, 353
market opportunity, **329**, 332, 333, 336, 342, 348, 349, 351
market segmentation, dynamic page generation and, 195
market strategy, 334–**335**, 336
marketing analytics software, 448
marketing automation systems, 372, **437**
marketing. *See also* online advertising; online marketing
      how multi-screen environment changes, 503–504
      multi-channel, 412–413
      prior to e-commerce, 53
      to children, 499–500
marketplace, **54**, 72, 171–172
marketspace, 43, **54**, 55, 57, 65, **329**
Markley, 118
Marktplaats, 738
markup languages, 137–140
Marriott, 253, 254–255, 788
Mashable, 659, 660
mashups, 210–211
massive machine-to-machine (M2M) connections, 121
massively multiplayer online (MMO) games, 685
MasterCard, 746
MasterCard Identity Check, 285–286
MasterCard MasterPass, 295
MasterCard RPPS, 305
Mastodon, 706
Matomo, 198
Mattel, 343
mattress industry, digital native verticals, 772
Mavrix Photographs LLC v. LiveJournal, Inc., 586
MBAGlobalNet, 791
McAfee, 237, 282
McDonald's, 508
McEnroe, John, 483
McGregor, Conor, 483
MCI, 98
McKesson, 833

McMaster-Carr, 848, 849
m-commerce (mobile e-commerce), 51, 52, 54, **60**, 61, 63, 154, 498, 501–504, 757, 766, 770, 775
    platform providers, 342
    m-commerce, retail, 61, 154, 501, 502
MD4, 271, 273
MD5, 271, 273
media
    average time spent per day, 412–413
    consumption of, 637, 638–639, 643
    mass, 57
media content industry, 645–646
media convergence, 646–648
Media Radar, 404
Media Rating Council, 407
MediaTek, 92
Medzilla, 791
Meeco, 573
Meerkat, 619
Meetup, 706
megabits per second (Mbps), 101, 116
Megaupload, 676
Meituan Waimai, 312
Melissa, 249
MENA (Middle East and North Africa), 745–747
menu costs, 53, 65, 195
Mercado Pago, 296
Mercedes Benz, 132, 415
MercExchange (Thomas Woolston), 591
merchant account, **293**
merchant server software package (e-commerce software platform), **197**–200
Merck, 235
Merkle, 342
mesh economy companies. *See* on-demand service companies
message digest. *See* hash digest
message encryption, 570
message integrity, 268
Metalshub, 63
metatag(s), 205–206
metatagging, 594, 595–596
Metcalfe, Bob, 97
Metcalfe's Law, 66
metered subscription, **656**
Metorik, 169
Metro-Goldwyn-Mayer Studios v. Grokster et al, 544
Metropolitan Area Exchanges. *See* MAEs
MeWe, 706
Mexico, 70, 351, 849
MGM, 544, 669
Mic, 660
Michael Kors, 510
Michelin, 866
Microsoft, 126, 233, 234, 417, 422, 437, 439, 842
    ActiveX and VBscript, 209
    advertising revenue, 707
    Airband Initiative, 125
    child pornography and, 608
    connected cars, 347
    digital crimes unit, 248
    fiber-optic network, 116
    Internet access, India 93
    LinkedIn acquisition, 701
    private industrial network, 857
    VR and AR, 151, 152
    Walmart partnership, 860
    web server software, 342
Microsoft Advertising, 556
Microsoft Azure, 184, 185, 342, 380, 768
Microsoft Bing. *See* Bing
Microsoft Cortana, 153
Microsoft Dynamics, 342
Microsoft Edge, 209
Microsoft Expression Web, 137
Microsoft Internet Information Services (IIS), 141, 193, 207
Microsoft Visual Studio, 182, 183
Microsoft Windows XP, 282
Microsoft Xbox, 685, 686
Microsoft Xbox Live, 328
Microsoft.Net, 207
Middle East, 40, 113–114, 161, 379, 634, 704, 745–747, 748, 767, 795–796
middlemen. *See* intermediaries
Middleware Services layer, 114, **115**
Midwest Internet Cooperative Exchange (MICE), 118
Millennial Media, 720
Millennials, 331, 490, 497, 639, 660, 661, 683, 684
    insurance services, 783
    mobile banking and, 779
    mobile investment services, 780
    online career services and, 793
    online content consumption, 640–642
Minitel, 63
Mint Bills, 304
Mint, 779, 781
Mirai botnet, 259, 267
Mishra, Kartikeya, 92
mission statement, 170, 175
MIT Center for Energy and Environment Policy Research, 42
MiTM (man-in-the-middle) attack, **259**, 261
Mitnick, Kevin, 250
Mixi, 704
MM. LaFleur, 772
MMAs (malicious mobile apps), 262
MMS (Multimedia Messaging Service), 143
Mobify, 342
mobile advertising, 51, 379–381, 411–412, 479, 479, 518, 501–512. *See also* mobile marketing
mobile app(s), 51, 95, 153–155. *See also* native app(s); hybrid app(s); mobile web apps; mobile platform; specific apps
    Android. *See* Android (Google), apps
    as marketing platform, 412
    B2B marketing, 845–846
    Blackberry Hub, 77
    developing, 214–219, 220–221
    development platforms, 154
    Facebook, 76–77
    fake, 264
    in-app ads, 502–503
    Internet access, 49
    iPad. *See* Apple iPad, apps
    iPhone. *See* Apple iPhone, apps
    Klook, 220–221
    malicious, 262–263, 264–265
    marketplaces, 154–155
    messaging, 51, 52, 61, 706

mobile shopping with, 154
Pinterest, 466–467, 491
privacy, 554
Puma, 84
top, 501, 503
Uber, 40–42
mobile B2B, 835–836
mobile bill payments, 303
mobile browser(s). *See* browser(s)
mobile device(s), 43, 45–47, 50, 52, 57, 73, 99, 124, 137, 142, 154–155, 158, 214–219. *See also* mobile platform; specific devices
basic features, 505–506
how people use, 501–502
impact on content industries, 67, 148, 636, 637, 638, 643
impact on growth of social networks, 61, 703, 706, 708
Internet access, 48, 95, 107, 214
marketing, 83, 498
m-commerce, 51, 60, 63, 338, 498, 501–504
privacy, 559–560, 576–578
security, 262–263, 264–265
mobile EBPP business model, 304
mobile e-commerce. *See* m-commerce
mobile first design, 175, **217**
mobile malware, 236
mobile marketing, 379–381, 411–412, 468–471, 498–512. *See also* mobile advertising
ad formats, 507–508
augmented reality advertising, 509–510
basic marketing features, 504–506
campaigns, 508, 510
display advertising, 507
expenditures, versus desktop, 504–505
Facebook, 470
measuring results, 511–512
search, 501, 507
top firms, 505
3D advertising, 509–510
Twitter, 470
mobile messaging, 51, 52, 61, 143, 507–508
mobile payments, 291, 296–297, 309–314
mobile phone(s), 107, 136. *See also* smartphones, mobile platform
surveillance, 575, 579
mobile platform, 43, 46, **47–48**, 51, 52, 68, 73, 74, 106–107. *See also* mobile apps; mobile devices; specific devices; specific apps
Akamai, 160
banking industry, 779–780
brokerage industry, 780
career services industry, 793
collaborative commerce, 844
constraints, 216, 218
entertainment industry, 668, 669
gaming industry, 683–687
growth, 47–48, 51, 52
home entertainment, 671, 673, 675
Internet access, 48, 121–124
Internet traffic, 158
magazine industry, 662–663
media consumption, 637, 638, 673, 685
music industry, 681
newspaper industry, 649–656, 659
Pinterest, 466–467
privacy, 559–560
publishing industry, 649, 666
retail industry, 749, 752, 756, 770, 775

security, 262–263, 264–265 travel industry, 787–788
mobile presence
cost considerations, 218–219
design considerations, 216–217
performance considerations, 218–219
planning and building, 215–216
mobile users, 469
mobile wallets, 296
mobile web app, **214**
mobile website, **214**
developing, 137, 149, 214, 215–219
Google search algorithm, 399
Mobilegeddon, 399
Mobissimo, 787
ModCloth, 756, 767
model-driven data mining, **436**
Mofuse, 218
Molbase, 852
MomentFeed, 518
Mondelez, 235
Monero, 302
monopoly, 605, 617–622
monopoly profits, 65
Monsoon, 342
Monster, 343, 348, 788, 791, 793
Moosejaw, 756, 767
Morgan Stanley, 347
Morphe Cosmetics, 772
Mosaic, 98, **134**
Mothercare, 328
motion picture industry. *See* movie industry
Motley Fool, 344
MOTO (Mail Order-Telephone Order) transactions, 292, 601, 750
Motors.co.uk, 738
Movable Type, 149
Moven, 779
movie industry, 636–639, 643–646, 648, 667–679, 691–695. *See also* Hollywood; home entertainment
movies, box office, 639, 668, 673, 675, 676, 677
Movinga, 39, 794
Mozilla Firefox, 142, 434
Mozilla Foundation, 135
MRO goods, 351, **825**, 845, 848, 849, 850
MSN, 343, 348, 726, 727, 728
MSN Money, 781
MSNBC, 687, 735
Mt. Gox, 301
MTV, 686
Multi Time Machine (MTM), trademark lawsuit against Amazon, 592
multi-channel marketing, 412–413, 530
Multimedia Messaging Service. *See* MMS
multiplayer online battle games, 687
multi-tier architecture, **192**
multi-tier supply chain, **826**
multivariate testing, **188**
music industry, 356–357, 636, 639, 650, 668, 670, 680–683
Music Modernization Act, 634, 683–684
music, streaming, 637, 642, 644, 645, 668, 669
mutually assured destruction. *See* MAD
My M&Ms, 419
MyCheckFree, 304
Mydoom, 249
MyPoints, as example of affiliate revenue model, 329, 332
Myspace, 345

MySQL, 198

N

Nakamoto, Satoshi, 299, 300
Name Your Own Price auction, **722**
Namshi, 70, 747
NAP of the Americas, 118
NAPs (Network Access Points), 117
Napster, 357, 681
narrowband, **117**, 120
NASA, 210
National Association of Realtors, 784
National Basketball Association (NBA), 85
National Center for Supercomputing Applications. *See* NCSA
National Consumers League, 832
National Cyber Security Centre (UK), 235
National Cybersecurity and Communications Integration Center (NCCIC), 289
National Fair Housing Alliance, 476
National Football League (NFL), 246
National Health Service (NHS), Great Britain, 234, 235, 483
National Informatics Centre, 277
National Information Infrastructure Protection Act, 288
National Public Radio (NPR), 148
National Science Foundation. *See* NSF
National Security Agency. *See* NSA
native advertising, 379, **403**
native app(s), 95, 154, 155, **214**–219
native digital news sites, 657–661
Naturebox, 749, 761
Natuzzi Italia, 151
Naver, 729
Nazi memorabila, 132
NBCUniversal, 646, 669, 678, 766
NCSA (National Center for Supercomputing Applications), 98, 134
near field communication. *See* NFC
neighborhood effects, 385–386
Neiman Marcus, 414–415
Nelson, Ted, 134
Nest Labs, 126, 556
Nest Weave, 126
net margin, **759**
Net marketplace(s), 59, 814, **819**, 846–819. *See also* specific types
net neutrality, 98, 99, **601**, 604
NetBank, 779
Netflix, 328, 332, 364, 426, 427, 604, 637, 644, 648, 669, 671–676, 677–679
    case study, 691–695
Netherlands, 291, 296, 340
NetQuote, 783
Netscape, 63, 98, 208
Netscape Navigator, **135**
Netscout Arbor, 259, 260
Netsky.P, 249
NetSuite, 199
Nettis Environment Ltd. V. IWI, Inc., 594
Network Access Points. *See* NAPs
Network Advertising Initiative (NAI), 432, 569
network effects, **66**, 720, 728, 803
network externalities, 55, 348
Network Interface Layer, of TCP/IP, **102**
network keyword advertising, **398**
network neutrality. *See* net neutrality
network notification, 61

Network Solutions Inc., 98, 342, 593
Network Technology Substrate layer, 114, **115**
Networkadvertising.org, 569
Neustar, 259
new concept test, 187
New York International Internet Exchange (NYIIX), 118
New York Stock Exchange, 301, 349
New York Times, 150, 419, 423, 433, 642, 650, 653, 654, 657
New York Times test, 546
New Yorker, 663
New Zealand, 92, 339, 603
Newegg, 591, 761
NeweggBusiness, 848
News Corp., 784
News Media Alliance, 657
news server, 196
NewsBlur, 140
newspaper industry, 636, 649–662. *See also* publishing industry, online newspaper industry, specific newspapers
    Facebook, 716–718
    privacy issues, 537–539
next generation firewalls, 280
NextBio, 437
Nextdoor, 706
NextRadioTV, 186
NFC (near field communication), **297**, 309, 519
Niantic, 683
NiceHash, 301
Nigeria, 131, 634
Nigerian letter e-mail scam, 250–251
Nike, 83, 343, 419, 499, 712, 772, 831, 857
Nintendo, 150, 686
Nissan, 687
Nissan Motor Co., Ltd. V. Nissan Computer Corp., 594, 596
No Free Lunch rule, 546
Node.js, 110, 209
NOGs (Internet Network Operators Groups), 130
Nokia, 92, 600, 857
nonrepudiation, **241**, 268
Noon.com, 747
Nordic Pay, 296
    Nordstrom, 425, 493, 752, 755, 774
North Africa, 745, 748, 795
North Korea, 235, 247, 599
Norway, 291, 296
NotPetya, 235
NSA (National Security Agency), 133, 233, 234, 235, 243, 253, 258, 261, 270, 290, 574, 575, 600
NSF (National Science Foundation), 96, 98
NSFNET, 96, 98
NTT Communications, 116, 484
Numa, 337
numeric address, 280
NuOrder, 852
Nurmagomedov, Khabib, 483
NuWar. *See* Storm
Nymex, 249

O

O2O (online-to-offline), 71
Objective C, 154, 217
Obrecht, Cliff, 323, 324
Ocado, 350
Oculus Rift, 95, 150, 152

ODBC (Open Database Connectivity), 195
OECD (Organization for Economic Cooperation and Development), 290
Office of Cybersecurity and Communications (CS&C), 289
offline commerce, 390
oil industry, 865–870
Oldandsold Antiques Auction, 719
Oliver, Jamie, 483–484
ologopolies, 616–622
Omidyar, Pierre, 98, 335
omni-channel, 83–85, 749, **752**, 753, 755, 756, 757, 760, 762, 767, 769–771
Onavo, 559
on-demand computing, 108
on-demand service, 43, 62, 73, 350, 794–798
1&1, 342
One Kings Lane, 756
OnePlus, 286
OneSpan Sign, 257
one-to-many markets, 845, 849
one-to-one marketing, **416**. *See also* personalization
one-way irreversible mathematical function, 270
OneWeb, 93, 120
online advertising, **395**. *See also* online marketing
    advertising networks/exchanges, 404–406
    affiliate marketing, 409–410
    behavioral targeting, 413, 416–418
    connected cars, 346–347
    content marketing, 404
    costs, 445–447
    display advertising, 401–407
    effectiveness, 443–445
    e-mail marketing, 407–409
    evolution, 454
    first banner ads, 63
    local advertising, 412, 513–521
    mobile advertising, 411–412, 498–512
    native advertising, 403–404
    pricing models, 445
    programmatic advertising, 406, 453–457
    real-time bidding, 406
    rich media ads, 402
    search engine advertising, 397–401
    social advertising, 411, 456–498
    spending, 395, 396
    sponsorships, 403
    strategies and tools, 392–427
    traditional tools, 395–411
    trends, 383
    video ads, 370–373, 402–403
    viral marketing, 410
online auctions, 424–425, 715, 719–726
online banking, 303, 304, 779–780
online bill payments, 303
online book publishing industry, 663–667
online brokerage, 779–780
online buyers, 389–390
online career services, 788, 791–793
online catalog, **197**, 198
online communities. *See* social networks
online consumer behavior, 382–392
online consumer purchasing model, 388, 443
online content and media, 636–695. *See also* specific industries
    a la carte revenue model, 644
    aggregators, 345
    attitudes about paying for, 644
    consumption, 643–645
    revenue models, 643–644
    syndication, 345
    tolerance of advertising, 644
    trends, 637
Online Copyright Infringement Liability Limitation Act, 584
online credit card fraud, 238
online entertainment industry, 667–687
    growth, 644, 670
    revenues, 639, 644, 668–670
online financial services, 778–785
    multi-channel vs. pure, 780
    robo-advisors, 780
online firms, analyzing viability of, 757–760
online forum. *See* online message board
online gambling, 608, 611–612
online game industry, 636, 637, 639, 644, 667, 668, 670, 683–687
online gamers, 684–685
online insurance services, 782–783
online lending services, 781–780
online magazine industry, 662–663
online marketing. *See also* online advertising, specific types
    advertising networks/exchanges, 404–406
    affiliate marketing, 409–410
    B2B, 845–846
    behavioral targeting, 413, 416–418
    content marketing, 404
    customer retention strategies, 415, 418–420
    display advertising, 401–407
    e-mail marketing, 407–409
    lead generation marketing, 410–411
    local marketing, 412, 513–521
    long tail marketing, 425, 426–427
    marketing analytics, 447–449
    metrics, lexicon, 440–443
    mobile marketing, 411–412, 498–512
    native advertising, 403–404
    other strategies, 413, 416–427
    pricing strategies, 422–425
    programmatic advertising, 406, 453–457
    real-time bidding, 406
    rich media ads, 402
    roadmap, 393
    SEM, 397–401
    social marketing, 411, 456–498
    sponsorships, 403
    strategic issues and questions, 392–394
    strategies and tools, 392–427
    technologies, 428–439
    traditional tools, 395–411
    trends, 383
    video ads, 402–403, 402–403
    viral marketing, 410
    website as marketing platform, 394–395
online marketing communications, costs and benefits of, 440–449
online marketing technologies, 428–439
    big data, 436–437
    cookies, 430–432, 433–434
    CRM systems, 438–439
    data mining, 435–436

data warehouses, 435–445
databases, 432, 435
marketing automation systems, 437–438
tracking files, 430–432, 433–434
web transaction logs, 428–430
online media, 146, 148
online message board, **143**
online mortgage services, 781–782
online music industry, 636, 639, 650, 668, 680–683
online newspaper industry, 649–662
online payments. *See* e-commerce payment systems
online publishing industry, 649–667
online purchasing decision, 387–389, 448
online real estate services, 784–785
online recruitment industry. *See* online career services
online retail, 51, 52, 59, 748–757. *See also* specific companies
advantages and challenges, 754, 755
business models, 760–773
common themes in, 773–775
history and evolution of, 750–752
omni-channel integration, 756–757
revenues, 752–754
sales, share by type of company, 760 761
specialty merchants, 749, 750, 752, 775
subscription sales revenue model, 749, 761
top firms, 755
trends, 749
virtual merchants, 760–769
worldwide, 59
online security. *See* e-commerce security
online shoppers, 389–390
online social network, **705**
online stored value payment system, **295**
online travel services, 785–788, 789–790
online video, 148, 342, 350
online video advertising, 148, 402
metrics, 441, 442
OnlineNIC, 593, 594
ooVoo, 144
Open Connectivity Foundation, 129
Open Database Connectivity. *See* ODBC
Open Interconnect Consortium, 129
open rate, 441, **442**
open set top boxes, FCC proposed regulations on, 99
open source software, **198**
Open Web Analytics, 198
OpenCms, 194
Opendoor, 785
OpenPGP, **276**
OpenSky, 812
OpenSSL, flaw, 261
OpenTable, 801–804
OpenText, 195
Opera Software, 92
operating margin, **759**
operating system security enhancements, 281–282
Operation Pangea, 609
opportunism, 391–392
Optimum WiFi hotspots, 124
opt-in model, **560**
opt-out model, **560**
Oracle, 195, 208, 342, 435, 437, 439, 510, 815, 816, 828, 830, 833, 861
Oracle ATG Web Commerce, 199

Oracle Commerce Cloud, 199
Oracle PeopleSoft, 227
Orange, 117
Orbitz, 72, 343, 357, 786, 787
order management software, providers, 342
organic search, **397**
Organization for Economic Cooperation and Development. *See* OECD
organizational development, **335**, 336
Osiris, 247
OTT services, 672
outsourcing, **180**
Overstock, 752, 761
over-the-top (OTT), 637, **671**, 672, 673, 693
Overture, 591. *See also* Goto.com
OVH (OVHcloud), 184, 185–186

P

P2P (peer-to-peer) e-commerce, 40
P2P file sharing, 544
P2P lending, 340
P2P mobile payment apps, **296**
P2P payments, 296–297
PaaS (platform as a service), 108
packet filters, 280
Packet Internet Groper. *See* Ping
packet switching, 96, 97, **100**–101, 102, 104
packets, **100**
page content, 189
page delivery, 189
page design, 189
page generation, 189
page views, **440**, 441
Page, Larry, 145–146
paid inclusion, **398**
PaineWebber Inc. v. Fortuny, 594, 595
Pakistan, 69, 311, 812
Pallas, 265
Panda, **399**
Pandora, 148, 328, 426, 515, 644, 645, 663, 669, 681, 682
PaperThin, 195
Parachute, 772
Paraguay, 634
Paramount, 499, 669
patches, 281–282
patent(s), **588**–590, 591
one-click purchasing, 357, 361, 363
pay for privacy (PFP), **572**, 573
pay TV. *See* cable television providers; satellite television providers
Payfort, 745–746
Payment Card Industry-Data Security Standard. *See* PCI-DSS
payment gateways. *See* Internet payment service providers
Payment Services Directive, EU, 286
payment systems. *See also* e-commerce payment systems
EBPP, 303 304
e-commerce, 290–302, 309–314
providers, 342
PayPal, 83, 252, 291, 292, 295, 296, 304, 342, 518, 563, 608, 737, 738
PayPal Credit, 295
pay-per-click (PPC) search ad, **398**
Paytm, 296, 313
Paytm Mall, 739
paywall, **657**
PC Connection, 752, 771

PCI-DSS (Payment Card Industry-Data Security Standard), **294**
PCProtect, 249
Peacomm. *See* Storm
Peering and Internet Exchange (PAIX), 118
peer-to-peer (P2P) e-commerce. *See* P2P e-commerce
Pegasus, 264
Penguin, **399**
Penguin Random House, 483
penny auction, **722**
Perfect 10, Inc., v. Amazon.com, Inc., 582
Perfect Commerce, 851
perfect competition model, 72
Perfect Information rule. *See* New York Times test
perfect market, 65, 68, **334**
Periscope, 148, 587, 645
Perkins, Melanie, 323, 324, 325
Perl, 198, 207, 210
perma-cookies. *See* supercookies
persistent location tracking, **559**
Personal Capital Corp, 780
personal computers, 97, 106, 107, 364
Personal Data Economy (PDE), 572, 573
personal profiles, **556**
personalization, **56**, 57, 211, 355, **416**, 429, 541. *See also* customization
PersonalizationMall, 756
personally identifiable information (PII). *See* PII
Peru, 125
pet food industry, 167–169
Petsmart, 171, 756
Petya/NotPetya, 235, 247
Pew Research Center, 384, 555, 641, 654
Pexels, 325
Pgconnectdevelop.com, 843
PGP (Pretty Good Privacy), 270, **276**
Pgshop, 772
pharmacies, online, 609–610
pharming, **257**
Philip Morris, 608
Philippines, 93
phishing, **250**–252
PhoneGap, 218
photo sharing, 350
PHP, 198, **209**
physical design, **180**, 181
piggyback strategy, 421
PII, 551, **553**, 558, 561, 566, 567, 568
Ping (Packet Internet Groper), 113
Pinsight Media, 380
Pinterest, 43, 52, 62, 67, 83, 146, 149, 210, 343, 344, 704–707, 712
    Apple Pay, 490
    apps, 491
    basic features, 490, 491
    boards, 490–495
    brand pages, 491–495
    Buyable Pins, 490, 492
    case study, 465–467
    Cinematic Pins, 466, 490, 492, 494
    embedding, 491
    Guided Search, 466
    hashtags, 491
    Image Hover, 491
    integration with Facebook and Twitter, 491, 492, 495
    keywords, 491
    Lens, 466, 491
    marketing campaigns, 493
    marketing tools, 490–492
    measuring marketing results, 495–496
    Pin It button, 491, 492, 494, 495
    pins, 490–496
    Product Pin, 490, 492, 494
    Promoted Pins, 466, 490, 492, 494
    Promoted Video, 490, 492
    repins, 491, 496
    Rich Pins, 465, 490, 492
    Shop the Look, 492
    social marketing, 335, 489–496
    URL links, 491, 492, 494
    web analytics, 496
    widgets, 210, 491, 493
piracy
    movie and television industry, 676
    music industry, 680, 681
Pixabay, 325
Pixar, 679, 694
Pizza Hut, 518
PKI (public key infrastructure), 274, **275**–277
PlasticsNet, 868
platform as a service. *See* PaaS
platform as a service (Paas) providers, 353
Playboy Enterprises, Inc., v. Global Site Designs, Inc., 594, 595
Playboy Enterprises, Inc., v. Netscape Communications, Inc., 591, 596
Playtonic Games, 339
Plusnet, 117
podcast, 128, **148**
Podesta, John, 252
Pokemon GO, 95, 150, 151, 683–684
Poland, 247
political issues
    model for organizing, 542–543
    overview, 540–547
    understanding in e-commerce, 540–547
Polycom, 145
polymorphic malware, 238, 248
Ponemon Institute, 237
POP3 (Post Office Protocol 3), **112**
pop-up blockers, 570
pornography, 606–608
portals, 726–733. *See also* specific portals
    business models, 732–731
    general-purpose, **728,** 731
    growth and evolution of, 727–728
    horizontal, 348
    revenue sources, 732
    top U.S, 728
    types of, 728, 731
    vertical market, 328, **731**
Porter's five forces, 355, 356
ports, 261
Possum, **400**
Post Office Protocol 3. *See* POP3
Postmates, 794
potentially unwanted application (PUA), 248–249
potentially unwanted programs. *See* PUPs
PowerReviews, 342
Powersourceonline, 848, 852

practice networks, **712**
predatory pricing, 616–622
predictive marketing, 777
PredictSpring, 342
PredictWallStreet, 712
Prensky, Marc, 640
Pretty Good Privacy. *See* PGP
Prevent All Cigarette Trafficking Act, 608
price competition, 357
price discovery, 55, 720
price discrimination, 56, 195, **422**
price dispersion, 71
price transparency, 56, 720
Priceline, 332, 349, 591, 722, 723, 787, 802. *See also* Booking Holdings
PriceWaterhouseCoopers, 780
pricing models, online advertising, 445
pricing, **420**
    discovery, 55
    discrimination, 56
    discriminatory, 616–622
    dynamic, 41, 53, 65
    flash, 72
    hit and run, 72
    predatory, 616–622
    price dispersion, 71
    transparency, 56
pricing strategies, 422–425
print industry. *See* publishing industry, online publishing industry; specific industries
printing press, 57
PRISM, 133, 574
privacy, 51, 52, 75, 76–77, 95, **241**, **547**–579. *See also* surveillance
    Apple and, 574, 576–578
    attitudes toward, 555–558
    behavioral targeting, 555–558
    consumer rights-based, 563
    encryption, 570, 572
    Facebook, 76–77, 537, 552, 553, 556–559, 563, 564–566, 568, 569, 572, 574, 576–578
    facial recognition technology, 556–5249
    FTC, 560–564
    government invasion of, 574–575, 576–578, 579
    impact of information-gathering tools, 553, 554
    information rights, 547–579
    Internet users' efforts to preserve, 555
    IoT, 129
    issues raised by marketing, 555–558
    key issues for consumers, 555
    location-based, 559
    mobile platform, 559–560
    private industry self-regulation, 568–569
    private sector, 549–572
    profiling, 555–558
    public sector, 548–549
    retargeting, 555–558
    right to be forgotten, 537–539, 547, 566, 567
    safe harbor, 568
    security and, 548
    social networks, 51, 52, 558, 712
    technological solutions, 569–572
    threats from government, 550–552
    threats from private institutions, 549–572
Privacy Act, 551, 552

privacy advocacy groups, 573
Privacy Badger, 570, 571
privacy default browsers, 570, **571**–572
Privacy International, 573
privacy issues, European Union, and 537–539, 566–568
privacy laws,
    federal, applicable to private institutions, 550, 551
    federal, applicable to U.S. government, 549, 550
    state, 551
privacy policies, **211**, 551, 561, 563, 564–566
Privacy Protection Act, 550, 551
privacy protection business, 572–573
Privacy Rights Clearinghouse, 573
privacy seal programs, 568–569
privacy shield agreements, **568**
private cloud, **110**, 185
private industrial network, **354**, **819**, 856–862
    collaborative commerce and, 858, 861
    implementation barriers, 861–862
    objectives of, 857–858
    Walmart, 859–860
private key, 270
private trading exchange (PTX). *See* private industrial network
pro forma earnings, 760
Proactis, 352
probabilistic cross-device tracking, **431**
Procter & Gamble, 352, 757, 772, 840, 843, 856–857
procurement managers, 826
procurement process, **822**–826
Professional and Amateur Sports Protection Act (PASPA), 611
profiling, **432**, 555, **556**–558
profit, **361**
profitability, 357–358
profits, monopoly, 65
programmatic advertising, 381, **406**
    case study, 453–457
programming/scripting languages, 198
progressive web apps. *See* PWA
Progressive, 783
property rights, 542
Prosper, 782
Protect Act, 607
Protect America Act, 258
protocol, **102**
prototyping, **190**
Proxama, 519
proximity marketing, **515**, 519–520
proximity mobile payments, 296–297, 309–314
proxy bidding, 726
proxy server (proxy), 196, **280**–281
PUA (potentially unwanted application), 248–249
public cloud, **108**, 110, 263, 266
public key cryptography, **270**–277
    digital certificates, 273–277
    digital envelopes, 273–274
    digital signatures, 270–274
    hash digests, 271–273
    PKI, 273–277
    simple case, 271
public key infrastructure. *See* PKI
public key, 270
public policy, e-commerce security and, 287–290
public safety and welfare, 542, 605–612

public safety vs anonymity, 242–243
public-private cooperation efforts, 289–290
publishing industry, 636, 649- 667. *See also* online publishing industry; specific industries
Puma, 82–85
PUPs (potentially unwanted programs), **248**–249
purchasing funnel, 448
pure digital news sites. *See* native digital news sites
PWA (progressive web apps), 50
Python, 110, 210

Q

Qihoo, 360, 145
QQ, 701, 704
QR codes, 221, 309, 310, 412, 498, 519
Qualcomm, 92, 126
query-driven data mining, **435**
QuiBids, 723
Quick Response (QR) codes. *See* QR codes
Quikr, 60
QuickQuote, 783
Qwant, 145
Qzone, 704

R

Rackspace, 184
radio, 46, 54, 55
radio industry, 636, 639, 650, 668, 682. *See also* music industry
Rails. *See* RoR
raising capital, 338, 339–340
Rakuten Linkshare, 342, 410
Ramnit, 247, 249
Randolph, Marc, 692
ransomware, 233–235, **247**, 249
Rasmussen, Lars, 324
Ratesetter, 340
Ravelry, 712
RC series encryption, 270
RDES, 270
reach, **54**, **440**, 441, 727
Real Player, 148
Really Simple Syndication. *See* RSS
real-time bidding (RTB), **406**, 454–456
real-time customer service chat systems, **419**
Realtor.com, 784
Reaper (IoTroop) botnet, 267
recency, **440**, 441
Reckitt Benckiser, 235
recommendation systems, 385–386, 426
Red Hat Linux (Apache), 342
Reddit, 658, 659
Redfin, 784
redundancy, **116**
Reeder, 140
Refinery28, 660
registration form, **428**
Regulation A+, JOBS Act, 338
REI, 341
relational database, **435**
release window, **675**–676, 677, 678
Rematch Live, 483
remote sales, taxation of, 601, 602–603
Renault, 234

Reserve, 803, 804
responsibility, **544**
responsive web design. *See* RWD
responsive web design with server-side components (RESS). *See* AWD
restaurant delivery industry, 795–796
Resy, 803, 804
retail e-commerce. *See* online retail
retail industry, 59, 342, 390, 502, 749–750. *See also* online retail
retailers, luxury, 414–415
retargeting, **417**
retention rate, 441, **442**
revenue model(s), 171, **328**–329, 332, 336
    advertising, 328, 332
    affiliate, 329, 332
    e-tailer, 342
    freemium strategy, 328
    market creator, 343, 349
    sales, 328, 332
    subscription, 328, 332
    transaction broker, 343, 349
    transaction fee, 328, 332
    community providers, 343, 344
    content providers, 343, 345
    online content, 644
    portals, 343, 348
    service provider, 343, 350
RFC, 112
RFID, 125, 566
Rheingold, Harold, 705
rich media ad, 342, **402**
richness, **55**, 57, 355, 429, 541
right to be forgotten (RTBF), 537–539, **547**, 566, 567
right to delist. *See* right to be forgotten
Right to Financial Privacy Act, 551
Rihanna, 710, 776
Riley v. California, 575
Riot Games, 687
Ripple, 302
risk assessment, **283**
risk aversion, 546
rivalry among existing competitors, 355, 356
Roberts, Larry, 97
Robertson, Nick, 776
Robins, Thomas, 552
ROBO (research online, buy offline), 71
robo-advisors, online financial services, 780
Rocket Internet, 68, 69–70, 337, 796
Rocket Mortgage, 782
RocketHub, 339
RocketLawyer, 343, 350
Roku, 671,
Romania, 603
root servers, 105
ROPO (research online, purchase offline), 385
RoR (Ruby on Rails), 198, **210**
Rosnoft, 235
Rosetta Stone, 596–597, 709
Rotana, 635
RoundMenu, 795
router, **101**
routing algorithm, **101**
Royal National Institute of the Blind, 213

RSA SecurID token, 284
RSS (Really Simple Syndication), **140**
Ruby on Rails. *See* RoR
Rue La La, 425, 761
Rupert, Johann, 414
Russia, 40, 69, 83, 130, 132, 233, 234, 235, 290, 600, 603, 701, 702, 704, 710, 716, 789, 796
Rustock botnet, 248
RWD (responsive web design), 137, **217**, 218

S

SaaS (software as a service), 108, 199, 815, 828, 835, 836, 861, 867
Saatva, 772
safe harbor agreements, **568**
Sailing Anarchy, 712
Sailnet, 343, 348
Sainsbury's, 185–186
Saint-Gobain, 235
sales revenue model, **328**, 329
sales tax, Amazon, 768–769
sales, measuring mobile location-based marketing effectiveness, 521
Salesforce, 108, 342, 439
Salesforce Commerce Cloud, 83, 199, 491
Salesjobs, 791
SalesPredict, 737
Sam's Club, 719
Samsclub.com Auctions, 719
Samsung, 92, 126, 342, 379, 488, 499
Samsung Australia, 488
Samsung Galaxy, 128, 154, 285
Samsung Gear, 95, 150
Samsung Pay, 285, 291, 292, 296, 297
Samsung S Voice, 153
Samwer, Alexander, 69
Samwer, Marc, 69
Samwer, Oliver, 69, 70
SAP, 195, 342, 439, 815, 828, 830, 833, 837, 839, 851, 861
SAP Ariba, 816, 821, 837, 840, 851
SAP Hybris Commerce Cloud, 199
satellite Internet, **120**
satellite television providers, 638, 646, 668, 671, 672, 673. *See also* specific providers
Saudia Arabia, 599, 746, 747, 796
Saudi Arabia Public Interest Fund, 747
scalability, **203**
scale economies, **353**
Scandinavia, 296
SCGI, 207
Schaeffler, 354
Schick, 370, 371
Sciarra, Paul, 465
SCM (supply chain management), **829**, **838**–839
  concepts and challenges, 827, 828
  trends in, 828–846
SCM systems, **838**–839
scope strategy, **363**
Scratch, 167–169
Scribd, 328, 329
Scrum, **190**
Scrum master, 190
SDLC (systems development life cycle), **178**
search, 95
search advertising. *See* search engine advertising

search costs, 55, 71, 72
search engine(s), 47, 64, **145**–146, 465–467. *See also* SEM (search engine marketing); SEO (search engine optimization)
  how Google works, 145–146, 147
  keyword indexes, 145
  natural language queries, 145
  organic search, 146
  privacy issues, 537–539, 553, 554, 558, 578
  sponsored links, 146
  tracking by, 553, 554, 558, 578
  visual, 146, 465–467
search engine advertising, **397**–401, 465–467 501, 507
search engine marketing. *See* SEM
search engine optimization. *See* SEO
Sears, 446, 756, 767, 769, 771
Seattle Internet Exchange (SIX), 118
SEC (Securities and Exchange Commission), 170, 338, 813
secret key cryptography. *See* symmetric key cryptography
secure negotiated session, **277**–278
Secure Sockets Layer. *See* SSL
Secure Sockets Layer (SSL)/Transport Layer Security (TLS), **113**, 141
Securities Act of 1970, 760
Securities and Exchange Commission. *See* SEC
security, online. *See* e-commerce security
security audit, **287**
security breach disclosure, state legislation, 551
security organization, **284**
security policy, **283**
security tokens, **284**
seed capital, **336**, 339-340
SeedRocket, 337
Seedrs, 340
SelectQuote, 783
self-driving cars, 126
Selfie Pay. *See* Mastercard Identity Check
seller's lament, **725**
seller-side solutions, **818**
SEM (search engine marketing), 146, 342, **397**–401
sensors, 125
SEO (search engine optimization), 205–206, **398**, 426, 483, 484
Sephora, 152, 510, 520
Sequoia Capital, 220
Sequoia China, 323, 701
Series A financing, 337
Sertifi, 273
server(s), **105**, 281–282
server-side programming, 194, 198, 197, 207–208, 209–210, 214, 217
service provider 343, **350**–351
service sector, 627, 778
SES, 93
session key, **277**
SFR, 117
SGML (Standard Generalized Markup Language), 134
Shadow Brokers, 233, 234, 235, 252–253
shadow economy market. *See* underground economy marketplace
Shadowcrew, 243
sharing economy companies, 40. *See also* on-demand service companies
Sharp, Evan, 465, 467
Shell, 866, 869
Shellshock, 207, 261
Sherman Antitrust Act, 616–617, 657
Sherpalo Investments, 379

shill bidding, 726
shill feedback, 726
ShoeBuy, 756, 761, 767
shopBeacon, 519
Shopgoodwill, 719
Shopify, 168–169, 183, 198, 210, 342, 491
Shopkick, 519
shopping cart, 179, 182, 190, 196, **197**, 198, 204, 207
    abandonment, 72, 420, 441, 442, 449
    privacy issues, 554
shopping cart database, **428**
Shopzilla, 345
Short Messaging Service. *See* SMS
Showbizjobs, 791
Showtime, 669, 671, 672, 674, 693
Siemens, 354, 600
signed certificate, 275
Silbermann, Ben, 465, 466
Silk Road, 609–610
SIM card hijacking, 265
SIMILE Widgets, 210
Simple, 779
Simple Mail Transfer Protocol. *See* SMTP
SimplyHired, 788, 791, 793
Singapore, 93, 119, 311, 313, 339, 340, 379, 599, 812
SingPost, 812
SingtelDASH, 313
Sirius XM, 682
site management tools, **194**
site transaction logs, 554
Sitecore, 195
Sitecore Commerce, 182, 183, 199
Sky Broadband, 117
Skype, 131, 143, 144, 422, 844
Slack, 61, 128, 150
Slammer, 246, 249
Slate, 659
Sling TV, 672
Slippery Slope, 546
smart cars. *See* cars, connected (smart)
smart contracts, blockchain, 299
smart credt cards. *See* EMV credit cards
smart houses, 126
smart speakers, 51
smart televisions, 125–126, 638, 673
smart things, 125–126
SmartBear, 342
smartphone(s). 95, 99, 106, 107, 111, 121, 132, 153, 154. *See also*
  mobile apps; mobile devices; mobile platform; specific devices
    disruptive technology, 365
    privacy issues, 554, 559–560, 576–578
smartwatches, 46, 126, 127–128. *See also* Apple Watch
SmartyPig, 779, 781
smishing, 263
SMS (Short Messaging Service), 143
SMS spoofing, 263
SMTP (Simple Mail Transfer Protocol), 102, **112**
SnagAJob, 791
Snapchat, 43, 51, 52, 61, 83, 143, 148, 471, 472, 483, 559, 563, 619, 704–708, 710
    Lenses, augmented reality, 150
    privacy issues, 559, 563
    social marketing, 496–497

3D World Lens, 509–510
Snapchat Lens Studio, 510
Snapchat Snapstreaks, 710
sniffer, **258**
Snowden, Edward, 133, 243, 258, 290, 574, 575
SOASTA, 161
social advertising, 411, 468–500. *See also* social marketing
social commerce. *See* social e-commerce
social contagion, 385–386
Social Contract rule, 546
social density, **474**
social e-commerce, 51, 52, **61**, 62, 63, 330–331, 466–467, 749, 756, 775
    Buy buttons, 473, 477, 479, 496, 508
social engineering, **250**
Social Finance Inc., 782
social issues. *See also* ethics
    model for organizing, 542–543
    overview, 540–547
    understanding in e-commerce, 540–547
social marketing, 411, 468–500. *See also* social advertising
    analytics, 482, 483–484
    downside, 498
    ExchangeHunterJumper.com case study, 525–530
    Facebook, 473–482
    Instagram, 471, 496
    LinkedIn, 496, 497–498
    Pinterest, 489–496
    players, 471–472
    process, 472–473
    Snapchat, 496–497
    to children, 499–500
    Twitter, 482, 485–489
social marketing services, providers, 342
social marketing specialist, careers, 733–7692
social media. *See also* social advertising, social marketing, social networks
    newspaper industry, 650–653, 655–656
    online travel industry, 788
social media associate, careers, 521–524
social network(s), 43, 51, 52, 55, 57, 61–62, 63, 67, 139, 703, **704**–715, 716–717. *See also* specific social networks
    advertising, 707, 708, 709
    B2B and, 844–845
    branding and, 708, 710–712
    business models, 707–709
    collaborative commerce and, 844–845
    dark side of, 710–711
    demographics, 705–706
    during Reinvention period of e-commerce, 67
    early, 703–704
    employee privacy protection, 712
    engagement, 473, 707
    features of, 713–715
    for professionals, 701–702
    growth, 705–707
    impact on businesses, 709
    marketing to children and, 499–500
    messaging, 706
    mobile devices, 706
    privacy, 51, 52, 558
    security, 261–262
    social contagion, 385–386
    technologies, 713–715

types of, 709, 712–713
U.S, top, 705
use as listening tool, 709
worldwide, 704
social recruiting, 792–793
social search, 62, **400**
social sign-on, 61
social technologies, 57, 355, 429, 541
social-mobile-local, 43, 44, 51, 62, 67, 68, 411–412
society, major e-commerce trends, 51, 52
Softbank, 120, 220, 379, 500, 729, 730
software. *See also* specific types
    copyright protection, 581
    poorly designed, 260–261
    supply chain attacks, 236
    vulnerabilities, 233–234, 260–261
software as a service. *See* SaaS
Sohu Sogou, 145
Solvay, 866
Sony, 247, 499, 678, 686
Sony BMG, 669
Sony PlayStation, 150, 685, 686
SoundCloud, 564
Souq.com, 745–747, 748
South Africa, 93, 603, 634
South Dakota v. Wayfair, 601
South Korea, 132, 301, 310, 311, 371, 379, 603, 704, 729
Southeast Asia, 40, 69, 70, 220, 221
Soverain Software, 591
Space Norway, 93
SpaceX, 93, 120
Spain, 70, 379, 537–538
spam (junk) Web sites, **258**
spam, 51, 143, 233, **408**–409
spammers, 408
Spark, 437
spear-phishing, 251
Spencerstuart, 791
Spider Webs Ltd., 593, 594
spiders, 145
Spiegelhauer, Doug, 167–169
split testing. *See* A/B testing
Spokeo v. Robins, 552
sponsored communities, **712**
sponsorship, **403**, 445
spoofing, **257**
Spoonfed, 796
sporting goods, 225–228
Sports Authority, 227, 756
spot purchasing, **826**, 847, 852
Spotify, 148, 328, 329, 345, 422, 427, 633–635, 636, 644, 669, 681, 682–683
Sprint, 98, 1172, 124, 380
spyware, **250**, 264–265, 551
spyware blockers, 570
SQL (structured query language), **435**
SQL injection attack, **260**
Square, 291, 292
Squarespace, 182, 323, 342
Sri Lanka, 124–125, 131
SSL (Secure Sockets Layer), 113, 141, 261, 277–278, 280, 290, 293
SSL/TLS, 277–278
Stack, Dick, 225
Stack, Edward, 225

StackPath, 160
Stacks Bowers, 719
Standard Generalized Markup Language. *See* SGML
Standard Oil Co. of New Jersey v. United States, 617
Staples, 341
Starbucks, 262, 263, 296, 297, 518, 843
startup(s), 69–70, 336–338. *See also* entrepreneur(s)
Starz, 679, 693
State Farm, 783
State Farm Bank, 779
State Street Bank & Trust v. Signature Financial Group, Inc., 589–590
stateless, **200**
static content, 172, 194, 200, 204
Sterling Commerce, 858
stickiness, 441, **442**
Stirling, Lindsey, 427
Stitch Fix, 373, 761
Stitcher, 635
stolen data, value and market for, 238–240
Storm, 249
strategic analysis, factors in, 758
StreamCast, 544
streaming media, **146**, 148, 342
streaming music, 633–635, 636, 637, 642, 644, 645, 668, 669
streaming video, 160
Stripe, 380
structured query language. *See* SQL
StubHub, 738
subscription revenue model, **328**, 332, 644
subscription services, examples of, 167–169, 328, 329
subscription video on demand. *See* SVOD
subscription-based sales revenue model, 329
substitute products, 172, 355, 356
substitution cipher, **268**
Subway, 842
.sucks domain, 592
SugarCRM, 439
Sukar.com, 746
Sumerian, 152
Sumitomo Chemical, 866
Sun Microsystems, 208
SunButter, 480
supercookies, 431, 433
Superfish adware, 250
Super Wi-Fi, 123
suppliers, in marketplace, 172
supply chain(s), **817**, 826–833
    accountable, 831–832
    adaptive, 830–831
    labor issues, 831–832
    multi-tier, 826–827
    risk, 823–824
    role of enterprise systems in, 828
    role of legacy computer systems in, 828
    sustainable, 832–833
    vulnerabilities, 823–824
supply chain competition, **815**
supply chain management. *See* SCM
supply chain management (SCM) systems. *See* SCM systems
supply chain simplification, **829**–830
supply chain visibility, **827**–828
SupplyOn, 352, 354, 848, 855
supply-push model, **772**

surge pricing, 424–425
surveillance
    e-commerce, 574–575, 576–578, 579
    government, 574–575, 576–578, 579
    Internet, 95, 131–133
    online communications, 51, 52
sustainable supply chains, 832–**833**
sustaining technologies, **365**
SVOD (subscription video on demand), 672
Sweden, 291, 379, 603
Swift, 154
Swift, Taylor, 683
Swiftic, 218
Swish, 296
switching costs, 66, 363
Switzerland, 83, 301
SWOT analysis, **173**–174
Sybase, 195
Symantec, 238, 245, 246, 250, 252, 262–263, 282
Symantec Norton AntiVirus, 282
symmetric key cryptography, **269**–270
SyndicateRoom, 340
syndication, of online content, 345
system architecture, **191**
system design specification, **180**
system design, 180
system functionalities, **179**
system testing, **187**
systems
    analysis/planning, 179–180
    building, 180–187
    design, 180
    development life cycle (SDLC), 178
    maintenance, 188
    testing, 187–188
systems analysis
    building a mobile presence, 215
    typical e-commerce site, 179, 180
systems development life cycle. *See* SDLC

T

T1, 117, **119–120**, 122
T3, 117, **119–120**
tablet computer(s). tablet computers, 95, 106, 107, 111, 121, 123, 154, 365. *See also* specific devices; mobile devices; mobile platform
Tagged, 700
tags, 137, 138, 139, 140
Tai, Bill, 324
Taiwan, 119, 301, 379, 603, 729
Takeaway, 39
takedown notices, 582, 583, 585, 586, 587, 595
Takis, 510
Talabat, 796
TalkTalk, 117
Tanzania, 93, 131
Tapad, 431
Target, 127, 343, 508, 518, 520, 625, 752, 755, 756, 763, 769, 774
    data breach, 238–239
    mobile payments, 296, 297
target audience, identifying, 171
Taringa!, 704
TaskRabbit, 794
Tastemade Indonesia, 493
taxation. *See also* sales tax; VAT (value-added tax)

    e-commerce, by states, 601
    Europe, 600, 602-603
    online sales, 52
taxi industry, Uber, 39–42, 49
Taxify, 39
TCP/IP, 96, 97, **102**, 103, 104, 105, 112, 113, 114, 115, 144
TCV, 220
TDEA (Triple DES Encryption Algorithm), 270
TE-Food, 841-842
technological convergence, **646**
technology, e-commerce
    infrastructure, 73–75
    unique features of, 52–57
    major e-commerce trends, 51, 52
technology, social, 57
Telefonica, 119, 120, 234
Telegram, 132
Telehouse, 118
Telephone Consumer Protection Act, 551
telephone, as a commerce technology, 55, 57
telepresence, 145 844
Telesat, 93
television, as commerce technology, 46, 54–56
television industry, 636–639, 643–646, 648, 667–679, 691–695. *See also* home entertainment
Telnet, **112**
template test, 187
Tencent, 132, 309, 311, 313, 704
Tencent Music, 634
Terms of Use policies, 548, 564–566, 585
Tesla, 126
Tether, 300
Tewari, Naveen, 379, 380, 381
textile industry, 833
Texture, 663
Thailand, 131, 311, 599, 729, 730
Thales, 263, 354
Thawte, 342
Theia Holdings, 93
The Atlantic Magazine, 657
The 5th, 167
The Hut Group, 186
The Iconic, 69
The Ringer, 635
The Seam, 352, 848, 855
The Washington Post et al., v. TotalNews, Inc., et al., 594, 597–598
The Well, 344, 703, 705
TheKnot, 170, 171
Thing Labs, 720
third-party cookies. *See* cookies
3.5G (3G+), 122
3G (Third Generation), 122
Ticketmaster Corp. v. Tickets.com, 594, 597
Tidal, 148, 682
Tide.com, 713
Tier 1 Internet Service Providers (Tier 1 ISPs), **116**, 160
Tier 3 Internet Service Providers (ISPs), **117**
Tiffany, 415, 775
tiger teams, 253
tight coupling, **829**
TikTok, 498, 499–500, 705, 707
Timberlake, Justin, 706
Time Magazine, 657
time starvation, 351

Time Warner, 646, 648
timeline, developing an e-commerce presence, 175
TimeLooper, 151
Tinba, 247
Tiscali, 117
Titan Aerospace, 124
TLS (Transport Layer Security), 113, 141, 277–278, 290, 293,
T-Mobile, 124, 152
T-Online, 145
TNT Express, 234, 235
Tomlinson, Ray, 97
Tor, 239, 248, 555, 570
TotalNews, 597
ToysRUs, 835
Tracert, **113**
trackbacks, blog, 149
tracking files, 430–432, 433–434
trade secret(s), **598**
Trade Secrets Directive (EU), 598
trade, restraint of, 617–622
Tradecomet, 620
trademark(s), **590**, 592–598
Trademark Dilution Revision Act (TDRA), 592
transaction broker, 343, **348**, 349
transaction brokering, **775**
transaction costs, 54, 65, 72, 353, 720
transaction fee revenue model, **328**, 332
transaction log, **428**
transaction(s)
 commercial, 45
 digitally enabled, 45
transit ISPs, 116, 117
Transmission Control Protocol (TCP), **102**
Transmission Control Protocol/Internet Protocol (TCP/IP). *See* TCP/IP
trans-organizational business process, **856**
transparency, cost, 56
transparency, price, 56
Transport Layer Security. *See* TLS
Transport Layer, of TCP/IP, **102**, 113
Transport Services and Representation layer, 114, **115**
transposition cipher, **268**
TransUnion Corporation, 579
travel industry, 357, 501, 785–788, 789–790. *See also* airline industry
Travelers, 783
Travelex, 312
Travelocity, 72, 332, 343, 357, 786, 787
Triguboff, Harry, 789
Tribune Company, 650
Trident, 264
TripAdvisor, 787, 789–790
Triple DES Encryption Algorithm. *See* TDEA
Trivago, 787,
Trojan downloaders and droppers, 247
Trojan horses, **247**–248, 249
True Value, 857–858
Trueffect, 437
Trulia, 784
Trump administration, 133, 604
Trunk Club, 373
trust, in online markets, 391–392
TrustArc, 568–569
TRUSTe. *See* TrustArc
Trustwave, 161

TruTV, 686
TUI AG, 787
Tumblr, 149, 704, 705, 707, 712, 732
Turkey, 812
tweet(s), 485
TweetDeck, 489
21st Century Communications and Video Accessibility Act, 213
Twenty-First Century Fox, 669, 691–692, 693
Twitalyzer, 489
Twitch.tv, 587, 686–687
Twitter, 43, 67, 83, 148, 149, 343, 344, 437, 457, 483, 484, 645, 704–709, 710, 712, 780
 Amplify, 486, 487
 basic features, 485
 business model, 708
 child pornography and, 608
 cybersquatting and, 594
 Do Not Track (DNT), 434
 followers, 489
 hashtag, 485
 Iran, 132
 links, 485
 marketing campaigns, 488
 marketing tools, 485–487
 measuring marketing results, 489
 mention, 485
 message (DM), 485
 mobile ads, 470, 487, 505
 mobile users, 469
 Moments tab, 485
 Periscope app, 587
 privacy, 537, 568, 572
 Promoted Accounts, 488, 489, 491
 Promoted Trends, 486, 487, 488, 489
 Promoted Tweets, 485–486, 487, 488, 489, 508
 Promoted Video, 486, 487
 reply, 485
 retweet, 485
 social marketing, 335, 482, 485–489
 Timeline, 482, 485, 487
 tweets, 85
 Twitter Cards, 486, 487
twofers, 423
two-tier architecture, **192**
2001: A Space Odyssey, 153
TypePad, 149
typosquatting, 595

U

U.S. Constitution, 549, 552, 564, 577, 579, 580, 600, 605
 Bill of Rights, 549, 600
 First Amendment, 549, 576, 582, 600, 606, 607
 Fourteenth Amendment, 549
 Fourth Amendment, 549, 579
U.S. Copyright Office, 581
U.S. Department of Commerce, 130
U.S. Department of Defense, 96, 97, 145
U.S. Department of Homeland Security, 116, 288, 289
U.S. Department of Justice, 235, 300, 608, 667
U.S. economy, 302
U.S. Federal Communication Commission. *See* FCC
U.S. Federal Trade Commission. *See* FTC
U.S. Foreign Intelligence Surveillance Court (FISC), 258
U.S. National Institute of Standards and Technology (NIST), 108

U.S. Postal Service, 143, 360, 766
U.S. SAFE WEB Act, 288
U.S. Supreme Court, 51, 544, 552, 559, 575, 577, 578, 579, 581, 583, 588, 589, 590, 600, 601, 606, 607, 611, 617
U.S. Treasury, 295
Uber, 43, 49, 52, 60, 63, 62, 68, 126, 350, 702, 748, 749, 794, 796, 797
    case study on, 39–42
    digital disruption, 365
    dynamic pricing, 424–425
    FTC privacy enforcement action, 563
UberBlack, 39
UberCargo, 39
UberEats, 39, 796
uberization, 39, 42
UberPool, 39, 40
UberRush, 39
UberX, 39
uBid, 719, 721
ubiquity, **54**, 57, 355, 429, 541
Ukraine, 235
Ulbricht, Ross, 610
Ultimate Fighting Championship, 483
Under Armour, 839
underground economy marketplace, 238–240
unfair competitive advantage, 65, **334**
unfit fitness, 366
Uniform Rapid Suspension (URS) system, 592
Uniform Resource Locator(s). *See* URL(s)
Unilever, 329, 371, 372, 373, 379
Union Square Hospitality Group, 804
UNIQLO, 493
unique visitors, **440**, 441, 468, 727–728
unit testing, **187**
United Arab Emirates (UAE), 379, 746, 747, 795
United Kingdom, 83, 117, 185, 186, 213, 233, 237, 330, 331, 339, 340, 351, 373, 379, 389, 412–413, 467, 483, 502, 538, 539, 608, 785, 789, 849. *See also* England, Great Britain
United Nations, 130, 213
United States
    freedom of expression, 538, 539, 547, 573, 584, 587, 600, 606, 607. *See also* First Amendment
    freedom of speech, 549, 576, 577, 582, 587 600, 604, 605, 606, 607. *See also* First Amendment
    freedom of the press, 538, 539, 550, 600. *See also* First Amendment
    government regulation and surveillance of Internet, 132
    views of privacy compared to Europe, 539
United States Computer Emergency Readiness Team. *See* US-CERT
United States Patent and Trademark Office (USPTO), 588, 590, 591
United States v. Jones, 575
universal computing, **134**
universal proximity mobile wallets, **296**
universal standards, 54–**55**, 57, 355, 429, 541
universalism, 546
University of Chicago, 790
Unix, 140, 193, 197, 207, 208
Unlawful Internet Gambling Enforcement Act, 608
unsubscribe rate, 442
UNTUCKit, 488
UPS (United Parcel Service), 360, 608
Urban Outfitters, 520, 752
URLs (Uniform Resource Locators), 47, **104**, 135, 263. *See also* domain name(s); hyperlink(s)

Us.jobs, 793
USA Freedom Act, 133, 550, 575
USA PATRIOT Act, 258, 288, 289, 574, 575, 600
USA Today, 653, 654
USAA, 779
Usablenet, 342, 770
USAJobs, 791
US-CERT (United States Computer Emergency Readiness Team), **289**
user interface design, 190
user-generated content, 173, 350
utility, in online markets, 391–392
utility computing, 108
utility program, 111–113
UUNet, 98
UX designer position, 219, 222–224

V

V.me. *See* Visa Checkout
value chain, **358**–359, 362, 758
value chain management (VCM) services, **850**
value proposition, 40, **326**–328, 336, 344, 351, 362, 364
value web, **360**–361
value-added taxes (VAT), 600, 602–603
variable costs, 420
VBScript, **209**
vCPM, 445
Vendio, 198
Venmo, 291, 292, 297, 563
venture capital, 39, 64, 66, 68, 69–70, 336–338, 373. *See also* startups
venture capital investor(s), **337**–338
VeriSign, 136, 276, 342
Verizon, 116, 252, 564, 593, 594, 645, 646, 648, 692, 694, 729
    as portal, 732
Verizon Media, 145, 348, 505, 507, 515, 728
Verizon Wireless, 406, 431
Vero, 706
versioning, **423**
vertical market, **819**
vertical market portals, 728, **731**–733
vertical marketplace, 353
vertical scaling, **203**
Viacom, 586
Viasat, 93
Viber, 143, 144
Vice, 642, 650, 658, 659
video ads, **402**–403
video chatting, 144
video conferencing, 144–145
Video Privacy Protection Act, 551
video server, **141**
Vietnam, 286
view time, 441, **442**
viewability. *See* ad viewability
viewability rate, **440**, 441
view-through rate. *See* VTR
view-to-cart ratio, 441, **442**
Viget, 84
Villeroy and Boch, 185
Vimeo, 148, 587
Vine, 499
Vinted, 60
Vipps, 296
viral marketing, **410**

Virgin Media, 117
virtual communities, 703, 705
virtual merchants, 343, 749, **760**–769, 773, 774, 775
virtual private network. *See* VPN
virtual reality (VR), 95, **150**, 151–152, 509–510, 749, 771
Virtualstream, 184
virus, **246**
Virut, 248
Visa Checkout, 295
vishing, 263
Vive, HTC, 150
VK, 704, 710
Vodafone, 119
voice assistants. *See* intelligent digital assistants
Voice over Internet Protocol. *See* VoIP
VoIP (Voice over Internet Protocol), **144**, 577
Vonage, 144
vortal, 343, 348
Vox Media, 658, 659
Vox Populi Registry Ltd., 592
VPN (virtual private network), 109, 131, 132, **278**
VR/AR Association, 151
Vroom, 753
VTR (view-through rate), **440**, 441
Vudu, 678
Vzaar, 528

W

W.W. Grainger, 351, 352, 363, 848, 849
W3C (World Wide Web Consortium), 112, 130, 139, 434
W3C (World Wide Web Consortium) Web Content Accessibility Guidelines (WCAG) 2.0, 212–213
W3Techs, 210
Wacker, 866
Waitrose, 350
Waldenbooks, 665
Wall Street Journal, 343, 446, 653, 654, 657,
walled garden, **645**
Walmart, 341, 343, 678, 752, 755, 756, 764, 767, 769, 774, 835, 843
    acquisition of online merchants, 756, 767,
    blockchain, 842
    competition with Amazon, 860
    cost competition strategy, 364
    e-commerce marketplace, 72
    Microsoft partnership, 860
    private industrial network, 352, 354, 857, 859–860
    supply chain issues, 824, 860
Walmart Global Replenishment System (GRS), 859–860
Walmart Retail Link, 859–860
WannaCry, 233–235, 246, 247, 249, 253, 282
Warby Parker, 364, 772
Warner Records, 669
Washington Post, 597–598, 645, 653, 654, 657
Wassenaar Arrangement, 290
watch lists, 726
Wave, 343, 350
Wayfair, 601, 752, 761
Waze, 620
Wealthfront, 780
wearable technology, 51, 95, 99, 125, 125–128, 737
Web (World Wide Web), 45, **47**, 49–50, **94**, 98, 134–153. *See also* websites; web pages
Web 2.0, **67**, 149–150

web analytics, 51, 342, 496
web application servers, 191, **196**–197
web attack kits, 238
web beacons (web bugs), 417, 430, 431, 432, 433, 554
web browser(s), 98, **142**. *See also* browser(s)
web camera. *See* webcam
web client, **141**–142
web development methodologies, 190–191
web performance management, 342
web server hardware, 141, 342
web server software, **140**–141, 193, 198, 342
web server performance, degradation, 202
web services, **190–191**
web surfing, anonymous, 570
web transaction logs, 428–430
webcam, 144, 145
Webcollage, 342
WebCrawler, 145
WebEx, 144
WebIntellects, 342
weblog. *See* blog
WebMD, 344, 403
webrooming, 71, 385
Webroot, 238
websites(s)
    architecture, simple vs multi-tier, 192
    as marketing platform, 394–395
    building in-house vs outsourcing, 180, 182–187
    choices in building and hosting, 182
    components of budget, 176
    content for, 172–173
    demand on, 200–201
    hosting own vs outsourcing, 184, 187
    implementation, 188
    maintenance, 188
    optimization, 188–189
    pre-built templates, 180, 182, 183, 184, 198
    scaling techniques, 203–204
    SDLC, 178
    site management tools, 194
    testing process, 187–188
    tools for building, 183
website design
    annoying features, 205
    basic considerations, 205, 206
    ExchangeHunterJumper.com, 529–530
    providers, 342
    Puma, 83–84
    tools for interactivity and active content, 206–211
website optimization, 188–189
website performance, 204
Webtrends, 194, 342, 449, 482
WebTrust, 568
Webvan, 72
WeChat, 131, 144, 311–314, 325, 701, 704, 729, 730
WeChat Pay, 296, 309, 310, 311–314
Weebly, 182, 323, 342
Weibo, 701, 704
Weiner, Jeff, 701
WEP (Wired Equivalent Privacy), 279
Westchestergov.com, 713
Westwing, 69
WeWork, 730

WhatsApp, 51, 52, 61, 131, 143, 144, 264, 290, 483, 577, 619, 621, 706
White-Fi, 123
white hats, **253**
Whole Foods, 518, 756, 764, 767
wholesale model, **666**
widgets, 182, **210**–211, 491, 493
Wi-Fi, 91–93, **122**–124, 125, 128, 279, 516, 517, 519
Wi-Fi Protected Access. *See* WPA
wiki, **149–150**
Wikibooks, 150
WikiLeaks, 252
Wikimedia Foundation, 150
Wikinews, 150
Wikipedia, 150, 357, 587
Wiktionary, 150
WiMax, 91, 122, 123
Wimbledon, 483
Wimdu, 70
Windows Media Player, 148
Windows Phone, 218, 466, 766
Wingspan Bank, 779
winner's regret, **725**
WIPO Copyright Treaty, 584
Wired Equivalent Privacy. *See* WEP
wireframing, 190
wireless access point (hot spot), 122, 124
wireless Internet access technologies, 121–124. *See also* mobile, Internet access
wireless local area network. *See* WLAN
WireLurker, 264
Wish.com, 72
Wix, 182, 218, 323, 342
Wixen Music, 633
WLAN (wireless local area network), Internet access, 122–124
Wolfram/Alpha Widgets, 210
WooCommerce, 168–169
WordPress, 149, 168–169, 175, **182**, 189, 194, 196, 210
working capital, **760**
World Bank, 339
World Commission on Environment and Development (WCED), 833
World Intellectual Property Organization (WIPO), 583, 592
World Trade Organization (WTO), 830, 831
World Wide Web. *See* Web
Worldwide Web Consortium. *See* W3C
worm, **246**, 247, 248, 249, 262, 282
WPA (Wi-Fi Protected Access), 279
WPA2, 262, **279**
WPA3, **279**
WPP, 380
Wyndham, 287, 788

X

Xanga, 149
X-cart, 198
Xerox Parc Labs, 97
Xiaomi, 380
Xing, 704
XKeyscore program, 133, 258
XML (eXtensible Markup Langauge), **139**, 140, 190, 193, 209, 868

Y

Yahoo, 145, 246, 328, 332, 343, 348, 434, 437, 454, 646, 648, 653, 692, 707
    acquisition by Verizon, 646, 729, 732
    as portal, 726, 731
    as search engine, 145, 727, 728, 732
    data breach, 253
    privacy, 550, 556, 565, 574
Yahoo Finance, 781
Yahoo Japan, 729–730
Yahoo Messenger, 143
Yahoo News, 659
Yahoo Small Business, 180, 183, 198
Yang, Jerry, 145
Yelp, 399, 417, 620, 657, 789–790, 803
yield management, 424
Yodlee. *See* Envestnet Yodlee
YoKart, 342
Yoox Net-a-Porter (YNAP), 414–415, 761
YouTube, 43, 62, 83, 148, 483, 484, 503, 527, 528, 529, 604, 620, 635, 637, 641, 643, 645, 648, 669, 671, 672, 679, 687, 706
    Internet traffic, 158
    live streaming, 587
    programmatic advertising, 457
    social network marketing strategy, 335
    Viacom lawsuit against, 586
YouTube Music, 635, 682
YP, 515
YTO Express, 812

Z

Zalando, 69
Zalora, 69
Zanui, 69
Zano, 339
Zappos, 403, 416
Zayo Goup, 116
Zcash, 302
Zelle, 291, 292, 297
Zen Cart, 198
zero-day vulnerability, **261**
zettabyte, 158
Zeus, 247, 248, 249
Ziegfeld, Ziggy, 423
ZigBee, 125
Zillow, 784
Zimmerman, Phil, 276
Zinio, 663
Zipjet, 39, 794
zombie computer, 248
zombie cookies. *See* supercookies
Zopa, 340
Zotob, 249
Zozo, 730
Zreality, 151
ZTE, 133, 286
Zuccarini, John, 595
Zuckerberg, Mark, 69, 76
Zulily, 761
Z-Wave, 125